Exploring
Corporate Strategy

Pearson Education

We work with leading authors to develop the strongest
educational materials in strategy bringing cutting-edge thinking
and best learning practice to a global market.

Under a range of well-known imprints, including
Financial Times Prentice Hall, we craft high quality print and
electronic publications which help readers to understand
and apply their content, whether studying or at work.

To find out more about the complete range of our
publishing, please visit us on the World Wide Web at:
www. pearsoneduc.com

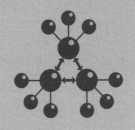

Exploring
Corporate Strategy

SIXTH EDITION

Gerry Johnson

University of Strathclyde
Graduate School of Business

Kevan Scholes

Sheffield Hallam University

FINANCIAL TIMES

Prentice Hall

An imprint of **Pearson Education**

Harlow, England · London · New York · Reading, Massachusetts · San Francisco
Toronto · Don Mills, Ontario · Sydney · Tokyo · Singapore · Hong Kong · Seoul
Taipei · Cape Town · Madrid · Mexico City · Amsterdam · Munich · Paris · Milan

To Jenny and Phyl

Pearson Education Limited

Edinburgh Gate
Harlow
Essex CM20 2JE

and Associated Companies throughout the world

Visit us on the World Wide Web at:
www.pearsoneduc.com

Previous editions published under Prentice Hall imprint 1984, 1988, 1993, 1997, 1999
Sixth edition published under the Financial Times Prentice Hall imprint 2002

© Prentice Hall Europe 1984, 1988, 1993, 1997, 1999
© Pearson Education Limited 2002

ISBN 0 273 65117 X (text only)
ISBN 0 273 65112 9 (text & cases)

British Library Cataloguing-in-Publication Data
A catalogue record for this book is available from the British Library

Library of Congress Cataloging-in-Publication Data
A catalog record for this book is available from the Library of Congress

10 9 8 7 6 5 4 3 2 1
07 06 05 04 03 02

Typeset in 10/12pt Garamond by 35
Printed and bound by Rotolito Lombalda, Italy

BRIEF CONTENTS

DETAILED CONTENTS

Part II • THE STRATEGIC POSITION   93

3 The Environment   97

7 Business-Level Strategy

LIST OF ILLUSTRATIONS

LIST OF EXHIBITS

PREFACE

It is now eighteen years since the first edition of *Exploring Corporate Strategy* was published. Both the world of business and the public services have seen vast changes over that time. There have also been major changes in the subject of corporate strategy. Central to this has been a widespread recognition of the importance of the subject to practising managers in both the public and private sectors. This has been reflected in the widespread inclusion of Strategy as a subject in educational programmes at undergraduate, postgraduate and professional levels as well as its adoption in short courses and consultancy assignments. It is now accepted that an understanding of the principles and practice of strategy is not just the concern of top managers, but essential for different levels of management – though clearly emphases within the subject will vary. We have consistently argued the importance of this wider 'uptake', so these are changes that we welcome.

The combined sales of our first five editions exceeded 500,000. This sixth edition is being published at a time when many, if not most, organisations are feeling the combined impact of globalisation, information technology and rapid changes in their business environment. Whereas the structure of the book remains broadly the same, we have tried to give more prominence to these 'new economy' issues whilst recognising that the divide between old and new in this respect is somewhat artificial. There is more attention to development of material to do with knowledge, learning and innovation, hypercompetition, the speed of strategic responses and new structural forms and the linkages between these. A number of other concepts and approaches have been updated and revised. These changes are in response to requests and observations by readers and adopters of the book, and we are most grateful for these.

The important changes that were made to layout and design in the fifth edition have been retained and further improved to increase clarity and 'navigation' and make reading the book an enjoyable experience. Each chapter has clear learning outcomes and a summary. Important 'definitions' are highlighted in the margins – there has been particular attention given to illustrations and case studies. The vast majority of these are new in this edition and the choice of examples reflects the issues mentioned above. All the 87 illustrations have questions, which allows them to be used as mini-cases by tutors and for students to check out their own progress on understanding the text. A new feature of the book last time was case examples at the end of each chapter. These have proved very popular – they allow a reflection back on the range of issues within the chapter and help students to see how they connect.

An important new feature of the book is the introduction of *critical commentaries* at the end of each part of the book. These are designed to achieve three things. First, to highlight the links between the separate chapter topics within a part. Second, to take a more holistic view of the strategic issues, for example about an organisation's strategic position (Part II). Both of these issues are fundamental to the essence of strategy – the importance of connections and the need to see the 'big picture'. The third purpose of the critical commentary is to reflect on the issues from that part of the book as viewed through the three different lenses: design, experience and ideas – introduced below. We intend these section commentaries to be especially important to managers and postgraduate students. Overall, our aim, then, has been to develop both the content and style of the book and we hope you will be pleased with the results of our efforts. *A guide on how to get the most from all the features and learning materials in/with* Exploring Corporate Strategy *follows this preface.*

Exploring Corporate Strategy is not a book of corporate planning techniques, but rather builds on the practice of strategic management, as researchers and practitioners in the area understand it. It is a book primarily intended for students of strategy on undergraduate, diploma and master's courses in universities and colleges; students on courses with titles such as Corporate Strategy, Business Policy, Strategic Management, Organisational Policy and Corporate Policy. However, we know that many such students are already managers who are undertaking part-time study: so this book is written with the manager and the potential manager in mind.

The style of the book reflects our personal experience as active teachers and consultants for more than twenty-five years. It is the blending of theory with practice that is at the heart of good strategic management, and the study of the subject should reflect that experiential learning, for example through case studies. It allows students both to apply concepts and theories, and – just as important – to build their own. However, it is also the case that the growing body of research and theory can be of great help in stimulating a deep understanding of strategic problems and strategic management. Our approach builds in substantial parts of such research and theory, and encourages readers to refer to more. But we also assume that readers will have the opportunity to deal with strategic problems through such means as case study work or projects, or, if they are practising managers, through their involvement in their own organisations. Our view in this respect is exactly the same as that of the writers of a medical or engineering text, and we encourage readers to take the same view. It is that good theory helps good practice, but that an understanding of the theory without an understanding of the practice is very dangerous – particularly if you are dealing with a patient, a bridge or, as with this book, organisations. Reinforcing this theory/practice link has been one of the reasons for introducing the critical commentaries mentioned above and the concept of the three strategy lenses – below.

So a major change has been introduced through our concept of the *three strategy lenses*. This is to underline the importance of exploring and understanding strategy in more than one way. As well as the 'traditional' *design* view of strategy we discuss how strategy can arise from *experience* and culture and also how it can be a product of *ideas* which emerge from the complex world within and around an organisation. These three strategy *lenses* are discussed fully in Chapter 2. As with real lenses they are different, but complementary, ways of viewing strategy and strategic management. All three views are relevant to the study of strategy, and the text reflects this.

For example, one of the themes running through the book is the importance of a clear analysis of the strategic situation facing the organisation and a rational assessment of the future options available to it. In considering such issues, the book includes, for example, discussion of the value of: environmental audits; structural and strategic group analysis of competitive environments; value chain analysis; models of strategic choice and the findings of those researchers who have tried to understand the relationship between strategic positioning of organisations and financial performance. In short, one of the themes is that the employment of rational models of analysis and choice in organisations is important to strategic management.

However, the book also draws on the growing research and literature on decision-making processes within a political and cultural context, and considers how such influences can be understood and what mechanisms exist for managing strategy within such a cultural and political context.

The ideas lens is also reflected in the content of the book – for example, in explaining the importance of innovation and how knowledge is created and shared within and around organisations. The advantage that organisations might gain from their organisational knowledge cannot be fully explained as an issue of planning and systems. The informal processes within and around an organisation will be important too.

The book also recognises that strategic management is as relevant to the public sector and to not-for-profit organisations as it is to the private sector of industry and commerce. Indeed, the period since the first edition was published has seen unprecedented changes in the recognition of strategic management in the public sector against the background of significant changes in their role and method of operation. This 'new era' is reflected in discussions and examples throughout the book. We also have many references, examples and illustrations of the application of strategic management concepts to the public sector. Since the last edition we have also edited and published a companion book devoted to public sector strategy (see 'Getting the Most from *Exploring Corporate Strategy*' which follows this preface). Many of these changes in the public sector are also mirrored in the larger private sector organisations and our coverage of the importance of structures and organisational processes reflects these changes.

The structure of the book is explained in some detail in Chapter 1. However, it might be useful to give a brief outline here. The book is in four parts.

Part I comprises an introduction to corporate strategy, first in terms of its characteristics and the elements of strategic management (Chapter 1), and then in terms of different ways in which strategy development in organisations can be understood and explained (Chapter 2).

Part II of the book is concerned with understanding an organisation's *strategic position*. Chapter 3 is concerned with organisations' position within their 'business' environment. This includes an organisation's competitive position. Chapter 4 considers the factors underpinning strategic capability – resources and competences. There is particular emphasis on the importance of knowledge. Chapter 5 is concerned with understanding organisational purposes. It is centred on the question of whom the organisation is there to serve and includes discussions of corporate governance, stakeholder relationships, business ethics and culture.

Part III deals with *strategic choice*. Chapter 6 is concerned with corporate-level strategy – how the corporate centre can add value to the business units (or, conversely, how it might destroy value). Chapter 7 deals with business-level (or competitive) strategy. The main issues are about the basis of competitive advantage and how to compete better in a fast-moving world. Chapter 8 looks at the more detailed choices of both strategic direction and method. It then looks at the criteria by which the likely success or failure of strategies could be assessed.

The final part of the book – Part IV – is about translating *strategy into action*. Chapter 9 is about organising for success and picks up recent literature about the connections between structures, organisation processes and the importance of establishing and maintaining internal and external relationships and boundaries. Chapter 10 is a completely new look at the relationship between an organisation's overall strategy and strategies in four key resource areas: people, information, finance and technology. Chapter 11 considers approaches to and methods of managing change and provides important links back to Chapters 2 and 5.

Many people have helped us with the development of this new edition. First and foremost have been the adopters of the current edition – many of whom we have had the pleasure of meeting at our annual seminars. Many of you have provided us with constructive criticism and thoughts for the new edition – we hope you are happy with the results! Also, our students and clients at Sheffield, Cranfield and Strathclyde and the many other places where we teach: they are a constant source of ideas and challenge and it would be impossible to write a book of this type without this direct feedback. Our own work and contacts have expanded considerably as a result of our book and we now both have important links across the world who have been a source of stimulation to us. Our contacts in Ireland, Holland, Denmark, Sweden, France, Canada, Australia, New Zealand and Singapore are especially valued.

We would like to thank those who have contributed directly to the book by providing case studies, and those organisations that have been brave enough to be written up as case studies. The growing popularity of *Exploring Corporate Strategy* has often presented these case study companies with practical problems in coping with direct enquiries from tutors and students. We hope that those using the book will respect the wishes of the case study companies and not contact them directly for further information. **Sheffield Theatres Trust has made this a proviso of releasing the case study for inclusion.**

There are many colleagues that we need to thank for assisting us in improving our understanding of particular aspects of the subject or related areas. Strategy is such a vast domain that this assistance is essential if the book is to remain up to date. So thank you to John Bessant, Julia Balogun, Graham Beaver, John Barbour, Andrew Campbell, Tony Clayton, Andrew Coleman, John Ellis, Jan Horwath, Phyl Johnson, Greg Parrish, Richard Schoenberg, Jill Shepherd, Steve Tallman, Joe Tidd, and Katarina Wass. Special thanks are due to all those who provided and helped develop illustrations; their assistance is acknowledged at the foot of those illustrations – thank you to all these contributors. Urmilla Lawson at Strathclyde has also assisted us in this process. Thanks are also due to the library staff at Strathclyde and Sheffield Hallam for their valuable assistance with references. Our thanks are also due to those who have had a part in preparing the manuscript for the book, in particular, Lesley Nixon at Strathclyde and Jenny Scholes in Sheffield.

Gerry Johnson
Kevan Scholes

November 2001

GETTING THE MOST FROM
EXPLORING CORPORATE STRATEGY

Through the various editions of *Exploring Corporate Strategy* we have tried to respond to the continuing demand for more material whilst keeping the size of the text manageable for readers. These demands have included more depth in topics, more coverage of particular sectors or simply more examples and tasks for students. We have already produced additional materials and publications and improved the cross-referencing to other material where it is relevant to a particular section of the text. This note gives some practical advice on how you might gain most advantage from this wide and varied range of materials.

Using *Exploring Corporate Strategy*

To get the most from *Exploring Corporate Strategy* and related materials, the broad advice to students and managers is to ensure that you have achieved three things:

- you understand the concepts;
- you can apply these concepts to practical situations – if you are a manager it is particularly important to apply the concepts to your own work context;
- you read more widely than this book alone.

Features of the text

- *Learning outcomes* are included at the beginning of each chapter which show what you should have achieved on completing the chapter. Check that you have understood all of these.
- *Key terms* are highlighted in the text and explained in the margins and listed alphabetically in the Glossary at the end of the book.
- *Illustration* boxes appear throughout the chapter and include questions so they can be used as mini-cases. Make sure that you read and answer these to check that you understand the theory/practice connection. If you are a manager, always ask yourself an additional question: 'what are the lessons for me and my organisation from this example?' Do this for the case examples and case studies too, if you can. The best strategic managers are those who can transfer learning from one situation to another.
- *Chapter summaries* help you to recap and review the main points of the chapter.

- *Recommended key readings* are listed at the end of each chapter. Make sure that you are familiar with those that are relevant to your course of study. There are extensive references for more detailed study and in depth research.

- *Work assignments* are organised in two levels of difficulty. Your tutors may have set some of these as course tests. In any case, you should treat these in the way you would previous examination papers – as a means of testing your own learning of both concepts and applications. If you are a manager, take the opportunity to work through these assignments for your own organisation and involve other members of your team if you can.

- *A case example* is included at the end of each chapter to help you consolidate your learning of the major themes. Answer the questions at the end of the example.

- *A commentary* appears at the end of each part of the book. Use them to ensure that you can see connections between issues in different chapters of that part of the book and that you can see the theme of that part in more than one way (through the strategy lenses as described in Chapter 2).

- If you are using the *Case Studies* edition try to read the cases relevant to the topics on your course – even if they are not set as class work or assessments. The *Guide to Using Case Studies* on page 587 indicates the main focus of each case and the relevant chapter. Case study introductions highlight which key learning points are covered by the case.

Check the *Exploring Corporate Strategy* website (see p. xxxi) regularly for updates and additional material and to use the multiple choice questions for each chapter. Ask if your tutor has a copy of the *Exploring Corporate Strategy* videos (see details on p. xxxi).

GUIDED TOUR

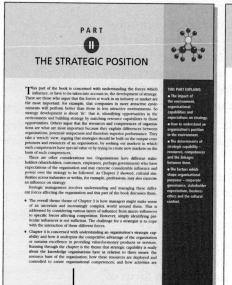

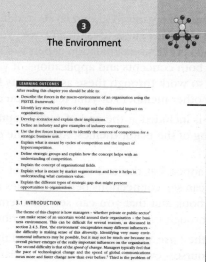

Learning outcomes
list what you should
have achieved or
understood by the
end of the chapter.

Part opening pages provide a brief explanation of
the topics covered in the following chapters.

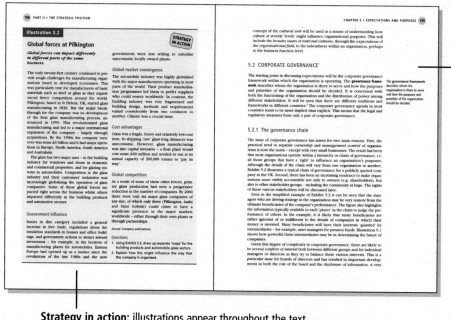

Key terms are high-
lighted in the text
with an explanation
in the margin to
emphasise some of
the most important
points.

Strategy in action: illustrations appear throughout the text
to illustrate the theory/practice connection.

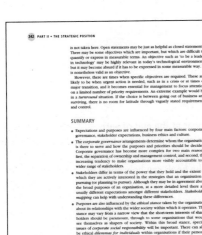

Recommended key readings provide sources for additional study on particular topics or concepts.

Summaries recap and review the main points of the chapter.

Case examples at the end of each chapter help consolidate your learning of the major themes.

Work assignments, now organised into two levels of difficulty, can be used as a means of testing your learning of theory and concepts.

GUIDED TOUR continued

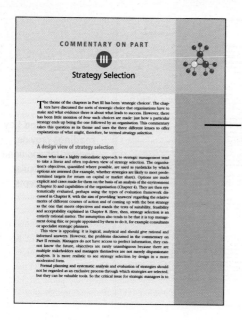

Part commentaries appear at the end of each major part of the book so that connections between issues in different chapters can be highlighted and the strategic themes of the book can be viewed in more than one way.

Exploring Corporate Strategy website (www.booksites.net/johnsonscholes), is updated on a regular basis and includes topical material relating to themes in the book, updates/cross-references to case studies; work assignments; multiple choice questions and tutor support material.

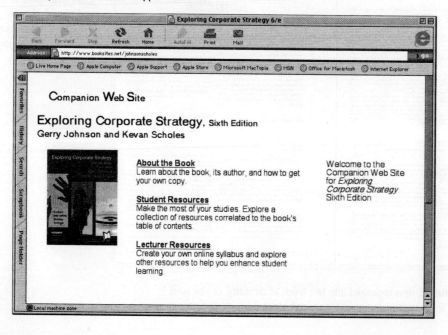

Teaching and learning resources

Exploring Corporate Strategy website (www.booksites.net/johnsonscholes)

A Companion Website accompanies
Exploring Corporate Strategy, 6th edition
by Johnson and Scholes

Visit the *Exploring Corporate Strategy*
Companion Web Site at *www.booksites.net/johnsonscholes*
to find valuable teaching and learning material including:

For students:
- Study material designed to help you improve your results
- Learning objectives for each chapter
- Multiple choice questions to test your understanding
- Minicase studies to take your study further
- Weblinks to journals, other sources and all organisations mentioned in the text
- Case updates
- Online glossary to explain terms
- Key concept definitions

For lecturers:
- A secure, password protected site with teaching material
- A downloadable version of the full Instructor's Manual, including:
  - how to plan programmes using the text
  - guide to using the case studies
  - case study teaching notes
  - tutor notes for chapter-end work assignments
  - questions linked to illustrations and case examples
- Downloadable PowerPoint slides of all figures from the book
- Minicase study teaching notes related to the cases on the student site
- Information on ordering the *Exploring Corporate Strategy* video
- A syllabus manager that will build and host your very own course web page

Exploring Corporate Strategy – the videos

There are two videos to support the text – they can be purchased from Sheffield Hallam University Press, Sheffield S1 1WB (telephone: 0114 225 4702)

Exploring Corporate Strategy – with the experts

This video runs for about 115 minutes. It consists of six separate key strategic topics from throughout the book and provides invaluable additional teaching material for the classroom or for private study. Each topic presents an up-to-date coverage of the issues – from leading academic or practitioner experts.

- CORE COMPETENCES *(Gerry Johnson)*
- COMPLEXITY THEORY *(Ralph Stacey)*
- GLOBALISATION *(George Yip)*
- STAKEHOLDER MAPPING *(Kevan Scholes)*
- CORPORATE PARENTING *(Andrew Campbell)*
- STRATEGY IN THE PUBLIC SECTOR *(CEOs from four public services)*

At the time of going to press, a new video is under preparation and relates to key issues included in the sixth edition.

The Exploring Strategic Management series

This series from FT/Prentice Hall builds on readers' knowledge of *Exploring Corporate Strategy* and provides more depth by topic or sector. All these books have been written in conjunction with Gerry Johnson and Kevan Scholes. Books available are:

- V. Ambrosini with G. Johnson and K. Scholes *Exploring Techniques of Analysis and Evaluation in Strategic Management*, 1998; ISBN: 0-13-570680-7
- T. Grundy with G. Johnson and K. Scholes *Exploring Strategic Financial Management*, 1998; ISBN: 0-13-570102-3
- J. Balogun and V. Hope Hailey with G. Johnson and K. Scholes *Exploring Strategic Change*, 1999; ISBN: 0-13-263856-8
- G. Johnson and K. Scholes (editors), *Exploring Public Sector Strategy*, 2001; ISBN: 0-273-64687-7

A note for tutors

Instructor's manual

A comprehensive set of supporting material for tutors, including:

- how to plan programmes using the text;
- using the case studies;
- tutor briefs for chapter-end work assignments and questions linked to illustrations and case examples;
- teaching notes for case studies;
- a CD containing all the exhibits from the book and some additional items that will be useful when preparing class sessions or presentations;
- multiple choice questions (on the website).

Since the first publication of the book we have always been concerned that good-quality practical support and advice to tutors is provided. This has been one of the driving forces behind the growth of the support material. The advice above for students and managers is also likely to be relevant to tutors.

Since 1989 we have run annual one-day workshops for tutors (also in Scotland since 1995). These have proved to be very popular with both experienced tutors and those who are new to the subject.

Details of forthcoming workshops are posted on our website. We hope that the exploitation of our website will make this support more comprehensive, more universal in coverage and more consistent in terms of the support tutors can expect, irrespective of their location.

We are always happy to receive feedback from users of the book. Contact us at KScholes@scholes.u-net.com or Gerry@gsb.strath.ac.uk

ENDORSEMENTS FOR
EXPLORING CORPORATE STRATEGY

Johnson and Scholes *is one of the outstanding texts in international management education. It combines clarity of structure and presentation with topical and enduring examples. It also has a depth of synthesis and critical reflection based on relevant research which is rare in text books.*

Andrew Pettigrew, Warwick University Business School

Exploring Corporate Strategy *is strong at integrating theory and practice . . . has a rare European orientation both in its theoretical coverage and its empirical illustrations and cases . . . is comprehensive and easy to combine with further theoretical readings.*

Prof. Leif Melin, Jönköping International Business School

With this new edition, Exploring Corporate Strategy *should be your first choice. Thorough, well written and packed with examples and cases. A student's dream textbook.*

Andrew Campbell, Director of Ashridge Strategic Management Centre, Co-author of *Corporate-level Strategy*

This text constitutes one of the most useful, incisive and complete resources for those students of strategy who are serious about the subject. In terms of breadth, depth and sheer insight, Johnson and Scholes is simply unsurpassed – a truly indispensable guide. The text, as ever, is rigorous, relevant and yet deliciously readable. A good balance of academic rigour and practical application that is bound together with an accessible and yet comprehensive style.

Prof. Lloyd C. Harris, Cardiff Business School, Editor of The *Journal of Strategic Marketing*

The great thing about Gerry Johnson's and Kevan Scholes' book is that it explicitly addresses the cultural dimension of strategy as well as the more analytic in ways that also make sense to non-Anglo-Saxons, indeed to non-western readers. I use the text to great effect in the strategy courses that I teach in China.

Max Boisot, ESADE, University of Ramon Llull, Barcelona

An ideal core text providing a well-structured framework for learning, understanding and application. The illustrations, cases, web-site and companion series of texts provide an excellent media to support and enhance strategic management programmes.

Ron Livingstone, MBA Programme Director, Caledonian Business School

THE AUTHORS

Gerry Johnson BA, PhD (left) is Professor of Strategic Management at the University of Strathclyde Graduate School of Business before which he was at Cranfield School of Management. He is author of numerous books and papers on Strategic Management, is a member of the editorial board of the Strategic Management Journal and referees for many European and US academic journals. His research work is primarily concerned with processes of strategy development and change in organisations. He is a regular visitor to universities throughout Europe, the USA and Australasia; and he works extensively as a consultant at a senior level on issues of strategy formulation and strategic change with many UK and international firms.

Kevan Scholes MA, PhD, DMS, CIMgt, FRSA (right) is Principal Partner of Scholes Associates, a consultancy specialising in strategic management. He is also Visiting Professor of Strategic Management at Sheffield Hallam University, UK. He has extensive lecturing and consultancy experience of both public and private sector organisations. This includes a wide range of ongoing international work in Ireland, Australia and New Zealand. He has a special interest in the strategic management of Professional Service Organisations. He has also been an adviser on management development to a number of national bodies and is a Companion of the Institute of Management.

ACKNOWLEDGEMENTS

We are grateful to the following for permission to reproduce copyright material:

Exhibit 1.1 reprinted by permission of Harvard Business School Press from *Competing for the Future* by Hamel & Prahalad, Boston, MA 1994. Copyright © 1994 by the Harvard Business School Publishing Corporation, all rights reserved; Exhibit 3.3 from *Total Global Strategy* by Yip, © 1995. Adapted by permission of Pearson Education, Inc., Upper Saddle River, NJ; Exhibit 3.4 adapted with the permission of The Free Press, a Division of Simon & Schuster, Inc., from *Competitive Strategy: Techniques for Analysing Industries and Competitors* by Michael E. Porter, Copyright © 1980, 1988 by The Free Press; Exhibits 3.6 and 3.7 adapted with the permission of The Free Press, a Division of Simon & Schuster, Inc., from *Hyper-Competitive Rivalries: Competing in Highly Dynamic Environment* by Richard A. D'Aveni, with Robert Gunther. Copyright © 1994, 1995 by Richard A. D'Aveni; Exhibits 4.3 and 4.4 adapted with the permission of The Free Press, a Division of Simon & Schuster, Inc., from *Competitive Advantage: Creating and Sustaining Superior Performance* by Michael E. Porter. Copyright © 1985, 1988 by Michael E. Porter; Exhibit 4.9 from *The Knowledge-Creating Company: How Japanese Companies Create the Dynamics of Innovation* by Ikujiro Nonaka and Hirotaka Takeuchi, copyright 1995 by Oxford University Press, Inc. Reprinted by permission of Oxford University Press, Inc.; Exhibit 5.5 adapted from A. Mendelow, *Proceedings of 2nd International Conference on Information Systems,* Cambridge, MA, 1991 reproduced by permission of Kluwer Academic/Plenum Publishers; Exhibit 5.10 adapted from E. Schein, *Organisation Culture and Leadership* (1997) Jossey-Bass and Exhibit 6.11 from M. Goold, A. Campbell and M. Alexander, *Corporate Level Strategy* (1994) Wiley. Reprinted by permission of John Wiley & Sons, Inc; Exhibit 6.7 adapted from J.R. Montanari and J.S. Bracker, *Strategic Management Journal*, Vol. 7, No. 3 (1986) and Exhibit 4.6 based on G. Hamel and A. Heene (eds.), *Competence-based Competition* (1994) John Wiley & Sons, and Exhibit 10.5 adapted from P. Timmers, *Electronic Commerce* (2000) John Wiley & Sons. Reproduced by permission of John Wiley & Sons Limited; Exhibit 7.5 reprinted with the permission of The Free Press, a Division of Simon & Schuster, Inc., from *Hypercompetitive Rivalries: Competing in Highly Dynamic Environments* by Richard A. D'Aveni with Robert Gunther. Copyright © 1994, 1995 by Richard A. D'Aveni; Illustration 8.2 (a, b, c and d) by courtesy of PIMS Associates Ltd. with special thanks to Keith Roberts, Tony Clayton and Tony Hillier, Senior Directors at PIMS Associates, for their help and insights into the interpretation of strategic issues and evidence contained in the PIMS section of this book; Exhibit 9.13: Figure from adapted from *Managing Across Borders* by C. Bartlett and S. Ghoshal published by Random House Business Books. Used by permission of The Random House Group Limited; Exhibit 10.3 from *Strategic Human Resource Management* by L. Gratton, V. Hope Hailey, P. Stiles and C. Truss, 1999, by permission of Oxford University Press; Exhibit 10.8 adapted from *Corporate Financial Strategy* by K. Ward. Reprinted by permission of Butterworth Heinemann; Exhibits 10.9, 10.11 and 10.12 adapted from *Managing Innovation: Integrating Technological Market and Organisational Change*, 2nd Edition (2001) J. Tidd, J. Bessant and K. Pavitt, reproduced by permission of the authors and John Wiley & Sons Limited.

All Illustrations and Cases are credited at source within the text.

Text extracts: The Economist Newspaper Limited for Chapter 6 case example adapted from 'Behind Branson' published in *The Economist* 21st February 1988 © The Economist Newspaper Limited, 1988 London, Illustration 7.6 'Easy does it' published in *The Economist* 18th November 2000 © The Economist Newspaper Limited, 2000 London, and Illustration 5.5 adapted from 'Stop signs on the web' published in *The Economist* 13th January 2001 © The Economist Newspaper Limited, 2001 London; EIASM for Illustration 2.1 adapted from 'Orchestral manoeuvres in the dark: discourse and politics in the failure to develop an artistic strategy' by S. Mailtlis and T. Lawrence, published in *Proceedings of the EIASM Workshop on Microstrategy and Strategising*; Elsevier Science for Illustration 3.3 adapted from *European Management Journal*, Vol. 17, No. 1 1999, and *Long Range Planning*, Vol. 28, No. 6, 1995; Financial Times Limited for Illustration 6.3 adapted from 'Tata may have allowed Tetley but "tea folk" will remain' by K. Merchant published in *Financial Times* 28th February 2000, and Illustration 11.8 on Pringle adapted from *Financial Times* 24th–25th February 2001; HarperCollins Publishers Ltd. for a table in Exhibit 5.3 from *Changing paradigms: transformation of management knowledge for the 21st century* by T. Clarke and S. Clegg; Harvard Business School Publishing for Illustration 7.5 adapted from 'From value chain to value constellation: designing interactive strategy' by R Norman and R Ramirez, published in *Harvard Business Review* Vol. 71, No. 4, 1993; Haymarket Business Publications for Illustration 5.6 adapted from 'Cross channel culture club' by A. Senter, published in *Management Today* February 1999; Information Today Inc. for Illustration 6.3 adapted 'About.com acquired by Primedia: sin or synergy?' by B. Quint, published in *Information Today* December 2000, Vol. 17, iII; John Wiley & Sons Limited for Illustration 10.7 adapted from 'The diffusion of robotics' by J. Tidd, J. Bessant and K. Pavitt, published in *Managing innovation: integrating technological, market and organisational change*, and Illustration 10.3 *Digital marketing; global strategies from the world's leading experts* by J. Wind and V. Mahajan (2001); Johnson Graduate School of Management for Illustration 2.8 adapted from 'Fading memories: a process theory of strategic business exit in dynamic environments' by R.A. Burgelman in *Administrative Science Quarterly* 39 (1994), and Illustration 2.9 'Architectural innovation: the reconfiguration of existing product technology and the failure of established firms' by R Henderson and K. Clarke, published in *Administrative Science Quarterly* 35 (1990); Philip McCosker for Chapter 6 case example adapted from his article 2 'Stretching the brand: a review of the Virgin Group', published in *European Case Clearing House Papers* 2000; Oxford University Press for Illustration 11.1 adapted from 'Contrasts in culture: Russian and western perspectives on organizational change' by S. Miichailova, published in *Academy of Management Executive* Vol. 145, No. 4, 2000; Oxford University Press Inc. for Exhibit 4.9 adapted from *The knowledge creating company* by J. Nonaka and H. Takeuchi (1995); Pulp and Paper Magazine for Illustration 9.3 adapted from 'ERP and e-procurement software assist strategic purchasing focus at Sonoco' by Monica Shaw, published in *Pulp and Paper*, Vol. 74, No. 2, 2000; The Regents of the University of California for Chapter 2 case example adapted from 'Perspectives on strategy; the real story behind Honda's success' by Richard T. Pascale, published in *California Management Review*, Vol. 26, No. 3, 1984, © 1984 by The Regents of the University of California; Sage Publications Ltd. for Illustration 9.2 from 'Team-based structures at Saab Training Systems' by Tomas Mullern, published in *The Innovating Organisation* edited by A. Pettigrew and E. Fenton; Sheffield City Council for Illustration 5.9 adapted from their *Strategic Plan 2000-2003*; Strategic Rail Authority for Illustration 9.7 adapted from their *Annual Report 1999-2000*; Times Newspapers Limited Illustration 5.1 adapted from *Sunday Times* 21st April 1996,

Illustration 6.6 *Sunday Times* 1st October 2000, Illustration 8.3 from *Sunday Times* 17th December 2000, Illustration 4.6 from *Sunday Times Hospital Guide* 14th and 21st January 2001, Illustration 8.1 adapted from *Sunday Times* 4th February 2001, 'Australia to overtake French wine sales' by Tom Robbins published in *Sunday Times* 11th February 2001, and Illustration 10.6 *Sunday Times* 18th March 2001; Patrizia Tiberi Vipraio for Illustration 9.5 adapted from her article 'Italy's craftmanship faces a global challenge', published in *QED* September 1997; and W.W. Norton & Company Inc. for Illustration 7.8 adapted from *Thinking strategically: the competitive edge in business, politics and everyday life* by Avinash K. Dixit and Barry J. Nalebuff, © 1991 by Avinash K. Dixit and Barry J. Nalebuff.

We are grateful to the Financial Times Limited for permission to reprint the following material: Illustration 3.8 adapted from Triumph wants a slice of the Japanese Market, and from Auto page VI, © *Financial Times*, 27 & 28 February, 2001; Illustration 6.5 adapted from Carmakers eye route to twin track revenues, © *Financial Times*, 28 February, 2001; Illustration 6.7 adapted from The Royal Bank of Scotland and the Take-over of NatWest, © *Financial Times*, 10 February, 2000; Illustration 7.3 adapted from Australian wines set to leapfrog the French, © *Financial Times*, 11 February, 2001 and 3 & 4 March, 2001; Illustration 7.7 adapted from NXT Learn Lessons from Dolby, © *Financial Times*, 6 February, 2001; Illustration 10.8 adapted from A fit and healthy leader of UK biotechnology, © *Financial Times*, 14 March, 2001; Illustration 11.4 adapted from Styles of Managing Change, © *Financial Times*, 20 March, 2001; Illustration 11.6 adapted from Symbolic Activity and Strategic Change, © *Financial Times*, 24–25 February, 2001; Case Study on UK Car Dealers caught in the headlights, © *Financial Times*, 20 March, 2001; Case Study on South African Breweries printed with permission; on Snappy Snaps, © *Financial Times*, 28 April, 2001; Case Study on ASM, © *Financial Times*, 18 April, 2001; Case Study on General Motors Brazil, adapted © *Financial Times*, 10 April, 2001; Case Study on Ericsson epilogue adapted from First aid rushed in as Ericsson bleeds, © *Financial Times*, 29 May, 2001.

PART

1

INTRODUCTION

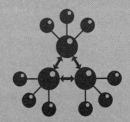

This opening part of the book provides an introduction to the study of the management of strategy in organisations. It also provides a guide to the structure and content of this book.

Chapter 1 explains why the study of strategic management is important, how it differs from other aspects of management and explains some of the main concepts and terms used throughout the rest of the book. It also provides a framework for thinking about strategic management in terms of understanding the *strategic position* of an organisation, *strategic choices* for the future and the ways in which strategies are *translated into action*. It goes on to show that different aspects of strategic management are likely to be important in different contexts; the small business context is, for example, very different from the multi-national business; public sector organisations and not-for-profit organisations will also be different.

The framework introduced in Chapter 1 is useful for thinking about the problems of strategic management. However, strategies followed by organisations do not come about solely as a result of managers thinking about strategic issues and carefully *designing* strategies for their organisation. Chapter 2 introduces a second major theme of the book; namely that we also need to understand how strategic management actually occurs in organisations. This chapter shows how strategy development can usefully be thought of in different ways. These are introduced in chapter 1 and discussed more fully in Chapter 2 as three strategy 'lenses'. The first lens is strategy as *design* – which has tended to be the orthodox way in which strategy development has been explained. Here top managers design carefully thought through strategies based on extensive analysis and execute them in an orderly planned way. The second lens sees strategy moving forward in an incremental fashion building on the basis of *experience* of the past – often bases of past success. This lens draws on cultural, institutional and cognitive theories. The third lens sees strategy development in terms of *ideas* that lead to innovation and change. Here strategies emerge and develop in an organisation less from top down direction and plans and more on the basis of the variety and diversity within and around organisations. This lens draws upon the evolutionary and complexity theories.

The challenge of strategic management is to be able to understand complex issues facing organisations and develop the capability for long term organisational success. These two chapters in Part I set out how this book can help readers address this challenge.

THIS PART EXPLAINS:

● The concepts and some of the main terminology necessary to understand the field of strategy and strategic management.

● The structure of this book: in particular what is meant by the strategic position, strategic choices and strategy into action, how these relate to each other and how they may differ by organisational context.

● The three strategy lenses: different explanations about how strategies develop in organisations

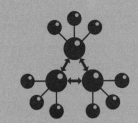

1

Introducing Strategy

LEARNING OUTCOMES

After reading this chapter you should be able to:

- Describe the characteristics of strategic decisions.
- Define what is meant by strategy and strategic management.
- Explain the difference between strategy as 'fit' and 'stretch'.
- Explain how strategic priorities vary by level: corporate, business and operational.
- Understand what distinguishes strategic management from operational management.
- Explain what is meant by strategic business units (SBUs) in organisations.
- Understand the vocabulary of strategy.
- Explain the elements of the *Johnson and Scholes* strategic management model.
- Understand which elements of the strategy model are likely to be most important in different contexts.

In January 2001 the Federal Communications Commission in the USA approved a $105 billion merger of AOL, the world's largest Internet service provider, with Time Warner – the multimedia empire. The intention to merge had been signalled by the two chief executives 12 months earlier. This was a defining moment for both companies. Business analysts hailed it as evidence that the previously separate sectors of computing, telecommunications and the world of media and entertainment were converging at a rapid rate. So it also had major implications for their competitors in each 'sector' and their customers and potential customers. Illustration 1.1 explains some of the background to the merger and the ways in which the new company intended to take advantage of the combined company.

The merger would clearly change the *direction* of the business, its justification was about developing a *long-term* position in the industry and it would have *far-ranging implications* for most parts of the business in terms of priorities and how the organisation would function. It also raised further challenges for the *future*. In short, this was a major *strategic* development.

All organisations are faced with the challenges of strategic development: some from a desire to grasp new opportunities, such as with AOL/Time Warner, others to overcome significant problems. This book deals with why changes in strategic direction take place in organisations, why they are important, how such decisions are taken, and some of the concepts that can be useful in understanding these issues. This chapter is an introduction and explanation of this theme, and deals with the questions of what is meant by 'strategy' and 'strategic management', why they are so important and what distinguishes them from other organisational challenges, tasks and decisions. In discussing these it will become clearer how the book deals with the subject area as a whole. The chapter draws on the AOL/Time Warner illustration for the purposes of discussion; and as the book progresses, other such illustrative examples are used to help develop discussion.

One other point should be made before proceeding. The term 'corporate strategy' is used here for two main reasons. First, because the book is concerned with strategy and strategic decisions in all types of organisation – small and large, commercial enterprises as well as public services – and the word 'corporate' embraces them all. Second, because, as the term is used in this book (discussed more fully in section 1.1.2), 'corporate strategy' denotes the most general level of strategy in an organisation and in this sense embraces other levels of strategy. Indeed Chapter 6, which looks at these higher-level issues, is entitled 'Corporate-level strategies'. Readers will undoubtedly come across other terms, such as 'strategic management', 'business policy' and 'organisational strategy', all of which are used to describe the same general topic.

1.1 THE NATURE OF STRATEGY AND STRATEGIC DECISIONS

Why are the issues facing AOL and Time Warner described as 'strategic'? What types of issues are strategic, and what distinguishes these from other types of issues in organisations – such as those that would be regarded as operational?

1.1.1 The characteristics of strategic decisions

The characteristics usually associated with the words 'strategy' and 'strategic decisions' are these:

● Strategy is likely to be concerned with the *long-term direction* of an organisation. The AOL/Time Warner merger set the new company on a path as a multimedia giant that would have lasting effects. Time Warner had already embarked on that path with its interests in film production, cable/television, music and publishing. Indeed, this empire had come together through a previous series of acquisitions and mergers. In contrast, AOL was a young company focused on Internet service provision so this was a big change in direction for them.

- Strategic decisions are normally about trying to achieve some *advantage* for the organisation over competition. For example, the AOL/Time Warner merger was justified in terms of providing 'content' (e.g. music or movies) to an Internet service provider – or (in reverse) giving a new distribution route to the content provider. It was also about moving before competitors did so and making it difficult for them to imitate. For example, the merger was expected to give major advantage in the music industry to the extent that it could transform the way in which music was sold and distributed and how artists received payments. In other situations advantage may be achieved in different ways and may also mean different things. For example, in the public sector, strategic advantage could be thought of as providing better value-for-money services than other providers, thus attracting support and funding from government. Strategic decisions are sometimes conceived of, therefore, as the search for effective *positioning* in relation to competitors so as to achieve advantage.

- Strategic decisions are likely to be concerned with the *scope of an organisation's activities*. For example, does (and should) the organisation concentrate on one area of activity, or should it have many? The issue of scope of activity is *fundamental* to strategy because it concerns the way in which those responsible for managing the organisation conceive the organisation's boundaries. It is to do with what they want the organisation to be like and to be about. This could include important decisions about product range or geographical coverage. The broadening of the scope of activities is an important reason for the AOL/Time Warner merger. This is particularly true for AOL managers who are likely to find themselves in the midst of the entertainment industry as against their previously narrower activities as an Internet service provider.

- Strategy can be seen as the *matching of the resources and activities of an organisation to the environment* in which it operates. This is sometimes known as the search for *strategic fit*.[1] The notion of **strategic fit** is developing strategy by identifying opportunities in the business environment and adapting resources and competences so as to take advantage of these. Here it would be seen as important to achieve the correct *positioning* of the organisation, for example in terms of the extent to which it meets clearly identified market needs. This might take the form of a small business trying to find a particular niche in a market, or a multinational corporation seeking to place most of its investments in businesses which have found successful market positions or have identified attractive markets. In the fast-moving world of the media and IT, customers might value providers who can provide a range of services through a set of complementary channels (e.g. Internet as well as physical retail outlets). This was certainly starting to happen in the music industry in the early 2000s. So, creating the ability to 'bundle' together services that were previously fragmented and offering new ways for customers to access products were clear priorities for the merged AOL/Time Warner. The nature of the music and entertainment markets provided opportunities not necessarily found in other markets. Customer tastes and requirements were relatively common between countries (particularly in

Strategic fit is developing strategy by identifying opportunities in the business environment and adapting resources and competences so as to take advantage of these

Illustration 1.1

AOL/Time Warner – the world's first Internet-powered media and communications company

STRATEGY IN ACTION

Managing strategy requires the consideration of a wide range of factors, which shift and change over time.

On 11 January 2001 the Federal Communications Commission in the USA approved the $105 billion merger of AOL – the world's largest Internet service provider (ISP) – with Time Warner (TW) – the media and entertainment empire with interests in magazines, film studios, cable TV and news and music production. The merger created a company with annual revenue of almost $40 billion and 85,000 employees. It brought together AOL's 26 million Internet customers with TW's different customer base which included 44 million magazine and 12 million cable TV subscribers.

It was a year and a day since the intention to merge had been announced by Steve Case of AOL and Gerald Levin of TW. *Business Week* reported the planned merger as follows:

> Case – who will become the chairman of AOL/TW – is making a huge bet that by melding the TW colossus with his Internet empire he will create a hybrid with unmatched advantages as the long-anticipated convergence of entertainment, information, communications and on-line services comes about in the next few years. It is a bid to define the future. By assembling more assets, audiences and advertisers for the new digital marketplace than anyone [else] . . . Case . . . sees a chance to move so far ahead that others won't catch up for years – the way that Alfred P. Sloan audaciously engineered the creation of General Motors in the 1920s – producing the corporation that dominated the auto age.

The merger brought together two quite different companies. AOL, only some 15 years old, had dominated the ISP market – being five times

bigger than the number two in the USA in terms of subscriber numbers and capturing an estimated 33 per cent of time online – three times as much as Microsoft or Yahoo!. It had become the *de facto* 'operating system' for the Internet – much to Microsoft's displeasure. It was much smaller than TW in terms of both revenue and employees (about one-fifth the size) and was an organisation that thrived on change. In contrast, TW went back to 1923 and had grown through a series of related diversifications (by mergers) and had enormous investments in movie, TV and music assets (such as best-selling TV shows (*Friends* and *ER*) and Madonna's CDs). It had a lot to lose from too much change.

AOL had a lot to gain from the merger – its stock had dropped substantially during 2000 in line with other high-tech stocks. TW might provide some solidity behind a dot.com image that was beginning to lose its initial gloss. It opened up the broadband cable network to an ISP – who were being held back technically by the slow speed of traditional telephone lines and, of course, there was all that TW content – movies, TV programmes and music. The TW customer base had not been 'exploited' in terms of selling a wider range of products and services. TW also had large advertising revenues through its magazines and TV channels.

Despite the fact that AOL made the running in the merger, there were benefits for TW too. They felt that they owned largely mature businesses with limited growth potential. TW's executives had consistently believed that technology would continue to transform the entertainment industry and that companies could not ignore major developments – like the Internet. They already had experience of how the Internet could disrupt their current businesses in publishing, music and TV. For example, they were part of the music industry lobby that eventually succeeded in 2001 in blocking the US Internet company Napster from providing music online to customers. But TW's own Internet efforts had flopped – they were simply not familiar with how to make an Internet company succeed. So they were attracted by AOL's 'Internet savvy' and proven track record in building revenue and market share. They also saw opportunities to cross-sell TW subscriptions to the younger AOL customers.

Not everyone was happy with the merger. Major rivals such as Disney, Microsoft and Yahoo! lobbied hard with the regulatory authorities to block the merger. In the end, all they achieved were some conditions. The most important was a requirement to make AOL's instant messaging service open to other providers. The regulators were trying to avoid a situation where AOL/TW customers found themselves in a 'walled garden' – benefiting from a wide range of services from AOL/TW but unable to communicate with non-AOL/TW customers or receive content from other providers. There were others who expressed concerns too – artists and composers in the music industry had campaigned in 2000 against the merging of TW and EMI music interests and they were further concerned that their interests would suffer from the stranglehold that AOL/TW would have on the music industry. For example, Roger Wallis, chairman of the Swedish Society of Popular Music composers, who claimed that Scandinavia would be particularly affected by the deal, said:

> We are concerned that [it] will put more control in the hands of the big music companies and make it difficult for all individual artists and composers to use the Internet as a great opportunity to spread music around the world. What we are pressing for is some form of . . . separation between the ownership of distribution channels and the ownership of music copyrights.

The thing that excited many observers about the merger was the creation of a platform to develop 'next-generation' services – such as interactive TV and digital music. During 2000, when the merger was still pending, the companies had worked together to launch 'AOL by Phone' (telephone access to the Internet) and 'AOL TV' (Internet by cable TV).

Those journalists who had experienced previous mega-mergers that had failed to deliver their promise were also cautious about AOL/TW. They reminded readers that more than 70 per cent of mergers fail and the 1990 merger that created TW had itself got off to a rocky start. AOL had a corporate culture that was speedy and collaborative whilst TW was slow and decentralised. Its reward structure emphasised performance at business-unit level and (by implication) discouraged collaborative efforts. Each of the TW business units was a multi-billion dollar business headed by a CEO and usually a leader in its own markets. So the trick would be to gain advantage from the synergies that the merger promised without undermining those qualities that had created leadership in publishing, film, cable TV and music. Delivering next-generation products – digital music and interactive TV – were what these synergies were about. This was a tough agenda.

Main sources: Adapted from *Business Week*, 8 May 2000, p. 65; *The Times*, 7 September 2000, p. 27; *Fortune*, 8 January 2001, p. 72.

Questions

1. Why were the issues facing AOL/TW described as strategic?
2. Identify examples of issues that fit each of the circles of the model in Exhibit 1.4 on page 17.
3. To what extent would you describe the strategy for AOL/TW in its various markets as 'fit' or 'stretch' as described in Exhibit 1.1 on page 8?

Exhibit 1.1	The leading edge of strategy: fit or stretch

ASPECT OF STRATEGY	ENVIRONMENT-LED 'FIT'	RESOURCE-LED 'STRETCH'
Underlying basis of strategy	Strategic fit between market opportunities and organisation's resources	Leverage of resources to improve value for money
Competitive advantage through . . .	'Correct' positioning Differentiation directed by market need	Differentiation based on competences suited to or creating market need
How small players survive . . .	Find and defend a niche	Change the 'rules of the game'
Risk-reduction through . . .	Portfolio of products/businesses	Portfolio of competences
Corporate centre invests in . . .	Strategies of business units or subsidiaries	Core competences

Source: Adapted from G. Hamel and C.K. Prahalad, *Competing for the Future*, Harvard Business School Press, 1994.

the Internet where universal standards had been adopted – but also in the media), allowing for rapid globalisation.

- However, strategy can also be seen as *building on or 'stretching' an organisation's resources and competences* to create opportunities or to capitalise on them.[2] Strategy development by '**stretch**' is the leverage of the resources and competences of an organisation to provide competitive advantage and/or yield new opportunities. For example, a small business might try to change the 'rules of the game' in its market to suit its own competences – which was the basis on which many 'dot.com' companies entered established sectors. A large multinational corporation may focus its strategies on those businesses with development potential. Here the emphasis is not just on ensuring that resources are available (or can be made available) to take advantage of some new opportunity in the marketplace, but also on identifying existing resources and competences that might be a basis for creating new opportunities in the marketplace. So the AOL/Time Warner merger should be viewed in terms not only of improved competitiveness in current 'arenas' – such as in the distribution of music – but also of exploiting strengths to create new offerings or to compete in new arenas. For example, the combined company could offer new subscription packages covering TV, movies, telephone and Internet services. It could then exploit this customer base to generate income from advertisers or other providers of complementary products or services. Of course, in practice, organisations develop strategies on the bases of both 'fit' and 'stretch'. Exhibit 1.1 contrasts the two approaches.

- Strategies may require *major resource* changes for an organisation. For example, decisions to expand geographically have significant implications in terms of the need to build and support a new customer base. Sometimes this

'**Stretch**' is the leverage of the resources and competences of an organisation to provide competitive advantage and/or yield new opportunities

might be seen as high risk – for example for AOL/Time Warner, entering markets where there is no tradition of subscription and where 'piracy' is prevalent. Strategies, then, need to be considered not only in terms of the extent to which the existing resource capability of the organisation is suited to opportunities, but also in terms of the extent to which resources can be obtained and controlled to develop a strategy for the future.

● Strategic decisions are likely to *affect operational decisions*: for example, the AOL/Time Warner strategy required a whole series of decisions at the operational level – even to get the merger approved by the regulatory authorities. After the merger, new structures and management controls would be needed to deal with the much more diverse set of activities. Human resource policies and practices would also have to be reviewed. This link between overall strategy and operational aspects of the organisation is important for two other reasons. First, if the operational aspects of the organisation are not in line with the strategy, then, no matter how well considered the strategy is, it will not succeed. Second, it is at the operational level that real strategic advantage can be achieved. AOL was successful as an Internet service provider not only because of a good strategic concept, but also because of the detail of how the concept was put into effect in terms of the logistics of accessing and servicing customers, generating advertising revenue etc. Indeed, competence in particular operational activities might determine which strategic developments might make most sense. For example, AOL's knowledge of how to provide service to the younger consumer was seen as particularly attractive to Time Warner as a major provider of popular music.

● The strategy of an organisation is affected not only by environmental forces and resource availability, but also by the *values and expectations* of those who have *power* in and around the organisation. In some respects, strategy can be thought of as a reflection of the attitudes and beliefs of those who have most influence on the organisation. Whether a company is expansionist or more concerned with consolidation, and where the boundaries are drawn for a company's activities, may say much about the values and attitudes of those who influence strategy – the *stakeholders* of the organisation. In the merger the running was set by AOL, reflecting the influence of the AOL chief executive Steve Case. But he was constrained by regulatory authorities and lobby groups (including performers) – not only in the USA but also in other major markets such as Europe – and the ability to persuade both sets of shareholders that the deal made commercial sense and would increase the long-term value of the company.

In general, of course, there are other stakeholders who have influence: financial institutions, the workforce, buyers and perhaps suppliers and the local community. The beliefs and values of these stakeholders will have a more or less direct influence on the strategy development of an organisation.

Overall, if a *definition* of a strategy is required, the most basic might be 'the long-term direction of an organisation'. However, the characteristics described above can provide the basis for a fuller definition:

Strategy is the *direction* and *scope* of an organisation over the *long term*, which achieves *advantage* for the organisation through its configuration of *resources* within a changing *environment* and to fulfil *stakeholder* expectations

Strategy is the *direction* and *scope* of an organisation over the *long term*, which achieves *advantage* for the organisation through its configuration of *resources* within a changing *environment* and to fulfil *stakeholder* expectations.

There are a number of consequences of these characteristics:

● Strategic decisions are likely to be *complex in nature.* It will be emphasised that this complexity is a defining feature of strategy and strategic decisions. This is especially so in organisations with wide geographical scope, such as multinational firms, or wide ranges of products or services. AOL/Time Warner needed to coordinate their activities over a wide geographical area.

● Strategic decisions may also have to be made in situations of *uncertainty*: they may involve taking decisions with views of the future about which it is impossible for managers to be sure. No one can really predict with much clarity where the industry convergence that AOL/Time Warner represent will lead or pace of change. This applies to the various sectors in which they are involved, such as music, cable TV and Internet service provision – the impact may not be the same or move at the same pace in each of these sectors.

● Strategic decisions are also likely to demand an *integrated* approach to managing the organisation. Unlike functional problems, there is no one area of expertise, or one perspective, that can define or resolve the problems. Managers, therefore, have to cross-functional and operational boundaries to deal with strategic problems and come to agreements with other managers who, inevitably, have different interests and perhaps different priorities. If AOL/Time Warner are to gain benefit from the merger then TW managers have to see the Internet as a major new distribution opportunity whilst AOL managers need to be more strategic as to how they might extend the portfolio of content offered to AOL customers.

● They may also have to manage and perhaps change *relationships and networks* outside the organisation, for example with suppliers, distributors and customers. AOL/Time Warner needed to decide to what extent their new internal relationship as content provider to Internet service provider should be exclusive. For example, should Time Warner customers be offered an alternative Internet service provider other than AOL and should AOL be able to source from other content providers such as Disney?

● Strategic decisions will very often involve *change* in organisations which may prove difficult because of the heritage of resources and because of culture. These cultural issues are heightened following mergers as two very different cultures need to be brought closer together – or at least learn how to tolerate each other. Indeed, this often proves difficult to achieve – up to 70 per cent of mergers fail to deliver their 'promise' for these reasons.

1.1.2 Levels of strategy

Strategies exist at a number of levels in an organisation. Individuals may say they have a strategy – to do with their career, for example. This may be relevant when considering influences on strategies adopted by organisations, but it is not the subject of this book. Taking AOL/Time Warner as an example, it is possible to distinguish at least three different levels of organisational strategy. **Corporate-level strategy** is concerned with the overall purpose and scope of an organisation and how value will be added to the different parts (business units) of the organisation. This could include issues of geographical coverage, diversity of products/services or business units, and how resources are to be allocated between the different parts of the organisation. For AOL/Time Warner, the most important corporate issues were about how new opportunities could be created by the merged company. This was the fundamental rationale for the merger. The corporate centre needed to play a crucial role in determining how the organisation should be structured, how resources should be allocated in setting targets and reviewing performance. The corporate centre should also be asking whether there are other ways in which they can add value to the separate business units within the company. It might be argued, for example, that a new corporate brand should be created. Corporate-level strategy is also likely to be concerned with the expectations of owners - the shareholders and the stock market. Being clear about corporate-level strategy is important: it is a *basis* of other strategic decisions. It may well take form in an explicit or implicit statement of 'mission' that reflects such expectations.

The second level can be thought of in terms of **business unit strategy**,[3] which is about how to compete successfully in particular markets. The concerns are therefore about how advantage over competitors can be achieved; what new opportunities can be identified or created in markets; which products or services should be developed in which markets; and the extent to which these meet customer needs in such a way as to achieve the objectives of the organisation - perhaps long-term profitability or market share growth. So, whereas corporate strategy involves decisions about the organisation as a whole, strategic decisions here need to be related to a strategic business unit (SBU). A **strategic business unit** is a part of an organisation for which there is a distinct external market for goods or services that is different from another SBU. In public sector organisations a corresponding definition of a SBU might be a part of the organisation or service for which there is a distinct client group. For example, ICI has a paints business that sells paints to various different types of customers, including industrial buyers and retail buyers. ICI Paints might choose to organise itself with an industrial division and a retail division. However, within those structural divisions there will be a need for different strategies according to different markets. Retailers could include huge multiple chain stores buying direct from ICI and small retailers buying through distributors. These are distinct markets that require different strategies, and are therefore different SBUs.

Confusion can often arise because an SBU may not be defined in terms of an organisational structure. It may not be a separate structural part of an organisation. For example, AOL/Time Warner had inherited separate companies structured around particular products (cable/TV, publishing, Internet service provision). Also, the customer bases of the two companies were different - particularly in terms of age profile. But the logic of the merger dictated that

Corporate-level strategy is concerned with the overall purpose and scope of an organisation and how value will be added to the different parts (business units) of the organisation

Business unit strategy is about how to compete successfully in particular markets

A strategic business unit is a part of an organisation for which there is a distinct external market for goods or services that is different from another SBU

'bundling' these services in different ways for different customer groups should be the basis of competitive advantage. So SBUs needed to be thought about in these terms – for example, businesses vs. households and by different demographic characteristics – such as age. The specific products that might be bundled into an attractive package for younger consumers and the extent to which the Internet is the dominant access and distribution channel will be very different from customers in older age groups. This emphasises the difference between an SBU and a division or a business within an organisation. An SBU is a unit of an organisation for strategy-making purposes. It may or may not be a separate structural part of the organisation.

The third level of strategy is at the operating end of an organisation. Here there are **operational strategies**, which are concerned with how the component parts of an organisation deliver effectively the corporate- and business-level strategies in terms of resources, processes and people. For example, in AOL/ Time Warner it was important that film production, TV scheduling, publishing titles and subscriber recruitment efforts dovetailed into higher-level decisions about service bundling and market entry. For example, it was important that the acquisition and distribution of content was planned to match the needs of the various customer groups that they were targeting. Indeed, in most businesses, successful business strategies depend to a large extent on decisions that are taken, or activities that occur, at the operational level. The integration of operational decisions and strategy is therefore of great importance.

> **Operational strategies** are concerned with how the component parts of an organisation deliver effectively the corporate- and business-level strategies in terms of resources, processes and people

1.1.3 The vocabulary of strategy

At the end of section 1.1.1, a definition of strategy was given. It can be dangerous to offer a definition, because lengthy semantic discussions can follow about whether or not it is precise enough, and whether everyone would agree with it. In fact, there are different definitions according to different authors. There are also a variety of terms used in relation to strategy, so it is worth devoting a little space to clarifying some of these.

Exhibit 1.2 and Illustration 1.2 employ some of the terms that readers will come across in this and other books on strategy. Exhibit 1.2 explains these in relation to a personal strategy readers may have followed themselves – becoming fit. Illustration 1.2 shows how these relate to an organisation – British Airways.

Not all these terms are always used in organisations or in strategy books: indeed, in this book the word 'goal' is rarely used. Moreover, it may or may not be that mission, goals, objectives, strategies and so on are written down precisely. In some organisations this is done very formally; in others it is not. As is shown in Chapter 2, a mission or strategy might sometimes more sensibly be conceived of as that which is implicit or can be deduced about an organisation from what it is doing. However, as a general guideline the following terms are often used.

- A *mission* is a general expression of the overall purpose of the organisation, which, ideally, is in line with the values and expectations of major

Exhibit 1.2	The vocabulary of strategy	
TERM	DEFINITION	A PERSONAL EXAMPLE
Mission	Overriding purpose in line with the values or expectations of stakeholders	Be healthy and fit
Vision or strategic intent	Desired future state: the aspiration of the organisation	To run the London Marathon
Goal	General statement of aim or purpose	Lose weight and strengthen muscles
Objective	Quantification (if possible) or more precise statement of the goal	Lose 5 kilos by 1 September and run the Marathon next year
Unique resources and core competences	Resources, processes or skills which provide 'competitive advantage'	Proximity to a fitness centre, supportive family and friends and past experience of successful diet
Strategies	Long-term direction	Associate with a collaborative network (e.g. join running club), exercise regularly, compete in marathons locally, stick to appropriate diet
Control	The monitoring of action steps to: • assess effectiveness of strategies and actions • modify strategies and/or actions as necessary	Monitor weight, kilometres run and measure times: if progress satisfactory, do nothing; if not, consider other strategies and actions

stakeholders and concerned with the scope and boundaries of the organisation. It is sometimes referred to in terms of the apparently simple, but actually challenging question: 'What business are we in?'

● A *vision* or *strategic intent* is the desired future state of the organisation. It is an aspiration around which a strategist, perhaps a chief executive, might seek to focus the attention and energies of members of the organisation.

● If the word *goal* is used, it usually means a general aim in line with the mission. It may well be qualitative in nature.

● On the other hand, an *objective* is more likely to be quantified, or at least to be a more precise aim in line with the goal. However, in this book the word 'objective' is used whether or not there is quantification.

● *Unique resources* and *core competences* are the bases upon which an organisation achieves strategic advantage in terms of activities, skills or know-how which distinguish it from competitors and provide value to customers or clients.

● The concept of *strategy* has already been defined. It is the long-term direction of the organisation. It is likely to be expressed in fairly broad statements of the direction that the organisation should be taking and the types of

Illustration 1.2

British Airways and the vocabulary of strategy

STRATEGY IN ACTION

Annual reports and public statements contain much of the vocabulary of this book.

Mission

To be the undisputed leader in world travel.

We are passionately committed to excellence and to the highest levels of customer service.

Goals

- *The customers' choice* – the airline of first choice in our key markets.
- *Strong profitability* – meeting investors' expectations and securing the future.
- *Truly global* – global network, global out-look: recognised everywhere for superior value in world travel.
- *Inspired people* – inspired teams of people, building and benefiting from the company's success.

Values

- Safe and secure
- Honest and responsible
- Innovative and team-spirited
- Global and caring
- A good neighbour

Competitive strategy

The airline's strategy is focused on a revised fleet strategy, aimed at targeting profitable passenger segments and on product develop-ments for all its brands.

Elements of strategy

- Reducing aircraft size to reduce dependence on unprofitable transfer passengers and other low-yielding business.
- Product and network improvements to main-tain share of key business markets.
- Cost cutting and efficiency programmes.
- Developing alliance relationships to strengthen the global network.
- Establishing the airline's low-cost subsidiary GO, which can serve a segment of the market that the mainline airline is not designed to meet.

Strategic initiatives

There are eight focus areas:

1. People: Employee numbers will reduce to reflect the reduction in capacity.
2. Distribution costs: Exploiting the opportunities offered by e-business and working with travel agents to manage the costs of distribution.
3. Gatwick: Review the destinations served from Gatwick and reduce costs.
4. Domestic routes: Select appropriate-sized aircraft; focus on point-to-point traffic and review of further product specification.
5. Product costs: Aim product offerings at customer needs to ensure value for money for the customer.
6. Aircraft utilisation: Improvements in aircraft use through changes to schedules, standby aircraft and maintenance downtime.
7. Subsidiaries: Review the role of subsidiary operations and their contribution to network revenue margin and group profitability.
8. Procurement: Work with suppliers to achieve cost savings through lower prices, more efficient methods of payment and optimum specification of items.

Prepared by Urmilla Lawson, University of Strathclyde.
Source: Adapted from BA Fact Book 2000 (from website).

Question

Find websites for other companies (including air-lines) and compare their use of strategic vocabulary. What conclusions do you draw from the similarities and differences?

action required to achieve objectives: for example, in terms of market entry, new products or services, or ways of operating.

● It is, then, important to exercise some degree of *strategic control* so as to monitor the extent to which the action is achieving the objectives and goals.

As the book develops, many other terms will be introduced and explained. These are the basics with which to begin.

1.2 STRATEGIC MANAGEMENT

What, then, is *strategic management*? It is not enough to say that it is the management of the process of strategic decision making. This fails to take into account a number of points important both in the management of an organisation and in the area of study with which this book is concerned.

Strategic management is different in nature from other aspects of management. Exhibit 1.3 summarises some of these differences. An individual manager is most often required to deal with problems of operational control, such as the efficient production of goods, the management of a salesforce, the monitoring of financial performance or the design of some new system that will improve the level of customer service. These are all very important tasks, but they are essentially concerned with effectively managing resources already deployed, often in a limited part of the organisation within the context of an existing strategy. Operational control is what managers are involved in for most of their time. It is vital to the effective implementation of strategy, but it is not the same as strategic management.

Exhibit 1.3	Characteristics of strategic management and operational management

STRATEGIC MANAGEMENT	OPERATIONAL MANAGEMENT
● Ambiguous/uncertain	● Routinised
● Complex	
● Organisation-wide	● Operationally specific
● Fundamental	
● Long-term implications	● Short-term implications

The scope of strategic management is greater than that of any one area of operational management. Strategic management is concerned with complexity arising out of ambiguous and non-routine situations with organisation-wide rather than operation-specific implications. This is a major challenge for managers who are used to managing on a day-to-day basis the resources they control. It can be a particular problem because of the background of managers who may typically have been trained, perhaps over many years, to undertake operational tasks and to take operational responsibility. Accountants find that they still tend to see problems in financial terms, IT managers in IT terms, marketing managers in marketing terms, and so on. Each aspect in itself is important, of course, but none is adequate alone. The manager who aspires to manage, or influence, strategy needs to develop a capability to take an overview, to conceive of the whole rather than just the parts of the situation facing an organisation. Because strategic management is characterised by its complexity, it is also necessary to make decisions and judgements based on the *conceptualisation* of difficult issues. Yet the early training and experience of managers is often about taking action, or about detailed *planning* or *analysis*. This book explains many analytical approaches to strategy, and it is concerned too with action related to the management of strategy. There is also, however, an emphasis on understanding concepts of relevance to the complexity of strategy which informs this analysis and action.

Nor is strategic management concerned only with taking decisions about major issues facing the organisation. It is also concerned with ensuring that the strategy is put into effect. It can be thought of as having three main elements within it, and it is these that provide the framework for the book. **Strategic management** includes *understanding the strategic position* of an organisation, *strategic choices* for the future and turning *strategy into action*.

The next sections of this chapter discuss each of these aspects of strategic management and identifies elements that make up each aspect. Exhibit 1.4 shows these elements and defines the broad coverage of this book. It is import- ant to understand why the exhibit has been drawn in this particular way. It could have shown the three aspects of strategic management in a linear form – understanding the strategic position preceding strategic choices, which in turn precede strategy into action. Indeed, many texts on the subject do just this. However, in practice, the elements of strategic management do not take this linear form – they are interlinked. One way of understanding a strategy better is to begin to implement it, so strategic choices and strategy into action may overlap. Similarly, an understanding of the strategic position may be built up from the experience of strategies in action. It is for structural convenience only that the subject has been divided into sections in this book; it is not meant to suggest that the process of strategic management must follow a neat and tidy path. Indeed, the evidence provided in Chapter 2 on how strategic manage- ment occurs in practice suggests that it usually does not.

Strategic management includes *understanding the strategic position* of an organisation, *strategic choices* for the future and turning *strategy into action*

1.2.1 The strategic position

The **strategic position** is concerned with the impact on strategy of the external environment, internal resources and competences, and the expectations and influence of stakeholders

Understanding the **strategic position** is concerned with impact on strategy of the external environment, internal resources and competences, and the expectations and influence of stakeholders. The sorts of questions this raises are central to future strategy. What changes are going on in the environment, and how will they affect the organisation and its activities? What are the resources and competences of the organisation and can these provide spe- cial advantages or yield new opportunities? What is it that those people and groups associated with the organisation – managers, shareholders or owners,

| Exhibit 1.4 | A model of the elements of strategic management |

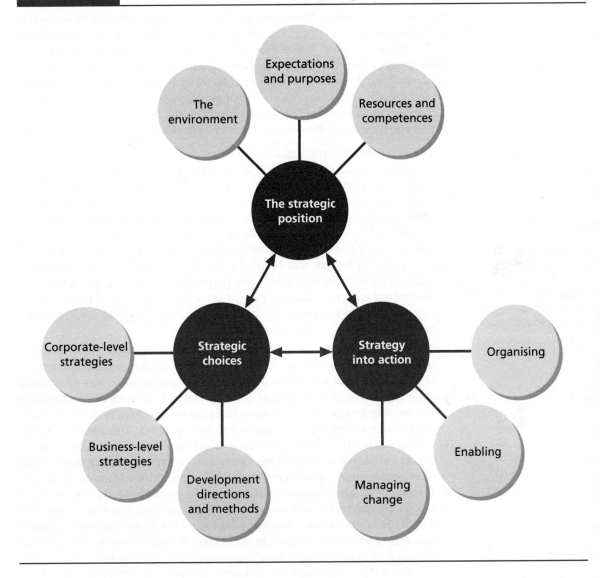

unions and others who are stakeholders in the organisation – aspire to, and how do these affect what is expected for the future development of the organisation?

These are clearly all important issues for AOL/Time Warner. Decisions to forge the merger no doubt required careful consideration about the convergence of technologies and consumer behaviour leading to views about future demand for new services in the market. An equally important issue was how the particular competences of the merged organisation might be configured to provide competitive advantage – perhaps by developing new services such as interactive TV or digital music online. Also, the expectations of stakeholders need to be understood, for example the concerns being shown by musicians and composers about the stranglehold that AOL/Time Warner might have on the music industry. These groups could lobby regulatory bodies to place restrictions on the company's activities in the music industry. So the reason for understanding the strategic position is to form a view of the key influences on the present and future well-being of an organisation, and what opportunities and threats are created by the environment, the competences of the organisation and the expectations of stakeholders. These are discussed briefly below.

- The *environment*. The organisation exists in the context of a complex commercial, political, economic, social, technological, environmental and legal world. This environment changes and is more complex for some organisations than for others. How this affects the organisation could include an understanding of historical and environmental effects, as well as expected or potential changes in environmental variables. Many of those variables will give rise to *opportunities* and others will exert *threats* on the organisation – or both. A problem that has to be faced is that the range of variables is likely to be so great that it may not be possible or realistic to identify and understand each one; and therefore it is useful to distil out of this complexity a view of the key environmental impacts on the organisation. Chapter 3 examines how this might be possible.

- The *resources and competences* of the organisation make up its *strategic capability*. Just as there are outside influences on the organisation and its choice of strategies, so there are internal influences. One way of thinking about the strategic capability of an organisation is to consider its *strengths* and *weaknesses* (what it is good or not so good at doing, or where it is at a competitive advantage or disadvantage, for example). The aim is to form a view of the internal influences – and constraints – on strategic choices for the future. On occasions, specific resources – for example, the particular location of an organisation – could provide it with competitive advantage. However, competences which provide real advantage – in this book we refer to these as *core competences* – are more likely to be activities, know-how and skills which *in combination* provide advantages for that organisation which others find difficult to imitate. In AOL/Time Warner, it is not one particular resource or activity that was of importance but the combination of many and the ability to manage the linkages between the different parts of the enlarged business that might provide the company with its competitive advantage. Chapter 4 examines resources and competences in detail.

- There are a number of influences on an organisation's *purpose*. Chapter 5 explores these. Formally, the issue of *corporate governance* is important. Here the question is: who *should* the organisation primarily serve and how should managers be held responsible for this? The *expectations* of different *stakeholders* affect purpose and what will be seen as acceptable in terms of strategies advocated by management. Which views prevail will depend on which group has the greatest *power*, and understanding this can be of great importance in recognising why an organisation follows the strategy it does. *Cultural influences* from within the organisation and from the world around it also influence the strategy an organisation follows, not least because the environmental and resource influences on the organisation are likely to be interpreted in terms of the assumptions inherent in that culture. Chapter 5 builds on the discussion in Chapter 2 to show how cultural influences on strategy can be examined. All of this raises *ethical* issues about what managers and organisations do and why. This array of influences also takes form in statements of *objectives*. These are also discussed in Chapter 5.

Together, a consideration of the *environment, strategic capability*, the *expectations* and the *purposes* within the *cultural* and *political* framework of the organisation provides a basis for understanding the strategic position of an organisation. Such an understanding needs to take the future into account. Is the current strategy capable of dealing with the changes taking place in the organisation's environment? Is it likely to deliver the results expected by influential stakeholders? If so, in what respects, and if not, why not? It is unlikely that there will be a complete match between current strategy and the picture which emerges from answering these questions. It may be that the mismatch is marginal, or it may be that there is a need for a fundamental realignment of strategy. Assessing the magnitude of required strategic changes and the ability of the organisation to effect such changes is another important aspect of the organisation's strategic position.

1.2.2 Strategic choices

Strategic choices involve understanding the underlying bases for future strategy at both the corporate and business unit levels (discussed above) and the options for developing strategy in terms of both the directions in which strategy might move and the methods of development.

> **Strategic choices** involve understanding the underlying bases for future strategy at both the corporate and business unit levels and the options for developing strategy in terms of both the directions and methods of development

● At the highest level in an organisation there are issues of *corporate-level strategy*, which are concerned with the scope of an organisation's strategies, the relationship between the separate parts of the business and how the corporate centre adds value to these various parts. For example, the corporate centre, as a parent to the business units, could add value by looking for synergies between business units, by channelling resources – such as finance – or through particular competences – such as marketing or brand building. There is a danger, of course, that the centre does not add value and is merely a cost upon the business units and is therefore destroying value. There are very different ways in which these issues might be resolved. For example, AOL/Time Warner could continue to operate as separate businesses with a very slim corporate centre simply 'policing' a market-like relationship between AOL and the separate business units within Time Warner as its content provider. In contrast, the corporate centre could integrate the businesses into a new single organisation and create divisions around target markets (e.g. geographically) or customer groups (e.g. by age group). These issues about the role of the centre and how it adds value are *parenting* issues and will be discussed in Chapter 6.

- There are strategic choices in terms of how the organisation seeks to compete at *business level.* This requires an identification of *bases of competitive advantage* arising from an understanding of both markets and customers, and special competences that the organisation has; for example, whether AOL/Time Warner will take advantage of the reduced costs that should result from the merger to reduce prices in its separate business units such as music, cable TV and Internet service provision or whether it will focus on investing in ways of differentiating itself from competitors through innovative new services, such as interactive TV, that others cannot match. Or perhaps they will choose to do both of these. These issues of business-level strategies will be discussed in Chapter 7.

- Strategy may develop in the future in different *directions.* For example, historically Time Warner had developed through diversification into related fields (publishing, film, music and television). Indeed, the merger with AOL is just the latest example of the dominance of this particular development direction. This would contrast with other organisations that might concentrate in a narrower field and seek to grow market share and/or progressively develop the product features and enter new geographical markets. AOL had developed through such a combination of directions.

- Organisations also have choices of the *method* of strategy development. The development *method* used by Time Warner had been merger or acquisition (as against internal development or strategic alliances, which are favoured by many other organisations). These options for development directions and methods are important and need careful consideration: indeed, in developing strategies, a potential danger is that managers do not consider any but the most obvious course of action – and the most obvious is not necessarily the best. These issues are discussed in Chapter 8 together with a discussion of the success criteria that determine why some strategic choices are likely to be better than others. These include the *suitability* of the strategy – whether it addresses the strategic position of the organisation; whether the strategy is *feasible* in terms of resources and competences required to implement it; and, finally, whether the strategy would be *acceptable* to the stakeholders. For example, in considering strategic choices for AOL/Time Warner further mergers might seem attractive in terms of further securing their ability to offer a differentiated portfolio of services. But this might not be feasible in terms of the further resources required or, indeed, there may not be a suitable partner. It may not be acceptable to shareholders for the reason of raised financial risk nor to regulators because of monopoly considerations or concerns over the types of services. It could be argued that they would be better advised to concentrate on consolidating the merger and allowing the separate business units to compete strongly and gain market share in their own sectors.

1.2.3 Strategy into action

Translating **strategy into action** is concerned with ensuring that strategies are working in practice. A strategy is not just a good idea, a statement or a plan. It is only meaningful when it is actually being carried out. How this occurs is typically thought of in terms of:

Strategy into action is concerned with ensuring that strategies are working in practice

- *Structuring* an organisation to support successful performance. This includes structures, organisational processes, boundaries and relationships (and the interaction between these elements). These issues will be discussed in Chapter 9. For example, if AOL/Time Warner remains structured around its current business units (music, film/TV, publishing, Internet) it will need to establish new roles and processes to facilitate those separate business units in working together to create new services like online digital music. This is the rationale for the merger. It will have the difficult problem of building relationships between separate groups of people (for example, music and Internet specialists) that have different cultures and who are used to working in different ways.

- *Enabling* success through the way in which the separate resource areas of an organisation support strategies; and also the reverse of this – the extent to which new strategies are built on the particular resource and competence strengths of an organisation. Chapter 10 will consider this two-way relationship between strategy and four important resource areas (people, information, money and technology). Clearly a central issue for AOL/Time Warner is how they can continue to get market advantage in publishing, music and TV through the exploitation of IT – particularly the Internet. But this will have implications for the people and financial resources of the organisation too.

- Strategy very often involves *change*, and Chapter 11 looks at how organisations might manage change processes. This will include the need to change day-to-day routines and cultural aspects of the organisation, and overcoming political blockages to change. Following mergers, such as AOL and Time Warner, an inability to manage one or more of these change issues results in the performance expectations of the merger not being met. This is a very common outcome of mergers and acquisitions.

1.3 STRATEGY AS A SUBJECT OF STUDY

An explanation of the history of strategy as a subject of study is helpful in understanding how it will be presented in this book. It will also introduce the important idea of the different *lenses* through which strategy might be viewed – an issue that will be explained in depth in Chapter 2 and will run through all the parts of the book.

The origins of the study and teaching of strategy can be traced to a number of major influences:

● The first is to do with the *task of the general manager* and, perhaps most obviously, took form in the *business policy*[4] courses run at universities such as Harvard going back to the 1960s. The continual question posed here was 'what would you do if you took over as chief executive of such and such an organisation?' It positioned strategy as the responsibility of the general manager (typically a CEO) and was based on the common-sense experience of executives and not so much on theory or research. Teaching was dominated by attempts to replicate real business situations in the classroom by the saturation exposure to case studies.

● In parallel there developed in the 1960s and 1970s the influence of books on *corporate planning*.[5] Here the emphasis was on trying to analyse the various influences on an organisation's well-being in such a way as to identify opportunities or threats to future development. It took the form of highly systematised approaches to planning. This analytic approach is a dominant legacy in the study of the subject. It assumes that managers can and should understand all they possibly can about their organisational world; and that by so doing they can make optimal decisions about the organisation's future. It was a highly influential approach and, for example, gave rise to specialist corporate planning departments in organisations in the private and public sectors, especially in the 1970s.

In the 1980s both of these approaches came in for considerable criticism. There developed a growing body of research addressing many key strategic questions which started to become influential in how the subject was seen and how students and managers should learn about strategy:

● Typically this took the form of examining *evidence* about the links between financial performance and the strategies followed by organisations on, for example, product development, market entry, diversification and associated decisions about organisational structure.[6] It was argued that managers benefit from lessons drawn from such research in order to make wiser strategic decisions. The continuing assumption was, of course, that strategic decisions should be driven by analysis and evaluation so as to make optimal decisions; but that an accumulation of research findings could provide evidence by which to do this.

● Others[7] argued that the world was simply not that straightforward. Its complexity and uncertainty meant that it was impossible to analyse everything up front, predict the future; and that the search for optimal decisions was futile. It was necessary to accept the messiness of organisational life, that managers made decisions which were as much to do with collective and individual experience, organisational politics and the substantial influence of organisational history and culture as they were to do with strategy. As evidence of this, they pointed to the adaptive nature of how strategies developed in organisations.[8] They argued that it would be fruitful to spend more time understanding *managerial processes* of decision making in dealing with the complexity of strategic management in the reality of their social, political and cultural contexts.

- The orthodox view has been that such social and political and cultural constraints on managers result in sub-optimal decisions, inertia and perhaps underperformance. In other words, that managers do need to be better at analysis and planning and can take optimal decisions but that their personal biases and the culture of their organisation get in the way. More recently, others have questioned this.[9] They suggest that organisations are not so very different from living organisms. These organisms do not just plan and analyse, they live, they experience, they interpret and between them and within them there is sufficient diversity and variety for them to be able to change and innovate to deal with their changing environments. There has grown up an argument that organisations and managers are better understood not so much as living in the world of planning and analysis, but as using their skills and senses within the more complex world of *social interaction* in their organisation and, more widely, in the world around them. Moreover, that this will better explain how organisations cope with fast-changing environments, how new ideas and innovation come about and therefore how more significant strategic transformations come about.

This book argues that it is useful to draw on all of these views. The sort of analysis, conceptual models, research evidence, and planning systems and tools employed by those who seek to *design* strategies are useful. They help strategists think through problems and issues so as to challenge and question and, indeed, inform decision making. No doubt such an approach played a large part in the partners in the AOL/TW merger thinking through its benefits and its problems. However, it is also important to understand how the *experience* of managers and the culture of organisations inform and constrain the development of strategies; and how differences between people and groups are resolved. Moreover, by understanding such phenomena, important insights can be gained into the management of strategic change. It would be unwise of the top management of AOL/TW to believe that the sorts of change they have in mind are likely to happen without addressing such issues in the businesses that comprise the new portfolio of the merged corporation. There is also much to be learned from understanding how new *ideas* might emerge in organisations from the variety of experience and behaviours that are to be found across a huge corporation such as AOL/TW. It is unrealistic to believe that all such ideas can be planned from the top. Given the purpose of the merger – to search for new opportunities by bringing the different businesses together – thinking about how such potential innovation can be encouraged and tapped would be important. So all three ways of looking at strategy development are useful. They will be referred to in this book as the *lenses* through which strategy in organisations can be viewed:

- *Strategy as design*: the view that strategy development can be a logical process in which economic forces and constraints on the organisation are weighed carefully through analytic and evaluative techniques to establish clear strategic direction and in turn carefully planned in its implementation is perhaps the most commonly held view about how strategy is developed and what managing strategy is about. It is usually associated with the notion that it is top management's responsibility to do this and that top management leads the development of strategy in organisations.

● *Strategy as experience*: here the view is that future strategies of organisations are based on the *adaptation* of past strategies influenced by the experience of managers and others in the organisation, and are taken-for-granted assumptions and ways of doing things embedded in the cultural processes of organisations. In so far as different views and expectations exist, they will be resolved not just through rational analytic processes, but also through processes of bargaining and negotiation. Here, then, the view is that there is a tendency for the strategy of the organisation to build on and be a continuation of what has gone before.

● *Strategy as ideas*: neither of the above lenses is especially helpful in explaining innovation. So how do new ideas come about? This lens emphasises the potential variety and diversity which exist in organisations and which can potentially generate novelty. If we are to understand how innovations and innovative strategies come about, it is necessary to understand how this potential diversity contributes to it. Here strategy is seen not so much as planned from the top but as *emergent* from within and around the organisation as people cope with an uncertain and changing environment in their day-to-day activities. New ideas will emerge, but they are likely to have to battle for survival against the forces for conformity to past strategies that the experience lens explains. Drawing on explanations from evolutionary and complexity theories, the ideas lens provides insights into how this might take place.

These 'lenses' will be introduced more fully in Chapter 2 and referred to regularly throughout the book – particularly in the commentaries, which are at the end of each part of the book. It is important to understand these different explanations because all three provide insights into the challenges that are faced in managing the complexity of strategy.

Illustration 1.3 shows an example of the three lenses as it might apply to decisions of individuals.

1.4 STRATEGIC MANAGEMENT IN DIFFERENT CONTEXTS[10]

The AOL/Time Warner merger has been used in this chapter to illustrate different aspects of strategic management. To a greater or lesser extent, all these aspects are relevant for most organisations. However, it is likely that different aspects will be more important in some contexts and in some organisations than in others. For example, the need to understand the convergence of previously separate industries (such as media and the Internet), to develop new 'routes to market' and to maintain a dominant market share in its various markets was of particular importance to AOL/Time Warner. This is a different emphasis from that of a steel or glass manufacturer supplying commodity-like materials into mature markets or a public sector service provider tailoring services to the needs of a local community within statutory requirements.

Illustration 1.3

Choosing a new car

The strategy lenses also apply to the personal strategies followed by individuals.

A manager was considering buying a new car. He had driven Jaguars for some time. However, he thought it would be a good idea to review the options systematically (*the design lens*). He obtained the brochures for a range of luxury car makes, identified the major factors that were important to him and considered all the performance indicators for each of the cars against these. He even allocated a weighted score to the factors that meant most to him. The analysis told him that a BMW or a Mercedes might be a better choice than a Jaguar.

This surprised him; and he didn't much like the answer. He had always driven a Jaguar, he was used to it, felt it had an especially English character and that it suited his personality (*the experience lens*). He was also looking forward to having the new model. So his inclination was to buy another Jaguar.

Actually he ended up buying an open-top Mercedes sports. This was because his wife thought he needed to liven up his image and liked the idea of driving it on holidays (*the ideas lens*). With some reluctance he bought the new Mercedes. This proved to be a good decision. They both liked the car and it depreciated in value much more slowly than a Jaguar.

So what are the lessons? The planning and analysis was there; and if it didn't end up informing the decision directly, it did indirectly. His wife justified the purchase of the Mercedes in part on the basis of that analysis. He would

have ended up with another Jaguar; a continuity of what he was used to. He actually chose what (to him) was a novel, innovative option that, in the long run, significantly changed his approach to car buying. Of course, if his wife had not intervened, his inclination to the Jaguar based on past experience would probably have prevailed. This depended on him and his circumstances – the context. Some ideas get through, some do not, depending how attractive the ideas were to him. Or it could have been that the power of analysis had been such as to overcome this. So it is with organisations. All these three lenses are likely to be there. The nature and context of the organisation are likely to determine which one prevails.

It is also difficult to say which lens was best. Who is to say that the analysis actually provided the optimal result? Maybe it was important that he should feel comfortable with his past.

Question

Choose a decision from your own personal life and consider how the three lenses impacted on the final choice that you made.

However, in AOL/Time Warner these current priorities are likely to shift over time as the industry convergence progresses and more parts of the market mature. Even within the one company, different business units may face quite different market conditions – Internet service provision and publishing are in different phases of technological and market development. It would, then, be wrong to assume that all aspects of strategic management are equally important in all circumstances. This section reviews some of the ways in which aspects differ in different contexts.

1.4.1 The small business context[11]

Small businesses are likely to be operating in a single market or a limited number of markets, probably with a limited range of products or services. The scope of the operation is therefore likely to be less of a strategic issue than it is in larger organisations. It is unlikely that small businesses will have central service departments to undertake complex analysis and market research; rather, it may be senior managers themselves, perhaps even the founder of the firm, who has direct contact with the marketplace and whose experience is therefore very influential. Indeed, in small firms the values and expectations of senior executives, who may themselves be in an ownership position, are likely to be very important, and even when current management are not owners, it may be that the values and expectations of the founders persist. It is also likely that, unless the firm is specialising in some particular market segment, it will be subject to significant competitive pressures; so issues of competitive strategy are likely to be especially important for the small firm. However, decisions on competitive strategies are likely to be strongly influenced by the experience of those running the business, so the questions posed and concepts discussed about the nature of competition in Chapter 3 and bases of competitive strategy in Chapter 6 are likely to be especially relevant.

Small firms are also likely to be private companies. This significantly affects their ability to raise capital. Combined with the legacy of the founder's influence on choice of product and market, this may mean that choices of strategy are limited. The firm may see its role as consolidating its position within a particular market. If it does not, and is seeking growth, then the raising of finance is crucial, so building or maintaining relationships with funding bodies such as banks becomes a key strategic issue.

1.4.2 The multinational corporation[12]

The key strategic issues facing multinationals such as AOL/Time Warner are substantially different from those facing the small business. Here the organisation is likely to be diverse in terms of both products and geographical markets. It may be that they have a range of different types of business in the form of subsidiary companies within a holding company structure, or divisions within a multidivisional structure. Therefore, issues of structure and control at the corporate level and relationships between businesses and the corporate centre are usually a major strategic issue for multinational companies. Indeed, a central concern is the extent to which the corporate centre adds to or detracts from the value of its businesses (see Chapters 6 and 9). At the business unit level, many of the competitive strategic issues will, perhaps, be similar to those faced by smaller firms – though the strength of the multinational within a given geographical area may be greater than for any small firm. However, for the multinational parent company, a significant issue will be how corporate business units should be allocated resources given their different, and often competing, demands and how this is to be coordinated. The coordination of operational logistics across different business units and different countries may become especially important. For example, a multinational manufacturing company such as Toyota or General Motors has to decide on the most sensible configuration of plants for the manufacture of cars. Most have moved from manufacturing a particular car at a particular location, and now manufacture different parts of cars in different locations, bringing together such components for the assembly of a given model in a given location. The logistics problems of coordinating such operations are immense, requiring sophisticated control systems and management skills far removed from those in the smaller firm. An important choice that a major multinational has to make is the extent to which it controls such logistics centrally, or devolves autonomy to operating units. It is, again, an issue of structure, management processes and relationships – the subject of Chapter 9 of this book.

1.4.3 Manufacturing and service organisations

Whilst differences exist between organisations providing services and those providing products, there is also an increasing awareness of similarities. For an organisation that competes on the basis of the services it provides – for example, insurance, management consultancy and professional services – there is no physical product. Here competitive advantage is likely to be much more related to the extent to which customers value less tangible aspects of the firm. This could be, for example, the soundness of advice given, the attitude of staff, the ambience of offices, the swiftness of service and so on. For manufacturing organisations the physical product itself has been regarded as central to competitive strategy and services are needed simply to support the product (such as product information, back-up service and so on). Managers in manufacturing organisations may therefore believe they exercise more direct control over competitive strategy than can be exercised in a service organisation. However, the computer hardware industry demonstrates that in a competitive commodity-like world the physical products of competitors are very similar, and competing by providing more functionality (storage and processor speed) fails to win new customers. Increasingly it is service that determines the winners – speed to market with new products, simplicity of the ordering process and effective helpline support make the difference. So, most have come to understand that, since physical products are often perceived by customers as very similar, other features such as service or brand image are just as important in achieving competitive advantage. Bases of competitive advantage related to resources, organisational competences and value to customers are discussed in Chapters 4 and 6.

1.4.4 The innovatory organisation[13]

There are an increasing number of organisations that claim to depend substantially on innovation for their strategic success, and still others that argue the importance of becoming more innovatory. Certainly businesses in the field of high technology products or those dependent on research and development, for example in the pharmaceutical industry, have long experienced the extent to which innovation is important. Innovation is seen as the ability to 'change the rules of the game'. The rapid developments in information technology have thrown up opportunities for organisations that can do business in new ways – the dot.com companies of the e-commerce revolution. The success of all these innovatory organisations is likely to be built on a willingness to challenge the status quo in an industry or a market and an awareness of how the organisation's resources and competences can be 'stretched' to create new opportunities. The need to see and act strategically against very short time horizons is another key feature of the innovatory context. Although the same strategic issues exist as with other companies, it is unlikely to be the formal procedures that matter so much as the type and quality of the people, the sources of knowledge in the organisation and the extent to which the prevailing culture encourages the transfer of knowledge and the questioning of what is taken for granted. Innovation will also be influenced by how people are managed and how they interact. For example, organisational structures that encourage interaction and integration, rather than formal divisions of responsibility, may encourage innovation.

Although the ideas lens is especially important in understanding strategy in innovatory organisations, there has been evidence that some of the difficulties of the dot.coms has been a failure to look at their development in other ways – particularly through the design lens – for example, to understand some of the basic ideas about competition and strategic capability.

1.4.5 Strategy in the public sector[14]

The concepts of strategy and strategic management are just as important in the public sector as in commercial firms. However, like the private sector, the public sector is diverse, as some examples show.

- *Nationalised companies* may be similar in many respects to commercial organisations; the differences are associated with the nature of ownership and control. Postal services in many countries are in, or moving towards, this position. There is likely to be a good deal of direct or indirect control or influence exercised from outside the organisation, by government in particular. A commercial enterprise that is state controlled may find not only planning horizons determined more by political than by market conditions, but also constraints on investment capital and therefore on bases of financing, and on the latitude that managers have to change strategies. It is for these reasons that there has been large-scale privatisation of previously state-run enterprises over the past 20 years – steel, telecommunications, rail services, airlines and many more. Understanding the power of different stakeholders (Chapter 5) and constraints on change (see Chapters 2 and 11) may be especially important here.

- A *government agency* has a labour market, and a money market of sorts; it also has suppliers and users or customers. However, at its heart lies a political market that approves budgets and provides subsidies. It is the explicit nature of this political dimension which managers – or officers – have to cope with which particularly distinguishes government bodies, be they national or local, from commercial enterprises. This may in turn change the horizons of decisions, since they may be heavily influenced by political considerations, and may mean that analysis of strategies requires the norms of political dogma to be considered explicitly. However, although the magnitude of the political dimension is greater, the model of strategic management discussed here still holds.

- *Public service* organisations – for example, health services and many of the amenities run by local government – face difficulties from a strategic point of view because they may not be allowed to specialise, and may not be able to generate surpluses from their services to invest in development. This can lead to a mediocrity of service where strategic decisions mainly take the form of striving for more and more efficiency so as to retain or improve services on limited budgets. Careful deployment and appropriate development of resources becomes very important (see Chapters 4 and 10).

- In the public sector, the notion of competition is usually concerned with competition for *resource inputs*, typically within a political arena. The need to demonstrate *best value* in *outputs* has become increasingly important. Many of the developments in management practices in the public sector, such as internal markets, performance indicators, competitive tendering and so on, were attempts to introduce elements of competition in order to encourage improvements in value for money. More recently there has been a shift of emphasis to cooperation and inter-agency working in an attempt to address *outcomes* of social importance. Examples would be tackling the drugs problem, crime and disorder or mental health, all of which require cooperative efforts to improve outcomes. This means that being able to build and sustain strategic alliances is a priority – as discussed in Chapter 8.

- Overall, the role of ideology in the development of strategy in the public sector is probably greater than that in commercial organisations. Putting it in the terminology of this book, the criterion of *acceptability to stakeholders* of strategic choices is probably of greater significance in the public sector than in the commercial sector.

1.4.6 The voluntary and not-for-profit sectors[15]

In the voluntary sector it is likely that underlying values and ideology will be of central strategic significance and play an important part in the development of strategy. This is particularly the case where the *raison d'être* of the organisation is rooted in such values, as is the case with organisations providing services traditionally not for profit, such as charities.

In not-for-profit organisations such as charities, churches, private schools, foundations and so on, the sources of funds may be diverse and are quite likely not to be direct beneficiaries of the services offered. Moreover, they may provide funds in advance of the services being offered – in the form of grants, for example. There are several implications. Influence from funding bodies may be high in terms of the formulation of organisational strategies. Competition may be high for funds from such bodies; but the principles of competitive strategy (see Chapter 7) nonetheless hold. However, since such organisations are dependent on funds which emanate not from users but from sponsors, there is a danger that they may become concerned more with resource efficiency than with service effectiveness (see Chapter 4). The fact that multiple sources of funding are likely to exist, linked to the different objectives and expectations of the funding bodies, might also lead to a high incidence of political lobbying, difficulties in clear strategic planning, and a requirement to hold decision making and responsibility at the centre, where it is answerable to external influences, rather than delegate it within the organisation.

1.4.7 Professional service organisations

Traditionally based values are often of particular importance in professional services such as medicine, accountancy, law and other professions. Private sector professional firms may also have a partnership structure. Partners may be owners and perhaps bear legal responsibility for advice and opinion offered by the firm; they may therefore carry considerable power; and there may be many of them – each of the top four accountancy firms now aspires to global strategies, but each may have thousands of partners. Traditionally, although interacting with clients and exercising actual or potential control over resources, these partners may not have regarded themselves as managers at all. As a partner in a major accountancy firm put it: 'We see ourselves as the largest network of sole traders in the world.' The problems of developing and implementing strategy within such a context are, therefore, heavily linked to the management of internal political influences (see Chapter 5) and the ability to take account of, and where necessary to change, organisational culture (see Chapters 5 and 11). Another factor is the pressure that those in the professions find themselves under to be more 'commercial' in their approach. Such pressure may come from government, as in the case of doctors; or it may be a function of size, as has been found in the growing accountancy and law firms. This has meant that

Illustration 1.4

Strategic issues in different contexts

The strategic issues faced by managers in different organisations depend on their business context.

Global organisations

Many companies today are struggling to achieve a globally integrated organisation that retains the capability for local flexibility and responsiveness. Virtually no company has achieved a totally satisfactory solution. . . . The task is achievable if managers break it down into digestible pieces and if they relate changes in organisation to the specific changes in global strategy.

> G. Yip, *Total Global Strategy*,
> Prentice Hall, 1995, pp. 161–162

A multi-business company

The business units of multi-business companies create value through direct contact with customers. They compete in their markets to satisfy customer needs and to generate revenues and profits. In contrast the parent [company] . . . acts as an intermediary influencing the decisions and strategies pursued by the businesses and standing between the businesses and those who provide capital for their use.

> M. Goold, A. Campbell and M. Alexander,
> *Corporate Level Strategy*, Wiley, 1994, p. 12

Professional services

The players [in accountancy] are broadly similar in size and in their range of resources, consequently there is no natural leader to direct and structure the market. Even where the professional offerings are similar . . . the ability to co-ordinate and integrate people to create a real benefit for the client can be a distinguishing factor. The result is that teamwork, relationship management and integration are the competences that may distinguish one firm from the pack.

> Colin Sharman, Senior Partner,
> KPMG, 1998

Not-for-profit sector

If your mission is, say, to eliminate poverty or save the planet, then almost anything you do can be justified. If management is weak and without legitimacy (which is too often the case), this means staff often set their own personal agendas. To a greater extent than most private organisations, there are also multiple stakeholders, and managers can find themselves buffeted by warring factions both outside and inside the organisation. Young staff often join with a view that they are going to change the world, and find out that many jobs are pretty routine. There is a great danger that they then invest their energy in trying to create their vision of the world within the organisation.

> Sheila McKechnie, Director of
> Shelter until 1995

Public sector

Efficient and effective public services are an essential part of a healthy democratic society. Many local authorities recognise this and successfully achieve high standards, often in difficult circumstances. Others are less successful, and provide services that fall well short of the best that can be achieved within the resources that are available. The Government's proposals for best value . . . will require councils to meet the aspirations of local people for the highest quality and most efficient services at a price that people are willing to pay.

> 'Modernising Local Government',
> DETR, 1998, p. 5

Question

Refer to Exhibit 1.4 and answer the following question separately *in relation to each of the contexts*:

Which element of the strategy model is being emphasised? Why?

such organisations have had to be concerned with competitive strategy (see Chapter 7).

Illustration 1.4 shows some examples of the different emphasis of strategy in different contexts.

SUMMARY

- Strategy is the *direction* and *scope* of an organisation over the *long term*, which achieves *advantage* for the organisation through its configuration of *resources* within a changing *environment* and to fulfil *stakeholder* expectations. So all organisations are faced with the challenge of managing strategy.

- Strategic decisions may be about a search for strategic 'fit' – trying to find ways to match the organisation's resources and activities to the environment in which it operates. Strategic decisions could also be based on trying to 'stretch' the resources and competences of the organisation to create new opportunities.

- Strategies will also be influenced by the values and expectations of stakeholders in and around the organisation, and the extent of the power they exert. The culture within and around an organisation will also influence its strategy.

- Strategic decisions are made at a number of levels in organisations. Corporate-level strategy is concerned with an organisation's overall purpose and scope; business level (or competitive) strategy with how to compete successfully in a market; and operational strategies with how resources, processes and people can effectively deliver corporate- and business-level strategies.

- The formulation of business-level strategies is best thought of in terms of strategic business units (SBUs) which are parts of organisations for which there are distinct external markets for goods or services. However, these may not represent formal structural divisions in an organisation.

- Strategic management is distinguished from day-to-day operational management by the complexity of influences on decisions, the fundamental, organisation-wide implications that strategic decisions have for the organisation, and their long-term implications. It can be problematic for managers not least because their strategic horizons are likely to be limited by their experience and organisational culture and most of their training may have been in operational management.

- Strategic management can be conceived of in terms of understanding the *strategic position*, *strategic choices* for the future and translating *strategy into action*. The strategic position of an organisation is influenced by the external environment, internal resources and competences, and the expectations and influence of stakeholders. Strategic choices include the underlying bases of choices at both the corporate and business levels and the directions and methods of development. Strategic management is also concerned with understanding which choices are likely to succeed or fail. Translating strategy into action is concerned with issues of structuring, resourcing to enable future strategies and managing change.

- How organisations develop strategies can be explained in different ways. A design view sees the process as planned from the top. An experience view sees it as the product of individual experience and organisational culture. The ideas view sees strategy as emerging from ideas within and around an organisation.

- Organisations in different contexts are likely to emphasise different aspects of the strategic management process. For some organisations the major challenge will be developing competitive strategy; for others it will be building organisational structures capable of integrating complex global operations; for yet others it will be understanding their competences so as to focus on what they are especially good at; and for still others it will be developing a culture of innovation. Strategic priorities need to be understood in terms of the particular context of an organisation.

RECOMMENDED KEY READINGS

It is useful to read about how strategies are managed in practice and some of the lessons that can be drawn from this which inform key themes in this book. For example:

- For readings on the concepts of strategy in organisations, John Kay's book, *Foundations for Corporate Success: How business strategies add value*, Oxford University Press, 1993, is a helpful explanation from an economics point of view. For a wider theoretical perspective, see R. Whittington, *What is Strategy and Does it Matter?*, 2nd edition, Routledge, 2001.

- It is also useful to read accounts of where the management of strategy in organisations has made an impact on organisational performance. Reference is also often made in this book to G. Hamel and C.K. Prahalad, *Competing for the Future*, Harvard Business School Press, 1994, which draws extensively on examples of successful strategies in organisations. Readers are encouraged to keep up to date with developments and strategies in organisations through newspapers, business magazines and dedicated business websites (such as FT.com).

- For a discussion of strategy in different types of organisations, see H. Mintzberg, J. Quinn and S. Ghoshal (eds), *The Strategy Process: Concepts, contexts and cases*, 4th edition, Prentice Hall, 1998.

REFERENCES

1. In the 1980s much of the writing and practice of strategic management was influenced by the writings of industrial organisations economists. One of the most influential books was Michael Porter, *Competitive Strategy*, Free Press, first published 1980. In essence, the book describes means of analysing the competitive nature of industries so that managers might be able to select among attractive and less attractive industries and choose strategies most suited to the organisation in terms of these forces. This approach, which assumes the dominant influence of industry forces and the over-riding need to tailor strategies to address those forces, has become known as a 'fit' view of strategy.

2. The notion of strategy as 'stretch' is perhaps best explained in G. Hamel and C.K. Prahalad, *Competing for the Future*, Harvard Business School Press, 1994.

3. The term 'SBU' can be traced back to the development of corporate-level strategic planning in General Electric in the USA in the early 1970s. For an early account of its uses, see W.K. Hall, 'SBUs: hot, new topic in the management of diversification', *Business Horizons*, vol. 21, no. 1 (1978), pp. 17–25.

4. See for example: C. Christensen, K. Andrews and J. Bower, *Business Policy: Text and cases*, 4th edition, Irwin, 1978.

5. For example, J. Argenti, *Systematic Corporate Planning*, Nelson, 1974 or H. Ansoff, *Corporate Strategy*, Penguin, 1975.

6. One of the important books that marked this shift was: D. Schendel and C. Hofer, *Strategic Management: A new view of business policy and planning*, Little, Brown, 1979.

7. See: C. Lindblom, 'The science of muddling through', *Public Administration Review*, vol. 19 (Spring 1959), pp. 79–88; J. Quinn, *Strategies for Change*, Irwin, 1980; A. Pettigrew, *The Awakening Giant*, Blackwell, 1985; H. Mintzberg, 'Crafting strategy', *Harvard Business Review*, vol. 65, no. 4 (1987), pp. 66–75.

8. See Quinn (reference 7 above).

9. See: R. Stacey, *Managing Chaos: Dynamic business strategies in an unpredictable world*, Kogan Page, 1992; S. Brown and K. Eisenhardt, *Competing on the Edge: Strategy as structured chaos*, HBR Press, 1998.

10. For an extensive discussion of strategy in different types of organisations, see H. Mintzberg, J. Quinn and S. Ghoshal (eds), *The Strategy Process: Concepts, contexts and cases*, 4th edition, Prentice Hall, 1998.

11. For strategy development in small businesses, see C. Barrow, R. Brown and L. Clarke, *The Business Growth Handbook*, Kogan Page, 1995.

12. There are now many books on managing strategy in multinationals. In this book we will refer often to C. Bartlett and S. Ghoshall, *Managing Across Borders: The transnational solution*, 2nd edition, Random House, 1998; and G. Yip, *Total Global Strategy*, Prentice Hall, 1995.

13. A good review of aspects of innovation and their organisational implications can be found in J. Tidd, J. Bessant and K. Pavitt, *Managing Innovations: Integrating technological, marketing and organisational change*, 2nd edition, Wiley, 2001.

14. See: G. Johnson and K. Scholes (eds.), *Exploring Public Sector Strategy*, FT/Prentice Hall, 2001, in particular J. Alford, 'The implications of publicness for strategic management theory' (Chapter 1) and N. Collier, F. Fisnwick and G. Johnson, 'The processes of strategy development in the public sector' (Chapter 2). Also: D. McKevitt and A. Lawton, *Public Sector Management: Theory, critique and practice*, Sage, 1994.

15. See J.M. Bryson, *Strategic Planning for Public and Nonprofit Organizations*, Prentice Hall, 1995.

WORK ASSIGNMENTS

* Refers to a case study in the Text and Cases edition. ✳ Denotes more advanced work assignments.

1.1 Using the characteristics discussed in section 1.1.1, write out a statement of strategy for Corus* or an organisation with which you are familiar.

1.2 Note down the characteristics of strategy development at AOL/Time Warner, or Microsoft/Netscape which would be explained by the notion of (a) strategic management as 'environmental fit', and (b) strategic management as the 'stretching' of capabilities.

1.3 Using Exhibit 1.2 and Illustration 1.2 as a guide, note down and explain examples of the vocabulary of strategy used in the annual report of a company of your choosing.

1.4✳ Using annual reports, press articles and the Internet, write a brief case study (similar to the AOL/Time Warner illustration or the Corus* case), which shows the strategic development and current strategic position of an organisation.

1.5 Using Exhibit 1.4 as a guide, note down the elements of strategic management discernible in the Corus* case or an organisation of your choice.

1.6✳ Using Exhibit 1.4 as a guide, show how the different elements of strategic management differ in:

(a) a multinational business (e.g. AOL/Time Warner, The News Corporation*)
(b) a professional services firm (e.g. KPMG*)
(c) a public sector organisation (e.g. CSA*)
(d) a small business (e.g. Coopers Creek*)
(e) a high technology business (e.g. Microsoft, Netscape, Amazon* or Freeserve*).

CASE EXAMPLE

Battle of the browsers: rounds one and two

In June 2000 a federal court judge upheld the US Justice Department's contention that the Microsoft Corporation was guilty of breaking the law by using its monopoly to stifle competition and crush its rivals. The court stated that Microsoft had violated anti-trust laws by using its position to monopolise the web browser market. They were accused of imposing 'technological shackles' on other software companies. The company was ordered to be split into two separate businesses – one owning the 'Windows' operating system and the other owning software applications and Internet browser developments. The company's shares had fallen by 50 per cent during the court hearings and Bill Gates, the Microsoft chairman, warned that this ruling would lead to disaster for Microsoft and America and immediately indicated that the company would appeal against the decision.

The seeds of the court case started some six years earlier in 1994 when Marc Andreesen, a 24-year-old from Silicon Valley, launched a new way to search and retrieve information from the Internet. His company Netscape invented the Navigator Internet browser. The world's press hailed the arrival of a cyber-genius, and predicted he would create a new computer standard that could make him as powerful as Bill Gates. Netscape grabbed 80 per cent of the booming browser market. It began building intranets, providing systems for companies to create their own web-like networks. It became the platform and promoter of Sun Microsystem's Java, a new software language that challenged Microsoft's Windows operating system for personal computers (PCs). When Netscape was listed on the stock market in August 1995 its shares took off like a rocket. Before the company had made a net profit it was valued at $2.7 billion (£1.7 billion).

Gates initially dismissed the Internet and Netscape as unimportant. But Netscape's surging sales, and the phenomenal growth and popularity of the Internet, quickly forced him to change his tune. Marshalling the vast resources of Microsoft, and spending hundreds of millions of dollars on research and development, he had 2,000 of his best programmers rush out a browser of his own, the Explorer, and then bombarded the public with free copies. Microsoft's share of the browser market soared from 2.9 per cent at the end of 1995 to more than 40 per cent by the end of 1997, while Netscape's share fell to 54 per cent. Netscape's financial performance suffered badly too. Some analysts believed that the company might be in terminal decline and might not be able to survive – at least as an independent company.

So Netscape looked for help from the US Justice Department, which in October 1997 charged Microsoft with using its monopolistic 90 per cent control of all PC operating systems to force computer manufacturers to install its browser on their machines. In December, Judge Thomas Jackson issued a preliminary injunction to force Microsoft to make available two versions of Windows to PC manufacturers, one including the browser and one without. The Justice Department wanted Microsoft to remove the Explorer icon that automatically appeared on the computer screen when a user started the Windows programme. Microsoft denied it used unfair business practices, and claimed that it was simply exercising its right to enhance its operating system. It said that an Internet browser was an integral part of its Windows software.

But Microsoft realised they were playing for big stakes. In May 1995, Bill Gates wrote: 'The Internet is the most important single development to come along since the IBM PC was introduced in 1981. It has enough users that it is benefiting from the positive feedback loop of the more users it gets, the more content it gets; and the more content it gets, the more users it gets.' He went on to say that it presented a huge threat to Microsoft, because rival companies, such as Netscape and Sun, were trying to use it to 'commoditise the underlying operating system'. In other words, Netscape might gain control of the desktop with its browser becoming an alternative to Windows.

This first battle of the browsers also brought to the surface some fundamental policy issues for governments about the fostering of technological development. It was a reminder that free-market forces do not necessarily guarantee the success of the best product in high-technology fields, as they usually do in other areas of commerce. Whenever a company gets ahead (in high technology) it had an increasing advantage over its rivals, made increasing returns, and was able to use its position to dominate other markets. So many 'inferior products' had beaten superior ones, such as the VHS video beating Betamax and Dos beating Apple's operating system. So the critical issue was to establish a user base more quickly than competitors. The more people that used a given technology, the more likely that technology was to beat its competitors. In the computer industry the first company to establish an industry standard and a large installed base of products invariably dominated its market, as Microsoft dominated PC operating systems. Moreover, it puts it in a position to expand into other markets and dominate them in the same way.

Microsoft was dismissive of such theories, which they claimed missed the realities in the computer industry. In particular the fact that life cycles were short and leaders vulnerable to their products being made obsolete by superior products from competitors. They argued that there were many examples of great successes that became failures, such as Word Perfect, dBase, Lotus 1-2-3, and it was simply to do with people taking their eye off the ball.

As the legal proceedings rolled on through 1999 and 2000 developments in browsers moved on at a rapid pace – in ways that perhaps made the court hearings look like 'yesterday's battle'. A new browser war was under way as software firms started to compete to provide browsers for 'information devices' such as set-top boxes (e.g. for digital cable or satellite TV), handheld computers and third-generation ('smart') mobile phones. These devices were widely expected to eventually out-number PCs. This second browser battle was shaping up very differently from the first one. The main difference being that Microsoft's ability to include browser software as part of the device's operating systems (as it could do with Windows on PCs) was no longer the case. Their cut-down version of Windows for these devices had failed. In the meantime Netscape had become part of AOL and was strongly in the running – but alongside dozens of new rivals such as Opera, OpenTV, Lineo, QNX and Plixo. Also, with these new devices the choice of browser was made by the appliance manufacturer and the service provider (such as the cable company) rather than, in the case of PCs, by the operating system supplier (Microsoft) or the individual user (downloading from the Internet). So the new rivals were courting the appliance manufacturers and service providers rather than targeting consumers. With so many potential suppliers it seemed much less likely that just one browser would dominate. Also, this resulting diversity meant that an important selling point for a browser was its conformity to the technical standards agreed by the World Wide Web Consortium. The existence of these standards would also reduce the switching costs for appliance makers if they decided to change browsers – a very difficult thing to achieve with the old browsers on PCs. Netscape seemed to have learnt lessons from its bruising encounter with Microsoft in the first browser battle. It was actively supporting these standardisation measures as a means of preventing a re-run – even though it left Netscape's new software (Gecko) facing more competitors.

Sources: Adapted from *The Sunday Times*, 11 January 1998; *The Economist*, 16 December 2000.

Questions

1. Refer to section 1.1 and explain why the issues facing Netscape and Microsoft were strategic.

2. List the main factors that you would identify in the strategic position of Netscape and Microsoft (separately and under the three headings of environment, resources and expectations).

3. Think about the strategic choices for the future for each company in relation to the issues raised in section 1.2.2.

4. This case example concerns global competition in an innovative industry. Refer to section 1.3 and decide how this particular context 'shapes' the relative importance of the elements of strategy – as shown in Exhibit 1.4.

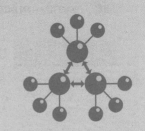

2

Understanding Strategy Development

2.1 INTRODUCTION

In Chapter 1 strategy was defined. This chapter provides explanations of how strategies come about in organisations. There are different explanations of this and these are discussed in terms of the three 'lenses' – or ways of seeing things – introduced in Chapter 1 (section 1.3), which employ and build on different organisational theories in order to enable the reader to consider strategy development processes critically.

| Exhibit 2.1 | Understanding strategy development |

How strategy development can be seen
THREE STRATEGY LENSES
Strategy as *design*
Strategy as *experience*
Strategy as *ideas*

How strategy development processes can be understood
Strategic planning systems
Strategic leadership
Organisational politics
Logical incrementalism
The learning organisation
Imposed strategy

Implications for strategy development
Intended and realised strategy
Strategic drift
Strategic management in uncertainty and complexity

Exhibit 2.1 summarises the structure of the chapter, and begins with the different lenses.

- First the *design* lens, the idea that strategy is formulated by top management through careful analysis and planning and implemented down through the organisation.

- Next the *experience* lens is discussed. This section draws on research which shows how strategic decisions are made and strategies develop as the outcome of people's *experience and cultural processes* in and around organisations.

- The next section examines the *ideas* lens: how quite new strategies can be explained, why some organisations are more innovative than others and why and how some organisations seem to cope with a fast-changing environment better than others.

Following a discussion of these three lenses, they are employed to shed light on strategy development processes evident in organisations. These processes include *planning*, *strategic leadership* (which encapsulates *entrepreneurial* processes and strategic *vision*), *political processes*, *logical incrementalism*, the idea of the *learning organisation* and that strategy might be *imposed* on organisations. In fact, it is rare to find organisations in which singular explanations are adequate to explain strategic decision making and strategy development: multiple explanations of strategy development are usually evident in organisations and these are illustrated at the end of this part.

The final part of the chapter builds on this review of processes to raise some *implications for strategy development.*

- The differences between formal planning resulting in *intended strategy* and *realised strategy* arising from emergent strategy development processes are considered and the implications discussed.

- Patterns of strategy development are also discussed, showing the ways in which strategies are observed to develop over time in organisations. The conclusion is that strategic changes may take different forms, but do not usually occur as major, one-off changes in direction. Rather, they are more gradual, incremental developments, with only occasional, more 'transformational' change. This is explained in relation to the previous discussion in the chapter. There is then a discussion as to why there is a tendency in organisations for *strategic drift*, in which strategies lose touch with the changing environment of the organisation.

- The final part of this section considers the appropriateness of the different lenses and different processes of strategy development in relation to the environmental *context of organisations*; in particular, how different approaches to strategy development may be more or less well suited to *stable, dynamic or complex* environments.

The *summary* at the end of the chapter draws together the lessons from the chapter and briefly discusses implications for the structure and content of this book.

2.2 THE STRATEGY LENSES

Most people make sense of complex situations in more than one way. Think of everyday conversations or discussions. It is not unusual for people to say: 'But if you look at it this way. . . .' It is useful to take more than one view of an issue, especially if it is complex. Taking one view can lead to a partial and perhaps biased understanding. A fuller picture, which might give different options or solutions, can be gained from viewing the issue in terms of multiple perspectives or, as employed here, through different lenses. This part of the chapter considers how the development and management of strategy can be viewed through the lenses of *design, experience and ideas*.[1]

2.2.1 Strategy as design

Tutors often start a strategy course by asking students what they mean by 'strategic management'. Typically the first few characteristics that come back from the class are: 'planning', 'setting objectives', 'analysis' and maybe 'evaluating options'. These are words associated with a *design* view of strategy.[2] Stated more fully, the assumptions underpinning a design approach to strategy development are these:

- Although the range of influences on an organisation's performance are many, they can be understood through careful analysis such as to identify those which are most likely to influence the organisation significantly. It may even be possible to forecast, predict or build scenarios about future impacts such that managers can think through the conditions in which their organisation is likely to operate. Strategy development is therefore seen as a process of systematic thinking and reasoning.

- This analysis permits the matching of organisational strengths and resources with the changes in the environment of the organisation so as to take advantage of opportunities and overcome or circumvent threats. The strategy of an organisation is, therefore, the result of decisions made about the positioning and repositioning of the organisation in terms of its strengths in relation to its markets and the forces affecting it in its wider environment.

- This analytic thinking precedes and governs action. So decisions about what the strategy should be in terms of its content come first and are cascaded down through the organisation to those who have to make things happen. Decisions about what the strategy should be are therefore separate from the implementation of that strategy.

- It is the responsibility of management – more specifically, top management – to plan the destiny of the organisation. So an assumption here is that an organisation is a hierarchy with top management who make important decisions, and lower levels of management, and eventually the population of the organisation, who carry out these decisions.

- All this is done logically. Objectives are clear and probably explicit, there is careful and thorough analysis of the factors internal and external to the organisation that might affect its future and inform management about the strategic position of the organisation, and a range of options for future strategic direction are considered and evaluated in terms of the objectives and the forces at work on the organisation. A strategic decision is then made on the basis of what is considered to be optimal, given all these considerations; and its implementation is planned in terms of how it will be cascaded down through the various functions and levels of the organisation.

- There are tools and techniques which enable managers to understand the nature and impact of the environment an organisation faces, the particular competences of that organisation, the influence of power within and around the organisation, the organisational culture and its links to strategy, the strategic choices an organisation has available to it, how decisions can be put into effect through project planning, and so on. In this book we explain many of them and discuss their usefulness.

- Associated assumptions are that since the complexity organisations face can be understood in this analytic way, logical conclusions will be reached by a rational group of top managers and people in the organisation will accept the consequent logic. The organisation is, then, seen as a rational system.

- This system can be controlled in a rational way too. The structure of the organisation should be suited to the strategy to be followed; and the various control systems, including budgets, variance analysis, management by objectives and so on will facilitate the control of strategic direction by providing means by which top management can assess whether or not others in the organisation are meeting expected objectives and behaving in line with the strategy.

Illustration 2.1 shows how such assumptions may take form; and Exhibit 2.2 shows data from a survey[3] which asked managers to report on how they saw strategies developing in their organisations. It shows that features of the design approach are seen as being present. However, it also shows that this differs in some important ways. For example, it differs by level of manager; and there are differences by context, with managers in more stable environments seeing more evidence of design than those in more uncertain environments. This perception of design processes managing strategy can be explained in a number of ways.

- First and most obvious is that objective setting, planning systems and the use of analytic and evaluative tools are found in most organisations. So there are visible signs of the design lens. However, the fact that such systems are present does not necessarily mean that they are actually the way in which strategy is managed (see below). There are other reasons why managers may perceive design as the means of strategy development.

- The design lens also provides the basis of an approach to managing complexity which is logical and structured. In this sense it helps provide a means of coping with such complexity.

- However, a third reason is to do with the desire to feel in control. Quite understandably managers, particularly CEOs, need to feel in control of the complex and often challenging situations they face. The assumptions, tools and techniques of design provide them with ways in which they can feel in control.

- Rationality is also deeply rooted in our way of thinking and in our systems of education over the past two thousand years. In this sense the design lens is deeply embedded in our human psyche. So, for example, even when managers do not report that strategy is actually developed in ways the design lens suggests, they often think it should be.

- It should be added, however, that managers typically do see other explanations. The elements of design are seen by them as *one* explanation, not as *the* explanation of how strategies develop in their organisations.

In summary, then, the **design lens** views strategy development as the deliberate positioning of the organisation through a rational, analytic, structured and directive process. The big question is whether this is an accurate or sufficient portrayal of strategic management. This book argues that the design lens is useful but not sufficient. Other explanations help a fuller understanding of the practice of strategic management and provide insights into how the complexity of strategic management can be handled.

The **design lens** views strategy development as the deliberate positioning of the organisation through a rational, analytic, structured and directive process

Illustration 2.1

The Management Charter Initiative (MCI)

STRATEGY IN ACTION

The strategic management competences identified by organisations often emphasise planning, analysis, evaluation and control.

After independent reports suggested that UK companies needed to be better at management development, the MCI was established in 1988. It was a system of management competence standards, and was the combined idea of the Confederation of British Industry, the British Institute of Management, and several companies, including Shell and BP. Its highly structured format identified competences that were required by managers.

The following is an extract from Strategic Management Level 5:

- *External and internal operating environments* involves reviewing your organisation's external operating environment, evaluating your competitors and potential partners, developing good relationships with your organisation's stakeholders, and reviewing your organisation's structures and systems.

- *Establish strategies to guide the work of your organisation* is about strategic planning. It involves helping to create a shared vision and mission to guide the work of your organisation, helping to define its policies and values, formulating objectives and strategies, and gaining support for the strategies you are proposing.

- *Evaluate and improve organisational performance* is about managing the strategic performance and achieving necessary improvements. This involves developing measures and criteria to evaluate your organisation's performance, carrying out evaluations, and finding the reasons for success and failure in your organisation's strategy.

- *Secure financial resources for your organisation's plans* covers examining the way your organisation generates and allocates financial resources, evaluating proposals from others on expenditure, and obtaining the financial resources which your organisation needs.

- *Enhance your own performance* is about continuously developing your own knowledge and skills and optimising your use of your time and other resources so that you can meet your objectives.

- *Enhance productive working relationships* is about enhancing relationships with your managers and other colleagues. It involves providing guidance on your organisation's values and how to work in accordance with these values.

- *Develop management teams* is about improving the performance of your management team. This involves analysing the strengths and weaknesses of your team and its members, and then taking steps to improve your teams effectiveness.

- *Delegate work to others*. It involves giving responsibility and authority for substantial pieces of work – whole programmes of work, part programmes of work and important one-off tasks – to others. It also covers agreeing with them the targets they need to achieve, advising and supporting them in what they do, and promoting and protecting them and their planned activities.

- *Chair and participate in meetings* is about leading and contributing to meetings so that the objectives of the meetings can be achieved.

- *Use information to take critical decisions* covers obtaining relevant information, analysing this information and taking decisions which are critical to your organisation's performance. It also covers advising and informing other people.

Source: Management Standards, courtesy of the Management Standards Unit. This material is Crown Copyright © and is reproduced under licence from the Controller of Her Majesty's Stationery Office. All rights reserved.

Questions

1. How do the MCI competences correspond to the explanation of the design lens?

2. Using the explanations of the experience and ideas lenses, suggest ways in which these competences may not be sufficient.

Exhibit 2.2	Managers' perceptions of elements of the design lens

Perceptions that there exists:	LEVEL IN ORGANISATION		ENVIRONMENTAL STABILITY	
	CEO	Middle management	Higher	Lower
Precision of objectives	Yes	No	Yes	No
Detailed planning	Yes	No	Yes	No
Systematic analysis of environment	Yes	No	Yes	–
Careful evaluation of strategic options	Yes	No	–	–

These findings are based on a survey of perceptions of strategy development processes undertaken at Cranfield School of Management in the 1990s. The findings indicate statistically significant differences.

2.2.2 Strategy as experience

Since strategy is about the long-term direction of an organisation, it is understandable that it might be thought of in terms of major decisions about the future taken at a point in time at the top of the organisation and resulting in one-off major changes. However, much of the evidence from research carried out into how strategies develop in organisations gives a different picture. It suggests that, more typically, strategies develop in an *adaptive* fashion building on the existing strategy and changing gradually. Strategy is better understood in terms of continuity, or 'momentum':[4] once an organisation has adopted a particular strategy, it tends to develop from and within that strategy, rather than fundamentally changing direction.

An apparently coherent strategy of an organisation may not be pre-planned in some grand fashion. It can develop on the basis of a series of strategic moves each of which makes sense in terms of previous moves. Perhaps a product launch, or a significant investment decision, establishes a strategic direction which, itself, guides decisions on the next strategic move – an acquisition perhaps. This in turn helps consolidate the strategic direction, and over time the overall strategic approach of the organisation becomes more established. As time goes on, each move is informed by this developing pattern of strategy and, in turn, reinforces it. Exhibit 2.3 shows this. This could, of course, lead to a quite significant shift in strategy, but *incrementally*. In many respects, such gradual change makes a lot of sense. No organisation could function effectively if it were to undergo major revisions of strategy frequently; and, in any case, whilst change occurs in the environment, it is unlikely that it will be so great that this would be necessary. In a positive sense, incremental change could therefore be seen as adaptation to the opportunities which arise in a continually changing environment. However, it can also be seen as heavily influenced by experience. The **experience lens** views strategy development as the outcome of individual and collective experience of individuals and the taken-for-granted assumptions most obviously represented by cultural influences.

The **experience lens** views strategy development as the outcome of individual and collective experience of individuals and the taken-for-granted assumptions

---

| Exhibit 2.3 | **Strategic direction from prior decisions** |

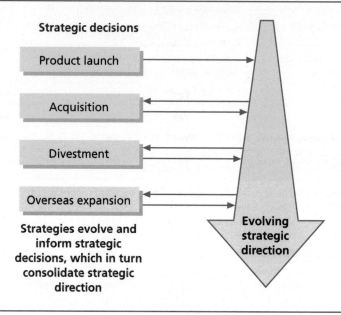

Strategic decisions

Product launch

Acquisition

Divestment

Overseas expansion

Strategies evolve and inform strategic decisions, which in turn consolidate strategic direction

Evolving strategic direction

Experience and bias

Human beings are able to function effectively not least because they have the cognitive capability to make sense of problems or issues they come across. They recognise and make sense of problems and issues on the basis of past experience and what they come to believe to be true about the world. More formally, **individual experience** can be explained in terms of the mental (or cognitive) models people build over time to help make sense of their situation. Managers are no exception to this. When they face a problem they make sense of it in terms of the mental models which are the basis of their experience.[5] This has major advantages. It means they are able to relate such problems to prior events and therefore have comparisons to draw upon. It means they can interpret one issue in the light of another; they therefore have bases for making decisions based on prior experience. If they did not have such mental models they could not function effectively; they would meet each situation as though they were experiencing it for the first time.

There are, however, downsides to this. The same mental models, the same experience, can lead to bias. People, managers included, make sense of new issues in the context of past issues; they are likely to address a problem in much the same way as they dealt with a previous one seen as similar. Moreover, they are likely to search for evidence which supports those inclinations. So some data will be seen as more important than other data and some may not be taken on board at all. For example, a profit downturn in a business might be interpreted differently by managers with different functional backgrounds.

Individual experience: mental (or cognitive) models people build over time to help make sense of their situation

A sales or marketing executive might see it as a result of increased competitor activity or a downturn in market demand, and may advocate increased promotional expenditure to put things right. The production manager may see it as a matter of quality or efficiency and advocate investment in more state-of-the-art manufacturing plant. The accountant may see it as matter of rising costs and advocate better cost control or reduction in expenditure. Such biases are not simply a matter of functional experience, however. They can result from any prior experience in organisational or personal terms. The important points are these:

- The interpretation of events and issues in terms of prior experience is bound to take place. The idea that managers approach problems and issues of a strategic nature entirely dispassionately and objectively is unrealistic.

- To some extent there will be different interpretations according to past experience; and this can give rise to bargaining and negotiation between influential individuals as to how to interpret issues and what to do about them. This is discussed more fully in section 2.3.3 below.

- Such interpretation and bias arise from experience of the past, not least in terms of what is seen to have worked or given rise to problems in the past. So the future is likely to be made sense of in terms of the past. This is one explanation of why strategies tend to develop incrementally from prior strategy.

However, managers do not operate purely as individuals; they work and interact with others in the organisation, and at this collective level there are also reasons to expect similar tendencies. This is now discussed.

Collective experience: organisational culture and strategy development

Organisational culture is the 'basic *assumptions and beliefs* that are shared by members of an organisation, that operate unconsciously and define in a basic taken-for-granted fashion an organisation's view of itself and its environment'.[6] The application of experience is rooted, not only in individual experience, as discussed above, but also in collective (group and organisational) experience reflected in organisational routines accumulated over time. So strategies can be seen as the outcome of the collective taken-for-granted assumptions and routines of organisations. It is therefore important to recognise the significance of organisational culture in strategy development.

This taken-for-grantedness is likely to be handed down over time within a group. Such groups might be, for example, a managerial function such as marketing or finance; an organisational unit such as a business; or more widely a professional grouping, such as accountants, an industry sector, or even a national culture. There are, then, several cultural frames of reference which influence managers: Exhibit 2.4 shows this graphically. Some of these, which are especially important in understanding how strategies develop, are now discussed.

Organisational culture is the 'basic *assumptions and beliefs* that are shared by members of an organisation, that operate unconsciously and define in a basic taken-for-granted fashion an organisation's view of itself and its environment'

Exhibit 2.4	Cultural frames of reference

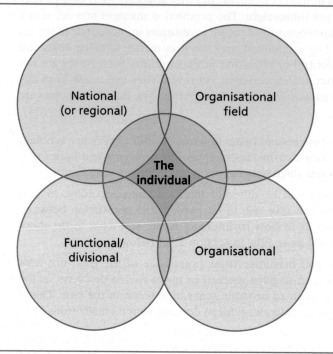

Institutional theorists[7] point to the similarities between organisations in terms of the assumptions and practices common between them and the strategies they follow: accountancy firms are similar, universities are similar, publishing firms are similar, and so on. Over time, similarities develop in terms of the way people in those organisation see their organisations and the environment in which the organisation operates, including the nature of customers, suppliers, competitors, and so on. Indeed, there develop **organisational fields** which are networks of related organisations which share common assumptions, values and ways of doing things so taken for granted, so *institutionalised*, that it is difficult for people to question or change them. Academics in traditional universities see academic research as the primary role of their organisation. Journalists see the reporting of news as the primary purpose of newspapers. Police see the maintenance of law and order as their primary purpose. They can come to be seen as *the* legitimate way to behave or think, so organisational strategies tend to develop within institutionally similar cultural parameters. The most obvious manifestations of this are professions such as accountancy, law and education; or similar firms within industries. Indeed, such institutionalised ways of thinking and behaving are sometimes called *industry recipes*. The implication of this is that, on the whole, managers think that they have more choice in developing strategies than they really do and that they tend to follow strategies similar to related organisations. Illustration 2.2 includes an example of institutional norms and practices in the accountancy profession.

Organisational fields are networks of related organisations which share common assumptions, values and ways of doing things

Illustration 2.2

STRATEGY IN ACTION

Taken-for-grantedness at organisational and institutional levels

Shared assumptions influence and may constrain the way business is done and strategy develops.

The paradigm at the organisational level

The managers from a large city-based newspaper were considering the future strategy of their organisation. They had analysed their competitive environment, concluded it was becoming more hostile and that substantial strategic changes were needed. In order to consider the challenge of strategic change they then considered what it was they tended to take for granted in their business. They realised that many of the assumptions and beliefs they held in common were rarely talked about but strongly influenced the way they approached their business. They tried to surface these and for each they considered what the assumption tended to discount or overlook. Here is their list:

'We assume that:

Our business is about news . . . although actually most of our revenue comes from the sale of advertising.

Our paid for daily newspaper will always be there . . . although free newspapers have made strong incursions into our market.

We are valued by the local community . . . although the demographics of that community have changed dramatically in the last 5 years so we're not sure what it is.

Ours is an immediate business: we re-make it every day. . . . What does this say about long-term strategic thinking and sustaining major change?'

Institutional norms[1]

Most accounting firms have been organised and managed as 'partnerships', along principles originating in law firms. Most managerial positions would be occupied by accountants, not by specialised managers, who spend only some of their time on managerial matters. Young accountants would join the firm and work towards partnership; after 7–10 years a decision would be made as to whether they would become a partner. If the decision were to be negative the candidate would be encouraged to leave the firm, irrespective of how productive he/she might be.

Firms were not required to govern themselves this way, they just did. Some firms found that this provided economic advantages: professionals were more content in partnerships and the up-or-out system enabled firms to continually replenish their talent pool. But others lost experienced professionals without being able to replace them. Partnerships are also difficult to manage, do not easily adapt to changing circumstances and find it hard to invest for the long term. So why did these arrangements become so widespread? The only explanation is that firms mimicked others and it became the expected way of doing things. Accountants came to believe that this was the way firms OUGHT to be managed.

[1] *Source*: Reprinted with permission of Royston Greenwood, University of Alberta, Canada.

Questions

1. Explain why the managers of the newspaper business thought their paradigm might be a problem. Give specific examples of how these problems might show themselves.

2. What other examples of institutionalised norms can you think of? Again consider the benefits and problems associated with them.

A **paradigm** is the set of assumptions held relatively in common and taken for granted in an organisation

Such taken-for-granted assumptions are also likely to exist at the organisational level – the organisational *paradigm*[8] – and can be especially important as an influence on the development of organisational strategy. In this book the word **paradigm** is frequently employed to mean the set of assumptions held relatively in common and taken for granted in an organisation. For a group or organisation to operate effectively there has to be such a generally accepted set of assumptions; in effect, it represents *collective experience* without which people would have to 'reinvent their world' for different circumstances that they face. Rather like individual experience, the paradigm allows the collective experience gathered over years to be applied to a given situation to make sense of it, to inform a likely course of action and the likelihood of success of that course of action. Illustration 2.2 also gives an example of an organisational paradigm. This paradigm may reflect institutional influences; so it may be particularly strong if the transfer of staff between firms tends to be within that industry, or organisational field, as it often is in engineering, banking and many parts of the public sector, for example. It is also likely that an organisation with a relatively stable management, and a long-term momentum of strategy, will have a more homogeneous paradigm than one in which there has been rapid turnover of management and significant change forced upon it.

This all may seem to be very obvious but there are some important implications.

- These are assumptions which are taken for granted; they are unlikely to be talked about as problematic. However, major problems arise if significant change in the organisation is needed or expected. Suppose universities come under pressure to raise revenue from teaching rather than concentrating on research. Suppose newspapers find their revenue coming mainly from advertising revenue rather than people buying the newspaper for the news. Suppose the government expects the police to concentrate more on prevention of crime than on 'catching criminals'. The problem is that the core assumptions of the paradigm will be difficult to change precisely because they are taken for granted; and the organisation might therefore find itself unable to adjust to such pressures.

- At the organisational level at least, the paradigm is likely to be linked to other aspects of organisational culture, such as organisational *rituals*, *stories* and the everyday *routines* of organisational life. Section 5.5.5 discusses this more extensively. These taken-for-granted organisational processes can further add to the conservative influence of organisational culture.

- There is an important relationship between the paradigm and how strategies develop. Exhibit 2.5 helps explain this. The forces at work in the environment, and the organisation's capabilities in coping with these, are made sense of in terms of the experience of managers and the collective assumptions within the paradigm. However, environmental forces and organisational capabilities, while having this indirect influence on strategy formulation, nonetheless impact on organisational performance more directly. For example, many commentators suggested that the problems that beset Marks and Spencer (M&S) in the late 1990s were the result of just such a situation. Their managers were accused of being over-wedded to M&S ways of thinking

Exhibit 2.5	The role of the paradigm in strategy formulation

and behaving, resulting in an inability to identify or take seriously changes in consumer expectations and the incursions of competitors on their traditional customer base.

- The taken-for-grantedness of an organisation, be it in terms of the paradigm or the organisational processes associated with it, may, however, also comprise many of the strengths (or competences) of an organisation (see section 4.4) and potentially provide bases of competitive advantage (see section 7.4.2). So this cultural dimension of organisational experience can be working both for and against the strategic development of an organisation.

- The paradigm is not the same as the explicit *values* of an organisation, nor is it the same as the *strategy* of an organisation, though it is likely to influence both. So it should not be assumed that the drawing up of some sort of value statement or the publishing of a document explaining a strategic direction will of itself change the paradigm. The notion that reasoned argument necessarily changes deeply embedded assumptions rooted in collective experience is flawed; readers need only think of their own experience in trying to persuade others to rethink their religious beliefs, or indeed, allegiances to sports teams to realise this. This poses a problem, not least in managing strategic change; and this is picked up in Chapter 11.

- The taken-for-grantedness in organisations or industries is also one of the major problems in trying to develop innovative strategies in organisations. The influence of the paradigm is conservative. Innovation is likely to require the questioning and challenging of basic assumptions, which can be uncomfortable for those who attempt it and threatening for those who do not welcome it.

2.2.3 Strategy as ideas

The careful reader will have gathered that the two lenses described so far have said very little about innovation and new ideas. Although the experience lens offers an explanation of change, it is change based on past strategy and existing organisational assumptions and practices. In so far as new ideas or practices occur, they are more likely to be borrowed or imitated. For example, when a new CEO from a private sector company takes charge in a public sector organisation, he or she may introduce all sorts of ideas which are 'new' to that organisation; but they may be just what he or she is familiar with from the private sector context. Notionally a design approach could result in innovation, but in fact tends to so emphasise control that it is likely to result in conformity rather than innovation. This leaves a problem: how to account for innovative strategies. How did Ericsson become a mobile phone company; where did innovative products such as Post-Its® and the Sony Walkman® come from? How do organisations faced with highly turbulent environments and short decision horizons, such as those in high-technology businesses or e-commerce, cope with the speed of change and innovation that is required? The two lenses discussed so far do not adequately explain this.

*The **ideas lens** sees strategy as the emergence of order and innovation from the variety and diversity which exist in and around organisations*

The **ideas lens** sees strategy as the emergence of order and innovation from the variety and diversity which exists in and around organisations. New ideas and therefore innovation may come from anywhere in an organisation, or indeed from stimuli in the world around it. The evidence is that innovation comes, not from the top, but quite likely from low down in an organisation.[9] There are links here to the experience lens. Sensing of an organisation's environment takes place throughout an organisation, not just at the top. People interpret issues in different ways according to their experience and may come up with different ideas based on personal experience. Such ideas may not be well formed or well informed and, at the individual level, they may be diverse. The greater the variety of experience, the more likely there will be innovation. Organisations in industry sectors which are developing and fragmented are more innovative than those in mature and concentrated industries,[10] because of the diversity of ideas that exist in such dynamic conditions; and innovation in large organisations often comes from outside their boundaries, often from smaller businesses.[11]

However, such variety of potential new ideas faces forces for conformity. The culture of the organisation acts as a filter of ideas; formal processes of control, planning and evaluation act to regularise what ideas will and will not go forward; the self-interest of powerful managers may block ideas counter to their own. So pressures for conformity may see off the novelty. There is also evidence that certain strategies, for example the pursuit of high levels of diversification, tend to result in low levels of innovation[12] since organisational resources and priorities are channelled towards the pursuit of that strategy rather than innovation.

Researchers have begun to examine and develop useful insights into how organisations can be innovative in conditions of uncertainty. For example, Brown and Eisenhardt[13] studied high-technology firms in Silicon Valley. In so doing they turned to explanations built on complexity theory and evolutionary theory, both of which are well established in the natural sciences but have hitherto received little attention in the social sciences or in management. The ideas lens draws on the principles of evolutionary theory and complexity theory because they help in the understanding of innovation and change.

The importance of variety and diversity

Both complexity and evolutionary theories emphasise the importance of variety and diversity within and around organisations and place a great deal less emphasis on top-down design. Such variety and diversity potentially exist for all organisations in the form of an ever-changing environment, different businesses within a corporation, different groups within businesses, and the variety of different individuals and their experience and ideas within an organisation. So, variety may exist at different levels and in different forms; what matters is that there is variety and diversity, and that they are encouraged rather than over-controlled.

How ideas are generated

Evolution explains how any living system, arguably including an organisation, evolves through natural selection acting upon variation and diversity. The basic principles are these.[14] Whether the concern is with species, as in the natural world, or people in societies, or indeed ideas in organisations, uniformity is not the norm; there exists variety. If an environment changes very little – as in the Amazonian rainforest – there is more stability than in environments that change a great deal. So the birds of the Amazonian rainforest have changed little over millennia, but other species, viruses are a good example, change much faster because their environments change a great deal. The parallel with organisations is that as their environments change, so too will the speed of change of organisations. However, this is not because of planning and design. In the natural world, change and newness come about because of what might appear to be imperfections – a mutation of a gene, for example – which may provide the basis for a 'fitter' organism in a changing environment. In organisations, ideas will be also copied imperfectly between individuals, between groups or between organisations and some of these will give rise to innovations better suited to the changing environment. An idea of the research chemist in the R&D laboratory may be taken up by a marketing executive, perhaps, but may be interpreted differently from the original idea; one organisation may seek to copy the strategy of another but will not do things in exactly the same way. Some of these imperfect copies will not be successful; but others may be. The famous exemplar of this is the Post-It®, which originated in an 'imperfect' glue being applied to paper but which resulted in a semi-adhesive for which the researcher saw market potential.

It is not possible to plan in detail or control for the 'right' amount of diversity, the content of the variety or what eventually emerges. The differences arise naturally and in an unpredictable way. However, there are conditions which foster such diversity, imperfect copying, change and therefore innovation and it may be possible for managers to design processes and make decisions which build on the principles described above so as to foster new ideas and innovation.

- A *changing and unpredictable environment* will, of itself, generate a diversity of ideas and innovations because it will demand responses from organisations and they will vary. An organisation that seeks to ensure that its people are in contact with and responsive to that change is likely to generate a greater diversity of ideas and more innovation than one that does not. On the other hand, one that tries to insulate itself from its environment, for example by trying to resist market changes or by relying on a particular way of doing or seeing things – sometimes known as a 'strong culture' – will generate less variety of ideas and less innovation.

- Similarly, high degrees of control and strict hierarchy are likely to encourage conformity and reduce variety; so innovation is less likely the more elaborate and bureaucratic the top-down control.

- Implicit in the design lens is that *consensus* is a 'good thing' because it facilitates collective action and a clear understanding about strategy. The ideas lens suggests that the environment is too complex and rapidly changing for this to be likely or even desirable. It may not always be comfortable, but a lack of consensus and diversity of ideas and views may be of benefit because innovation requires just such variety and benefits from the challenging and questioning of taken-for-granted assumptions and the possibility of experimentation.[15]

- In line with this, new ideas are likely to advance most where they are allowed and encouraged to compete with each other.

- Complexity theorists also argue that innovation and creativity emerge when there is sufficient order to make things happen but not when there is such rigidity of control as to prevent such innovation. This is the idea of 'adaptive tension' or 'edge of chaos'.[16] Innovations are most likely to occur when the organisation never quite settles down into a steady state or equilibrium and the volatility and diversity are given sufficient rein (Exhibit 2.6), though of course not to the extent that it cannot function.

- They also argue that in the context of uncertainty and complexity, too little recognition is given to the *intuitive capacity* of people:[17] that people have the ability to sense changes in and appropriate responses to changes in their environment; that this needs to be encouraged; and that the ideas that they come up with as a result usefully contribute to strategy development.

- The more the boundaries between the organisation and its environment are reduced, the more innovation is likely to occur. For example, for some high-technology businesses it is difficult to see quite what are their boundaries. They are networks rather than clearly bounded organisations (see section 9.4.3 in Chapter 9). These are organisations intimately linked to a wider environment; and as that environment changes, so do the ideas in the network. A good example of this is Formula One motor racing where the different teams are intimately linked with the wider motor industry as well as other areas of advanced technology; and indeed are so networked between themselves that new ideas get imitated (but changed) very rapidly.

Exhibit 2.6	Conditions of adaptive tension

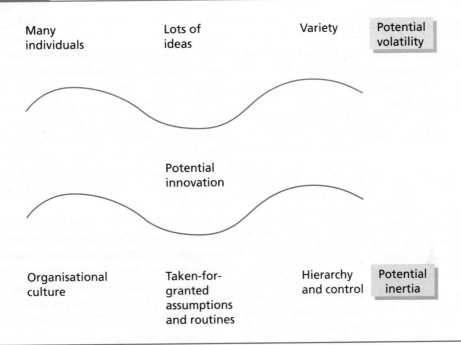

- Similarly, within organisations what matters is appropriate interaction and cooperation to encourage variety and the spread of ideas. There is evidence of the 'strength of weak ties',[18] by which is meant that it is the variety of informal contacts rather than formally structured contacts that gives rise to new ideas. For example, it is not unusual to hear people say that they find the informal electronic networks they themselves set up for knowledge sharing and exchange in organisations to be more valuable than those set up formally by the organisation.

- Since speed of change is important, some writers[19] have emphasised the importance of 'time pacing' of new ideas in organisations. They point to the fact that in some organisations with high rates of innovation of new products, these new products are not brought on stream when old products become redundant; rather the rate of new product innovation is paced such that new products and ideas are coming to the fore even when existing ones are successful.

Illustration 2.3 shows how some of these principles take form in Digital Animations Group.

How new ideas take root in organisations

Evolutionary theory suggests that the extent to which ideas manifest themselves at an organisational level as a new product, service or process will be

Illustration 2.3

Managing by ideas

Managing new ideas and the development of ideas in situations of change and uncertainty is central to future success in some organisations; and may require top management to rethink the approach to strategy development.

Digital Animations Group (DAG) is a global player in the application of digital technology to the future of everyday life. It became widely known as the company behind Ananova, the virtual newscaster, sold to Orange in 2001, but has many more applications and characters in its development pipeline. Based in Scotland, its growing workforce includes animators and programmers who work together, merging creativity with leading-edge use of hardware and the development of conceptually advanced software. The company brings what is possible in the virtual world into the real world in the form of life-like digital motion video of apparently real-life but impossible stunts. However, in development terms it spends more time bringing the real world into the virtual world in the form of Avatars: digitally created but life-like, and, in the future, intelligent people. It plays within the two worlds of reality and virtuality, recombining them digitally into exciting new mixtures at the human/computer interface.

DAG patents its ideas, since the worth of such intangibles is now legally recognised. However, the company is aware that, whilst patents play a role in securing sustainable competitive advantage, the major part of the game is constant reinvention and recombination: and that managing this intellectual property company involves managing ideas by managing the conditions and climate in which they are exchanged.

Senior management know that in such a fast, novel field, the organisation needs to be strategically flexible and adaptable. They actively encourage both the cross-over of ideas and the competition of ideas, knowing the result in some cases will be pure fun and silliness whereas in others the outcome will have great potential commercial value. Sometimes silly ideas can turn into sensible ones if allowed to struggle to survive next to others. What counts is both diversity of ideas and the competition of those ideas.

By promoting the recombination of ideas between animators and programmers and between the different national cultures of the highly skilled, globally sourced staff, variety and a competitive selection environment are created. Staff are also allowed to take a month off each year and play with any idea that is lurking in their minds. According to the CEO some of the best ideas arise from this period.

Having the ability to generate the space for such idea creation and the sensitivity to discern the market opportunities that arise from it is how strategy develops. Ask management for a conventional strategic plan and they will not be able to provide you with one. Ask them to talk about how their ideas are generated and allowed to evolve, and they will not stop for breath.

Source: Company.

Questions

1. Which characteristics of the ideas lens described in section 2.2.3 do you see in DAG?
2. What problems might the CEO find in managing the strategy of the business?

dependent on *selection mechanisms*. These selection mechanisms may take different forms but are all to do with how attractive the ideas are and how capable they are of surviving, or overcoming, the obstacles in their way.

- At the *organisational level* a key selection mechanism is the market; a strategy will develop and prosper according to whether it is more attractive to customers than the strategies of other organisations. This is, of course, a conventional measure of strategic success to do with competitive strategy (see Chapter 7). Whilst this is often discussed in terms of the economics of markets and may, therefore, appear to be all very rational, it is important to emphasise that customer preferences are not always to do with economic attractiveness. Customers may be attracted to one product over another for highly subjective, personal and emotional reasons.

- At the level of the *strategic initiative* within an organisation, a selection mechanism could, of course, be a project evaluation, planning or budgetary process; but the political and cultural context of the organisation will also act as a selection mechanism. Some initiatives will be sufficiently attractive to enough people to overcome cultural inertia and political barriers; and others will not (see section 2.3.3 below).

- At the level of the *idea* it is the extent to which one idea is more or less attractive than other ideas to individuals or groups of people. This could be for rational reasons, demonstrated analytically; or it might be for more subjective, emotional reasons. In line with this, complexity theory emphasises the need for sufficient support or 'positive feedback'. For example, a new product idea in a science-based research-intensive company received widespread support because it addressed 'green' issues; research scientists were attracted to the idea that their work was being put to good use; and senior managers, who were also scientists by background, admitted that it was also attractive because, unusually for their business, its application and potential benefits were the sort of thing that interested their colleagues in other divisions, their friends and their families. The new product idea persisted despite strong evidence of its lack of commercial viability. Of course, in time this positive feedback at this level would probably not be enough for it to persist because it would run into market selection mechanisms; but emotional attraction had carried the idea forward within the organisation.

- This also illustrates that *communities of interest* – groups with similar interests – such as the scientific community in the example above are important for the promotion of ideas and initiatives. The new product idea may continue to develop within that science-based community but be unattractive to the executives at corporate level or to customers.

- However, it is unlikely that an innovation at whatever level will initially find widespread support; so it may matter that there exists *sufficient initial support*. For example, in the marketplace this might take the form of a niche market; for the innovative entrepreneur, it may be the backing of a risk-taking venture capitalist; for the innovative scientist in the R&D lab, it may be sufficient support from a senior manager as champion of the idea against the objections of other senior management colleagues.

● At whichever level, however, the idea of selection suggests that there may be a *fight for survival*; so it may well be that conflict is inevitable in the marketplace, between individuals or between ideas.

How innovative strategies come about

Complexity theory and evolutionary theory explain strategy development as emerging patterns of strategic direction from within organisations. For example, using an example from the natural sciences, the ordered pattern and direction of a flock of birds does not exist because of some plan set down by a leader and communicated through a hierarchy. Complexity theorists argue that so it is in organisations: ideas and patterns of behaviour form strategies, but not necessarily through top-down plans and control.

Organisations consist of many individuals with the capacity to take different directions, undertake different activities, think different thoughts and so on: they are complex systems with potentially very high diversity. Ordered patterns of behaviour come about not because of tight and specific control, but because of a limited number of 'order-generating rules'. For example, the flocking of birds can be simulated on a computer with just three such rules:

● maintain minimum distance from other birds and objects in the environment;

● match velocity with other birds;

● move towards the centre of mass of the surrounding birds.[20]

So in organisations, patterns of behaviour which may be seen as consistent strategic direction can emerge because of a number of guiding principles or rules. Research is now beginning to establish the nature of these.[21] Exhibit 2.7 summarises the types of rules which have been identified as important in organisations facing fast-changing environments; and gives some examples from such organisations of how they take form and their effects. A number of observations can be drawn from the research:

● As suggested earlier, the number of rules does not need to be many to result in consistent patterns of behaviour. It appears that the number may be between 2 and 7.

● It is argued that older, more established organisations may need fewer rules than younger organisations with less experience.

● It may be that top managers deliberately seek to establish such rules (as in Illustration 2.4), or it may be that they form within the organisation.

Complexity theorists also like to talk about 'strange attractors'. These are patterns that, whilst not entirely predictable, are recognisable in their form. The flocking of birds never takes on quite the same form, but is recognisable. Similarly, patterns of behaviour of organisations that we call strategies may never be entirely the same, but are recognisable and tend to be similar between organisations. In this sense there is a similarity with the explanations given by institutional theorists. Strategies for organisations within an organisational field (see page 46 above and section 5.5.2) tend to be similar; and this should be expected because the 'rules' within that field have come to be similar.

Exhibit 2.7	Simple rules

Turbulent markets require strategic flexibility to seize opportunities – but flexibility can be disciplined. Different types of simple rules help.

TYPE	PURPOSE	EXAMPLE
How-to rules	Spell out key features of how a process is executed – 'What makes our process unique?'	Dell focuses on the process of rapid reorganisation around focused customer segments. A key how-to rule for this process is that a business must be split in two when its revenue hits $1 billion.
Boundary rules	Focus managers on which opportunities can be pursued and which should not	Miramax has boundary rules that guide their movie-picking process: first, every movie must revolve around a central human condition, such as love (*The Crying Game*) or envy (*The Talented Mr Ripley*). Second, a movie's main character must be appealing but deeply flawed – the hero of *Shakespeare in Love* is gifted and charming but steals ideas from friends and betrays his wife. Third, movies must have a very clear story line with a beginning, middle and end. Finally, there is a firm cap on production costs.
Priority rules	Help managers rank the accepted opportunities	Intel's rule for allocating manufacturing capacity: allocation is based on a product's gross margin. Without this rule, the company might have continued to allocate too much capacity to its traditional core memory business rather than seizing the opportunity to dominate the nascent and highly profitable microprocessor niche (see Illustration 2.8).
Timing rules	Synchronise managers with the pace of emerging opportunities and other parts of the company	Nortel, the Internet service company, has rules for product development. First, project teams must know when a product has to be delivered to the leading customer to win, which keeps Nortel in touch with cutting-edge customers, who represent the best opportunities. Second, product development time must be less than 18 months, which forces Nortel to move quickly into new opportunities.
Exit rules	Help managers decide when to pull out of yesterday's opportunities	Danish hearing aid company Oticon has a rule which avoids its getting trapped in project developments which are 'yesterday's opportunities'. If a key team member – manager or not – chooses to leave the project for another within the company, the project is killed.

Source: Adapted from K.M. Eisenhardt and D.N. Sull, 'Strategy as simple rules', *Harvard Business Review*, January 2001, pp. 107–116.

Illustration 2.4

Boundarylessness and success at GE

STRATEGY IN ACTION

Leaders of complex organisations may focus on a limited number of guiding principles or 'rules'.

GE has been one of the fastest-growing, most profitable and highly rated conglomerates in the world, with a market capitalisation in the range of US$250 billion. GE has constantly outperformed its rivals and has consistently topped the polls as the world's most admired company.

At a time when many firms have focused on only a few core businesses, it is highly diverse. Between 1981 and 1997, GE made 509 acquisitions totalling $53 billion, and 310 divestitures of $16 billion. In 1999 there were 108 acquisitions worth US$21 billion. Its businesses are as varied as light bulbs, home appliances, jet engines and financial services. GE has also successfully managed multiple brands simultaneously and chosen to maintain separate identities for their acquired brands, such as Hotpoint, NBC and RCA.

Many commentators have tried to explain the success of GE. Most agree that major factors are the management style of the CEO, Jack Welch, and the importance of the mission and principles which guide the businesses and the managers. These principles are few:

- Be number one or two in the market in every business, or exit it. In most of its businesses, GE is no.1, not just in market share, but in expanding the scope of its markets.
- Share and adopt successful new ideas across businesses; the pursuit of 'boundarylessness'. A business CEO is expected to try out ideas successful in other GE businesses and to promote the sharing of successful ideas from his/her own business. Groups of employees from all levels regularly meet to propose means of improving efficiency and solving problems. And pay and promotion are tied to boundaryless behaviour via the sharing of

ideas and transfer of knowledge. GE's success appears to be rooted in this movement of ideas and also management talent around a diverse corporation.

- Challenge and question the status quo. Welch regularly meets with his managers and insists that they challenge him about his policies and initiatives; this is filtered down the corporation by sessions of lower-level employees questioning their managers face-to-face.

These principles provide challenging, even ambiguous, demands on management. A business CEO may naturally wish to focus on that business rather than spending time and effort sharing ideas across businesses, experimenting with the ideas of other businesses, or being challenged about bases of success. However, it is not enough for the CEO to point to high business performance; sharing is seen as equally important even if potentially time consuming. Nor can managers claim that the requirement for sharing is an excuse for poor performance of their business; Welch's management control systems require high levels of performance in terms of market share, financial targets and shareholder value.

Prepared by Urmilla Lawson, Graduate Business School, University of Strathclyde.
Sources: Jack Gordon, 'My leader, myself: faux freethinkers and the new cult of the CEO', *Training*, Nov. 1998, v.35 i.11; Henry Beam, 'Jack Welch and the GE way' (Review), *Business Horizons*, May–June 1999, v.42, i.3; 'The house that Jack built', GE Company Profile, *The Economist (US)*, 18 Sept. 1999; Presentation by Professor Bill McKelvey at *The Fifth International Conference on Competence Based Management*, Helsinki, June 2000.

Questions

1. Complexity theorists suggest that adaptive tension (or edge of chaos) helps generate new ideas (see page 52). What elements and sources of adaptive tension are to be found in GE's management style?
2. Would you like to be a CEO of a GE business? Why?

Implications for management

The implications of complexity theory and evolutionary theory as applied to innovation in the context of strategic management are these:

- It is not possible for top management to know or understand and plan the future. The future will emerge. Nor is it realistic to expect new ideas and innovations to be planned in a top-down fashion.

- It does matter, however, that management needs to be aware of and sensitive to the wider environment which will affect the organisation and will itself throw up new ideas and challenges. Management also need to find ways of encouraging the variety within the organisation that will generate new ideas.

- This will not be achieved by determining 'tight' strategies and control systems. It is more likely to be managed by creating forms of organisation and cultures of organisation which encourage variety, diversity and informal networking. Evolutionary theorists, in particular, emphasise the importance of imperfections in the development of new ideas; very different from emphasising regularisation through control and tight planning.

- There is, then, a de-emphasis of formal planning and systems; and a greater emphasis on the day-to-day aspects of organisational life and organisation design which encourages the social interaction of people and their intuitive sensing and awareness of what is going on around them. Emerging stimuli in the organisational world and ideas within the organisation are less likely to be developed through formal analysis and objectivity and more likely to be developed by a reliance on 'pattern recognition' based on experience and intuition.

- There is a recognition that strategic change will normally take place incrementally, but that occasionally change may be sudden and more dramatic as new ideas surface and take organisational form (see section 2.4.2 below).

- Complexity theory emphasises the importance of order-generating rules. There are, however, differences in the extent to which these just emerge or to which managers can proactively influence them. One view emphasises the inevitability of the adaptive tension or 'edge of chaos' that exists in organisations, stressing that this results in the emergence of order-generating rules and that innovation, itself, is emergent. It de-emphasises the role of top management in all this.[22] The role of management here is not to do with trying to establish clarity of direction or intervene in creating order-generating rules; rather it is to be sensitive to emergent patterns in organisations, to foster these by acting in a more coaching role. Strategic management is, then, about identifying order as it emerges rather than directing that order.

- Others take a more managerial view. They argue that it is the role of top management to ensure that adaptive tension exists, for example by seeking to establish the sort of rules that will generate such adaptive tension,[23] as in Illustration 2.4. They argue that managers may usefully generate the sort of overarching mission, intent or vision explained in Chapter 1 and provide a few guiding 'rules' or principles. However, they need to understand that too much order is dangerous; that the creation of ambiguity may be important as a means of creating adaptive tension; and that they have a role to play here (again see Illustration 2.4). In so far as top management can exercise control, this may be limited to monitoring some key measures, perhaps linked to the overall mission of the organisation or the few key guiding rules. For example, how many new products have been developed, accounting for what additional percentage of revenue or profits? How many new networks or new joint ventures have been formed, and so on?

2.2.4 A summary of strategic lenses

Exhibit 2.8 summarises the three lenses discussed above. In many respects it has to be recognised that the design lens, especially in its emphasis on analysis and control, is the orthodox approach to strategy development most commonly written about in books, taught at business schools and verbalised by management when they discuss the strategy of their organisations. As explained in Chapter 1, it is also a convenient lens by which to structure this book. However, the other lenses are important because they raise significant challenges in thinking about and managing strategy. The experience lens is rooted in evidence of how strategies develop incrementally based on experience and the historical and cultural legacy of the organisation; and suggests that it is much more difficult to make strategic changes than the design lens might imply. The ideas lens helps an understanding of where innovative strategies

Exhibit 2.8	Three strategy lenses		
	STRATEGY AS:		
	DESIGN	**EXPERIENCE**	**IDEAS**
Overview/ Summary	Deliberate positioning through rational, analytic, structured and directive processes	Incremental development as the outcome of individual and collective experience and the taken for granted	Emergence of order and innovation through variety and diversity in and around the organisation
Assumptions about organisations	Mechanistic, hierarchical, logical	Cultures based on history, legitimacy and past success	Complex systems of variety and diversity
Role of top management	Strategic decision makers	Enactors of their experience	'Coaches', creators of context and 'champions' of ideas
Implications for change	Change = implementation of planned strategy	Change incremental with resistance to major change	Change incremental but occasionally sudden
Underpinning theories	Economics; decision sciences	Institutional theory; theories of culture; psychology	Complexity and evolutionary theories

come from and how organisations cope with dynamic environments. It also poses questions about whether or not top management really have control over strategic direction to the extent the design lens suggests. In the rest of the book the three lenses are employed in commentaries at the end of Parts II, III and IV in particular to examine critically the coverage of each part.

2.3 STRATEGY DEVELOPMENT PROCESSES IN ORGANISATIONS

The previous sections have dealt with different explanations of how strategies develop. These are not mutually exclusive explanations. They are different lenses through which it is possible to understand and explain what goes on in organisations. People who work in, or observe, organisations (for example, consultants or students) are likely to see a variety of processes occurring which contribute to strategy development. These lenses help provide a means of understanding and interpreting the causes and the effects of such processes. The sections which now follow consider some of these observable strategy development processes and use the different lenses to explain them.

2.3.1 Strategic planning systems

Often, strategy development is equated with strategic planning systems. In many respects they are the archetypal manifestation of the design approach to managing strategy. Such processes may take the form of highly systematised, step by step, chronological procedures involving many different parts of the organisation, as shown in Illustration 2.5. Organisations which have sophisticated and extensive planning systems may well be populated with managers who believe that strategies can and should be developed in such ways and who may argue that a highly systematic approach is *the* rational approach to strategy formulation. The evidence of the extent to which the formalised pursuit of such a systemised approach results in organisations performing better than others is, however, equivocal[24] – not least because it is difficult to isolate formal planning as the dominant or determining effect on performance. This is not to say that formalised planning does not have its uses.

- It can provide a structured means of *analysis and thinking* about complex strategic problems, at its best requiring managers to *question and challenge* the received wisdom they take for granted.

- It can encourage a *longer-term view* of strategy than might otherwise occur. Planning horizons vary, of course. In a fast-moving consumer goods company, 3–5-year plans may be appropriate. In companies which have to take very long-term views on capital investment, such as those in the oil industry, planning horizons can be as long as 14 years (in Exxon) or 20 years (in Shell).

- It can be used as a means of *control* by regularly reviewing performance and progress against agreed objectives or previously agreed strategic direction.

Illustration 2.5

Strategic planning systems in BT:
BT's business planning cycle 2000/01

Planning cycles in large corporations can involve iteration between different organisational levels over many months.

In BT the development of corporate and business plans, supporting operating plans and budgets, started at Group level but iterated between the corporate level (Group), lines of business (e.g. BT Wireless) and business units within lines of business (e.g. BT Cellnet) over a 12-month period.

	GROUP[1,2]	LINE OF BUSINESS (LoB)	BUSINESS UNIT (BU)
April	Broad strategic direction (with press announcement)		
June	Board review of strategy		
August	Strategic planning guidance and financial goals issued	Planning guidance and goals to BUs	
September			Draft BU strategic plans
October		Draft LoB strategic plans to Group	
November	Group review of LoB strategic plans Updated strategic direction (press announcement)		
December	Complete Group strategic plan	Finalise LoB strategic plans	Finalise BU strategic plans Prepare draft operational plan and budget
January	Board meeting to agree strategic plan	Submit draft operational plan and budget to Group	
February	Complete Group operational plan and budget		
March	Board meeting to agree operational plan and budget	Finalise LoB budget and operational plan	Finalise BU budget and operational plan

1. The Group Investment Committee meets monthly to agree capital expenditure and investment proposals which exceed the LoBs' delegated authority.
2. The Group Executive Committee meets three times a month to consider strategic and operational issues.

Source: Company (with permission).

Questions

1. What might be the benefits of such a planning system?
2. What might be the problems and disadvantages?

- It can be a useful means of *coordination*, for example by bringing together the various business unit strategies within an overall corporate strategy, or ensuring that resources within a business are coordinated to put strategy into effect.
- Strategic planning may also help to *communicate* intended strategy.
- It can be used as a way of involving people in strategy development, therefore perhaps helping to create *ownership* of the strategy.
- Planning systems may provide a sense of security and logic for the organisation and, in particular, management who believe they *should* be proactively determining the future strategy and exercising control over the destiny of the organisation.

Whilst, on the face of it, planning is most obviously explained through the design lens, it can also be explained through the other lenses, and these suggest other possible benefits.

- The experience lens suggests that strategy actually develops on the basis of more informal sensing of the environment on the basis of people's experience or through the cultural systems of the organisation, as described in the previous section. Here, planning is not seen as directing the development of strategy so much as drawing together the threads of a strategy which emerges on the basis of that experience and, perhaps, post-rationalising it. So the strategy comes to look as though it has been planned. Of course, even if the formally stated strategy of an organisation is post-rationalised, it may nonetheless be important to ensure effective communication of it, and this can be aided by a systematic planning system.
- The ideas lens also emphasises the emergence of strategy from within the organisation rather than from the top; so again planning may be seen here as making sense of that emergent strategy. Planning systems also provide a selection mechanism by which new ideas can be evaluated. Plans typically embody the strategy as it is generally accepted, so, in a sense, new ideas and innovations have to compete for their survival, or prove their worth, against such plans and planning processes.

There are, however, dangers in the formalisation of strategic planning,[25] and some of these can be understood by reference to the different lenses.

First, looking through the design lens itself, there are evident problems in the way in which strategic planning systems are put into effect in some organisations.

- The managers responsible for the implementation of strategies, usually line managers, may be so busy with the day-to-day operations of the business that they cede responsibility for strategic issues to specialists. However, the specialists do not have power in the organisation to make things happen. The result can be that strategic planning becomes an *intellectual exercise* removed from the reality of operation. As General William Sherman said in 1869 in the context of the American Civil War: 'I know there exist many good men who honestly believe that one may, by the aid of modern science, sit in comfort and ease in his office chair and, with figures and algebraic symbols, master the great game of war. I think this is an insidious and most dangerous mistake.'[26]

- The process of strategic planning may be so cumbersome that individuals or groups in the firm might contribute to only part of it and *not understand the whole.* This is particularly problematic in very large firms. One executive, on taking over as marketing manager in a large multinational consumer goods firm, was told by his superior: 'We do corporate planning in the first two weeks of April, then we get back to our jobs.'

- There is a danger that strategy becomes thought of as *the plan.* Managers may see themselves as managing strategy because they are going through the processes of planning. Strategy is, of course, not the same as 'the plan': strategy is the long-term direction that the organisation is following, not a written document on an executive's shelf. This highlights the difference between *intended* and *realised* strategies (see section 2.4.1 below).

- Strategic planning can become over-detailed in its approach, concentrating on extensive analysis which, whilst sound in itself, may miss the major strategic issues facing the organisation. For example, it is not unusual to find companies with huge amounts of information on their markets, but with little clarity about the strategic importance of that information. The result can be *information overload* with no clear outcome.

The experience lens also highlights dangers.

- Planners can *overlook the importance of the experience of those in an organisation* and see centrally planned strategy as determining what goes on in an organisation. As was explained in discussing the experience lens, the individual and collective experience of an organisation will influence its strategy; and the experience of those responsible for strategy implementation will affect how a strategy is implemented. If formal planning systems are to be useful, those responsible for them need to ensure that they draw on such experience. This may account for why more and more organisations are changing to more inclusive ways of developing strategy, involving different levels of management. However, the sorts of danger highlighted next, remain.

- The strategy resulting from deliberations of a corporate planning department, or a senior management team, may not be *owned* more widely in the organisation. In one extreme instance, a colleague was discussing a company's strategy with its planning director. He was told that a strategic plan existed, but found it was locked in the drawer of the executive's desk. Only the planner and a few senior executives were permitted to see it!

- Strategies are more or less successfully implemented through people. Their behaviour will not be determined by plans. So the *cultural and political dimensions* of organisations have to be taken into account. Planning processes are not typically designed to do this.

The ideas lens also adds to an understanding of the pitfalls of formal planning.

- Formal systems of planning, especially if linked to very tight mechanisms of control, can result in an inflexible, hierarchical organisation with a resultant *stifling of ideas and dampening of innovative capacity.*

● Planning can become obsessed with the search for a definitively *right strategy*. It is unlikely that a 'right' strategy will naturally fall out of the planning process. It might be more important to establish a more generalised strategic direction within which there is the sort of flexibility that the ideas lens would emphasise. As Mintzberg puts it: 'If you have no vision, but only formal plans, then every unpredicted change in the environment makes you feel your sky is falling in.'[27]

Certainly there has been a decline in the use of formal corporate planning departments. For example, a study of corporate planning in the oil industry found that, between 1990 and 1996, corporate planning staff had declined from 48 to 3 in BP, 60 to 17 in Exxon, 38 to 12 in Mobil and 54 to 17 in Shell.[28] On the other hand, there has been a growth of *strategy workshops* where participants remove themselves from day-to-day responsibilities to tackle strategic issues facing their organisation. Such events may well use the sorts of techniques of analysis and planning described in this book. However, rather than just relying on these to throw up strategic solutions, a successful workshop process works through issues in face-to-face debate and discussion, drawing on and surfacing different experiences, assumptions, interests and views. In this respect it is seeking to tackle the design of strategy, whilst facing up to the realities of the cultural and political processes of the organisation. Whilst such events are typically for groups of senior managers, perhaps the board of an organisation, organisations are beginning to see benefits in similar events across other levels of management.

2.3.2 Strategic leadership

Strategy development may also be strongly associated with an individual. A **strategic leader** is an individual upon whom strategy development and change are seen to be dependent. They are individuals personally identified with and central to the strategy of their organisation: their personality or reputation may result in others willingly deferring to such an individual and seeing strategy development as his or her province. In other organisations an individual may be central because he or she is its owner or founder; often the case in small businesses. Or it could be that an individual chief executive has turned round a business in times of difficulty and, as such, personifies the success of the organisation's strategy.

*A **strategic leader** is an individual upon whom strategy development and change are seen to be dependent*

Again the three lenses help explain and raise questions about how such individuals develop their ideas about strategy, and how they influence strategy development.

● The design lens suggests that individuals have thought this all through analytically. Whilst a plan may not exist as a written document, it exists in terms of analysis and evaluation carried out by that individual. This could be by using the sorts of technique associated with strategic planning and analysis; or it might simply be that the individual has consciously, systematically and on the basis of their own logic worked through issues their organisation faces and come to their own conclusions.

- The experience lens suggest that the strategy advanced by the individual is formed on the basis of that individual's experience, perhaps within the organisation or perhaps from some other organisation. The strategy advanced by a long-established chief executive may strongly reflect or be informed by his or her organisation's paradigm; and the strategy advanced by a chief executive new to an organisation may be based on a successful strategy followed in a previous organisation.

- The strategy of an organisation might also be associated more symbolically with an individual, for example the founder of a business. Such a figure may come to embody the strategic direction of the organisation. In effect the strategy and the individual become embedded in the history and culture of that organisation. This is often the case in family-controlled businesses.

The ideas lens provides additional insights to the role of the strategic leader:

- Evolutionary theorists emphasise the way in which strategies develop from competing ideas, so tend to diminish the role of so-called strategic leaders. However, the potential importance of an overall vision, mission or intent and the (perhaps few) guiding rules associated with these are recognised as important; and some writers see this as *the* role of the strategic leader.[29] Indeed, it is a role for which successful strategic leaders are often applauded because such a vision can provide sufficient clarity within which the discretion of others in the organisation can be exercised.

- However, some complexity theorists would argue for the importance of recognising the importance of high intuitive capacity and would accept that strategic vision can be associated with an executive with such a capacity, who sees what others do not see and espouses new ways of working.

- Others point out that new businesses or business activities are usually created by individual entrepreneurs. They may be correct, but evolution suggests that for every successful entrepreneur there are likely to be many who fail. The few that succeed will, indeed, be applauded as innovatory and creative, but they were the product of a diverse population of ideas most of which did not succeed.

2.3.3 Organisational politics

Managers often suggest that the strategy being followed by the organisation is really the outcome of the bargaining and power politics that go on between important executives. Such executives are continually trying to position themselves such that their views prevail or that they control the resources in the organisation necessary for future success. The **political view**[30] of strategy development is, then, that strategies develop as the outcome of processes of bargaining and negotiation among powerful internal or external interest groups (or stakeholders). This is the world of boardroom battles often portrayed in film and TV dramas. What do the lenses have to say about this?

The design lens suggests that such political activity gets in the way of thorough analysis and rational thinking. On the whole it is seen as an inevitable

The **political view** of strategy development is, that strategies develop as the outcome of processes of bargaining and negotiation among powerful internal or external interest groups (or stakeholders)

but negative influence on strategy development. Certainly, the interests of different stakeholders and the protection of those interests can get in the way of strategy development, as Illustration 2.6 shows.

It is, however, the experience lens which most helps explain the likelihood of political activity and some of the implications that flow from this.

- If people in organisations are rooted in their experience, it is not surprising that, in approaching problems – often major problems – from that point of view, they seek to be protective of their views in the face of different views based on different experience. This may be linked to the exercise of power. It is not surprising that the conductor in Illustration 2.6 takes a different position from the marketing director and others in the organisation: they are approaching the problem with different experience bases and are interested in preserving or enhancing the power of their positions.

- The outcome of such political processes may well be the sort of inertia shown in Illustration 2.6. So political activity may then be seen as one explanation of incremental, adaptive strategy development. There are at least two reasons for this. First, if different views prevail in the organisation and different parties are exercising their political muscle, compromise may be inevitable. Second, it is quite possible that it is from the pursuit of the current strategy that power has been gained by those wielding it. Indeed it may be very threatening to their power if significant changes in strategy were to occur. In such circumstances it is likely that a search for a compromise solution which accommodates different power bases may well end up with a strategy which is an adaptation of what has gone before.

- The experience lens also suggests that the analytic processes that go into planning may not be entirely based on objective and neutral facts. Views of the world – of the marketplace, of technological development, of organisational competences and so on – that are stated and regarded as important in a plan will have been espoused and supported by a group of managers. The fact that that a view is accepted and is in the plan may be the result of the powerful influence they have and may, in turn, provide them with added power. The objectives which are set may reflect the ambitions of powerful people. Information is not politically neutral, but rather can be a source of power for those who control what is seen to be important; so the withholding of information, or the influence of one manager over another because that manager controls sources of information, can be important. Powerful individuals and groups may also strongly influence the identification of key issues and indeed the strategies eventually selected. Differing views may be pursued, not only on the basis of the extent to which they reflect environmental or competitive pressures, for example, but also because they have implications for the status or influence of different stakeholders. Planning is, in this sense, political, or at least has a political dimension.

- All of this suggests that political activity has to be taken seriously as an influence on strategy development. The problems of the orchestra are unlikely to be resolved by relying on a formalised planning system; whatever thinking goes into the strategy will need to go hand in hand with activity

Illustration 2.6

ASO: UK Symphony Orchestra

Stakeholders' interests and expectations can create problematic circumstances for the development of strategy.

Developing an artistic strategy for the ASO was a complex process, due largely to the interests and involvement of its numerous stakeholders. The process was prompted by a critical report from the Arts Council, the orchestra's main funder, in late 1996. Commenting on the 'audience resistance to new initiatives' brought in by the Conductor, the report argued that the organisation needed 'clearer artistic and audience focus'. It called for a change in strategic leadership, recommending 'that the CEO should take overall responsibility for the artistic direction'. The Conductor defended his previous decisions, arguing that he had been criticised both for having programmes that were too conservative and too adventurous. At the same time, his Artistic Advisor suggested the confusion over strategic focus was partly due to a 'clash of ideals' with the previous Marketing Director, who 'went off in her own direction'.

Other individuals expressed concerns about the orchestra's artistic direction, including members of the management, board, and the orchestra itself. The musicians' representative, for example, expressed the need for a change from 'churning out Tchaikovsky', but felt they had now gone too far the other way, playing lesser known repertoire which was neither the orchestra's strength, nor popular with their audiences.

Despite the widely shared concern over the orchestra's artistic direction, developing a strategy proved difficult. In late 1997, the CEO responded to the widespread disquiet with an announcement that he intended to appoint an Artistic Director who would 'own the artistic policy in future'. In the meantime, the Chairman commented, 'We haven't got an artistic strategy

. . . the people struggling to find one are the conductor, the CEO, the Artistic Advisor, and the band.' He said that some months earlier he had also produced a 'strategic framework' document, which he had discussed with the orchestra because 'it was terribly important that it was owned by everybody'. The Board of Directors sought to contribute their views too and so an Artistic Sub-committee was formed. When the Artistic Director was appointed some months later, however, he decided that it was impractical to involve a committee in repertoire issues and instead worked with the Conductor on artistic planning.

Because of the number and diversity of stakeholder groups seeking input to the artistic strategy, the process was drawn out, with some difficult dynamics. Six months after his appointment, the Artistic Director still believed the big issue was 'to get the policy together', and at the Board's away-day in early 1999, he announced, 'I've been here for one year and I don't think I've made any impression at all.' At the same meeting, the Chairman said, 'We're accused of losing coherence in what we do and who we are. A compromise of what the Conductor wants and what's financially possible is what happens. It's impossible to create good concerts and certainly a long term strategy.' He concluded, 'We need agreement, even if it's not exactly to everyone's liking.'

Source: Adapted from S. Maitlis and T. Lawrence, 'Orchestral manoeuvres in the dark: discourse and politics in the failure to develop an artistic strategy', *Proceedings of the EIASM Workshop on Microstrategy and Strategising*, Brussels, 2001.

Questions

1. Write a brief report to the chief executive explaining what the problem is and what he should do.

2. How important is a written strategic plan in such circumstances? Why?

to address the political processes at work. This is addressed in other parts of this book, in particular sections 5.3.3 and 11.4.4, as well as in the commentaries at the end of each part of the book.

The ideas lens also suggests that organisational politics can be seen as a manifestation of the sort of conflict that results from innovation and new ideas. The variety and diversity that exist in organisations takes form in new ideas supported or opposed by different 'champions'. In this sense such battling over what is the best idea or the best way forward is to be expected as an inevitable manifestation of innovatory organisations. Indeed, arguably, if such conflict and tensions did not exist, neither would innovation. However, this lens would warn against the excesses of this. In so far as differences and conflict help spawn new ideas they can be productive: but there comes a point where this is not so, where the sort of inertia shown in Illustration 2.6 is the likely outcome.

2.3.4 Logical incrementalism

In a study of major multinational businesses, Quinn[31] concluded that the management process could best be described as *logical incrementalism*. Managers have a view of where they want the organisation to be in years to come and try to move towards this position incrementally. They do this by attempting to ensure the success and development of a strong, secure, but flexible core business, building on the experience gained in that business to inform decisions about the development of the business and perhaps experimenting with 'side bet' ventures. Such experiments cannot be expected to be the sole responsibility of top management – they have encouraged to emerge from lower levels, or 'subsystems', in the organisation. Effective managers realise that they cannot do away with the uncertainty of their environment by trying to 'know' about how it will change. Rather, they try to be sensitive to environmental signals through constant scanning and by testing changes in strategy in small-scale steps. Commitment to strategic options may therefore be tentative in the early stages of strategy development. There is also a reluctance to specify precise objectives too early, as this might stifle ideas and prevent experimentation. Objectives may therefore be fairly general in nature. Overall, **logical incrementalism** can be thought of as the deliberate development of strategy by 'learning through doing' or the 'crafting' of strategy.[32]

Logical incrementalism is the deliberate development of strategy by 'learning through doing'

This view of strategy making is similar to the descriptions that managers themselves often give of how strategies come about in their organisation. Illustration 2.7 provides some examples of managers explaining the strategy development process in their organisation. They see their job as 'strategists' as continually, proactively pursuing a strategic goal, countering competitive moves and adapting to their environment, whilst not 'rocking the boat' too much, so as to maintain efficiency and performance. Quinn himself argues that 'properly managed, it is a conscious, purposeful, pro-active, executive practice'.[33]

Again the strategy lenses help explain and interpret these findings. First the design lens.

Illustration 2.7

STRATEGY IN ACTION

An incrementalist view of strategic management

Managers often see their job as managing adaptively: continually changing strategy to keep in line with the environment, whilst maintaining efficiency and keeping stakeholders happy.

● 'You know there is a simple analogy you can make. To move forward when you walk, you create an imbalance, you lean forward and you don't know what is going to happen. Fortunately, you put a foot ahead of you and you recover your balance. Well, that's what we're doing all the time, so it is never comfortable.'[1]

● 'The environment is very fast changing. You can set a strategic direction one day and something is almost certain to happen the next. We do not have a planning process which occurs every two years because the environment is stable, but a very dynamic process which needs to respond to the unexpected.'[1]

● 'I begin wide-ranging discussions with people inside and outside the corporation. From these a pattern eventually emerges. It's like fitting together a jigsaw puzzle. At first the vague outline of an approach appears like the sail of a ship in a puzzle. Then suddenly the rest of the puzzle becomes quite clear. You wonder why you didn't see it all along.'[2]

● 'The real strength of the company is to be able to follow these peripheral excursions into whatever . . . one has to keep thrusting in these directions; they are little tentacles going out, testing the water.'[3]

● 'We haven't stood still in the past and I can't see with our present set-up that we shall stand still in the future; but what I really mean is that it is a path of evolution rather than revolution. Some companies get a successful formula and stick to that rigidly because that is what they know – for example, [Company X] did not really adapt to change, so they had to take what was a revolution. We hopefully have changed gradually and that's what I think we should do. We are always looking for fresh openings without going off at a tangent.'[3]

● 'The analogy of a chess game is useful in this context. The objective of chess is clear: to gain victory by capturing your opponent's king. Most players begin with a strategic move, that assumes a countermove by the opponent. If the countermove materialises, then the next move follows automatically, based on a previous winning strategy. However, the beauty of chess is the unpredictability of one's opponent's moves. To attempt to predict the outcome of chess is impossible, and therefore players limit themselves to working on possibilities and probabilities of moves that are not too far ahead.'[4]

Sources:

1. Quotes from interviews conducted by A. Bailey as part of a research project sponsored by the Economic and Social Research Council (Grant No.: R000235100).
2. Extract from J.B. Quinn, *Strategies for Change*, Irwin, 1980.
3. Extracts from G. Johnson, *Strategic Change and the Management Process*, Blackwell, 1987.
4. From a manager on an MBA course.

Questions

1. With reference to these explanations of strategy development, what are the main advantages of developing strategies incrementally?
2. Is incremental strategy development bound to result in strategic drift (see section 2.4.2)? How might this be avoided?

- Logical incrementalism does not fit a neat sequential design approach to strategy development. The idea that the implementation of strategy somehow follows a choice, which in turn has followed analysis, does not hold. Rather, strategy is seen to be worked through in action.

- However, whilst strategy is not designed in terms of being pre-planned, it is nonetheless rationally thought through, taking account of the forces in the environment and the competences of the organisation.

The experience and ideas lenses help provide an understanding of how this happens and some of the benefits. Both these lenses emphasise the importance in strategy development of the activities and contribution of people throughout the organisation, in the 'subsystems' of the organisation, rather than just at the top.

- Sensing of environmental changes is done through these subsystems, drawing on the experience and sensing of people at different levels and in different roles in the organisation.

- The variety of these people's experience, emphasised by the ideas lens, is critical because it ensures sufficient diversity in the way the complexities of the environment and organisational capabilities are understood and interpreted. The top management role of providing overarching vision rather than tight control is also in line with the ideas lens.

- It can be argued that if strategies are developed in such a way, it has considerable benefits. Continual testing and gradual strategy implementation provides improved quality of information for decision making, and enables the better sequencing of the elements of major decisions. Since change will be gradual, the possibility of creating and developing a commitment to change throughout the organisation is increased. Because the different parts, or 'subsystems', of the organisation are in a continual state of interplay, the managers of each can learn from each other about the feasibility of a course of action. Such processes also take account of the political nature of organisational life, since smaller changes are less likely to face the same degree of resistance as major changes. Moreover, the formulation of strategy in this way means that the implications of the strategy are continually being tested out. This continual readjustment makes sense if the environment is considered as a continually changing influence on the organisation.

2.3.5 The learning organisation

The concept of the *learning organisation*,[34] and strategy development as a learning process, became popularised in the 1990s. In many respects it corresponds to the aspects of logical incrementalism described above, especially in so far as it starts with the argument that the uncertainty and complexity of the world of organisations cannot readily be understood purely analytically. The world to which organisations have to adapt appears to be so turbulent and unpredictable that traditional approaches to strategic management are simply not appropriate; there is little to be gained from formalised planning approaches with predetermined fixed objectives and analysis that may take weeks or months to work through. The idea that top managers can formulate strategies implemented by others also becomes redundant because top managers are less in touch with such a complex and turbulent world than others within the organisation.

It is the characteristics of the experience and ideas lenses that more closely match those of the learning organisation.

- There is a need for the continual challenge of that which is taken for granted in the organisation; so there is a need to develop organisations which are *pluralistic*, in which different, even conflicting ideas and views are welcomed; in which such differences are surfaced and become the basis of debate.

- *Experimentation* is the norm, so ideas are tried out in action and in turn become part of the learning process.

- This is more likely to take place where *informality* of working relationships is found. New ideas emerge more through *networks* of working relationships than through hierarchies; more through dialogue, even storytelling, than through formal analysis. If organisations are seen as *social networks*,[35] the emphasis is not so much on hierarchies as on different interest groups which need to cooperate with each other, negotiate what should be done and find ways of accommodating different views. For example, a multinational firm working on a global scale is unlikely to be solely reliant on formal structural processes to make things happen. It is likely that it will be dependent on the network of contacts that builds up over time between different parts of the organisation across the world.

- This is also a political process of *bargaining and negotiation*, so conflict and disagreement will occur; but this is an inevitable outcome of diversity and variety in organisations and should not necessarily be regarded as negative in the process of strategy development. The dangers are at the extremes; that conflict and disagreement become so pronounced that they get in the way of the benefits of diversity; or that the fear of diversity leads to formalised systems of planning and control that can dampen innovation and learning.

- Within this view, the job of top management is to create this sort of organisation by building teams and networks that can work in such ways; by allowing enough *organisational slack* that there is time for debate and challenge; and by releasing control rather than holding on to it. This may be done, for example, through the development of different types of organisational structure (see Chapter 9) and through the development of the everyday behaviour and culture of the organisation (see Chapters 10 and 11).

The **learning organisation** is capable of continual regeneration from the variety of knowledge, experience and skills of individuals within a culture which encourages mutual questioning and challenge around a shared purpose or vision

The **learning organisation** is, then, one capable of continual regeneration from the variety of knowledge, experience and skills of individuals within a culture which encourages mutual questioning and challenge around a shared purpose or vision.

2.3.6 Imposed strategy

There may be situations in which managers face what they see as the imposition of strategy by agencies or forces external to the organisation. Government may dictate a particular strategic course or direction – for example, in the public sector, or where it exercises extensive regulation over an industry – or choose to deregulate or privatise an organisation previously in the public sector. This may not be the choice or even the wish of the managers. Businesses in the private sector may also be subject to such imposed strategic direction, or significant constraints on their choices. The multinational corporation seeking to develop businesses in some parts of the world may be subject to governmental requirements to do this in certain ways, perhaps through joint ventures or local alliances. An operating business within a multidivisional organisation may regard the overall corporate strategic direction of its parent as akin to imposed strategy. Increasingly, managers in long-established businesses see themselves as having little choice but to change the way they do business as a result of the development of new forms of e-business and radical changes in the business environment, not least of which are new ways of doing business.

The different lenses also provide useful insights here.

- Whilst an imposed strategy may not be developed by the managers in the organisation concerned, the strategy has presumably been developed elsewhere and the sorts of explanation of strategy development already given may help explain how that has occurred.

- It might be argued – indeed governments have argued – that such imposed strategy is a way of overcoming the sort of strategic inertia that had arisen as a result of strategies developing incrementally on the basis of history, experience, existing cultural norms or the compromises that result from bargaining and negotiation of powerful groups in an organisation.

- The argument may also be put forward that the imposition of a general strategic direction can provide impetus for innovation and creativity. It creates the sort of overall declaration of intent and provides sufficient principles and guidelines for change to create 'adaptive tension' and competition of ideas, whilst avoiding overprescription and control of behaviours and solutions.

2.3.7 Multiple processes of strategy development

This discussion of different lenses and different strategy development processes raises three further important points:

- First, it has to be recognised that there is no one right way in which strategies are developed. This is discussed more fully below but it is sufficient here to point out that, for example, the way in which strategies develop in a fast-changing environment is not likely to be the same – nor should it be – as in an environment in which there is little change. (See section 2.4.3 below.)

- Second, it is very likely that the way in which strategies are developed will be seen differently by different people. For example, as Exhibit 2.2 shows,

Exhibit 2.9	Some configurations of strategy development processes

The findings below are based on a survey of perceptions of strategy development processes undertaken at Cranfield School of Management in the 1990s.

DOMINANT DIMENSIONS	CHARACTERISTICS	RATHER THAN	TYPICAL CONTEXTS
Planning Incrementalism (Logical incrementalism)	Standardised planning procedures Systematic data collection and analyses Constant environmental scanning Ongoing adjustment of strategy Tentative commitment to strategy Step-by-step, small-scale change	Intrusive external environment Dominant individuals Political processes Power groups	Manufacturing and service sector organisations Stable or growing markets Mature markets Benign environments
Incremental Cultural Political	Bargaining, negotiation and compromise amongst conflicting interests of groups Groups with control over critical resources more likely to influence strategy Standardised 'ways of doing things' Routines and procedures embedded in organisational history Gradual adjustments to strategy	Deliberate, intentional process Well-defined procedures Analytical evaluation and planning Deliberate managerial intent	Professional service firms (e.g. consultancy or law firms) Unstable, turbulent environment New and growing markets
Imposed Political	Strategy is imposed by external forces (e.g. legislation, parent organisation) Freedom of choice severely restricted Political activity likely within organisation and between external agencies	Strategy determined within the organisation Planning systems impact on strategy development Influence on strategic direction mainly by managers within the organisation	Public sector organisations, larger manufacturing and financial service subsidiaries Threatening, declining, unstable and hostile environments

senior executives tend to see strategies more in terms of design whereas middle management tend to see strategies rather more as the result of cultural political processes. Managers who work for government organisations or agents of government tend to see strategy as more imposed than those in the private sector.[36] People who work in family businesses tend to see more evidence of the influence of powerful individuals, who may be the owners of the businesses.

● Indeed, it is unlikely that any one process described above singularly explains what is occurring in the development of strategy in any organisation. There will be multiple processes at work. For example, if a planning system exists, it will not be the only process at work in the development of strategy. There will undoubtedly be some level of political activity, and elements of the strategy could well be imposed. Exhibit 2.9 shows how different processes take form in different organisational contexts.

2.4 IMPLICATIONS FOR STRATEGY DEVELOPMENT

The discussion so far has some important implications for the development of strategies and for managers involved in this. In this section some of these are discussed.

2.4.1 Intended and realised strategies

Conceiving of organisations' strategies in the different ways explained in this chapter means it is important to be careful about just what is meant by the concept of strategy.

- Typically, strategy has been written about as though it is developed by managers in an *intended*, planned fashion. **Intended strategy** is an expression of desired strategic direction deliberately formulated or planned by managers; or by a strategic leader. It may be that the implementation of this intended strategy is also planned in terms of resource allocation, control systems, organisational structure and so on. Strategy is here conceived of as a deliberate, designed process of development and implementation (see route 1 in Exhibit 2.10).[37] However, as the discussion on strategy development processes in this chapter shows, this does not necessarily explain how the **realised strategy**, that is, the strategy actually being followed by an organisation in practice, actually comes about.

- In many organisations that attempt to formulate detailed intended strategies, much of what is intended follows route 2 in Exhibit 2.10 and is *unrealised*; it does not come about in practice, or only partially so. There may be all sorts of reasons for this; the plans are unworkable; the environment changes after the plan has been drawn up and managers decide that the strategy, as planned, should not be put into effect; or people in the organisation or influential stakeholders do not go along with the plan. (Also see the discussion of the drawbacks of planning systems in section 2.3.1 above.)

- As discussed in section 2.3.6 above, strategies could also be *imposed* on an organisation (route 3 in Exhibit 2.10).

- If strategy is regarded as the long-term direction of the organisation, which develops over time, then it can be *emergent* (route 4 in Exhibit 2.10).[38] How this happens has been explained in different ways in section 2.3. The management of organisations depends a great deal on the *experience* of those involved, individual or collective, and embedded in organisational culture. Managers typically reconcile different views through *negotiation* and *political activity*, or by falling back on established ways of doing things, or *routines*, that make up the culture of the organisation. So strategy could develop in an emergent fashion as the *outcome of cultural and political processes.*

- Strategy development as explained in terms of *logical incrementalism* or *learning* may also take form in emergent strategies. Again the strategy

Intended strategy is an expression of desired strategic direction deliberately formulated or planned by managers

Realised strategy, the strategy actually being followed by an organisation in practice

| Exhibit 2.10 | Strategy development routes |

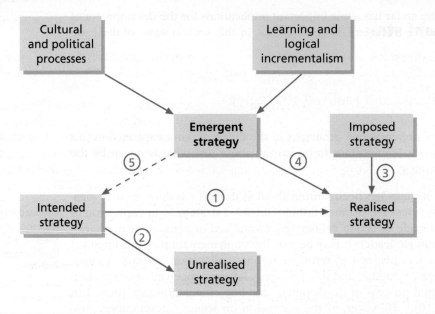

that develops is not predetermined by a plan, but grows from the interpretation by people in the organisation of their situation and the interaction, debate, and sometimes conflict between them.

● If plans exist, they may perform the role of monitoring the progress or efficiency of a strategy which emerges as the outcome of such experience and ways of doing things, or more proactive influencing of strategic direction from within the organisation (route 5 in Exhibit 2.10). Or, more cynically, they may do little more than pull together the views and 'wisdom' built up over time in the organisation. Indeed, it is often a complaint of chief executives that the planning systems in their organisation have degenerated into little more than post-rationalisations of where the organisation has come from. It can be dangerous because the organisation appears to be taking a proactive, systematic approach to strategy development when it is not.

There are a number of important practical implications for managers here.

● There may be a gap between what top managers think strategy is, or should be – the intended strategy, perhaps as stated in a strategic plan – and what is actually going on in practice – the realised strategy. Illustration 2.8 shows how Intel's top management believed the organisation was following one strategy in the 1980s when it was in fact developing another.

● The organisational effort, in terms of systems and management time, may be going into designing the intended strategy, when more effort needs to be

Illustration 2.8

Emergent strategy

Strategic direction may emerge from actions taken by middle management, and organisational routines rather than by strategy as designed by top management.

Intel, the world's largest manufacturer of microprocessors (MPs), was widely regarded as a highly innovative and skilfully managed high-technology company. However, Intel originated as a memory company, in the business of DRAMs – Dynamic Random Access Memory – and EPROMS – Erasable Programmable Read Only Memory. So how did the core business of Intel get transformed from DRAMs to MPs in the 1980s, and how did this happen, despite top management clinging to the view that DRAMs were the core strategic business of Intel?

Initially, the distinctive competences of Intel included design and process technology, in line with the basis of the competitive environment at that time. However, the industry was in a state of rapid change and fierce competition, and as such, the basis of competition shifted to manufacturing and commoditisation. Intel faced increasing turbulence in this new environment and attempted to solve their manufacturing problems by entering into the business of producing microprocessors.

One of the regulations within Intel was with respect to the allocation of manufacturing capacity: the different product divisions competed for manufacturing resources from the centre. Intel's resource allocation strategy criteria attempted to manifest the external competitive realities of the different businesses by allocating manufacturing capacity in proportion to the sectors that displayed the highest profit margins. Although the official corporate strategy was committed to memory, and top management continued to allocate R&D funds to work on memory, the reality of the cumulative events was that, as MPs gradually became more

profitable, manufacturing capacity was increasingly allocated away from memory and towards MPs.

Furthermore, Intel had a tradition and a culture of 'constructive confrontation'; candid discussions regarding the merits and demerits of the different strategic initiatives and allocation of resources were encouraged. Middle managers had a mandate to respond to the external competitive pressures of the environment. When several middle managers took the initiative to use a new process technology which favoured logic and MPs rather than memory, this resulted in the rapid growth of the MP business.

Despite the fact that the official corporate strategy was inherently committed to memory, Intel's external and internal environment produced a major shift in the allocation of resources away from the memory business to the emerging MP business. Although there was still heavy investment in DRAMs, the actual allocations for the manufacturing capacity were decided at lower levels in the organisation. By the time top management realised this, DRAMs' market share had diminished to such an extent that it needed an investment of several hundred million dollars in order to survive, and a decision was made to exit the memory business.

Prepared by Urmilla Lawson Graduate Business School, University of Strathclyde.

Source: R.A. Burgelman, 'Fading memories: a process theory of strategic business exit in dynamic environments', *Administrative Science Quarterly*, 39 (1994), pp. 24–56.

Questions

1. Identify the processes at work in strategy development at Intel in terms of those described in section 2.3.

2. Compare the change at Intel with the inertia at Kasper (Illustration 2.9). Suggest reasons why the strategy changed at Intel and not at Kasper.

spent on attending to the processes that give rise to the realised strategy, especially if significant strategic change is needed; and this may mean understanding and addressing cultural and political processes. Managing strategy does not just mean formulating intended strategy.

- It may be that the intentions of top management are not the best way forward. It could be that the direction of strategy that emerges from lower in the organisation is more appropriate to the needs of the organisation. The strategic contribution of middle and lower-level management is, for example, being increasingly recognised by researchers[39] and there exist well-documented accounts of significant changes in strategy occurring in this way, as Illustration 2.8 shows again in relation to Intel.

2.4.2 Strategic drift

Punctuated equilibrium is the tendency of strategies to develop incrementally with periodic transformational change

Historical studies of organisations have shown the prevalence of processes leading to emergent strategy.[40] There are usually long periods of relative *continuity* during which established strategy remains largely unchanged or changes *incrementally*, and there are also periods of *flux* in which strategies change but in no very clear direction. *Transformational* change, in which there is a fundamental change in strategic direction, does take place but is infrequent. This pattern has become known as **punctuated equilibrium**[41] – the tendency of strategies to develop incrementally with periodic transformational change – and is illustrated in Exhibit 2.11. In understanding this pattern the experience lens is particularly helpful.

| Exhibit 2.11 | Patterns of strategy development |

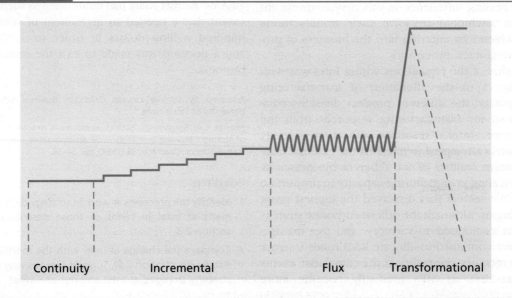

Continuity   Incremental   Flux   Transformational

Exhibit 2.12	The dynamics of paradigm change

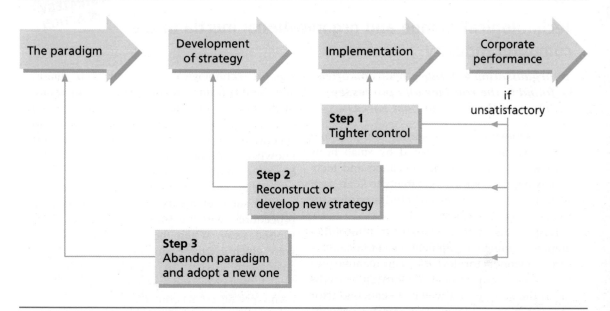

Source: Adapted from P. Grinyer and J-C. Spender, *Turnaround: Managerial recipes for strategic success*, Associated Business Press, 1979, p. 203.

There are strong forces at work which are likely to push organisations towards this pattern. Incremental strategic change is a natural outcome of the influence of experience. The influence of the paradigm and 'the way we do things around here' is likely to mean that, faced with pressures for change, perhaps because of changes in the environment, managers try to minimise the extent to which they are faced with ambiguity and uncertainty, by looking for that which is familiar. There are, however, dangers. Environmental change may not be gradual enough for incremental change to keep pace: if such incremental strategic change lags behind environmental change, the organisation will get out of line with its environment and, in time, need more fundamental, or transformational, change. Indeed, transformational change tends to occur at times when performance has declined significantly. There is another danger: that organisations become merely reactive to their environment and fail to question or challenge what is happening around them or to innovate to create new opportunities; in short, they become complacent.

All this raises difficulties when managing strategic change because it may be that the action required is outside the scope of the paradigm and the existing culture, and that members of the organisation would therefore be required to change substantially their core assumptions and ways of doing things. Desirable as this may be, the evidence is that it does not occur easily, as Illustration 2.9 shows. Managers are more likely to attempt to deal with the situation by searching for what they can understand and cope with in terms of the existing paradigm. Exhibit 2.12 shows how this might occur.[42] Faced with

Illustration 2.9

Technological change and organisational inertia in the computer industry

An organisation's 'Achilles heel' can often be found in the routines and processes which were the bases of past success.

In a fast-moving, technologically complex and innovative industry dominated by small firms with well-developed communication and technology transfer, one firm's inability to keep pace with innovations in manufacturing processes forced it out of business.

Kasper Instruments produced photolithographic alignment equipment, used to manufacture semiconductor devices. Their manufacture required the transfer of small, intricate patterns on to the surface of a wafer of semiconductor material such as silicon. This transfer process, called lithography, required only certain areas of the wafer to be exposed to light, with masks used to provide the appropriate shield.

Contact aligners were the first form of mask to be used commercially and, as the name suggests, these made contact with the wafers. Kasper Instruments' position as industry leader was because of its expertise in the contact alignment technique. However, as technology became more advanced, proximity masks were able to be used which did not come into contact with the wafer, so the risk of damage was reduced. Technology within the industry continued to develop incrementally until a quite different process of electron beam alignment was developed in which a focused beam wrote directly on to the wafer. Yet the industry leader was unable to make the technological transition; in the switch from contact to proximity aligners Kasper Instruments lost its position of industry leader to Canon and was ultimately forced to leave the industry.

The technological change needed for Kasper to keep pace with Canon and introduce the more efficient proximity alignment technique

was, in technological terms, relatively minor; and the top team at Kasper were keenly aware of the need to change. However, they seemed unable to rise to Canon's challenge, refusing to accept the obsolescence of their own expert knowledge in the contact technique. Whilst Kasper continually held on to the past, trying to modify its own production technique to include some elements of Canon's innovative procedures, with no success, its market share slipped away. When the engineers at Kasper were given a Canon proximity aligner to take apart with a view to producing their own model, they dismissed it as a mere copy of their own (very different) contact.

What seemed to be a small incremental development in technology required Kasper to totally rethink the way it did business, from its production processes to its sales and marketing strategies. In its failure to translate its technical understanding of the need for change by changing the routinised processes existing in the organisation, it was not alone. Throughout the history of technological change within this industry, each innovation has been a harbinger of doom for the market leader.

Prepared by Phyl Johnson Graduate Business School, University of Strathclyde.

Source: Adapted from R. Henderson and K. Clark, 'Architectural innovation: the reconfiguration of existing product technology and the failure of established firms', *Administrative Science Quarterly*, vol. 35 (1990), pp. 9–30.

Questions

1. Which processes of strategic management described in this chapter might have helped to avoid Kasper's problems?

2. Would these processes be suited to organisations facing less innovatory or changing environments?

Exhibit 2.13	The risk of strategic drift

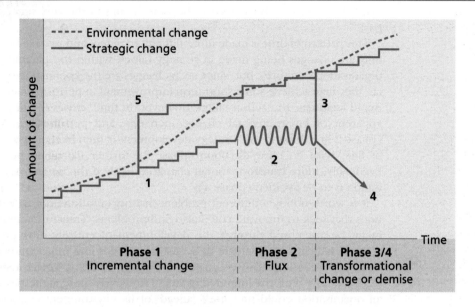

a stimulus for action, such as declining performance, managers first try to improve the implementation of existing strategy. This could be through tightening controls and improving accepted ways of operating. If this is not effective, a change of strategy may occur, but a change in line with the existing paradigm and ways of doing things. For example, managers may seek to extend the market for their business, but assume that it will be similar to their existing market, and therefore set about managing the new venture in much the same way as they have been used to. Alternatively, as shown in Illustration 2.9, even where managers know intellectually that they need to change, indeed know technologically how to do so, they find themselves constrained by organisational routines, assumptions or political processes. What is occurring is the predominant application of the familiar and the attempt to avoid or reduce uncertainty or ambiguity. This is likely to continue until there is, perhaps, dramatic evidence of the redundancy of the paradigm and its associated routines.

As observed earlier in the chapter, this is also an explanation of incremental strategy development. Indeed, it could be that changing the strategy within the paradigm makes sense: after all, it does encapsulate the experience of people in the organisation, and permits change to take place within what is familiar and understood. However, the outcome of processes of this kind may not keep strategy in line with environmental change. Rather, it may be adaptation in line with the experience enshrined in the organisational culture. Nonetheless, the forces in the environment will have an effect on performance. Over time, this may well give rise to the sort of **strategic drift** shown in Exhibit 2.13 (phase 1) in which the organisation's strategy gradually moves away from relevance to

Strategic drift occurs when the organisation's strategy gradually moves away from relevance to the forces at work in its environment

the forces at work in its environment. Even the most successful companies may drift in this way. Indeed, there is a tendency – which has become known as the Icarus Paradox – for businesses to become victims of the very success of their past.[43]

This pattern of drift is made more difficult to detect and reverse because, not only are changes being made in strategy (albeit within the parameters of the organisation's culture), but, since such changes are the application of the familiar, they may achieve some short-term improvement in performance, thus tending to legitimise the action taken. However, in time, either the drift becomes apparent or environmental change increases, and performance is affected (phase 2 in Exhibit 2.13). Strategy development is then likely to go into a state of flux, with no clear direction (phase 3), further damaging performance. Eventually, more transformational change is likely if the demise of the organisation is to be avoided (phase 4).

It is worth noting a different problem that organisations can face. Organisations that seek to innovate could also find problems. Transformational change might be attempted through the development of entirely new products or services which seek to create new customer needs and expectations not previously in existence. This could succeed and in so doing create a shift in the market in line with the intended strategy. However, there is the risk that such an organisation could find itself 'ahead' of its environment (represented by phase 5 in Exhibit 2.13). In the exhibit, the strategy and the environment eventually realign, but in reality this might not happen and the lag in time before such realignment could cause significant problems, not least in performance.

All this goes to emphasise the delicate balance that an organisation faces in developing its strategy. It has internal cultural pressures which tend to constrain strategy development, and environmental forces, not least in terms of its markets, with which it must cope. How it might do so is the central theme of this book.

2.4.3 Strategic management in uncertain and complex conditions

The different lenses and strategy development processes described in this chapter can also be seen to be more or less useful and applicable in different contexts. Not all organisations face similar environments and they differ in their form and complexity; therefore different ways of thinking about strategy development and different processes for managing strategy may make sense in different circumstances. Since one of the main problems of strategic management is coping with uncertainty, it is useful to consider this issue in terms of organisations facing different contexts.[44]

Exhibit 2.14 shows how organisations may seek to cope with conditions which are more or less stable or dynamic, and simple or complex.

● In *simple/static* conditions, the environment is relatively straightforward to understand and is not undergoing significant change. Raw materials suppliers and some mass-manufacturing companies are examples, at least from the

Exhibit 2.14	Strategy development in environmental contexts

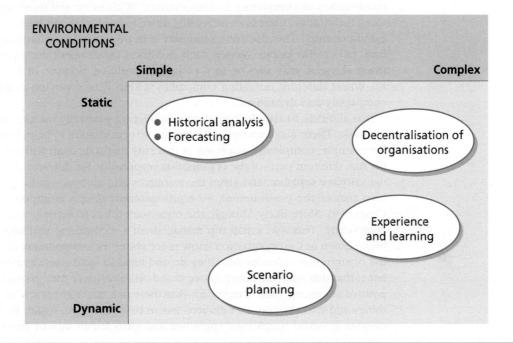

past. Technical processes may be fairly simple, and competition and markets remained the same over time. In such circumstances, if environmental change does occur, it may be predictable, so it could make sense to analyse the environment extensively on an historical basis as a means of trying to forecast likely future conditions. In situations of relatively low complexity, it may also be possible to identify some predictors of environmental influences. For example, in public services, demographic data such as birth rates might be used as lead indicators to determine the required provision of schooling, health care or social services. So in simple/static conditions, seeing strategy development in design terms may make sense.

- In *dynamic* conditions, managers need to consider the environment of the future, not just of the past. The degree of uncertainty therefore increases. They may employ structured ways of making sense of the future, such as *scenario planning*, which is discussed in the next chapter (see section 3.2.4), or they may rely more on encouraging active sensing of environmental changes low down in the organisation and the sort of *diversity and variety* seen as necessary through the ideas lens. Or they may do both. Change will need to be seen as normal and not reliant on lengthy reference up and down decision-making hierarchies. The emphasis is on creating the organisational conditions necessary to encourage individuals and groups to be intuitive and challenging in their thinking about possible futures through the sort of *learning organisation* described above.

- Organisations in *complex* situations face an environment difficult to comprehend. They may, of course, face dynamic conditions too, and therefore a combination of complexity and uncertainty. With more and more sophisticated technology, there is an increasing move towards this condition of greatest uncertainty. The electronics industry is in this situation. A multinational firm, or a major public service such as a local government authority with many services, may also be in a complex condition because of its diversity, whilst different operating companies within it face varying degrees of complexity and dynamism.

It is difficult to handle complexity by relying primarily on analysis and planning. There may be ways of designing the organisation to help, however: for example, complexity as a result of diversity might be dealt with by ensuring that different parts of the organisation responsible for different aspects of diversity are separate, and given the resources and authority to handle their own part of the environment. So *organisational design* is important (see Chapter 9). More likely, though, the organisation has to *learn* to cope with complexity. This may entail top management's recognising that specialists lower down in the organisation know more about the environment in which the organisation operates than they do and have to have considerable influence; that this strategic competence based on *experience* may provide competitive advantage (see Chapter 4); that there are not 'right ways' of doing things and that the taken-for-granted has to be challenged. Again, then, the insights gained through the experience and ideas lenses may be helpful.

Even from this brief review of different contexts, it should be clear why it is important to view strategy development processes in different ways. Indeed, arguably, organisational environments are becoming more dynamic and more complex; so holding to the design lens, and a reliance on analysis and planning as *the* way of developing strategy, would be very unwise.

2.5 SUMMARY AND IMPLICATIONS FOR THE STUDY OF STRATEGY

This chapter has dealt with different ways in which strategy development can be understood. These help to make sense of what is seen in organisations and also ways of thinking about how strategy should be developed. Some of the lessons of the chapter are now summarised and related to what follows in the rest of the book.

- There are different ways of making sense of the strategies of organisations. This chapter has provided three *lenses* by which to do so; strategy as *design*, as *experience* and as *ideas*.
- Most often the process of strategy development is described in terms of design; as a result of *analysis, evaluation and planning systems* carried out by top management objectively and dispassionately. However, there is evidence to show that this is not an adequate explanation of what occurs in practice.

- In explaining this, the *experience* lens can be helpful because it shows how the individual and collective experience of people and the taken-for-granted assumptions and routines of organisations (which take form in the *culture* of the organisation) tend to lead to future strategies being adaptations of strategies of the past.

- However, in order to understand how really innovatory strategies come about, or to see how some organisations are coping with rapidly changing and unpredictable environments, the *ideas* lens is also useful. Here the emphasis is on the *diversity and variety* of people and ideas in organisations and their environments, and therefore the potential for new ideas and initiatives emerging and creating new strategies rather than being designed.

- These lenses can be helpful in explaining and providing insight into different processes of strategy development observable in organisations. This chapter has considered:
  - the arguments for and against formal *strategic planning*;
  - how *strategic leaders* may influence the strategy of their organisations;
  - the way in which the bargaining and negotiation associated with *political activity* plays a part in strategy development;
  - how organisations may proactively try to cope with dynamic and uncertain environments through processes of *logical incrementalism* relying on strategies emerging from within the organisation and less on hierarchy and top-down control and direction; or more open *learning* systems in which the surfacing of assumptions, explicit debate about them and a diversity of views are encouraged;
  - how strategies might also be *imposed* on organisations by external agencies.

- It is unlikely that any one of these explanations sufficiently describes the strategy development processes in an organisation. Rather, it is likely that a mixture, or *configuration of processes*, accounts for how strategies develop.

- It is important to distinguish between the *intended* strategy of managers – that which they say the organisation should follow – and the *realised* strategy of an organisation – that which it is actually following. This is particularly important when considering how relevant the current strategy of an organisation is to a changing and competitive environment: it is likely to be more useful to consider the relevance of realised strategy than that of intended strategy.

- The realised strategies of organisations usually evolve *incrementally*, as a continual process of relatively small adjustments to existing strategy. Over time, the organisation may become out of line with a changing environment (*strategic drift*), eventually reaching a point of crisis. At this time, more fundamental or transformational change may occur. The result tends to be a pattern of *punctuated equilibrium* in which long periods of incremental strategy development are interrupted by periodic transformational change.

- Whilst processes of strategy development reliant on analysis of historical data may be helpful in *stable environments*, they will be less useful in *dynamic environments*, in which more attention needs to be given to ways of responding throughout the organisation to change; and *complex environments* in which, again, there is likely to be a need to recognise the strategic contributions of people throughout the organisation.

The approach taken in this book has been influenced by this understanding of how strategies develop in organisations. As has been said in Chapter 1, the idea of a purely sequential model of strategic management has been rejected. The sequence of understanding the strategic position, considering strategic choices and translating strategy into action is a useful structure for the book, and for thinking about the problems of strategy, but readers are urged to regard these aspects of strategic management as interdependent and an influence on one another; and just as likely to occur in terms of social, political and cultural processes as through formal planning systems. Nonetheless, the book also contains examples of, and references to, many techniques of quantitative and qualitative analysis. The value of such analytical approaches is not to be diminished. Not only do they provide an essential tool for managers to think through strategic problems and analyse possible solutions, but they can provide means whereby the taken-for-granted wisdom of the organisation and assumed courses of action can be questioned and challenged.

This chapter has highlighted the importance of viewing the processes of strategy development in different ways, through different lenses. These lenses will be employed throughout the rest of the book, but particularly at the end of Parts II, III and IV as a means of encouraging readers to do just this, and by so doing gain a fuller and more critical understanding of the management of strategy.

The overall aim is, then, to provide a framework for strategy and strategic management which usefully combines the rigour of analysis with the reality of the processes of management.

RECOMMENDED KEY READINGS

- For insights into the design lens see the debate between Henry Mintzberg and Igor Ansoff on the merits of different approaches to strategic management which appeared in the *Strategic Management Journal* in 1990 and 1991. These papers were 'The design school: reconsidering the basic processes of strategic management' by H. Mintzberg (vol. 11, no. 3, 1990), a critique of this by I. Ansoff (vol. 12, no. 6, 1991) and a riposte by Mintzberg entitled 'Learning 1, Planning 0' in the same volume.

- For further insights into discussions on processes of strategy development which relate to this chapter's explanation of the experience lens see the following:
  - A.M. Pettigrew, *The Awakening Giant*, Basil Blackwell, 1985, remains the fullest account of such processes in an organisation;
  - G. Johnson, 'Managing strategic change: strategy, culture and action', *Long Range Planning*, vol. 25, no. 1 (1992), pp. 28–36;
  - On incremental strategic change, see J.B. Quinn, *Strategies for Change: Logical incrementalism*, Irwin, 1980; also summarised in H. Mintzberg, J.B. Quinn and S. Ghoshal (eds), *The Strategy Process*, 4th edition, Prentice Hall, 1998;
  - Compare this with G. Johnson, 'Rethinking incrementalism', *Strategic Management Journal*, vol. 9, no. 1 (1988), pp. 75–91;
  - K. Daniels and J. Henry (1998) 'Strategy: a cognitive perspective', in S. Segal-Horn (ed.), *The Strategy Reader*, Blackwell, for a discussion of the influence of individuals' mental models on strategy.

- For a book on strategic management which builds on the concept of understanding and eliciting managers' mental models as a basis for addressing many of the issues raised in this text, see C. Eden and F. Ackerman, *Making Strategy: The journey of strategy*, Sage Publications, 1998.

- *Competing on the Edge* by S.L. Brown and K.M. Eisenhardt, Harvard Business School Press, 1998, employs evolutionary theory and complexity theory to re-examine strategy; and is therefore a good example of the application of the ideas lens. Also see R.D. Stacey, *Strategic Management and Organisational Dynamics. The Challenge of Complexity*,

3rd edition, Pearson Education, 2000, for a detailed discussion of complexity theory in relation to strategic management.

- Other writers also take multiple perspectives on the study of strategic management. Two good examples are: R. Whittington, *What is Strategy - and does it matter?*, Thomson Learning, 2001, and H. Mintzberg, *The Strategy Safari: A guided tour through the wilds of strategic management*, Free Press, 1998.

REFERENCES

1. There are numerous explanations of strategic management from a multiple perspective approach, for example: R. Whittington, *What is Strategy - and does it matter?*, Thomson Learning, 2001; H. Mintzberg, *The Strategy Safari: A guided tour through the wilds of strategic management*, Free Press, 1998; E.E. Chaffe, 'Three models of strategy', *Academy of Management Review*, vol. 10, no. 1 (1985), pp. 89-98; and C.R. Schwenk, *The Essence of Strategic Decision Making*, Lexington Books, 1988.

2. The design view is represented in most strategy textbooks. For example, see A.J. Rowe, R.O. Mason, and K.E. Dickel, *Strategic Management: A methodological approach*, Addison-Wesley Publishing, 1987, and R. Grant, *Contemporary Strategic Analysis: Concepts, techniques, applications*, 4th edition, Blackwell, 2002.

3. V. Ambrosini with G. Johnson and K. Scholes, *Exploring Techniques of Analysis and Evaluation in Strategic Management*, Prentice Hall, 1998, contains a paper by A. Bailey and C. Avery entitled 'Discovering and defining the process of strategy development', which shows the research approach used in this survey and provides a means of analysing processes of strategy development in organisations. For a more detailed explanation of the research see A. Bailey, G. Johnson and K. Daniels, 'Validation of a multi-dimensional measure of strategy development processes', *The British Journal of Management*, vol. 11 (2000), pp. 151-162.

4. The idea of strategy 'momentum' is explained more fully in D. Miller and P. Friesen, 'Momentum and revolution in organisational adaptation', *Academy of Management Journal*, vol. 23, no. 4 (1980), pp. 591-614.

5. Though the term 'experience' is used in this chapter, studies which have examined this at the individual level are often referred to as research in managerial cognition. For an explanation and examples of such work, see A. Huff, *Mapping Strategic Thought*, Wiley,

1990; and for a discussion of individual cognition and relationships to strategy see K. Daniels and J. Henry, 'Strategy: a cognitive perspective', in S. Segal-Horn (ed.), *The Strategy Reader*, Blackwell, 1998. For an example of a study which looks at how managers' mental models influence strategy see R. Calori, G. Johnson, and P. Sarnin, 'CEOs' cognitive maps and the scope of the organization', *Strategic Management Journal*, vol. 15, no. 6 (1994), pp. 437-457.

6. This definition is taken from E. Schein, *Organisational Culture and Leadership*, 2nd edition, Jossey-Bass, 1992, p. 6.

7. For a good summary of institutional theory, see W.R. Scott, *Institutions and Organizations*, Sage, 1995.

8. 'Paradigm' is a term used by a number of writers: see, for example, J. Pfeffer, 'Management as symbolic action: the creation and maintenance of organisational paradigms', in L.L. Cummings and B.M. Staw (eds), *Research in Organisational Behaviour*, JAI Press, 1981, vol. 3, pp. 1-15, and G. Johnson, *Strategic Change and the Management Process*, Blackwell, 1987.

9. See 'Everyday innovation/everyday strategy', G. Johnson and A.S. Huff, in *Strategic Flexibility - Managing in a Turbulent Environment*, G. Hamel, G.K. Prahalad, H. Thomas and D. O'Neal (eds), Wiley, 1998, pp. 13-27.

10. See Z.J. Acs and D.B. Audretsch, 'Innovation in large and small firms - an empirical analysis', *American Economic Review*, vol. 78, September (1988), pp. 678-690.

11. See E. von Hippel, *The Sources of Innovation*, Oxford University Press, 1988.

12. See M.A. Hitt, R.E. Hoskisson and H. Kim, 'International diversification: effects of innovation and firm performance in product-diversified firms', *Academy of Management Journal*, vol. 40, no. 4 (1997), pp. 767-798.

13. The most extensive use of evolutionary and complexity theories in the discussion of strategy is to be found in S.L. Brown and K.M. Eisenhardt, *Competing on the Edge*, Harvard Business School Press, 1998.

14. For those who want to read more on evolutionary theory, a simple introduction is J. Miller and V. Van Loom, *Darwin for Beginners*, Icon Books, 1992. A more challenging read is D.C. Dennett, *Darwin's Dangerous Idea*, Penguin, 1995.

15. Evidence on the importance of consensus in organisations can be found in G. Dess and N. Origer, 'Environment, structure and consensus in strategy formulation: a conceptual integration', *Academy of Management Review*, vol. 12, no. 2 (1987), pp. 313–330, and G. Dess and R. Priem, 'Consensus-performance research: theoretical and empirical extensions', *Journal of Management Studies*, vol. 32, no. 4 (1995), pp. 401–417.

16. See Brown and Eisenhardt, reference 13.

17. For a fuller discussion of complexity theory see R.D. Stacey, *Strategic Management and Organisational Dynamics. The Challenge of Complexity*, 3rd edition, Pearson Education, 2000.

18. See M.S. Granovetter, 'The strength of weak ties', *American Journal of Sociology*, vol. 78, no. 6 (1973), pp. 1360–1380.

19. See Brown and Eisenhardt, reference 13.

20. C.W. Reynolds, 'Flocks, herds and schools: a distributed behaviour model', *Proceedings of SIGGRAPH '87, Computer Graphics*, vol. 21, no. 4 (1987), pp. 25–34, as quoted in R.D. Stacey, reference 17, p. 277.

21. This discussion is based on research by K.M. Eisenhardt and D.N. Sull reported in 'Strategy as simple rules', *Harvard Business Review*, January 2001, pp. 107–116.

22. See Stacey, reference 17.

23. See Brown and Eisenhardt, reference 13.

24. L.C. Rhyne, 'The relationship of strategic planning to financial performance', *Strategic Management Journal*, vol. 7, no. 5 (1986), pp. 423–36, indicates that, whilst most research on the subject does show some benefits from financial planning, other studies give contrary or non-conclusive findings on the relationship between formal planning and performance. P. McKiernan and C. Morris, 'Strategic planning and financial performance in the UK SMEs: does formality matter?', *Journal of Management*, vol. 5 (1994), pp. S31–S42, also conclude that there is little evidence of direct links between formal planning and performance.

25. These conclusions are drawn from H. Mintzberg, *The Rise and Fall of Strategic Planning*, Prentice Hall, 1994.

26. Sherman's quote is taken from B.G. James, *Business Wargames*, Penguin, 1985, p. 190.

27. Also from Mintzberg, reference 25.

28. 'Strategic planning in oil and gas companies' is a study carried out by Rob Grant. His findings are available in R.M. Grant, 'Strategic planning among the major oil and gas corporations', Working Paper, McDonough School of Business, Georgetown University, Washington, DC, 1999.

29. See Brown and Eisenhardt, reference 13.

30. There has been relatively little published which has examined strategic management explicitly from a political perspective, but it is a central theme of D. Buchanan and D. Boddy, *The Expertise of the Change Agent: Public performance and backstage activity*, Prentice Hall, 1992.

31. J.B. Quinn's research involved the examination of strategic change in companies and was published in *Strategies for Change*, Irwin, 1980. See also J.B. Quinn, 'Strategic change: logical incrementalism', in H. Mintzberg, J.B. Quinn and S. Ghoshal (eds), *The Strategy Process* (European edition), Prentice Hall, 1995.

32. See H. Mintzberg, 'Crafting strategy', *Harvard Business Review*, vol. 65, no. 4 (1987), pp. 66–75.

33. See J.B. Quinn, *Strategies for Change*, reference 31, p. 58.

34. The concept of the learning organisation is explained in P. Senge, *The Fifth Discipline: The art and practice of the learning organisation*, Doubleday/Century, 1990.

35. The concept of the organisation as a set of social networks is discussed by, for example, M.S. Granovetter, 'The strength of weak ties', *American Journal of Sociology*, vol. 78, no. 6 (1973), pp. 1360–80, and G.R. Carroll and A.C. Teo, 'On the social networks of managers', *Academy of Management Journal*, vol. 39, no. 2 (1996), pp. 421–40.

36. For a discussion of the differences between strategy development in the public and private sectors see N. Collier, F. Fishwick and G. Johnson, 'The processes of strategy development in the public sector' in *Exploring Public Sector Strategy*, G. Johnson and K. Scholes (eds), Pearson Education, 2001.

37. The framework used here is, in part, derived from the discussion by H. Mintzberg and J.A. Waters, 'Of strategies, deliberate and emergent', *Strategic Management Journal*, vol. 6, no. 3 (1985), pp. 257–272.

38. There are now numerous books and papers which show the significance of cultural and political processes: for example, the books published by researchers at the Centre for Corporate Strategy and Change at Warwick Business School, including A. Pettigrew, *The Awakening Giant*, Blackwell, 1985; and A. Pettigrew, E. Ferlie and L. McKee, *Shaping Strategic Change*, Sage, 1992. See also G. Johnson, *Strategic Change and the Management Process*, Blackwell, 1987. Institutional theorists also emphasise the extent

to which managers are 'captured' by their institutional culture; see W.R. Scott, *Institutions and Organizations: Foundations for organizational science*, Sage, 1995.

39. For a discussion of the role of middle management in strategy development, see S. Floyd and W. Wooldridge, *The Strategic Middle Manager*, Jossey-Bass, 1996.

40. The origins of this explanation of emergent strategy are a paper by H. Mintzberg and J.A. Waters, 'Of strategies deliberate and emergent', *Strategic Management Journal*, vol. 6, no. 3 (1985), pp. 257–272.

41. The concept of punctuated equilibrium is explained in E. Romanelli and M.L. Tushman, 'Organisational transformation as punctuated equilibrium: an empirical test',

Academy of Management Journal, vol. 37, no. 5 (1994), pp. 1141–1161.

42. This figure is based on that shown in P. Grinyer and J-C. Spender, *Turnaround: Managerial recipes for strategic success*, Associated Business Press, 1979, and *Industry Recipes: The Nature and Sources of Management Judgement*, Blackwell, 1989.

43. See D. Miller, *The Icarus Paradox*, Harper Business, 1990.

44. R. Duncan's research, on which this classification is based, could be found in 'Characteristics of organisational environments and perceived environmental uncertainty', *Administrative Science Quarterly*, vol. 17, no. 3 (1972), pp. 313–327.

WORK ASSIGNMENTS

* Refers to a case study in the Text and Cases edition. ✻ Denotes more advanced work assignments.

2.1 Using the three lenses explained in section 2.2, give different explanations for the development of the strategy followed by Honda (see chapter case example).

2.2 Using the different explanations in section 2.3, characterise how strategies have developed in different organisations (e.g. Honda, Ericsson,* KPMG A *).

2.3✻ Planning systems exist in many different organisations. What role should planning play in a public sector organisation such as local government or the National Health Service and a multinational corporation such as AOL/Time Warner (see Illustration 1.1) or The News Corporation.*

2.4 With reference to the explanations of incremental strategy development in Illustration 2.7, what are the main advantages and disadvantages of trying to develop strategies incrementally?

2.5 Read the annual report of a company with which you are familiar as a customer (for example, a retailer or transport company). Identify the main characteristics of the intended strategy as explained in the annual report, and the characteristics of the realised strategy as you perceive it as a customer.

2.6✻ Incremental patterns of strategy development are common in organisations, and managers see advantages in this. However, there are also risks of strategic drift. Compare how lessons from both the design lens and the ideas lens suggest such drift might be avoided whilst retaining the benefits of incremental strategy development.

2.7 Suggest why different approaches to strategy development might be appropriate in different organisations such as a university, a fashion retailer and a high-technology company.

CASE EXAMPLE

Honda and the US motorcycle market in the 1960s

In 1984, Richard Pascale published a paper which described the extraordinary success Honda had experienced with the launch of their motorcycles in the US market in the early 1960s. It was an article that has generated discussion about strategy development processes ever since.

The US market had been served by Harley Davidson of the USA, BSA, Triumph and Norton of the UK and Moto-Guzzi of Italy. In 1959 Harley was the market leader with total sales of $16.6 million. But the total British share of the US industry was 49 per cent at that time. By 1973, however, the British share had dropped to only 9 per cent. This was largely the result of the incursions of Honda in the 1960s, following the setting up in 1959 of the American Honda Motor Company. Honda sales rose from $500,000 in 1960 to $77 million in 1965.

In his paper, Richard Pascale provided not one, but two accounts of how this extraordinary market success had occurred. What follows are extracts from his paper.

The Boston Consulting Group's and Harvard Business School's accounts of the success

Following the dramatic decline in the British share of the US motorcycle industry from 1959 to 1973, in 1975 the Boston Consulting Group (BCG) issued a report to the British Government summarising their findings of their study into Honda's strategy in the motorcycle industry.

> The success of the Japanese manufacturers originated with the growth of their domestic market during the 1950s. This resulted in a highly competitive cost position which the Japanese used as a springboard for penetration of world markets with small motorcycles in the early 1960s. (BCG, 1975: xiv)

Other studies, for example by the Harvard Business School, explained Honda's success in the USA.

After the second world war, motorcycles in the USA attracted a very limited group of people other than police and army personnel who used motorcycles on the job. While most motorcyclists were no doubt decent people, groups of rowdies who went around on motorcycles and called themselves by such names as 'Hell's Angels', 'Satan's Slaves', gave motorcycling a bad image. A 1953 movie called 'The Wild Ones' starring a 650cc Triumph, a black leather jacket and Marlon Brando gave the rowdy motorcyclists wide media coverage. The stereotype of the motorcyclist was a leather-jacketed, teenage troublemaker.

Honda's marketing strategy was described in the 1963 annual report as 'With its policy of selling, not primarily to confirmed motorcyclists but rather to members of the general public who had never before given a second thought to a motor-cycle. . . .' Honda started its push in the US market with the smallest, lightweight motorcycles. It had three-speed transmission, an automatic clutch, five horse-power (the American cycle only had two and a half), an electric starter and step-through frame for female riders. And it was easier to handle. The Honda machines sold for under $250 in retail compared with $1,000–$1,500 for the bigger American or British machines.

By June 1960 Honda's Research and Development effort was staffed with 700 designers/engineers. This might be contrasted with 100 engineers/draftsmen employed by . . . [European and American competitors]. In 1962 production per man-year was running at 159 units, [a figure not reached by Harley-Davidson until 1974]. Honda's fixed asset investment was $8170 per employee . . . [more than twice that of its European and American competitors]. With 1959 sales of $55 million Honda was already the largest motorcycle producer in the world.

In 1961 they lined up 125 distributors and spent $150,000 on regional advertising. Their advertising was directed to the young families, their advertising theme was 'You Meet the Nicest People on a Honda'. This was a deliberate attempt to dissociate motorcycles from rowdy, Hell's Angels type people.

Again, quoting from the Boston Consulting Group report:

> The Japanese motorcycle industry, and in particular Honda, the market leader, present a [consistent] picture. The basic philosophy of the Japanese manufacturers is that high volumes per model provide the potential for high productivity as a result of using capital intensive and highly automated techniques. Their market strategies are therefore directed towards developing these high model volumes, hence the careful attention that we have observed them giving to growth and market share.

The Honda executives

The second version of events was based on interviews with the Japanese executives based in the US who actually launched the motorcycles. This was quite different:

> There were only 3,000 motorcycle dealers in the United States at that time and only 1,000 of them were open 5 days a week. The remainder were open on nights and weekends.
>
> My other impression was that everyone in the United States drove an automobile – making it doubtful that motorcycles could ever do very well in the market. However, with 450,000 motorcycle registrations in the US and 60,000 motorcycles imported from Europe each year, it didn't seem unreasonable to shoot for 10 per cent of the import market.
>
> In truth, we had no strategy other than the idea of seeing if we could sell something in the United States. It was a new frontier, a new challenge, and it fit the 'success against all odds' culture that Mr. Honda had cultivated. We did not discuss profits or deadlines for breakeven. Fujisawa (the co-founder of Honda) told me if anyone could succeed, I could and authorised $1 million for the venture.
>
> We knew our products at the time were good but not far superior. Mr. Honda was especially confident of the 250cc and 305cc machines. The shape of the handlebar on these larger machines looked like the eyebrow of Buddha, which he felt was a strong selling point. Thus, after some discussion and with no compelling criteria for selection, we configured our start-up inventory with 25 per cent of each of our four products – the 50cc Supercub and the 125cc, 250cc and 305cc

machines. In dollar value terms, of course, the inventory was heavily weighted toward the larger bikes.

> We chose Los Angeles where there was a large second and third generation Japanese community, a climate suitable for motorcycle use, and a growing population. We were so strapped for cash that the three of us shared a furnished apartment that rented for $80 per month. Two of us slept on the floor.
>
> We were entirely in the dark the first year. We were not aware the motorcycle business in the United States occurs during a seasonable April-to-August window – and our timing coincided with the closing of the 1959 season. Our hard-learned experiences with distributors in Japan convinced us to try to go to the retailers direct. By spring of 1960, we had forty dealers and some of our inventory in the stores – mostly larger bikes. Then disaster struck.
>
> By the first week of April 1960, reports were coming in that our machines were leaking oil and encountering clutch failure. As it turned out, motorcycles in the United States are driven much farther and much faster than in Japan. Our testing lab worked twenty-four-hour days bench testing the bikes to try to replicate the failure. Within a month, a redesigned head gasket and clutch spring solved the problem. But in the meantime, events had taken a surprising turn.
>
> Throughout our first eight months, following Mr. Honda's and our own instincts, we had not attempted to move the 50cc Supercubs. While they were a smash success in Japan (and manufacturing couldn't keep up with demand there), they seemed wholly unsuitable for the US market where everything was bigger and more luxurious.
>
> We used the Honda 50s ourselves to ride around Los Angeles on errands. They attracted a lot of attention. One day we had a call from a Sears buyer. But we still hesitated to push the 50cc bikes out of fear they might harm our image in a heavily macho market. But when the larger bikes started breaking, we had no choice. And surprisingly, the retailers who wanted to sell them weren't motorcycle dealers, they were sporting goods stores.

Pascale went on to explain:

> In the spring of 1963, an undergraduate advertising major at UCLA submitted, in fulfilment of a routine course assignment, an ad campaign for Honda. Its theme: You Meet the Nicest People on a Honda. Encouraged by his instructor, the student passed his

work on to a friend at Grey Advertising. Grey attempted to sell the idea to Honda.

The President and Treasurer favoured another proposal from another agency. The Director of Sales, however, felt strongly that the Nicest People campaign was the right one - and his commitment eventually held sway. Thus, in 1963, through an inadvertent sequence of events, Honda came to adopt a strategy that directly identified and targeted that large untapped segment of the marketplace that has since become inseparable from the Honda legend.

By 1964, nearly one out of every two motorcycles sold was a Honda. As a result of the influx of medium income leisure class consumers, banks and other consumer credit companies began to finance motor-cycles - shifting away from dealer credit, which had been the traditional purchasing mechanism available. Honda, seizing the opportunity of soaring demand for its products, took a courageous and seemingly risky position. Late in 1964, they announced that there-after, they would cease to ship on a consignment basis but would require cash on delivery. Honda braced itself for revolt. While nearly every dealer questioned, appealed, or complained, none relinquished his fran-chise. In one fell swoop, Honda shifted the power relationship from the dealer to the manufacturer.

Making sense of the success

Clearly these two separate accounts are very different, yet they describe the same market suc-cess. Since the publication of the paper, many writers on strategy have hotly debated what these accounts actually represent.

Source: This case example is based on R.T. Pascale, 'Perspectives on strategy: the real story behind Honda's success', *California Management Review*, vol. 26, no. 3 (Spring 1984), pp. 47–72.

Questions

1. Which characteristics of the three lenses discussed in section 2.2 apply to the different accounts in the case?

2. Are the different accounts mutually exclusive? Explain your view.

3. Do you think Honda would have been more or less successful if they had adopted a more formalised strategic planning approach to their launch?

4. The Harvard account refers to the statement of strategy in the 1963 Honda annual report (see page 90 above). If this statement was based on a strategic plan, what was the plan based on?

PART

II

THE STRATEGIC POSITION

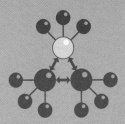

This part of the book is concerned with understanding the forces which influence, or have to be taken into account in, the development of strategy. There are those who argue that the forces at work in an industry or market are the most important: for example, that companies in more attractive environments will perform better than those in less attractive environments. So strategy development is about 'fit': that is, identifying opportunities in the environment and building strategy by matching resource capabilities to those opportunities. Others argue that the resources and competences of organisations are what are most important because they explain differences between organisations, potential uniqueness and therefore superior performance. They take a 'stretch' view, arguing that strategies should be built on the unique competences and resources of an organisation, by seeking out markets in which such competences have special value or by trying to create new markets on the basis of such competences.

There are other considerations too. Organisations have different stakeholders (shareholders, customers, employees, perhaps government) who have expectations of the organisation and may exercise considerable influence and power over the strategy to be followed. As Chapter 2 showed, cultural similarities across industries or within, for example, professions, may also exercise an influence on strategy.

Strategic management involves understanding and managing these different forces affecting the organisation and this part of the book discusses them.

- The overall theme theme of Chapter 3 is how managers might make sense of an uncertain and increasingly complex world around them. This is addressed by considering various layers of influence from macro influences to specific forces affecting competition. However, simply identifying particular influences is not sufficient. The challenge for a strategist is to cope with the interaction of these different forces.

- Chapter 4 is concerned with understanding an organisation's strategic capability and how it underpins the competitive advantage of the organisation or sustains excellence in providing value-for-money products or services. Running through the chapter is the theme that strategic capability is really about the knowledge organisations have in relation to three issues: the resource base of the organisation; how these resources are deployed and controlled to create organisational competences; and how activities are

THIS PART EXPLAINS:

● The impact of the environment, organisational capabilities and expectations on strategy.

● How to understand an organisation's position in the environment.

● The determinants of strategic capability – resources, competences and the linkages between them.

● The factors which shape organisational purposes – corporate governance, stakeholder expectations, business ethics and the cultural context.

linked together, both inside the organisation and in the 'supply' and 'distribution' chains. Core competences are also explained as those activities and processes – and indeed the organisational knowledge about these – which underpin the competitive edge of the organisation and are difficult for others to imitate.

● Chapter 5 is about how expectations 'shape' organisational purposes and strategies. This is considered within four main themes. Corporate governance is concerned with understanding whom the organisation is there to serve. Stakeholder influence raises the important issue of power relationships on and in organisations. A discussion of ethics raises the question of what organisations should be doing strategically. And a discussion of cultural influences helps explain how national, institutional and organisational cultures affect organisational purposes and strategy.

Although this part of the book is divided into three chapters, it should be stressed that there are strong links between these different influences on strategy. Environmental pressures for change will be constrained by the resources available to make changes, or by an organisational culture which may lead to resistance to change; and capabilities yielding apparent opportunities will be valuable only if opportunities in the environment can be found. The relative importance of the various influences will change over time and may show marked differences from one organisation to another. However, the ability of an organisation to find ways to integrate these different influences in such a way as to create value is vitally important. This notion of integration is encapsulated

---

Exhibit IIi   **The business idea**

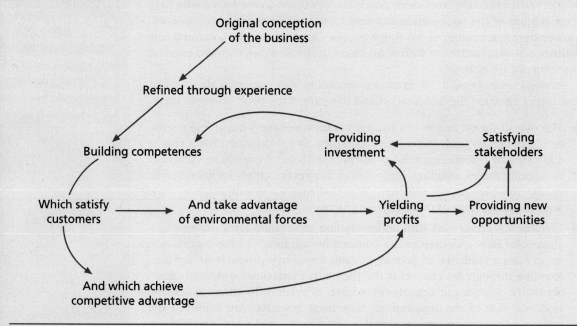

in the concept of the business idea,* a model of why and how an organisation has been successful by reconciling the different forces and influences on strategy. This is represented in Exhibit IIi. It shows schematically how an original idea for a business which has developed successfully will have found a way of operating such that environmental forces, organisational resources and competences, and stakeholder expectations mutually reinforce one another. Less successful organisations would not be experiencing the same sorts of reinforcing cycles: the different forces would be pulling in different directions rather than being mutually reinforcing. The business idea is a concept to which we return in the commentary at the end of Part II to emphasise the important lesson of integration, but also to ask how organisations might achieve it.

* The business idea is developed in *Scenarios: The art of strategic conversation*, by Kees van der Heijden, J. Wiley, 1996.

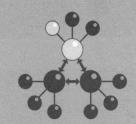

3

The Environment

LEARNING OUTCOMES

After reading this chapter you should be able to:

- Describe the forces in the macro-environment of an organisation using the PESTEL framework.
- Identify key structural drivers of change and the differential impact on organisations.
- Develop scenarios and explain their implications.
- Define an industry and give examples of industry convergence.
- Use the five forces framework to identify the sources of competition for a strategic business unit.
- Explain what is meant by cycles of competition and the impact of hypercompetition.
- Define strategic groups and explain how the concept helps with an understanding of competition.
- Explain the concept of organisational fields.
- Explain what is meant by market segmentation and how it helps in understanding what customers value.
- Explain the different types of strategic gap that might present opportunities to organisations.

3.1 INTRODUCTION

The theme of this chapter is how managers – whether private or public sector[1] – can make sense of an uncertain world around their organisation – the business environment. This can be difficult for several reasons, as discussed in section 2.4.3. First, 'the environment' encapsulates many different influences – the difficulty is making sense of this *diversity*. Identifying very many environmental influences may be possible, but it may not be much use because no overall picture emerges of the really important influences on the organisation. The second difficulty is that of the *speed of change*. Managers typically feel that the pace of technological change and the speed of global communications mean more and faster change now than ever before.[2] Third is the problem of

| Exhibit 3.1 | Layers of the business environment |

complexity. Managers are no different from other individuals in the way they cope with complexity; they try to simplify what is happening by focusing on those few aspects of the environment which have been important historically. It is important to find ways to avoid these tendencies whilst achieving an understanding of the environment which is both usable and oriented towards the future.

In this chapter, frameworks for understanding the environment of organisations are provided with the aim of helping to identify key issues and ways of coping with change and complexity. These frameworks are provided in a series of 'layers' briefly introduced here and summarised in Exhibit 3.1.

- The most general 'layer' of the environment is often referred to as the *macro-environment*. This consists of broad environmental factors that impact to a greater or lesser extent on almost all organisations. It is important to identify these issues and particularly those that are likely to have a differentially large impact on a specific organisation. The PESTEL (and similar) frameworks can help this discussion since they look at the way in which future trends in the *political, economic, social, technological, environmental and legal* environments might impinge on organisations.

- Any specific factor in the general environment will affect some organisations more than others. Also, it will affect some organisations favourably whilst posing a threat to others. So a key question is whether it is possible to identify the *structural drivers* which might affect individual organisations or organisations of particular types.

● If the future environment is likely to be very different from the past it is helpful to construct pictures – or *scenarios* – of possible futures. This helps managers consider the different ways in which strategies might need to change depending on how the business environment might unfold. Of course, for many organisations there may be a problem of knowing whether the future is likely to be very different from the past.

● Within this broad general environment the next 'layer' would be called an industry. This is a group of organisations producing the same products or services. However, it is also important to understand how previously separate industries might converge, as seen in the AOL/Time Warner illustration in Chapter 1. The *five forces* framework and the concept of *hypercompetition* can be useful in understanding how the competitive dynamics within and around an industry are changing.

● Within most industries or sectors there will be many different organisations with different characteristics and competing on different bases. So there is a need to understand some intermediate 'layer' between the industry and the individual organisation. The concept of *strategic groups* can help this understanding. These are organisations within an industry that have similar characteristics to each other but are quite different from those in other strategic groups.

● These discussions of industries and strategic groups will highlight the fact that organisations are networked with and economically tied to a whole series of other organisations and not just to other 'producers'. For example, the fortunes of an organisation are intimately linked with those in their supply and distribution chains; a local government housing department in a major city is part of a complex network of organisations all concerned with 'regeneration' (private developers, central government agencies, venture capitalists) and so on. The concept of *organisational fields* will be introduced as a way of understanding this wider network of influences and relationships in the business environment.

● The customers and consumers of an organisation's products or services are of critical importance. So the concept of *markets* and how they are structured is equally important to the understanding of the structure of production. The concepts of *market segmentation, customer value* and *life cycles* are discussed.

● All of these concepts can contribute to answering the key managerial question, namely the extent to which the business environment is likely to help or hinder an organisation's competitive position and performance and how opportunities and threats might arise in the future. This will be reviewed in the final part of the chapter.

3.2 THE MACRO-ENVIRONMENT

3.2.1 The PESTEL framework[3]

Illustration 3.1 shows some of the macro-environmental influences which might affect organisations. It is not intended to provide an exhaustive list, but

Illustration 3.1

Examples of environmental influences

A wide range of environmental influences can affect organisational strategies and performance.

Government action
In 1999, the UK government set up the National Institute for Clinical Excellence (NICE). NICE was part of the NHS and used teams of experts to provide patients, health professionals and the public with authoritative, robust and reliable guidance on the current 'best practice'. This guidance covered both individual health technologies and the clinical management of specific conditions (including approving the use of specific drugs).

Capital markets
In 1999 and the early part of 2000 the world stock markets were driven higher and higher by investors' love affair with technology stocks. But then came the crash. Stock markets lost some 20 per cent of their value by early 2001 and technology stocks lost far more. The hardest hit were Internet and telecommunications companies – many losing 90 per cent of their market valuation. This forced them to scale down their development plans drastically and many smaller companies went bankrupt (see Illustration 10.6 for further details).

Demographics
By the year 2000, the trend of an ageing population was well established in the western economies. This provided many companies with an easily identifiable target market for their goods and services.

Other markets, such as Asia, however, had been experiencing a population explosion and a resulting reduction in the average age of their population, which gave these markets their own particular needs and opportunities.

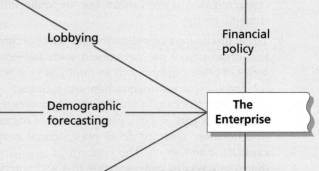

Sociocultural
Growing health consciousness and social pressures on smokers in western countries have adversely affected the sales of tobacco products in these markets. Public pressure has also led to stringent regulations relating to tobacco advertising, methods of promotion, and packaging. Coupled with heavy taxes and court cases, which have bitten into their profits and share prices, tobacco companies have recently concentrated their marketing efforts on the developing world.

Technology
The introduction of new multimedia mobile services such as data, entertainment and text messaging has been more than just the next level of telecommunications achievements – it has also been the driving force behind many changes in other industrial and service sectors. These new data services require secure transactions over mobile networks, more processing power and increased memory capacity. As a result, smart-card manufacturers, banking applications developers and billing software developers have all increased their investment in R&D in order to capitalise on this technology.

Questions

1. Using this illustration and Exhibit 3.2 as a guide, draw up an andit for an 'industry' environment of your choice

2. Which of the influences you identified are likely to be the main 'drivers for change' in future? Why?

Prepared by Urmilla Lawson, Graduate Business School, University of Strathclyde.

Labour markets
In 2001 the UK government attempted to remedy labour shortages in some public services by new approaches to recruitment and retention of nurses and teachers. This included offering higher salaries with bonuses and allowances, hiring from abroad, making home ownership more available in expensive parts of the country (through initiatives such as shared ownership and equity schemes), and encouraging those who had left the profession, taken early retirement or let their registration lapse to return to work.

Competition
Deregulation of the UK financial services sector led to intense competition within the industry. In the 1990s, there were a vast number of new entrants in the form of supermarkets, retail outlets and Internet banks, and many building societies shed their mutual ownership status, converting to public companies. In response, many banks merged or acquired other financial service providers in order to obtain the critical mass required to be successful, reduce costs and expand into new markets. Most notable were Royal Bank of Scotland's takeover of NatWest Bank and HSBC's takeover of Midland Bank.

Labour policy and industrial relations

Marketing policy

The Enterprise

Economic forecasting

Environmental sensing and R&D policy

Purchasing

Economy
Taiwan, with a population of 22 million people, has played a key role in the electronics industry. This has assisted it in eluding the economic recession that has hit much of Asia. In the 1990s, Taiwan's electronics factories evolved from contract manufacturers into designer-manufacturers. This shift to design and creation of products has led to the outsourcing of manufacturing to China. This capability to move steadily into higher-value information technology products has been the basis of Taiwan's export-driven and thriving economy. Taiwan's prosperity as an electronics workshop has been the result of partnering with the US computer industry – in 2000, Compaq, Dell and IBM all outsourced approximately 65 per cent of their notebook computer requirements to Taiwan.

Ecology
Huntingdon Life Sciences (HLS), the biggest drug-testing company in Europe, was targeted by anti-vivisection protesters and animal-rights groups following a documentary about the company in 2000. HLS used about 70,000 animals a year to test the effectiveness of pharmaceuticals. Animal-rights militants launched an offensive of intimidation and violence against employees of the company and any organisation connected with HLS. During their campaign, Barclays, Royal Bank of Scotland, Citibank and Merrill Lynch all severed ties with HLS. As a result of the protesters' tactics and negative publicity, many shareholders sold their shares and banks called in their loans, leaving HLS on the verge of bankruptcy.

Suppliers
In autumn 2000, the price of oil products leapt in response to a combination of surging crude oil values, tension in the Middle East and the onset of a heavy refinery maintenance season. This led to an attendant rise in heating oil and gasoline as consumption rose whilst inventories were at a minimum. As a result, there was an increase in the price of airline tickets, pigments, inks, waxes and resins – anything that used crude oil. It also created record profits for oil companies and triggered unprecedented public protests in many European countries.

Exhibit 3.2	Macro-environmental influences – the PESTEL framework

1. **What environmental factors are affecting the organisation?**
2. **Which of these are the most important at the present time? In the next few years?**

Political
- Government stability
- Taxation policy
- Foreign trade regulations
- Social welfare policies

Sociocultural factors
- Population demographics
- Income distribution
- Social mobility
- Lifestyle changes
- Attitudes to work and leisure
- Consumerism
- Levels of education

Environmental
- Environmental protection laws
- Waste disposal
- Energy consumption

Economic factors
- Business cycles
- GNP trends
- Interest rates
- Money supply
- Inflation
- Unemployment
- Disposable income

Technological
- Government spending on research
- Government and industry focus on technological effort
- New discoveries/development
- Speed of technology transfer
- Rates of obsolescence

Legal
- Monopolies legislation
- Employment law
- Health and safety
- Product safety

it gives examples of ways in which strategies are affected by such influences and some of the ways in which organisations seek to handle aspects of their environment.[4]

The **PESTEL framework** categorises environmental influences into six main types: political, economic, social, technological, environmental and legal

Exhibit 3.2 shows the **PESTEL framework**, which categorises environmental influences into six main types: political, economic, social, technological, environmental and legal. It provides a summary of some of the questions to ask about key forces at work in the macro-environment.

It is particularly important that PESTEL is used to look at the *future* impact of environmental factors, which may be different from their past impact. Scenarios may help with this and are discussed in section 3.2.4 below. Also, environmental forces which will be especially important for one organisation may not be so important for another. For example, a multinational corporation might be especially concerned with government relations and understanding future policies of individual country governments, since it may be operating plants or subsidiaries within many different countries with different political systems. It is also likely to be concerned with how labour costs and exchange rates might change, as these factors will affect its ability to compete with multinational rivals. A retailer, on the other hand, may have been primarily concerned with local customer tastes and behaviour. But the situation might be changing as commonality of consumer tastes develops across old (national) boundaries, providing both an opportunity and threat to retailers depending on how they respond. A computer manufacturer is likely to be concerned with developments in the technological environment that lead to product innovation and obsolescence. Public sector managers and civil servants are likely to be especially concerned with changes in public policy, public funding levels and demographic changes.

3.2.2 Structural drivers of change

The items in Exhibit 3.2 are of limited value if they are merely seen as a listing of influences. It is, therefore, important that the implications of the PESTEL factors are understood. It may be possible to identify a number of **structural drivers of change**, which are forces likely to affect the structure of an industry, sector or market. It will be the *combined effect* of some of these separate factors that will be so important, rather than the factors separately. A good example can be found in the forces which are increasing the globalisation of some industries and markets (see Exhibit 3.3).[5]

Structural drivers of change are forces likely to affect the structure of an industry, sector or market

- There is an increasing *convergence of markets* worldwide for a variety of reasons. In some markets, customer needs and preferences are becoming more similar. For example, there is increasing homogeneity of consumer tastes in goods such as soft drinks, jeans, electrical items (e.g. audio equipment) and personal computers. The opening of McDonald's outlets in most countries of the world signalled similar tendencies in fast food. As some markets globalise, those operating in such markets become *global customers* and may search for suppliers who can operate on a global basis. For example, the global clients of the major accountancy firms may expect the accountancy firms to provide global services. In turn, this may provide opportunities for *transference of marketing* across countries. Marketing policies, brand names and identities, and advertising may all be developed globally. This further generates global demand and expectations from customers, and may also provide marketing cost advantages for global operators. Nor is the public sector immune from such forces. For example, universities are subject to similar trends reinforced by changing delivery technologies through the Internet.

- There may be *cost advantages* of global operations. This is especially the case in industries in which large volume, standardised production is required for optimum *economies of scale*, as in some components of the electronics industry. Other cost advantages might be achieved by central *sourcing efficiencies* from lowest-cost suppliers across the world. *Country-specific costs*, such as labour or exchange rates, encourage businesses to search globally for low cost in these respects as ways of matching the costs of competitors which have such advantages because of their location. For example, given increased reliability of communication and cost differentials of labour, some software companies base their customer service departments in India, where there is highly skilled but low-cost staff. A telephone

Exhibit 3.3   Drivers of globalisation

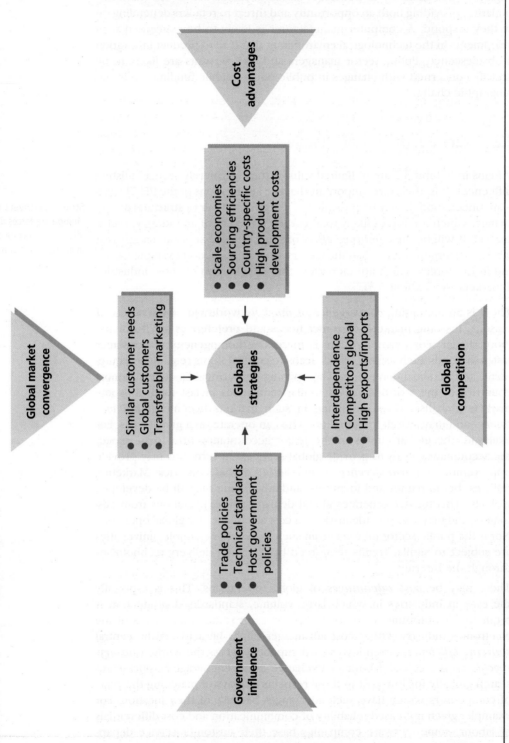

Source: Based on G. Yip, *Total Global Strategy*, Prentice Hall, 1995, chapter 2.

enquiry from Holland could well be routed to Bombay. The strength of the British currency against the newly introduced euro in 1999/2000 further drove the trend of 'offshore' sourcing by manufacturers and retailers. Other businesses face high *costs of product development* and may see advantages in operating globally with fewer products rather than incurring the costs of wide ranges of products on a more limited geographical scale.

- The activities and policies of *governments* have also tended to drive the globalisation of industry. Political changes in the 1990s meant that almost all trading nations function with market-based economies and their *trade policies* have tended to encourage free markets between nations. This has led to major concerns (and public demonstrations) about the impact on developing countries. This has been further encouraged by *technical standardisation* between countries of many products, such as in the automobile, aerospace and computing industries. However, it is worth noting that in many industries country-specific regulations still persist and reduce the extent to which global strategies are possible. It may also be that particular *host governments* actively seek to encourage global operators to base themselves in their countries.

- *Global competition* is therefore becoming increasingly evident, and as it does, it encourages further globalisation. If the levels of *exports and imports* between countries are high, it increases interaction between competitors on a more global scale. If a business is competing globally, it also tends to place globalisation pressures on competitors, especially if customers are also operating on a global basis. It may also be that the *interdependence* of a company's operations across the world encourages the globalisation of its competitors. For example, if a company has sought out low-cost production sites in different countries, these low costs may be used to subsidise competitive activity in high-cost areas against local competitors, thus encouraging them to follow similar strategies.

3.2.3 Differential impact of environmental influences

Understanding how PESTEL factors might impact on and drive change in general is only really a starting point. Managers need to understand the *differential impact* of these external influences and drivers on particular industries, markets and individual organisations. For example, some industries (such as telecommunications) may have more potential for global development than others (such as some sectors of retailing).

The example of globalisation used above may be particularly important in some industries. But, as shown in Illustration 3.2, the impact may be different in different parts of the business. However, the same process of identifying key drivers and their differential impact could be applied to other important environmental themes. For example, the public services might be particularly influenced by the impact of an ageing population. This would have several drivers (as with the globalisation example), such as medical advances, social/political stability, economic advancement and so on. Also, the impact on

Illustration 3.2

Global forces at Pilkington

Global forces can impact differently in different parts of the same business.

The early twenty-first century continued to provide tough challenges for manufacturing organisations based in developed economies. This was particularly true for manufacturers of basic materials such as steel or glass as they experienced fierce competition around the world. Pilkington, based in St Helens, UK, started glass manufacturing in 1826. But the major breakthrough for the company was its development of the float glass manufacturing process, announced in 1959. This revolutionised glass manufacturing and led to a major international expansion of the company – largely through acquisitions. By the 1990s the company turnover was some £3 billion and it had major operations in Europe, North America, South America and Australasia.

Flat glass has two major uses – in the building industry for windows and doors in domestic and commercial properties, and for glazing systems in automobiles. Competition in the glass industry and their customers' industries was increasingly globalising the operation of glass companies. Some of these global forces impacted right across the business whilst others impacted differently in the building products and automotive sectors:

Government influence

Issues in this category included a general increase in free trade, regulations about the insulation standards in houses and office buildings, and government actions to attract inward investment – for example, in the location of manufacturing plants for automobiles. Eastern Europe had opened up as a market since the revolutions of the late 1980s and the new

governments were less willing to subsidise uneconomic locally owned plants.

Global market convergence

The automobile industry was highly globalised with the major manufacturers operating in most parts of the world. Their product standardisation programmes led them to prefer suppliers who could source worldwide. In contrast, the building industry was very fragmented and building design, methods and requirements varied considerably from one continent to another. Climate was a crucial issue.

Cost advantages

Glass was a fragile, heavy and relatively low-cost item. So shipping 'raw' glass long distances was uneconomic. However, glass manufacturing was also capital intensive – a float plant would cost some £60 million and needed to run at its annual capacity of 200,000 tonnes to 'pay its way'.

Global competition

As a result of some of these other forces, primary glass production had seen a progressive reduction in the number of companies. By 2000 there were only six major glass companies of any size, of which only three (Pilkington, Asahi and Saint Gobain) could claim to have a significant presence in the major markets worldwide – either through their own plants or through partnerships.

Source: Company publications (with permission).

Questions

1. Using Exhibit 3.3, draw up separate 'maps' for the building products and automobile glass sectors.
2. Explain how this might influence the way that the company is organised.

particular parts of the public services is different – increasing (in *relative* terms) the need for health care and reducing services aimed at or driven by younger people (such as primary schools and courts).

3.2.4 Scenarios[6]

When the business environment has high levels of uncertainty arising from either complexity or rapid change (or both), different approaches will be needed to understand the future impact of the environment. *Scenarios* are especially useful in circumstances where it is important to take a long-term view of strategy, probably a minimum of five years; where there are a limited number of key factors influencing the success of that strategy; but where there is a high level of uncertainty about such influences. A **scenario** is a detailed and plausible view of how the business environment of an organisation might develop in the future based on groupings of key environmental influences and drivers of change about which there is a high level of uncertainty. For example, in the oil industry there is a need for views of the business environment of up to 20 years; and whilst a whole host of environmental issues are of relevance, a number of these, such as raw material availability, price and demand, are of crucial importance. Obviously, it is not possible to forecast precisely such factors over a 20-year time horizon, but it can be valuable to have different views of possible futures. In other industries the level of uncertainty is very high even for much shorter time horizons and scenario planning may be valuable too. Scenario planning does not attempt to predict the unpredictable and, therefore, considers multiple, equally plausible, futures. These scenarios are not just based on a hunch; they are logically consistent but different from each other as shown in Illustration 3.3.

A **scenario** is a detailed and plausible view of how the business environment of an organisation might develop in the future based on groupings of key environmental influences and drivers of change about which there is a high level of uncertainty

Sharing and debating these scenarios improves organisational learning by making managers more perceptive about the forces in the business environment and what is really important. For example, scenarios can be used to examine the *Business Idea*[7] (which was explained in the introduction to Part II).

Scenarios have three key ingredients: first, the building of the scenarios around the key drivers; second, the development of strategies (or contingency plans) for each scenario; third, the monitoring of the environment to see how it is actually unfolding, and adjusting strategies and plans accordingly. It is not inconceivable that several scenarios could unfold over time, requiring significant adjustments to the team strategy. Illustration 3.3 shows how the scenario planning process can be undertaken.

It can be seen that assumptions about the key drivers in the business environment are essential to the process of building scenarios. It is important that the number of assumptions is kept to just a few, since the complexity in drawing up scenarios rises dramatically in proportion to the number of assumptions included; this can be done, for example, by focusing on the factors which (i) have high potential impact and (ii) are uncertain (as with the four factors identified in Illustration 3.3(a) on the book publishing industry). Each of these factors may have different futures (again see Illustration 3.3a). These factors may 'combine' to create scenarios of the future, such as the three

Illustration 3.3

Building scenarios

The book publishing industry and oil industry both face changing environments which are hard to predict on the basis of experience or historical analysis.

(a) The Book Publishing Industry: scenarios from configurations of factors

Step 1: Identify high-impact, high-uncertainty factors in the environment

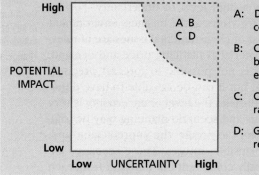

A: Development of electronic communications market

B: Consumer perceptions of books compared with electronic substitutes

C: Costs of paper and other raw materials

D: Government spending and regulation

Step 2: Identify different possible futures by factor

A: (i) Rapid change
   (ii) Measured change
B: (i) Favourable
   (ii) Unfavourable
C: (i) High and increasing
   (ii) Stabilising
D: (i) In support of books
   (ii) In support of electronic media

Step 3: Build scenarios of plausible configurations of factors

Scenario 1: No great change

Favourable consumer perceptions of books compared with electronic substitutes (B(i)) are supported by government spending and regulation (D(i)). There is measured change in the development of electronic communications markets (A(ii)) and stable costs of paper and other raw materials (C(ii)).

Scenario 2: Electronic chaos

Rapid change in the development of the electronic communications market (A(i)) is encouraged by government spending and regulation in support of electronic media (D(ii)). Further-more, unfavourable consumer perceptions of books compared with electronic substitutes (B(ii)) are combined with high and increasing costs of paper and other raw materials (C(i)).

Scenario 3: Information society

Stable consumer perceptions of books compared with electronic substitutes (B(ii)), measured change in the development of electronic communications markets (A(ii)) and government spending and regulation in support of books are favourable (D(i)). However, there is concern over the high and rising cost of paper and other raw materials (C(i)).

(b) Thematic scenarios at Shell

The oil industry faces an ever-changing environment which is hard to predict on the basis of past experience.

In an attempt to develop strategies for the 25 years between 1995 and 2020, the companies of the Royal Dutch/Shell Group developed two global scenarios. Whilst at an initial reading these scenarios might appear as 'favourable' and 'unfavourable', they can be seen as more complex in their implications.

New frontiers

In this scenario, economic and political liberalisation increase wealth creation in the societies which adopt them. However, enormous upheavals are also experienced as long-standing barriers are dismantled and poor countries assert themselves, claiming a larger role on the world's economic and political stage. Whilst rapid economic growth of 5-6 per cent is sustained in these developing countries, there is slow erosion of the comparative wealth of the developed world, which produces problems as new priorities and lifestyles are gradually established. Big companies find themselves increasingly challenged, as cheaper capital and fewer international barriers lead to an environment of relentless competition and innovation. This creates a high level of energy demand, and substantial new resource development and improvements in efficiency are required to fuel this growth and prevent demand outstripping supply.

Barricades

In this scenario, liberalisation is resisted and restricted because people fear they might lose what they value most - jobs, power, autonomy, religious traditions, cultural identity. This creates a world of regional, economic, cultural and religious division, and conflict in which international business cannot operate easily. Markets are constricted and difficult for outsiders to enter, as reforms are structured to help insiders. Oil prices are depressed because of instability, followed by a huge rise as trouble flares in the Middle East. There is increasing divergence between rich and poor economies as many poor countries become marginalised, partly due to a lack of foreign investment. In the developed world, coalitions of 'green' and other political interests increasingly cause energy to be regarded as something bad, other than for its tax-raising potential. The unfavourable investment climate which this produces is reinforced by the deep divides around the world. Widespread poverty and environmental problems are experienced in poorer countries, whilst in richer nations, a shrinking labour force and ageing population are causes for concern.

Prepared by Sara Martin, Cranfield School of Management, and Tony Jacobs, Bristol Business School.

Sources: Adapted from *Long Range Planning*, vol. 28, no. 6 (1995), pp. 38–47; *Accountancy*, March 1995, pp. 54–55.

Question

Choose another industry with which you are familiar (or the brewing industry from the Case example of this chapter) and construct two or three scenarios for the future using one or both of the approaches in this illustration.

in Illustration 3.3(a). If the number of factors is large, scenarios may not 'emerge' easily in this way. They may be more concerned with the 'tone' of the future – for example, (i) an optimistic future and a pessimistic future, or (ii) according to dominant themes, as in Shell (Illustration 3.3b). In either case, the proponents of scenarios argue that the allocation of probabilities to factors should be avoided: it endows the scenarios with spurious accuracy, which can be unhelpful given the purpose of the scenarios.

3.3 INDUSTRIES AND SECTORS

The previous section looked at how general forces in the environment might influence an organisation and the success or failure of strategies. But the impact of these general forces tends to surface in the more immediate environment through changes in the competitive forces on organisations. An important aspect of this for most organisations will be competition within their industry or sector. Readers who have some knowledge of economic theory will be familiar with the notion of an **industry** as 'a group of firms producing the same principal product'[8] or, more broadly, 'the group of firms producing products that are close substitutes for each other'.[9] This concept of an industry can be extended into the public services through the idea of a *sector*. Social services, health care or education also have many producers of the same kinds of services. From a strategic management perspective it is useful for managers in any organisation to understand the competitive forces acting on and between organisations in the same industry or sector since this will determine the attractiveness of that industry and the way in which individual organisations might choose to compete. It may inform important decisions about product/market strategy and whether to leave or enter industries or sectors. However, it is important to remember that the boundaries of an industry may be changing – for example, by *convergence* of previously separate 'industries' such as between computing, telecommunications and entertainment as seen in the AOL/Time Warner illustration in Chapter 1 (Illustration 1.1). **Convergence** is where previously separate industries begin to overlap in terms of activities, technologies, products and customers.[10] Illustration 3.4 shows how one company was anticipating and adapting to convergence.

The boundaries of an industry might also be destroyed by forces in the macro-environment. For example, e-commerce is destroying the boundary of traditional retailing by offering manufacturers new or complementary ways to trade – what are now being called new 'business models'[11] – such as websites or e-auctions (as discussed in section 10.3). So the frameworks discussed below need to be considered against a future situation rather than historically. The subsections below will address three issues about competitive forces in an organisation's industry or sector:

- *Sources* of competition – using the five forces framework (section 3.3.1).
- The *dynamics* of competition and hypercompetition (section 3.3.2).
- An industry or sector is made up of a significant number of 'players' who are different from each other in terms of their characteristics and the strategies

An industry is 'a group of firms producing the same principal product'

Convergence is where previously separate industries begin to overlap in terms of activities, technologies, products and customers

Illustration 3.4

Chapter 2 at Pearson

STRATEGY IN ACTION

Changes in the business environment can create opportunities as industries converge.

By 2001 – four years after Marjorie Scardino became CEO – Pearson was transforming itself from a stodgy publisher into a global force in the media and education sectors. The transformation started with disposals – including the Tussaud Group of wax museums and shares in investment-banking interests. This was followed by more than 100 deals to pull together an empire more clearly focused on a vision for being a '21st century learning company, capable of delivering its products and services to any audience, on paper or on-line'. The rationale behind this was to service a transforming education market where people were not only in formal education longer but were re-educating themselves continuously – lifelong learning.

But to take advantage of this convergence of publishing, education and online technologies required some bold acquisitions. It started with the $4.6bn purchase of Simon & Schuster's education business – which instantly transformed Pearson into the educational publishing leader with 27 per cent of the key US school and college market. A further $3bn was spent on a collection of other education and publishing assets – including Britain's children's and illustrated book publisher Dorling Kindersley Holdings (which fell on hard times after a disastrous commercial misjudgement). Their boldest and most controversial move was to pay $2.5bn for National Computer Systems (NCS), a little-known educational testing company. Pearson reorganised itself into three groups:

- **Pearson Education** with sales of $3.3bn in 2000 and comprising: Prentice Hall, Scott Foresman, Addison-Wesley, Longman, National Computer Systems and Learning Network.
- **Penguin Group** with sales of $1.1bn in 2000 and comprising: Penguin, Putnam, Dorling Kindersley and Viking.
- **Financial Times Group** with sales of $1.3bn in 2000, and comprising: *Financial Times, Les Echos* (a French business newspaper), the Spanish newspaper group Recoletos, and Financial Times online.

But after all this frantic deal-making 'chapter 2' was beginning – getting financial results from the vision. Analysts conceded that Pearson probably had the most coherent strategy in publishing but worried as to whether the drive to introduce online technology into schools would be slowed by the bureaucracy and funding limitation of the education sector. Competitors also were claiming that Pearson had bitten off more than they could chew and were underestimating the difficulties of making 'electronic learning' work.

Source: Adapted from *Business Week*, 22 January 2001.

Questions

1. What factors are driving the opportunity for 'electronic learning'?
2. What dangers are Pearson running in their proactive approach to transforming these two industries (publishing and education)?
3. How might you change their approach?

that they are pursuing. There is a need for an intermediate level between that of the industry and the individual organisations that make up that industry. These are called *strategic groups* and are discussed in section 3.3.3.

Later sections of the chapter will look at how the competitive environment is also shaped by forces other than the producers within an industry or sector. First is a wider network of organisations, such as customers, suppliers and partners, called the *organisational field* and discussed in section 3.4 below. Also, because an industry or sector is defined in terms of producers rather than users of products and services, it is inward looking. Section 3.5 provides ways of looking at the structure of the competitive environment in terms of *customers and markets*.

3.3.1 Sources of competition – the five forces framework

Inherent within the notion of strategy is the issue of competitiveness. In business, this is about gaining advantage over competitors; in the public sector, it might be demonstrable excellence within a sector and/or advantage in the procurement of resources (the two will probably be linked). A problem is that managers often will take a far too parochial view as to the sources of competition, usually focusing their attention on direct competitive rivals (as discussed below). But there are many other factors in the environment which influence this competitiveness. The **five forces framework**[12] helps identify the sources of competition in an industry or sector (see Exhibit 3.4). Although initially used with businesses in mind, it is of value to most organisations.

The **five forces framework** helps identify the sources of competition in an industry or sector

When using this framework to understand competitive forces it is essential to bear the following in mind:

- It must be used at the level of *strategic business units* (as defined in Chapter 1 and discussed extensively in Chapters 6 and 7) and not at the level of the whole organisation. This is because organisations are diverse in their operations and markets. For example, an airline might compete simultaneously in several different arenas such as domestic and long haul, and target different customer groups such as leisure, business and freight. The impact of competitive forces is different in each of these.

- The framework must not be used just to give a snapshot in time. It is important not just to describe these forces but also to understand how they can be countered and overcome in the *future*.

- These competitive forces will not only be subject to steady changes into the future but, more importantly, to *discontinuities* caused by changes in the macro-environment discussed above. So understanding the connections between competitive forces and these structural drivers is essential. For example, technological changes can destroy many of the competitive advantages and barriers that have protected organisations historically. In the public services the same could be true with political discontinuities (such as a change of government).

- The five forces are *not independent* of each other. Pressures from one direction can trigger off changes in another in a dynamic process of shifting

| Exhibit 3.4 | The five forces framework |

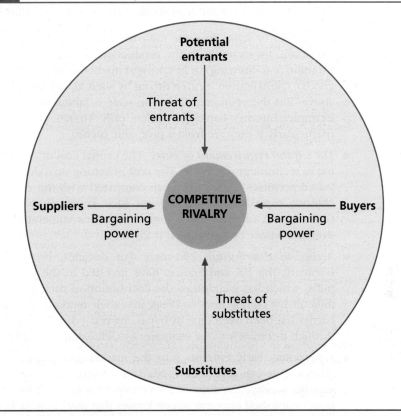

Source: Adapted from M.E. Porter, *Competitive Strategy: Techniques for Analyzing Industries and Competitors* © 1980, Free Press, 1980, p. 4. Copyright by The Free Press, a division of Simon & Schuster Inc. Reproduced with permission.

sources of competition. For example, potential new entrants finding them-selves blocked may find new routes to market by bypassing traditional distribution channels and selling directly to consumers. The discontinuity created by the rapid development of the Internet would, of course, favour such action.

● Competitive behaviour may be concerned with *disrupting* these forces and not simply accommodating them. This dynamic picture of competition will be discussed more fully in section 3.3.3 and has been referred to as hyper-competition.[13]

Bearing these caveats in mind, the five forces is a useful starting point in under-standing competitive forces.

The threat of entry

Threat of entry will depend on the extent to which there are **barriers to entry**. These are factors that need to be overcome by new entrants if they are to

Barriers to entry are factors that need to be overcome by new entrants if they are to compete successfully

compete successfully. These should been seen as providing *delays* to entry and not as permanent barriers. Also, they may deter many potential entrants but probably will not deter them all. Typical barriers are as follows:

- *Economies of scale.* In some industries, economies of scale are extremely important: for example, in the production of electrical components, in distribution (e.g. brewing) or in sales and marketing (e.g. fast-moving consumer goods). Globalisation is often driven by such global advantages as discussed above. But the economically viable scale is falling in some industries – for example, Internet banking requires only 10,000 customers to be viable (particularly if they are from a profitable niche).

- *The capital requirement of entry.* The capital cost of entry will vary according to technology and scale. The cost of setting up a dot.com business with leased premises is minimal when compared with the cost of, for example, entering capital-intensive industries such as chemicals, power or mining. Globalisation can also leave some companies vulnerable to entrants from overseas whose cost of capital is lower.

- *Access to distribution channels.* For decades, brewing companies, in Germany, the UK and France, have invested in the financing of bars and pubs, which has guaranteed the distribution of their products and made it difficult for competitors to break into their markets. In some markets this barrier has been overcome by bypassing retail distribution and direct selling through e-commerce (for example, by Dell Computers and Amazon).

- *Experience.* Early entrants into the market gain experience sooner than others. This can give them advantage in terms of cost and/or customer/ supplier loyalty. It is difficult for a competitor to break into a market if there is an established operator which knows that market well, has good relationships with the key buyers and suppliers, and knows how to overcome market and operating problems. Indeed in some cases they may have created a proprietary industry standard to the extent that the brand is synonymous with the product category (historically, *Hoover* for vacuum cleaners, *Reuters* for online news, and, more recently, *Microsoft* for computer operating systems). This phenomenon is related to the concept of the 'experience curve' and is dealt with in more detail in Chapter 4 (section 4.4.1). Of course, this experience will be less valuable when product life cycles are shortening and may be of no value at all when a major discontinuity occurs. The opening up of the public services to competitive forces is a good example of how the accumulated experience of negotiating with the providers of funds was rapidly eroded by a lack of experience in 'customer care' as this rose up the political agenda and became of prime importance when seeking funds and justifying budgets.

- *Expected retaliation.* If an organisation considering entering a market believes that the retaliation of an existing firm will be so great as to prevent entry, or mean that entry would be too costly, this is also a barrier. Entering the breakfast cereal market to compete with Kellogg's would be unwise unless very careful attention was paid to a strategy to avoid retaliation. This dynamic interaction between incumbents and potential new entrants will be discussed more fully in section 3.3.2 below. In global markets this retaliation can take place at many different 'points' or locations, as also discussed in section 3.3.2.

● *Legislation or government action.* Legal restraints on competition vary from patent protection, to regulation of markets (e.g. pharmaceuticals and insurance), through to direct government action. Of course, managers in hitherto protected environments might face the pressures of competition for the first time if governments remove such protection. For example, in the 1990s many public services such as telecommunications, electricity and gas supply and rail systems, traditionally operated as state monopolies, increasingly faced deregulation and/or privatisation.

● *Differentiation.* By differentiation is meant the provision of a product or service regarded by the user as different from and of higher perceived value than the competition; its importance will be discussed more fully in Chapter 7. However, here it is important to point out that organisations able to achieve strategies of differentiation provide for themselves barriers to competitive entry. However, this barrier can rapidly be eroded, for a number of reasons. Competitors may simply imitate the offering – so robustness to imitation may be an important consideration, as discussed in Chapters 4 and 6. Previously passive customers may become more educated about the choices available and more willing to exercise choice. This has happened with many services, such as legal services. Customers' needs may shift and competitors find new bases of differentiation. For example, reliability or speed of delivery may become more valued as the other product features become more similar between providers.

Illustration 3.5 shows the barriers to entry and the other cometitive forces in the mobile phone industry.

The threat of substitutes

Substitution reduces demand for a particular 'class' of products as customers switch to the alternatives – even to the extent that this class of products or services becomes obsolete. This depends on whether a substitute provides a higher perceived benefit or value. Substitution may take different forms:

● There could be *product-for-product substitution* – for example, e-mail substituting for a postal service. This is evidence that previously different sectors are converging, as mentioned above.

● There may be *substitution of need* by a new product or service, rendering an existing product or service redundant. For example, more reliable and cheaper domestic appliances reducing the need for maintenance and repair services. IT is already impacting significantly in this area – giving individuals the tools to undertake jobs for which they previously needed a service provider (e.g. from secretarial services or printing, through to e-commerce transactions).

Substitution reduces demand for a particular 'class' of products as customers switch to the alternatives

Illustration 3.5

The mobile phone industry

The five forces framework provides an understanding of the competitive nature of an industry.

Competitive rivalry

By 2000 the competitive rivalry between network operators was becoming intense. In the UK numerous different packages were on offer. If a customer threatened to withdraw, operators would offer a new free phone and several free months of line rental as an enticement to stay. In markets approaching saturation, emphasis was placed on cost, coverage, the offering of new products and services, and on general customer service.

Buying power

Buying power of consumers was high. The danger for providers was confusing consumers with over-complex offers. Independent firms (e.g. in the UK, Carphone Warehouse) competed with retailers owned by network operators (e.g. Vodaphone). Others offered cheaper deals through newspaper adverts and the Internet.

Power of suppliers

Equipment manufacturers competed for market share. Manufacturers with a considerable presence, Nokia, Motorola and Ericsson, had concerns about market saturation. The initial failure of WAP phones compared with the success of text messaging meant that to some extent customers had lost faith in the ability of equipment manufacturers to develop new functionality. Areas of potential growth were multi-task chips and smart cards in phones to aid m-commerce. Upgrading was now more important than market penetration.

Threat of substitutes

In the 1990s the main threat of substitution was 'technological regression' where customers returned to fixed line telephony because of high mobile call charges. By 2000, price decreases and the 'need' for everyone to have a mobile phone reduced this threat. More threatening was the convergence of mobile telephony with PDAs (personal digital assistants) and with the Internet. This was threatening because of the difficulty in predicting how these new technologies would be accepted in the market. The other threat was location technology in mobile phones, making you easy to find. An opportunity for marketers, in emergencies and personal safety if lost, but bringing big brother cons as well.

Threat of entrants

The threat of entrants was low because of the enormous cost in both licences (£22 billion in the UK alone) and in the general investment needed to be a player in new 3G (broadband) technology. Power was a function of who was ahead of the game in 3G. Future power struggles were likely to be a function of deregulation, upgrading and the uptake of new functionality.

Prepared by Jill Shepherd, Graduate Business School, University of Strathclyde.

Questions

Viewing this industry through the eyes of a network operator (such as BT Cellnet):

1. Which would you regard as the three most important threats to your business?

2. How could you respond to each of these to lessen their impact?

3. Answer questions 1 and 2 for an equipment manufacturer – such as Nokia.

4. What are the main benefits and limitations of the five forces framework?

- *Generic substitution* occurs where products or services compete for disposable income; for example, furniture manufacturers compete for available household expenditure with (amongst others) suppliers of televisions, videos, cookers, cars and holidays.

The power of buyers and suppliers

The next two forces can be considered together because they are linked. The relationship with buyers and sellers can have similar effects in constraining the strategic freedom of an organisation and in influencing the margins of that organisation.

Buyer power is likely to be high when some of the following conditions prevail:

- There is a concentration of buyers, particularly if the volume purchases of the buyers are high. This is the case in grocery retailing in France and the UK (and increasingly in other European countries), where just a few retailers dominate the market.
- The supplying industry comprises a large number of small operators.
- There are alternative sources of supply, perhaps because the product required is undifferentiated between suppliers or, as for many public sector operations, when the deregulation of markets spawns new competitors.
- The component or material cost is a high percentage of total cost, since buyers will be likely to 'shop around' to get the best price and therefore 'squeeze' suppliers.
- The cost of switching a supplier is low or involves little risk – for example, if there are no long-term contracts or supplier approval requirements.
- There is a threat of backward integration by the buyer (e.g. by acquiring a supplier) if satisfactory prices or quality from suppliers cannot be obtained.

Supplier power is likely to be high when:

- There is a concentration of suppliers rather than a fragmented source of supply. This is usually the case in the provision of finance by central government to public corporations such as the National Health Service or the BBC in the UK and has been seen as a major constraint to their development.
- The 'switching costs' from one supplier to another are high, perhaps because a manufacturer's processes are dependent on the specialist products of a supplier, as in the aerospace industry, or a product is clearly differentiated.
- The brand of the supplier is powerful – for example, a retailer might not be able to do without a particular brand.
- There is the possibility of the supplier integrating forwards if it does not obtain the prices, and hence the margins, it seeks.
- The supplier's customers are highly fragmented.

It is interesting to understand the *dynamics* of how organisations seek to change the balance of power between buyers and suppliers. For example:

- Many manufacturers, faced with competitive demands for lower prices and hence the need to reduce costs, have significantly reduced the number of suppliers of components. The remaining suppliers gained in volume orders but have had to prove themselves against strict criteria of price, quality and delivery.

- In the light of this trend, some suppliers might attempt to seek out market segments with less powerful buyers or to differentiate products so that buyers become more dependent on that product.

- A growing trend is to view the supplier/buyer relationship as a collaborative one of mutual interest – a point discussed in section 3.4 below. In the public sector, and now in some e-commerce businesses, this collaboration is often described as *co-production* since the buyer increasingly takes on activities previously undertaken by the supplier.

Competitive rivalry

Competitive rivals are organisations with similar products and services aimed at the same customer group

These wider competitive forces will impinge on the direct competitive rivalry between an organisation and its most immediate competitors. **Competitive rivals** are organisations with similar products and services aimed at the same customer group. There are a number of factors that affect competitive rivalry:

- The extent to which competitors are *in balance*. Where competitors are of roughly equal size, there is the danger of intense competition as one competitor attempts to gain dominance over another. Conversely, the less competitive markets tend to be those with dominant organisations within them and the smaller players have accommodated themselves to this situation (for example, by confining activities to certain niches).

- Market *growth rates* may affect rivalry. The idea of the life cycle suggests that conditions in markets, primarily between growth stages and maturity, are important, not least in terms of competitive behaviour. For example, in situations of market growth, an organisation might expect to achieve its own growth through the growth in the marketplace; whereas when markets are mature, this has to be achieved by taking market share from competitors. Exhibit 3.5 summarises some of the conditions that can be expected at different stages in the life cycle.

- *High fixed costs* in an industry, perhaps through high capital intensity, may result in price wars and very low-margin operations as capacity-fill becomes a prerogative.

- If the addition of *extra capacity is in large increments*, the competitor making such an addition is likely to create at least short-term overcapacity and increased competition.

- Again, *differentiation* is important. In a commodity market, where products or services are undifferentiated, there is little to stop customers switching between competitors.

- Where there are *high exit barriers* to an industry, there is again likely to be the persistence of excess capacity and, consequently, increased competition. Exit barriers might be high for a variety of reasons. For example, high investment in non-transferable fixed assets or high redundancy costs.

| Exhibit 3.5 | The life-cycle model |

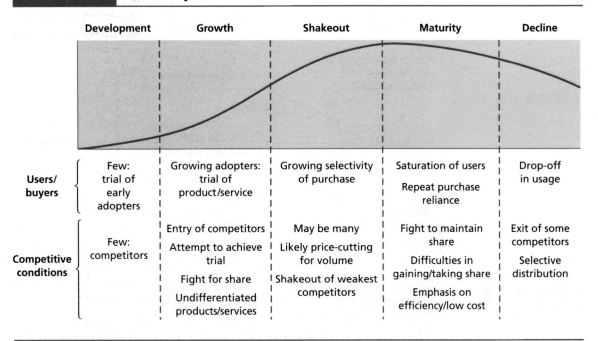

		Development	Growth	Shakeout	Maturity	Decline
Users/ buyers		Few: trial of early adopters	Growing adopters: trial of product/service	Growing selectivity of purchase	Saturation of users Repeat purchase reliance	Drop-off in usage
Competitive conditions		Few: competitors	Entry of competitors Attempt to achieve trial Fight for share Undifferentiated products/services	May be many Likely price-cutting for volume Shakeout of weakest competitors	Fight to maintain share Difficulties in gaining/taking share Emphasis on efficiency/low cost	Exit of some competitors Selective distribution

Key questions arising from the five forces framework

The five forces framework can be used to gain insights into the forces at work in the industry environment of an SBU which need particular attention in the development of strategy. It is important to use the frame for more than simply listing the forces. The following questions help focus on the implications of these forces:

- What are the *key forces* at work in the competitive environment? These will differ by type of industry as discussed earlier.

- What are the *underlying forces* in the macro-environment that are driving competitive forces? For example, the lower labour costs for software and service operators located in India are both an opportunity and a threat to European and US companies.

- Is it likely that the forces will *change*, and if so, how? For example, pharmaceutical businesses built strong market positions on their expertise in marketing branded drugs to a highly fragmented set of buyers – the doctors. However, government action in many countries, such as the promotion of generic drugs and the introduction of new treatment protocols, buying procedures and price regulation, has had the effect of significantly increasing competitive pressures on such firms and forcing them to reconsider their competitive strategies.

- How do particular competitors stand in relation to these competitive forces? What are their strengths and weaknesses in relation to the key forces at work?

| Exhibit 3.6 | Cycles of competition |

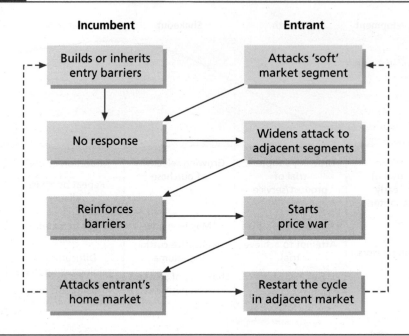

Source: Adapted from R.A. D'Aveni with Robert Gunther, *Hyper-Competitive Rivalries: Competing in a Highly Dynamic Environment* © 1994, Free Press, 1995, p. 115.

- What can managers do to *influence* the competitive forces affecting an SBU? Can barriers to entry be built, power over suppliers or buyers increased, or ways found to diminish competitive rivalry? These are the fundamental questions relating to *competitive strategy* and will be a major concern of Chapter 7.

- Are some industries more *attractive* than others? It can be argued that some industries are intrinsically more profitable than others because, for example, entry is more difficult, or buyers and suppliers are less powerful.

3.3.2 The dynamics of competition and hypercompetition[14]

The previous section has looked at how competition might arise but has not looked in detail at the process of competition *over time*, in particular the fact that competitive advantage will eventually be eroded because the forces discussed above will change and/or competitors will manage to overcome adverse forces. This process of erosion will be speeded up by changes in the macro-environment such as new technologies, globalisation or deregulation. So advantage is more or less always *temporary* – though time-scales will differ. Organisations will then respond to this erosion of their competitive position, creating what has been called a *cycle of competition* as shown in Exhibit 3.6 and exemplified in Illustration 3.6.

Illustration 3.6

Cycles of competition

Changes in the business environment and moves by competitors erode the competitive position of organisations who, in turn, respond by countermoves. Competition moves through cycles and any competitive advantage is temporary.

A market leader in a consumer goods sector of the French market, having achieved significant barriers to entry, was enjoying the benefits of good financial returns. This success attracted the attention of a German consumer goods company that was wishing to become a significant Europe-wide player (see Exhibit 3.6).

The German's first competitive move was to target a consumer age group where consumption and brand awareness were both low. The French had limited their marketing efforts to the over-25 age groups – the Germans saw a possibility of extending the market into the 18–25 group and aimed their promotional efforts at the group with some success. This first move was ignored by the French company as it did not impact on their current business. However, from this bridgehead the second move was to attack the segments (age groups) covered by the French. This triggered a competitive response to contain the entrant to their original niche. They did this by an advertising campaign reinforcing brand awareness in their traditional segments.

The entrant responded by counter-advertising and price reductions – undermining the margins earned by the French company. Competition then escalated with a counterattack by the French into the German market. This wider competitive activity played itself out, resulting in the erosion of both of the original

strongholds and a progressive merger of the French and German markets.

It is possible at this stage that this whole cycle of competition could have repeated itself in an adjacent market – such as the UK. However, what happened was that the German firm saw an opportunity to move away from this *cost/quality* basis of competition by adapting the product for use by businesses. Their core competences in R&D allowed them to get the adapted product to market faster than their French rival. They then consolidated these first-mover advantages by building and defending barriers. For example, they appointed key account salespeople and gave special offers for early adoption and three-year contracts.

However, this stronghold came under attack by the French firm and a cycle of competition similar to the consumer market described above was triggered off. However, the German firm had built up significant financial reserves to survive a price war, which they then initiated. They were willing and able to fund losses longer than the French competitor – who were forced to exit the business user market.

Questions

1. Could the French firm have slowed down the cycle of competition shown in Exhibit 3.6?

2. How could the French firm have prevented the German firm escalating competition, to their advantage, in the business user market?

For large global organisations another consideration about the dynamics of competition is also illustrated in Illustration 3.6. Moves and countermoves by organisations and their competitors may take place simultaneously in several locations. So a competitive move in one arena, the German company's aggressive move into France, did not trigger off a countermove in that arena (France) but in their competitor's home territory (Germany). So the competitive dynamics between these two organisations needs to be understood as multi-point competition. There is some evidence that multi-point competition can reduce the competitive rivalry by raising the costs and risks of these moves and countermoves[15] – say in the airline industry.

The illustration also shows that the cycle of competition may escalate on to a new basis. So the various moves and countermoves on the basis of cost/quality competition (Exhibit 3.6) resulted in a merging of markets where one player then shifted the basis of competition. The ways in which market conditions can influence strategic choices (competitive moves) will be discussed in section 7.5.

An important issue to understand is the speed at which these cycles of competition might move. Organisations are increasingly operating in situations where the speed of the cycle is very high – this has been called *hypercompetition*. **Hypercompetition** occurs where the frequency, boldness and aggressiveness of dynamic movements by competitors accelerate to create a condition of constant disequilibrium and change.[16] The implications of how competition is understood and how organisations might respond are extremely important. Whereas competition in slower-moving environments is primarily concerned with building and sustaining competitive advantages that are difficult to imitate, hypercompetitive environments require organisations to acknowledge that advantages will be temporary. Competition is also about disrupting the status quo so that no one is able to sustain long-term advantage on any given basis. So longer-term competitive advantage is gained through a sequence of short-lived moves.

Hypercompetition occurs where the frequency, boldness and aggressiveness of dynamic movements by competitors accelerate to create a condition of constant disequilibrium and change

3.3.3 Strategic groups[17]

An industry may be too generic a concept to provide a basis for understanding competition. For example, Ford and Morgan Cars are in the same industry (automobiles) but are they competitors? The former is a publicly quoted multi-national business; the latter is owned by a British family, produces about 500 cars a year and concentrates on a specialist market niche where customers want hand-built cars and are prepared to wait up to four years for one. In a given industry there may be many companies each of which has different interests and which compete on different bases. There is a need for some intermediate basis of understanding the relative position of organisations between the level of the individual organisation and the industry. This is the concept of *strategic groups*.

Strategic groups are organisations within an industry with similar strategic characteristics, following similar strategies or competing on similar bases

● **Strategic groups** are organisations within an industry with similar strategic characteristics, following similar strategies or competing on similar bases.

| Exhibit 3.7 | Some characteristics for identifying strategic groups |

It is useful to consider the extent to which organisations *differ* in terms of **characteristics** such as:

- Extent of **product (or service) diversity**

- Extent of **geographical coverage**

- Number of **market segments served**

- **Distribution channels used**

- Extent (number) of **branding**

- **Marketing effort** (e.g. advertising spread, size of salesforce)

- **Extent of vertical integration**

- Product or service **quality**

- **Technological leadership** (a leader or follower)

- Relationship to **influence groups** (e.g. government, the City)

- **Size** of organisation

Sources: Based on M.E. Porter, *Competitive Strategy*, Free Press, 1980; and J. McGee and H. Thomas, 'Strategic groups: theory, research and taxonomy', *Strategic Management Journal*, vol. 7, no. 2 (1986), pp. 141–160.

These characteristics are different from those in other strategic groups in the same industry or sector. There may be many different characteristics which distinguish between strategic groups.[18] For example, size, breadth of product range, geographical coverage, quality or service levels or marketing spend. Which of these characteristics are especially relevant in terms of a given industry needs to be understood in terms of the history and development of that industry and the forces at work in the environment (see Exhibit 3.7). Illustration 3.7, Figure 1, shows a strategic group map of the major providers of MBAs in the Netherlands in 2000.

This concept is useful in several ways:

- It helps understand who are the most direct competitors of any given organisation, on what basis competitive rivalry is likely to take place within each strategic group and how this is different from one group to another. For example, traditional universities were competing on the value of their degrees and their research record.

- It raises the question of how likely or possible it is for an organisation to move from one strategic group to another. Mobility between groups depends on the extent to which there are barriers to entry between one group and another. In Illustration 3.7, Figure 2 shows examples of mobility barriers for the groupings identified in the industry. These may be substantial.

Illustration 3.7

Strategic groups in Dutch MBA education

STRATEGY IN ACTION

Mapping of strategic groups can provide insights into the competitive structures of industries or sectors and the opportunities and constraints for development.

There are three kinds of institution offering MBA courses in the Netherlands: traditional universities, for-profit business schools (FPBS) and polytechnics.

- Traditional universities offer a wide range of subjects, do research, and attract students both nationally and internationally. Their programmes are more academic than vocational. A university degree is generally valued more highly than one from a polytechnic.

- FPBSs are relatively new, and provide MBA degrees only. Usually they are located close to the centre of the country. MBA education at FPBSs is generally more of the action learning type, which makes it attractive for practising managers. Many students already have diplomas of a university or a polytechnic. Several of these schools receive accreditation of the Dutch Validation Council.

- Polytechnics (in the Netherlands named HogeScholen) often attract students from the region and provide education more aimed at application of theory than at developing conceptual thinking. Some of the polytechnics provide MBA degrees, in some cases in cooperation with universities from the UK.

Figure 1 gives an indication of how these three types of institution were positioned in terms of geographical coverage and 'orientation'.

Figure 2 shows the barriers that prevent organisations moving from one group to another (they show the barriers *into* a group) For example, if the FPSBs tried to 'enter' the strategic group of Traditional universities they would need to build up a reputation in research or innovation. They may not be interested in doing research, since there would be high costs and little pay-off for their effort. In reverse, for traditional universities to move in the direction of the FPBSs may be difficult since the faculty may not have skills in action learning and may be inexperienced at working with older students.

Figure 1 Strategic groups in MBA education in the Netherlands

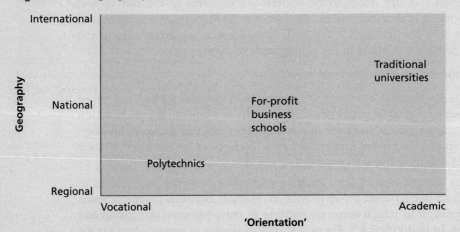

Figure 2 Mobility barriers

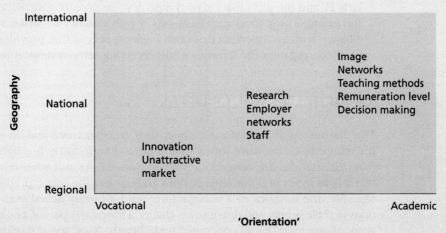

Figure 3 Strategic space

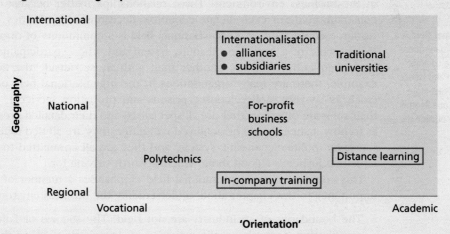

Figure 3 shows where 'strategic space' might exist. These spaces are created by changes in the macro-environment – particularly globalisation and information technology. This could provide opportunities for Dutch business schools to seek more international business. However, the reverse threat of international competitors entering the Dutch market is a major concern. Information and communication technology helps students study at their own place of work or at home, and also enables them to tap into an international network. So an American or British school could provide content over the Internet and local student support through partnerships with Dutch institutions.

Source: J. Eppink and S. de Waal, 'Global influences on the public sector', in G. Johnson and K. Scholes (eds), *Exploring Public Sector Strategy*, FT/Prentice Hall, 2001, Chapter 3.

Question

How might this analysis influence the next strategic moves by each of the three types of institution?

- In identifying potential opportunities and threats to organisations, Illustration 3.7, Figure 3, shows that changes in the macro-environment – particularly IT and the globalisation of companies – are creating strategic 'spaces'; for example, for local providers (say a polytechnic) to strike a strategic alliance with an American or British business school that provides students with content over the Internet whilst receiving tutorial support locally.

3.4 ORGANISATIONAL FIELDS

The discussions about industries, how they are structured and, in particular, the nature of competitive forces in and around an industry highlight the fact that organisations are networked with economic links and other relationships to a whole series of other organisations and not just the other 'producers'. For example, the fortunes of a manufacturer are intimately linked with organisations in their supply and distribution chains; a hospital is part of a complex network of organisations all concerned with 'health' (GPs, social workers, fitness centres, drugs companies, and so on). The concept of *organisational fields* is a way of understanding this wider network of influences and relationships in the business environment. These relationships matter because they will constrain, guide or even dictate economic decisions and priorities – such as resource deployment. An **organisational field** is a community of organisations that partake of a common meaning system and whose participants interact more frequently with one another than with those outside the field.[19] For example, there are many organisations in the organisational field of 'justice' (such as lawyers, police, courts, prisons and probation services). Although their roles are different (they are all specialists) and their detailed prescriptions as to how justice should be achieved will differ, they are all tied together into the same 'politico-economic system' and they are all committed to the principle that justice is a good thing which is worth striving for.

This concept of an organisational field emphasises a number of issues of importance to this chapter about understanding the business environment:

- The boundaries of an industry are not rigid. The success or failure of an organisation depends on the activities of organisations other than direct competitive rivals – this was also a key message from the five forces framework discussed above.

- An organisational field may also be 'permeable'. This means that the boundaries are changed or eroded by the influence of adjacent fields – even to the extent that two fields start to merge. For example, the norms of the accountancy profession have changed as they embrace consultancy and bring new types of people into the accountancy firms.

- The various organisations in the organisational field are often tied to each other by economic relationships (such as buyer–supplier relationships, or regulator–regulatee and so on), therefore their successes or failures are intertwined. This is an important message from the concept of the value chain, which looks at how these relationships add to, or detract from, an organisation's strategic capability and will be discussed in Chapter 4.

An **organisational field** is a community of organisations that partake of a common meaning system and whose participants interact more frequently with one another than with those outside the field

- A critically important feature of an organisational field is that the various parties are tied together in ways beyond this economic dependency.[20] They share a common set of purposes (at least at a generic level) and more crucially they are likely to share a set of taken-for-granted beliefs and assumptions (e.g. 'justice matters'). These may be deeply embedded and hard to surface and concern the 'legitimacy' of an organisation within an organisational field as discussed in section 2.2.2. These are also issues at the centre of the discussions in Chapter 5 – so the concept of organisational fields will be revisited there.

- The implication of this institutionalisation is that any individual organisation's strategies are likely to change slowly – the organisational field creates inertia. However, this is not always the case. When boundaries do get eroded the change can be quite rapid, as many public sector organisations experienced in the 1990s.

3.5 MARKETS

The concept of strategic groups discussed in section 3.3.3 helps with understanding the similarities and differences in the characteristics of 'producers' – those organisations that are actual or potential competitors. However, the success or failure of organisations is also concerned with how well they understand customer needs and are able to meet those needs. So an understanding of markets is important.

3.5.1 Market segments

In most markets there is a wide diversity of customers' needs, so the concept of **market segmentation**[21] can be useful in identifying similarities and differences between groups of customers or users. It will be seen in Chapter 4 that this understanding of what customers (and other stakeholders) value and how competitors are positioned to meet these needs is a critical element in understanding strategic capability.

Market segmentation identifies similarities and differences between groups of customers or users

The concept of market segmentation should remind managers of several important issues:

- Customer needs may vary for a whole variety of reasons – some of which are identified in Exhibit 3.8. Theoretically, any of these factors could be used to understand market segments. However, in practical terms it is important to consider which bases of segmentation are most important in any particular market. For example, in industrial markets, segmentation is often thought of in terms of industrial classification of buyers – e.g. 'we sell to the domestic appliance industry'. However, it may be that this is not the most relevant basis of segmentation when thinking about the future. Segmentation by buyer behaviour (for example, direct buying versus those users who buy through third parties such as contractors) or purchase value (for example, high-value bulk purchasers versus frequent low-value purchasers) might be

Exhibit 3.8	Some bases of market segmentation	

TYPE OF FACTOR	CONSUMER MARKETS	INDUSTRIAL/ ORGANISATIONAL MARKETS
Characteristics of people/ organisations	Age, sex, race Income Family size Life-cycle stage Location Lifestyle	Industry Location Size Technology Profitability Management
Purchase/use situation	Size of purchase Brand loyalty Purpose of use Purchasing behaviour Importance of purchase Choice criteria	Application Importance of purchase Volume Frequency of purchase Purchasing procedure Choice criteria Distribution channel
Users' needs and preferences for product characteristics	Product similarity Price preference Brand preferences Desired features Quality	Performance requirements Assistance from suppliers Brand preferences Desired features Quality Service requirements

more appropriate in some markets. Indeed, it is often useful to consider different bases of segmentation in the same market to help understand the dynamics of that market and how these are changing. Illustration 3.8 shows three different examples of how companies have concentrated on particular segments in order to get a dominant position.

● Relative market share (i.e. share in relation to that of competitors) within market segments is an important consideration. There is an important relationship between market power and performance in commercial organisations. This is not just because of scale benefits of size, but also because of 'experience curve' effects which are discussed more fully in the next chapter (see section 4.4.1). The organisation which has built up most experience in servicing a particular market segment should not only have lower costs in so doing, but also have built relationships which may be difficult for others to break down.

● The earlier discussion on life cycles of markets (see section 3.3.1 and Exhibit 3.5) makes the point that opportunities and threats will vary over time from the embryonic stage through growth to maturity and decline.

The issue of overriding importance is that what customers value will vary by market segment and therefore 'producers' are likely to achieve advantage in segments that are especially suited to their particular core competences, as discussed in Chapter 4. They may find it very difficult to compete on a broader

Illustration 3.8

Bases of market segmentation

Markets can be segmented in many different ways but segmentation must always relate to customer need.

Triumph

Until the late 1960s, Triumph and other UK companies dominated the UK motorcycle industry. However, the market was invaded by Japanese manufacturers – such as Honda – offering sophisticated and, more importantly, reliable machines. This led to the bankruptcy of most of the domestic manufacturers. However, in 1991 Triumph was revived by the property developer John Bloor who recognised the value of the Triumph brand – it was synonymous with high performance – having featured in the famous 1950s Marlon Brando film *The Wild One*. This allowed the company to attack the biking enthusiasts, who bought powerful bikes – such as the Harley Davidson. The company went from strength to strength and by 2000 they were manufacturing 30,000 bikes, 80 per cent of which were exported to countries such as USA, Germany, France and Japan.

Saga

Founded in 1951, Saga gained national attention by providing affordable holidays and tours for British pensioners – particularly offering 'off-season' deals. This was so successful that the company soon developed into a full-service travel company aiming at the older customer (the over-50s). The holidays on offer were described as for those who are 'mature in years but young at heart'. They opened up in Boston USA in 1979.

Progressively the company expanded its portfolio of activities as it became clear that this group was growing in size and also becoming more affluent. By 2000, as well as its travel services the company offered a wide range of insurance services, a credit card, share dealing and investments, and provided information and products relating to health – such as medical insurance and food supplements.

Volkswagen

When the Berlin wall came down in 1989, to many western companies this marked a major opportunity for development in eastern European markets. But it was not good enough to see eastern Europe as an export opportunity or as a market where tried and tested 'formulae' in western Europe would work. The levels of disposable income were very low and consumers, distributors and producers had very different expectations regarding product and service quality and prices.

In the automobile market, Volkswagen moved quickly with its acquisition of Skoda in the Czech Republic. This provided the basis for VW to become the dominant supplier into eastern Europe. By 2000 they were selling some 275,000 vehicles in the region – representing 23.7 per cent market share in the region. This was significantly ahead of second-place Fiat (14.8 per cent). Significantly, over 60 per cent of the VW group sales in the region were through Skoda – a different approach from any of VW's rivals.

Sources: Financial Times, 27 and 28 February 2001; Saga website.

Questions

1. What was the basis of segmentation in each of the three examples and why was it useful?

2. What were the dangers of each company's approach?

| Exhibit 3.9 | Perceived value by customers in the electrical engineering industry |

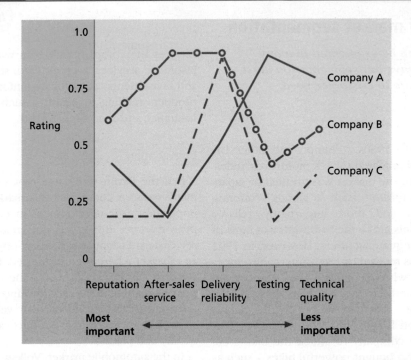

basis. For example, a small local brewery competing against the big brands on the basis of its low prices underpinned by low costs of distribution and marketing is confined to that segment of the local market that values low price. Its geographical 'reach' is limited as distribution costs will rise steeply with distance. Other small brewers may compete in different segments where they command premium prices because their products are tailored to local tastes.

3.5.2 Understanding what customers value

Although market segmentation is a useful concept, managers may fail to be realistic about how markets are segmented and the strategic implications of that segmentation. It will be seen in the next chapter that an understanding of customer needs and how they differ between segments is crucial to developing the appropriate strategic capability in an organisation. However, value is multi-dimensional and the idea of perceived customer value is useful in understanding this complexity (see Exhibit 3.9).[22] The exhibit relates to one segment of the electrical engineering industry – company-based buyers of electrical engineering equipment – and illustrates the following:

● In this market segment there were many factors valued by customers, most of which were taken for granted (for example, that the product is fit for its purpose). These were the threshold requirements (product features) which would be expected from any provider into this segment.

- The factors shown in Exhibit 3.9 (the reputation of a producer, after-sales service, delivery reliability, testing facilities and technical quality) were seen as particularly important. These were the features which would determine which provider was preferred (from amongst those that met the threshold requirements). Indeed, reputation, after-sales service and reliable delivery were *especially* valued by customers in this segment. It will be seen in Chapter 4 (section 4.2) that from the potential providers' viewpoint these would be seen as the *critical success factors*.

- The exhibit profiles different providers against these factors that customers value. For example, it is clear that the particular strengths that company A possesses are not the factors *most* valued by customers; whereas B's strengths appear to have a better match.

- This provides a link into the issues of strategic capability discussed in Chapter 4 (see Exhibit 4.1). For example, company A needs to consider if it should attempt to switch its resources to improve customer service and delivery. Alternatively, it might focus on a different market segment in which customers value technical features more.

The key message from this example is that it is important to see 'value' through the eyes of the customer (or stakeholder). Although this might be a self-evident statement, it may not be easy to achieve this for several reasons:

- Organisations may not be able to make sense of the complex and varied behaviours they experience in their markets. Often they will have vast amounts of raw data about customer behaviour, preferences and purchasing patterns but they lack the capability to draw useful conclusions out of these data (for example, to spot trends or connections). So an ability to use IT systems to understand customer needs better could be an important source of competitive advantage in many sectors (as discussed in section 10.3).

- Many manufacturers may be distanced from the final users by several intermediaries – other manufacturers and distributors. Although these direct customers may be the strategic buyers – in the sense that they are dictating product features and service levels – there is a danger that what value means to the final consumer is not understood. In other words, many manufacturers may be out of touch with what is ultimately driving demand for their product or service. However, there is not much point understanding the needs of the final consumer if the needs of the strategic buyer are ignored.

- Value of the product or service is often conceived of internally (e.g. by groups of professionals such as designers, engineers, teachers or lawyers) and not tested out with customers or clients. This is an important criticism of many public service organisations. It can result in a false view of what is really valued by customers (and other stakeholders) and, therefore, of the competences needed to succeed.

- Customers' concept of value changes over time – either because they become more experienced (through repeat purchase) or because competitive offerings become available which offer better value. The concept of the product life cycle discussed earlier (see Exhibit 3.5) also suggests that conditions in markets change over time in terms of customer behaviour.

3.6 OPPORTUNITIES AND THREATS

The concepts and frameworks discussed above should be helpful in understanding the factors in the macro-, industry and market environments that might impact on an organisation. However, there is usually a need to understand in a more detailed way how this collection of environmental factors might influence strategic success or failure. This can be done in more than one way.

3.6.1 Strategic gaps

By using some of the frameworks described in this chapter, managers can begin to identify and/or create 'new market space'[23] to gain competitive advantage. There may be different opportunities to do this:

Looking across substitute industries

As well as competing in their own industry, organisations also face competition from industries that are producing substitutes, as discussed in section 3.3.2 above. So substitution provides opportunities for organisations which are often overlooked. This can be because competitive moves made by direct rivals tend to trigger a stronger response than potential substitutes and also because managers tend to see substitutes as threatening rather than as an opportunity.

An example would be software companies attempting to substitute electronic versions of reference books and atlases for the traditional paper versions. If this opportunity is to be realised then a realistic assessment has to be made of the relative merits of the two products/technologies *in the eyes of the customer*. The paper versions have more advantages than meets the eye: no hardware requirement (hence greater portability) and the ability to browse are two important benefits. This means that software producers would need to design features to counter the strengths of the paper versions; for example, the search features in the software. Of course, if computer hardware develops into a new generation of portable handheld devices, this particular shortcoming of electronic versions might be rectified.

Looking across strategic groups

It is also possible to identify new market space by looking across strategic groups – particularly if changes in the macro-environment make new market spaces economically viable. For example, deregulation of markets (say in electricity generation and distribution) and advances in IT (say with educational study programmes) could both create new market space. In the first case, the locally based smaller-scale generation of electricity becomes viable – possibly linked to waste incineration plants. In the latter case, geography can be 'shrunk' and educational programmes be delivered across continents through the Internet and teleconferencing (together with local tutorial support). New strategic groups emerge in these industries/sectors.

Looking across the chain of buyers

In section 3.5.1 above, it was emphasised that identifying who is the target customer is critical for a business. It was also noted that this can be confusing, as there may be several people involved in the overall purchase decision. The user is one party but they may not buy the product themselves; so the buyer may not use the product themselves and there may be other influencers on the purchase decision too. Importantly, each of these parties may value different aspects of the product or service. These distinctions are often quite marked in business-to-business transactions, say with the purchase of capital equipment. The purchasing department may be looking for low prices and financial stability of suppliers. The user department (production) may place emphasis on special product features. Others – such as the marketing department – may be concerned with whether the equipment will speed throughput and reduce delivery times. By considering who is the 'most profitable buyer' an organistion may shift its view of the market and aim its promotion and selling at *those* 'buyers'.

Looking across complementary product and service offerings

This involves the organisation's considering the potential value of complementary products and services. For example, computer hardware cannot function without the complementary software applications. Another example is in book retailing where the overall 'book-buying experience' is much more than just stocking the right books. It also includes an ambience conducive to browsing (such as reading areas or coffee bars) and opening hours to suit busy customers. Staff who are themselves 'book oriented' could be employed so they could use their own experience as a customer to pass on recommendations.

Looking for new market segments

Looking for new market segments can be helped by contradicting the traditional appeal of products or services. If the emphasis is on selling emotional appeal, the alternative may be to provide a no-frills model which costs less and would appeal to another potential market. The opposite can also be true, where a product is given a new lease of life by appealing to the emotions rather than its functionality.

The Starbucks coffee chain created new market space by transforming drinking coffee into an emotional experience rather than merely functional. A special atmosphere was created within the coffee bars. In contrast, The Body Shop, operating in the highly emotional cosmetics industry, challenged the accepted viewpoint. This was achieved by the production of purely functional products, noted for their lack of elaborate packaging or heavy advertising. This created new market space by attracting the consumer who wanted quality skin-care products without the added frills.

Looking across time

When predicting the impact of changes in the macro- or competitive environments it is important to consider how they are going to affect the consumer.
Organisations can gain first-mover advantages that way. Cisco Systems realised
that the future was going to see a significant need for high-speed data exchange
and were at the forefront of producing equipment to address this future need.
They identified new market space because no one else had assessed the likely
implications of the Internet boom. This meant that they could offer specially
designed products well ahead of their rivals, giving them an important competitive edge.

3.6.2 SWOT[24]

A **SWOT** analysis summarises
the key issues from the
business environment and the
strategic capability of an
organisation that are most
likely to impact on strategy
development

The key 'strategic messages' from both the business environment (this chapter)
and concerning strategic capability (Chapter 4) can be summarised in the form
of a SWOT analysis. A **SWOT** analysis summarises the key issues from the business environment and the strategic capability of an organisation that are most
likely to impact on strategy development. This can be useful as a basis against
which to judge future courses of action, as seen in Chapters 6, 7 and 8. The
aim is to identify the extent to which the current strengths and weaknesses are
relevant to, and capable of, dealing with the threats or capitalising on the
opportunities in the business environment. SWOT analysis will be discussed in
section 4.8.

SUMMARY

- *Environmental influences* and trends can be thought of as being in *layers*
  around an organisation. The most general layer is the macro-environment
  where an understanding of political, economic, social, technological, environmental and legal influences (PESTEL) can provide an overall picture of the
  variety of forces at work around an organisation. This can also cast light on
  the key influences and *structural drivers of change* and provide the basis of
  examining the extent to which these will have differential impact on both
  industries (or sectors) and organisations within industries in the future.

- When there are long-term strategic horizons but high levels of uncertainty
  around key environmental forces, *scenarios* can be a useful way of understanding the implications of these influences on strategy. This includes the
  need for organisations to be ready and prepared to face more than one situation in their future environment.

- Within the more general environment sit *industries* or *sectors*. However,
  the boundaries of these are not sharp and certainly change over time, for
  example through the convergence of previously separate industries.

- *The five forces framework* helps understand the sources of competition
  within and around an industry especially in terms of barriers to entry, the

power of buyers and suppliers, the threat of substitutes and other reasons for the extent of competitive intensity.

- The basis of competition within an industry is *dynamic*. The way in which competition is played out varies over time – sometimes changing very rapidly. This is called the cycle of competition. For large global organisations competition will be taking place in several arenas simultaneously and moves in one arena might trigger countermoves in a different arena.

- Many industries and sectors are now characterised by rapid pace of change to the extent that competitive advantage on one particular basis will not last for any significant period of time. This is *hypercompetition* and the implications for organisations are significant. Since advantages are temporary and quickly eroded, it is essential continuously to find new bases for competing. Putting effort into sustaining old advantages might be a distraction from developing new advantages. Long-term advantage is sustained through a series of temporary advantages.

- Within an industry or sector *strategic groups* are usually found. These are organisations with similar strategic characteristics, following similar strategies or competing on similar bases.

- Organisations are networked through economic links and other relationships with a series of other organisations and not just the other 'producers'. For example, there are important relationships with suppliers, distributors, trade associations or regulatory bodies. This network is called the *organisational field*. These relationships matter because they will constrain, guide or even dictate economic decisions and priorities – such as resource deployment. They also matter in terms of an organisation's legitimacy, which will be discussed in Chapter 5.

- The success or failure of organisations is also concerned with how well they understand customer needs and are able to meet those needs. So an understanding of markets is important. The concept of market segments can be useful in understanding similarities and differences between groups of customers or users.

- *Opportunities* and *threats* arise in the environment for many different reasons. The frameworks and concepts in this chapter can help build up a picture of the competitive position of an organisation and how it might change in the future.

RECOMMENDED KEY READINGS

- A good general text on international business and global organisations is: C. Hill, *International Business: Competing in the global marketplace*, 3rd edition, McGraw-Hill, 2000. G. Yip, *Total Global Strategy*, Prentice Hall, 1995, Chapter 2, explains in more detail the forces for globalisation in industries.

- To understand scenarios in detail see: K. van der Heijden, *Scenarios: The art of strategic conversation*, Wiley, 1996, and G. Price's chapter, 'The why and how of scenario planning' in V. Ambrosini with G. Johnson and K. Scholes (eds), *Exploring Techniques of Analysis and Evaluation in Strategic Management*, Prentice Hall, 1998.

- M.E. Porter, *Competitive Strategy: Techniques for analysing industries and competitors*, Free Press, 1980, is essential reading for those who are faced with an analysis of an organisation's competitive environment.

● R. D'Aveni (with R. Gunther), *Hypercompetitive Rivalries*, Free Press, 1995 is an authoritative source on the dynamics of competition and hypercompetition.

● V. Ambrosini with G. Johnson and K. Scholes (eds), *Exploring Techniques of Analysis and Evaluation in*

Strategic Management, Prentice Hall, 1998, contains relevant papers entitled 'Scenarios made easy' by D. Mercer, and 'Competitor analysis' by G. Johnson, C. Bowman and P. Rudd.

REFERENCES

1. For a discussion on how environmental forces – particularly *global forces* – impact on the public sector see: J. Eppink and S. de Waal, 'Global influences on the public sector', in G. Johnson and K. Scholes (eds), *Exploring Public Sector Strategy*, Financial Times/Prentice Hall, 2001, Chapter 3.

2. Henry Mintzberg argues that environmental change is not now faster than it was: see *The Rise and Fall of Strategic Planning*, Prentice Hall, 1994, Chapter 4.

3. Previous editions of this book have used the PEST framework. However, this can lead to an underemphasis on ('green') environmental issues. This is the reason for the change to PESTEL.

4. Of the books which review environmental influences on organisations, L. Fahey and V.K. Narayanan, *Macroenvironmental Analyses for Strategic Management*, West, 1986, remains one of the best.

5. See G. Yip, *Total Global Strategy*, Prentice Hall, 1995, Chapter 2. Also, a good general text on international business and global organisations is: C. Hill, *International Business: Competing in the global marketplace*, 3rd edition, McGraw-Hill, 2000.

6. See K. van der Heijden, *Scenarios: The art of strategic conversation*, Wiley, 1996, and G. Price's chapter, 'The why and how of scenario planning' in V. Ambrosini with G. Johnson and K. Scholes (eds), *Exploring Techniques of Analysis and Evaluation in Strategic Management*, Prentice Hall, 1998. The use of scenarios by Shell is described in G. Ringland, *Scenario Planning*, Wiley, 1998.

7. The business idea is discussed in the section commentary. The source is: K. van der Heijden, *Scenarios: The art of strategic conversation*, Wiley, 1996.

8. D. Rutherford, *Routledge Dictionary of Economics*, 2nd edition, Routledge, 1995.

9. See M.E. Porter, *Competitive Strategy: Techniques for analysing industries and competitors*, Free Press, 1980, p. 5.

10. See: J. Sampler, 'Redefining industry structure for the information age', *Strategic Management Journal*, vol. 19 (1998), pp. 343–355.

11. In business books the term 'business model' has traditionally been used to refer to the types of framework and concepts discussed in this book and shown in the exhibits. In the e-commerce world it is used more narrowly to describe the relationships and information flows in an 'industry' or sector. This will be described more fully in section 10.3 and readers can refer to the references given there.

12. Porter (reference 9 above), Chapter 1.

13. R. D'Aveni (with R. Gunther), *Hypercompetitive Rivalries*, Free Press, 1995.

14. For a full discussion of the dynamics of competition see D'Aveni (reference 13 above).

15. J. Gimeno and C. Woo, 'Hypercompetition in a multi-market environment: the role of strategic similarity and multi-market contact on competition de-escalation', *Organisation Science*, vol. 7, no. 3 (1996), pp. 323–341.

16. This definition is from D'Aveni (reference 13 above) p. 2.

17. For examples of different uses of strategic group analysis, see P. Lewes and H. Thomas, 'The linkage between strategy, strategic groups and performance in the UK retail grocery industry', *Strategic Management Journal*, vol. 11, no. 5 (1990), pp. 385–397; J. McGee and S. Segal-Horn, 'Strategic space and industry dynamics', *Journal of Marketing Management*, vol. 6, no. 3 (1990), pp. 175–193; and R. Reger and A. Huff, 'Strategic groups: a cognitive perspective', *Strategic Management Journal*, vol. 14, no. 2 (1993), pp. 103–124.

18. The characteristics listed in Exhibit 3.8 are based on those discussed by Porter (reference 9 above) and by J. McGee and H. Thomas, 'Strategic groups: theory, research and taxonomy', *Strategic Management Journal*, vol. 7, no. 2 (1986), pp. 141–160. This paper also provides a useful background to strategic group analysis.

19. This definition is taken from W. Scott, *Institutions and Organisations*, Sage Publications, 1995.

20. Institutional theory describes and explains these dependencies. See: P. DiMaggio and W. Powell, 'The iron cage revisited: institutional isomorphism and collective rationality in organisational fields', *American Sociological Review*, vol. 48 (1983), pp. 147–160.

21. A useful discussion of segmentation in relation to competitive strategy is provided in M.E. Porter, *Competitive*

Advantage, Free Press, 1985, Chapter 7. See also the discussion on market segmentation in P. Kotler, *Marketing Management*, 8th edition, Prentice Hall, 1994.

22. This approach and the example shown in Exhibit 3.9 are dealt with more extensively in G. Johnson, C. Bowman and P. Rudd's chapter, 'Competitor analysis' in V. Ambrosini with G. Johnson and K. Scholes (eds), *Exploring Techniques of Analysis and Evaluation in Strategic Management*, Prentice Hall, 1998.

23. See: W. Kim and R. Mauborgne, 'Creating new market space', *Harvard Business Review*, vol. 77, no. 1 (1999), 83–93.

24. The idea of SWOT as a common-sense checklist has been used for many years: for example, S. Tilles, 'Making strategy explicit', in I. Ansoff (ed.), *Business Strategy*, Penguin, 1968. See also T. Jacobs, J. Shepherd and G. Johnson's chapter on SWOT analysis in V. Ambrosini with G. Johnson and K. Scholes (see reference 22 above). SWOT will be discussed more fully in section 4.8 and Illustration 4.8.

WORK ASSIGNMENTS

* Refers to a case study in the Text and Cases edition. ✳ Denotes more advanced work assignments.

In the assignments that follow, an example of an industry is normally required. For this purpose, the European brewing industry, the pharmaceutical industry,* the media/entertainment/Internet industry (see AOL/Time Warner, Pearson, News Corporation*), or an industry of your choice could be useful.

3.1 Using Illustration 3.1 and Exhibit 3.2 as a guide, undertake an audit of the macro-environment of a chosen industry or sector. What are the key environmental influences on organisations in that industry? What are the main drivers of change?

3.2 Identify the main changes likely in an industry. Following the guidelines in section 3.2.4 and Illustration 3.3, construct scenarios for the industry for an appropriate time period.

3.3 Assume you have just become personal assistant to the chief executive of a major pharmaceutical company. She knows you have recently undertaken a business management degree and asks if you would prepare a brief report summarising how scenario planning might be useful to a company in the pharmaceutical industry.

3.4 Drawing on section 3.3, carry out a five forces analysis of an industry or sector. What are the key competitive forces at work in that industry? Are there any changes that might occur that would significantly affect bases of competition in the industry?

3.5 ✳ Compare two industries in terms of the key environmental influences and competitive forces in them. Assess and compare the entry barriers, and the extent of competitive rivalry in the two industries.

3.6 ✳ Building on section 3.3.3 and Illustration 3.7:
(a) Identify the strategic characteristics that most distinguish organisations in an industry or sector of your choice. Construct one or more strategic group maps on these bases.
(b) Assess the extent to which mobility between strategic groups is possible. (If you have constructed more than one map for the industry, do the mobility barriers you identify differ amongst them? What does this signify?)
(c) Identify any vacant strategic spaces in the maps. Do any represent viable strategic positions? What would be the characteristics of an organisation competing in such a space?

3.7 To what extent are the models discussed in this chapter appropriate in the analysis of the environment of a public sector or not-for-profit organisation? Give examples to support your arguments.

3.8 ✳ Using the concepts and frameworks in this chapter, write a report for an organisation (e.g. A brewing company (see chapter-end case example), Corus,* Thorntons,* News Corporation*) which assesses its industry environment and its competitive position within that environment.

CASE EXAMPLE

The European brewing industry

At the beginning of the twenty-first century Europe was the major centre of beer consumption and production in the world. The European alcoholic drinks market was dominated by beer, which accounted for over 60 per cent of the total alcohol market by volume (30 per cent by value). Annual beer consumption was about 300 million hecto-litres (a hectolitre is 100 litres) as shown in Table 1, although rates of consumption varied considerably from country to country as shown in Table 2.

As a production entity, European output was more than 50 per cent greater than that of the USA, the world's largest beer-producing country. Table 3 shows beer production by country.

Industry structure

Table 4 shows the top ten European brewing companies by their output in 1998. The European market, taken as a whole, was not very concentrated; the top five brewers had a combined market share of less than 40 per cent. The European brewers were also relatively insular. Only four of the top ten had sales of any significance outside Europe (i.e. over 1 million hectolitres per annum) and for the majority of them, the bulk of their output was produced in their country of origin. On a global comparison, Anheuser-Busch of the USA, the largest brewing company in the world, had an annual output more than three times that of

Table 1 European beer consumption by country and year ('000 hectolitres)

COUNTRY PAYS LÄNDER	1980	1992	1993	1994	1995	1996	1997	1998	1999
Belgique	12 945	11 269	10 860	10 720	10 513	10 284	10 243	10 011	10 203
Danmark	6 698	6 630	6 541	6 619	6 505	6 363	6 165	5 707	5 562
Deutschland[1]	89 820	114 424	110 338	112 386	110 999	107 987	107 679	104 550	104 629
España	20 065	27 572	26 229	26 642	26 963	26 199	26 238	26 417	27 120
France	23 745	23 022	22 585	22 686	22 690	23 133	21 655	22 663	22 833
Greece		4 130	4 130	4 200	4 005	3 885	3 940	4 211	4 354
Ireland	4 174	4 410	4 364	4 832	4 932	5 196	5 406	5 592	5 699
Italia	9 539	13 524	14 324	15 010	14 530	13 758	14 535	15 501	15 555
Luxembourg	417	436	413	407	477	469	466	453	472
Nederland	12 213	13 692	13 019	13 231	13 265	13 276	13 475	13 225	13 309
Österreich	7 651	9 673	9 326	9 364	9 309	9 185	9 145	8 736	8 810
Portugal	3 534	6 646	6 347	6 162	6 416	6 136	6 318	6 494	6 475
Suomi (Finland)	2 738	4 444	4 364	4 293	4 153	4 074	4 170	4 084	4 087
Sverige	3 935	5 475	5 537	5 886	5 687	5 228	5 459	5 077	5 258
United Kingdom	65 490	60 973	59 177	60 575	59 129	59 894	61 114	58 835	58 917
EU – UE – EU	262 964	306 320	297 554	303 013	299 573	295 067	296 008	291 556	293 283
Norge	1 961	2 172	2 137	2 187	2 284	2 299	2 330	2 203	2 260
Schweiz/Suisse	4 433	4 789	4 568	4 550	4 431	4 305	4 249	4 277	4 212
TOTAL[2]	269 358	313 281	304 259	309 750	306 288	301 671	302 587	298 036	299 755

1. 1980 and 1990 excluding GDR, sans RDA, ohne DDR.   2. 1980 excluding, sans, ohne Greece.
Source: CBMC.

TABLE 2 Annual consumption per capita by country and year (litres)

COUNTRY PAYS LÄNDER	1980	1992	1993	1994	1995	1996	1997	1998	1999
Belgique	131.0	112.0	108.0	106.0	104.0	102.0	101.0	98.0	100.0
Danmark	130.7	128.2	126.0	126.7	124.4	120.9	116.7	107.7	104.6
Deutschland[1]	145.9	142.0	135.9	138.0	135.9	131.9	131.2	127.5	127.5
España	53.7	70.5	66.0	66.2	66.6	66.1	66.7	66.3	68.8
France	44.3	40.9	39.2	39.3	39.1	39.6	37.0	38.6	38.7
Greece	☐	42.0	42.0	42.0	40.0	39.0	39.0	42.0	43.0
Ireland	121.7	124.0	123.0	112.6	112.7	118.0	123.7	124.2	126.0
Italia	16.7	23.8	25.1	26.2	25.4	24.0	25.4	26.9	27.1
Luxembourg	115.8	112.0	103.8	101.7	118.0	114.0	112.0	107.0	110.0
Nederland	86.4	90.2	85.2	86.0	85.8	85.1	86.4	84.3	84.4
Österreich	101.9	122.6	116.7	116.6	115.7	114.0	113.3	108.1	108.9
Portugal	35.0	65.3	64.4	62.3	64.7	61.9	63.6	63.3	64.9
Suomi (Finland)	56.6	88.8	86.9	84.4	82.7	82.2	84.0	80.0	80.1
Sverige	47.4	62.4	63.8	67.3	64.5	59.1	61.7	57.3	59.3
United Kingdom	118.3	105.1	101.7	103.7	100.9	101.9	103.6	99.3	99.0
EU – UE – EU	☐	☐	**80.1**	**81.7**	**80.6**	**78.9**	**79.2**	**77.8**	**78.3**
Norge	48.1	50.8	50.0	50.5	52.5	52.6	52.9	49.7	50.7
Schweiz/Suisse	69.5	69.4	65.5	64.8	62.7	60.6	59.5	59.9	58.8
TOTAL[2]	**82.5**	**82.7**	**80.0**	**81.0**	**79.9**	**78.2**	**78.6**	**77.2**	**77.6**

1. 1980 & 1990 excluding GDR, sans RDA, ohne DDR.   2. 1980 excluding, sans, ohne Greece.
Source: CBMC.

Table 3 European beer production by country and year ('000 hectolitres)

COUNTRY PAYS LÄNDER	1980	1992	1993	1994	1995	1996	1997	1998	1999
Belgique	14 291	14 259	14 182	14 743	14 528	14 232	14 014	14 015	☐
Danmark	8 169	9 775	9 435	9 410	10 058	9 591	9 181	8 075	8 024
Deutschland[1]	92 342	120 158	115 800	118 300	116 900	114 200	114 800	111 700	112 800
España	20 027	26 082	24 278	25 024	25 313	24 716	24 773	24 991	25 852
France	21 684	21 296	20 833	20 445	20 634	20 441	19 483	19 807	19 866
Greece	☐	3 900	3 900	4 250	4 005	3 945	3 945	4 022	4 359
Ireland	6 000	6 680	6 910	7 186	7 402	7 764	8 152	8 478	8 648
Italia	8 569	10 923	11 715	12 098	11 990	11 117	11 455	12 193	12 137
Luxembourg	729	569	558	531	518	484	481	469	450
Nederland	15 684	20 659	20 431	22 175	23 118	23 494	24 701	23 988	24 502
Österreich	7 606	10 014	9 823	10 144	9 662	9 547	9 366	8 830	8 869
Portugal	3 557	6 874	6 568	6 637	6 928	6 713	6 623	6 784	6 760
Suomi (Finland)	2 823	4 576	4 588	4 538	4 726	4 669	4 804	4 697	4 700
Sverige	3 759	4 973	5 140	5 430	5 309	4 805	4 858	4 568	4 673
United Kingdom	64 830	57 617	56 746	58 333	56 800	58 072	59 139	56 652	57 854
EU – UE – EU	**270 070**	**318 355**	**310 907**	**319 244**	**317 891**	**313 790**	**315 775**	**309 359**	**299 494**
Norge	2 001	2 186	2 146	2 202	2 256	2 274	2 299	2 169	2 181
Schweiz/Suisse	4 127	4 128	3 907	3 891	3 763	3 627	3 563	3 586	3 599
TOTAL[2]	**276 198**	**324 669**	**316 960**	**325 337**	**323 910**	**319 691**	**321 637**	**315 114**	**305 249[3]**

1. 1980 excluding GDR, sans RDA, ohne DDR.   2. 1980 excluding, sans, ohne Greece.   3. 1980 excluding, sans, ohne Belgique.
Source: CBMC.

Table 4 **Top ten brewers in Europe, 1997 and 1998**

	1997 ESTIMATED MARKET SHARE (% BY VOLUME)	1998 ESTIMATED MARKET SHARE (% BY VOLUME)
1. Carlsberg (Denmark)	8.7	8.7
2. Heineken (Holland)	8.4	8.3
3. Danone (France)	8.1	8.1
4. Diageo (Eire)	6.6	7.0
5. Interbrew (Belgium)	5.7	5.8
6. Bass (UK)	4.5	4.7
7. Fosters Brewing (Australia)	3.0	3.1
8. Private Label	3.1	3.0
9. Whitbread (UK)	2.9	3.0
10. Bräu & Brunnen (Germany)	2.8	2.8
	46.4	45.5
TOTAL	100.0	100.0

Volumes include those companies in which the relevant brewer has a financial interest.

Source: Euromonitor from trade sources.

Carlsberg and 50 per cent greater than Heineken worldwide.

Individual European countries had substantially different industry structures. They varied from the highly concentrated to the highly fragmented. For example, sales in Denmark and the Netherlands were dominated by one company (Carlsberg and Heineken respectively); Italy, Belgium and France were dominated by two producers; Spain and the United Kingdom had more competitors whilst Germany was very fragmented. Some countries, such as the United Kingdom, had regulations which limit the degree of concentration allowed in industries. Other countries did not have these rules, and in fact some encouraged concentration to help the creation and development of significant international competitors.

There was little ownership of breweries by other European companies in Germany and none in Denmark. However, significant proportions of the Italian and Spanish industries were owned by foreign brewers as a result of cross-border acquisitions since the 1970s, driven by small domestic markets causing ambitious brewers to seek international expansion. Table 5 shows the major European cross-border ownership stakes.

There was little ownership in Europe by non-European brewers. There were, however, licensing arrangements whereby brewers in one country brew a brand from another country. This principally took place in the United Kingdom. A good example had been Whitbread, which brewed and sold both Stella Artois and Heineken under licence in the UK. This provided them with an expanded portfolio of brands with which to compete. In 2000 there were some important changes in ownership. Interbrew acquired Bass and Whitbread of the UK for £2.3 billion for Bass alone. This gave them 32 per cent market share in the UK. But the UK government ruled against the deal and required Interbrew to sell off Bass. The company had appealed against the decision, claiming that UK competition law was much tougher than the European Commission expected in Europe and the sale of Bass would leave them with only 10 per cent market share – way behind Scottish and Newcastle with 28 per cent. Also in 2000 the French brewer Danone combined their brewing interests in France, Belgium and Italy with the brewing businesses of Scottish and Newcastle of the UK under the name Brasseries Kronenbourg/Alken Maes. Danone held a minority 25 per cent stake.

Table 5 Cross-European ownership stakes

	HEINEKEN	DANONE[1]	CARLSBERG	INTERBREW
France	*	**		*
Germany			*	
Belgium		*		**
Netherlands	**			*
Denmark			**	
Spain	*	*		
Italy	*	*	*	*
Greece	*			
United Kingdom		*	*	*
Ireland	*			

* Denotes an ownership presence.
** Denotes country of origin.

1. In March 2000 Danone combined its brewing interests with Scottish and Newcastle (UK), trading as Kronenbourg/Alken Maes. Danone held a minority 25 per cent stake.

Brands and market segments

With low growth, or decline, in consumption in the European markets, branding had become increasingly important. Brewers had intensified their brand development policies and very high brand awareness existed amongst consumers, principally due to high-profile (and high-cost) advertising.

In a saturated market, segmentation was also significant. For example, in the United Kingdom, total beer sold since the 1970s had not fluctuated substantially but in the same period lager's share of the market had increased from 7.5 to 55 per cent. Distinct segments of the European market also developed – paradoxically both premium (strong) and low-alcohol segments were important. Also, supermarket chain own-label beers had increased as a result of their low price and the distribution power of the supermarket chains.

Distribution

European consumers purchased their beer in two main ways. They either purchased beer in stores to drink at home (known as the 'off trade') or they purchased it, principally on draught, in an outlet such as a bar, pub, café, restaurant or hotel to be consumed immediately. There were large differences between countries in draught beer sales, with the UK, Ireland and Germany being particularly high and Denmark and Greece particularly low. The type of container in which beer is purchased also varies significantly from country to country.

Channels of distribution also varied. For example, in France, Holland, Spain, Italy, Belgium and Denmark brewers did not own many of the retail outlets and tended to distribute through wholesalers, which may or may not be owned by the brewers. The supermarket chains had substantial power, which was growing across Europe as more beer was sold through supermarkets. In the UK and to a lesser extent Germany, the brewing companies owned a significant proportion of the retail outlets and distributed direct to the pubs and bars. However, in the UK there had been a drastic reduction in brewery-owned pubs and by 2000 independent groups were the major owners of pubs.

Imports and exports

Table 6 shows imports as a percentage of consumption and exports as a percentage of production by country.

Table 6 **Imports and exports of beer by country (1999)**

COUNTRY	IMPORTS (% OF CONSUMPTION)	EXPORTS (% OF PRODUCTION)
Belgique	N/A	34 (est.)
Danmark	2	29
Deutschland	3	8
España	7	2
France	23	11
Greece	4	5
Ireland	10	41
Italia	25	4
Luxembourg	31	27
Nederland	8	50
Österreich	5	5
Portugal	3	7
Suomi (Finland)	2	6
Sverige	1	N/A
United Kingdom	9	6
EU	8	12
Norge	3	2
Schweiz/Suisse	15	1
TOTAL	8	12

Source: CBMC.

Four brewing companies

Heineken

Heineken was far the biggest and most global of the European brewery companies, yet was still a family business. There had been three generations of Heineken, each with its own approach to building the business. Heineken had become Europe's favourite brand of beer and the most international beer in the world. Heineken beer was available in over 170 countries and the company's product portfolio consisted of over 80 brands. With more than 110 breweries in over 50 countries and export activities all over the world, Heineken was the most international brewery group in the world. In 1999, the total beer volume of Heineken Group was 90.9 million hectolitres, ensuring the Heineken Group second place in world rankings. In Europe, Heineken had been the leading brewer, with leading positions in the Netherlands, Ireland, Spain, Poland and France. This international orientation

had been part of Heineken's identity since its early days. In the 1870s, it was already exporting Heineken to the UK and France, followed by markets in the Caribbean and West Africa. Export had proved to be an excellent way of exploring new markets and building up the brand name and image. This had enabled Heineken to support strong local brands whilst remaining true to the original export philosophy by positioning Heineken in the premium segment.

Grolsch

Royal Grolsch NV was a medium-size international brewing group – less than one-tenth the size of Heineken. Its key products included Grolsch Premium Lager, Grolsch Amber Ale and Grolsch Blond. Grolsch's premium lager was the only beer available in the distinctive 'swingtop' bottle used by Grolsch for more than 100 years. The Grolsch brewery was established in 1615 in Groenlo, in the

Netherlands. Grolsch was first exported in 1946 and by 2000 was available in over 100 countries. Grolsch was renowned as a producer of premium beers. It had been the number one brand in the premium segment in the Netherlands. Globally, Grolsch beer had occupied a leading position in several important markets, such as the UK, USA, Canada, France and Australia. Its strategy was to export to countries with well-developed markets, and in some countries, Grolsch beer was brewed under licence. Grolsch had achieved strong market position by giving top priority to professionalism and quality. In 2000, Grolsch's export sales were up 9 per cent, reflecting growth in its target markets of Europe and North America. The company's quality philosophy applies to the product and also to their financial and social obligations.

Bass Brewers

In August 2000, Bass sold its brewing interests to Interbrew. Ever since its first exports to St Petersburg in 1784, Bass Breweries had been the UK's biggest beer exporter. It exported to five continents and over 79 countries. Brands included Caffrey, Carling, Worthington and Tennants. The combination of its strong brands and the ability to invest in them meant that Bass Brewers accounted for 24 per cent of the UK beer market. By continuously investing time, energy and a great deal of money, Bass Brewers managed to keep their brands fresh and at the top of the best-seller list. In 2000, Bass Brewer's off-trade volume increased by 19.6 per cent and there was also good performance from worldwide sales. By focusing on brand management and as a result of a sustained and integrated packaging of advertising, sponsorship and promotion, Bass Brewers had taken every opportunity to reinforce its relationship with customers, for example by sponsoring the FA Carling Premiership, the Worthington Cup and T in the Park. These activities, combined with a marketing investment in excess of £75 million a year, helped the brands realise their full potential. The opening of Bass-branded pubs outside the UK had further strengthened its overseas position. As well as exporting brands, Bass had been committed to increasing its presence abroad through joint ventures and acquisitions.

Scottish and Newcastle

In March 2000, Scottish and Newcastle announced a major partnership with Group Danone's beer interests (Kronenbourg in France and Alken Maes in Belgium). They were the majority partner in a new European beer group called Brasseries Kronenbourg/Alken Maes. The company was the UK market leader with 28 per cent market share – although the contested purchase of Bass and Whitbread had taken Interbrew to 32 per cent share.

The company's turnover in 2000 was £3.6 billion with pre-tax profits of £409 million. The company owned seven breweries (six in the UK and one in Ireland). Its brands included John Smiths, Courage, Newcastle Brown and Theakston's. It also brewed other famous brands under licence, including Becks, Miller Pilsner and Fosters. Its top five brands accounted for 68 per cent of sales. Scottish and Newcastle also owned a portfolio of retail businesses in the leisure market which together accounted for £1.1 billion of the 2000 turnover and £246 million of the profits. They had more than 2,700 outlets, including specialist bars (such as Bar 38), pub food outlets (e.g. Chef and Brewer – acquired from Grand Metropolitan in 1993), theme restaurants (e.g. Old Orleans) and budget accommodation (Premier Lodges).

Sources: As shown on tables. Also the previous case study by Tony Jacobs and Murray Steele in the fifth edition of *Exploring Corporate Strategy* (1999) and company websites.

Questions

Using the data from the tables:

1. What are the major trends in the European beer industry?

2. For the four brewing companies outlined above (or brewers of your choice) explain:
   - how these trends will impact differently on these different companies;
   - how their strategy should change.

3. Why do you think Bass sold their brewing interests to Interbrew?

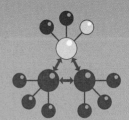

4

Strategic Capability

LEARNING OUTCOMES

After reading this chapter you should be able to understand:

- The importance of knowledge and knowledge management.
- The meaning and importance of critical success factors.
- The strategic importance of resources and the concept of unique resources.
- The importance of competences and the meaning of core competences.
- The factors that create value for money in products or services.
- The importance of performing better than 'competitors' and the concept of benchmarking.
- Why some strategies are more difficult to imitate than others – the concept of robustness.
- How key issues can be summarised (SWOT).

4.1 INTRODUCTION

Chapter 3 outlined how the external environment in which an organisation is operating can influence its strategic development by creating both opportunities and threats. But successful strategies are also dependent on the organisation having the *strategic capability* to perform at the level that is required for success. So the first reason why an understanding of strategic capability is important is concerned with whether an organisation's strategies continue to *fit* the environment in which the organisation is operating and the opportunities and threats that exist. Many of the issues of strategy development are concerned with changing strategic capability better to fit a changing environment. The major upheavals in many manufacturing industries during the 1990s were examples of such adjustments in strategic capability, involving major gains in labour productivity and the adoption of new technologies. The early twenty-first century is dominated in industry, commerce and the public services by the struggle to understand and exploit the capabilities offered by IT even just to stay in business.

Exhibit 4.1   The roots of strategic capability

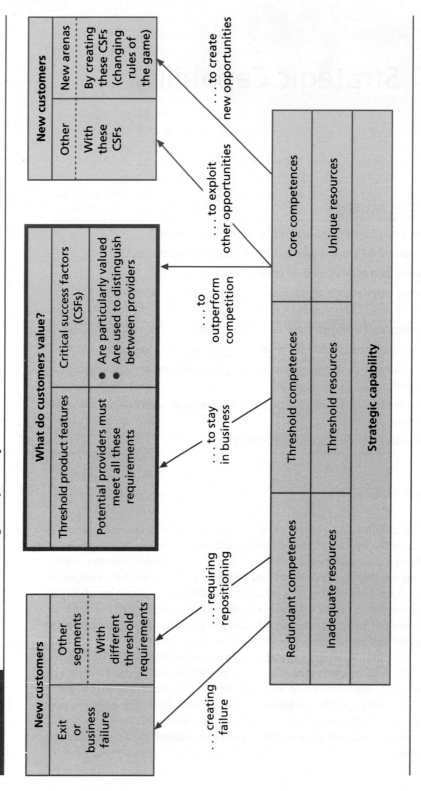

However, understanding strategic capability is also important from another perspective. The organisation's capability may be the leading edge of strategic developments, in the sense that new opportunities may be created by *stretching* and exploiting the organisation's capability either in ways which competitors find difficult to match or in genuinely new directions, or both. This requires organisations to be *innovative* in the way they develop and exploit their capability. This has been called the resource-based view of strategy.[1] As mentioned in Chapter 3, in a fast-moving (hypercompetitive) world the only really enduring capability is the ability to change strategy as the basis of competition moves on through different phases of the cycle of competition. Indeed, stretching IT capabilities and hypercompetitive behaviour have been the basis on which the dot.com companies not only challenged the incumbent organisations in many service industries but also created whole new services and areas of economic activity.

4.1.1 The roots of strategic capability

This chapter is concerned with understanding strategic capability with both these 'fit' and 'stretch' perspectives in mind. There will be a particular emphasis on *knowledge* and *knowledge management* as increasingly important resources and competences for successful organisations. Exhibit 4.1 shows how the discussion is structured and Illustration 4.1 outlines the terminology and uses the example of an Olympic relay running team (four athletes each running 100 metres) to show what each term means. Readers are encouraged to follow these definitions and example from the illustration as the structure of this chapter is described in the following paragraphs in relation to Exhibit 4.1:

- Strategic capability is about providing products or services to customers that are valued – or might be valued in the future. An understanding of *what customers value* is the starting point and this has already been introduced in Chapter 3 (section 3.5.2). This is concerned with the *product features* – remembering that this includes not just the product itself but aspects of service too. First are the threshold product features that all potential providers must be able to offer if they are to stay in a particular market or market segment. Second are the *critical success factors*, which are the product features that are particularly valued by a group of customers and, therefore, where the organisation must excel to outperform competition. For the Olympic team the 'customer' is the International Olympic Committee (IOC) and their threshold requirements for any team entering the games are explicit – the qualifying standards, drug tests and so on as shown in the illustration. The critical success factors (needed to win a gold medal) are very simply defined – to run faster than the other teams (although in some sports there are subjective criteria too).

- The discussion then moves to whether an organisation has the *resources and competences* to provide products/services that meet these customer requirements:

Illustration 4.1

Strategic capability – the terminology

TERM	DEFINITION	EXAMPLE (THE OLYMPIC RELAY TEAM)
A. What customers value		
Threshold product features	Product features and performance standards all of which must be met by providers	Meet qualifying standard Pass drug tests Be selected into national team (for individuals)
Critical success factors	Features that are particularly valued by customers and used to distinguish between potential providers	Run fastest in final (In some events, e.g. gymnastics, there are subjective factors too)
B. Strategic capability		
Strategic capability	The ability to perform at the level required for success. It is underpinned by the resources and competences of the organisation	Athletic ability in chosen sport
Threshold resources	Resources needed to stay in the business	A healthy body (for individuals) Medical facilities and practitioners Training venues and equipment Food and supplements
Unique resources	Resources that create competitive advantage and are difficult to imitate	Individuals with: ● Exceptional heart and lungs ● Height or weight World-class coach
Inadequate resources	Resources that do not adequately underpin the meeting of threshold product features. They may be adequate for other segments	Injured body Poor training facilities Poor coaches
Threshold competences	Activities that underpin the meeting of threshold product features	Individual training regimes Physiotherapy/injury management Diet planning
Core competences	Activities that underpin the meeting of critical success factors and hence give competitive advantage	Squad coaching Teamwork
Redundant competences	Activities where performance standards are below the level needed to stay in business. They may be adequate for other segments	Psychological therapy
C. Outcomes and responses		
Business failure	Failure to meet threshold requirements	Not selected for games
Repositioning	Addressing other segments with different threshold requirements	Try for selection to European or Commonwealth games
Staying in business	Meeting the threshold product features	Selected for the games
Outperforming competitors	Satisfying the critical success factors better than competitors	Winning the gold medal
Exploiting other opportunities	Other arenas that *already* value the same CSFs	Playing American Football
Creating new opportunities	Where the CSFs *could be* valued	Presentations to managers

- What resources are *available* to an organisation, from both within and outside, to support its strategies?
- What is the *threshold* level of resources needed to support particular strategies? If an organisation does not possess these resources it will be unable to meet customers' threshold requirements on one or more product feature. For the relay team these are healthy athletes, medical and training facilities etc.
- What *unique resources* might organisations have to meet the critical success factors of a particular segment and gain competitive advantage? The relay team may have individuals with exceptional physical characteristics that help them run faster.
- Some organisations might have *inadequate resources* and be unable to meet the threshold requirements of customers. This occurs not only because resources dissipate (for example, the individual runners get older or injured) but, more importantly, because customer requirements are constantly rising. But these resources may be adequate for meeting the requirements of customers in other market segments. So a relay team may not have the individual athletes needed to achieve Olympic qualifying standards but they may be adequate to meet the lower standards for regional games.
- *Competence* is created when resources are 'deployed' into the separate activities of the organisation and into the processes through which these activities are linked together. So competence is about the *activities* of an organisation and the *processes* that link activities together both within and beyond the organisation. Usually, the key to good or poor performance is found here rather than in the resources *per se.* This is because activities and processes may be more difficult to imitate than is the acquisition of resources, as discussed below; for example, training regimes and diet planning for the athletes are more difficult to imitate than acquiring training facilities and food/supplements.
- Although an organisation will need to reach a *threshold level* of competence in *all* the activities that it undertakes, only some of these activities are *core competences*. Core competences are those competences that underpin the organisation's ability to outperform competition by meeting the critical success factors better than competitors. There may be many relay teams that have great individual runners but the squad coaching and teamwork (baton exchange) may decide who wins the gold medal. This also involves the intuitive understanding between the athletes based on experience of working together on baton exchange.
- Core competences might also provide the basis on which strategies may be built to exploit *opportunities in other markets* where the same critical success factors are valued. Olympic athletes are often signed up by other sports where speed is important - such as American football.
- Core competences might also be the basis of creating *opportunities in new arenas* where the same CSFs would be valued above those that currently prevail. In other words, to change the rules of the game in those new arenas. Olympic athletes sometimes exploit the fame that comes from success to break into new careers. For example, they are employed

to help 'break the mindset' about teamwork, coaching and endurance in management development programmes.

- As with resources, some organisations may have inadequate (redundant) competences as customer requirements move on. This could lead to *business failure*. However, these competences may be adequate to serve customers in different segments (*repositioning*), for example in developing markets. The reason why a relay team might fail to win at the Olympics could be to do with psychological preparation. However, they still might be a good enough team to win at regional games.

● The later sections of the chapter look at how organisations might develop the strategic capability to succeed. This will include a discussion of the following:
- Delivering products that are valued by customers. This requires the ability to manage both cost and product features.
- Competitive advantage is about performing better than other organisations, so there is a need to understand performance standards and what good and poor performance means.
- The importance of robustness of resources and competences – the extent to which these are easy or difficult to imitate.
- The chapter concludes with a brief discussion of how an organisation's strengths and weaknesses might be summarised and related to the opportunities and threats discussed in Chapter 3.

4.1.2 The importance of knowledge[2]

Knowledge is important to all organisations and in a knowledge-based economy the capability of individual organisations is critically underpinned by knowledge. **Knowledge** is defined as awareness, consciousness or familiarity gained by experience or learning. The concept of knowledge relates to all of the issues listed above and shown in Exhibit 4.1:

Knowledge is awareness, consciousness or familiarity gained by experience or learning

● Knowledge of what *customers value* is important – both their threshold requirements and the things they especially value.

● Knowledge links to *resources* too. There are resources that underpin knowledge without which it may be impossible to meet customer requirements. For example, acquiring or developing adequate hardware and software for information systems infrastructure is a threshold requirement for most organisations in the twenty-first century.

● Some knowledge will be a *unique resource* – for example, the knowledge of a particularly talented individual, such as a research scientist, or the intellectual property of an organisation (e.g. its patents).

● Knowledge may be captured by a system or a business process (such as market research or procurement processes), which may be an important *competence*. Since important knowledge will rest outside an organisation, the processes which integrate knowledge between organisations are also important. This is a threshold requirement for doing business – for example, the knowledge to procure supplies and distribute products is as important as the knowledge on how to manufacture those products. The concept of the *value chain* will look at this issue. Unlike resources, which might dissipate over time, knowledge-based competences are likely to improve with time[3] as experience is accumulated.

● Knowledge may also be an organisational *core competence* in that it provides competitive advantage. But for this to occur it must be difficult to imitate, as will be discussed below. For example, the processes through which knowledge is shared and/or integrated could give competitive advantage. This would be important in new product development where knowledge about product feature development and market knowledge need to be blended to create commercially successful products. It will be seen below that knowledge that is embedded in an organisation's culture will be difficult for competitors to imitate and, therefore, may well be a core competence.

This theme of knowledge and knowledge 'management' processes as important sources of competitive advantage, therefore, will run through the discussions that follow. As seen in Chapter 3, a key capability in hypercompetitive markets is the ability to move from one temporary advantage to another through the cycle of competition rather than dissipating resources in defending a particular basis of advantage. So the speed at which knowledge is developed and exploited will be of particular importance in fast-changing environments.[4]

It is useful at the outset to flag up how the concept of knowledge is connected to a traditional resourced-based view of strategy. As will be seen, a resource-based view of strategy is centred around the ways in which competitive advantage can be gained through the exploitation of resources and competences – particularly those unique resources and core competences that competitors will find difficult to imitate. This inevitably leads to the conclusion that sustainable advantage is most likely to be built around a combination of activities and processes that are embedded in an organisation's way of doing things. Whilst this can be thought of in cultural terms, it is also organisational knowledge and it cannot all be captured in explicit systems. It is the knowledge that is embedded in organisational processes and may well be taken for granted (tacit). This is why it is so difficult for competitors to imitate.

4.2 CRITICAL SUCCESS FACTORS (CSFs)[5]

Exhibit 4.1 showed that the starting point for understanding strategic capability is an understanding of what customers value, as introduced in section 3.5.2. It shows that customers in any market segment will have threshold requirements on all features of the product or service. If one or more of these are not met a provider will drop out of that part of the market. But customers are likely to value some features above others and this will vary by market segment. Some customers may be particularly interested in price, others in reliability and yet others in delivery time, and so on. They will use this smaller 'list' of features to distinguish amongst those producer organisations that all meet the threshold requirements. These are known as **critical success factors (CSFs)** and are those product features that are particularly valued by a group of customers

Critical success factors (CSFs) are those product features that are particularly valued by a group of customers and, therefore, where the organisation must excel to outperform competition

and, therefore, where the organisation must excel to outperform competition. They will differ from one market segment to another.

Since different customer groups value different product features, organisations will need to compete on different bases and through different resources and competences. For example, consider how small shops compete with supermarkets in grocery retailing. The major supermarkets are pursuing strategies which provide lower prices and 'one-stop shopping' to consumers through their resources (store location, product range) and competences (knowledge of merchandising, securing lower-cost supplies and computerised logistic systems). These give a supermarket competitive advantage over smaller shops with those customers who particularly value low prices and one-stop shopping. It is difficult for smaller shops to imitate these resources and competences. So a 'corner shop' grocery store gains competitive advantage over supermarkets by concentrating on those customers whose critical success factors are different aspects of service (for example, personal service, extended opening hours, informal credit, home deliveries, etc.). This strategy may be underpinned by unique resources (such as shop location, the market knowledge of the owner) and core competences (the personal style and customer relationships sustained by the owner).

It is important to understand that those resources and competences which allow supermarkets to gain competitive advantage over corner shops are threshold resources and competences to survive as a supermarket. Competitive advantage over other supermarkets is achieved through other unique resources (perhaps a prime location or unique products such as home-baked bread) or core competences (perhaps in the management of own-brand supply). However, industry experience shows that these resources and competences tend to be easy to imitate in the medium term. Consequently, competitive advantage needs to be secured by continually shifting the ground of competition. So a core competence could be the processes of innovation – which requires the knowledge to link together many separate areas of knowledge such as brand development, marketing and financial services.

In the public services the concept of critical success factors is also valid except that it may relate to a stakeholder other than the customer, for example the providers of funding. Sometimes the requirements of both customers and funders matter but they may value different things. Perhaps the funder is particularly interested in 'price' (i.e. the unit costs) with a threshold quality requirement whereas the recipient of the service might wish to see a higher quality of service. These may be difficult pressures to reconcile.

The issues about resources and competences introduced in this section will now be discussed more fully.

4.3 THE STRATEGIC IMPORTANCE OF RESOURCES

4.3.1 Available resources[6]

Strategic capability is underpinned by the resources *available* to an organisation since it is resources that are deployed into the activities of the organisation to create competences. From a strategic perspective an organisation's resources include both those that are owned by the organisation and those that can *accessed* to support its strategies. Some strategically important resources may be outside an organisation's ownership, such as its network of contacts or customers.

Typically, resources can be grouped under the following four headings:

- *Physical resources* – such as machines, buildings or production capacity. The nature of these resources, such as the age, condition, capability and location of each resource, will also determine the usefulness of the resources.

- *Human resources* – including knowledge, skills of people and adaptability of human resources. This applies both to employees and to other people in an organisation's networks. In knowledge-based economies people do genuinely become 'the most valuable asset'. But to gain advantage of this will require a strong link between overall business strategies and human resource strategies, as discussed in section 10.2.

- *Financial resources* – such as capital, cash, debtors and creditors, and suppliers of money (shareholders, bankers, etc.). The relationship between financial strategies and business strategies will be looked at in section 10.4.

- *Intellectual capital* is the intangible resources[7] of an organisation and is often overlooked or undervalued. This would include the knowledge that has been captured in patents, brands, business systems, customer databases and relationships with partners. There should be no doubt that these intangible resources have a value, since when businesses are sold part of the value is 'goodwill'. In a knowledge-based economy, intellectual capital is likely to be the major asset of many organisations and there are pressures to find ways of assessing and accounting for the value of intangibles.[8] An important issue is the extent to which the knowledge of individual employees is personal to, and owned by, them or whether this is the legal property of the organisation. This often surfaces when individuals leave to work for a competitor and confidentiality clauses (and patents) attempt to protect companies against loss of this knowledge.

4.3.2 Threshold resources

A set of *threshold resources* are needed to exist as a provider to any market segment (see Exhibits 4.1 and 4.2). But this threshold tends to rise with time (through the activities of competitors and new entrants) so there is a need continuously to improve this resource base just to stay in business. So some industries or sectors have seen progressive shakeout of providers as the processes of competition make these resource requirements an increasingly difficult barrier to achieve. The way in which the Premier Soccer League in England developed during the 1990s created a gulf between those who were able to spend money on expensive squads of players and ground improvements and those who could not. The latter group tended to be relegated to lower divisions. (See *Manchester United* case example at the end of Chapter 5.)

Exhibit 4.2	Resources, competences and competitive advantage

	Same as competitors' or easy to imitate	Better than competitors' and difficult to imitate*
RESOURCES	Threshold resources	Unique resources
COMPETENCES	Threshold competences	Core competences

* Provides the basis to outperform competitors or demonstratably provide better value for money

The problem for established organisations is that they may experience step changes in the business environment that can make a large part of their resource base redundant. But unless an organisation is able to dispose of those redundant resources they may be unable to free up sufficient funds to invest in the new resources that are needed and their cost base will be too high. For example, traditional banks continue to struggle with their legacy of a vast array of branches in a world where new competitors do not have branches and have invested heavily in call centres and online Internet banking. In 2000, the average transaction cost through a branch was £1 compared with 54p via telephone and only 15p on the Internet. Also, branch transaction costs were rising as volumes fell and the more profitable customers migrated to e-banking (via telephone and/or Internet). So the message is that organisations may have to change their resource base considerably just to stay in business.

4.3.3 Unique resources

The ability of an organisation to meet the critical success factors in a particular market segment may be underpinned by unique resources as shown in Exhibits 4.1 and 4.2. **Unique resources** are those resources which critically underpin competitive advantage. They sustain the ability to provide value in the product, are better than competitors' resources and are difficult to imitate. This is shown in Exhibit 4.2. Economists would refer to the benefits derived from this advantage as the *economic profit (rent)*.[9] For example, some libraries have unique collections of books which contain knowledge unavailable elsewhere; retail stores with prime locations can charge higher than average prices. Illustration 4.2 shows how the Ordnance Survey were able to exploit

Unique resources are those resources which critically underpin competitive advantage

Illustration 4.2

The Ordnance Survey

Some organisations have unique resources in their intellectual capital – but these still need to be exploited.

The Ordnance Survey (OS) has existed in the UK for over 200 years as the national mapping agency. Its core functions have included producing, maintaining and marketing maps and managing computer data and geographical information. These are used for leisure, educational and administrative purposes. Its activities were progressively commercialised during the 1990s, and in 1999 the government changed its status from a government body to a trading fund – it then had to run its own finances and make a 9 per cent return on capital. The OS earned income from selling products and services, including issuing licences for others to utilise copyright material. As a result, in 2000 OS made a profit of £12.7m on a turnover of £99.6m.

Although the public perception of OS had been as a provider of maps, OS had kept ahead in the market by utilising technology, as computers replaced the need for drawing by hand, and quicker and more accurate revisions could be made. It realised the importance and potential of geographical information systems, which allow a wide variety of information to be synthesised more rapidly. This had the effect of making maps more interactive, and therefore more responsive to consumer needs.

Competitive advantage had been gained by OS being able to license its data. OS had worked with several private sector partners who incorporated OS data into their software products. Innovation had been crucial, as OS attempted to provide a comprehensive service via their Solution Centre, which operated as a consultancy. Computerised data evolved into the biggest part of the business and OS utilised its experience in data collection by providing services to many public and private organisations. This included aiding the police in mapping crime patterns, locating derelict land for development, targeting marketing efforts, calculating insurance risks, and managing property portfolios. OS had also benefited from the growing telecom industry and adopted an e-strategy to turn its maps into digital data for use in mobile phones, mapping websites, and in-car navigation systems.

OS also ensured that it maintained its leading position in the market by capitalising on and investing in new technology and developments – some 3,000 changes were entered into its database daily, ensuring consistent relevance and accuracy. The National Topographic Database, which recorded over 2 million features of the UK landscape, proved to be a successful product. It was also fiercely protective of their copyright – in March 2001 the Automobile Association agreed to pay OS £20m for alleged copyright infringement.

Sources: Adapted from *Financial Times*, 19 August 2000, 3 October 2000 and 22 December 2000; *Computer Weekly*, 5 October 2000.

Questions

1. What are the unique resources that OS possesses?

2. What competences are needed to exploit these resources?

3. How might a competitor undermine these unique resources?

their intellectual capital to advantage. Some organisations have patented products or services that give them advantage – but these resources may need to be defended by a willingness to bring litigation against illegal imitators. Mining companies own a particular outcrop of minerals. But it will become exhausted. For service organisations, unique resources may be particularly talented individuals – such as surgeons or teachers or lawyers. But they may leave the organisation or be poached by a rival. So trying to sustain long-term advantage only through unique resources may be very difficult.

4.4 COMPETENCES AND CORE COMPETENCES[10]

4.4.1 What is a core competence?

The difference in performance between organisations in the same market is rarely explainable by differences in their resource base since resources can usually be imitated or traded. Superior performance will also be determined by the way in which resources are deployed to create competences in the organisation's activities. For example, the knowledge of an individual will not improve an organisation's performance unless he or she is 'assigned' (or allowed) to work on particular tasks which exploit that knowledge or, more importantly, is able to share that knowledge with others who can build on it. Performance is also affected by the processes of linking separate areas of knowledge and activities together both inside and outside the organisation. Although an organisation will need to achieve a threshold level of competence in all of the activities and processes that underpin the product and service, only some will be core competences, as shown in both Exhibits 4.1 and 4.2.
Core competences are activities or processes that critically underpin an organisation's competitive advantage. They create and sustain the ability to meet the critical success factors of particular customer groups better than other providers in ways that are difficult to imitate. In order to achieve this advantage, core competences must fulfil the following 'criteria' (see Exhibit 4.2):

> **Core competences** are activities or processes that critically underpin an organisation's competitive advantage

- The competence must relate to an activity or process that fundamentally underpins the value in the product or service features – *as seen through the eyes of the customer* (or other powerful stakeholder). As was mentioned in Chapter 3, this is not easy for managers to understand since they are likely to have a very internal view of value – even to the extent that they regard customers as being ungrateful for not appreciating the things which they (the insiders) value.

- The competence leads to levels of performance from an activity or process that are significantly better than competitors (or similar organisations in the public sector). *Benchmarking* may help in understanding performance standards and what constitutes good or poor performance.

- The competence must be *robust* – i.e. difficult for competitors to imitate. It has already been seen that in a fast-moving world, advantage gained in specific ways (such as a new marketing campaign or a superior product feature) is not likely to be robust but is short-lived. So core competences are unlikely to be about how these specific improvements are achieved but about the whole process by which continuous change and improvement occur. It will also be seen that robustness will be greater where competences are embedded – to the extent that managers themselves have difficulties in fully explaining what underpins success.

Exhibit 4.1 also shows that a core competence may be the basis on which new strategies are built – for example, by extending into new markets. It may also be the basis on which opportunities in new arenas can be created – by breaking the established 'rules of the game' – as was seen with dot.com companies in the early 2000s.

4.4.2 Where core competences reside

Managers often find it difficult to specify the core competences of their organisation, as mentioned above. This could be for several reasons:

● First, they may come up with things that are, in fact, critical success factors (product features that are particularly valued by customers) like 'good service' or 'reliable delivery'. But core competences are about the activities that underpin the ability to meet these critical success factors, not the factors themselves.

● Second, they are likely to look at too generic a level. Core competences may be embedded deep in an organisation at an operational level in the work routines of the organisation, as discussed below (section 4.7.4).

● Third, they are hidden even to the extent that managers themselves may not explicitly understand them. Indeed, if they are to be difficult to imitate this is likely to be an important attribute. So before proceeding to a detailed discussion it is helpful to look at an example (see Illustration 4.3) to see exactly where core competences might reside in organisations.

The organisation in Illustration 4.3 manufactured and sold consumer goods to major UK retailers. It had won several major retail accounts and increased its profits significantly.

The *critical success factors* with the major customers were the reputation of brand, excellence of service, delivery, product range and innovation. In relation to competitors the organisation was seen as particularly successful in terms of its level of service and its range.

The illustration shows that this success can be understood better by being more specific as to what these CSFs actually mean. For example, good service meant flexibility and rapid response but also finding ways of solving the problems that buyers in the retailers might have – getting the wrong order mix or over-ordering. These can be regarded as the *reasons for success.*

But the reasons why the organisation outperformed competitors do not emerge until these reasons are 'unpacked' by identifying the resources and competences that underpin these items:

Illustration 4.3

STRATEGY IN ACTION

Core competences for a consumer goods business

Core competences underpinning competitive success can be embedded in linked organisational activities at an operational level.

From 1996 to 1998 a consumer goods company had won several major retail accounts from competitors. In order to identify the core competences underpinning its competitive advantage it analysed how it uniquely met the retailers' criteria of supplier selection by 'unpacking' them in terms of its organisational processes as shown below.

Questions

1. Why would it be difficult for competitors to imitate the competences that the company identified?

2. What competences might this company need to have in order to be seen as a successful innovator in consumer goods?

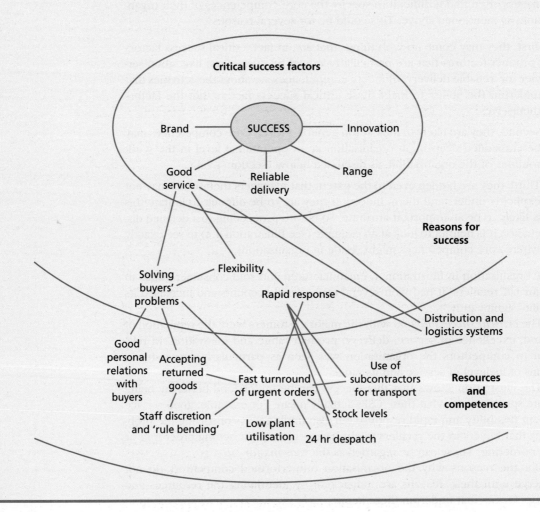

● A good deal of their success was underpinned by their distribution and logistics systems. These were essential resources and competences to service these particular customers. However, these could be (and were) matched by all competitors. Indeed the retailer would not deal with suppliers who could not meet these requirements. So even though they were important to staying in business, they were *not* unique resources or core competences. They were threshold resources and competences.

● It was important to understand how this company was able to be flexible and to solve buyers' problems. This is more difficult because it requires getting down to details at operational levels that may not be immediately obvious. In this company several explanations emerged, some of which were readily identified by managers (such as automated production lines and standardised product range) but several were not. For example:
  - 'bending the rules' – for example, taking back goods from major retailers when, strictly speaking, the policies and systems of the business did not allow it;
  - using 'organisational slack' (that top management was trying to do away with) to create flexibility in changing production runs – such as production lines with low utilisation;
  - 'custom and practice' rather than company policy, for example in prioritising the solving of problems of the buyers of the major retailers (such as taking product returns). This knowledge of 'how to work the system' is a good example of organisational knowledge being embedded in the culture rather than vested in a system.

So here knowledge was about the whole system and the experience to make it work. Newcomers (and certainly competitors) would have difficulty knowing what was going on, and competitors would find this very difficult to imitate.

● Out of this unpacking might emerge an understanding of where core competences reside. Here, what emerged was that the relationship between the sales personnel and the retail buyers encouraged buyers to 'ask the impossible' of the company when difficulties arose; and the combination of sound logistics, stock levels, spare capacity and staff discretion to the point of rule-bending resulted in competitive advantage. It was this *combination* of activities that gave superior performance and not just one or two items in isolation. Moreover, much of this was embedded in operational levels of activity in the organisation which were not evident to competitors – indeed, had not been clear to the managers themselves.

4.4.3 The importance of linkages

The example in Illustration 4.3 has looked in detail at the issue of providing value in products or services. But in doing so it focused narrowly on one specific relationship of a manufacturer and its immediate customer (the retailer). In reality, of course, value will also be created (and cost incurred) outside this particular linkage, for example in the supply chain of the manufacturer and in the activities that the supermarket performs in serving its customers. So individual organisations are part of a bigger 'system' of resources, activities and processes that link organisations together. This is called the value chain and will now be discussed. Where activities are located in the value chain, how they are performed and managed and how they are linked together will determine the value that customers receive in the final product. A good value product could result from how a set of linked activities are performed from design, component manufacture, assembly processes, care and speed of distribution, the way the product is stored and displayed, right through to support on installation and after-sales service.

So an organisation's competences can contribute to the delivery of customer value in two ways. First is competence in separate activities (for example, concerned with production or marketing). Second is the competence in linking activities together, which includes the ability to ensure that all these separate activities (both inside and outside an organisation) are helping to deliver the same customer value and are not working to different agendas. For example, an organisation may be competent in manufacturing processes that produce products to engineering specifications that competitors find difficult to match. But it will not gain advantage from this unless it is able to maintain the quality of its raw materials or if its distributors fail to handle and store finished products carefully. It is the combined effect of all of these activities that creates or destroys value and which also creates cost.

The value chain concept can be helpful in understanding how value is created or lost. The **value chain**[11] describes the activities within and around an organisation which together create a product or service, as mentioned above. It is the cost of these *value activities* and the value that they deliver that determines whether or not best value products or services are developed. In turn this underpins competitiveness, as discussed above. Exhibit 4.3 is a representation of a typical value chain within an organisation. **Primary activities** are *directly* concerned with the creation or delivery of a product or service and can be grouped into five main areas: inbound logistics, operations, outbound logistics, marketing and sales, and service.

- *Inbound logistics* are the activities concerned with receiving, storing and distributing the inputs to the product or service. They include materials handling, stock control, transport, etc.
- *Operations* transform these various inputs into the final product or service: machining, packaging, assembly, testing, etc.
- *Outbound logistics* collect, store and distribute the product to customers. For tangible products this would be warehousing, materials handling, transport, etc. In the case of services, they may be more concerned with arrangements for bringing customers to the service if it is a fixed location (e.g. sports events).
- *Marketing and sales* provide the means whereby consumers/users are made aware of the product or service and are able to purchase it. This would include sales administration, advertising, selling and so on. In public services, communication networks which help users access a particular service are often important.
- *Service* includes all those activities which enhance or maintain the value of a product or service, such as installation, repair, training and spares.

The **value chain** describes the activities within and around an organisation which together create a product or service

Primary activities are *directly* concerned with the creation or delivery of a product or service

| Exhibit 4.3 | The value chain within an organisation |

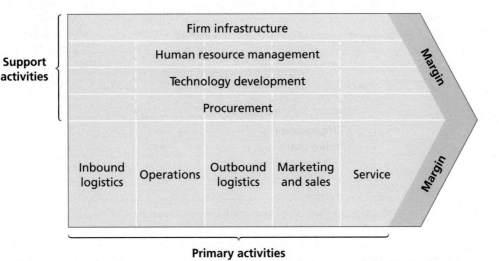

Source: M.E. Porter, *Competitive Advantage: Creating and Sustaining Superior Performance*, Free Press, 1985. Used with permission of The Free Press, a division of Simon & Schuster, Inc. © 1985, 1988 by Michael E. Porter.

Each of these groups of primary activities is linked to support activities. **Support activities** help to improve the effectiveness or efficiency of primary activities. They can be divided into four areas:

Support activities help to improve the effectiveness or efficiency of primary activities

- *Procurement.* This refers to the *processes* for acquiring the various resource inputs to the primary activities. As such, it occurs in many parts of the organisation.

- *Technology development.* All value activities have a 'technology', even if it is just know-how. The key technologies may be concerned directly with the product (e.g. R&D, product design) or with processes (e.g. process development) or with a particular resource (e.g. raw materials improvements). This area is fundamental to the innovative capacity of the organisation.

- *Human resource management.* This is a particularly important area which transcends all primary activities. It is concerned with those activities involved in recruiting, managing, training, developing and rewarding people within the organisation.

- *Infrastructure.* The systems of planning, finance, quality control, information management, etc. are crucially important to an organisation's performance in its primary activities. Infrastructure also consists of the structures and routines of the organisation which sustain its culture.

In most industries it is rare for a single organisation to undertake in-house all of the value activities from the product design through to the delivery of the final product or service to the final consumer. There is usually specialisation of role and any one organisation is part of the wider *value system*. The **value system** is the set of inter-organisational links and relationships which are necessary to

The **value system** is the set of inter-organisational links and relationships which are necessary to create a product or service

| Exhibit 4.4 | The value system |

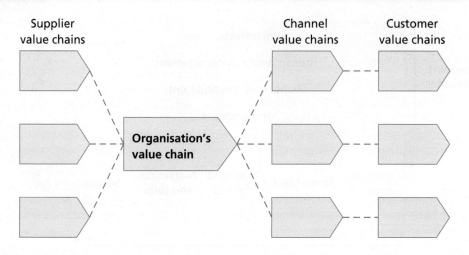

Source: M.E. Porter, *Competitive Advantage: Creating and Sustaining Superior Performance*, Free Press, 1985. Used with permission of The Free Press, a division of Simon & Schuster Inc. © 1985, 1988 by Michael E. Porter.

create a product or service (see Exhibit 4.4). It is this process of specialisation within the value system on a set of linked activities that often underpins excellence in creating best-value products. So an organisation ought to be clear about what activities it ought to undertake itself. However, since much of the cost and value creation will occur in the supply and distribution chains, managers need to understand this *whole process* and how they can manage these linkages and relationships to improve customer value. It is not sufficient to look at the organisation's internal position alone. For example, the quality of a consumer durable product (say a cooker or a television) when it reaches the final purchaser is not only influenced by the linked set of activities which are undertaken within the manufacturing company itself. It is also determined by the quality of components and the performance of the distributors. The ability of an organisation to influence the performance of other organisations in the value chain may be a crucially important competence and a source of competitive advantage. As (through IT) organisations gain improved knowledge about this wider value system and understand better where cost and value are created, they are able to make more informed choices on issues such as:

● whether they should 'make' or buy a particular activity or component (this is the outsourcing decision);

● who might be the best partners in the various parts of the value system;

● what kind of relationship to develop with each partner (e.g. supplier or strategic alliance).

Again the collective know-how in an organisation on how to make all of this work is organisational knowledge which might give competitive advantage to some organisations over others. Illustration 4.4 shows how one company

Illustration 4.4

Solectron

STRATEGY IN ACTION

Some businesses specialise in value chain integration.

The Solectron Corporation was established in 1977 and rapidly became the world's biggest electronics manufacturing services company. Their primary activity was to provide integrated supply chain operations to original equipment manufacturers such as Ericsson, Mitsubishi, Motorola, Nokia, Cisco, Compaq, Dell, IBM and NCR. Solectron would work in partnership with the manufacturers in designing and producing electronics products. In 1999 the organisation made the decision to create three integrated business units, which would form the basis of an efficient operation governing the whole supply chain.

Technology solutions

Solectron provided Technology Solutions which involved partnerships with customers, offering services principally centred on component design as well as circuit board design. This meant that Solectron could manage the whole process from the initial concept to volume manufacture. Technology roadmaps were also offered, which outlined the whole design process, such as sourcing the best components, materials management and the final distribution. It involved utilising their global expertise in procurement so that customers could improve the availability, reliability and flexibility of their materials. The emphasis was placed on lowering costs without losing any quality or speed of operation. Additionally, the Vendor Managed Inventory Programme allowed more accurate stock forecasts which facilitated capacity planning and minimised incidences of idle stock.

Manufacturing and operations

The New Product Introduction team within Solectron offered a wide range of pre-production services. Prototyping was carried out, so that the customer could assess the products' suitability for volume production. This had significant savings for the customer in terms of time and money. Systems assembly services were also offered, which were linked to the customer and then distributed by Solectron. Orders could then be fulfilled without the customer being required to take any action. By making use of their global facilities Solectron could offer a package of manufacturing and distribution services, eliminating the need for the customer to manage problems such as customs clearance, local requirements or freight tariffs.

Global services

Solectron's involvement didn't cease at the assembly point. The customer was offered a further wide range of services which could be implemented at any point in the product life cycle. This included product repair, upgrades, remanufacturing and maintenance, carried out by means of the global service centres operated by Solectron. The services provided also focused on the end user, such as helpdesk facilities, warehousing, returns processing. It was also Solectron's intention to expand the global services facility which would allow customers to make use of service centres which were located nearby, thus saving both time and money. It also freed up the customer's resources for more product innovation.

Sources: Adapted from *Electronic News*, 7 August 2000, *Electronic Buyers' News*, 30 October 2000, *Forbes*, 8 January 2001.

Questions

Imagine that you are an electronics OEM (original equipment manufacturer):

1. Why might you use the services of Solectron?
2. What other alternatives do you have?

Illustration 4.5

Criminal justice . . . a value network

Value networks consist of a range of different 'players' undertaking specialist activities.

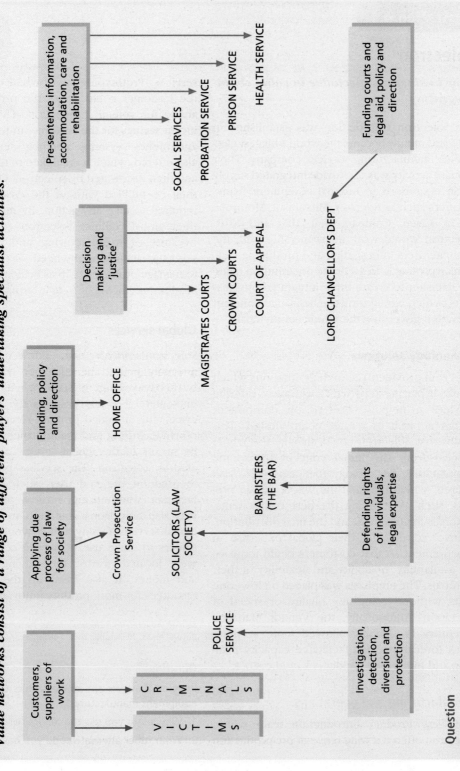

Question

How could you improve the value-for-money 'delivered' by this value network?

resolved these issues as part of a strategy to supply high-quality technical and other services within the electronics industry.

As organisations build e-commerce relationships within the value system, there may be shifts in the 'architecture' of the value system towards a value network. A **value network**[12] is a value system where the inter-organisational relationships are more fluid. For example, a particular activity or component may be available from several 'members' of the network on an entirely interchangeable basis. However, the members of the network are tied together through their commitment to particular product and service standards, shared data (say about customers), IT/communication systems and protocols and, not least, shared values and trust. As factors change in the macro-environment – such as deregulation or information technology advances – there are opportunities to reconfigure the value network in ways that improve customer value or provide that value in different ways – through what, in the world of e-commerce, have become known as new business models.[13] For example, a travel company may decide to provide its products directly to end users through the use of post, telephone and Internet. This cuts out the traditional intermediaries – the travel agents. Of course, new business models may also create roles for new kinds of third parties (such as those discussed in section 10.3.2) to ensure that the value network functions effectively and develops and changes its 'members'.

Illustration 4.5 shows that in some sectors value networks have been the normal *modus operandi* for some time. In Chapter 9 (section 9.4.3) some of the organisational implications of this will be discussed in considering how networks are built and sustained. Competence in understanding and managing these links and relationships – both inside and around an organisation – is an essential aspect of creating and delivering customer value and may be the source of competitive advantage for some organisations.

Sections 4.2 to 4.4 have looked at the importance to organisations of possessing appropriate resources and competences. But strategic capability is about how these resources and competences might create competitive advantage. This is concerned with three related issues: delivering products/services that are *valued*; performing *better* than other organisations; and the *robustness* of the resources and competences (to imitation). The next three sections will look at these issues in turn.

> A **value network** is a value system where the inter-organisational relationships are more fluid

4.5 DELIVERING VALUE FOR MONEY

It has already been emphasised that if organisations are to survive they must be competent to provide the product features required by customers at the threshold level. If they are to outperform competitors they must be able to meet the critical success factors, as discussed above. But customers do not value product features at any price. Price is also an important product feature and, therefore, organisations must be competent in managing cost. Otherwise they will not be able to meet customer price expectations and/or generate sufficient profit and therefore, in the long run, survive financially. This section will look at these issues of managing cost and providing product features that are valued.

Exhibit 4.5	Sources of cost efficiency

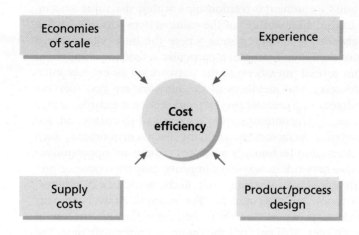

4.5.1 Sources of cost efficiency[14]

Cost efficiency is a measure of the level of resources needed to create a given level of value

Cost efficiency is a measure of the level of resources needed to create a given level of value. Customers can benefit from cost efficiency in terms of lower prices or more product features for the same price. In some public services the key stakeholder may be the budget provider who wishes to maintain levels of service provision and quality but at reduced cost. Cost efficiency is determined by a number of factors called *cost drivers* (see Exhibit 4.5). It is important to understand the knowledge and competences associated with each of these factors and whether or not they might be core competences (i.e. as a basis for competitive advantage).

- *Economies of scale* are traditionally an important source of cost advantage in manufacturing organisations, since the high capital costs of plant need to be recovered over a high volume of output. In other industries, similar economies are sought in distribution or marketing costs. So some organisations will sustain their competitive position through core competences in activities which maintain these scale advantages. This could include the knowledge and ability to secure funding for large-scale investments, competence in mass-consumer advertising (to maintain volume) or the ability to develop and sustain global networks of partners or distributors. Capacity utilisation also influences economies of scale and the knowledge and systems of production planning could be important, as mentioned below.

- *Supply costs* influence an organisation's overall cost position. Location may influence supply costs, which is why, historically, steel or glass manufacturing was close to raw material or energy sources. In some instances, ownership of raw materials gave cost advantage too. How supplier relationships are fostered and maintained is of major importance in sustaining this position.

Supply costs are of particular importance to organisations which act as intermediaries, where the value added through their own activities is low and the need to identify and manage input costs is critically important to success. For example, in commodity or currency trading, the key resource is knowledge of how prices might move and hence competitive advantage can be gained through competences that maintain higher-quality information than that of competitors. Traditionally, this was concerned with personal contacts and networks that were often difficult to imitate. But now information technology capability is critical to their success. Since all traders now have access to similar information systems, advantage will be eroded and staying ahead will be about the innovative ways in which those systems are exploited – all of which will be short-lived. So the core competences are the processes of innovation and development and not any particular system.

● *Product/process design* also influences the cost position. Efficiency gains in production processes have been achieved by many organisations over a number of years through improvements in *capacity-fill, labour productivity, yield* (from materials) or *working capital* utilisation. The important issue is having the knowledge to understand the relative importance of each item to competitive advantage in a particular situation. For example, managing capacity-fill has become a major competitive issue in many service industries. For example, an unfilled seat in a plane, train or theatre cannot be 'stocked' for later sale. So marketing special offers (whilst protecting the core business) and having the IT capability to analyse and optimise revenue are important competences. In contrast, much less attention has been paid to how product *design* may contribute to the overall cost competitiveness of an organisation. Where it has been undertaken, it has tended to be limited to the production processes (e.g. ease of manufacture). However, product design will also influence costs in other parts of the value system – for example, in distribution or after-sales service. Canon gained advantage over Xerox photocopiers in this way – they eroded Xerox's advantage (which was built on the Xerox service and support network) by designing a copier that needed far less servicing. The ability to conceive of the design/cost relationship in this more holistic way and to gain the information needed for such an understanding requires successful organisations to have good knowledge of where and how cost is added throughout the value chain.

● *Experience*[15] can be a key source of cost advantage and there have been many studies concerning the important relationship between the cumulative experience gained by an organisation and its unit costs – described as the *experience curve*. The premise of these findings is that, in any market segment of an industry, price levels tend to be very similar for similar products. Therefore, what makes one company more profitable than the next must be the level of its costs. The experience curve suggests that an organisation undertaking any activity learns to do it more efficiently over time, and hence develops core competences in this activity. Since companies with higher market share have more cumulative experience, it is clearly important to gain and hold market share, as discussed in Chapter 3. It is important to remember that it is the *relative market share* in definable market segments that matters.

There are three important implications of the experience curve concept that could influence an organisation's competitive position:

- Growth is not optional in many markets. If an organisation chooses to grow more slowly than the competition, it should expect the competitors to gain cost advantage in the longer term – through experience.
- Organisations should expect their real unit costs to decline year on year. In high-growth industries this will happen quickly, but even in mature industries this decline in costs should occur. Organisations that fail both to recognise and to have the competence to respond to this are likely to suffer.
- It may be possible to reduce cost by outsourcing those activities where an organisation is not very experienced. Historically, one of the criticisms of public services was that their quasi-monopoly status had tended to shield them from the pressures to push down unit costs, resulting in a preference to keep everything in-house even where experience was low and costs high.

4.5.2 Product features[16]

The success of an organisation is also related to how well it is able to provide product features that are valued – at a given price. If organisations are to be profitable this requires an ability to operate effectively. **Effectiveness** is the ability to meet customer requirements on product features at a given cost. Effectiveness will be achieved only if managers are able to do the following:

Effectiveness is the ability to meet customer requirements on product features at a given cost

- They must be clear which product features will be valued by customers in the future. Understanding threshold product features and critical success factors (as discussed in section 4.2) is crucial.
- They must understand what are the drivers of uniqueness[17] within their organisation or wider value system and how they can create and sustain this uniqueness. For example, this may relate to the knowledge of employees – for example in craft industries. Or it could be about the competence to manage the linkages between activities as discussed in section 4.4.3 above.
- Whether any added costs of providing better features are more than recovered through the value which customers place on this uniqueness – the price they are prepared to pay. Customers will pay a premium for features that they especially value. They will not pay for features that are above their threshold requirements. An over-engineered product will not recover the additional costs through the prices that can be charged.
- Since value is often about perception, the ways in which a product's features are communicated are important and in some circumstances could constitute a core competence. For example, this could apply to the processes through which brand names or corporate image is built and communicated.
- In a fast-changing world, competitive advantage is increasingly concerned with service rather than the product *per se*. So business processes that

provide information to potential customers, the ordering process, billing and after-sales service are where the difference between competitors might lie. This is particularly true in those markets where products are becoming commodity-like – such as computer hardware. The implication is that manufacturers need to see themselves more as service organisations that deliver a product rather than a product company with services to support the product. The exploitation of IT is crucial to improved service and will be discussed more fully in section 10.3.

4.5.3 What is valued varies with time

Strategic capability cannot be regarded in a static way. What customers value will vary over time – particularly the critical success factors discussed in section 4.2 above. So competences will become redundant if not changed and core competences will be matched by others and become threshold competences to stay in business. The development of global competition in the motor industry[18] over recent decades illustrates this issue of changing customer requirements and the need to develop and change resources and competences (see Exhibit 4.6). During the 1950s and 1960s, the US giants such as Ford and General Motors dominated the global market through the critical success factor of *achieving market access* supported by core competences of negotiating dealer networks and, later, gaining approval for and funding overseas production plants. Meanwhile, Japanese manufacturers were developing competences in defect-free manufacture. This was based on new competences in managing factories and supply chains. By the mid-1970s they were significantly outperforming Ford on *quality and reliability* – which proved to be critical success factors allowing them to achieve global sales. By the mid-1980s, although maintaining a global network continued to distinguish Ford and the Japanese from many European companies such as Peugeot, the manufacturing and supplier management processes underpinning quality and reliability were becoming threshold competences – i.e. requirements to remain in the industry. So the previous CSFs became the new industry standards. The competitive arena then switched to the critical success factor of uniqueness of product in an increasingly 'commodity-like' industry (without raising prices). This required competences of agility in design and manufacturing techniques and 'lifestyle niche' marketing (e.g. companies like Mazda). For a time these were core competences, giving competitive advantage to those companies that possessed them. However, those advantages were also eroded as others caught up, and so on.

This example of the motor industry is provided to demonstrate the need for constant review and innovation. The impact of technological change can be profound in many industries, 'changing the rules of the game' and providing opportunities for new entrants to succeed as incumbent players fail to respond. In a hypercompetitive world, advantage is temporary and very short-lived. This should influence the way in which strategic choices are made – as discussed in section 7.5.

Most service industries are currently experiencing this need to innovate in relation to the impact of information technology. Innovative ways of redesigning

Exhibit 4.6	Critical success factors and core competences change over time

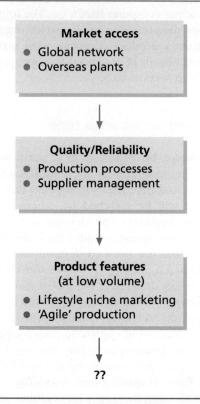

Market access
● Global network
● Overseas plants

↓

Quality/Reliability
● Production processes
● Supplier management

↓

Product features
(at low volume)
● Lifestyle niche marketing
● 'Agile' production

↓

??

Source: Based on G. Hamel and A. Heene (eds), *Competence-based Competition*, Wiley, 1994, pp. 16–18.

services and their delivery abound. These new business models range from 'direct-line selling' to full e-commerce applications, as seen in Chapter 10 (section 10.3). IT is also a source of many new services previously impractical or too costly with older technologies and is an example of the issues to be discussed in the next section.

4.5.4 Providing value in new markets and new arenas

At the beginning of the chapter, Exhibit 4.1 showed that core competences might also allow an organisation to build strategies in new markets through the stretching and exploitation of such competences. This is because customers elsewhere already value the features which that core competence underpins (for example, speed of delivery, product reliability or whatever).

A core competence may also underpin the ability to create opportunities in new arenas where these CSFs *would be valued* above those that currently prevail. In other words, they can be used to change the 'rules of the game' in those new arenas. It could be argued that the success of Richard Branson's Virgin in such varied arenas is built around the fact that a significant number of customers value simplicity – particularly in markets which are shrouded in 'producer' jargon and complexity, such as financial services or mobile phones. The ability to develop a simplified offering and to communicate in simple language gave advantage over the incumbent suppliers who were tied up in their 'professional' view of the product – rather than a customer perspective.

4.6 PERFORMING BETTER THAN COMPETITORS

An organisation's strategic capability is a *relative* issue since it concerns the ability to meet and beat the performance of competitors. This means that managers need to understand performance standards, i.e. what constitutes good and poor performance, and *benchmarking*[19] is now widely used to assist this understanding. The importance of benchmarking is not in the detailed 'mechanics' of comparison but in the impact that these comparisons might have on behaviours. It can be usefully regarded as a process for gaining momentum for improvement and change. But it has dangers too. The mechanics of the process can take over and it can also result in changes in behaviour that are unintended and certainly dysfunctional. For example, benchmarking in the form of sector league tables, as with schools or health services, can lead to problems. The university sector in the UK has been subjected to rankings in league tables on research output, teaching quality and the success of graduating students in terms of employment and starting salaries. This has resulted in staff being 'forced' to orientate their published research to certain types of journal and, in some cases, weighting their recruitment towards students who are more able to 'help' meet performance standards. Little of this is to do directly with the quality of the education in universities. So the general point is that if the basis of benchmarking is flawed it can set off a reorientation of strategies that are flawed – in the sense that they do not lead to genuinely better performance.

Since benchmarking compares inputs (resources), outputs or outcomes it is also important to remember that it will not identify the reasons for the good or poor performance of organisations since the process does not compare competences directly. However, if it is well directed it should encourage managers to seek out these reasons and hence understand how their competences could be improved. Managers would need to observe and understand how top-performing organisations undertook their activities and to assess if these could be imitated or improved upon. Again, this relies on the basis of the benchmarking being valid. It may be that improvements in outputs or outcomes can be achieved by a radical reconfiguration of how activities and processes are undertaken. The move away from traditional business models to e-commerce models that will be discussed more fully in Chapter 10 (see Exhibit 10.6) is an example of this. So the power of benchmarking is the impetus it might give to 'breaking the frame' and conceiving of new ways of meeting and beating the performance of the best.

This section will look at a number of different bases for *benchmarking* (assessment) of performance standards: improvements on *historical* performance; *industry (or sector) norms/standards*; and *'best in class'* beyond the industry in which an organisation currently operates.

4.6.1 Historical comparison

Historical comparison looks at the performance of an organisation in relation to previous years in order to identify any significant changes

Organisations should be concerned with improving their performance over time, otherwise they are likely to lose their competitive advantage or even drop out of the market as customer expectations and the performance of competitors rise.[20] So, looking at how much an organisation is improving over time can be useful. **Historical comparison** looks at the performance of an organisation in relation to previous years in order to identify any significant changes. The danger with historical comparison alone is that it can lead to complacency since it is the rate of improvement compared with that of competitors that is important.

4.6.2 Industry norms/standards

Industry norms compare the performance of organisations in the same industry or sector against a set of agreed performance indicators

Some valuable insights about performance standards can be gleaned by looking at the comparative performance of other organisations in the same industry or between similar public service providers. These **industry norms** compare the performance of organisations in the same industry or sector against a set of agreed performance indicators. Illustration 4.6 shows that these comparisons (particularly in the public services) are often in the form of league tables, as mentioned above. This comparison needs to be understood in relation to the organisation's separate activities and not just its overall performance. In the late 1990s the UK public services introduced more systematic approaches to benchmarking[21] through the Best Value Initiative and Clinical Governance (for health care). One feature of these initiatives was that organisations were required to develop plans that showed how they would improve their outputs or outcomes over a five-year period, with a minimum level of improvement being specified. This minimum was usually to meet the performance standards (on *all* performance outputs/outcomes) in five years' time that the top 25 per cent were already achieving.

The danger of industry norm comparisons (whether in the private or public sector) is that the whole industry may be performing badly and losing out competitively to other industries that can satisfy customers' needs in different ways. So a benchmarking regime needs to look wider than a particular industry or sector, as discussed below.

Another danger with benchmarking within an industry is that the boundaries of industries are blurring through competitive activity and industry convergence. For example, supermarkets are (incrementally) entering retail banking and their benchmarking needs to reflect this (as does the benchmarking of the traditional retail banks).

Illustration 4.6

Benchmarking health care

STRATEGY IN ACTION

The performance of similar organisations can be compared by using a range of different benchmarking data concerned with inputs, outputs and outcomes.

In January 2001 the *Sunday Times* published the first guide to hospitals in Britain and Ireland using data compiled by an independent agency (Dr Foster). In England alone there were 174 hospital trusts – organised into eight regions. Below are comments on some of the data used in these inter-hospital comparisons.

Mortality index

Mortality rate is a measure of the proportion of patients that die during or shortly after treatment. This index was used to compare the rates of mortality between hospitals once the differences in the types of patient being treated were taken into account. It was an average over a five-year period. An average performance had an index of 100. The highest mortality rate was 119 in Walsall and the lowest 68 in University College Hospitals, Central London.

Doctors per 100 beds

This was the number of full-time doctors per 100 beds across all levels of seniority. It was shown to have a strong inverse correlation with mortality rates. Numbers ranged from 17 in Greenwich (London) to 70 in Oxford.

Nurses per 100 beds

This was the number of full-time qualified nurses employed per 100 beds. This did not have a strong relationship with mortality index but affected patient satisfaction. Numbers ranged from 70 in Newham (London) to 180 at University College Hospitals (Central London).

Waiting time for in-patient treatment

This was the time that patients had to wait from the decision to admit to hospital to the actual admission. The best-performing hospitals admitted 99 per cent of patients within 6 months – the worst only 51 per cent. The average waiting time was 29 weeks. The NHS Plan set a target that by 2008 no patient would wait more than 8 months for any treatment.

Waiting time for outpatient treatment

This was the time to see a specialist from the day the patient got an appointment. The commitment (in the Patients Charter) was 13 weeks maximum waiting time. The best performance in terms of patients seen within this 13 weeks was 92 per cent and the worst 58 per cent. There were significant variations between specialisms too. For example, in the Eastern Region (17 hospitals) the figures for gynaecology ranged from 96 to 65 per cent; paediatrics from 95 to 60 per cent, and cardiology from 93 to 36 per cent.

Patients' trust in doctors

Surveys of patients showed that the proportion of patients having trust in their doctors ranged from 94 to 76 per cent.

Source: Adapted from *The Sunday Times Hospital Guide* (in association with Dr Foster), 14 and 21 January 2001.

Questions

1. Which of these benchmark data refer to inputs, which outputs and which outcomes?

2. What conclusions might the chief executive of an individual hospital draw from these data?

3. What are your conclusions about the benefits and drawbacks of benchmarking exercises of this type? Use other examples to support your case.

4.6.3 Best-in-class benchmarking

Best-in-class benchmarking compares an organisation's performance against 'best in class' performance – wherever that is found

The shortcomings of industry norm comparisons have encouraged organisations to seek comparisons more widely through the search for *best practice wherever it may be found*. The potential for change is enhanced by (benchmarking) partnerships across industries or sectors. **Best-in-class benchmarking** compares an organisation's performance against 'best in class' performance – wherever that is found. As mentioned above, the real power of the benchmarking approach is not just 'beyond industry/sector' comparisons. It is concerned with shaking managers out of the mindset that improvements in performance will be gradual as a result of incremental changes in resources or competences, which is not the reality that many organisations face in the twenty-first century. They face threats from other organisations that achieve *dramatic* improvements in performance on particular value activities or through how activities are linked together. But benchmarking will only provide the 'shock' that should encourage managers to understand better how to improve their competences. They will then need to observe how activities might be performed better. For example, British Airways improved aircraft maintenance, refuelling and turnround time by studying the processes surrounding Formula One Grand Prix motor racing pit stops.[22] A police force wishing to improve the way in which it responded to emergency telephone calls studied call centre operations in the banking and IT sectors.

For service organisations in particular, the critical issue is that improved performance in one sector – particularly on issues like speed and reliability – shifts the *general level* of expectations in customers about speed or reliability from all companies and public sector organisations. So benchmarking these issues could 'break the frame' within organisations about the performance standards to be achieved. Of course, organisations can view this in a positive rather than a threatening light. Benchmarking can be used to spot opportunities to dramatically outperform the incumbent providers by organisations who are particularly competent at certain activities or business processes. This is an example of stretching core competences to exploit opportunities in different markets or arenas, discussed above.

4.7 ROBUSTNESS

The previous two sections have been concerned with the ability to provide best value to customers (or to stakeholders) and to perform better than competitors. A further important consideration about core competences is the extent to which they are robust, i.e. difficult for competitors to imitate. Imitation may be difficult for one of four main reasons (see Exhibit 4.7):

● The resource or competence is *rare*. This has already been mentioned in the discussion of unique resources above.

● The competence is concerned with managing *complex* activities or processes rather than being vested in separate activities such as a new product feature or an innovative advertising campaign that may be easier to imitate.

Exhibit 4.7 Four sources of robustness

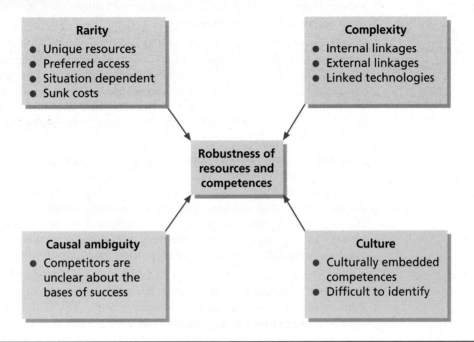

- Competitors are not clear which resources or competences have underpinned the success of their better-performing rivals. This is known as *causal ambiguity*.
- One of the reasons for causal ambiguity might be that the competence is *embedded in the culture*. In other words, organisations themselves are unable to explain the basis of their superior performance, as was seen in the example in Illustration 4.3 at the beginning of this chapter.

4.7.1 Rarity

Robustness could be related to the nature of an organisation's resources or competences, which may be rare (or unique). For example:

- Rarity may depend on who owns the competence and whether it is easily transferable. For example, in professional service organisations some services are built around the competence of specific individuals – such as the doctor in 'leading edge' medicine. Using the terminology of this chapter, this is a *unique resource* and not an organisational core competence. But since these individuals are 'tradeable', they may leave and join competitors, this unique resource is usually not robust. The organisation is vulnerable to the loss of these individuals' services. Core competences *may* be found in the activities that exist for recruiting, training, motivating and rewarding these rare individuals – ensuring that they do not defect to 'competitors'. Or a core competence may be embedded in the culture that attracts them to work for the particular organisation.

● An organisation may have secured *preferred access* to customers or suppliers – perhaps through an approval process or by winning a bidding process (as with broadcasting or mobile phone licences). This may be particularly advantageous if this approval for access cannot be obtained without a specified history of operation or having followed a specified development programme – say with pharmaceutical products. This means that a competitor cannot find a short-cut to imitation.

● Some competences are not transferable because they are only of value if used in a particular organisation. They are *situation dependent*. For example, the systems for operating particular machines are not applicable to organisations that do not use those same machines. It might also be the case that the transfer costs of moving competences from one organisation to another are too high. This is a problem that global companies face when trying to bring the performance of all of their locations up to the standards of the best.

● Sometimes incumbent organisations have advantage because they have *sunk costs* (say in set-up) that are already written off and they are able to operate at significantly lower overall cost.

Managers may fail to understand how rarity can be built and lost. For example:

● Most organisations have difficult decisions to make about which activities (in the value chain) they should own and undertake themselves and which should be outsourced. Usually, it is advisable to ensure that core competences are owned by the organisation (i.e. are undertaken internally). The problem is that organisations may not understand adequately which of their competences are core competences, as explained above. Or, perhaps more frequently, they may not regard 'new' competences as core – even if they are rare – and hence may continue to access them from external sources, inhibiting the organisation's ability to learn and to develop these competences and increasing their vulnerability to these 'suppliers'. IT developments in organisations have been blighted by this problem, in the sense that managers in the organisation have failed properly to comprehend how IT investments can transform the way in which activities are performed. In turn, the external suppliers, or consultants, do not understand the business well enough to tailor their advice and ensure that it becomes properly embedded in the organisation – driving strategic change and creating new opportunities. So the outcome is that IT is imported to run the business processes that currently exist rather than a radical rethink of how the organisation does business and competes.

● In some sectors – particularly amongst professional groups in public services – there is an ethos (and often a requirement) that organisations should not hang on to rare knowledge but disseminate it for the wider good, perhaps through publication in professional and academic journals. This can lead managers and professionals in those fields to question whether 'difficult to imitate' is an appropriate aspiration in those circumstances. The position taken in this book is that the criterion is nonetheless valid and that this does not cut across the duty to spread best practice and raise the knowledge base and performance standards of the whole sector. Competitive advantage from innovation cannot be protected (for example, through patents), therefore the fruits of any individual improvement will give only short-term advantage (or recognition of excellence). So the excellent organisations *long term* are those whose processes of innovation and change deliver continuous improvements which are valued by customers and are ahead of competitors. These processes of innovation are the core competences.

● In reality this is not that far away from what happens in most competitive market situations in the private sector (hypercompetition as discussed in Chapter 3). Products and processes can be patented but ideas cannot – they are in the public arena. So advantage will be short-lived and those organisations that are good at learning, adapting and moving to new bases of competition are likely to be the long-term winners.

4.7.2 Complexity

One of the most complex aspects of an organisation is its knowledge base because it is distributed or shared knowledge. It is not just the knowledge of individuals, technologies etc., it is knowledge which is gained over time about how to get things done. It is difficult for this type of knowledge to be codified and built into computer-based systems. It is therefore difficult to imitate.

So robustness may be created through competence in managing the linkages that assist knowledge sharing. For example (see Exhibit 4.8):

● Links between the separate activities *within* an organisation. This includes primary–primary links; primary–support links and support–support links in the value chain (see Exhibit 4.4). Sometimes advantage is gained because

Exhibit 4.8 Competitive advantage through managing linkages

TYPE OF LINKAGE	TYPE OF ACTIVITY	EXAMPLE
Internal linkages	Primary–primary	Interdepartmental coordination
	Primary–support	Computer-based operational systems
	Support–support	Managing innovation through people
External linkages	Vertical integration	Extend ownership of activities in supply/distribution chain
	Specification and checking	. . . of supplier/distributor performance
	Total quality management	Working with suppliers/distributors
	Merchandising activities	to improve their performance
	Reconfigure value chain	. . . by deleting activities
Integrating competences	Internal and/or external	Combining separate technologies

particular resources and competences are interconnected – for example, they must be used together. So software may have been custom-built for particular systems and cannot be transferred to competitors.

● Links with activities in the *wider value system*.[23] As mentioned in section 4.4.3, one impact of IT and e-commerce is that traditional value systems are emerging into more fluid value networks. The implication is that organisations have more choice of partners and are less bound to their traditional relationships. So this source of advantage may be eroded and replaced by competences needed to build and sustain strong relationships in this wider network (as discussed in Chapter 9).

● Competence in separate technologies can be integrated to create new products or different levels of service. Companies such as Canon, Hewlett Packard or Xerox illustrate how their product range developed over time around core technologies of microelectronics, precision engineering and optics – supplemented by software development. So three organisations that were focused on different products (cameras, printers and copiers) became competitive rivals in new arenas. This is because, unlike products and resources that deteriorate and become redundant over time, competences have the potential to improve over time as experience accumulates.

So, overall, the message is that competences may be robust because they are complex – simpler competences may be easily imitated.

4.7.3 Causal ambiguity[24]

One reason why competences might be robust is that competitors find it difficult to diagnose the cause and effect underpinning an organisation's advantage. So, high levels of uncertainty exist on how to imitate a successful strategy. This is called causal ambiguity. This uncertainty could relate to any or all of the aspects of strategic capability discussed in the preceding sections of this chapter. For example, rivals may be unclear on:

● what are the critical success factors (those factors that customers *particularly* value) from amongst the many *threshold* product features. For example, are customers particularly interested in product quality or flexibility or speed of delivery?

● the resources on which the success is based – whether the organisation has any unique resources or not. For example, is brand name crucial to success?

● the competences that underpin the organisation's success and which are the core competences. For example, do they succeed through strong personal relationships or state-of-the-art scheduling systems?

If it is difficult for rivals to answer these questions, an organisation may gain advantage in two ways. First, rivals waste resources in attempting to understand how they should compete and trying out competitive strategies. Second, they choose the wrong strategic responses.

4.7.4 Culture

One reason why competitors might find it difficult to understand cause-and-effect is that managers within an organisation do not understand this *explicitly* themselves. In most organisations this knowledge and these competences are embedded in the culture and are not explicit. This is what is known as organisational knowledge. So coordination between various activities occurs 'naturally' because people know their part in the wider picture or it is simply 'taken for granted' that activities are done in particular ways. Competences which are embedded within the culture are difficult to imitate and therefore may be core competences if they also deliver better value to customers (or stakeholders).[25] The implication of this is that a critically important issue in sustaining competitive advantage is how the embedded knowledge and routines[26] within the organisation are maintained and developed in ways which match the intended strategies. This includes how knowledge is shared to create effective performance – even if this bends the rules as previously seen in Illustration 4.3.

There are some practical problems and dilemmas here. First, if competences are not visible, how can they be managed? Therefore, second, to 'manage' competences that are embedded in the culture might require making them simpler and more transparent or codified. But then they become visible to competitors too, therefore they can be more easily imitated and cease to be a source of advantage (although this may not be easy for competitors because it may not fit their way of doing things – their culture). Third, armed with the power of modern IT there are many third parties whose business is to codify knowledge that was previously embedded in organisations. So expert systems are now available to competitors, again eroding advantage. This demystification of professional work in many sectors is one of the major impacts of IT. Fourth, a significant potential downside of culturally sustained core competences is that they can become *key rigidities*.[27] **Key rigidities** are activities that are deeply embedded and difficult to change and out of line with the requirements of new strategies. Illustration 2.9 is an example of such inertia.

Key rigidities are activities that are deeply embedded and difficult to change and out of line with the requirements of new strategies

4.7.5 Knowledge creation and integration

Knowledge is an important theme in this chapter about strategic capability. It can take all the various forms discussed in this chapter. In a complex and dynamic environment, organisations that are able to create and integrate knowledge better than competitors are likely to gain advantage. Knowledge creation can occur through different processes, and knowledge application will entail the integration of different types of knowledge and the ability to use different processes to achieve this.

Exhibit 4.9 provides Nonaka and Takeuchi's[28] view on how knowledge creation processes can be categorised. It is important to distinguish between two types of knowledge, as discussed above. *Explicit knowledge* is codified, 'objective' knowledge that is transmitted in formal systematic language. In contrast, *tacit knowledge* is personal, context-specific and therefore hard to formalise and communicate. Usually, competence requires both kinds of knowledge. For example, a driving instructor can drive a car through tacit knowledge, but to

Exhibit 4.9	Knowledge creation processes

	To Tacit knowledge	To Explicit knowledge
From Tacit knowledge	Socialisation (sympathised knowledge)	Externalisation (conceptual knowledge)
Explicit knowledge	Internalisation (operational knowledge)	Combination (systematic knowledge)

Source: I. Nonaka and H. Takeuchi, *The Knowledge-Creating Company*, Oxford University Press Inc., © 1995. Reprinted by permission of Oxford University Press.

teach others requires explicit knowledge of the driving process and this is what is first of all communicated to the learner driver. The learner must use this explicit knowledge to develop his or her tacit knowledge on how to drive a car. This tacit knowledge is achieved through practice and feedback on performance from the instructor whilst driving a car in a variety of situations.

Nonaka and Takeuchi also argue that truly innovative companies are ones that can modify and enlarge the knowledge of individuals to create a 'spiral of interaction' between tacit and explicit knowledge through the four processes shown in Exhibit 4.9.

- *Socialisation* is a process of sharing experiences between individuals and thereby allowing them to acquire tacit knowledge from others without a formal system or the use of language. The apprenticeship model in craft industries is a good example.
- *Externalisation* is the process of articulating tacit knowledge into explicit concepts. This can be very difficult. It may require a combination of different methods such as model building, metaphors or analogies.
- *Combination* is the process of systematising concepts into a 'knowledge system', for example by linking separate bodies of explicit knowledge. Individuals achieve this through formal methods of meetings, documents or computer networks.
- *Internalisation* is the process of embodying explicit knowledge into tacit knowledge. It is closely related to 'learning by doing'.

Illustration 4.7 gives examples of all four processes and how important it is to manage the interaction and linkages between these two types of knowledge (through the four processes).

Illustration 4.7

Innovation and knowledge creation

Truly innovative companies have high levels of competence in managing the 'spiral of interaction' through the four processes shown in Exhibit 4.9.

Socialisation

Honda set up 'brainstorming camps' to solve problems in development projects. The meetings were usually away from the workplace and were open to every employee who was interested in the project; status and credentials were never challenged. Such camps were not just a forum for creative dialogue but also a medium for sharing experiences and enhancing mutual trust among participants. The camps reoriented the 'mental models' of all individuals but not in a forceful way.

Externalisation

Canon's mini-copier is a good example of how an analogy was used effectively for product development. The major barrier to lowering costs was the internal drum. In the end a disposable drum was used. The origin of this idea came from Hiroshi Tanaka (team leader of the taskforce) who explored how the technology for manufacturing beer cans could be used for a copier drum.

Combination

Kraft was a manufacturer of dairy and processed foods and utilised EPOS (electronic point of sale) data from retailers to create new sales systems and methods. Kraft developed an information-intensive marketing programme called 'micromerchandising', which provided supermarkets with timely and detailed recommendations on the optimal merchandise mix – supported by sales promotions based on the analyses of their EPOS data. Their analyses of data produced a unique classification of stores and shoppers and were capable of pinpointing who shopped where and how.

Internalisation

General Electric documented all customer enquiries and complaints (more than 14,000 per day) and then 'programmed' them into 1.5 million potential problems and their solutions. The system is equipped with an online diagnosis function that used artificial intelligence technology to provide telephone operators with quick answers to enquiries. If solutions are not found, 12 full-time specialist repair experts produced solutions on the spot and these are then programmed into the database. Crucially, new product development staff regularly spend time with the telephone operators to 're-experience' the customer problem-solution knowledge.

The spiral of knowledge creation

New product development often occurs from a spiral through the four modes above. Socialisation processes can help define the broad 'field' or boundaries within which the product will sit. Externalisation will take this rich mix of tacit knowledge and convert it to a 'product concept' which is 'tested' and 'justified' against other bodies of explicit knowledge – such as market analysis – i.e. the process of combination. Out of this comes the product prototype. The organisation's commercialisation of the new product then depends on internalisation of this knowledge, perhaps through piloting.

Source: I. Nonaka and H. Takeuchi, *The Knowledge-Creating Company*, Oxford University Press Inc., © 1995.

Questions

1. Why is tacit knowledge important to competitive advantage?
2. What are the advantages and disadvantages of trying to make tacit knowledge explicit?
3. Does the spiral of knowledge have to start with 'socialisation'?

Illustration 4.8

SWOT analysis of Renault

STRATEGY IN ACTION

A SWOT analysis explores the relationship between the main environmental influences and the strategic capability of an organisation.

The table below shows a SWOT analysis of the car manufacturer Renault around the end of 1998. After having been close to bankruptcy in the mid-1980s, Renault had managed to establish a good reputation in Europe, thanks to their TQM policy, numerous Formula One victories, and a range of products that were both attractive and innovative (Espace, Twingo, Scenic, Kangoo, etc.), centred around the concept 'Lifestyle Cars'. The company regained its financial health in 1994, despite the failure of an alliance with the Swedish car manufacturer Volvo, and made a net profit of €1.6bn in 1998. The National Renault Automobile company was privatised in 1996 and became anonymously the Renault Company. However, in 1998,

only 16 per cent of sales were made outside Europe, and its success was due solely to newly launched mid-range cars. Unlike almost all other car manufacturers, Renault had one single brand/make, which was supposed to meet the expectations of the purchasers of Twingo at €8,000, as well as the buyers of the Safrane at €45,000. Moreover, Renault's luxury models (the Baccara then Initiale series) were not well known. Finally, the limited size of the firm did not allow it to realise economies of scale to the same extent as those of its largest competitors, General Motors, Ford, Toyota, Volkswagen or Daimler-Chrysler.

Source: The French translation of *Exploring Corporate Strategy* by F. Frery, Publi Union, 2000, p. 219.

STRENGTHS AND WEAKNESSES	KEY ENVIRONMENTAL DEVELOPMENTS				
	Saturation of developed markets	Growing environmental and fiscal pressure in Europe	Potential for growth in developing markets (Asia, Latin America)	Growing demand for recreational vehicles	+ −
Main strengths					
● Product range	+		++	+++	6
● Capacity for innovation	++		+	+	4
● Formula One image	+		+	+	3
Main weaknesses					
● Sales concentrated in Europe	− − −	− −	− −		7
● Small size compared with main competitors	− −		−		3
● Poor performance in the top-of-the-range sector	−			−	2
+	4	0	4	5	
−	6	2	3	1	

Questions

1. Are the items with the highest scores (positive or negative) in the two right-hand columns of the table the principal strengths and weaknesses of the company?

2. What can you tell from the scores on the bottom two lines with respect to the company's ability to keep pace with and react to changes in its environment?

3. Amongst the main environmental changes, can you clearly identify which are the opportunities and the threats?

4.8 STRENGTHS AND WEAKNESSES[29]

The issues discussed in the preceding sections provide insights into the strategic capability of an organisation. The key 'strategic messages' from both the business environment (Chapter 3) and this chapter can often be summarised in the form of a SWOT analysis. SWOT stands for strengths, weaknesses, opportunities and threats. A **SWOT** analysis summarises the key issues from the business environment and the strategic capability of an organisation that are most likely to impact on strategy development. This can also be useful as a basis against which to judge future courses of action, as seen in Chapters 6, 7 and 8. The aim is to identify the extent to which the current strengths and weaknesses are relevant to, and capable of, dealing with the changes taking place in the business environment. It can also be used to assess whether there are opportunities to exploit further the unique resources or core competences of the organisation. For example, Illustration 4.8 shows that Renault already has many of the competences needed to meet a changing market; in particular, its track record in innovation and its development of new models (such as people carriers and leisure vehicles). It also reveals that its involvement in Formula One motor racing was largely beneficial. But the company had some real weaknesses too, given important trends in the environment. For example, it was heavily committed to European markets, which were mature and highly competitive and where fiscal cuts and ecological issues were becoming important pressures on car manufacturers. They were less well represented in developing markets such as Asia or Latin America – though, interestingly, the strengths mentioned above could be exploited in these new arenas and would assist entry.

Overall, this SWOT analysis should help focus discussion on future choices and the extent to which Renault is capable of supporting these strategies.

> A **SWOT** analysis summarises the key issues from the business environment and the strategic capability of an organisation that are most likely to impact on strategy development

SUMMARY

- Strategic capability is about the ability to provide products or services with features that are valued by customers. Competitive advantage will be achieved by organisations that are able to do this better than their competitors and in ways that are difficult to imitate.

- Understanding what customers value – or might value in the future – is important. This includes customers' *threshold* requirements – which must be met by every potential provider. Even these are changing and becoming more demanding over time. It also includes *critical success factors* – those factors that customers particularly value and, therefore, where an organisation must excel to outperform competition.

- Strategic capability starts with resources. A lack of the threshold level of resources will preclude organisations from serving particular markets. Some resources may be unique to an organisation and be the basis of competitive advantage.

- Resources are important because they need to be 'deployed' into the activities that an organisation undertakes in order to create competence in those activities. Organisations must reach a threshold level of competence in all activities to stay in business and this threshold 'standard' rises with time.

- Some activities or processes may be *core competences* that underpin an organisation's competitive advantage. To achieve this, an activity or process must satisfy three criteria. First, it fundamentally contributes to value for money in the product, in the eyes of the customer; second, it must be performed better than competitors; and third, it must be relatively difficult to imitate.

- Delivering value for money requires the management of both cost and product features. There are several sources of potential advantage on each of these factors.

- Value for money is also determined by activities that are undertaken outside an organisation – in the value chain (or supplies or channels). Competence is needed in managing these linkages in the value chain.

- What customers value will change with time, so core competences will be eroded. However, there may be opportunities to exploit core competences in new markets or new arenas.

- It is important to understand the performance standards that need to be achieved to outperform competitors. This can be done by benchmarking – but this must not be done in a narrow or parochial way.

- There may be several reasons why competences might be robust (difficult to imitate). For example, rarity, complexity, uncertainty as to how and why advantage is gained or because competence is embedded in the organisational culture (tacit).

RECOMMENDED KEY READINGS

- The importance of analysing and understanding knowledge is discussed in: I. Nonaka and H. Takeuchi, *The Knowledge Creating Company*, Oxford University Press, 1995; V. von Kroch, K. Ichijo and I. Nonaka, *Enabling Knowledge Creation: How to unlock the mystery of tacit knowledge and release the power of innovation*, Oxford University Press, 2000; K. Fisher and M. Fisher, *The Distributed Mind: Achieving high performance through the collective intelligence of knowledge work teams*, AMACOM, 1997. Also, a collection of articles can be found in *Harvard Business Review on Knowledge Management*, HBR Press, 1998.

- There are a number of books and articles about the importance of understanding core competences. For example: G. Hamel and C.K. Prahalad, 'The core competence of the corporation', *Harvard Business Review*, vol. 68, no. 3 (1990), pp. 79–91; G. Hamel

and A. Heene (eds), *Competence-based Competition*, Wiley, 1994.

- A number of the chapters in V. Ambrosini with G. Johnson and K. Scholes (eds), *Exploring Techniques of Analysis and Evaluation in Strategic Management*, Prentice Hall, 1998, provide further discussion of concepts introduced in this chapter. Specifically: M. Tampoe on core competences; A. Shepherd on the value chain; G. Tomlinson on benchmarking; T. Jacobs, J. Shepherd and G. Johnson on SWOT.

- An extensive discussion of the value chain concept and its application can be found in M.E. Porter, *Competitive Advantage*, Free Press, 1985.

- J. Kay, *Foundations of Corporate Success*, Oxford University Press, 1993, discusses many aspects of the links between strategic capability and competitive success.

REFERENCES

1. The concept of resource-based strategies was discussed by B. Wernerfelt, 'A resource-based view of the firm', *Strategic Management Journal*, vol. 5, no. 2 (1984), pp. 171–180. The idea of driving strategy development from the resources and competences of an organisation is discussed in G. Hamel and C.K. Prahalad, 'Strategic intent', *Harvard Business Review*, vol. 67, no. 3 (1989), pp. 63–76; G. Hamel and C.K. Prahalad, 'Strategy as stretch and leverage', *Harvard Business Review*, vol. 71, no. 2 (1993), pp. 75–84; and D.J. Teece, G. Pisano and A. Shuen, 'Dynamic capabilities and strategic management', Harvard Business School Working Paper, 1992.

2. The importance of analysing and understanding knowledge is discussed in I. Nonaka and H. Takeuchi, *The Knowledge Creating Company*, Oxford University Press, 1995; V. von Kroch, K. Ichijo and I. Nonaka, *Enabling Knowledge Creation: How to unlock the mystery of tacit knowledge and release the power of innovation*, Oxford University Press, 2000; K. Fisher and M. Fisher, *The Distributed Mind: Achieving high performance through the collective intelligence of knowledge work teams*, AMACOM, 1997: D. Neef, *A Little Knowledge is a Dangerous Thing: Understanding the global knowledge economy*, Butterworth-Heinemann, 1998. Also, a collection of articles can be found in *Harvard Business Review on Knowledge Management*, HBR Press, 1998.

3. See M. Peteraf, 'The cornerstones of competitive advantage: a resource-based view', *Strategic Management Journal*, vol. 14, no. 3, (1993), p. 179.

4. See R. D'Aveni, *Hypercompetitive Rivalries*, Free Press, 1995, Chapter 2.

5. See M. Hardaker and B. Ward, 'Getting things done', *Harvard Business Review*, vol. 65, no. 6 (1987), pp. 112–120, for a full discussion of how critical success factors can be identified.

6. A systematic way of assessing the resources of an organisation would be a *resource audit*. This topic is covered in a number of papers and texts: for example, R. Grant, *Contemporary Strategy Analysis*, 3rd edition, Blackwell, 1998, Chapter 4; and R.B. Buchelle, 'How to evaluate a firm', *California Management Review* (Fall 1962). The latter provides extensive checklists under functional areas.

7. Intangible resources have become increasingly recognised as being of strategic importance. See: T. Clarke and S. Clegg, *Changing Paradigms: The transformation of management knowledge for the 21st century*, Harper Collins, 2000, p. 342 (this outlines Arthur Andersen's classification of intangible assets); R. Hall, 'The strategic analysis of intangible resources', *Strategic Management Journal*, vol. 13, no. 2 (1992), pp. 135–144; and 'A framework linking intangible resources and capabilities to sustainable competitive advantage', *Strategic Management Journal*, vol. 14, no. 8 (1993), pp. 607–618.

8. An example is the need to develop human resource accounting. This is discussed in: Y. Baruch, 'HR accountancy: the issue can no longer be ignored', *The International Journal of Applied Human Resource Management*, vol. 1, no. 1 (2000), pp. 66–76.

9. Economic profit is sometimes referred to as Ricardian rent and is a long-established economic concept. See: D. Ricardo, *Principles of Political Economy and Taxation*, Murray, 1817.

10. There are a number of books and articles about the importance of understanding core competences. For example: G. Hamel and C.K. Prahalad, 'The core competence of the corporation', *Harvard Business Review*, vol. 68, no. 3 (1990), pp. 79–91; G. Hamel and A. Heene (eds), *Competence-based Competition*, Wiley, 1994; M. Tampoe's chapter, 'Getting to know your organisation's core competences' in V. Ambrosini with G. Johnson and K. Scholes (eds), *Exploring Techniques of Analysis and Evaluation in Strategic Management*, Prentice Hall, 1998, Chapter 1.

11. An extensive discussion of the value chain concept and its application can be found in M.E. Porter, *Competitive Advantage*, Free Press, 1985. See also A. Shepherd's chapter, 'Understanding and using value chain analysis' in V. Ambrosini with G. Johnson and K. Scholes, Chapter 2 (see reference 10 above).

12. P. Timmers, *Electronic Commerce*, Wiley, 2000, pp. 182–193, provides an interesting discussion of how value networks are being created and changed by IT (this issue will be discussed more fully in section 10.3).

13. In business books the term 'business model' has traditionally been used to refer to the types of framework and concepts discussed in this book and shown in the exhibits. In the e-commerce world it is used more narrowly to describe the relationships and information flows in an 'industry' or sector. This will be described more fully in section 10.3 and readers can refer to the references given there.

14. See Grant (reference 6 above), pp. 200–209.

15. P. Conley, *Experience Curves as a Planning Tool*, available as a pamphlet from the Boston Consulting Group. See also A.C. Hax and N.S. Majluf, in R.G. Dyson (ed.), *Strategic Planning: Models and analytical techniques*, Wiley, 1990.

16. A useful reference on creating 'added value' product features is: J. Kay, *Foundations of Corporate Success*, Oxford University Press, 1993, Chapter 2.

17. See Grant (reference 6 above) pp. 228-234.

18. This example is from Hamel and Heene (reference 10 above), pp. 16-18.

19. Benchmarking is used extensively in both private and public sectors. G. H. Watson, *Strategic Benchmarking*, Wiley, 1993, and S. Codling, *Benchmarking Basics*, Gower, 1998, are a practical guide to benchmarking. See also G. Tomlinson's chapter, 'Comparative analysis: benchmarking' in V. Ambrosini with G. Johnson and K. Scholes (see reference 10 above).

20. Corporate failure and corporate recovery are discussed in: S. Slatter and D. Lovett, *Corporate Turnaround: Managing companies in distress*, Penguin, 1999.

21. For a good overall review of the use of benchmarking in the public sector see: M. Wisniewski, 'Measuring up to the best: a manager's guide to benchmarking', in G. Johnson and K. Scholes (eds.), *Exploring Public Sector Strategy*, Financial Times/Prentice Hall, 2001, Chapter 5. The specific initiatives are reviewed in other chapters: S. Speller, 'The best value initiative' in Chapter 6; D. Herbert, 'Clinical governance' in Chapter 7.

22. A. Murdoch, 'Lateral benchmarking, or what Formula One taught an airline', *Management Today*, November 1997, pp. 64-67. See also the Formula One case study in the case study section of this book (Text and Cases version only).

23. The importance of managing vertical relationships has been stressed by Porter (reference 11 above) and Kay (reference 16 above), Chapter 17.

24. See Grant (reference 6 above, p. 183, and S. Lippman and R. Rumelt, 'Uncertain imitability: an analysis of interfirm differences in efficiency under competition', *Bell Journal of Economics*, vol. 13 (1982), pp. 418-438.

25. J.B. Barney, 'Organisational culture: can it be a source of competitive advantage?', *Academy of Management Review*, vol. 11, no. 3 (1986), pp. 656-665.

26. See Nonaka and Takeuchi (reference 2 above) for a discussion of embedded (tacit) knowledge.

27. D. Leonard-Barton, 'Core capabilities and core rigidities: a paradox in managing new product development', *Strategic Management Journal*, vol. 13 (Summer 1992), pp. 111-125.

28. Reference 2 above.

29. The idea of SWOT as a common-sense checklist has been used for many years: for example, S. Tilles, 'Making strategy explicit', in I. Ansoff (ed.), *Business Strategy*, Penguin, 1968. See also T. Jacobs, J. Shepherd and G. Johnson's chapter on SWOT analysis in V. Ambrosini with G. Johnson and K. Scholes (see reference 10 above).

WORK ASSIGNMENTS

* Refers to a case study in the Text and Cases edition. ✳ Denotes more advanced work assignments.

4.1 Undertake a resource audit of an organisation with which you are familiar. Then identify which resources, if any, are unique in the sense that they are difficult to imitate (see Exhibit 4.2). Has the organisation gained competitive advantage as a result of this uniqueness? Why/why not? You can answer this in relation to Amazon* or Formula One* if you so wish.

4.2 Use Exhibits 4.3 and 4.4 to map out the key value activities for Amazon* or a Formula One team* or an organisation of your choice, both within the company and in the wider value system/network in which it operates.

4.3 Explain how the organisation you have analysed in assignment 4.2 does or does not gain competitive advantage from:

(a) competence in separate value activities;
(b) managing linkages within the value chain and wider value system/network.

4.4 ✳ Explain how changing the way in which relationships in the value system/network are managed could improve the efficiency or effectiveness, or both, of an organisation. Illustrate your answer by reference to an organisation of your choice, the Criminal Justice System (Illustration 4.5) or Amazon.*

4.5 ✳ Take any industry and public service and sketch out a map of how core competences have changed over time (use Exhibit 4.6 as an example). Why have these changes occurred? How did the relative strengths of different companies or service providers change over this period? Why?

4.6 ✳ It has been said that the power of benchmarking is in understanding how value for money is created or lost in the separate activities of the organisation against the 'best in class' organisations for each activity. To what extent do you feel this is a universal prescription for improving competitive performance? Make a critical assessment of the dangers or pitfalls in this approach?

4.7 Prepare a SWOT analysis for an organisation of your choice (see Illustration 4.8). Explain carefully why you have chosen each of the key items in your shortlists.

CASE EXAMPLE

Competences, knowledge management and competitiveness at Pliva

By the new millennium, Pliva, a Croatian pharmaceutical company, founded in 1921, had evolved from a regional distributor to a firm with global ambitions. Operating mainly in eastern Europe and in Russia, in 2001 it opened an office in London. Selling predominantly generic pharmaceuticals, it had an ambitious R&D department that had previously discovered an antibiotic, azithromycin. Marketed under the name Sumamed by Pliva, the product had been outlicensed to the global pharmaceutical giant Pfizer, which marketed it under the name Zithromax within western markets whilst Pliva retained the rights over eastern markets. The year 2001 saw the culmination of the R&D department having reinvented itself and the placing of a number of new compounds in the clinical trials that are required to test and prove safety and efficacy before new drugs can be marketed.[1] Once a nationalised company, Pliva, after the Balkan war, was quoted on both the new Croatian Stock Exchange and the London Stock Exchange. Accustomed to change, the company set itself a target of achieving double-digit sales growth in the period from 2001 to 2007.

The future was set to include further transformation. Having accumulated substantial wealth courtesy of this global product, Pliva knew that as patent expiry of azithromycin approached[2] in 2007 it needed to concentrate on how to sustain and indeed improve upon its level of performance. It had already begun to approach this challenge in many ways, two of which were medium term. Firstly, it had acquired two eastern European companies, Polfa Krakow in Poland and Lachema in the Czech Republic. The second medium-term action it had taken was to acquire the technology to

produce generic[3] versions of five biotechnology products. Although these drugs were generic, they were the first of their kind. Throughout their patent life they had sold less than they could have done on the basis of disease prevalence, as some countries and health authorities had constrained the prescribing of these expensive medicines. Institutions such as the National Centre for Clinical Excellence[4] in the UK had deliberated on whether they should be made fully available on the UK's free at the point of consumption National Health Service. Despite this, or indeed because of this, in strategic terms the acquisition of these drugs represented a huge opportunity not only to enter a large global market but also to increase that market. This was an unusual situation to be in, however, as in the pharmaceutical industry markets historically reached saturation prior to patent expiry.

Thus in 2001 the company was poised to enter a new and exciting phase in its history but also a challenging one. On the one hand, these biotechnology products and their development (known in the firm as 'The Big Five Project') represented a way of showing that Pliva was capable of developing global, innovative, albeit generic, products – a competence on which they could fruitfully build as their own new products proceeded through clinical trials. To open their new Research Institute in 2002, having successfully developed these generic products, would show shareholders that they could compete in the new millennium. On the other hand, Pliva knew that these products required careful and fast development to ensure that they could be feasibly marketed globally ahead of, or at least in line with, the competition and in a way that would expand the market. As capable as the company was of achieving this, in 2001 it had yet to develop and launch products on a global basis.

The CEO, Mr Covic, knew that these products represented an opportunity to develop world-class

This case study was prepared by **Jill Shepherd**, *Graduate School of Business, University of Strathclyde, UK.*

competences in new product development and strategic marketing. He also was aware of the fact that as western pharmaceutical companies entered Croatia, staff who had been previously restricted in their choice of employer would be increasingly able to move to find new jobs. He wanted to introduce more exciting and challenging managerial practices and wondered whether the new concepts of competences and knowledge management might help. Equally, there was the specific challenge Pliva faced of knowledge management in terms of patent law. The generic versions of these drugs were destined to set a precedent in terms of the owners of the patents fighting more ferociously than normal to defend their patents given the different life-cycle dynamics of these more innovative and revolutionary drugs when compared with non-biotech compounds. This was an issue that was set to become much more topical as companies developed drugs on the basis of genomics.[5]

In the spring of 2001 Jill Shepherd, an academic specialising in organisational knowledge and strategic management, was asked by the management board of Pliva to visit the company to look at competences and knowledge management. Jill had been previously involved in a large corporate transformation project within the company led by a Big Five consulting firm, so was well known by the senior management. During a few days in the head office of Pliva in Zagreb, Jill made a presentation to the board, held meetings with staff, interviewed senior and middle managers and generally walked the corridors to find out how best to proceed. On her return to the UK she wrote to the CEO:

Dear Mr Covic,

Thank you for the hospitality shown to me during my recent visit. As ever, it was a pleasure to return to Zagreb and to your company. Below you will find some suggestions as to how I think you might proceed.

The Biotech Big Five Project

This is a hugely exciting prospect that needs to be celebrated throughout the firm. Targets for the timing of launches in different countries need to be set as well as financial targets for commercial success. Milestone plans need to generated backwards from these final cross-

functional goals to work out what needs to be done by when to achieve them. A highly motivated cross-functional team needs to be set up that reports into the Product Portfolio Committee set up in the earlier transformation programme. In each functional area, supporting milestone plans need to be generated. Information about patents, pricing, purchase patterns and processes as well as market size needs to be collected and built into market models. In each launch country knowledge needs to gained on medical practices to make the case for spending hard-pressed budgets on these generic formulations. Registration requirements need to be established; these products will set registration as well as patenting precedents. In time, negotiations on price with the relevant authorities will be critical. Lessons learnt from developing these products in the East where they are not under any type of patent protection need to be exploited when western markets are considered.

Competence development

The Big Five Biotech project is a golden opportunity to develop world-class competences and to 'leapfrog' many western firms. This is because you have a very intelligent workforce that are loyal, at least for the moment, to the one national pharmaceutical Croatian company. Furthermore, you have a challenge in these products that is very interesting and novel. Before competence development can start, senior management need to openly show their enthusiasm for the project's potential not only in terms of future earning power but also in terms of what they offer as regards competence development. An air of expectation, challenge and excitement needs to be created.

Specifically, there is room for competence development in the areas of cross-functional knowledge-based milestone planning, strategic marketing, especially dynamic market modeling,[6] patent law, biotech manufacturing and all the competences needed to produce high quality, ethical documentation to support the marketing applications. Decisions need to be made now as to whether you will obtain these competences from outside in the form of subcontractors, outside in the form of external advisers who can work alongside your staff, transferring their competences, or whether you are able to develop the competences in-house through a mixture of training, mentoring of middle management by senior management, and experience. The criteria you need to consider when making these decisions include risk of failure, competence transfer in-house and cost. You also need to consider that your staff is more willing than most in western firms to learn.

Knowledge management

The infrastructure is already well established in Pliva to begin to share knowledge on a much larger scale. The Biotech Big Five project can be an exemplar of knowledge management going beyond sharing to encompass the more strategic activity of dynamic knowledge creation. This can be in terms of producing, as you already have done, dynamic market models that incorporate unknowns and therefore assumptions that can gradually be refined.

Knowledge management can also be a way of accumulating all the learning from the project to aid the process of competence development in people not engaged in the Big Five project. Those that will be involved in global product development, as your own new products move out of phase I clinical trials into the bigger phase II and phase III trials[7] which involve much more strategic thinking and coordination and integration, need to learn from the Biotech Big Five. Thus the strategic intrapreneurship within the Biotech Big Five project can be made contagious through knowledge management.

The intranet you have can serve you well in generating ways of obtaining market knowledge from your affiliate staff, sharing learning and interfacing with the Internet to obtain external information. Much more can be done, however, to introduce the concept of self-organising communities on the intranet such that strategy formulation and implementation can involve more staff and be more flexible and adaptable.

Many leading-edge companies are also using the concept of knowledge management to communicate in more efficient and effective ways with their shareholders. This can include promoting the worth of intellectual capital and knowledge workers in the annual report and showing how both are being managed, as well as communicating using e-mail and the Internet on a much more regular basis with shareholders. Thus part of knowledge management becomes ensuring that Corporate Communications promotes Pliva's developing knowledge advantage courtesy of a more willing than average workforce.

Human resource management

HR needs to support competence development and knowledge management. It needs to be involved in promoting the development of new competences and the advocating of more knowledge sharing between hierarchies and more dynamic knowledge transformation within cross-functional project teams and within self-organising communities of interest and practice. HR needs to plan exactly how it will help in this regard. It needs as a function to support the way core business processes add value.

The one advantage the company has is a willing and dedicated workforce that has not been subjected to many years of downsizing and the constant threat of substantial reorganisation post mergers and hostile takeovers. Related to this is a willingness to learn and, through learning, a willingness to change. If care is not taken, however, that willingness will be lost. Staff will become demotivated by a lack of freedom to achieve and will achieve less as a result. Equally, it has to be realised that staff are not used to taking initiative and will need great encouragement. HR must become more strategic in how it supports the organisation to tread this fine balance.

Senior management

These suggestions represent a challenge to Pliva: one I feel the company can meet. There is, however, one proviso, which is that senior management style must be able to support the role of middle management in delivering these products to market in a way that makes them the huge commercial success they can be. Senior management must spend less time managing things themselves and more time creating the conditions in which middle management can be inspired to achieve this. Increasingly, competitive advantage is about developing unique competences and a way of constantly transforming knowledge rather than adopting a secretive long-term strategy. To achieve this, senior management need to manage more the conditions in which their managers operate and spend less time on dictating strategy themselves.

I wish you well in your new ambitions for the company and remain at your disposal for further clarification and help should you so require.

Yours sincerely,
Jill Shepherd

Notes

1. All prescription drugs need to be subject to extensive trials to prove to national regulatory bodies that they are both safe and effective before they are launched. The ability to do this effectively on a global scale and within tight time and cost constraints is a major entry barrier to the pharmaceutical industry.

2. Whilst under patent protection of 25 years, prescription pharmaceuticals cannot be sold by any other company. This creates a monopoly situation during that time for that particular chemical, albeit drugs that achieve the same or similar effect might also be available either in patented or non-patented (generic) form.

3. Generics are products no longer under patent protection that may be produced by anyone with the technology and know-how to produce them and to prove they work as safely and as effectively as the original product. Normally, once drugs become generic they are considered of low innovative content and compete with others of higher innovative content. Pricing is a key issue.

4. The National Centre for Excellence (NICE) was set up to provide fast access to modern treatments, deciding which drugs should (or should not) be available on the NHS and to which patients. At the time of writing, NICE was deliberating on whether the biotech product Beta-interferon should be available to all MS (multiple sclerosis) sufferers.

5. Genomics is the process by which disease is managed through an understanding of how genes work. This possibility has arisen from the advances within molecular biology, the Human Genome Project and the patenting of innovations related to it, all of which allows genes to be identified, their functionality determined and the knowledge used to treat and even prevent disease. Ownership is an issue in this field, as is what can and should be patentable. Working in this area requires new, highly specialised competences.

6. Dynamic market modelling involves starting with the prevalence and incidence of a disease in a market and working backwards from this to a projected market value for a certain company's product. Assumptions are incorporated in the model about how the market can be changed. These assumptions are reduced in time by collecting knowledge about the marketplace from the whole company, especially affiliates, as well as proactively developing and influencing the way in which patients are diagnosed, treated and monitored. The model becomes the centre of the cross-functional development team's attention around which they base their work.

7. Phase I trials are small and involve low, non-therapeutic quantities of drugs whereas Phase II and to a greater extent Phase III trials are larger, more complex and often global.

The author would like to thank Mr Covic, Zelimir Vuksic, Radan Spaventi, Branca Scaramuca, Ranka Markov, Ivo Friganovic and Mislav Jursic and Gerry Cole of Pliva for their collaboration in creating this case. With permission from Dubravko Merlić, Director, Corporate Communications.

Questions

1. Identify the areas of knowledge that you feel are essential to underpin Pliva's strategy.

2. In which areas can knowledge and knowledge management underpin core competences at Pliva?

3. Why, in terms of knowledge and knowledge management, might Pliva fail to improve performance?

4. If you were CEO, what would you do next in terms of knowledge management and competence development?

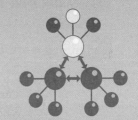

5

Expectations and Purposes

LEARNING OUTCOMES

After reading this chapter you should be able to understand:

- The importance of corporate governance, the governance chain and the different corporate governance arrangements in different countries.
- The meaning of organisational stakeholders and how their expectations shape strategy.
- Stakeholder mapping – the importance of stakeholder power and interest.
- Ethical issues and their impact on strategy.
- Cultural frames of reference and their impact on organisational culture.
- The concept of an organisational field.
- The meaning and importance of legitimacy.
- The cultural web and how to use it to diagnose and describe culture.
- How culture can be characterised and the impact on strategy.
- How organisational purposes can be communicated.

5.1 INTRODUCTION

The previous two chapters have looked at the influence of the environment and resources respectively on an organisation's strategic position. However, this fails to recognise the complex role that people play in the evolution of strategy as introduced in Chapter 2. Strategy is also about what people *expect* an organisation to achieve and, therefore, what influence people can have over an organisation's purposes. This chapter will look at these issues by examining the *political and cultural contexts* of an organisation.

Exhibit 5.1 summarises how the theme of expectations and purposes will be progressed through the chapter:

- The most fundamental questions are *whom should* the organisation be there to serve and *how should* the direction and purposes of an organisation be determined? This is the province of *corporate governance* and the *regulatory framework* within which organisations operate. This relates not only to the power to influence purposes, but also to the processes of supervising

Exhibit 5.1 **Expectations and purposes**

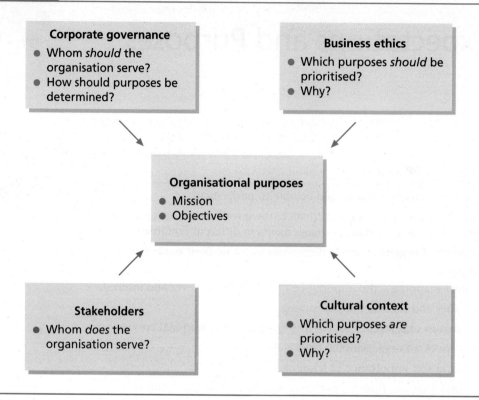

Corporate governance
- Whom *should* the organisation serve?
- How should purposes be determined?

Business ethics
- Which purposes *should* be prioritised?
- Why?

Organisational purposes
- Mission
- Objectives

Stakeholders
- Whom *does* the organisation serve?

Cultural context
- Which purposes *are* prioritised?
- Why?

executive decisions and actions, and the issues of *accountability.* So these are the *formal* expectations of organisations. There are significant differences in the approach to corporate governance in different countries and these will be reflected in the discussion.

- *Whom* the organisation *does actually* serve in practice is the second important issue. This will be addressed through the concept of *organisational stakeholders* and the extent to which they are interested in, or able to influence, an organisation's purposes. Stakeholders are those individuals or groups who depend on the organisation to fulfil their own goals, and on whom, in turn, the organisation depends. This requires an understanding of both the *power* and *interest* of different stakeholder groups.

- *Which purposes* an organisation *should* fulfil is influenced by *ethical* considerations. This is concerned with the expectations of society at large. At the broadest level, these issues impinge on corporate governance – particularly in relation to the accountability of organisations. The ethical agenda is also concerned with *corporate social responsibility* to the various stakeholders – particularly those with little formal power.

- *Which purposes are actually* prioritised above others is related to a variety of factors in the *cultural context* in which the organisation is operating. The concept of the *cultural web* will be used as a means of understanding how culture at several 'levels' might influence organisational purposes. This will include the broader issues of *national cultures*, through the expectations of the *organisational field*, to the *subcultures* within an organisation, perhaps at the business function level.

5.2 CORPORATE GOVERNANCE[1]

The starting point in discussing expectations will be the corporate governance framework within which the organisation is operating. The **governance framework** describes whom the organisation is there to serve and how the purposes and priorities of the organisation should be decided. It is concerned with both the functioning of the organisation and the distribution of power among different stakeholders. It will be seen that there are different traditions and frameworks in different countries.[2] The corporate governance agenda in most countries tends to be more implicit than explicit. This means that the legal and regulatory measures form only a part of corporate governance.

The **governance framework** describes whom the organisation is there to serve and how the purposes and priorities of the organisation should be decided

5.2.1 The governance chain

The issue of corporate governance has arisen for two main reasons. First, the practical need to separate *ownership* and *management control* of organisations is now the norm – except with very small businesses. The result has been that most organisations operate within a hierarchy or chain of governance, i.e. all those groups that have a 'right' to influence an organisation's purposes. Although the details of the chain will vary from one organisation to another, Exhibit 5.2 illustrates a typical chain of governance for a publicly quoted company in the UK. Second, there has been an increasing tendency to make organisations more visibly accountable not only to owners (e.g. shareholders), but also to other stakeholder groups – including the community at large. The rights of these various stakeholders will be discussed later.

Even in the simplified example of Exhibit 5.2 it can be seen that the managers who are driving strategy in the organisation may be very remote from the ultimate beneficiaries of the company's performance. The figure also highlights the information typically available to each 'player' in the chain to judge the performance of others. In the example, it is likely that many beneficiaries are either ignorant of or indifferent to the details of companies in which their money is invested. Many beneficiaries will have their interests 'guarded' by intermediaries – for example, asset managers for pension funds. Illustration 5.1 shows how powerful these intermediaries may be in determining the future of companies.

Given this degree of complexity in corporate governance, there are likely to be several *conflicts of interest* both between different groups and for individual managers or directors as they try to balance these various interests. This is a particular issue for boards of directors and has resulted in important developments in both the role of the board and the disclosure of information. A very

Exhibit 5.2	The chain of corporate governance: typical reporting structures

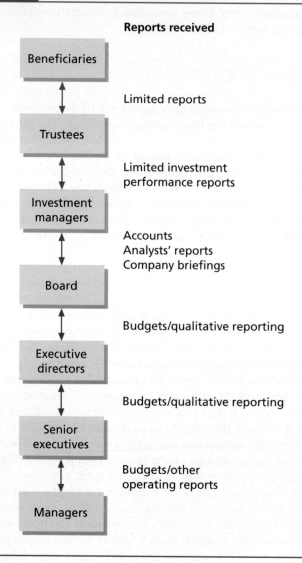

Reports received

Beneficiaries

↕ Limited reports

Trustees

↕ Limited investment performance reports

Investment managers

↕ Accounts
Analysts' reports
Company briefings

Board

↕ Budgets/qualitative reporting

Executive directors

↕ Budgets/qualitative reporting

Senior executives

↕ Budgets/other operating reports

Managers

Source: Adapted from David Pitt-Watson, Braxton Associates.

important question in large publicly quoted corporations is whether corporate managers should regard themselves as solely responsible to shareholders and, if so, which shareholders – individuals or institutional shareholders (or analysts who advise shareholders)? Or should they have a wider responsibility as 'trustees of the assets of the corporation' on behalf of a wider range of stakeholders?[3] The Hampel Committee[4] in the UK concluded that boards of directors were responsible *to* shareholders but must only be responsible *for relationships with* other stakeholders and *take into account* their interests. This is an

Illustration 5.1

STRATEGY IN ACTION

Sir Rocco Forte, Granada and the 'Ice Maiden'

Pension fund managers have become increasingly powerful players in determining the future of companies – sometimes shown dramatically during takeover bids.

By 2001 Sir Rocco Forte had picked himself up from the devastating blow in 1996 of losing to Granada his £4 billion family empire of 800 hotels, 1,000 restaurants and 100,000 employees. He had set up RF hotels – a collection of six luxury hotels worldwide bought with the family £300m funds from the takeover. He had learnt three lessons from the takeover. First, owning only 8 per cent of the shares is not enough to prevent a hostile takeover; second, to use bank loans to fund RF hotels rather than the stock market; and third, that pension fund managers have considerable power to make or break companies, or rather those who manage those businesses.

In 1996 it was Carol Galley, vice-chairman and fund manager of Mercury Asset Management (MAM), who brought down the Forte empire. She had been dubbed the 'Ice Maiden' by the tabloid press who described her as the most powerful woman in the UK. Galley controlled over 900 pension funds throughout Britain. Even though Rocco Forte had a high profile in the business world, sentiment meant little to Galley who told him coolly that she had examined the £3.8 billion bid for Forte by Granada and considered it to be good. MAM voted its 14.6 per cent shareholding in Forte in favour of Granada. This action was seen as decisive by other shareholders.

Sir Rocco was devastated, but Galley had no regrets. She had done what she was paid to do – she was responsible to pension fund holders for the value of their stake in Forte.

Although, traditionally, pension fund managers had been discreet, barely visible players in the financial world, all this changed after the 'Big Bang' in the City of London in the 1980s. The pension fund plutocrats emerged from the shadows and became regarded as the key power players in the 'governance chain' and the most deadly beasts in the corporate jungle.

Sources: Adapted from *Sunday Times*, 21 April 1996 and 28 January 2001.

Questions

1. Refer to Exhibit 5.2 and list for each of the 'players' in the corporate governance chain:
   (a) the pros and cons of the takeover from their point of view;
   (b) whether you feel they would have favoured or feared a takeover.

2. What are your own views about the benefits and dangers of investment managers having as much power as described in the illustration?

3. What are the drawbacks of keeping a company privately owned and relying on bank loans for additional capital (refer to section 5.2.5 of the text)?

important distinction that will be discussed more fully in section 5.4 below about the ethical stance of organisations.

5.2.2 Shareholders and the role of the governing bodies

The primary statutory responsibility of the governing body of an organisation is to ensure that the organisation actually fulfils the wishes and purposes of the 'owners'. In the private sector, this would be the board of directors working on behalf of shareholders. In the public sector, the governing body would be accountable to the political arm of government – possibly through some intermediate 'agency' such as a funding body. There are important differences between countries regarding the role, composition and *modus operandi* of the board of directors.[5] In the UK, the USA and Australia, the wide spread of shareholdings tends to limit the power of the individual shareholders and heighten that of intermediaries (such as pension fund managers). In most other European countries (e.g. Belgium, the Netherlands and France), shareholding is more closely held and often minority led – perhaps by the founding family, financial institutions or other interests either acting together or using protective mechanisms such as preference shares. The board is strongly controlled by these particular shareholder interests. In Japan, the board tends to be viewed as just one part of a multi-layered corporate decision-making process, and hence is usually dominated by corporate executives. Japanese banks tend to have shareholdings in organisations, as against simply providing loan capital. There is also likely to be a complex web of cross-shareholdings between companies. These latter two factors tend to reduce the pressure for short-term results[6] as against longer-term performance, in marked contrast to US/UK companies. In turn, this influences the approach to important aspects of strategy, such as investment. Short-termism is also driven by the directors and managers – who emphasise short-term financial measures such as return on investment, and who may have a vested interest through remuneration packages tied to these short-term measures.

These different traditions naturally bring with them different structures and compositions of the board. In the UK and USA, there is a single-tier board usually incorporating both executive and non-executive directors. The board supervises the activities and performance of managers to a greater or lesser extent. Many organisations have adopted a subcommittee structure which allows for a more detailed involvement of the board with the work of the managers of the organisation. Non-executive directors sometimes represent the interests of key stakeholders (e.g. institutional investors).

In many other European countries (notably Germany, the Netherlands and France), the *two-tier board* is either mandatory or prevalent. For example, in Germany, the 'upper-tier' or supervisory board oversees the work of the 'lower-tier' board, which is entrusted with the day-to-day management of the organisation. Importantly, the composition of this supervisory board is built around the principles of *co-determination* – half of the members being elected by shareholders, the other half by employees. However, the shareholders maintain the final say through the chairman's casting vote.

The main potential benefit of the two-tier form of governance is the counterbalancing of the power of managers, which is often a feature of management-dominated unitary boards in the UK and the USA – particularly where non-executive directors are weak or ineffective. There has been particular concern that managerial interests have dominated strategic decisions on issues such as diversification and acquisitions – decisions which have proved unsuccessful and not in the best interests of shareholders. There has been much debate as to whether a legally prescribed balance of power is or is not beneficial. There were similar proposals for industrial democracy in the UK[7] in the 1970s but they were not acted on by government. In France, the two-tier system is optional.

In Japan, the composition of the board is heavily weighted towards executive members. However, as membership of the board is seen as a tier in the management hierarchy, the entry of executives on to the board is controlled by the chairman, who will often take external advice (for example, from bankers) before a manager is promoted to director. In Japanese corporate culture, a prerequisite of a good director is someone who is able to continue to promote the interests of employees. So, in contrast to Germany, employees in Japan have power through cultural norms (trust and the implicit 'duties' of directors) rather than through the legal framework of governance. The different corporate governance traditions and frameworks in different countries tend to result in a different prioritisation of many of the corporate governance issues discussed in this section of the book, as shown in the critique given in Exhibit 5.3.

The role of the board in nationalised industries is – in theory – very similar to the private sector, except that capital expenditure and borrowings are directly controlled by the minister responsible. In reality, the power of boards is often curtailed by political priorities and the involvement of ministers in management decisions (for example, prices, wages and plant closures). The desire to remove this conflict between political expediency and the need for longer-term strategic direction was an important reason behind the major privatisation programmes in many countries during the 1980s and 1990s.

The public services have a wide variety of arrangements for governing bodies, but there are some commonalities. There has been a move in many countries to increase the proportion of (so-called) independent members on governing bodies. These independent members are the nearest equivalent of the non-executive director in the private sector. Governing bodies are often factional, or representational, in practice even if not by regulation. This particularly applies to the place of employees and unions on governing bodies.

5.2.3 Rights of creditors and lenders

One of the reasons why the corporate governance situation varies so much from one country to another is the differing arrangements for corporate finance. There are the different 'traditions' regarding *equity/debt* ratios and the extent to which the *relationship* with bankers is regarded as one of partnership or simply 'contractual'. At one extreme, particularly in the USA and UK,

| Exhibit 5.3 | Strengths and weaknesses of governance systems |

Anglo-Saxon Model (US and UK)

Strengths
- Dynamic market orientation
- Fluid capital investment
- Extensive internationalisation

Weaknesses
- Volatile instability
- Short-termism
- Inadequate governance structures

European Model (Germany)

Strengths
- Long-term industrial strategy
- Very stable capital investment
- Robust governance procedures

Weaknesses
- Internationalisation more difficult
- Lack of flexibility
- Inadequate investment in new industries

Asian Model (Japan)

Strengths
- Very long-term industrial strategy
- Stable capital investment
- Major overseas activity

Weaknesses
- Financial speculation
- Secretive, sometimes corrupt governance procedures
- Weak accountability

Source: Adapted from T. Clarke and S. Clegg, *Changing Paradigms: The transformation of management knowledge for the 21st century*, HarperCollins Business, 2000, Table 6.5, p. 324.

equity is the dominant form of long-term finance and commercial banks provide debt capital; relationships with bankers are towards the contractual end of the spectrum. In contrast, in Japan (and to a lesser extent Germany), banks often have significant equity stakes and may be part of the same parent company, and the lead banks may organise the activities of other banks. The power of lenders in these two extremes is very different and exercised in different ways. UK and US banks may exercise their power through *exit* (i.e. withdrawing funds) even if this liquidates the company. Japanese banks are more concerned to steer the longer-term strategy of the organisation and to use their power to make their voice heard.

The trade creditor is the least protected stakeholder in the trading process and there is little in the corporate governance framework to redress this. So creditors need to mitigate their risk through prudence in their dealings.

5.2.4 Relationships with customers and clients

The legal framework of many countries enshrines the principle of *caveat emptor*, placing the burden of risk on the customer and giving the balance of power to the company. However, there have been some significant moves to change this. Legislation to protect consumers' interests grew substantially from the 1960s onwards. In situations of natural monopolies, many governments created 'watchdog' bodies to represent the customers' interests. In the case of the privatised utilities in the UK and elsewhere, this has become enshrined in the office of the regulator (Oftel, Ofwat, etc.), whose powers of regulation set them up as a surrogate for the market and who exert control over prices and services through a set of performance targets. This has important implications for how the companies construct their competitive strategies.

Even without the use of a legally binding framework, there have been other attempts to give more rights and voice to individual consumers. In the 1990s the *Citizen's Charter Initiative* in the UK public services was one such attempt. Each public service had to develop and publish a charter which stated the rights of clients and the performance standards which they could expect from the organisation. These performance standards raised the visibility to users of the organisation's performance, creating some measure of 'market pressure' (see Illustration 5.2). Following the election of a Labour government in 1997 these were supplemented by the *Best Value Initiative* which placed a duty on public service organisations to identify and move towards the standards reached by the best providers. Crucially, this benchmarking had to be made beyond the public services – hence upholding the customers' right to get genuinely best value from public services (see section 4.6.3).

5.2.5 Forms of ownership

The form of ownership can have a fundamental effect on the purposes of an organisation and the strategies that are pursued. There may also be issues as to whether the form of ownership is appropriate to the strategic purposes of an organisation.

- In the life cycle of many commercial organisations, a major strategic choice has to be made about whether it is appropriate to move from a *privately owned* organisation – for example, a family business – to a *publicly quoted* corporation. Such a decision might be made because the owners decide that increased equity is required to finance the growth of the business. The family members who own the business need to recognise that their role will change. They become answerable to a much wider group of shareholders and to institutions acting for those shareholders.

- The board of directors of a business has a responsibility to shareholders to provide them with a reasonable rate of return on their investment. It may be that the board arrives at the view that the sale to a different *corporate parent* may be to the advantage of a company or a business within the corporation. For example, a family-controlled firm might consider selling

Illustration 5.2

The Patient's Charter revisited

STRATEGY IN ACTION

The public services have been attempting to increase the rights and voice of individual 'clients'. But alongside this must go responsibilities too.

In the 1990s, in many public services in the UK and elsewhere, governments were keen to increase the voice of the client through various means, including, in the UK, what became known as the *Citizen's Charter*. These charters outlined the rights of citizens and the standards they should expect from the public services. Each public service adopted their own charter. In the National Health Service, this was known as the *Patient's Charter* and was launched in 1991. The Labour government elected in 1997 decided to revise and extend the charter and in 2001, after extensive consultation, *Your Guide to the NHS* was published for this purpose. Importantly, they wanted to use the opportunity to restate some values on which the NHS had been built and to emphasise the idea of partnership between the NHS and patients. So patients must accept responsibilities as well as receiving rights. The two key sections of the guide were:

NHS Core Principles (Commitments)

- Health care on the basis of clinical need, not the ability to pay
- Comprehensive services
- Services shaped by needs of patients, families and carers
- Different responses to different populations
- Continuous improvement of quality and minimisation of errors
- Valuing staff
- Public funds only to be used for NHS patients

- Work with others to create seamless services
- Keep people healthy and reduce inequities in health
- Confidentiality and open access to information

Responsibilities of patients

- Lead a healthy lifestyle
- Care for yourself where possible
- Give blood and carry a donor card
- Listen to advice on treatment
- Treat NHS staff with respect
- Keep your appointments
- Return equipment after use
- Pay charges promptly
- Use this guide to find services

This guide was part of a wider programme of change for patients set out in the NHS Plan. The guide also laid out national standards, which included both quantitative targets (e.g. to be seen at outpatients' clinics within 30 minutes of appointment time) and qualitative standards (e.g. standards of cleanliness). Importantly, NHS organisations were required to develop a local Patient's Prospectus to reflect local priorities.

Sources: Adapted from *Your Guide to the NHS*, Department of Health, 2001. Department of Health website (www.doh.gov.uk).

Question

Make your own critique of the benefit of the Patient's Charter as a means of increasing the power ('voice') of clients of the health service by asking what happens if the clients' rights are not honoured (e.g. guaranteed admission for treatment).

out to a corporation as a way of realising its assets. Or it may be that the board of a firm decides that it is not able to compete as an independent unit as well as it might within a corporate body, perhaps because it is trading nationally within increasingly global markets. The sale of the business might therefore make sense.

- Some sectors have a tradition of *mutual ownership* by their members – for example, insurance companies and building societies. Customers (for example, those with savings accounts and/or mortgages) are members of the organisation in place of shareholders. As many UK building societies became banks in the late 1990s they tended to change their form of ownership by de-mutualising and issuing windfall shares to members. This changes the governance arrangements for the organisation to be more similar to companies. Interestingly, as Illustration 5.3 shows, some organisations were, at the same time, trying to move in the other direction – to mutualise.

- Businesses also become the targets for acquisitions and a board might decide that such an offer is more attractive to shareholders than the returns they can promise in the future. On occasions, businesses decide to merge, perhaps because the executives believe that the synergies resulting from coming together are greater than the businesses would achieve by operating independently. These decisions are, then, the outcome of considerations of strategy where a decision is reached that the business would be better off under other ownership. The corporate governance framework within which acquisitions and mergers might take place is discussed in section 5.2.6 below.

- Historically, most public sector bodies have been tightly controlled by their 'owners', the central or local government or government departments. However, latterly this has changed in a number of respects in many countries, notably by the *privatisation* of such public bodies.[8] In the UK, this process began in the 1980s with the government selling British Telecom and gas, water and electricity utilities. The government took such decisions in order to require organisations to face up to market forces, to become more aware of customer needs and competitive pressures and to provide access to private sector capital. In turn, managers found more latitude in terms of strategic choice – what they could provide in terms of product or services; the ability to diversify, raise capital for expansion and so on. In some other countries (for example, Ireland and New Zealand), governments retained ownership but created state-owned enterprises with considerable commercial freedom.[9]

- In both publicly quoted and state-owned companies, another example of changing ownership is when all or part of the organisation is sold to management – a *management buyout*. This has happened, for example, in commercial organisations when managers of a business have been faced with a corporate decision to close or dispose of that business. Those who work in the organisation may have sufficient faith in its future to raise capital to buy the business themselves. In the public sector, too, buyouts have occurred: for example, when a public corporation has chosen to withdraw from a particular market or when the government has sold off a nationalised enterprise, such as the railways in the 1990s.

Illustration 5.3

Mutualisation or de-mutualisation?

Many financial service organisations have de-mutualised – whilst in other sectors mutualisation is being considered.

De-mutualisation in financial services

Mutual ownership had a long tradition in the UK and was associated with organisations that had some 'social purpose' – particularly building societies and life assurance companies.

However, in the late 1990s the members of many of these organisations in the UK voted to become companies by issuing shares to members and seeking a flotation on the stock market. The Halifax, Britain's largest building society, de-mutualised in 1997 and became a bank – developing its services accordingly. This left its previous building society competitors uncertain as to whether to follow the Halifax's example or to remain mutually owned. In December 2000 the Bradford and Bingley Building Society de-mutualised and at the same time the largest remaining building society, The Nationwide, announced that it would hold a vote on de-mutualisation in July 2001. Standard Life, a major life insurer, was also facing a campaign to de-mutualise. The problem faced by management was that it required only 50 votes from qualifying members to force a vote. Members usually consisted of customers who held insurance policies, mortgages or particular types of savings accounts. Historically, members were said to benefit from mutual ownership through lower mortgage rates or higher savings rates since funds were not being paid out to shareholders as dividends. However, flotation had its attractions too since all members received free 'windfall' shares – amounting to £620 in the case of Bradford and Bingley.

Proposals for mutual ownership in the water industry

In June 2000, Kelda (previously known as Yorkshire Water) unveiled radical plans to sell its assets to a customer-owned mutual company. This was a response to tough regulatory requirements to cut costs and reduce prices. Under the plan, Kelda would sell its physical assets (pipelines, sewage works and reservoirs) to a 'community-owned corporation' for about £2.6 billion. The new entity would be listed under provident society rules, which governed cooperatives. This was described as a hybrid between the old public sector ownership (pre-privatisation) and a stock market listed company. The company would be entirely debt financed. It was claimed that this would help reverse the company's declining shareholder value and profits. However, Ofwat – the industry regulator – was unimpressed by the proposals and, mindful of the likelihood of other water companies following suit, turned down the proposals. There was also a court ruling that any supplier that hived off ownership of its assets had to tender immediately for the management of those assets.

Sources: Financial services: *The Guardian*, 21 December 2000, *The Independent*, 6 December 2000. Kelda: *Daily Telegraph*, 15 June 2000; *The Independent*, 6 December 2000.

Questions

1. List the benefits and disadvantages of mutual ownership from the point of view of managers and customers.

2. What other alternatives does Kelda have for improving its financial performance?

- Even when a change in ownership has not been made, public sector organisations have been required to face questions of corporate purpose by other means such as deregulation, market testing and the creation of quasi-markets, as discussed in section 9.3.4. These have usually required changes in the corporate governance and regulatory framework.

5.2.6 Mergers and takeovers

The impact of corporate governance on strategy, and the differences between the USA and UK, and Continental European countries such as Germany, is shown clearly in the area of takeovers (particularly hostile takeovers). In the USA and UK, the exposure of managers to the threat of takeover (i.e. a market-pressure-based system) is regarded as a primary means of ensuring the good performance of organisations. In contrast, in Germany the performance of companies is seen as being primarily controlled through institutional mechanisms such as equity ownership by banks, two-tier boards and co-determination. Therefore, the corporate governance issues around (hostile) takeovers are largely confined to those countries which have adopted the Anglo-Saxon market-based approach to governance. The specific issue has been the extent to which a free market in buying and selling shares and companies – over the head of the board of directors – should be constrained in law and codes of conduct, to produce a semi-regulated framework for takeovers. Equally important has been a concern with the *conflict of interest* which directors face in defending against a hostile bid, and the extent to which *defensive measures* should be regulated. Often, bids are regarded as hostile by boards of directors because they might jeopardise their *personal* position (as executives), whereas a takeover may actually be in the longer-term interests of the shareholders and positively beneficial to other stakeholders, such as employees or customers.

Similar questions have been asked in other sectors about the role of managers and board members faced with privatisation or de-merger (for example, in the public services) or de-mutualisation (of building societies and insurance companies). The organisation's executive board members may well gain or lose considerably depending on the outcome of these big decisions. This raises difficult ethical issues for managers, as will be discussed below (section 5.4.3).

5.2.7 Disclosure of information

Once ownership and control are separated in organisations, an important aspect of corporate governance is to establish a framework about *disclosure of information* to various stakeholder groups. This clearly has to be balanced with the commercial prerogative for confidentiality on certain aspects of an organisation's operation.

In the 1990s in the UK, there was mounting criticism of the quality of financial reporting and the effectiveness of the independent auditing. This led to the establishment of the Cadbury Committee,[10] which reported in late 1992 and again in 1996. The first report, which had the backing of the Bank of England, the London Stock Exchange and the accounting bodies, sought to establish a code of best practice on disclosure and audit arrangements. Companies listed on the Stock Exchange were required to make a statement in their annual report that they complied with the code of best practice. So this aspect of corporate governance was exercised not through statute but in a 'voluntary' way, albeit with severe penalties (delisting) for non-compliance.

It is interesting to note that the issue that attracted most attention was the disclosure of *directors' pay*. This was the subject of a separate report in the UK – the Greenbury Report. Again, this indicated the need for corporate governance arrangements to address issues where there is potentially a conflict of interest. Of course, disclosure can be a costly and time-consuming business and is an important consideration for privately owned businesses when thinking about public flotation.

5.3 STAKEHOLDER EXPECTATIONS[11]

The corporate governance framework provides the formal requirements and boundaries within which strategy is being developed. It is also important to understand the expectations of different stakeholders in more detail and the extent to which they are likely to seek influence over an organisation's purposes and strategies.

Stakeholders are those individuals or groups who depend on the organisation to fulfil their own goals and on whom, in turn, the organisation depends.

Stakeholders are those individuals or groups who depend on the organisation to fulfil their own goals and on whom, in turn, the organisation depends. Few individuals have sufficient power to determine unilaterally the strategy of an organisation. Influence is likely to occur only because individuals share expectations with others by being a part of a stakeholder group. Individuals tend to identify themselves with the aims and ideals of stakeholder groups, which may occur within departments, geographical locations, different levels in the hierarchy, etc. Also important are external stakeholders of the organisation, typically financial institutions, customers, suppliers, shareholders and unions. They may seek to influence company strategy through their links with internal stakeholders. For example, customers may pressurise sales managers to represent their interests within the company. Even if external stakeholders are passive, they may represent real constraints on the development of new strategies.

Individuals may belong to more than one stakeholder group and stakeholder groups will 'line up' differently depending on the issue or strategy in hand. For example, marketing and production departments might be united in the face of proposals to drop certain product lines, whilst being in fierce opposition regarding plans to buy in new items to the product range. Often it is specific strategies that trigger off the formation of stakeholder groups. For these reasons, the stakeholder concept is valuable when trying to understand the political context within which specific strategic developments (such as the introduction of a new product or extension into a new geographical area) would take place. In this sense it is also concerned with strategic choice, as will be seen in Chapter 8.

Exhibit 5.4	Some common conflicts of expectations

- In order to grow, short-term profitability, cash flow and pay levels may need to be sacrificed.
- 'Short-termism' may suit managerial career aspirations but preclude investment in long-term projects.
- When family businesses grow, the owners may lose control if they need to appoint professional managers.
- New developments may require additional funding through share issue or loans. In either case, financial independence may be sacrificed.
- Public ownership of shares will require more openness and accountability from the management.
- Cost efficiency through capital investment can mean job losses.
- Extending into mass markets may require a decline in quality standards.
- In public services, a common conflict is between mass provision and specialist services (e.g. preventive dentistry or heart transplants).
- In public services, savings in one area (e.g. social security benefits) may result in increased spending elsewhere (e.g. school meals, medical care).
- In large multinational organisations, conflict can result because divisions 'belong' to two organisational fields – the company and the host country.

5.3.1 Conflicts of expectations

The differing forms of corporate governance discussed in the previous section are intended to provide a framework within which the interests of different stakeholder groups are given formal power of decision within organisations. Although this may prove useful in smoothing the strategic decision-making process, it will not remove conflict of interests. Since the expectations of stakeholder groups will differ, it is quite normal for conflict to exist regarding the importance or desirability of many aspects of strategy. In most situations, a compromise will need to be reached between expectations that cannot all be achieved simultaneously.

Exhibit 5.4 shows some of the typical stakeholder expectations that exist and how they might conflict. They include the conflicts between growth and profitability; growth and control/independence; cost efficiency and jobs; volume/mass provision and quality/specialisation; and the problems of sub-optimisation, where the development of one part of an organisation may be at the expense of another. 'Short-termism' is often driven by the career aspirations of managers at the expense of the long-term health of the organisation. As mentioned earlier, there maybe an overemphasis on short-term financial performance measures linked to remuneration packages.

Arguably, the likelihood of conflict is greatest where expectations from different organisational fields collide. This could occur when an organisation is privatised, a market deregulated, a CEO moves from one type of organisation to another or where pressure groups start raising 'new' issues (such as corporate social responsibility). These issues were mentioned in section 2.2.2 and will be discussed more fully in sections 5.4.2 and 5.5.2 below.

Large global organisations inevitably find themselves operating in multiple arenas. For example, an overseas division is part of the parent company, with all that implies in terms of expectations about behaviour and performance. But it is also part of the local community, which has different expectations, and these two 'worlds' may not sit comfortably alongside each other.[12] For example, in recent years, overseas outlets of McDonald's have often been targeted in anti-capitalist protests (even in the UK). Back at head office the division is expected to behave like 'any other division' even though this may conflict with the ability to meet local expectations of behaviour.

5.3.2 Stakeholder mapping[13]

Stakeholder mapping
identifies stakeholder
expectations and power
and helps in understanding
political priorities

Stakeholder mapping identifies stakeholder expectations and power and helps in understanding political priorities. It underlines the importance of two issues:

● How *interested* each stakeholder group is to impress its expectations on the organisation's purposes and choice of strategies.

● Whether they have the means to do so. This is concerned with the *power* of stakeholder groups (see section 5.3.3 below).

Power/interest matrix

The power/interest matrix can be seen in Exhibit 5.5. It seeks to describe the political context within which an individual strategy would be pursued by

---

Exhibit 5.5 | **Stakeholder mapping: the power/interest matrix**

LEVEL OF INTEREST

		Low	High
POWER	**Low**	**A** Minimal effort	**B** Keep informed
	High	**C** Keep satisfied	**D** Key players

Source: Adapted from A. Mendelow, *Proceedings of the Second International Conference on Information Systems*, Cambridge, MA, 1991.

classifying stakeholders in relation to the power they hold and the extent to which they are likely to show interest in supporting or opposing a particular strategy. The matrix indicates the type of relationship which organisations typically might establish with stakeholder groups in the different quadrants. Clearly, the acceptability of strategies to *key players* (segment D) is of major importance. Often the most difficult issues relate to stakeholders in segment C (institutional shareholders often fall into this category). Although these stakeholders might, in general, be relatively passive, a disastrous situation can arise when their level of interest is underrated and they suddenly *reposition* to segment D and frustrate the adoption of a new strategy. A view might be taken that it is a *responsibility* of strategists or managers to raise the level of interest of powerful stakeholders (such as institutional shareholders), so that they can better fulfil their expected role within the corporate governance framework. Also, this could be concerned with how non-executive directors could be assisted in fulfilling their role, say, through good information and briefing.

Similarly, organisations might address the expectations of stakeholders in segment B through information – for example, to community groups. These stakeholders can be crucially important 'allies' in influencing the attitudes of more powerful stakeholders: for example, through *lobbying*.

Stakeholder mapping might help in understanding better some of the following issues:

- Whether the levels of interest and power of stakeholders properly reflect the corporate governance framework within which the organisation is operating, as in the examples above (non-executive directors, community groups).

- Who are likely to be the key *blockers* and *facilitators* of a strategy and how this could be responded to – for example, in terms of education or persuasion.

- Whether organisations should seek to *reposition* certain stakeholders. This could be to lessen the influence of a key player or, in certain instances, to ensure that there are more key players who will champion the strategy (this is often critical in the public sector context).

- The extent to which stakeholders may need to be assisted or encouraged to *maintain* their level of interest or power. For example, public 'endorsement' by powerful suppliers or customers may be critical to the success of a strategy. Equally, it may be necessary to discourage some stakeholders from repositioning themselves. This is what is meant by *keep satisfied* in relation to stakeholders in segment C, and to a lesser extent *keep informed* for those in segment B. The use of *side payments*[14] to stakeholders as a means of securing their acceptance of new strategies has traditionally been regarded as a key maintenance activity.

These questions raise some difficult ethical issues for managers in deciding the role they should play in the political activity surrounding strategic change. For example, are managers really the honest brokers who weigh the conflicting expectations of stakeholder groups? Or are they answerable to one stakeholder

Illustration 5.4a

Stakeholder mapping at Tallman GmbH

Stakeholder mapping can be a useful tool for determining the political priorities for specific strategic developments or changes.

Tallman GmbH was a German bank providing both retail and corporate banking services throughout Germany, Benelux and France. There were concerns about its loss in market share in the corporate sector which was serviced from two centres – Frankfurt (for Germany and Benelux) and Toulouse (for France). It was considering closing the Toulouse operation and servicing all corporate clients from Frankfurt. This would result in significant job losses in Toulouse, some of which would be replaced in Frankfurt alongside vastly improved IT systems.

Two power/interest maps were drawn up by the company officials to establish likely stakeholder reactions to the proposed closure of the Toulouse operation. Map A represents the likely situation and map B the preferred situation – where support for the proposal would be sufficient to proceed.

Referring to map A it can be seen that, with the exception of customer X and IT supplier A, the stakeholders in box B are currently opposed to the closure of the Toulouse operation. If Tallman was to have any chance of convincing these stakeholders to change their stance to a more supportive one, the company must address their questions and, where possible, alleviate their fears. If such fears were overcome, these people might become important allies in influencing the more powerful stakeholders in boxes C and D. The supportive attitude of customer X could be usefully harnessed in this quest. Customer X was a multinational with operations throughout Europe. They had shown dissatisfaction with the inconsistent treatment that they received from Frankfurt and Toulouse.

The relationships Tallman had with the stakeholders in box C were the most difficult to manage since, whilst they were considered to be relatively passive, largely owing to their indifference to the proposed strategy, a disastrous situation could arise if their level of interest was underrated. For example, if the German minister were replaced, her successor might be opposed to the strategy and actively seek to stop the changes. In this case they would shift to box D.

The acceptability of the proposed strategy to the current players in box D was a key consideration. Of particular concern was customer Y (a major French manufacturer who operated only in France – accounting for 20 per cent of Toulouse corporate banking income). Customer Y was opposed to the closure of the Toulouse operation and could have the power to prevent it from happening, for example by the withdrawal of its business. The company clearly needed to have open discussions with this stakeholder.

– such as shareholders – and hence is their role to ensure the acceptability of their strategies to other stakeholders? Or are they, as many authors suggest, the real power behind the throne, constructing strategies to suit their own purposes and managing stakeholder expectations to ensure acceptance of these strategies?

These are important issues for managers and other stakeholders to consider. The corporate governance arrangements for the organisation will answer these questions only at the most general level. Against that backdrop, the balancing of the conflicting interests of different stakeholders is strongly determined by

Map A: The likely situation

A	Shareholder M (–) Toulouse office (–) Customer X (+) French minister (–) Marketing (–) IT supplier A (+) B
Customer Z German minister C	Customer Y (–) Frankfurt office (+) Corporate finance (+) D

Map B: The preferred situation

French minister A	Shareholder M (–) Toulouse office (–) Marketing (–) IT supplier A (+) B
Customer Z German minister C	Customer X (+) Customer Y (+) Frankfurt office (+) Corporate finance (+) D

By comparing the position of stakeholders in map A and map B, and identifying any changes and mismatches, Tallman could establish a number of tactics to change the stance of certain stakeholders to a more positive one and to increase the power of certain stakeholders. For example, customer X could be encouraged to champion the proposed strategy and assist Tallman by providing media access, or even convincing customer Y that the change could be beneficial.

Tallman could also seek to dissuade or prevent powerful stakeholders from changing their stance to a negative one: for example, unless direct action were taken, lobbying from her French counterpart may well raise the German minister's level of interest. This has implications for how the company handles the situation in France. Time could be spent talking the strategy through with the French minister and also customer Y to try to shift them away from opposition at least to neutrality, if not support.

Questions

To ensure that you are clear about how to undertake stakeholder mapping, produce your own complete analysis for Tallman GmbH against a different strategy, i.e. *to service all corporate clients from Toulouse*. Ensure that you go through the following steps:

1. Plot the most likely situation (map A) – remembering to be careful to *reassess* interest and power for each stakeholder in relation to this *new* strategy.

2. Map the preferred situation (map B).

3. Identify the mismatches – and hence the political priorities. Remember to include the need to *maintain* a stakeholder in its 'opening' position (if relevant).

4. Finish off by listing the actions you would propose to take and give a final view of the degree of political risk in pursuing this new strategy.

the ethical stance of the organisation and the individual managers. This will be discussed fully in section 5.4 below.

Illustration 5.4a shows some of the practical issues of using stakeholder mapping to understand better the political context surrounding a new strategy. The example relates to a German bank with headquarters in Frankfurt (Germany) and providing corporate banking services from head office and a regional office in Toulouse (France). It is considering the closure of its Toulouse office and providing all corporate banking services from Frankfurt. The example illustrates several issues.

- Stakeholder groups are not usually 'homogeneous' but contain a variety of subgroups with somewhat different expectations and power. In the illustration, *customers* are shown divided into those who are largely supportive of the strategy (customer X), those who are actively hostile (customer Y) and those who are indifferent (customer Z). So when using stakeholder mapping, there is clearly a balance to be struck between describing stakeholders too generically – hence hiding important issues of diversity – and too much subdivision, making the situation confusing and difficult to interpret.

- Most stakeholder groups consist of large numbers of individuals (such as customers or shareholders), and hence can be thought of largely independently of the expectations of individuals within that group. With some stakeholder groups this is not the case: they consist of a small number of individuals or even single individuals (e.g. the chairperson of the company or the minister of a government department). It is essential to distinguish between the role *per se* and the individual who is currently undertaking that role. It is useful to know if a new individual in that role would shift the positioning. Serious misjudgements can be made if proper care is not paid to this point.

  In the example, it has been concluded that the German minister (segment C) is largely indifferent to the new development – it is very low in her priorities. However, a change of minister might shift this situation overnight. Although it will be impossible for the bank to remove such uncertainties entirely, there are implications for the political priorities. For example, those permanent officials who are advising the minister need to be kept satisfied, since they will outlive individual ministers and provide a continuity which can diminish uncertainty. It is also possible, of course, that the German minister's level of interest will be raised by lobbying from her French counterpart. This would have implications for how the company handles the situation in France.

Illustration 5.4a shows how an organisation could establish political priorities from stakeholder mapping.

5.3.3 Power[15]

The previous section was concerned with understanding stakeholder expectations and highlighted the importance of power. Power is the mechanism by which expectations are able to influence purposes and strategies. It has been seen that, in most organisations, power will be unequally shared between the various stakeholders.

Before proceeding, it is necessary to understand what is meant here by 'power'. In particular, a distinction needs to be drawn between, on the one hand, the power that people or groups derive from their position within the organisation and through the formal corporate governance arrangements, and on the other, the power that they possess by other means. For the purposes of this discussion, **power** is the ability of individuals or groups to persuade, induce or coerce others into following certain courses of action. This is the

Power is the ability of individuals or groups to persuade, induce or coerce others into following certain courses of action

Exhibit 5.6	Sources and indicators of power

SOURCES OF POWER

(a) Within organisations
- Hierarchy (formal power),
  e.g. autocratic decision making
- Influence (informal power),
  e.g. charismatic leadership
- Control of strategic resources,
  e.g. strategic products
- Possession of knowledge and skills,
  e.g. computer specialists
- Control of the environment,
  e.g. negotiating skills
- Involvement in strategy implementation,
  e.g. by exercising discretion

(b) For external stakeholders
- Control of strategic resources,
  e.g. materials, labour, money
- Involvement in strategy implementation,
  e.g. distribution outlets, agents
- Possession of knowledge (skills),
  e.g. subcontractors
- Through internal links,
  e.g. informal influence

INDICATORS OF POWER

(a) Within organisations
- Status
- Claim on resources
- Representation
- Symbols

(b) For external stakeholders
- Status
- Resource dependence
- Negotiating arrangements
- Symbols

mechanism by which one set of expectations will dominate strategic development or seek compromise with others.

Exhibit 5.6 summarises the various sources of power for both internal and external stakeholders and can be used to understand how powerful each stakeholder is in influencing a particular strategy (as part of stakeholder mapping). It should be noted that the relative importance of these sources will vary over time. Indeed, major changes in the business environment – such as deregulation or the advent of cheap and powerful IT – can drastically shift the power balance between organisations and their stakeholders. For example, consumers' knowledge of different companies' offerings through Internet browsing has increased their power considerably. Deregulation and 'citizen empowerment' have required public service organisations to adopt more customer-focused strategies.

Since there are a variety of different sources of power, it is often useful to look for *indicators of power*, which are the visible signs that stakeholders have been able to exploit one or more of the sources of power listed in Exhibit 5.6. There are four useful indicators of power: the *status* of the individual or group (such as job grade or reputation); the *claim on resources* (such as budget size); *representation* in powerful positions; and *symbols* of power (such as office size or use of titles and names).

No single indicator is likely fully to uncover the structure of power within a company. However, by looking at all four indicators, it may be possible to

Illustration 5.4b

Assessment of power

Assessing the power of stakeholders is an important part of stakeholder mapping.

The corporate finance department is seen as powerful by all measures, and the marketing department universally weak. Equally, the Frankfurt operation is particularly powerful compared with Toulouse. This analysis provides important data in the process of stakeholder mapping, since the strategic importance of power is also related to whether individuals or groups are likely to exercise their power. This assessment thus helped in deciding where to locate the stakeholders on the power/interest maps.

Combining the results of this analysis with the stakeholder mapping exercise, it can be seen that Toulouse's only real hope is to encourage supplier A to reposition by convincing it of the increased IT opportunities which a two-centre operation would provide. Perhaps shareholder M could be helpful in this process through lobbying the supplier.

Internal stakeholders

INDICATORS OF POWER	CORPORATE FINANCE	MARKETING	FRANKFURT	TOULOUSE
Status				
Position in hierarchy (closeness to board)	H	L	H	M
Salary of top manager	H	L	H	L
Average grade of staff	H	M	H	L
Claim on resources				
Number of staff	M	H	M	M
Size of similar company	H	L	H	L
Budget as % of total	H	M	H	L
Representation				
Number of directors	H	None	M	None
Most influential directors	H	None	M	None
Symbols				
Quality of accommodation	H	L	M	M
Support services	H	L	H	L

H = high   M = medium   L = low

External stakeholders

INDICATORS OF POWER	IT SUPPLIER A	CUSTOMER Y	SHAREHOLDER M
Status	M	H	L
Resource dependence	M	H	H
Negotiating arrangements	M	H	L
Symbols	M	H	L

H = high   M = medium   L = low

understand which people or groups appear to have power by a number of these measures. It should be remembered that the distribution of power will vary *in relation to the particular strategy under consideration*. For example, a corporate finance function will be more powerful in relation to developments requiring new capital or revenue commitments than in relation to ones which are largely self-financing or within the financial authority of separate divisions or subsidiaries. Illustration 5.4b shows these indicators of power in the bank from the previous illustration. The corporate finance department was seen as powerful by all indicators and the marketing department as universally weak. Equally, Frankfurt was particularly powerful in relation to Toulouse.

A similar understanding of the power held by external stakeholders can be useful. The indicators of power here are slightly different:

● The *status* of an external stakeholder can often be inferred by the speed with which the company responds.

● *Resource dependence* in terms of the relative size of shareholdings or loans, or the proportion of a company's business tied up with any one customer, or a similar dependence on suppliers. A key indicator could be the ease with which a supplier, financier or customer could switch or *be switched* at short notice.

● *Symbols* are also valuable clues about power. For example, whether the management team wines and dines a customer or supplier, or the level of person in the company who deals with a particular supplier.

Again, no single indicator will give a full understanding of the extent of the power held by external stakeholders. Illustration 5.4b shows these indicators of power for the bank from the previous illustration. It can be seen that Toulouse's only real hope of survival is to encourage supplier A to 'reposition' by convincing it of the increased IT opportunities that a two-centre operation would provide. Perhaps shareholder M could be helpful in this process through lobbying the supplier.

5.4 BUSINESS ETHICS[16]

The previous sections have discussed the formal obligations of organisations imposed through the regulatory and corporate governance frameworks and also the expectations of those stakeholders who are most interested and powerful. However, there has been little discussion so far about the societal expectations of organisations and how these impact on an organisation's purposes. This is the province of *business ethics* and exists at three levels:

● At the *macro* level, there are issues about the role of businesses and other organisations in the national and international organisation of society. Expectations range from laissez-faire free enterprise at one extreme and organisations as shapers of society at the other. There are also important issues of international relationships and the role of business on an international scale. Managers need to understand the factors which influence these societal expectations of organisations – particularly in relation to how inclusive or exclusive they are expected to be to the influence of the various stakeholders discussed in the previous section. This is the first issue – the broad *ethical stance* of an organisation.

● Within this macro framework, *corporate social responsibility* is concerned with the *specific* ethical issues facing corporate entities (private and public sector). This concerns the extent to which the organisation should move beyond the minimum obligations provided through regulation and corporate governance, and how the conflicting demands of different stakeholders can be reconciled.

● At the *individual* level, it concerns the behaviour and actions of individuals within organisations. This is clearly an important issue for the management of organisations, but it is discussed here only in so far as it affects strategy, and in particular the role of managers in the strategic management process.

5.4.1 The ethical stance

The regulatory environment and the corporate governance arrangements for an organisation determine the minimum obligations of an organisation towards its various stakeholders. Therefore, a key strategic issue within organisations is the *ethical stance* which is taken regarding obligations to stakeholders. The **ethical stance** is the extent to which an organisation will exceed its minimum obligations to stakeholders and society at large. Different organisations take very different stances and there is likely to be a strong relationship between the ethical stance and the character of an organisation.

Exhibit 5.7 outlines four *stereotypes*[17] to illustrate these differences They represent a progressively more inclusive 'list' of stakeholder interests and a greater breadth of success criteria:

The **ethical stance** is the extent to which an organisation will exceed its minimum obligations to stakeholders and society at large

● At one extreme there are organisations which have taken the narrow view that the only responsibility of business is the short-term interests of shareholders. Their ethical stance is that it is the domain of government to prescribe, through legislation, the constraints which society chooses to impose on businesses in their pursuit of economic efficiency (i.e. the legal and regulatory environment and the arrangements for corporate governance). The organisation will meet these minimum obligations but no more. The presence of many new-economy organisations of this type is creating dilemmas for governments as they consider whether and how they might try to regulate the Internet (see Illustration 5.5). It is also argued that expecting companies to exercise social duties can, in extreme cases, undermine the authority of government and give business organisations even more power: for example, multinationals operating in developing countries.

● The ethical stance of category 2 is similar to that of the previous group, but it is tempered with a recognition of the *long-term financial benefit to the shareholder* of well-managed relationships with other stakeholders. Many of the issues are therefore managed proactively and carefully as a matter of long-term self-interest. For example, external sponsorships or welfare provision

Exhibit 5.7	Four possible ethical stances

1. Short-term shareholder interests

2. Longer-term shareholder interests

3. Multiple stakeholder obligations

4. Shaper of society

might be regarded as sensible expenditures akin to any other form of investment or promotion expenditure. The avoidance of 'shady' marketing practices is necessary to prevent the need for yet more legislation in that area. It is argued that, if managers wish to maintain discretion in the long run over issues such as marketing practices, then they are wise to operate responsibly in the short term. This group would also take a similar view to the Hampel Committee[18] mentioned earlier that organisations not only have responsibility *to* their shareholders but they also have a responsibility for *relationships* with other stakeholders.

● The third category is that stakeholder interests and expectations (wider than just shareholders) should be more *explicitly incorporated in the organisation's purposes* and strategies, and usually they will go beyond the minimum obligations of regulation and corporate governance. They also argue that the performance of the organisation should be measured in a much more pluralistic way than just through its financial bottom line. The Quaker companies of the nineteenth century are a good example: to a considerable extent, the attitudes of these companies have remained more socially progressive than others during the twentieth century. Some authors[19] have described this stance as seeing organisations as a 'forum for stakeholder interaction' as against being the private property of shareholders. Companies in this category might argue that they would retain uneconomic units to preserve

Illustration 5.5

Regulating the Internet?

If organisations believe that their only duty is to maximise profits for their owners then their actions might result in changes in regulation.

The Internet was meant to be about freedom. The great triumph of innovation on the Internet had been because of its unregulated or self-regulated nature. But 2000 was probably the year when governments started seriously to regulate the Internet and challenge the rights to transmit information in an unrestricted manner. In Britain, the new Regulation of Investigatory Powers Act gave the police access to e-mail and other online services. South Korea had outlawed access to gambling websites. The United States had passed a law requiring schools and libraries that received federal funds for Internet connections to install software to block material 'harmful to the young'. In France the courts required Yahoo! to find a way of blocking French users from receiving information about Nazi memorabilia. Under EU law, consumers could now sue EU-based Internet sites in their own countries and this might be extended internationally. Many of these regulations were justified as means of preventing so-called abusive uses of the Internet such as child pornography.

There were those who argued against this drift towards regulation – claiming that since the Internet does away with geographical boundaries it also does away with territorially based laws. Since individuals and companies can decide in which country to site their websites, this creates competition between different countries' jurisdiction. For example, because of its constitutional guarantee of the right of free speech, the United States had become the home

and safe haven for many of the most controversial websites.

But governments are not helpless against such tactical behaviour. They have some potentially powerful tools at their disposal. Filtering, through software at Internet service provider level or international 'gateways', is possible. In some countries, such as Burma, regulation is much simpler – long prison sentences for unauthorised accessing of the Internet. But perhaps the most promising approach (from governments' point of view) is coordinated action. For example, the Council of Europe – a group of 41 countries – is producing the draft of an international treaty on cybercrime. This will include issues such as copyright and taxation. So the battle for freedom on the Internet will go on – with both sides attempting to exploit technology to its advantage. It is far from clear who will win.

Source: Adapted from *The Economist*, 13 January 2001, pp. 25–7.

Questions

1. Imagine that you were establishing an e-commerce business. What would be the practical implications to the way that you ran your business for each of the different ethical stances shown in Exhibit 5.7?

2. What would be the implications for governments and regulators if most businesses followed each of these stances?

3. How would these actions by businesses and governments affect citizens and consumers?

jobs, would avoid manufacturing or selling 'anti-social' products and would be prepared to bear reductions in profitability for the social good. However, there are clearly important issues of balance. Many public sector organisations are, rightly, positioned within this group. They are subject to a wide diversity of expectations and unitary measures of performance are often inadequate in reflecting this diversity.

- The final group represents the *ideological* end of the spectrum. They have purposes that are concerned with *shaping society*, and the financial considerations are regarded as of secondary importance or a constraint. The extent to which this is a viable ethical stance clearly depends upon issues of regulation, corporate governance and accountability. Arguably, it is easier for a private, family-owned, organisation to operate in this way, since it is not accountable to external shareholders. Some would argue that the great historical achievements of the public services in transforming the quality of life for millions of people were largely because they were mission driven in this way, and supported by a political framework in which they operated. In many countries since the mid-1980s, there has been a major challenge to the legitimacy of this mission-driven stance within public services and a reassertion of the rights of citizens (as taxpayers) to expect demonstrable best value from its public services. This has severely curtailed the ability of public services – particularly at the local level – to be proactive shapers of society.

  Charitable organisations face similar dilemmas – it is often fundamental to their existence that they have zeal to protect and improve the interests of particular groups in society. But they also need to remain financially viable, which can bring problems with their image – sometimes being seen as over-commercial and spending too much on administration or promotional activities.

Some authors[20] have discussed the relationship between the stance that organisations take towards their stakeholders and society at large and the types of institutional arrangements that are prevalent at various levels around the organisation. They conclude that the more inclusive stances (types 3 and 4 in Exhibit 5.7) are most likely to occur:

- When social justice is prominent in the sociocultural norms and political agenda. So some forms of capitalism are concerned with property rights of owners whilst others overtly expect a more inclusive stakeholder agenda for businesses.

- In more economically developed nations which have usually progressed to a state of economic strength which allows a more inclusive agenda. The way in which the green issues have risen in importance over 50 years is an example.

- In industries or sectors that are in the public eye – for example, consumer goods and services as against institutional/industrial/primary goods.

- Where the degree of competitive rivalry is high (the reverse point being that oligopolies often 'collude' to exclude stakeholder influences).

- In younger industries – since attitudes are formed 'at birth' and become institutionalised (as will be discussed in section 5.6 below). Young industries start with values of a more socially inclusive era.

- Organisational values and culture are also important, as are the personal values of powerful individuals in organisations. These will be discussed in section 5.6 below.

5.4.2 Corporate social responsibility[21]

> **Corporate social responsibility** is concerned with the ways in which an organisation exceeds the minimum obligations to stakeholders specified through regulation and corporate governance

Within this broad ethical stance **corporate social responsibility** is concerned with the ways in which an organisation exceeds the minimum obligations to stakeholders specified through regulation and corporate governance. This includes considerations as to how the conflicting demands of different stakeholders can be reconciled. Since the legal and regulatory frameworks pay uneven attention to the rights of different stakeholders it is useful[22] to distinguish between contractual stakeholders – such as customers, suppliers or employees – who have a legal relationship with an organisation, and community stakeholders – such as local communities, consumers (in general) and pressure groups – who do not have the protection of the law to the same extent as the first group. Therefore the corporate social responsibility policies of companies will be particularly important to these community stakeholders.

Exhibit 5.8 outlines a number of these issues, both internal and external to the organisation, and provides a checklist against which an organisation's actions on corporate social responsibility can be assessed. Although a large number of companies produce guidelines on some or all of the issues, a significant number have no programme at all. Some authors[23] recommend social auditing as a way of ensuring that these issues of corporate social responsibility get systematically reviewed.

5.4.3 The role of individuals and managers

It should be clear from the preceding discussion that business ethics – as part of strategic management – raises some difficult dilemmas for individuals and managers within organisations:

- What is the responsibility of an individual who believes that the strategy of his or her organisation is unethical (for example, its trading practices) or is not adequately representing the legitimate interests of one or more stakeholder groups? Should the individual report the organisation; or should he or she leave the company on the grounds of a mismatch of values? This has often been called *whistleblowing*.[24]

- Managers are usually in a powerful position within organisations to influence the expectations of other stakeholders. They have access to information and channels of influence which are not available to many other stakeholders. With this power comes an ethical responsibility to behave with *integrity*.

Exhibit 5.8	Some questions of corporate social responsibility

Should organisations be responsible for . . .

INTERNAL ASPECTS	EXTERNAL ASPECTS
Employee welfare . . . providing medical care, assistance with mortgages, extended sick leave, assistance for dependants, etc.?	**Green issues** . . . reducing pollution to below legal standards if competitors are not doing so? . . . energy conservation?
Working conditions . . . enhancing working surroundings, social and sporting clubs, above-minimum safety standards, etc.?	**Products** . . . danger arising from the careless use of product by consumers?
Job design . . . designing jobs to the increased satisfaction of workers rather than for economic efficiency?	**Markets and marketing** . . . deciding not to sell in some markets? . . . advertising standards?
Intellectual property . . . respecting and not claiming corporate ownership of the private knowledge of individuals	**Suppliers** . . . 'fair' terms of trade? . . . blacklisting suppliers?
	Employment . . . positive discrimination in favour of minorities? . . . maintaining jobs?
	Community activity . . . sponsoring local events and supporting local good works?

Given that strategy development can be an intensely political process, managers can often find real difficulties establishing and maintaining this position of integrity. As has been seen, there is a potential conflict for managers between what strategies are best for their own career and what strategies are in the longer-term interests of their organisation. Integrity is particularly threatened by the potential for insider-trading prior to acquisitions. The international business community was beset by a series of such cases in the 1990s.

Integrity is a key ingredient of professional management and is included in the code of conduct of professional bodies, such as the Institute of Management. Best practice is shared through the international links between these professional bodies.

5.5 THE CULTURAL CONTEXT

The earlier section about stakeholder expectations sought to explain why differences in expectations might arise between stakeholders. It would be easy to conclude that such political pressures would result in a vast variation in the types of strategy individual organisations would be pursuing – even in the same

Exhibit 5.9	Cultural frames of reference

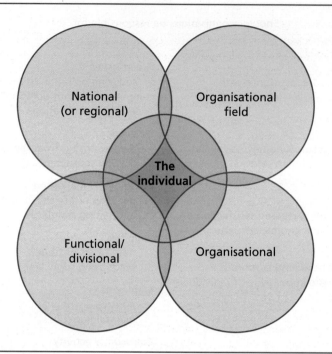

industry or market. But this is rarely the case, as has already been observed in Chapter 3 in the discussion of strategic groups. Importantly, the experience lens (introduced in section 2.2.2 and used throughout the book) introduced the idea that strategy is shaped by institutionalisation and expectations of conformity. So in practice there is a much higher level of commonality between the strategies of different organisations than might be expected. In some instances this may be deemed necessary to protect the interests of particular stakeholders and becomes enshrined in regulation or in corporate governance (for example, in pharmaceuticals or financial services). However, this uniformity is more often explained in cultural terms. In section 2.2.2 it was seen that organisations can be captured by their culture, which is the product of history, and/or by institutional forces that exist across organisations. So trying to understand culture is clearly important; but it is not straightforward.

Exhibit 2.4 showed that there are a variety of cultural frames of reference which might impinge on individuals (and through them the organisation). This is reproduced here as Exhibit 5.9. The sections that follow will build on that introductory discussion of culture in two ways:

● To identify the important factors and issues in each of the cultural *frames of reference.*

● To show how organisational culture can be *characterised*, as a means of understanding the influences of culture on both current and future organisational purposes and strategies.

5.5.1 National and regional cultures[25]

The national cultural context influences the expectations of stakeholders directly. For example, attitudes to work, authority, equality and a number of other important factors differ from one location to another.[26]

It is important to understand these influences, for two reasons. First, values of society change and adjust over time, and therefore strategies which were acceptable and successful twenty years ago may not be so today. For example, there has been an increasing trend within many countries for the activities of companies to be constrained by legislation, public opinion and the media. Second, organisations that operate *internationally* have the added problem of coping with the very different standards and expectations of the various countries in which they operate.[27] Illustration 5.6 shows how this can create issues and difficulties in mergers between British and French companies.

Although they are not shown separately in Exhibit 5.9 (for reasons of simplification), it may often be necessary to identify important *subnational* (usually regional) cultures. For example, attitudes to some aspects of employment, supplier relationships and, certainly, consumer preferences would differ significantly at a regional level even in a relatively small and cohesive country like the UK, and quite markedly elsewhere in Europe (e.g. between northern and southern Italy). There also are developing aspects of *supranational* culture beyond a single nation. For example, moves towards a 'Euro-consumer' with converging tastes and preferences are of crucial strategic importance to many organisations in planning their product and distribution strategies.

5.5.2 The organisational field

The concept of the *organisational field* was introduced in Chapters 2 and 3. An **organisational field** is a community of organisations that partake of a common meaning system and whose participants interact more frequently with one another than with those outside the field.[28] Organisations within a field tend to cohere around common norms and values. For example, there are many organisations in the organisational field of 'justice' (such as lawyers, police, courts, prisons and probation services), as mentioned in Chapters 3 and 4 (see Illustration 4.5). Although their roles are different (they are all specialists) and their detailed prescriptions as to how justice should be achieved will differ, they are all tied together into the same 'politico-economic system' and they are all committed to the principle that justice is a good thing which is worth striving for. In Chapter 3 the 'economic implications' of these relationships were discussed. The discussion here will be about how these relationships influence an organisation's purposes and strategies (and place boundaries around what is desirable or even possible).

Each organisation in the field may exercise a different type of influence. Some may exercise regulatory authority over other organisations – for example, a state agency. Others may reflect the influence of societal norms – for example, the local community. Others, including customers, suppliers and competitors,

*An **organisational field** is a community of organisations that partake of a common meaning system and whose participants interact more frequently with one another than with those outside the field*

Illustration 5.6

Cross-Channel mergers

National cultures can get in the way of successful cross-border mergers.

French and British companies approach business in different ways – strongly shaped by the different national cultures. This can be an important impediment to successful mergers unless managers are aware of these differences and able to manage their impact within the merged companies. The first difference shows in attitudes to ownership. In the late 1990s, France still had more companies in state-ownership than Britain. This created a greater closeness between the public and private sectors. Also, some of the best brains from the Grandes Ecoles will have worked both in the civil service and in companies – whereas in Britain these tend to be two different career paths. British managers are strongly driven by shareholder value whereas their French counterparts tend to take more of an inclusive stakeholder approach. This is reflected in differences in regulations and procedures – for example, in UK insolvency procedures, banks stand above most creditors whereas in France under *redressment judiciaire* the interests of employees rank above those of banks.

The impact of national culture is also seen in the day-to-day ways that companies function. The French are much more committed to rational, analytical approaches to decision making whereas the British tend to get straight to the point and rely more on 'gut feel'. Meetings in France are held mainly to rubber stamp what has already been decided by 'the boss'. The British expect to go to meetings to influence decisions. The membership of meetings tends to reflect these different purposes. The French have more people involved – since it is part of the education and communication process. In Britain the membership is usually confined to those who have a 'right' to influence the decision.

There is also the difficult issue of which language should be used – which is particularly difficult with British/French mergers because of the chauvinistic attitudes in both countries. Then there are the issues of allocation of senior management posts and so on. A commonly used resolution to this problem is the 'pairing' of French MDs with British deputies (and vice versa). This may be a short-term political necessity but usually doesn't work for long.

Source: Adapted from A. Senter, 'Cross Channel culture club', *Management Today*, February 1999, pp. 73–5.

Questions

1. Imagine that you work for a French company that is considering a merger with a British company. Write a short executive report to your CEO listing the cultural clashes that might arise and how they could be handled.

2. Now write another report to the British CEO.

3. Do you feel that the rights of bankers as creditors should be high or low priority (as in the UK and France respectively)?

4. What might be the consequence to the development strategies of British companies of changing the situation in the UK to align with French law?

are likely to share common assumptions about acceptable or wise practice; what makes sense in terms of the strategic direction of organisations and how they go about pursuing that strategy.

But the point is that the organisational field is both the organisations comprising it and the assumptions they adhere to. So operating in that field means that organisations typically conform to those assumptions in order to be considered legitimate. This will be referred to in this book as the recipe.

A **recipe**[29] is a set of assumptions held in common within an organisational field about organisational purposes and a 'shared wisdom' on how to manage organisations. It may prove difficult for individual organisations to step out of line from this recipe without being dubbed mavericks, i.e. not legitimate. Such cultural influences can be advantageous – say to customers – in maintaining standards and consistency between individual providers. The danger is that managers become 'institutionalised' and do not see the lessons that can be learnt from outside their organisational field. Professions, or trade associations, can often be thought of as an attempt to formalise and institutionalise an organisational field where the membership is exclusive and the behaviours of members become regulated.

Because the dominant culture varies from one field to another, the transition of managers between sectors can prove quite difficult. A number of private sector managers were encouraged to join public services during the 1990s in an attempt to inject new cultures and outlooks into the public sector. Many were surprised at the difficulties they experienced in adjusting their management style to the different traditions and expectations of their new organisation – for example, in issues like consensus building as part of the decision-making process. Many public sector organisations were privatised, creating important changes to their organisational field (as shown in Illustration 5.7) and requiring new behaviours within the privatised companies.

Of course, these same problems can occur when switching between cultures at any of the levels shown in Exhibit 5.9. So managers in multinational companies experience this when switching between geographical divisions (in different regions/countries). Others experience problems if they change functions in the organisation (say from engineering to manufacturing).

The practical implication of these comments is that *legitimacy* is an important influence on an organisation's purposes and strategies in the following ways:

- Legitimacy can be shaped by several factors, most notably coercive regulation (e.g. legislation or other forms of regulative influence), normative expectations (e.g. what society expects), or simply that which is taken for granted as being appropriate.

- Over time, there tends to develop a consensus amongst managers in an organisational field about strategies that will be successful or that are legitimate – this is the recipe discussed above.

- Strategies themselves become legitimised. An organisation's strategy is acceptable if it is recognised as such by the organisational field. Stepping outside that strategy may be risky because important stakeholders may not go along with it.

A **recipe** is a set of assumptions held in common within an organisational field about organisational purposes and a 'shared wisdom' on how to manage organisations

Illustration 5.7

Rail privatisation – changing organisational fields

STRATEGY IN ACTION

Major changes in the business environment, such as privatisation, can create – indeed may be intended to create – significant changes to the organisational field.

Prior to privatisation in the mid-1990s the UK railway network was run by a single public sector operator – British Rail (BR). The organisation was vertically integrated, from heavy manufacturing and engineering through rail operations to computer services and travel agency, railway police and telecommunications. It was inextricably linked to government policy, financial subsidy and political constraints on capital expenditure. The relationships of BR to industrial customers such as electricity generators, coal mining and steel producers (themselves within the public sector) was set by government policy and regulated accordingly. The expression of expectations placed upon BR by customers and through the media became virtually ritualised. Labour relations were heavily politicised in terms of rival postures of political parties and centralised negotiations with trade unions. Under the stewardship of BR the railway had become a highly institutionalised public sector organisation. Most BR staff enjoyed lifelong careers in the railway and identified themselves as 'railwaymen'. Senior staff careers moved around BR and there was a 'club' ambience to their interrelationships. In addition, the interdependent nature of rail operations had evolved a network of mutual obligations between the various parts

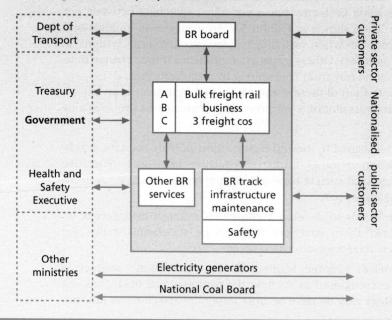

Figure 1 A representation of the organisational field of British Rail bulk freight business: pre-privatisation

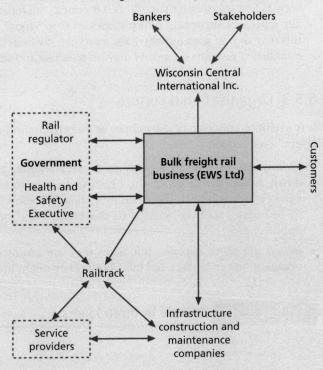

Figure 2 A representation of the organisational field of British Rail bulk freight business: post-privatisation

of the railway system. Figure 1 shows this organisational field for one part of the business – bulk freight.

The privatisation of BR freight's major customers (coal, steel and electricity) and the process of BR privatisation inevitably exposed the management teams to alternative institutional templates. Not least were the market-based changes that took form in the demands of powerful buyers and competition, as well as other reconstituted relationships within the railway's organisational field. By 1997 BR no longer existed in a substantial form and the bulk freight companies were in direct negotiated relationships with customers, government and providers of rail services (see Figure 2). This was a difficult period

for managers and employees as they tried to make sense of the forces unleashed upon them.

Source: 'Games people play: exploring micro processes of institutional change in the privatization of British Rail'; a working paper by Gerry Johnson, Stuart Smith and Brian Codling.

Question

1. Given the changes in the organisational field for the bulk freight business, use the cultural web (Exhibit 5.11 on page 230) to map out the key changes in behaviours that would be needed in the company.

2. How could those changes be achieved?

- Therefore, organisations tend to mimic each other's strategies; this is discussed in Chapter 6. This is so particularly in times of uncertainty. There will be differences in strategies between organisations but within bounds of legitimacy;[30] or if some organisations differ markedly they are likely to be seen as less legitimate than others. Of course, such fringe players may actually represent successful future strategies (e.g. Virgin, Direct Line etc.), but this may not be seen initially – for example, customers may remain loyal to established providers; bankers may be reluctant to fund these ventures.

5.5.3 Organisational culture

It is useful to conceive of the culture of an organisation as consisting of three layers[31] (see Exhibit 5.10):

- *Values* may be easy to identify in an organisation, and are often written down as statements about the organisation's mission, objectives or strategies (which will be as discussed in section 5.6 below). However, they tend to be vague, such as 'service to the community' or 'equal employment opportunities'.

- *Beliefs* are more specific, but again they are issues which people in the organisation can surface and talk about. They might include a belief that the

---

Exhibit 5.10   Culture in three layers

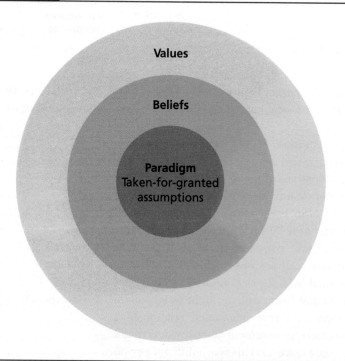

Source: Adapted from E. Schein, *Organisation Culture and Leadership*, Jossey-Bass, 1997.

company should not trade with particular countries, or that professional
staff should not have their professional actions appraised by managers.

● *Taken-for-granted assumptions* as the core of an organisation's culture.
They are the aspects of organisational life which people find difficult to
identify and explain. Here they are referred to as the organisational *paradigm*
– the importance of which was discussed in section 2.2.2. It will be seen
below, in the discussion of the cultural web, that the paradigm is maintained and reinforced by the taken-for-granted ways of doing things in the
organisation.

As organisations increasingly make visible their carefully considered public
statements of their values, beliefs and purposes – for example, in annual
reports, mission statements and business plans – there is a danger that these
are seen as useful and accurate descriptions of the organisational paradigm. But
they are likely to be at best only partially accurate, and at worst misleading.
This is not to suggest that there is any organised deception. It is simply that the
statements of values and beliefs are often statements of the aspirations of a particular stakeholder (such as the CEO) rather than accurate descriptions of the
culture as it exists in terms of what goes on in and around the organisation.
This 'real' culture is evidenced by the way the people in the organisation actually behave: it is the taken-for-granted assumptions about 'how you run an
organisation like this' and 'what really matters around here'. For example, an
outside observer of a police force might conclude from its public statements of
purpose and priorities that it had a balanced approach to the various aspects
of police work – catching criminals, crime prevention, community relations,
etc. However, a deeper probing might quickly reveal that (in cultural terms)
there is the 'real' police work (catching criminals) and the 'lesser work' (crime
prevention, community relations).

5.5.4 Functional and divisional cultures

In seeking to understand the relationship between culture and an organisation's strategies, it may be possible to identify some aspects of culture that
pervade the whole organisation. However, there may also be important *subcultures* within organisations. These subcultures may arise in a number of
ways – some of which are concerned with one or more of the external frames
of reference already mentioned, such as unions or professions. The subcultures may also relate directly to the structure of the organisation. For example,
the differences between geographical divisions in a multinational company,
or between functional groups such as finance, marketing and operations, can
be very powerful, to the extent that they can be self-perpetuating (see section 5.5.6 below) and exclusive. These differences between divisions may be
particularly evident in organisations that have grown through acquisition. Also,
different divisions may be pursuing different types of strategy, as discussed in
Chapter 7. These different market positionings require or foster different cultures. Indeed, it will be seen later (Chapter 11) that aligning strategic positioning and organisational culture is a critical feature of successful organisations.

Exhibit 5.11   The cultural web

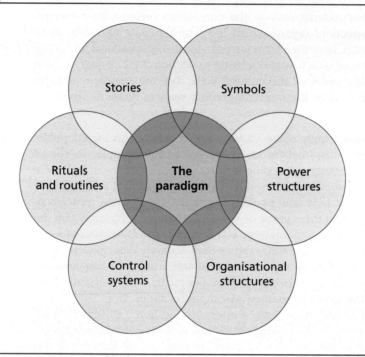

5.5.5 The cultural web[32]

Trying to understand the culture at all of these levels is clearly important, but it is not straightforward. For example, it has already been noted that even when a strategy and the values of an organisation are written down, the underlying assumptions which make up the paradigm are usually evident only in the way in which people behave day-to-day. To understand the taken-for-grantedness may mean being very sensitive to what is signified by the physical manifestations of culture evident in an organisation. Indeed, it is especially important to understand these wider aspects because not only do they give clues about the paradigm, but they are also likely to reinforce the assumptions within that paradigm. In effect, they are the representation in organisational action of what is taken for granted (i.e. they are also taken for granted). As mentioned in section 2.4.2, it is these taken-for-granted assumptions that can result in strategic drift. The concept of the **cultural web** is a representation of the taken-for-granted assumptions, or paradigm, of an organisation and the physical manifestations of organisational culture (see Exhibit 5.11). The cultural web can be used to understand culture in any of the frames of reference discussed above.[33]

Culture can be analysed by observing the way in which the organisation (or organisational field or nation) actually behaves – the cultural artefacts (the

The **cultural web** is a representation of the taken-for-granted assumptions, or paradigm, of an organisation and the physical manifestations of organisational culture routines, rituals, stories, structures, systems, etc.). Out of these will also come the *clues* about the taken-for-granted assumptions. To use an analogy, it is like trying to describe an iceberg (which is mainly submerged). This is done by observing the parts of the iceberg that show and also (from these clues) inferring what the submerged part of the iceberg must look like.

Illustration 5.8 shows a cultural web drawn up by trust managers in the National Health Service in the UK.[34] It would be similar to many other state-owned health care systems in other countries. It should, however, be borne in mind that this is the view of managers; clinicians might well have quite different views.

Exhibit 5.12 outlines some of the questions that might help build up an understanding of culture through the elements of the cultural web:

- The *routine* ways that members of the organisation behave towards each other, and towards those outside the organisation, make up 'the way we do things around here'. At its best, this lubricates the working of the organisation, and may provide a distinctive and beneficial organisational competence. However, it can also represent a taken-for-grantedness about how things should happen which is extremely difficult to change and protective of core assumptions in the paradigm.

- The *rituals* of organisational life are the special events through which the organisation emphasises what is particularly important and reinforces 'the way we do things around here'. Examples of ritual can include relatively formal organisational processes – training programmes, interview panels, promotion and assessment procedures, sales conferences and so on. An extreme example, of course, is the ritualistic training of army recruits to prepare them for the discipline required in conflict. However, rituals can also be thought of as relatively informal processes such as drinks in the pub after work or gossiping around photocopying machines. A checklist of rituals is provided in Chapter 11 (see Exhibit 11.7).

- The *stories* told by members of the organisation to each other, to outsiders, to new recruits and so on, embed the present in its organisational history and also flag up important events and personalities. They typically have to do with successes, disasters, heroes, villains and mavericks who deviate from the norm. They distil the essence of an organisation's past, legitimise types of behaviour and are devices for telling people what is important in the organisation.

- *Symbols*[35] such as logos, offices, cars and titles, or the type of language and terminology commonly used, become a shorthand representation of the nature of the organisation. For example, in long-established or conservative organisations it is likely that there will be many symbols of hierarchy or deference to do with formal office layout, differences in privileges between levels of management, the way in which people address each other, and so on. In turn this formalisation may reflect difficulties in changing strategies within a hierarchical or deferential system. The form of language used in an organisation can also be particularly revealing, especially with regard to customers or clients. For example, the head of a consumer protection agency

Illustration 5.8

The cultural web of the NHS

The cultural web can be used to identify the taken-for-granted aspects of an organisation.

The diagram shows a cultural web produced by managers in the NHS in the 1990s.

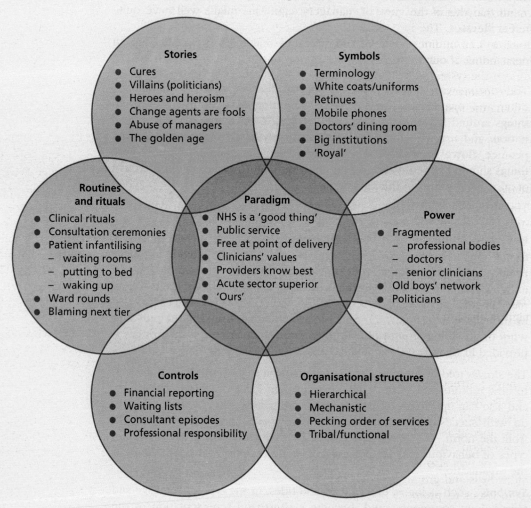

Stories
- Cures
- Villains (politicians)
- Heroes and heroism
- Change agents are fools
- Abuse of managers
- The golden age

Symbols
- Terminology
- White coats/uniforms
- Retinues
- Mobile phones
- Doctors' dining room
- Big institutions
- 'Royal'

Routines and rituals
- Clinical rituals
- Consultation ceremonies
- Patient infantilising
  - waiting rooms
  - putting to bed
  - waking up
- Ward rounds
- Blaming next tier

Paradigm
- NHS is a 'good thing'
- Public service
- Free at point of delivery
- Clinicians' values
- Providers know best
- Acute sector superior
- 'Ours'

Power
- Fragmented
  - professional bodies
  - doctors
  - senior clinicians
- Old boys' network
- Politicians

Controls
- Financial reporting
- Waiting lists
- Consultant episodes
- Professional responsibility

Organisational structures
- Hierarchical
- Mechanistic
- Pecking order of services
- Tribal/functional

Routines and rituals

This took form, for example, in routines of consultation and of prescribing drugs. Rituals had to do with what the managers termed 'infantilising', which 'put patients in their place' – making them wait, putting them to bed, waking them up and so on. The subservience of patients was further emphasised by the elevation of clinicians with ritual consultation ceremonies and ward rounds. These are routines and rituals which emphasise that it is the professionals who are in control.

Stories

Most of the stories within health services concern developments in curing – particularly terminal illnesses. The heroes of the health service are in curing, not so much in caring. There are also stories about villainous politicians trying to change the system, the failure of those who try to make changes and of heroic acts by those defending the system (often well-known medical figures).

Symbols

Symbols reflected the various institutions within the organisation, with uniforms for clinical and nursing staff, distinct symbols for clinicians, such as their staff retinues, and status symbols such as mobile phones and dining rooms. The importance of the size and status of hospitals was reflected, not least, in the designation of 'Royal' in the name, seen as a key means of ensuring that it might withstand the threat of closure.

Power structures

The power structure was fragmented between clinicians, nurses and managers. However, historically, senior clinicians were the most powerful and managers had hitherto been seen as 'administration'. As with many other organisations, there was also a strong informal network of individuals and groups that coalesced around specific issues to promote or resist a particular view.

Organisational structures

Structures were hierarchical and mechanistic. There was a clear pecking order between services,

with the 'caring' services low down the list – for example, mental health. At the informal level there was lots of 'tribalism' between functions and professional groups.

Control systems

In hospitals the key measure has been 'completed clinical episodes', i.e. activity rather than results. Control over staff is exerted by senior professionals. Patronage is a key feature of this professional culture.

The paradigm

The assumptions which constitute the paradigm reflect the common public perception in the UK that the NHS is a 'good thing'; a public service which should be provided equally, free of charge at the point of delivery. However, it is medical values that are central and the view that 'medics know best'. This is an organisation concerned with curing illness rather than preventing illness in the first place. For example, pregnancy is not an illness, but pregnant women often argue that hospitals treat them as though they are ill. It is the acute sector within hospitals that is central to the service rather than, for example, care in the community. Overall, the NHS is seen as belonging to those who provide the services.

Questions

1. Read through section 5.5.5 of the text and ensure that you understand what are the elements of the cultural web (using this NHS managers example).

2. From all the detail in this web, develop up to four statements, which together you feel would encapsulate the culture of the NHS at that time.

3. What are the implications of this analysis in terms of the ease or difficulty with which new strategies might be developed?

Exhibit 5.12	The cultural web: some useful questions

Stories
- What core beliefs do stories reflect?
- How pervasive are these beliefs (through levels)?
- Do stories relate to:
  - strengths or weaknesses?
  - successes or failures?
  - conformity or mavericks?
- Who are the heroes and villains?
- What norms do the mavericks deviate from?

Routines and rituals
- Which routines are emphasised?
- Which would look odd if changed?
- What behaviour do routines encourage?
- What are the key rituals?
- What core beliefs do they reflect?
- What do training programmes emphasise?
- How easy are rituals/routines to change?

Organisational structures
- How mechanistic/organic are the structures?
- How flat/hierarchical are the structures?
- How formal/informal are the structures?
- Do structures encourage collaboration or competition?
- What types of power structure do they support?

Control systems
- What is most closely monitored/controlled?
- Is emphasis on reward or punishment?
- Are controls related to history or current strategies?
- Are there many/few controls?

Power structures
- What are the core beliefs of the leadership?
- How strongly held are these beliefs (idealists or pragmatists)?
- How is power distributed in the organisation?
- Where are the main blockages to change?

Symbols
- What language and jargon are used?
- How internal or accessible are they?
- What aspects of strategy are highlighted in publicity?
- What status symbols are there?
- Are there particular symbols which denote the organisation?

Overall
- What is the dominant culture?
- How easy is this to change?

in Australia described his clients as 'complainers', and in a major teaching hospital in the UK, consultants described patients as 'clinical material'. Whilst such examples might be amusing, they reveal an underlying assumption about customers (or patients) which might play a significant role in influencing the strategy of an organisation.

Although symbols are shown separately in the cultural web, it should be remembered that many elements of the web are symbolic, in the sense that they convey messages beyond their functional purpose. Routines, control and reward systems and structures are symbolic in so far as they signal the type of behaviour valued in an organisation.

- *Power structures* are also likely to be associated with the key assumptions. The paradigm is, in some respects, the 'formula for success', which is taken for granted and likely to have grown up over years. The most powerful groupings within the organisation are likely to be closely associated with this set of core assumptions and beliefs.

  For example, accountancy firms may now offer a whole range of services, but typically the most powerful individuals or groups have been qualified chartered accountants with a set of assumptions about the business and its market rooted in the audit practice. Power may be based not just on seniority. In some organisations, power could be lodged within other levels or functions: for example, with technical experts in a high-tech firm.

- The *control systems*, measurements and reward systems emphasise what it is important to monitor in the organisation, and to focus attention and activity upon. For example, public service organisations have often been accused of being concerned more with stewardship of funds than with quality of service. This is reflected in their procedures, which are more with accounting for spending than with regard for outputs. Reward systems are important influences on behaviours, but can also prove to be a barrier to success of new strategies. For example, an organisation with individually based bonus schemes related to volume could find it difficult to promote strategies requiring teamwork and an emphasis on quality rather than volume.

- *Organisational structure* is likely to reflect power structures and, again, delineate important relationships and emphasise what is important in the organisation. Formal hierarchical, mechanistic structures may emphasise that strategy is the province of top managers and everyone else is 'working to orders'. Highly devolved structures (as discussed in Chapter 9) may signify that collaboration is less important than competition and so on.

- *The paradigm* of the organisation encapsulates and reinforces the behaviours observed in the other elements of the cultural web. The illustration shows that the overall picture of the NHS was of a system fundamentally about medical practice, fragmented in its power bases historically, with a division between clinical aspects of the organisation and its management; indeed, a system in which management had traditionally been seen as relatively trivial. As one executive put it: 'there is an arrogance of clinicians, but it is a justifiable arrogance; after all, it is they who deliver on the shopfloor, not management'.

The cultural web is, then, a useful concept for understanding the underlying assumptions linked to political, symbolic and structural aspects of an organisation.

5.5.6 Characterising an organisation's culture

In understanding the influence of culture on organisational purposes, it is important to be able to characterise culture. It is in this way that judgements can be made about the ease or difficulty the organisation would experience in pursuing different kinds of strategy. Three different ways of characterising culture will be briefly described.

The graphic descriptor

Sometimes it is possible to capture the essence of an organisation's culture in a simple graphic descriptor. For example, the NHS cultural web in Illustration 5.8 could be summed up as 'The National Sickness Service'. Sometimes this can be done to define the dominant culture of different strategic groups within a sector. For example, comparing cultural webs for old and new universities in the UK, they could be characterised as 'Boffins and Gurus' and 'Teaching Factories' respectively. The cultural webs of even large companies sometimes would deserve the cultural characterisation of 'The Family Firm'. Although this approach is rather crude and unscientific, it can be very powerful in terms of organisational members seeing the organisation as it really is – which may not be immediately apparent from all of the detailed points in the cultural web. The importance of this is in getting people to understand that culture drives strategies – for example, a 'national sickness service' would clearly prioritise strategies that are about spectacular developments in curing sick people above health promotion strategies. So those favouring health promotion strategies need to understand how they can gain support in such a cultural context rather than assuming that rational processes like planning and resource allocation will be adequate in themselves.

Miles and Snow[36]

Miles and Snow categorised organisations into three basic types in terms of how they behave strategically (Exhibit 5.13A). A *defender* organisation will behave quite differently from a *prospector* organisation. For example, defender cultures find change threatening and tend to favour strategies which provide continuity and 'security'. This is supported by a bureaucratic approach to management which may make the organisation averse to innovation. In contrast, a prospector culture thrives on change, favouring strategies of product and market development supported by a more creative and flexible management style. It is a culture in which innovation can prosper. Again, the importance of this characterisation is to make managers aware that an organisation will lean towards those strategies that best fit the culture. Adoption of other strategies must be supported by efforts to shift culture – at least in the part of the organisation that will be driving that strategy. This will be discussed more fully in Chapter 11.

Exhibit 5.13	Characterising culture

A. Miles and Snow

TYPE OF CULTURE	CHARACTERISTICS OF STRATEGIC DECISION MAKING		
	DOMINANT OBJECTIVES	PREFERRED STRATEGIES	PLANNING AND CONTROL SYSTEMS
Defender	Desire for a secure and stable niche in market	Specialisation; cost-efficient production; marketing emphasises price and service to defend current business; tendency to vertical integration	Centralised, detailed control; emphasis on cost efficiency; extensive use of formal planning
Prospector	Location and exploitation of new product and market opportunities	Growth through product and market development (often in spurts); constant monitoring of environmental change; multiple technologies	Emphasis on flexibility; decentralised control; use of ad hoc measurements
Analyser	Desire to match new ventures to present shape of business	Steady growth through market penetration; exploitation of applied research, followers in the market	Very complicated; co-ordinating roles between functions (e.g. product managers); intensive planning

Source: Adapted from R.E. Miles and C.C. Snow, *Organizational Strategy, Structure and Process*, McGraw-Hill, 1978.

B. Handy

TYPE OF CULTURE	CHARACTERISTICS		
	STRATEGY DRIVEN BY:	MODUS OPERANDI	SUITED TO DELIVER:
Role culture	Committees	Structures and systems	Efficiency Repetitive tasks
Task culture	Teams	Shared values Ad hoc procedures	Projects or tasks Innovation
Power culture	Leaders	Command	Rapid response
Personal culture	Individuals	Personal creativity Expert power	Innovation

Source: Adapted from C. Handy, *Understanding Organisations*, 4th edition, Penguin, 1993.

Handy[37]

Handy characterised culture in terms of the relationship between the organisation and individuals and also the importance of power and hierarchy. Again, different cultures will behave differently, as shown in Exhibit 5.13B. For example, each of these four cultures would approach a strategy such as product development in different ways. A *role culture* would have well-sorted arrangements for interdepartmental meetings and a schedule of tasks against time-scales to ensure the development and launch goes smoothly. A *task culture* may prefer to create an ad hoc project team to see the 'project' through. A *power culture* would support the strategy by the chief executive (or other senior figure) personally and actively issuing instructions indicating who does what and by when. Finally, a *personal culture* would rely on the personal motivation and inventiveness of individuals. The implications again are the same as those discussed above. Culture will drive strategies which best fit these characteristics. For example, power or personal cultures will drive strategies that are 'manageable' in a defined part of an organisation and avoid strategies that require complex coordination and collaboration with others.

When characterising organisational cultures it is important to understand:

- There is not a 'best' and 'worst' culture. The issue is that culture is likely to drive strategy, as shown above, and therefore cutural mismatches are likely to occur when organisations are trying to change strategy. For example:
  - A 'low-price' positioning (on the strategy clock – see Exhibit 7.2) – for example, a *commodity* product or service is likely to be matched to a *defender, role or process* culture. The innovative nature of some other cultures could make it difficult to contain costs within an acceptable level without demotivating people.
  - In contrast, a positioning of differentiation – perhaps through product features or service quality – requires more creative behaviours and this will match well with a *prospector or personal* culture.

- This matching of strategy and dominant culture is likely to become embedded in successful organisations over a period of time. In other words, the key elements of the strategy become taken for granted and may represent core competences of the organisation, as mentioned in Chapter 4. Indeed, the relationship between strategy and dominant culture is usually *self-perpetuating*. So not only does a defender culture match well with a 'commodity' positioning, but it is likely to seek out those parts of the market which secure such a positioning. This is called reinforcing cycles and will be discussed in Chapter 9. Moreover, the organisational routines – for example, *selection and recruitment* – are likely to perpetuate the dominant culture by not selecting individuals who will 'rock the boat'.

- In many organisations, *cohesiveness* of culture is found at a level below the corporate entity, as discussed in section 5.5.5 above. There is a continuing debate about the extent to which cohesiveness or diversity of culture is a strength or a weakness in organisations.

5.6 COMMUNICATING ORGANISATIONAL PURPOSES

The previous sections have looked at the factors that influence organisational purposes – the corporate governance framework, stakeholder relationships, ethical standards and culture. This section will look at ways in which organisations attempt to explicitly communicate purposes, for example through statements of *mission, vision, intent* and *objectives*. In some instances such statements may be a formal requirement of corporate governance. In others they may be expected of the organisation by one or more stakeholders. Illustration 5.9 is an example for a social services department of a local government authority. Despite this, it must be remembered that these statements may not be an accurate reflection of the priorities within the organisation, for the political and cultural reasons discussed above.

5.6.1 Mission statements

A **mission statement** is a generalised statement of the overriding purpose of an organisation. It can be thought of as an expression of its *raison d'être.* If there is substantial disagreement within the organisation or with stakeholders as to its mission, it may well give rise to real problems in resolving the strategic direction of the organisation.

> A **mission statement** is a generalised statement of the overriding purpose of an organisation

Although mission statements have become much more widely adopted in the 1990s and 2000s, many critics regard them as bland and wide-ranging. However, this may be necessary given the political nature of strategic management, since it is essential *at that level* to have statements to which most, if not all, stakeholders can subscribe. They need to emphasise the common ground amongst stakeholders and not the differences.

Mission statements usually attempt to address some of the following issues:[38]

- A *vision*[39] that is likely to persist for a significant period of time as a 'beacon in the distance' towards which an organisation can strive.

- Provide clarity on the main *intentions and aspirations* of an organisation. Hamel and Prahalad[40] prefer the term *strategic intent* to that of vision or mission; they see it as an 'animating dream'. They argue that a powerful **strategic intent** is one that encapsulates the desired future state or aspiration of an organisation – the sense of discovery and destiny – that motivates managers and employees alike throughout the organisation. The view taken here is that, in practice, mission, vision and strategic intent are used fairly interchangeably by managers.

> **Strategic intent** is the desired future state or aspiration of an organisation

- Describe the organisation's main activities and the position it wishes to attain in its industry. Many statements talk about being 'the leader' or 'the best'.

- Be a statement of the key *values* of the organisation, particularly regarding attitudes towards stakeholder groups and the ethical agenda discussed earlier.

Mission statements are used differently by organisations in different circumstances (see Exhibit 5.14):

- If strategy is driven by managers who see other stakeholders and the corporate governance requirements largely as constraints, they may be *secretive* about organisational purposes and see little value in mission statements.

Illustration 5.9

STRATEGY IN ACTION

Organisational purposes for a social services department

Organisations are finding it useful to publish a statement of their purposes. This is usually done at several levels of detail.

As part of its strategic plan for 2000–2003, Sheffield City Council Social Services Department outlined its purposes, priorities and targets. The following are extracts from this plan.

1. Statement of purpose
We will work within the framework of the law and our resources to:
- protect and strengthen the well-being of people and families in Sheffield, focusing on the most vulnerable;
- work together with people, their families and with other organisations to ensure the provision of helpful, timely and good value social services.

2. Primary objectives for 2000–2003
We will:
- ensure all our statutory duties are fulfilled;
- ensure that people can easily and quickly contact us for advice and help;
- make timely and accurate assessments of need, taking into account people's circumstances, culture, age, sex, health, disability and sexuality;
- apply the rules for arranging services (eligibility criteria) fairly and consistently;
- provide clear care plans [to clients] to explain how we will arrange and provide help and support;
- regularly check that help and support are being provided and are of an acceptable standard;
- ensure our workforce is effectively supported and managed and that expenditure is controlled within cash limits.

3. Service priorities – people with mental health problems[1]
Priorities for 2000/2001 are to:
- develop an integrated adult mental health service with Community Health Sheffield;[2]

- reorganise community mental health teams to focus on access and assessment and provide effective services for people with serious mental illness;
- continue implementation of the Government's National Service Framework Development Plan[3] in conjunction with our partners;
- ensure that investment from the mental health grant is allocated in line with this government framework.

4. Targets (mental health)
We will be meeting our objectives if we see:
- fewer people readmitted to hospital;
- all service users with an identified care co-ordinator;
- an increase in the number of community support and short-term care places.

Notes
1. There were annual service plans for each area – this is one example.
2. This is a health care agency.
3. This plan concerned improvements in mental health care through better inter-agency working.

Source: Sheffield City Council.

Questions
1. How useful are these various statements of purpose to the shaping and implementation of the department's strategy? In answering the question, ensure that you give a critique of each of the various 'levels' of statement in order to establish:
   (a) what it is meant to achieve;
   (b) whether you feel that it does so;
   (c) any improvements you would suggest.
2. Comment on the extent to which these various levels of purpose are consistent with each other.

Exhibit 5.14	The role of mission statements

		ETHICAL STANCE	
		Legal minimum	**Ideological**
DRIVERS OF STRATEGY	**Internal managers**	Secretive	Evangelical
	External stakeholders	Regulations and procedures	Political

When they do exist, they are simply paid lip-service and are not powerful influences on the strategic development of the organisation.

- In contrast, managers who have a missionary zeal for the organisation are likely to use the mission statement in an *evangelical* way to 'sell' purposes to other stakeholders. The mission of the organisation is closely aligned to the *strategic intent* of these managers.

- Where strategy is dominated by powerful external stakeholders whose main concern is that the organisation *complies* with the corporate governance arrangements. Complying with regulations and procedures becomes the purpose and any sense of mission may be lost. This is the classic faceless bureaucracy found in the centrally planned economies of eastern Europe prior to 1990.

- In contrast, if strategy is dominated by external stakeholder(s) with missionary zeal, the purposes of the organisation may become highly politicised. So the ability to produce a mission statement acceptable to all stakeholders can be difficult.

5.6.2 Objectives

Objectives are statements of specific outcomes that are to be achieved. Objectives – both at the corporate and business unit level – are often expressed in financial terms. They could be the expression of desired sales or profit levels, rates of growth, dividend levels or share valuations. But organisations also have market-based objectives, many of which are quantified as targets – such as market share, customer-service, repeat business and so on. Also, objectives might relate to how the organisation intends to address the expectations of other stakeholders, such as customers, suppliers, employees and the community at large.

Many writers[41] have argued that objectives are not helpful unless they are capable of being measured and achieved, i.e. unless they are closed. This view

> **Objectives** are statements of specific outcomes that are to be achieved

is not taken here. Open statements may be just as helpful as closed statements. There may be some objectives which are important, but which are difficult to quantify or express in measurable terms. An objective such as 'to be a leader in technology' may be highly relevant in today's technological environment, but it may become absurd if it has to be expressed in some measurable way. It is nonetheless valid as an objective.

However, there are times when specific objectives are required. These are likely to be when urgent action is needed, such as in a crisis or at times of major transition, and it becomes essential for management to focus attention on a limited number of priority requirements. An extreme example would be in a *turnround* situation. If the choice is between going out of business and surviving, there is no room for latitude through vaguely stated requirements and control.

SUMMARY

- Expectations and purposes are influenced by four main factors: corporate governance, stakeholder expectations, business ethics and culture.

- The *corporate governance* arrangements determine whom the organisation is there to serve and how the purposes and priorities should be decided. Corporate governance has become more complex for two main reasons: first, the separation of ownership and management control, and second, the increasing tendency to make organisations more visibly accountable to a wider range of stakeholders.

- Stakeholders differ in terms of the power that they hold and the extent to which they are actively interested in the strategies that an organisation is pursuing (or planning to pursue). Although they may be in agreement about the broad purposes of an organisation, at a more detailed level there are usually different expectations amongst different stakeholders. *Stakeholder mapping* can help with understanding these differences.

- Purposes are also influenced by the *ethical stance* taken by the organisation about its relationships with the wider society within which it operates. This stance may vary from a narrow view that the short-term interests of shareholders should be paramount, through to some organisations that would see themselves as shapers of society. Within this broad stance, specific issues of *corporate social responsibility* will be important. There can also be ethical *dilemmas for individuals* within organisations if their personal values come into conflict with the ethical standards and behaviours in the organisation.

- Purposes are strongly influenced by cultural frames of reference at various 'levels'. This ranges from the national culture, through the organisational field to the organisational culture and subcultures. All of these influence whether strategies are regarded as legitimate.

- Culture consists of 'layers' of values, beliefs and taken-for-granted assumptions and ways of doing things in organisations. The *cultural web* is a useful concept for understanding how these connect and influence strategy.

- It is useful to understand and characterise both the culture and the subcultures in an organisation. This can help in understanding the ease or difficulty with which new strategies could be adopted.

- Organisational purposes can be communicated at different levels of detail, from an overall mission statement through to detailed operational objectives for the various parts of the organisation.

RECOMMENDED KEY READINGS

- R.I. Tricker, *International Corporate Governance: Text, cases and readings*, Prentice Hall, 1999, remains the most comprehensive book on corporate governance. Also useful is A. Davies, *A Strategic Approach to Corporate Governance*, Gower, 1999.

- For more about the stakeholder concept, read I.I. Mitroff, *Stakeholders of the Organisational Mind*, Jossey-Bass, 1983, or R.E. Freeman, *Strategic Management: A stakeholder approach*, Pitman, 1984, or K. Scholes' chapter in V. Ambrosini with G. Johnson and K. Scholes (eds), *Exploring Techniques of Analysis and Evaluation in Strategic Management*, Prentice Hall, 1998.

- Readers should be familiar with the political context of strategic decision making by reading J. Pfeffer, *Managing with Power: Politics and influence in organisations*, HBS Press, 1994.

- Readers can gain some useful insights into business ethics by reading: P. Werhane and R.E. Freeman, 'Business ethics: the state of the art', *International Journal of Management Research*, vol. 1, no. 1 March (1999), pp. 1–16.

- A useful book on corporate social responsibility is: W. Frederick, J. Post and K. Davis, *Business and Society: Management, public policy, ethics*, 7th edition, McGraw-Hill, 1992.

- E. Schein, *Organisation Culture and Leadership*, Jossey-Bass, 1997, is useful in understanding the relationship between organisational culture and strategy.

- An important paper on institutional theory and the concept of organisational fields is: P. DiMaggio and W. Powell, 'The iron cage revisited: institutional isomorphism and collective rationality in organizational fields', *American Sociological Review*, vol. 48 (1983), pp. 147–160.

- A full explanation of the cultural web can be found in G. Johnson, 'Managing strategic change: strategy, culture and action', *Long Range Planning*, vol. 25, no. 1 (1992), pp. 28–36. G. Johnson's chapter 'Mapping and re-mapping organisational culture' in V. Ambrosini with G. Johnson and K. Scholes (eds), *Exploring Techniques of Analysis and Evaluation in Strategic Management*, Prentice Hall, 1998, shows how to carry out a cultural web exercise.

- A comprehensive coverage of the influence of national culture on strategy can be found in R. Mead, *International Management: Crosscultural dimensions*, Blackwell, 1994. See also S. Schneider and J-L. Barsoux, *Managing Across Cultures*, Financial Times/Prentice Hall, 1997, Chapter 4.

REFERENCES

1. Useful general references on corporate governance are: A. Davies, *A Strategic Approach to Corporate Governance*, Gower, 1999; N. Bain and D. Band, *Winning Ways through Corporate Governance*, Macmillan, 1996; and R.I. Tricker, *International Corporate Governance: Text, cases and readings*, Prentice Hall, 1999 (which remains the most comprehensive book on the subject). Also, *Harvard Business Review on Corporate Governance*, HBS Press, 2000, is a collection of eight papers published in the journal during the 1990s. CIMA, *Corporate Governance:*

History, Practice and Future, 2000, is a guide for practising managers.

2. These differences between countries are discussed in the general books (reference 1 above) and also in: T. Clarke and S. Clegg, *Changing Paradigms: The transformation of management knowledge in the 21st century*, HarperCollins, 2000, Chapter 5.

3. This issue of to whom corporate managers should be accountable is discussed by J. Charkham, *Keeping Good Company: A study of corporate governance in five countries*, Clarendon Press, 1994, and J. Kay, 'The

stakeholder corporation', in G. Kelley, D. Kelly and A. Gamble, *Stakeholder Capitalism*, Macmillan, 1997.

4. Hampel Committee on Corporate Governance, 1997.

5. See reference 2 above and J. Charkham (reference 3 above).

6. Short-termism as an issue in the Anglo-American tradition is contrasted with the 'Rhine model' more typical of Germany, Switzerland, Benelux and northern European countries by M. Albert, 'The Rhine model of capitalism: an investigation', in W. Nicoll, D. Norburn and R. Schoenberg (eds), *Perspectives on European Business*, Whurr Publishers, London, 1995.

7. *Report of the Committee of Inquiry on Industrial Democracy*, Chairman: Lord Bullock, HMSO, 1977.

8. The privatisation of public utilities is discussed in P. Jackson and C. Price, *Privatisation and Regulation: A review of the issues*, Longman, 1994, Chapter 3.

9. E. Doyle, 'Implications of ownership for strategy: the example of commercial semi-state bodies in Ireland, in G. Johnson and K. Scholes (eds), *Exploring Public Sector Strategy*, Financial Times/Prentice Hall, 2001, Chapter 10.

10. The Report of the Committee on the Financial Aspects of Corporate Governance, 1992 and 1996 (The Cadbury Reports). CIPFA, *Corporate Governance in the Public Services: A discussion paper*, CIPFA, 1994, initiated a discussion as to how recommendations of the Cadbury Report might be translated into the public sector.

11. The early writing about stakeholders was concerned with 'coalitions' in organisations: for example, the seminal work by R.M. Cyert and J.G. March, *A Behavioural Theory of the Firm*, Prentice Hall, 1964. Later, stakeholder analysis became central to strategic analysis: for example, I.I. Mitroff, *Stakeholder of the Organisational Mind*, Jossey-Bass, 1983; R.E. Freeman, *Strategic Management: A stakeholder approach*, Pitman, 1984; J. Harrison and H. Caron, *Strategic Management of Organisations and Stakeholders: Concepts*, West Publishing, 1993.

12. T. Kostova and S. Zaheer, 'Organisational legitimacy under conditions of complexity: the case of the multinational enterprise', *Academy of Management Review*, vol. 24, no.1 (1999), pp. 64–81.

13. This approach to stakeholder mapping has been adapted from A. Mendelow, *Proceedings of 2nd International Conference on Information Systems*, Cambridge, MA, 1981. See also K. Scholes' chapter, 'Stakeholder analysis' in V. Ambrosini with G. Johnson and K. Scholes (eds), *Exploring Techniques of Analysis and Evaluation in Strategic Management*, Prentice Hall, 1998. For a public sector explanation see K. Scholes, 'Stakeholder mapping: a practical tool for public sector managers', in G. Johnson and K. Scholes (eds), *Exploring Public*

Sector Strategy, Financial Times/Prentice Hall, 2001, Chapter 9.

14. See Cyert and March (reference 11 above).

15. J. Pfeffer, *Managing with Power: Politics and influence in organisations*, HBS Press, 1994 (particularly part II, pp. 69–165), and C. Hardy (ed.), *Power and Politics in Organisations*, Ashgate, 1995, both provide a useful analysis of the relationship between power and strategy.

16. There is a prolific flow of literature on business ethics. Readers can gain some useful insights into the field by reading: P. Werhane and R.E. Freeman, 'Business Ethics: the state of the art', *International Journal of Management Research*, vol. 1, no. 1 March (1999), pp. 1–16. This is a useful summary of recent publications on business ethics. Practising managers might wish to consult: B. Kelley, *Ethics at Work*, Gower, 1999, which covers many of the issues in this section and includes the Institute of Management guidelines on ethical management.

17. Some authors propose more categories. For example, Marcus (reported in M. Jones, 'The institutional determinants of social responsibility', *Journal of Business Ethics*, vol. 20, no. 2 (1999), pp. 163–179) suggests five categories: narrow, financial, utilitarian, social justice and social harmony.

18. See reference 4 above.

19. H. Hummels, 'Organizing ethics: a stakeholder debate', *Journal of Business Ethics*, vol. 17, no. 13 (1998), pp. 1403–1419.

20. M. Jones – reference 17 above.

21. A useful book on corporate social responsibility is: W. Frederick, J. Post and K. Davis, *Business and Society: Management, public policy, ethics*, 7th edition, McGraw-Hill, 1992.

22. J. Charkham, 'Corporate governance lessons from abroad', *European Business Journal*, vol. 4, no. 2 (1992), pp. 8–16.

23. D. Clutterbuck, 'Corporate responsibility audit', in V. Ambrosini with G. Johnson and K. Scholes (eds), *Exploring Techniques of Analysis and Evaluation in Strategic Management*, Prentice Hall, 1998, Chapter 11.

24. R. Larmer, 'Whistleblowing and employee loyalty', *Journal of Business Ethics*, vol. 11, no. 2 (1992), pp. 125–128; M. Miceli and J. Near, *Blowing the Whistle: The organisational and legal implications for companies and employees*, Lexington Books, 1992.

25. One of the earlier works on the influence of national culture was G. Hofstede, *Culture's Consequences*, Sage, 1980. A comprehensive coverage of this topic can be found in R. Mead, *International Management: Cross-cultural dimensions*, Blackwell, 1994.

26. See S. Schneider and J-L. Barsoux, *Managing Across Cultures*, Financial Times/Prentice Hall, 1997. The

differences between national cultures are explained – particularly in Chapter 4.

27. See R. Lewis, *When Cultures Collide: Managing successfully across cultures*, 2nd edition, Brealey, 2000, a practical guide for managers. It offers an insight into different national cultures, business conventions and leadership styles. C. Buggy, 'Empathy is the key to cultural communication', *Professional Manager*, vol. 8, no. 1 (1999) argues that understanding cultural differences is crucial to success.

28. This definition is taken from W. Scott, *Institutions and organizations*, Sage, 1995.

29. The term 'recipe' was introduced to refer to *industries* by J. Spender, *Industry Recipes: The nature and sources of management judgement*, Blackwell, 1989. We have broadened its use by applying it to *organisational fields*. The fundamental idea that behaviours are driven by a collective set of norms and values remains unchanged.

30. D. Deephouse, 'To be different or to be the same?: It's a question (and theory) of strategic balance', *Strategic Management Journal*, vol. 20, no. 2 (1999), pp. 147-166.

31. E. Schein, *Organisation Culture and Leadership*, 2nd edition, Jossey-Bass, 1997.

32. A fuller explanation of the cultural web can be found in G. Johnson, *Strategic Change and the Management Process*, 1987, and G. Johnson, 'Managing strategic change: strategy, culture and action', *Long Range Planning*, vol. 25, no. 1 (1992), pp. 28-36.

33. A practical explanation of cultural web mapping can be found in G. Johnson, 'Mapping and re-mapping organisational culture', in V. Ambrosini with G. Johnson and K. Scholes (eds), *Exploring Techniques of* Analysis *and Evaluation in Strategic Management*, Prentice Hall, 1998.

34. A detailed public sector example of cultural web mapping can be found in G. Johnson, 'Mapping and re-Mapping organisational culture: a local government example', in G. Johnson and K. Scholes (eds), *Exploring Public Sector Strategy*, Financial Times/Prentice Hall, 2001, Chapter 17.

35. The significance of organisational symbolism is explained in G. Johnson, 'Managing strategic change: the role of symbolic action', *British Journal of Management*, vol. 1, no. 4 (1990), pp. 183-200.

36. R.E. Miles and C.C. Snow, *Organisational Strategy: Structure and process*, McGraw-Hill, 1978. Although this is now an old reference, it is still a useful way of characterising culture.

37. C. Handy, *Understanding Organisations*, 4th edition, Penguin, 1997.

38. See A. Campbell and K. Tawadey, *Mission and Business Philosophy*, Butterworth/Heinemann, 1993; A. Campbell, M. Devine and D. Young, *A Sense of Mission*, Financial Times/Pitman, 1990; J. Abrahams, *The Mission Statement Book*, Ten Speed Press, 1995.

39. The importance of vision is discussed in I. Wilson, 'Realising the power of vision', *Long Range Planning*, vol. 25, no. 5 (1992), pp. 18-28; and R. Whittington, *What is Strategy and Does it Matter?*, Routledge, 1993, Chapter 3.

40. See G. Hamel and C. Prahalad, 'Strategic intent', *Harvard Business Review*, vol. 67, no. 3 (1989), pp. 63-76.

41. For example, I. Ansoff, *Corporate Strategy*, Penguin, 1968, p. 44, argued that objectives should be precise and measurable.

WORK ASSIGNMENTS

* Refers to a case study in the Text and Cases edition. ✳ Denotes more advanced work assignments.

5.1 ✳ For an organisation of your choice, map out a governance chain that identifies all the key players through to the beneficiaries of the organisation's good (or poor) performance. To what extent do you think managers are:
(a) knowledgeable about the expectations of beneficiaries?
(b) actively pursuing their interests?
(c) keeping them informed?
How would you change any of these aspects of the organisation's operations? Why?

5.2 ✳ Undertake a critique of the different traditions of corporate governance in the UK/USA, Germany and Japan in terms of your own views of their strengths and weaknesses. Is there a better system than any of these? Why?

5.3 Choose any organisation which does not operate a two-tier board (or the public sector equivalent).
(a) Would a two-tier board be a better form of governance? Why?
(b) What would you need to do to move to a two-tier system?
(c) Is this likely to be possible?

5.4 ✳ Write a discussion paper explaining how a change in ownership of an organisation with which you are familiar (private or public sector) might benefit shareholders or other stakeholders.

5.5 Using Illustration 5.4 as an example, identify and map out the stakeholders for Manchester United, CSA,* Sheffield Theatres,* KPMG* or an organisation of your choice in relation to:
(a) current strategies;
(b) a number of different future strategies of your choice.
What are the implications of your analysis for the management?

5.6 For the News Corporation* or an organisation of your choice, use Exhibit 5.7 to establish the *overall stance* of the organisation on ethical issues.

5.7 ✳ Identify the key corporate social responsibility issues which are of major concern in an industry or public service of your choice (refer to Exhibit 5.8). Compare the approach of two or more organisations in that industry, and explain how this relates to their competitive standing.

5.8 Use the questions in Exhibit 5.12 to plot out a tentative cultural web for KPMG* or an organisation of your choice.

5.9 Use Exhibit 5.13 to identify organisations with which you are familiar which are close to the Miles and Snow or Handy stereotypes. Justify your categorisation.

5.10 ✳ By using a number of the examples from above, critically appraise the assertion that 'culture can only really be usefully analysed by the symptoms displayed in the way the organisation operates'. Refer to Schein's book in the recommended key readings to assist you with this task.

CASE EXAMPLE

Playing the game? Manchester United

Introduction

Initial interpretation of the first reported financial results of a new century for Manchester United, the world's biggest club, could have been that the 'bubble' of confidence in football had burst. The City had reacted nervously to the announcement of reduced profits, so wiping one-third off the plc's stock market valuation. Closer examination, however, suggested such an interpretation to be premature: the club itself was justifiably arguing the financial performance to be 'solid' (annual turn-over had, after all, increased by 5 per cent to £116 million, producing a £16.8 million profit, whilst United spent over £50 million on facilities and new players).

Table 1
Manchester United's financial performance

	1997 £m	1998 £m	1999 £m	2000 £m
Turnover	87.9	87.9	110.7	116.0
Pre-tax profit	27.6	27.8	22.4	16.8
(financial year to 31 July)				

Source: Adapted from Manchester United plc annual reports.

The year began with United the darling of the money market and, on the playing side, undisputed domestic and European champions. The previous season they had completed a domestic League and Football Association (FA) Cup 'double' and capped the achievement by beating Bayern Munich to be christened champions of Europe.

This case study was prepared by Bob Perry, University of Wolverhampton Business School, in collaboration with Professor Kevan Scholes, Sheffield Hallam University. It is intended as a basis for class discussion and not as an illustration of either good or bad management practice.

Later, they had also competed in the inaugural World Club championship in Brazil (at the expense of entry to the FA Cup). The withdrawal from the FA Cup may have cost £5 million in lost gate receipts but television income had soared to £30.5 million. By March 2000, with share prices standing at 402p in the stock market, valuation had reached the 'magical' milestone of £1 billion. Coinciding with this record-breaking valuation was the announcement of the opening of a 15,000-square-foot store and Internet-related Red Café in the heart of Asia.

Manchester United plc, despite reduced profitability, was still in the best of health.

English football's sea-change

United's position looked decidedly less rosy a decade and a half earlier. A corporate transformation from provincial English football club to global corporation likened to the fast-food giant McDonald's in this space of time was remarkable.

The club's resurgence should be set within the context of a dramatic turnround in English football industry fortunes themselves. The mid-1980s were *the* low point for a game blighted by rampant crowd disorder, the smallest post-war attendances, and failure to agree a television contract (meaning no televised coverage). Matters were, however, to worsen still further. The mere mention of *Bradford* and *Heysel* invoke the tragedy of lost life in an 18-day period during May 1985 (one clearly attributable to a decaying stadium, the other to a combination of 'hooliganism', poor facilities and inept policing). The Heysel repercussions involved a ban on all English clubs competing in European competition. Domestically, an unsympathetic government proposed legislation to intervene in the affairs of a 'beautiful game' with a tarnished image and seemingly in terminal decline.

These events, however, were to provide the impetus to review and then pursue a number of fresh initiatives spawning greater commercialisation, supporter involvement and a new role for clubs in the wider community. Many would cite the recommendations embodied in a report into the Hillsborough stadium disaster of 1989 (the so-called Taylor Report) as the catalyst for such a turnaround.

By the year 2000, football was radically altered, with undreamed-of social respectability, finance and media attention. In 1992 a 'kiss of life' was administered by a BSkyB-funded FA 'super league' and effectively football was repackaged for a mass television audience. There had since this time been clear signs of growth in attendances whilst the home audience's appetite for the televised game appeared insatiable, and resultant deals with television companies had showered money upon the game. (England's Premier League alone received £540 million annually from 2001 for television rights.) Flotations on financial markets and product merchandising had contributed to massive overall increases in income.

Football showed little sign of stabilising from these major developments. The 1995 (Bosman) ruling of the European Court of Justice had freed constraints on the negotiation of players' personal terms and loosened restrictions on the number of foreigners a team could field, invoking a form of 'player liberation'. Consequently, there had been an influx of non-British talent into the game and top players had commanded substantial financial rewards.

Manchester United's transformation

The mid-1980s similarly were a period of mediocrity for Manchester United, just one of several slumbering giants unable to compete in European competition and failing to recapture past playing glories. In terms of the club's pedigree, the 1960s had marked a pinnacle, when under the ownership of Louis Edwards and the management of Sir Matt Busby the club won the European Cup in 1968. Edwards became a director in 1958 (the

same year as the Munich air disaster) and presided over a remarkable recovery. The disaster had meant death and injury to several of the club's and the country's best players but the dogged determination to continue to compete at the very highest level of international football had attracted to the club many admirers, some far outside the Manchester region. In 1980 Martin Edwards inherited the club from his father.

By 1989, Martin (by now chief executive) was about to sell his majority shareholding in the club to Michael Knighton for £10 million. Resistance from fellow directors and a failure by Knighton to attract sufficient financial backing meant the takeover was aborted. Two years later, the club was floated on the stock exchange (primarily to raise funds for ground improvements) at a price of 32p per share and with a valuation of £40 million. The corporate body now comprised three subsidiaries of Merchandising, Catering and Football. Further share issues followed in 1994 and 1997, with Edwards accumulating £71 million for shares he sold, so reducing his stake to 6.5 per cent. By 1997 Manchester United had become the world's wealthiest club, exceeding the turnover of others by some distance, and Edwards' wealth had grown accordingly.

Takeover speculation

In 1998, a breakaway proposal for a fully constituted European super league by Italian-based company Media Partners was given advanced consideration by Europe's big clubs, including United.

Speculation concerning the formation of a fully constituted European super league coincided with a possibility of a media takeover deal. On 8 September 1998 the board announced that they had received an offer of £623.4m from BSkyB – the satellite broadcasting company (in which Rupert Murdoch's News International has a 40 per cent stake). They unanimously recommended that shareholders accept the bid. When the news of these negotiations leaked out there was an uprising of indignation from supporters and others who felt that the club should not fall into the hands of a media empire. There were concerns that media ownership would ruin the football industry as they had known and loved it for generations. In an open joint letter from Mark Booth, chief executive of BSkyB, and Edwards, appreciation was expressed that football was not just another business but was 'part of the cultural fabric of Manchester and the nation'. The letter also said that the acquisition would create one of the great partnerships in sport.

In April 1999, Stephen Byers, the government Trade and Industry Secretary, blocked the plan, ruling the proposal against the public interest. The club's shares at that stage stood at 186p, but United's marketing drive, particularly into so-called new media, continued unabated. This was allied to the club's outstanding on-field successes in the FA Cup, Premiership and the Champions' League.

The European dimension

The 1998 super league breakaway attempts were thwarted by Uefa (the European football body), by offering major concessions to the big clubs, including expanding the league to 32 clubs, so doubling

Table 2 Europe's most powerful clubs

		TURNOVER £m
Manchester United	England	**87.9**
Real Madrid	Spain	72.2
Bayern Munich	Germany	65.2
Juventus	Italy	55.3
Barcelona	Spain	48.6
Milan	Italy	48.6
Internazionale	Italy	48.2
Liverpool	England	45.5
Borussia Dortmund	Germany	41.5
Paris St-Germain	France	32.9
PSV Eindhoven	Holland	26.2
Ajax	Holland	25.2
Marseilles	France	15.4
Porto	Portugal	8.5

(The so-called G14 clubs' turnover based on 1997–98 financial returns)

Source: Adapted from *The Independent*, September 2000.

the group-stage and thereby increasing individual clubs' share of revenues.

The Uefa-organised Champions' League may have been a means of directing £330 million to Europe's richer clubs, yet Uefa continued to face demands from the big clubs for more money and power, backed by the ultimate threat of a breakaway. The so-called G14 clubs, formed following the Media Partners talks, continued to meet periodically and collectively pressed for more concessions. The clubs believed they could obtain more for the Europe-wide television rights than Uefa obtains. Also on the agenda was the distribution of the money, and the frustrations of having to release key players for international duty.

The new ethos

'We strive to ensure that shareholders, loyal supporters, customers and key commercial partners alike benefit from our performance.'
        (*Manchester United plc annual report*)

'Getting in to watch a game is like a military campaign. A seat is like a commodity to be exploited. The "added-value" package includes lunch (with an ex-player), a walk on the pitch and perhaps a word with a current team member. All for £200. Despite the fact that there are 63 corporate boxes there is still a waiting list of 100 companies. For individuals to get a match ticket you have to pay £10 a year to join a list – and no refund if you never get in. There are 100,000 on this list – so that's £1 million up-front to start with.'
        (*A fan*)

In 1996, finance director Robin Launders was interviewed in *Accountancy* magazine about the goals of Manchester United. He was keen to stress that he was not a football man – which proved no barrier to being recruited (as long as he didn't actually *dislike* football). His formula for success was expressed as follows:

'Running a football club is easy; all you've got to do is to make enough profit year after year to do three things: develop your team, develop your stadium and – if you're a quoted company – to pay a dividend. If you can do all these things, year on year, then life is good.'

Such a prescription was not universally supported by other interested parties. Many supporters resented the way in which the traditionally working-class game had evolved and the replacement of standing males chanting songs by seated, well-heeled corporate guests. As one journalist summarised,

> 'Football used to be about glory, romance, loyalty and the national game, and not about exploitation and multinational corporations. But that is exactly what Manchester United now is.'

The issue of constantly changing replica kit had caused some considerable resentment amongst parents of young fans who felt pressured into spending large amounts on these. A television programme revealed that the UK replica kit market was worth as much as £200 million per annum, and that mark-up was as high as 200 per cent. Tommy Docherty (a former manager) described the practice as 'stealing' from the public: 'when Dick Turpin [an infamous highwayman] took your money – at least he wore a mask!' The launch of another new kit in time for Christmas 2000 was the nineteenth in eight years. Doubtless mindful of a newly established Government Football Task Force out to protect supporters, the club promised that the kit would stay for two years.

Peter Kenyon was appointed deputy chief executive in May 1997 with a brief to broaden United's supporter base. For United, the commercial logic was faultless: the greater the support, the greater the potential to sell club merchandise. A former chief executive of the sportswear company Umbro International, Kenyon recruited Peter Draper, also from Umbro, to spearhead a clinical brand-marketing campaign. As if to prove they had a warmer side too, during 2000 they established a three-year partnership to raise £1 million for Unicef, the United Nations children's fund. The tie-up was perceived as fitting the ethos of Manchester United as reaching out to 'global children'. This involved visits by players and officials to some of the poorest communities in the world, including Inner Mongolia, Brazil and Uganda where they encountered some families surviving on less than £200 a year. Thanks to links with

Trafford Borough Council, local schoolchildren and disabled groups make use of some of the facilities at the club's breathtaking training centre.

In August 2000 Kenyon succeeded Edwards as chief executive. Edwards was not always at one with the manager, Sir Alex Ferguson, and unpopular with the fans for his attempts to sell the club. Kenyon promised a more communicative people-centred change of style.

Marketing the brand

United became less dependent upon gate receipts alone (they accounted for the majority of turnover in 1990, ten year on it had fallen to a third), now that merchandising and related activities had expanded rapidly – with over 1,500 items in the on-site shop and hundreds of outlets throughout the world. There was Manchester United mail order and a deal with BSkyB saw the launch of the Manchester United satellite channel (MUTV) which by 1998 was broadcasting six hours per day. October 2000 saw the premiere of the feature-length movie *Manchester United: Beyond the Promised Land.* Manchester United Insurance credit cards, savings accounts, hotel and leisure facilities, even weddings at the ground, and investments in other European clubs meant that the range of interests the plc pursued was diverse. Pre-season tours to places as far away as Australia, the Far East and Asia cemented Manchester United as a genuinely international brand.

Financial analysts believed, however, that the club had only exploited the more obvious income streams and that even more lucrative areas offered themselves. Future investment plans were well advanced in new-media technology, principally the Internet. United's strategy had been to enter robust business partnerships and harness the benefits of new technology. The official website was launched in August 1998, with a modest 16 million hits a month initially recorded. By the year 2000, the figure soared to a staggering 77 million. The club were said to be looking forward to the possibilities of relaying matches live across the globe.

A database compiled from match ticket applications and merchandising had a listing of 700,000 names, but this represented the tip of a very large iceberg. A survey of their supporter base is likely to reveal something like 40 million people worldwide. This is likely to grow still further, particularly in countries late to embrace the game. North America, for instance, with the distractions of baseball, American football and netball has yet to acknowledge football in the same way that the rest of the world does. Similarly, a market of an estimated 20 million potential Chinese customers, accustomed to a diet of the Premiership on television, had yet to be exploited. According to private research the United brand has 79 per cent 'name awareness' in China. If evidence of potential existed it could be found in the Thai-language edition of the United Magazine, which sold a respectable 20,000 copies a month.

For organisations wishing to associate themselves with Manchester United, sponsorship did not come cheaply. Vodafone paid £30 million for a four-year deal for the privilege of shirt sponsorship. Imaginatively, a deal with a Coral-backed betting website, eurobet.com, provided finance and additional promotion opportunities. The website was one of the sponsors of a Formula One racing car team, which will feature the club's official website prominently on their cars.

Despite sell-out crowds and a waiting list for season tickets, the club attempted to 'peg' admission prices and, of twenty Premiership clubs, only six charged less. The club's home ground since 1910, Old Trafford (the so-called Theatre of Dreams) increased its capacity by 12,400 to 67,500, making it the largest in Britain and yielding an extra £176,000 every home game.

Factors influencing United's future

Smaller clubs in the English football league were dismayed by this growing financial rift between the top few clubs and the rest. As one chairman remarked:

'Matches can be rescheduled at short notice to suit satellite stations and their exclusive audiences. There is a disregard for the little clubs. The gap between the haves and the have-nots is too great. Manchester United is now marketed as the national team – which has taken it away from its roots and its local community. Football should be a love affair otherwise you are just a business. The big clubs have forgotten their roots and are isolating themselves.'

There were also concerns that not enough money was recycled to schools and junior football – from where the next generation of players would come.

Despite such concerns, Manchester United appeared to grow stronger, exhibiting awesome negotiating 'muscle'. In terms of income from television rights, an increased share of the £2 billion, five-year renegotiation by the FA announced in June 2000 represented the tip of an iceberg. The demand and consequently the price to broadcast United games was huge, not just domestically but also worldwide, with the potential advertising income from MUTV apparent. If individual clubs were allowed to negotiate their own deals, particularly as part of a European super league, United would be stronger still. Further, a long-term deal with Nike to begin in August 2001 was reported to be worth £22 million a year. Then, in February 2001, United announced a unique marketing alliance with the world's wealthiest baseball team, the New York Yankees. This involved agreement on shared market information, joint sponsorship and promotional programmes and the sale of goods. United can now use the Yankees' huge merchandising network to target the elusive North American market. (In return, the Yankees, through United, get access to Europe and the Far East.)

Players contracted to the club can benefit from the best training facilities at the purpose-built £14 million Trafford Training Centre, Carrington, set in 70 acres. (Further expenditure of £8.5 million was also planned.) Potentially they could also enjoy huge salaries (club captain Roy Keane was successful in negotiating a staggering £50,000 per week income). The club was better placed than any to pay the top dollar in terms of wage demands and at the same time keep operating expenses a 'reasonable' proportion of revenues. The team represented a combination of big-money buys and players who have progressed through, thanks to the club's youth policy. Investment in a thriving playing academy, after all, should ensure a steady supply of home-grown stars, potentially saving millions in acquiring top footballing talent.

United, like others, were relieved that approved plans to further modify the transfer system post Bosman in accordance with European Union law were modest. The European Commission had expressed concern that, by tying players to clubs, the transfer system restricts players' freedom of movement, hence the need for some reform. Uefa and Fifa, the game's two leading governing bodies, responded by outlining a plan including a new type of playing contract, protection of 'poaching' of players by other clubs, and compensation for clubs for developing young players. United could continue to buy new players and keep them contracted to the club.

On the downside, inspirational team manager Sir Alex Ferguson was approaching retirement age. The retirement of one of his predecessors, Sir Matt Busby, coincided with a period in the doldrums on the playing side. The financial wherewithal of the plc suggests that such a repetition would be unthinkable.

The pace of change in the sport, leisure and entertainment industries was frantic throughout many parts of the world in the late 1990s. Manchester United perhaps epitomised this change more than most. But had it got it right?

Sources: D. Conn, 'Europe's richest clubs launch power play', *The Independent*, 14 September 2000; S. Curry, 'Netting a billion', *The Sunday Times*, 12 March 2000; I. Hawkey, 'Transfers face shake-up', *The Sunday Times*, 29 October 2000; G. Otway, 'Gold Trafford expanding to cash in on the dream', *The Sunday Times*, 30 May 1999; J. Rowley, 'Can Man U save the world?' *The Sunday Times*, 6 August 2000; *Soccer Investor Weekly*, no. 18 (7 November 2000). Also company annual reports, other corporate data (www.manutd.com home page), industry data, e.g. Deloitte and Touche's football analysis (www.deloitte.co.uk), financial media, sports media, *Without Walls*, Channel 4, 1995, *Panorama*, BBC, December 1997. Thanks also to the research and efforts of past Wolverhampton University MBA student groups.

Questions

Questions related to Chapter 5

1. Do you feel that the various aspects of corporate governance discussed in section 5.2 are appropriate for a football club? What changes in governance would you like to see?

2. Refer to section 5.3.2 and Exhibit 5.5 and undertake a stakeholder mapping exercise for any strategic development which is likely to be under consideration by the board (for example, 'The formation of a European super league of major clubs'). How would you use this analysis if you were: (a) a board member wishing to support the strategy, (b) an opponent of the strategy?

3. Refer to Exhibit 5.7 and decide which ethical stance you feel best describes Manchester United now and how you would wish to see the club. Justify your own position.

4. Refer to section 5.5.4 and decide what you feel were the key cultural characteristics of Manchester United in terms of values, beliefs and taken-for-granted assumptions: (a) pre-1990, and (b) today. What are the implications of these changes for current and future strategies?

5. If you were allowed to write a short mission statement for Manchester United, what would it be? Does it properly reflect your answers to the questions above? Refer to Exhibit 5.13 for different types of mission statement.

Other questions

6. How, organisationally, has Manchester United aligned itself to external environmental factors? Identify key opportunities, commenting on how well placed United is to maximise them, and major threats and their significance to the plc.

7. Analyse the intensity of competition, commenting specifically upon:
   - In which market(s) does United operate?
   - On what basis are they competing, and which strategies present themselves?
   - Who are their competitors?
   - How sustainable is corporate growth?

8. Consider the role of football within the plc. Does it matter whether United continues to win matches, whether the club has a dip in form and is relegated, or indeed if it needs to play football at all!

9. In terms of United's external environment, how free are they to operate as they please? Who are the regulatory bodies, and what dilemmas does United face?

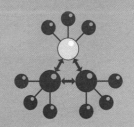

Coping with Complexity: The 'Business Idea'

A repeated theme in the book so far has been that the management of strategy involves coping with uncertainty, change and complexity. This is evident from the discussion in the preceding three chapters which have reviewed many of the forces at work on the strategies of organisations, from macro environmental trends, to forces of competition, internal capabilities and competences, organisation culture and stakeholder influences. These different forces do not tend to act singly on organisations; they are likely to be interdependent. They may also exert influence in different directions. Shareholders may require year on year increasing returns, the government may be demanding increasing expenditure on environmental protection, competitive pressures may be demanding heavy investment in more efficient plant and more attention to customer service, whilst the competences of the organisation may historically lie in its technical engineering excellence. Clearly this is a complex problem. How organisations – especially successful ones – and their managers cope with this complexity is the theme for this chapter.

This commentary uses the three lenses of design, experience and ideas, introduced in section 2.2 of Chapter 2, to consider this key issue. It does so first by briefly revisiting the concept of the 'business idea' presented in the introduction to Part II; then by discussing what each of the three lenses has to say about that concept; and finally by drawing the insights from the three lenses together to help provide an understanding of how managers might handle such complexity.

The business idea

In the introduction to this part of the book, the business idea[1] was introduced as a model of why an organisation has been successful (see Exhibit IIi on page 94). The key point is that some organisations have found ways of reconciling the complexity of different forces they face such that these become positive feedback loops which provide for success. To take an example, Exhibit IIii is a representation of the business idea for Kindercare, which grew to be a highly successful child care centre in the USA.[2] The exhibit shows how Kindercare was built around the concept of 'innovative child care'. More innovative child care leads to more teacher satisfaction, which leads to retention of motivated ex-schoolteachers and in turn to more innovative child care. It also

Exhibit IIii

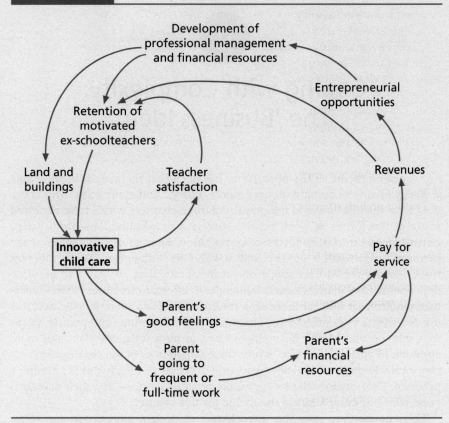

Source: Prepared by Michel Bougon, Bryant College, Smithfield, USA.

gives parents good feelings such that they are prepared to pay rather more for the services. In turn this leads to the sorts of revenues which allow the setting up of professional management services at the centre, thus freeing up teachers to concentrate on teaching and further innovation, as well as funds for acquiring land and buildings. Less successful organisations would not be experiencing the same sort of positive feedback. The different forces would be pulling in different directions rather than being mutually reinforcing.

However, as it stands this is no more than a description of why a business is successful. It does not explain *how* such a self-reinforcing business idea comes about; and as an extension of this, what managers might do about it, if anything. The different lenses are now used to explore this.

Complexity and design

Chapters 3, 4 and 5 have shown that the organisational world is, indeed, a complex place, but has presented concepts and frameworks by which managers can unpack this complexity. The design view suggests that such analysis also allows managers to go further: that on the basis of such analytic understanding they can build a sufficiently clear picture to deliberately position and direct their organisation in such a way as to benefit from environmental opportunities, circumvent threats, build on or develop competences and proactively manage the sometimes conflicting interests and influences of stakeholders.

Most of the frameworks discussed in these chapters could, for example, be used to provide data based on analysis for more or less formalised strategic decision making, to feed into a corporate planning exercise or a strategic workshop, for example. Indeed, the sequencing of the chapters might be used as a logical way of doing this. This is a view of strategic management which is underpinned by the sorts of assumption discussed in section 2.2.1: essentially that this complex organisational world is sufficiently stable, predictable or at least discernible for such analysis to be useful for the purposes of strategy design.

The design lens therefore suggests that managers can and should analyse and plan the integration of the different forces represented by the business idea. A starting point for such analysis might be historical. Over time, all organisations must have developed a business idea which accounts for their current or past success. So analysing what this business idea is could be very useful in order to understand the basis for success that exists (or existed) but also to understand ways in which it might be built on. Systems thinking can help such analysis. The components of the business idea can be broken down in a systematic, analytic way, much as has been done in Exhibit IIi. This could further draw on much of the discussion in Chapters 3, 4 and 5; for example, the competences of the organisation, key drivers in the environment, key stakeholders and their influences, and aspects of organisational culture.

Managers might then ask questions such as:

- What are the core elements of the business idea that must be protected and defended?

- What is there within the business idea that is difficult for other organisations to copy and therefore provides distinctiveness and is the basis of core competences?

- Is the business idea likely to be relevant in the future, for example in terms of scenarios that have been built?

- What are the strengths and weaknesses of the current business idea?

- Is the business idea capable of extension into other areas, for example new markets or possible acquisitions? (See Chapter 8.)

- If not, is it possible to conceive of other mutually reinforcing cycles developed from or extending the existing business idea that might be suited to the challenges and opportunities of the future? This would entail designing new activities and processes complementary but additive to those that currently exist.

Looking at the complexity of integrating different forces and influences on strategy through this lens, the business idea becomes manageable, indeed it becomes a planning tool. It could be used as part of a strategic planning process, a strategy workshop by managers or, indeed, a project assignment by students.

Complexity and experience

The second lens, strategy as experience, begins from a different starting point. As explained in section 2.2.2 of Chapter 2, this emphasises the influence of the personal experience of individuals, the culture of organisations and the institutional norms in which those organisations exist.

Beginning first with managers as individuals, it is important to understand that they have to simplify the complexity they face: it is not possible for them to operate in terms of 'perfect knowledge'. Understanding the effect of such *simplification processes* is important. Research shows that, even if a manager has a very rich understanding of his or her environment, for example, it is unlikely that he or she will bring that complex understanding to bear on for all situations and all decisions – rather, the manager will access part of that knowledge.[3] This is called *selective attention*: selecting from total understanding the parts of knowledge which seem most relevant. Managers also use *exemplars* and *prototypes* as a way of making sense of, for example, competition. It is not unusual for managers to refer to a dominant competitor rather than a list of competitive characteristics: 'We compete against the Japanese . . .' or 'The service on Singapore Airlines . . .' are ways of encapsulating quite complex sets of characteristics. Over time, this partial representation of reality can become fixed. The Japanese become a generic competitor; Singapore Airlines *is* competition. The risk is that the 'chunk' of information most often used becomes the only information used and that stimuli from the environment are selected out to fit these dominant representations of reality. Information that squares with Singapore Airlines being the main competitor is taken on board, whilst information counter to this is not. Sometimes this distortion can lead to severe errors as managers miss crucial indicators because they are, in effect, scanning the environment for issues and events that are familiar or readily recognisable.[4] Managers then become sensitive to information that confirms or reinforces such a bias, rather than to other information that counters it.

In terms of the experience lens, then, the business idea can also be seen as a mental model of what an organisation is about. As such, it is both useful, because it provides managers with short-cuts in their making sense of complexity, but also potentially dangerous because the evidence is that such mental models become fixed and begin to dictate how new stimuli are made sense of.

At the level of organisational culture, the experience lens suggests that there also exists an organisational way of doing things akin to the business idea, but that it is not constructed analytically or in a planned fashion. The business idea may have originated in the mind of an entrepreneur and been developed over many years through trial and error as that entrepreneur grew the business and experienced success and failure. Some initiatives worked; others did not. Some skills proved to be important; others were not. Opportunities arose which were suited to the skills of the business; other opportunities were not. Over time and through experience the business idea developed. How it was delivered gradually became embedded in organisational processes and routines around which people learned to cohere. The integration of the different forces and influences on strategy were not developed by design but rather through the experience of individuals and groups of people working together, gradually building into a culture, reinforced by success. The organisation's paradigm (see Chapter 2) and culture web (see Chapter 5) are, in effect, the business idea in taken-for-granted form. What are the consequences?

- The experience lens emphasises the importance of history and culture. Organisations that are successful develop ways of doing things which lead to that success; and they continue to build on that success: so the business idea becomes more and more embedded in organisational culture. The greater the success, the more this culturally embedded business idea ends up driving the future strategy of the organisation; it becomes a ready-made solution to circumstances which arise. However, there may – some would argue there must – come a time when this business idea becomes less and less relevant to the environment; and this is what is referred to in Chapter 2, section 2.4.2, as strategic drift.

- This is because, in effect, the business idea becomes so routinised that it leads to myopia. To continue the example above, the organisation's systems become so attuned to understanding and dealing with *the* competition of Singapore Airlines and educating major stakeholders – shareholders, analysts, staff, the press – that this is what matters, that there is a danger that other key forces at work are overlooked or ignored.

- The degree of this embeddedness may also be magnified as forces of institutionalisation (see Chapters 2 and 5) grow. A whole organisational field may come to take for granted a business idea. Indeed, airline operators together with governments in Europe and the USA, manufacturers and airports did just this prior to the 1980s, leading to protection of existing operators, barriers to new entrants, accusations of price fixing and a failure to take customer disquiet seriously.

- The embededness of this 'cultural business idea' may mean that it is very difficult to change. If strategies are to be developed effectively there must, therefore, be means of questioning and challenging that which is taken for granted. The experience lens suggests that the major role of the frameworks of analysis described in Chapters 3, 4 and 5 is to do just this. It may be at least as important to surface the assumptions that managers have as to undertake careful economic analysis, because it is likely to be these assumptions that are driving strategic decisions. Indeed, there are those[5] who argue that strategy discussions between managers should be largely about identifying such assumptions and using the agenda which emerges for the purposes of debate.

- However, there is a challenge and a paradox here. The taken-for-grantedness of the business idea helps explain why some organisations achieve competitive advantage which is difficult for others to copy. Imitation of the bases of advantage is difficult because those bases are difficult to identify, precisely because they are embedded in the culture (see section 4.7.4) in the form of routines, control systems and so on.

- The challenge is this. Is it really conceivable that the deeply embedded, taken-for-granted, perhaps everyday routines that make up the bases of success can be readily analysed? Outsiders would have difficulty identifying them; and so too would senior executives who are unlikely to be involved in such activities. For example, whilst the sort of mapping of competences illustrated in Illustration 4.3 did get to detail far greater than that shown in this book, it took managers two days; and that within a culture of openness and trust.

● The paradox is this: if one of the reasons that competences lodged in an organisation's culture yield advantage is because they are so natural to the firm concerned and so difficult for others to see, does trying to manage them mean that there is a risk that they lose their advantage? To manage them means to simplify them; potentially to codify them. In this way they become more visible internally, but arguably less taken for granted, less complex, less causally ambiguous and more visible and potentially imitable by others.[6]

The message from the experience lens is that a reliance on analysis and planning for making sense of complexity might well underestimate the problems of managing the business idea. Surfacing and challenging the taken-for-granted components of that idea may well be an important way of understanding the strategic situation the organisation is in and deliberating on ways to go forward. However, it needs to be recognised that it will not be easy to do. Executives who wish to do so will need to invest substantial time, not only of their own and other senior executives, but also of people in the organisation whose day-to-day lives are engaged with such processes.

Complexity and ideas

Looking through the ideas lens, there is an acceptance of the way in which the business idea might have become embedded in the culture of an organisation: in this sense there is an overlap with the experience lens. However, whereas the experience lens emphasises uniformity and conformity, the ideas lens additionally helps to explain innovation and how new business ideas come about.

The ideas lens emphasises variety and diversity at different levels, across and within organisations. First, at the level of a population of organisations, for every successful business idea there were probably many unsuccessful ones. The successful ones proved to be more attractive to the conditions of their environment – to buyers in the market, to investors, to communities, to potential and actual employees and so on. However, for every successful entrepreneur there are many who do not succeed. In the market for cheap flight airlines, Laker Air of the 1980s failed but easyJet has succeeded. Firms compete with others; in this sense one business idea competes with the business ideas of competitors; some survive and some do not. This is the position taken by 'population ecologists'[7] who study strategy in terms of the births and deaths of populations of businesses, and who tend to emphasise a good deal less the centrality, influence and control of managers on all of this than do adherents of the design school of thinking.

The recognition by the experience lens of the importance of trial and error also receives support, with particular emphasis on the importance of imperfect copying. Remember the institutionalist view described in Chapter 2 (page 46): a successful business idea, evident in the strategy of an organisation, will tend to be imitated by others. However, it will not be imitated perfectly; organisations will have a very imperfect notion of the components of the business idea of competitors: they will copy parts of the strategy of successful organisations and add their own dimensions based on their own business idea; and the result could be success or it could be failure. Arguably this is just what has happened with the success of Virgin Air; Richard Branson copied the basics of transcontinental flights but introduced his own version of it. The important point to understand is that through such imperfect copying, ideas are always recombining to produce new ideas; and in this way successful innovatory strategies may develop. Here is an explanation of how successful organisations lose out and others take over from them: but the explanation is not founded so much on the design capabilities of managers as on the results of imperfect copying and the resulting variety of new business ideas eventually giving rise to a winning strategy.

Another level at which the ideas lens sheds light on the business idea is within an organisation itself. Whilst organisations are cultures which embed a business idea and around which people cohere, there will also be elements of diversity and variety. There will be some individuals or groups within the organisation who have different ways of doing things or see things differently. Or they will be networked with others outside their organisation who do. This accounts for why new ideas, in effect amendments to the dominant business idea, come up within the organisation. This could happen quite low down in the organisation; the routine of taking back unwanted goods from major retailers in the company in Illustration 4.3 was not originated at the top of the organisation but by a relatively junior despatch manager seeking to help a sales executive, who in turn was trying to satisfy a concern of a buyer in a major retailer. The lessons drawn from studies of strategic innovations reported in Chapter 2 emphasise the importance of this variety and diversity of ideas within organisations rather than a reliance on top-down strategic planning.[8]

There are lessons here for managers.

- In a context in which the environment is changing rapidly and innovation matters, Chapter 4 argued that the only competences that are really core in achieving competitive advantage are those of innovation and the development of new ideas. Managers have some choices here. They may block ideas, perhaps because they are not seen to fit with their experience of the business idea, or they may encourage variety and tolerate those who do not conform. They may champion what might at first appear to be mavericks, or demand that they conform. They can set up rigid hierarchies which ensure conformity, or create the conditions which will encourage new ideas and tolerate apparent inefficiencies and the failure of new ideas. They can set up control systems solely concerned with measuring variance against plans and budgets; or they can monitor what happens to ideas, when they succeed and fail, and so help the organisation learn from them.

- There needs to be a recognition, then, that innovation could come from anywhere in the organisation and is likely to take form, at least initially, in deviations from the prevailing norms; and that means deviations from the apparently positive feedback loops that might represent the successful business idea of the past. This may not be comfortable and the experience lens would suggest that it is likely to be resisted. The strategic manager who seeks innovation is likely to have to be tolerant of this and allow the sort of latitude that permits and facilitates it.

- The ideas lens suggests that creating this latitude will not be helped by a detailed prescribing or specification of the business idea, as the design lens would suggest. Rather there is a need to create an overarching vision of what the organisation is about, or is seeking to achieve. It may also be helped by developing the few 'rules' which are needed to establish organisational coherence but which are sufficiently flexible to allow and encourage variety and diversity: and some would say that these need to be sufficiently ambiguous to create the sort of 'adaptive tension' required for innovation (see pages 59–60 in Chapter 2).

- For managers in organisations that rely on innovation it is also important to accept that the knowledge and understanding of their bases of success can never be perfect, and that they cannot gain advantage by trying to make it so. Rather, advantage lies in continually transforming what they have faster than their competitors.

The key point is that the ideas lens sheds light on the sources and bases of variety and diversity, and therefore innovation and change in the business ideas of organisations, and suggests ways in which managers may facilitate this.

Our view

This section commentary has addressed an important challenge that strategic managers face: the integration of different influences and forces on strategy development, here referred to as the 'business idea'. It is accepted that successful organisations have found ways to integrate such forces in such a way as to achieve the sort of positive feedback shown in Exhibit IIii. However, what the lenses show is that this can be understood in different ways. We argue that these different ways are not incompatible but are usefully complementary.

The complexity of an organisation's business idea has very likely developed over time through managerial experience, experimentation and gradual embeddedness in culture. It represents the basis of success of the organisation; but it also potentially contains the seeds of downfall because it becomes so embedded that it cannot easily be changed. In this respect it provides explanations of strategic drift and the Icarus paradox[9] explained in section 2.4.2.

The design lens argues that these complex, mutually reinforcing interactions can be understood, analysed and planned. We would argue that that may be more problematic than some adherents to this school of strategy would admit. However, this does not mean that the tools of analysis are wasted, because they also provide a basis upon which managers can challenge and question taken-for-grantedness and thus help manage the development of the business idea, or at least question it.

The ideas lens says that it is not just a matter of top-down management. There will be variety within and between business ideas. Imperfect copying and deviation from the business idea will throw up new ideas. The challenge is for managers to accept that they cannot expect to control all this; that they themselves are one of the forces which select for and against new ideas; but that they can and should cultivate the potentially positive effects of the imperfection and deviation that will exist in and around their organisations through the way in which they design and control their organisations.

Brown and Eisenhardt[10] argue that organisations potentially face two opposite problems. Some managers and some organisations may be too wedded to a view of the future – they call this the Foresight Trap – based on their experience or a detailed plan which results in a rigidity of views. For other managers or organisations there is too little attention to the forces that will affect the future, leading to no view at all about what it might be like; and therefore chaos. They suggest that managers need to avoid falling into either of these traps and accept the inevitability of the ambiguity and uncertainty of the complexity they face. The lessons they draw are these:

- Rather than trying to identify a definitive future, managers need to have an overall view of the environment of their organisation, broad enough to accommodate different futures, and a vision about the identity of their organisation which they can adjust as the future unfolds. In terms of the business idea, this suggests that it is indeed important to have views about how different forces, internal and external to the organisation, interlink and are integrated; but not a view which is over-rigid. Rather than seeing the business idea as a fixed system, it needs to be seen as an adaptive one.

- Managers need to avoid major one-off exercises looking at their environment and likely futures. There should be 'constant but thin' attention to the future. In other words, managers should constantly keep in touch with their environment and how it is changing but they should not spend a lot of time doing it and certainly not assume that such attention can take the form of one-off analytic exercises.

- Experimentation is important; the future will be understood through action, through doing. Organisations need to try out new ideas and see if they work and in so doing learn about the future as it changes. So encouraging the variety within the organisation that gives rise to such ideas is important.

REFERENCES

1. For a full explanation of the business idea see Kees van der Heijden, *Scenarios: The art of strategic conversation*, Wiley, 1997.
2. This example is adapted from M.G. Bougon and J. Komocar, 'Directing strategic change: a dynamic holistic approach', in A. Huff (ed.), *Managing Strategic Thought*, Wiley, 1990.
3. For a review of these points see the introduction to J. Dutton, E. Walton and E. Abrahamson, 'Important dimensions of strategic issues: separating the wheat from the chaff', *Journal of Management Studies*, vol. 26, no. 4 (1989), pp. 380–395.
4. See A. Tversky and D. Kahnemann, 'Judgements under uncertainty: heuristics and biases', *Science*, vol. 185 (1975), pp. 1124–1131.

5. This is the approach taken by C. Eden and F. Ackerman in *Making Strategy: The journey of strategy*, Sage Publications, 1998.

6. This argument is similar to that taken by J.B. Barney, 'Organizational culture: can it be a source of sustained competitive advantage?', *Academy of Management Review*, vol. 11, no. 3 (1986), pp. 656–665.

7. An example of the approach taken by the population ecologists can be found in M.T. Hannan and J. Freeman, *Organizational Ecology*, Harvard University Press, 1988.

8. See S.L. Brown and K.M. Eisenhardt, *Competing on the Edge*, Harvard Business School Press, 1998.

9. See D. Miller, *The Icarus Paradox*, HarperCollins, 1990.

10. See reference 8.

PART

III

STRATEGIC CHOICES

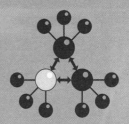

Strategic choices are concerned with decisions about an organisation's future and the way in which it needs to respond to the many pressures and influences discussed in Part II of the book. In turn, the consideration of future strategies must be mindful of the realities of translating strategy into action which, themselves, can be significant constraints on strategic choice.

Chapter 1 (section 1.1.2) explains different levels of strategy and strategic decisions. At these different levels executives are faced with choices as to how to meet the expectations of stakeholders whilst satisfying the needs and expectations of users, often in competition with another organisation. For example:

- Investment analysts and pension fund managers have expectations of corporations about how they create value for shareholders in comparison with other corporations. To meet these expectations, corporate executives have to take decisions about which businesses it makes sense to have in their portfolio and how they can add more value to those businesses in comparison with other corporations who might seek to own them. Choices therefore have to be made about corporate strategy.

- Business-level executives, in turn, must take decisions about how to satisfy the expectations of their corporate parents whilst also satisfying the needs of customers or users; and again how they can do this better than competition. This requires choices to be made about business (or competitive) strategy.

- In turn, these executives face decisions about how they will develop these strategies in terms of the products and markets they might develop; does it make sense to launch new products, enter new markets and should this be done through organic development, alliances or mergers and acquisitions?

There are, then, common themes in the choices that have to made to do with *satisfying expectations* of stakeholders by *creating value* in the context of actual or potential *competition*.

The overall challenge, which is the theme of Part III as a whole, is the extent to which these different levels of strategic choice are consistent with each other. In other words, how do strategic decisions at the corporate level affect those at the business-unit level; and, in turn, how do the decisions at the

THIS PART EXPLAINS:

- Corporate-level strategies and the role of the corporate parent.

- Portfolio decisions and diversification.

- Bases of business level competitive strategies – the strategy clock.

- Other bases of strategic choice – including game theory and strategies for hypercompetitive conditions.

- Strategic options – in terms of both directions and methods of development.

- Evaluating the suitability, acceptability and feasibility of strategies.

| Exhibit IIIi | Strategic choices |

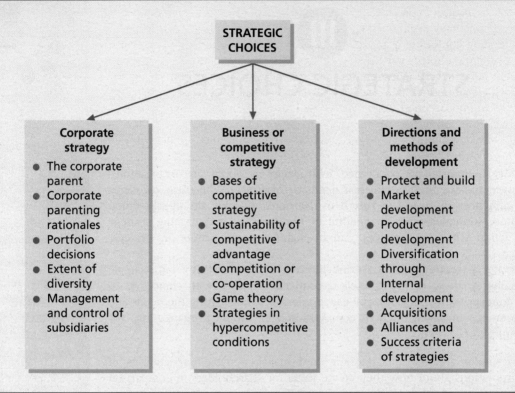

business-unit level affect those at the corporate level? And, in turn, how do they both create value for stakeholders? In the chapters that follow we return to these questions repeatedly.

The discussion of strategic choice has been divided into three chapters to reflect the three areas of strategic choice shown in Exhibit IIIi.

● Chapter 6 is concerned with corporate-level strategy; and, in particular, how corporate parents who manage multiple business units might create or destroy the value created by those businesses. In order to address this, four interrelated issues are addressed. First, the overall rationale of the corporate parent: what is its purpose in managing a multi-business corporation? Different possible rationales are discussed. Second, what is the logic of the portfolio of businesses within the corporation? Different logics are considered in relation to the different rationales that might be adopted by corporate parents. Third, the extent of corporate diversity is discussed together with the arguments for and against diversification strategies; and again this is considered in the light of the possible corporate rationales and portfolio logics. Finally, the question is raised as to whether the way the corporate parent relates to and seeks to control its businesses or subsidiaries makes sense when all the other issues are considered.

- Chapter 7 is concerned with business-level or competitive strategy. How might business unit managers compete successfully in markets so as to meet the needs of customers (or users) and create value for stakeholders, of which one may well be a corporate parent? This is first considered by examining choices of generic bases of competitive strategies: what are the fundamental choices available by which competitive advantage in markets might be achieved? Questions are also raised as to the extent to which sustainable competitive advantage is possible to achieve; and when it makes sense to choose co-operative rather than competitive strategies. The contribution of game theory to ways of thinking about competitive strategy is then discussed and the chapter concludes by considering the implications of turbulent, fast-changing 'hypercompetitive' environments on choices of competitive strategy.

- Chapter 8 deals with choices of both strategic direction and method. This includes considerations of how directions of strategic development can be built around market opportunities; developments of product; development of competences; and the various combinations of these three parameters. Development methods ranging from internal development, through strategic alliances to acquisitions and mergers are explained. The chapter then moves on to discuss why some strategies might succeed better than others. It does this by introducing the concepts of suitability, acceptability and feasibility. *Suitability* is a broad criterion concerned with whether a strategic option addresses the circumstances in which the organisation is operating – the strategic position as discussed in Part II. *Acceptability* is concerned with the expected performance outcomes (such as return or risk) of a strategic option, and the extent to which these would be in line with expectations. *Feasibilty* is concerned with whether a strategy could be made to work in practice, and therefore with the practicalities of resourcing and strategic capability.

6

Corporate-Level Strategy

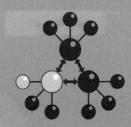

LEARNING OUTCOMES

After reading this chapter you should be able to explain:

● What is meant by the corporate parent in a multi-business organisation.

● The arguments for and against the value-adding capabilities of corporate parents.

● Different rationales of corporate parents, including the portfolio manager, the restructurer, the synergy manager and the parental developer.

● Different bases for explaining the portfolio logic of corporations; for example, in terms of balance, business attractiveness and 'fit'; and different frameworks for thinking about these.

● The differences between related and unrelated diversification; and the links between diversification and corporate performance.

● The importance of the compatibility of the corporate parenting rationale, the logic of the corporate portfolio, the nature and extent of diversification and the nature of corporate control exercised by the parent.

6.1 INTRODUCTION

The central concern in this chapter is the strategic decisions at the corporate level of organisations; decisions which may affect many business units. Managers at this level are acting on behalf of shareholders, or other stakeholders, to provide services and, quite possibly, strategic guidance to business units which, themselves, seek to generate value by interacting with customers (the subject of Chapter 7). In these circumstances a key question is to what extent and how might the corporate level add value to what the businesses do; or at the least how it might avoid destroying value.

Exhibit 6.1 represents a simplified multi-business company structure. It shows a number of business units grouped within divisions and a corporate centre or head office providing, perhaps, legal services, financial services and the staff of the chief executive. There are different views as to what is meant by corporate strategy and what, indeed, represents corporate as distinct from business-level strategy. Here the view is that anything above the business-unit

Exhibit 6.1	The multi-business company

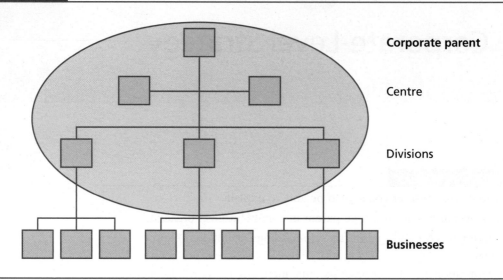

Corporate parent

Centre

Divisions

Businesses

The levels of management above that of the business units and therefore without direct interaction with buyers and competitors are referred to as the **corporate parent**

level represents corporate activity and is the subject of the discussion in this chapter. In this chapter the levels of management above that of business units and therefore without direct interaction with buyers and competitors are often referred to as the **corporate parent**. So, for example, the divisions within a corporation which look after several businesses act in a corporate parenting role. Of course it could be that there are parts of the corporate centre that do indeed interact with customers: a central call centre or a customer service department in a commercial organisation; or a special crime squad or specialist helicopter unit in a police force, for example. But where this is the case the same lessons apply as discussed in Chapter 7 relating to business units.

The relevance of this discussion does not only relate to large conglomerate businesses. Even small businesses may consist of a number of business units; for example, a local builder may be undertaking contract work for local government, work for industrial buyers and for local homeowners: not only are these different market segments, but the mode of operation and competences required for competitive success are also likely to be different. Moreover, the owner of that business has to take decisions about the extent of investment and activity in each segment. Public sector organisations such as local government or health services also provide different services, which correspond to business units in commercial organisations. So corporate level strategy is relevant to them too.

The discussion on corporate level strategy begins in section 6.2 by considering the arguments which have been advanced as to why and how a corporate parent might or might not be able to create value or add value to the business units within it. The chapter then moves on to consider this in more

Exhibit 6.2	Four key questions of corporate strategy

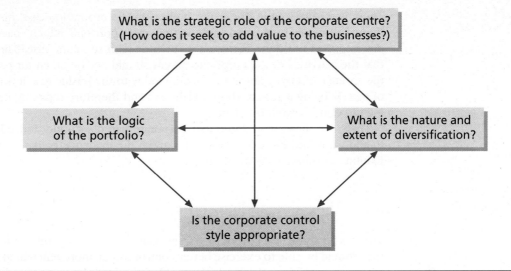

detail by considering the four key questions shown in Exhibit 6.2 which form the basis for the structure of the rest of the chapter.

● What is the overall *rationale* of the corporate parent in terms of how it envisages itself enhancing the value created by the business units for its shareholders/stakeholders? This is the focus of section 6.3 which considers four possible corporate roles, the portfolio manager, the restructurer, the synergy manager and the parental developer.

● What is the logic of the mix of business units in the *corporate portfolio*; and how does this make sense in terms of the corporate rationale? This is the focus of section 6.4 and is examined by reviewing a number of frameworks for considering such portfolios.

● Section 6.5 then asks whether the extent and type of *diversity* of the corporation are sensible given the corporate rationale and logic of the portfolio. Here, then, the focus is on the nature and extent of diversification.

● Finally, section 6.6 introduces the important issue of how corporate parents and business units interact; in particular, the way in which the centre seeks to manage business units. Here the question is whether the nature of *corporate control* of subsidiaries is appropriate in terms of the previous issues discussed, namely the corporate rationale, the logic of the portfolio and the extent of diversity. It is a question which is also taken up more fully in Chapter 9.

The four questions posed in Exhibit 6.2 are, therefore, interrelated. There is no absolute right or wrong answer to them: rather the key issue is the extent to which there is a consistency between the answers to them.

6.2 THE CORPORATE PARENT: VALUE ADDING OR VALUE DESTROYING?

There is a story told in one major multinational corporation that, historically, there had never been a business within their portfolio which, having been divested, had not done better on its own or with someone else. The point is that the activities of the corporate parent should not be taken for granted. In the absence of clarity about how it adds value to the businesses, it is in danger of merely being a cost to those businesses and therefore reducing or destroying the value created by them.

There are those who argue that corporate parents should, indeed, be able to add value and there are those who argue the evidence is that they do not. Exhibit 6.3 summarises these views.

6.2.1 The value-adding corporate parent[1]

Those who argue that corporate parents can create value point to the fact that they should be able to exercise better control and be more efficient at resource allocation than financial markets would if the businesses operated independently. After all, the corporate parent should have ready access to internal information within the businesses not available to external financial analysts: so the corporate parent should be able to take decisions with regard to those businesses, for example, in terms of allocation of resources, increasing or decreasing investment or changing management in times of poor performance. Moreover, they should have the co-operation of the managers in doing this since the managers work for the corporation. The corporate parent should also be able to enhance potential between the businesses. If one business is doing particularly well, other businesses should be able to learn from it; if management

Exhibit 6.3	The multi-business corporation: value creation or destruction?

VALUE CREATING?	OR DESTROYING?
● Beneficial control on businesses and better resource allocation through: – ready access to internal information – co-operation of business executives – real-time (not lagged) decision-making	● Businesses would be better off on their own subject to 'market' mechanisms
● Enhanced potential for exploitation of slack, synergies, transferences and learning between businesses	● The Centre: – adds cost – creates 'bureaucratic fog' – delays decisions and market responsiveness – buffers businesses from investment realities – provides a focus for managerial ambition
● Intervention in managerial appointments and development	● Managerial ambition and empire building is a better explanation of corporate growth and development

Exhibit 6.4	Potential added value roles of the corporate parent

ADDING VALUE THROUGH:

- Efficiency/leverage
- Expertise
- Investment and competence building
- Fostering innovation – coaching/learning
- Mitigating risk
- Image/networks
- Collaboration/co-ordination/brokerage
- Standards/performance assessment
- Intervention (e.g. acquisition, disposal, change agency)
- Acting in a visionary capacity

in one business has particular skills, other businesses might be able to benefit from this; there may also be synergies between businesses in terms of common usage of resources; and so on.

At the heart of this is the 'transaction cost' argument put forward by economists.[2] These potential ways of adding value are surely more efficiently and effectively carried out within the boundaries of a corporation. The alternative would, presumably, be to rely on contractual relationships of some sort to achieve such benefits, with their associated costs; and the mechanisms of financial markets to deal with underperformance. Advocates of the benefits of the corporate entity would say that financial markets could do little more than wait for poor performance, reduce share value, wait for takeovers to occur and hope that improvement would take place because of such changes. So, on the face of it the costs of achieving such benefits should be less within a corporate structure.

Certainly corporate centres have claimed to add value in many ways (see Exhibit 6.4); they include the following:

- Improving *efficiency* – perhaps through scale advantages from resource sharing, particularly in the use of infrastructure, support services and other overhead items. The corporate parent may have more *leverage* in either purchasing or market access.

- Providing *expertise* and *services* not available within smaller units – for example, personnel and financial services, estates management and IT infrastructure. Some of the most successful corporate parents have competences in market analysis, or cost analysis, which help fundamentally to reassess the role and future of divisions or subsidiaries. Human resource and management developments and succession planning may be important ways in which the parent adds value.

- Providing *investment*, particularly during the early days of new ventures. This investment could be in resources and infrastructure, but could also be concerned with developing or changing the core competences within businesses.

- *Fostering innovation* through the management of the knowledge creation processes. This could involve *coaching* of people and managers in divisions and the important role of providing a larger *peer group* through which individuals improve their own knowledge and skills, and where organisational *learning* occurs.

- *Mitigating risk* which smaller units inevitably run, and easing the problems created by the variety and variability of demands from customers. Arguably bigger or more diverse organisations can smooth out these problems more easily.

- Providing a strong *external image* from which smaller units can benefit, and accessing *external networks* better than any separate unit.

- Encouraging *collaboration* and *co-ordination* of effort which could result in products or services which a single unit could not deliver. The corporate parent may also be able to *broker* external linkages or collaborations which may be essential to the processes of innovation.

- Setting *standards*, assessing *performance* of individuals and units, and *intervening* to improve performance (for example, by replacing managers, selling off businesses or ensuring turnaround of poorly performing divisions or businesses).

- As Hamel and Prahalad[3] have highlighted, the importance of clear strategic intent can help galvanise motivation and enthusiasm throughout the organisation by providing what they call a sense of destiny and discovery. The idea is that by providing the businesses and those who work in them an attractive challenge of the future, managers will seek to 'stretch' their businesses beyond the day-to-day operations and short-term requirements imposed on them by their competitive environments and become more creative and innovative in developing business-level strategy. Arguably this *visionary role* is one which, to a greater or lesser extent, all corporate parents should play, not least because of the importance of providing clarity internally and externally about the logic and purpose of the organisation.

6.2.2 The value-destroying corporate parent[4]

There are, however, contrary arguments; that corporate centres actually tend to destroy value and that businesses would be better off on their own subject to market mechanisms, not least financial markets. Here the argument is that not only is there a real and sometimes very large financial cost of the centre, but that it may also create diseconomies in other ways.

- Corporate parents can add cost with bureaucratic mechanisms and hierarchies that delay decisions, create a 'bureaucratic fog' and hinder market responsiveness. Not least this is because there may be several levels of corporate parent above the business unit, each with executives who have a decision-making influence over the business units.

- It is not clear that the cost of these levels of management above the business unit are offset by the benefits they provide.

- Corporate parents buffer the executives in businesses from the realities of financial markets by providing a financial 'safety net' that mean that executives are not truly answerable for the performance of their businesses.

- Far from having a clear overall vision of what is trying to be achieved, the diversity and size of some corporations make it very difficult to see what they are about.

- Corporate hierarchies provide a focus for managerial ambition. Managers aspire to be at the top of the corporate ladder, rather than performing the value creation role of the business-unit level. The corporate centre is rather more seen as a vehicle for empire building in which executives seek to grow the number of businesses and the size of the corporation for motives of personal ambition.

Increasingly, analysts and commentators are beginning to raise questions about the extent to which corporate parents really do add value.[5] An example of the questions raised about the value-adding capabilities of BT as a corporate parent is given in Illustration 6.1. However it should not be thought that this is only a private sector issue. In the public sector, too, similar questions about the value-adding capabilities of parents also arise. In the UK there has been much questioning of the extent to which it makes sense for local government authorities to control many services that, historically, they had within their portfolios. For example, traditionally schools were managed through local education authorities (LEAs) who allocated government funds and provided certain services. However, in the 1990s both central government and many head teachers and governing bodies of schools began to question the value-adding role of this level of management. Central government, wishing to improve education standards, began to centralise education policy; and the schools themselves wanted more flexibility in decision making. The result was that many schools opted out of LEA control and for direct funding from central government.

The view taken in this chapter is that, indeed, there is a very great risk that corporate parents will destroy value: but that this is not inevitable. If parents do have the information about business units such that they can provide the sorts of benefit shown in Exhibit 6.4, then a well-managed parent should be able to add value. The real issue is, then, not whether a business unit should have a parent or be independent, but which parent is most appropriate and what the corporate strategy of the parent is such that it enhances the value created at business-unit level. The components of that corporate strategy can be informed by addressing the four questions raised in the introduction to this chapter and set out in Exhibit 6.2.

6.3 THE CORPORATE RATIONALE

The first question posed in Exhibit 6.2 is: what is the strategic rationale of the corporate parent? What is it there for? What role in value creation does it see for itself and, informed by this, how will it answer the other three questions posed in Exhibit 6.2? Being clear about this is important for at least three reasons.

Illustration 6.1

BT in the bunker[1]

A key issue of corporate-level strategy is the value-adding role of the corporate centre.

British Telecom (BT) was part of the nationalised UK Post Office until 1984, when it was floated as a public limited company. Following an initial period of cost cutting, it pursued a strategy of development into mobile communications and international expansion. By 2000 its share price was over £15; however, by March 2001 it was at £1.15, and BT's corporate management was being heavily criticised.

Its borrowings of £30 billion were often quoted as a main concern. This had arisen from huge expenditure since 1999 on mobile phone licences in Germany and Britain and in consolidating BT's position in Japan, Germany, Ireland and Norway. However, the FT[2] reported that: 'France Telecom and Deutsche Telecom have bigger debts; Vodafone's fall has cost investors more money; and the shares of Colt and Energis have performed more poorly of late.' Yet the concerns of institutional investors contributed to the chairman's, Sir Iain Vallance, standing down; and there were questions as to whether Sir Peter Bonfield should remain as chief executive. So why did BT and its executives take so much flak?

Clarity of international strategy

Investors were concerned that BT's international strategy had lost its direction. BT had been preparing to merge with MCI Communications, the US telecoms group, when, in 1997, a bid from WorldCom meant that BT was forced to sell its 20 per cent stake. Whilst this made a huge profit for BT, it left its international strategy unclear. BT had also lost out in acquisition activity (e.g. Vodafone had acquired Japan Telecom), and had been left in a weak position in alliances in which it had taken an interest.

Clarity of ownership strategy

BT had also proposed to float 25 per cent of its subsidiaries, Wireless (mobile communications), Yell (Yellow Pages and directories) and Wholesale (land line capacity and call terminations), all of Ignite (corporate and wholesale broadband network); and refocus its activities on western Europe and Japan. But there was confusion on this. The finance director, Philip Hampton, who was said to favour a more far-reaching break-up of the group, argued against the plans to float a 25 per cent stake in Yell in favour of a full de-merger: 'At the end of the day we could not justify why it was important . . . to hold 75 per cent of Yell'.[4] Commentators wondered why it had been proposed in the first place and went on to ask why the restructuring proposals even contemplated turning BT into a telecoms 'investment trust', with 75 per cent stakes in separately quoted companies.

Corporate culture

In addition to all this, the view was that the corporate centre of BT was slow to respond, cumbersome and hamstrung by its past in terms of its structures and its approach to understanding markets. Newspapers used words such as 'BTs lingering civil service culture'.

Notes

1. This was the headline for the article on BT in *The Sunday Times* of March 25, 2001.
2. *Financial Times*, 25 March 2001.
3. Quoted in *The Sunday Times*, 11 March 2001.

Questions

1. Using the checklist in section 6.2.1, consider how BT corporate centre might add value to its subsidiaries.

2. Revisit this illustration when you have read the chapter and consider if the concerns about BT as a corporate parent were justified.

- Because in the absence of such clarity it is likely that the corporate parent will undertake activities and bear costs that have nothing to do with adding value to the business units, and are therefore just costs which diminish value. This is discussed more extensively in sections 6.3.1 to 6.3.4 below.

- Because corporate managers need to be able to make clear to the stakeholders what the corporation as a whole is about. In the absence of doing so, investors can become confused as to what a corporation is trying to achieve or how it is going about doing it; and they might not understand the argument for the presence of certain businesses within a portfolio, or how a corporate parent might add value to them. Certainly this has been the case for highly diversified firms. Financial institutions have begun to question what value is added by the corporate centre and to take the view that the different businesses might be better divested from existing corporate parents.

- Internally, if business unit managers are not be able to make sense of what their corporate parent is there for, they inevitably feel as though the corporate centre is either little more than a cost burden on them, or that corporate executives lack clarity of direction. In either case they are likely to become demotivated. They will also wish to know whether their business is seen as central to corporate aspirations or peripheral. If they are not clear, it is unlikely that they will manage the business in ways to enhance the overall aspirations of the corporation. Indeed, strategic decisions at the business level could run counter to corporate strategy. Of course, the reverse is the case. Clarity at the corporate level can provide a basis on which strategic choice is made at the business level.

The discussion which follows considers four corporate rationales,[6] summarised in Exhibit 6.5.

6.3.1 The portfolio manager

The **portfolio manager** is, in effect, a corporate parent acting as an agent on behalf of financial markets and shareholders with a view to enhancing the value attained from the various businesses in a more efficient or effective way than financial markets could. Their role is to identify and acquire under-valued assets or businesses and improve them. They might do this, for example, by acquiring another corporation, divesting low-performing businesses within it and encouraging the improved performance of those with potential. They may well seek to keep the cost of the centre low, for example by having a small corporate staff with few central services, leaving the businesses alone so that the chief executives of those businesses have a high degree of autonomy, but setting clear financial targets for those chief executives with very high rewards if they achieve them and the expectation of low rewards, or loss of position, if they do not.

Such corporate parents could, of course, manage quite a large number of such businesses because they are not directly intervening in the strategies of those businesses. Rather they are setting financial targets, making central

A **portfolio manager** is a corporate parent acting as an agent on behalf of financial markets and shareholders

Exhibit 6.5	Portfolio managers, restructurers, synergy managers and parental developers

	Portfolio managers	Restructurers	Synergy managers	Parental developers
Logic	● 'Agent' for financial markets	● Value creation at SBU level: limited role to create SBU 'fitness'	● The achievement of synergistic benefits	● Central competences can be used to create value in SBUs
Strategic requirements	● Identifying and acquiring undervalued assets ● Divesting low-performing SBUs quickly and good performers at a premium	● Identifying restructuring opportunities ● Intervention in SBU to transform performance ● Sale of SBU when restructuring complete or unfeasible or market conditions favourable	● Sharing activities/ resources or transferring skills/ competences to enhance competitive advantage of SBUs ● Identification of appropriate bases for sharing or transferring ● Identification of benefits which outweigh costs	● SBUs not fulfilling their potential (a parenting opportunity) ● The Centre has clear and relevant resources or capabilities to enhance SBU potential ● The portfolio is suited to Centre's expertise
Organisational requirements	● Autonomous SBUs ● Small, low-cost corporate staff ● Incentives based on SBU results	● Autonomous SBUs ● Small, specialist Centre ● Turnround skills of corporate staff ● Incentives based on acquired SBU results	● Collaborative SBUs ● Corporate staff as integrators ● Overcoming SBU resistance to sharing or transferring ● Incentives affected by corporate results	● Centre manages understand SBUs ('sufficient feel') ● Effective structural and control linkages from Centre to SBUs ● SBUs may be autonomous unless collaboration is required ● Incentives based on SBU performance

evaluations about the well-being and future prospects of such businesses and investing or divesting accordingly.

A good example of such a corporation was GEC, the industrial conglomerate so powerful under Lord Weinstock in the 1980s and 1990s. Weinstock did not pretend to have a direct involvement in the businesses. He saw his role as setting clear and challenging financial targets and letting the executives get on with their jobs in their businesses. They were examined minutely about the performance of those businesses in financial terms, but were left to get on with it strategically. A successful chief executive in GEC could look forward to running his or her own business provided the targets were met. The central costs imposed upon that chief executive were low but, if successful, he or she could draw on the substantial financial resources of the group for purposes of investment.

A parallel situation in the public sector is that the parent would be acting on behalf of the government in the allocation of financial resources. For example, the Higher Education Funding Council is responsible on behalf of government for the allocation of research funds to universities in England and Wales. It sets criteria and establishes procedures by which to evaluate universities' research activities, and funds are allocated according to the ratings which result. But it does not intervene in the universities themselves with regard to the strategies they choose to follow.

6.3.2 The restructurer

In some respects **restructurers** are similar to portfolio managers in so far as they are likely to have low central costs with relatively minimal involvement at business unit level. However, they are also adept at identifying restructuring opportunities in businesses and have the skills to intervene to transform performance in those businesses. They may well hold a diverse range of businesses within their portfolio. However, they do have a limited role at business-unit level, which is to identify ways in which businesses can be turned round or fitness improved and to manage the restructuring period. This might take effect in some ways similar to the activities of the portfolio manager. They will acquire another corporation and sell off businesses which do not have restructuring or improvement opportunities through their skills opportunities; but they will also move specialist managers from the centre into the businesses they keep to set them on a profitable course. They will then leave the businesses alone. So again the emphasis is on autonomous business units with a small corporate centre, but, in this case, with specialist turnround skills of corporate staff. The incentives for the businesses will, again, be based on SBU performance and little attention will be paid to integrating the businesses or achieving synergies across those businesses. In its heyday of acquisitions, Hanson[7] was often thought of as a portfolio manager, but would more accurately be described as a restructurer. It did more than buy and sell businesses: it targeted businesses in which it could see opportunities for restructuring and therefore value creation.

Of course, in this case it is likely that the business restructuring opportunities that will be sought will be those that match the skills of the corporate centre. In this sense there are some similarities with the parental developers discussed in section 6.3.4. below.

Some would argue that the days of the portfolio manager and restructurer are gone. They are certainly not popular corporate rationales with financial analysts and there are many fewer such corporations than there used to be. For example, the corporate strategies of both GEC and Hanson have changed since

Restructurers are adept at identifying restructuring opportunities in businesses

the departures of Lord Weinstock and Lord Hanson, with extensive divestment and a search for greater focus, and, as Illustration 6.2 shows, the once powerful and hugely diverse Lonhro has gone through similar changes. Even Tomkins, which built a business with a portfolio described as 'from buns' (Hovis bread) 'to guns' (Smith and Wesson) sold its bakery business in 2000 to focus more on its engineering businesses.

The decline of the portfolio managers and restructurers could be because financial analysts and investors have become more adept at analysing for themselves the opportunities that businesses present and identifying underperforming businesses. There are also increasing signs that financial institutions such as pension funds are becoming more interventionist in the affairs of corporations: if the pension fund Hermes sees opportunities for improving returns to shareholders through the reconfiguration of businesses within a portfolio, it will approach corporate executives direct. The role of corporate parents acting as 'agents' on behalf of investors is therefore being reduced.

6.3.3 The synergy manager

Synergy can occur in situations where two or more activities or processes complement each other, to the extent that their combined effect is greater than the sum of the parts

Synergy is often seen as *the* raison d'être of the corporate parent. Potentially, **synergy** can occur in situations where two or more activities or processes complement each other, to the extent that their combined effect is greater than the sum of the parts.[8] In terms of corporate strategy, the logic is that value can be enhanced across business units. This might be done in a number of ways:[9]

● Activities might be shared: for example, common distribution systems might be used for different businesses; overseas offices may be shared by smaller business units acting in different geographical areas; common brand names may provide value to different products within different businesses.

● There may exist common skills or competences across businesses. For example, on the face of it there may be diverse products or technologies within an industrial products business; but the value-adding capabilities of service offered to industrial customers may be a common thread through such businesses. If this is so, then the skills and competences learned in one business may be shared by another, thus improving performance. Or there may exist expertise built up, for example, in marketing or research, which is transferable to other businesses within a portfolio less capable in such ways, again enhancing their performance.

However, there are problems in achieving such synergies:

● The skills or competences on which argued synergy is supposed to be based may not really exist or, if they do, may not add value. It is not unusual for managers to claim, either at the business level or the corporate level, that particular competences exist, are important and are useful to share, when they are little more than the inherited myths in the business, or are not really valued by customers.

Illustration 6.2

From Lonrho to Lonmin

STRATEGY IN ACTION

The highly diversified, decentralised conglomerate form of corporation is becoming less common.

At its peak, Lonrho controlled 900 subsidiary companies in Africa, Europe, Asia and North America with a turnover in excess of $7bn and a workforce of over a quarter of a million. For much of this time it was dominated by its chairman, Roland 'Tiny' Rowland.

Lonhro's 1993 annual report listed its principal activities as embracing:

- Mining of gold, platinum, rhodium and coal; it was the third-largest producer of platinum in the world through its ownership of mines in South Africa and a major gold producer from mines in Ghana and Zimbabwe.

- Agriculture, including ranching and production of cotton, sugar and tea; Lonrho ranked as the largest single producer of food in Africa, owner of 1.5 million acres of land and 125,000 cattle spread across ten countries.

- Agricultural equipment and motor vehicle distribution and assembly; the company was one of the world's largest automobile distributors, selling Rolls-Royces, Volkswagens, Audis, Mercedes and French, Japanese and American vehicles in Britain, Europe and Africa.

- Other interests included engineering and manufacturing; printing; insurance; exporting; property management; hotels; finance and general trading; production and retailing of textiles. It also owned the *Observer* newspaper and 23 provincial newspapers in the UK.

As the 1993 annual report explained, at that time the company was 'divisionalised into 30 management regions . . . principally organised on a territorial basis in Africa and on an activity basis outside Africa'. Lonhro insisted that decentralisation was the key to its management philosophy. Each region was highly autonomous, with a chief executive and finance director being responsible for the efficient day-to-day operations of its business, and its own specialist personnel. It was the group's policy 'to grant each region sufficient capital and revenue autonomy to operate a successful business', though capital expenditure was monitored and controlled by the centre. The performance of each region was then monitored centrally through the medium of budgetary control based on an annual budget, updated through revised forecasts.

However, after investor confidence began to decline in the early 1990s, there was a protracted battle between a major shareholder, Dieter Boch, a German financier, and Tiny Rowland. The output of this was that Boch eventually took control of the business in 1994, Rowland resigned in 1995 and Boch began to unravel the complex corporation. By 2000, the corporation was renamed Lonmin; much of its diversified portfolio had been divested such that it had come to be focused on the mining of platinum, coal and gold mainly in Southern and Central Africa.

Questions

1. What parenting rationale and portfolio logic might apply to a group as diversified as Lonhro?

2. How might this differ for the more focused Lonmin?

● There also needs to be a benefit in such sharing or transference of skills which outweighs the costs involved in doing so. There will be a cost – whether financial or in terms of opportunity cost – in such sharing, not least because it will require central resources to undertake the integration.

In terms of practical realities:

● Managers in the businesses have to be prepared to co-operate in such transference and sharing: and there are reasons they may not wish to do so, not least of which is that such sharing detracts from focusing on the primary concerns they have for their own businesses. Also, for managers in the businesses to be collaborative in achieving such synergistic benefits, rewards may have to be tailored to encourage such sharing. The problem is that rewards to business managers are typically on business unit performance, whereas under this strategy they are being asked to co-operate in sharing activities between businesses. It is quite possible that the business unit manager will respond by asking 'what's in it for me?' and conclude that there is very little.

● There also needs to be compatibility between the systems and culture of the business units that are to do the sharing. A business may have been acquired with the logic of gaining synergistically from an existing business in a firm's portfolio, only to find that the two businesses are quite different in cultural terms such that sharing between the two is problematic.

● Finally, the corporate parent needs to be determined to achieve such synergies. The need here, at a minimum, is for central staff to act as integrators, and therefore to understand the businesses well enough to do so. The centre may also need to be prepared to intervene at the business level in terms of strategic direction and control to ensure that such potential synergies bear fruit. However, in turn this raises questions as to whether such detailed understanding of businesses and hands-on directive influence from the corporate centre makes sense for other reasons. This relates to the sorts of issues discussed in section 6.6 below and in section 9.3 of Chapter 9.

The notion of synergy has long been a justification used by corporate bodies for their value-adding capabilities. However, this has become less so. It has been realised that synergistic benefits are not as easy to achieve as would appear, can be costly to the extent that the benefits do not outweigh the costs, and in any case the basis of synergies may be mythical. However, it remains a dominant theme in corporate-level strategy, as Illustration 6.3 shows.

6.3.4 The parental developer[10]

The **parental developer** seeks to employ its own competences as a parent to add value to its businesses

The **parental developer** seeks to employ its own competences as a parent to add value to its businesses. Here, then, the issue is not so much about how it can help create or develop benefits across business units or transference between business units, as in the case of managing synergy: rather parental developers have to be clear about the relevant resources or capabilities they have to enhance the potential of business units. Suppose, for example, it has a

Illustration 6.3

Espoused synergies in acquisitions

STRATEGY IN ACTION

Many companies cite synergy as one of the justifications for mergers and acquisitions.

Primedia and About

In December 2000, About.com, a US Internet portal, was acquired by Primedia, a magazine publisher based in the USA. About.com covered over 50,000 subjects and was the seventh most frequently visited Internet site, with 60 million users each month. Primedia published 220 magazines, including periodicals and trade publications, and owned a television network as well as 200 websites and other Internet properties.

The CEO of Primedia, Thomas Rogers, said, 'The Primedia and About merger creates the leading model for the integration of traditional and new media niche content and the resulting delivery of targeted marketing vehicles . . . Primedia is the leading traditional media company in the delivery of highly targeted niche print and video products to consumers. About is the leading online company in the delivery of niche content. This is the most synergistic combination either of these two companies could enter into and creates a one-of-a-kind company that no two other companies could create.'

Primedia planned to take advantage of cross-marketing and shared content with the new merger. Rogers argued that, as well as the benefits from sheer scale in market niches, there would be major cost-saving synergies. Revenue would be generated by applying 'Primedia's 1,600-person sales force and 60,000 advertisers . . . to About's niche-based sites [and] driving Primedia magazine subscriptions on these sites'. Cost synergies would result from cutting back About's marketing expenses whilst significantly cutting back Primedia's own spending on Internet businesses.

Tata Tetley

In March 2000, Tata Tea, India's largest producer of tea, acquired the Tetley Group, the second-biggest tea brand in the world. According to the vice-chairman of Tata Tea, Mr Kumar, 'the synergies will produce a global leader'. Tata would supply produce to Tetley for the manufacture of teabags and it would gain from Tetley's skills in blending, packaging, inventory management, cost control and distribution.

Kumar argued that in an industry in which brand strength is a critical business success factor, Tetley's flair for product development and marketing would allow Tata to gain a larger share of the tea market and opportunities to achieve synergies and higher added value. Tata's activities would also benefit from standardised management practices, including the quality performance norms and consumer focus of Tetley. The two organisations would work under a unified global strategy, and their combined strength would help to create opportunities to expand sales in existing and new markets.

The breadth of experience and vertical integration would equip Tata to compete anywhere in the world. With the globally recognised Tetley brand and other regional brands, Tata would have a product portfolio of over 100 varieties of teas (margins for which were higher than for traditional tea) and this would make it possible to tap into markets effectively and increase market share.

Prepared by Urmilla Lawson, University of Strathclyde Graduate School of Business

Sources: B. Quint, 'About.com acquired by Primedia: sin or synergy?', *Information Today*, Dec. 2000, vol. 17, i. 11, p. 22; K. Merchant, 'Tata may have swallowed Tetley but "tea folk" will remain', *The Financial Times*, 28 Feb. 2000, p. 26.

Questions

1. What would the corporate parent need to do to ensure the realisation of the sorts of synergy described above?

2. What might prevent the realisation of these synergies?

great deal of experience in globalising domestically based businesses; or a valuable brand that may enhance the performance of image of a business; or perhaps specialist skills in financial management, brand marketing or research and development. If such parenting competences exist, corporate managers then need to identify a 'parenting opportunity': a business or businesses which are not fulfilling their potential but where improvement could be made by the application of the competences of the parent – for example, a business which could benefit by being more global, by brand development or by central R&D support.

The competences that parents have will vary. Shell would argue that it is not just their huge financial muscle that matters but also that they are particularly adept at negotiating with governments as well as developing high-calibre internationally mobile executives who can work almost anywhere in the world within a Shell corporate framework, and that this allows them to develop businesses globally. 3M are single-mindedly concerned with inculcating a focus on innovation in their businesses. They try to ensure a corporate culture based on this, set clear innovation targets for their businesses and elevate the standing of technical personnel concerned with innovation. Unilever have increasingly sought to focus on developing their core expertise in global branding and marketing in the fast-moving consumer goods company, with supporting state-of-the-art research and development facilities to back it up. They would argue that this is where they can add greatest value to their businesses, and that it has significantly affected the shape of their corporation over the years (see Illustration 6.4 on page 294). Of course, it could be that some corporate parents become adept at developing networking for learning across their businesses – Canon would claim they do this – and in this sense they may be encouraging synergy benefits; but this horizontal benefit is not necessarily the core rationale of the parental developer.

Running an organisation on this basis does, however, pose some challenges. For example:

- If the corporate parent identifies that it has value-adding capabilities in particular and limited ways, the implication is that it should not be providing services in other ways, or if it does they should be at minimal cost. For example, some corporate centres have decided to outsource a great many services that were once seen as a traditional role of the centre: legal services, payroll services, training and development and so on. One chief executive, following such a course of action, claimed that his head office workforce would be reduced by over 50 per cent with a saving of over 60 per cent of the costs of that centre. Moreover, he claimed, by so doing it focused the attention of corporate executives on management time in areas that really could add value as distinct from merely administrative functions.

- Following the same logic in the public sector can create a dilemma. On the one hand, keeping such central services in the public sector ensures political control over social purposes – for example, ensuring service coverage to all sections of the community. On the other hand, a private sector company might be a better parent, in the sense that they might be more skilled at providing the service or doing it more efficiently.

- Another and very challenging responsibility of the corporate parent is being sure about just how it can add value to business units. If the value-adding capabilities of the parent are wrongly identified then, far from the businesses benefiting, they will be subject to interference from the centre in ways which are counter-productive. There needs to be some hard evidence of such value-adding capabilities.

- The corporate parent may realise that there are some business units within its portfolio where it can add little value. This may help identify businesses that should not be part of the corporate portfolio. More uncomfortably, however, such business units could be high-performing businesses, successful in their own right and not requiring the competences of the parent. The parent may argue that other businesses in the portfolio can learn from them; but this is the logic of synergy management rather than parental development. The question the parental developer has to ask is how it is adding value to *that* business. The logic of the parental development approach is that since the centre cannot add value, it is a cost and is therefore destroying value; that the parent should therefore consider divesting such a business, realising a premium for it and reinvesting it in businesses where it can add value. Logical as this may seem, it is unlikely to find favour, not least because the executives at the centre might be indicted by their own shareholders for selling the 'crown jewels'.

- This, in turn, raises the question as to whether the parent could adopt multiple rationales in its parenting. For example, could it simultaneously act as a parental developer for some of its businesses with a hands-off, almost portfolio approach, for those in which it cannot add further value? Or could it be both a synergy manager and a parental developer? The dangers are, of course, that the rationale becomes confused, the centre unclear as to what it is trying to achieve, the business unit managers confused as to their role in the corporation and the cost of the centre escalates. A multiple approach also raises the issue of multiple control styles in corporate bodies (see section 6.6 below), and in particular whether this is feasible.

- If the logic of the parental developer is to be followed then the executives of the corporate parent must also have 'sufficient feel' or understanding of the businesses within the portfolio to know where they can add value and where they cannot: this is an issue taken up in section 6.3.4 below in relation to the logic of portfolios. It is also necessary that there has to be effective structural and control linkages from the centre to the businesses; an issue taken up in section 6.6 below and in section 9.3.

6.4 THE CORPORATE PORTFOLIO

So far the discussion has been about the rationales that corporate parents might have in relation to the management of a multi-business organisation. It should be seen that each of these rationales has implications in terms of the number and nature of the businesses within such a group; or vice versa, the

Exhibit 6.6	The growth share matrix (or BCG box)

MARKET SHARE

		High	Low
MARKET GROWTH	High	Stars	Question marks
	Low	Cash cows	Dogs

number and nature of businesses will have implications for the rationale the parent might adopt. To take two examples: a parent acting as a portfolio manager might be able to manage a very diverse set of businesses with no particular similarities between them, largely by setting financial targets, whereas a synergy manager needs to understand the businesses well and can therefore probably only cope with a limited number of related-type businesses. The rest of the issues which now follow are to do with the nature and diversity of the businesses within the group, given the different rationales described above. The first concern is with the basis upon which the portfolio of the business is considered.

A number of tools have been developed for helping managers choose what businesses to have in a portfolio. Each tool gives more or less focus on one of three criteria:

● the *balance* of the portfolio;

● the *attractiveness* of the businesses in the portfolio in terms of how profitable they are or are likely to be and how fast they are growing; and

● the degree of '*fit*' that the businesses have with each other in terms of potential synergies or the extent to which the corporate parent will be good at looking after them.

6.4.1 The growth share matrix (or BCG box)[11]

One of the most common and long-standing ways of conceiving of the balance of a portfolio of businesses is in terms of the relationship between market share and market growth identified by the Boston Consulting Group (BCG). Exhibit 6.6 represents this approach and shows the terms typically used to refer to the types of businesses in such a portfolio.

- A **star** is a business unit which has a high market share in a growing market. The business unit may be spending heavily to gain that share, but experience curve benefits (see section 4.3.3) should mean that costs are reducing over time and, it is to be hoped, at a rate faster than that of competitors.

- A **question mark** (or problem child) is a business unit in a growing market, but without a high market share. It may be necessary to spend heavily to increase market share, but if so, it is unlikely that the business unit is achieving sufficient cost reduction benefits to offset such investments.

- A **cash cow** is a business unit with a high market share in a mature market. Because growth is low and market conditions are more stable, the need for heavy marketing investment is less. But high relative market share means that the business unit should be able to maintain unit cost levels below those of competitors. The cash cow should then be a cash provider (e.g. to finance question marks).

- **Dogs** are business units with a low share in static or declining markets and are thus the worst of all combinations. They may be a cash drain and use up a disproportionate amount of company time and resources.

A **star** is a business unit which has a high market share in a growing market

A **question mark** (or problem child) is a business unit in a growing market, but without a high market share

A **cash cow** is a business unit with a high market share in a mature market

Dogs are business units with a low share in static or declining markets

The growth share matrix permits business units to be examined in relation to (a) market (segment) share and (b) the growth rate of that market and in this respect the life cycle development of that market. It is therefore a way of considering the balance and development of a portfolio.

It is argued that market growth rate is important for a business unit seeking to dominate a market because it may be easier to gain dominance when a market is in its growth state. In a state of maturity, a market is likely to be stable, with customer loyalties fairly fixed, so it is more difficult to gain share. But if all competitors in the growth stage are trying to gain market share, competition will be very fierce: so it will be necessary to invest in that business unit in order to gain share and market dominance. Moreover, it is likely that such a business unit will need to price low or spend high amounts on advertising and selling, or both. This strategy is one of high risk unless this low-margin activity is financed by products earning higher profit levels. This leads to the idea of a balanced mix of business units.

Of course, other firms might take a different view. For example, if the corporate aspiration is one of high growth in income and the business is prepared to invest to gain that growth, then it may be prepared to support more *stars* and *question marks* than a parent who is concerned with stable cash generation and who may concentrate on preserving or building its *cash cows*.

There could be links between the businesses in such a portfolio in terms of perceived synergies; but this is not necessary for the logic to hold. The idea is that the corporate parent will be good at spotting investment opportunities in line with this matrix. They could be less concerned about managing the businesses themselves; so in this sense it would correspond to the logic of the portfolio manager or restructurer. It is not always the case that the matrix is used with this in mind: but if the corporate parent envisages itself as having some more proactive logic associated with it, then it might wish to ask whether a portfolio logic more appropriate to its purpose may be helpful; some of which are discussed below.

It is worth noting that some caution needs to be exercised in the use of the BCG matrix:

- There can be practical difficulties in deciding what exactly 'high' and 'low' (growth and share) can mean in a particular situation.

- The analysis should be applied to *strategic business units*, not to products or to broad markets (which might include many segments).

- In many organisations the critical resource to be planned and balanced will not be cash, but the innovative capacity, which consists of the time and creative energy of the organisation's managers, designers, engineers, etc. *Question marks* and *stars* are very demanding on these types of resource.

- The position of *dogs* is often misunderstood. Certainly, there may be some business units which need immediate deletion – but even then there may be political difficulties if they are the brainchild of people with power within the organisation. However, other dogs may have a useful place in the portfolio. They may be necessary to complete the product range and provide a credible presence in the market. They may be held for defensive reasons – to keep competitors out. They may also be capable of revitalisation.

- Little is said about the behavioural implications of such a strategy. How does central management motivate the managers of *cash cows*, who see all their hard-earned surpluses being invested in other businesses? Indeed, perhaps the single factor which makes the creation and management of a balanced portfolio difficult in practice is the jealousy that can arise between the various strategic business units.

6.4.2 Balance in a public sector portfolio

The different services offered by public sector organisations can also be considered in terms of the balance of a portfolio, as seen in Exhibit 6.7. Here the key judgements are concerned with (a) the organisation's 'ability to serve effectively' by providing perceived value for money with the resources which are available to it, and (b) the political attractiveness of its services in terms of the extent to which they can gain stakeholder and public support for funding. Not all services will be public sector 'stars' in this respect. Some may be services required politically or because of public need, but for which there are limited resources – the 'political hot box'. In many respects this is where the National Health Service in the UK finds itself. Similarly – and a point often forgotten by public sector managers when reviewing their portfolio of activities – a provider of public services may be mandated to provide some statutory services and find resources 'locked up' in so doing. There are still other services that a public sector provider may have undertaken effectively for many years but for which there is little popular public support or funding attractiveness. Somewhat strangely these are referred to as the 'golden fleece' in the matrix.

Exhibit 6.7	Public sector portfolio matrix

ABILITY TO SERVE EFFECTIVELY

	High	Low
High	Public sector star	Political hot box
Low	Golden fleece	Back drawer issue

PUBLIC NEED AND SUPPORT + FUNDING ATTRACTIVENESS

Source: J.R. Montanari and J.S. Bracker, *Strategic Management Journal*, vol. 7, no. 3 (1986), reprinted by permission of John Wiley & Sons Ltd.

'Back drawer issues' are the equivalent of dogs in the BCG matrix; they have neither political (or public) support, nor sufficient resources. In a review of the public sector portfolio, they are the sorts of service which, if possible, should be dropped.

Another problem may arise for managers in public sector organisations. They may find it difficult to develop services with real growth potential or generate surpluses to be reinvested, because this may not be their brief from government. They may be expected to manage services which cannot make money, but which are public necessities. Further, if they seek to develop services which can grow and make money, these may be privatised or put out to private tender. It may be seen as legitimate for a local government leisure department to manage public parks and recreation grounds, but the development of indoor tennis and swimming pools with profit potential may be seen as an inappropriate activity. The definition of the appropriate portfolio of activities therefore requires a clarity of corporate purposes and aspirations.

Exhibit 6.8	Indicators of SBU strength and market attractiveness

INDICATORS OF SBU STRENGTH COMPARED WITH COMPETITION	INDICATORS OF MARKET ATTRACTIVENESS
• Market share • Salesforce • Marketing • R&D • Manufacturing • Distribution • Financial resources • Managerial competence • Competitive position in terms of, e.g. image, breadth of product line, quality/reliability, customer service	• Market size • Market growth rate • Cyclicality • Competitive structure • Barriers to entry • Industry profitability • Technology • Inflation • Regulation • Workforce availability • Social issues • Environmental issues • Political issues • Legal issues

6.4.3 The directional policy matrix

The **directional policy matrix** positions SBUs according to (a) how attractive the relevant market is in which they are operating, and (b) the competitive strength of the SBU in that market

Another way to consider a portfolio of businesses is by means of the *directional policy matrix*,[12] which categorises business units into those with good prospects and those with less good prospects. Sometimes known as the *attractiveness matrix*, it provides a way of considering a portfolio of business units in terms of their attractiveness by directing attention to the attractiveness of both the environment for SBUs and their competitive position. Specifically, the **directional policy matrix** positions business units according to (a) how attractive the relevant market is in which they are operating, and (b) the competitive strength of the SBU in that market. Each business unit is positioned within the matrix according to a series of indicators of attractiveness and strength. The factors typically considered are set out in Exhibit 6.8. However, these should not be thought of as pre-ordained. The factors should be those most relevant to the organisation and its market: for example, as identified by PESTEL or five forces analysis for attractiveness and through competitor analysis to identify business unit strength. Some analysts also choose to show graphically how large the market is for a given business unit's activity, and even the market share of that business unit, as shown in Exhibit 6.9. For example, managers in a firm with the portfolio shown in Exhibit 6.9 will be concerned that they have relatively low shares in the largest and most attractive market, whereas their greatest strength is in a market with only medium attractiveness and smaller markets with little long-term attractiveness.

The matrix also provides a way of considering appropriate corporate-level strategies given the positioning of the business units as shown in Exhibit 6.10. It suggests that the businesses with the highest growth potential and the greatest strength are those in which to invest for growth; and those which are the

Exhibit 6.9	Market attractiveness/SBU strength matrix

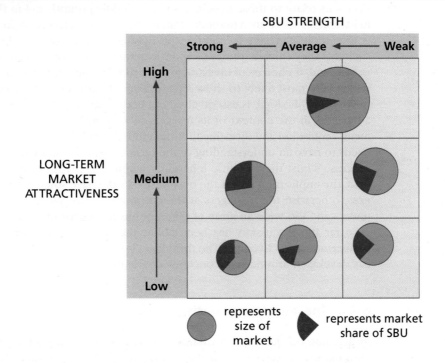

Exhibit 6.10	Strategy guidelines based on the directional policy matrix

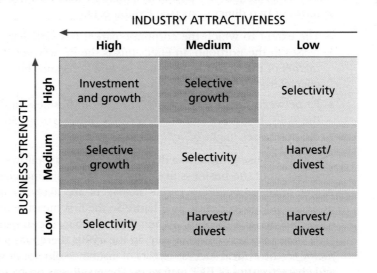

weakest and in the least attractive markets should be divested or harvested (i.e. used to yield as much cash as possible before divesting or closure). The difficult decisions relate to those businesses in the middle ground; and in the example in Exhibit 6.9 there are a number of these. Where the matrix helps in this respect is in getting managers to identify the reasons for the positions in the matrix such that they can ask questions about whether it is possible to grow such businesses; and, if choices of investment have to be made between the businesses, which look most likely to show a pay-off on the basis of such evidence.

This portfolio logic is essentially about understanding the relative strength of a business in the context of its markets so as to make decisions about investment, acquisition and divestment. It therefore assumes that the corporate centre needs to have an understanding of the businesses, their strategies and bases of success. Whilst there is little inherently within this matrix to do with relatedness, the implication is that the businesses should have some degree of relatedness, otherwise the managers at the corporate centre would be expected to understand too wide an array of different businesses for investment purposes.

So far the discussion has been about the logic of portfolios in terms of balance and attractiveness. The third logic is to do with 'fit'. Thinking about fit has developed around two concepts – parenting and core competences.

6.4.4 The parenting matrix

In deciding on the appropriateness of the role of the parent and the mix of business units best suited to the parent, the *parenting matrix* (or Ashridge Portfolio Display[13]) can be useful. This builds on the ideas set out in section 6.3.4 above which discussed the *parental developer* corporate rationale. It suggests that corporations should seek to build portfolios that fit well with their corporate centre parenting skills and that the corporate centre should in turn build parenting skills that are appropriate for their portfolio. By juggling these two principles, corporations should be able to move towards greater fit in terms of two dimensions (see Exhibit 6.11):

● The extent to which the corporate parent has sufficient '*feel*' for the businesses in the portfolio. In effect this is the fit between the *critical success factors* of the business units (see section 4.2) and the skills, resources and characteristics of the corporate parent.

● Fit between the *parenting opportunities* of business units (see below) and the skills, resources and characteristics of the parent. So this is about how the businesses might *benefit* from the parent.

The logic for using these two dimensions of fit is as follows. If the critical success factors of the business fit badly with the skills and characteristics of the parent organisation, then parent managers are likely to misunderstand the business and inadvertently do it harm. So the first measure of fit is about avoiding problems. For example, when BAT, a tobacco company, acquired Eagle Star, a financial services company, in the 1990s there was low *critical success factor fit*: the critical success factors of insurance did not fit well with the skills and characteristics of BAT managers. The result was problematic. BAT encouraged Eagle Star to gain market share (a normal strategy in tobacco) with the

| Exhibit 6.11 | The parenting matrix: the Ashridge Portfolio Display |

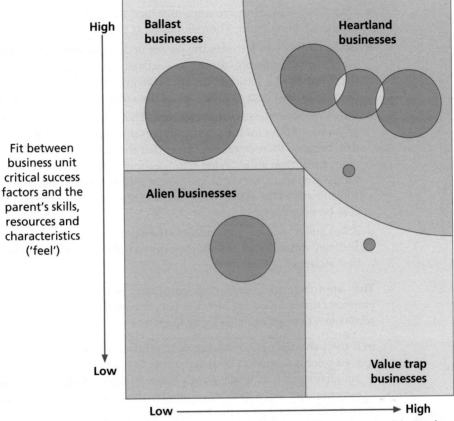

Source: Adapted from M. Goold, A. Campbell and M. Alexander, *Corporate Level Strategy*, Wiley 1994.

consequence that Eagle Star took on inappropriate insurance risks, incurring some big losses a few years later. The lack of fit was partly the cause of these subsequent losses. Fit between critical success factors of the business and the characteristics of the parent is therefore about downside risk. High fit means low risk of problems. Low fit means high risk of problems.

Fit between the parenting opportunities of the business and the characteristics of the parent is about benefit and opportunity. High fit means high potential for added value. Low fit means low potential. A 'parenting opportunity' is an opportunity for the business to improve that which can be better exploited with help from a parent organisation. For example, the business may need to cut costs and could be helped by a parent organisation with experience of doing this; the business may need to expand in Asia and would be helped by a parent with good Asian contacts; the business may need to improve its marketing skills and could be helped by a parent with strong marketing skills; and so on.

Exhibit 6.11 shows what a resulting portfolio might look like.

- *Heartland* businesses are ones to which the parent can add value without danger of doing harm. They should be at the core of future strategy.

- *Ballast* businesses are ones the parent understands well but can do little for. They would probably be just as successful as independent companies. If they are part of a future corporate strategy, they need to be managed with a light touch and bear as little cost of the corporate bureaucracy as possible.

- *Value trap* businesses are dangerous. They appear attractive because there are opportunities for the parent to add value. But they are deceptively attractive, because there is a high danger that the parent's attentions will result in more harm than good. Value trap businesses should only be included in the future strategy if they can be moved into the heartland. Moreover, some adjustments to the skills, resources or characteristics of the parent will probably be necessary.

- *Alien* businesses are clear misfits. They offer little opportunity to add value and they rub awkwardly with the normal behaviour of the parent. Exit is the best strategy.

This approach to considering corporate portfolios therefore places the emphasis firmly on asking how the parent benefits the business units, and this results in a number of challenging questions.

- If the parent is not enhancing the performance of the business units, what is its role? A corporate body has a role to play with regard to purely corporate affairs, such as dealing with financial institutions and negotiating with governments. But if its role is limited to this, the cost of delivering these functions should be low to the business unit. A large and costly corporate headquarters which does little to enhance the strategies of its business units can be a great cost burden to them, thus undermining potential market-based competitive advantage, and so reducing the overall returns for shareholders.

- Where, then, is greatest value to be added? An overall pattern has emerged in the past decade or so which suggests that organisations throughout the world are attempting to drive responsibility for strategic decisions nearer and nearer to markets. There is an attempt to ensure that business-specific competences are directed at developing successful competitive strategies. The trend towards deregulation and privatisation of public utilities and government authorities, increasing throughout the world, has a similar rationale underlying it. The aim is to give the responsibility for developing strategic capability and achieving competitive advantage in markets to the business unit level – to managers who are most closely in touch with their markets. The role of the parent has therefore been increasingly seen as one of facilitation, or of taking a hands-off approach as far as possible.

- If the corporate parent seeks to enhance the strategies of the businesses it must, then, be very clear that there is a match between its skills in so doing and the help which the businesses require to achieve competitive advantage. It must also avoid undertaking roles which do not enhance strategies at the business unit level. For example, the corporate parent may impose cumbersome strategic planning more to do with providing information to the centre than with aiding the strategic development of the units; it may retain a large head office staff which duplicate the roles of executives in business units; or it may make demands on business unit strategy that are not sensible in terms of competitive strategy at that level.

- The concept of fit has equal relevance in the public sector. The implication is that public sector managers should control directly only those services and activities that fit services and activities for which they have special managerial expertise. Other services should be outsourced or set up as independent agencies. Whilst outsourcing, privatising and setting up independent agencies is driven as much by political dogma as by corporate-level strategy analysis, the trend has been in this direction.

- The corporate parent should also assess which businesses should most sensibly be within its portfolio given these considerations. Illustration 6.4 shows how Unilever reviewed its role as a corporate parent and, in consequence, its portfolio.

- If the corporate parent does, indeed, seek to enhance business strategies, it needs to consider the number of business units for which it can sensibly do so. For this the parent has to have sufficient feel for the businesses, so the number cannot be great unless they are similar businesses in terms of technology, products or competences; or in similar markets.

6.4.5 A relatedness matrix[14]

The idea of synergy, discussed in section 6.3.3 above, presupposes that there are capabilities, resources or competences across a portfolio of businesses which, when put together, yield benefits greater than the sum of their parts. If this is applied to portfolio management, it suggests the importance of the two dimensions shown in Exhibit 6.12. First, the extent to which the portfolio

| Exhibit 6.12 | The relatedness matrix |

DEGREE OF RELATEDNESS OF BUSINESS UNITS

MANAGEABILITY		Low	High
	High	Distractions	Heartland businesses
	Low	Aliens	Value traps

Illustration 6.4

Unilever's parenting

If the role of the parent is to add value to business units, it needs to be clear about how it can do this for which businesses.

Unilever, the consumer products company, involved in food, detergents and personal products, has built particular skills, resources and characteristics which make it an effective parent of certain kinds of business, but a less effective parent of others.

Unilever had developed as a decentralised organisation, traditionally setting great store in the country or regional manager. It had a strong technology base and centralised corporate research laboratories; a strong marketing focus, built around skills in product development and branding for mass market consumers; and an unusual human resource management process, monitoring the progress of 20,000 managers, a large portion of whom were expatriates.

The skills, resources and characteristics of Unilever's corporate centre fitted well with the parenting opportunities and critical success factors of its businesses. Regionally focused consumer products businesses needed help to access product and market knowledge from across the globe. Consumer products businesses also benefited from the type of support Unilever provided in product marketing, basic technical research and new product development. Unilever found from long experience that continuous new product development was the right policy. The company therefore pressed its subsidiaries to push harder in this area than they would probably choose to do on their own.

For the past 20 years, Unilever has been focusing its portfolio. It has disposed of businesses such as animal feed, tea plantations and speciality chemicals that were not in its heartland (see figure). A speciality chemical business is often global, operating from one site in serving a global market, whereas consumer goods businesses are multi-local, having many sites serving the slightly different needs of different regions. Unilever is more knowledgeable about multi-local businesses than global businesses. The needs of a speciality chemicals business and tea plantations were also different from Unilever's consumer products businesses. Unilever's skills in marketing, fat technology and new product development were of little relevance here.

In the figure, Unilever's food businesses are identified as having the best fit because the combination of centralised skill management and decentralised decision making that Unilever was most comfortable with suits food businesses best. The detergents businesses were becoming increasingly global, particularly in developed economies, and Unilever has been losing market share to companies more comfortable with a centralised management philosophy. The detergents businesses were therefore moving to the edge of Unilever's heartland. The perfume and up-market cosmetics businesses, part of the personal products division, were also global, requiring a management approach that Unilever was less comfortable with. This led to the personal products businesses as a group being positioned differently from the food businesses.

In 2000 Unilever reorganised in a way that reflects these differences. In essence the company

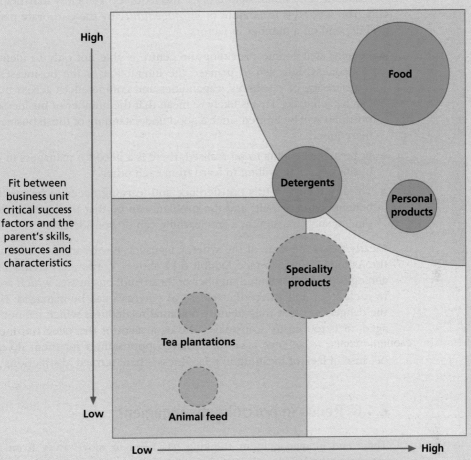

High

Low

Fit between business unit critical success factors and the parent's skills, resources and characteristics

Food

Detergents

Personal products

Speciality products

Tea plantations

Animal feed

Low ——————————————→ High

Fit between business unit parenting opportunities and the parent's skills, resources and characteristics

split into two divisions – a food business and a home and personal care business – enabling the management teams of the two divisions to develop different parenting skills reflecting the different needs of these two product areas.

Prepared by Andrew Campbell, Ashridge Strategic Management Centre.

Questions

1. How might the results of this parenting matrix exercise differ from a portfolio exercise using the growth/share matrix?

2. What are the benefits and disadvantages of keeping the two divisions set up in 2000 in one company? Should Unilever consider a de-merger?

consists of businesses which are *related* to each other in such terms; the sorts of competence analysis suggested in section 4.4.2 and the questions on bases of relatedness raised in section 6.5.1 and Exhibit 6.14 below may help identify this. The second is the extent of *manageability* by the corporate parent; this will depend on a number of factors.

- Benefits will accrue providing the centre is able not only to identify such relatedness, but also to manage the interaction of the businesses so that transference of resources, capabilities and competences across businesses can be achieved. This is likely to mean that the number of businesses in the portfolio will be limited since a good understanding of those businesses will be required.

- In turn, for benefits to be realised, there is a need for managers in different businesses to be willing to learn from each other.

- Third, the cost of this transference and learning needs to be less than the benefits which result; and the problem can be that the cost in managerial time of such transference and learning can be considerable.

Clearly this is the logic of the synergy manager. Borrowing the terminology of the Ashridge portfolio (see Exhibit 6.11 above), corporate parents should be aiming to identify a limited number of 'heartland' businesses which are related to each other and where the release of synergies can be managed. However, the dangers are that they identify potential relatedness which cannot be managed, or is too costly to manage (the equivalent of the value trap); or spend time trying to achieve synergies where opportunities for them do not exist because of lack of meaningful relatedness – here termed 'distractions'.

6.4.6 Trends in portfolio management

The trend in management thinking has been to move away from focusing mainly on the balance and attractiveness criteria (i.e. sections 6.4.1 and 6.4.3 above) towards focusing more on the fit criterion (i.e. 6.4.4 and 6.4.5 above). In other words, the challenge the corporate parent increasingly faces is to justify how a portfolio of businesses achieves greater value than the sum of its parts either because of the synergistic fit between the businesses, or the fit between business needs and parental competences, or both. Many companies diversified in the 1970s and 1980s in order to get into more attractive businesses and balance their portfolios. Most of these initiatives failed and the late 1980s and 1990s were periods of unbundling, break-ups, and de-mergers of portfolios that had, at best, spurious relatedness. Corporate parents sought to achieve greater focus on technologies or markets they could understand and in which there were greater chances of achieving such fit.

   The increasing sophistication of the capital markets has, in turn, encouraged this trend. As explained at the beginning of the chapter, shareholders no longer need corporate managers in conglomerates to act on their behalf to smooth earnings over a portfolio of businesses because they can smooth their returns themselves by investing in a selection of companies with different earnings profiles. Moreover, shareholders can move money into attractive sectors, such as health care or emerging technologies, more easily than corporate parents can. The argument is that corporate parents should stop doing tasks that shareholders can more easily do for themselves and focus on creating additional value from the application of management expertise.

There has been a parallel trend in the public sector, with increasing political pressure by governments to challenge what large and often bureaucratic bodies have to offer to more local delivery of services. Here the driving forces have been the combination of a desire to reduce the cost of central government and the demand for more local accountability for services.

Each of the portfolio logics discussed in this section assumes a role of the centre. In turn, the role of the centre and the logic of the portfolio make assumptions about the diversity of businesses within a corporate portfolio. This is the subject of the next section.

6.5 THE EXTENT OF CORPORATE DIVERSITY

The different rationales of corporate parents discussed in section 6.3 have different implications about the diversity of portfolios. As suggested above, a portfolio manager or restructurer may have a very diverse portfolio because they are not seeking to intervene in or even know a great deal about those businesses. On the other hand, a synergy manager and parental developer need to know about the businesses in order to add value. To do so, it is unlikely that they can cope with high degrees of diversity. Moreover, they are likely to need to manage businesses which have a degree of relatedness in some way. The converse of this argument is also important; the extent of diversity of a corporate portfolio should inform the role played by the corporate parent. For example, it would be foolish for managers of a highly diverse, unrelated portfolio to try to adopt the role of a synergy manager; unless of course they chose to radically change the portfolio.

The nature of diversity and the degree of relatedness of business units in a portfolio are therefore important issues to examine. The rest of this section therefore considers the topic of diversification. **Diversification** is typically defined as a strategy which takes the organisation away from its current markets or products or competences (also see the discussion in section 8.2.4). The extent to which this occurs can be thought of in terms of the relatedness (or unrelatedness) of diversification.

> **Diversification** is typically defined as a strategy which takes the organisation away from its current markets or products or competences

6.5.1 Related diversification

Related diversification is strategy development beyond current products and markets, but within the value system (see section 4.5) or 'industry' in which the company operates. For example, Unilever is a diversified corporation, but virtually all of its interests are in the fast-moving consumer goods industry. Beginning with this definition, related diversification could take different forms, as Exhibit 6.13 shows.

> **Related diversification** is strategy development beyond current products and markets, but within the value system or 'industry' in which the company operates

| Exhibit 6.13 | Related diversification options for a manufacturer |

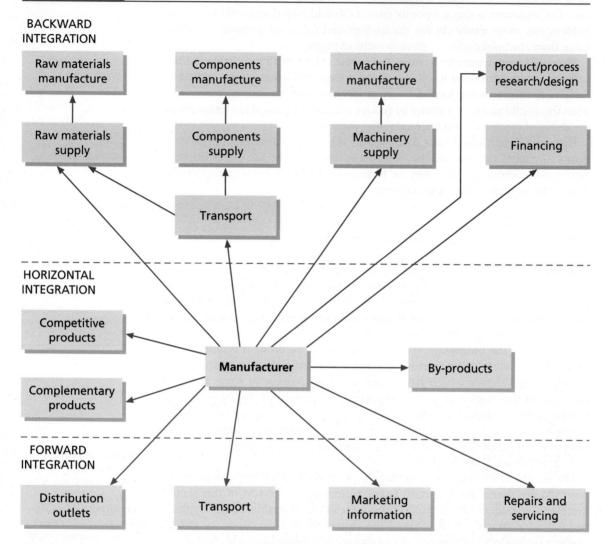

Note: Some companies will manufacture components or semi-finished items. In those cases there will be additional integration opportunities into assembly or finished product manufacture.

Vertical integration
describes either backward
or forward integration into
adjacent activities in the
value system

● **Vertical integration** describes either backward or forward integration into adjacent activities in the value system. *Backward integration* refers to development into activities which are concerned with the inputs into the company's current business (i.e. are further back in the value system). For example, raw materials, machinery and labour are all important inputs into a manufacturing company, so the acquisition by a car manufacturer of a component manufacturer would be related diversification through backward integration. *Forward integration* refers to development into activities

Exhibit 6.14	Some reasons for related diversification

POSSIBLE ADVANTAGES	EXAMPLES/COMMENTS

● Control of supplies
  – Quantity
  – Quality
  – Price
	Tea processors own plantations to secure continuity of supply.
	Components for motor cars may need to be manufactured by the company.
	Printing facilities can be cheaper if in-house.

● Control of markets	Manufacturers own retail outlets to gain guaranteed distrubution.
● Access to information	Car manufacturers own credit services, car hire firms and servicing firms to access information on customer preferences.
● Cost savings	Fully integrated steel plants save costs of reheating and transport.

● Building on:
  – Core competences
  – Technology
	Firm of accountants moving into tax advice or corporate recovery.
	Precision engineering equipment manufacturer in one market entering another with similar technical requirements.

● Spreading risk	Avoids over-reliance on one product or market, but builds on related experience.
● Resource utilisation	Manufacturer acquiring company for compatible products to fill capacity.
● Parenting	So the corporate parent can understand business units.

which are concerned with a company's outputs (i.e. are further forward in the value chain), such as transport, distribution, repairs and servicing. Illustration 6.5 shows how car manufacturers have begun to diversify through forward integration.

● **Horizontal integration** is development into activities which are competitive with, or complementary to, a company's present activities. For example, many organisations have realised that there are opportunities in other markets for the *exploitation* of the organisation's competences – perhaps to displace the current providers as a new entrant. For example, the Automobile Association (AA) had been founded as a members' club for motorists in the UK and extended into providing rescue services for breakdowns. As this market came under fierce attack from specialist breakdown organisations in the 1990s, the AA extended into new markets by exploiting its expertise in *rapid response to crisis*. It launched a home service for electrical and plumbing emergencies, a development pioneered by similar motoring organisations in Australia.

Horizontal integration is development into activities which are competitive with, or complementary to, a company's present activities

Exhibit 6.14 summarises some reasons given for related diversification or, conversely, could be used to give reasons why highly diversified companies might divest activities to increase their degree of specialisation on more related activities.

However, potentially the definition of related diversification so far employed masks a problem of significant strategic importance. Should relatedness be

Illustration 6.5

Diversification through forward integration in the car industry

Companies may see benefits in diversifying by means of forward integration.

A global downturn in automobile sales led manufacturers to rationalise their operations by decreasing production, brands, jobs and capacity. However, they also geared up to exploit new opportunities to earn revenue and decrease costs by diversifying into downstream activities. Margins from such downstream activities as selling vehicle financing, leasing and insurance, and providing parts, servicing and repair are higher than those of vehicle sales. But there are other advantages too.

Ford has been attempting to redefine itself as 'the world's leading consumer company for automotive products and services', rather than solely as a manufacturer of vehicles. In addition to Ford's traditional business units, the company has been seeking higher returns from their downstream activities, which include Ford Credit, Hertz, and direct sales and e-business initiatives. The most pertinent features of these ventures are that the companies can collate information on customer preferences, which can be fed to the manufacturing plants. In fact, one of Ford's motives for its 1999 acquisition of KwikFit was to access its database of customers.

In an attempt to lift their service, repair and maintenance businesses to a more prominent role, both General Motors (Europe) through its Vauxhall MasterFit operations and Ford through its RapidFit division have launched initiatives to enable their franchised dealers to win back some of the servicing and repair business for older cars. There has also been an increasing trend of manufacturers buying formerly independent dealerships in their own brands, with some manufacturers taking large equity stakes in the super-dealers.

As cars become more sophisticated, the accompanying technology has also become more advanced. Manufacturers have been exploring new business opportunities in in-car Internet and telematics systems. The most promising technologies are those being explored in navigation systems, safety and security controls, and mobile multimedia functions. This could become the interface for customer contact; for example, General Motor's *OnStar* mutimedia business offers voice-activated services, emergency assistance, stolen vehicle tracking and e-mail.

The focus is on accessing customers and selling directly to them, rather than centring on the car as a one-time sale. Manufacturers want to develop customer relationship strategies whereby the purchaser of the vehicle is retained in a long-term relationship with the manufacturer for the duration of ownership. The manufacturers also want to establish links with the used vehicle's future owners, ensuring that they capture more of the life cycle of the product. In this way, they can leverage their customer base to cross-sell and promote other products and services, such as repair, mortgages and credit.

Prepared by Urmilla Lawson, University of Strathclyde Graduate School of Business

Source: Adapted from T. Burt, 'Carmakers eye route to twin track revenues', *The Financial Times*, 28 Feb. 2001, Auto Section, p. 1.

Questions

1. What other areas of forward integration might car manufacturers consider and why?

2. How might the resources and competences of a car manufacturer differ from the downstream activities they are moving into?

3. Bearing in mind the answer to question 2, is the diversification downstream related or unrelated diversification?

thought of in terms of the value system of organisations, as described above, or should it be thought of in other terms, for example in terms of competences of organisations? To continue an example given above: which is more useful, to conceive of Unilever's related diversification in terms of moves into products and markets within the fast-moving consumer goods industry, or in terms of moves into companies in which competences such as marketing and research and development are crucial? In the case of Unilever these may go hand in hand, but for other organisations they may well not. For example, a firm may justify backward integration into financing or raw material manufacturing (see Exhibit 6.13) as related diversification when in fact the competences required for such businesses are fundamentally different. Certainly historically this has led to some strangely diversified businesses. In the 1980s, UK brewing companies followed diversification strategies justified by them as related developments. Historically brewers had been vertically integrated forward from production into pubs. Diversification then took the form of buying hotel businesses and opening restaurant chains on the grounds that these were related to pubs. This then took the brewers further into the leisure industry; and diversification into holiday companies and bookmakers followed. Each move in itself was arguably related to the activities of the business as it progressively diversified; and was justified in terms of potential synergies. However, it was difficult to see how the resulting overall portfolio was related, not least in terms of the sorts of competences required to brew beer as compared with those required to run a bookmaker! Unsurprisingly, many of these diversified brewing conglomerates have now been broken up. Indeed, over the past decade there have been many instances of large conglomerates choosing to de-merge to form more focused corporations; a tendency which appears to have improved profits, net worth and reduced risk of takeovers.[15]

A problem which many established firm are finding in the new millennium further illustrates the same point. Diversification into e-businesses which, on the face of it, are highly related in terms of product can prove problematical in terms of the competences required to develop business ideas suited to that medium and keep pace with changes in it. The products may be related to the original core business but the competences are not.

The 'ownership' of more value activities within the value system through vertical or horizontal integration does not therefore guarantee improved performance for the organisation, or better value for money for the consumer or client. Some of the reasons why related diversification could be problematical have already been raised. Others include:

- The time taken up by top management on trying to ensure that the benefits of relatedness are achieved through sharing or transference across business units.

- The reluctance of business unit managers to share and learn from other business units: this is particularly likely if they are incentivised and rewarded on the basis of the performance of their own business alone.

- A lack of new ideas or innovation because of the lack of diversity and the focus on a limited number of technologies and markets.

The received wisdom that relatedness matters has therefore been questioned.[16] There has been increasing emphasis on improving performance within the value system through external linkages and the management of relationships with the various parties in the supply and distribution chains. Arguably, the ability to achieve this could itself be a core competence. It would include the need to ensure that innovation and improvement of value for money are occurring within other organisations in the value system on which the organisation depends, such as suppliers and distributors.

6.5.2 Unrelated diversification

Unrelated diversification is an organisation moving beyond its current value system or industry

Typically, **unrelated diversification** is thought of as an organisation moving beyond its current value system or industry. So unrelatedness has tended to be defined in somewhat narrow terms: that is, opportunities beyond the current product and market base of the organisation and outside the current industry (or value system). However, as the discussion above has revealed, this narrow definition tends to hide important differences in the degree of relatedness of diversification opportunities and the basis of such relatedness. Again, this is where considering organisational competences could be important. If the competence perspective is taken into account, then the traditional notion of unrelated diversification might be thought of in terms of degrees of relatedness and unrelatedness as follows.

● Diversification into quite new markets and new products by *exploiting* the current competences of the organization. For example, a university business school might argue that it could build on its research and teaching skills to develop consultancy services for industry; or a manufacturer might seek to exploit its distribution and logistics skills, as in Illustration 6.6.

● To continue the discussion of corporate rationales (see section 6.3 above), the global development of conglomerate businesses is more likely to work if subsidiaries are related such that they are conducive to effective parenting from the centre. This might be by means of (a) building a portfolio of businesses with sufficient common competences between them to allow for effective 'synergy management' (see section 6.3.3 above) or (b) by ensuring that the businesses are such that they can benefit from the competences at the centre of a 'parental developer' (see section 6.3.4).

● Diversification by the exploitation of competences may go beyond simply moving into markets which already exist: it may involve the *creation* of genuinely new markets. There are some elements of this in relation to the AA example above. It was the absence of an efficient and reliable means for individual households to access the fragmented suppliers of electrical and plumbing services which created the AA's opportunity. Another example is the way in which research and development based on microelectronics technology has progressively spawned whole new markets, such as personal electronic organisers, interactive video games, and so on which did not exist twenty years ago. However, such diversification requires very good market

Illustration 6.6

Standard Photographic's diversification

A diversification programme may build on its historical competences but is takes a company far from its origins.

Based in Leamington Spa in the UK, Standard Photographic's business was originally based on the production of photographic film, though this ceased in 1967. Up to then it had about 10 per cent of the market in the UK under the Standard brand. However, following competition from Kodak, Fuji and Agfa it turned to film packaging. By 1999 it was buying over 40 million rolls of film a year and repackaging these for own-brand labels for Boots, Dixons, Superdrug and Tesco, achieving a 60 per cent share of the own-brand film market in Europe. The turnover of the packaging operation was £9.4 million (at margins of 5 per cent) of the firm's £23.5 million but was expected to decline.

Standard also moved into other businesses, including the conversion of photographic paper (7 per cent margins on sales of £7.8 million) and film processing (8 per cent margins on £1.8 million turnover). However, the latter was under threat from digital photography. Standard also had a logistics business turning over £9 million (11 per cent margins) and a 20 per cent growth record. This business provided a maximum 36-hour delivery of film to retailers. Orders transmitted before 5.30 p.m. were packed in the evening and delivery guaranteed to more than 2,500 retail outlets by 9 a.m. the next day. Standard had built up skills to handle this rapid delivery. Gordon Bott, the managing director, explained that inventory levels were kept to a minimum: 'Stock management is the key to the process because of the cash flow implications. It is difficult to forecast levels of buffer stock

because of market volatility caused by promotion campaigns, in-store activities and the weather'; and cash flow management was vital since retailers did not pay Standard till two months after delivery. In 1999 it built on this logistics business by delivering printing and publishing products, floppy discs as well as cosmetic products to 250 high street Boots shops.

By 2000, Standard Photographic had decided on a further area of diversification into 'order fulfilment for e-businesses'. Gordon Bott: 'The heaviest criticism of dotcoms is their order fulfilment service. We strongly believe the consumer increasingly wants reliable delivery more than next day delivery . . . We have proven expertise in handling rapid fulfilment of orders received electronically . . . the challenge of fulfilment companies will be to be flexible enough to offer delivery at a specific time when the customer wants it.' However, the company recognises that in moving into this area it will be competing against established competitors such as Exel, Parcel Force and White Arrow Express.

Source: Adapted from *The Sunday Times*, 1 October 2000.

Questions

1. What are the reasons for the diversification strategy of Standard Photographic?

2. Compare the diversification programme of Standard with that of the car manufacturers in Illustration 6.5 in terms of (a) product/market relatedness and (b) competence relatedness. Consider which of the diversification programmes is more or less related.

Exhibit 6.15	Some reasons for unrelated diversification

POSSIBLE ADVANTAGES	EXAMPLES/COMMENTS
● Exploiting underutilised resources and competences	Farmers use fields for camp sites. Local authorities use plastic waste for new materials.
● Escape from present business	A company's products may be in decline and unrelated diversification presents the only possible 'escape'.
● Spreading risk	Some companies believe that it is good sense not to have all their 'eggs in one basket' and so diversify into unrelated areas.
● Even out cyclical effects in a given sector	Toy manufacturers make subcontract plastic moulded products for industry.
● Need to use excess cash or safeguard profits	Buying a tax loss situation.
● Personal values or objectives of powerful figures	Personal image locally or nationally may be a motive for high-profile diversification.

knowledge and the creativity to better provide for market needs. Arguably, it is these competences on which such apparently unrelated diversification may be built.

● The most extreme form of unrelated diversification is where *new competences* are developed for new market opportunities. This extreme end of the diversification spectrum is less common, though it is tempting to argue that firms that have tried to move from traditional ways of operating to e-business have found themselves in just this position. However, if a pedantic definition of unrelatedness were taken, entirely new competences might never be observed at all since it usually proves possible to identify some degree of relatedness in the market or resources or competences in any development opportunity.

Exhibit 6.15 summarises some of the reasons for unrelated diversification. It is worth noting that *synergy* is a commonly cited reason for both *related* and *unrelated diversification*. It should be evident from the discussion above why this is the case: because synergy can be thought of in terms of products, markets, technology and also competences.

6.5.3 Diversification and performance

Diversification has been one of the most frequently researched strategic issues of business. In particular, there have been a number of studies which have investigated the relationship between the choice of diversification as a strategy and the performance of the organisation in financial terms. Overall, it needs to be said that the various attempts to demonstrate the effects of diversification on performance are inconclusive. Early research[17] suggested that firms which developed through *related diversification* outperformed both those that remained specialised and those which developed through *unrelated diversification.* These findings were later questioned.[18] The sum total of all of the research work linking patterns of diversification to financial performance remains somewhat unclear. This is, perhaps, not surprising since so many studies rely on measures of relatedness whilst acknowledging that it is difficult to be precise as to what related and unrelated diversification means or to measure accurately what constitutes organisational competences. However, there are some insights from the research over the years.

- The balance of evidence is that relatedness of diversification is financially beneficial in so far as it allows an organisation to build on and leverage common resources and competences.[19]

- There are, however, limits to the extent to which diversity is advantageous. The costs and complexity of managing diversity are considerable; imagine attempting to act as a synergy manager across a large portfolio of related businesses. The cost and time of corporate managers involved in trying to understand and involve themselves in managing synergies across the businesses would be not only high, but probably highly inefficient. So whilst profitability does increase with diversity, this is only up to a *limit of complexity*, beyond which this relationship reverses.[20] Complexity, as measured by customer numbers or communication costs, also reduces profit potential, particularly for service-based businesses.[21]

- Similar patterns are also found when it comes to international diversification. Whilst geographic diversification tends to increase profitability, the combination of diverse locations and diverse business units again gives rise to level of complexity beyond which benefits are not gained.[22] Interestingly, there is also evidence that, as international diversity grows, levels of innovation internal to the firm also decline, as the focus becomes more and more to do with co-ordination of the portfolio and diversified growth through acquisition.[23]

- Other studies[24] argue that a key factor is the resource situation of the organisation – particularly the area of underutilised resources. Underutilisation of physical resources or intangible resources (brand name, etc.) is likely to encourage related developments, whereas excess financial resources may well be used to underwrite unrelated developments (e.g. through acquisition), particularly if other resources and competences are difficult to develop or grow quickly. This raises the question of whether successful performance is a *result* of choosing diversification or if the relationship is, in fact, the reverse. Perhaps successful organisations *choose* diversification because opportunities in their current product or market domain look limited.

The final point that needs to be made here is to do with the theme of this chapter. The extent to which diversification is likely to enhance performance will also depend on whether the nature and extent of diversification are compatible with the other challenges of corporate strategy, namely:

- the compatibility with the corporate parenting rationale (see section 6.3);
- the logic of the corporate portfolio (see section 6.4); and
- the nature of corporate control exercised by the parent and therefore the relationship of the parent with its business units: this is the subject of the next section.

6.6 CORPORATE CONTROL[25]

Clearly much of the above also has implications for how a multi-business corporation is organised and managed. In particular there are implications about the way in which the corporate centre interacts with and seeks to exercise more or less control over the businesses. Much of this has already been intimated above. A portfolio manager or restructurer is likely to be focusing on minimal strategic control, leaving business-level strategy to chief executives of the businesses, and exercising control more through clear and challenging financial targets. On the other hand, the synergy manager and parental developer may be intervening a good deal in the businesses in order to achieve synergies across the business units or provide parental benefits. What would be very counterproductive is for the means of control to be inconsistent with the logic of the corporate centre. For example, if a portfolio manager were to have a diverse portfolio but try to intervene in the strategies of the businesses, it would very likely lead to disaster. Conversely, if a synergy manager tried to make transferences between business units without having an understanding of those businesses and involving themselves in the strategy of those businesses, it could be chaos.

In Chapter 9 (section 9.3.2) this issue of corporate control is discussed more fully. What matters here is to understand that there is a necessary link between organisational design, corporate control and the logic of the corporate entity.

6.7 CORPORATE-LEVEL COMPETITION

The chapters that follow go on to focus on competitive strategy at the business level. However, before doing so it is important to emphasise that competition also occurs at the corporate level. At the business level the competition is, in effect, between businesses for the right to serve customers. At the corporate level the competition takes place between corporate parents for the right to own businesses. Investors and potential investors are continually seeking ways to achieve better returns, and this means that they are reviewing not only the performance but also the corporate strategies of the sorts of organisation discussed in this chapter. In so doing they make choices between one corporation and another, and do so on the basis of many of the issues discussed in this chapter.

This competition is most visible during a hostile takeover. The managers in one parent company are saying to the shareholders of another, 'We can do a better job of managing these businesses than their current parent has

Illustration 6.7

The Royal Bank of Scotland and the takeover of NatWest

STRATEGY IN ACTION

Investors may decide who would make the best parent for a business on the basis of corporate rationale, portfolio logic and managerial track record.

In autumn 1999, fund managers had to decide between three competing groups of parent managers, all of whom wanted to run the financial services businesses that made up the National Westminster Group. The Bank of Scotland bid for National Westminster in September 1999. By Christmas 1999, the existing managers at National Westminster had resigned or been dismissed and a new team with a new strategy was in place. In addition, the Royal Bank of Scotland (RBS) had made a counter-offer. All three sets of managers were trying to persuade the shareholders that they could do the best job of parenting the NatWest businesses.

The decision facing the shareholders was not straightforward. There was no obvious higher bidder and the financial case for the takeover was much the same for RBS as for the Bank of Scotland. They both claimed roughly the same potential cost savings, proposed to sell off businesses worth more to others and argued similar revenue increases could be found. As a result the fund managers could not avoid deciding which of the three they thought would be the best parent. RBS, who eventually succeeded, was able to base its case on three advantages over its rivals.

First, the combined RBS/NatWest would represent a portfolio of businesses with more market power within each business unit. Sir George Mathewson, then RBS's chief executive, argued that the business portfolio of Natwest was more

'congruent' with RBS than with the Bank of Scotland and would increase market power in key sectors substantially. The combined bank would be the largest corporate bank in the UK, in retail banking it would stand second to Lloyds TSB; with Direct Line it would be the largest UK motor insurer; and even on life assurance and pensions it would not be far behind other banks such as Lloyds TSB and Abbey National.

Second, RBS was clear that the businesses would be organised in customer-focusing divisions, leaving the branch networks largely intact to ensure substantial geographic presence throughout the country. The corporate centre would take responsibility for only a limited number of roles, including treasury and setting up a 'central manufacturing unit' to ensure that financial products were aligned.

Investment bankers also believed the RBS management's track record to be more credible when it came to cost savings. One investment banker offered another reason for preferring RBS management. 'Investment bankers don't like to be proved silly: the share growth of RBS had been better than the Bank of Scotland; that's much the same as saying that the management is better.'

Source: Adapted from *Financial Times*, 10 February 2000.

Questions

1. Based on the content of the chapter, identify the main ways in which corporate executives might argue for parenting advantage over rival corporations.

2. Choose another example of a takeover battle and identify reasons why the successful bidder won.

done.' This is shown in Illustration 6.7 with regard to the takeover battle for the National Westminster Group. Indirectly this competition between parent companies is going on all the time. Almost every company is being considered as a possible takeover target by some other company. What the aggressor has to be able to argue is that he or she can create more value than the incumbent. How parent managers create value is, therefore, central not only to the performance of companies but also to their survival. It helps identify which businesses they should buy and sell, it guides how they should 'parent' these businesses and it determines whether they should be taken over by another company.

SUMMARY

- Corporate strategy is the concern of the corporate parent, by which is meant levels of management above that of business units.

- There is no 'best' corporate strategy. What matters is the consistency with which a corporate strategy is developed in terms of (a) clarity of the rationale of the corporate parent in seeking to add value to business units; (b) the logic of the corporate portfolio; (c) the nature and extent of the diversity of the portfolio; and (d) the nature of corporate control exercised by the corporate parent.

- Different roles of the corporate parent could include portfolio managers, restructurers, synergy managers and parental developers.

- Portfolio logic might focus on achieving (a) balance between types of business units; (b) business units which are more or less attractive in terms of industry characteristics and their market positions; or (c) fit between competences of the business units or between the business units and the competences of the corporate parent.

- The nature and extent of diversification can be considered in terms of the degree of relatedness of business units within the portfolio. Bases of relatedness have traditionally been considered with regard to linked activities within the organisation's value system; but increasingly, relatedness is being considered in terms of similarities or compatibilities of organisations' competences.

- The extent of diversification should also be considered in relation to the rationale of the corporate strategy, the diversity of the portfolio and the relationship of the business units with the parent. Portfolio managers and restructurers may be able to handle diverse portfolios employing largely financial control mechanisms. Synergy managers and parental developers are likely to require less diverse portfolios and closer relationships with business units.

- Corporate control is concerned with the way in which the corporate parent interacts with and guides the business units within its portfolio. It is important that the nature of this control is compatible with the other aspects of corporate strategy discussed in this chapter.

RECOMMENDED KEY READINGS

- For an overview of strategic issues facing multibusiness firms and readings (some of which are referenced in this chapter) which provide an extensive coverage of ways of understanding these, see M. Goold and K.S. Luchs, *Managing the Multibusiness Company*, Routledge, 1996.

- The issue of parenting is covered in detail with many examples in M. Goold, A. Campbell and M. Alexander, *Corporate Level Strategy*, Wiley, 1994.

- A summary of different portfolio analyses, their benefits and limitations, is provided in D. Faulkner, 'Portfolio matrices', in V. Ambrosini (ed.) with G. Johnson and K. Scholes, *Exploring Techniques of Analysis and Evaluation in Strategic Management*, Prentice Hall, 1998.

- The issue of corporate diversity and corporate strategy is discussed extensively in D.J. Collis and C.A. Montgomery, *Corporate Strategy: Resources and the scope of the firm*, Irwin, 1997.

REFERENCES

1. The opening chapters of M. Goold and K.S. Luchs, *Managing the Multibusiness Company*, Routledge, 1996, provide a good introduction to the theories underpinning the value-adding capabilities of multiproduct firms.

2. Transaction cost economics was developed by Oliver Williamson: see *Markets and Hierarchies*, Free Press, 1975. However, key arguments are summarised in the book by M. Goold and K.S. Luchs (see reference 1 above).

3. For a discussion of the role of a clarity of mission, see A. Campbell, M. Devine and D. Young, *A Sense of Mission*, Hutchinson Business, 1990. However, G. Hamel and C.K. Prahalad argue in Chapter 6 of their book, *Competing for the Future*, Harvard Business School Press, 1994, that mission statements have insufficient impact for the competence of a clarity of 'strategic intent'. This is more likely to be a brief but clear statement which focuses more on clarity of strategic direction (they use the word 'destiny') than on how that strategic direction will be achieved. See also Hamel and Prahalad on strategic intent in the *Harvard Business Review*, vol. 67, no. 3 (1989), pp. 63–76.

4. M. Goold, A. Campbell and M. Alexander, *Corporate Level Strategy*, Wiley, 1994, is concerned with both the value-adding and value-destroying capacity of corporate parents.

5. The extent and means of the value-adding capabilities of corporate parents is the theme of M. Goold, A. Campbell and M. Alexander (see reference 4 above).

6. The first three rationales discussed here are based on a paper by Michael Porter, 'From competitive advantage to corporate strategy', *Harvard Business Review*, vol. 65, no. 3 (1987), pp. 43–59.

7. For an account of Hanson see A. Brummer and R. Cowe, *Hanson: A biography*, Fourth Estate, 1994.

8. See A. Campbell and K. Luchs, *Strategic Synergy*, Butterworth/Heinemann, 1992.

9. Here the rationales of the 'synergy manager' and 'skills transferer' described by Porter (see reference 6 above), have been combined.

10. The logic of parental development is explained extensively in Goold, Campbell and Alexander (see reference 4 above).

11. For a more extensive discussion of the use of the growth share matrix see A.C. Hax and N.S. Majluf in R.G. Dyson (ed.), *Strategic Planning: Models and analytical techniques*, Wiley, 1990; and D. Faulkner, 'Portfolio matrices' in V. Ambrosini (ed.), *Exploring Techniques of Analysis and Evaluation in Strategic Management*, Prentice Hall, 1998; for source explanations of the BCG matrix see B.D. Henderson, *Henderson on Corporate Strategy*, Abt Books, 1979.

12. See A. Hax and N. Majluf, 'The use of the industry attractiveness–business strength matrix in strategic planning', in R. Dyson (ed.), *Strategic Planning: Models and analytical techniques*, Wiley, 1990.

13. The discussion in this section draws on M. Goold, A. Campbell and M. Alexander, *Corporate Level Strategy*, Wiley, 1994, which provides an excellent basis for understanding issues of parenting.

14. For a useful discussion of relatedness as applied to corporate portfolios see D. Collis, 'Related corporate portfolios', in Goold and Luchs (see reference 1 above).

15. See P. Comment and G. Jarrell, 'Corporate focus and stock returns', *Journal of Financial Economics*, vol. 37 (1995), pp. 67–87, and C.C. Markides, *Diversification, Refocusing and Economic Performance*, MIT Press, 1995.

16. This question is raised in the discussion on synergy by Campbell and Luchs (see reference 8 above).

17. R.P. Rumelt, *Strategy, Structure and Economic Performance*, Harvard University Press, 1974.

18. C.A. Montgomery, 'The measurement of firm diver-sification: some new empirical evidence', *Academy of Management Journal*, vol. 25, no. 2 (1982), pp. 299-307; and R.A. Bettis, 'Performance differences in related and unrelated diversified firms', *Strategic Management Journal*, vol. 2 (1981), pp. 379-393.

19. For example, see C.C. Markides and P.J. Williamson, 'Related diversification, core competencies and cor-porate performance', *Strategic Management Journal*, vol. 15 (1994), pp. 149-165; D.D. Bergh, 'Size and relatedness of units sold: an agency theory and resource based perspective'. *Strategic Management Journal*, vol. 16 (1995), pp. 221-239.

20. For example, R.M. Grant, A.P. Jammine and H. Thomas, 'Diversity, diversification and profitability among British manufacturing companies, 1972-84', *Academy of Management Journal*, vol. 31, no. 4 (1988),

pp. 771-801; and D.J. Collis and C.A. Montgomery, *Corporate Strategy: Resources and the scope of the firm*, Irwin, 1997.

21. See T. Clayton, 'Services in focus', *PIMSletter no. 49*, PIMS Europe Ltd, 1992.

22. A useful review of the international dimension is: M. Hitt, R.E. Hoskisson and H. Kim, 'International diver-sification: effects on innovation and firm performance in product-diversified firms', *Academy of Management Journal*, vol. 40, no. 4 (1997), pp. 767-798.

23. See reference 22 above.

24. S. Chatterjee and B. Wernerfelt, 'The link between resources and type of diversification', *Strategic Management Journal*, vol. 12, no. 1 (1991), pp. 33-48.

25. The discussion here and in section 9.3 in Chapter 9 builds on the work of M. Gould and A. Campbell, *Strategies and Styles*, Blackwell, 1987.

WORK ASSIGNMENTS

* Refers to a case study in the Text and Cases edition. ✳ Denotes more advanced work assignments.

6.1 Drawing on evidence from your reading in the financial press, do you believe that corporate parents of multi-business firms add or destroy the value created by those businesses? Give examples to support your arguments.

6.2 Identify the corporate rationales for a number of different multi-business corporations: e.g.

(a) Virgin
(b) News Corporation*
(c) Royal Bank of Scotland*
(d) CRH*.

6.3 ✳ Choose a number of companies with portfolios of business units (e.g. Virgin, The News Corporation*, CRH* or South African Breweries*). Identify and explain the role of the corporate parent and how, if at all, the parent enhances or could enhance business unit strategies.

6.4 ✳ Obtain the annual report of a major multi-business corporation and apply different techniques of portfolio analysis to understand and explain the logic

for the mix of businesses. Which portfolio approach is most appropriate given the corporate rationale you think is being followed by the corporate parent?

6.5 Based on the discussion in section 6.5, explain what is meant by related and unrelated diversification. Bearing in mind your explanation, is related diver-sification a more sensible strategy than unrelated diversification?

6.6 Many corporate parents argue that they search for synergies between the businesses in their portfolio. Do you think this is a realistic aspiration? Give examples from organisations with which you are familiar to support your arguments.

6.7 Using the framework in Exhibit 6.2 and the argu-ments in this chapter, evaluate the corporate strategy of:

(a) The News Corporation*
(b) CRH*
(c) An organisation of your choice.

CASE EXAMPLE

The Virgin Group

Introduction

The Virgin Group is one of the UK's largest private companies, with an annual turnover estimated at £3bn per annum by 2000. Virgin's highest-profile business was Virgin Atlantic, which had developed to be a major force in the international airline business. However, the group spanned over 200 businesses from financial services through to railways; from entertainment megastores and soft drinks to cosmetics and condoms. (Figure 1 shows the breadth of the group's activities.) Its name was instantly recognisable. Research showed that the Virgin name was associated with words such as 'fun', 'innovative', 'daring' and 'successful'. The personal image and personality of the founder, Richard Branson, were high profile; in British advertisements for Apple Computers, together with Einstein and Gandhi, he was featured as a 'shaper of the 20th century'.

Origins and ownership

Virgin was founded in 1970 as a mail order record business and developed as a private company

in music publishing and retailing. In 1986 the company was floated on the stock exchange with a turnover of £250 million. However, Branson became tired of the public listing obligations. Compliance with the rules governing public limited companies and reporting to shareholders were expensive and time-consuming, and he resented making presentations in the City to people whom, he believed, did not understand the business. The pressure to create short-term profit, especially as the share price began to fall, was the final straw: Branson decided to take the business back into private ownership and the shares were bought back at the original offer price, which valued the company at £240 million.

Virgin had grown fast, becoming profitable and entering and claiming a significant share of new markets without the traditional trappings of the typical multinational. There was little sense of management hierarchy and there seemed to be a minimum of corporate bureaucracy. There was no 'group' as such; financial results were not consolidated either for external examination or, so Virgin claimed, for internal use. Its financial operations were managed from Geneva.

Figure 1 **The Virgin Group**

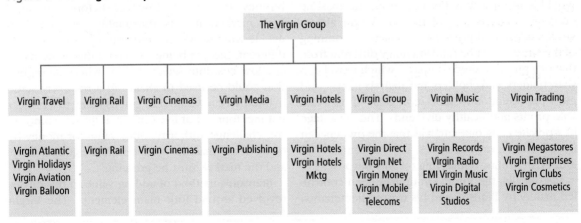

Each business or group of businesses ran its own affairs but they were tied together through a degree of shared ownership and shared values. Some argued that Virgin's ownership structure enabled it to take long-term views, free from investors' fixation with short-term returns. Indeed, Branson argued that, as he expanded, he would rather sacrifice short-term profits for long-term growth and the capital value of the various businesses. Others argued that financing purely through equity slowed the group's ability to expand. Still others suggested that the complex web of businesses, with ownership in offshore trusts in the Channel Islands and the British Virgin Islands, did little to support Branson's image of honesty and openness.

Corporate structure

The structure of Virgin Group was so opaque that the true financial position of Virgin Group was unclear. Due to its status as a private company, the complex group structure, and unavailability of consolidated accounts, it was difficult to arrive at accurate figures for the Group's collective turnover and profit. Companies within the group did not even share a common accounting year-end.

The Group has been described as a 'keiretsu' organisation – a structure of loosely linked autonomous units run by self-managed teams that use a family brand name. Branson's philosophy was that if a business got to a certain size, he would spin off a new business from the existing one. Branson has argued that, as Virgin almost wholly comprised private companies, the running of the Group must be fundamentally different from that of a public limited company, which must keep shareholders, stakeholders and analysts happy, and must pay attention to short-term goals of high taxable profits and healthy dividends. The advantage of a private conglomerate was that the owners can ignore short-term objectives and concentrate on long-term profits, reinvesting for this purpose.

Historically, the Virgin Group had been controlled mainly by Branson and his trusted lieutenants, many of whom had stayed with him for more than twenty years. The approach to management was one that decentralised decision making, with an emphasis on autonomous business-level decision making and responsibility for their own development.

In 2000 the head office consisted of about 30 people. Senior staff had often had successful careers in large, multinational corporations. With businesses scattered across a wide range of industries and markets, the approach was hands-off, and until he was needed to finalise big deals or to settle strategy, Branson ruled with a loose rein by delegating to managers and giving them leeway to use their initiative. However, when it came to marketing and promotion, Branson would take a more involved role. And when it came to the financing of the group and its deals, Branson's operating style was expressed in his autobiography: 'In the early 1970s I spent my time juggling different banks and suppliers and creditors in order to play one off against the other and stay solvent. I am now juggling bigger deals instead of the banks. It is only a matter of scale.'

Corporate rationale

Whilst the diversity of Virgin's business interests has been questioned, Branson has insisted that their core values and approach have remained the same. The name Virgin was chosen to represent the idea of the company being a virgin in every business they enter. However, before entering a new market, it was thoroughly researched to decide whether Virgin could offer something truly different: the aim being to extend the brand name at a low cost into selected areas where its reputation could be used to shake up a relatively static market. Virgin would only put its name to a project if it met four out of five criteria: it must be innovative, challenge authority, offer value for money by being better than the competitors, be good quality, and the market must be growing.

Branson's method of adding value to businesses revolved around four main elements. The Virgin brand was the single most important asset of the company. Based on a set of attributes and values rather than a market sector, it was about being the consumer's champion. But this was underpinned by their public relations and marketing skills; Virgin's understanding of the opportunities presented by 'institutionalised' markets; and their experience with greenfield start-ups. Virgin saw an 'institutionalised' market as one dominated by few competitors, not giving good value to customers because they had become either inefficient or preoccupied with each other; and Virgin did well when it identified complacency in the marketplace and offered more for less. Virgin had taken on one established industry after another, from British Airways to Coca-Cola and railways, in an effort to shake up 'fat and complacent business sectors'.

The Virgin brand made it possible to overcome barriers to entry in various industries and sectors. Branson and his business development team reviewed about 50 business proposals a week, with about four new projects under discussion at any one time. Good prospects would be those that addressed institutionalised markets, fitted the Virgin brand, could respond to the Virgin method of treatment, offered an enticing reward-to-risk ratio, and could be represented by a capable management team.

Some have described the Virgin Group as a branded venture capital house, with the use of partners providing flexibility and limiting risk. Each business was 'ring-fenced', so that lenders to one company had no rights over the assets of another, even if that company went bankrupt. Virgin's expansion into new markets had been through a series of joint ventures whereby Virgin provided the brand and its partner provided the majority of capital. For example, Virgin's stake in Virgin Direct required an initial outlay of only £15m, whilst its partner, AMP, ploughed £450m into the joint venture. Virgin Group's move into clothing and cosmetics required an initial outlay of only £1,000, whilst its equal partner, Victory Corporation, invested £20m. With Virgin Mobile, Virgin built a business in the wireless industry by

forming partnerships with existing operators to sell mobile services under the Virgin brand name. The carriers' competences lay in network management, not branding. Virgin set out to differentiate itself by offering innovative services such as no line rentals, no monthly fees and cheaper prepaid offerings. Although it did not operate its own network, Virgin won an award for the best wireless operator in the UK.

Management style

Branson has sought out people with innovative ideas who are willing to start new businesses, want to be the best at whatever they do, and with a strong desire to beat the competition. Organisational participants must share certain values specific to the Group and everyone was expected to be familiar with the corporate culture. Within the business units, Branson adopted his own personal style of management, priding himself on actively involving employees and seeking their ideas on ways of further adding value to his customers. Employees were expected to internalise values and behave accordingly. This internalisation of corporate values meant a greatly reduced need for external controls, but employees were still held accountable for their performance. Human resource management systems were in place to keep people committed by stock options, bonuses and profit sharing, and wherever possible, there was promotion from within.

Challenges for the future

By 2001 commentators had a number of concerns. Virgin appeared to be highly dependent on the profits of Virgin Atlantic; this was troubling as the airline industry was cyclical and facing increased competition as a result of deregulation. There were also few other businesses making substantial profits and many seemed to be operating at a loss. For example, both Virgin Express and Virgin Sun had reported continuous losses since their inception. In 1999, Virgin Direct Banking reported losses of £20.4m. Virgin Cinema, Virgin Cola and Virgin Clothing all made losses. Virgin Vodka, launched in 1994, was to be found in just a few duty-free shops and on Virgin Atlantic flights. In 2000, Branson finally folded his UK clothing line, Virgin Clothing.

Selling chunks of some businesses to fund new and existing businesses had become a familiar story at Virgin – they sold off their UK and Irish cinema houses, sold Virgin Music, sold a 49 per cent stake in Virgin Atlantic to Singapore Airlines, and in 2001 were seeking buyers for Virgin Sun and Virgin Express.

The most public problem was Virgin Rail, whose Cross Country and West Coast lines were ranked 23rd and 24th out of 25 train operating franchises according to the Strategic Rail Authority's Review in 2000. It was cited as one of the most unpopular and inefficient train operators in Britain, with complaints that the service was worse than it had been prior to privatisation. It was estimated that Virgin needed to double the number of passengers to be a success and spend £750 million on new rolling stock and service improvements. There were other costs too. Government subsidies would decline up to 2002 from around £77 million in 1998 and it would be necessary for Virgin to be paying the UK government annual franchise fees rising from £3.9 million to £220 million in 2012. The loss of rail passengers in 2001, following rail disasters and the consequent national disruption to rail traffic as a result of emergency upgrading of track, did nothing to help this situation.

Another concern was whether Virgin had become purely an endorsement brand, rather than one that could offer real expertise to the businesses with whom it was associated. Because Branson was so closely linked to the Virgin brand, there was also a risk he could undermine Virgin's value if some of his high-publicity ventures failed spectacularly. Critics also argued that Branson's foray into so many diverse products and services could dilute the strength of the brand, and the Virgin brand, arguably its most precious asset, could become associated with major problems, even failure. At the end of 2000, Branson was struck a blow when his People's Lottery consortium failed in their bid to run the UK National Lottery and Virgin Rail failed to win the East Coast main line franchise.

Sources: The Economist, 21 February 1998; P. McCosker, 'Stretching the brand: a review of the Virgin Group', *European Case Clearing House*, 2000.

This case was updated and revised by Urmilla Lawson, University of Strathclyde Graduate School of Business.

Questions

1. What is the corporate rationale of the Virgin Group?

2. Are there any relationships of a strategic nature between businesses within the Virgin portfolio?

3. Does the Virgin Group, as a corporate parent, add value to its businesses? If so how?

4. What are the main issues facing the Virgin Group and how should they be tackled?

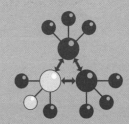

7

Business-Level Strategy

LEARNING OUTCOMES

After reading this chapter you should be able to explain:

- Different bases of achieving competitive advantage in terms of 'routes' on the strategy clock.
- The meaning and importance of differentiation strategies.
- The relationship of differentiation strategies to core competences.
- The extent to which competitive advantage is sustainable.
- When co-operation rather than competition makes sense.
- The principles of game theory in relation to business strategy.
- The implications of hypercompetition to competitive strategy.

7.1 INTRODUCTION

In Chapter 1 the idea of the business unit (or SBU) was introduced as a part of an organisation with a distinct external market for goods or services. In most organisations there are a number of business units. Clearly this is so in a large, maybe multinational, corporation where business units may be defined by product, service or geographical region. But even a small business is likely to be competing in different markets, which have different needs, and very likely with different products or services. In the public sector too there are the equivalent of business units; for example, the different services provided by local government and the different courses (undergraduate, postgraduate, distance learning and so on) offered by universities.

This chapter is concerned with the bases of strategic choice at this level; in particular, if it is possible to generate levels of profit (or as a public sector equivalent, best-value services) such that they are not eroded by competition. This is sometimes referred to as the generation of 'rents', 'superprofits' or 'economic profit'. Such **rents**[1] (or more strictly Ricardian rents) result from an organisation having resources or capabilities which permit it to produce at lower cost or generate a superior product or service at standard cost, in relation to firms with inferior resources and capabilities (see section 4.3.3 in Chapter 4). This in turn raises the issue of whether such a position of competitive advantage is sustainable. It is an important question for several reasons:

Rents result from an organisation having resources or capabilities which permit it to produce at lower cost or generate a superior product or service at standard cost, in relation to firms with inferior resources and capabilities

- It is the focus of what business-level strategy is about: how to compete effectively in a market.

- It is the core issue of how value is realised in a business; after all, value is realised only when a buyer is prepared to pay for goods or services. The extent to which they are prepared to pay a price which provides profits superior to those of competitors will therefore determine the extent to which that business is highly regarded by its owners and ultimately investors.

- A key question, therefore, is the extent to which it is possible to achieve bases of competitive advantage which are sustainable; or are managers faced with the need continually to rethink how such advantage is to be achieved?

- In the end the extent to which that multi-business corporation is well regarded by those who invest in it is dependent on the extent to which value is created by its constituent business units. (Of course, there is a corollary to this: the choices at the corporate level may or may not enhance value created at the SBU level; these were the issues addressed in Chapter 6.)

- Whilst these concerns are expressed in terms of commercial businesses in competitive markets, very similar issues arise for public sector organisations. How might it be possible to provide best value services in ways which demonstrably and sustainably meet the expectations of users, compete effectively for scarce resources and meet the ever-growing pressures for better value for money from the providers of those resources, such as government? However, in this chapter the terms 'business' and more often 'business unit' are used because they connote a part of the organisation with direct interface with customers or users, whereas 'organisation', for example, can suggest a corporate entity with many such units.

Exhibit 7.1 provides an outline of how these issues are discussed in the chapter.

- The chapter begins by reviewing briefly the implications arising from the issues discussed in Part II of the book on the bases of strategic choice at the business level. In particular, how choices need to be made taking into account the forces at work in the environment, the capabilities of the organisation and the expectations of stakeholders. The question posed is the extent to which these are influences which are likely to be in conflict or compatible with one another.

- The chapter then moves to a discussion of generic *competitive strategies*. These are the fundamental bases on which a business unit might seek to achieve a lasting advantageous position by meeting the expectations of buyers, users or other stakeholders. In particular, different bases of achieving competitive advantage are considered. These include price-based strategies, differentiation strategies and focus strategies. This section concludes by revisiting the concept of competitive advantage in the context of the sorts of stakeholder and institutional expectations discussed in Chapter 5: here the question is raised as to what extent organisations actually do, or should, follow the single-minded pursuit of achieving competitive advantage. These considerations in turn inform considerations discussed in Chapter 8 about

| Exhibit 7.1 | Bases of strategic choice at the business level |

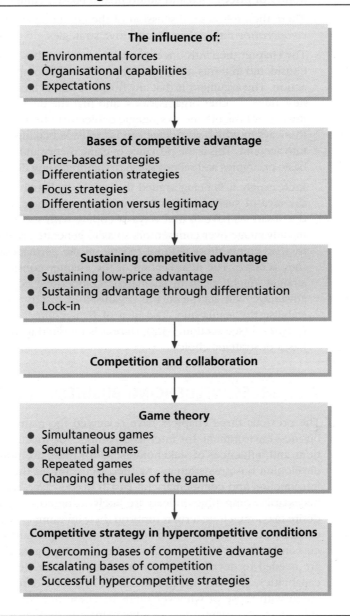

The influence of:
- Environmental forces
- Organisational capabilities
- Expectations

Bases of competitive advantage
- Price-based strategies
- Differentiation strategies
- Focus strategies
- Differentiation versus legitimacy

Sustaining competitive advantage
- Sustaining low-price advantage
- Sustaining advantage through differentiation
- Lock-in

Competition and collaboration

Game theory
- Simultaneous games
- Sequential games
- Repeated games
- Changing the rules of the game

Competitive strategy in hypercompetitive conditions
- Overcoming bases of competitive advantage
- Escalating bases of competition
- Successful hypercompetitive strategies

the *directions* which business units may follow, such as developing new products or new markets, and the different *methods* by which these might be achieved, for example through internal development, acquisition or alliances. This again highlights the interlinked nature of considerations of corporate and competitive strategy, as was shown in Exhibit IIIi in the introduction to Part III.

- The next section of the chapter considers specifically the issue of *sustainability* of price-based and differentiation-based competitive strategies.

- There then follows a discussion of the conditions and potential benefits of *co-operative* rather than competitive strategies.

- The chapter then introduces *game theory*. Here bases of strategic choice are considered in terms of the interdependence of competitors and competitive action. The argument is that any business unit is faced with competing business units in other organisations; and that the decisions and actions of one must affect the others; so strategic choices can be aided by thinking through the ways in which advantage can be achieved taking such interdependence into account. This is the province of game theory and this section outlines the basic principles and relates these to the preceding discussion in the chapter.

- Increasingly it is being argued that in a fast-changing and uncertain world, the idea of sustainability of competitive advantage is problematic. Rather, organisations have to find ways of coping with such conditions and achieving advantage over competitors so as to generate greater levels of profitability than competitors without relying on the permanence of the advantages they achieve. The next section of the chapter considers what competitive strategy might mean in such hypercompetitive conditions; in effect that advantage will accrue to the organisation that is able to disrupt and destabilise the status quo. The idea of *hypercompetition* was introduced in Chapter 3 (see section 3.3.2). Here it is revisited to consider lessons for the bases of strategic choice.

7.2 FORCES INFLUENCING BUSINESS STRATEGY

The previous three chapters have reviewed the many forces at work in the business environment, the internal capabilities of organisations and the expectations and influences of stakeholders. All of these are potentially important in developing business strategy. As the discussion on the 'business idea' in the introduction and commentary on Part II makes clear, these influences are not necessarily compatible; indeed are likely to be conflicting. Shareholders may desire maximum long-term returns on their investment, whilst bankers are concerned with shorter-term cash flow; competitive pressures may be forcing price cuts and reduced margins whilst at the same time greater levels of investment are needed to develop new products or reinforce developing organisational capabilities. The user of a public service will have different expectations compared with those of whoever funds it. These potential conflicts are unavoidable; in many respects they are what managing strategy is about; and successful organisations reconcile them better than unsuccessful ones. However, it helps to be able to focus on some important issues. One of these is to what extent, and how, it might be possible to achieve competitive advantage. This question focuses the strategist's attention on a number of key questions:

- What is the nature of the competitive environment? Is it stable and mature or fast changing and uncertain (section 2.4.3). How competitively intense is it? The discussion in section 3.3.1 is especially relevant here.

- In order to consider if there is a strategy which might achieve competitive advantage, it is important to begin by asking what is especially valued by customers or users. Here section 3.5.2 will be useful. In terms of achieving rents or superprofits the question is, then, whether there is a strategy which will be valued more by the buyer or user than that which is on offer by a competitor such that the buyer is prepared to pay a price above that of competitors.

- Does the business unit have competences which allow it to deliver the desired competitive strategy; and are these competences likely to provide a sustainable advantage or might competitors quickly be able to imitate, or improve on them? Sections 4.4 to 4.7 are relevant here.

- Are there constraints placed upon the choice of competitive strategy; for example, in terms of stakeholder expectations? Discussions in sections 5.2 and 5.3 of Chapter 5 help here.

7.3 BASES OF COMPETITIVE ADVANTAGE: THE 'STRATEGY CLOCK'

The rest of this chapter reviews different ways in which managers in a business might think about **competitive strategy**, the bases on which a business unit might achieve competitive advantage in its market.[2] For public service organisations, the concern is with an equivalent issue: the bases on which the organisation chooses to sustain the quality of its services within agreed budgets; how it provides 'best value'.

Competitive strategy is the bases on which a business unit might achieve competitive advantage in its market

The discussion begins here by introducing generic market-facing options based on the principle that organisations achieve competitive advantage by providing their customers with what they want, or need, better or more effectively than competitors; and in ways which their competitors find difficult to imitate. Assuming that the products or services of different businesses are more-or-less equally available, customers may choose to purchase from one source rather than another because either (a) the price of the product or service is lower than a competitor's or (b) the product or service is perceived by the customer to provide better 'added value' or benefits than that available elsewhere.[3] Although these are very broad generalisations, important implications which represent the generic strategic options for achieving competitive advantage flow from them. These are shown in Exhibit 7.2 and portrayed in Illustration 7.1 in the context of the history of Japanese car firms in the European car market. They are now discussed.

7.3.1 Price-based strategies (routes 1 and 2)

Route 1 may seem unattractive, but there are successful organisations following it. It is the **'no frills' strategy** which combines a low price, low perceived added value and a focus on a price-sensitive market segment. It can be viable because there may well exist a segment of the market which, whilst recognising

A **'no frills' strategy** combines a low price, low perceived added value and a focus on a price-sensitive market segment

Exhibit 7.2	**The strategy clock: competitive strategy options**

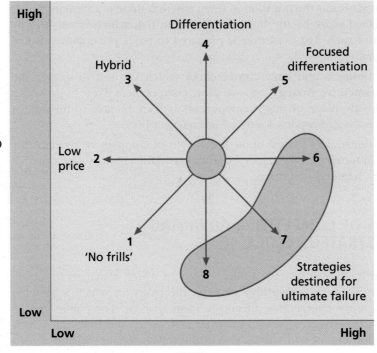

PRICE

		Needs/risks
1	'No frills'	Likely to be segment specific
2	Low price	Risk of price war and low margins; need to be cost leader
3	Hybrid	Low cost base and reinvestment in low price and differentiation
4	Differentiation (a) Without price premium	Perceived added value by user, yielding market share benefits
	(b) With price premium	Perceived added value sufficient to bear price premium
5	Focused differentiation	Perceived added value to a particular segment, warranting price premium
6	Increased price/standard value	Higher margins if competitors do not follow; risk of losing market share
7	Increased price/low value	Only feasible in monopoly situation
8	Low value/standard price	Loss of market share

Note: The Strategy clock is adapted from the work of Cliff Bowman (see D. Faulkner and C. Bowman, *The Essence of Competitive Strategy*, Prentice Hall, 1995). However, Bowman uses the dimension 'Perceived Use Value'.

Illustration 7.1

Competitive strategies of Japanese car firms in Europe

STRATEGY IN ACTION

The strategy clock helps explain bases of competitive strategy as well as how these might change over time.

Route 1

During the 1960s and early 1970s, the Japanese car manufacturers entered the European market by targeting the low-cost/low-added-value sector, which they believed would not be defended by European manufacturers. Their 'no frills' products were seen as cheap, and bought with few added-value expectations. The sales volume that this produced and the experience gained from this market entry strategy allowed them to form a bridgehead into Europe and develop other, more profitable, strategies.

Route 2

By the late 1970s and early 1980s, the improved quality and reliability of their products changed the perception of their cars to that of being as good as their European competitors. However, the Japanese cars continued to be sold at a cheaper price than their rivals, which allowed them to increase sales volume further.

Route 3

Following their earlier success, the late 1980s saw the Japanese further advance their position by producing competitively priced cars that were more reliable and of better quality than their rivals. Competitors followed the Japanese and attempted to maintain their position by improving the quality and reducing the relative prices of their own cars.

Route 4

By the mid-1990s, the main Japanese manufacturers, in common with other car firms, were seeking ways to differentiate their products on the basis of providing extra features such as air-bags, air conditioning and longer-term warranties. For much of this period the Japanese lead times for such innovations were less than most of their competitors'. However, by 2000, competitors were catching up and sustainable differentiation was becoming more difficult.

Route 5

Toyota's Lexus model – which stands alone from the rest of its range and does not use the Toyota name – is competing against manufacturers such as Jaguar and Mercedes in the luxury market segment. Because it is a new entrant, it does not have the 'pedigree' of its competitors; advertising campaigns aim to persuade buyers that they should be buying cars not on name, but on features.

Prepared by Tony Jacobs, Bristol Business School.

Questions

1. Why do new entrants to industries often enter 'through' point 1 on the strategy clock?

2. Why did the incumbent market leaders not respond to the Japanese 'trading up' through positions 2 and 3 on the clock?

3. Would it be feasible to enter the market through route 5 and then move to other positions? Which other positions would be more or less difficult and why?

that the quality of the product or service might be low, cannot or chooses not to afford to buy better-quality goods. The most profitable clothing retailer (in 2000) in the UK, Matalan, follows this strategy, as do the grocery retail chains Aldi and Netto in Europe. Their stores are basic, their merchandise range is relatively limited with few speciality or luxury products, and their prices are very low. As Illustration 7.1 shows, a business may also seek to achieve market entry through route 1 and use this as a bridgehead to build volume before moving on to other strategies. The strategy may also be a viable means of competing in an industry in which major firms are following a different strategy, as shown in Illustration 7.2.

A **low price strategy** seeks to achieve a lower price than competitors whilst trying to maintain similar value of product or service to that offered by competitors

Route 2, the **low price strategy**, seeks to achieve a lower price than competitors whilst trying to maintain similar value of product or service to that offered by competitors. In the public sector, costs are, in effect, the 'price' of a service to government as the provider of funds. Here the expectation may, indeed, be that there will be year-on-year efficiency gains and that these will be achieved without loss of quality.

If a business unit aims to achieve competitive advantage through a low price strategy it has two basic choices in trying to achieve sustainability. The first is to try to identify and focus on a market segment which is unattractive to competitors; and in this way avoid competitive pressures to erode price below levels which would achieve acceptable returns. In effect this is route 1 described above. A more challenging situation is where there is competition on the basis of price. This is a common occurrence in the public sector and for many firms with commodity-type products and services. Here tactical advantage may be gained by reducing price; but it is likely to be followed by competitors, with the danger of a slide into margin reduction across an industry as a whole, and an inability to reinvest to develop the product or service for the long term. Clearly a low price strategy cannot be pursued without a low cost base. However, low cost in itself is not a basis for advantage if competitors can also achieve the same low costs. The need is for a low cost base which competitors cannot match. The key challenge is how costs can be reduced in ways which others cannot match such that a low price strategy might give sustainable advantage. The evidence is that this is difficult to achieve, but some ways in which it might be possible are discussed in section 7.4.1 below.

7.3.2 Added value, or differentiation strategies (route 4)

A **differentiation strategy** seeks to provide products or services unique or different from those of competitors in terms of dimensions widely valued by buyers

The next option is a broad **differentiation strategy** which seeks to provide products or services unique or different from those of competitors in terms of dimensions widely valued by buyers. The aim is to achieve higher market share than competitors (which in turn could yield cost benefits) by offering better products or services at the same price; or enhanced margins by pricing slightly higher. In public services, the equivalent is the achievement of a 'centre of excellence' status which could attract higher funding from government: for example, universities try to show that they are better at research or teaching than other universities. This strategy might be achieved through the following:

Illustration 7.2

easyJet's 'no frills' strategy

Multiple bases for keeping costs down can provide a basis for a successful no-frills strategy.

Launched in 1995, easyJet were seen as the brash young upstart of the European airline industry and widely tipped to fail. In 2001, this Luton-based airline has done more than survive. From a start point of six hired planes working one route, by 2000 they had nineteen fully owned aircraft flying from four bases to sixteen cities. By 2004, they planned to have 44 Boeing 737s operating their low-price routes.

easyJet had largely seen off the big national airlines (known as flag carriers) such as British Airways' Go and KLM's Buzz operations that tried to compete alongside them in the European low-price, no-frills niche. Debonair went bust in 1999 when they tried to expand too fast. Ryanair remained easyJet's most closely competitive rival.

Stelios Haji-Ioannou, founder of easyJet, explained that their strategy was 'based on the belief that demand for short-haul air transport is price elastic – in simple English, if you reduce your price, more people will fly'. easyJet forces the consumer to consider the wider implications of purchasing luxury: 'The question is not should I fly BA or easyJet to Nice, it's should I fly BA to Nice or buy another pair of jeans.'

Beneath the surface of easyJet's cosmetic cost savings of not offering free in-flight refreshments or different first, business and economy classes, is a philosophy of cost saving that permeates through the whole company, from its paperless office to its no-ticket flights. For example, easyJet had not entered the market for connecting flights and simply transported customers from A to B and back again. Consequently, they were able to dispense with costly ticketing procedures along with the ticket vendors such as travel agents. easyJet's customers simply ring the number on the side of their aircraft, or increasingly access their website and book by credit card. Customers then check-in with a code, not a ticket. Air crew pick up rubbish from each flight in plastic bags. The absence of the need for connections also allowed easyJet to operate out of cheaper airports such as London Luton and Liverpool. These savings alone decreased the price of a flight by 25 per cent. easyJet also made the most of their locations by using the lack of competition for time slots to keep their aircraft off the tarmac and in the air, so earning substantially more hours of revenue per aircraft than airlines operating out of busier airports.

easyJet floated a quarter of their shares in November 2000 and were valued at £1.2 billion. The future challenge for easyJet, in the words of Stelios, was to find the six million passengers to fill his new aircraft.

Prepared by Phyl Johnson, University of Strathclyde, Graduate School of Business.

Questions

1. Read sections 7.3.1 and 7.4.2 and identify the bases of easyJet's no-frills strategy.
2. How easy would it be for a large airline such as BA to imitate the strategy?

- Uniqueness or improvements in products: for example, by investment in R&D, design expertise or building on the innovatory capabilities in the organisation. This is often the basis upon which manufacturing firms such as those in the car industry seek to compete, by investing in technology or design to achieve greater reliability, product life or performance. However, it should be noted that such improvements are often not durable: competitors are able to catch up.

- Marketing-based approaches – in effect, demonstrating better than the competition how the product or service meets customer needs. Here the strategy is likely to be built on the power of the brand or by powerful promotional approaches – for example, see Illustration 7.3.

- Competence-based approaches in which an organisation tries to build differentiation on the basis of its competences. If these really are competences which are peculiar to the organisation then it may well be very difficult for competitors to imitate them. However, identifying core competences as a basis for building a differentiation strategy is a challenging task (see sections 4.4 to 4.7 in Chapter 4 and section 7.4.2 below).

The extent to which these approaches will be successful is likely to be dependent on a number of factors.

- Has the organisation clearly identified *who the customer is*? This is not always straightforward. For example, for a newspaper business, is the customer the reader of the newspaper, the advertiser, or both? They are likely to have different needs and values. If a strategy of differentiation is to be followed, what will it be based upon? Public sector organisations face a similar issue. It may be very important that they offer perceived added value; but to satisfy whom? There may be no market-based mechanisms for users to buy services, so perceived added value may be measured in terms of the extent to which pressure groups, institutions or politicians are satisfied.

- The extent to which the organisation understands *what is valued by the customer*, user or perhaps a stakeholder group (such as a provider of funds or politicians in the public sector) can be dangerously taken for granted by managers. As explained in Chapters 2 and 4, managers may pursue strategies either on the basis of traditional ways of operating and taken-for-granted assumptions rooted in experience, or on the basis of resources and skills that the organisation has. Managers may therefore fail to address the most basic of questions: what does the customer value? A manager may conceive of a strategy of differentiation in technical terms: for example, as a better-engineered product. Whilst the uniqueness may be real in technical terms, it is of no value in achieving competitive advantage unless it is of greater perceived value to the user than products or services of competitors. Indeed, a differentiating factor for an organisation may be the ability of the managers to be closer to the market than competitors, so that they can better sense and respond to customer needs.

- It is important to be clear *who the competitors are*. For example, is the business competing with a wide competitor base or with a much narrower base, perhaps within a particular market segment? In the latter case, a

Illustration 7.3

Differentiation in the wine industry: an Australian success story

Successful differentiation needs to be based on what customers value.

By 2001 the traditional dominance of French wines in the UK had ended, with sales of Australian wine outstripping them for the first time. By 2000, Australian wines accounted for 19.5 per cent of UK wine sales in terms of value (up 25 per cent over 1999), with French wines showing a steady decline. And for wines over £5.00, Australian wine had already overtaken French wines. In the prestigious 2000 wine sampling contest in London, the Australians had won awards for three-quarters of the wines entered.

However, many wine experts still regarded Australian wines as inferior to French wines. For example, in some top London restaurants such as Le Gavroche, Australian wines were not served because they believed that customers preferred the quality of French wine over 'something more than a chemist's blend' (*FT*, 11 February 2001). Whilst French wine still tended to be favoured for eating out, Australian wine was favoured by take-home drinkers – and 84 per cent of all wine sold in the UK was drunk at home.

The success of Australian wines with retailers was put down to several factors. The quality was consistent, compared with French wines that could differ by year and location. Also, whilst the French had always highlighted the importance of the local area of origin of the wine within France, Australia had, in effect, 'branded' the country as a wine region and then concentrated on the variety of grape – a Shiraz or a Chardonnay, for example. This avoided the confusing details of the location of vineyards and the names of chateaux that many customers found difficult about French wines. Terry Davies, managing director of Beringer Blass, explained: 'you can pronounce the name on the bottle on our wines', the inference being that people often could not on a bottle of French wine.

Historically the European wine makers had also focused on their home markets. This was particularly the case in Italy, but French producers also tended to assume that consumers overseas would buy wine in much the same way as in France. This was changing, however. French wine makers were becoming less insular. Caroline Gilby, a consultant to the industry, explained that one well-known Chablis producer had spent time working in Chile, the US and Australia before taking up his present job. 'Wine makers interested in quality will have travelled. That's quite a change and it has started to happen only in the last five years.' Mike Paul of Destination Wine also believed that 'there are signs that there could be a backlash from the old world as France and Italy get their act together' (*FT*, 3/4 March 2001).

Sources: Adapted from *Financial Times*, 11 February and 3/4 March 2001.

Questions

1. What other reasons might account for the success of Australian wines?

2. What would you advise French wine producers to do to counter the Australian success?

strategy of focused differentiation may be appropriate (see section 7.3.4 below). In the case of broad-based differentiation, it is likely that the business will have to concentrate on bases of differentiation commonly accepted across the industry or a market. For example, it is unlikely that a car manufacturer trying to compete in the broadly based saloon car market could achieve competitive advantage without recognising the buyers' concern with quality and reliability, which have become threshold requirements. The emphasis must, then, be on how to achieve an advantage in other ways, requiring a much more sophisticated understanding of customer needs and how these can be met by building on core competences. Reference back to sections 4.4 to 4.7 and Illustration 4.3 will help demonstrate this.

- Another problem in identifying relevant competitors occurs as markets globalise. For example, a company may find its bases of differentiation eroded by another company which it did not previously see as a competitor because it did not share common geographical markets. As the two competitors increase their geographical scope, they may become competitors. Or it could be that a competitor develops a basis of differentiation in one market and then enters another on the basis of this, thus challenging an established operator's strategic position.

- The extent to which the basis of differentiation is *difficult to imitate* also needs to be considered. This is addressed more fully in section 7.4.2 below.

- The idea that competitive advantage through differentiation can be achieved on a static basis is questionable. There are two reasons for this. In many markets, customer needs change, and therefore *bases of differentiation may need to change*. However, even if relatively constant customer needs can be identified, over time competitors may be able to imitate bases of differentiation; and the signs are that this is speeding up (see section 7.7 below). The implication is that a business following a differentiation strategy may have to review bases of differentiation continually, and keep changing, as is the case for those car manufacturers following strategies of broad differentiation.

Some of these problems of identifying appropriate bases of differentiation are demonstrated in Illustration 7.4.

7.3.3 The hybrid strategy (route 3)

A **hybrid strategy** seeks simultaneously to achieve differentiation and a price lower than that of competitors

A **hybrid strategy** seeks simultaneously to achieve differentiation and a price lower than that of competitors. This is the position that Japanese saloon car manufacturers were able to occupy for much of the 1980s and 1990s (see Illustration 7.1). Here the success of the strategy depends on the ability both to understand and to deliver enhanced value in terms of customer needs, whilst also having a cost base that permits low prices and is sufficient for reinvestment to maintain and develop bases of differentiation.[4] This should not be confused with just trying to keep costs down in general whilst seeking to achieve differentiation; after all, presumably managers should always be trying to operate at the lowest cost commensurate with the strategy they are following.

Illustration 7.4

Crinkly biscuits as competitive advantage?

STRATEGY IN ACTION

In building a competitive strategy, executives need to be wary of spurious bases of competitive advantage.

Senior executives of an international food manufacturing company were taking part in a strategy workshop, discussing bases of competitive advantage for their strategic business units. The issues of competitive advantage based on perceived customer needs was raised, and one of the executives, the quality assurance manager for a biscuit business, commented as follows:

> I totally agree. In our business we know what customers want and we have invested to provide it. Our research shows that customers care a lot about the crinkles on the edges of their biscuits. They like neat regular crinkles. We have just invested £1 million in equipment that will deliver just that with very little wastage. We are the leader in this field.

In the discussion which followed, it became clear that there were at least three flaws in what the manager had said. First, his point of reference for considering his strategy was the end user, the consumer. In fact, the company referred to grocery retailers as 'competitors' because such retailers sold own-brand goods. Yet if the major retailers, which controlled 50 per cent of the distribution of biscuits, did not stock the product, it never reached the consumer. Whilst consumers were, of course, very important, the strategic customer was the retailer; but the business had no clear strategy for achieving competitive advantage with regard to retailers.

Second, it became clear that the identification of customer need was based on a survey which had pre-specified certain characteristics of biscuits, one of which was 'regular crinkles'. The quality assurance manager's colleagues were of the opinion that the fact that 'consumers had ticked a few boxes to do with ideas thought up by some guys in the R&D department' was a spurious basis upon which to build a strategy, let alone invest large amounts of capital.

Third, when challenged, the manager had to admit that there was nothing to stop a competitor buying similar equipment and achieving just the same quality of crinkles. If there was any competitive advantage – and this was dubious – it was easily imitable.

Questions

This example illustrates three common shortcomings in differentiation strategies:

(a) Value-for-money is incorrectly assessed by focusing on the wrong customer (or 'stakeholder').

(b) Inappropriate research to identify benefits.

(c) Easy imitation of the supposed sources of differentiation.

Bearing in mind these shortcomings identified in the claim for differentiation made in the illustration:

1. Do the bases of differentiation explained in Illustration 7.3 on the Australian wine industry overcome these shortcomings?

2. What *might have been* sustainable bases of differentiation for this biscuit business?

It might be argued that, if differentiation can be achieved, there should be no need to have a lower price, since it should be possible to obtain prices at least equal to competition, if not higher. However, the hybrid strategy could be advantageous in the following circumstances:

- If much greater volumes than the competition can be achieved, and margins still kept attractive because of a low cost base.

- If it is possible to be clear about the core competences on which differentiation can be built, and then reduce costs on other activities. IKEA recognised that it could achieve a high standard of production, but at a low cost, whilst concentrating on building differentiation on the bases of its marketing, range, logistics and store operations (see Illustrations 7.5).

- If there is a market segment with particular needs which also facilitates a low-price approach. IKEA offers good quality but to a market segment that is prepared to build and transport its products.

- As an entry strategy in a market with established competitors. This is a strategic approach to new market development that Japanese firms have used in the past on a global basis. They would search for the 'loose brick'[5] in a competitor's portfolio of businesses – perhaps a poorly run operation in a geographical area of the world – then enter that market with a superior product and, if necessary, a lower price. The aim was to take share, divert the attention of the competitor, and establish a foothold from which they could move further. However, in following such a strategy it is important to ensure that (a) the overall cost base is such that low margins can be sustained, and (b) a clear follow-through strategy has been considered for when entry has been achieved.

7.3.4 Focused differentiation (route 5)

A **focused differentiation** strategy seeks to provide high perceived value justifying a substantial price premium, usually to a selected market segment

A **focused differentiation** strategy seeks to provide high perceived value justifying a substantial price premium, usually to a selected market segment. In the market for saloon cars, Ford, Rover, Peugeot, Renault, Volkswagen and Japanese competitors are all competing within the one market, trying, often with some difficulty, to convince customers that their product is differentiated from their competitors'. A Lexus is also a saloon car, but it is not seeking to compete directly with these other manufacturers. It is offering a product with higher perceived value at a substantially higher price than in the saloon car market. It is therefore trying to attract different sorts of customers; a different market segment. However, this strategy raises some important issues:

- The choice may have to be made between broad differentiation across a market or a more focused strategy. This may take on global proportions, as managers have to decide between a broad approach in increasingly global markets, or more selective focus strategies. Indeed, in the 1990s many global businesses decided to sell off businesses in their portfolio and reduce the extent of their diversification in order to achieve such focus (see section 6.5).

Illustration 7.5

IKEA's hybrid strategy

Combining perceived low price with perceived added value can be a highly successful strategy but one which requires innovative thinking.

Since IKEA began in 1953 it has grown into a highly successful global network of stores but retained the same retailing concept: 'to offer a wide range of furnishing items of good design and function at prices so low that the majority of people can afford to buy them'.

The product offering was clearly different. The products were simple, high-quality Scandinavian design. They were also provided in knock-down furniture kits that the customers transported and assembled themselves, thus saving the often lengthy time that other stores required for delivery. The huge suburban stores had plenty of parking and amenities such as cafés, restaurants, wheelchairs and supervised childcare facilities. The customers expected styling and quality readily available at reasonable prices. IKEA met this expectation by encouraging customers to create value for themselves by taking on certain tasks traditionally done by the manufacturer and retailer, for example the assembly and delivery of the products. Of course, this also reduced cost. So too did the fact that customers were supplied with tape measures, pens and notepaper when they visited the stores; thus reducing the number of sales staff required.

To deliver low-cost yet high-quality products consistently, IKEA had buying offices around the world whose prime purpose was to identify potential suppliers. Designers at headquarters then reviewed these to decide which would provide what for each of the products, their overall aim being to design for low cost and ease of manufacture. The most economical suppliers were always chosen over traditional suppliers, so a shirt manufacturer might be employed to produce seat covers. Although the process through which acceptance to become an IKEA supplier was not easy, it was highly coveted for, once part of the IKEA system, suppliers gained access to global markets and received technical assistance, leased equipment and advice on how to bring production up to world-quality standards. By the mid-1990s, IKEA was offering a range of 12,000 items from suppliers in 45 countries at prices 20–40 per cent lower than for comparable goods.

The whole philosophy of keeping costs down ran through the company. IKEA had always been frugal in its approach. In its early years it had relocated to Denmark to escape Swedish taxation. Echoes of the same philosophy and style could be seen in Anders Moberg, the chief executive. He drove a Nissan Primera, dressed in informal clothes and clocked in just as the other employees did. When abroad he travelled economy class and stayed in modest hotels. He also expected his executives to do likewise.

Source: Company data, newspaper articles and R. Norman and R. Ramirez, 'From value chain to value constellation: designing interactive strategy', *Harvard Business Review*, vol. 71, no. 4 (1993), pp. 65–77.

Questions

1. Which other businesses can you think of that follow a hybrid strategy?

2. Why might businesses find it difficult to follow a hybrid strategy?

3. What basic guidelines would you propose for a business considering such a strategy?

- Because an organisation choosing to follow a focus strategy is likely to be targeting a particular market segment, it is important to realise that, within that segment itself, the strategy clock is just as relevant so managers face further choices. Lexus competes in the luxury car segment, but within that segment it is following a strategy distinct from other luxury car companies. Its competitors might be seen as top-of-the-range Mercedes and BMW. Against these competitors in this segment, Lexus is following a low-price or perhaps hybrid strategy. Its quality is just as good, but relative to those other models, its prices are lower.

- It is again important to be clear about which market segment (or segments) is being targeted, defined in terms of a coherent set of customer needs; and this needs to be translated into action which satisfies those customers. This may be difficult to do, if the organisation is attempting to compete in different market segments, with different needs. For example, department stores attempt to sell a wide range of products in one store. They may also attempt to appeal to different customer types in so doing. But they run into problems because the store itself, the fixtures and fittings, the décor and store ambience, and the staff, may not be differentiated according to the different market segment needs.

- Focus strategies may conflict with stakeholder expectations. For example, a public library service could probably be run more cost efficiently if it were to pull out of low-demand market niches and put more resources into its popular branch libraries. It might also find that an extension of its services into audio and video tapes or new forms of public information service would prove popular. However, the extent to which these strategies would be regarded as within the library's remit might be hotly debated.

- New ventures often start in very focused ways – for example, new 'leading-edge' medical services in hospitals. It may, however, be difficult to find ways to grow such new ventures. Moving from route 5 to route 4 will mean a lowering of price and therefore cost, whilst maintaining differentiation features. On the other hand, maintaining a highly focused (route 5) approach may not be easy because users may not be prepared, or able, to pay the price or, as in the public sector, provide funding support to subsidise such projects.

- The advantages of the focused approach have to be carefully monitored because the market situation may change. Differences between segments may be eroded, leaving the organisation open to much wider competition. This was a concern for the manufacturers of luxury cars, such as Jaguar, as the top end of the executive car range came closer and closer to the style of luxury cars. Or the market may be further segmented by even more differentiated offerings from competitors.

7.3.5 Failure strategies (routes 6, 7 and 8)

The strategies suggested by routes 6, 7 and 8 are probably destined for failure. Route 6 suggests increasing price without increasing value to the customer. This is, of course, the very strategy that monopoly organisations are accused of following. However, unless the organisation is protected by legislation, or high economic barriers to entry, competition is likely to erode market share. Route 7 is an even more disastrous extension of route 6, involving the reduction in value of a product or service, whilst increasing relative price.

Route 8, reduction in value whilst maintaining price, is also dangerous, though firms have tried to follow it. There is a high risk that competitors will increase their share substantially.

Arguably there is another basis of failure, which is for a business to be unclear as to its fundamental generic strategy such that it ends up being 'stuck in the middle' – a recipe for failure.

The strategy clock is, then, a market-based model of generic strategy options rooted in the question: what is of value in the product or service to the customer, user or provider of funding? It does not deny that the cost base of an organisation is crucially important, but it sees this as a means of developing generic strategies, and not as a basis for competitive advantage in itself.

7.3.6 Differentiation versus legitimacy

The considerations discussed so far in this section have had a major impact on the debates about competitive strategy which take place in organisations. It is common to hear discussions in businesses about 'competitive advantage' and 'bases of differentiation', for example: and they are terms which have found their way into an increasingly market-driven public sector. However, it is important to pause and consider the extent to which such debates have actually influenced practice – realised strategy if you like – or the performance of organisations. If the lessons of the previous sections are to be taken at face value, then the search for truly differentiated strategies would be of paramount importance, and the most succesful organisations would be those clearly differentiated from others. In fact the evidence on both of these counts is equivocal.

It is not differences of strategy but similarity of strategies which often describes competitors. Accountancy firms offer similar services, seek to enhance those services in similar ways, build relationships with clients in particular ways and so on. The airlines who compete on long-haul flights or car manufacturers tend to follow similar strategies and imitate each other when one introduces new features or services. Indeed, the whole idea of strategic groups (see section 3.3.3) builds on the idea of similarity of strategies amongst directly competing firms. The evidence is that successful strategies tend to be copied, especially where organisations face uncertainty and ambiguity.[6] There are two main reasons for this. The first is the obvious one: that where one organisation has achieved success, others see a short-cut to the same success – or at least they have the hope of doing so. The second reason is less obvious and goes back to the observations about organisational fields and legitimacy made in Chapter 5 (see section 5.5.2). There may well be pressures to conform to the norms and practices of that organisational field – pressures to be 'legitimate' in the eyes of members of that field – and these may include powerful stakeholders such as government, professional bodies, customers and so on.

There is, moreover, evidence that such conformity and mimicry may make sense in terms of enhancing performance in at least two respects:

● In the long term, organisations that conform to the strategic norms of the organisational field tend to stand more chance of survival. For those that choose the path of differentiation, some may outperform others, but for some it will be their demise. So imitation and conformity may be a safe bet.

● Other organisations, for example suppliers, or financiers, or potential employees, may also see such organisations as safe bets too. So the organisations may benefit in terms of cost of supplies or finance or calibre of staff, for example.

It has been argued that strategic balance – balance between differentiation and similarity with others – may be a sensible approach and there is some evidence that it does result in higher levels of return for firms than those that follow more extreme differentiation or imitation strategies.[7]

7.4 SUSTAINING COMPETITIVE ADVANTAGE

If the lessons of searching for competitive advantage as discussed in section 7.3 above are to be taken seriously, the issue of sustainability is important. Is it possible to achieve competitive advantage in such a way that it can be preserved over time? There are those who argue that it can and others who argue it cannot. In this section the arguments for sustainability are addressed. In section 7.7 an alternative view is put forward: that organisations have to reconcile themselves to a world of increasing turbulence and uncertainty in which sustainability is not possible.

A good deal of what follows builds on the earlier discussion in Chapter 4 (section 4.7) on the robustness of core competences. The argument that was put forward there was that the core competences on which successful strategies are based are more likely to be durable, in the sense of being difficult for others to imitate, if they are rare, complex, causally ambiguous or culturally embedded. It is a lesson which is reinforced when considering the sustainability of generic strategies.

7.4.1 Sustaining low price advantage

It was said earlier that achieving and sustaining competitive advantage through low price is dependent on low cost but that it is difficult to sustain. So, how might it be achieved and what are the problems?

● The most ambitious aim is for an organisation to seek to sustain reduced prices over competition on the basis of having *the lowest* cost base such that competitors cannot hope to emulate it – of being a *cost leader* – and being prepared to sustain and win a price battle if necessary. However, cost leadership is very difficult to achieve. It has been argued that it can be achieved by means of substantial *relative market share advantage* because this provides a firm with cost advantages through economies of scale and market power (for example, buying power). Experience curve effects (see section 4.5.1) can also be important: a firm that moves fastest down the experience curve such that it achieves a market share position significantly greater than that of competitors by the time the market is mature should be operating at substantially lower unit costs and should be able hold on to that advantage. Although there is evidence that firms that have achieved such a position do have lower costs, it is not clear what 'substantial relative market share advantage' means.[8] The likelihood is that it needs to be very substantial. The firm with 60 per cent of its market with the nearest competitor at 15 per cent may be able to rely on lowest cost; but a firm with 20 per cent with competitors hovering around 15 per cent may not. There are, however, not that many markets with firms with such dominant share positions; and still fewer in which firms with such dominant positions rely on low price strategies – why should they if they dominate the market? Instead they tend to benefit from low cost positions by reinvesting profits into bases of differentiation. For example, Kelloggs or Mars may well be the lowest cost operators in their markets, but they reinvest their profits into branding and product and service differentiation.

● In developing strategy, it is in any case dangerous to assume a direct link between relative market share advantage and sustainable advantage in the market because there is little evidence of sustainability; dominant firms lose market share and others overtake them. Moreover, if the idea of cost leadership is to be taken seriously as an industry-wide strategy, it is problematic for all but a very few firms – indeed, arguably in a given industry, for all but one firm. In its literal form, it is therefore not a basis for an industry-wide strategy.

● Porter actually defines[9] cost leadership as '*the* low-cost producer in its industry . . . a low-cost producer must find and exploit all sources of cost advantage'. So here the concern is with cost advantages through organisationally specific competences driving down cost throughout the value chain[10] (see Chapter 4, section 4.5.1 and Exhibit 4.5). For example, cost advantage might be achieved because a business is able to obtain raw materials at lower prices than competitors, or able to produce more efficiently, or because it is located in an area where labour cost is low, or because its distribution costs provide advantages. A business purchasing large quantities of a given material from a supplier is likely to obtain better prices, have greater negotiating power to ensure that deliveries are on time (and therefore reduce stocks), and build up knowledge and experience amongst its buyers that lead to greater internal efficiencies. In effect the business is seeking to move down its experience curve faster than competitors and therefore achieve lowest cost *in particular areas of its operations*. Of course, if this approach is to be followed it matters that the operational areas it chooses do truly bestow cost advantages which yield real price advantages over competition. There would be no point in aiming to reduce costs in operational areas of minimal impact on price; nor would it be sensible to focus on operational areas where competitors could just as readily follow suit. However, it may be possible to identify where competitors are vulnerable; for example, where they have a lower market share and consequent higher costs (e.g. in cost of sales or distribution) or inherently higher costs, perhaps because of location or labour costs. It may then be possible for the business to concentrate on driving down its costs in these areas as a further means of gaining competitive advantage. All of this requires a mindset where innovation (in cost reduction) is regarded as essential to survival.

- There are dangers here, however. The single-minded focus on cost reduction in all these different ways may result in the customer perceiving a lower added value product or service and an intended route 2 strategy slipping to route 1 by default. Indeed, Porter observes that such 'low-cost producers typically sell a standard, or no frills, product . . . [Such a firm] will be an above-average performer in its industry provided it can command prices at or near the industry average'. It is therefore actually likely to be following a strategy which is somewhere between routes 1 and 2.

- It may also be possible to achieve competitively advantageous low costs by careful examination of capabilities and competences in parts of the value chain. Suppose it is possible to identify which capabilities and competences are needed to compete effectively at low price. It may be that these are much less sophisticated than those required to achieve advantage through differentiation. They may be capable of being so standardised and routinised that the cost of their provision can be substantially reduced. A worldwide example of this is McDonald's; another is easyJet (see Illustration 7.2). Or it may be possible to reduce substantially the costs of activities by outsourcing their provision. The organisation would then focus on managing what it can control best to keep down costs and looking for low-cost outsourcing for the rest (see section 4.4.3).

- There are, however, risks here too. Competitors may be able to do the same, so no advantage is gained. Or, still more problematic, the organisation may outsource activities which it has failed to recognise as actual or potential value-enhancing activities and are thus the basis of a differentiation strategy (see section 7.3.2 above).

- It may be feasible to follow a strategy of low price to achieve competitive advantage within a market segment in which (a) low price is important; and (b) a business has cost advantage over competitors *operating in that segment*. An example here is the success of dedicated producers of own-brand grocery products for supermarkets. They are able to hold prices low because they can avoid the high overhead and marketing costs of major branded manufacturers. However, they can only do so provided they focus on that product or market segment.

- However, whilst all of these are potential advantages, if low cost is the basis of a strategy of low price, managers need to be sure that competitors cannot easily imitate or catch up with their cost advantages. This is problematic, not least because most businesses have very little accurate information about the cost base of their competitors.

The main points that need to be emphasised are, then, that:

- sustaining competitive advantage through low price based on lower costs than competitors is difficult. Illustration 7.6 revisits easyJet's strategy to consider some of the problems;

Illustration 7.6

Sustaining a low price strategy: easyJet revisited

Sustainability of competitive advantage raises major challenges for the long-term success of an organisation.

Undoubtedly easyJet has been a huge success (see Illustration 7.2). However, following its successful flotation, some commentators suggested there were threats looming on the horizon. In fact, easyJet's 2000 prospectus for its flotation had fourteen pages on risk alone.

The acquisition of over 30 new Boeing 737s and the search for the passengers to fill them could ramp up the pressure on themselves. Analysts pointed to the fact that Debonair went bust by trying to grow too fast and suggested that there might not be much more volume to squeeze out of the low-price intra-European routes. As they tried do so, might this also mean easyJet would face increasing competition from rivals such as Ryanair whom hitherto they had largely avoided: and increasing competition would mean pressures on already modest margins.

A second risk revolved around their corporate ambition. By 2001 the portfolio included easyEverything, an Internet café operation, easyRentacar.com, an Internet-only car rental company, easyValue.com, comparison online shopping, easydot.com, a free web-based e-mail service and, being planned, easyMoney.com, an online financial services business. The extension of their brand into these other areas at the same time as trying to extend their core operation would inevitably increase the complexity of their business: and complexity costs money to manage, not least in management time and corporate overhead, as easyJet's flag-carrier competitors would testify.

In their in-flight magazine, easyJet proudly profiled their young, all-737 fleet. Although known as the reliable workhorse of the skies, the 737 is an old aircraft. A serious design fault on this aircraft (remember Concorde) could ground easyJet's entire operation. So by buying only 737s easyJet had taken another risk by putting all their eggs in one basket.

In addition to this, 2000 saw easyJet enter a dispute with the owners of its base at Luton airport, who wished to raise the landing charges. By 2001 a customer booking online with easyJet found increased charges identified separately on their quotation as a 'fat cat' charge; and there were reports that Stelios Haji-Ioannou had considered moving easyJet's base from Luton to Liverpool.

Others suggested that easyJet were leaving themselves open to being the victim of their own success. Successful strategies can become set in stone, whereas the strategic innovator has to stay open to new and potentially different opportunities. easyJet appeared to be totally engaged with and very happy playing the game they had learned to play well. Its committed workforce, who provided enthusiastic support for its no-frills strategy, might find future change difficult.

Prepared by Phyl Johnson, University of Strathclyde, Graduate School of Business.

Sources: Adapted from *The Economist*, 'Low-cost airlines: easy does it', 18 November 2000, pp. 122–124; D. Sull, 'Easy-Jet's $500 million gamble', *European Management Journal*, vol. 17, no. 1 (1999), pp. 20–38.

Questions

1. Do you think easyJet's successful no-frills strategy is sustainable?

2. What recommendions would you make to Stelios Haji-Ioannou to ensure the future success of easyJet?

● in so far as it is possible to achieve, it is likely to require the management of low cost across multiple points in the value chain and continual attention to finding new ways to reduce those costs.

7.4.2 Sustaining differentiation-based advantage

Differentiation is often espoused by managers as central to the strategy of their organisation; but too often they simply mean 'being different'. This may not be enough; the lessons from section 7.3.2 earlier in this chapter need to be borne in mind; but the specific concern here is that of sustainability. If the aim is sustainable differentiation, there is little point in striving to be different if others can imitate readily.

For example, the investment in state-of-the-art production equipment by the biscuit manufacturer in Illustration 7.4, even if it were really meeting an important customer need, and therefore providing for a meaningfully different product, could be imitated readily by a competitor who could make the same investment. Or a firm of accountants which carries out a relatively standardised audit procedure will find it difficult to differentiate its services based on variations of those procedures. Even if it can develop such variations, they are likely to be copied rapidly by others. This is not to say that such actions are not important; they may be vital just to be able to compete effectively with others who are also improving their businesses; but that is not the same as *sustainable differentiation*. Sustainable differentiation needs to be based on less imitable aspects of competitive advantage. For example, for the accountants it is more likely that differentiation can be achieved on the basis of the extent to which those involved in the firm understand the needs of their clients, build relationships with individuals within the client base, and can ensure that their own services are integrated to meet clients' needs. And for the biscuit manufacturer a combination of strong branding to the consumer and high levels of service to the retailer with assured delivery on time, up-to-date information on the progress of orders and rapid and flexible response to their needs will be a more likely basis of sustainable advantage.

It is, then, not likely to be one specific advantage or difference that matters, but a mix of linked activities, relationships and competences throughout different parts of the value chain – the core competences of an organisation – that provides the basis of sustainability. This was the theme developed in Chapter 4 (section 4.7) which discussed the robustness of core competences.

Leaving aside the possibility that an organisation might have resources or competences that are rare, i.e. are difficult for others to obtain at all, conditions to sustain differentiation[11] include the following:

● *Difficulties of imitation* based on core competences. The reasons for this include:
  - *Complexity*: the competences upon which successful strategy is based are too complex for competitors to comprehend.
  - *Causal ambiguity*: associated with complexity might be the difficulty of competitors understanding cause and effect. Even if a potential imitator

can discern what the linked competences of a successful strategy are, it may still be difficult to see why they give rise to the success that they do.
- And these may be especially difficult to imitate when competences are *culturally embedded* deep down in the organisation.

● *Imperfect mobility* is another reason why sustainability may be possible: this is concerned with whether or not the capabilities and competences of an organisation could be traded. If they can be traded, then differentiation may not be sustainable. A pharmaceutical firm may gain great benefits from having top research scientists, or a football club star players, but these valuable assets may be poached by competitors: they are tradable. On the other hand, some bases of advantage are very difficult to trade and imperfect mobility will be more likely. For example:
- More *intangible assets* such as brand image or reputation are difficult for a competitor to obtain. Even if the competitor acquires the company to use the brand, the reputation of the brand may not readily transfer given new ownership.
- *Switching costs* are the actual or perceived cost for a buyer of changing the source of supply of a product or service. The buyer might be dependent on the supplier for particular components, services or skills; or the benefits of switching may simply not be worth the cost or risk.
- *Co-specialisation* may also help achieve imperfect mobility: for example, if one organisation's resources or competences are intimately linked with the buyers' organisation. It could be, for example, that a whole element of the value chain for one organisation, perhaps distribution or manufacturing, is undertaken by another.

A combination of the difficulties of imitation and imperfect mobility is of course especially helpful. In its most effective form it can give rise to the possibility of 'lock in', explained in the next section and illustrated in Illustration 7.7.

7.4.3 The delta model and lock-in

Another approach to thinking about sustainability, whether it be for price-based strategies or differentiation strategies, is the idea of 'lock-in'.[12] Here an organisation has achieved a proprietary position in its industry; it has become an industry standard. For example, IBM was an industry standard; Microsoft became an industry standard, as did the Pentium processor from Intel. In the university sector, Oxford and Cambridge universities occupy this position. As industry standards, they are not necessarily the best products. For example, technically speaking, many argue that the Apple Macintosh had a better operating system than Microsoft; as did Betamax over VHS. But this did not stop Microsoft and VHS becoming the industry standards by achieving a lock-in position. In all of these cases the achievement of this position meant that other businesses had to conform to or relate to that standard in order to prosper; the architecture of the industry came to be built around this dominant player. For example, software applications by other businesses were written around the Microsoft standard for Pentium processors, making it very difficult for other

Illustration 7.7

NXT learn lessons from Dolby

Becoming the industry standard requires a strong brand, patent protection and close relationships with other companies.

NXT believed its flat screen loudspeakers could find their way into everything from conventional hi-fi systems and public address systems, to tiny loudspeakers for mobile phones and stereo equipment for cars. Their ideas came from military research into soundproofing aircraft. The flat screen speakers were based on techniques related to materials and audio processing in which flat objects (such as pieces of cardboard or plastic) radiate soundwaves and give sound reproduction on a par with top-quality conventional loudspeakers.

Strategically, NXT took its model as Dolby, the creator of specialist audio technologies whose name appears on screen credits in most cinemas. Dolby is privately owned; by 2000 its turnover was only around £85 million but the profit levels were 'thought to be substantial'. Most of Dolby's business came from licensing related audio technologies to around 500 consumer goods companies, including most of the large Japanese electronics manufacturers. In the past 20 years, these businesses had sold about 800 million products that relied on Dolby's audio ideas. Their value to much larger companies began by Dolby feeding them its own technology – backed by strong branding and patent protection. As these relationships became successful and well established they began to be used by other firms, so Dolby became a conduit for related technologies.

NXT had also started to build its connections: it had sold 200 licences for ideas to companies including Philips, Daimler, Chrysler and Siemens. The result was that, despite operating at a loss on sales of just £13 million in 2000, its stocks were highly rated. Its approach had parallels to Dolby in several ways:

- To protect their technology, NXT had taken out 1,500 patents in 70 countries, many more than Dolby. Patents covered not only the technical works of the flat screen loudspeakers but their application for ideas such as talking birthday cards.

- It insisted that licensees work closely with them when they adapted their ideas for their own use. NXT could veto production of goods that used its ideas if they believed they were not up to scratch.

- It ensured its brand name appeared on products made by licensees. Like Dolby, the logo stood for sound quality, so inventors were more likely to come to NXT with their ideas and competitors were less likely to persuade companies to take their technology.

- NXT was moving on to other ideas to license to companies such as speech recognition.

However, there were differences from Dolby. One-third of Dolby's revenue came from making systems used in production studios and cinemas as part of projection machinery. They argued that this gave 'an ability to follow trends in areas such as film or video content creation' and to pick up ideas relevant to the consumer side of the business. NXT did not wish to be in manufacturing, saying, 'we don't want to compete with our licensees'.

Source: Adapted from *Financial Times*, 6 February 2001.

Questions

1. Using the checklists in sections 7.4.2 (on sustaining differentiation) and 7.4.3 (on lock-in), identify the ways in which NXT and Dolby attempt to sustain competitive advantage.

2. Do you think NXT's aspirations are realistic? What might threaten them?

organisations to break into the market. In the public sector in the UK, reference is made to the 'gold standard', by which is meant an exemplar organisation. If other organisations choose to provide services significantly differently they run the risk of a loss of legitimacy.

The achievement of lock-in is likely to be dependent on a number of factors:

- The first is likely to be size or market dominance. It is unlikely that other organisations seek to conform to such standards unless they perceive the organisation that promotes it to be dominant in its market.

- However, it is more likely that such standards will be set earlier rather than later in life cycles of markets. In the volatility of growth markets it is more likely that the single-minded pursuit of lock-in will be achieved than when the market is mature. This was the case for Microsoft and Intel. Similarly, it was the same for the dominance of Sky over its rivals. Sky, with the financial support of the News Corporation, was able to undercut and invest heavily in technology, sustaining substantial losses over many years, in order to achieve that target. This is not to say it had, inherently, a better product; what it had was management and investors with a more single-minded drive and commitment to get to market fast and achieve dominance.

- Once this position is achieved, it may be self-reinforcing and escalating. When one or more firms support the standard, then more come on board; then others are obliged to; and so on.

- There is likely to be rigorous insistence on the preservation of that lock-in position. Rivals will be seen off fiercely; insistence on conformity to the standard will be strict. This can of course lead to problems as Microsoft found in the American courts when it was deemed to be operating against the interests of the market (see the case example at the end of Chapter 1).

Illustration 7.7 shows how one company set out to achieve a lock-in position in its industry in some of these ways, and by building barriers to imitation and the sorts of switching cost and co-specialisation with customers explained in section 7.4.2 above.

7.5 COMPETITION AND COLLABORATION

So far the emphasis has been on competition and competitive advantage. However, the concept of the organisational field (see sections 3.4 and 5.5.2) is a reminder that advantage may not always be achieved by competition alone; and Chapter 8 (section 8.3.3) discusses the importance of strategic alliances. Collaboration between organisations[13] may be a crucial ingredient in achieving advantage or avoiding competition.[14] Also, organisations may compete in some markets and collaborate in others or even simultaneously compete and collaborate.

Collaboration between potential competitors or between buyers and sellers is likely to be advantageous when the combined costs of purchase and buying transactions (such as negotiating and contracting) are lower through collaboration than the cost of operating alone. Such collaboration also helps build switching costs (see section 7.4.2 above). This can be illustrated by briefly returning to the five forces framework[15] from section 3.3.1. For example:

- *Buyer–seller collaboration.* Component manufacturers might build close links with customers so as to reduce lead times for delivery, to help in research and development activities, to build joint information systems and reduce stock, and even to take part in planning teams to design new products. This is now facilitated by IT systems even to the extent that some suppliers may be linked into a manufacturer's enterprise resource planning (ERP) system (as discussed in section 9.3.2). Indeed, manufacturers have actively sought out suppliers who are able to collaborate in these ways and in many cases made it an essential requirement to become an accredited supplier.

- *Collaboration to increase buying power.* For many years the power and profitability of pharmaceutical companies were aided by the fragmented nature of their buyers – in the main, individual doctors. In the 1990s many governments have promoted, or required, collaboration between doctors and centralised government drug-specifying agencies, the result of which has been more co-ordinated buying power.

- *Collaboration to build barriers to entry or avoid substitution.* Faced with threatened entry or substitute products, organisations in an industry may collaborate to invest in research and development or marketing. For example, marketing boards in agriculture have been set up to promote the joint interests of producers; trade bodies have been established to promote an industry's generic features such as safety standards or technical specifications in order to speed up innovation and pre-empt the possibility of substitution. These efforts to prevent entry may be frustrated by the collaborative efforts of other organisations seeking to gain entry.

- *Collaboration to gain entry and competitive power.* Organisations seeking to develop beyond their traditional boundaries (for example, geographical expansion) may need to collaborate with others to gain entry into new arenas. The only way of gaining local market knowledge may be to collaborate with local operators. Indeed, in some parts of the world, governments require entrants to collaborate in such ways. Collaboration may also be advantageous for purposes of developing required infrastructure such as distribution channels, information systems or research and development activities. It may also be needed for cultural reasons: buyers may prefer to do business with local rather than expatriate managers.

- *Collaboration to share work with customers.* An important trend in the public services is a move towards more *co-production* with clients.[16] For example, self-assessment of income tax: the motives may be varied but include cost efficiency, quality/reliability improvement or increased 'ownership/responsibility' from the clients. E-commerce allows more organisations to take this approach on board. For example, websites can be designed to assist customers with self-service (the virtual shopping basket is an example) or to allow them to design/customise a product or service to their own specification (for example, when ordering a new computer or the decoration and furnishing of a room). At a more mundane level, the use of e-mail attachment of documents has transformed 'who does what' in preparing for meetings or even writing books!

7.6 GAME THEORY

The origins of game theory can be traced back to the study of war. The central idea is that the general, or in our case the strategist, has to anticipate the reaction of others – for the general, the enemy; for the manager, competitors. There are two core assumptions in this. First, that the competitor will behave rationally. The idea of rationality in this sense is simply that competitors will always try to win to their own benefit. Second, that the competitor is in an interdependent relationship with other competitors. So all competitors are affected by what other competitors do; one competitor's move will galvanise response from another competitor, and the outcome of choices made by one competitor is dependent on the choices made by another. The assumption in game theory is that to a greater or lesser extent competitors are aware of the interdependencies that exist and of the sorts of move that competitors could take. Arguably, this is especially so within strategic groups (see section 3.3.3) where competitors are following similar strategies or have similar characteristics or where competitors are targeting the same market segments.

The key principle for the strategist as game theorist is the need to put themselves in the position of the competitor or competitors such that they can take an informed, rational view about what that competitor is likely to do; and therefore choose their best course of action in this light. The principle is simple enough, but the study of game theory based on these simple principles has become very complex and elaborate. Readers who wish to follow this up will have to do so separately.[17] In the space available here, some basic guiding principles of game theory are illustrated. Certainly their application can have major impact; to take a spectacular example, many of the government auctions around the world for third-generation mobile phone licences have been based on game theory principles: in the UK auction the revenue raised was £22 billion after more than 100 rounds of bidding![18]

7.6.1 Simultaneous games

A simultaneous game is where the players involved – for example, competitors – are faced with making decisions at a point in time. Perhaps the most famous example of game theory is a simultaneous game, the Prisoner's Dilemma, represented in Exhibit 7.3. This is usually shown in terms of individuals, but here as companies, that have to choose whether to co-operate or not. Suppose, for example, that two firms dominate a market and have to decide whether to try to gain market share through spending heavily on marketing to try to achieve a still higher share. They may know that the returns from such heavy expenditure would not offset its cost. Therefore, the logical course of action would be for both parties to keep marketing expenditure at the current low level to

Exhibit 7.3	A 'Prisoner's Dilemma'

		Competitor A	
		Heavy marketing spend	Low marketing spend
Competitor B	Heavy marketing spend	B = 5 A = 5	B = 12 A = 2
	Low marketing spend	B = 2 A = 12	B = 9 A = 9

preserve their current shares: in a sense to collude tacitly to keep the situation as it is for mutual benefit. If both players select this strategy, the payoff to each firm is represented in the bottom right-hand quadrant of Exhibit 7.3. However, there is likely to be a temptation by one or the other competitor to try to steal an advantage over the other. Each knows that if it alone spent more on marketing it would achieve substantial returns. This is represented in the top right and bottom left quadrants. The danger is, of course, that, knowing this, both parties decide they must spend heavily on marketing to ensure that the other competitor does not get an advantage. The result is the top left quadrant which is a much worse return than would have happened had they both decided to keep marketing expenditures at the current level. The Prisoner's Dilemma model suggests that the incentives open to both parties (in this case to spend heavily on marketing) may lead to a pay-off which is much worse for both.

In fact, in practice this is not likely to occur if there are a limited number of competitors, as will be seen later. But it could well occur if there are many competitors jostling for position in a fragmented market. In such circumstances it might be most logical for competitors to hold prices at a relatively high level, but no one expects anyone else to do so, and price wars result.

Nonetheless, the example of the Prisoner's Dilemma illustrates some important principles. It may well be that the end result is a lesser pay-off than could logically be achieved: but it is the *dominant strategy*. A **dominant strategy** is one that outperforms all other strategies whatever rivals choose, so it makes sense to use it if it exists. In the Prisoner's Dilemma example it would be much better for co-operation to exist between the two parties. However, the fact is that if either of the competitors breaks rank on this the other one will suffer badly. So the dominant strategy is to spend heavily on marketing.

Illustration 7.8a introduces another dimension. Here competitors also face a decision on investment; this time to do with research and development. However, they are not equal. They have different resource bases and competences. Also, one firm has a dominant strategy and the other does not. If a firm does

A **dominant strategy** is one that outperforms all other strategies whatever rivals choose

not have a dominant strategy, as in the illustration, game theory suggests that it is important to identify if there are any *dominated* strategies; and, if there are, to eliminate the possibility of that situation occurring. The third principle says that if there is not a dominant or dominated strategy, look for an *equilibrium*. In game theory, **equilibrium** is a situation where each competitor contrives to get the best possible strategic solution for itself given the response from the other.

Illustration 7.8a shows these principles, examines the choices available to the firms, identifies the likely pay-offs and considers how the firms might resolve the situation.

In game theory, **equilibrium** is a situation where each competitor contrives to get the best possible strategic solution for itself given the response from the other

7.6.2 Sequential games

In the simultaneous games discussed so far the competitors were making decisions or moves at the same time and without knowing what each other was doing. However, this is not always the case; a strategic decision may well be sequential, one party making a move, followed by the other. In such circumstances there is a need to think differently. The guiding principle here is to *think forwards and reason backwards*. In other words, to try to think through the sequence of moves that competitors might make based on a reasonable assumption about what that competitor desires as the outcome; and on that basis decide the most advantageous moves you can make. Assuming a simultaneous sequence of moves, Illustration 7.8b shows how Innova might set about making a strategic decision.

As the illustration shows, some important lessons arise; for example:

- the importance of timing in strategic moves;
- the importance of the careful weighing of risk;
- the importance of establishing credibility and commitment: for example, in the illustration here Innova could not achieve its desired outcome unless it had a reputation for sticking to its decisions.

7.6.3 Repeated games[19]

The example given in Illustration 7.8a ended up with both parties sub-optimising the outcome. In fact, if there were only two competitors involved this would probably be unlikely because, over time, they would learn to ensure a better outcome. In repeated games, competitors interact repeatedly and it has been shown that in such circumstances the equilibrium outcome is much more likely to favour co-operation. This is not necessarily because of explicit collusion, but because they learn to do so through experience. The presence or absence of implicit co-operation will, however, be dependent upon a number of factors. These include:

- The number of competitors in a market. If it is low, there is likely to be co-operation; but the greater the number of competitors the more it is likely that someone will break rank.

Illustration 7.8

Simultaneous and sequential games in strategic decision making

Game theory can provide useful means of thinking through appropriate strategic moves in competitive strategy.

(a) A simultaneous game

Innova and Dolla are competitors in the market for computer games. Innova is known to have highly innovative designers but is short of the sort of finance required to invest heavily in rapid development of products. Dolla is strong financially but relatively weak in terms of its research and design. Each faces the crucial choice of investing heavily in research and design or not: investing heavily would shorten the development time but would incur considerable costs. These choices can be thought of in terms of the sort of matrix shown in Figure 1.

Each of them probably regards high levels of investment by both as the worst outcome: Innova because their financial position is weak and it could be a risky route to follow; Dolla because if they can raise the finance, Innova have better

chances of winning given their design capabilities. This is represented by a low pay-off (bottom right) in Figure 1.

Innova has a dominant strategy, which is to keep its investment low. If Dolla were to invest low, Innova would get a better pay-off by also investing low (top left). On the other hand, if Dolla were to go for a high level of investment, Innova would suffer, but not as much by keeping investment on the low side as they would if they went for a high level of investment (top right is better than bottom right for Innova).

Dolla, on the other hand, does not have a dominant strategy. However, it knows that Innova does and therefore probably expects that Innova will keep levels of investment down. Dolla also knows that if it goes for a low level of investment, it loses whether or not Innova adopts the same strategy or goes for a high level of investment (top and bottom left). So it does not make sense for Dolla to go for a low level of investment; it is a *dominated strategy*. Knowing all this, the likelihood is that Dolla will decide to go for high levels of investment.

Figure 1 A simultaneous move game

DOLLA

		LOW Invest	HIGH
INNOVA	LOW Invest	3 4	
		4 2	
	HIGH	2 1	
		3 1	

Figure 2 A sequential move game

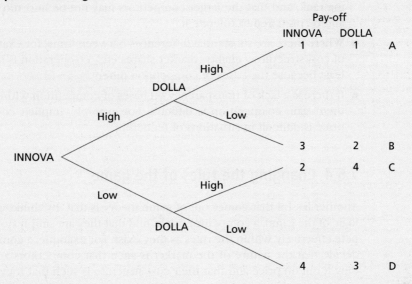

This is not what Innova wants ideally; but the best it can do is follow its dominant strategy of investing low which results in the least worst pay-off – the *equilibrium* solution (the top right in Figure 1). It does not result in high pay-off but a high pay-off for Innova is only possible if Dolla invests low. Of course, the temptation would be to imitate Dolla but it would result in a worse pay-off.

(b) A sequential game

Innova will not be happy with this outcome: so is it able to avoid the situation? Considering the problem as a sequential game helps. Figure 2 sets out possible moves in a sequential manner from Innova's point of view.

If Innova decides to invest low, it knows that Dolla is likely to respond high and gain the advantage (pay-off C). However, if Innova moves first and invests high, then it places Dolla in a difficult position. If Dolla also invests high, it ends up with a low pay-off as well as Innova (pay-off A). In these circumstances – provided of course that Dolla's strategist is a game theorist – Dolla would reject that strategy as a *dominated strategy* and choose to invest low (with pay-off B). In this (sequential) game, this is the *equilibrium*.

By working through these different game logics, Innova comes to realise that if it waits for Dolla to make a move, it is bound to lose out; if it moves first and invests high, then it stands a chance of winning the competitive game. Of course there are risks here, not least the financial risks for Innova. There are also risks in that Dolla may not believe that Innova will really invest high; so Innova needs to recognise the importance of being credible in its move. If it appears to waver in its decision, perhaps by delaying, or by not making a substantial enough investment, very likely Dolla will invest high too and both lose out (pay-off A). Of course, if there is some way of Innova appearing to be credible in a decision to invest high, whilst actually investing low, thus persuading Dolla to invest low too, then Innova achieves its *dominant strategy* (pay-off D). So game theory is also about bluff and counter-bluff.

Source: Adapted from A.K. Dixit and B.J. Nalebuff, *Thinking Strategically*, W.W. Norton & Co., 1991.

Questions

1. Suggest other strategic decision situations where game theory approaches might be useful.

2. What might prevent strategic decisions being made in this way? (Rereading Chapter 2 might help here.)

- If there are small competitors competing with larger competitors it is quite possible that the smaller competitors will gain disproportionately by breaking rank; and that the larger competitors may not be hurt too much by this and be prepared to tolerate it.

- Where there are substantial differences between firms, for example in terms of cost structures, quality, market shares etc., co-operation is less likely, not least because the bases of competition differ.

- If there is a lack of transparency on bases of competition within the market, then again co-operation is difficult. For example, implicit co-operation on price is difficult in situations of tendering.

7.6.4 Changing the rules of the game

Another lesson that comes out of game theory is that, by thinking through the logic of the game, a competitor might find that they are simply not able to compete effectively within the rules as they exist. For example, a competitor might decide that the nature of the market is such that competitors are always battling it out on price and that their cost structure is such that they cannot hope to compete effectively. Or, as with the examples given here, that competition always seems to be played out on the basis of heavy marketing expenditure or heavy investment in research and development. An alternative approach for a competitor who decides they cannot win on such bases is to try to change the rules of the game. For example, in a market dominated by price-based strategies, a competitor might try to shift the rules of the game towards:

- Bases of differentiation based on clearer identification of what customers value (see section 7.3.2 above).

- Building incentives for customer loyalty. Frequent-flier programmes on many airlines are a good example of this.

- Making pricing more transparent, for example by trying to get published price lists established as the norm in the industry. On the face of it, this may not seem to avoid price competition, but the principles of game theory would suggest that greater transparency is likely to encourage co-operative behaviour amongst competitors.

Game theory does of course rely on the principle of rationality; and it may well be that competitors do not always behave rationally. However, it does provide a useful way of thinking through the logic of interactive competitive markets and, in particular, when it makes sense to compete, on what bases, and when it makes sense to co-operate.

7.7 COMPETITIVE STRATEGY IN HYPERCOMPETITIVE CONDITIONS[20]

As Chapter 3 made clear, strategists face increasingly turbulent, fast-changing, uncertain situations and increased levels of competition; the sort of environment described in Chapter 3 (section 3.3.2) as *hypercompetitive*. Whereas competition in slower-moving environments may be primarily concerned with building and sustaining competitive advantages that are difficult to imitate, hypercompetitive environments require organisations to acknowledge that advantages may be temporary. Indeed, competition may become more to do with disrupting the status quo so that no one is able to readily achieve long-term advantage. As such situations have become more common, the idea of sustainable competitive advantage has itself come to be questioned. Other approaches, which do not consider competitive strategies as the fixed positioning of an organisation over time, but emphasise more the importance of change, of speed, flexibility, innovation and disruption of markets, have gained currency. Of course, game theory can be helpful in such circumstances, since it provides a basis for thinking through competitors' likely decisions and moves. Here, however, the idea of strategies in hypercompetitive situations is considered.

7.7.1 Overcoming traditional bases of competitive advantage

Many markets and industries are not stable any longer because the forces at work in the environment are rapidly changing. New technology, in particular, is reshaping industries, and organisations are busily trying to disrupt the status quo rather than preserve it. Organisations will therefore try to build barriers to preserve advantage in different ways discussed in this book; but others will be trying to circumvent or overcome these bases of advantage and barriers. This happens in various ways.

Advantage based on price or differentiation

The discussion on the strategy clock has reviewed various market-facing bases of competitive advantage pursued by organisations. These are rooted in the cost base of the organisation (for price) or the value added for customers (for differentiation). However, that section pointed out that these bases of advantage are likely to be eroded. Organisations will therefore seek other bases of advantage too. These may be other market-facing options within the strategy clock, such as greater focus, or they may make other strategic moves by trying to build barriers against competition. Some of these other moves are now reviewed (see Exhibit 7.4), together with how such moves may be overcome; following which the likely escalation of competition based on such moves is explained.

Seeking advantage through market-based strategic moves

- A firm may try to achieve advantage by *first-mover advantage* – by being the first to make a strategic move in a market: perhaps by launching a product first. On the face of it, this can give considerable benefits. It may take time for competitors to catch up; allow the first mover to gain benefits of economies of scale and experience curve effects; and build customer loyalty and therefore switching costs. However, in a hypercompetitive environment it is more difficult to sustain first-mover advantage. The time available to gain advantage

Exhibit 7.4	Market moves and building barriers for competitive advantage

FIRMS SEEK COMPETITIVE ADVANTAGE THROUGH:

Market moves
- Low price or differentiation strategies (see the strategy clock)
- First-mover advantage
- Developing new products and new markets

Building barriers
- Resource-based advantage
- Strongholds
- 'Deep pockets'
- Scale

from the first move is reduced and in some markets technology allows, indeed encourages, rapid response and innovation. Obviously it is easier for an e-commerce business to respond quickly to a first move than it is for a manufacturing firm that may need to invest in plant and equipment, for example.

Competitors realise the importance of not allowing a first mover to establish a dominant product or design before they make a move. They have also learned lessons about how to achieve advantage over the first mover. Instead of launching an imitation product, a competitor may launch a product with enhanced features, seeking to further differentiate and thus leapfrog or outflank the first mover. Or it could be that they attack a particular segment, eroding the market power of the first mover; or perhaps choose a 'no frills' strategy to capture a downmarket segment with a cheaper product before moving into the main market of the first mover.

- Firms also often seek to achieve advantage by *developing new products or entering new markets*. This is discussed more fully in section 8.2. However, such moves may be relatively easily imitated. The firm is faced with exactly the same problems of sustaining advantage as they would in their original product market arena.

Seeking advantage by building barriers

Firms also try to sustain advantage by building barriers to prevent competitors entering their domains or against them succeeding if they do:

- Section 7.4.2 above and section 4.7 in Chapter 4 explained how firms may try to build competitive advantage through the robustness of their resource and competences. In other words, they are seeking to build *resource-based advantage*. However, as was explained, this is no easy matter; and especially in markets where technological advance is rapid, or where advantage is based on technical know-how, it may be unwise to rely on the continued benefits of existing or past resource-based advantage.

- Another way of trying to hold on to competitive advantage is to build *strongholds*. A firm may try to dominate particular areas – e.g. a geographic area or market segment. By doing so they seek to achieve market power in that area. However, such strongholds can be undermined. The benefits of economies of scale built up in one area can be undermined by another competitor using the economies of scale from their own home territory to enter a market. This is what the Japanese car producers did in the 1970s and repeated it, together with other Far Eastern producers, in the semiconductors market. Indeed, it is becoming more and more common as markets globalise.

  Domination of strongholds may also have built switching costs for buyers. However, these can be overcome too. Entrants into such strongholds may be prepared to buy their way in, either by low price, or by sampling their products, or even providing their services free for a period of time. It does of course require them to have sufficient resources to do this, so it is likely to mean that they have, themselves, some dominant position in another stronghold; or it may mean that the cost of entry is relatively low, as it is in some e-com businesses.

  Firms have also often tried to build strongholds by tying up distribution channels. Entrants may be able to get round this too, for example by using different distribution channels: mail order instead of retailing, for example; or e-business rather than retailing. Acquisition may also be a route into a stronghold. An entrant may acquire an existing firm, or even be able to acquire the dominant firm in that stronghold.

- The advantage of '*deep pockets*', or substantial surplus resources, is that a competitor can withstand an intensive competitive war. Such deep pockets may take different forms: most obviously financial, but also conceivably in terms of talent or perhaps global reach which gives an organisation the opportunity to gain competitive knowledge worldwide and also move resources wherever they are necessary either to preserve their own interests or to tackle competition. However, smaller firms have found ways of neutralising the power of these giants. They may avoid direct competition by concentrating on market niches. They may co-operate with other smaller firms. Smaller firms also merge or build alliances so that they can compete with larger firms. For example, retail organisations such as SPAR are a way of bringing together smaller retailers to combat the power of major retailers. However, such co-operation may not be overt. It could be that the combined, though tacit, effort of smaller firms could undermine larger firms. For example, major consultancy firms have found that smaller boutique-type consultancy firms, particularly in the strategy area, have eroded their market power. Such smaller firms find ways of providing more specialised or customised services rather than the more commodity-type approach of larger firms. It is not that these smaller consultancies collude, but rather that they become a perceived collective alternative to the larger players.

- Of course, deep pockets may be linked to the *scale of the operation*. The argument for high market share has already been rehearsed; firms are also increasingly arguing that global scale in certain markets is necessary to be a credible competitor. So firms may seek to build the scale of their operation. However, especially in markets with relatively few competitors, they will all

Exhibit 7.5	Escalation of bases of competition

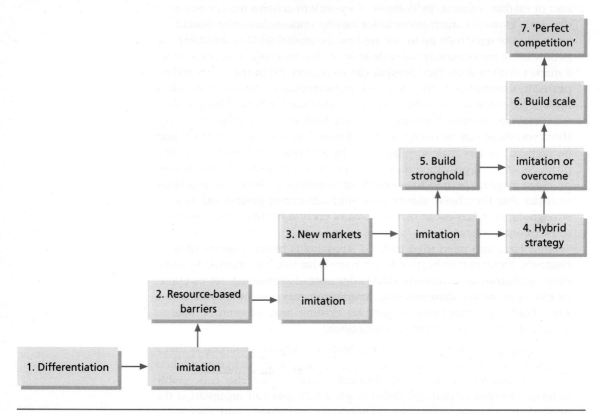

Source: Adapted from R. D'Aveni, *Hypercompetitive Rivalries: Competing in highly dynamic environments,* Free Press, 1995, p. 235.

be trying to do the same. This does of course explain why large mergers of firms take place – to achieve global scale and coverage (see section 8.3.2).

7.7.2 Escalating bases of competition

Chapter 3 (section 3.3.2) explained that in hypercompetitive conditions cycles of competition will speed up. As this happens, bases of competition are likely to escalate as firms seek to make different market moves and build different barriers. Exhibit 7.5 shows how this might happen.

A firm may develop a product or service and seek to achieve advantage by its distinctiveness, or *differentiation*, in its market (1). However, this will be imitated, and in hypercompetitive conditions, this may happen rapidly. The firm may try to build barriers, perhaps based on the greater exploitation of its *resource base or competences* (2). However, this may prove difficult in conditions where know-how and technical advance are moving fast. The next move may be to try to stretch competences and resources to find *new markets* (3); but if this is successful competitors will follow. There may be an attempt to drive down costs to achieve a low price, differentiation (i.e. *hybrid strategy*) basis of advantage (4); or perhaps the firm will try to focus on building barriers to competition in *stronghold* areas (5). But competitors can also drive down their costs; and strongholds may be difficult to preserve in fast-changing market conditions. It may be at this stage that the firm seeks to build *scale*: it might dispose of peripheral businesses to raise funds to build global reach; or it may seek to merge with a competitor (6). The ultimate outcome of such escalation may be a few dominant players in the market, with little competitive advantage between them and consequently little upon which to build the creation of rents (7).

7.7.3 Successful hypercompetitive strategies

The overall message is that, increasingly, whatever the bases of competitive advantage – differentiation, moving first, building and protecting strongholds or having 'deep pockets' – competitors can find ways round them. Together with the development of new ways of doing business (e.g. e-business), the result is increasingly hypercompetitive market conditions. In such circumstances, the argument[21] is that managers need to rethink their approach to strategic management. It is no longer possible to plan for sustainable positions of competitive advantage. Indeed, planning for long-term sustainability will destroy competitive advantage because it will slow down response. Rather, some uncomfortable, even paradoxical, principles emerge.

- Every advantage is temporary and will be eroded. However, long-term advantage may be sustained through a series of temporary advantages.

- Disruption of the status quo is strategic behaviour, not mischief. The ability constantly to 'break the mould' could be a core competence.

- Sustaining old advantages can be a distraction from developing new advantages. A leader's willingness to cannibalise the basis of their own success could be crucial. In order to gain advantages, firms must be prepared to destroy the bases of their own competitive advantage. Instead of trying to protect competitive advantage, the firm has to be prepared to pre-empt imitation by others, by identifying niches which can be exploited, or developing and launching new products or services. In all of this, choosing to compete on other than the normal bases of competition can be useful.

- Predictability is dangerous. Surprise is important. So unpredictability and apparent irrationality may be logical. If competitors come to see a pattern in the behaviour of another competitor, then they can predict the next moves to be taken and can quickly learn how to imitate or outflank. Managers must learn ways of at least appearing to be unpredictable or even irrational to the external world whilst, internally, thinking this through carefully.

- Similarly, beware of attacking competitors' weaknesses. If a competitor gets used to being attacked in the same sort of way, that competitor can learn about the strengths of the firm and how they will compete.

- Competing is necessary but makes winning more difficult. Whilst it is absolutely necessary to compete in the hypercompetitive environment, doing so

Illustration 7.9

Intel's hypercompetitive strategy

STRATEGY IN ACTION

In a fast-changing business environment, a company's competitive strategy may show characteristics of hypercompetitive strategies.

Intel's history was one of pursuing alternative technologies, including microprocessors, other chips, flash memories and personal computers. The result was that competitors were not clear as to where its next move would take place. However, after 10 years of 30 per cent per annum compound growth, 1998 saw a slow-down. Intel's success in the field had led to its becoming more and more focused on micro-processors and more and more centralised. Craig Barrett, who took over as CEO in 1998, embarked on a programme of activity that signalled the days of the hypercompetitive stra-tegy were back. Here's how *Business Week* described the chronology:

April 1997: Barrett wants the troops to break their old habits and diversify. He compares Intel's micro-processor business to a creosote bush, a plant that kills off nearby vegetation.

July 1997: Barrett . . . kicks off the first of eight seminars for Intel's top brass . . . aimed at getting them to dream up new businesses.

October 1997: buys DEC's chip unit . . . The deal contains . . . rights to the zippy StrongARM pro-cessor, which Intel adopts for some mobile and networking products.

January 1998: surveys 2,000 Internet service providers and discovers they want simple servers that do jobs such as encryption. So Intel develops server appliances that debut two years later.

February 1998: to kick-start a networking business, Intel hosts a press event in San Francisco and unveils dozens of products, including routers and switches.

March 1998: to reclaim lost share (because of lower chip prices in the market), Intel launches the cheap Celeron chip. But it's poorly received.

July 1998: the launch of a new-business group to fund internal start-ups.

August 1998: forms a home-products group to develop Web appliances and Internet-enabled TVs and set-top boxes.

September 1998: . . . studies the Web-hosting business . . . a risky leap from making chips. The board gives it the O.K. six weeks later.

November 1998: completes a crash, 12-month program to set up Web-based order taking for its customers. In 1999, online revenues soar quickly to $1 billion per month.

February 1999: unveils plans to co-develop a digital signal processor with Analog Devices . . . to help it gain ground in markets such as cell phones and consumer electronics.

March 1999: acquires networking chipmaker Level One . . . specializing in chips that connect network cards to wiring.

April 1999: announces a home networking kit, the first product it will sell directly to consumers over the Web. The product sends data over phone wiring in homes.

June 1999: buys Dialogic, a maker of PC-based phone systems, [giving] Intel technology for the convergence of voice and data networks.

September 1999: unveils 13 networking chips and opens its first Web-hosting center . . . with a capa-city for 10,000 servers: it could serve hundreds of e-commerce companies.

October 1999: acquires DSP Communications, a leader in wireless phone technology, and IPivot, a maker of gear for speeding up secure e-commerce transactions.

February 2000: launches a line of seven server appliances, called the NetStructure family, that speed up and manage Web traffic. This puts Intel in competition with Cisco Systems.

Source: Adapted from *Business Week*, 13 March 2000, pp. 56–61.

Questions

1. What characteristics of hypercompetitive strat-egies are discernible in Intel's approach?

2. What are the risks of Barrett's approach?

simply accelerates the speed of hypercompetition and makes winning more difficult. However, there is no alternative. Managers just have to learn to be better at doing it and faster than competitors.

● Rather than trying to identify and implement a 'grand plan' in the form of a one-off change in strategy, smaller strategic initiatives which develop into a longer-term shift in overall strategy have their advantages. The longer-term direction is not as easily discernible by competitors and they allow flexibility in the management of strategy.

● Signalling, or more usefully misleading signalling, of strategic intentions may also be useful. In this the strategist may draw on the lessons of game theory (see section 7.6 above) to signal moves which competitors may expect but which are not the surprises that actually occur.

Many of these characteristics of hypercompetitive strategies are shown in Illustration 7.9.

An implication that arises out of this discussion is the extent to which sustainability of competitive advantage is possible. In addressing this question, it may be useful to ask the following questions:

● What is the nature of the competitive environment that is faced? Not all business environments are fast-moving, hypercompetitive environments. Some are more stable than others. The more stable the environment, the more the lessons in section 7.3. hold. The less stable the environment, the more the lessons in this section may hold.

● However, it is also important to recognise that the lessons of hypercompetitive strategies are essentially about the importance of timing, speed, innovation, flexibility and risk taking. Arguably these are competences which, themselves, are sustainable. The more the business environment demands such speed and flexibility, the more it will be the organisations that can build cultures of such flexibility in innovation that will win. These organisations are unlikely to be traditional hierarchies with heavy top-down planning and control. They are more likely to involve devolution of responsibility for sensing of buyer expectations and competitive moves; active debate across a non-hierarchical network; encouragement of variety and diversity of views and ideas; acceptance of responsibility for action at levels in the organisation well below top management; latitude to try things out and tolerance of things going wrong. This is a description of the sort of 'learning organisation' discussed in section 2.3.5. The point that needs to be emphasised here is that the basis of an effective competitive strategy becomes one of organisational culture and design for flexibility, innovation and speed rather than about analysis, positioning and sustainability.

SUMMARY

● Bases of strategic choice need to take account of the *environment* in which the organisation operates: for example, competitive advantages may be eroded as technology changes or as new competitors enter markets.

- It is important to recognise the role of organisational resources, capabilities and *core competences* in terms of the bases on which competitive strategy and advantage may be built.

Market-facing choices of business unit strategies to achieve *competitive advantage* include:

- A *'no frills'* strategy combining low price and low perceived added value.

- A *low price* strategy providing lower price than competitors at similar added value of product or service to competitors.

- A *differentiation* strategy which seeks to provide products or services which are unique or different from competitors.

- A *hybrid* strategy which seeks simultaneously to achieve differentiation and prices lower than competitors.

- A *focused differentiation* strategy which seeks to provide high perceived value justifying a substantial price premium.

- Sustaining bases of competitive advantage is likely to require a linked set of organisational competences which competitors find difficult to imitate.

- Or the ability to achieve a 'lock-in' position to becoming the 'industry standard' recognised by suppliers and buyers.

- Strategies of collaboration may offer alternatives to competitive strategies.

- Game theory provides a basis for thinking through competitors' strategic moves in such a way as to pre-empt or counter them.

- In hypercompetitive conditions sustainable competitive advantage is difficult to achieve. Speed, flexibility, innovation and the willingness to change successful strategies are important bases of competitive success.

- In such circumstances the competences of the organisation required for success are likely to be found in organisational cultures and structures which encourage such speed, flexibility, innovation and the capacity to change.

RECOMMENDED KEY READINGS

- The foundations of the discussions of generic competitive strategies are to be found in the writings of Michael Porter, which include *Competitive Strategy* (1980) and *Competitive Advantage* (1985), both published by Free Press. Both are recommended for readers who wish to understand the background to discussions in sections 7.3 to 7.5 of this chapter on competitive strategy and competitive advantage.

- A good paper to read on the sustainability of competitive strategies is 'Competing on resources: strategy in the 1990s', by David Collis and Cynthia Montgomery, *Harvard Business Review*, July–August, 1995.

- There is much written on game theory but a good deal of it can be rather inaccessible to the lay reader. An exception is the book by A.K. Dixit and B.J. Nalebuff, *Thinking Strategically*, W.W. Norton & Co, 1991 which provides a fascinating insight to its applications.

- Hypercompetition, and the strategies associated with such conditions are explained in Richard D'Aveni, *Hypercompetitive Rivalries: Competing in highly dynamic environments*, Free Press, 1985.

REFERENCES

1. For a fuller discussion of rents see R. Perman and J. Scoular, *Business Economics*, Oxford University Press, 1999, pp. 67-74.

2. The debate on bases of competitive strategy, as a key issue in the consideration of business strategy, has been strongly influenced by the writings of Michael Porter and, in particular, his book *Competitive Advantage*, Free Press, 1985. There are a number of papers which provide useful critiques of Porter's competitive strategies: M. Cronshaw, E. Davis and J. Kay, 'On being stuck in the middle, or Good food costs less at Sainsburys', working paper, Centre for Business Strategy, London School of Business, 1990; C.W.L. Hill, 'Differentiation versus low cost or differentiation and low cost: a contingency framework', *Academy of Management Review*, vol. 13, no. 3 (1988), pp. 401-412; A. Karnani, 'Generic competitive strategies: an analytical approach', *Strategic Management Journal*, vol. 5, no. 4 (1984), pp. 367-380; S.S. Mathur, 'How firms compete: a new classification of generic strategies', *Journal of General Management*, vol. 14, no. 1 (1988), pp. 30-57, 'Generic strategies and performance: an empirical examination with American data. Part 1: Testing Porter', *Organisation Studies*, vol. 7, no. 1 (1986), pp. 37-55; D. Miller and P.H. Friesen, 'Porter's (1980) generic strategies and performance: an empirical examination with American data. Part 2: Performance implications', *Organisation Studies*, vol. 7, no. 3 (1986), pp. 255-261; R.E. White, 'Generic business strategies, organisational context and performance: an empirical investigation', *Strategic Management Journal*, vol. 7, no. 3 (1986), pp. 217-231; and D. Faulkner and C. Bowman, *The Essence of Competitive Strategy*, Prentice Hall, 1995.

3. Exhibit 7.2 is based on a framework developed at Cranfield School of Management by Cliff Bowman (see D. Faulkner and C. Bowman, *The Essence of Competitive Strategy*, Prentice Hall, 1995). However, they use the term 'perceived use value' rather than 'perceived added value'. A similar framework is also used by Richard D'Aveni, *Hypercompetitive Rivalries: Competing in highly dynamic environments*, Free Press, 1995.

4. The researchers and writers who argue that cost-based strategies are not incompatible with differentiation include D. Miller, 'The generic strategy trap', *Journal of Business Strategy*, vol. 13, no. 1 (1992), pp. 37-42; and C.W.L. Hill, 'Differentiation versus low cost or differentiation and low cost': a contingency framework', *Academy of Management Review*, vol. 13, no. 3 (1998), pp. 401-412. Their arguments are supported by the work of PIMS (see reference 8), who argue for the benefits of a 'virtuous circle' in strategy, by which they mean the search for low cost which provides surpluses to reinvest in differentiation and product advantages.

5. See G. Hamel and C.K. Prahalad, 'Do you really have a global strategy?', *Harvard Business Review*, vol. 63, no. 4 (1985), pp. 139-148.

6. Mimicry of strategies in conditions of uncertainty is noted by P.J. DiMaggio and W.W. Powell, 'The iron cage revisited: institutional isomorphism and collective rationality in organizational fields', *American Sociological Review*, vol. 48 (1983), pp. 147-160.

7. The idea of strategic balance is developed by D. Deephouse, 'To be different, or to be the same? It's a question (and theory) of strategic balance', *Strategic Management Journal*, vol. 20 (1999), pp. 147-166.

8. The debate on the benefits of relative market share are complicated. There are perhaps three key points: (a) a firm with a high absolute market share may not have a high relative share because there may be a competitor which also has a comparable share; (b) arguments differ as to whether relative market share should be measured in terms of the nearest individual competitor, or the nearest two or three competitors; and (c) estimates of the relative market share necessary to achieve sustainable market power advantage vary between about 40 and 70 per cent. For discussion on this debate, see, for example, R.D. Buzzell and B.T. Gale, *The PIMS Principles*, Free Press, 1987, Chapter 5. See also R.D. Buzzell, 'Are there natural market structures?', *Journal of Marketing*, vol. 45, no. 1 (1981), pp. 42-51.

9. These quotes concerning Porter's three competitive strategies are taken from his book *Competitive Advantage*, Free Press, 1985, pp. 12-15.

10. Cost advantage is discussed in R. Grant, *Contemporary Strategy Analysis*, 3rd edition, Blackwell, 1998, Chapter 7; and B. Karloff, *Strategic Precision*, Wiley, 1993, Chapter 3.

11. There is much written on the issue of sustainability of competitive advantage. For an early contribution see C.K. Prahalad and G. Hamel, 'The core competence of the corporation', *Harvard Business Review*, May-June, 1990. Also see D. Collis and C. Montgomery, 'Competing on resources: strategy in the 1990s', *Harvard Business Review*, July-August, 1995.

12. The Delta Model is explained and illustrated more fully in A.C. Hax and D.L. Wilde II, 'The Delta Model', *Sloan Management Review*, Winter 1999, pp. 11-28.

13. See *Creating Collaborative Advantage*, edited by Chris Huxham, Sage Publications, 1996.

14. See G. Hamel, Y. Doz and C.K. Prahalad, 'Collaborate with your competitors and win', *Harvard Business Review*, vol. 61, 1989, pp. 133-139.

15. The five forces model was first introduced in M. Porter, *Competitive Strategy*, Free Press, 1980.

16. See reference 18 in Chapter 8 relating to section 8.3.3 of that chapter.

17. For readings on game theory see: A.K. Dixit and B.J. Nalebuff, *Thinking Strategically*, W.W. Norton & Co., 1991; also J. McMillan, *Games, Strategies and Managers*, Oxford University Press, 1992.

18. A specialist in the field of auction design is Paul Klemperer of Oxford University. Material related to the subject can be accessed on his website: www.nuff.ox.ac.uk/economics/people/klemperer.htm

19. To understand more on repeated games, see R. Axelrod, *The Evolution of Cooperation*, Penguin, 1990.

20. This section is based on the work of Richard D'Aveni, *Hypercompetitive Rivalries: Competing in highly dynamic environments*, Free Press, 1995. For readers who want to read more on the topic, there is a special edition of *Organization Science* (vol. 7, no. 3, 1996) devoted to it.

21. This is the radical conclusion reached by D'Aveni (see reference 20 above).

WORK ASSIGNMENTS

* Refers to a case study in the Text and Case edition. ✳ Denotes more advanced work assignments.

7.1 Using Exhibit 7.2, the strategy clock, identify examples of organisations following strategic routes 1 to 5. If you find it difficult to be clear about which route is being followed, note down the reasons for this, and consider if the organisations have a clear competitive strategy.

7.2 ✳ Michael Porter argues that a business must have a clear competitive strategy. Assess the extent to which any, or all, of the following have a clear competitive strategy:

(a) Barclaycard*
(b) Marks and Spencer* (throughout its existence)
(c) an organisation of your choice.

7.3 You have been appointed personal assistant to the chief executive of a major manufacturing firm, who has asked you to explain what is meant by 'differentiation' and why it is important. Write a brief report addressing these questions.

7.4 ✳ How appropriate are bases of competitive advantage explained in section 7.3 for considering the strategies of public sector organisations? Illustrate your argument by reference to a public sector organisation your choice.

7.5 Applying the lessons from section 7.4, consider how sustainable are the strategies of any of:

(a) Ryanair*
(b) Brewery Group Denmark*
(c) an organisation of your choice.

7.6 Drawing on sections 7.5 (on collaborative strategies) and 7.6 (on game theory), write a report for the chief executive of a business in a competitive market (e.g. Pharmaceuticals* or Formula One*) explaining when and in what ways co-operation rather than direct competition might make sense.

7.7 ✳ Follow up the key reading on game theory (Dixit and Nalebuff). To what extent and how do you consider game theory approaches useful in developing competitive strategy for organisations?

7.8 Discuss the view that hypercompetitive conditions and hypercompetitive strategies are relevant to only a few industries.

7.9 ✳ Choose an industry which is becoming more and more competitive (e.g. banking). How might the principles of hypercompetitive strategies apply to that industry?

Madonna: The reign of the queen of pop

The music industry is full of one-hit wonders and brief careers. Pop stars that remain at the top for decades are very few; and even fewer can claim to be one of the wealthiest women in the world, running a highly successful business: this is Madonna's story of sustained competitive success.

Madonna's business success

Described by *Billboard Magazine* as the smartest businesswoman in show business, Madonna Louise Ciccone began her music career in 1983 with the hit single 'Holiday' and in late 2000 enjoyed critical acclaim for her latest album 'Music'. By 2001, Madonna had produced 51 single tracks, 14 albums, had undertaken four world tours and had major roles in five films.

It is estimated that this twice-married mother of two had a personal fortune of over £135 million. She owns Chelsea Girl LLC, a limited liability company, and one-third of the record company Maverick. Maverick, formed in 1992, has been a highly successful partnership between Madonna and Warner Bros whose roster includes Prodigy and Alanis Morrisette. It has generated over $775 million in revenue since 1992. Madonna's stake was estimated to be much more than £30 million in 2000.

Madonna was also one of the first media icons to realise the power of the Internet and that she needed control of the madonna.com domain name, and she engaged in a court battle to secure it. But it was her record-breaking web-cast deal with Microsoft in late November 2000 that was widely reported as a shining example of her business acumen. Microsoft got exclusive access to her one-off gig in Brixton and beamed it live across

the World Wide Web; she got £30 million of promotion for her album and 2001 tour in return.

Sustained success

By 2001 Madonna had sustained her reign as the 'queen of pop' over a seventeen-year period. Along with many others, Phil Quattro, the president of Warner Brothers, has argued that the foundation of her success is that: 'She always manages to land on the cusp of what we call contemporary music, every established artist faces the dilemma of maintaining their importance and relevance, Madonna never fails to be relevant.' (*Billboard*, 21 February 1998). Madonna's chameleon-like ability to change persona, change her music genre with it and yet still achieve major record sales has been the hallmark of her success. She has consistently inhabited and achieved success with one persona, thrown it off before it faded and created a new and equally profitable image.

Madonna's early poppy style was aimed at young 'wannabe' girls. The image that she portrayed through hits such as 'Holiday' and 'Lucky Star' was picked up by Macy's, the US-based department store. They produced a range of Madonna look-alike clothes that mothers were happy to purchase for their daughters. Madonna then underwent her first image change and in doing so, offered the first hint of the smart cookie behind the media image. In the video for her hit 'Material Girl', she deliberately mirrored the glamour-based, sexual pussycat image of Marilyn Monroe whilst simultaneously mocking both the growing materialism of the late eighties and the men fawning after her. Media analysts Sam and Diana Kirschner commented that with this kind of packaging, Madonna allowed the record companies to keep hold of a saleable 'Marilyn image' for a new cohort of fans, but also allowed her original fan base of now growing-up wannabe girls to take the more critical message from

This case was prepared by Phyl Johnson, University of Strathclyde Graduate Business School.

the music. The theme of courting controversy but staying marketable enough has been recurrent throughout her career.

Madonna's subsequent image changes have been more dramatic. First she took on the Catholic Church in her video 'Like a Prayer' where, as a red-dressed 'sinner', she kissed a black saint easily interpreted as a Jesus figure. Her image had become increasingly sexual whilst also holding on to a critical social theme: e.g. her pointed illustration of white-only imagery in the Catholic Church. At this point in her career, Madonna took full control of her image in the $60 million deal with Time Warner that created her record company, Maverick.

In 1991, she published a coffee-table soft-porn book entitled *Sex* that exclusively featured pictures of herself in erotic poses. Her image and music also reflected this erotic theme. In her 'Girlie' tour, her singles 'Erotica' and 'Justify my Love' and her fly-on-the-wall movie *In Bed with Madonna* she played out scenes of sadomasochistic and lesbian fantasies. Although allegedly a period of her career she would rather forget, Madonna more than survived it. In fact, she gained a whole new demography of fans, who not only respected her artistic courage, but also did not miss the fact that Madonna was consistent in her message: her sexuality was her own and not in need of a male gaze. She used the media's love affair with her, and the *cause célèbre* status gained from having MTV ban the video for 'Justify my Love', to promote the message that women's sexuality and freedom is just as important and acceptable as men's.

Changing gear in 1996, Madonna finally took centre stage in the lead role in the film *Evita* that she had chased for over five years. She beat other heavyweight contenders for the role, including Meryl Streep and Elaine Page: both with more conventional credentials for the part than Madonna. Yet she achieved the image transition from erotica to saint-like persona of Eva Peron and won critical acclaim to boot. Another vote of confidence from the 'establishment' came from Max Factor, who in 1999 signed her up to front their relaunch campaign that was crafted around a glamour theme. Procter and Gamble (owners of the Max Factor

make-up range) argued that they saw Madonna as 'the closest thing the 90s has to an old-style Hollywood star . . . she is a real woman'.

With many pre-release leaks, Madonna's keenly awaited album 'Ray of Light' was released in 1998. Radio stations worldwide were desperate to get hold of the album being billed as her most successful musical voyage to date. In a smart move, Madonna had teamed up with techno pioneer William Orbit to write and produce the album. It was a huge success, taking Madonna into the super-trendy techno sphere, not the natural environment for a pop star from the early 80s. Madonna took up an 'earth mother / spiritual' image and spawned a trend for all things eastern in fashion and music.

By 2001, her next persona was unveiled with the release of her album 'Music'. Here her style has moved on again to 'acid rock'. With her marriage to British movie director Guy Ritchie, the ultimate 'American Pie' had become a fully fledged Brit babe. Her collaboration with Brits such as comedian Ali G, dress designer Stella McCartney, her friendships with prominent Brits such as Sting and Trudie Styler as well as her Guinness drinking, church-going, weekend family car washing and settled lifestyle have endeared her to her new home nation.

Throughout her seventeen-year career, Madonna has therefore consistently changed image. Indeed, many commentators have argued that it is this ability to consistently change that is attractive in itself. She is not just growing up with her fans and changing to appeal to their life-stage changes, but also continually picking up new generations of fans as she goes: fans who wait to see what her next incarnation will be.

Collaboration for success

It would seem that, in part, cleverly chosen collaborators go some way to account for her currency. For instance, her 'Ray of Light' collaboration with musician and producer William Orbit gave her a direct line into the epicentre of the techno club scene. Bringing new innovative artists such as Alanis

RELEASES	YEAR	IMAGE	TARGET AUDIENCE
Lucky Star	1982	Trashy pop	Young wannabe girls, dovetailing from fading disco to emerging 'club' scene
Like a Virgin Like a Prayer	1984	Originally a Marilyn glamour image, then became Saint & Sinner in lace, challenging sexual & religious imagery	More grown up – rebellious – fan base, more critical female audience and male worshippers
Vogue Erotica Bedtime Stories	1990 1992 1994	Erotic porn star, sadomasochistic, sexual control, more Minelli in *Cabaret* than Monroe	Peculiar mix of target audiences: gay club scene, 90s women taking control of their own lives, also pure male titillation
Something to remember Evita	1995	Softer image, ballads preparing for glamour image of Evita film role	Broadest audience target, picking up potential film audiences as well as regular fan base. Most conventional image. Max Factor later used this mixture of Marilyn and Eva Peron to market their glamour image
Ray of Light	1998	Earth mother, eastern mysticism, dance music fusion	Clubbing generation of the 90s, new cohort of fans plus original fan base of now 30-somethings desperately staying trendy
Music	2000	Acid rock, tongue in cheek Miss USA / cow girl, cool Britannia	Managing to hit the changing club scene and 30-something Brits

Morrisette in 1997 on to her Maverick record label also allowed her to take part in their sphere of artistic influence and feed off it.

In addition, Madonna has collaborated in business to help her sustain her position in the music industry. For instance, in 1992, after much criticism for her controversial Catholic and erotic themes, she made the decision to reach out to protect her artistic control and created her record company, Maverick, alongside potential competitors Warner Bros. Industry commentators note that whereas most musicians create their own record company to get more royalties, Madonna did it for control: a more profitable commodity in the long term. A big enough star to have a strong voice, Madonna was able to insist that Maverick run its own operation independent of Warner Bros but still receive their considerable support. For example, when Madonna wanted to replace Freddy De Mann, her former manager and 17 per cent owner of Maverick, it was Warner Bros who under-wrote the deal and allowed Madonna to appoint her preferred candidates.

In amongst all the image changes, there is a part of Madonna that remains certain and predictable. There are messages from which she has never wavered throughout her whole career: control of her own sexuality, control of her own image, the independence of women and breaking established gender norms. Whatever face she chooses to wear, it is certain that it will be her choice and she will decide when it's time to change.

Sources: 'Bennett takes the reins at Maverick', *Billboard Magazine*, 7 August 1999; 'Warner Bros expects Madonna to light up international markets', *Billboard Magazine*, 21 February 1998; 'Maverick builds on early success', *Billboard Magazine*, 12 November 1994; Jardine, A. (1999) 'Max Factor strikes gold with Madonna', *Marketing*, vol. 29, pp. 14–15; Kirschner, S. and Kirschner, D. (1997) 'MTV, adolescence and Madonna: a discourse analysis', in *Perspectives on Psychology & the Media*, American Psychological Association, Washington, DC; 'Warner to buy out maverick co-founder', *Los Angeles Times*, 2 March 1999; 'Why Madonna is back in Vogue', *New Statesman*, 18 September 2000; 'Madonna & Microsoft', *The Financial Times*, 28 November 2000.

Questions

1. Describe and explain the strategy being followed by Madonna in terms of the explanations of competitive strategy given in Chapter 7.

2. Why has she experienced sustained success over the past two decades?

3. What might threaten the sustainability of her success?

4. What lessons might she learn from her music career that she could employ in running Maverick?

8

Directions and Methods of Development

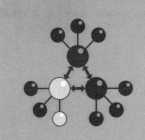

8.1 INTRODUCTION

The previous two chapters were concerned with the broad issues of strategic choices at both the corporate and business unit levels in organisations. Within this broad 'steer' there are a number of specific options concerning both the *direction* (e.g. new products, new markets) and the *method* (e.g. internal, merger/acquisition, alliances) of developing an organisation's strategies, as previously indicated in Exhibit IIIi in the introduction to Part III. This chapter is about these directions and methods of development and will address three key issues:

● What directions and methods of development are '*available*' to organisations.

● Why some directions and methods might be *preferred* over others.

● Why some directions and methods might *succeed better* than others.

It should be clear from Part II of this book that the survival and success of organisations are influenced by their ability to respond to the competing pressures described in Chapters 3, 4 and 5. First are changes in the business environment (Chapter 3); second, the strategic capability of an organisation – its resources and competences (Chapter 4); and third, the cultural and political context – the expectations and purposes (Chapter 5). So in reviewing the way

Exhibit 8.1	Strategy development directions

PRODUCTS

		Existing	**New**
MARKETS	**Existing**	**A** PROTECT/BUILD ● Consolidation ● Market penetration	**B** PRODUCT DEVELOPMENT ● On existing competences ● With new competences ● Beyond current expectations
	New	**C** MARKET DEVELOPMENT ● New segments ● New territories ● New uses ● With new competences ● Beyond current expectations	**D** DIVERSIFICATION ● On existing competences ● With new competences ● Beyond current expectations

in which strategies develop in the future it is important to understand how these three 'pressures' might shape strategic choices. They can be thought of as the *motives* for pursuing some strategies and not others:

● *Environment-based motives* – fitting new strategies to a changing business environment.

● *Resource-based motives* – stretching and exploiting the competences of an organisation.

● *Expectations-based motives* – meeting the expectations created by the regulatory and governance framework, powerful stakeholders, ethical considerations and culture.

These motives will be used to describe and explain both the development directions and methods commonly found in organisations. Exhibit 8.1 is an adaptation of the product/market matrix[1] often used for conceiving of *directions* for strategic development. It considers the development directions 'available' to an organisation in terms of the *market coverage, products, competence base* and *expectations* about an organisation's strategies. These range from strategies concerned with protecting and building an organisation's position with its existing products and competences through to diversification requiring changes of products, competences and entering or creating new market opportunities which take the organisation into arenas in which it is currently not a credible player. Each of the development directions shown in Exhibit 8.1 is discussed below. It should be noted that the business idea (discussed in the introduction to Part II of this book) could provide a focus for the identification of strategic directions for an organisation since it contains all of these three dimensions (motives).

In the long run, of course, developments in any of the boxes are likely to require the development of competences and credibility to cope with a changing situation. Illustration 8.1 shows that a combination of development directions is usually pursued.

The middle part of the chapter considers the issue of development *methods*. Whatever the broad strategy and development direction, there will be different methods by which a strategy could be pursued. For example, an organisation may be pursuing a broad strategy of growth, through positioning itself as the cheapest provider of 'regular' quality products (route 2 on the strategy clock in Exhibit 7.2). The development direction within this generic approach could be one of gaining market share (*market penetration*) through continued reduction of costs (to remain the lowest cost producer) passed on to customers in lower prices. However, there are still issues as to the *method* by which this might be achieved. The cost improvements may be achieved *internally* by increasing the efficiency of current operations or through *strategic alliances* – perhaps to share distribution outlets with another (non-competing) company; or it may be achieved by *acquisition* of a competitor to gain market share and to benefit from the associated economies of scale.

Since the purpose of this chapter is also to understand why some strategies might succeed better than others, the final part of the chapter will introduce the *success criteria* by which strategies can be judged. The aim of this final part of the chapter is to help readers understand these criteria and some of the ways of exploring each criterion.

8.2 DIRECTIONS FOR STRATEGY DEVELOPMENT

This section reviews the different directions in which organisations' strategies develop. The section is structured around the categories of development direction represented by the boxes in Exhibit 8.1. Many of the points discussed in this section are summarised in Exhibit 8.4 later in the chapter, which will be used when discussing success criteria in section 8.4.

8.2.1 Protect and build on current position

Box A in Exhibit 8.1 represents strategies which are concerned with protecting, or building on, an organisation's current position. Within this broad category there are a number of options.

Consolidation

Consolidation is where organisations protect and strengthen their position in their current markets with current products. Since the market situation is likely

Consolidation is where organisations protect and strengthen their position in their current markets with current products

Illustration 8.1

Pret à Manger hits the States – with help from McDonald's

STRATEGY IN ACTION

Sometimes the development directions of organisations can complement each other. So working together may make sense.

In January 2001 McDonald's – the global fast-food burger chain – snapped up one-third of the shares in Pret à Manger, the company that brought upmarket sandwiches and snacks into London's high streets and gained a loyal following with busy professionals. This made McDonald's the company's major shareholder and was seen by the management of Pret à Manger as a big boost to their plans to develop business in the USA where their first outlets had only recently opened in New York's financial district.

The move into New York had initially been with the same concept and range of products as they sold in London – with the vital addition of key lime pie – made by a specialist in Brooklyn but seen as a typical Pret à Manger product. There was a feeling that McDonald's help would be invaluable in spreading beyond New York – particularly their understanding of planning issues (for sites) and the complexities of labour relations.

However, the relationship was not going to be a one-way street. McDonald's core business was massive – nearly 30,000 outlets in 120 countries. But the burger chain's sales were flagging in a mature market. Whilst burgers would remain the core of their business operations, investments in the like of Pret à Manger were seen as an attempt to reduce their dependence on beef (with problems like BSE scares) and develop their 'other-brands' cat-

egory. Early attempts in this direction were through changes in the McDonald's menus. But Happy Meals and Chicken Nuggets had been the only successes in 15 years. There were many failures like McDLT, McLean and McPizza. So they had changed strategy and slowly started investing in rivals in other parts of the food industry such as Boston Chicken, Chipotle Mexican Grill, Donatos Pizza and Aroma (a British chain of coffee and sandwich bars). This was seen as a way of capitalising on their core competences in franchising, operations, marketing and property management. Indeed these were all areas from which Pret à Manger expected to benefit in their geographical expansion in the USA.

Some analysts were cautious about this marriage of a mainstream global giant with a the likes of Aroma and Pret à Manger – top-of-the - market niche players from Europe. They pointed to Aroma's underperformance against its rivals like Starbucks and also wondered if their image in the market would be dented by the association with the McDonald's brand.

Source: Adapted from *The Sunday Times*, 4 February 2001.

Questions

1. Referring to Exhibit 8.1, classify the various developments for Pret à Manger and McDonald's mentioned above.

2. List the arguments for and against each development.

to be changing (e.g. through improved performance of competitors or new entrants) consolidation does not mean standing still. Indeed, it may require considerable reshaping and innovation to improve the value of an organisation's products or services. In turn, this will require attention to how an organisation's resources and competences should be adapted and developed to maintain the competitive position of the organisation:

- Consolidation may require reshaping by *withdrawal* from or *downsizing*[2] of some activities. For example:
  - The concept of the product life cycle (see Exhibit 3.5) is a reminder that demand for any product or service has a finite life. Even where demand remains strong, the ability to compete profitably will vary through the stages of the life cycle. Knowing when to withdraw from markets can be crucial.
  - In some markets, the *intrinsic value* of a company's products or assets is subject to changes over time, and a key issue may be the astute acquisition and disposal of these products, assets or businesses. This is particularly important for companies operating in markets that are subject to *speculation*, such as energy, metals, commodities, land or property.
  - Perhaps the most compelling reason for withdrawal from particular markets is that the organisation is unable to secure the resources or achieve the competence levels of the leaders in the market overall or the niches or segments of the market.
  - Since an organisation's resources are limited, there may need to be a review of the *priorities* for their deployment. So withdrawal from some activities releases resources for others. The shift in a local government authority's range of services over time is a good example of such a policy.
  - The expectations of dominant stakeholders may be a reason for withdrawal. For example, the objective of a small entrepreneur may be to 'make a million' and then retire. This would lead to a preference for strategies that make the company an attractive proposition to sell, rather than being guided by longer-term considerations of viability.
- Consolidation may also be concerned with the *maintenance of market share* in existing markets. It is worthwhile exploring *why* the maintenance of market share might be an important consideration for organisations. The link between performance and relative market share, which is emphasised by the experience curve work (see Chapter 4, section 4.5.1), is supported by the findings of the PIMS database as shown in Illustration 8.2 (Figure 1). (The PIMS – Profit Impact of Market Strategy – database[3] contains the experiences of over 3,000 businesses – both products and services.)

The conclusions from these findings are important for managers to understand when considering consolidation as a strategy. Good financial performance is concerned with creating and exploiting a more favourable resource and competence base than competitors:

- The major factor seems to be *asset turnover*, with low-share businesses showing substantially higher investment/sales ratios than high-share

Illustration 8.2

STRATEGY IN ACTION

PIMS findings on various types of consolidation strategies

Research evidence shows the link between choice of strategies and financial performance.

Figure 1 **On average, market share has an important, positive, influence on profits[1]**

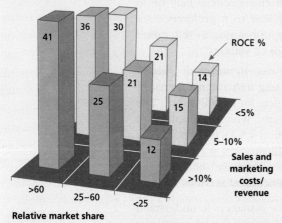

Figure 2 **A market leader with premium products has a strong competitive advantage[1]**

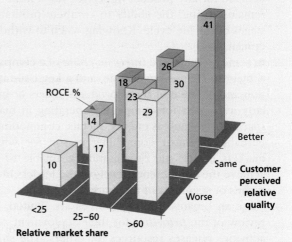

Figure 3 **Market share is critical when marketing intensity is high[1,2]**

Figure 4 **Heavy marketing is not a substitute for quality[1,2]**

Notes:
1. All columns in these charts show the scale/profit margin relationship at the 99 per cent significance level, both across the graph as a whole and from one share group to the next.
2. Detailed form of these relationships depends on market structure and business strategy.

Source: PIMS Associates Ltd. Reproduced with permission.

businesses (sometimes nearly 25 per cent poorer). This can be attributed to scale economies in the use of fixed assets.

- The purchase/sales ratio differences between high- and low-market-share firms are also startling – high-market-share companies are able to buy more competitively or add more value to purchases. Economies of scale also show up in some other cost categories, such as marketing, but not in R&D. High-share businesses have higher R&D/sales ratios, largely because they are better placed to exploit innovation, as discussed below.

- A PIMS study of fast-moving consumer goods businesses[4] showed a strong interaction between *brand rank*, the *mix* of advertising and promotion activities, and profitability. The evidence showed that it is difficult to make profits unless the company has one of the leading three brands.

- High-market-share firms are more likely to develop strategies of higher price/ higher quality than low-share competitors and this may be self-sustaining (see Figure 2). Longer-term PIMS evidence shows that this phenomenon may be self-sustaining. High-share firms tend to be more profitable, providing extra resources for R&D to improve and differentiate products, enhancing their market position and also justifying higher prices, which in turn increase profits. However, it must be remembered that high market share and size are not always the same. There are large firms which do not dominate the markets in which they operate; and there are small firms which dominate market segments.

- Quality is important in the improvement of profit performance (see Figures 2 and 3). The best situation appears to be a combination of high share and high product/service quality, but even firms with low market shares demonstrate significantly higher profit performance if they have offerings of superior quality. (In this sense, quality can be a partial substitute for market share in sustaining advantage.)

- High marketing expenditure is not a substitute for quality (see Figure 4). Indeed, it appears that high marketing expenditure damages ROI most when quality is low. It must be concluded that simply gearing up marketing expenditure, as a means of consolidating a company's position, is not sufficient.

- Another implication is that gaining and holding market share during the growth phase of the product life cycle is important since it will give advantages during the maturity phase.

Market penetration

Within the broad category of protecting and building an organisation's position, there may be opportunities for **market penetration**, which is where an organisation gains market share. Much of the previous discussion is relevant to this direction, since, for example, competences which sustain or improve quality or innovation or increasing marketing activity could all be means of achieving market penetration. So, too, are the arguments concerning the long-term desirability of obtaining a dominant market share. However, it needs to be noted that the ease with which an organisation can pursue a policy of market penetration will be dependent on:

Market penetration is where an organisation gains market share

- The nature of the market – in particular, whether it is growing or declining. When the overall market is growing, or can be induced to grow, it is easier for organisations with a small market share, or even new entrants, to gain share. This is because the absolute level of sales of the established organisations may still be growing, and in some instances those companies may be unable or unwilling to meet the new demand. Import penetration into some industries has occurred in this way. In contrast, market penetration in static markets can be much more difficult to achieve.

- There may be *resource issues* driving or preventing market penetration. Building market share can be a costly process for weakly positioned businesses. Short-term profits are likely to be sacrificed, particularly when trying to build share from a low base. A PIMS study of competitiveness in Europe and North America[5] showed that the key drivers of market share were an organisation's competences to sustain quality, innovation and intellectual property (e.g. patents). All these factors impact on the perceived value for money of the organisation's products or services, and can also act as barriers to entry for new competitors.

- Sometimes the *complacency of market leaders* can allow lower share competitors to catch up because they are not regarded as serious competitors (i.e. they are not like the current competitors). But the growth and development of markets redefines the 'definition' of a credible player. Also, a low-share competitor may build a reputation in a market segment of little interest to the market leader, from which it penetrates the wider market.

8.2.2 Product development

Product development is
where organisations deliver
modified or new products to
existing markets

Changes in the business environment may create demand for new products or services at the expense of established provision. **Product development** is where organisations deliver modified or new products to existing markets. At a minimum, product development may be needed to survive but may also represent a considerable opportunity. Sometimes this may be achieved *with existing competences*. For example:

- Retailers tend to follow the changing needs of their customers by introducing new product lines; and public services shift their pattern of services as the needs of their communities change.

- When product life cycles are short – as with software or consumer electronics – product development becomes an essential requirement of an organisation's strategy. An organisation's advantage might lie in the processes of knowledge creation and integration (as discussed in Chapter 4). Illustration 4.7 showed how these processes can be combined to produce a 'spiral of knowledge creation' for successful product development.

- An organisation may have developed a core competence in market analysis that it is able to exploit. With the advent of cheap and powerful IT, those organisations which are good at *data-mining*[6] may gain advantage in this way, as discussed in section 10.3. Successful product development requires high-quality information about changing customer needs and the creativity to know how better to provide for these needs.

However, product development may require the *development of new competences*:

● There may be a need to respond to a *change of emphasis* amongst customers concerning the importance of product/service features. This can occur because customers become more experienced at judging value for money – for example, through repeat purchase or because new choices become available in the market. One of the stated purposes behind the privatisation measures in the public services (described in Chapters 5 and 9) was to empower customers in this way – through increasing choice and raising consumers' awareness and expectations about best value in public services.

● The critical success factors (CSFs – see section 4.2) may change if the previous CSFs can be met by many providers. Competition moves to meeting new CSFs and advantage will be gained by those organisations that are competent to deliver these other aspects of the customer experience. For example, functionality of the product may become a threshold requirement (which all providers must meet) and other factors such as the quality of information provided to clients, the clarity of billing, the ease of payment methods and so on may become the CSFs. It may be that customers or suppliers would value a new e-commerce business model – such as Internet selling or sourcing. So organisations would need competences in activities that underpin these new CSFs. As mentioned in Chapters 4 and 5, even the recognition of the need for such change can prove difficult, since the dominant culture and distribution of power are not attuned to such radical thinking.

Despite the attractiveness of product development, it may not always be in line with *expectations* and may raise uncomfortable dilemmas for organisations:

● Whilst new products may be vital to the future of the organisation, the process of creating a broad product line is expensive, *risky* and potentially *unprofitable*, because most new product ideas never reach the market; and of those that do, there are relatively few that succeed. Product development may require a commitment to high levels of spending on R&D. Whilst high-market-share companies may benefit in profit terms from relatively high levels of R&D expenditure, companies in a weak market position with high expenditure may suffer. Profitability can be depressed by over-rapid rates of new product introductions, as organisations struggle to learn new competences needed to debug production, train salespeople, educate customers and establish new channels.

● The need to develop products, even to survive in existing markets, is underlined by the consequences of not doing so. It is likely that performance may become so poor in relation to that of competitors or other providers that the organisation becomes a target for acquisition by organisations which have core competences in *corporate turnround*.

8.2.3 Market development

Market development is where existing products are offered in new markets

Normally organisations will be selective in their market coverage. This may lead to a situation where there are no further opportunities within the current market segments. In these circumstances an organisation may develop by **market development**, where existing products are offered in new markets. Both *resource and market considerations* might drive an organisation's development into new markets. For example:

● Whether products can be exploited in other *market segments* where similar critical success factors exist. For example, this was one reason for allowing public service providers 'commercial freedom' to seek out paying customers to complement the publicly funded provision.

● Development of *new uses* for existing products. For example, manufacturers of stainless steel have progressively found new applications for the products, which were originally used for cutlery and tableware. Nowadays the uses include aerospace, automobile exhausts, beer barrels and many applications in the chemical manufacturing industry.

● *Geographical* spread, either nationally or internationally, into new markets. Chapter 3 discussed how in many industries there are increasing market pressures for globalisation and that companies need to know how to respond and have the resources and competences to do so. Often it is those organisations with small home markets which 'lead' globalisation (as can be seen in the chapter-end case example in Chapter 3 about the European Brewing Industry – where Heineken (Holland), Carlsberg (Denmark) and Guinness (Ireland) are the most globalised companies). Increased global market participation – as against simply selling more goods into a few new countries – requires an organisation to consider three main issues[7] (see Exhibit 8.2):
  - The benefits of high market share (in a single market) have already been discussed in section 8.2.1 and illustrated in Illustration 8.2. These benefits of *market share* can be even more important in global markets – for example, by concentrating manufacturing on a small number of locations, both cost and quality benefits may result.
  - High global market share is important, but not sufficient for global market participation. There also needs to be a *global balance* of revenues within the global market. This is one feature that historically tended to distinguish Japanese companies in global markets from their competitors. For example, in the automobile industry, companies like Toyota and Nissan had a significant presence in all three of the major 'arenas' (North America, Europe and Asia Pacific). In contrast, the major American companies (Ford and GM) were strong in two arenas (North America and Europe), whilst the major European players (e.g. Peugeot) tended to be strong only in Europe.
  - There is also a need to be participating in *globally strategic markets*. These are countries that are important beyond their stand-alone attractiveness. This could occur for a number of reasons. For example, to be involved in at least one *large* market may be essential to get the cost

Exhibit 8.2	Three elements of a globalisation strategy

Source: Adapted from G. Yip, *Total Global Strategy*, Prentice Hall, 1995, Chapter 3.

structure or experience which is to be exploited elsewhere. It may be necessary to have a presence in the *home market of global customers* to gain access to, or credibility with, their global divisions or subsidiaries. In order to gain advantage over competitors there may be a need to operate in *competitors' home countries* or the countries where *competitors have a major presence*. Finally, a market may be strategically important because it is a source of industry innovation – for example, the USA for computer software, Germany for industrial control equipment, or the UK for popular music.

● Globalisation will usually require some adjustment to product features or development methods.[8] For example, it may be necessary to use agents or Internet selling for new territories whilst sales volumes are low. It will also require other competences, for example in market analysis and language and cultural awareness. There may be a need to reassess the way in which an organisation's structure, processes and relationships are managed (as discussed in Chapter 9).

Illustration 8.3 shows how Wal-Mart, the US-based retailer, expanded internationally. This continued, profitable growth also required competences in reducing opening costs of new outlets.

● In reality market development usually requires some degree of product development as well as *competence development*. For example, a manufacturer of branded grocery products for the premium market may enter the mainstream market through own-brand sales to supermarkets. This will

Illustration 8.3

Wal-Mart moves into Europe

STRATEGY IN ACTION

Globalisation through acquisition can be quick – but results may take longer to accrue.

In July 1999 Wal-Mart – the US retail giant, which operated in eight countries outside the USA (with annual sales of $200bn – more than twice its nearest rival) – took over ASDA – Britain's third-largest grocery supermarket. The move was publicly welcomed by the UK Labour government who were investigating UK supermarkets for allegedly having high prices (by international comparisons). Share prices in UK supermarkets plummeted with investors' fear of a Wal-Mart revolution in the industry. But not much changed in the short run and the company was pinning its hopes on non-food products and the prices which Wal-Mart's size can bring. Lee Scott, the Wal-Mart CEO explained:

> The opportunity is in the soft side of the home and electronics. As you look at global sourcing, there is an opportunity to provide tremendous value to customers in Britain. The transition will happen incrementally as Asda buyers get more familiar with the opportunities that exist and as they have more exposure to Wal-Mart stores. There is product this year that is globally sourced and there will be more next year. We're not talking about meat or produce. It's televisions, DVD players, pillow cases.

However, press comment was not favourable. One analyst's research paper argued that

'Wal-Mart has not yet succeeded in markets that it cannot drive a truck to and it has certainly had little impact as yet on the UK . . . we believe that ASDA's growth is now running into sand'. Others pointed to problems that Wal-Mart was experiencing in Germany. Scott explained that, as well as inheriting poor-quality properties:

> Germany is difficult. Building a supply chain that is willing to take costs out to pass on to the consumer does not happen overnight. It's [also] about convincing German management . . . that a motivated staff really determines our success. We will continue to focus on Germany to bring it up to the standard it can operate at.

Some analysts believed that there would be a second stage of Wal-Mart acquisitions in Britain with Safeway (the no. 4 grocery retailer) or Boots (a personal care/pharmacy-based retailer) as possible targets. Meanwhile Wal-Mart was embarked on its strategy of price cutting, and Scott was pleased that Wal-Mart had been singled out in the supermarket competition report as having had a downward impact on costs in Britain.

Source: Adapted from *The Sunday Times*, 17 December 2000.

Questions

1. Referring to section 8.2.3 and Exhibit 8.2, explain why Wal-Mart chose to develop into Europe.

2. What are the advantages and disadvantages of market development by acquisition?

3. How could Wal-Mart's difficulties be overcome?

require the development of new competences in (for example) key account selling.

● Organisations also may encounter some difficulties around credibility and *expectations* as they attempt to enter new markets or market segments. For example, a specialist may not been seen as a credible 'mainstream' supplier. The reverse may be even more problematic where a mainstream provider attempts to develop sales in specialist niches.

8.2.4 Diversification[9]

Diversity was discussed in Chapter 6 as an important issue at the corporate level in organisations. **Diversification** is typically defined as a strategy which takes the organisation away from its current markets or products or competences (i.e. box D in Exhibit 8.1). Diversification will increase the diversity that a corporate centre must oversee and Chapter 6 discussed the various forms of related and unrelated diversification and the reasons why they might make sense in terms of corporate-level strategy. Even small (single SBU) organisations may find themselves in circumstances where diversification may be a real option – or even a necessity. Many of the motives for diversification are similar to those for product or market development so the arguments will not be repeated again in detail. However, *in general*, diversification might occur because:

Diversification is typically defined as a strategy which takes the organisation away from its current markets or products or competences.

● The business *environment* changes, both threatening the future of current strategies and throwing up new opportunities – some of which might be 'related' in the senses discussed in Chapter 6. For example, as seen in Chapter 1, AOL (an Internet service provider) and Time Warner (a content provider) merged as a response to what they perceived as industry convergence, as discussed in Chapter 3.

● An organisation has *resources and competences* that can be exploited in new arenas. For example, the psychology department of a hospital may be able to offer a service to defence lawyers in the courts in preparing psychological reports on offenders.

● The *expectations* of powerful stakeholders might drive diversification. For example, investors may press for excess cash to be invested *somewhere* even if the current product and market development opportunities seem limited (often non-executive directors will push for such moves to 'sweat the assets' and they may be able to spot diversification opportunities through their wider contacts). But expectations can also limit the ability to diversify. For example, an organisation may not be seen as a credible player in a new arena by customers, distributors, the labour market and so on. Or, quite frequently, the organisational culture is unable to adapt to the requirements of successful operation in new arenas.

It should be remembered that a single SBU that diversifies is, in effect, creating a new set of management challenges akin to those dealt with by a corporate centre in larger organisations (as discussed in Chapter 6). So diversification may lead to a decline in performance if an organisation does not have the parenting competences to manage a more diverse set of activities.

8.3 METHODS OF STRATEGY DEVELOPMENT

The previous section of this chapter reviewed the *directions* in which organisations might develop. However, for any of these directions there are different *methods of development*. These methods can be divided into three types: internal development, acquisition (or disposal) and joint development (or alliances). Many of the points discussed in this section are summarised in Exhibit 8.4 later in the chapter, which will be used when discussing success criteria in section 8.4.

8.3.1 Internal development

Internal development is where strategies are developed by building up an organisation's own resource base and competences

Internal development is where strategies are developed by building up an organisation's own resource base and competences. For many organisations, internal development (sometimes known as 'organic development') has been the primary method of strategy development, and there are some compelling *resource* reasons why this should be so:

- For products that are highly technical in design or method of manufacture, businesses may choose to develop new products themselves, since the process of development is seen as the best way of acquiring the necessary competences to compete successfully in the marketplace. Indeed, it has been seen above that these competences may also spawn further new products and create new market opportunities.

- A similar argument may apply to the development of new markets by direct involvement. For example, many manufacturers still choose to forgo the use of agents, since they feel that the direct involvement gained from having their own salesforce is of advantage in gaining a full understanding of the market. This market knowledge may be a core competence in the sense that it creates competitive advantage over other organisations that are more distant from their customers.

- In fast-moving environments (whichever strategic directions of development are being pursued) an organisation needs to have competence in the processes of knowledge creation and integration as discussed in Chapter 4. If these competences are not present then internal development may be an inappropriate development method. Perhaps these competences should be acquired – either by acquisition of, or an alliance with, another organisation (see below).

- Although the final cost of developing new activities internally may be greater than that of acquiring other companies, the spread of cost may be more favourable and realistic. This is a strong motive for internal development in small companies or many public services that may not have the resources available for major investment. The slower rate of change which internal development brings may also minimise the disruption to other activities.

There may also be issues about the business *environment* which would create a preference for internal development:

- An organisation may have no choice about how new ventures are developed. In many instances those breaking new ground may not be in a position to develop by acquisition or joint development, since they are the only ones in the field.

- This problem is not confined to such extreme situations. Organisations wishing to develop by acquisition may not be able to find a suitable target for acquisition. For example, this is a particular difficulty for foreign companies attempting to enter Japan.

Internal development also may avoid the often traumatic political and cultural problems arising from post-acquisition integration and coping with the different traditions and incompatible *expectations* of two organisations.

8.3.2 Mergers and acquisitions

Acquisition is where an organisation develops its resources and competences by taking over another organisation. Development by acquisition tends to go in waves[10] and also tends to be selective in terms of industry sector. For example, in the UK, the early 1990s saw a wave of mergers in professional service organisations, such as law firms, property services, accountancy firms and financial services. This was followed by mergers in pharmaceuticals, electricity and information technology sectors. For example, in 2000, 25 per cent of the takeovers involving British companies were in the IT sector – amounting to almost 900 deals.[11] International developments through acquisition have been critically important in some industries, such as newspapers and media, food and drink, many sectors of the leisure industries and, in the early 2000s, in the telecommunications sector. Globally the number of completed acquisitions doubled between 1991 and 1997 to about 14,000 per annum.[12] In 1998 there were 3,000 cross-border acquisitions in Europe, valued at $220 billion (representing 45 per cent of the total value of European mergers and acquisitions).

Acquisition is where an organisation develops its resources and competences by taking over another organisation

Motives for acquisitions & mergers[13]

The need to keep up with a changing *environment* often dominates the thinking about acquisitions:

- A compelling reason to develop by acquisition is the speed with which it allows the company to enter new product or market areas. In some cases the product or market is changing so rapidly that acquisition becomes the only way of successfully entering the market, since the process of internal development is too slow. This remains a key motive in many e-commerce businesses.

- The competitive situation may influence a company to prefer acquisition. In markets that are static and where market shares of companies are reasonably steady, it can be a difficult proposition for a new company to enter the market, since its presence may create excess capacity. If, however, the new company enters by acquisition, the risk of competitive reaction is reduced.

- The same arguments also apply when an established supplier in an industry acquires a competitor either for the latter's order book to gain market share, or in some cases to shut down its capacity to help restore a situation where supply and demand are more balanced and trading conditions are more favourable. This is clearly more likely to happen in industries that have low levels of concentration – providing opportunities for industry rationalisation if some of the other advantages cited here prevail.

- Deregulation was a major driving force behind merger and acquisition activities in many industries such as telecommunications, electricity and other public utilities such as water. This was because regulation (or the process/type of deregulation) created a level of fragmentation which was regarded as sub-optimal. So this was an opportunity for acquisitive organisations to rationalise provision and/or seek to gain other benefits (for example, through the creation of 'multi-utility' companies offering electricity, gas, telecommunications and other services to customers).

- There may be financial motives for acquisitions. If the share value or price/earnings (P/E) ratio of a company is high, the motive may be to spot and acquire a firm with a low share value or P/E ratio. Indeed, this is one of the major stimuli for the more opportunistic acquisitive companies. An extreme example is asset stripping, where the main motive for the acquisition is short-term gain by buying up undervalued assets and disposing of them piecemeal.

There may be *resource considerations* too:

- A lack of resources or competences to compete successfully and the reality that the necessary innovations cannot be put in place quickly enough – they must be acquired. For example, a company may be acquired for its R&D expertise, or its knowledge of a particular type of production system or business processes or of market needs. International developments are often pursued through acquisition (or joint development) for this reason of market knowledge.

- Sometimes there are reasons of cost efficiency which make acquisition look favourable. This cost efficiency could arise from the fact that an established company may already be a long way down the experience curve and have achieved efficiencies which would be difficult to match quickly by internal development. The necessary innovation and organisational learning would be too slow. In public services, cost efficiency is usually the stated reason for merging units or rationalising provision (often by cutting out duplication or by gaining scale advantages).

Acquisition can also be driven by the *expectations* of key stakeholders:

- Institutional shareholders may expect to see continuing growth and acquisitions may be a quick way to deliver this growth. But there are considerable dangers that acquisitive growth may result in value destruction rather than creation – for some of the reasons discussed in Chapter 6. For example, the 'parent' does not have sufficient feel for the acquired businesses and, accidentally, destroys value. This is clearly more likely where acquisition is the method of pursuing diversification.

● There are some stakeholders whose motives are speculative rather than strategic. They favour acquisition which might bring a short-term boost to share value. Other stakeholders are usually wary of the speculators since their short-term gain can destroy longer-term prospects.

Making acquisitions work[14]

Problems may be encountered with acquisitions for a number of reasons. For example, the acquirer may pay too much or may be unable to add any value to its purchases (the parenting issue as discussed in Chapter 6). The expected synergistic benefits, which are often the cited reasons for acquisitions, are not realised because of the inability to integrate the new company into the activities of the old. This often centres round problems of cultural fit. Where acquisition is being used to acquire new competences, this 'clash of cultures' may simply arise because the organisational routines are so different in each organisation. For example, a company that has grown and succeeded by dominating a particular segment of the market may feel the need to extend into the 'mainstream' and decide to do this by acquisition. It is likely that many of the strategically important routines of these two organisations will be very different: in manufacture, continuous flow versus batch production; in customer communications, advertising versus personal selling; in distribution, the use of intermediaries versus direct delivery; and so on. Cultural fit can be even more problematic with cross-border mergers. This is because of the added complication of different national cultures (as discussed in section 5.5.1).

Mergers are more typically the result of organisations coming together voluntarily because they are actively seeking synergistic benefits, perhaps as a result of the common impact of a changing environment in terms either of opportunities or threats or of the excessive costs of innovation. This may encourage managers in both organisations to work harder at overcoming problems of post-merger integration.

There are three broad approaches to issues of post-merger cultural fit. First is the decision that the 'parent' culture will remain and effort will be put into the process of *assimilating* the 'joiners' into that culture. Second is the attempt to build a *hybrid* culture that combines the features of both organisations – this is probably the most difficult to achieve. Third is the decision to keep the previous cultures intact and *separate*. This could be appropriate where the reasons for acquisition were financial rather than strategic – so integration of activities is not important.

The research evidence on the financial consequences of acquisitions is inconclusive, in a similar way to the research on diversification discussed in Chapter 6 (of course, diversification is often achieved through acquisition). However, some of the findings do act as a reminder that acquisition is not an easy or guaranteed route to improving financial performance. It may take the acquiring company some considerable time to gain any financial benefit from acquisitions, if at all. As many as 70 per cent of acquisitions end up with lower returns to shareholders of both organisations. Some studies confirm the importance of non-economic factors such as previous experience of acquisitions; decisions on whether to remove or retain executives of the acquired company;

the management of post-acquisition cultural issues and the level of employee resistance to the change of ownership. Where the motive was about knowledge and competence transfer it can be difficult to know exactly which knowledge to transfer. This is because of causal ambiguity, as discussed in section 4.7.3. Managers themselves in the acquired organisation may be unclear about the reasons for their success (or failure).

8.3.3 Joint developments and strategic alliances[15]

A **joint development** is where two or more organisations share resources and activities to pursue a strategy

A **joint development** is where two or more organisations share resources and activities to pursue a strategy. Joint development of new strategies has become increasingly popular. This is because organisations cannot always cope with increasingly complex environments (such as globalisation) from internal resources and competences alone. They may see the need to obtain materials, skills, innovation, finance or access to markets, and recognise that these may be as readily available through co-operation as through ownership. Alliances vary considerably in their complexity, from simple two-partner alliances created to co-produce a product to one with multiple partners created to provide complex products and solutions.[16]

Motives for alliances[17]

Alliances may be formed either to *exploit* current resources and competences or to *explore* new possibilities. There are many detailed motives for alliances but they tend to fall into three broad categories:

- The need for *critical mass* which alliances can achieve by co-option of either competitors or providers of complementary products. This can lead to cost reduction and an improved customer offering.
- *Co-specialisation* – allowing each partner to concentrate on activities that best match their resources and competences. For example, alliances are often used to enter new geographical markets where an organisation needs local knowledge and expertise in distribution, marketing and customer support.
- *Learning* from partners and developing competences that may be more widely exploited elsewhere. For example, first steps into e-commerce may be achieved with a partner that has expertise in website development and similar competences. However, as e-commerce takes a growing proportion of sales, the intention might be to bring those activities in-house.

Strategic alliances are also important in the public sector. For example, Illustration 8.4 shows how the problem of drug abuse was tackled by collaborative arrangements between the different agencies involved (health, police, social services and education). There have also been many public/private partnerships in the UK; for example, the Public Finance Initiative (PFI) was established to allow public sector organisations to gain advantage through partnerships for the development and maintenance of capital items – particularly property.

Illustration 8.4

UK anti-drug strategy

STRATEGY IN ACTION

The ability to co-ordinate the activities of different public and voluntary sector agencies can be the key to successful 'social welfare' strategies.

In the late 1990s, Britain, like most western countries, was facing growing social problems from the misuse of drugs. The government's strategy to tackle this issue was published in 1998 and had four objectives:

1. Young people are to be helped to resist drug use in order to achieve their full potential in society.

2. Communities are to be protected from drug-related anti-social and criminal behaviour.

3. Treatment should enable people with drug problems to overcome them and live healthy and crime-free lives.

4. Stifle the availability of illegal drugs on the streets.

But the practical question was how to organise to meet these objectives as the responsibilities were split across several 'agencies':

● *Health* was responsible for diagnosing and treating patients of drug abuse.

● *Criminal Justice* (police, prisons, probation and customs/excise) was responsible for enforcing the law and the rehabilitation of offenders.

● *Social Services* were responsible for the social care and protection of drug users and their families.

● *Education* was responsible for drug education.

● *Voluntary sector* (mainly charities) ran services alongside and in partnership with many of these public sector agencies – such as information, counselling and support.

The following structures and processes were put in place to promote and support the collaborative working that was necessary if the drug problems were to be contained or reduced:

● At ministerial level in central government there was a cabinet sub-committee devoted to the issue including ministers from the main 'involved' departments.

● Keith Hellawell, the ex-chief constable of West Yorkshire Police, was appointed as a full time 'drugs czar' to spear-head efforts and reported to this committee.

● At local levels, *Drug Action Teams* were established comprising senior people from the local public and voluntary agencies concerned. They advised on and informed strategies and actions that were taken in local areas.

The overall approach to tackling drugs was emphasised in a comment by South Yorkshire Police:

Whenever we take a dealer out we simply create a void, an opportunity for someone else to move in and take over his pitch. The only realistic chance we have of making any long-term inroads into the problem is to work in partnership to change the culture and attitudes of society, and so to reduce demand. We can only do that through better education and by providing treatment services for those suffering.

Sources: Adapted from UK Anti-Drug Co-ordination Unit; South Yorkshire Police.

Questions

1. What are the alternative ways in which the anti-drug strategy could be delivered other than this particular approach of alliances?

2. Compare the benefits and problems of these various approaches.

Exhibit 8.3	Types of and motives for strategic alliances

	Form of Relationship		
	Loose (Market)	*Contractual*	*Ownership*
EXAMPLES	● Networks ● Opportunistic alliances	● Licensing ● Franchising ● Subcontracting	● Consortia ● Joint ventures
Influencing Factors			
A The Market			
● Speed of market change	Fast change	⟶	Slow change
B Resources			
● Asset management	Managed separately by each partner	⟶	Managed together
● Partners assets	Draws on 'parent's' assets	⟶	Dedicated assets for alliance
● Risk of losing assets to partner	High risk	⟶	Low risk
C Expectations			
● Spreading financial risk	Maintains risk	⟶	Dilutes risk
● Political climate	Unfavourable climate	⟶	Favourable climate

Forms of alliance

There are a variety of arrangements for joint developments and alliances (see Exhibit 8.3). Some may be very formalised inter-organisational relationships; at the other extreme, there can be loose arrangements of co-operation and informal networking between organisations, with no shareholding or ownership involved:

● *Joint ventures* are typically thought of as arrangements where organisations remain independent but set up a newly created organisation jointly owned by the parents. The joint venture was a favoured means of beginning collaborative adventures between eastern and western European firms in the early 1990s, with eastern European firms providing labour, entry to markets and sometimes plant; and western companies providing expertise and finance.

● *Consortia* may well involve two or more organisations in a joint venture arrangement, and will typically be more focused on a particular venture or project. Examples include large civil engineering projects, such as the Channel Tunnel, or major aerospace undertakings, such as the European Airbus. They might also exist between public sector organisations: for example, functions such as public transport which cross administrative boundaries often are run by co-ordinating consortia involving both private and public sector organisations. *Joint ventures or consortia* usually involve formalised inter-organisational relationships in the form either of shareholding or of agreements specifying asset sharing and distribution of profits.

- At the other extreme, *networks* are arrangements whereby two or more organisations work in collaboration without formal relationships, but through a mechanism of mutual advantage and trust. Such networks can be enduring and provide considerable mutual benefit to the organisations involved. Network organisations are discussed more fully in Chapter 9 (section 9.4.3). Networks have been created in the airline industry by 'code-sharing' arrangements, allowing passengers to use several 'partner' airlines whilst travelling on a single ticket. These then progressed to somewhat more formal alliances (such as 'One World' – still largely for marketing purposes but with some cross-equity involvement between (some) partners in the alliance).

- *Opportunistic alliances* might also arise focused around particular ventures or projects, but again may not be highly formalised. In this sense, these arrangements are much nearer to market relationships than to contractual relationships.

- Many intermediate arrangements exist. One such is *franchising*, perhaps the best-known examples of which are Coca-Cola and McDonald's. Here the franchise holder undertakes specific activities such as manufacturing, distribution or selling, but the franchiser is responsible for the brand name, marketing and probably training. *Licensing* is common in science-based industries, where, for example, the right to manufacture a patented product is granted for a fee. With *subcontracting*, a company chooses to subcontract particular services or part of a process: for example, increasingly in public services responsibility for waste removal, cleaning and IT services may be subcontracted to private companies. All these intermediate arrangements are likely to be contractual in nature, but are unlikely to involve ownership.

- An important issue for many public service organisations is the involvement of the customer in *co-production*[18] of the service. This has been a long-standing arrangement in some services, for example the PAYE system for tax collection where most of the work and responsibility lies with employers. In other services co-production is increasingly possible with modern IT and seen as a way of more fully involving communities in 'customising' services. Nor is this confined to the public sector. Many e-commerce companies are trying to move beyond customisation of products/services (which assumes a prior knowledge of customer needs) to customerisation[19] where the customer 'designs' the product/service online and the service provider creates the product/service from their supply chain. For example, e-commerce-based interior design companies can offer such a service.

Factors influencing the form of alliance

Exhibit 8.3 shows the factors that can influence the form of alliance:

- Many organisations will find themselves operating in *business environments* where alliances are most likely to secure their success. For example:

- Opportunistic moves into new arenas may need to be done quickly before the best partners form relationships with competitors. The globalisation of telecommunications has been characterised by this. Of course, in reverse, alliances may be thrust on to organisations as they become the dominant arrangement in the industry (such as airlines or public/private partnerships).
- Market entry (overseas) may require a local partner – not just for their knowledge and contacts but to appear a serious and credible 'player' in the market or with the host government.

● As with acquisitions, there may also be *resource reasons* why organisations prefer to develop through alliances – the issues of scale economies and complementary competences mentioned above being central. The difference from acquisitions often is found in the desire to learn from partners. This is particularly true where partnerships are being used to enter new countries, work with new technologies (such as IT) or operate in new regulatory regimes (such as deregulation of public services). Resource considerations often are the dominant influence on the form of alliance that emerges. In particular:
- Asset *management*: the extent to which assets do or do not need to be managed jointly.
- The extent to which resources will be drawn from the 'parent's' operations on an ongoing basis or whether *dedicated assets* will be required for the alliance.
- The extent to which there is a risk of one or other of the parties involved *losing assets or competences* to the partner.

For example, formal alliances (such as joint ventures or consortia) usually fit situations where the assets involved need to be jointly managed and where these assets can be separated from the parent companies without damaging knock-on effects to those companies; for example, setting up a dedicated production unit where the assets and expertise can be specifically devoted to the joint venture without its removal harming the parents. At least in theory, there is a low risk that the assets could be appropriated by one or other party involved. Having said this, some organisations enter joint ventures specifically to obtain know-how and expertise for their own internal developments (as mentioned above).

In contrast, informal alliances (such as networks) match situations where assets do not need joint management and where they cannot be easily separated from the parent organisations without harm being done. So capital, expertise, know-how and so on can come together more informally. For example, it may be that one partner is providing access to distribution channels which are part of the company's operation as a whole. If the assets involved were split off into a separate organisation, there would be a high risk of their being appropriated by another party.

● Some organisations will operate in situations where there are *expectations* that alliances should be the preferred development method:
- Alliances may dilute risk for each partner and some stakeholders may prefer this as it spreads their financial risk.

- Many public sector ventures either require or 'prefer' alliances[20] - often with the private sector.[21] The political climate is more favourable to such arrangements.
- In some industries - and parts of the public sector too - it has simply become fashionable or taken for granted that alliances are a good thing. So those that don't 'join the club' run the risk of missing the opportunities - even where the environmental or resource-based 'case' for the alliance is weak.

Ingredients of successful alliances

There has been a great deal written about the ingredients of successful alliances.[22] Although organisations may see many of the benefits of alliances (outlined above), it is not necessarily easy to make alliances work. The success of alliances tends to be dependent on how they are managed and the way in which the partners foster the evolution of the partnership. For example, the following are found to be important:

- *Trust* is probably the most important ingredient of success and a major reason for failure if it is absent. But trust has two separate elements to it. Trust can be *competence based* in the sense that each partner is confident that the other has the resources and competences to fulfil their part in the alliance. This would include competences in business processes such as decision making and motivation of staff as well as 'technical' operational competences. Trust is also *character based* and concerns whether partners trust each other's motives and are compatible in terms of attitudes to integrity, openness, discretion and consistency of behaviour. It is for these reasons that relationships between family companies are often based on long-standing social relationships between the families.
- *Senior management support* is important since alliances require a wider range of relationships to be built and sustained. This can create cultural and political hurdles which senior managers must help to overcome.
- Defining and meeting *performance expectations*. This requires the willingness to exchange performance information. For example, a manufacturer in alliance with its distributors in overseas markets would wish to understand their performance in the market in relation to *their* competitors.
- Clear *goals and organisational arrangements* - particularly concerning activities that cross or connect the partners.
- *Compatibility* at the operational level requiring efforts by partners to achieve strong interpersonal relationships at these lower levels and not just between senior managers of the partners. In cross-country partnerships this will include the need to transcend national cultural differences (for example see Illustration 11.1).
- Allowing the alliance to *evolve and change* rather than prescribing it too parochially at the outset. For example, this could include an agreement between partners that regular reviews will be undertaken of how the partnership operates with the purpose of agreeing changes or adjustments to the *modus operandi*.

8.4 SUCCESS CRITERIA

This section of the chapter looks at why some strategies might succeed better than others by introducing the concept of *success criteria* by which strategies can be judged. The aim of this final part of the chapter is to help readers understand these criteria and introduce some frameworks which cast light on each criterion.[23] These criteria can also be used explicitly to evaluate strategies as part of a process of strategy selection.

There are three main *success criteria*:

- *Suitability* is a broad criterion concerned with whether a strategy addresses the circumstances in which an organisation is operating – the *strategic position* as discussed in Part II of this book. For example, the extent to which new strategies would *fit* with the future trends and changes in the environment, how the strategy might *stretch* and exploit the core competences of an organisation.

- *Acceptability* is concerned with the expected *performance outcomes* (such as the *return* or *risk*) of a strategy and the extent to which these would be in line with *expectations*.

- *Feasibility* is concerned with whether a strategy could be made to work in practice. Assessing the feasibility of a strategy requires an emphasis on more detailed practicalities of *resourcing* and strategic capability.

Each of these criteria will now be discussed in more detail.

8.4.1 Suitability

Suitability is concerned with whether a strategy addresses the circumstances in which an organisation is operating – the strategic position

Suitability is concerned with whether a strategy addresses the circumstances in which an organisation is operating – the strategic position. This relates back to the discussions in Part II of the book so the concepts and frameworks already discussed in these chapters can be helpful in understanding suitability. So suitability can be thought as the *rationale* of a strategy and whether it 'makes sense' in relation to the strategic position of an organisation. The discussions of development directions and methods in the sections above were concerned with not only understanding what directions and methods were 'available' but also explaining some reasons why each might be preferred. So the various examples in those sections illustrated why strategies might be regarded as *suitable* from the point of view of:

- exploiting *opportunities* in the environment and avoiding *threats*;
- capitalising on an organisation's *strengths* and avoiding or remedying *weaknesses*;
- addressing *expectations*.

Exhibit 8.4 summarises these points from the earlier sections and provides a checklist of typical reasons why specific directions or methods of development might be regarded as suitable.

Exhibit 8.4   Some examples of suitability

STRATEGIC OPTION	WHY THIS OPTION MIGHT BE SUITABLE IN TERMS OF:		
Directions	**Environment**	**Resources/Competences**	**Expectations**
Consolidation	Withdraw from declining markets Sell valuable assets (speculation) Maintain market share	Build on strengths through continued investment and innovation	Better returns at low risk by exploiting current strategies
Market penetration	Gain market share for advantage	Exploit superior resources and competences	
Product development	Exploit knowledge of customer needs	Exploit R&D	Better returns at medium risk by exploiting current strengths or market knowledge
Market development	Current markets saturated New opportunities for: geographical spread, entering new segments or new uses	Exploit current products	
Diversification	Current markets saturated or declining	Exploit core competences in new arenas	Better returns at higher risk by 'sweating the assets'
Methods			
Internal development	First in field Partners or acquisitions not 'available'	Learning and competence development Spread of cost	Cultural/political ease
Merger/Acquisition	Speed Supply/Demand P/E ratios	Acquire competences Scale economies	Returns: growth or share value Problems of culture clash
Joint development	Speed Industry norm	Complementary competences Learning from partners	'Required' for entry Dilutes risk Fashionable

Exhibit 8.5	Understanding the relative suitability of strategic options

The relative suitability of strategic options can be understood by:

METHOD	APPROACH
Ranking	• Options are assessed against key factors in the environment, resources and expectations • A score (and ranking) is established for each option
Decision trees	• Options are 'eliminated' by progressively introducing further requirements to be met
Scenarios	• Options are matched to different future scenarios

However, it is also important to understand why strategies might be *unsuitable* (particularly if managers might prefer these strategies):

- They do not properly address all (three) of the factors about an organisation's situation. They are unduly shaped by one aspect at the expense of others. For example, the desire to chase market opportunities without the necessary competences or funding, the failure to acknowledge the need for product development or the pursuit of a strategy against the wishes of a powerful stakeholder would be examples.

- There may be strategies 'available' to an organisation that are *more suitable*. So suitability should be judged in *relative* terms. There are some useful frameworks that can assist in understanding this better (see Exhibit 8.5). Illustrations 8.5 to 8.7 show how these frameworks can be used:
  - *Ranking* strategic options against a set of factors concerning an organisation's strategic position as discussed above – see Illustration 8.5.
  - *Decision trees*, which also assess strategic options against a list of key factors. However, preferred options emerge by progressively introducing requirements which must be met (such as growth, investment or diversity) – see Illustration 8.6.
  - *Scenarios*, which attempt to match specific options with a range of possible future situations and are particularly useful where a high degree of uncertainty exists (say, in the environment, as discussed in section 3.2.4 – see Illustration 3.3).

- The elements of the strategy are not *internally consistent*. The *competitive strategy* (such as low price or differentiation), the development *direction* (such as product development or diversification) and the development *method* (internal, acquisition or alliances) need to be consistent. Strategies are unlikely to succeed if these three elements do not work together as a 'package'. Since organisations are likely to be developing and changing elements of a strategy incrementally over time, it is quite probable that strategies will become internally inconsistent resulting in declining performance.
  For example, a manufacturer of consumer durable goods was competing on the *basis* of commodity products (position 1 on the strategy clock –

Illustration 8.5

Ranking options: Churchill Pottery

STRATEGY IN ACTION

Ranking can usefully build on a SWOT analysis by comparing strategic options against the key strategic factors from the SWOT analysis.

In 1990 Churchill Pottery, based in Stoke-on Trent, UK, was one of the subjects of a BBC series entitled *Troubleshooter*, where the management teams of a number of companies were invited to discuss their organisation's strategic development with Sir John Harvey-Jones (ex-chairman of ICI). Like many traditional manufacturing companies at the time, Churchill found itself under increasing pressure from cheaper imports in its traditional markets, and was considering whether to move 'up market' by launching a new range aimed at the design-conscious end of the market. The ranking exercise below was done by a group of participants on a management programme, having seen the Churchill Pottery video.

The results of the ranking are interesting. First, they highlight the need to do *something*. Second, the radical departures in strategy – such as moves into retailing or diversification – are regarded as unsuitable. They do not address the problems of the core business, do not fit the capabilities of Churchill and would not fit culturally. This leaves related developments as the front runners – as might be expected in a traditional manufacturing firm like Churchill. The choice boils down to significant investments in cost reduction to support an essentially 'commodity' approach to the market (options 2 and 5) or an 'added value' attack on the growing 'up-market' segments. The company chose the latter and with some success – presumably helped by their wide television exposure through the *Troubleshooter* series.

Source: Adapted from the *Troubleshooter* series, BBC, 1990, 1993.

Questions

1. Has option 4 been ranked above the others because:
   (a) it has the most ticks
   (b) it has the least crosses
   (c) a combination of these
   (d) other reasons?
   Justify your answer.

2. List the main strengths and limitations of ranking analysis.

Ranking exercise

STRATEGIC OPTIONS	KEY STRATEGIC FACTORS						
	FAMILY OWNERSHIP	INVESTMENT FUNDS	LOW PRICE IMPORTS	LACK OF MARKETING/ DESIGN SKILLS	AUTOMATION LOW	CONSUMER TASTE (DESIGN)	RANKING
1. Do nothing	✓	?	✗	?	✗	✗	C
2. Consolidate in current segments (investment/ automation)	✓	✗	✓	?	✓	?	B
3. Expand overseas sales (Europe)	✗	✗	✗	✗	✗	?	C
4. Launch 'up-market' range	✓	✓	✓	✗	?	✓	A
5. Expand 'own-label' production (to hotel/ catering industry)	✓	✓	✓	?	✗	?	B
6. Open retail outlets	✗	✗	?	✗	?	?	C
7. Diversify	✗	✗	?	?	?	✓	C

✓ = favourable; ✗ = unfavourable; ? = uncertain or irrelevant.   A = most suitable; B = possible; C = unsuitable.

Illustration 8.6

STRATEGY IN ACTION

A strategic decision tree for a law firm

Decision trees evaluate future options by progressively eliminating others as additional criteria are introduced to the evaluation.

A law firm had most of its work related to house conveyancing where profits had been significantly squeezed. Therefore, it wanted to consider a range of new strategies for the future. Using a strategic decision tree it was able to eliminate certain options by identifying a few key criteria which future developments would incorporate, such as growth, investment (in premises, IT systems or acquisitions), and diversification (for example, into matrimonial law which, in turn, often brings house conveyancing work as families 'reshape').

Analysis of the decision tree reveals that if the partners of the firm wish growth to be an important aspect of future strategies, options 1–4 are ranked more highly than options 5–8. At the second step, the need for low investment stra-

tegies would rank options 3 and 4 above 1 and 2, and so on.

The partners were aware that this technique has limitations in that the choice at each branch of the tree can tend to be simplistic. Answering 'yes' or 'no' to diversification does not allow for the wide variety of alternatives which might exist between these two extremes, for example *adapting the 'style' of its conveyancing service* (this could be an important variant of options 6 or 8). Nevertheless, as a starting point for evaluation, the decision tree provides a useful framework.

Questions

1. Try reversing the sequence of the three parameters (to diversification, investment and growth) and redraw the decision tree. Do the same eight options still emerge?

2. Add a fourth parameter to the decision tree. This new parameter is development by *internal methods* or by *acquisition*. List your sixteen options in the right-hand column.

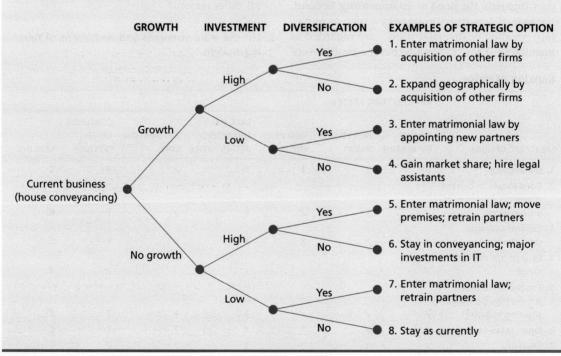

GROWTH	INVESTMENT	DIVERSIFICATION	EXAMPLES OF STRATEGIC OPTION
Growth	High	Yes	1. Enter matrimonial law by acquisition of other firms
		No	2. Expand geographically by acquisition of other firms
	Low	Yes	3. Enter matrimonial law by appointing new partners
		No	4. Gain market share; hire legal assistants
No growth	High	Yes	5. Enter matrimonial law; move premises; retrain partners
		No	6. Stay in conveyancing; major investments in IT
	Low	Yes	7. Enter matrimonial law; retrain partners
		No	8. Stay as currently

Current business (house conveyancing)

Illustration 8.7

Sewerage construction project

Investment in items of infrastructure –
such as sewers – often requires a careful
consideration of the wider costs and
benefits of the project.

In the 1990s, Britain's recently privatised water companies were monopolies supplying water and disposing of sewage. They needed to invest in new sewerage systems to meet the increasing standards required by law. They often used cost–benefit analysis to assess projects. The figures below are from an actual analysis.

Benefits

Benefits result mainly from reduced use of rivers as overflow sewers. There are also economic benefits resulting from construction. The following benefits are quantified in the table:

COST/BENEFIT	£m	£m
Benefits		
Multiplier/linkage benefits		0.9
Flood prevention		2.5
Reduced traffic disruption		7.2
Amenity benefits		4.6
Investment benefit		23.6
Encouragement of visitors		4.0
Total benefits		42.8
Costs		
Construction cost	18.2	
Less: Unskilled labour cost	(4.7)	
Opportunity cost of construction		(13.5)
Present value of net benefits (NPV)		29.3
Real internal rate of return (IRR)		15%

Note: Figures discounted at a *real* discount rate of 5 per cent over 40 years.

- The multiplier benefit to the local economy of increased spending by those employed on the project.
- The linkage benefit to the local economy of purchases from local firms, including the multiplier effect of such spending.

- Reduced risk of flooding from overflows or old sewers collapsing – flood probabilities can be quantified using historical records, and the cost of flood damage by detailed assessment of the property vulnerable to damage.
- Reduced traffic disruption from flooding and road closures for repairs to old sewers – statistics on the costs of delays to users, traffic flows on roads affected and past closure frequency can be used to quantify savings.
- Increased amenity value of rivers (e.g. for boating and fishing) can be measured by surveys asking visitors what the value is to them or by looking at the effect on demand of charges imposed elsewhere.
- Increased rental values and take-up of space can be measured by consultation with developers and observed effects elsewhere.
- Increased visitor numbers to riverside facilities resulting from reduced pollution.

Construction cost

This is net of the cost of unskilled labour. Use of unskilled labour is not a burden on the economy, and its cost must be deducted to arrive at opportunity cost.

Net benefits

Once the difficult task of quantifying costs and benefits is complete, standard discounting techniques can be used to calculate net present value and internal rate of return, and analysis can then proceed as for conventional projects.

Source: Adapted from G. Owen, formerly of Sheffield Business School.

Questions

1. What do you feel about the appropriateness of the listed benefits?

2. How easy or difficult is it to assign money values to these benefits?

Exhibit 7.2). Their concern was to grow market share in the home market (*market penetration*), gain scale economies and fight off the threat of cheap imported goods. They were pursuing this by *acquisitions* of smaller-share companies. This strategy was working well until there were no more small players to acquire and the threat of cheap imports remained significant unless costs could be further reduced. So the *method* of gaining market share had to switch to *internal* efforts to win customers from competitors and a major cost reduction programme commencing with the rationalisation of the production facilities they had inherited from the acquisitions. So the search for internal consistency is a continuous and not a one-off process.

8.4.2 Acceptability

Acceptability is concerned with the expected performance outcomes of a strategy

Acceptability is concerned with the expected performance outcomes of a strategy. These can be of three broad types: *return*, *risk* and *stakeholder reactions*. Exhibit 8.6 summarises some frameworks that can be useful in understanding the acceptability of strategies together with some of the limitations of each of these. In general, it is helpful to use more than one approach in building up a picture of the acceptability of a particular strategy.

Return

An assessment of the returns likely to accrue from specific strategies could be a key criterion of acceptability of a strategy – at least to some stakeholders.

Exhibit 8.6	Some criteria for understanding the acceptability of strategic options		
CRITERIA	**USED TO UNDERSTAND**	**EXAMPLES**	**LIMITATIONS**
Return			
Profitability	Financial return of investments	Return on capital Payback period Discounted cash flow (DCF)	Apply to discrete projects Only tangible costs/ benefits Difficulties of quantification
Cost–benefit	Wider costs/benefits (including intangibles)	Major infrastructure projects	Quantification
Real options	Sequence of decisions	Real options analysis	Technical detail often difficult
Shareholder value analysis (SVA)	Impact of new strategies on shareholder value	Mergers/acquisitions	
Risk			
Financial ratio projections	Robustness of strategy	Break-even analysis Impact on gearing and liquidity	
Sensitivity analysis	Test assumptions/robustness	'What if?' analysis	Tests factors separately
Stakeholder reactions	Political dimension of strategy	Stakeholder mapping Game theory	Largely qualitative

There are a number of different approaches to understanding return. This section looks briefly at four of these approaches. It is important to remember that there are no absolute standards as to what constitutes a good or poor return. It will differ between industries, countries and also between different stakeholders. There are also arguments as to which measures give the best assessment of return, as will be seen below.

Profitability analyses[24]

Traditional financial analyses have been used extensively in assessing the acceptability of strategies. Three of the more commonly used approaches are as follows (see Exhibit 8.7):

- Forecasting the *return on capital employed* (ROCE) a specific time after a new strategy is implemented (e.g. the new strategy will result in a return on capital of 15 per cent by year 3). This is shown in Exhibit 8.7(a).

- *Payback period* has been used where a significant capital injection is needed to support a new venture. In Exhibit 8.7(b), the payback period is calculated by finding the time at which the cumulative net cash flow becomes zero – in the example, three and a half years.

  The judgement is then whether this is regarded as an adequate outcome and if the organisation is prepared to wait that long for a return. This will vary from one industry to another. Major public sector ventures such as bridge building may well be assessed on a payback period of up to 60 years.

- *Discounted cash flow* (DCF) is a widely used investment appraisal technique, and is essentially an extension of the payback period analysis. Once the net cash flows have been assessed for each of the years (see Exhibit 8.7c), they are discounted progressively to reflect the fact that funds generated early are of more real value than those in later periods (years). In the example, the discounting rate of 10 per cent reflects the value placed on money tied up in the venture. So the projected net cash flow of £2m in year 2 is discounted to £1.82m and so on. The net present value (NPV) of the venture is then calculated by adding all the discounted annual cash flows (after taxation) over the anticipated life of the project. DCF is particularly useful for comparing the financial merits of strategies which have very different patterns of expenditure and return.

Although the assessment of return may be assisted by the use of one or more of these financial methods, it is important to recognise some of the implicit assumptions which inevitably limit their use. In particular, it is important not to be misguided by the tidiness or apparent thoroughness of these approaches. Most of these methods were developed for the purposes of capital investment appraisal and, therefore, focus on discrete *projects* where the incremental costs and cash inflows are easily predicted. Neither of these assumptions is necessarily valid in many strategic developments. The precise way in which a strategy might develop, and the costs and income flows, tend to become clearer as the implementation proceeds rather than at the outset.

Exhibit 8.7	Assessing profitability

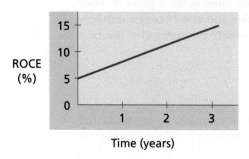

(a) Return on capital employed

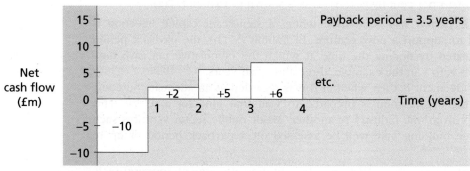

(b) Payback period

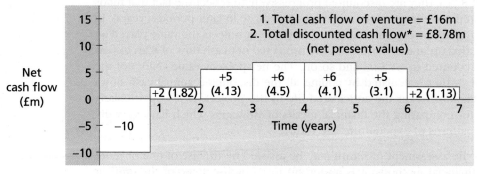

* Using a discounting rate of 10%.
Figures in brackets are discounted by 10% annually.

(c) Discounted cash flow (DCF)

Also, there are often significant time lags between *revenue* expenditures and income benefits. Nor are strategic developments easy to isolate from the ongoing business activities in accurately assessing costs and projected income.

Additionally, financial appraisals tend to focus on the direct *tangible* costs and benefits, and do not set the strategy in its wider context. For example, a new product launch may look unprofitable as an isolated project, but may make real strategic sense through the market acceptability of other products in the company's portfolio. Or, in reverse, the intangible cost of losing *strategic focus* through new ventures is readily overlooked. These are crucial considerations for organisations where investment in innovation (either products or processes) is a major element of cost.

In an attempt to overcome some of these shortcomings, other approaches to assessing return have been developed.

Cost–benefit[25]

In many situations, profit is too narrow an interpretation of return, particularly where intangible benefits are an important consideration, as mentioned above. This is often the case for major public infrastructure projects, such as the siting of an airport or a sewer construction project, as shown in Illustration 8.7, or in organisations with long-term programmes of innovation (e.g. pharmaceuticals or aerospace). The *cost–benefit* concept suggests that a money value can be put on all the costs and benefits of a strategy, including tangible and intangible returns to people and organisations other than the one 'sponsoring' the project or strategy.

Although in practice monetary valuation is often difficult, it can be done, and, despite difficulties, cost-benefit analysis is an approach which is valuable if its limitations are understood. Its major benefit is in forcing people to be explicit about the various factors which should influence strategic choice. So, even if people disagree on the value which should be assigned to particular costs or benefits, at least they are able to argue their case on common ground and decision makers can compare the merits of the various arguments.

Real-options-based approaches

The previous three approaches tend to assume some degree of clarity about the directions and outcomes of a strategic option. In many situations the precise costs and benefits of particular strategies tend to become clear only as implementation proceeds. Luehrman[26] says that this is because 'executing a strategy almost always involves making a sequence of decisions. Some actions are taken immediately, while others are deliberately deferred. . . . The strategy sets the framework within which future decisions will be made, but at the same time it leaves space for learning from ongoing developments and for discretion to act based on what is learnt'. This suggests that a strategy should be seen as a *series* of 'real' options (i.e. choices of direction at particular points in time as the strategy takes shape, as a result of the previous choices that were made). The benefit of this approach is that it can provide a clearer

Exhibit 8.8	Real options framework

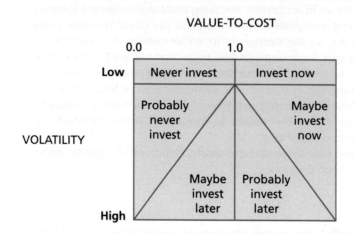

Source: Adapted from T.A. Luehrman. 'Strategy as a portfolio of real options', *Harvard Business Review*, September–October, 1998, p. 3.

understanding of both strategic and financial return and risk of a strategy by examining each step (option) separately as it 'occurs'. The degree of volatility surrounding a strategy will change over time as a result of this partial implementation (i.e. the previous steps (options)). So strategic and financial evaluation are brought more closely together than is often the case. Exhibit 8.8 shows that high levels of volatility should have two effects. Firstly, to defer decisions as far as possible because (secondly) the passage of time will clarify the expected returns – even to the extent that apparently unfavourable strategies might prove viable at a later date (the category 'maybe invest later' in the exhibit). This can help in deciding whether to pursue the strategy at all and whether it should be pursued immediately or deferred to a later date.

Shareholder value analysis[27]

During the 1980s, attempts were made to address many of the limitations and criticisms of traditional financial analyses. At the same time, renewed attention was paid to the primary legal responsibility of company directors: namely, the creation of value and benefits for the shareholders. The takeover boom of the 1980s caused both corporate raiders and victims alike to look at how corporate development strategies were, or were not, generating shareholder value. Together, these factors spawned *shareholder value analysis* (SVA). This was taken up in the 1990s as managing for shareholder value (MFV), which is an approach to corporate and business unit management which is founded on the central concept that companies should be managed with the specific objective of maximising the value of the company to its owners. This may seem to be an obvious objective for managers to adopt but there was an absence of an effective value-based management framework which managers could use to operationalise the concept of managing for value – to help them to take value-based decisions on a day-to-day basis. A number of well-known companies from around the world now claim to have taken various steps towards managing for value. These include Coca-Cola, Lloyds TSB, Cadbury-Schweppes, Lufthansa, Boots, Reuters and Telstra.

The shareholder value measure used most commonly is total shareholder returns (TSRs), which in any year is equal to the increase in the price of a share over the year plus the dividends per share earned in the year, all divided by the share price at the start of the year. Value-based businesses use this measure to set themselves performance goals (e.g. to earn TSRs of 20 per cent each year, or for TSRs to be in the top quartile of a peer group of companies, or to double the value of the business in four years). They also use TSRs to reward managers – typically the most senior managers – for the performance the business has achieved for its owners. Used effectively, TSR goals align the interests of owners and managers.

However, it is also important to understand which factors will lead to increased TSR. Since shareholder value is determined by the long-term cash-generating capability of the business (see section 10.4.1), managers need to use financial measures in their decision making that reflect cash flow as well as more traditional measures such as profitability, as discussed above. One such measure is economic profit (EP). This is defined as net operating profit after tax, less a charge for the capital employed in the business. EP indicates where value has been created or destroyed in the period. EP is a better measure of value creation since it includes all the costs of doing business, including the cost of the capital needed for the businesses to function (which can often be a significant proportion of total costs). Traditional accounting measures – such as operating profit – ignore the cost of capital completely. This means that traditional measures can give managers very misleading signals about where value is being created or destroyed. This can produce completely new perspectives on the performance of the business; for example, a realisation that all products may be profitable (by traditional measures) but only some produce a positive economic profit. This means that other products are destroying value.

Although MFV has done much to address the shortcomings of traditional financial analyses, it does not remove many of the inherent uncertainties surrounding strategic choices. Nevertheless, the idea of valuing a strategy may serve to give greater realism and clarity to otherwise vague strategies. It is an important way in which business and financial strategies should overlap and is discussed further in section 10.4.

Risk

The likely return from a particular strategy is an important aspect of the acceptability of that strategy. However, another aspect of acceptability is the *risk* that an organisation faces in pursuing a particular strategy. This risk can be particularly high for organisations with major long-term programmes of innovation or where high levels of uncertainty exist about key issues in the environment. This section outlines some ways in which this risk can be understood.

Illustration 8.8

STRATEGY IN ACTION

Sensitivity analysis

Sensitivity analysis is a useful technique for assessing the extent to which the success of a preferred strategy is dependent on the key assumptions which underlie that strategy.

In 2001 the Dunsmore Chemical Company was a single-product company trading in a mature and relatively stable market. It was intended to use this established situation as a cash cow to generate funds for a new venture with a related product. Estimates had shown that the company would need to generate some £4m cash (at 2001 values) between 2002 and 2007 for this new venture to be possible.

Although the expected performance of the company was for a cash flow of £9.5m over that period (the *base case*), management was concerned to assess the likely impact of three key factors:

● Possible increases in *production costs* (labour, overheads and materials), which might be as much as 3 per cent p.a. in real terms.

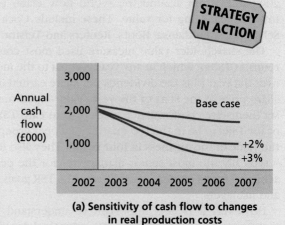

(a) Sensitivity of cash flow to changes in real production costs

● *Capacity-fill*, which might be reduced by as much as 25 per cent owing to ageing plant and uncertain labour relations.

● *Price levels*, which might be affected by the threatened entry of a new major competitor. This could squeeze prices by as much as 3 per cent p.a. in real terms.

It was decided to use sensitivity analysis to assess the possible impact of each of these factors on the company's ability to generate £4m. The results are shown in the graphs.

Financial ratios[28]

The projection of how key financial ratios might change if a specific option were adopted can provide useful insights into risk. At the broadest level, an assessment of how the *capital structure* of the company would change is a good general measure of risk. For example, options which would require the extension of long-term loans will increase the gearing of the company and increase its financial risk.

At a more detailed level, a consideration of the likely impact on an organisation's *liquidity* is important in assessing risk. For example, a small retailer eager to grow quickly may be tempted to fund the required shopfitting costs by delaying payments to suppliers and increasing bank overdraft. This reduced liquidity increases the financial risk of the business. The extent to which this increased risk threatens survival depends on the likelihood of either creditors or the bank demanding payments from the company – an issue that clearly requires judgement.

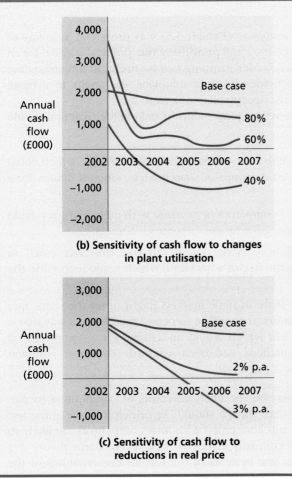

(b) Sensitivity of cash flow to changes in plant utilisation

(c) Sensitivity of cash flow to reductions in real price

From this analysis, the management concluded that its target of £4m would be achieved with *capacity utilisation* as low as 60 per cent, which was certainly going to be achieved. Increased *production costs* of 3 per cent p.a. would still allow the company to achieve the £4m target over the period. In contrast, *price* squeezes of 3 per cent p.a. would result in a shortfall of £2m.

The management concluded from this analysis that the key factor which should affect their thinking on this matter was the likely impact of new competition and the extent to which they could protect price levels if such competition emerged. They therefore developed an aggressive marketing strategy to deter potential entrants.

Source: The calculations for the sensitivity test utilise computer programs employed in the Doman case study by P.H. Jones (Sheffield Hallam University).

Question

What should the company do if its marketing campaigns fail to stop real price erosion?

(a) Push to achieve more sales volume/capacity-fill?
(b) Reduce unit costs of production?
(c) Something else?

Sensitivity analysis[29]

Sensitivity analysis is sometimes referred to as *what if?* analysis. It allows each of the important assumptions underlying a particular strategy to be questioned and challenged. In particular, it seeks to test how sensitive the predicted performance or outcome (e.g. profit) is to each of these assumptions. For example, the key assumptions underlying a strategy might be that market demand will grow by 5 per cent p.a., or that the company will stay strike-free, or that certain expensive machines will operate at 90 per cent loading. Sensitivity analysis asks: what would be the effect on performance (in this case, profitability) if, for example, market demand grew at only 1 per cent, or by as much as 10 per cent? Would either of these extremes alter the decision to pursue that particular strategy? A similar process might be repeated for the other key assumptions. This can help develop a clearer picture of the risks of making particular strategic decisions and the degree of confidence managers might have in a given decision. Illustration 8.8 shows how sensitivity analysis can be used.

Stakeholder reactions

In Chapter 5, *stakeholder mapping* (Exhibit 5.5) was presented as a way of understanding the political context and prioritising the 'political agenda' for an organisation. Therefore, stakeholder mapping can be useful in understanding the likely reactions of stakeholders to new strategies, the ability to manage these reactions, and hence the acceptability of a strategy.

There are many situations where judgements of stakeholder reactions could be crucial. For example:

● A new strategy might require a substantial issue of *new shares*, which could be unacceptable to powerful groups of shareholders, since it dilutes their voting power.

● Plans to *merge* with other companies or to *trade* with new countries could be unacceptable to unions, government or some customers.

● A new e-commerce business model might cut out *channels* (such as retailers), hence running the risk of a backlash, which could jeopardise the success of the strategy.

● Attempts to gain market share in static markets might upset the status quo to such an extent that competitors will be forced to retaliate in a way that is damaging to all parties, but which would undermine the assumptions on which a strategy's acceptability had been assessed. The most common example of this would be a price war.

Since an important issue may be the likely reactions of competitors to particular strategic changes, *game theory* should, in principle, have some use in understanding risk since it is concerned with how competitors are likely to react to any moves which a company makes (or vice versa). Game theory lays out and quantifies the costs and benefits of the various combinations of the company moves and competitor reactions and was discussed in detail in Chapter 7 (section 7.5). Both governments and telecom companies allegedly used game theory to guide their bidding for the so-called third generation mobile telephone licences in Europe in 2000. Of course, the winners were governments as licences brought in £22 billion in the UK alone.

8.4.3 Feasibility

Feasibility is concerned with whether an organisation has the resources and competences to deliver a strategy

Feasibility is concerned with whether an organisation has the resources and competences to deliver a strategy. A number of approaches can be used to understand feasibility.

Financial feasibility

A useful way of assessing financial feasibility is *funds flow forecasting*,[30] which seeks to identify the funds which would be required for any strategy and the likely sources of those funds, as shown in Illustration 8.9.

Illustration 8.9

STRATEGY IN ACTION

Funds flow analysis: a worked example

A funds flow analysis can be used to assess whether a proposed strategy is likely to be feasible in financial terms. It does this by forecasting the funds which would be required for the strategy and the likely sources of those funds.

Kentex plc (a UK electrical goods retailer) was considering pursuing a strategy of expansion which in the immediate future would involve opening new stores in the Irish Republic. To evaluate the financial feasibility of this proposal and establish what funds would be required and how these funds may be sourced, the company decided to undertake a funds flow analysis.

Stage 1: Identification of sources

Opening of the new stores was estimated to increase the sales revenue from the current £30m to £31.65m per annum over the following three years. This was expected to generate funds from operations totalling £15m over the three years. This was the estimate of future profits corrected for non-fund items such as depreciation and represents real flow of funds into the company for a three-year period.

Stage 2: Identification of uses

There would be a number of costs associated with the new stores. First, Kentex decided to purchase rather than lease property so there would be the direct costs of the capital investment required for purchasing and fitting out the stores. This was forecast to be £13.25m. Also,

there will be additional working capital costs to cover stock, etc. This was not calculated by separate consideration of each element, e.g. stock increases, increased creditors; instead the forecasts were based on a simple pro rata adjustment. On the previous sales level of £30m a working capital level of £10m was required, so the expected increase in sales of £1.65m would require an additional £0.55m in working capital. Tax liability and expected dividend payments were estimated at £1.2m and £0.5m respectively.

Stage 3: Identification and funding of shortfall

These calculations show a shortfall in funds of £0.5m. The company then finalised the forecast by looking at alternative ways of funding the shortfall. Whilst it could raise funds through the issue of new share capital, it chose to seek a short-term loan of £0.65m. It should be noted that this in turn would incur interest payments of £0.15m over the three-year period assuming simple interest at 7.5 per cent per annum, hence leaving a net income of £0.5m.

Questions

1. Which parts of this assessment are likely to have the greatest probability of error?

2. What are the implications of your answer to question 1 for how the analysis should be presented to the decision makers?

3. How might this uncertainty influence the management of the implementation phase if approval is given?

SOURCES	£	USES	£
Funds from operations	15,000,000	New fixed assets	13,250,000
		Working capital	550,000
		Tax	1,200,000
		Dividends	500,000
Subtotal	15,000,000	Subtotal	15,500,000

Note: Shortfall between sources and uses amounting to £500,000.

Exhibit 8.9	Resource deployment – some important questions
Staying in business	• Do we lack any necessary resources? • Are we performing below threshold on any activity?
Competing successfully	• Which unique resources already exist? • Which core competences already exist? • Could better performance create a core competence? • What new resources or activities could be unique or core competences?

It should be remembered that funds flow forecasting is subject to the difficulties and errors of any method of forecasting. However, it should highlight whether a proposed strategy is likely to be feasible in financial terms and the *timing* of new funding requirements. It can normally be undertaken using a spreadsheet. This issue of funding strategic developments is an important interface between business and financial strategies and is discussed more fully in section 10.4.

Financial feasibility can also be assessed through break-even analysis,[31] which is a simple and widely used approach to assessing the feasibility of meeting targets of return (e.g. profit) and, as such, combines a parallel assessment of acceptability. It also provides an assessment of the risk of various strategies, particularly where different strategic options require markedly different cost structures.

Resource deployment[32]

Although financial feasibility is important, a wider understanding of the feasibility of *specific* strategies can be achieved by identifying the resources and competences needed for a particular strategy. For example, geographical expansion in the home market might be critically dependent on marketing and distribution expertise, together with the availability of cash to fund increased stocks. In contrast, a different strategy of developing new products to sell to current customers is dependent on engineering skills, the capability of machinery and the company's reputation for quality in new products.

A resource deployment assessment can be used judge two things (as discussed in Chapter 4 and shown in Exhibit 8.9): first, the extent to which an organisation's current resources and competences would need to change to reach or maintain the threshold requirements for a strategy, and second, the unique resources and core competences required to sustain competitive advantage. The issue is whether these changes are *feasible* in terms of scale, quality of resource or time-scale of change.

The final section of the book will look at the practical issues of translating strategy into action. In practice, the implementation of strategies may throw up issues which might make organisations reconsider whether particular strategic options are, in fact, feasible. This may lead to a reshaping, or even abandonment, of strategic options.

SUMMARY

- A development strategy for the future has three elements: the broad *competition strategy* (already discussed in Chapter 7), the *direction* of development and the *method* of development. These three elements must be compatible with each other.

- Development directions can be identified in four broad categories; *protect* and *build* (current products in current markets); *product development* (for existing markets); *market development* (with existing products); and *diversification* (away from existing products and markets).

- An organisation's *competences* and the *expectations* in and around the organisation will also create (or limit) development directions. For example, core competences may provide a basis on which to develop into new arenas provided an organisation can establish its credibility in that new arena.

- For any development direction there is a further element of strategy – the *method* of development (*internal* development, *acquisition* or *joint* development).

- Internal development has the major benefit of building organisational competences through learning. However, it can result in overstretched resources and the loss of the advantages of specialisation.

- Mergers and acquisitions are a common method of development, largely because of speed and the ability to acquire competences not already held 'in-house'. However, the track record of acquisitions is not good, largely owing to cultural differences and a failure of the 'parent' to understand (and influence) the businesses it has acquired.

- Strategic alliances have many different forms and are an increasingly popular method of development. The most successful alliances appear to be those where partners have positive attitudes to managing and developing the partnership. In particular, there is trust between partners in both the competence and the integrity of each party.

- The success or failure of strategies will be related to three main *success criteria*: suitability, acceptability and feasibility.

- Suitability is concerned with whether a strategy addresses the circumstances in which the organisation is operating – the strategic position as discussed in Part II of this book. It is about the *rationale* of a strategy.

- The acceptability of a strategy relates to three issues: the expected *return* from a strategy, the level of *risk* and the likely *reaction of stakeholders*. There are no absolute standards as to what constitutes a good or poor return or what is an acceptable level of risk. It will differ between industries, countries and also between different stakeholders.

- Feasibility is concerned with whether an organisation has the resources and competences to deliver a strategy. It is important to assess the organisation's capability to deliver a strategy – in terms of all the resources and competences needed to succeed. Financial measures can assist as part of this assessment. Feasibility is also informed by implementation of a strategy. So strategies may need to be reshaped as implementation proceeds.

RECOMMENDED KEY READINGS

● M.E. Porter, *Competitive Advantage*, Free Press, 1985, discusses the logic of how strategies can be chosen dependent on the situation of the organisation.

● A good discussion of the reasons for, and problems with, mergers and acquisitions can be found in D. Jemison and P. Haspeslagh, *Managing Acquisitions: Creating value through corporate renewal*, Free Press, 1991, and A. Grundy, *Breakthrough Strategies for Growth*, Pitman, 1995.

● A useful book on strategic alliances is Y. Doz and G. Hamel, *Alliance Advantage*, Harvard Business School Press, 1998.

● A companion book which explores techniques more fully is V. Ambrosini with G. Johnson and K. Scholes (eds), *Exploring Techniques of Analysis and Evaluation in Strategic Management*, Prentice Hall, 1998. See, for example, the chapter on shareholder value analysis by R. Mills.

● Useful texts on financial analyses for both strategic analysis and strategy evaluation are: A.N. Grundy with G. Johnson and K. Scholes, *Exploring Strategic Financial Management*, Prentice Hall, 1998, and J. Ellis and D. Williams, *Corporate Strategy and Financial Analysis*, Pitman, 1993.

REFERENCES

1. This figure is an extension of the product/market matrix: see H. Ansoff, *Corporate Strategy*, Penguin, 1988, Chapter 6.

2. E. Fenton and A. Pettigrew, 'Theoretical perspectives on new forms of organising', in A. Pettigrew and E. Fenton (eds), *The Innovating Organisation*, Sage, 2000, cite 'downscoping' as a major factor that has driven changes in how organisations are structured and organised. Whether downsizing delivers results has been questioned in: W. McKinley, C. Sanchez and A. Schick, 'Organisational downsizing: constraining, cloning, learning', *Academy of Management Executive*, vol. 6, no. 3 (1995), pp. 32–44.

3. The PIMS data are collected from organisations which subscribe to the services offered by the Strategic Planning Institute. The data shown here are aggregate data, but subscribers are able to access data more specific to their industry sector. More details of the PIMS methodology can be found in R.D. Buzzell and B.T. Gale, *The PIMS Principles*, Free Press, 1987.

4. PIMS, 'Marketing: in pursuit of the perfect mix', *Marketing*, 31 October 1991.

5. A. Clayton and C. Carroll, 'Building business for Europe', *Panorama of EU Industry*, 1995. This was a study of competitiveness undertaken jointly by PIMS Associates and the Irish Management Institute for the European Commission.

6. Data-mining is discussed in: B. Gates, *Business @ the Speed of Thought*, Penguin, 1999, pp. 225–233.

7. For a full discussion of building global market participation, see G. Yip, *Total Global Strategy*, Prentice Hall, 1995, Chapter 3.

8. See Yip (reference 7 above), Chapter 4.

9. References on diversification can be found in section 6.5.

10. G. Muller-Stewens, 'Catching the right wave', *European Business Forum*, issue 4, Winter 2000, pp. 6–7, illustrates the major waves of mergers over the last 100 years.

11. *The Sunday Times*, 7 January 2001 ('Top deals in 2001').

12. R. Schoenberg and R. Reeves, 'What determines acquisition activity within an industry?', *European Management Journal*, vol. 17, no. 1 (1999), pp. 93–98.

13. Useful discussions of the reasons for, and problems with, mergers and acquisitions can be found in D. Jemison and P. Haspeslagh, *Managing Acquisitions: Creating value through corporate renewal*, Free Press, 1991; P. Haspeslagh, 'Maintaining momentum in mergers', *European Business Forum*, issue 4, Winter 2000, pp. 53–56: B. Savill and P. Wright, 'Success factors in acquisitions', *European Business Forum*, issue 4, Winter 2000, pp. 29–33. R. Schoenberg, 'Knowledge transfer and resource sharing as value creation mechanisms in inbound continental European acquisitions', *Journal of Euromarketing*, vol. 9, no. 4 (2001). A practical guide for managers is: T. Galpin and M. Herndon, *The Complete Guide to Mergers and Acquisitions*, Jossey-Bass, 2000.

14. See: Haspeslagh, and Savill and Wright (both from reference 7 above); R. Schoenberg, 'The influence of cultural compatibility within cross-border acquisitions: a review', *Advances in Mergers and Acquisitions*, vol. 1, (2000), pp. 43–59; S. Sudarsanam, P. Holl and A. Salami (1996) 'Shareholder wealth gains in mergers: effect of synergy and ownership structure', *Journal of Business Finance and Accounting*, Vol. 23, pp. 673–698. A. Gregory, 'An examination of the long term performance of UK acquiring firms', *Journal of Business Finance and Accounting*, vol. 24 (1997), pp. 971–1002; G. Bruton, B. Oviatt and M. White, 'Performance

of acquisition of distressed firms', *Academy of Management Journal*, vol. 37, no. 4 (1994), pp. 972–989; A. Cannella and D. Hambrick, 'Effects of executive departures on the performance of acquired firms', *Strategic Management Journal*, vol. 14 (Summer 1993), pp. 137–152; R. Larsson and S. Finkelstein (1999) 'Integrating strategic, organisational, and human resource perspectives on mergers and acquisitions: a case survey of synergy realization', *Organization Science*, Vol. 10, no. 1, pp. 1–26.

15. Useful books on strategic alliances are: Y. Doz and G. Hamel, *Alliance Advantage*, Harvard Business School Press, 1998; D. Faulkner, *Strategic Alliances: Co-operating to compete*, McGraw-Hill, 1995; and P. Lorange and J. Roos, *Strategic Alliances: Formation, implementation and evolution*, Blackwell, 1992. A practical guide for managers is: E. Rigsbee, *Developing Strategic Alliances*, Crisp, 2000. See also: J. Whipple and R. Frankel, 'Strategic alliance success factors', *Journal of Supply Chain Management*, vol. 39, no. 3 (2000), pp. 21–31.

16. Doz and Hamel (reference 15 above) p. 6.

17. See: Doz and Hamel (reference 15 above, Chapters 1 and 2; M. Koza and A. Lewin, 'The co-evolution of strategic alliances', *Organisation Science*, vol. 9, no. 3 (1998), pp. 255–264.

18. See: J. Brudney and R. England, 'Towards a definition of the co-production concept', *Public Administration Review*, vol. 43, no. 10 (1983), pp. 59–65, and J. Alford, 'A public management road less travelled: clients as co-producers of public services', *Australian Journal of Public Administration*, vol. 57, no. 4 (1998), pp. 128–137.

19. See: J. Wind and V. Mahajan, *Digital Marketing: Global strategies from the world's leading experts*, Wiley, 2001.

20. S. Hill, 'Public sector partnerships and public/voluntary sector partnerships: the Scottish experience', in G. Johnson and K. Scholes (eds), *Exploring Public Sector Strategy*, Financial Times/Prentice Hall, 2001, Chapter 12.

21. R. Butler and J. Gill, 'Formation and control of public–private partnerships: a stakeholder approach', in G. Johnson and K. Scholes (eds), *Exploring Public Sector Strategy*, Financial Times/Prentice Hall, 2001, Chapter 11.

22. See reference 15 above.

23. For a companion book which explores techniques more fully, see V. Ambrosini with G. Johnson and K. Scholes (eds), *Exploring Techniques of Analysis and Evaluation in Strategic Management*, Prentice Hall, 1998.

24. Useful texts on financial analyses for both strategic analysis and strategy evaluation are: A.N. Grundy with G. Johnson and K. Scholes, *Exploring Strategic Financial Management*, Prentice Hall, 1998, and J. Ellis and D. Williams, *Corporate Strategy and Financial Analysis*, Pitman, 1993.

25. Cost-benefit analysis is discussed in A. Williams and E. Giardina, *Efficiency in the Public Sector: The theory and practice of cost-benefit analysis*, Edward Elgar, 1993. (Despite the title, the book covers the private sector too.)

26. T. Luehrman, 'Strategy as a portfolio of real options', *Harvard Business Review*, vol. 76, no. 5 (1998), pp. 89–99.

27. The main proponent of shareholder value analysis was A. Rappaport, *Creating Shareholder Value: The new standard for business performance*, Free Press, 1986. See also J. Kay, *Foundations of Corporate Success*, Oxford University Press, 1993, Chapter 13, and A. Grundy, *Breakthrough Strategies via Growth*, Pitman, 1995. See also R. Mill's chapter, 'Understanding and using shareholder value analysis', in V. Ambrosini with G. Johnson and K. Scholes (see reference 23), Chapter 15.

28. See Ellis and Williams (reference 24 above), Part III.

29. Computer spreadsheets are ideally suited for sensitivity analysis. Ellis and Williams (reference 24 above) give an example on pp. 348–349 in relation to share price.

30. See Ellis and Williams (reference 24 above), pp. 188–193, for a discussion of the funding of strategies.

31. Break-even analysis is covered in most standard accountancy texts. See, for example, E. McLaney and P. Atrill, *Accounting: an Introduction*, Prentice Hall, 1999.

32. This relates to the idea of 'resource-based strategies' discussed in Chapter 4. Useful references are B. Wernerfelt, 'A resource-based view of the firm', *Strategic Management Journal*, vol. 5, no. 2 (1984), pp. 171–180, and D. Collis and C. Montgomery, 'Competing on resources: strategy in the 1990s', *Harvard Business Review*, vol. 73, no. 4 (1995), pp. 118–128; M. Peteraf, 'The cornerstones of competitive advantage: a resource-based view', *Strategic Management Journal*, vol. 14, no. 3 (1993), p. 179.

WORK ASSIGNMENTS

* Refers to a case study in the Text and Cases edition. ✻ Denotes more advanced work assignments.

8.1 Identify possible development strategies in terms of their combination of *direction* and *method* of development in one of the following:

(a) Barclaycard*
(b) Coopers Creek*
(c) an organisation of your choice.

8.2 In the case of Lonely Planet, Barclaycard* or an organisation of your choice, write a brief for the management explaining how the PIMS findings in Illustration 8.2 should influence their choice of strategies.

8.3 ✻ Referring to sections 8.3.2 and 6.3.3 and using additional examples of your own, criticise the argument that 'synergy is a sound basis for acquisition'.

8.4 Write a short (one paragraph) statement to a chief executive who has asked you to advise whether or not the company should develop through mergers/acquisitions. Write a similar statement to the chief executive of a hospital who is considering possible mergers with other hospitals.

8.5 ✻ 'Strategic alliances will not survive in the long term if they are simply seen as ways of "blocking gaps" in an organisation's resource base or competences.' Discuss this in relation to any alliances which have recently featured in the business press.

8.6 Undertake a ranking analysis of the choices available to Coopers Creek,* Barclaycard,* W.H. Smith* or an organisation of your choice similar to that shown in Illustration 8.5.

8.7 ✻ Bearing in mind your answers to the questions in Illustration 8.7:

(a) What is your feeling about the overall 'validity' of cost–benefit analysis?
(b) How could it be improved?

8.8 Using Illustration 8.8 as an example, what would you propose as the most important parameters to include in a sensitivity analysis in the case of each of the following organisations?

(a) The News Corporation*
(b) Sheffield Theatres*
(c) Barclaycard*
(d) an organisation of your choice.

8.9 ✻ Using examples from your answer to previous assignments, make a critical appraisal of the statement that 'Strategic choice is, in the end, a highly subjective matter. It is dangerous to believe that, in reality, analytical techniques will ever change this situation.' Refer to the commentary at the end of Part III of the book.

CASE EXAMPLE

Lonely Planet Publications:
Personal passion to business success

By the beginning of the 21st century Lonely Planet had come a long way from the husband and wife operation working on a kitchen table in 1972. The company produced more than 350 titles (some of which were in their ninth edition), covering some of the most inaccessible regions in the world. It employed nearly 300 staff in four offices in three continents, though the largest proportion were employed in Melbourne, Australia, where the company continued to undertake the production of most of its English-language books. Titles covering the Americas, Caribbean, Micronesia and Antarctica were produced in the US office. Lonely Planet also had more than 100 contracted authors and an annual turnover of some A$40m. The financial performance of Lonely Planet was impressive by almost any measure. During the 1990s the company enjoyed rapid growth and high profitability. For example, in 1998 sales were up 22 per cent over the previous year's A$27 million. Over 90 per cent of sales came from guidebooks (Shoestrings and Travel Survival Kits), the remainder coming from its newer lines such as city guides and phrase books, diving guides, atlases and travel literature. Each year, Lonely Planet donated a percentage of its profits to organisations which benefit the people and places it covers. In the past, contributions have been made to famine relief organisations in Africa, health care co-operatives in Central and South America and environmental groups working to stop nuclear testing in the Pacific.

In spite of the change in the nature of the organisation as it grew, the books retained their chatty style and practical format, with much material being sent in from backpackers on the road.

Early days

A newly married English couple, Tony and Maureen Wheeler, had founded the company after walking, hitching and backpacking their way to Australia in 1972. Soon the numerous 'how did you do it?' enquiries inspired them to write down their travel experiences and produce a 'cut and paste' publication called *Across Asia on the Cheap*. It was an instant success, which encouraged them to postpone their return to England and return to their first love of being 'on the road'. Tony Wheeler reflected on the early successes: 'Now I can look back and think that was a really clever idea, but at the time I didn't realise it. It was just a nice thing to do. As soon as we saw how well the first book went, we thought "Lets do another". We grew very slowly at first. It took us five years to get to ten titles.'

Jim Hart: a new partner

The year 1980 was an important one for Lonely Planet. Jim Hart, a friend of the Wheelers, with a mixture of travel and publishing experience, joined Lonely Planet from a major publishing house in Adelaide, South Australia. With Jim's involvement, the Wheelers' shoestring operation gradually took on more permanence, allowing them more time to travel and to undertake the intensive year-long research effort necessary for the production of an India guide. When the first edition of *India: A Travel Survival Kit* came out in 1981, it marked a major turning point for Lonely Planet. Previously, books priced at A$3.95 had sold up to 30,000 copies: by 1981 books priced at A$14.95 sold 100,000 copies. The India guidebook provided the steady income desperately needed for the company to finance its operations. By the time Jim joined, Tony and Maureen had already established the Lonely Planet name and set up the beginning of an international distribution system. With Jim's involvement and with the publication of the India guide, Tony and Maureen could look forward to a period of stability.

In 1984/85 they set up a US office, which proved to be both difficult and costly. Nonetheless, it eventually worked, and in 1991 they were ready for further international expansion. The UK was the natural choice given the English language and its proximity to Continental European markets too.

This expansion into Europe was another major test for the company. Lonely Planet, had created a name for itself by publishing guidebooks to the world's more out-of-the-way places, and did not have an image as a provider of travel information about the industrialised countries of the West. Lonely Planet expected to meet fierce competition in the European market, which was dominated by the big American-produced guides.

In 1993, heartened by its UK experience, Lonely Planet set up an office in France. The French office marked a significant development for the company in that, unlike its other overseas offices, its role was not limited to promotion and distribution but included production of French translations. It also marked the company's first attempt to diversify into non-English-speaking markets and to control the content, presentation and marketing of its products and brand in those markets. Until this time, Lonely Planet had considered itself to be exclusively an English-language publisher. Foreign publishers had undertaken the translation of its books into other languages under various licensing arrangements.

On the road again: the Wheelers in the 1990s

Whilst continuing to run the business, much of the Wheelers' time was still spent on the road researching, which they described as 'dawn to dusk hard work and not without some annoyances'. Typically they travelled overseas half-a-dozen times a year, investigating new places, double-checking facts from one of their books, or simply enjoying life on the road.

The primary passion of the Wheelers was always to produce good travel information. Profit was important, but mainly because it was the means to grow and do more for travellers.

Publishing industry changes

The move towards global consolidation of publishing interests appeared to be part of the large players' corporate strategies. Control of newspapers, printing works, film libraries and production, databases, book retailing and publishing, radio and television broadcasting, satellite television and magazines began to converge in the expectation of massive economies of scale.

These global companies were also at the forefront of the implementation of new technologies that offered the possibility of increasing audience size and, hence, further levering the returns from their information stores. In this climate, smaller publishers survived by catering for specialist markets, which the large corporates could not service economically.

There were also important changes in distribution channels. In the late 1980s, the owner-operators of independent bookstores dominated the market numerically. In Australia, for instance, 75–80 per cent of bookstores were owner-operated stores or were small chains with two to five stores. The majority of these were not commercially aggressive and books were generally sold at the publisher's recommended retail price. This pricing structure was supported by a 100-year-old international publishing cartel. Book retailers competed on the basis of convenience and service rather than price.

By the early 1990s, however, bookstore chains and large department stores were becoming increasingly dominant in the book-retailing segment throughout the world. Book superstores had emerged in the USA to compete with discount stores – Wal-Mart alone had 18 per cent of the US book retail market. These stores were very commercially oriented. They offered a wide selection of books, and their size and buying power allowed them to negotiate large margins with publishers, who often had no choice but to comply or be denied access to their readers. Lower prices were in part passed on to consumers through heavy discounting of many titles.

Technology was changing too. The basic concept of presenting prepackaged information via the printed page in book form, the primary method of communicating information since the invention of the printing press, was being challenged. Further, the Internet allowed virtually free access to information from anywhere in the world and, significantly for Lonely Planet with its two-year recycle time, allowed users to gain instant access to current information (for example on current train timetables and weather patterns).

Lonely Planet went its own way in developing applications in response to these rapid developments in technology. In 1994 it had gathered a small group of editors and cartographers to develop applications for a Lonely Planet Internet site. In a few months, this group of half-a-dozen 'experimenters' had developed what became one the largest Internet sites in Australia. By the late 1990s the website was receiving 6 million hits per month and Lonely Planet was also providing travel information to other major sites such as Yahoo!, Travelocity and AOL.

Into the 21st century

Lonely Planet attributed its success to a large range of titles, brand loyalty and the best form of advertising that accompanied the loyalty: word of mouth. Lonely Planet guidebooks were thoroughly revised every two to three years on average. By contrast, most of the company's competitors updated only small sections of their books, some on a yearly basis. Each Lonely Planet book was in a constant state of revision.

Most printing and binding of finished books was done in Hong Kong and Singapore. Apart from cost considerations and delivery time to major overseas markets, printers had to be able to 'section sew' books. This type of binding, which prevents pages from falling out and book spines from being broken, guaranteed that Lonely Planet books stood up to the hard treatment that they receive on the road.

Whilst Lonely Planet initially covered far-flung destinations for budget travellers, its scope had widened to cover the most popular spots and to offer good-value options for travellers of all ranges. The typical Lonely Planet reader was now hard to define by age or income. Lonely Planet built its reputation covering Asia, Africa and Latin America, but with new travel guides, videos and phrasebooks on Europe and the USA, Lonely Planet has now covered the entire globe.

Between editions, travellers can access instant online updates through 'Upgrades', which can be downloaded at no charge from the company's website. These online supplements extend the usefulness of existing guidebooks. Whilst Lonely Planet's main product continued to be guidebooks, the company's product offerings had been greatly extended and included: travel guides, shoestring guides, condensed guides, French language editions, phrasebooks, walking guides, cycling guides, wildlife guides, diving and snorkelling guides, first time travel guides, healthy travel guides, travel journal, world food guides, restaurant guides, illustrated pictorial books, videos, travel atlases, city maps, and free newsletters. They also had non-print products such as videos, Internet content and an online photo service, 'Lonely Planet Images', which was the largest travel-exclusive online photo library in the world. Lonely Planet's extensive travel information resources were also customised for use by other companies and organisations – for example, American Express and Swiss Air.

Lonely Planet had also focused on integrating content on the Internet and developing mapping capabilites to provide geographical data in digital and print form. They saw themselves as a travel information provider, not just a guidebook publisher. This had required an ongoing assessment of how to capture, store and communicate information and a commitment to seeking better and faster ways to deliver and receive that information. Lonely Planet offered many such products and services, including its online Upgrades, 'CitySync', which let travellers use their Palm or Visor handheld computer to quickly search and sort hundreds of detailed hotel and restaurant reviews, major sights, shopping and entertainment options – all pinpointed on scrollable street maps in major cities; and 'eKno' – a communication card for travellers with low phone rates, free e-mail, and a toll-free voicemail service.

A valuable asset

Lonely Planet's successes attracted the attention of the corporate giants of the publishing industry. During the late 1980s the Wheelers began to receive lucrative buyout offers from a number of large organisations, including the software giant Microsoft, with an approach about joint development of multimedia travel publications. Although flattered by Microsoft's interest, Tony, Maureen and Jim declined the offer, feeling that an association with such a large and powerful organisation could compromise Lonely Planet's independence. As Tony said, 'It really felt like we would be going to bed with an elephant and if it rolled over we would be crushed'. When asked why they didn't 'take the money and run', Maureen said: 'I don't know if I'd like to travel without a reason, and I really, really like the books we do. I always did, right from the very first book. On a day-to-day basis, I really like all the people who work here, and who still enjoy working here. I suppose I just love the books.'

Sources: Adapted from 'Lonely Planet Publications' in G. Lewis, A. Morkel and G. Hubbard, *Australian and New Zealand Strategic Management: Concepts, context and cases*, Prentice Hall, 1998; the company website www.lonelyplanet.com

Questions

1. Refer to Exhibit 8.1 and section 8.2 and describe in chronological order the development directions taken by Lonely Planet between 1972 and 2001.

2. Why were other directions *not* pursued?

3. Repeat the analysis in relation to methods of development (refer to section 8.3).

4. What are the choices on direction and method of development for the period ahead? Which would you recommend? Why?

COMMENTARY ON PART

III

Strategy Selection

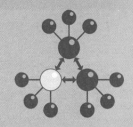

The theme of the chapters in Part III has been 'strategic choices'. The chapters have discussed the sorts of strategic choice that organisations have to make and what evidence there is about what leads to success. However, there has been little mention of *how* such choices are made: just how a particular strategy ends up being the one followed by an organisation. This commentary takes this question as its theme and uses the three different lenses to offer explanations of what might, therefore, be termed *strategy selection*.

A design view of strategy selection

Those who take a highly rationalistic approach to strategic management tend to take a linear and often top-down view of strategy selection. The organisation's objectives, quantified where possible, are used as yardsticks by which options are assessed (for example, whether strategies are likely to meet predetermined targets for return on capital or market share). Options are made explicit and cases made for them on the basis of an analysis of the environment (Chapter 3) and capabilities of the organisation (Chapter 4). They are then systematically evaluated, perhaps using the types of evaluation framework discussed in Chapter 8, with the aim of providing 'answers' regarding the relative merits of different courses of action and of coming up with the best strategy as the one that meets objectives and stands the tests of suitability, feasibility and acceptability explained in Chapter 8. Here, then, strategy selection is an entirely rational matter. The assumption also tends to be that it is top management doing this; or people appointed by them to do it, for example consultants or specialist strategic planners.

This view is appealing: it is logical, analytical and should give rational and informed answers. However, the problems discussed in the commentary on Part II remain. Managers do not have access to perfect information, they cannot know the future, objectives are rarely unambiguous because there are multiple stakeholders and managers themselves are not merely dispassionate analysts. It is more realistic to see strategy selection by design in a more moderated form.

Formal planning and systematic analysis and evaluation of strategies should not be regarded as an exclusive process through which strategies are selected, but they can be valuable tools. So the critical issue for strategic managers is to ensure that an organisation's planning and evaluation activities assist, however strategy selection takes place. For example, *sensitivity analysis* (section 8.4.2 above) is a useful technique for allowing decision makers to understand the risks and uncertainties surrounding specific strategies, but it does not select strategies for those decision makers. Formal planning systems used appropriately might involve people in the organisation in thinking through strategy and therefore can be a useful means of *raising the level of debate* amongst a wider group of decision makers or people who may influence decisions about the eventual strategy followed. *Scenario planning* can get people not only thinking about uncertain futures, but challenging preconceptions they might have about what strategy their organisation should follow in the future. *Option theory* provides means of evaluating and monitoring strategic options as they develop – it quite literally allows organisations to keep options open. *Game theory* requires people to put themselves in the place of their competitors and think options through from their point of view as well as their own, again potentially challenging preconceptions about the strategy to follow. *Strategy workshops* or future search conferences which employ any of these analytic tools can fulfil a similar purpose and allow many more people in the organisation to contribute to the quality of thinking about future strategies.

Much of what has been discussed in Chapters 6, 7 and 8 are, then, concepts, models and tools which allow and encourage rational, analytic thinking. However, this is not just about top-down planning of strategy; it is as much to do with enriching discussions and debates about the strategy of organisations; and therefore about strategic thinking and learning.[1] If this moderated view about the contribution of these approaches is taken, then the question of how strategies are actually selected still remains. The concepts, tools and techniques discussed so far may contribute to the processes by which strategy selection takes place: but it would be simplistic to suggest that they are *the* means of strategy selection. So it is useful to look at different explanations of this.

Strategy selection and experience

The experience lens sees organisations in terms of individual and collective experience. It positions individual judgement and the influence of organisational culture as more central; and sees political processes as ways in which such differences may be reconciled.

Selection by doing: the logical incrementalist view

If selection does not take place as part of a formal planning process or by means of a particular evaluative device, this does not, of itself, necessarily mean there is an absence of rationality. Managers in organisations know well enough that it is impossible to plan everything up-front. Strategy selection often occurs 'in the doing'. For example, a retailer introduces a new range of products in some stores and monitors their success: if they succeed they are extended to other stores: if they fail, they are dropped. E-commerce businesses do not try to plan up-front all possible new developments – it would be impossible in the turbulent world in which they exist; but managers of such businesses would argue that they may, for example, look for acquisition opportunities of new start-up businesses with the very rational purpose of developing new options for the future. The corporate centre of a multinational may monitor local initiatives for ones which might be potential winners internationally. This may then be followed by a geographical region's being encouraged to test the wider acceptability of the innovation with modifications required for different local circumstances. If this proves successful, the innovation could then be adopted internationally. The selection of these strategies has not necessarily been the result of a detailed formal planning process but of experimentation and learning by doing. What works is developed further; what does not, is not. It is, however, considered and intentional, corresponding to what was referred to in Chapter 2 as *logical incrementalism.*[2] Furthermore, it could be that analytic tools are used as part of the selection process at any of the stages in the experimentation process as a way of checking *why* a strategy might be worth following or developing. Of course, it is also possible that a strategy developed in such a way might eventually be built into a formal strategic plan, which is a statement of the future direction of the organisation; but this is not the same as saying that the plan gave rise to or played a central part in selecting, the strategy.

The role of cultural and political processes

Studies which have traced how particular strategic decisions are made in organisations[3] show how cultural and political processes play an important part in strategy selection. They also show that it is difficult to separate out selection as a distinct process as it occurs in practice (see Exhibit IIIii). Selection needs to be seen as part of an iterative process much more based on experience and cultural and political processes in organisations.

The *awareness* of strategic issues is not necessarily an analytical process; rather, people get a 'gut feeling' based on their previous experience or received wisdom. This awareness 'incubates' as various stimuli help build up a picture of the extent to which circumstances deviate from what is normally to be expected, perhaps in terms of internal performance measures such as turnover or profit performance; or perhaps customer reaction to the quality and price of service or products. This accumulation of stimuli eventually reaches a point where the presence of a problem cannot be ignored. Typically, a *triggering point* is reached when the formal information systems of the organisation highlight the problem; a variance against budget becomes undeniable or a number of sales areas consistently report dropping sales. At this stage, however, issues may still be ill-defined.

Issue formulation involves information gathering, but not always in a highly structured, objective manner. Information is gathered on a verbal and informal basis, perhaps supplemented by more formal analysis. However, making sense of information draws heavily on *experience* – individual and collective – and the assumptions encapsulated in the paradigm. The role of information generated from analysis is often to post-rationalise or legitimise managers' emerging views of the situation.

Exhibit IIIii | **Phases of strategic decision making**

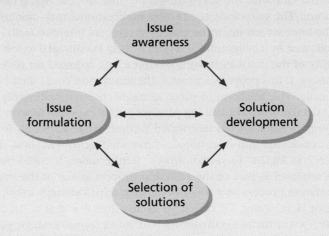

Through *debate and discussion* there may be an attempt to reach an organisational view on the problem to be tackled. An emerging view therefore takes shape in terms of both individual and collective experience, with different views resolved through political processes of negotiation. It may also be that these processes of issue formulation trigger a different problem. So the process tends to be iterative.

In *developing solutions*, managers typically 'search' for known, existing or tried solutions; or wait for possible solutions to emerge, drawing on their experience. Managers begin with a rather vague idea of a possible solution and refine it by recycling it through selection routines (see below) back into problem identification or through further search routines. The process is again based on debate and discussion and collective management wisdom and experience.

The process of developing solutions therefore overlaps with processes of *selecting solutions*. A number of potential solutions get reduced until one or more emerges. It is not formal analysis which plays the major role, but judgement, negotiation and bargaining. It should also be remembered that the process might well be taking place below the most senior levels of management, so referring possible solutions to a higher hierarchical level may be required; indeed, another way of selecting between possibilities may be to seek such *authorisation*.

Studies of how strategic decisions are made therefore suggest that they emerge as the *outcome* of managerial experience within a social, political and cultural context, even if formal planning procedures exist; and in this process the individual and collective experience of managers plays an important role.

In some respects, this is reflected in the different ways in which many organisations now set about the development of strategy. For example, there has been a substantial growth of *strategy workshops*, typically for groups of senior managers, perhaps the board of an organisation, in which participants remove themselves from day-to-day responsibilities to tackle strategic issues facing their organisation. Such events may well employ the sorts of techniques of analysis and planning described in this book. However, rather than just relying on these to throw up strategic solutions, a successful workshop process works through issues in face-to-face debate and discussion, drawing on and surfacing different experiences, interests and views.

Mimicry and the institutionalisation of strategies

Researchers who look at patterns of strategies followed by organisations add a different dimension to this. They point to the evidence that a great deal of similarity of strategies exists between organisations within organisational fields; strategies become institutionalised. For example, professional service firms such as accountants and lawyers follow similar strategies; retailers follow similar strategies; so too do universities, and so on. A number of observations arise.

First, this may be because the individual and collective experience of managers in organisations tends to be from within those organisational fields (see section 5.5.2); they have common experience, compete according to the same sorts of 'rules', and therefore follow similar strategies.[4] Second, it may make a lot of sense for one organisation to mimic a successful strategy of another; so there develops an 'orthodoxy' of strategy: this was pointed out in section 7.3.6. Third, mimicry may not be so much to do with imitating success as striving for legitimacy. Universities strive for research excellence because it is commonly accepted that that is what universities are about. The major firms of accountants have all been trying to develop globally: no doubt there are economically reasoned arguments for this, but there is also the fear that without doing so they would cease to be taken seriously as 'a major player'.

Another explanation for such similarities of strategies being followed across organisations is the faddish nature of strategic logic. In the 1980s the emphasis, for example, was on competing on the basis of finding suitable markets in which to do so. This was the result of a marketing orthodoxy of the time and, more specifically, Porter's work on competitive forces at work in markets. In the 1990s the emphasis swung towards the importance of core competences, unique to the organisation upon which competitive advantage can be built. In the 1980s everyone was sure of the wisdom of the former; in the 1990s they became convinced of the wisdom of the latter. Since at any one time, everyone seems to have been convinced of the wisdom of one or the other, there was a general uniformity about the very bases and questions being asked about competitive strategy.

All of this suggests that it is the tendency of organisations to conform, to follow the strategy being followed by others, especially if that is successful: so another explanation of strategy selection is that it is to do with mimicry and organisational legitimacy. This is not to say that those involved in strategic management in organisations might not talk as though choice will be made about real differences which bestow real advantages; in other words, they may employ the rhetoric of competitive strategy and differentiation, and may use tools of analysis and evaluation as part of that rhetoric, but in the end for many organisations the strategy selected will be on the basis of conformity.

The ideas lens: strategy selection or evolution?

Much of what has been said so far suggests the strong influence of forces for conformity: careful analysis or the influence of experience. As the researchers in institutional theory point out, innovation is not common; similarity is. And there is little evidence that the formal planned design of strategies gives rise to innovation. When it occurs, how then do more innovative strategies get selected; and how are the activities of more innovative organisations to be explained? The discussion above, describing how experimentation and logical incrementalism occur, is a useful starting point. Here there is less emphasis on selection at a point in time or, indeed, formal evaluation, and more emphasis on the emergence of a strategy through tentative steps, driven as much by people from within the organisation as by people at the top of it.

Both complexity theorists and evolutionary theorists argue that innovation tends to arise from below (though they differ somewhat in their explanations of how it occurs). It is not top-down planning that creates innovation; it is activity within an organisation. New ideas tend to arise more through entre-preneurial behaviour than through plans. To borrow from previous examples, a small business unit within a multinational might come up with new ideas; or a new e-business might develop a product or service that is sufficiently attrac-tive in a market for it to develop to a size where it might be bought out by a bigger one. One way of thinking about this is that such innovations succeed to the extent that they 'fit' an opportunity in a wider environment. However, innovation can also be seen as evolving in tandem with the environment itself. As the environment changes, most obviously the market, so new ideas emerge; some get picked up and some do not through the selection processes explained through the experience lens. In this sense, the ideas and innovations are part of the very environment in which they exist – the idea of co-evolution.[5]

Another explanation of how such innovation comes about is through the collaboration and networking between individuals and organisations. It is not tight, mechanistic organisations that are innovatory, but rather organisations that foster 'weak ties' and networks. This is, of course, evident in the social relations between people. It is not typically the formal meetings and gather-ings that give rise to the energy that sparks ideas and new thinking, but the informal and more relaxed social activities.

Of course, it may be that in any organisation, or any community of organisa-tions, very few truly innovative products or services succeed. For every one that does, there may be many that fail. So what matters is the variety of ideas, some of which may come to fruition but many of which will not. How then does this process of innovation from below come to develop into a fully fledged organisational strategy? There are a number of explanations.

Selection of such new ideas need not be seen in formalised planning and evaluative terms. There are other, less formal, but nonetheless powerful selec-tion mechanisms.

- New ideas will be competing against powerful influences to preserve the status quo. They will have to compete within the existing culture of the organisation and that culture may reject such new ideas. There will be powerful vested interests in the preservation of the status quo. So managers and other stakeholders, collective and individual, and their experience, biases and emotions are themselves selection mechanisms. Some new initiatives will be appealing and some will not. For example, it is not unusual to see ideas associated with a better environment, or the social good, or the well-being of children, progressing faster and receiving more support than others.

- Innovations will also have to show some sign of success in some way. One way in which innovatory strategies progress is for their champions to find ways of demonstrating such success. The adoption of Post-Its® as a possibly viable product by 3M was initially the result of a failure – a glue that did not stick as it was intended to do – and its initial development was not through formal processes but by their inventor using them within 3M and building a demand for them internally within the firm, thus showing their market attractiveness.

- In addition, the sort of market experimentation described earlier as a 'logical incrementalist' approach, or trial and error, can be seen as a selection mechanism through this lens.

- And of course there will be the formal planning and budgeting processes of the organisation; and since the new idea is unlikely to be immediately profitable and could be risky, it will have to put up a good case to get over such hurdles.

Organisations therefore have selection mechanisms, but not just the formal selection mechanisms conceived of in terms of rational, analytic evaluative exercises.

What, within all this, is the role of senior managers, traditionally seen as the planners and selectors of strategy? The role of top management here is to be much more aware of changes that are happening in the environment, to encourage variety within the organisation so that new ideas might emerge, suited to such changes, and to monitor those new ideas as they develop to see to what extent they are progressing and surviving and to foster those that are. In this sense they are not so much directors of strategy as coaches and 'talent spotters'. They must also know when and how to intervene in the process. For example, there could be dangers if experimentation within the parts of the organisation only results in tinkering around at the edges through a fragmented approach to innovation without ever really making fundamental evaluations or reappraisals of what is appropriate to take forward and invest in. This view of strategic choice does not, then, do away with the role of top management so much as put that role in a different perspective.

Our view

As in the commentary to Part II, our view is that these different lenses shed light and provide guidance to the issue of strategy selection in usefully different but complementary ways.

It is important to be realistic about how strategies develop and how they are selected. Strategic choice based on, or strongly influenced by, experience and cultural and political processes is the norm. This does suggest that strategies are probably better thought of as emerging rather than being selected at a point in time. It also suggests that the strong influence of experience and organisational culture can lead to problems of strategic drift (see section 2.4.2). This explanation also makes it difficult to explain how more innovative strategies come to exist, and this is where explanations are helpful from evolutionary and complexity theory since they focus attention on the generation of ideas and see cultural and political processes as selection mechanisms. Formal planning and evaluation processes can play an important part too. Not only are they another selection mechanism, but they can be means of raising challenging, analytic and evaluative questions which perform the role of changing minds, not just making plans.

REFERENCES

1. Future search conferences are discussed by M. Weisbord, *Productive Workplaces*, Jossey-Bass, 1987, p. 285.
2. See J.B. Quinn, *Strategic Change: Logical Incrementalism*, Irwin, 1980.
3. This section brings together the work of a number of researchers. For a thorough discussion of the problem of awareness and diagnosis stages of the decision-making process, see M.A. Lyles, 'Formulating strategic problems: empirical analysis and model development', *Strategic Management Journal*, vol. 2, no. 1 (1981), pp. 61–75; H. Mintzberg, O. Raisinghani and A. Theoret, 'The structure of unstructured decision processes', *Administrative Science Quarterly*, vol. 21, no. 2 (1976), pp. 246–275; and L.M. Fahey, 'On strategic management decision processes', *Strategic Management Journal*, vol. 2, no. 1 (1981), pp. 43–60.
4. The classic account of institutionalisation is by P. DiMaggio and W. Powell, 'The iron cage revisited: institutional isomorphism and collective rationality in organizational fields', *American Sociological Review*, vol. 48 (1983), pp. 147–160.
5. The idea of co-evolution of organisations is discussed in J.A.C. Baum and J.V. Singh, 'Organization-environment co-evolution', in Baum and Singh (eds), *Evolutionary Dynamics of Organization*, Oxford University Press, 1994. The same book also includes other papers on co-evolution.

PART

IV

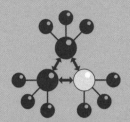

STRATEGY INTO ACTION

Understanding the strategic position of an organisation and considering the strategic choices open to it are of little value unless the strategies managers wish to follow can be turned into organisational action. Indeed, strategies cannot take effect until they take shape in action. Such action takes form in the day-to-day processes and relationships that exist in organisations; and these need to be managed, desirably in line with the intended strategy. Such processes will very likely be within resource areas or functions of the organisation; how these relate to the overall strategy is therefore important. The development of a new strategy may also require significant strategic change for the organisation. Such change does not take place simply because it is considered to be desirable; it takes place if it can be made to work and put into effect by members of the organisation. Part IV deals with the vital issues of translating strategy into action and the difficulties and methods of managing strategic change. This discussion includes a range of related issues:

- Chapter 9 is about *organising* for success. It looks at three separate strands of this topic and how they can contribute to successful strategies. These strands are organisational structures, organisational processes, and the management of relationships. The chapter reviews the various types of organisational structure and looks at the advantages and disadvantages of each one. Organisational processes are concerned with different forms of 'control' within organisations, ranging from direct supervision and centralised planning to self-control and the personal motivation of staff. The section on relationships looks at the important issue of centralisation or devolution of both strategic and operational decision making. It is also concerned with the boundaries of an organisation and how external relationships need to be established and maintained. So it includes issues such as networking, outsourcing and alliances. In discussing these topics the chapter highlights the importance in organising for success of how these various elements work together to create configurations that are well matched to an organisation's strategies.

- Chapter 10 is a new look at the relationship between an organisation's overall strategy and the strategies in four key resource areas: people, information, finance and technology. The two questions that are pursued through the chapter are these. First, whether the separate resource areas of an organisation are capable of *enabling* strategies to be executed successfully. For example, if the management of information is adequate to support a move into e-commerce activities, or whether the competences of staff and the organisational culture are in line with new strategies – perhaps a strategic alliance in a new country. The second question is whether the strategies of an organisation are being shaped to capitalise on the expertise in a particular resource area. For example, an organisation may have access to funds that its competitors do not. Or perhaps it has developed new technologies that could transform product features or reduce the cost of operational processes. Importantly, success or failure of strategies will also depend on how these separate resource areas are integrated together – for example, to support a new product launch.

● Chapter 11 examines more specifically how *strategic change* might be managed. This is done in several ways. First, by acknowledging that it is important for the means of managing change to suit an organisation's specific needs; and therefore that it is important to understand organisational change contexts and organisational barriers to change. Then by looking at the different approaches to managing change, including the styles of management and roles managers and others play in managing strategic change. Finally by considering a range of levers that can be employed to help manage change in organisations, including changes to organisational routines, the management of political and symbolic processes, the importance of communication, and other specific tactics for managing change.

This part of the book concludes by re-examining some of these themes through the three lenses of design, experience and ideas; and also by employing these to briefly review themes from the book as a whole.

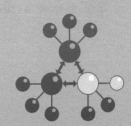

9

Organising for Success

LEARNING OUTCOMES

After reading this chapter you should be able to:

- Describe the main structural types of organisations and their strengths and weaknesses.
- Describe the most important organisational processes (such as planning systems, performance targets) and the circumstances where they will be most appropriate.
- Describe how the management of internal and external relationships might help or hinder success.
- Define centralisation and devolution.
- Describe strategic planning, financial control and strategic control and the circumstances to which they are best matched.
- Describe different types of network both within and between organisations.
- Describe how structure, processes and relationships combine to produce different configurations.
- Describe Mintzberg's six organisational configurations and how these might match to different circumstances.
- Compare and contrast different configurations of global companies.
- Define reinforcing cycles and give examples.
- Outline some common dilemmas about organising for success.

9.1 INTRODUCTION

Perhaps the most important resource of an organisation is its *people*. So the roles people play, how they interact through formal and informal processes and the relationships that they build are crucial to the success of strategy. Traditionally this has been seen as the province of organisation design, and views about regulation through organisation can be traced back to early twentieth-century management scientists and beyond.[1] These approaches were commensurate with a view of strategy making as essentially top-down and the rest of the organisation was seen as concerned with implementation. So organisation

| Exhibit 9.1 | Organising for success |

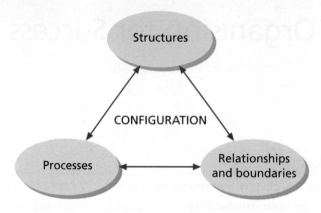

design was seen as a means of top-down control. Such principles of control are known as *bureaucratic* or *mechanistic*.[2] However, as was seen in Chapter 2 and in the commentaries at the end of each part, the idea that strategy is formulated in a top-down way is questionable, and the extension of this, that mechanistic structures and controls are necessarily appropriate, is therefore also questionable. Indeed, in a fast-moving world it is better to think about these issues of organising in an active and fluid way rather than the more static concepts of organisational design. For this reason some authors have suggested that the terminology should not be around the *noun* 'organisation' but around the *verb* 'organising', which more accurately reflects the nature of the challenge.[3]

This chapter has taken on board this important thought and the theme of the chapter is the way in which an organisation's *configuration* can help or hinder strategies. An organisation's **configuration** consists of the structures, processes, relationships and boundaries through which the organisation operates[4] – as shown in Exhibit 9.1 The early 21st century is characterised by important changes that are influencing the way that people are thinking about these organisational issues and how they are actually being lived out in practice. This chapter considers the issues of *organising for success* in the light of the following trends:

An organisation's **configuration** consists of the structures, processes, relationships and boundaries through which the organisation operates

- The *speed of change* and the increased levels of *uncertainty* in the business environment, as discussed in Chapter 3.

- The heightened importance of *knowledge* creation and knowledge sharing as a fundamental ingredient of strategic success. So the organisational issues are both how to foster knowledge creation and how to share and use that knowledge. These are different challenges. For example, the creation of knowledge often requires specialisation whereas its sharing and use invariably require the integration of different 'streams' of knowledge. Anyone who has had the responsibility for bringing new products to market knows how challenging it can be to integrate market knowledge with knowledge on how to create improved product features.

- *Globalisation* continues to grow in importance. Whether this relates to a more international customer base, competitors, suppliers, employees or sources of finance, few organisations are untouched by global forces. Organising for a globalising world has many challenges: communicating across wider geography, co-ordinating more diversity and building relationships across diverse cultures are some examples.

- A consequence of these three (and other) factors has been the growth in importance of *networks* both within and between organisations as an organisational response and diminishing attention to the formal structural hierarchy and the roles within those structures. In other words, processes and relationships have been forced to centre-stage as organisations address these issues of uncertainty, knowledge 'management' and globalisation.

Exhibit 9.1 shows the strands of an organisation's configuration and provides the structure for the chapter:

- The broad *structural design* (of roles, responsibilities and lines of reporting) in organisations may have moved from centre-stage but it is still an important influence on the success or failure of strategy. Failure to address issues of structure can, at a minimum, constrain strategy development and performance. But structure is not the panacea for success, as too many managers have tended to believe.

- The *processes* that connect, drive and support the people within and around an organisation will have a major influence on success or failure. These processes include formal systems and controls but also, importantly, the informal ways in which people interact and the behaviours needed for success.

- How *relationships* within and beyond the organisation are fostered and maintained will also influence performance. An important part of this will be how the *boundaries* between various 'players' are defined and sustained. This is a big agenda and the chapter will look at three aspects of relationships:
  - How responsibility for strategic and operational decisions can be divided – issues of *centralisation and devolution* (this relates to discussions in Chapter 6 about the role of corporate parents).
  - Where, within the wider value chain, activities are best located – the issues of *outsourcing*. There are links with discussions in Chapter 4.
  - Relationships with partners – issues of *strategic alliances* raised in Chapter 8.

In looking at these three strands (structures, processes and relationships) of an organisation's configuration the discussions will try to reflect the following:

- The relative importance of each strand will vary with circumstances and with time – but all three strands matter. As mentioned above, processes and relationships may be receiving particular attention at the moment – but structure is still an important element in organising for success.

- The essence of organising for success is to ensure that these issues about structures, processes, relationships and boundaries are working in harmony and not just being driven along by the latest thinking about a single strand (such as outsourcing or flatter structures or new IT systems). This need for *consistency* of configuration will be discussed at the end of the chapter.

● There are important connections to the issues raised in Chapter 10 about the enablers of success. For example, how information technology or human resource developments also underpin success. Similarly, managing change (Chapter 11) is intimately tied up with these issues of organising for and enabling success.

9.2 STRUCTURAL TYPES

Managers asked to describe their organisation usually respond by drawing an organisation chart, in an attempt to map out its structure. These structures define the 'levels' and roles in an organisation. In turn, structures facilitate or constrain how the processes and relationships work. This chapter begins with a review of these basic structural types, and their advantages and disadvantages. In doing so, particular attention will be paid to how well suited each structure might be to the type of business environment discussed above, where rapid change, growing uncertainty, the power of knowledge and globalisation are the norm rather than the exception. Since structures are just one strand of an organisation's configuration, in many circumstances structure will be 'determined' by the other elements of relationships, boundaries and processes rather than vice versa as has traditionally been thought to be the case.

9.2.1 The simple structure

In a **simple structure** the organisation is run by the personal control of an individual

A simple structure can be thought of as no formal structure at all. In a **simple structure** the organisation is run by the personal control of an individual. The configuration of the organisation centres on the relationships that individual can foster and maintain (both inside and outside the organisation) and the largely informal processes by which this is done. It is commonly the way in which very small businesses operate. There may be an owner who undertakes most of the responsibilities of management, perhaps with a partner or an assistant. However, there is little division of management responsibility, and probably little clear definition of who is responsible for what if there is more than one person involved.

The main problem here is that the organisation can operate effectively only up to a certain size, beyond which it becomes too cumbersome for one person to control alone.

9.2.2 The functional structure

A **functional structure** is based on the primary activities that have to be undertaken by an organisation such as production, finance and accounting, marketing, human resources and information management

A **functional structure** is based on the primary activities that have to be undertaken by an organisation such as production, finance and accounting, marketing, human resources and information management. Exhibit 9.2 represents a typical organisation chart for such a business. This structure is typically found in smaller companies, or those with narrow, rather than diverse, product

Exhibit 9.2   A functional structure

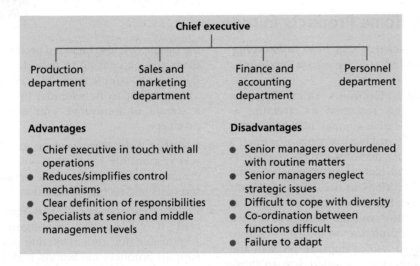

Chief executive

- Production department
- Sales and marketing department
- Finance and accounting department
- Personnel department

Advantages

- Chief executive in touch with all operations
- Reduces/simplifies control mechanisms
- Clear definition of responsibilities
- Specialists at senior and middle management levels

Disadvantages

- Senior managers overburdened with routine matters
- Senior managers neglect strategic issues
- Difficult to cope with diversity
- Co-ordination between functions difficult
- Failure to adapt

ranges. Also, within a multidivisional structure (see below), the divisions themselves may be split up into functional departments.

Exhibit 9.2 also summarises the potential advantages and disadvantages of a functional structure. There are advantages in that it allows greater operational control at a senior level; and linked to this is the clear definition of roles and tasks (see Illustration 9.1). However, there are disadvantages, particularly as organisations become larger or more diverse. In such circumstances, senior managers might be burdened with everyday operational issues, or rely on their specialist skills rather than taking a strategic perspective on problems. Perhaps the major concern in a fast-moving world is that managers remain functionally focused and can neither see the need for an overall strategic view nor find it very easy to deliver a co-ordinated response quickly. The focus of individuals is the *separate business processes* and no one (other than the most senior managers) has any real ownership of the whole product or client group. It proves difficult to integrate the knowledge of the functional specialists.

Similarly, because a functional structure is built around business processes it can be very problematic in coping with diversity. For example, there may be attempts to impose an unhelpful uniformity of approach between an organisation's SBUs. So lead times in production, debt control in finance, advertising expenditure in marketing, bonus systems in human resources, may be too rigid to reflect the diversity which the organisation faces.

Of course, processes and relationships can be used to minimise these problems with the functional structure, for example by improving *co-ordination* between functions either through systems or relationship building. This will be discussed more fully below. Some functions might address the problem in their substructure; for example, within sales and marketing, there might be *roles* such as product managers or key account sales staff.

Illustration 9.1

Electrolux Home Products Europe

Functional structures can help in bringing uniformity and simplicity into a business.

In January 2001, Electrolux Home Products Europe completely realigned its structure as part of its competitive strategy in Europe. The Swedish multinational company manufactured a range of consumer durables – such as cookers and fridges – and had grown through several decades of acquisitions to become a dominant player in Europe. But the market in Europe was fiercely competitive and the company needed to find a way to capitalise on its size – both to reduce costs and also to improve product and service standards. Their solution was to introduce a Europe-wide functional structure to replace the geographical structure (resulting from its acquisitions). The new structure is shown in the diagram.

The management explained the rationale for the restructuring: 'the realignment of EHP Europe is a part of a programme to ensure profitable growth as the organisation drives more simplicity into its business, while reducing the number of organisational hand-offs, and creating more focus on areas where increased effort is required to meet the tougher challenges of the market-place'.

The functional departments would operate as follows:

● **Purchasing, Production and Product Development** was the manufacturing arm of

the business. It also included product development and purchasing to provide a 'seamless flow' from supplies to finished products. This was felt to be essential to maintaining a stream of innovative and cost effective products.

● **Supply Chain Management and Logistics** was responsible for getting products to the customer and was the link between sales forecasts and factory production.

● **Product Businesses, Brand Management and Key Account Management** was responsible for the marketing activities to support products and brands. It also included key account management, service and spare parts.

● **Sales clusters** were the sales divisions and were grouped geographically into seven clusters.

The first three divisions were managed as cost centres whilst the sales clusters were focused on sales revenue.

Source: Adapted from *The Electrolux Executive*, December 2000.

Questions

1. Compare the advantages and disadvantages of a functional structure (above) with alternative structures such as product or geographical divisions.

2. Why do you think Electrolux chose this particular structure?

```
                          EHP
                         Europe
  ┌──────────────┬──────────────┬──────────────┬──────────────┐
Purchasing,      Supply Chain    Product Businesses,   Sales
Production       Management      Brand Management     clusters
and Product      and Logistics   and Key Account
Development                      Management
```

9.2.3 The multidivisional structure

A **multidivisional structure** is built up of separate divisions on the basis of products, services or geographical areas (see Exhibit 9.3). Divisionalisation often comes about as an attempt to overcome the problems that functional structures have in dealing with the diversity mentioned above.[5] So divisionalisation allows a tailoring of the product/market strategy to the requirements of each separate division and can improve the ownership of the strategy by divisional staff. A similar situation exists in many public services, where the organisation is structured around *service departments* such as recreation, social services and education. Within these departments further divisionalisation might occur, although on different bases.

In practice, the creation of divisions which closely match strategic business units (SBUs as defined in Chapter 1) can prove difficult – for example, for reasons of size and efficiency (there would simply be too many divisions). So the divisional structure, in reality, is usually much broader than any one SBU. However, whilst the diversity within a division is less than in the organisation as a whole, nevertheless diversity still exists and can be difficult to manage. One way of coping with this in larger divisions is for divisionalisation to be rolled down to a next tier of subdivisions – sometimes by geography, sometimes by client group. A police force usually has territorial divisions. An education department often has subdivisions for primary, secondary and tertiary education.

A **multidivisional structure** is built up of separate divisions on the basis of products, services or geographical areas

Exhibit 9.3   A multidivisional structure

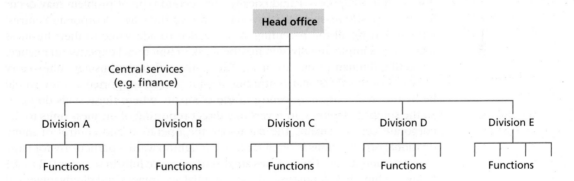

Advantages

- Concentration on business area (e.g. product/market)
- Facilitates measurement of unit performance
- Ease of addition and divestment of units
- Facilitates senior management's attention to strategy
- Encourages general management development

Disadvantages

- Possible confusion over locus of responsibility (centralisation/devolution confusion)
- Conflict between divisions
- Basis of intertrading
- Costly
- Divisions grow too large
- Complexity of co-operation if too many divisions

A common problem in creating divisions is in deciding the *basis* of division-alisation – should it be based on products or markets or technologies? The result can, of course, be a complex organisation: for example, a company may decide that it needs a number of levels of divisions in order to break up business activities sensibly. A first level of divisions based on broad product groups might be created. Within each of these divisions, there may be separate businesses, which in turn have their own divisional structure. At this level in the organisation, a division will then have a functionally based structure of departments dealing with the specialist tasks of that division.

This raises the problems of which businesses should be in each division, which functions are to be included at each level of divisionalisation, and which functions are properly placed within the corporate head office rather than within any one of the divisions. For example, where should a function such as financial planning be placed? Presumably, this is required both at a corporate level and at some level within an operating division. This issue has already been introduced in the discussion about corporate-level strategy in Chapter 6 and will be discussed more fully in section 9.4.1 below, which is concerned with choices about centralisation or devolution of decision making.

The potential advantages of divisional structures mainly centre on the benefits of specialisation within a division, allowing competences to develop with a clearer focus on a particular product group, technology or customer group. It can also make it easier to monitor the activities of a division as a separate business. However, there can be disadvantages and difficulties of three main types. First, divisions become so specialised and self-sufficient that they are *de facto* independent businesses – but carrying the costs of the corporate centre of the company. So it may make more sense to split the company into independent businesses, and de-mergers of this type have been very common, as discussed in Chapter 6. Paradoxically, the second type of problem may occur for the opposite reason. Divisions have created their own 'corporate centres' without having all the parenting skills needed to add value to their business units. For example, the division may be weak in functional expertise in finance, marketing, human resources or IT. The result is that the business units carry the costs of this divisional centre but are not as well supported as they would be by the 'real' corporate centre of the company where these skills do exist. So the solution might be to revert to a direct reporting of business units to the corporate centre. Finally, the day-to-day the operation and control of multi-divisional organisations is often far from straightforward – particularly for large global organisations. These issues are discussed more fully in sections 9.3 to 9.5 below. Exhibit 9.3 summarises these potential advantages and disadvantages of a multidivisional structure.

9.2.4 The holding company structure

A **holding company** is an investment company consisting of shareholdings in a variety of separate business operations

A **holding company** is an investment company consisting of shareholdings in a variety of separate business operations. Although part of a parent company, these businesses may operate independently and may retain their original company names. As mentioned in Chapter 6, the role that the parent company takes may be limited to decisions about the buying and selling of subsidiaries with little involvement in their product or market strategy. The processes and relationships between the corporate centre and the separate businesses is confined to financial issues such as investment and financial performance. This is the way in which many traditional conglomerates were run (such as Hanson, Lonrho or BTR).

A holding company structure is based on the idea that the constituent businesses will operate their product/market strategy to their best potential if left alone, particularly as business environments become more turbulent. However, the businesses can benefit from their membership of the group in any of the ways discussed in Chapter 6 (such as cheaper finance for investment) without having to carry the burden of a high central overhead. The holding company itself may also claim benefits, such as the spreading of risk across many business ventures and the ease of divestment of individual companies. Perhaps the greatest weaknesses of this structure are the lack of internal strategic cohesion and duplication of effort between businesses.

The fact that many of these conglomerates have been de-merged into their separate companies suggests that these benefits are often not enough to hold the 'federation' together. They have become unpopular in the eyes of financial institutions who fail to see how the holding company can add value to the separate companies better than the stock market, as discussed in Chapter 6.

9.2.5 The matrix structure[6]

A **matrix structure** is a combination of structures which could take the form of product and geographical divisions or functional and divisional structures operating in tandem. Exhibit 9.4 gives examples of such a structure. Matrix structures may be adopted because there is more than one factor around which knowledge needs to be built whilst ensuring that these separate areas of knowledge can be integrated. For example, a global company may prefer geographically defined divisions as the operating units for local marketing (because of their specialist local knowledge of customers). But at the same time they may still want global product divisions responsible for the worldwide co-ordination of product development, manufacturing and distribution to these geographical divisions (because of their specialist knowledge of these issues). However, matrix structures do not occur only in large, complex, organisations. For example, they are common in professional service organisations (both public and private sector). Exhibit 9.4 shows how in a school the separate knowledge of subject specialists needs to be combined to create programmes of study tailored differently to different age groups. Because a matrix structure replaces formal lines of authority with (cross-matrix) relationships, this often brings problems. In particular, it will typically take *longer to reach decisions* since they may result from bargaining or consensus rather than imposition. There may be a good deal of *conflict* because of the lack of clarity of role definition and responsibility.

As with any structure, but particularly with the matrix structure, the critical issue in practice is the way in which it is operated (i.e. the processes and

A **matrix structure** is a combination of structures which could take the form of product and geographical divisions or functional and divisional structures operating in tandem

Exhibit 9.4	Two examples of matrix structures

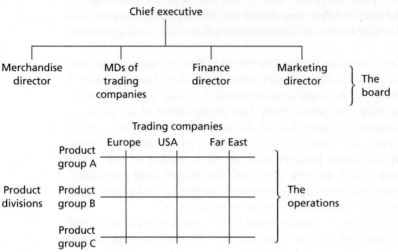

(a) Multinational organisation

Head teacher

Subject leadership			
	Head of languages	Head of science	Head of social studies	etc.

Pupil groups — Head of lower school / Head of upper school / Head of sixth form

(b) School

Advantages
- Quality of decision making where interests conflict
- Direct contact replaces bureaucracy
- Increases managerial motivation
- Development of managers through increased involvement in decisions

Disadvantages
- Length of time to take decisions
- Unclear job and task responsibilities
- Unclear cost and profit responsibilities
- High degrees of conflict
- Dilution of priorities
- 'Creeping bureaucracy'

relationships). For example, one 'arm' of the matrix may need to *lead* in the sense that it dictates some key parameters (such as economic production volumes) within which the other 'arm' of the matrix must work (for example, when offering local variation). Another practicality concerns ownership of strategy by staff. This may require the 'designation' of specialist staff to some products or client groups and not others. For example, the IT department may designate individuals to support particular front-line divisions. They may be physically located in that division and have a two-way reporting arrangement (to the head of IT and to the divisional manager). Perhaps the key ingredient in a successful matrix structure is that senior managers are good at sustaining collaborative relationships (across the matrix) and coping with the messiness and ambiguity which that can bring.

9.2.6 Team-based structures[7]

Although matrix structures may be less fashionable than previously, the principles around which they are built are very relevant to the challenges of the 21st century outlined in the introduction to this chapter, in particular the need for fluidity, the fostering of specialist knowledge whilst being able to integrate that knowledge and the need to cope with wider geography. However, management thinking and practice have moved on and these issues have resurfaced in the shape of team-based structures. But team-based structures are not new. The proponents of total quality management (TQM) had often supported team-based structures (as against activity-based structures) at the operational level – for example, at Volvo in the automobile industry. This included the idea that *self-managed teams* might deliver better-value products or services than a traditional regime with strict division of labour and extensive formal controls (as in production-line working). The issue for strategic management is whether it is suitable as an overall approach for organisations (or perhaps for divisions within a organisation). A **team-based structure** attempts to combine both horizontal and vertical co-ordination through structuring people into cross-functional teams – often built around business processes. For example, an information systems company might have development teams, product teams and applications teams who, respectively, are responsible for: (a) new product development, (b) service and support of standard products, and (c) customising products to particular customers (or customer groups). Each of these teams will have a mix of specialists within it – particularly software engineers and customer service specialists so they are able to see the issues holistically. Illustration 9.2 shows an example of a team-based structure.

Sometimes team-based structures are adopted to reflect the diversity of customers. For example, in a university department different teams of lecturers and administrators may be created to support separately the undergraduate and postgraduate students. But lecturers are still connected to their academic subject group too. In many public services there are concerns that traditional structures (into separate professional departments or organisations such as social services, health and education) hinder the ability to address major strategic issues of social concern. For example, mental health requires professional expertise from each of these areas. So *cross-cutting* (diagonal slice) teams are being created to tackle these major issues. Another example is drug abuse (police, social services and health care).

*A **team-based structure** attempts to combine both horizontal and vertical co-ordination through structuring people into cross-functional teams*

Illustration 9.2

Team-based structures at Saab Training Systems

STRATEGY IN ACTION

A change in structure may be needed to improve competitive performance.

In the 1990s Saab Training Systems was a high-tech company working in the defence industry. It was a fully owned subsidiary of the Swedish company Saab. In 1997 the company had 260 employees and a turnover of about £52 million. It sold computer-aided equipment for military training – for example, laser-based simulators. The market was characterised by long, complicated and politicised negotiations with clients, fierce global competition and overcapacity as defence budgets reduced as a result of the 'peace dividend'. This high degree of uncertainty and need for flexibility had forced the company to react. It shunned external alliances, which were common in the industry, and focused on exploiting its core competence in laser-based simulation. But it also needed to drastically speed up throughput times in both development and production to get new product to commercialisation faster and then to shorten delivery times.

The company decided to abandon its traditional functional structure in favour of a more flexible team-based structure and a more business-process-oriented way of doing business. Before these changes the company was organised into functions (production, development, marketing and purchasing). Each function had its own internal hierarchy. This structure created problems with cross-functional co-ordination and communication. In the new structure 40 teams were created that reported directly to the senior management team. Team sizes were between 6 and 8. If they got bigger they were split. The teams were built around the business processes. There were five *business teams*

who negotiated contracts with customers and monitored contracts. Each team was responsible for one or more products and particular geographical markets. When a contract was signed it became a 'project' to which other teams were assigned: a *delivery team* (who planned production and tested products prior to shipping); a *purchasing team* (responsible for sourcing materials and components); and an *applications team* (who adapted the company's 'standard' products to the need of particular customers). Finally, production was assigned to one of 14 *product teams* (who were also responsible for product development). In addition to these 'front-line' teams there were central functions such as personnel and finance.

Co-ordination of the various teams involved in a customer's order was very important since the particular mix of teams assigned to that order was temporary. It was dissolved as soon as the order was delivered to the customer. Also, product teams were working on more than one project at any time. The responsibility for co-ordination of any project was shared between the business team (commercial responsibility) and delivery teams (production planning).

Source: Adapted from T. Mullern, 'Integrating the team-based structure in the business process', in A. Pettigrew and E. Fenton (eds), *The Innovating Organisation*, Sage, 2000, Chapter 8.

Questions

1. Why did the functional structure not suit the company's strategy?

2. How did the team-based structure help?

3. What problems could the team-based approach create?

9.2.7 Project-based structures[8]

For some organisations, teams are built around projects that have a finite life span. A **project-based structure** is one where teams are created, undertake the work (e.g. internal or external contracts) and are then dissolved. This is clearly appropriate for organisations that deliver large, expensive and durable goods or services (civil engineering, information systems) or those delivering time-limited events – such as conferences, sporting events or even management development programmes. So the organisation structure is a constantly chang-ing collection of project teams created, steered and glued together loosely by a small corporate team. There is most likely to be cross-membership of teams (which, if prevalent, starts to resemble a matrix). Many organisations use such teams in a more ad hoc way to complement the 'main' structure. For example, *taskforces* are set up to make progress on new elements of strategy or to provide momentum where the regular structure of the organisation is not effective.

As with other structures, there are some important practical considerations in project-based structures concerning the other organising issues of processes, relationships and boundaries. For example, if project teams are short-lived, where do the team members come from and where do they go to on project completion? Hence the boundaries issue is crucial – should they be employees or contracted or something between the two? Relationships are a concern too. If teams are transient, how are they made to operate as a team and how do they gain understanding and ownership of the organisation's strategies?

Overall, team-based and project-based structures have been growing in importance because of their inherent flexibility which is seen as so important in a fast-moving world where individual knowledge and competences need to be redeployed and integrated quickly and in novel ways.

> A **project-based structure** is one where teams are created, undertake the work and are then dissolved

9.2.8 Intermediate structures

In reality, few organisations adopt a structure that is just like one of the pure structural types discussed above. There exists a whole range of 'shades of grey' between these pure types of structure. The skill is in blending together these pure types to match the organisation's circumstances; in ensuring that struc-tures can change with time; and in ensuring that the various strands of an organisation's configuration (structure, processes and relationships) work well together. For example, a company that is developing both new products and new markets and is organised in a functional structure will ultimately find the functional structure inappropriate for supporting this increased diversity (as discussed above). A change to a multidivisional structure would almost certainly assist this changing strategy. However, since the strategic change is incremental rather than transformational it is more than likely that this struc-tural change (from functional to divisional) will also occur incrementally in a series of intermediate steps through changes in the processes and relation-ships (discussed below). The first challenge that the diversity might bring is competition for resources between established products and markets and the new ones. Initially, these conflicts might be resolved by pushing the decision upwards until a sufficiently *senior executive* makes the decisions. When too many conflicts need to be resolved in this way, new *rules*, guidelines and procedures may develop to guide how resources are to be shared between products. It may become necessary to *formalise* these procedures in the planning process by, for example, allocating a budget to the new products or markets. So the configuration addresses the changing circumstances by changes to processes and relationships rather than a change from a functional structure.

As the new products or markets become more important and create more competition for resources, it may be necessary to create *interdepartmental liaison roles* – often team-based as discussed above. For example, a committee or a taskforce may be set up to advise on priorities. This may lead either to permanent teams of co-ordinators or special *co-ordinating roles* (the product manager is a good example). It may also prove necessary to create a department with the sole function of co-ordination, for example *centralised planning*. Ultimately, as the diversity increases, the costs of maintaining the functional structure (in terms of processes and relationship maintenance) will be unacceptably high and the organisation will divisionalise. Or alternatively, the new ventures will be created as a separate division or subsidiary, and the functional structure in the 'parent' reverts to its previous *modus operandi* as the 'problem' of diversity is removed.

9.3 PROCESSES

Structure is a key ingredient of organising for success. But within any structure, what makes organisations work are the formal and informal organisational processes.[9] These processes can be thought of as controls on the organisation's operations and can therefore help or hinder the translation of strategy into action. They range from formal controls (systems, rules and procedures), through social controls (culture and routines as discussed in Chapters 2 and 5), to self-controls (the personal motivation of individuals). This section will look at how these processes can help or hinder strategy and how they might fit with the other elements discussed in this chapter. The extent to which these processes are more or less effective in addressing the issues outlined in the introduction about rapid change, knowledge and globalisation will also be borne in mind. Several stereotypical processes will be discussed:

- Direct supervision
- Planning and control systems
- Performance targets
- Market mechanisms
- Social/cultural processes (norms)
- Self-control (personal behaviour and motivation)

It needs to be remembered that in reality a blend of these processes will operate (although some will dominate others). The important issue is that the processes match the strategy and the other organisational elements (structures, relationships and boundaries).

9.3.1 Direct supervision

Direct supervision is the direct control of strategic decisions by one or a few individuals. It is a dominant process in small organisations. It can also exist in larger organisations where little change is occurring and if the complexity of the business is not too great for a small number of managers to control the strategy *in detail* from the centre. This is often found in family businesses and in parts of the public sector with a history of 'hands-on' political involvement (often where a single political party has dominated for a long period).

Direct supervision may also be appropriate during major change – for example, an organisational *crisis* or a major transformation occurring in the business environment. Here the survival of the organisation may be threatened and autocratic control through direct supervision may be necessary. The appointment of receivers to companies in financial difficulty by their creditors is also a good example.

Direct supervision is the direct control of strategic decisions by one or a few individuals

9.3.2 Planning and control systems

Planning and control is the archetypal administrative control, where the successful implementation of strategies is achieved through *systems* that plan and control the allocation of resources and monitor their utilisation. A plan would cover all parts of the organisation and show clearly, in financial terms, the level of resources allocated to each area (whether that be functions, divisions or business units). It would also show the detailed ways in which this resource was to be used. This would usually take the form of a *budget*. For example, the marketing function may be allocated £5m but will need to show how this will be spent, e.g. the proportions spent on staff, advertising, exhibitions and so on. These cost items would then be monitored regularly to measure actual spend against plan. Revenue generation will also form part of the plan and actual sales will be monitored against plan. Of course, there will need to be some degree of flexibility in these plans and budgets to meet the unexpected or to adapt to what is actually being achieved. For example, if revenues are running behind plan it may be necessary to reduce spending budgets in some areas and/or increase them in others – such as advertising.

The strengths and weaknesses of a planned approach to strategy were introduced in section 2.3.1 where one of the strengths was identified as this ability to monitor and control the implementation of strategy. Many of the major strides forward in manufacturing efficiency and reliability in the early parts of the twentieth century were achieved through this 'scientific management', which is still an important approach in many such organisations. Such a dominance of detailed planning and co-ordination is particularly useful where the

Planning and control is where the successful implementation of strategies is achieved through *systems* that plan and control the allocation of resources and monitor their utilisation

degree of change is low. However, the detailed way in which planning would support strategy can vary:

- Planning can be 'top-down' and accompanied by *standardisation of work processes* or *outputs (such as product or service features)*. Sometimes these work processes are subject to a rigorous framework of assessment and review – for example, to meet externally audited quality standards (such as ISO 9000). In many service organisations such 'routinisation' has been achieved through IT systems leading to de-skilling of service delivery and significant reductions in cost. This can give competitive advantage where organisations are positioning on low price with commodity-like products or services. For example, the cost of transactions in Internet banking are a fraction of transactions made through branches.

- Many larger organisations have now exploited IT systems extensively through the introduction of enterprise resource planning (ERP) systems[10] supplied by software specialists such as SAP, Oracle, Epicor or Baan. These systems aim to integrate the entire business operations, including personnel, finance, manufacturing operations, warehousing etc. For example, this started with the use of EPOS (electronic point of sale) systems in retail outlets, which linked back into stock control. Further advantage may be gained if these systems can stretch more widely in the value-system beyond the boundaries of the organisation into the supply and distribution chains – for example, in automatic ordering of supplies to avoid 'stockout'. E-commerce operations are taking the integrative capability further (this is discussed more fully in section 10.3). Illustration 9.3 shows an example of enterprise resource planning.

- Centralised planning approaches often use a *formula* for controlling resource allocation within an organisation. For example, in the public services, budgets might be allocated on a per capita basis (e.g. doctors' patients). There may then be some room for *bargaining* and fine-tuning around this formula – for example, in *redefining* the formula – by weightings or introducing additional factors. The danger is that the need for change is underestimated and the formula inhibits the ability to redeploy resources within an organisation.

- Many organisations face situations where these top-down planning and control processes may not be appropriate, for example in a rapidly changing environment and/or if there is significant diversity in circumstances between the various business units. It will be seen in section 9.4 below that in these situations 'bottom-up' planning from business units is an important process – but within central guidelines (see Exhibit 9.5). If this approach is to work there need to be processes of *reconciliation* to ensure that the sum total of business unit plans can be resourced. This may be resolved through processes of *bargaining* and hopefully a revisiting of some of the central policies and guidelines, which should be regarded as movable (to a greater or lesser extent) through these planning processes. There may need to be several iterations of this process, as shown in Exhibit 9.5. The danger of bottom-up planning is that key aspects of strategy are not addressed in the

Illustration 9.3

Enterprise resource planning (ERP) at Sonoco

ERP systems aim to create a more integrated and strategic approach to business operations.

Millions of consumers and businesses across the world have depended on the packaging materials produced by Sonoco Products Co. based in Hartsville, South Carolina. Sonoco has been producing packaging for everything from bulk agricultural products to plastic bags used for groceries, and by 2000, had annual revenues of US$2.5bn.

Over time, Sonoco's operating resource purchases (for maintenance, repair and operating (MRO), janitorial, safety and office supplies) utilised a transaction-based rather than a strategic-based purchasing approach. This resulted in higher prices, inefficient processes, fragmented contacts with suppliers, and low data visibility.

In the 1990s Sonoco embarked on a plan to increase their earnings by expanding their existing markets and developing new ones, and focusing on more efficient operations. One of its aims was to ensure that the right systems, processes and people were in place for a strategic-based purchasing and cost control system. Furthermore, it also sought to automate transactions and to consolidate data.

As part of this focus, in 1998, Sonoco invested in IT systems that allowed them to maintain and view data more effectively. The initial component of this was a PeopleSoft ERP system for financial and human resource applications. The purchase of operating resources and certain commodities was centralised at its corporate headquarters in Hartsville. Although Sonoco standardised PeopleSoft for their financial and HR requirements throughout the company, this had not been done for all purchasing activities. The various divisions had been allowed to choose their own ERP systems for production and materials requirement planning. The ultimate goal was to have the central data interfaced from the various division-level ERP systems to the central PeopleSoft system in Hartsville.

Sonoco initially decided to reduce the number of suppliers for the MRO category. They examined the data from the ERP purchasing module and identified the key suppliers within each of its operating resources categories. By September 1998, they had lowered supplier numbers from 1,200 to three. Subsequently the ERP accounts payable module automated many purchasing and payment tasks, and the purchasing module was also used to perform complex tasks such as blanket orders and capital purchases. As a result of the system, the skill set of the employees shifted from clerical work to more analytical and supplier-negotiation work.

As a result of the 10 per cent reduction in spending on operating resources, the investment for the system had been more than recovered. Sonoco had been able to achieve a more strategic purchasing focus.

Prepared by Urmilla Lawson, Graduate Business School, University of Strathclyde.

Source: Adapted from Monica Shaw, 'ERP and e-procurement software assist strategic purchasing focus at Sonoco', *Pulp & Paper*, vol. 74, no. 2 (2000), p. 45.

Question

What could be the next steps in further exploiting ERP at Sonoco?

| Exhibit 9.5 | 'Bottom-up' business planning |

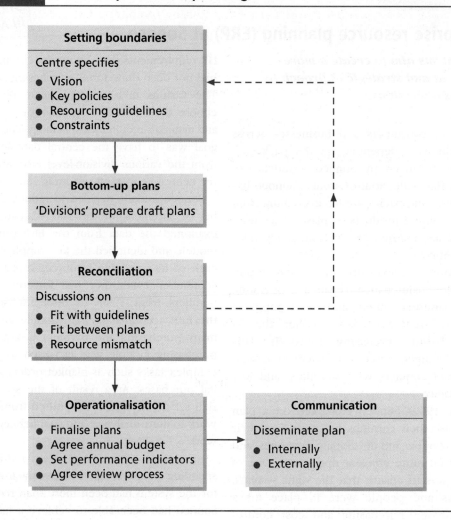

plans of business units; for example, the need to invest in new technologies, infrastructure or intellectual capital.

9.3.3 Performance targets

Performance targets
relate to the *outputs* of an organisation (or part of an organisation), such as product quality, prices, or its *outcomes* such as profit

Performance targets can be an important process through which successful strategies are fostered. Unlike planning processes discussed above, where targets tend to be about resource *inputs* (e.g. budgets) these targets relate to the *outputs* of an organisation (or part of an organisation), such as product quality, prices, or its *outcomes* such as profit. The performance of an organisation is judged, either internally or externally, on its ability to meet these targets. However, within specified boundaries, the organisation remains free on how targets should be achieved. This approach can be particularly appropriate in certain situations:

- It will be seen below (section 9.4) that targets of this type are commonly used by the corporate centre of organisations in controlling the strategies and performance of business units in order to ensure that corporate objectives are achieved. In large organisations there is likely to be a cascade of targets down through divisions, business units and functions. They will often be translated into targets for individuals too.

- In the absence of a genuine market, many of the privatised utilities in the UK and elsewhere were controlled through the appointment of regulators until such time as a market could be developed.[11] These regulators controlled the organisations through a mechanism of *price-capping* (the so-called K-factors), which imposed a ceiling on prices related to the retail price index (RPI). As competition developed in the market, regulation moved towards a series of agreed *performance indicators* (PIs) as a means of ensuring that 'competitive' performance was maintained.

- In the public services, where control of resource inputs was the dominant approach historically, there are continuing attempts to move the control processes towards outputs (such as quality of service) and, more importantly, towards outcomes (for example, patient mortality rates in health care, as previously seen in Illustration 4.6).

Many managers find the process of developing a useful set of PIs for their organisations difficult. One reason for this is that many indicators give a useful but only partial view of the overall picture. Also, some indicators are qualitative in nature, whilst the hard quantitative end of assessing performance has been dominated by financial analysis. In an attempt to cope with this very heterogeneous situation, *balanced scorecards*[12] have been used as a way of identifying a useful, but varied, set of key measures. **Balanced scorecards** combine both qualitative and quantitative measures, acknowledge the expectations of different stakeholders and relate an assessment of performance to choice of strategy (as shown in Exhibit 9.6 and Illustration 9.4). Importantly, performance is linked not only to short-term outputs but also to the way in which processes are managed – for example, the processes of innovation and learning which are crucial to long-term success.

Balanced scorecards combine both qualitative and quantitative measures, acknowledge the expectations of different stakeholders and relate an assessment of performance to choice of strategy

Exhibit 9.6 is an example of a balanced scorecard for a small start-up company supplying standard tools and light equipment into the engineering industry. The owner-manager's financial perspective was simply one of survival during this start-up period, requiring a positive cash flow (after the initial investments in plant, stock and premises). The strategy was to compete on customer service for both initial delivery and maintenance back-up. This required core competences in order processing and maintenance scheduling underpinned by the company's IT system. These core competences were open to imitation, so, in turn, the ability to improve these service standards continuously was critical to success.

<table>
<tr><td colspan="2">**Exhibit 9.6**</td><td colspan="2">**The balanced scorecard: an example**</td></tr>
</table>

FINANCIAL PERSPECTIVE		CUSTOMER PERSPECTIVE	
CSF*	**Measures**	**CSF***	**Measures**
Survival	Cash flow	Customer service (standard products)	• Delivery time • Maintenance response time

INTERNAL PERSPECTIVE		INNOVATION AND LEARNING PERSPECTIVE	
CSF*	**Measures**	**CSF***	**Measures**
IT systems development • Features • Cost	Performance per £ invested (vs. competitors)	Service leadership	• Speed to market (new standards) • Speed of imitation (robustness)

*CSF = critical success factor

9.3.4 Market mechanisms[13]

Market mechanisms have been the dominant process through which organisations have related to their external suppliers, distributors and competitors in most sectors of free market economies. Therefore, it is perhaps not surprising that managers (and indeed politicians) have attempted to use market mechanisms internally within organisations. **Market mechanisms** involve some formalised system of 'contracting' for resources or inputs from other parts of an organisation and for supplying outputs to other parts of an organisation. It might be started in small ways with *competitive bidding* – perhaps through the creation of an *investment bank* or 'top-sliced' resources held at the corporate centre for which business units can bid for additional resources to support particular projects or developments. This can be a successful way of supporting innovative ventures in their early phase, where otherwise they may be starved of resources.

Over the recent past, many organisations have introduced a formal *internal market*. For example, a customer–supplier relationship may be established between a central service department, such as training or IT, and the operating units. It then becomes an important management task to regulate and manage this internal market. An important feature of internal markets is the 'right' of the internal customer to specify their requirements. This may be done in the

Market mechanisms involve some formalised system of 'contracting' for resources

Illustration 9.4

The balanced scorecard: Rockwater

STRATEGY IN ACTION

Balanced scorecards attempt to reflect the interdependence of different performance factors – which together will determine success or failure.

Rockwater, a wholly owned subsidiary of Brown and Root/Halliburton, a global engineering and construction company, is a worldwide leader in underwater engineering and construction. The table below shows how the company transformed its vision and strategy into a balanced scorecard with four sets of performance measures. The ultimate aim of this exercise was to create value for the whole organisation.

Source: R.S. Kaplan and D.P. Norton, 'Putting the balanced scorecard to work', *Harvard Business Review*, vol. 71, no. 5 (1993), pp. 134–147.

Questions

1. Imagine yourself as the chief executive of Rockwater and draw up a table that shows:
   (a) the various ways in which you would plan to use the balanced scorecard (e.g. establishing targets, assessing individual performance, bonuses, etc.);
   (b) the ways in which the balanced scorecard will assist you;
   (c) any shortcomings of the scorecard approach.
2. Give other examples of how a scorecard approach, in general, could build both positive and dysfunctional behaviours in organisations.

THE VISION	STRATEGY	OBJECTIVES	BALANCED SCORECARD
'As our customers' preferred provider, we shall be the industry leader. This is our mission.'	Services that surpass needs Customer satisfaction Continuous improvement Quality of employees Shareholder expectations	**Financial** Return on capital Cash flow Project profitability Reliability of performance **Customer** Value for money Competitive price Hassle-free relationship High-performance professional Innovation satisfaction **Internal** Shape customer requirement Quality service Safety/loss control Superior project management Tender effectiveness **Growth** Product and service innovation Empowered workforce Continuous improvement	**Financial perspective** Return on capital employed Cash flow Project profitability Profit forecast reliability Sales backlog **Customer perspective** Customer ranking survey Customer satisfaction index Market share Pricing index **Internal business perspective** Hours with customers on new work Tender success rate Rework Safety incident index Project performance index Project closeout cycle **Innovation and learning perspective** Revenue per employee % revenue from new services Rate of improvement index Staff attitude survey No. of employee suggestions

form of a *service-level agreement* with the internal supplier. This agreement should ideally reflect the best performance that would be achieved by third-party suppliers from outside the organisation. At a practical level, there are some problems that can be created by internal markets. These are largely concerns about the behaviours that market mechanisms can trigger off. First is an escalation in *bargaining* between units, which can consume important management time. Second is the creation of a new bureaucracy monitoring all of the *internal transfers* of resources between units. An overzealous use of market mechanisms can also have a profound impact on the dominant culture of an organisation, shifting it from one of collaboration and relational processes to competition and contractual relationships, which may prove dysfunctional.

It was for a number of these reasons that the new Labour government in the UK made changes to the operation of the internal market in health care in 1997. The internal market had created supplier–purchaser relationships – for example, family doctors (GPs) were given their own budgets and were free to buy hospital treatment for their patients (rather than the old system of simply referring them 'free of charge'). In turn, hospitals built up their income through these 'charges' (rather than simply being allocated a budget). There were particular concerns about the effects of overcompetitive behaviour and the emergence of a two-tier standard of provision as some GPs became more astute purchasers than others. Symbolically, the language was also changed, for example 'purchasers' became 'commissioners' of health care and all parties were required to work collaboratively to develop health plans for their districts (this led to the creation of Primary Care Trusts).

9.3.5 Social/cultural processes

Historically, perhaps too much emphasis may have been placed on the formal processes of co-ordination used to implement successful strategies. They may have been successful in a slower-moving, less complex, environment but by themselves they may be inadequate in meeting the challenges of the 21st century. The 'softer' processes within organisations – the social processes and self-controls – are of major (and probably growing) importance in most organisations. This section looks at how social processes can play an important part in delivering successful strategies. **Social processes** are concerned with organisational culture and the *standardisation of norms*. Knowledge integration occurs through the taken-for-granted assumptions of the organisation (as discussed in Chapter 5). Social processes are particularly important in organisations facing complex and dynamic environments. The fostering of innovation is crucial to survival and success in these circumstances – but not in bureaucratised ways. It must be allowed to flourish through the social processes which exist within and between what has been called the 'community of communities'[14] – in other words, the informal processes whereby individual specialists and groups interact to share and integrate their knowledge.

Social processes can also be important *between* organisations in their approach to competition and collaboration. Illustration 9.5 shows how important

Social processes are concerned with organisational culture and the *standardisation of norms*

Illustration 9.5

Italy's craftsmanship faces a global challenge

STRATEGY IN ACTION

Well-functioning networks between small companies have been a source of competitive advantage for many craft industries – but can they survive and adapt to globalisation and new technologies?

Industrial commentators, of a variety of nationalities, looking for a key to success among small and medium-sized companies (SMEs), have often portrayed 'Third Italy' (in the centre and north east of the country) as a model. It is an area where there are networks of smaller firms, producing the best of Italian craftsmanship in specialist sectors such as textiles, footwear or kitchen equipment. Relying on an atmosphere of loyalty and trust, the networks are based on a mixture of competition and co-operation and involve informal agreements on pricing. They believed this helped to obviate exploitation by large customers or suppliers, 'stealing of good ideas or excessive financial risk'.

The real secret of the success of Third Italy was flexibility. A good example was to be seen in the craft of goldworking. In this specialist sector, ancient traditions and personalised designs were coupled with collective information on new techniques. The result was products that gave satisfaction to a sophisticated market. Technology was also helping production cycles to be shortened, and small firms were able to produce a much larger range of products. This was particularly seen in districts like Prato (textiles), Sassuolo (ceramics) or Mirandola (biomedical instruments).

That was the picture until a few years ago. Then a change occurred as the forces of globalisation began to take effect. The challenge was now for the local, integrated community of each district to compete with large organisations which enjoyed the benefits of a different kind of integration – international organisations, which could site their various activities in different countries and overcome geographical separation with the aid of modern information technology. Also, the IT revolution means that information that used to be guarded within the local community is now freely available around the world. Big players today are able to impose their will on what used to be local decision making.

Meanwhile, small, specialist firms' sense of 'belonging' (to a geographically defined district) clearly does not work in the way it once did. Small groups of firms compete for global success separately from the district as a whole. This change from local to global networking is difficult and dangerous. Small manufacturing enterprises can no longer rely, as they once did, on social processes that defended them against the opportunism of stronger organisations.

Source: P.A. Vipraio, 'Italy's craftsmanship faces a global challenge', *QED*, September 1997, pp. 14–17.

Questions

1. How did the relationships *between* small firms help in providing value-for-money products for customers?
2. What are the dangers in this?
3. What do you think are the key changes in processes which must be made to make a successful transition from local to global networks?

this can be in craft industries and how other forces – globalisation and new technologies – can undermine these processes.

In was seen in Chapters 2 and 5 that social processes can also create *rigidities* if an organisation is needing to change strategy.[15] Resistance to change may be 'legitimised' by the cultural norms. For example, plans to de-skill service delivery through routinisation (IT systems) and the use of 'non-professional' staff may be a logical strategy to pursue in terms of improving value to customers, but it is likely to be resisted by professional staff. The social processes may work against such a change. However, this need not be the case. Since these professionals are likely to be strongly influenced by the behaviour of their peer group in other organisations, they may accept the need for change if they see it working successfully elsewhere. It is for these sorts of reasons that many organisations commit significant resources to maintaining *professional networks*, both inside and between organisations, as a method of keeping in touch with best practice.

Training and development is another way in which organisations invest in maintaining the social processes within an organisation. It provides a common set of reference points (norms) to which people can relate their own work and priorities, and a common language with which to communicate with other parts of the organisation.

9.3.6 Self-control and personal motivation

With rapid change, increasing complexity and the need to exploit knowledge, the motivation of individuals and their self-control is becoming critically important to performance and raises some issues about organising for success:

Processes of **self-control** achieve the integration of knowledge and co-ordination of activities by the direct interaction of individuals without supervision

- Processes of **self-control** achieve the integration of knowledge and co-ordination of activities by the direct interaction of individuals without supervision (this is sometimes referred to as mutual adjustment).[16] The contribution of managers to this process is to ensure that individuals have the *channels* to interact (perhaps by improving the IT and communications infrastructure), and that the social processes which this interaction creates are properly *regulated* to avoid the rigidities mentioned in section 9.3.5 above. So managers are concerned with shaping the *context*[17] in which others are working – particularly to ensure that knowledge creation and integration is working. If individuals are to have a greater say in how they perform their work and achieve the organisation's goals, they need to be properly *supported* in the way in which resources are made available to them. One of these key resources is likely to be information, and it will be seen in Chapter 10 that an organisation's IT strategy is a critical ingredient in this process of supporting individuals.

- Personal motivation of individuals is strongly influenced by the type of leaders and leadership style. The credibility of leaders is important and can be built in more than one way. For example, credibility may arise from being a member of the peer group – as a professional role model. This is why so many leaders in professional service departments or organisations continue their own professional work as well as overseeing the work of others. Credibility may also be built by demonstrably shaping a favourable context for individuals to work and interact. Finally, credibility might arise from the way in which leaders interface with the business environment – for example in winning orders or securing a budget (from the corporate centre or, in the public sector, the funding body). These three leadership roles – of the professional role model, supporting individuals and securing resources – have been called the grinding, minding and finding roles[18] respectively which are so important in knowledge-based organisations.

9.4 RELATIONSHIPS AND BOUNDARIES

A key aspect of an organisation's configuration is the ability to integrate the knowledge and activities of different parts of an organisation (both horizontally and vertically) and with other organisations (particularly within the value chain, as discussed in Chapter 4). Structures and processes are an important part of this, as discussed in the previous sections. However, there is also a need to decide 'who does what' – so the *boundaries* within an organisation (between its constituent parts) need to be 'defined', as do external boundaries (on issues such as outsourcing). Within these broad 'demarcations' there are *relationships* to be built and maintained both internally and externally in ways that are fluid enough to respond to an uncertain environment. This section looks at the following issues (see Exhibit 9.7):

● Where responsibility and authority for operational and strategic decisions should be vested inside an organisation. Also, how these divided

---

| Exhibit 9.7 | **Relationships and boundaries** |

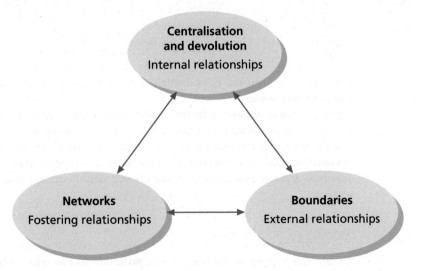

responsibilities can be connected and integrated. This is the debate about *centralisation and devolution*, which will build on the discussions about parenting in Chapter 6.

● Some important organisational implications about external relationships – the *boundaries* of an organisation.

● *Networks* and how they can foster relationships.

9.4.1 Centralisation vs. devolution

Devolution concerns the extent to which the centre of an organisation delegates decision making to units and managers lower down in the hierarchy

One of the important continuing debates in both public[19] and private sector organisations has been concerned with *devolution*. **Devolution** concerns the extent to which the centre of an organisation delegates decision making to units and managers lower down in the hierarchy.

It is probably no accident that this interest in the importance of devolution coincided with a sustained period of market and financial pressure for most large organisations. It has been further fuelled by globalisation and the opportunities presented by cheaper and more powerful communication technologies. This has triggered senior managers to take action to address a number of issues:

● The danger of top managers becoming out of touch with the 'sharp-end' action in the markets and operations of the business. Overcentralisation in large organisations can result in managers losing their way and becoming too concerned with internal matters at the expense of serving the customer or client. In fast-moving markets, or during periods of significant change in the public services, there was a feeling that more authority was needed *close to the action* in order to improve corporate performance.

● The increased speed at which decisions need to be made and the inability of traditional multi-layered hierarchies to cope with this. Although de-layering can be an important structural response, by itself it can create other problems such as increased spans of control so that senior managers became overstretched. They needed to devolve many more of their decisions to others.

Illustration 9.6 shows how British Telecom restructured in 2000/2001 to address these issues.

Despite these reasons why increased devolution might make sense, there is a worry that devolution can become a 'fad' and simply a reaction to a previous era of overcentralisation. To avoid this risk the issue of centralisation vs. devolution needs to be seen as a *continuum* from highly centralised to highly devolved and not as a black or white choice. This is the approach taken in this section.

Dividing responsibilities

Section 6.3 looked at the question of whether and in what ways a corporate parent can add value to its constituent business units or departments (see

Illustration 9.6

British Telecom restructures for the 21st century

Increasing diversity and speed of change usually require a rethink of the centralisation–devolution of strategy in organisations.

In November 2000, BT, the ex-state-owned UK telecommunications company, announced that it was changing its structure from a centralised to a much more devolved structure. The chief executive, Sir Peter Bonfield, explained this in the annual review to shareholders:

The communications industry is changing faster than ever before and, if BT is to stay ahead of the wave, it has to continue to change – in quite fundamental ways.

Developments in information and communications technology – the Internet, mobility and multimedia – are transforming all our lives – at work, at home and in between. And it's only just begun. It's rapidly becoming a broadband world. New types of network and new methods of access, via cable, fibre, satellite and wireless, will bring information, communications and entertainment to customers, wherever they are, faster than ever before.

Customers will be 'always-on', always connected. And this requires a whole new response – a new way of thinking about what customers want and need, and how BT can supply it.

To succeed in this new world, we must:

● continue to increase our focus on our customers, whose expectations and requirements are becoming ever more sophisticated and demanding;
● bring new communications possibilities to our customers everywhere, at the right price; and
● get even better at spotting new opportunities and developing new business models.

And we have to do so at speed. It is in response to these challenges that we are radically restructuring BT by creating a number of new international businesses, each with its own character and priorities but working together to meet customers' needs. (These are called *lines of business*) and are:

● *Ignite*, our international broadband network business, focused primarily on corporate and wholesale markets;
● *BT Openworld*, our international, mass-market Internet business;
● *BT Wireless*, our international mobile business, with a particular emphasis on mobile data; and
● *Yell*, our international directories and associated e-commerce business, which we have announced we will be listing this year.

These new businesses will work alongside *Concert*, our global venture with AT&T, which will continue to serve global communications needs of multinational customers.

We also intend to separate the UK fixed business into a *wholesale business*, using our fixed-network assets, and a *retail business* wholly focused on meeting customers' needs with an array of packages and propositions. Increasingly, the UK retail business will serve its customers using e-business technologies and channels.

The wholesale UK business will also benefit from the freedom to concentrate on its customers among the other operators in the UK.

Questions

1. List the advantages and disadvantages of BT's moving from a centralised bureaucratic structure to this family of businesses.

2. How will the management processes between centre/business unit and business unit/business unit need to change to support the structural change?

| Exhibit 9.8 | Strategic planning |

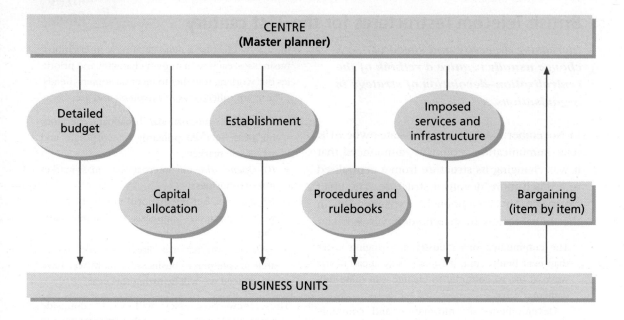

Exhibit 6.4). An important determinant of organising for success is clarity around how responsibilities for decision making are to be *divided* between the centre and the business units. Goold and Campbell[20] provide three valuable *stereotypes* (or management styles) of different ways of dividing these responsibilities. The organisational processes and the way that relationships work is very different in each case.

Strategic planning

Strategic planning (Exhibit 9.8) is the most centralised of the three approaches. In a **strategic planning style**, the relationship between the centre and the business units is one of a parent who is the *master planner* prescribing detailed roles for departments and business units, which are seen as *agencies* whose role is confined to the operational delivery of the plan. In the extreme form of strategic planning, the centre is expected to add value in most of the ways outlined in Exhibit 6.4. The centre orchestrates, co-ordinates and controls all of the activities of the departments and business units through the extensive use of the formal planning and control systems (as discussed in section 9.3 above) shown in Exhibit 9.8. The centre also directly manages the infrastructure and provides many corporate services. This is a style suited to the synergy manager or parental developer roles adopted by corporate centres, as discussed in Section 7.3. This is the classic bureaucracy familiar to many managers in large public and private sector organisations. Multinational fast-food chains,

In a **strategic planning style**, the relationship between the centre and the business units is one of a parent who is the *master planner* prescribing detailed roles for departments and business units

| Exhibit 9.9 | Financial control |

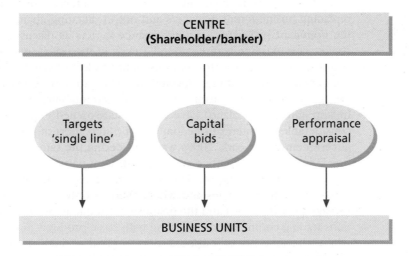

such as McDonald's, would arguably come closest to this stereotype. They have globalised a service delivery concept and maintain standards across the world through standardisation and routinisation of activities.

Strategic planning can be a useful approach and one in which corporate managers add value, but only if they are able to have a detailed working knowledge of each business unit. Where attempts are made to extend beyond this arena, strategic planning as a management style becomes difficult to operate and often dysfunctional. Essentially, corporate managers run the risk of holding back the development of business areas that they do not understand or, even worse, steering them in inappropriate directions. The potential costs of bureaucracy are also dangers with this style, both in money and in lost opportunities.

This brand of devolution fosters relationships between the centre and business units or departments that tend to become tactical and characterised by a 'special pleadings' mentality (bargaining item by item) in the business units. This can hold back strategy development in a changing business environment.

Financial control

Financial control (Exhibit 9.9) is the most extreme form of devolution – short of dissolution of the organisation into separate businesses. The relationship between the centre and the business units is as a parent who is a *shareholder or banker* for those units. As the name suggests, the relationship is financial and there is little concern for the detailed product/market strategy of business units – even to the extent that they can compete openly with each other provided they deliver the financial results. They might even have authority to raise funds from outside the company. This is a style suited to the portfolio manager or restructurer roles of a corporate centre, as discussed in section 6.3.

In **financial control** the role of the centre is confined to setting financial targets, allocating resources, appraising performance and intervening to avert or correct poor performance

In **financial control** the role of the centre is confined to setting financial targets, allocating resources, appraising performance and intervening to avert or correct poor performance. Importantly, these interventions would usually be replacing business unit managers and not in dictating changes in strategy. So the dominant processes are performance targets as discussed in section 9.3 above. This extreme is rarely found – even in the private sector. Some public sector managers appear to hold this as their ideal of what devolution means, but in reality, such extreme devolution is likely to remain unacceptable within the public sector for reasons of political accountability. Some countries (e.g. Ireland and New Zealand) have created state-owned enterprises (SOEs) with considerable commercial freedom but one step short of privatisation. The UK government in the early 2000s was considering the same issue of commercial freedom for The Post Office and its constituent parts.

This style is most appropriate to organisations operating in stable markets with mature technologies and where there is only a short time lag between management decisions and the financial consequences: for example, organisations trading commodities or dealing with basic products. It is also appropriate where the diversity of business units is great – since the other two styles require some measure of relatedness between business units. A major concern with financial control can be the dominance of short-termism. No one has responsibility for fostering innovation and organisational learning. The business units are focused on meeting tough short-term targets set by a centre that does not have the resources or the competences to manage the knowledge creation and integration processes. So competence development can only really happen through acquisitions and disposals.

Strategic control

Strategic control is concerned with shaping the *behaviour* in business units and with shaping the *context* within which managers are operating

Strategic control (Exhibit 9.10), which lies between these two extremes, necessarily defines the way in which most organisations operate. In a sense it is not a single stereotype, since it bridges all of the space between strategic planning and financial control. The relationship between the centre and the business units is one of a parent who behaves like a *strategic shaper*. **Strategic control** is concerned with shaping the *behaviour* in business units[21] and with shaping the *context* within which managers are operating. This is a style suited to the synergy manager or parental developer roles of a corporate centre as discussed in section 6.3. So, referring back to Exhibit 6.4, the centre would expect to add value in a variety of ways and Exhibit 9.10 provides a *checklist* against which an organisation can establish its own particular brand of strategic control. For example, the centre might expect to add value by:

● Defining and shaping the *overall* strategy of the organisation.

● Deciding the *balance* of activities and the role of each business unit.

● Defining and controlling organisational *policies* (on employment, market coverage, etc.).

● Defining the 'rules of engagement' between the various business units. For example, whether competition in the marketplace between business units

Exhibit 9.10	Strategic control

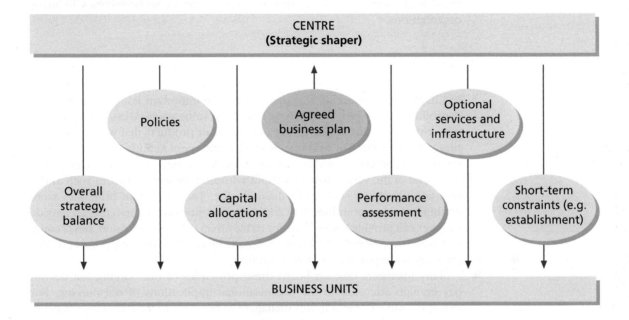

will be allowed. This may also include the use of internal market mechanisms, as discussed in section 9.3 above.

- Deciding 'boundary' issues; for example, whether business units are able to source their inputs (e.g. IT services) from outside the organisation. This is discussed more fully below (section 9.4.2).

- Fostering innovation and organisational learning.

- Defining standards and assessing the *performance* of the separate business units and intervening to improve performance (i.e. the processes of performance targeting discussed in section 9.3 above).

However, the centre does not fulfil these roles through an imposed master plan. Rather, strategic control is built through the processes of agreeing strategies of business units (perhaps through their business plans) – but within central boundaries and guidelines. Perhaps the biggest concern with this style is that the centre tries to shape strategy in these ways without being clear about the 'corporate logic' or having the competences to actually add value in these ways.

9.4.2 Boundaries

There have been a number of discussions of boundaries in earlier chapters and it is not the intention to repeat that detail here. So this section will look at how the definition and establishment of boundaries within and around organisations is an important consideration in organising for success and how there have been important strategic changes to these boundaries in many organisations.

Outsourcing

In Chapter 4, outsourcing was presented as an important issue about strategic capability that arises from the concept of the value chain. Outsourcing occurs where organisations decide to buy in services or products that were previously produced in-house. For example, payroll, component manufacture, IT services, training, are all commonly occurring examples of outsourced activities. At the other end of the value chain it is about withdrawing from activities such as distribution, customer services or maintenance. Two important principles were established when searching for candidates for outsourcing: first, that an outside supplier can provide better value for money than in-house provision, but second, that core competences should not normally be outsourced since these activities critically underpin competitive advantage.

Many managers take on board these principles of outsourcing but do not pay enough attention to the organisational implications of outsourcing. For example, outsourcing requires managers to be much more competent at maintaining performance through their management of supplier (or distributor) *relationships* rather than through management control systems within their own organisation. This may take some considerable attention. For example, suppliers or distributors will need to be educated about the organisation's strategies, priorities and standards and how their work influences the final performance of the product or service. They need to be motivated to perform consistently to these required standards. It should be clear from section 9.3 that there are different processes by which this might be achieved. At one extreme, suppliers might be 'tied in' through enterprise resource planning systems. This might be possible and desirable where the requirements of the supplier are clear and unlikely to change quickly. At the other extreme, the relationship may be maintained through social processes and norms – for example, working with suppliers who know the company well and are tuned into the cultural norms. This would be important where suppliers are adding creative input to the product or service (such as designers) where the two-way interaction needs to be much more fluid. Between these extremes, market mechanisms and/or performance targets could be used if a contractual approach to the relationship is felt to be appropriate – for example, for one-off projects or where there is a range of potential suppliers.

Illustration 9.7 shows how the UK railway system – which had been a single company (British Rail) running the railways through a 'command and control approach' – was divided into smaller specialist companies separately responsible for the infrastructure (Railtrack), service provision (Train Operating Companies) and rolling stock (ROSCOs). This arrangement was blamed for the disastrous situation that happened in the autumn of 2000.

Illustration 9.7

British railways in crisis

Sometimes a command and control system might be the best way to deliver reliable service.

In the autumn of 2000 the British railway system nearly reached 'meltdown'. The aftermath of a fatal accident caused by poor track maintenance and the worst autumn rainfall for 400 years together created chaos – described by some of the press as a 'nervous breakdown'. Many were suggesting that this was an inevitable result of privatisation (in 1995) and the way in which the previously managed 'command and control' integrated system had been split into a 'quasi-market' with more than 100 service providers tied together through legal contracts, performance measures and penalty payments. It was felt to be impossible to cope with crisis when management, ownership and operation of the industry was divided between numerous unco-operative companies and institutions who had contractual relationships with each other.

Indeed, an outsider often had difficulty understanding how the industry was structured. At privatisation the previously integrated functions of the railway were divided into:

- *Railtrack* – who owned and ran the infrastructure and directly managed 14 major stations.
- Train operating companies (*TOCs*) – 28 companies that ran the trains under a renewable franchise.
- Rolling stock companies (*ROSCOs*) – who owned the trains and leased them to the TOCs.
- Maintenance companies – who undertook most of the track maintenance under contract to Railtrack.
- There were also several *regulatory* and similar bodies who were involved in railways:

The Office of Rail Regulation (ORR) – who regulated the activities of Railtrack and the TOCs, and Passenger Transport Executive (PTEs) (in seven major urban connurbations) who specified service levels and provided subsidies.

Earlier criticism of the fragmented system had led to the government's creating the *Strategic Rail Authority* (SRA) to provide a focus and direction for Britain's railways and take over the function of awarding franchises. It was pledged to introduce longer franchises to encourage a more strategic approach from TOCs.

In his first annual report in July 2000, Sir Alastair Morton, chairman of the Shadow Strategic Rail Authority,[1] described the SRA's role: 'We shall emphasise service, to be delivered by private sector operations and suppliers to provide what the consumers and the areas served want. The SRA will be not an operations-driven, command-and-control authority managing the railways.'

Three months later, the system approached 'meltdown' and many were asking whether, in fact, there ought to be a command-and-control management of the rail industry. Some were even suggesting that the railways should be renationalised.

Note

1. The SRA operated as a 'shadow' authority before the legislation was approved by Parliament in 2001.

Sources: Adapted from Strategic Rail Authority Annual Report 1999–2000 and website; *The Times*, 30 November 2000.

Questions

1. What problems does a 'quasi-market' structure create?

2. Why was the SRA created and why was it reluctant to operate in a command-and-control mode?

Strategic alliances

This debate about defining boundaries and managing relationships with other organisations (or other parts of the same organisation) resurfaced in Chapter 8 in the discussion about strategic alliances. The organisational concerns are similar to those with outsourcing except that a strategic alliance may be much more overtly relational in the way the alliance is constructed (as against the contractual nature of many supplier–customer relationships). Readers are referred to Exhibit 8.3, which shows the spectrum of strategic alliance types from entirely contractual to essentially relational. The important organisational issue is finding the balance between the best sources of specialist knowledge (which would suggest many members of an alliance) and the competence to integrate these strands of specialist knowledge to create a best-value product or service to customers. The more members of an alliance, the more complex this integration task becomes and the more effort that needs to be put into the ingredients of successful alliances, as discussed in section 8.3.3 – such as trust. This will be discussed further below when considering networks and the ability of some organisations to achieve a nodal position in a network of multiple partners.

Virtual organisation[22]

Virtual organisations are held together not through formal structure and physical proximity of people, but by partnership, collaboration and networking

The logical extension of much of this thinking would be an organisation whose in-house (owned) resources and activities are minimised and nearly all resources and activities reside outside the organisation. These so-called **virtual organisations** are held together not through formal structure and physical proximity of people, but by partnership, collaboration and networking. The important issue is that this organisation feels 'real' to clients and meets their needs at least as adequately as other organisations. It has been argued[23] that such extreme forms of outsourcing are likely to result in serious strategic weakness in the long run, as the organisation becomes devoid of core competences and cut off from the learning which can exist through undertaking these activities in-house. This is now an important consideration in many industries such as civil engineering, publishing and specialist travel companies, all of which are highly dependent on outsourcing aspects of their business which hitherto were considered as core. The concern is whether short-term improvements are being achieved at the expense of securing a capacity for innovation. The danger of 'virtuality' is that knowledge creation and innovation only occur within the specialist 'boxes' represented by the activities of separate partners. There is no one who has the competence or authority to integrate these pockets of knowledge.

9.4.3 Networks[24]

The various issues and trends that are redefining the boundaries of organisations are important responses to the changes outlined at the beginning of this chapter (particularly knowledge creation, communication technologies and globalisation). Taken together, they mean that more organisations have become dependent on internal and external networks to ensure success. So *co-operation* has become a key aspect of organising for success. Networks can take different forms:

● The nature of work activities in many organisations has now changed such that many activities no longer need to take place in a particular location such as a factory or an office. The result is that many more people are able to carry out their work *independently* but remain connected to key corporate resources (such as databases and specialist advice) and to colleagues, suppliers and clients through the telecommunications and computing infrastructure. This has been called teleworking, where at least part of an organisation's work is delivered by a network of independent operators who may be employees, self-employed or a mixture of both. Since the exploitation of the Internet remains a major strategic issue for many organisations (see Chapter 10), new ways of organising will be essential. The Internet allows many formal structures to be dismantled and replaced with well-functioning networks supported by this information infrastructure.

● Networks may simply be loose 'federations' of experts who voluntarily come together to integrate their expertise to create products or services. In the entertainment business, musicians, actors and other creative artists sometimes come together in this way as well as through the more formal processes of agents and contracts. Some organisations make their living by maintaining databases of resources (people) in the network and possibly facilitating social contact through organising networking events.

● A critical test of any strategy is whether it will provide best-value products or services to customers. Part of this concerns the way in which a customer interfaces with an organisation before, during and after purchase. On the whole, customers wish to experience this interface as being smooth and 'joined up', and traditionally this has often not been the case. Since most products and services are produced by integrating different components, knowledge and activities, all too often customers experience a service which is disjointed. They get passed around in a search for information about the product. The delivery and after-sales support processes may be disjointed too. This criticism has applied to both private and public sector organisations. The question is, how can the network of knowledge and activities be made to work more smoothly? There are several 'solutions' (see Exhibit 9.11):

- A **one-stop shop** is a *structural* solution where a physical presence is created through which all client enquiries are channelled. The function of the one-stop shop is to put together a complete package of products or services by co-ordinating the various services. A 'turnkey' contractor (say, in civil engineering) might operate in this way – using their own expertise in project management and managing a network of suppliers, but not actually undertaking any of the detailed work themselves. With the growth of e-commerce, the one-stop shop may, in fact, be *virtual* in the sense that clients enter via a 'gateway' (say a website) but the physical services or products that are being integrated into the customer's

A **one-stop shop** is where a physical presence is created through which all client enquiries are channelled

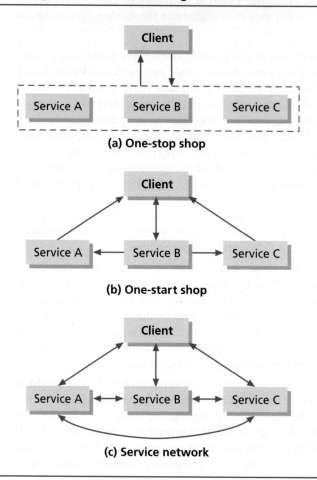

| Exhibit 9.11 | 'Joined-up' services: smoothing the network |

(a) One-stop shop

(b) One-start shop

(c) Service network

product or service are actually dispersed (in physical terms). The critical issue is that it feels joined-up to the customer whose needs can be satisfied through this one gateway.

A **one-start shop** deals with client enquiries by *diagnosing* the client's needs and *referring* them to the most appropriate provider

- A second option is a **one-start shop** which deals with client enquiries by *diagnosing* the client's needs and *referring* them to the most appropriate provider. This is referred to as 'pigeon-holing'. The role of primary health care practitioners (GPs) has traditionally been concerned with this process. Many advice services for small businesses have been established in this way – whether it be by banks or by government-sponsored agencies (e.g. Business Link (Small Business Service) in the UK). The critical issues at the one-start gateway are full *knowledge* of all the capabilities throughout the whole network and *authority* to refer clients to particular providers. The relationship with the providers in the network must be maintained to ensure that these two things can happen.

- In a **service network** the client may access all of the services of the network through any of the constituent members of the network. A well-functioning network may not be easy to achieve, since it requires all members of the network to be fully informed, capable and willing to 'cross-sell' other people's products and to act collaboratively. Above all else, it requires *trust and respect* between members of the network.

     Some service networks also have a one-start shop facility. For example, Best Western is an international network of independent hotels, where customers can receive information or make bookings at any hotel in the network or through central booking points. This facility has the clear advantage of encouraging travellers to 'book on' their next destination with Best Western.

- Many networks are essentially multiple strategic alliances and the ingredients of successful alliances outlined in section 8.3.3 would be relevant considerations for the success of networks in both the public and private sectors. It has been suggested[25] that multiple alliances are often characterised by one organisation having achieved a *nodal position* from which they drive the other partners along. This may be an important ingredient of successful networks and requires the organisation at the nodal position to have three strengths:
  - A compelling *vision* that legitimises the need for the network and entices in partners. In the public sector this may be a vision of politicians who then set up the network to deliver – for example, on drugs, crime and disorder, social exclusion and so on.
  - *Unique resources or core competences* to establish and hold the nodal position – such as a proprietary system as seen with technologies such as VHS video or the Windows computer operating system.
  - *Networking skills* to sustain and develop the network.

9.5 CONFIGURATIONS

Exhibit 9.1 at the outset of this chapter was a reminder that organising for success is not achieved through the separate strands (structures, processes and relationships) discussed in the previous sections of this chapter but by the way in which the elements work together consistently and how they match an organisation's strategies. This is called an organisation's **configuration** and consists of the structures, processes, relationships and boundaries through which the organisation operates. Recent research[26] supports the view that it is this type of holistic change that drives organisation success and not fads and fashions around the separate strands. This notion has also been called *complementarity*[27] – that performance is dependent on a set of complementary changes. But configurations should also be *contingent* on circumstances (for example, size, nature of the environment and so on). It should be clear from previous discussions in this book that any configuration is likely to *emerge* over time as an organisation finds ways of adjusting to the context in which it is operating. So it is unlikely to be a carefully considered choice as such. This final section will look at the following issues about configurations and strategy:

In a **service network** the client may access all of the services of the network through any of the constituent members of the network

An organisation's **configuration** consists of the structures, processes, relationships and boundaries through which the organisation operates

Exhibit 9.12 | Mintzberg's six organisational configurations

	SITUATIONAL FACTORS		DESIGN PARAMETERS	
Configuration	Environment	Internal	Key part of organisation	Key processes
Simple	Simple/dynamic Hostile	Small Young Simple tasks CEO control	Strategic apex	Direct supervision
Machine bureaucracy	Simple/static	Old Large Regulated tasks Technocrat control	Technostructure	Planning and control systems
Professional bureaucracy	Complex/static	Simple systems Professional control	Operating core	Planning systems Social control
Divisionalised	Simple/static Diversity	Old Very large Divisible tasks Middle-line control	Middle line	Performance targets
Adhocracy	Complex/dynamic	Often young Complex tasks Expert control	Operating core Support staff	Social processes Self-control
Missionary	Simple/static	Middle-aged Often 'enclaves' Simple systems Ideological control	Culture	Social processes

Source: Adapted from H. Mintzberg, *The Structuring of Organizations*, Prentice Hall, 1979.

- typical configurations and how they change;
- global organisations – as an example of changing configurations;
- reinforcing cycles – the links with other aspects of strategy.

9.5.1 Stereotypes

Mintzberg[28] has described six pure configurational stereotypes. These can be described in terms of the different 'mix' of structures, processes and relationships discussed above. It is useful for managers to reflect on the extent to which they see a match or mismatch between their organisational configuration and the context in which they are operating[29].

Exhibit 9.12 summarises the key features of Mintzberg's six configurations, in terms of the circumstances or situations to which each is best suited and also the structure, processes and relationships of the organisation.

● The *simple* configuration is likely to have no formal structure (like the simple structure discussed earlier). Few of the processes are formalised, and it makes minimal use of planning. It has a small management hierarchy, dominated by the chief executive (often the owner) and a loose division of work. The organisation is driven forward by the vision and personality of the chief executive, probably through direct supervision and personal relationship building. This configuration can prove highly effective in small entrepreneurial organisations where flexibility to changing circumstances is critical to success.

● The *machine bureaucracy* is often found in mature organisations operating in markets where rates of change are low. It is characterised by a large staff function – or *technostructure* – which develops planning and control systems to standardise work routines. The major improvements in cost efficiency in manufacturing industries early in the twentieth century were largely achieved through machine bureaucracies. More recently, the exploitation of IT to routinise service delivery is an example. This configuration is very appropriate for organisations producing commodity products or services where cost leadership is critical to the organisation's competitive perform-ance (postal services would be an example).

● The *professional bureaucracy* is bureaucratic without the centralisation found in the machine bureaucracy. Professional work is complex, but it can be standardised through ensuring that the professional staff have the same core knowledge and competences. An emphasis on the processes of training and peer group interaction is important to sustaining this standardisation. The activities of different groups will be integrated through planning systems.

● The *divisionalised* configuration is often found as a response to diversity in the products and markets of the organisation. The structure is divisionalised (as discussed earlier in the chapter) and there are key decisions establishing centre/division relationships, as discussed in section 9.3. In particular, the corporate centre will specify levels of performance output expected from divisions or subsidiaries. These might be generic, such as overall profit per-formance, and might be found when *financial control* is the management style. In contrast, in organisations closer to *strategic control*, this specifica-tion of outputs is more likely to be expressed as a series of *performance indicators*, such as market share, efficiency ratios and a 'league table' posi-tion. Market mechanisms might be used between divisions if they have a customer–supplier relationship.

● The *adhocracy* is found in organisations whose competitive strategy is largely concerned with innovation and change. This configuration is highly organic, relying on direct interaction between individual workers and a management style that assists and promotes these processes of social and self-control. Many professional service organisations (when providing cus-tomised services) may configure themselves in this way.

● *Missionary* organisations are dominated by cultural issues that are clear, focused, inspiring and distinctive. These ideals dominate the organisation's purposes and its *modus operandi.* Many voluntary organisations operate in this way: they attract like-minded individuals who share the missionary

| Exhibit 9.13 | **Configurations in multinational companies** |

GLOBAL CO-ORDINATION

		Low	High
LOCAL INDEPENDENCE AND RESPONSIVENESS	**Low**	International divisions	Global product companies
	High	International subsidiaries	Transnational corporations

Source: Adapted from C. Bartlett and S. Ghoshal, *Managing Across Borders: The transnational corporation*, 2nd edition, Random House, 1998.

vision, and as such rely little on structures and formal processes to drive the organisation along.

Although few organisations will fit neatly into just one of these stereotypes, they can be used to think through how closely an organisation's configuration matches the situation in which it is operating and whether change might improve performance.

9.5.2 Configurations and globalisation[30]

The growth in the size and importance of multinational businesses warrants some special mention, since the organisational implications can be significant. The way in which these organisational issues have changed *over time* with increasing globalisation[31] also provides a good example of how organising for success is about the various strands of structure, processes, relationships and boundaries need to change as strategies and circumstances change:

● When the degree of globalisation of markets was low, the most basic form of configuration for a multinational was the retention of the 'home' structure and the creation of overseas subsidiaries, which were managed through *direct supervision* between the top manager of the subsidiary and the chief executive of the parent company. This was common in single-product companies or where the overseas interests were relatively minor. Beyond this simple configuration, the critical issue is the extent to which local independence and responsiveness should take precedence over global co-ordination (see Exhibit 9.13). In other words, it is an example on a global scale of the more general issues of co-ordination discussed in this chapter. How this is addressed will vary with circumstances and over time.

- A common form of multinational configuration was *international divisions*. Here the home-based structure may be retained at first – whether functional or divisional – and the overseas interests managed through separate international divisions. These draw on the products of the home company, with the disadvantage of lack of local tailoring of services. Strategy is determined centrally (close to Goold and Campbell's *strategic planning*) and formal processes (of planning and performance targets) dominate. Although vertical co-ordination is strong, there is no attempt to co-ordinate horizontally between the separate geographical divisions. This configuration tends to work best where there is a wide geographical spread and a portfolio of closely related products.

- Geographically based *international subsidiaries* often evolved from the previous structure These subsidiaries were part of a multinational whole, but operated independently by country. In these companies, virtually all the management functions were nationally based, allowing for higher degrees of local responsiveness. Many of the multinationals founded in colonial days operated this way, such as Inchcape, Shell or Burmah. In such circumstances, the control of the parent company is likely to be dependent on some form of planning and reporting system, and perhaps the ultimate veto over national strategies; but the level of global co-ordination is likely to be low. The relationship would be close to Goold and Campbell's *financial control*.

- With the increasing globalisation of many industries there has been a move away from international divisions or subsidiaries to what has become known as a *global product* or integrated structure. Here the multinational is split into product divisions that are then managed across the world with a style close to Goold and Campbell's *strategic planning*. The logic of such an approach is that it should promote cost efficiency (particularly of production) on an international basis, and provide enhanced transfer of resources and competences (such as technology and brands) between geographical regions. The network of plants, each one in a separate country, may be making parts of cars, for example, which are assembled in yet another country: this manufacturing network may be supported by an international research and development network. The international development of many Japanese companies – for example, in electronics – was managed in this way. A key requirement to support this structure is planning mechanisms to co-ordinate the various operations, and it is in these organisations that the planning and formal control systems are likely to be most sophisticated.

  The obvious danger with a global product strategy is that local needs and differences may be ignored. Also, it is likely that the multinational will have several companies or divisions selling into the same country and these may be uncoordinated – perhaps creating inefficiencies through duplication of effort and confusing customers.

- As globalisation has become more pervasive some organisations have tried to address the organisational issues more fundamentally in terms of redefining all of the issues of structure, boundaries, relationships and processes that are

A **transnational corporation** combines the local responsiveness of the international subsidiary with the advantages available from co-ordination found in global product companies

discussed in this chapter. They have attempted to become what has been termed a **transnational corporation**, which combines the local responsiveness of the international subsidiary with the advantages available from co-ordination found in global product companies. This is achieved by creating an integrated *network* of interdependent resources and competences. Specifically, the transnational exhibits the following features:

- Each national unit operates independently, but is a source of ideas and capabilities for the whole corporation.
- National units achieve global scale through specialisation on behalf of the whole corporation.
- The corporate centre manages this global network by first establishing the role of each business unit, then sustaining the systems, relationships and culture to make the network of business units operate effectively.

The success of a transnational corporation is dependent on the ability *simultaneously* to achieve global competences, local responsiveness and organisation-wide innovation and learning. This requires some degree of clarity as to boundaries, relationships and the roles that the various managers need to perform. For example:

- Those responsible for *global products or businesses* have the overriding responsibility to further the company's global competitiveness, which will cross both national and functional boundaries. They must be the *product/market strategist*, the *architect* of the business resources and competences, the driver of product innovation and the *co-ordinator* of transnational transactions.

- Managers of *countries or territories* must act as a *sensor* of local needs. They must be able to *build* unique competences: that is, become a centre of excellence which allows them to be a *contributor* to the company as a whole.

- Managers of *functions* such as finance or IT have a major responsibility for ensuring worldwide innovation and learning across the various parts of the organisation. This requires the skill to recognise and spread best practice across the organisation – a form of *internal benchmarking*. So they must be able to *scan* the organisation for best practice, *cross-pollinate* this best practice and be the *champion* of innovations.

- The critical issue is the role played by the *corporate managers*, which is vital in the transnational corporation in integrating these other roles and responsibilities. Not only are they the *leaders*, but they are also the *talent spotters* among business, country and functional managers, facilitating the interplay between them. For example, they must foster the processes of innovation and knowledge creation. They are responsible for the *development* of a strong management centre in the organisation.

Illustration 9.8 shows ABB's experience with transnational configurations during the 1990s.

There are interesting differences between countries in the way that global strategies have developed[32] over time. Companies which originated in many European countries (such as Unilever or Nestlé) needed to internationalise their activities at an early stage, owing to the small size of their home markets. This

Illustration 9.8

The network organisation: Asea Brown Boveri

STRATEGY IN ACTION

Network organisations need to change and develop with circumstances.

In 1997, Percy Barnevik, whose vision had originally created the giant ABB engineering company and made of it a model for management worldwide, retired as chief executive, remaining only as chairman. His successor was Goran Lindahl, former head of Power Transmission and one of Barnevik's key lieutenants over the previous decade.

Lindahl inherited an organisation that had been steadily developing from the early days of the ABB merger. During the early 1990s, the organisation had been led by a group executive in which were represented the six main business segments – plus six regions and major countries. Some regional heads were also segment heads. In 1993, this group executive had been rationalised, so that the geographical representation was standardised around the three big regions of the Americas, Europe–Middle East–Africa and Asia-Pacific. A new executive board organised around the three regional heads and the heads of the three core businesses (power generation, power transmission and distribution, and industrial and building systems) was created. This reorganisation was intended to reflect the increasingly regional scope of business.

However, soon ABB came under several new pressures. Regional heads had become seen as regional barons, whilst middle managers were leaving the organisation with complaints of the complexity of the organisation. During 1998, the Asian crisis disrupted many of the key markets in which ABB was operating. Between May and August 1998, the ABB stock price fell by a quarter. In April, Martin Ebners, the aggressive

Swiss shareholder activist, had taken a 12 per cent shareholding and was arguing loudly for a change in share structure and a partial break-up of the Group.

In August 1998, Goran Lindahl announced a major change in the organisational structure of the Group. The regional management structure was abolished, taking out one of the axes of ABB's famous matrix, and saving 100 management jobs. This reflected the increasingly global scope of the business. The biggest core business – industrial and building systems – was split into three separate divisions (automation, oil, gas and petrochemicals). Seven divisions emerged, each reporting detailed financial performance figures. Each division continued to contain clusters of business areas and local country units. Countries were declared important for local customer contacts, but investment and technology decisions would now take place on a global basis.

Lindahl described the reorganisation as 'an aggressive move aimed at greater speed and efficiency by further focusing and flattening the organisation'.

Prepared by Richard Whittington, Said Business School, Oxford.

Sources: Adapted from *Financial Times*, 13 August 1998; *Finanz und Wirtschaft*, 15 August 1998; *Cash*, 14 August 1998; Leona Achtenhagen *et al.*, Beyond the matrix structure of ABB, Universitat St. Gallen; www.abb.ch/abbgroup

Questions

1. What were the strengths and weaknesses of the network approach adopted by ABB in the early 1990s?

2. How did the subsequent structural changes address these issues?

typically took the form of international subsidiaries. As globalisation increased, their challenge was to reduce local autonomy and increase global integration. For example, the glass manufacturer Pilkington (see Illustration 3.2) responded to the global forces outlined in the illustration by a major increase in the global co-ordination of its automotive glass business (where global forces were very strong). However, with building products, glass co-ordination was strengthened regionally (e.g. within Europe) rather than globally – reflecting the significant differences between regions.

In contrast, US companies with a large domestic market historically tended to favour international divisions. Therefore they faced two challenges in globalisation: first, the issues of local autonomy; and second, the barriers between their separate strategic views of the domestic and international business. Japanese companies had traditionally been strongly domestically focused, and their international activities first developed through exporting. This resulted in strong global product strategies, and the subsequent need to relocate some production facilities overseas strengthened this position. The challenge then became one of increasing local autonomy without losing the benefits of the global product strategies.

9.5.3 Reinforcing cycles

Part II of the book introduced the *business idea* as an explanation of how the elements of an organisation's strategic position (environment, resources and expectations) were interconnected and reinforced each other. This idea of a reinforcing cycle of related factors is useful here too. Whereas an organisation's configuration may be thought of as 'following' strategy either in a planned or incremental way, in reality the relationship also works in the opposite direction: that is, organisations operating with particular configurations tend to seek out strategies that best fit that configuration and 'reject' those which require change. Also, the fact that it is possible to identify a limited number of stereotypes for organisational configurations, as described above, is a reminder that the separate organisational strands (structure, relationships, boundaries and processes) are not independent variables – they tend to occur in particular groupings. Indeed, configurations found in practice tend to be very *cohesive*, *robust* and *difficult to change*.[33] The explanation of this draws together the issues which have been discussed above.

Reinforcing cycles are created by the *dynamic interaction* between the various factors of environment, configuration and elements of strategy; they tend to preserve the status quo

Reinforcing cycles are created by the *dynamic interaction* between the various factors of environment, configuration and elements of strategy. Reinforcing cycles tend to preserve the status quo. Exhibit 9.14 shows two examples from the stereotypes in section 9.5.1 above. The machine bureaucracy is a configuration often adopted in stable environmental conditions and can help create a position of cost leadership. This can underpin a positioning of 'low price' (or cost efficiency in the public services), requiring standardised work processes which, in turn, are well supported by a defender culture. This culture *seeks out* stable parts of the environment and the whole cycle is self-perpetuating. A similar reinforcing cycle can occur with the adhocracy, as seen in the same exhibit.

Exhibit 9.14	Reinforcing cycles: two examples

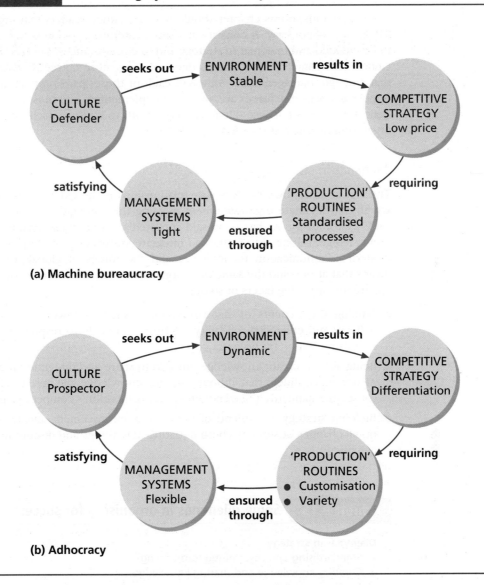

(a) Machine bureaucracy

(b) Adhocracy

None of this may be a problem for an organisation – in fact, the matching of these various organisational issues to each other may prove to be a source of great strength to the organisation. However, it should be remembered from Chapter 2 and the concept of the business idea that this is also likely to be an explanation of why *strategic drift* is so common. The organisation may need the capability to 'break out' of these reinforcing cycles if it is to survive and succeed in the long term. This will be discussed fully in Chapter 11, which is concerned with managing change.

9.6 ORGANISATIONAL DILEMMAS

The discussions in this chapter should have reminded readers that organising for success is not easy. It consists of a set of interlinking strands, which need to be blended and matched to strategy and to circumstances. This section concludes with some of the practical dilemmas (or, more correctly, *dualities*[34]) that strategic managers face. Although each of these 'pairs' appears to be of opposing forces, the forces are, in fact, complementary and must be balanced against each other. These dilemmas relate both to strategy itself and then to organising for success (see Exhibit 9.15).

Dilemmas in strategy

The test of structures, processes or relationships is the extent to which they are able to facilitate organisations in meeting the strategic challenges of the early 21st century. As has been said repeatedly above, these challenges are: rapid change, the need to foster and integrate knowledge, the exploitation of modern communication technologies and the forces of globalisation. This means that at one and the same time organisations may have to accommodate apparently opposing facets of strategy:

- Gaining the benefits of standardisation – such as lower cost, speedier delivery and enhanced reliability – whilst being able to respond to desires for customisation (at no extra cost!).

- Being able to create knowledge but also to share and integrate knowledge. Also to be confident that although sharing knowledge will raise the industry (or sector) standards it need not erode an organisation's competitive position.

- Building strategy as a blend of continuous improvement and transformational changes of strategy (both initiating new things and discontinuing old activities).

Exhibit 9.15   Some dilemmas in organising for success

Dilemmas in strategy
- Standardising and customising (positioning)
- Creating knowledge and sharing knowledge
- Continuity and change
- Innovation and stability

Leading to . . .

Dilemmas in organising for success
- Hierarchies and networks
- Vertical accountability and horizontal integration
- Empowering but holding the ring (tight–loose)
- Centralising and devolving (devolution style)
- Holistic solutions and best practice on each element (but not fads)

● The need to innovate – but from a stable base which mitigates the risks inherent in innovation.

These strategic dilemmas, in turn, throw up a set of organisational dilemmas. It is organisations that can master these dilemmas that are likely to perform best:

● *Heirarchies* and *networks* need not be incompatible, for a number of reasons. Firstly, an organisation may be pursuing a range of strategies at the same time. So some parts of the organisation may require configurations close to machine bureaucracies as they standardise their products, reduce costs through routinisation of processes, and compete fiercely on low prices and 'no frills', reliable products or services. Other parts of the organisation may be competing on differentiation of product or service strongly supported by a configuration similar to the adhocracy. Secondly, circumstances change with time – for example, through the stages of the product life cycle.

● Goold and Campbell's stereotypes should remind readers that relationships may need to be established both *vertically* and *horizontally* in organisations. Decisions on one dimension will affect the other. For example, their stereotype of 'strategic planning' attempts to master-plan both dimensions simultaneously whereas financial control is strong on vertical control processes and weak on horizontal co-ordination. Strategic control fills the middle ground.

● These stereotypes also emphasise the importance of being clear about the *'tight-loose'* agenda. This is what was referred to above as 'who does what?' – between the centre and the business units. But it also applies to other key relationships that have been discussed, such as outsourcing and strategic alliances.

● Perhaps the key organising dilemma is how to get the balance right between excellence that derives from *specialisation* and the ability to *integrate* knowledge and activities to provide best value products and services. This has been seen both in terms of fostering and integrating knowledge and also in the various roles and relationships needed in large global organisations.

SUMMARY

● Structuring for success is about an organisation's configuration. This is built up of related strands: structures, processes, relationships and boundaries. Configuration is a means to an end (improved performance). All too often it is seen as an end in itself. An inappropriate configuration can impede an organisation's strategies. However, the reverse is not true – a change of configuration will not guarantee success.

● There are many stereotypical structures (such as functional, divisional, matrix). It is important to be familiar with the strengths and weaknesses of each structural type and to understand that real organisation structures are usually a blend of these pure stereotypes.

- There is a range of different organisational *processes* to facilitate strategy. These processes range from formal controls (systems, rules and procedures), through social controls (culture and routines as discussed in Chapters 2 and 5), to self-controls (the personal motivation of individuals). These will be more or less appropriate to different circumstances and strategies.

- Relationships and boundaries are also important to success. Internally, a key issue is the 'style' of *centralisation/devolution*. Externally, there are choices around outsourcing, alliances and networks which may help or hinder success.

- The separate organisational strands will come together to form an organisational configuration. Usually this emerges as a response to the circumstances in which an organisation is operating. Mintzberg's stereotypical configurations are useful in showing the relationship between the organisation's circumstances and the organisational strands discussed in this chapter.

- *Globalisation* presents a special problem for organisations in trying to balance the competing forces of global uniformity and local responsiveness. There are several different configurational 'solutions' to this problem depending on circumstances.

- Finally, the most successful organisations are likely to be those whose managers can master the strategic and organisational dilemmas that the modern competitive world creates.

RECOMMENDED KEY READINGS

- A comprehensive review of structuring issues in the modern economy is A. Pettigrew and E. Fenton (eds), *The Innovating Organisation*, Sage, 2000.

- The centralisation/devolution considerations are discussed in M. Goold and A. Campbell, *Strategies and Styles*, Blackwell, 1987, and more fully in M. Goold, A. Campbell and M. Alexander, *Corporate Level Strategy: Creating value in the multibusiness company*, Wiley, 1994.

- For a discussion of issues of structuring in the public sector context see: K. Scholes, 'Strategy and structure in the public sector', in G. Johnson and K. Scholes

(eds), *Exploring Public Sector Strategy*, Financial Times/Prentice Hall, 2001, Chapter 13.

- Organisational configurations are covered comprehensively in H. Mintzberg, *The Structuring of Organizations*, Prentice Hall, 1979, and H. Mintzberg and J.B. Quinn, *The Strategy Process: Concepts and cases*, 3rd edition, Prentice Hall, 1995.

- Configurations in multinational corporations are covered in C. Bartlett and S. Ghoshal, *Managing Across Borders: The transnational corporation*, 2nd edition, Random House Business Books, 1998, and G. Yip, *Total Global Strategy*, Prentice Hall, 1995, Chapter 8.

REFERENCES

1. Some of these early writings are to be found in D. Pugh, *Organisation Theory*, Penguin, 1984.
2. These definitions come from T. Burns and G. Stalker, *The Management of Innovation*, Tavistock, 1968.
3. The point has been argued by E. Fenton and A. Pettigrew, 'Theoretical perspectives on new forms of organising' in A. Pettigrew and E. Fenton (eds), *The*

Innovating Organisation, Sage, 2000, Chapter 1, and also by C. Handy, 'Rethinking organisations', in T.Clark (ed.), *Advancement in Organisational Behaviour: Essays in honour of Derek S. Pugh*, Ashgate, 1996.
4. This idea of configuration is similar to that of *Strategic Architecture*, as discussed by G. Hamel and C.K. Prahalad, *Competing for the Future*, Harvard

Business School Press, 1994, Chapter 10, and J. Kay, *Foundations of Corporate Success*, Oxford University Press, 1993, Chapter 5.

5. This view of divisionalisation as a response to diversity was originally put forward by A.D. Chandler, *Strategy and Structure*, MIT Press, 1962.

6. Matrix structures are discussed by C. Bartlett and S. Ghoshal, 'Matrix management not a structure, a frame of mind', *Harvard Business Review*, vol. 68, no. 4 (1990), pp. 138–145.

7. T. Mullern, 'Integrating the team-based structure in the business process: the case of Saab Training Systems', in A. Pettigrew and E. Fenton (eds), *The Innovating Organisation*, Sage, 2000, Chapter 8.

8. See reference 7, page 238.

9. For example, this is the theme that runs through Pettigrew and Fenton's book – see reference 3.

10. For readers who would like to read more about ERP the following are useful: P. Bingi, M. Sharma and J. Godla, 'Critical issues affecting an ERP implementation', *Information Systems Management*, vol. 16, no. 3 (1999), pp. 7–14; N. Bancroft, *Implementing SAP/R3: How to introduce a large system into a large organisation*, Manning/Prentice Hall, 1996.

11. See P. Jackson and C. Price, *Privatisation and Regulation: A review of the issues*, Longman, 1994, Chapter 3. M. Bishop, J. Kay and C. Mayer, *Privatisation and Economic Performance*, Oxford University Press, 1994, provides a number of in-depth case studies of deregulation.

12. See R. Kaplan and D. Norton, 'The balanced scorecard: measures that drive performance', *Harvard Business Review*, vol. 70, no. 1 (1992), pp. 71–79, and 'Putting the balanced scorecard to work', *Harvard Business Review*, vol. 71, no. 5 (1993), pp. 134–147.

13. Market mechanisms of several types were introduced into many large organisations, particularly previously administered monopolies in the public sector in many countries. See Jackson and Price (reference 11 above), Chapters 5 and 8.

14. J.S. Brown and P. Duguid, 'Organisational learning and communities of practice: towards a unified view of working, learning and innovation', *Organisational Science*, vol. 2, no. 1 (1991), pp. 40–57.

15. For example, D. Leonard-Barton, 'Core capabilities and core rigidities: a paradox in managing new product development', *Strategic Management Journal*, vol. 13 (Summer 1992), pp. 111–125.

16. H. Mintzberg, *The Structuring of Organizations*, Prentice Hall, 1979.

17. The idea of top managers as 'shapers of context' is discussed in S. Ghoshal and C. Bartlett, 'Linking organisational context and managerial action: the dimensions of the quality of management', *Strategic Management Journal*, vol. 15 (1994), pp. 91–112; C. Bartlett and

S. Ghoshal, 'Changing the role of top management: beyond strategy to purpose', *Harvard Business Review*, vol. 72, no. 6 (1994), pp. 79–88; S. Ghoshal and C. Bartlett, 'Changing the role of top management', *Harvard Business Review*, vol. 73, no. 1 (1995), pp. 86–96.

18. This description of the three roles in professional service organisations was originally introduced by: D.H. Maister, 'Balancing the professional service organisation', *Sloan Management Review*, vol. 24, no. 1 (1982).

19. For a discussion of these issues in the public sector context see: K. Scholes, 'Strategy and structure in the public sector', in G. Johnson and K. Scholes (eds), *Exploring Public Sector Strategy*, Financial Times/Prentice Hall, 2001, Chapter 13, and T. Forbes, 'Devolution and control within the UK public sector: National Health Service Trusts', ibid., Chapter 16.

20. M. Goold and A. Campbell, *Strategies and Styles*, Blackwell, 1987.

21. C. Bartlett and S. Ghoshal, 'Changing the role of top management: beyond strategy to purpose', *Harvard Business Review*, vol. 72, no. 6 (1994), pp. 79–88; S. Ghoshal and C. Bartlett, 'Changing the role of top management', *Harvard Business Review*, vol. 73, no. 1 (1995), pp. 86–96.

22. Virtual organisations and the extensive use of sub-contracting have been widely discussed. For example, W. Davidow and M. Malone, *The Virtual Corporation*, Harper Business, 1992. Also, Handy (reference 3 above) who describes the extreme form of virtual organisation as 'a bag of contracts'.

23. J.C. Jarillo, *Strategic Networks: Creating the borderless organisation*, Butterworth/Heinemann, 1993.

24. See W. Ruigrok, L. Achtenhagen, M. Wagner and J. Ruegg-Sturm, 'ABB: beyond the global matrix towards the network organisation', in A. Pettigrew and E. Fenton (eds), *The Innovating Organisation*, Sage, 2000, Chapter 4. Also Jarillo (reference 23).

25. Y. Doz and G. Hamel, *Alliance Advantage*, Harvard Business School Press, 1998, p. 235.

26. See Pettigrew and Fenton – reference 3 above. A summary of the research project (INNFORM) on which the book was based can be found in *Hottopics*, vol. 1, no. 5, Warwick Business School, 1999.

27. P. Milgrom and P. Roberts, 'Complementarities and fit: strategy, structure and organisational change in manufacturing', *Journal of Accounting and Economics*, vol. 19, no. 2 (1995).

28. See reference 16 above.

29. For further reading on the relationship between configuration and organisational context, see D. Miller, 'The genesis of configuration', *Academy of Management Review*, vol. 12, no. 4 (1987), pp. 686–701, D. Jennings and S. Seaman, 'High and low levels of

organisational adaptation: an empirical analysis of strategy, structure and performance', *Strategic Management Journal*, vol. 15, no. 6 (1994), pp. 459-475.

30. Good general texts on global organisations are G. Yip, *Total Global Strategy*, Prentice Hall, 1995; C. Hill, *International Business: Competing in the global marketplace*, 3rd edition, McGraw-Hill, 2000.

31. See C. Bartlett and S. Ghoshal, *Managing Across Borders: The transnational corporation*, 2nd edition, Random House Business Books, 1998, and C. Bartlett and S. Ghoshal, *Transnational Management: Text cases and readings in cross-border management*, Irwin, 1995.

32. Yip (reference 30 above, Chapter 8).

33. This idea of configurations being cohesive is discussed in D. Miller, 'Organisational configurations: cohesion, change and prediction', *Human Relations*, vol. 43, no. 8 (1990), pp. 771-789. There is also a collection of research on configurational approaches to organisation in the *Academy of Management Journal*, vol. 36, no. 6 (1993), pp. 1175-1361.

34. A. Pettigrew and E. Fenton, 'Complexities and dualities in innovative forms of organising', in A. Pettigrew and E. Fenton (eds), *The Innovating Organisation*, Sage, 2000, Chapter 10.

WORK ASSIGNMENTS

* Refers to a case study in the Text and Cases edition. ∗ Denotes more advanced work assignments.

9.1 Draw up organisation charts for a number of organisations with which you are familiar and/or any of the case studies in the book. Why are the organisations structured in this way?

9.2 Referring to section 9.2.3 on the multidivisional structure, consider the advantages of creating divisions along different bases – such as product, geography or technology. Do this for an organisation with which you are familiar or AOL/Time Warner (Illustration 1.1), the BBC (the case example in this chapter) or The News Corporation.*

9.3 ∗ Referring to Exhibit 9.6 and Illustration 9.4, write a short executive brief to the CEO of a multidivisional organisation explaining how balanced scorecards could be a useful management process to monitor and control the performance of divisions. Be sure you present your critique of both the advantages and pitfalls of this approach.

9.4 ∗ Make a critical appraisal of the importance of the centre/division relationship in underpinning the strategic development of organisations (see Exhibits 9.8 to 9.10). Illustrate your answer by describing (with justification) the relationships which you feel would be most appropriate for the following organisations:

(a) The News Corporation*
(b) AOL/Time Warner (Illustration 1.1)
(c) British Telecom (Illustration 9.6)
(d) an organisation of your choice.

9.5 ∗ Referring to Exhibits 9.8 to 9.10, choose an organisation with which you are familiar and discuss the following two situations: (i) increasing centralisation, (ii) increasing devolution. In each case, explain and justify:

(a) examples of the circumstances in which you would recommend each change;
(b) how the change would assist the organisation to improve its performance;
(c) any potential dangers of the change and how these might be avoided.

9.6 By referring to Exhibit 9.12, explain which of Mintzberg's organisational configurations best fits the situation of each of the organisations in assignment 9.4. To what extent is the actual configuration of the organisation in line with this expectation, and what are the implications of any mismatches?

9.7 ∗ By referring to the elements of organising for success (structures, processes and relationships), compare the key difference you would expect to find in an organisation operating in a relatively simple/static environment and another organisation operating in a complex/dynamic environment (see Exhibit 9.14).

9.8 ∗ By using specific examples from your answers to the previous assignments, explain how the various aspects of structures, processes and relationships need to fit together to support an organisation's strategies (see Exhibit 9.15). How close are theory and practice? Refer to Pettigrew and Fenton and Mintzberg and Quinn in the recommended key readings to assist with your answer.

CASE EXAMPLE

Building One BBC

The BBC was founded in 1922 as a public service broadcaster of radio and, subsequently, television. It is independent of government and overseen by a board of governors. Its income is derived from a licence fee paid by 22 million households in the UK raising revenue of some £2 billion. As such the BBC remained one of the few large broadcasters in the world which did not carry advertising, although it did derive commercial income of almost £100 million from the sale of programme rights and branded products worldwide. In Britain, and to some extent in other parts of the world, the BBC was seen more as an institution than a company. Its broadcasts reached over 50 million people domestically each week and almost 300 million worldwide. It had a global reputation for the diversity, depth and quality of its programming – particularly in drama, documentaries and news.

In April 2000 in a speech to 400 managers, which was subsequently relayed to all staff, Greg Dyke, the new Director-General, laid out his vision for the BBC and how he planned to restructure the way in which the organisation worked. One newspaper reported his speech as follows:

> Under Lord Birt [the previous Director-General] the BBC was about performance graphs, bar charts and endless spending lists. The new BBC as unveiled by Greg Dyke yesterday, is a many-petalled flower. . . . – contained in a BBC booklet, *Building One BBC*, published to explain the changes to staff [which] sums up what observers have dubbed Mr. Dyke's 'happy clappy' approach to running a notoriously unhappy organisation . . .
>
> . . . 'I have a different style of management to John. In the end I think we live in a world where if you want to get and keep the most talented people, you want an organisation that is happy with itself' [said Dyke].

Not surprisingly, such a prominent institution was constantly in the public eye – not only in terms of its broadcasting output but also in how it was financed and managed. The appointment of Greg Dyke as Director General was something of a shock to many people. He did not fit the 'establishment figure' image of most of his predecessors. He had a background in commercial television and was more flamboyant and 'street wise'. Like many new leaders, his first steps in stamping his brand on the BBC was to review its structure and management processes and this is what was announced in April 2000 and published in the booklet *Building One BBC*.

Structure prior to 2000

John Birt's structure for the BBC was built on the principles being adopted by many parts of the public sector at the time. He created an internal market by separating the management responsibilities into divisions covering the three major aspects of broadcasting: Resources (such as studios, outside broadcast equipment etc.), Programme Production and Programme Broadcasting (see Figure 1).

Each of these divisions had its own 'headquarters', several business units[1] and traded with each other in an internal market and also with third parties outside the BBC. For example, those broadcasting programmes would commission services both internally and from external production companies. The programme producers would hire infrastructure from BBC resources but also use external studios and equipment. They would sell their programmes both internally and to other broadcasters. BBC Resources would hire its facilities externally as well as to the BBC programme producers. This structural arrangement was designed to bring some 'market discipline' to the organisation and to ensure the each of these three major areas was delivering value for money when tested against its competitors. In this BBC internal market John Birt saw the role of the centre as the regulator of the market – defining the 'rules' and setting up the

Figure 1 John Birt's structure (pre-2000; simplified)

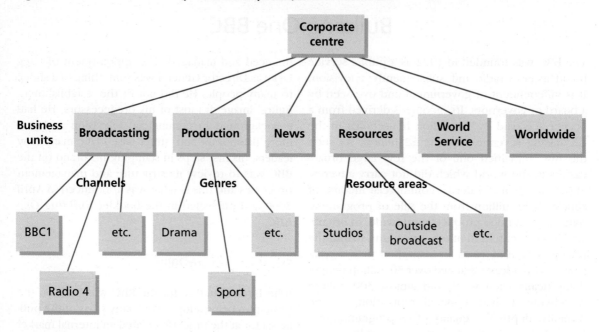

systems and procedures to manage this internal market. This included targets and transfer prices between the 'customers' and 'suppliers'. But most things that might be centralised in other organisations were devolved and duplicated, such as financial management. Significantly, because of the very fast nature of News, that area of the BBC's activities was excluded from this internal market and both production and broadcast were managed as a single unit. Indeed, live news was broadcast as it was produced.

New goals for the future – Building One BBC

In his introduction to *Building One BBC*, Greg Dyke explained the background to the structural changes:

> Our aim is for the BBC to be a place where people work collaboratively, enjoy their job and are inspired and united behind a common purpose – to create great television programmes and outstanding on-line services. If the BBC is to be a magnet for the best talent in Britain, then it must be an exciting and creative place to work.

. . . People are proud to work for the BBC, but want to see change. They believe that the BBC has taken bold steps towards a strong position in the digital age, but think it has too many managerial layers and costly processes, and that too much time is spent on negotiating within the BBC. As a result, as an organisation, we simply move too slowly. People also comment on a culture of division and of internal – rather than audience – focus.

He then went on to list five goals that the changes were designed to address:

- *To put audiences first [and] creativity and programme making at the heart of the BBC.* This was seen as the only way in which the BBC could win and retain its audiences in the digital age - where there would be vast choice for consumers.

- *Over time to raise the proportion of BBC funding that is spent on programmes from 76 per cent to 85 per cent.* Put another way, this meant reducing management overhead from 24 per cent to 15 per cent.

- *Create a culture of collaboration, in which people work together to make great programmes.* The implication was that the current structure bred a divisive culture.

- *To change the way the organisation works so that we can take decisions quickly and act decisively, while retaining sufficient checks and balances to avoid damaging mistakes.* This was contrasted with the way in which the digital world was spawning new entrants who acted decisively (such as Microsoft or AOL).[2]

- *To make sure that the BBC is properly equipped with the skills it needs to compete effectively in the digital world.* New skills were needed in things like cross-media brand-building, distribution, gateway and rights management.

Greg Dyke's proposed changes

Building One BBC went on to explain the nine changes that would help achieve these goals:

- *A flatter structure will be introduced* in which BBC Broadcast and BBC Production headquarters disappear, bringing programme and channel interests closer to the centre of the BBC and resulting in a substantial reduction in overhead. This structure was symbolically depicted as a flower (see Figure 2).

- *A more inclusive top-team will be created* where the number of programming and broadcasting people on the Executive Committee[3] will rise from four to nine. The top 50–60 managers will join them in a Leadership Group. The purpose of this was to raise the strategic importance of programming and broadcasting issues and to gain more ownership of BBC strategies.

- *BBC Production will be replaced* by three programming divisions (Drama, Entertainment and Children (DEC); Factual and Learning (FL) and Sport). They will report directly to the Director-General and be represented on the Executive Committee.

- *In Sport, Children and Education[4] commissioning and programme making will be reintegrated to create a single BBC division for each area.* Previously it was only News that was integrated in this way. The reasons for this change were that Sport was similar to News in having a high proportion of live coverage. Children and Education were felt to be two market segments where integrated management of all the products for that segment would be beneficial and give the managers 'cross-media capability'. For example, Sport would manage the online sports service as well as broadcasting of events.

- Similar arguments were used to justify *the reintegration of music commissioning and production in radio* (for Radios 1, 2, and 3).

- Over the whole corporation *a more collaborative commissioning process will be introduced, with programme guarantees in most areas.* This meant that broadcasters and programme-makers would work more closely together in planning their activities over a sensible time period – such as a season or a year. It was an attempt to eliminate the worst of the internally competitive behaviour that the internal market had generated.

- *A New Media division will be set up.* BBC Online and interactive television will be brought together, as well as 'blue skies' developments. This was a response to merging technologies and a desire to ensure that the BBC had an integrated vision about new technologies and, more importantly, would develop and deliver a coherent rather than fragmented strategy.

- *Duplication of cental and support functions will be eliminated (e.g. Marketing, Strategy, Finance and Human Resources).* If divisions need support they will draw on resources provided centrally.

- *Internal trading will be simplified* with a reduction in business units from 190 to about 40. This would vastly simplify and reduce the cost of internal financial transactions between internal customers and suppliers in the internal market.

Figure 2 Greg Dyke's new structure (2000)

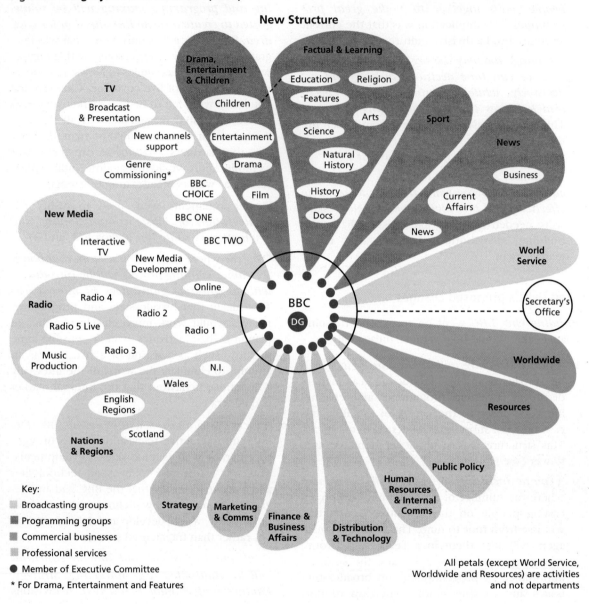

Key:
- ▢ Broadcasting groups
- ■ Programming groups
- ▢ Commercial businesses
- ▢ Professional services
- ● Member of Executive Committee

* For Drama, Entertainment and Features

All petals (except World Service, Worldwide and Resources) are activities and not departments

Finally the Director-General reminded staff that '. . . it is important to remember that this will not mean the end of change at the BBC. . . . agility and flexibility are key objectives [of these changes]. We will need to continue to adapt our structures and processes to face our changing environment: this structure is a beginning not an end'.

Notes

1. For example, Programme Broadcasting included the various radio and television channels.

2. See Illustration 1.1 in Chapter 1 of this book.
3. The Executive Committee had 18 members.
4. The latter two are units within DEC and FL respectively.

Sources: BBC Annual Reports; *Building One BBC* – April 2000 (by permission); *Daily Telegraph*, 4 April 2000.

Questions

1. What would you see as the strengths and weaknesses of John Birt's structure? Why were there exceptions within the internal market structure (particularly News)?

2. Undertake a critique of the changes in structures that Greg Dyke proposed, and justify each of them in terms of its contribution to creating better value for money in the BBC's services.

3. Discuss how the role of the corporate centre will change and compare it with Goold and Campbell's stereotypes. Do you have any concerns about the way in which the relationships between the centre and its new divisions will work?

4. How will the relationships between divisions change? How has the internal market been modified and why? Why hasn't Greg Dyke chosen to dismantle the internal market completely?

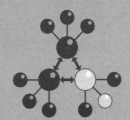

10

Enabling Success

LEARNING OUTCOMES

After reading this chapter you should be able to:

- Explain why resource management issues are important in enabling strategic success.
- Describe how human resource strategies might develop people that can enable successful strategies.
- Explain how human resource strategies might ensure that the cultural and political context of an organisation is a strength rather than a weakness.
- Understand how HR strategies can assist in changing the structures, roles, processes and relationships in organisations.
- Explain how developments in access to and processing of information can build or destroy core competences.
- Describe new business models and assess their appropriateness to different industries or sectors.
- Explain the relationship between information management and organisational structures and processes.
- Understand the issues about managing strategies to create financial value.
- Explain how different strategies will need to be funded in different ways.
- Understand the differing financial expectations of stakeholders.
- Describe how technology can change the competitive forces on an organisation and its strategic capability.
- Understand how the way that technology development is managed can influence the success of strategies.

10.1 INTRODUCTION

Strategy is about how organisations perform *overall*. Since very few individuals sit at the very top of organisations, their experience of, and contribution to, strategic success is from 'below'. They will operate in parts of an organisation where their day-to-day work is dominated by issues about that function,

---

Exhibit 10.1 **Enabling strategic success**

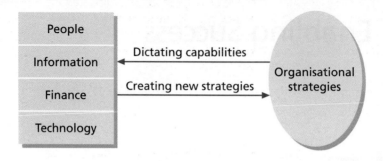

---

department, division or project team. It should be clear from discussions earlier in this book that in all organisations except the very smallest, *specialisation* is usually a key factor underpinning success. This specialisation might be reflected in the formal structures of the organisation as discussed in Chapter 9 or it might be concerned with the different contributions that individuals make within teams. In either case, managers and individuals lower down in organisations may control resources and competences that are crucial in *enabling* strategic success – even if this is simply their own knowledge or the specialist knowledge of the group in which they work. They are also likely to be the most knowledgeable about changes in parts of the business environment with which they interface. For example, HR specialists should understand the labour market, finance managers the money markets, marketing the customers and so on. So many of the issues in the parts of the organisation will be strategic too. In fact, with the continuing move to flatter structures and the adoption of new organisational forms – such as networks and project teams – more 'responsibility' for strategy is found at lower levels, as discussed in Chapter 9. The efforts, decisions and priorities of those managers in the parts of the business are crucial to success or failure of the overall strategies.

The purpose of this chapter is to help readers to understand better the crucial role that managers and individuals in the parts of an organisation (whether that be business functions, departments, divisions or project teams) play in *enabling* the success of strategies. Those managers and individuals can enable the success of strategy in action in two different ways as shown in Exhibit 10.1:

- changing and developing resources and competences to fit changing strategies;

- developing unique resources or core competences in the part of the organisation in which they work on which successful new strategies can be built.

So ideas and initiatives from within the parts of an organisation can shape strategy.

A major danger in organisations is that resource management is only identified with the first of these two issues. Indeed, even there, resource management becomes so enshrined in the systems and procedures of the organisation's business functions that changing strategy is difficult. The second issue is of crucial importance in enabling successful strategies and requires managers to think more about the strategic purposes of resource management and beyond the narrow confines of the systems and procedures in their part of the organisation. This chapter will look at four key resource areas: people, information, money and technology and the ways in which they might enable strategic success. In each case two related questions will be considered:

- Are the parts of the organisation capable of *enabling* strategies to be executed successfully?

But also . . .

- Are the strategies of the organisation being shaped to capitalise on the expertise in that resource area?

To take one example to illustrate this point at the outset, many organisations at the beginning of the 21st century are rightly concerned about whether they are 'missing the boat' in terms of the use of IT and the exploitation of information in their business. But to understand properly this relationship between information and strategy it is important to ask not just how information processing capability might be 'grafted' into the business to improve the competitiveness of current strategies but also how the whole business process might be transformed by IT. The danger of asking only the first question is that strategy moves forward as a set of adjustments to an old business idea – to perform things a little better, a little cheaper and a little faster. It does not ask the radical question as to changing the business idea to capitalise on the new capabilities that IT offers. These same two-way considerations apply to the other resource areas too, as will be seen below.

10.2 MANAGING PEOPLE[1]

10.2.1 Introduction

An important theme running through this book is that people are at the heart of strategy. The knowledge and experience of people can be the key factors enabling the success of strategies. But they can also hinder the successful adoption of new strategies too. So human resource issues are a central concern and responsibility of most managers in organisations and are not confined to a specialist human resource function. Indeed, although formal HR systems and structures may be vitally important in supporting successful strategies, it is quite possible that they may hinder strategy if they are not tailored to the types of strategies being pursued. For example, highly bureaucratic recruitment procedures may deter applications from creative individuals who do not see themselves working in a bureaucratic environment. For companies whose strategies are built around high rates of innovation in products or processes this could prove disastrous as they fail to attract the right kind of recruit. Also, the relationship between people and successful strategies goes beyond the traditional agenda of the HR function and is concerned with behaviours as much as

Exhibit 10.2	Strategy and people

competences. The ability to change behaviours may be the key ingredient for success.

Bearing this in mind, it is helpful to think about the people dimension of strategy as being concerned with three related aspects (see Exhibit 10.2):

● people as a resource (which relates to Chapter 4);

● people as the cultural/political context (which relates to Chapters 2 and 5);

● the need to organise people (which relates to Chapter 9).

Before discussing each of these issues in detail, it is important to look at a few overall considerations about the way in which an organisation's human resources might enable success.

The importance of context

The 'HR agenda' is clearly going to vary depending on a range of both external and internal issues for any individual organisation. However, it is worth noting that over the past decade there have been a number of important trends which have affected many organisations and to which both overall strategies and HR strategies need to respond:

- Changing demographics and rising educational levels affect both consumer behaviour and the nature of the labour market.

- Structural changes in the economy – such as a shrinking public sector, deregulation and a shift to service sector employment – have had major impacts on attitudes to work and the power of unions.

- Political and legal changes have also diminished the power of organised labour and sought to empower other stakeholders such as individual employees and customers.

- Information technology is transforming the way that public and private sector organisations 'do business'. This will be discussed more fully in section 10.3 below – but here it needs to be noted that it is transforming the nature of work, the types of jobs, and the competences that people need.

Within these general external factors there are a number of issues about the internal context of an organisation that will influence (or constrain) how the relationship between strategy and human resources is managed. For example:

- The stage of an organisation's products in their life cycle. The strategic priorities are quite different when products are new and markets embryonic as against the issues in mature markets.

- Similarly, organisations pursuing low price strategies face different challenges from differentiators.

- The management style and employee relations will be inherited and can severely constrain strategic development unless changed. Issues such as decision-making styles, trust, openness, attitudes to risk-taking are crucially important.

So when thinking through the issues raised below it is important to interpret them in the context of specific organisational strategies and the circumstances that a particular organisation or sector faces.

Soft and hard human resource approaches

Human resource management is about both 'hard' and 'soft' approaches. **Hard human resource approaches** are about people as a resource and how systems and procedures can be used to acquire, utilise, develop and retain people to the strategic advantage of the organisation. The needs of the organisation are dominant. **Soft human resource approaches** are concerned with people's behaviour, both individually and collectively, i.e. culture, how this helps or hinders strategies and how it can be changed. It is also about a commitment to meeting the needs of individuals as well as the organisation. In the modern economy the need for organisations to create and share knowledge is crucial to success and can be strongly influenced by how trust is built and sustained within organisations – what has been called 'fair process'.[2] As mentioned above, HR in organisations often underplays the soft side and concentrates on hard systems and structures. Since the soft side is about changing behaviours, if it is neglected strategic development and change will be hindered. Research with a collection of large companies[3] has shown that there is rarely any overarching human resource strategy that pulls these two strands together and incorporates

Hard human resource approaches are about how systems and procedures can be used to acquire, utilise, develop and retain people

Soft human resource approaches are concerned with people's behaviour, both individually and collectively

a set of complementary initiatives. Rather, human resource strategies tend to consist of a mix of broad principles and statements and new initiatives developed on an ad hoc basis as a response to external or internal pressures. A more strategic approach would be helpful.

These introductory comments about the current state of human resource strategy in organisations provide a background against which the relationship between business and human resource strategies can be explored.

10.2.2 People as a resource

An important message from Chapter 4 of this book is that the possession of resources (including people) does not guarantee strategic success. Strategic capability is essentially concerned with how these resources are deployed, managed, controlled and, in the case of people, motivated to create competences in those activities and business processes needed to run the business. The concept of core competences goes beyond this in a search for those few activities that underpin competitive advantage or demonstrable excellence.

Nevertheless, the starting point of successful strategies is acquiring, retaining and developing resources of at least a threshold standard and this clearly applies to people as a resource. Much of the 'hard' side of HR is concerned with ensuring that this 'baseline' is maintained in the organisation. It is about *performance management*. This is a tough agenda in a rapidly changing world since the threshold standards are constantly shifting in an upward direction. So HR activities can help enable successful strategies in the following ways:

- Audits to assess HR requirements to support strategies and/or identify people-based core competences on which future strategies might be built.

- Goal-setting and performance assessment of individuals and teams. Most organisations will expect line managers to undertake these tasks, usually within a centrally designed appraisal scheme. This improves the chances of appraisals being linked to strategy. Also, there has been a move towards so-called 360° appraisals (i.e. from multiple perspectives – not just the line manager but also from other parts of the organisation on which their work impacts) so that the full scope and impact of an employee's work on the success of strategy can be judged.

- In many organisations the use of rewards has had to take on board the reality of more teamworking in delivering strategy. Highly geared individual incentives (often found in salesforces) may undermine this teamwork. But team incentives tend to have complemented individual incentives rather than replaced them.

- Recruitment is a key method of improving strategic capability in many organisations – particularly where new competences are needed in the organisation. So, many public sector organisations are needing to recruit people with marketing and IT skills as they try to get closer to their customers and exploit IT. Similarly, redeployment and redundancy planning are important in all organisation's facing change. Succession planning has had to be refocused away from preparing people for particular jobs in a hierarchy to simply ensuring that a sufficiently large pool of talented individuals exists to meet future senior leadership requirements.

● The existence of uniquely competent individuals in an organisation, such as a top surgeon in a hospital, criminal lawyer or leading academic in a university, will not be a robust source of long-term strategic advantage since those individuals may leave or retire or die. So if excellence is to be sustained, a major concern for HR policy should be how those persons' knowledge can be spread in the organisation, for example through using them in mentoring roles or by 'codification' of their knowledge into work routines. However, these processes of spreading knowledge may educate competitors too (for example, as employees move organisations). So innovation and creativity must be *continuously* nurtured in the organisation.

● In training and development there has been a reduction in the use of formal programmes and more coaching and mentoring to support self-development. These are important skills for individuals if their organisation's strategies are changing and developing constantly.

In order to put in place and execute HR strategies in all these areas, managers and HR professionals need to be familiar with the organisation's strategies, how these might be changing in the future and the implication to people's competences. Indeed, most HR thinking would go further and argue that it is important for employees *themselves* to understand these issues. For example, in the UK this thinking spawned major national initiatives such as Investors in People (IiP). This is a scheme which helps organisations define, in detail, the development needs of each employee in line with the organisation's strategies but ideally in a way which gains ownership by individuals of their own development. So each individual needs to see how their job contributes to the success or failure of the organisation's strategies. Those managers who have been involved in IiP will know what a major task this can be.

However, it is not enough simply to adjust the performance management processes to support changing strategies. Managers need to be able and willing to envisage a future where the strategies and performance of the organisation are transformed by stretching the HR capabilities of the organisation better than their competitors. For example, a capability in mentoring and coaching could provide an environment that will attract creative people who like to be challenged and to learn. In turn, this creates a workforce that is much more able than competitors to 'think out of the box' and to produce innovative product features and new ways of competing in the market. This will require organisation structures and processes to support these behaviours, as mentioned in Chapter 9 and discussed further below.

Illustration 10.1 shows how one organisation needed to adjust its approach to performance management as strategies changed.

10.2.3 People as the cultural and political context

This book has a whole chapter (Chapter 5) on the need to understand the cultural and political context within which strategy is developed and delivered.

Illustration 10.1

Human resource strategies at Hewlett Packard

Human resources and business strategies need to match – but this will change over time.

Hewlett Packard's reputation for innovation and enlightened people management is lauded not only amongst academics and management gurus but also by other major companies. From its origin as a garage business producing technical equipment in 1937 to its present-day status as a $47 billion-a-year company, the emphasis has been on fast-paced innovation together with a highly sophisticated performance management process and a set of cultural values enshrined in the 'HP Way'.

The major strength of HP has been the manner in which it strongly links business and human resource strategies. This gains clarity from the business planning process. Both the long-term plan and the annual plan have clear HR elements. For the long term, strong leadership and organisational development processes are combined with detailed scanning of demographic trends to ensure capabilities will align with long-term aims. For the annual plan, the performance management system uses various mechanisms to plan, monitor and assess individual performance. Because HP is operating in a high-velocity environment, performance targets at the individual level are determined largely between manager and employee in negotiation and these are subject to high revisability in case environmental conditions make existing targets in appropriate or unrealistic. 360° appraisal is used because of the importance of teamwork. In addition to the annual formal appraisal, HP is committed to the practice of continuous appraisal, encouraging informal feedback combined with coaching and counselling to develop employees.

But growth has brought issues of increased bureaucracy, which has sapped innovation and reduced knowledge transfer. HP responded in two ways: the first was to split the firm into two with the computing side of the business retaining the name and Hewlett Packard brand. Second, they announced the move into 'e-services'. A consequence is that the traditional style of people management based on cultural control through internalisation of the HP Way is under threat. A key pillar of the HP Way, 'management by walking about', is seen by some as anachronistic given the global and virtual character of teams and the number of people working from home. The paradox of HR systems is that they must provide a high degree of continuity and consistency so that employee expectations of the effort–reward bargain are reasonably consistent, whilst at the same time they must be flexible to adapt to changing environmental conditions. HP has a long history of change management and HR excellence, but even for them, resolving their present tensions represents a considerable challenge.

Prepared by Philip Stiles, Judge Institute of Management Studies (see Chapter 3 of reference 3).

Question

What are the specific changes that Hewlett Packard should make to its performance management framework to support its move into e-services?

Chapter 11 will also emphasise that many of the problems of managing change result from a failure to understand, address and change this context. But still this is an area of significant weakness in the strategic management of organisations. As mentioned above, this softer side of changing behaviours is very often neglected in favour of the 'harder' issues discussed in the previous section. So it is an area where HR strategies can contribute significantly in enabling the success of business strategies. They can attempt to turn the cultural and political context into a strength rather than a weakness. This could be done in a number of ways:

● Educating managers in how these 'softer' aspects of strategy can be understood – for example, using the tools and checklists from Chapter 5 – particularly the cultural web (Exhibit 5.11) and stakeholder mapping (Exhibit 5.5). Many organisations have 'values statements' in an attempt to highlight these issues and/or change behaviours. The evidence from the research[4] is that a values statement is likely to be more effective if its use is judged 'locally' for different types of staff, geographical locations or divisions and the types of strategy being pursued. Values statements that are open to such flexible interpretation are much less likely to be received cynically and their impact on culture is through slow osmosis rather than imposed requirements.

● Encouraging debate on the relationship between culture and strategic choices. This should be done in both directions. Since culture may hinder new strategies, decisions may need to be made about whether or not to pursue those strategies and/or whether culture can be changed. Equally important, however, is the debate about what types of strategy are particularly suited to an organisation's culture. Indeed, there may be some strategies where an organisation's culture gives unique advantage over other organisations.

● Championing the debate about the cohesiveness or diversity of culture (as discussed in Chapter 2) and the impact on success or failure of strategies. This may be a key ingredient of successful strategy formulation and implementation in organisations and assisting managers in understanding the role of challenge in organisations can be invaluable.

● Ensuring that the change agenda is not underestimated in terms of difficulty and time-scales. Culture change is a long process of changing behaviours. The hard change tools (structures and systems) if used alone are unlikely to deliver, as seen in Chapter 11.

● Raising the awareness, as to how *styles* of managing change need to vary with circumstances, as will be discussed in Chapter 11. So helping managers develop their relationship management skills as a key ingredient of managing the political relationships with both internal and external stakeholders is important. Also, *teams* in organisations must between them be capable of operating different styles simultaneously. Therefore, building and maintaining teams of different personality types is just as important as the mix of competences in teams.[5]

One key issue in HR policy is the extent to which the organisation is espousing 'soft' HR approaches and yet managing only in 'hard' ways. A key example is the extent to which the rhetoric of 'concern for each individual and their personal development' is actually followed through or whether the reality is that individuals are simply seen as 'just another resource'. The reason this is an ethical question is that in a fast-changing world this could make a crucial practical difference to individuals in at least two ways. First, since lifelong jobs are disappearing rapidly, individuals need to be prepared and competent to face the external labour market at several times in their careers. So possessing competences that have value in this external labour market is important to the individual and a responsibility of employers who espouse soft-side approaches to HR. Second, most organisations benefit from the personal knowledge of individual employees and have a moral responsibility not to exploit this to the extent that the individual has no marketability outside the company, for example through restrictive clauses in employment contracts. In sectors where skills are in short supply, employers are having to pay more attention to the softer issues. For example, Illustration 10.2 shows the importance of HR issues in attracting and retaining knowledge workers.

10.2.4 Organising people

Chapter 9 was concerned with the issues of organising for success with particular emphasis on how the balance of this agenda is needing to change in the 21st century. It is not the intention to repeat that detail here but to highlight some of the implications to HR strategy in enabling success in the modern world.

The HR function

There are a number of important considerations concerning the HR function in organisations. The most challenging question is whether a specialist HR function is needed at all, or at least whether its traditional scale and functions are appropriate. In principle (and in practice in many organisations), people can be managed strategically without a specialist HR function. The alternative is that these HR activities are devolved in the organisation to line managers. Exhibit 6.4 provided a systematic way of addressing the question as to the added value that the organisation might accrue through the central organisation of activities – such as HR. This can be used item by item through the whole HR agenda such as recruitment, training, rewards etc. to continually retest whether the inherited split of responsibilities between the HR specialists and business units remains appropriate. For example, if recruitment is undertaken centrally, how is that justified? Is it cheaper? Will it be done better? Will it reduce risk? And so on. Readers may expect that in a faster-moving world there might be a movement away from specialist HR teams. This may make sense for many items – for example, the dismantling of across-company grades and payscales as organisations globalise – to reflect the much greater diversity in the labour markets. But for other aspects the reverse might be true. For example, a major problem of highly devolved organisations is the failure of the devolved units to understand and put in place competence development (through training, mentoring etc.)

Illustration 10.2

The power of the knowledge worker

STRATEGY IN ACTION

In a knowledge-based economy people are truly the most valuable asset. human resource policies need to reflect this.

How to recruit and retain knowledge workers is one of the biggest challenges organisations face in the knowledge era. Where there is no longer a shortage of ideas, there is, however, invariably a shortage of the right type of people to execute them. Whether they are ICT specialists, engineers familiar with the latest CAD-CAM, middle managers able to work virtually and without taking into consideration geographical boundaries, or front-line service workers able to deal with any customer enquiry, knowledge workers are invaluable.

Organisations, especially in America, have seen prime staff leave to set up their own dot.com companies. Even after the crash of dot.com stocks, turnover of staff remains a problem. Knowing how valuable they are and that there is no longer such a stigma attached to a CV characterised by many employers, such workers are changing jobs rapidly, often increasing their salaries substantially each time. Organisations are beginning to respond. Some companies are making a point of becoming an employer of choice by offering better pensions, loyalty bonuses, flexible working and help with child care. Employers are beginning to put these 'work–life' policies on the board's agenda.

ARM Holdings in the UK was a case in point. The company is a leading intellectual property provider, licensing processors, peripherals and chip designs to leading electronics companies. In all its communications, ARM emphasises that people are important, empowered and well looked after. An alternative approach is to make workers more knowledgeable either through training, especially through the web, or, as Ford has done, by offering a PC, printer and Internet access to all employees for a $5 monthly fee. The logic being that workers will be able to communicate amongst themselves more easily, be more able to use computers at work and will become more acquainted with the mindset of e-consumers which will help make the whole organisation more customer focused.

The knowledge worker, a term first coined by the management guru Peter Drucker in 1988, is here to stay. There is the potential to create a win–win relationship, with employees gaining job security, interesting work and an improved work–life balance and the best organisations gaining competitive advantage from the best workers.

Prepared by Jill Shepherd, University of Strathclyde.

Sources: Adapted from ARM company report and website; *Business Week*, 21 February 2000, p. 41; *The Economist*, 25 March 2000, pp. 101–103; *The Sunday Times*, 29 October 2000, section 7, p. 24.

Question

Referring to Exhibit 10.3 (page 489), identify the different ways in which human resource strategies can give competitive advantage to knowledge-based organisations.

that matches overall corporate strategies. This may be because managers at that level are unfamiliar with corporate-level strategies – such as globalisation – and extremely busy ensuring that their business unit survives the next quarter's trading and performance review. They may also not have the professional HR knowledge to resolve some of these HR issues. HR develops in a fragmented way through the efforts of busy 'gifted amateurs'. So someone needs to be the guardian of this crucial investment in competence, knowledge and innovation in HR practice and be able to interpret and translate it in the circumstances of the organisation.

If an HR function is felt to be valuable against these measures then the expectations as to its broad role must be clear and consistent with the discussion above.[6] The strategic responsibility for HR could be entirely devolved to line managers and the HR function remain as a *service provider* – for example, undertaking recruitment or arranging training. Alternatively its role could be to 'set the rules' within which line managers operate, for example on pay and promotions (i.e. *the regulator*). If an HR function is to have a strategic role this could be either in an *advisory* role (fulfilling the benchmarking of best practice role mentioned above) or as *change agents* moving the organisation forward.

The determinants of the most appropriate role for an HR function are, again, the context. The type of staff, the nature of the strategy and the broad structural arrangements in the organisation are all important. For example, some aspects of HR strategy need to be controlled centrally because they are central to the delivery of corporate-level strategies, whilst other aspects can be usefully devolved since they need to be interpreted differently in different parts of the organisation.

Middle (line) managers

It has been mentioned above that there has been a significant move towards line managers being centrally involved in managing HR issues themselves. This has the clear advantage of more ownership and a better chance of blending HR and business strategies. But there are also concerns – some of which have already been surfaced. Research[7] confirms the concerns as to whether the circumstances in which line managers operate are conducive to their doing a good job on HR issues and hence the risk that strategic success is not enabled as much as it could be:

- Whether it is realistic to expect line managers to be competent HR professionals. Handled badly, this could be a formula for mediocrity. This same concern could equally be applied to other areas such as information management (discussed in section 10.3 below).
- The short-term pressures to meet targets do not help line managers in taking a more strategic view of HR issues. Downsizing and de-layering have left the remaining managers too busy.
- Trade unions and professional associations have tended to resist a dispersion of HR responsibility. From a union's point of view it is much easier to deal with a single, centralised authority. Professional bodies may take a similar view.

- Managers may lack the incentive to take on more HR activities, either directly in their pay or grade or indirectly in their judgement as to which competences make them more marketable outside the company.

There has been criticism of middle managers as the 'gatekeepers' who maintain the status quo and block strategic change whereas, in reality, their active involvement in change programmes is crucial. It has been suggested that it is better to think of their management role more as a *change relayer*[8] *or an intermediary* as discussed in Chapter 11. This better describes the role than either of the traditional descriptors of change implementor or change recipient. It is a more strategic view of how middle managers can help change work through people by undertaking the following roles simultaneously:[9]

- First and foremost is undertaking and living the change themselves. So their influence as a *role model* is important.
- To help and assist their staff in understanding and adjusting to change. This is the role of the *mentor or coach*.
- Third is the *translator* of top-down strategies into practical strategies that work on the ground in their part of the organisation.
- They also need to be able to manage the detailed implementation of strategy – this is the *project manager role*.
- Fifth is the *instigator* or champion of ideas and initiatives. This is a reminder that many successful strategies are driven bottom-up and not top-down. They are likely to synthesise information for this purpose and to influence top management perceptions by the slant they put on that information. This is a significant source of power for middle managers – the information gatekeeper.
- Finally, and often forgotten, is the need to keep the organisation functioning whilst new strategies and changes are brought in. This is the role of the *guardian* of the organisation's performance and reputation.

It can be seen that each of these roles will have a crucial influence on the ability of people to adjust to change. The implication for top managers is not to bypass middle managers in the strategy development process, otherwise the changes may not stick with the people in the organisation.

Structures and roles

People may be held back from enabling strategic success because the traditional structures and roles do not match future strategies. For example, many service organisations have inherited a job demarcation and grading structure that worked well historically but is not suited to a world where service organisations are driven by IT systems as well as people. So most of the clerical roles that were needed to 'push paper' should be replaced by IT systems that take over and routinise that work. This would then allow those staff to spend more time supporting the professionals (say, teachers in a school) or in advising customers. However, these changes are not quite as easy to effect as it might seem, as organisations are driven by the old structures and roles – shored up by relationships with unions that reinforce the past rather than looking towards the future. These may mean that the issues of mismatch between strategy and these aspects of managing people are tackled by incremental adjustments to the current arrangements rather than by radical HR interventions such as:

● Creating new jobs and grades – for example, the professional administrator to take a more professional responsibility for the organisation's systems and infrastructure.

● Funding some of these posts by reductions elsewhere – both the at clerical and the professional levels. So, for example, one less teacher to free all the teaching staff from administrative duties.

● Creating teams of mixed professional groups to own product/service improvement to particular groups of customers. Significant effort has been put into this in health care – the clinical teams in the separate specialisms in hospitals and the creation of Primary Care Trusts in community-based health care are examples.

● Retraining, redeploying and offering redundancy in those areas which need to shrink.

Those organisations that are able to envisage and implement such changes are likely to significantly outperform others.

Processes and relationships

As circumstances and strategies change, organisations may need to change the processes and relationships discussed in Chapter 9 as well as organisational structures. For example, the divisionalisation of previously centralised organisations (perhaps as a response to more diversity in the marketplace) will mean that collaborative ventures between divisions may become optional rather than mandatory within the new devolved structures. So divisional managers need to improve their relationship management skills as they can no longer rely on a central 'policing' of these relationships between divisions. For example, divisions may have been compelled to work collaboratively to develop products or to support key customers. Once this compulsion is removed, managers in one division need to persuade other divisions to collaborate – they cannot compel them. This can also happen where there have been 'supplier–customer' relationships within the company – for example, operating divisions have been compelled to source their services internally (such as IT services). In more devolved regimes those managing these internal services will need to improve their relationship management skills if they are to retain this internal 'business'. They need to spend more time with managers in the operating divisions in order to understand their needs better and to improve the service levels to the best that could be provided by an external supplier.

This is also a reminder that another challenge is whether HR expertise should reside in the organisation or be bought in from specialist suppliers (e.g. consultants). This is the issue of organisational boundaries, discussed in Chapter 9. External agencies will have the advantage of a wider experience and

Exhibit 10.3	Competitive advantage through people

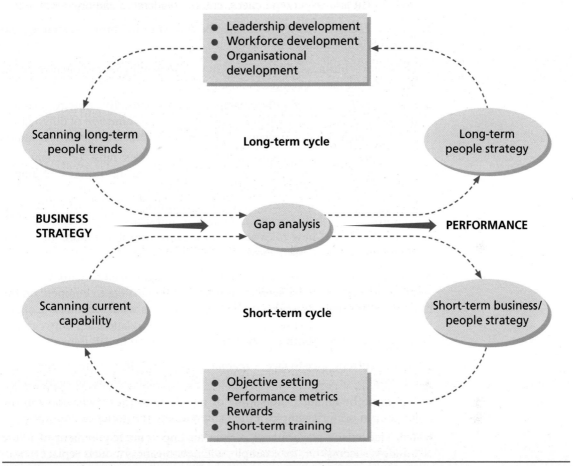

Source: Adapted from L. Gratton, V. Hope Hailey, P. Stiles and C. Truss, *Strategic Human Resource Management*, Oxford University Press, 1999, p. 185.

knowledge of HR practices but the disadvantage of being unfamiliar with the detailed circumstances of specific organisations.

10.2.5 Competitive advantage through people

The various separate points about the relationship between business and human resource strategies have been brought together and summarised in the model shown in Exhibit 10.3. This model emphasises the importance of the two-way relationship between business and HR strategies:

● HR strategies must be able to support the current strategies of an organisation through the short-term cycle of HR activities of objective setting, performance appraisal, rewards and training.

- *Simultaneously* they must be able to transform the organisation and be a platform from which new strategies can be built – through the long-term cycle of HR issues – competences, culture, leadership and organisation.

These two cycles of HR activities must be *linked* to the business strategy and to each other in a number of ways:

- *Vertically* – business strategy and HR activities must be complementary in the ways that have been exemplified above.
- *Horizontally* – between the separate elements of the HR strategy. Enabling the success of a strategy will normally require a *combination* of different HR activities such as training, changed performance measures and new rewards.
- Over *time* – the short-term and long-term cycles must be connected. Achieving short-term delivery goals must not be at the expense of longer-term HR capability. For example, using reward systems as the main tool to stimulate short-term success – say through individual bonus schemes – may compromise the ability to take more radical and strategic interventions, such as the creation of new roles and relationships to enable a more innovative organisation as discussed above.

An example of how these various connections might need to work to enable strategic success could be seen in an organisation wishing to compete on the basis of improved face-to-face customer service. This would require the organisation to resolve the following questions about the relationship between this business strategy and both the short-term and longer-term HR issues:

- Is the current face-to-face capability adequate? If not, how can it be improved? For example, should it be done through training or recruitment?
- Will there be an adequate supply of people with these behaviours in the longer run or, for example, if they entered new territories or countries?
- Will face-to-face performance remain an important requirement of future business success? Or, for example, will new business models replace it with telephone or Internet customer service?
- If so, do they have HR strategies to shift the balance of skills and behaviours through recruitment, redundancy and training?

In these ways, the feedback processes and redirection of both business and HR strategies can occur. Those organisations that are competent in managing these processes are likely to gain competitive advantage. So these processes may represent core competences of an organisation.

10.3 MANAGING INFORMATION[10]

In the early 21st century, knowledge creation and information management are issues at the front of managers' minds as the potential source of improved competitiveness, as discussed in Chapter 4 and in the introduction to this chapter. Within this wider agenda, considerations have naturally focused on IT and the extent to which it can transform competitiveness. But therein lies the danger

Exhibit 10.4	Strategy and information

that was flagged up in the introduction to this chapter. IT and information systems start to take on a purpose of their own – disconnected from the organisation's strategies. From a strategic point of view the issue is the extent to which improvements in information processing capability (through IT and information systems) can improve and assist the way in which knowledge is created and shared both within and around an organisation. Chapter 4 made the important point that not all of this knowledge will be captured in systems. Indeed, the tacit knowledge embedded in organisations is difficult to capture yet is usually the basis on which competitive advantage is built. This will be reflected in the discussions in this section, which will look at three main connections between information, IT developments and strategy (see Exhibit 10.4):

● information and strategic capability – particularly the impact of IT and information systems developments on core competences (as discussed in Chapter 4);

● information and changing business models within and across industries and sectors;

● information and structures/management processes (as discussed in Chapter 9).

10.3.1 Information and strategic capability

Since a large part of business activity is concerned with processing and transmitting information within and between organisations (and individual customers), information processing capability can improve an organisation's strategic capability in several ways:

- Reducing the direct cost of transactions between an organisation and its customers, suppliers or channels. This is particularly true for service organisations. For example, Internet banking reduces the cost of a banking transaction with a customer to a few pence compared with traditional branch banking where each transaction costs about £1.

- Improving service quality – for example, the speed and accuracy of real-time booking systems.

- Improving business processes in order to reduce cost or increase service quality indirectly. For example, electronic point of sale (EPOS) systems in retail outlets have not only improved efficiency and service in the store, but also provided high-quality information on which to plan stocking, purchasing and sales promotions.

But the wider availability of information will also accelerate the learning of competitors, so advantages gained through experience may be shorter-lived than hitherto. This will inevitably mean that organisations will need to revisit and redefine the basis on which they are competing more frequently, as discussed in Chapters 3 and 7. In turn, this will put more information demands on the organisation.

Chapter 4 introduced the concept of core competences as a way of understanding how competitiveness of organisations was related to their capability. Information strategies can have a profound influence on creating and destroying core competences. This will be demonstrated by looking at examples of how information and IT might impact on the three 'elements' of a core competence as described in Chapter 4, namely ensuring that products/services *are valued by customers*, *outperforming competitors* and *robustness* of competences (to imitation).

Information and product/service features

The enhanced capabilities of IT are already enabling organisations to provide product/service features that are valued by customers. First, *lower prices* (through reduced costs) – particularly where the product is information, such as in financial services. Second, improved pre-purchase information (e.g. website browsing, customer bulletin boards). Third, easier and faster purchasing processes (e.g. online ordering) and delivery. This can allow customers to move closer to just-in-time with their business processes. Fourth, shorter development times for new features. These, in turn, might give purchasers advantage with *their* customers. Fifth, product or service reliability and diagnostics are being improved (e.g. engine management systems in cars). Sixth, personalised products are increasingly being offered without price premium (e.g. customising PC architecture for each purchaser). Finally, improved after-sales service can be provided by better information systems (e.g. automatic service reminders). The strategic importance of this list is that if customers value some or all of these improved features, and if competitors learn quickly how to provide them by exploiting information and IT, then the threshold standards that need to be achieved to survive in a market will rise rapidly. So providers who are unable to deliver these higher standards will fall out of the market. Illustration 10.3 shows an example of this in how 'digital marketing' is becoming increasingly important.

Information and competitive performance

Chapter 4 reminded readers that competitiveness and standards of performance are determined not just within a particular industry or sector. Customer expectations of service standards, for example on speed or reliability, become the *universal benchmarks* crossing all industries and public services. So, for example, public service providers become 'compelled' to develop websites because the expectations of the general public have been raised through the levels of service they experience as consumers of products and services purchased from the private sector.

A key implication of the IT revolution for organisations producing or distributing physical products is that, in future, competitive advantage is more likely to be achieved through service performance (e.g. speed and reliability of delivery or maintenance) than in product features *per se*. So managers need to conceive of their business not as a product company with support services but as a service company which supplies a product. This is a profound mindset shift for some managers when considering which competences are most crucial to competitive performance. In particular, their ability to process information and to build their market knowledge becomes much more important than previously.

Another implication is that, at least for a period of time, competitive advantage might be gained by organisations that are able to build a much more detailed knowledge of the market. This knowledge would result from competences in analysing the subtle differences between customer needs in different parts of the market and building product or service features to meet these needs (as mentioned in Chapters 3 and 7). Most organisations now have colossal amounts of raw data about these issues and the IT processing capacity to analyse the data. But they are not good at this data-mining process, which will convert this data into market knowledge. **Data mining**[11] is about finding trends and connections in data in order to inform and improve competitive performance. For example, building up individual customer purchasing history as a basis for promoting offers (as many websites are now attempting); identifying connected purchases (for example, readers of particular newspapers or magazines have similar purchasing patterns for other goods and services); or simply finding underlying drivers of demand (such as demographic factors as discussed in Chapter 3).

Data mining is about finding trends and connections in data in order to inform and improve competitive performance

Illustration 10.3

The new rules of digital marketing

IT can offer product and service features that are valued by customers. But marketing activities must change to take advantage of this.

Marketing is primarily about an organisation's relationship with its customers. If IT can create better product or service features, marketing activities may need to respond in a number of ways.

Customisation or customerisation?

Many organisations already pursued strategies of customisation – where product or service features are varied for different segments in the market (e.g. strategies at positions 4 or 5 on the strategy clock (Exhibit 7.2)). In some industries position 3 on the clock has been achieved by some providers – this is mass customisation where a basic product 'platform' can be quickly varied for different customers at little cost. But IT presents an opportunity beyond this into customerisation – moving away from this passive customer role to an active involvement in product/service design. So the relationship management roles of marketing become crucial to success. The challenge is to integrate the traditional face-to-face roles with e-relationships that IT builds.

Brands

IT can destroy brands, as consumers become more knowledgeable about the various offerings in the marketplace. This need not be the case. Indeed, if brands can be shifted to reflect customer lifestyles rather than product features, they may be enhanced by IT. The wide geographical reach of IT channels means that brands should be less parochial. They are also cheaper and quicker to build than previously.

Pricing

Better-informed consumers can commoditise markets. So creative approaches to pricing are important. This might include, for example, tying the suppliers' prices to prices that the company is achieving in *its* market.

Advertising

IT and the Internet are a major challenge to the power of the major advertising agencies and the media barons. It allows marketeers to move away from mass broadcast media to more personalised and interactive communications with customers. So website design could be crucially important. This would include an understanding that customer 'browsing' has a recreational element to it as well as simply searching out the 'best buys'. So an innovative and even challenging website might engage customers more.

Market research

IT puts masses of data into the hands of companies at very low cost. So the prizes are there for the market researchers who can develop data-mining skills (as discussed in the text). Since interactive relationships will be developed with customers, it opens up possibilities for more experimentation as a key way of learning how customers and markets behave.

Source: Adapted from J. Wind and V. Mahajan, 'The challenge of digital marketing', in J. Wind and V. Mahajan, *Digital Marketing: Global strategies from the world's leading experts*, Wiley, 2001, Chapter 1.

Question

Choose an organisation with which you are familiar (or a case study in this book) and write a short report to the marketing director highlighting how marketing activities should change as a result of new information technologies.

Information and robustness

Chapter 4 (section 4.7) considered several reasons why resources or competences might be robust. Information processing capability can have an influence of any of these factors – hence changing the vulnerability of an organisation to imitation of its core competences:

- First, a resource or competence might be *rare*. When IT infrastructure costs were high this used to be a reason why a few larger organisations gained advantage over others through their IT infrastructure and competences. Others could not afford the capital costs. On the whole, this is no longer true. IT is now pervasive even in very small companies. In some sectors, being a first mover can create rarity advantage even to the extent of setting the propriety standards for the industry (as discussed in section 7.4.3). Microsoft itself with its Windows computer operating system is a good example.

- Core competences may also be difficult to imitate because they are *complex*. Here the situation has moved on. The mastery of the hardware and standard software needed to build information systems used to be complex – now it is not. The current areas of complexity are more in the data-mining activities (discussed above), the activities which underpin speed to market and in 'e-relationship management'[12] with customers (joining up all the different routes through which customers interface with a company). In other words, the processes of learning and innovation within an organisation on how to *exploit* information could be a core competence.

- Core competences may be robust because of *causal ambiguity* – competitors find it hard to understand the reasons why an organisation is successful. Similarly, robustness may result from the nature of core competences – they are *embedded* in the way an organisation works and not explicit. Many IT developments – particularly intelligent systems – are essentially concerned with attempting to codify the tacit knowledge in organisations to make it explicit. For example, helplines use every customer query and its solution to progressively build up knowledge as to what can go wrong with a product and how it is solved. This ability to codify previously tacit knowledge removes barriers to imitation and undermines core competences. Of course, some types of organisational knowledge are difficult to codify – such as intuition and experience which is shared knowledge based on interactions across many parts of an organisation – the 'ways of doing things'. As mentioned in the introduction to this section, there is a danger in becoming over-dependent on systems and ignoring this type of knowledge simply because it is difficult to codify and build into the system. But this is the very reason why it is difficult to imitate and may be crucial to competitive advantage.

Information and competitive strategy

The strategic role of information in organisations will need to be different depending on the way in which the organisation is positioning its products or services in the market (as described by the strategy clock from Chapter 7 – Exhibit 7.2). The reverse is also true – competence in information management might be the platform for new bases of competition through the creation of different product/service features. Since larger organisations will tend to have a collection of strategic business units pursuing different strategies, there must be the information capability to support all SBUs but in different ways. The role of information in enabling different competitive strategies is as follows:

- *Routinisation (positions 1 and 2 on the strategy clock)* – where the role of information, usually through IT systems, is to reduce drastically the cost of transactions with customers, suppliers or channels. For example, by moving the customer towards self-service (for example, websites replacing face-to-face selling).

- *Mass customisation (position 3 on the strategy clock)* – where IT can create more product features that are valued (as discussed above) at the same or lower price. This is a major battleground in many sectors at the present time.

- *Customisation (positions 4 and 5 on the strategy clock)* – where information can be provided to customers (say, through websites) in advance of any face-to-face or telephone contact, which is reserved for advising a much more knowledgeable customer.

- *The IT laggards* – who do not value the features that IT can offer and will remain significant parts of the market in most sectors. This provides a continuing opportunity for those providers who are especially good at providing information in more traditional ways, for example personal face-to-face service.

10.3.2 Information and changing business models

The impact that information processing capability has on competences and business processes as exemplified above is transforming the way in which organisations build their relationships with others in their value network (as discussed in section 4.4.3). In both the private and public sectors it is transforming business models.[13] A **business model** describes the structure of product, service and information flows and the roles of the participating parties. This includes potential benefits and sources of revenue to each of the parties. The value chain framework discussed in section 4.4.3 can be used to identify many traditional business models. For example, the linear supply chain from component manufacturers, to finished product assemblers, primary distributors, retailers and finally the consumer. Even in this case – where the product 'flows' in a linear fashion through the chain – information and other services may exist in branches of the chain. For example, market research and after-sales service may be undertaken by other parties from outside this linear chain. Exhibit 10.5 shows how e-commerce models are emerging out of traditional business models based on the degree of *innovation* from traditional approaches and the *complexity* (mainly the level of integration of activities). It can be seen that IT is impacting in three main ways:

- By replacing physical or paper-based processes with electronic processes. For example, *e-shops* shift marketing and 'display' to websites. *E-procurement*

A **business model** describes the structure of product, service and information flows and the roles of the participating parties

Exhibit 10.5	New business models

DEGREE OF INNOVATION

DEGREE OF INTEGRATION		Same as before	Extended	New
	Single function	E-shop E-procurement	E-auction Value chain services (e.g. payment systems, logistics) Trust services	Information brokerage (e.g. search engines)
	Integrated functions	E-mall	Third-party marketplace (e.g. web hosting)	Virtual communities Collaboration platforms Value chain integrator

Source: Adapted from P. Timmers, *Electronic Commerce*, Wiley, 2000, Chapter 3.

shifts tendering, negotiation and purchasing processes to websites. In both cases the advantages are in reduced costs and wider choice. An *e-mall* takes the concept a little further by creating a collection of e-shops with a common umbrella – such as a brand.

● By significantly extending the functions that traditional business models can offer. For example, sourcing or selling through setting up *e-auctions* is both easy and cheap and can lead to significantly reduced purchasing costs or increased revenues. *Trust services* (such as supplier or customer certification or vetting) extends the kinds of information services often available to members of trade associations. Other information functions in the value chain can be provided more efficiently or effectively by *value chain service specialists* – such as payments or logistics. Some organisations see benefits in leaving a number of value chain activities to specialists who create *third-party marketplaces* and may offer web-based marketing, branding, payment systems, logistics and so on. Often this would be viewed as a complementary route to market rather than a complete replacement.

● It could be argued that these first two categories are little more than the exploitation of IT to enable improvements in the efficiency and effectiveness of information processing within 'old' business models. Some of the most exciting developments are where IT is enabling business models that are not possible without IT. So IT is genuinely transformational in driving strategic changes in and between organisations. Perhaps the most well established example is the *information brokerage* role of companies like Yahoo! with their search engines. *Virtual communities* can be sustained by IT – as Amazon tries to do in bringing authors, readers and publishers into dialogue on their website. Sometimes IT can provide a *collaboration platform*, for example allowing customers and suppliers to work together on product design using specialist IT design tools. *Value chain integration* may be made possible through IT if separate activities can be knitted together by faster and more reliable information flows. For example, sales staff can discuss requirements with customers using both 'real-time' information about manufacturing capability, availability and production scheduling and also 'straight through' information about the same issues in the supply chain. Sometimes integration allows customers to change their specification and delivery schedules themselves – which then automatically reconfigures requirements back in the supply chain.

From a strategic point of view the important considerations of any of these e-commerce business models is the extent to which they are able to create better value for money for customers. In doing so they will threaten the position of some organisations and provide opportunities to others – including new entrants. But to suggest that IT will simply lead to the demise of intermediaries is not true. Some intermediary roles will be redundant, as customers are able to gather information more freely and 'talk' directly to potential suppliers. At the same time, new intermediary roles will be spawned if they add value or reduce cost. Many of the roles discussed above have that potential, such as third-party marketplaces, virtual communities or information brokerage.

Illustration 10.4 uses the five forces framework from Chapter 3 (Exhibit 3.4) to summarise some of the impacts of these changing business models on the competitive position of organisations.

10.3.3 Information and structuring

Chapter 9 was concerned with organising to create and support successful strategies. Improvements in information processing capability are making a significant contribution to better ways of organising. But this must fit the organisational approach and vice versa. Again a few examples illustrate this point:

- It has already been pointed out in the previous chapter that organisations competing with low price strategies (positions 1 or 2 on the strategy clock, Exhibit 7.2) may find a centralised bureaucratic configuration to be appropriate (see Exhibit 9.8). This bureaucracy must deliver routinised business processes, which reduce cost whilst maintaining threshold quality levels. IT can facilitate this cost reduction through routinisation whilst also enabling quite complex co-ordination.

- Highly devolved organisations (operating close to Goold and Campbell's *financial control* – Exhibit 9.9) are less concerned with complex co-ordination and require accurate and timely information about the performance of business units against pre-agreed targets. This is the core of the relationship between the corporate centre and the business units.

- In the middle ground of *strategic control* (see Exhibit 9.10) information may assist in a number of ways. First, the bottom-up planning from business units is likely to be important and the corporate centre needs to be able to co-ordinate and reconcile these plans. High-quality reliable information is

Illustration 10.4

Information technology and the five competitive forces

STRATEGY IN ACTION

Information technology can transform the competitive forces in an industry

In Chapter 3, the five forces framework was introduced as a way of mapping out the competitive forces in an industry.

New entrants

Barriers to entry may be raised because of the up-front investment needed to operate and compete – although this continues to decline. More importantly, incumbents may have tied suppliers and/or customers into their particular systems, creating inertia to change. Barriers may be lowered for a number of the reasons mentioned below, such as better-informed consumers leading to less customer loyalty.

Power of suppliers

A major threat for many organisations is that their suppliers are able to forward integrate using IT and take over some or all of the functions undertaken by the organisation. This is particularly threatening for intermediaries – such as travel agents – where IT is increasing the number of companies dealing directly with the end customers. But suppliers may have power without forward integration, in particular where they own the 'technology platform' around which a business's systems and operations are built. Microsoft's Windows operating system is still hugely powerful in this respect.

Power of buyers

It has been claimed that one of the most important social impacts of the Internet is to empower consumers by giving them easy access to market information and, therefore, making them more knowledgeable and discerning consumers. The same would apply to business-to-business transactions – e-auctions being an obvious example.

Substitutes

IT is impacting at all three levels of substitution. It is creating direct product-for-product substitution (e.g. Internet vs. branch banking). But it is also substituting the need for certain products and services as consumers are able to undertake those tasks themselves using IT software packages (e.g. some legal services) or satisfy the need in a different way (e.g. tele-conferencing instead of business travel). At the level of generic substitution, IT hardware, software and IT-related services are capturing a growing percentage of consumer spending – at the expense of sectors whose products/services are seen as less exciting.

Competitive rivalry

As consumers become more knowledegeable about the offerings of different providers it is driving many markets to be commodity-like – in the sense that consumers regard the offerings as much the same. Of course, IT can assist providers in their attempts to differentiate themselves from competitors – largely in terms of improved service. But IT software and systems are widely available to competitors – so they may catch up quickly. So IT is fuelling hyper-competition, as discussed in Chapters 3 and 6.

Questions

1. Choose an organisation with which you are familiar (or one of the case studies in this book) and analyse how IT will impact on each of the five forces.

2. What are the implications for the organisation's future strategies?

needed to support those processes. Second, it may be that parts of the organisation have customer–supplier relationships with each other – perhaps in an internal market. This too requires high-quality information. Finally, information is required about the performance of business units and the corporate centre.

● Better information through IT can allow managers and external stakeholders to bypass some of the traditional 'gatekeepers', who gained power from their gatekeeping of information. Within organisations, many middle management roles have been as information conduits between the senior managers and the front line. For example, IT can create direct communication between the top and the bottom of an organisation and many chief executives are introducing their own websites for that purpose. (Readers are reminded that middle managers play other important roles in the strategy of their organisation as well as being an information gatekeepers (see section 10.2.4 above)). The issue could also apply to the bypassing of unions as information conduits to employees. The same is true externally – the sales-force is no longer the primary route through which customers gain their product knowledge or even place orders. So their role will move from 'closing deals' to relationship management and advice. In the public sector politicians are able to put in place two-way communication with their communities rather than relying on managers as the conduit and filter. There are already challenging implications for the whole way in which the political and service provision processes work.

In summary, IT is creating a world with fewer 'gatekeepers' – so flattened structures, with more direct communication of strategy to and from the front line and more direct interaction at much lower levels across the organisation (and with external stakeholders). But this interaction is informed by a common database and 'regulated' by guidelines or rules within these information systems. It is also a world where the key decision makers are much better informed about the impact of past strategies and outside influences through the accumulation of knowledge from the front line on day-to-day issues like customer queries (for example, on helplines).

10.3.4 Implications for managers[14]

The practical implications of these previous discussions for managers and those responsible for information strategy in organisations are as follows:

● Managers need to realise that IT can transform the organisation, not just fine-tune current strategies and processes. They need to move away from seeing information management as a support function and place it on a par with other business functions.

● Information managers need to understand the full potential of IT from their professional knowledge and external networks (i.e. be the company benchmarker). They need to understand the limitations of IT too – for example, it cannot replace certain types of knowledge (such as intuition). They need to be involved in and credible on business strategy as part of the corporate team (and not sit on the sidelines) and to see new business opportunities that IT could open up. They also need to have the influencing skills to educate and persuade senior colleagues about these opportunities.

10.4 MANAGING FINANCE[15]

Money and the way that it is managed can be a key determinant of strategic success. From a shareholder's point of view, what matters is the cash-generating capability of the business since this determines the ability to pay dividends in the short term and to reinvest for the future (which, in turn, should enable a future flow of dividend payments).[16] The public sector equivalent is the need to deliver best value within financial limits (as mentioned in section 4.6). However, as highlighted in previous sections in this chapter, strategic success – in this case enabled through good financial management – cannot be achieved through a set of 'rules' and priorities which apply in equal measure to all organisations and at all times. The relationship between finance and strategic success is dependent on context. Nonetheless, there are three broad issues that organisations of all types face (see Exhibit 10.6):

Exhibit 10.6	Strategy and finance

Exhibit 10.7	The determinants of value creation

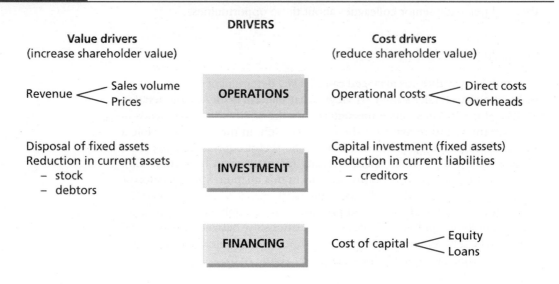

DRIVERS

Value drivers
(increase shareholder value)

Cost drivers
(reduce shareholder value)

Revenue —< Sales volume / Prices

OPERATIONS

Operational costs —< Direct costs / Overheads

Disposal of fixed assets
Reduction in current assets
   – stock
   – debtors

INVESTMENT

Capital investment (fixed assets)
Reduction in current liabilities
   – creditors

FINANCING

Cost of capital —< Equity / Loans

- *Managing for value*, whether this is concerned with creating value for shareholders or ensuring the best use of public money, is an important consideration for and responsibility of managers.

- *Funding* strategic developments is clearly important too: in particular, that the nature of the funding is appropriate for the type of strategy – and vice versa. This is concerned with balancing business and financial risks.

- The *financial expectations* of stakeholders will vary – both between different stakeholders and in relation to different strategies. This should influence managers in both strategy development and implementation.

10.4.1 Managing for value[17]

There has been a continuing theme through this book, that the long-term success of strategies is determined by the extent to which they deliver best value in the eyes of major stakeholders. Two examples of this are competitiveness in the marketplace and the ability to provide value to shareholders (through the returns they receive in dividend and share price movement – see section 8.4.2). In competitive markets these two issues are closely linked in the long term since the returns to shareholders are driven by market success. However, this broad connection between competitiveness and shareholder value is too simplistic and needs exploring in more detail. Shareholder value is determined by the long-term cash-generating capability of the organisation which, in turn, is determined by the ways in which a wide number of factors are managed. It is important that managers understand what 'managing for value' means and how it might be achieved. As shown in Exhibit 10.7, value creation is determined by three main issues: funds from operations, investment in (or disposal of) assets, and financing costs.

- *Funds from operations* are clearly a major contributor to value creation. In the long term, this concerns the extent to which the organisation is operating profitably. This is determined by:
  - Sales revenue - made up of sales volume and the prices that the organisation is able to maintain in its markets.
  - 'Production' and selling costs - both made up of fixed and variable elements.
  - Overhead or indirect costs.
- *Investment in assets* - the extent to which assets and working capital are being stretched is also a key consideration. Some organisations have developed competences in supporting much higher levels of business from the same asset base than others. This will affect value creation as follows:
  - The costs of capital investment or, in some cases, the disposal of redundant assets.
  - The management of the elements of working capital such as stock, debtors and creditors will increase or decrease shareholder value as indicated.
- *Financing costs* - the mix of capital in the business - between debt (requiring interest payments) and equity will determine the cost of capital (and also the financial risk).

The issues in the public sector are very similar. The problem for most public sector managers is that their financial responsibilities are usually confined to managing their budget (i.e. the cash outflows of operations). They will usually be doing this with little understanding of the other financial issues from the diagram, which will be managed by the corporate financial function. There is a real need for managers to be much more familiar with the impact of their day-to-day management decisions on the wider financial health of the organisation. For example, the use of fixed assets or the incurring of bad debts.

Key value and cost drivers

It is not the intention in this book to discuss the detailed issues concerning the management of each of the separate items shown in Exhibit 10.7. From a business strategy point of view the critical issue is to understand what are the *key value and cost drivers*. The value chain concept (section 4.4.3) is important in helping managers understand how and where value may be created within an organisation and in the wider value network. Importantly, it is likely that costs and value creation are spread *unevenly* across the activities in the value chain and value network. So some activities are more crucial to value (or cost) creation than others but this will vary with the type of business and with the circumstances in which it is operating, as will be seen below. Financial analysis can sharpen up an understanding of the significance of this by quantification of *value drivers* (which drive cash inflows) and *cost drivers* (which drive cash outflows).

Some examples illustrate the importance of this identification of key cost and value drivers:

- *Sources of capital* are usually of major importance, for two reasons. The cost of capital is a major cost driver and will vary with source. So the relative cash outflows which result from servicing loans as against equity would be an important strategic consideration. However, debt and equity also bear different levels of risk. So the gearing of an organisation should also be determined by the financial and business risks. This will be discussed more fully in section 10.4.3 below.

- *Capital expenditure* (capex) can be a major cash outflow that can destroy shareholder value unless it contributes to improving the revenues or reducing the costs elsewhere in Exhibit 10.7. In principle, the business cases for capex items should address this issue before expenditure is approved. Commonly the case for expenditure would relate to *enhanced product features* leading to increased sales and/or better prices; or *reduced costs* (for example, through increased labour productivity) or *decreased working capital* (for example, through stock reduction by streamlining production or distribution).

- New capital expenditure increases the *capital intensity* of the business which will influence the importance of fixed asset turnover and will also affect the ratio of fixed to variable costs and hence the relative importance of sales volume.

- As mentioned above, cost and value creation are spread unevenly through the activities in the value chain. So the detailed *cost structure* of businesses varies considerably from sector to sector and hence the relative importance of specific cost items. For example, service organisations are generally more labour intensive than manufacturing – underlining the importance of wage levels. Retailers are concerned with stock turnover and sales volume per square metre – reflecting two major cost drivers.

- Sometimes the crucial cost or value drivers are *outside the organisation* (in the supply or distribution chain). The strategic implication is that the organisation needs to be competent in maintaining the performance of its key suppliers or distributors. This means the ability to select, motivate and 'control' suppliers and distributors. It may also mean a reconsideration as to whether any of these activities should be taken 'in house' if they are so critically important to cost and value creation. This was discussed in Chapters 4 and 9 (outsourcing).

- Since suppliers' prices are the buyers' costs, there may also be an unevenness in the shareholder value creation being achieved by different organisations in the value network. This will be a result of the relative *bargaining power* of suppliers and buyers (as discussed in the five forces framework – section 3.3.1). For example, a manufacturer simultaneously facing a scarcity of supply of a raw material and powerful distributors for their product will find it difficult to maintain shareholder value creation. Since supply costs and product prices may be dictated by others, shareholder value creation will need to centre on managing the costs of in-house activities and/or the other items listed above (cost of capital and investment costs).

- The *type of strategy* being pursued is also important since this shifts the 'mix' of cost and value needed to support a competitive product or service. It may be that an organisation is successfully differentiating itself from its competitors by extra spending in selected areas (e.g. advertising). Provided this spending results in added value (possibly through prices) or relative cost reductions elsewhere (say in production through greater volume from increased sales), this may well be a defensible cost.

- The extent to which managers are able to *control* items of cost and value creation will vary with context. For example, in commodity markets price is externally determined – so managing for value must concentrate on other items. At divisional level in both the private and public sectors the cost of capital may be determined by decisions at the corporate level. So divisional managers must focus on other items.

- The key cost and value drivers may change *over time*. For example, during the introduction of a new product, the key factor may be establishing *sales volume*; once established, *prices and unit costs* might be most important; during decline, improving cash flow through *stock and debtor reduction* may be essential to support the introduction of the next generation of products.

Overall, the message is that managers can benefit considerably from a detailed understanding of the value creation processes within their organisation and the wider value network – it can help them be more strategic in how they prioritise their efforts for performance improvement. Illustration 10.5 shows how one organisation did just this.

10.4.2 Funding strategic development[18]

A basic issue which has to be faced by all organisations is how they will be financed. Decisions on finance will be influenced by ownership – for example, whether the business is privately held or publicly quoted – and by the overall corporate intent of the organisation. For example, there will be a different financial need if a business is seeking rapid growth by acquisition or development of new products compared with if it is seeking to consolidate its past performance. Managers also need to recognise that the financial strategy they choose to follow could be helpful or could hinder strategies at SBU level, as mentioned briefly above. This section uses the growth/share matrix (see Exhibit 6.6) to illustrate how financial strategies would need to vary for the different 'phases' of development of an SBU – see Exhibit 10.8.

This is just one example of how financial and business strategies need to match and is concerned with the relationship between financial risk and financial return to investors. The greater the risk to shareholders or lenders, the greater the return these investors will require. Therefore, from an organisation's point of view, the important issue is how they should balance the business risk with the financial risk *to the organisation*. Debt carries greater financial risk than equity since it carries an obligation to pay interest. As a generalisation, the greater the business risk the lower should be the financial risk

Illustration 10.5

Managing for shareholder value at Cadbury-Schweppes plc

Companies use 'managing for value' as a platform for improving their performance.

In 1996, Cadbury-Schweppes – the UK-based confectionery and drinks company – appointed John Sunderland as CEO. This move heralded a significant change in how the business was to be managed. In the following year he launched a group-wide initiative to make the business value-based with the objective of maximising shareholder value over time.

The key early steps in the transition involved:

- Preparing a multi-year blueprint for the many changes that would be required in order to make the business value-based.

- Using new financial and operational performance measures to identify and understand sources of value creation and destruction; to set performance targets; and to manage day-to-day performance. These measures included: economic profit; return on total invested capital; earnings growth; and free cash flow.

- Focusing business unit strategies on the search for profitable growth, i.e. growth in which returns exceed the cost of capital.

- Creating new short- and long-term incentive plans for senior managers. Rewards were based on achieving annual economic profit and multi-year total shareholder return targets compared with the performance of a peer group of similar companies.

- Reviewing the value performance of all the businesses in the Group in order to enable a value-based group corporate strategy to be developed.

- Delivering awareness and training sessions on managing for value to the top 300 executives worldwide.

- Carrying out two pilot studies in core group businesses. These were designed to:
  - demonstrate that managing-for-value tools and techniques could be used successfully in Cadbury-Schweppes;
  - produce 'value champions' – managers who would serve as role models for individuals in other business units.

- Establishing the first 'rolling strategic management agenda' for the board. This agenda comprised a short list of the highest value-at-stake issues faced by the company. Each issue was allocated to an individual director, and board meetings made decisions on the value-maximising way of resolving each issue.

The performance of the business improved dramatically as the group portfolio of businesses was restructured and individual business units developed and implemented superior strategies. Average annual total shareholder returns from 1987 until 1997 were 9 per cent, which represented uninspiring performance compared with the FTSE and to peer companies. Returns leapt to 14 per cent for 1997 and 57 per cent for 1998, which represented superior performance for shareholders.

Prepared by John Barbour, John Barbour Management Consulting Ltd.

Questions

1. Why are all publicly quoted companies not managed with the explicit objective of maximising shareholder value over time?

2. What are the obstacles that most companies face when making the change to becoming value-based and how might they be overcome?

Exhibit 10.8 Funding strategies in different circumstances

Growth (Stars)	Launch (Question marks)
Business risk: *High* Financial risk needs to be: *Low* Funding by: *Equity* *(growth investors)* Dividends: *Nominal*	Business risk: *Very high* Financial risk needs to be: *Very low* Funding by: *Equity* *(venture capital)* Dividends: *Zero*
Maturity (Cash cows)	**Decline (Dogs)**
Business risk: *Medium* Financial risk can be: *Medium* Funding by: *Debt and equity* *(retaining earnings)* Dividends: *High*	Business risk: *Low* Financial risk can be: *High* Funding by: *Debt* Dividends: *Total*

Source: Adapted from K. Ward, *Corporate Financial Strategy*, Butterworth/Heinemann, 1993, Chapter 2.

taken by the organisation, and the growth/share matrix is a convenient way of illustrating this:

- *Question marks* (or *problem children*) are clearly high business risk. They are at the beginning of their life cycle and are not yet established in their markets; moreover, they are likely to require substantial investment. For those who wish to invest in them, therefore, there is a need to understand the nature of risk and a desire to seek high returns. A stand-alone business in this situation might, for example, seek to finance such growth from specialists in this kind of investment, such as venture capitalists who, themselves, seek to offset risk by having a portfolio of such investments.

- The degree of business risk remains high in high-growth situations even if relatively high market shares are being achieved – as is the case with *stars*. The market position here remains volatile and probably highly competitive. It could be that a business has been financed on the basis of venture capital initially, but as it grows and becomes established it needs to seek other financing. Since the main attractions to investors here are the product or business concept and the prospect of future earnings, equity capital is likely to be appropriate; a business might seek to raise equity by public flotation.

- Businesses that operate in mature markets with high shares (*cash cows*) should be generating regular and substantial surpluses. Here the business risk is lower and the opportunity for retained earnings is high, and in the case of a portfolio of businesses, the corporation may be seeking to recycle such a surplus into its growth businesses. In these circumstances, it may make sense to raise finance through debt capital as well as equity, since reliable returns can be used to service such debt and, in any case, the return expected by lenders is likely to be less than that expected by those providing equity. (Since interest on debt has to be repaid, the financial risk for the business itself is higher than with equity finance, so it is also reasonable for the business to expect the cost of debt to be lower than with equity.) Provided increased debt (*gearing* or *leverage*) does not lead to an unacceptable level of risk, this cheaper debt funding will in fact increase the residual profits achieved by a company in these circumstances. The danger is that an organisation overstretches itself, takes on too much debt, increases its financial risk by so doing, suffers a downturn in its markets and is unable to service its interest payments.

● If a business is in decline, in effect a *dog*, then equity finance will be difficult to attract. However, borrowing may be possible if secured against residual assets in the business. At this stage, it is likely that the emphasis in the business will be on cost cutting, and it could well be that the cash flows from such businesses are quite strong. These businesses may provide relatively low-risk investments.

Illustration 10.6 shows how funding sources need to match circumstances.

Conglomerates face a problem if they seek to develop a financial strategy for a portfolio of businesses where there is a mix of businesses more or less growing and in high- or low-share positions. What is the appropriate financial strategy? This cannot be answered in isolation from a consideration of overall corporate strategy. The organisation needs to consider its overall risk/return position. For example, if an organisation is seeking to follow a high-growth strategy by diversification and acquisition, then it may be perceived by the investing community as a high (business) risk business; as such, it may have difficulty raising debt capital, and those who provide equity may expect high returns. Organisations that have sought high growth through an acquisitive diversification strategy have suffered because they have not had appropriate financial strategies. They have been either unable to attract equity investment or unwilling to do so, and have sought to finance growth out of borrowings, in effect relying on ever-growing cash to finance such borrowing. A decline in such growth means that debt cannot be serviced and could lead to bankruptcy. The crucial point is that financial strategy of conglomerates should be driven by portfolio strategy. For example:

● A company focusing on a portfolio of high-growth, high-risk investments in emerging industries would need to have more equity and less debt, as is common with venture capital funded companies.

● A company focusing on a portfolio of mature cash cow businesses with reliable cash flows would need the opposite – more debt and less equity.

● A company seeking to develop new and innovative businesses on a regular basis might, in effect, be acting as its own venture capitalist, accepting high risk at the business level and seeking to offset such risk by encouraging new and innovative ideas. If it does so, it should consider if it has a role to play as those businesses mature, or if it needs to consider selling them on to other organisations, not least to raise capital for further investment.

Illustration 10.6

High-technology companies struggle to pay their debts

STRATEGY IN ACTION

The mix of funding in a business must reflect the nature of the market.

In early 2001 the stock markets around the world had a major 'shakeout' of technology shares. Some companies saw their market valuation drop by 90 per cent from a year before. This included some major household names such as Amazon and Yahoo! and many of the big telecom companies. But the ones who were really struggling were the smaller operators – such as Kingston Communications, Atlantic and Redstone Telecom in the telecom section and many smaller Internet and 'dot.com' companies too. These smaller companies were finding it difficult, if not impossible, to raise debt finance to offset this dramatic fall in their stock market valuation and inject much-needed cash to fund developments in their fiercely competitive sectors. These developments were crucial to their future strategies and included laying infrastructure (such as fibre-optic cables) and brand building.

The chairmen of these small companies were trying to reassure potential investors that they were not building their businesses beyond their capabilities. They had been reshaping their businesses to cut overheads. Some were forced to drastically reschedule the speed of rollout of new services. For example, Redstone had been planning to offer new DSL[1] services to 80 per cent of UK small businesses – but had to scale it back to just four areas (Solent, Newbury, Nottingham and Cambridge). So the speed of business development was dependent on how much finance was available – even to the extent that developments had to come into positive

cash flow before services could be extended further.

Most companies were suffering from a drastic change in attitude from their financiers as market conditions changed. In particular, they became especially nervous about the high level of debt being carried by companies – raising questions as to whether the interest payments on this debt could be met. But the owners of the smaller companies were fiercely protective about their independence and were trying to avoid any possibility of being swallowed up by the major telecom companies such as British Telecom. Analysts were not sure that this was achievable unless market conditions took a turn for the better. So the irony could be that the small players fall victim to the major operators – whose stranglehold on the market was the reason for the small companies' existence following deregulation of the telecom markets.

Note

1. DSL is a technology that enables traditional copper wires to be used for high-speed Internet services.

Source: Adapted from *The Sunday Times*, 18 March 2001.

Questions

1. Referring to section 10.4.2 and Exhibit 10.8, explain why many companies ended up with the financial difficulties described above.

2. If you were managing one of these companies, how would you ensure that there was a closer match between company strategy and funding?

Exhibit 10.8 also shows that dividend policy might also need to change with the nature of the business. In the launch phase investors may be mainly concerned with growth potential and cash will be limited for dividend payments. This would still be largely true during growth – though some dividend payments may be needed. During maturity the cash flow of the business should be strongly positive; opportunities for reinvestment to create further value may be limited so shareholders might receive most value by dividend payments. During decline the argument for providing shareholder value through dividends is even stronger.

Finally, it should be remembered that although the discussion in this section has been concerned with how funding should match strategy, the reverse is a key consideration too. This concerns how strategic developments might be driven by the funding circumstances of the organisation. A number of examples have appeared earlier in this book:

● The ownership of an organisation – in particular, whether it is privately owned, publicly quoted, a charity or a public sector organisation will dictate the sources and amounts of funding available. It has previously been seen (Chapter 5) that a common motive for changing the form of ownership is the need to open up new funding sources. However, ownership may in reality be a limitation on strategic development by dictating the funding environment within which strategy will *actually* develop.

● Although the potential motives for an acquisition are varied (as outlined in Chapter 8), often the driving force can be financial rather than strategic. For example, the need to reinvest excess funds or to show continuing growth to hold up share price. So an organisation may get driven into 'unholy alliances' creating all sorts of strategic problems (such as cultural clash) because of this shorter-term financial prerogative. The longer-term result is declining performance and destruction of shareholder value.

10.4.3 The financial expectations of stakeholders

The discussions in section 10.4.1 looked at how business strategies might create or destroy value for shareholders of a business. The public sector equivalent is the extent to which *politicians* (as the owners or guardians of public money) would regard public money to have been well spent. But it was seen in Chapter 5 that the owners are not the only ones who have a stake in organisations. So other stakeholders will have financial expectations of organisations. The issue is the extent to which business strategies should address these considerations and how they can be squared with creating value for the owners. For example:

● Chapter 5 introduced the idea of the governance chain (Exhibit 5.2) and made the point that the real beneficiaries of a company's performance usually have their financial interests represented by powerful intermediaries – institutional shareholders such as asset managers of pension funds. So strategy is strongly influenced by the financial expectations of these intermediaries who can become the key players on major strategic changes – such as mergers or takeovers.

- *Bankers* and other providers of interest-bearing loans are concerned about the *risk* attached to their loans and the competence with which this is managed. A consistently good track record in managing that risk could be regarded (in itself) as a reason for bankers to invest further with some companies and not others. The risk would be influenced by the capital structure of the company – particularly the gearing ratio (of debt to equity), which determines how sensitive the solvency of the company is to changes in its profit position. Interest cover is a similar measure which relates interest payments to profit.

- *Suppliers* and *employees* are likely to be concerned with the *liquidity* of the company, which is a measure of its ability to meet short-term commitments to creditors and wages. Bankers will share this concern because a deteriorating liquidity position may require correction through additional loans and the increased risk profile discussed above. Again, a track record in this area could be a competence underpinning good supplier relationships, resulting in discounts or improved credit.

- The *community* will be concerned with the *social cost* of an organisation's strategies, such as pollution or marketing. This is rarely accounted for in traditional financial analyses, but it is an issue of growing concern. Matters of business ethics were discussed in Chapter 5 (section 5.4). Failure to pay proper attention to these issues could be a source of strategic weakness.

- *Customers* are concerned about best-value products or services. This assessment is rarely made in traditional financial analyses, the implication being that companies which survive profitably in a competitive environment *must* be providing value for money. However, as mentioned above, cost and value creation tends to be distributed unevenly across the various activities and 'players' in the value chain. The relative 'winners' and 'losers' at any time are determined by circumstances which change the relative bargaining power of buyers and suppliers in the chain (as discussed in the five forces framework – section 3.3.1). Commodity-like industries (such as oil, steel or glass) show this very clearly in the way that prices swing with market conditions (supply/demand). In turn, this creates large swings in the shareholder value creation between peaks and troughs in demand. Where competitive pressures have not existed, such as in many public services, there have been attempts to develop performance measures more related to best value. However, many management information systems are not geared to such a detailed analysis of separate value activities, making this process difficult. In the UK in the late 1990s, political weight was put behind this process through the *Best Value Initiative* which defined a range of performance indicators and set standards against a benchmark of best performance (beyond the public sector) as discussed in section 4.6.

Overall, managers need to be conscious of the financial impact on various stakeholders of the strategies they are pursuing or planning to pursue. They also need to understand how these expectations could enable the success of some strategies whilst limiting the ability of an organisation to succeed with other strategies.

10.5 MANAGING TECHNOLOGY[19]

This section is about the relationship between technology, innovation and strategic success. As with previous sections of this chapter, it is important to start with a warning. The key strategic issue is innovation, and technology should be seen as a means of underpinning innovation in organisations. But it is easy for organisations to get distracted by technology development itself without asking how the technology will assist in the creation and sharing of knowledge in an organisation. Crucial is the question as to how this process will provide competitive advantage. As mentioned in Chapter 4, the technology itself may be easy to acquire by competitors so is not necessarily a source of advantage. The exploitation of that technology is where advantage may be created.

Technological innovation can take several forms, each of which might give organisations advantage in a particular way, as shown in Exhibit 10.9. It can be seen from this list how important technological developments might be in creating (or destroying) core competences in an organisation, as discussed in Chapter 4. This will be discussed more fully below.

As with the other issues in this chapter, the link between business strategy and technology is likely to be *dependent on context*. So factors such as company size, industry sector and product type will shape the relationship. However, it is useful to identify a number of different types of innovation where the strategic implications are different. These are called technological paths or trajectories:[20]

- *Supplier-dominated innovation* – such as in agriculture, with advances in machinery, fertilisers and pesticides. The strategic issue for an agricultural producer is rapid learning on how these new technologies might transform business processes in 'their' part of the value chain. Capitalising on this type of supplier-led innovation remains the current challenge for organisations in many different sectors in exploiting computer hardware and software developments (as discussed in section 10.3 above).

- *Scale-intensive innovation* – such as complex manufacturing systems in automobiles and other sectors – where advantage is gained from economies of scale and learning results from that scale, as discussed in Chapter 4. Here the strategic challenge is to ensure that incremental learning *does* occur and best practice is diffused through the organisation.

- *Information-intensive innovation* – such as in financial services, retailing or travel – where the exploitation of IT is the central strategic issue. This has already been discussed in section 10.3 above.

- *Science-based innovation* is still important in many sectors such as pharmaceuticals, electronics, materials and engineering. The strategic challenges are to monitor academic research, develop products and acquire the resources to achieve commercial-scale production. An associated task is the assessment and management of risk.

Exhibit 10.9	Strategic advantage through innovation

MECHANISM	STRATEGIC ADVANTAGE	EXAMPLES
Novelty in product or service	Offering something no one else can	Introducing the first . . . Walkman®, fountain pen, camera, dishwasher . . . to the world
Novelty in process	Offering it in ways others can't match – faster, lower cost, more customised, etc.	Pilkington's float glass process, Bessemer's steel process, Internet banking, online bookselling, etc.
Complexity	Offering something which others find difficult to master	Rolls-Royce and aircraft engines – complex machining and metallurgy
Legal protection of intellectual property	Offering something which others cannot do unless they pay you a licence or other fee	Blockbuster drugs like Zantac®, Viagra®, etc.
Robust design	Offering something which provides the platform on which other variations and generations can be built	Boeing 737 – over thirty years old the design is still being adapted and configured to suit different users
Rewriting the rules	Offering something which represents a completely new product or process which makes the old ones redundant	Typewriters vs. computer word processing, Ice vs. refrigerators Electric vs. gas or oil lamps

Source: Abridged version from J. Tidd, J. Bessant and K. Pavitt; *Managing Innovation: Integrating technological, market and organisational change*, 2nd edition, Wiley, 2001.

Bearing in mind these introductory comments about the types of innovation, this section of the chapter will now look at the following issues about the relationship between business strategy and technology and how innovation can enable strategic success (see Exhibit 10.10):

● how technology changes the competitive situation;

● technology and strategic capability;

● organising technology to achieve advantage.

10.5.1 Technology and the competitive situation

In Chapter 3, the five forces framework was used as a checklist for understanding the competitive forces within an industry and how they might determine the competitive position of different organisations. Technology can have a significant impact on these forces and this should influence how the strategies of individual organisations develop in the future, as the following examples illustrate:

● Barriers to new entrants may be lowered by reducing the economies of scale, for example in publishing, or the capital requirements for set-up, e.g. in computing. In some cases, barriers may be raised as technologies become

Exhibit 10.10 | **Strategy and technology**

more difficult to master and products more complex, for example in the aerospace industry.

- Substitution may be assisted by technology at several levels. New products may displace old, e.g. DVDs for videotape; the need may be displaced, for example using video conferencing rather than travelling to meetings, or technological developments in other sectors may 'steal' consumer demand through an array of exciting products, e.g. electronic goods displacing consumer spending on household durables such as kitchens and carpets. Sometimes technology can stop substitution, for example by tying the usage of one product to another – the 'debate' about Microsoft's success in tying software developments into the Windows operating system continues (see the case example at the end of Chapter 1).

- The relative power of suppliers and buyers can also be changed by technology. The Microsoft example applies here too since the questions being raised in court are the extent to which they (as a supplier to most businesses and households) have unreasonably high levels of power over their customers. But technological developments can work in the favour of buyers by freeing them from a single source of supply. This often happens when international specifications and standards are agreed (say for steel).

- Competitive rivalry amongst organisations can be raised through this process of generic specifications or diminished if one firm develops a new product or process which it is able to patent. The difference in the level of competitive rivalry in generic pharmaceuticals as against ethical (proprietary) pharmaceuticals is markedly different.

The strategic issues raised for individual organisations through these examples are two-fold. First, some organisations may be technological leaders and trying to gain advantage in some of the ways outlined above. Second, many other organisations may be needing to assess the likely impact on their competitive position of technological developments led by others.

10.5.2 The diffusion of innovation

If technological innovation is to enable success then an organisation needs to be able to assess how quickly new product and service features are likely to be adopted. Since technological innovation can be expensive, its commercial attractiveness can hinge on the extent and pace at which a market is likely to adopt new products – or the improved performance of existing products. This is called the **diffusion** of innovations. Diffusion is influenced by a number of factors to do with two main issues:[21] the *nature* of the innovation and the *processes* of bringing the innovation to market. Clearly these are issues which should strongly link business strategy and technology strategies together. Research on the pace of diffusion centres on two views of what determines the pace of diffusion:

> **Diffusion** is the extent and pace at which a market is likely to adopt new products

- *Supply-side models* which emphasise the importance of product features such as:
  - *Degree of improvement* in performance above current products (from a customer's perspective) – to provide sufficient incentive to change. For example, whether wide-screen television will encourage TV set replacement by consumers earlier than otherwise.
  - *Compatibility* with other factors, e.g wide-screen TV is more attractive when the broadcasting networks change more of their programmes to that format.
  - *Complexity* can discourage uptake. This can be complexity in the product itself or in the marketing methods being used to commercialise the product (e.g. unduly complex pricing structures as with mobile phones or many financial service products).
  - *Experimentation* – the ability to test products before commitment to a final decision – either directly or through the availability of information about the experience of other customers. This is why new product marketing often features satisfied customers and/or endorsements from suitable role models such as sports or pop celebrities.
- *Demand-side models* – which describe the processes that exist in markets between consumers that drive adoption of new products or product features.

The two types of model differ in their detailed explanations but at a practical level the implications for strategy are similar. Customers are different from each other and range from innovators (the first to adopt) through to laggards (the last to adopt). Also, the likelihood and extent of adoption by the slower groups is influenced by the response of the faster groups. This requires a sophisticated approach to new product launch – particularly where a company is introducing a new-generation product and wishing simultaneously to win new customers whilst progressively moving its current customers from old to new product or service.

The practical importance of the various factors listed above is as a checklist against which the technology strategies (for product/service improvements) can be matched to the market conditions in which the new or improved products will need to compete. This integration of these two sets of knowledge is of critical importance to the commercial success of technological innovations. For example, a manager writing a 'business case' to secure funds for improving particular product features would need to address many of the issues listed above. They would start by showing why the improved features might be valued by customers sufficiently to switch purchase or upgrade. It might also address issues of compatibility with other equipment that the consumer or distributor uses in conjunction with the product. The marketing plan would address how these attributes would be communicated and who would be the initial target audiences. It would address how initial adoptions would then be 'rolled out' into wider uptake in the market.

Illustration 10.7 shows how technology diffusion occurred in one sector.

10.5.3 Technology and strategic capability

Core competences

Chapter 4 underlined the importance of identifying core competences as the basis of an organisation's competitive advantage. A core competence is an activity or a process that gives advantage because it fundamentally underpins value in the product, is performed better than competitors and is difficult for competitors to imitate. As mentioned in the introduction to this section, technology itself is usually easy to imitate by competitors and is, therefore, not usually a unique resource or a core competence. There are, of course, exceptions to this, where technological breakthroughs have been carefully patented. However, from a strategic point of view the importance of technology lies in the potential both to create and to destroy core competences (as seen in the case of IT in section 10.3.1 above). So if technology is to enable success there are some important implications for business and technology strategies:

● To tie future developments to a single technology that an organisation has mastered can be both inappropriate and unduly risky. So expecting market development, new uses and diversification based on this technology to dominate the strategic choices could be imprudent. For example, the opportunities to stretch the technologies may be exhausted or be outflanked by other technological developments. For example, stainless steel was

Illustration 10.7

The diffusion of robotics

STRATEGY IN ACTION

Technology diffusion is driven by the behaviour of users.

The first commercial industrial robots were developed in the 1960s, and in the 1980s many believed that robots would replace most forms of manual work. However, in 1995 the number of robots per 10,000 workers was only 21 in the UK, 33 in the United States, 69 in Germany and 338 in Japan. This raises two questions: why has the diffusion of robots been so slow, and why are there such large differences in the rates of diffusion in different countries? Economists tend to argue that the level of investment in industrial robots, like all capital equipment, is a function of labour costs: the higher the labour costs, the more likely firms are to substitute robots for labour. This is clearly part of the explanation, as rankings of labour costs are similar to those for robot density in Japan, Sweden, Germany, the United States, France and the UK. However, more detailed studies reveal other factors affecting the diffusion of robots, such as industry structure and work organisation.

The automobile industry has traditionally been the largest customer for robots. The most common applications in this sector are in spot welding, machine loading and surface treatment. The main requirement is high accuracy, or rather repeatability. Therefore in those countries with the largest automobile sector, the electronics industry has begun to employ large numbers of robots in assembly, changing the rate and pattern of diffusion. Work organisation has also affected the number and types of robot used in different countries. Expensive, sophisti-

cated robots are common in the UK and United States in firms characterised by low levels of training. Therefore robots have to be made 'idiot proof' in order to minimise operator involvement. In contrast, cheaper, less complex robots are more common in Japan where operators are trained to work with the robots and to perform routine programming and maintenance. Moreover, many firms which have poor quality control of materials and components have been forced to adopt sophisticated component feeding and sensor systems to allow for component variability, whereas firms which have made investments in quality management have been able to use cheaper, simpler equipment. Thus the diffusion of industrial robots has not followed a simple logistics curve based on some cost function. Rather, patterns of adoption have varied as industrial robots and users' needs have co-evolved. Robots were originally conceived as being direct replacements for workers – so-called steel collar workers, or universal automation – but have become increasingly specialised such that there are now robots designed specifically for assembly, spraying or welding applications. At the same time, users have grown sophisticated and their needs have fragmented, some demanding 'turnkey' integrated solutions, others preferring to build their own systems from various components.

Source: Adapted from J. Tidd, J. Bessant and K. Pavitt, *Managing Innovation: Integrating technological, market and organisational change*, 2nd edition, Wiley, 2001, Chapter 7, with permission.

| Exhibit 10.11 | Developing or acquiring technology |

METHOD	INFLUENCING FACTORS					
	Importance of the technology	Prior knowledge and reputation	Complexity	Willingness to take risk	Desire to lead or follow	Speed
In-house	Key	High	Low/Medium	High	Lead	Slow
Alliances	Threshold	Low	High	Medium	Follow	Medium
Acquisition	Key or threshold	Very Low	High	Low	Follow	High

Source: Adapted from J. Tidd, J. Bessant and K. Pavitt, *Managing Innovation: Integrating technological, market and organisational change*, 2nd edition, Wiley, 2001.

the wonder material of the 1960s, substituting for other materials in many consumer and industrial applications. But, in turn, it has been substituted in some applications by developments in polymers, ceramics and composite materials.

- Core competences may be found in the processes of linking technologies together rather than the technologies *per se*. Indeed, many advances in process technology are concerned with how computer process control can be grafted to the technologies of the plant and machinery – not in being excellent in just one or other technology.

- In a rapidly changing and competitive world the fruits of any particular innovation are likely to be shorter-lived than hitherto. So core competences are not found in separate technological developments, but in the processes that ensure a constant flow of improvements and in the ability to bring improvements to market quickly and gain first-mover advantages. So the way in which technology is organised is likely to be of strategic importance, and this will be discussed below in section 10.5.4.

Developing or acquiring technology

An important strategic decision for many organisations is how technology is developed or acquired. This can be a key determinant in the success or failure of strategies. This is a detailed and complex subject given that many different variables could influence these decisions.[22] However, for the purposes of illustrating the link between business and technology strategies a few general principles are important (see Exhibit 10.11):

- *In-house development* will be favoured if the technology is key to competitive advantage and an organisation has expectations of gaining first-mover advantages. This will be feasible if the organisation already has a good knowledge of both the technology and the market opportunities and the complexity is not too great – it is within current organisational knowledge domains. Finally, it is important that the organisation is willing to take commercial and financial risk.

- *Alliances* are likely to be appropriate for 'threshold' technologies rather than ones on which competitive advantage is to be built. For example, a manufacturer of branded drinks may seek a partner to improve bottling and distribution processes. These are both important activities but competitive advantage is concerned with the product itself and brand maintenance. Alliances might also be appropriate where there is an intention to follow and imitate rather than lead. This would be particularly the case where the complexity of product or market knowledge is beyond the current knowledge base – so organisational learning is an important objective. Alliances also help to limit financial risk.

● *Acquisition of current players or rights* may be particularly appropriate if speed is important and there is no time for learning. It may also be essential if the level of complexity, both in technology and market application, is beyond current organisational knowledge and where credibility of the technology is essential to business success – so the source of the technology matters. So production under licence of an established technology may be more successful than developing an alternative.

Illustration 10.8 shows how one company developed through a combination of these processes.

10.5.4 Organising technology development

The location and funding of technology development

An important debate in many larger organisations is who within the organisation should be driving technology development and who should be funding it. This is part of the wider strategic debate about how strategic responsibilities could be divided between the corporate centre and divisions/departments of an organisation – discussed in section 6.3 and expanded in section 9.4. Decisions on this could be important in enabling strategic success through technology.

| Exhibit 10.12 | Funding and location of R&D |

LOCATED AT

		Corporate	Divisional
FUNDED BY	**Corporate**	Assessing new technologies	Commercialising new technologies
	Divisional	Exploratory development of new technologies	Incremental product or process improvements

Source: Adapted from J. Tidd, J. Bessant and K. Pavitt, *Managing Innovation: Integrating technological, market and organisational change,* 2nd edition, Wiley, 2001.

Illustration 10.8

Celltech – technology development in the biotechnology industry

STRATEGY IN ACTION

Many companies will use a combination of in-house development and acquisition of technology.

In early 2001 Celltech, the UK-based bio-technology company, signed an agreement with Pharmacia, the US drug company, worth £190 million up-front and a share of profits. This gave Pharmacia the rights to use CDP 870 – an injectable medicine for rheumatoid arthritis. That Celltech could extract such generous terms said much about the strength of their scientific knowledge. Indeed Pharmacia had beaten off fierce competition from many other drug companies to acquire these rights.

Celltech had come a long way since its foundation only 20 years previously. Its success had been built on its scientific expertise – focusing mainly on antibody remedies for inflammatory diseases (such as arthritis). This expertise had been built up painstakingly over those 20 years and not without setbacks. Celltech's core scientific strength was in understanding antibodies, which the human body uses to 'tag' invading pathogens – disease-producing substances or micro-organisms – prior to destroying them. They began to look at how antibodies could be used as a therapy for acute illnesses – such as cancers. This research ended in a series of products that allowed cancers to be targeted very specifically – rather than the more broad-based approach of chemotherapy. This research also led on to ways of tackling chronic (as against acute) diseases, such as arthritis, or Crohn's disease. CDP 870 was one of the products of this research. It had two main advantages over its

rivals. First, it was cheap, and second, it only had to be injected once each month (as against the more normal twice weekly).

But injectable medicines have their limitations. Patients would always prefer tablets or small molecule drugs. It was for this reason that in 1999 Celltech purchased Chiroscience for £696 million. Chiroscience had been built around improving existing small molecule drugs and discovering new ones. Celltech was seeking to harness those skills to build a comprehensive pipeline of small molecule drugs. The purchase of Chiroscience also included the Seattle-based 'gene hunting' unit, whose job was to identify new targets for drugs – both antibodies and small molecules.

So Celltech management had pursued a 'mixed' policy of organic growth and acquisitions. Following the Pharmacia deal, analysts were speculating if Celltech might be gearing up for another big strategic move. Of course, there was another possibility altogether, that Celltech's scientific expertise might make it a target for acquisition itself.

Source: Adapted from *Financial Times*, 14 March 2001.

Questions

1. Referring to section 10.5.3, explain how technology underpinned core competences at Celltech.

2. How did this affect the way in which they had balanced organic growth and acquisition?

3. What approach should they use for the future?

Exhibit 10.12 shows that different arrangements are likely to be suitable for different aspects of technology development. For example, at one extreme, new technologies are best assessed and funded corporately whilst at the other, incremental product and process improvements are best undertaken and funded locally. Between these extremes, the commercialisation of new technologies is often best done locally but funded corporately since others will learn and benefit from the first moves. Experimentation with new technologies might remain corporate but be funded by divisions who see commercial potential in their arena.

These same principles might lead to conclusions that some technology development activities might be outsourced where the technological expertise is inadequate in both divisions and the corporate centre but the particular technology development is crucial to securing current and future business.

Sometimes the technological expertise of an organisation might be greater than the current business can exploit – leading to considerations of spin-off of R&D (in whole or in part) to allow new commercial opportunities to be exploited (by licensing technology to third parties).

Enabling processes

Chapter 9 underlined the importance of organisational processes in enabling the success of strategies. This is particularly true in technology development where there are real dangers that an organisation's competence in technology fails to be exploited commercially. Since these processes are often difficult to manage, they may prove to be core competences that underpin competitive advantage, as mentioned above. Some of the following processes may be of crucial importance in enabling success through technology:

- Scanning the business environment (both technology and market developments) and spotting the opportunities for gaining advantage and the potential threats to current business. Related to this is the ability to select projects or developments that have a good strategic fit with the business. But this is not as easy as it sounds. Good strategic fit does not mean giving preference to incremental developments; it means addressing the future circumstances that the organisation will face. So it may well mean giving preference to transformational technologies – which could be very challenging in terms of both competences and culture of the organisation.

- Resourcing developments adequately, but not overgenerously, so as to ensure a good return for the investment. This is much easier to see in hindsight than in advance, but past experience and good benchmarking can help. This also includes the ability to monitor and review projects through their various stages – many organisations now use stage-gate processes to good effect.[23] This is a structured review process to assess progress on meeting product performance characteristics during the development process and ensuring that they are matched with market data. These processes must also include the ability to terminate and accelerate projects, to capture the learning from both successes and failures, and to disseminate results and best practice.

Of course, behind these processes is a set of much more detailed activities which will determine the success or failure of these processes. This would include activities ranging from forecasting, concept testing and option screening to communication, negotiation and motivation.

Gaining advantage through technology[24]

The preceding sections were intended to underline the importance of 'aligning' business and technology strategies in organisations as a way of enabling strategic success. Successful organisations will be those where there is a strong commitment to innovation from senior management and a business acumen based on an understanding of the business strategy and technology relationship.

There needs to be a creative climate where innovation is fostered, communication is extensive and where there is a culture of a learning organisation. Structures and processes must facilitate the creation of this environment and provide a commitment to individual and team development. In particular, it must support key individuals who will champion and facilitate the exploitation of technology for strategic success.

10.6 INTEGRATING RESOURCES

The sections above have looked at how resources and competences in separate resource areas need to support an organisation's strategies and may also be the basis on which new strategies can be built. However, there is a third issue that has only partly emerged from the consideration of the separate resource areas above. As discussed in Chapter 4, most organisational strategies not only require competences in separate resource areas, they require an ability to pull a range of resources and competences together – both inside the organisation and in the wider value chain. For example, Exhibit 10.13 shows some of the resources and activities that need to be integrated by an organisation hoping to gain competitive advantage through its competence in bringing new products to the market more quickly than competitors. This can be a complex matter and, therefore, may be the basis of competitive advantage. Competence in new product launches requires an ability to integrate and co-ordinate the separate activities of R&D, manufacture, etc. – each of which, in turn, involves bringing together a complex mixture of resources. It is not sufficient simply to own these resources or to be competent in these separate activities. It is the ability to link these together effectively and quickly that determines the success or failure of the strategy and could be a source of real competitive advantage.

The concluding message of the chapter as a whole is the same as for the separate resource areas. Systems developments have made important contributions to the performance of many organisations – for example the way in which enterprise resource planning (ERP) has helped with resource integration, as discussed in section 9.3.2 (see also Illustration 9.3). However, it is not sufficient to regard resource management and resource integration as being solely about the systems and procedures of an organisation's business functions. It has been seen in the sections above that although these systems and

| Exhibit 10.13 | Resource integration in a new product launch |

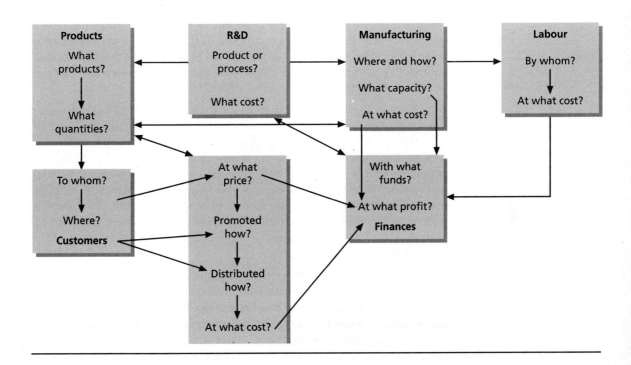

procedures may be vitally important in all resource areas, they can hold back strategic change and will not, by themselves, achieve resource integration. Integration also results from people's embedded behaviours and 'the way things are done' in an organisation. This is likely to be a potential benefit, since this embedded knowledge will be difficult to imitate, as discussed above. However, it can also prove to be the Achilles heel of an organisation as managers find it difficult to challenge and change this knowledge and the behaviours in the organisation and fail to respond to change.

SUMMARY

● Managers and individuals lower down in organisations usually control resources and competences that are crucial in *enabling* strategic success and are also likely to be the most knowledgeable about changes in parts of the business environment with which they interface. So understanding the relationship between resource management and strategic success is important.

- This is a two-way relationship. Resource management and development must support an organisation's strategies. But the development of unique resources and core competences in parts of an organisation may provide the 'springboard' from which new strategies are developed.

- The 'hard' side of resource management – systems and procedures – are vitally important in enabling success. But in all resource areas the critical question is how these systems contribute to the creation and integration of knowledge. Only part of this knowledge can be captured in systems. Indeed, competitive advantage is more likely to be gained from knowledge that cannot be codified since it will be more difficult to imitate.

- People are at the heart of strategy in most organisations. So understanding the relationship between business and human resource strategies is important. This must be about the informal ways in which people behave as well as formal systems and procedures. This involves issues about how people should be developed as a resource – such as recruitment, training and performance management. It is also concerned with understanding, managing and gaining advantage from the cultural and political context that people create. It is also concerned with how people can be organised for success – the structures, roles, processes and relationships discussed in Chapter 9.

- Information is also a key resource of particular attention at the moment with the rapid advances in information technology. These developments in the ability to access and process information can build or destroy an organisation's core competences, so are crucial to competitive advantage. IT is also spawning new business models – where traditional 'value networks' are being reconfigured. This is a serious threat to some organisations and an opportunity for others. Changing capability in access to and processing of information also has important implications for issues of structures and processes within and between organisations.

- Money is a resource of central importance in all organisations. So it is particularly important to understand whether and how business strategies might deliver financial value to shareholders or owners. Most strategic developments need funding which, in turn, creates risk. So the types of funding need to vary with strategy. In reverse, the type and availability of funds will determine which strategies best suit an organisation or, indeed, whether access to these funding sources might give competitive advantage. This will be influenced by the form of ownership. Stakeholders other than owners have financial expectations that will also influence an organisation's business strategies.

- The final resource area considered in this chapter is technology development. This will affect the competitive forces on an organisation and also its strategic capability. So the ways that technology is developed, exploited, organised and funded will all influence the success or failure of strategy.

- Competence in separate resource areas is not enough. Organisations need to be able to integrate resources to support current strategies or to develop new strategies.

RECOMMENDED KEY READINGS

- A useful book on Human Resource Management is: D. Torrington and L. Hall, *Human Resource Management*, 4th edition, Prentice Hall, 1998.

- L. Gratton, V. Hope Hailey, P. Stiles and C. Truss, *Strategic Human Resource Management*, Oxford University Press, 1999, is about the realities of people management in large, complex companies – based on collaboration with a number of high-profile organisations in the 'Leading Edge Forum'.

- A good general reference on information management is: J. Ward and P. Griffiths, *Strategic Planning for Information Systems*, 2nd edition, Wiley, 1996.

- The relationship between information and strategy and the power of IT is covered in: P. Timmers, *Electronic Commerce*, Wiley, 2000, and B. Gates, *Business @ the Speed of Thought*, Penguin, 1999.

- T. Grundy (with G. Johnson and K. Scholes), *Exploring Strategic Financial Management*, Prentice Hall, 1998, and K. Ward, *Corporate Financial Strategy*, Butterworth/Heinemann, 1993, explore the relationship between financial and business strategies.

- The relationship between technology and strategy is extensively reviewed in: J. Tidd, J. Bessant and K. Pavitt, *Managing Innovation: Integrating technological, market and organisational change*, 2nd edition, Wiley, 2001.

REFERENCES

1. A good general reference book on human resource management is: D. Torrington and L. Hall, *Human Resource Management*, 4th edition, Prentice Hall, 1998.

2. W. Kim and R. Mauborgne, 'Fair process: managing in the knowledge economy', *Harvard Business Review*, vol. 75, no. 4 (1997), pp. 65–75, argues that the right climate has to be created for employees to 'volunteer' their creativity and expertise.

3. L. Gratton, V. Hope Hailey, P. Stiles and C. Truss, *Strategic Human Resource Management*, Oxford University Press, 1999, is about the realities of people management in large, complex companies – based on collaboration with a number of high-profile organisations in the 'Leading Edge Forum'. This source was used extensively in preparing this section.

4. See reference 3 above.

5. The seminal work on this issue of balanced teams was: R. Belbin, *Management Teams: Why they succeed or fail*, Heinemann, 1981.

6. J. Storey, *Developments in the Management of Human Resources*, Blackwell, 1992, used this categorisatin of the roles of HR functions. D. Ulrich, *Human Resource Champion*, Harvard Business School Press, 1997, presents a slightly different categorisation based on the two dimensions of change vs. maintenance *and* people vs. processes.

7. For example, downsizing creates problems in this respect. See R. Thomas and D. Dunkerley, 'Careering downwards? Middle managers' experience in the downsized organisation', *British Journal of Management*, vol. 10 (1999), pp. 157–169.

8. J. Balogun and V. Hope Hailey (with G. Johnson and K. Scholes), *Exploring Strategic Change*, Prentice Hall, 1999, p. 218.

9. S. Floyd and B. Wooldridge, 'Dinosaurs or dynamos: recognising middle management's strategic role', *Academy of Management Executive*, vol. 8, no. 4 (1994), pp. 47–57.

10. A good general reference on information management is: J. Ward and P. Griffiths, *Strategic Planning for Information Systems*, 2nd edition, Wiley, 1996. Two books have been used as background on the issues of information management and the power of IT: P. Timmers, *Electronic Commerce*, Wiley, 2000, and B. Gates, *Business @ the Speed of Thought*, Penguin, 1999. Readers might also find R. Kalatoka and M. Robinson, *E-business: Roadmap to success*, Addison-Wesley, 1999; A. Hartman and J. Sifonis, *Net Ready: Strategies for success in the e-conomy*, McGraw-Hill, 2000; and M. Porter, 'Strategy and the internet', *Harvard Business Review*, vol. 79, no. 2 (2001), pp. 63–78, to be useful.

11. Gates (reference 10 above), pp. 225–233.

12. The need to join up the different customer interfaces (such as salesforce, websites, call centres) is discussed in: *Customer Essentials*, CBR Special Report, 1999, pp. 7–20.

13. See Timmers (reference 10 above), Chapter 3.

14. Readers should find the following article useful: 'E-management', *The Economist*, 18 November 2000.

15. Readers may wish to consult one or more standard texts on finance. For example: J. Samuels and F. Wilkes, *Financial Management and Decision Making*, Thomson, 1998, or M. Glautier and B. Underdown, *Accounting Theory and Practice*, 7th edition, Pearson Education, 2000.

16. J. Ellis and D. Williams, *Corporate Strategy and Financial Analysis*, Pitman, 1993, pp. 334–341, provide a detailed and clear explanation of how this cash generation leads to shareholder value.

17. T. Grundy (with G. Johnson and K. Scholes), *Exploring Strategic Financial Management*, Prentice Hall, 1998, Chapter 2, and Ellis and Williams (reference 16 above) Chapter 10, are useful references on managing for value.

18. For readers who wish to follow up the discussion in this section, see K. Ward, *Corporate Financial Strategy*, Butterworth/Heinemann, 1993, and T. Grundy and K. Ward (eds), *Developing Financial Strategies: A comprehensive model in strategic business finance*, Kogan Page, 1996.

19. The major source for this section is: J. Tidd, J. Bessant and K. Pavitt, *Managing Innovation: Integrating technological, market and organisational change*, 2nd edition, Wiley, 2001.

20. K. Pavitt, 'What we know about the strategic management of technology', *California Management Review*, vol. 32 (1990), pp. 17–26.

21. E. Rogers, *Diffusion of Innovations*, Free Press, 1995.

22. See Tidd *et al.* (reference 19 above) p. 222, and J. Tidd and M. Trewhella, 'Organisational and technological antecedents for knowledge acquisition', *R&D Management*, vol. 27, no. 4 (1997), pp. 359–375.

23. The stage-gate process is discussed in: R. Cooper, 'Third generation new product processes', *Journal of Product Innovation Management*, vol. 11, no. 1 (1994), pp. 3–14, or R. Thomas, *New Product Development: Managing and forecasting for strategic success*, Wiley, 1993.

24. See Tidd *et al.* (reference 19 above), p. 306.

WORK ASSIGNMENTS

✽ Denotes more advanced work assignments.

10.1 Choose a strategic development for an organisation with which you are familiar and list the key human resource changes that will be needed to enable success (refer to Exhibit 10.2 as a checklist).

10.2 ✽ Write an executive report to your CEO advising on whether or not the HR function should be closed and the work devolved to middle (line) managers. Centre your arguments on the impact on the strategic performance of the organisation.

10.3 Find examples of all of the new business models outlined in Exhibit 10.5. Explain in which sectors you feel each business model is most likely to grow quickly. Why?

10.4 ✽ (a) Choose an organisation which is shifting its generic competitive strategy from low price to differentiation. Describe how the information strategies will need to change to support this new strategy.

(b) Choose an organisation which is attempting the opposite shift (differentiation to low price) and undertake the same analysis.

10.5 Referring to Exhibit 10.7, give as many reasons as you can why profitable companies might be destroying shareholder value (with examples). Now repeat the exercise for organisations with poor levels of profitability that are nonetheless creating shareholder value (with examples).

10.6 ✽ Write an executive report on how sources of funding need to be related to the nature of an industry and the types of strategies that an organisation is pursuing.

10.7 Choose an industry or sector with which you are familiar and describe the ways in which new technologies and products have diffused into the market (refer to section 10.5.2). Who have been the winners and losers? Why?

10.8 ✽ By referring to Exhibit 10.11, write a report advising your CEO how technology should be acquired by your organisation. Remember to justify your conclusions.

10.9 Refer to the new product launch example in Exhibit 10.13. If you were project managing this launch, identify the specific ways in you would ensure resource integration between the various resource areas. Remember to identify both 'hard' and 'soft' ways in which you would achieve this integration.

CASE EXAMPLE

NHS Direct: A new gateway to health care

'NHS phone lines "put lives at risk"'. This headline in *The Sunday Times* on 3 December 2000 was an unwelcome early Christmas present for the UK Secretary of State for Health, coming just two weeks after the final 'rollout' of NHS Direct, the new telephone helpline service of the National Health Service (NHS) staffed by nurses.

Lord Winston, a well-known 'media figure' and one of the most prominent and respected doctors in the country, gave journalists a warning that this flagship reform of the NHS may be putting lives at risk. He claimed that nurses who staffed the helpline were less likely to identify patients with dangerous symptoms than if the patient had seen their own doctor. The newspaper quoted him as saying: 'No matter how well you train a nurse, they don't have medical qualifications, and it is that [which] will tell you what questions to ask.'

Several recent cases had inspired Lord Winston's comments, including failures to diagnose callers with meningitis and malaria. Indeed a number of family doctors (GPs) felt sufficiently concerned that they had openly advised their patients to avoid using the services of NHS Direct. Many doctors felt its annual cost of some £80 million could have been better spent in other ways, although NHS Direct cost less than 0.1 per cent of the annual NHS expenditure.

The National Health Service and NHS Direct

The UK National Health Service is one of the largest public sector organisations in Europe. In September 2000 there were over 991,000 staff in the NHS Hospital and Community Health Services (amounting to over 801,000 full-time equivalents). This included over 346,000 nursing, midwifery and health

---

This case was prepared by Alex Murdock, of South Bank University Business School. It is intended as a basis for class discussion and not as an illustration of either good or bad management practice. © A. Murdock, 2001. Not to be reproduced or quoted without permission.

visiting staff and 110,000 scientific, therapeutic and technical staff. Under the Labour government, annual spending on the NHS had reached over £42 billion by 2000 and was planned to increase. NHS expenditure formed the vast majority of total health care spending in the UK.

The unit costs of NHS Direct were comparable with other NHS services. In May 2000 the Royal College of Nursing reported that an NHS Direct enquiry cost £8 whilst an attendance at an accident and emergency department cost £42. The cost per contact with a GP was £10.55.

Background to NHS Direct

The NHS Direct Service emerged from the UK Government White Paper *The New NHS: Modern, dependable* in December 1997. A White Paper is a formal written proposal drafted by the government and setting out a plan of action or change. The White Paper promised that: 'we will provide easier and faster advice and information through NHS Direct, a new 24-hour telephone advice line staffed by nurses. We will pilot this through three care and advice helplines to begin in March 1998. The whole country will be covered by 2000.'

The White Paper also promised a range of other reforms in the NHS, including the expansion of information technology and shorter waiting lists. This envisaged a more patient-focused service providing ' "integrated care", based on partnership and driven by performance. It forms the basis for a ten-year programme to renew and improve the NHS through evolutionary change rather than organisational upheaval. These changes will build on what has worked, but discard what has failed.'

NHS Direct was seen as offering a means of diverting pressure from primary care services (GPs), ambulance services and hospital services. These were all seen as under considerable pressure, much of which was felt to be associated with calls that could be handled by a helpline. The development of a telephone advice service was part of much broader innovations in the delivery of healthcare services. This included providing 'walk-in' clinics where people did not need to make an appointment to see a doctor. Other health-related services such as pharmacy and dentistry were also regarded as having the potential to be linked to NHS Direct telephone advice services. The growth of the Internet also offered a potential to put more health information services on the Web. NHS Direct Online was developed to convey information to the public about such matters as influenza inoculations, local healthcare services and general healthcare issues.

NHS Direct thus represented the first step in a process that sought to radically reconfigure the delivery of healthcare services and healthcare information. It provided both opportunities and challenges to all the actors in the healthcare environment. The UK government hoped that NHS Direct would become a well-used and well-regarded '24/7' gateway to the NHS in people's own homes.

The introduction of NHS Direct[1]

The introduction of the service was, in public sector terms, very rapid with the three pilot sites taking calls as of March 1998 and by November 2000 NHS Direct had been progressively extended to the entire population of England, Scotland and Wales.

The phone service was run through 22 call centres, employed about 1,000 full-time equivalent nurses and possessed a capacity to handle 500,000 calls per month. There were also some 23 walk-in centres in town and city high streets, shopping centres and airports open 7 a.m. to 10 p.m. on weekdays and 9 a.m. to 10 p.m. at weekends, with no appointment necessary. They offered fast, convenient access to a range of services and consultations with experienced NHS nurses and local information on out-of-hours family doctors, dental and pharmacy services.

NHS Direct centres had successfully recruited nurses who had a wide variety of nursing experience, including both hospital and community settings. About 60 per cent of the nurses worked part-time for the service – often combining it with work elsewhere in the NHS. The provision of flexible hours and, in one case, a workplace crèche also had a positive impact on staff recruitment. However, over time there would be issues of career structure and the need to 'refresh' professional skills. A national competence framework had been developed together with a planned rotation of staff between call centres and walk-in centres.

There were some concerns that planned expansion might impact negatively on other employers of nurses (both within and outside the NHS). The inducements offered to attract nurses to NHS Direct may be insufficient to retain them – especially if their image was of 'protocol-driven call centre workers' rather than trained health care professionals. There were also issues of how NHS Direct nursing staff were kept up to date on developments within the hospital and community care settings.

NHS Direct was supported by a considerable amount of technology, including extensive use of diagnostic software which prompted the nurses staffing the service to ask particular questions of callers and suggested possible diagnoses and appropriate action.

Patterns of demand

Figure 1 shows the distribution of calls throughout the day in August 2000. It showed a significant pattern of 'peaks' and 'troughs' in demand during the day and different patterns between weekdays and weekends.

The government forecast that annual call volumes would increase steadily from 5 million per annum (in 2000) to some 20 million in 2003. The nature of the service meant that users had to feel confident that a nurse would be available to speak with them as and when they called. Therefore the

Figure 1 **Average number of calls by hour**

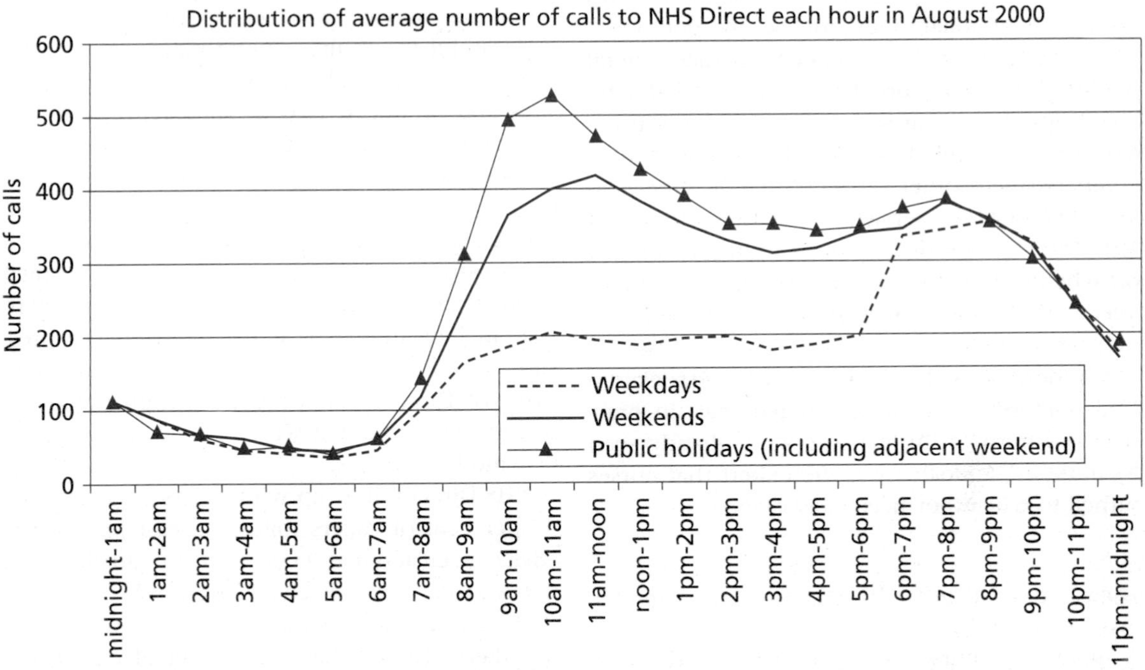

Distribution of average number of calls to NHS Direct each hour in August 2000

Source: Adapted from NHS Direct: A new gateway to healthcare.

service had to be able to deal with variations in demand in terms of growth, time of day and time of the year.

The mixed reaction of the Medical profession to NHS Direct

The original idea for NHS Direct was inspired by a report written by the Chief Medical Officer. So it was likely to be more favourably received by doctors than if it had been produced by politicians, political advisers or civil servants.

The speed of growth of the service concerned a number of doctors. GPs in the pilot areas reported local concerns that NHS Direct was adding to doctors' workload by advising patients to contact their doctor for further advice. The doctors were also concerned about a diversion of nurses away from direct care in hospitals. In the professional medical journals NHS Direct was variously accused

of being 'a cosmetic front', 'parasitic and destructive of the NHS' and based on 'political dogma'. A common thread was a concern that it might be used to mask a shortage of doctors.

In April 1999 the General Practitioners Committee (GPC) raised concerns about possible legal liability issues if doctors provided information on NHS Direct to their patients. The GPC felt NHS Direct represented 'a fundamental shift towards a demand led rather than a needs-based health service' and was 'a potential threat to the central role of GP's' and a possibly inappropriate diversion of resources. However, more positively, they suggested that NHS Direct could benefit family doctors by dealing with 'trivial queries', reducing the burden of their out-of-hours commitments and dealing with very demanding patients.

However, some doctors believed they had to come to terms with a demand (i.e. consumer) led primary healthcare system which was replacing the earlier producer (doctor) driven system. The Royal College of General Practitioners (RCGP) – the professional body for family doctors – acknowledged a political perception that general practice (family doctors) had not responded sufficiently to changes in society over the past three decades – particularly with their 'opening hours' compared with other services such as supermarkets and financial services. They suggested that NHS Direct and walk-in centres should be judged on whether they increase access for *appropriate* needs, whilst not fuelling *inappropriate* demands on primary care.

A report from the British Medical Association (the doctors' 'trade union') noted that, in practice, one-third of the patients were already seen by nurses. The doctor was the expert that nurses turned to when they needed assistance.

The attitude of other healthcare professionals

A number of nurses were attracted to the new roles as they represented an opportunity for greater professional discretion, an alternative to the stresses and constraints of hospital regimes and, in some cases, more cash. Nurses with disabilities or family responsibilities were attracted. Indeed, some 5 per cent of NHS Direct nursing staff were drawn back into nursing mainly due to the nature of the NHS Direct service itself.

Christine Hancock, the general secretary of the Royal College of Nursing, saw the enthusiasm of nurses for NHS Direct as a possible answer to the increase in demand for out-of-hours primary care. She described nurse-led services such as NHS Direct as cost effective and good for patients.

The ambulance services were also supportive of NHS Direct. One of the most respected ambulance service managers, Laurie Caple, observed: 'Already our experience in Northumbria, before NHS Direct goes live, has shown a breaking down of professional barriers, improved collaboration and partnership towards a common goal, and an overriding desire to make the pilot a success.'

The impact of the NHS Direct service

When the service was set up the government was careful to set up a monitoring process. The University of Sheffield followed up the three pilot sites and produced two detailed reports on the impact and operation of NHS Direct. The second of these two reports noted[2] the positive uptake of the service but also the report concluded that there was little evidence of NHS Direct having reduced the pressure on ambulance services or on hospital accident and emergency services, although there was an indication that it had reduced the pressure on GP services. The researchers suggested that NHS Direct had improved the appropriateness of services demanded without reducing the total demand for services.[3]

NHS Direct follow-up with callers indicated that 97 per cent of callers follow at least part of the advice given and that 95 per cent are satisfied with the service they received. Research by Kings College in London also indicated that 50 per cent of callers claimed that, as a result of calling the service, they felt more able to deal with the problem themselves in the future. Other research suggested that 92 per cent of the referrals made by NHS Direct to accident and emergency hospital departments were judged to be appropriate.

The UK Consumer magazine *Which?* tested the NHS Direct service by submitting a range of 'test' queries to it. The results of the *Which?* survey received considerable media attention. The media made much of the fact that three of the ten cases received less than optimal advice. The service also received a lot of positive attention from the media but was vulnerable to 'bad news' stories involving any cases which nurses handled inappropriately.

Further developments

In May 2000 the government announced that it planned to extend the remit of NHS Direct to include accepting referrals from the 999 emergency services operators that would previously have led to the despatch of an ambulance.

The service had the potential to monitor disease prevalence through the use of 'real time' data collected in the operation of the service. It might also be in a position to play a major role in public health, for example by identifying possible epidemics or changes in health circumstances locally and nationally.

In principle, NHS Direct could be involved more in 'interfacing' between the user and the NHS in general – reminding people of medical appointments and checking up on people coming out of hospital. As aspects of the NHS and other parts of the public sector came closer together (social services for example) perhaps the role of NHS Direct might extend even further.

Notes

1. The author acknowledges Monro *et al.*, 'Evaluation of NHS Direct first wave sites', 2nd interim report to Dept of Health, March 2000, as source for much of the information in this section of the case study.
2. Source: Monro *et al.*, 'Evaluation of NHS Direct first wave reports', 2nd interim report, p. 10.
3. Ibid., p. 65.

Questions

1. What are the human resource implications of an extension of NHS Direct services?

2. What are the major benefits and difficulties of using IT to change the 'business model' of the provider–customer relationships in the NHS?

3. From the government (taxpayers') perspective, what are the arguments for and against NHS Direct being a good *financial* investment?

4. What are the issues that will help or hinder the diffusion of information technology in the NHS (see section 10.5.2)? Include ways in which these technologies could/should be used beyond the current NHS Direct services.

11

Managing Strategic Change

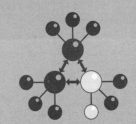

LEARNING OUTCOMES

After reading this chapter you should be able to:

- Understand differences in the scope of strategic change.
- Explain how different aspects of organisational context might affect the required design of strategic change programmes.
- Undertake a forcefield analysis based on cultural web mapping to identify forces blocking and facilitating change.
- Describe the main styles of managing change.
- Explain the role that 'strategic leaders', middle managers and outsiders play in the management of strategic change.
- Explain how organisational routines and symbols can be managed to facilitate change.
- Understand how political processes might facilitate change.
- Understand how different forms of communication are important in the management of strategic change.
- Consider the role of other change tactics that might be employed in organisations.

11.1 INTRODUCTION

This chapter is concerned with the management tasks and processes involved in changing strategies. It builds on a number of underlying premises (some of which are examined and questioned in the commentary on Part IV of the book following the chapter).

The first is that there is some *clarity of strategy* for the organisation; that people in the organisation can envisage what the future direction of the organisation is. As previously explained, this may be as a result of some sort of strategic plan; or perhaps a mission statement or the vision of a chief executive.

The need for such clarity has been a theme throughout the book, and will be returned to in parts of this chapter. However, this assumption does need to be qualified. Achieving such clarity in terms of the ownership of strategic direction by all of the stakeholders in the organisation is no easy matter; and in the sort of fast-changing environments discussed in various parts of the book, it is even more difficult. It must be recognised that whilst this is a vitally important role of strategic leadership (see section 11.3.2. below), change may be going on, and may need to go on, in situations where different stakeholders (including managers) have different conceptions about what the organisation is trying to achieve; and where, in consequence, there is disagreement. The lessons about managing stakeholders in section 5.3 and the discussion on political activity in this chapter are therefore important.

So, knowing or envisaging what a strategy is and designing a structure and processes to put this into effect does not in itself mean that people will make it happen. There is an assumption in most of what is written about strategic change[1] that there will be a tendency towards *inertia* and *resistance to change*; people will tend to hold on to existing ways of doing things and existing beliefs about what makes sense, as explained in Chapters 2 and 5. Managing strategic change must therefore address the powerful influence of the *paradigm* and the *cultural web* on the strategy being followed by the organisation.

If change is to be successful it also has to *link the strategic and the operational* and everyday aspects of the organisation. This emphasises the importance not only of translating strategic change into detailed resource plans, critical success factors and key tasks, and the way the organisation is managed through control processes (Chapter 9), but also of how change is communicated through the everyday aspects of the organisation discussed in this chapter.

The approach taken to managing strategic change will also need to be *context dependent*. It will not be the same for all situations in all types of organisation. Managers need to consider how to balance the different approaches to managing strategic change according to the circumstances they face. Moreover, managers need to be able to help create the sort of organisational context which will facilitate change.

These themes provide a background to the content of this chapter. Exhibit 11.1 provides a structure for the chapter. Section 11.2 begins by explaining important issues that need to be considered in *diagnosing the situation* an organisation faces when embarking on strategic change, in terms of the *scope of change* required, the variety of *contextual factors* that need to be taken into account and the *cultural forces blocking or facilitating change*.

Section 11.3 then discusses the management of strategic change in terms of the *styles of management* used to manage change and the roles played by *strategic leaders* and other *change agents* in managing strategic change. Section 11.4 then goes on to consider in more detail the means they might employ for *managing change*. Elements of the cultural web, including changes in *structure and control*, organisational *routines*, *symbols* and *political activity*, are discussed, as are the roles of different forms of *communication* and more specific *tactics* for managing change.

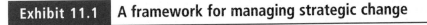

Exhibit 11.1   A framework for managing strategic change

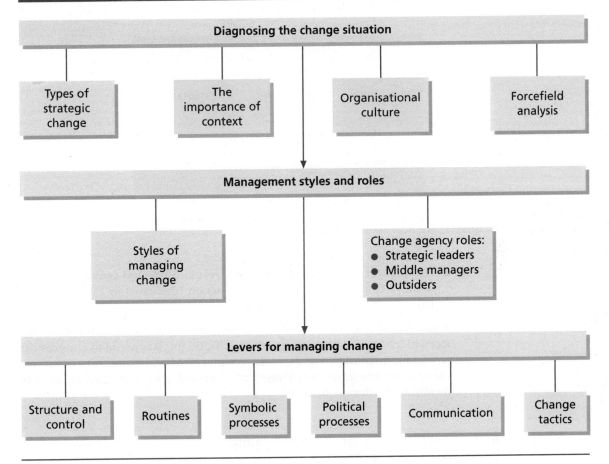

11.2 DIAGNOSING THE CHANGE SITUATION

It is important to remember that, in managing strategic change, much of what has been written in previous chapters in this book is usually seen as an essential precursor in identifying the need for and direction of strategic change. It will not be repeated in any detail here, but it is important to remember the need to understand the following:

● Why strategic change is needed (discussed in Chapters 3, 4 and 5 of the book).

● The basis of the strategy in terms of strategic purpose, perhaps encapsulated in the form of a statement of strategic intent and bases of competitive advantage or activity (discussed in Chapters 6 and 7).

● The more specific possible directions and methods of strategy development (discussed in Chapter 8).

Exhibit 11.2   Types of change

SCOPE

NATURE	Transformation	Realignment
Incremental	Evolution	Adaptation
Big Bang	Revolution	Reconstruction

Source: Adapted from J. Balogun and V. Hope Hailey, *Exploring Strategic Change*, Prentice Hall, 1999.

- The changes in structures, processes, relationships and activities required to move from strategic thinking into action (discussed in Chapters 9 and 10).

However, there is also a need to understand the magnitude of the challenge faced in trying to effect strategic change. To do this it is useful to consider the *scope* of change required, the wider *context* in which change is to occur and the specific *blockages* to change that exist and what forces might exist to *facilitate* the change process.

11.2.1 Types of strategic change

Chapter 2 showed that strategies develop in different ways. In the main, strategy development in organisations is *adaptive* in the way it occurs, with occasional more *transformational* changes.[2] Balogun and Hope Hailey[3] develop this further to identify four types of strategic change (see Exhibit 11.2), and these have implications for how change might be managed.

Arguably, it is beneficial for the *nature of change* in an organisation to be incremental. In this way it will build on the skills, routines and beliefs of those in the organisation, so that change is efficient and likely to win their commitment. A '*big bang*' approach to change might be needed on occasions, for example if the organisation is facing crisis or needs to change direction very fast; but it can be disruptive and painful. In terms of the *scope* of the change process, the issue is whether it can occur within the current paradigm (i.e. current organisational beliefs and assumptions). This can be thought of as a *realignment* of strategy rather than a fundamental change of strategic direction. Or does it require paradigm change? This is more *transformational* change. Combining these two axes shows that there are four types of strategic change:

- *Adaptation* is change which can be accommodated within the current paradigm and occur incrementally. It is the most common form of change in organisations.

- *Reconstruction* is the type of change which may be rapid and could involve a good deal of upheaval in an organisation, but which does not fundamentally change the paradigm. For example, an organisation may make major structural changes or embark on a major cost-cutting programme to deal with difficult or changing market conditions.

- *Evolution* is a change in strategy which requires paradigm change, but over time. It may be that managers anticipate the need for transformational change, perhaps through the sorts of analytical technique described earlier in the book. They may then be in a position of planned evolutionary change, with time in which to achieve it. Another way in which evolution can be explained is by conceiving of organisations as 'learning systems', continually adjusting their strategies as their environment changes. This has given rise to the idea of the *learning organisation*, which has been discussed elsewhere in the book (see section 2.3.5 and the commentary to Part IV of the book).

- However, as Chapter 2 points out, within incremental change may lie the dangers of strategic drift,[4] discussed in Chapter 2 (section 2.4.2), because change is based on, or bounded by, the existing paradigm and routines of the organisation, even when environmental or competitive pressures might suggest the need for more fundamental change. *Revolution* is change which requires rapid and major strategic and paradigm change, perhaps in circumstances where such drift has resulted in circumstances where pressures for change are extreme – for example, if profits decline or a takeover threatens the continued existence of a firm.

It is therefore helpful to have a view about the scope of change required. The sort of cultural analysis explained in Chapter 5 can be useful here. For example, if the cultural web is used, the central question becomes whether or not the change required could be accommodated within the bounds of the culture as it is and, in particular, the paradigm as it is; or whether it would require a really significant shift in this regard. For example, a retailer may launch quite new products without requiring fundamental changes in the assumptions and beliefs of the organisation. On the other hand, some changes in strategy, even if they do not take the form of dramatic product changes, may require fundamental changes in core assumptions in the organisation. For example, the shift from a production or focus for a manufacturer to a customer-led, service ethos may not entail the visible output of the firm in the form of its products to be changed, but will very likely require significant culture change.

11.2.2 The importance of context

There is no one right 'formula' for the management of change. The success of any attempt at managing change will also be dependent on the wider context in which that change is taking place. Take an obvious example. Managing

Exhibit 11.3	Contextual features
● **Time**	How quickly change is needed
● **Scope**	What degree of change is needed
● **Preservation**	What organisational resources and characteristics need to be maintained
● **Diversity**	How homogeneous are the staff groups and divisions within the organisation
● **Capability**	What is the managerial and personal capability to implement change
● **Capacity**	What is the degree of change resource available
● **Readiness**	How ready for change is the workforce
● **Power**	What power does the change leader have to impose change

change in a small, perhaps relatively new, business, where a motivated team are themselves driving change, would be quite different from trying to manage change in a major corporation, or perhaps a long-established public sector organisation, with established routines, formal structures and perhaps a great deal of resistance to change. The contexts are completely different and the approach to managing change therefore needs to be different.

Balogun and Hope Haley[5] build on this point to highlight a number of important contextual features that need to be taken into account in designing change programmes. One of these is, indeed, the scope of change required and this has been discussed in section 11.2.1 above. Exhibit 11.3 also summarises others. It is useful, then, to consider these contextual characteristics before embarking on a programme of change. Illustration 11.1 gives an example of Russian firms as a context in which such understanding has been shown to be very important.

Consider some examples of how the contextual features shown in Exhibit 11.3 might require different approaches to change:

● The *time* available for change could be dramatically different. For example, a business facing immediate decline in turnover or profits from rapid changes in its markets has a quite different context for change compared with a business where the management may see the need for change coming in the future, perhaps years away, and have time to plan it carefully as a staged process.

● No matter how significant the change, it may be that there is a need for the *preservation* of certain aspects of the organisation, in particular those that are to do with the competences on which changes need to be based. Suppose, for example, that a fast-growing computer business needs to become more formally organised because of its growth. This could well upset technical experts who have been used to rapid access to senior management: but it could be vital to preserve their expertise and motivation.

● Change may be helped if there is a *diversity* of experience, views and opinions within an organisation: but supposing that organisation has followed a strategy for many decades, leading to a very homogeneous way of seeing the world. Change could be hampered by this. So gauging the nature and extent of diversity is important.

Illustration 11.1

The change context for western ventures in Russian companies

STRATEGY IN ACTION

Westerners working in alliances with companies in other parts of the world frequently fail to understand the importance of cultural context.

The challenge for Russian firms of moving from a centrally planned economy with state controlled production units to a market-based economy is huge in scope. Russian firms have often looked to the West for the injection of capital and as alliance partners to help with this. How western managers might engage with such a challenge needs to bear the Russian context in mind.

Perhaps paradoxically for a once centrally planned economy, Russian managers have tended not to take the idea of long-term plans very seriously. Time horizons can be very limited; a Russian manager is quite likely to think of time horizons in days. Moreover, the notion of five-year plans has, of itself, connotations of the central planning and unfulfilled promises of the Communist past.

Russian managers also tend to emphasise continuity and tradition more than westerners. Their orientation is towards history and the preservation of what they have, rather than the necessity for changes. Hand in hand with this goes an emphasis on conformity. They are wary of independent thinking or openness, regarding such behaviour as potentially anti-social and promoting conflict. There is also a mistrust of change which can be explained, not least, as a result of their aversion to risk and uncertainty.

Managers in Russia have traditionally been concerned with the development of and maintenance of rules and procedures, rather than the management of change. The role of senior managers, in particular, has been seen as exercising a top-down, directive style with an expectation of high degrees of clarity and a dislike of ambiguity. The experience and capability in change management is limited. The extent to which resources are available to put change into practice may also be dependent upon whether external investment, often from the West, can be obtained. However, western managers may be seen in just that role; as investors rather than as agents of, or role models for, change.

There are also differences between Russian and western cultural assumptions both in business and personally. In business there remains a disquiet about the primacy of profits and of market forces; and also of the western emphasis on efficiency, professionalism and modernity. Russians tend to emphasise fate, destiny and faith in the Russian context.

All this can raise problems for western managers who may see themselves as trying to change the system, introduce a market focus, longer-term strategic thinking and more participative styles of management.

Source: Adapted from S. Miichailova, 'Contrasts in culture: Russian and western perspectives on organisational change', *Academy of Management Executive*, vol. 145, no. 4 (2000), 99–111.

Questions

1. Use the discussion of context in section 11.2.2 to identify key contextual issues which need to be taken into account in influencing change in Russian firms.

2. What problems do you think western managers might face?

3. Read the rest of the chapter and suggest the approach to change that western managers might follow, bearing in mind the Russian context.

- To what extent is there any experience or *capability* in managing change in the organisation? It could be that one organisation has managers who have managed change effectively in the past, or a workforce that has been used to and has accepted past changes in their work practices, whilst another has little experience of change.

- Change can be costly, not only in financial terms, but in terms of management time. Does the organisation have the *capacity* for change in terms of available resources?

- In some organisations there could be a *readiness* for change throughout different levels in the organisation. In others there could be widespread resistance or pockets or levels of resistance. One chief executive referred to his middle level of management as the 'concrete ceiling': it was filled with people who had been in the organisation for years, most of them going no further, and unwilling to contemplate change.

- Is there anyone in the organisation who has the *power* to effect change? Too often it is assumed that the chief executive has such power, but in the face of resistance from below, or perhaps resistance from external stakeholders, this may not be the case. And it may be that the chief executive supposes that others in the organisation have the power to effect change when they do not.

Pulling this together, the sorts of questions which emerge are these:

- Does the organisation in question have the sort of capacity, capability and readiness to achieve the scope of change required?

- Does the context need to be changed before the strategic change itself can occur? In other words, does there need to be an interim programme of change to get the organisation to a point where it is ready to embark on a more significant strategic change programme? Such an interim situation is described in Illustration 11.2.

- How does the context inform the choices about the means by which change can be managed? These choices about means are reviewed later in the chapter.

11.2.3 Organisational culture as context

Chapters 2 and 5 have already shown how the many aspects of the culture of the organisation work to shape and guide strategy, and how its influence can result in strategic drift. The *cultural web* is therefore a useful way of considering the cultural context for change.

Illustration 11.3 shows the cultural webs produced as part of a strategic change workshop by managers in the technical services department of a local government authority in the UK.[6] What emerged was a strong belief about high-quality service. However, the emphasis was on professional standards, with service being defined in these terms rather than as satisfying users of the service. This was, in turn, linked to the departmental structure. Departments

Illustration 11.2

Preparing for change at Daler-Rowney

STRATEGY IN ACTION

Managing strategic change may involve preparing the ground to achieve an organisational context with adequate capability and readiness for strategic change.

Daler-Rowney Ltd is one of the leading manufacturers and distributors of fine art materials in the world. It produces colours, brushes, paper and board as well as other material for artists.

Since 1983 Daler-Rowney has been a family business run by Jim Daler. In the 1990s he faced a problem. The market for artists' materials was changing. Traditionally artists had bought materials through small specialist shops, and the Daler-Rowney salesforce had concentrated on building relationships with the specialists who ran and often owned these shops. However, large multiple retailers, including Wal-Mart and WH Smith, were starting to sell artists' and craft materials. The problem was that it was unclear where the volume split would end up between the old and new customer base, so management had to be aware of the potential shift, and able to react accordingly.

However, most of Jim Daler's senior management team were wedded to the belief that the specialist retailer was where the future lay as well as the past. To implement any change in strategy required a management team open to such change and, in the mid-1990s, Jim Daler began to prepare the way for this.

First he organised a strategy workshop for the top team which surfaced and debated the changes taking place in the market and their implications. This was followed by a series of projects led by members of that team to consider in detail what should be done. Both exercises confirmed his own views of the need for change, but confirmed the resistance to change of others. There followed a period of internal debate and arguments. This was followed by the departure of the most intransigent opponents of change, despite their longevity of employment and the cost of their going. This sent a message that the commitment to change was serious.

Jim Daler also discussed with other family firms their experiences in dealing with similar challenges. There followed a restructuring of Daler-Rowney's top management, including the appointment of a new chief executive from outside the industry, and new sales and operations directors. In addition, he established a family board with the specific brief of long-term strategy formulation, bringing together the chief executive with family members and also non-executive directors.

By 2000 it was clear that many of the market changes which had been discussed were becoming reality, but that within the firm, there existed the commitment and know-how to tackle the changes needed to address these.

Source: Company, with permission.

Questions

1. In what ways might the interim changes made at Daler-Rowney have prepared the way for more substantial changes?

2. If Daler-Rowney's business were to shift markedly from small retailers to major multiple retail buyers, what might be the major organisational changes required?

Illustration 11.3

Understanding the cultural context for change in local government

The cultural web can be used as a way of understanding current organisational culture and desired future culture.

STRATEGY
IN ACTION

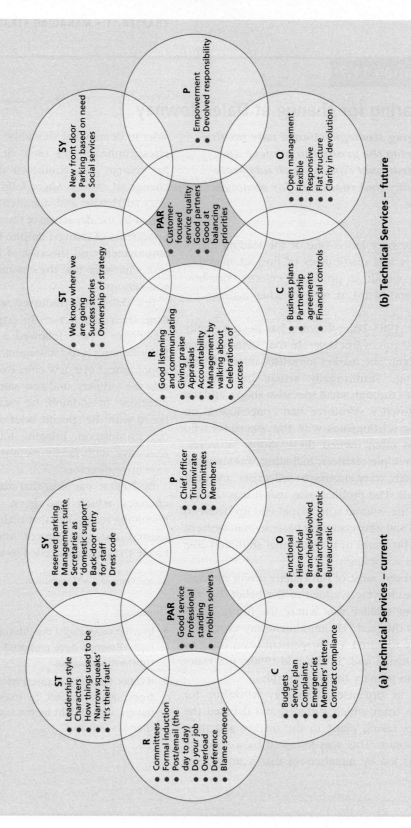

(a) Technical Services – current

ST
● Leadership style
● Characters
● How things used to be
● 'Narrow squeaks'
● 'It's their fault'

SY
● Reserved parking
● Management suite
● Secretaries as 'domestic support'
● Back-door entry for staff
● Dress code

P
● Chief officer
● Triumvirate
● Committees
● Members

PAR
● Good service
● Professional standing
● Problem solvers

R
● Committees
● Formal induction
● Post/email (the day to day)
● Do your job
● Overload
● Deference
● Blame someone

O
● Functional
● Hierarchical
● Branches/devolved
● Patriarchal/autocratic
● Bureaucratic

C
● Budgets
● Service plan
● Complaints
● Emergencies
● Members' letters
● Contract compliance

(b) Technical Services – future

SY
● New front door
● Parking based on need
● Social services

ST
● We know where we are going
● Success stories
● Ownership of strategy

P
● Empowerment
● Devolved responsibility

PAR
● Customer-focused service quality
● Good at balancing priorities
● Good partners

R
● Good listening and communicating
● Giving praise
● Appraisals
● Accountability
● Management by walking about
● Celebrations of success

O
● Open management
● Flexible
● Responsive
● Flat structure
● Clarity in devolution

C
● Business plans
● Partnership agreements
● Financial controls

Source: Adapted from G. Johnson, 'Mapping and re-mapping organisational culture: a local government example', in G. Johnson and K. Scholes (eds), *Exploring Public Sector Strategy,* Prentice Hall, 2001.

Questions

1. How might a change manager use the cultural web to help manage change?

2. What are likely to be the main problems in making changes indicated by the future web?

tended to be organisational silos within which services were delivered and the conventions of service preserved. These departments were headed by chief officers who tended to control access to and influence by elected members of local government and, inevitably, filter or translate elements of overall strategy to determine departmental response. The organisation was also characterised by a hierarchical and mechanistic approach to management with a strong emphasis on structuring, budgeting and bureaucracy. There was also an emphasis on being reactive rather than proactive. Managers saw themselves as problem solvers – indeed overloaded problem solvers – reacting to the wishes of elected members, or to complaints; attempting to avoid mistakes and often only doing so narrowly. The way of dealing with this was to 'get your head down and get on with the job'; and if anything did go wrong, try to blame someone else.

Clearly there were also linkages throughout this web. For example, powerful individuals or groups were closely associated with organisational structures that preserved power bases, with dominant routines which tended to persist, with symbols of hierarchy or authority and with stories about their power or the origins of their power. The dominant influence of the chief officer was preserved in an essentially hierarchical structure, formal committees for decision making, control over budgets (in formal terms); but more informally this took form in symbols of hierarchy such as privileges for senior managers (e.g. parking, offices and secretarial services). On the other hand, more junior staff entered their offices through a different door and from their early induction understood the importance of deferring to senior personnel and keeping focused on *their* job tasks. Technical services people also identified with counterparts from other local government authorities; so professional functionalism was preserved not only within the culture of the department, but by the institutionalised nature of the profession.

This was not compatible with the strategy being espoused by the organisation. The chief executive had been trying to develop a strategy focusing on major local issues which crossed department responsibilities and therefore required co-operation across departments. The problem with the sort of culture described here was that it was not only inherently departmental and functional, but that functionalism was preserved and legitimated by a professional ethos, protected by powerful departmental heads. These departmental heads did take part in discussions on overall local government strategy; they might agree to the logic of such a strategy; but back in their departments their focus was on preserving service standards strongly influenced by professional norms and established procedures. The danger was a local government strategy on paper only and a continuation of departmental strategies driven by the long-established culture and powerful individuals dedicated to its preservation.

Exhibit 11.4	Forcefield analysis

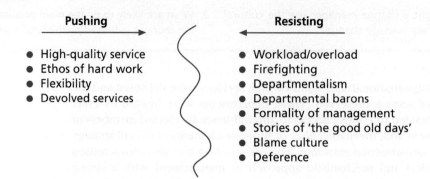

Source: Adapted from G. Johnson, 'Mapping and re-mapping organisational culture: a local government example', in G. Johnson and K. Scholes (eds), *Exploring Public Sector Strategy*, Prentice Hall, 2001.

11.2.4 Forcefield analysis

A **forcefield analysis** provides an initial view of change problems that need to be tackled, by identifying forces for and against change

A **forcefield analysis** provides an initial view of change problems that need to be tackled, by identifying forces for and against change. In fact, by building on a cultural web analysis, rather more extensive questions can be asked:

● What aspects of the current culture might aid change in the desired direction, and how might these be reinforced?

● What aspects of the current culture would block such change, and how can these be overcome?

● What needs to be introduced or developed to aid change?

Exhibit 11.4 is a representation of the sorts of blockage to change discussed above, and identified in the exercise using the cultural web. Whilst the blockages identified constituted a significant problem, the forcefield analysis also identified aspects of the culture that might facilitate change. The managers saw the dedication to good service, the ethos of hard work and the flexibility in service delivery that had developed as potentially positive, if only some of the blockages could be overcome. Moreover, the devolved nature of some services (to local offices) might be harnessed positively in a different culture.

Conceiving of what the culture would need to look like if a different strategy were being followed is also useful and the culture web can be used for this too (see Illustration 11.3b). This helps identify what needs to be added or introduced if change is to occur. Technical services managers recognised that there would be a need for a greater focus on what they called 'the customer' rather than just a professional definition of good service, and much more emphasis on being partners across departments. Changes in the way the organisation was structured were needed, as were more effective control systems. A key issue was the very powerful influence of chief officers of departments; more devolved responsibility was required. But all this meant that the way things were done on a day-to-day basis needed to change. The managers were able to identify several possibilities of changes of a symbolic, ritual or routine nature. There should be a good deal more emphasis on project or task groups which would be transient; more social events which brought together different levels of managers; more direct exposure to 'customers'; car parking by need rather than by rank; direct feedback from customers, not just in the form of complaints, but by more systematic surveys. Letters of thanks should be shared and circulated. Senior executives, in particular, needed to have much more exposure to staff and be prepared to listen to them in informal gatherings. The chief executive in particular needed to come across as more friendly, outgoing and in touch with the day-to-day concerns and problems of staff. There needed to be much more giving of praise, rather than blame, and willingness to talk about successes rather than near-failures. It ought to be normal to question and challenge ways of doing things.

What typically emerges from such an exercise in diagnosing a change situation is that the routines, control systems, structures, symbols and power or dependency relationships can be both important blockages and facilitators to change. Changes in the structure, design and control systems of organisations have already been reviewed in Chapter 9. In the next two sections (11.3 and 11.4), processes for managing change are discussed and the different roles in the change process are reviewed.

11.3 CHANGE MANAGEMENT: STYLES AND ROLES

This section of the chapter is concerned with the role managers can and do play in managing strategic change; and how they do it. It begins by considering different *styles of managing change* that might be employed. It then goes on to examine the role in strategic change played by *strategic leaders*; the role *middle managers* have in effecting change; and the influence of *outsiders* such as consultants and external *stakeholders*.

11.3.1 Styles of managing change

Whoever is in the position of managing change will need to consider the style of management they adopt; and again this is likely to be more or less appropriate according to organisational context.[7] These styles are summarised in Exhibit 11.5.[8]

- **Education and communication** involve the explanation of the reasons for and means of strategic change. It might be appropriate if there is a problem in managing change based on misinformation or lack of information. However, there are problems here. If large numbers of people are involved in the change, managers may try to communicate by mass briefings. But they are likely to find this ineffective, not least because those being briefed may not get a chance to assimilate the information, or because there is a lack of mutual trust and respect between managers and employees. Relying on processes of communication in a top-down fashion may be problematic: involvement of those affected by changes in strategy development and planning change processes may therefore be important.

- **Collaboration** or *participation* in the change process is the involvement of those who will be affected by strategic change in the identification of

Education and communication involve the explanation of the reasons for and means of strategic change

Collaboration or *participation* in the change process is the involvement of those who will be affected by strategic change in the identification of strategic issues, the setting of the strategic agenda, the strategic decision-making process or the planning of strategic change

| Exhibit 11.5 | Styles of managing strategic change | | | |

STYLE	MEANS/CONTEXT	BENEFITS	PROBLEMS	CIRCUMSTANCES OF EFFECTIVENESS
Education and communication	Group briefings assume internalisation of strategic logic and trust of top management	Overcoming lack of (or mis)information	Time consuming Direction or progress may be unclear	Incremental change or long-time horizontal transformational change
Collaboration/ participation	Involvement in setting the strategy agenda and/or resolving strategic issues by taskforces or groups	Increasing ownership of a decision or process May improve quality of decisions	Time consuming Solutions/outcome within existing paradigm	
Intervention	Change agent retains co-ordination/control: delegates elements of change	Process is guided/controlled but involvement takes place	Risk of perceived manipulation	Incremental or non-crisis transformational change
Direction	Use of authority to set direction and means of change	Clarity and speed	Risk of lack of acceptance and ill-conceived strategy	Transformational change
Coercion/edict	Explicit use of power through edict	May be successful in crises or state of confusion	Least successful unless crisis	Crisis, rapid transformational change or change in established autocratic cultures

strategic issues, the setting of the strategic agenda, the strategic decision-making process or the planning of strategic change. This can be helpful in increasing ownership of a decision or change process, and in increasing commitment to it. It may entail the setting up of project teams or taskforces. The outcome may be of higher quality than decisions taken without such an approach. Strategy workshops can also usefully cross levels of management to work on particular strategic problems, provide proposed solutions within a broad strategic framework, and drive change mechanisms down to routine aspects of organisational life. However, there is the inevitable risk that solutions will be found from within the existing paradigm. Anyone who sets up such a process, therefore, may need to retain the ability to intervene in the process.

Intervention is the co-ordination of and authority over processes of change by a change agent who delegates elements of the change process

● **Intervention** is the co-ordination of and authority over processes of change by a change agent who delegates elements of the change process. For example, it might be that particular stages of change, such as idea generation, data collection, detailed planning, the development of rationales for change and the identification of critical success factors, are delegated to project teams or taskforces. Such teams do not take full responsibility for the change process, but they do become involved in it and see their work building towards it. The sponsor of the change ensures the monitoring of progress and that change is seen to occur.[9] An advantage here is that it involves members of the organisation not only in originating ideas, but also in the *partial implementation* of solutions. For example, those who originate ideas might be given responsibility for co-ordinating or overseeing the implementation of such aspects of the strategic change. This involvement is likely to give rise to greater commitment to the change.

- **Direction** involves the use of personal managerial authority to establish a clear future strategy and how change will occur. It is essentially top-down management of strategic change. It may be associated with a clear vision or strategic intent developed by someone seen as a leader in the organisation; but it may also be accompanied by similar clarity about the sorts of critical success factors and priorities discussed in Chapter 10.

- In its most extreme form, a directive style becomes **coercion**, involving the imposition of change or the issuing of edicts about change. This is the explicit use of power and may be necessary if the organisation is facing a crisis, for example.

Direction involves the use of personal managerial authority to establish a clear future strategy and how change will occur

Coercion is the imposition of change or the issuing of edicts about change

There are some overall observations that can be made about the appropriateness of these different styles:

- Styles of managing change are not mutually exclusive in a change programme. For example, in a large commercial organisation strategic change will have implications for different stakeholders. Education and communication may be appropriate for some stakeholders, such as City institutions; but other styles may be more appropriate to galvanise change internally within the organisation.

- Different stages in the change process may require different styles of managing change. Clear direction may be vital to motivate a desire to change whilst participation or intervention may be more helpful in gaining wider commitment across the organisation, identifying blockages to change and planning specific action programmes.

- The evidence is that participative styles are most appropriate for incremental change within organisations, but that where transformational change is required, directive approaches may be more appropriate. It is also worth noting that even where top management see themselves adopting participative styles, their subordinates may perceive this as directive and, indeed, may welcome such direction.[10]

- If the organisation corresponds more to the sort of adhocracy, network or learning organisation described elsewhere in this book, it is likely that *collaboration* and *participation* will be not only desirable but also inevitable. This can of course lead to difficulties if there is disagreement; and such organisations have found that here too there may be times when stronger *direction* is needed in some form.

- Undoubtedly different styles suit different personality types. However, these observations suggest that those most effective at managing change may have the ability to adopt different styles in different circumstances. Indeed, there is evidence for this when it comes to the effectiveness of strategic leaders (see section 11.3.2 below).

Illustration 11.4

Styles of managing change

Executives use different styles of managing change.

Intervention in the oil industry

A Dutch executive of an oil company was appointed as chief executive in a national subsidiary in southern Europe, which had long been subject to government regulation on prices. 'I faced a sleepy management team which had simply managed the distribution of oil products; there was no thought about competition. Within a year we had to face a free market and all that meant in competitive terms. It was tempting to try to tell them what to do, but it would not have worked. They knew they had to change, but they did not know what it meant or how to do it. I set up project teams to tackle some of the major issues. I gave them the questions; they had to come up with the answers. I made it clear that the questions were based around the performance levels achieved in other businesses in the group, so they knew they could be achieved. For example, how do we reduce costs by 30 per

cent? How do we increase share by 50 per cent? Members of the project team visited companies in other countries to see what they were doing; they came to me and asked questions, and I offered some suggestions; consultants I brought in argued with them and challenged them. Their task was to come up with recommendations for the future within a six-month period. This they did and we debated them; I then led a team to pull it all together and identify specific plans of action to make it happen.'

Central direction in the British Labour Party

Following its defeat by the Conservatives in 1979, the British Labour Party became factionalised and, some commentators said, unelectable. When Tony Blair took over as leader, he made it clear that his aim was electoral victory. His challenge to his party colleagues was whether they wanted this or a role of perpetual opposition; and his strategy was to shift 'New Labour' to the centre of British politics. Although some complained that a lack of debate

---

- It also needs to be remembered that managing change will very likely involve a team of managers, not just an individual. So the question here is whether the team adopts a single style, or different styles for different members. Either might be appropriate depending on circumstances. For example, it might be very important that a single style is adopted in relation to external investors and when it comes to promoting the overall strategic direction of the organisation: but it might also be appropriate for different members of the team to adopt different styles if they are dealing with particular stakeholder groups who have greater or less resistance to change.

Illustration 11.4 shows how chief executives use different styles in different contexts.

11.3.2 Roles in managing change

It is, perhaps, important at the outset to say that, when it comes to discussing strategic change, there is too often an overemphasis on individuals at the top of an organisation. Certainly 'strategic leaders' are important, but when differ-

and democracy had developed in the party, there was general agreement that 'something had to be done' and a desire for clear direction, even though differences in policy remained. In the 1997 election, the Labour Party was seen by voters as unified around a strong leader, and won by its biggest-ever majority. By 2000, a growing number of party members were asking whether the time had come for less central direction and greater influence of party activists. Nonetheless, the 2001 general election was won by the Labour Party with a similar majority to that gained in 1997.

Collaboration in the travel industry[1]

In 2001, Hal Rosenbluth was chief executive of Rosenbluth International, one of the largest travel management companies in the world, operating in 24 countries, with a turnover of almost £4 billion. 'I have always had this dream of creating a company built on friendship.' His belief was that this approach helped the 5,000 'associates' who work for the firm to provide truly sustainable competitive advantage: 'You have to have an open, honest, trusting company that believes strongly in collaboration because

otherwise information is hoarded for political reasons. That's when a company slows down.'

His approach was to keep the business continually flexible by involving the associates. For example, he organised a 'Crayola' survey where associates sent him crayoned drawings about their feelings on the company; and an 'ambassador's council' where randomly selected employees from across the world flew to the Philadelphia headquarters to discuss with senior management how to improve business.

Sources:

1. Adapted from *Financial Times*, 20 March 2001.

Questions

Read section 11.3.1 of the text and Exhibit 11.5, then answer the following questions in relation to each of the three examples above.

1. Does the style match the circumstances? In what circumstances would it not be appropriate?

2. What might be the problems of each of the styles?

3. Only some stakeholders are specifically mentioned in the examples. Does this mean that the style should be the same towards all stakeholders of the organisation?

---

ent organisational contexts, types of change and change processes found in organisations are taken into account, it is useful to think of change agency more broadly. A '**change agent**' is the individual or group that effects strategic change in an organisation. For example, the creator of a strategy may, or may not, also be the change agent; and it may be that a middle manager is also change agent in a particular context. Some strategic leaders may need to rely on others to take a lead in effecting the changes. It may be that there is a group of change agents from within the organisation or perhaps from outside, such as consultants, who have a whole team working on a project, together with managers from within the organisation. So change agency does not necessarily correspond to one individual.

A **change agent** is the individual or group that effects strategic change in an organisation

Strategic leadership

The management of change is often directly linked to the role of a strategic leader. **Leadership** is the process of influencing an organisation (or group within an organisation) in its efforts towards achieving an aim or goal.[11] Within this definition, a leader is not necessarily someone at the top of an organisation, but

Leadership is the process of influencing an organisation (or group within an organisation) in its efforts towards achieving an aim or goal

rather someone who is in a position to have influence. However, the 'strategic leaders' who are typically written about are top managers. They are often categorised in two ways:

- Charismatic leaders, who are mainly concerned with building a vision for the organisation and energising people to achieve it, and are therefore usually associated with managing change. The evidence suggests that these leaders have particularly beneficial impact on performance when the people who work for them see the organisation facing uncertainty.[12]

- Instrumental or transactional leaders,[13] who focus more on designing systems and controlling the organisation's activities, and are more likely to be associated with improving the current situation.

Leadership literature often suggests that successful leaders have particular personal characteristics or traits. These include visionary capacity, being good at team building and team playing, a capacity for self-analysis and self-learning, mental agility and the ability to cope with complexity; self-direction and self-confidence; and charismatic leaders in particular are good at expressing complex ideas simply, creating commitment and channelling people's energy.[14] Peters and Waterman[15] argue that the most successful strategic leaders are 'masters of two ends of the spectrum'. By this they mean that such people are able to be both charismatic and instrumental, which may entail coping with potentially conflicting ways of managing.

- In strategy creation, an ability to undertake or understand detailed analysis and, at the same time, to be visionary about the future.

- In achieving organisational credibility for a strategy, they need to be seen as having insight about the future, and yet action-oriented about making things happen.

- In challenging the status quo in an organisation, an ability to maintain credibility and carry people with the change, whilst attacking the taken-for-granted and current ways of doing things.

- In communicating strategic intent, an ability to encapsulate often quite complex issues of strategy in everyday ways which people can understand.

- In consolidating a strategy, and making it happen, an ability to maintain organisational performance whilst breaking down old assumptions and old ways of doing things.

It is a challenging task, demanding the abilities to cope with ambiguity, to demonstrate flexibility, insight and sensitivity to strategic context, relate to others and manage change whilst achieving current performance.

Actually the evidence is that strategic leaders adopt different approaches to managing strategy and change; that is, they attend more to some aspects of strategic management than to other aspects. This is shown in Exhibit 11.6. In some respects this evidence suggests the adoption of different approaches which correspond to the different change management styles discussed in the previous section of the chapter. The approaches vary from a focus on personal responsibility in the search for future opportunities and the development of overall strategy (the *strategy approach*); a focus on developing people who can take responsibility for strategy at the market interface (the *human assets*

| Exhibit 11.6 | Strategic leadership approaches |

	STRATEGY	HUMAN ASSETS	EXPERTISE	CONTROL (BOX)	CHANGE
Focus of attention	Strategic analysis and strategy formulation	Developing people	Disseminating expertise as source of competitive advantage	Setting procedures and measures of control	Continual change
Indicative behaviour	Scanning markets, technological changes etc.	Getting the right people; creating a coherent culture	Cultivating and improving area of expertise through systems and procedures	Monitoring performance against controls to ensure uniform, predictable performance	Communicating and motivating through speeches, meetings etc.
Role of other managers	Day-to-day operations	Strategy development devolved	Immersion in and management of expertise area	Ensure uniform performance against control measures	Change agents; openness to change
Implications for managing change	Delegated	Recruiting/ developing people capable of managing strategy locally	Change in line with expertise approach	Change carefully monitored and controlled	Change central to the approach

Source: Adapted from C.M. Farkas and S. Wetlaufer; 'The ways chief executives lead', *Harvard Business Review*, May–June 1996, pp. 110–123.

approach); a focus on a particular area of *expertise* that will be a source of competitive advantage; the development, communication and monitoring of a set of *controls* to ensure uniform organisational behaviour and standards (the box approach); and on *strategic change* and the continual reinvention of the organisation. A distinctive focus on strategic change is certainly one of these approaches, but only one. Faced with the need for change, each of the approaches would have implications for how change might be managed by such strategic leaders, as also shown in Exhibit 11.6. The strategic leader who takes personal responsibility for the formulation of strategy may delegate responsibility for managing specific change processes, whereas another for whom change is *the* approach will see it as a personal responsibility. The strategic leader who focuses on control or a particular area of expertise may seek to manage change through those control mechanisms or on the back of that expertise; whilst the human assets approach may well lead to extensive involvement, indeed leadership of change, by local mangers. Such differences of approach are also discernible in Illustration 11.4, with Blair exhibiting more of the strategy and change approaches and Rosenbluth a more human assets approach.

Again there is debate as to whether the approaches described above are a function of the personality of individual strategic leaders or not. Ideally what is required is the ability to tailor the strategic leadership approach to context.

There is evidence[16] that the most successful strategic leaders are able to do just this. Indeed with regard to the management of change, it would seem to be a problem if they cannot. After all, some approaches are more to do with creating strategy, or with control rather than the management of change, and might well lead to approaches to change not suited to the particular needs of the specific change context.

Middle managers

A top-down approach to managing strategy and strategic change sees middle managers as implementers of strategy: their role is to put into effect the direction established by top management by making sure that resources are allocated and controlled appropriately, monitoring performance and behaviour of staff and, where necessary, explaining the strategy to those reporting to them. Those who take such an approach often tend to view middle managers not as facilitators of the strategy, but as blockages to its success. Indeed, this is sometimes seen as one reason for reducing the numbers and layers of management, so as to speed up communication between top management and organisational members, and to reduce potential blockages and filters.

However, there is evidence that middle managers can and do provide a real benefit in both the development and the implementation of strategy.[17] Their wider involvement in strategic management has been discussed in Chapter 10 (section 10.2.4). In the context of managing strategic change it is important to emphasise four important roles they play.

- The first is the systematic role of implementation and control: this does reflect the idea of top-down change in which they are monitors of that change.

- The second is the reinterpretation and adjustment of strategic responses as events unfold (e.g. in terms of relationships with customers, suppliers, the workforce and so on) – a vital role they are uniquely qualified for because they are in day-to-day contact with such aspects of the organisation.

- They are the crucial bridge between top management and members of the organisation at lower levels. Again, because they are in touch with the day-to-day routines of the organisation which can so easily become blockages to change and the climate for change that can help or hinder change, they are in a position to translate change initiatives into a locally relevant form or message.

- They are also in a position to advise more senior management on what are likely to be the organisational blockages and requirements for change; an example is that of the technical services managers given in Illustration 11.3.

Middle managers may therefore contribute substantially either to galvanising commitment to strategy and the change process, or to blocking it. Such involvement could help to achieve a positive role of commitment. Lack of commitment can result in serious blockages and resistance. The involvement of middle management in strategy development, the planning of and implementation of strategic change programmes and feedback on strategic change can therefore be very important.

Outsiders

Whilst existing managers have important roles to play, there is a good deal of evidence that 'outsiders' are important in the change process.

● A new chief executive from outside the organisation may be introduced into a business to effect change. He or she brings a fresh perspective on the organisation, not bound by the constraints of the past, or the everyday routines and ways of doing things which can prevent strategic change. *Hybrid* new chief executives seem to be especially successful. These are chief executives who are not part of the mainline culture of the organisation, but who have experience and visible success from within the same industry or even the same company. For example, they might have been a successful change agent with a competitor or some other part of a conglomerate.

● The introduction or arrival of new management from outside the organisation can also increase diversity of ideas, views and assumptions which can help break down cultural barriers to change; and they may help increase the experience of and capability for change. The success of introducing outsiders in middle and senior executive positions is, however, likely to depend on how much explicit *visible backing* they have from the chief executive. Without such backing they are likely to be seen as lacking authority and influence. With such backing, however, they can help galvanise change in the organisation.

● *Consultants* are often used in change processes. This may be to help formulate the strategy or to plan the change process. However, consultants are increasingly used as facilitators of change processes: for example, in a co-ordinating capacity, as facilitators of project teams working on change, or of strategy workshops used to develop strategy and plan the means of strategic change. The value of consultants is twofold: first, they too do not inherit the cultural baggage of the organisation and can therefore bring a dispassionate view to the process; and second, they signal symbolically the importance of the change process, not least because their fees may be of a very high order. For example, a consultancy project undertaken by some of the major strategy consultancy firms might involve large numbers of consultants on a worldwide basis and fees running into millions of pounds.

● It should also be remembered that there are likely to be key influencers of change external to an organisation within its *stakeholder* network and organisational field. Government, investors, customers, suppliers and business analysts all have the potential to act as change agents on organisations.

11.4 LEVERS FOR MANAGING STRATEGIC CHANGE

So far the chapter has looked at differences in the scope of change required, the importance of understanding other aspects of the change context and the management roles and styles in effecting change. The rest of the chapter examines different 'levers' that can be employed to manage strategic change. It is worth noting that most of these levers correspond to the outer rings of the cultural web; the implication is that the forces that act to embed and protect current ways of doing things and the current paradigm (see section 5.5.5) can also be levers for changing the ways things are.

11.4.1 Structure and control systems

Changing aspects of organisational structure and control, including reward systems, are important aspects of strategic change, but they have been covered elsewhere (see Chapter 9) and so will not be discussed in detail here. These aspects of change tend to position top managers as the paramount agents or controllers of change, with organisational members responding to the systems they install. The danger is, however, that changes in structure and control systems may not affect the everyday existence of members of the organisation: that whilst there may be a conformity towards such structures and systems, people will just carry on doing what they previously did on a day-to-day basis. Top management may think they have set up systems to implement strategy, but behaviour and assumptions may not have changed. So it is important to utilise other means of managing strategic change.

11.4.2 Organisational routines

Routines are the organisationally specific 'ways we do things around here' which tend to persist over time and guide people's behaviour

Routines are the organisationally specific 'ways we do things around here'[18] which tend to persist over time and guide people's behaviour. As has been seen in the discussion in Chapters 4 and 6, it may be that an organisation which becomes especially good at carrying out its operations in particular ways achieves real competitive advantages. However, there is also the risk that the same routines act to block change and lead to strategic drift (see section 2.4.2).

The power of such routines is clear enough when they need changing in order to accommodate a new strategy. Managers can make the mistake of assuming that because they have specified a strategy which requires operational changes in work practices, and explained to more junior management what such changes are, the changes will necessarily take place. They may find that the reasons which emerge as to why such changes should be delayed or cannot occur have to do with the persistent influence of long-standing organisational routines. A manager in a hospital trust in the UK, determined to make the hospital services more 'client friendly', tried to persuade a medical consultant both to adhere to appointment times so as to cut down waiting time and not to require patients to change into the white gowns traditional in that hospital: 'People could be sitting or lying around for an hour in very scanty gowns; it was embarrassing for them.' After much debate, the consultant agreed to more diligent appointment timing, but insisted the gowns were imperative. The manager instructed the white gowns to be removed from the consulting room. The following week, the consultant had purchased his own gowns and was bringing them into the hospital every morning.

It is important to drive the planning of strategic change down to the identification of critical success factors and competences underpinning these factors. In so doing, the planning of the implementation of the intended strategy is being driven down to operational levels, and it is likely this will require changes in the routines of the organisation. It is at this level that changes in strategy become really meaningful for most people in their everyday organisational lives. Moreover, as mentioned above, routines are closely linked to the taken-for-grantedness of the paradigm, so changing routines may have the effect of questioning and challenging deep-rooted beliefs and assumptions in the organisation. Running through this chapter, indeed through the whole book, has been the theme that changing strategy requires making changes in the taken-for-granted assumptions and the taken-for-granted routines and ways of doing things that are the elements of culture. Richard Pascale argues: 'It is easier to act your way into a better way of thinking than to think your way into a better way of acting',[19] that it is easier to change behaviour and thus change taken-for-granted assumptions than to try to change taken-for-grated assumptions as a way of changing behaviour. If this advice is to be taken seriously, it would argue that the style of change employed (see section 11.3.3 above) needs to take this into account; that education and communication to persuade people to change may be less powerful than involving people in the activities of changing; and that changing routines to change behaviour may itself help change people's beliefs and assumptions.

Managers who are trying to effect strategic changes need to take personal responsibility not only for identifying such changes in routines, but also for monitoring that they actually occur. The changes may appear to be mundane, but they can have significant impact. Illustration 11.5 gives some examples.

11.4.3 Symbolic processes[20]

Change processes are not always of an overt, formal nature: they may also be symbolic in nature. Chapter 5 (section 5.5.5) explained how symbolic acts and artefacts of an organisation help preserve the paradigm, and how their relationship to culture and strategy can be analysed. Here the concern is how they can be managed to signal change.

Symbols are objects, events, acts or people which express more than their intrinsic content. They may be everyday things which are nevertheless especially meaningful in the context of a particular situation or organisation. It is argued that the creation or manipulation of symbols has impact, to the extent that changing symbols can reshape beliefs and expectations because meaning becomes apparent in day-to-day experience in the organisation. This is one reason why changes in routines (discussed above) are important, but other such everyday or 'mundane' aspects include the stories that people tell, the status symbols such as cars and sizes of office, the type of language and technology used, and organisational rituals.

> **Symbols** are objects, events, acts or people which express more than their intrinsic content

- Many of the *rituals* of organisations are implicitly concerned with effecting or consolidating change. Exhibit 11.7 identifies such rituals.[21] They are capable of being managed proactively: new rituals can be introduced or old rituals done away with. *Rites of enhancement* might include the spreading of 'good news' of transformation and the rewarding of those contributing to it. Corporate newsletters are often used for this purpose. There could be *rites of integration*, such as conferences which applaud change and 'change heroes', or which involve or associate members of the organisation with

Illustration 11.5

Changes in organisational routines

STRATEGY
IN ACTION

Changes in organisational routines can be a powerful signal of and stimulus for change.

- In a retail business with an espoused strategy of customer care, the chief executive, on visiting stores, tended to ignore staff and customers alike: he seemed to be interested only in the financial information in the store manager's office. He was unaware of this until it was pointed out; and his change in behaviour afterwards, insisting on talking to staff and customers on his visits, became a 'story' which spread around the company, substantially supporting the strategic direction of the firm.

- Public sector organisations have been obsessed with the stewardship of public funds, often resulting in very risk-averse cultures. Some have tried to break this by setting up internal 'investment banks' so that staff can 'bid' for the funding of new ventures.

- Given that a drug can only be promoted on launch on the basis of claims substantiated by clinical data, how pharmaceutical firms conduct clinical trials is strategically important. The traditional approach has been to base extensive data collection on a scientific research protocol; and then write a report explaining why all these data had been collected. It was a highly time-consuming and costly process. Some firms changed their procedures to ensure that scientific tests addressed regulatory and medical need. They created ideal claims statements and drafted the report they would need. Only then did they create research protocols and data collection forms, specifying the data required from the trials to support the claims.

- The chief executive of Oticon, the Danish company manufacturing hearing aids, sought

to transform the organisation into a 'knowledge-based' company. He introduced an open-plan office with mobile seating arrangements, and put everyone to work in project-based teams. Traditional job responsibilities were broken down and all head office staff were required to do up to five jobs, deciding themselves what they should prioritise and working in frequently changing project teams. The new office had no walls, but only workbenches with computer terminals. People moved between desks according to the projects they were working on, taking a set of drawers with them. Incoming mail was scanned on to the computer; if someone wanted to view something on paper, they went to the mail room, and it was then shredded.

- The members of an operating board of a subsidiary of a major multinational had offices in different sites of its operation in the UK. They had a tendency to blame each other for the problems of the firm. The result was over-defensiveness and low-quality decision making. Eventually the board members relocated to one site with offices in the same building. The day-to-day contact with each other resulted in more open personal relationships, a greater readiness to sort out day-to-day problems and, eventually, a greater understanding of strategic issues.

Questions

1. Using the examples above, explain why changes in routines might help achieve strategic change.

2. Extend the list of examples in the illustration by suggesting routines that might be changed in order to effect change in some organisations with which you are familiar.

| Exhibit 11.7 | Organisational rituals and culture change | |

TYPES OF RITUAL	ROLE	EXAMPLES
Rites of passage	Consolidate and promote social roles and interaction	Induction programmes Training programmes
Rites of enhancement	Recognise effort benefiting organisation Similarly motivate others	Awards ceremonies Promotions
Rites of renewal	Reassure that something is being done Focus attention on issues	Appointment of consultants Project teams
Rites of integration	Encourage shared commitment Reassert rightness of norms	Christmas parties
Rites of conflict reduction	Reduce conflict and aggression	Negotiating committees
Rites of degradation	Publicly acknowledge problems Dissolve/weaken social or political roles	Firing top executives Demotion or 'passing over'
Rites of sense making	Sharing of interpretations and sense making	Rumours Surveys to evaluate new practices
Rites of challenge	'Throwing down the gauntlet'	New CEO's different behaviour
Rites of counter-challenge	Resistance to new ways of doing things	Grumbling Working to rule

new approaches, activities or belief systems. *Rites of conflict reduction* to minimise or contain disunity may take the form of structural change or personnel appointments that demonstrate which executive groups have significant influence and which have been marginalised. *Rites of passage* can signal change from one stage of the organisation's development to another: for example, the departure of the old and introduction of new management, perhaps the replacement of senior board members or even a whole board, can signify much more than individual personnel changes as an indication of the passing from one era to another.

● Symbolic significance is also embedded in the *systems and processes* discussed elsewhere in this chapter and in Chapter 9. Reward systems, information and control systems, and the very organisational structures that represent reporting relationships and often status are also symbolic in nature. For example, the way selection interviews are conducted is likely to signal to those being interviewed the nature of the organisation, and what is expected of them. A highly formal interview procedure may signal a mechanistic, hierarchical organisation, whereas a more informal dialogue is likely to signal an environment and expectation of challenge and questioning. If selection processes are changed, different types of managers are appointed, and visible encouragement to challenge and questioning is given; this can signal within the organisation the commitment to strategic change. In this sense, selection processes are symbolic in nature.

- Changes in *physical aspects* of the work environment are powerful symbols of change. Typical here is a change of location for the head office, relocation of personnel, changes in dress or uniforms, and alterations to offices or office space.

- The most powerful symbol of all in relation to change is the *behaviour of change agents* themselves, particularly strategic leaders. Their behaviour, language and the stories associated with them can signal powerfully the need for change and appropriate behaviour relating to the management of change. Having made pronouncements about the need for change, it is vital that the visible behaviour of change agents is in line with such change because, for most people in an organisation, their organisational world is one of deeds and actions, not of abstractions.

- *Stories* can be managed to some extent. The use of corporate newsletters and newspapers is an example. There are, however, more subtle examples. One chief executive claimed that the most effective way of spreading a story in his business was to get his secretary to leave a memo from him marked 'strictly confidential' by the photocopier for ten minutes: 'Its contents would be all over the office in half an hour and round the regions by the end of the day.'

- Also important in effecting change is the *language* used by change agents.[22] Either consciously or unconsciously, change agents may employ language and metaphor to galvanise change. Some examples are included in Illustration 11.6. In this context, language is not simply concerned with communicating facts and information; language is also powerful because it is symbolic and is able to carry several meanings at once. For example, it may link the past to the future: it may attack or undermine an image of the past, and therefore carry a very serious message, yet do so in a play-ful way; and it may evoke emotional feelings more strongly than rational understanding. Of course, there is also the danger that change agents do not realise the power of language and, whilst espousing change, use language that signals adherence to the status quo, or personal reluctance to change. Those involved in change need to think carefully about the language they use, and the symbolic significance of their actions.

Illustration 11.6 gives other examples of such symbolic signalling of change.

11.4.4 Power and political processes[23]

It may well be that there will be a need for the reconfiguration of *power structures* in the organisation, especially if transformational change is required. In order to effect this reconfiguration of power, it is likely that the momentum for change will need *powerful advocacy* within the organisation, typically from the chief executive, a powerful member of the board or an influential outsider: indeed, an individual or group combining both power and interest, as described in Chapter 5 (see section 5.3.3).

Chapter 5 discussed the importance of understanding the political context in and around the organisation. Having established this understanding, there is

Illustration 11.6

Symbolic activity and strategic change

STRATEGY IN ACTION

Symbolic aspects of management can aid the change process in organisations.

Language that challenges and questions

The chief executive of a retailing firm facing a crisis addressed his board: 'I suggest we think of ourselves like bulls facing a choice: the abattoir or the bull ring. I've made up my mind: what about you?'

In another company, the chief executive described the threat of a takeover in terms of pending warfare: 'We've been targeted: they've got the hired guns [merchant bankers, consultants, etc.] on board. Don't expect chivalry: don't look for white knights; this is a shoot-out situation.'

Physical objects that signal change[1]

The head nurse of a recovery unit for patients who had been severely ill decided that, if nurses wore everyday clothes rather than nurses' uniforms, it would signal to patients that they were on the road to recovery and a normal life; and to nurses that they were concerned with rehabilitation.

However, the decision had other implications for the nurses too. It blurred the status distinction between nurses and other non-professional members of staff. Nurses preferred to wear their uniforms. Whilst they recognised that uniforms signalled a medically fragile role of patients, they reinforced their separate and professional status as acute care workers.

The British Labour Party had always had a red flag as its motif, symbolising its socialist heritage. When Tony Blair took over as leader he not only coined the phrase 'New Labour' to connote the repositioning of the party towards the centre of British politics, but also changed the motif to a red rose, long associated with traditional British values and lifestyle.

Confirmatory action signalling change[2]

In a textile firm in Scotland, equipment associated with the 'old ways of doing things' was taken into the yard at the rear of the factory and physically dismantled in front of the workforce.

London's Metropolitan Police were heavily criticised for 'institutionalised racism'. In 2000 Brian Paddick was appointed to commander in charge of policing in an area at the heart of previous problems. He was committed to tackling racist attitudes and ensuring the police did not discriminate against minorities. This was underlined by his decision to be the first senior officer to state openly that he was gay. 'I knew that simply because I was gay I was likely to be over policed and under protected': an approach he believed his appointment signalled had to change.

Sources:

1. M.G. Pratt and E. Rafaeli, 'The role of symbols in fragmented organisations: an illustration from organisational dress', presented at the Academy of Management Meeting, Atlanta, GA, 1993.

2. *Financial Times*, 24/25 February 2001.

FT

Questions

For an organisation with which you are familiar (or for the chapter-end case study on joined up government):

1. Identify at least five important symbols or rituals in the organisation.

2. In what way could they be changed to support a different strategy? Be explicit as to how the symbols might relate to the new strategy.

3. Why are these potential levers for change often ignored by change agents?

Exhibit 11.8   Political mechanisms in organisations

ACTIVITY AREAS	MECHANISMS				
	RESOURCES	ELITES	SUBSYSTEMS	SYMBOLIC	KEY PROBLEMS
Building the power base	Control of resources Acquisition of/ identification with expertise Acquisition of additional resources	Sponsorship by an elite Association with an elite	Alliance building Team building	Building on legitimation	Time required for building Perceived duality of ideals Perceived as threat by existing elites
Overcoming resistance	Withdrawal of resources Use of 'counter-intelligence'	Breakdown or division of elites Association with change agent Association with respected outsider	Foster momentum for change Sponsorship/reward of change agents	Attack or remove legitimation Foster confusion, conflict and questioning	Striking from too low a power base Potentially destructive: need for rapid rebuilding
Achieving compliance	Giving resources	Removal of resistant elites Need for visible 'change hero'	Partial implementation and collaboration Implantation of 'disciples' Support for 'Young Turks'	Applause/reward Reassurance Symbolic confirmation	Converting the body of the organisation Slipping back

also a need to consider the implementation of strategy within this political context. The approach developed here draws on the content of Chapter 5 and also some of this chapter to provide a framework. Exhibit 5.6 in Chapter 5 lists sources of power in organisations. These also provide indicators of some of the mechanisms associated with power which can be used for change. Summarised in Exhibit 11.8, these include the manipulation of *organisational resources*; the relationship with powerful groupings and *elites*; activity with regard to *subsystems* in the organisation; and again, *symbolic activity*. All of these may be used to: (1) build a power base; (2) encourage support or overcome resistance; and (3) achieve commitment to a strategy or course of action.

- Acquiring additional *resources* or being identified with important resource areas or areas of expertise, and the ability to withdraw or allocate such resources, can be a valuable tool in overcoming resistance or persuading others to accept change.

- Powerful groupings in the organisation are of crucial importance and may, of course, correspond to powerful *stakeholder groups.* Association with such groupings, or their support, can help build a power base, and this may be necessary for the change agent who does not have a strong personal power base from which to work. Similarly, association with a change agent who is respected or visibly successful can help a manager overcome resistance to change.

- It may be necessary to remove individuals or groups resistant to change. Who these are can vary - from powerful individuals in senior positions, to loose networks within the organisation and sometimes including external stakeholders with powerful influence, to whole layers of resistance perhaps in the form of senior executives in a threatened function or service - the 'concrete ceiling' referred to earlier in the chapter.

- Building up *alliances* and a *network* of contacts and sympathisers, even though they may not be powerful themselves, may be important in overcoming the resistance of more powerful groups. Attempting to convert the whole organisation to an acceptance of change is difficult - it is likely that there will be parts of the organisation or individuals in it more sympathetic to that change than others. The change agent might sensibly concentrate on these to develop momentum, building a team strongly supportive of the activities and beliefs of the change agent. He or she may also seek to marginalise those who are resistant to change.

  The danger is that powerful groups in the organisation may regard the building of such a team, or acts of marginalisation, as a threat to their own power, and this may lead to further resistance to change. An analysis of power and interest similar to the stakeholder mapping described in Chapter 5 might, therefore, be especially useful to identify bases of alliance and likely political resistance.

- As has been seen, the employment of *symbolic mechanisms* of change can be useful. From a political point of view, this may take several forms. To build power, the manager may initially seek to identify with the very symbols which preserve and reinforce the paradigm - to work within the committee structures, become identified with the organisational rituals or stories that exist and so on. On the other hand, in breaking resistance to change, removing, challenging or changing rituals and symbols may be a very powerful means of achieving the questioning of what is taken for granted. Symbolic activity can also be used to consolidate change by concentrating attention or 'applause' and rewards on those who most accept change, thus making its wider adoption more likely; and there may be means of confirming change through symbolic devices such as new structures, titles, office allocation and so on, so that the change is to be regarded as important and not reversible.

Political aspects of management in general, and change specifically, are unavoidable; and the lessons of organisational life are as important for the manager as they are, and always have been, for the politician (see Illustration 11.7.). However, the political aspects of management are also difficult, and potentially hazardous. Exhibit 11.8 also summarises some of the problems.

One problem in building a power base is that the manager may have to become so identified with existing power groupings that he or she either actually comes to accept their views or is perceived by others to have done so, thus losing support amongst potential supporters of change. Building a power base is a delicate path to tread.

In overcoming resistance, the major problem may simply be the lack of power to be able to undertake such activity. Attempting to overcome resistance from a lower power base is probably doomed to failure. There is a second major danger: in the breaking down of the status quo, the process becomes so destructive and takes so long that the organisation cannot recover from it. If the process needs to take place, its replacement by some new set of beliefs and the implementation of a new strategy is vital and needs to be speedy. Further, as already identified, in implementing change the main problem is likely to be carrying the body of the organisation with the change. It is one thing to change the commitment of a few senior executives at the top of an organisation; it is quite another to convert the body of the organisation to an acceptance of significant change. The danger is that individuals are likely to regard change as temporary: something with which they need to comply only until the next change comes along.

11.4.5 Communicating change

Managers faced with effecting change typically underestimate substantially the extent to which members of the organisation understand the need for change, what it is intended to achieve, or what is involved in the changes. Some important points to emphasise are as follows.

● The reasons for a change in strategic direction may be complex, and the strategy itself may therefore embrace complex ideas. However, to be effective it is important that it is communicated in such a way that complexity has a meaning and vitality which can be assimilated across the organisation. This message has already been discussed elsewhere in the book, when considering the importance of *vision* and *strategic intent* in Chapters 5 and 6.

Illustration 11.7

Machiavelli on political processes

STRATEGY IN ACTION

'It should be borne in mind that there is nothing more difficult to handle, more doubtful of success, and more dangerous to carry through, than initiating changes in a state's constitution.'

The innovator makes enemies of all those who prospered under the old order, and only lukewarm support is forthcoming from those who would prosper under the new. Their support is lukewarm partly from fear of their adversaries, who have the existing laws on their side, and partly because men are generally incredulous, never really trusting new things unless they have tested them by experience. In consequence, whenever those who oppose the changes can do so, they attack vigorously, and the defence made by the others is only lukewarm. So both the innovator and his friends come to grief.

(Niccolò Machiavelli, *The Prince*, 1513)

Many writers on management argue that, when it comes to politics, the examples and principles given by the 16th-century writer Niccolò Machiavelli remain relevant to the manager of the 21st century.

Machiavelli's prince is precariously balanced between four interest groups: the army, the nobility, the populace and the state. Gauging the relative power of these and devising strategies which take this into account become crucial, as Machiavelli illustrates.

Scipio's *army* rebelled against him in Spain for allowing too much licence. Commodus and Maximinus (two Roman emperors) both exhibited excess cruelty, and both were killed by their armies.

The *nobility*'s desire is to command and oppress the people. Bentivogli, Prince of

Bologna, was killed by the Canneschi (nobility) who conspired against him. However, after the murder, the people rose up and killed the Canneschi. The Canneschi misjudged the goodwill of the people towards Bentivogli.

It is necessary for a prince to possess the friendship of the *populace*, particularly in times of adversity. Nabis, prince of the Spartans, sustained a siege by the rest of Greece and a victorious Roman army, defended his country against them, and maintained his own position through unifying the populace.

Machiavelli commends three principles:

- Establish whether you are in the position, in case of need, to maintain yourself alone, or whether you need the protection of others.

- Esteem your nobles, but do not make yourself hated by the populace.

- Follow the example of Ferdinand, King of Aragon and Spain, who 'continually contrived great things which have kept his subjects' minds uncertain and astonished, and occupied in watching their result'.

Prepared by Roger Lazenby, Middlesex University.

Questions

1. Do you agree that Machiavelli's three principles apply to effecting strategic change in organisations? Discuss this in relation to the power/interest matrix (Exhibit 5.5).

2. How might the political mechanisms outlined in Exhibit 11.8 be used to put the three principles into effect?

Exhibit 11.9	Effective and ineffective communication of change

CHANGES

TYPE OF MEDIA	Routine	Complex
Face-to-face (one-to-one or group)	Overly rich communication causes confusion	Rich communication for complex changes
Interactive (e.g. telephone, video conferencing)		**EFFECTIVE COMMUNICATION**
Personal 'memoing' (e.g. tailored memos, letters)	Routine communication for routine change	
General bulletins (e.g. circulars, announcement on noticeboards)		Too little information and sensitivity leads to mistrust and lack of commitment

Source: Adapted from R.H. Lengel and R.L. Daft, 'The selection of comunication media as an executive skill', *Academy of Management Executive*, vol. 2, no. 3 (1988), pp. 225–232.

These should not be banal statements of strategy, but rather should encapsulate the significance and challenge of that strategy.

- It may be important to clarify and simplify further the priorities of the strategy. Some writers argue[24] that a *three-theme* approach is useful, emphasising a limited number of key aspects of the strategy, rather than expecting to be able to communicate overall complexity and ramifications.

- There are *choices of media* by which to communicate the strategy and the elements of the strategic change programme.[25] Exhibit 11.9 summarises some of the choices and the likely effectiveness of these in different circumstances. Choices of media richness vary from face-to-face, one-to-one communication through to routine bulletins on noticeboards and circulars sent round the organisation.

  The extent to which these different forms of media are likely to be effective depends on the extent to which the nature of the change is routine or complex. To communicate a highly complex set of changes, it would be inappropriate to use standardised bulletins and circulars with no chance of any feedback or interaction. In situations of strategic change, members of the organisation not involved in the development of the strategy may see the effects of change as non-routine even when senior executives regard them as routine. So communication which provides interaction and involvement is likely to be desirable.

- The *involvement* of members of the organisation in the strategy development process or the planning of strategic change is also, in itself, a means of communication and can be very effective. Those who are involved might be used to cascade information about the change programme into the organisation, in effect becoming part of the change agency process themselves. This is an important element of the *intervention* style described in section 11.3.3 above.

● Communication needs to be seen as a two-way process. *Feedback* on communication is important, particularly if the changes to be introduced are difficult to understand or threatening or if it is critically important to get the changes right. It is rare that changes have been thought through in ways which have meaning to or can be put into effect at lower levels in the organisation. In addition, the purpose of the changes may be misunderstood or misconstrued at such levels.

These problems can be tackled in various ways. If there has been a cascading process in the organisation, this can also be used to obtain feedback. It may be useful to set up 'focus groups' which give feedback to senior executives on the implementation and acceptance of change. Some organisations employ survey techniques to check the extent to which change processes are being followed, understood or welcomed. In other organisations, senior executives invite feedback by 'walking the talk', ensuring that they meet with those responsible for implementing change, perhaps on an informal basis in their workplace.

● There is, however, another reason why communication is very important. Communication occurs in organisations not simply because managers trying to effect change wish to communicate, but because members of the organisation need to make sense of what is happening for themselves. They therefore communicate with each other. This takes the form of *rumours*, *gossip* and *storytelling*. In managing change, the task is not only to communicate change, but to do it sufficiently powerfully to overcome the inevitable *counter-communication* which is likely to take place.

11.4.6 Change tactics

There are also some more specific tactics of change which might be employed to facilitate the change process.

Timing

The importance of timing is often neglected in thinking about strategic change. To some extent this has already been covered in Chapter 10, when considering issues such as network analysis. However, network analysis has mainly to do with the scheduling tasks within a change project. Timing also refers to choosing the right time tactically to promote change. For example:

● The greater the degree of change, the more it may be useful to build on actual or perceived *crisis*. If members of the organisation perceive a higher risk in maintaining the status quo than in changing it, they are more likely to change. For example, the management of a company threatened by takeover may be able to use this as a catalyst for transformational strategic change. Indeed, it is said that some chief executives seek to elevate problems to achieve perceived crisis in order to galvanise change.

- There may also be *windows of opportunity* in change processes. For example, the period following the takeover of a company may allow new owners to make more significant changes than might normally be possible. The arrival of a new chief executive, the introduction of a new, highly successful product, or the arrival of a major competitive threat on the scene may also provide such opportunities. These windows of opportunity may, however, be brief; and the change agent may need to take decisive action during these periods.

- It is also important that those responsible for change do not provide conflicting messages about the timing of change. For example, if they see that rapid change is required, they should avoid the maintenance of procedures and signals which suggest long time horizons. For example, managers may exhort others to change whilst maintaining the same control and reward procedures or work practices that have been in place for many years. So the *symbolic signalling of timeframes* becomes important.

- Since change will be regarded nervously, it may be important to choose the time for promoting such change to avoid unnecessary fear and nervousness. For example, if there is a need for reduction in personnel or the removal of executives (see below), it may make sense to do this before rather than during the change programme. In such a way, the change programme can be seen as a potential improvement for the future rather than as the cause of such losses.

Job losses and de-layering

Change programmes are often associated with job losses, from the closure of units of the organisation, with hundreds or thousands of job losses, to the removal of a few senior executives. In the 1990s, in some countries change was associated with de-layering: the removal of whole layers of management. As indicated above, the timing of such job losses in relation to the change programme can be important. There are other considerations which can affect a change programme:

- The tactical choice of where job losses should take place related to the change programme may be important. For example, it could be that there is a layer of management or particular individuals who are widely recognised in the organisation as *blockers* of change. Their removal may indicate powerfully the serious nature and intent of the change. The removal of one layer of management may also provide perceived opportunities to management below. As one chief executive commented: 'If I have to lose people, then I will choose the most senior levels possible: they're the ones most usually resistant to change; and it provides a wonderful incentive for those below.'

- It may also be important to avoid 'creeping' job losses. If the change programme is continually associated with a threat to security, it is less likely to be successful. The same chief executive continued: 'It is better to cut deeply and quickly than hack away remorselessly over time.'

- It is also important, however, that if job losses are to take place, there is a visible, responsible and caring approach to those who lose their jobs. Not only are there ethical reasons for this, but tactically it signals to those who remain that the organisation cares. There are now many examples of companies which have successful redeployment, counselling services, outplacement arrangements, retraining facilities and so on. Indeed, British Coal Enterprise was set up with this purpose and was very successful in helping past employees in the coal-mining industry in all these respects.

Visible short-term wins

Strategy may be conceived of as having to do with long-term direction and major decisions. However, the implementation of strategy within a change programme will require many quite detailed actions and tasks. It is important that some of these tasks are seen to be put into place and to be successful quickly. This could take the form, for example, of a retail chain quickly developing a new store concept and demonstrating its success in the market; the effective breaking down of old ways of working and the demonstration of better ways; the speeding up of decisions by doing away with committees and introducing clearly defined job responsibilities; and so on.

In themselves, these may not be especially significant aspects of a new strategy, but they may be visible indicators of a new approach associated with that strategy. The demonstration of such wins will therefore galvanise commitment to the strategy.

Illustration 11.8 shows how a new chief executive in the long-ailing knitwear manufacturer Pringle employed tactics and symbolic changes to galvanise change in line with the new strategy for the business.

SUMMARY

A recurrent theme in this chapter has been that approaches, styles and means of change need to be tailored to the context of that change. Bearing in mind this general point, this chapter has then emphasised a number of key points in the management of strategic change:

- There are different *types of strategic change* which can be thought of in terms of their *scope* – the extent to which they involve paradigm change or not – and their *nature* in terms of whether they can be achieved through incremental change or require urgent, immediate action (the 'big bang' approach). Different approaches and means of managing change are likely to be required for different types of change.

- It is also important to diagnose other aspects of the change situation. Wider aspects of organisational context such as *resources and skills that need to be preserved*, the degree of *homogeneity or diversity* in the organisation, the *capability, capacity and readiness* for change and the *power* to make change happen are important.

Illustration 11.8

Tactics for strategic change at Pringle

STRATEGY
IN ACTION

In achieving strategic change it may be important to ensure that short-term actions signal long-term intentions.

Pringle, the long-established cashmere knitwear manufacturer, had endured a decade of losses and seen its workforce decline from over 2,000 in the early 1990s to 180 by 2000: the result of adverse exchange rates, an unsuccessful move into mass market sportswear and a decline in manufacturing quality. In 2000 the company was acquired by Hong Kong based Fang Brothers for just £6 million. The new owners recruited Kim Winser, a senior executive from Marks and Spencer, as chief executive.

The new chief executive decided Pringle's range was too big and poorly designed; and sought to reposition it away from its rather staid, middle-aged image towards a designer fashion brand. This was a major challenge, but the current situation, whilst of crisis proportions, nonetheless provided an opportunity. Her arrival, together with the state the company was in, ensured that everyone knew there was the need for radical change.

She decided on a relaunch of the fashion range of knitwear in just twelve weeks, a target that had never been achieved before – and one that was later reduced to nine. This, she argued, was essential in order to present a new range at the forthcoming Italian trade fair.

Most of the workforce that was left expected the factory to close, perhaps with manufacturing moving to the Far East. Instead she confirmed the manufacturing would remain in Hawick in Scotland. She further reinforced the Scottish link by branding the fashion merchandise 'Pringle Scotland' and explained: 'I have added Scotland to the name because in a lot of countries worldwide, it is definitely a bonus – people trust Scottish cashmere.'

New young designers were recruited; and the design function moved from Scotland to London. She also moved the company headquarters from the prestigious Saville Row in London to a new, more modern building

Others left the company. The contract of the existing manufacturing director was terminated: and the contract of Nick Faldo, the golfer, who had been Pringle's celebrity face for almost 20 years, was not renewed: instead the merchandise was shown on young and trendy models.

The process of change was helped with the visit of the Princess Royal to the Hawick factory at around the same time as the redesigned sweaters were seen worn publicly by David Beckham, the internationally famous football star.

The target of the Italian trade fair was met, one-sixth of the existing retail outlets were dropped and new retailers recruited, including Harvey Nichols and Selfridges. By the end of 2000 sales were increasing, the workforce had been increased and there had been investment in new machinery at Hawick. The spring 2001 sales were 30 per cent up on the previous year and Kim Winser expected the company to be profitable within two years.

Sources: Adatpted from *Trouble at the Top*, BBC2, 28 February 2001; and *Financial Times*, 24/25 February 2001.

Questions

1. Referring to section 11.4.6, identify the tactics used by Kim Winser.

2. In what ways were the short-term tactics in line with the longer-term strategy?

3. Using frameworks and concepts from the rest of the chapter, consider other ways in which Kim Winser might manage strategic change at Pringle.

- The *cultural web* and *forcefield analysis* are also useful as means of identifying blockages to change and potential levers for change.

- Different *styles* of managing strategic change are likely to be necessary according to different contexts and in relation to the involvement and interest of different groups.

- The management of strategic change is likely to involve different *roles in the change* process, including those of strategic leaders, middle managers and outsiders.

- Levers for managing strategic change include the importance of changes in *structure and control*, the need to change organisational *routines* and *symbols*, and the importance of *political processes, communication* and other change *tactics*.

RECOMMENDED KEY READINGS

- J. Balogun, V. Hope Hailey (with G. Johnson and K. Scholes), *Exploring Strategic Change*, Prentice Hall, 1999, builds on and extends many of the ideas in this chapter. In particular, it emphasises the importance of tailoring change programmes to organisational context.

- G. Johnson, 'Mapping and re-mapping organisational culture', in V. Ambrosini with G. Johnson and K. Scholes (eds), *Exploring Techniques of Analysis and Evaluation in Strategic Management*, Prentice Hall, 1998, and in *Exploring Public Sector Strategy*, Prentice Hall, 2001.

- For a discussion of styles of managing strategic change, see D. Dunphy and D. Stace, 'The strategic management of corporate change', *Human Relations*, vol. 46, no. 8 (1993), pp. 905-920.

- For a discussion of effective strategic leadership, see D. Goleman, 'Leadership that gets results', *Harvard Business Review*, March-April 2000, pp. 78-90, and C.M. Farkas and S. Wetlaufer, 'The ways chief executive officers lead', *Harvard Business Review*, May-June 1996, pp. 110-121.

- There are surprisingly few readings which focus on aspects of political management. The best book remains Machiavelli's sixteenth-century work, *The Prince*.

- A useful and interesting discussion is provided in J. Thornbury, *Living Culture*, Random House, 2000, which provides insights into managing culture change through an extended account of the change processes in KPMG in the 1990s.

REFERENCES

1. Many books and papers on strategic change build on the idea that the current state of the organisation is likely to be one of inertia or resistance to change; and that there is, then, a need to 'unfreeze' this situation. The dominance of this idea can be traced back to the work of K. Lewin; see 'Group decision and social change', in E.E. Maccoby, T.M. Newcomb and E.L. Hartley (eds) *Readings in Social Psychology*, Holt, Reinhart and Winston, 1958, pp. 197-211.

2. See E. Romanelli and M.L. Tushman, 'Organisational transformation as punctuated equilibrium: an empirical test', *Academy of Management Journal*, vol. 37, no. 5 (1994), pp. 1141-1161.

3. *Exploring Strategic Change* by J. Balogun and V. Hope Hailey, Prentice Hall, 1999, is a sister text to this book; this part of the chapter draws on their Chapter 3 on the context of strategic change.

4. The explanation of strategic drift and the implications for strategic change can be found in G. Johnson, 'Rethinking incrementalism', *Strategic Management Journal*, vol. 9 (1988), pp. 75-91, and G. Johnson, 'Managing strategic change - strategy, culture and action', *Long Range Planning*, vol. 25, no. 1 (1992), pp. 28-36.

5. See reference 3 above.

6. Approaches to how to use the cultural web for the purposes outlined here are dealt with in detail in the

chapter, 'Mapping and re-mapping organisational culture', in V. Ambrosini with G. Johnson and K. Scholes (eds), *Exploring Techniques of Analysis and Evaluation in Strategic Management*, Prentice Hall, 1998, and the similar chapter in G. Johnson and K. Scholes (eds), *Exploring Public Sector Strategy*, Prentice Hall, 2000.

7. See, for example, J.P. Kotter and L.A. Schlesinger, 'Choosing strategies for change', *Harvard Business Review*, vol. 57, no. 2 (1979), pp. 106-114.

8. The styles of managing change described here differ from those discussed in J. Balogun and V. Hope Hailey (see reference 3).

9. The intervention style is discussed more fully in P.C. Nutt, 'Identifying and appraising how managers install strategy', *Strategic Management Journal*, vol. 8, no. 1 (1987), pp. 1-14.

10. Evidence for this, as well as a discussion of different styles, is provided by D. Dunphy and D. Stace, 'The strategic management of corporate change', *Human Relations*, vol. 46, no. 8 (1993), pp. 905-20.

11. This definition of leadership is based on that offered by R.M. Stodgill, 'Leadership, membership and organization', *Psychological Bulletin*, vol. 47 (1950), pp. 1-14. For a more recent and more comprehensive discussion of leadership, see G.A. Yukl, *Leadership in Organizations*, 4th edition, Prentice Hall, 1998.

12. For this evidence see D.A. Waldman, G.G. Ramirez, R.J. House and P. Puranam, 'Does leadership matter? CEO leadership attributes and profitability under conditions of perceived environmental uncertainty', *Academy of Management Journal*, vol. 44, no. 1 (2001), pp. 134-143.

13. For fuller explanations of the distinction between charismatic and instrumental and transactional leadership see M.F.R. Kets de Vries, 'The leadership mystique', *Academy of Management Executive*, vol. 8, no. 3 (1994), pp. 73-89, and the paper by Waldman *et al.* (reference 12 above).

14. For a fuller discussion of leadership traits, see M.F.R. Kets de Vries (reference 13 above).

15. Peters and Waterman argue that 'An effective leader must be the master of two ends of the spectrum: ideas at the highest level of abstraction and actions at the most mundane level of detail.' See *In Search of Excellence*, Harper and Row, 1982, p. 287.

16. The discussion on different approaches of strategic leaders and evidence for the effectiveness of the adoption of different approaches can be found in D. Goleman, 'Leadership that gets results', *Harvard Business Review*, March–April 2000, pp. 78-90, and C.M. Farkas and S. Wetlaufer, 'The ways chief executive officers lead', *Harvard Business Review*, May–June 1996, pp.110-112.

17. See S. Floyd and W. Wooldridge, *The Strategic Middle Manager: How to create and sustain competitive advantage*, Jossey-Bass, 1996.

18. T. Deal and A. Kennedy refer to 'the way we do things around here', in *Corporate Cultures: The rights and rituals of corporate life*, Addison-Wesley, 1982.

19. This quote is taken from R. Pascale, *Managing on the Edge*, Viking, 1990.

20. For a fuller discussion of this theme, see G. Johnson, 'Managing strategic change: the role of symbolic action', *British Journal of Management*, vol. 1, no. 4 (1990), pp. 183-200.

21. See H.M. Trice and J.M. Beyer, 'Studying organisational cultures through rites and ceremonials', *Academy of Management Review*, vol. 9, no. 4 (1984), pp. 653-669; H.M. Trice and J.M. Beyer, 'Using six organisational rites to change culture', in R.H. Kilman, M.J. Saxton, R. Serpa and associates (eds), *Gaining Control of the Corporate Culture*, Jossey-Bass, 1985.

22. The importance of the language used by corporate leaders has been noted by a number of writers, but particularly L.R. Pondy, 'Leadership is a language game', in M.W. McCall, Jr and M.M. Lombardo (eds), *Leadership: Where else can we go?*, Duke University Press, Durham, NC. See also J.A. Conger and R. Kanungo, 'Toward a behavioural theory of charismatic leadership in organizational settings', *Academy of Management Review*, vol. 12, no. 4 (1987), pp. 637-647.

23. This discussion is based on observations of the role of political activities in organisations by, in particular, H. Mintzberg, *Power in and around Organisations*, Prentice Hall, 1983, and J. Pfeffer, *Power in Organisations*, Pitman, 1981.

24. See D.A. Nadler and M.L. Tushman, 'Organisational frame bending: principles for managing reorientation', *Academy of Management Executive*, vol. 3, no. 3 (1989), pp. 194-204.

25. See R.H. Lengel and R.L. Daft, 'The selection of communication media as an executive skill', *Academy of Management Executive*, vol. 2, no. 3 (1988), pp. 225-232

WORK ASSIGNMENTS

* Refers to a case study in the Text and Cases edition. ✳ Denotes more advanced work assignments.

11.1 Drawing on sections 11.2.1 and 11.2.2 assess the key contextual dimensions of an organisation (e.g. as for the case example on Joined-up Government) and consider how they should influence the design of a programme of strategic change.

11.2 ✳ Draw up a cultural web and use forcefield analysis to identify blockages and facilitators of change for an organisation (e.g. one for which you have considered the need for a change in strategic direction in a previous assignment). Redraw the web to represent what the organisation should aspire to given the new strategy. Using the cultural webs and forcefield analysis, identify what aspects of the changes can be managed by a change agent and how.

11.3 Identify and explain the styles of managing change (section 11.3.1. and Exhibit 11.5) and approaches to strategic leadership (section 11.3.2 and Exhibit 11.6) employed by different change agents (e.g. Kim Winser in Illustration 11.8., Colin Sharman in KPMG* or Luc Vandevelde of Marks and Spencer*.

11.4 Using Exhibit 11.7, give examples of rituals which signal (or could be used to signal) change in an organisation with which you are familiar.

11.5 ✳ Consider a process of strategic change that you have been involved in or have observed. Map out the steps in the change process in the following terms:
(a) new rituals introduced or old rituals done away with, and the impact of these changes;
(b) the means of communication employed by change agents, and how effective they were.

11.6 ✳ In the context of managing strategic change in a large corporation or public sector organisation, to what extent, and why, do you agree with Richard Pascale's argument that it is easier to act ourselves into a better way of thinking than it is to think ourselves into a better way of acting? (References 19 and also 15, 20 and 21 will be useful here.)

11.7 ✳ There are a number of books by renowned senior executives who have managed major changes in their organisation. Read one of these and note the levers and mechanisms for change employed by the change agent, using the approaches outlined in this chapter as a checklist. How effective do you think these were in the context that the change agent faced, and could other mechanisms have been used?

CASE EXAMPLE

Joined-up government:
Mental health provision in the UK[1]

In the 1990s the UK public services had experienced significant changes in what government expected of them and the way they were organised. The Conservative government prior to 1997 had followed a policy of trying to achieve greater efficiency and service through market forces, setting up structures within public services to promote competition. With the election of the Labour government in 1997 this policy changed. Rather than emphasising competition, the emphasis switched to co-operation and what became know as 'joined-up government'. Different services should work together to make them more accessible to their communities and improve quality. It was a theme with which Tony Blair, the Prime Minister, became personally identified.

Mental health services

The policy of joined-up government would affect the health service and social services substantially; and within these, one area that would be particularly affected would be the provision of mental health services. In health care, co-operation meant that the different parts of the service such as family doctors, hospitals and health authorities should be able to work with each other and other agencies to the benefit of the community. In 2000 the government published a White Paper entitled the *National Service Framework for Mental Health* which focused on the relationship between health care and social services. It argued that people needing help and advice on mental health were at risk of getting passed from one service to another; and that the different services should be co-ordinated in such a way as to be 'customer

facing', such that people should be provided a 'one-stop shop' experience – a co-ordinated, smooth approach to their care.

Up to 2000, mental health provision was made in two ways: first, through the National Health Service itself, and second, through Social Services. These were two very different structures with different lines of responsibility to government. The National Health Service was the responsibility of a central government minister and, in that sense, directly answerable to central government. Social Services were organised locally by local government. So although there was central government oversight of Social Services, the delivery of the services was largely managed locally. A patient who required mental health treatment might find themselves dealing with either the NHS or Social Services. For example, their need for care might be picked up by their doctor, or by a social worker if their behaviour was causing family disruption. Care itself could also be provided by both services: health services dealing with psychological needs and Social Services with support or rehabilitation.

Joined-up government meant that these two different services would need to co-operate to provide a seamless mental health service. But how was this to be done?

The workshop

Late in 2000 a strategy workshop took place between managers in the NHS and Social Services responsible for mental health. The brief was: how to provide a co-ordinated, one-stop shop for mental health services. In the workshop they discussed the strategy for co-operation, identified the resources and competences they would require to deliver this and then went on to consider the sorts of strategic change necessary.

This case was prepared by Jan Horwath, University of Sheffield.

Figure 1 **Cultural web for the NHS (current culture)**

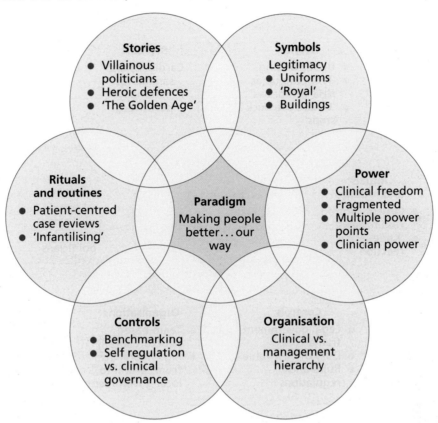

They were able to identify a number of basic competences that had to be provided for a co-operative service. These were:

- It would be necessary to identify a shared vision.

- There must be 'client' feedback processes. 'Joined-up' services could not be ensured if there was no understanding of the extent to which expectations were being met.

- There should be clear protocols and standards of such service. If these existed then it would be possible to empower staff at lower levels to ensure that clients' needs were being met. However, without such standards, such empowerment could lead to disjointed services, lack of efficiency and, at worst, chaos.

- There would be a need for clear information which should be shared, appropriate, accurate and available. Both services already centred their client information on case notes and case plans, but they were not shared.

- There would need to be effective communications with key stakeholders who should receive common messages from the two services. Without this there would be significant confusion.

- There should be a unified management structure with clear leadership and clear roles and responsibilities for managers within that common structure.

Participants on the workshop felt that, whilst some of these competences were common already and

Figure 2 **Cultural web for Social Services (current culture)**

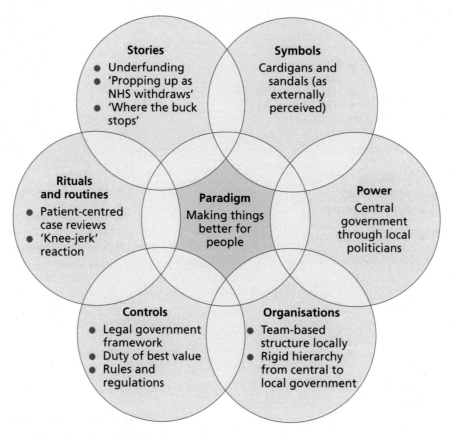

they could see how others might be brought together reasonably easily, the real problem was a gulf in values and behaviours rooted in the different cultures of the two services. As a means of examining this and considering the strategic changes needed, they used the cultural web.

The cultural webs

The participants drew up cultural webs for both the NHS and for Social Services in relation to mental health. In so doing they tried to identify where differences and similarities lay; and also what might get in the way of co-operation, and what might help. The resulting cultural webs are shown as Figures 1 and 2. (Readers may also like to refer to the NHS cultural web shown as Illustration 5.8

in Chapter 5). The interpretation of these webs by the participants led to the following conclusions.

The paradigm

The NHS was really a national sickness service which cures people – often in spectacular fashion; the result was that mental health care was a low status 'Cinderella' service in the NHS. Moreover, in the NHS, although patients' care was centrally important, it was medical values that were central and those providing them who believed they knew best.

On the other hand, Social Services was about making things better for people. Social Services saw themselves as managing risk on behalf of society. However, in this, Social Services personnel regarded themselves as working on long-term solutions whereas they saw health care focusing on short-term interventions and then withdrawing to leave Social Services to 'mop up'.

Power

In the NHS there were two key aspects of power. First, it was fragmented, with multiple power points such as clinicians, nursing and so on. Within this there was a good deal of emphasis on the freedom of clinicians – rather like academic freedom in universities; and it was the clinicians who were seen as having the greatest power of all. Managers in the NHS had traditionally not had a great deal of power and there were plenty of stories about conflict between clinicians and managers.

When it came to power, the history of Social Services was one of control from central government through local politicians. It was very procedurally driven through this hierarchy.

Organisation structure

In health services there were parallel hierarchies, one to do with clinicians and one to do with management. Whilst these did come together (for example, in a clinical specialism there would be a clinical director with managerial support), the fact remained that these two hierarchies were underpinned by power differences.

Social Services was dominated by the rigid hierarchy from central to local government. At the operational level, however, there was more emphasis on teams focusing on particular cases.

Controls

In health care the history had been self-regulation: this was now being questioned. Central standards were being set under 'clinical governance' arrangements. In effect this was a benchmarking exercise which set standards and asked for explanations of variances from those standards. Many clinicians saw it as an intrusion on their freedom to act and undue central interference.

Social Services operated within a local government framework controlled by central government. There were rigid standards and performance indicators set by central government. The feeling was that this was very restrictive to their ability to use professional judgement and to reflect local needs. Moreover, Social Services only seemed to get into the public light when they made mistakes, either intervening too much or not intervening at all in matters of welfare. The result was that it was a very nervous sort of culture, always referring back to rules and regulations and trying to cover its back. Social Services personnel had often lost their confidence in their ability to use professional judgement because of such criticism. Social Services also operated within the local government 'Best Value Initiative', a benchmarking framework, with a requirement to produce plans to show how, as a minimum, within five years they would reach the standards of the current 25 per cent best performing departments in the country. Participants did not much like this bureaucracy, but had become resigned to it.

Rituals and routines

The participants identified a number of similar rituals and routines, and some that were different. One common ritual, centrally important to both the NHS and Social Services, was the clinical review of patients. In the NHS many of the rituals were to do with 'infantilising' patients: making them wait, putting them to bed, waking them up and so on. The subservience of patients was further emphasised by the elevation of clinicians with ritual consultation ceremonies and ward rounds.

In Social Services they wanted to see themselves having a more 'adult' relationship and working in partnership with 'clients' rather than 'patients'. But the feeling was that the wider system in which Social Services was operating largely precluded this and they were forced back to a more dependent patient-type relationship. Another ritual throughout Social Services was the knee-jerk reaction to reorganise every time they faced a new problem.

Stories and symbols

In the NHS, stories and symbols were all about the legitimacy of the system. The stories were about villainous politicians trying to change things, heroic acts by those defending the system (often well-known medical figures) and stories about the golden age of the NHS. There were symbols which reflected the various institutions, such as nurses' uniforms and the importance of the size and status of physical buildings, reflected for example in the designation of 'Royal' to hospital names which was believed to ensure that a hospital could withstand the threat of closure.

In Social Services the symbols and stories were different. It was a Cinderella service, propping up the NHS. It was driven by procedures and populated by 'woolly thinkers'. It felt that the system forced them to make grey issues into either black or white. There were stories about how underfunding made it impossible to do a proper job. The key story was how social service was the end of the line – where the buck stopped; they saw others (e.g. health care) intervening then opting out to leave social services mopping up. As for symbols, they were aware that others tended to see them as '1960 hippies wearing cardigans and sandals'.

The implications

The participants reviewed the cultural webs. In trying to think through how to design a co-operative organisation and bring together the two cultures, they asked three questions:

- What positives could be built on?
- What were the negatives that had to be overcome?
- What were the behaviours that were needed but currently not there?

There were some other questions which the workshop raised:

- How were people to be convinced of the need and desirability of such co-operation? Some of the participants felt that a big education programme was what was needed, and that this again meant a clear identification of common starting points. Others felt that the way to start was to get a common training programme going so that behaviours changed as fast as possible.

- Participants also felt the need for some short-term wins that could be communicated and publicised. Not least here was the need for some important symbolic signals of a co-operative service. Here it was felt that role models were particularly important. But who?

- There was also the structural issue. What structures would be most appropriate? The mental health legislation called for structural changes and the creation of mental health trusts. These would bring together social services and NHS staff into the same organisations. But it was not clear to the group how exactly these would operate, how it would affect their lines of reporting and if, indeed, they would achieve anything better than would occur through two separate services working better together.

They agreed they had some major issues to tackle at their next meeting.

Questions

1. Drawing on other explanations in section 11.2, analyse the needs and problems of change in mental health provision.

2. In particular, draw up another web showing what a 'joined-up' provision of services would look like.

3. What programme of change should be developed to deliver such provision?

4. If you were a manger trying to achieve change in the NHS or Social Services to promote such provision, what would you concentrate on first, and why?

5. What problems do you think you would face and how might you seek to overcome them?

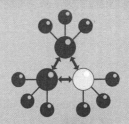

In Chapter 1 a framework for this book was presented (see Exhibit 1.4). The subsequent structure of the book has been based on that. The different parts of the book have discussed how the *strategic position* of the organisation can be understood (Part II), what *strategic choices* might be made and how (Part III) and in this part (Part IV) how organisations might translate *strategy into action*. However, Chapter 1 also explained that, although these themes are dealt with separately in the structure of this book, it is an artificial divide. That message has been repeated throughout the book. For example, understanding the strategic position, in so far as it is about making sense of issues in the environment, an organisation's resources and competences or stakeholder expectations, may very well take place in action rather than through data analysis alone. Similarly, strategic choice might take place in action, by trying things out and experimenting. Chapter 2 and the commentaries on Parts II and III have made these points. Nonetheless, as authors we are aware that structuring the book the way helps readers think about strategic management more clearly: and for some managers a linear, sequential view of strategic management is seen as *the* logical approach to managing strategy. For these reasons this commentary returns to the three lenses to consider the implications for translating strategy into action.

Designing strategic action

The design view of strategy encapsulates this linear view. Putting strategy into action is seen as an extension of the planning process: a strategy is first formulated and then it is implemented. The emphasis is on getting the *logic* of the strategy right and then *persuading* people of that logic; designing *structures and control systems* appropriate to the strategy and using them as mechanisms of change; putting in place the *resources* required; and planning the *timing and sequencing* of changes required. *Control* mechanisms and feedback systems also need to be in place so that the strategies can be refined, amended and so on, but nonetheless the linear sequence remains. It is a conception of strategic management based on the notion that thinking precedes organisational action.

There are associated assumptions about who does all this. There are those who are responsible for the formulation of strategy, usually seen as top management. They determine what the strategy should be through careful analysis of their internal and external organisational context, they carefully evaluate strategic options and then they translate those into implementation plans.

Much of what was discussed in Chapters 9, 10 and 11 could be seen as providing the bases for this approach. Chapter 9 was concerned with structuring the organisation. The design lens would suggest that 'structure follows strategy'; and there is evidence that structures of organisations have indeed changed following significant shifts in organisational strategies. For example, multidivisional structures followed the development of multi-product firms.[1] Control systems need to monitor how the implementation of strategy is progressing: these are likely to include financial systems such as budgets, reward systems and other ways of ensuring that the behaviour of those in the organisation corresponds to the strategy. So they need to focus on measures that are vital to strategy delivery. For example, the way a corporate parent relates to a subsidiary in terms of the means of control it exercises needs to correspond to its parenting rationale (see section 9.3.2): the performance targets that are set in a business need to be compatible with its competitive strategy (section 9.3.3). The organisation's structure and its control systems therefore need to be appropriate to deliver the strategy: if they are not, the effectiveness of the strategy will suffer.

A lesson that might be drawn from Chapter 10 is that it also matters that what goes on within major resource areas corresponds to the overall strategy. So strategies for areas such as finance, HR and information should correspond to the overall plan; and the priorities and key tasks being pursued in these areas should be in line with overall strategy.

Chapter 11 provides frameworks whereby a strategic change programme can be designed. Such design presupposes that there is a designer, the change agent, who will carefully think through which style of change management and which levers for managing change are most appropriate and will have most effect in what organisational context.[2] There are then others, the rest of the organisation, who will be the subject of this programme of change.

To repeat, much of this is what has been explained in the previous chapters of this book; and it makes a lot of sense. Without it an organisation and those within it could find themselves in a state of confusion with no clarity of direction, no way of knowing whether they were being successful and quite probably with a disenchanted group of shareholders and demotivated workforce. Some clarity of strategic direction and matching of overall strategy to the day-to-day workings of the organisation is clearly important. However, there are other lessons to be drawn about the links between the development of strategies and organisational action. The previous chapters have raised some of these already but using the experience and ideas lenses can help emphasise their importance as well as provide additional insights.

Strategic action and experience

Throughout this book there has been an attempt to explain strategic management both in terms of concepts and frameworks, and in terms of the behaviours and assumptions associated with individual experience, organisational cultures and institutionalisation. This highlights a point that is obvious when stated, but all too easy to overlook. Ultimately the success of translating strategy into action depends on the extent to which people are committed to it. This raises significant challenges.

Strategic inertia

The first challenge relates to the problem of strategic inertia. The discussion of the experience lens in Chapter 2 and its implications in terms of strategic drift, and the subsequent use of this lens to explain the persistence of the business idea (commentary on Part II) and strategy selection (commentary on Part III) emphasise the problem of strategic inertia. There is a very real danger that people in organisations become captured by their collective experience rooted in past success and organisational and institutional norms. Chapters in Part IV of the book have flagged up related problems.

Chapter 9 points out that organisations can become captured by their structures and systems. Some organisations, such as accountancy firms (see Illustration 2.2), universities, large public sector bureaucracies and arguably even some e-businesses of the new millennium, have become as much defined by the *way* they are organised as by what they do. In a sense in such organisations 'strategy follows structure';[3] they pursue strategies constrained by their structures and systems. The explanation in Chapter 2 of how strategies develop in organisations makes a similar point: it may well be the culture driving the strategy rather than the other way round (see section 2.2.2). Similarly, Chapter 10 points out that organisations may be captured by their resource legacy;[4] or by assumptions people make about what resource priorities really matter. A high-technology company becomes fixated on technology as the driving force of its business; a financially oriented chief executive focuses on financing issues to the detriment of wider issues; the HR function sets up 'state of the art' HR systems without ensuring that they are compatible with the strategic direction of the organisation.

Viewing strategic change (Chapter 11) through this lens emphasises the challenge of overcoming such inertia: indeed, much of the analysis of change needs and context suggested in section 11.2 is about seeking to establish the nature and extent of inertia; for example, is it the result of passive inertia through embeddedness in the existing culture, or more active, perhaps politicised resistance to change? The rest of that chapter suggests that managing change is about finding ways of overcoming this.

Many frameworks for designing change programmes have started from the position that breaking down cultural inertia and overcoming resistance to change are key requirements for putting strategy into action. Some argue that there is a need to 'unfreeze' the organisation before a new strategy can be followed;[5] and that this involves challenging the prevailing paradigm so that inertial constraints on following a new strategy are reduced. The organisation will therefore go through processes of change in which the mechanisms discussed in this part of the book may play a part.

- A change in the environment of the organisation – new technology, changes in customer tastes, or the entry of new competitors leading to a deteriorating market position – may act as an *unfreezing* mechanism. However, in the absence of a clear and dramatic external force for change, there may be other ways to achieve the unfreezing process. Managers may emphasise, even exaggerate, external signs of problems or threats, make structural changes, set up different control systems, remove long-established management or switch resources to different priorities as ways of signalling that existing ways of doing things are under challenge.

- There may develop a situation of *flux* in the organisation, in which competing views surface about causes of, and remedies for, the problems. It is likely to be a time of high political activity. Not least, there is likely to be a defence of boundaries and investment in resources, perhaps controlled by functional departments. Whilst such processes give rise to conflict and appear to be disruptive, they may actually be useful because they can facilitate the debate of different points of view and help surface and challenge what is taken for granted.[6]

- The way forward might be resolved by planned strategic direction coming from the top. Or it may be that individuals or groups within different parts of the organisation start to try new ways of doing things – a process of *experimentation*. This might be because a change agent is deliberately using a change style of participation or intervention (see section 11.3.1 of Chapter 11) or perhaps because people in a department sees themselves potentially benefiting from structural change in the organisation. The result could be that there is growing commitment to a new strategy direction. It might also mean that managers trying to instigate the new strategy learn from such experiments and refine the strategy they had planned.

- Members of the organisation, faced with a new strategy, may require a 'safety net' for the future. *Refreezing* processes may be needed to confirm the organisational validity of the new strategy, so managers may need to consider ways of signalling this: for example, by changing organisational structures (see Chapter 9), investment in resource areas central to that strategy (Chapter 10), by changing everyday routines (section 11.4.2) or by finding symbols of change (see section 11.4.3).

So here the whole emphasis of managing strategic change is how managers can utilise the sorts of processes discussed in Part IV of the book to overcome the inevitable inertia which exists.

The experience of middle management

The important role of middle management was discussed in Chapters 10 and 11. Imagine a situation where the top management of an organisation is trying to develop a new strategic direction. If they take the design view literally, they could assume that they can plan strategy implementation such that it will cascade down through the organisation. They will see middle management as part of this cascade, responsible for doing what the plan instructs them to do and monitoring its progress. There is another way of looking at this, however. If strategy is viewed as coming down through the organisation from the top, it is inevitable that those below top management must make sense of strategic direction in terms of their existing experience, both individual and collective: they will translate the strategic intention through their own experience lens.[7] Indeed, they must do this in order to try to put the new strategy into effect, since it is impossible for a top-down strategic plan to cover every detailed aspect of the operations of any organisation. It has to be translated into action within the organisation; and usually by managers responsible for resource areas of the organisation. If this is recognised, it throws a different light on the idea of putting strategies into action.

- Top managers need to recognise that they cannot plan everything; that strategies are bound to be translated into action within the organisation. Indeed, many strategic leaders have adopted approaches to managing strategy and styles of strategic change which explicitly recognise this (see sections 11.3.1 and 11.3.2). So they may manage through being clear about overall strategic intent rather than high levels of specificity of how strategies should be put into effect; or they may select key subordinates whom they believe will closely align with them on what they are trying to achieve; or they may involve subordinates in strategy development so that they become so aligned.

- Indeed, a second lesson is that it may be important that the translators of strategy – mostly the middle management – are involved in developing the strategic plans: if they are not, they must find themselves in the position of interpreting those plans on a different basis from those formulating them. Arguably this accounts for attempts to flatten organisational hierarchies, do away with levels of senior executives in central offices and devolve responsibility for strategy to customer-facing business managers (see section 9.4.1).

- However, it has to be recognised that how top managers conceive of strategies is not the same as how those lower down in the organisation conceive of them. Therefore there needs to be ways of relating the desired strategic direction to the everyday realities of people in the organisation; to build a bridge between the intentions of top management and the experience of those who will carry out those intentions in operational terms. This is why it is important to ensure that organisational routines and operating processes, day-to-day control systems and HR systems are in line with the intended strategy. Again, it is unlikely that top management can do all this; it is therefore vital that middle managers are engaged with and committed to such strategies so that they can perform this translation process.

- Desirable as all this may be, however, it also needs to be recognised that such perfection of translation is not likely. What is intended from the top rarely comes about in action in its entirety, or in the form in which it was originally conceived. This 'imperfection' moves the discussion forward to the ideas lens.

Strategic action, ideas and the learning organisation

The ideas lens accepts imperfections in organisational systems and highlights the importance of diversity and variety. In drawing on evolutionary theory and complexity theory it sees strategies as the emergence of patterns of order from that variety. Here the division between strategy formulation and strategy implementation disappears. Strategies are seen as developing from ideas that bubble up from within and around an organisation. They may arise because people are interacting with a changing environment which itself promotes new ideas; or they may arise because diverse, even maverick, ideas become attractive. These ideas may become absorbed or be post-rationalised into strategic plans, but their origins are not from the planning process. The ideas themselves are created and emerge in the everyday activity and social interaction that goes on in organisations and the world that surrounds those organisations. Strategies emerge through doing.

This raises questions about issues raised in this part of the book and some of the insights of both the design and experience lenses.

- The emphasis here is on the importance of interaction within the organisation and across the boundaries of the organisation. The greater such interaction, the more will new ideas and innovation come about. Whilst organisational structures and systems are unavoidable necessities, they tend to build barriers and boundaries and, consequently reduce such interaction. The ideas lens suggests that this is one of the reasons why inertia and resistance to new ideas and new strategies take place.

- The potential for new ideas, innovation and change is already there in an organisation and needs to be released. Far from seeing lower levels in the organisation as blockages to new strategies, they should be seen as the potential source of innovation. It is the formalised systems (the result of a design approach) and the experience embedded in culture that gets in the way.

- The ideas lens would suggest that the notion of a planned strategy being translated in such a prescriptive and precise way that it will be replicated in the detail of organisational action is unrealistic. Such planned intentions will be translated differently by people in the organisation; this is *imperfect copying* and, whilst the design lens would see it as inefficient, the ideas lens sees it as a source of new ideas and originality.

- There is, however, a recognition of the need for guidelines and rules. Without these there would be chaos. Those who are thinking about the direction of strategy should recognise the importance of clarity in overarching strategic purpose or intent and a few key guiding principles, around which measurement and monitoring might be built. However, they should avoid making these so prescriptive and constraining as to prevent interaction, sharing, questioning and innovative behaviour.

- Some organisations are learning such lessons because their organisational environments are changing so fast that traditional ways of organising and an embeddedness of culture do not exist in the same way as they do in more stable environments. Here there is no need for *unfreezing* mechanisms because the organisation is in a state of continual change.

All of this reflects the sort of arguments put forward by those that promote the idea of the *learning organisation*.

Traditionally, organisations have been seen as hierarchies and bureaucracies set up to achieve order and maintain control; as structures built for stability rather than change. Arguably, this conception of the organisation is not suited to the dynamic conditions for change of the 21st century. The organisation needs to be seen not as a stable hierarchy, but as an adaptive, continually changing **learning organisation** (see section 2.3.5) capable of continual regeneration from the variety of knowledge, experience and skills of individuals through a culture which encourages mutual questioning and challenge around a shared purpose or vision.

Advocates of the learning organisation point out that the collective knowledge of all the individuals in an organisation usually exceeds what the organisation itself 'knows' and is capable of doing; the formal structures of organisations typically stifle organisational knowledge and creativity. As suggested in Chapter 9 (section 9.3.6), in certain contexts the aim of management should be to encourage processes which unlock the knowledge of individuals, and encourage the sharing of information and knowledge, so that each individual becomes sensitive to changes occurring around them and contributes to the identification of opportunities and required changes. This is not the same as setting up a formal, 'hard wired' knowledge management system. The organisation then becomes capable of taking an holistic view of its environment rather than being reliant on partial, filtered information from its various functions. There is an absence of power plays and blocking routines, so that a shared vision of the future can be created and reinforced by mutual support by organisational members. Such an organisation, it is argued, will be creative and continually changing, and be able to cope with the ambiguity and contradictions it faces.

These kinds of organisations do not operate with the sorts of 'organisational silo' that can develop in highly departmentalised structures. Information flows and relationships between people are lateral as well as vertical. So as ideas bubble up from below, the risk of their fizzling out because of lack of interest from other parts of the organisation is reduced. There is also more likelihood that the sort of integration required for the idea to develop will occur. (The need for such integration was emphasised in section 10.6).

When it comes to strategic change this is less likely to be a situation of top-down change, nor should there be a need for unfreezing corresponding to the descriptions of change in the previous section. Here managers would be playing a less directive and more facilitative role. Arguably, an organisational form such as adhocracy, explained section 9.5.1, aspires to this rather than to the more traditional notions of stability and control. Where this exists, organisations should be well positioned to manage strategic change through continual *adaptation or evolution* (see section 11.2.1) such that proactive incremental change – or logical incrementalism – might come about. Indeed the organisation is all about change.

A **learning organisation** is capable of continual regeneration from the variety of knowledge, experience and skills of individuals through a culture which encourages mutual questioning and challenge around a shared purpose or vision

Our view

As with the two previous commentaries, we argue that these lenses are not mutually exclusive.

At its extreme, the design lens does indeed place too much emphasis on top-down management, all-knowing top executives who determine strategy and the idea that strategy can be masterminded from on high. However, this does not remove the need for strategic direction and care in thinking through the structuring of organisations, the management of key resource areas or the role of managers in promoting change. Even if the true learning organisation exists, with extraordinary powers of self-regeneration, there is nonetheless the requirement to pull together the energy for such change and direct it meaningfully. In all this, the design lens has much to offer.

However, the importance of individual experience and organisational culture is also of central importance. The experience lens certainly sheds light on the problems of change. However, it does more than this; in explaining barriers to change, it also provides insights into how those barriers can be removed or overcome and therefore into how change can be managed. It also highlights the fact that organisations are communities of experience within which lie competences and insights that can, themselves, form the basis of advantage and benefit for organisations.

The ideas lens highlights the potential for new ideas and innovation, but it also argues for the relevance of the other lenses. Certainly individuals are captured within their own experience and their own cultures, but they also differ; they are the source of potential variety, and the challenge is to release the energy of that variety. However, the ideas lens also points to the importance of sufficient clarity of direction and the importance of a sufficiency of rules. Innovation in organisations does not occur because of unbridled and anarchic individuality, but because of a balance between diversity and variety and a clarity of direction and a sufficiency of control.

Our argument is that understanding strategy in action requires the three lenses, not that one is more important than another.

Reviewing strategy

At the end of this book, it is timely to review the subject of strategy as a whole; and again useful to do so by employing the three lenses.

The book began by emphasising that the management of strategy is distinctly different from operational management in its complexity; this is perhaps its most distinguishing feature. When people talk about strategy or strategic management, that is what they imply. Because it is to do with the management, of the future direction of the organisation, the coping with uncertainty, the competition of potentially irreconcilable influences, it is about an area of management denoted by its complexity.

Our encouragement in this book has been to cast a critical eye on understanding the management of strategy. The dominant influence of the design lens can be put down to its perceived potential to simplify, or at least place order on, that complexity; and in this book we recognise the attraction and value of that. In thinking through this challenging topic, the design lens is especially useful. It draws on models and explanatory frameworks which allow for analysis and build on empirical findings from research. However, the challenge is not just to think about strategy but also to manage strategy: and managers and students alike should not delude themselves that a model which provides order means that the complexity is done away with.

It is because of this complexity and the importance of strategy as a management activity that the other two lenses are important. The experience lens helps explain how managers actually cope with such complexity, helps explain barriers and blockages to change and in so doing sheds light on how change programmes might be designed and managed. However, neither of these two lenses says enough about innovation; and that is where the ideas lens is especially useful. It also provides a useful counterbalance to the design lens, gives an alternative model for conceiving of how organisations and people cope with uncertainty and complexity, and explains how, in so doing, novelty and innovation may arise.

REFERENCES

1. The evidence that 'structure follows strategy' was provided in the historical studies of strategy development and organisational structures by A.D. Chandler, *Strategy and Structure*, MIT Press (1962).
2. *Exploring Strategic Change* by J. Balogun and V. Hope Hailey (Prentice Hall, 1999) specifically acknowledges that it takes this design approach to change.
3. For an argument and evidence that strategy may follow structure, see D. Hall and M.A. Saias, 'Strategy follows structure', *Strategic Management Journal*, vol. 1, no. 2 (1980), pp. 149-163.
4. For an exposition of a 'resource dependency' approach see J. Pfeffer and G.R. Salancik, *The External Control of Organisations: A resource dependence perspective*, Harper and Row, 1978.
5. The unfreezing model of change is widely used. It has its origins in the work of K. Lewin, 'Group decision and social change', in E.E. Maccoby, T.M. Newcomb and E.L. Hartley (eds), *Readings in Social Pschology*, Holt, Reinhart and Winston, 1958, pp. 197-211; but, for example, also see the paper by Isabella (reference 7 below) which uses the model to explain change.
6. The argument that conflict can bring about useful debate is developed by J.M. Bartunek, D. Kolb and R. Lewicki, 'Bringing conflict out from behind the scenes: private informal and non-rational dimensions of conflict in organizations', in D. Kolb and J. Bartunek (eds), *Hidden Conflict in Organizations: Uncovering behind the scenes disputes*, Sage, 1992.
7. For an explanation and example of the role middle managers play in translating strategic intent, see L.A. Isabella, 'Evolving interpretations as a change unfolds: how managers construe key organizational events', *Academy of Management Journal*, vol. 33, no. 1 (1990), pp. 7-41.

CASE STUDIES

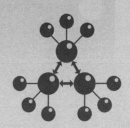

A guide to using the case studies

The main text of this book includes 86 short illustrations and 11 case examples which have been chosen to enlarge specific issues in the text and/or provide practical examples of how business and public sector organisations are managing strategic issues. The case studies which follow allow the reader to extend this linking of theory and practice further by analysing the strategic issues of specific organisations in much greater depth – and providing 'solutions' to some of the problems or difficulties identified in the cases.

The case studies are intended to serve as a basis for class discussion and not as an illustration of either good or bad management practice. They are not intended to be a comprehensive collection of teaching material. They have been chosen (or specifically written) to provide readers with a core of cases which, together, cover most of the main issues in the text. As such, they should provide a useful backbone to a programme of study but could sensibly be supplemented by other material. We have provided a mixture of longer and shorter cases to increase the flexibility for teachers. Combined with the *illustrations* and the short *case examples* at the end of each chapter (in both versions of the book) this increases the reader's and tutor's choice. For example, when deciding on material for Chapter 3, the case example *The European Brewing Industry*, tests a reader's understanding of the main issues influencing the competitive position of a number of organisations in the same industry with a relatively short case. For a case that permits a more comprehensive industry analysis, *The Pharmaceutical Industry* and the associated case study on the *GlaxoWellcome/SmithKlineBeecham* merger could be used. However, if the purpose is more focused – illustrating the use of the 'five forces' framework – the Illustration on *The Mobile Phone Industry* could be used.

Some cases are written entirely from published sources but most have been prepared in co-operation with and approval of the management of the organisation concerned. Case studies can never fully capture the richness and complexity of real-life management situations and we would also encourage readers and tutors to take every possible opportunity to explore the *live* strategic issues of organisations – both their own and others.

The following brief points of guidance should prove useful in selecting and using the case studies provided:

- The summary table that follows indicates the main focus of each of the chosen case studies – together with important subsidiary foci (where appropriate). In general, the sequence of cases is intended to mirror the chapter sequence. However, this should not be taken too literally because, of course, many of these cases cover a variety of issues. The 'classification' provided is therefore guidance only. We expect readers to seek their own lessons from cases, and tutors to use cases in whichever way and sequence best fits the purpose of their programmes.

- Where cases have been chosen to illustrate the issues of strategic choices and strategy into action covered later in the book, it will normally be a prerequisite that some type of analysis of the strategic position is undertaken, using the case material. When planning the use of these cases within programmes, care needs to be taken to balance the time taken on such strategic analysis so as to allow the time required to analyse the main issues for which the case has been chosen.

- Where the text and cases are being used as the framework for a strategy programme (as we hope they will), it is essential that students are required to undertake additional reading from other sources and that their 'practical' work is supplemented by other material as mentioned above.

A guide to the main focus of cases

Case	Introduction to strategy	Strategic management process	Business environment	Five forces	Resource and competence analysis	Stakeholder expectations/purposes	Culture	Overall strategic analysis	Corporate strategy/parenting	Competitive strategy	Strategic options	Diversification	Acquisitions	Overall strategic analysis	Global management	Structure, organisation design	Enabling	Managing change	Strategic leadership	Public sector management
Corus	●●																			
ASM Lithography	●●		●					●												
Ericsson		●●				●	●												●	
ST Electronics		●●																		
Pharmaceuticals			●●	●●																
Irish Ports			●●						●									●		●
KPN			●●							●●		●		●						
Amazon.com					●●					●●										
Car Dealers				●	●●															
Formula One					●●												●			
Broken Hill				●	●●															
Viking Sewing Machines					●●						●							●	●	
Tomkins						●●			●											
Sheffield Theatres						●●	●													●
Child Support Agency						●●														●●
Thorntons					●				●●		●●									
Burmah/BP		●			●				●●			●		●	●					
The News Corporation									●●			●●		●					●	
Royal Bank of Scotland									●●	●			●							
CRH									●				●●							
Ryanair		●							●	●●										
BMW		●	●							●●										
South African Breweries		●	●							●●	●●		●		●●					
Brewery Group Denmark										●●	●●			●	●●				●	
Barclaycard							●			●●				●						
WH Smith									●	●●										
GlaxoSmithKline									●				●●							
Snappy Snaps		●	●								●				●●					
Coopers Creek															●●	●				
Topps International					●											●●	●●			
General Motors Brazil																●●	●●			
Scottish Power Learning																●●				
Tetra Pak																●●				
KMPG (A)		●					●●									●		●●	●	
KMPG (B)															●●	●				
Marks and Spencer		●			●		●●			●								●●	●	
Xerox						●●													●●	

Key: ●● = Major focus
      ● = Important subsidiary focus

Corus

Kevan Scholes

This case study is the continuing story of one of the UK's largest and best-known manufacturing companies – British Steel, which merged with Hoogovens from the Netherlands to form Corus, the fifth largest steelmaker in the world. It covers the period before and after the privatisation of British Steel in 1989, through the merger of 1999 and into troubled times by 2001. In reviewing the history of the company it seeks to highlight many of the reasons for good or poor performance. The period from 1993 saw the company attempting to become a truly global steel company – leading to the 1999 merger. But the business environment remained difficult, with the high value of sterling against the euro since 1997 and excess world steel capacity both leading to price reductions for bulk steels. This required a continued driving down of costs, increased productivity and the resultant loss of jobs. Mergers between competitors within Europe may also weaken the company's competitive position.

• • •

February 2001 was a black month for the steel industry in the UK and the Netherlands. On 2 February, Corus, the Anglo/Dutch company, formed in October 1999 by the merger of British Steel plc and Koninklijke Hoogovens, announced 6,050 job losses by 2003 as a result of radical restructuring of its bulk steel operations. This followed some 4,500 job losses in the UK in 2000 – a relentless continuation of the reduction of the UK workforce to 22,000 from almost 300,000 in 1970. To make matters worse, on 16 February three of Corus's European rivals, Usinor (France), Arbed (Luxembourg) and Aceralia (Spain), agreed a merger, which would create the world's biggest steelmaker – valued at £3.8 billion, with annual production of some 46 million tonnes and sales of almost £20 billion. This made Corus seem relatively small with annual production of about 20 million tonnes and sales of less than £10 billion. The chairman of Usinor commented that a good size for a global steel company over the next five years was an annual production of 40–80 million tonnes.

THE WORLD STEEL INDUSTRY

Steel was one of the world's major industries and in 1999 the world production was 788 million tonnes. Appendix 1 to this case study shows the top 25 steel-producing countries. Traditionally most countries had produced for home consumption and levels of imports and exports were low between countries that had their own industry. There were exports to countries without a steel-making capability. The last quarter of the twentieth century saw significant changes in this pattern and the UK was typical of developed economies. In 1970 UK consumption of steel was 20 million tonnes, 95 per cent sourced from the UK. As this demand dropped to 13.9 million tonnes by 2000, imports had also increased to 6.6 million tonnes. In turn the UK producers were exporting more than half of their production. Appendix 2 shows the top 20 steel producers – with Corus at number five.

Around the world, production capacity exceeded demand by more than one-third, creating downward pressure on prices for commodity bulk steel products – favouring manufacturers in low-cost economies. In turn this had pressurised steelmakers in developed countries to press harder for cost reductions and productivity improvements, which averaged 4–5 per cent per annum in the 1990s. But difficult times were not new to steelmakers. The changes in the industry had been monumental over the previous quarter century. For example, the 'steel intensity' in many products (e.g. motor cars) had declined remarkably – with average steel thickness (for the same performance) reducing from 2 mm to 0.8 mm. In the reverse direction, improvements in metallurgical properties and reductions in cost were allowing steel beams to make major inroads into the construction market at the expense of concrete.

PRIVATISATION BRINGS SUCCESS

In the 10 years following the creation of British Steel plc in 1989 the company was seen as an example of how to transform an ailing nationalised company (BSC) with cumulative losses of some £7bn between 1975 and 1984 into a successful and profitable privatised manufacturing company (see Appendix 3 for details of financial results). These improvements in performance had resulted from a combination of increased investment, changes in management structures (reducing overheads and devolving decision making) and, most importantly, a revolution in working practices. Although the basic process of steel-making was long established, there were still important competitive advantages to be gained by both product development and the management of the logistics of the supply and distribution chains. Following acquisitions in the late 1980s, British Steel was also a major player in the distribution (stockholding) of steel in the UK, with over 30 per cent market share. Here the exploitation of information technology to reduce costs and increase customer service was critical to success.

CASE STUDIES

NEW DIRECTIONS

In 1993, Brian Moffat was appointed chairman and embarked on an ambitious and well-communicated strategy to be a genuinely internationally based steel company, which did not exist anywhere in the world at that time. It was recognised that globalisation, in some form was an important ingredient in adjusting to a changing business environment. Exchange rates were of critical importance to international businesses, and the combination of a strong pound against the US dollar and weakness against the Deutschmark in the mid-1990s was almost an ideal situation for British Steel (as an exporter to continental Europe and an 'offshore' manufacturer in the USA). But the uncertainties of international trade turned against the company. In January 1996, the pound sterling stood at DM 2.22 – by July 1997 it was DM 3.07 and it remained over DM 3.0 for most of the following four years. This was largely due to a weak euro – a new currency established for the European Union – which the UK government had declined to join. Sterling's strength against the US dollar declined slowly over the same period. Although the company's policy of hedging exchange rates reduced the impact of currency movements, the weak euro was a serious challenge since 80 per cent of sales were still in Europe (including the UK) where Germany was the biggest producer.

The impact was also felt indirectly, as the company's UK-based customers also came under competitive pressure in their own industries. So as UK-based manufacturing industries using steel – particularly the automobile industry – lost out in world markets their need for steel declined. The advent of Japanese transplants in the UK had reversed this trend a little. Another encouraging aspect of the late 1990s was the new willingness – at least in Europe – of national governments to remove their subsidy of state-owned steel firms and to move towards privatisation. Over the previous decade, British Steel had cited this as a major problem – the unwillingness to tackle the excess capacity in Europe.

Against this background British Steel's approach to achieving their globalisation vision was:

- To use a range of different approaches to global development, such as joint ventures (western Europe and USA); overseas transplants (USA, eastern Europe and possibly Asia and South America); and continued exports of high added-value products.
- To continue to achieve efficiency gains and remain one of the most cost-efficient producers globally.
- To target capital investment carefully and to keep a strong balance sheet (good cash management and low gearing) to ride out the fierce cycles in demand.

This globalisation of the company's activities culminated in the merger with Hoogovens in October 1999.

THE 1999 MERGER – CORUS IS BORN

Given the globalisation pressures it was no surprise when in June 1999 British Steel and Hoogovens announced their intention to merge and Corus was born in October of that year. The merger brought together British Steel's £6.3 billion sales and 15 million tonnes output with Hoogoven's £3.2 billion sales and 6.2 million tonnes. Hoogovens also had interests in aluminium production. Both companies were predominantly based in and servicing Europe whilst having holdings elsewhere – particularly in North America. British Steel had 44,200 employees and Hoogovens 22,100. The new company, Corus, was headed by Brian Moffat (from British Steel) as chairman and had joint chief executives (John Bryant from British Steel and Fokko van Duyne from Hoogovens). They explained the reasons for the merger as follows:

> [The merger is] intended to benefit our customers, our employees and our shareholders. **Our customers** are looking for a wider range of products tailored to their needs; they want more service, often with suppliers' teams working alongside them; they want the latest technology; they want more international coverage; and they want different metals for different purposes sometimes in combination with each other . . . Individually we already help [customers] design and optimise the manufacture of their products – such as aeroplanes, cars, engines, buildings, cans and white goods. Now, together, we will provide services and solutions more internationally and over a wider range of metal activities. . . . We believe that for **our employees** and their local communities, this exciting international structure will . . . help us ensure prosperity for our people . . . [and] . . . continue to attract quality people to our industry by offering them challenging and stimulating career opportunities. For **our shareholders** this is a strategy for growth. We will be a financially strong group, with the capacity to achieve synergy benefits from a variety of sources, which we are convinced could not be realised by any other means.

They went on to say that the two companies would be completely integrated at the business unit level. A new group would be created from the merger with a new approach, culture and style. They were not in the business of continuing with British Steel and Hoogovens as separate entities under the Corus umbrella.

A FURTHER DRIVE ON COSTS

Towards the end of the 1990s the management at British Steel, and subsequently Corus, again had to revisit the company's costs as an important response to falling prices and unfavourable exchange rates. They had a three-pronged attack: productivity gains, exploitation of information technology (IT), and significant reduction in costs of supplies.

Productivity gains were not to be of the old style – reductions in blue-collar workers – but to consist of management reductions to achieve overhead ratios more in line with the best in the world. Secondly, a move towards a multi-skilled technician as the model of the shopfloor worker was seen as essential to cost improvement by exploiting IT. Without investments in IT these productivity improvements could not be achieved.

IT was also essential to the third strand of reducing supply costs. Key suppliers were invited to a series of seminars on how they could both reduce prices and improve service. There was a view in the company that too many UK suppliers to major globalising companies such as Corus were shielded from the harsh realities of the global marketplace – such as exchange rate shifts – and needed to bear some of the burden. Brian Moffat felt that the likely outcome of reviewing supply chain management would be a substantial reduction in the number of suppliers as some suppliers reduced prices for guaranteed volumes and long-term contracts.

CRISIS

The combination of industry overcapacity, price pressures and the need to further increase productivity created the crisis of early 2001 at Corus. The signs were building up during 2000 with 4,500 jobs lost in the UK, eventually leading to the resignation of the joint CEOs in December – with Brian Moffat stepping in to run the company himself. Nonetheless, the announcements of 2 February 2001 caused a storm. Everyone had their own opinion on the reasons for the crisis and whom to blame. Press commentary at the time reflected this:

> Where Corus has also suffered is a lack of long term vision. While Arbed and Usinor have organised global alliances that have given them strong positions in developing markets such as Brazil, Corus's operations outside Europe are mainly concentrated on small steel ventures in the US, whose success has been patchy. Analysts also believe that in terms of strategy Corus compares poorly with ThyssenKrupp – which has concentrated most of its activities in high-value sheet steel for the automotive industry where it is regarded as having a technological lead. . . . According to critics the former British Steel missed a trick in the mid-1990's . . . in not using its financial strength to spread its operations globally.
>
> (*Financial Times*, 3 February 2001)

> The appointment of joint Chief Executives did not help . . . the company's command structure was cumbersome and decision-making slow . . . The different corporate culture in the UK and the Netherlands did not help. Unlike Anglo-Saxon companies, where chief executives take decisions and boards have an advisory role, in continental European boards, directors tend to have a greater influence on the day-to-day running of the company.
>
> (*Financial Times*, 3 February 2001)

The government, in the shape of Stephen Byers, trade and industry secretary, accused the company of refusing to engage in dialogue. 'Corus should think again and work with trade unions [and] the government . . . to identify alternatives [to closures].' Unions were appalled at the announcement. John Edmonds, general secretary of the GMB union, said the behaviour of Corus had been 'nothing short of disgusting'. Other union leaders accused the company of short-termism and of betraying the workforce. In sharp contrast, the stock market reacted favourably to the announcement, despite no final dividend payments – the share price rose by 10 per cent. The feeling was that a slimmer Corus would quickly bounce back to profit if it could push through cost reductions without industrial unrest.

Brian Moffat hit back at his critics, saying that the main reason for the cutbacks was Britain's economic climate, which no longer made it an attractive place for manufacturing industry to invest. He said that Britain's absence from the euro had also exacerbated the problems, resulting in a loss of £60 on every tonne of steel exported to Europe. He even went so far as to point out to politicians that Corus was not a nationalised company so there was no reason why he should tell the prime minister the details of his plans. He knew that there was no point in going to the government for money – which the European Union would probably veto anyway. This incensed MPs and their trade and industry committee claimed that the company had no strategy. Some MPs even called for Brian Moffat to be stripped of his knighthood – awarded in 1995 for services to the steel industry.

FINANCIAL GLOOM?

The company's results for the 15 months ending 31 December 2000 were published on 15 March 2001 and confirmed the urgency of the closures. The headline financial figures were depressingly bad – an operating loss of some £1.15 billion on a turnover of £11.7 billion (see Appendix 3). But the majority of this loss was put down to restructuring costs (£1.033 billion – including a write-down of assets of £701 million). In his statement Brian Moffat said:

> The operating loss masks good performances from the group's aluminium and stainless steel activities with profits of £109 million and £150 million respectively . . . The market scene for carbon (bulk) steels was one of over-supply and the resultant reduced prices, although demand remained reasonably buoyant . . . The current year presents some critical challenges for Corus both in terms of restoring the competitiveness of its integrated carbon steel assets in the UK and the Netherlands, and in ensuring it maintains the loyalty of its customer base. Concurrently, we will be focusing on the development and growth of our downstream carbon steel businesses (i.e. distribution and further processing), most of which remain profitable, together with aluminium operations and stainless steel interests. Key market areas will be construction, transportation, engineering, and distribution. Over time, therefore, the growth in our downstream activities will mean that we will become less dependent on our [production of basic steel product].

Indeed the detailed financial results showed that there were marked differences both between different product groups and between territories (see Appendices 4 and 5). Perhaps the future was not as gloomy as many thought – this seemed to be the view of the stock market.

APPENDIX 1 MAJOR STEEL-PRODUCING COUNTRIES BY CRUDE STEEL OUTPUT (MILLION TONNES), 1999

RANK	COUNTRY	PRODUCTION	RANK	COUNTRY	PRODUCTION
1	Mainland China	123.7	14	Taiwan	15.4
2	United States	97.3	15	Mexico	15.3
3	Japan	94.2	16	Spain	14.9
4	Russia	51.5	17	Turkey	14.3
5	Germany	42.1	18	Belgium	10.9
6	Korea	41.0	19	Poland	8.8
7	Ukraine	27.5	20	Australia	8.2
8	Brazil	25.0	21	South Africa	7.3
9	Italy	24.9	22	Netherlands	6.1
10	India	24.3	23	Iran	6.1
11	France	20.2	24	Czech Republic	5.6
12	United Kingdom	16.3	25	Austria	5.2
13	Canada	16.2			

Source: IISI Steel Statistics Yearbook, 2000.

APPENDIX 2 MAJOR STEEL-PRODUCING COMPANIES BY CRUDE STEEL OUTPUT (MILLION TONNES), 1999

	COMPANY	COUNTRY	OUTPUT
1	POSCO	Korea	26.5
2	Nippon Steel	Japan	25.2
3	Arbed	Luxembourg	22.2
4	Usinor	France	22.2
5	Corus	UK/Netherlands	21.3
6	LNM	*See footnote	20.0
7	Baoshan	China	16.7
8	Thyssen/Krupp	Germany	16.1
9	Riva	Italy	14.1
10	NKK	Japan	12.8
11	USX	USA	11.3
12	Kawasaki	Japan	11.1
13	SAIL	India	11.0
14	Nucor	USA	9.4
15	Sumitomo	Japan	9.9
16	China Steel	China	9.3
17	Severstal	Russia	9.0
18	Magnitogorsk	Russia	8.9
19	BHP	Australia	8.5
20	Bethlehem Steel	USA	8.5

* LNM head office is in the UK, its shares are quoted in Amsterdam and New York and its operations are in Kazakhstan, Indonesia, Germany, France, Ireland, Mexico and the USA.

Source: IISI Steel Statistics Yearbook, 2000.

APPENDIX 3 TURNOVER AND PRE-TAX PROFITS (£M)

	REVENUE	PRE-TAX PROFIT(LOSS)
1980/1	2,954	(1,800)
1981/2	3,443	(492)
1982/3	3,231	(866)
1983/4	3,358	(253)
1984/5	3,736	(378)
1985/6	3,735	(42)
1986/7	3,461	177
1987/8	4,116	419
1988/9	4,906	593
1989/90	5,113	733
1990/1	5,000	254
1991/2	4,600	(55)
1992/3	4,300	(149)
1993/4	4,190	80
1994/5	4,780	578
1995/6	7,050*	1,100
1996/7	7,224	451
1997/8	6,947	315
1998/9	6,455	(196)
1999(6 months)[†]	2,790	(189)
1999/00 (15 months)[†]	11,698	(1,152)

* This figure includes about £1,800m as a result of the reincorporation of United Engineering Steels (UES) and 51 per cent ownership of Avesta Sheffield.
[†] Previous years are March–March. Accounting practices at Corus moved to a December year-end. So 1999/00 was reported in two parts: 6 months to end September 1999 and 15 months to end December 2000.

APPENDIX 4 ANALYSIS OF TURNOVER AND OPERATING PROFIT (15 MONTHS ENDING 31 DECEMBER 2000)

	TURNOVER (£MILLION)	OPERATING PROFIT (£MILLION)
A. Segment		
Carbon steels	8,725*	(1,411)
Stainless steels	1,746	150
Aluminium	1,227	109
B. Destination		
UK	3,274	N/A
Europe (excluding UK)	6,018	N/A
North America	1,647	N/A
Other areas	759	N/A
TOTAL GROUP	**11,698**	**(1,152)**

* Includes revenues from distribution, further processing and other activities of £2,156m.
Source: Company preliminary report for the 15 months ending 31 December 2000.

APPENDIX 5 ANALYSIS OF TURNOVER AND SALES VOLUMES BY PRODUCT AND DESTINATION

| | PRODUCT SEGMENT | | | | | |
| | TURNOVER (£MILLION) | | | SALES VOLUME ('000 TONNES) | | |
DESTINATION	CARBON	STAINLESS	ALUMINIUM	CARBON	STAINLESS	ALUMINIUM
UK	2,450	201	123	8,566	150	74
Europe (excluding UK)	2,971	1,138	817	10,878	756	500
North America	863	258	201	2,436	149	87
Other areas	285	149	86	1,181	131	44
GROUP TOTAL	6,569*	1,746	1,227	23,061	1,186	705

* The Carbon figure excludes revenues from distribution, further processing and other activities that were included in Appendix 4.

Source: Company preliminary report for the 15 months ending 31 December 2000.

ASM Lithography

This case study is an article that appeared in the Financial Times *on 18 April 2001 which explains the development and underlying technology of the high-technology company ASM Lithography. It provides an opportunity to consider the strengths, weaknesses, opportunities and threats facing that company as it embarks on a major growth strategy in a competitive and changing high-technology environment.*

• • •

An anonymous-looking set of low-rise buildings outside Eindhoven in the Netherlands represents one of Europe's biggest hopes in high technology. It is the headquarters of ASM Lithography, a company poised, on the back of an agreed takeover of a US rival, to become the world's biggest maker of wafer-steppers, machines that play a vital role in manufacturing microchips.

The go-ahead for ASM's $1.6bn (£1.1bn) takeover of Silicon Valley Group, which is being delayed by a US government inquiry, would continue a success story that has few parallels in Europe, where in the past 25 years companies in electronics-related technologies have generally been outmanoeuvred by competitors from the US and south-east Asia.

WAFER-STEPPER TECHNOLOGY

The mass proliferation of digital devices – from personal notebooks to mobile telephones – is the result of increasingly powerful and cheap silicon chips. Driving on these changes has been the ability of engineers to cram more electronic devices on to a small piece of silicon. The wafer-stepper is the key to this development. Largely because of advances in wafer-steppers, the number of transistor-equivalents that can be squeezed on to a microchip has increased 250,000-fold over the past 30 years, while the price paid by the customer for each bit of information stored on the chip has fallen 30,000-fold (see Exhibit 1). The wafer-stepper takes its name from the step-and-repeat process by which the lens system in the machine shuttles across the surface of a 300mm-diameter wafer. This is how it can expose, with light passed through a photo-mask, each small part of the wafer. In a typical high-speed photo-lithography procedure,

Exhibit 1	How the performance and price of microchips have changed		
YEAR	MINIMUM FEATURE SIZE FOR AN ADVANCED CHIP (MICROMETRES)	PRICE PER BIT OF RANDOM ACCESS MEMORY (1,000TH OF US¢)	BIT CAPACITY FOR RANDOM ACCESS MEMORY
1970	10.00	492	1,000
1980	1.30	15	64,000
1990	0.50	0.48	4m
2000	0.18	0.015	256m
2010 (forecast)	0.05	0.00047	64bn

Source: ASM Lithography.

each wafer (which will later be dissected to give between 100 and 1,000 identical chips, depending on size) stays inside the wafer-stepper for only about half a minute for each process to print a specific layer of circuitry.

In most microcircuits, a wafer will have to return to the machine several times, to print further layers of circuits that are built up on top of the first one. This means that, each time the wafer is inside the machine, it may have to make a slight sideways movement every half a second or so, while the lens system also moves, possibly in a different direction and at a different speed. This translates into an almost unbelievably complicated mechanical problem. The lens system and wafer have to be aligned with a precision of one nanometre and in a fraction of a second, immediately after the wafer has been shifted with a force equivalent to several times gravitational acceleration. The wafer is then flooded with ultraviolet light, before a further step-and-repeat process takes place.

Under ASM Lithography's partnership strategy, it does not tackle all the technology behind this by itself. Devising the precision mechanics of ASM's wafer system is left to one of its four main partners – Philips, the Dutch electrical goods and electronics company that was ASM's original parent and continues to hold a small stake. The sensor and positioning technology (metrology) is the preserve of Agilent, a US instrumentation company, formerly part of the Hewlett-Packard computer company. While the optics in each wafer-stepper is left to Zeiss of Germany, the light sources in ASM's machines come mainly from a fourth partner – Cymer, a US manufacturer of high-frequency lasers that emit light in the ultraviolet range at a wavelength of 248 nanometres.

ASM AND WAFER STEPPERS

Behind ASM's success is the brain-box model: an approach apparent in other areas of high-tech manufacturing. It involves the company maintaining strong links with customers and retaining a crucial role in technology development while leaving to partner businesses much of the manufacturing and design of subcomponents.

Incongruously, an important contributor to ASM making this strategy work in the microelectronics age turns out to be a 155-year-old German business steeped in the mechanical engineering principles of the nineteenth century. Carl Zeiss, a large, privately owned optics group, is the Dutch company's sole supplier of the complex lens systems that are an essential part of its machines and account for about a quarter of its manufactured costs.

Costing up to $10m and weighing about 15 tonnes, wafer-steppers are among the most complicated machines on earth. They use optics, precision engineering and lasers to define with mind-boggling precision the dimensions of integrated circuits. 'Just about everything we do involves technologies at the limits of human capability,' says Doug Dunn, ASM's chief executive.

Worldwide sales of wafer-steppers – also called silicon lithography machines – last year came to nearly $6bn. The machines radiate ultraviolet light through a lens system and photographic mask. The light rays print (using a photo-resist) complicated patterns on to silicon wafers in which the lines are about 0.15 micrometres thick. The lines define the positions of transistors – of which tens of millions, assuming the lithographic patterns are fine enough, can be positioned through manufacturing steps on to a thumb-nail-sized chip. Because the accuracy and operating efficiency of wafer-steppers are vital to microchip production, the companies that make them influence the global $1,500bn-a-year electronics business.

Wafer-stepper manufacture is dominated by four companies, accounting for more than 95 per cent of world sales. With a market share estimated at 34 per cent, ASM is number two behind Nikon of Japan, with 37 per cent. But through the deal announced last October to buy Silicon Valley Group – now in number four position – ASM is due to become the world leader, with a share of more than 40 per cent, roughly twice as much as Canon of Japan. The deal is being delayed by an investigation into whether US national security would be endangered by allowing foreign control of Tinsley, a small subsidiary of Silicon Valley Group. As well as making lenses for lithography applications, Tinsley produces optical systems for surveillance satellites, including those operated by the US Defense Department. The results of the inquiry are expected in late April or early May (2001).

Assuming the deal goes through – and ASM is hopeful, saying it is ready to guarantee to the US government that the availability of Tinsley's technology will not be compromised – ASM hopes it can build on its position to take more than 50 per cent of the world market within a few years.

The company remains confident about the longer-term prospects, in spite of warnings in March that profits would be hit this year by the expected slow-down in investment in the $200bn-a-year microchip industry.

ASM'S DEVELOPMENT

ASM's strong run started only relatively recently. Formed in 1984 as a unit of Philips, the Dutch electronics company, it was spun out as a quoted company in 1995. Since then, revenues have risen fivefold to £2.2bn (£1.35bn) last year – with sales outside the Netherlands accounting for 85 per cent of its revenues. The company has more than doubled its market share in wafer-steppers since the early 1990s, when its US and Japanese competitors were in the ascendancy.

ASM's story underlines that in high technology, early movers do not necessarily end up strongest. Microchip lithography was invented by Perkin-Elmer, a US instrumentation business, which brought out its first machine in 1973. The machines defined lines 4 micrometres thick, making their resolving power roughly one-twenty-fifth of today's systems.

In the mid-1980s, GCA, a US company, was dominant in wafer-steppers, having entered the business in 1976. But both companies lost their lead in the 1990s to Nikon (which introduced its first machine in 1980) and Canon. A key to this was that the Japanese companies offered superior lens systems to the US competitors (both of which later quit the wafer-stepper business). Both Nikon and Canon had in-house optics technologies, developed as a result of their respective backgrounds in cameras and office equipment.

It is in this context that the ASM/Zeiss partnership, which started in the late 1980s, has been vital. The durability of this partnership – and the world-class optics technology that Zeiss provides – has been crucial to ASM's success.

Zeiss, whose centre for semiconductor optics technology is at its headquarters in Oberkochen, a small town near Stuttgart, employs several hundred people who work solely for ASM. They make lens stacks: 1-metre-tall systems of up to 30 lenses, each ground, sometimes with ion beams, to immense accuracy. The lens stacks are at the heart of each wafer-stepper, making sure the radiation is directed on to the wafers with the required precision.

The nature of the link with Zeiss has caused some heart-searching at ASM. Mr Dunn, an Englishman who took the top job at ASM in January 2000 after a career in the electronics industry with Plessey, Motorola and Philips, says it is 'risky' to have just one supplier for such a critical sub-component – 'but we don't have any other choice'.

Such is the rarefied nature of this technology, Mr Dunn explains, that it would be virtually impossible to have a back-up supplier that could provide the same quality as Zeiss. Also, by guaranteeing to Zeiss that it will buy lenses from no one else, ASM has made the importance of the link transparent, which Mr Dunn thinks spurs the German company to greater effort on its behalf. 'We fight a lot but underneath we have a good relationship', he says.

ASM has three other critical partnerships, as a result of which, under its brain-box strategy, it can divert most of its energies into machine development, marketing and building up links with customers, leaving in-depth technical know-how in the area of precision mechanics, metrology and light sources to others.

Of ASM's 4,300 employees (a figure that has increased by 2,000 in the past two years and of which 1,000 are based outside the Netherlands), nearly one in three works in research and development – a field that accounted for 10.8 per cent of sales last year. A similar number is in marketing or customer support, liaising with the big semiconductor companies that are the company's customers. Only about 800 work in manufacturing – and of these only half are traditional manufacturing and assembly workers, with the rest involved in buying subcomponents or organising shipments of finished goods.

ASM'S FUTURE CHALLENGES

Mr Dunn says that one of his biggest challenges is to make sure that the spirit of the company – where the average age is only 32 – is kept at the same high pitch as during these years of rapid high growth.

Meanwhile, he says that – assuming his US deal is approved and he is left, in effect, with just two competitors – he cannot afford to relax. He says: 'Every day when I wake up I am paranoid about what the Japanese are doing.'

The next few years, Mr Dunn intimates, are unlikely to be easy for ASM – even if its record in building up a rare European strength in high technology is second to none.

Ericsson and the creation of the mobile telephony systems business

Patrick Regnér

The case describes the history of the Swedish telecommunications company Ericsson's entry into the mobile telephone systems market. It examines the characteristics of strategic change from a public telecommunication to a mobile telephony focus, and shows how strategic innovation may emerge from the periphery of an organisation. The case describes how a small and insignificant unit in Ericsson turned the company into the world's largest supplier of mobile telephone systems. The focus is therefore on the dynamics of strategy innovation from the beginning of the 1980s to the turn of the century.

· · ·

Ericsson delivered the first commercial mobile telephone system in the world to Saudi Arabia in 1981. The company sold the system despite Saudi Tel, Saudi Arabia's PTT,[1] not specifying it at all in its order of telecommunication networks and equipment. Furthermore, Ericsson did not actually have a mobile phone system to sell or the required products for its infrastructure. This was, however, the first step towards making Ericsson the largest mobile telephony company in the world.

SRA – AN AUTONOMOUS AND SELF-RELIANT COMPANY WITH A VISION

It was a small and autonomous subsidiary of Ericsson, SRA, which insisted on selling a mobile telephone system to Saudi Arabia. SRA led a rather languishing life as a radio communication supplier at the time and, basically, was an independent company. The company's focus had been on radio products for military as well as civilian use (radio receivers, gramophones, TVs, radio systems for aviation and shipping, radar installations, etc.). From the 1960s the company had consolidated into communication and military radio equipment, leaving consumer goods. Its major business was in the military market. SRA's

---

[1]PTT refers to Post, Telephone and Telegraph, which were the traditional government organisations or monopolies responsible for running a country's postal and telecommunications services.

This case was prepared by Patrick Regnér, Stockholm School of Economics. It is intended as a basis for class discussion and not as an illustration of either good or bad management practice. © Peter Regnér, 2001. Not to be reproduced or quoted without permission.

independence from Ericsson was not only due to its small size, unrelated technology and generally microscopic role in Ericsson, but reflected the fact that British GE-Marconi owned 29 per cent of the company at the time.

The president of SRA, Åke Lundqvist, was extremely enthusiastic about mobile telephony. He had joined SRA in the mid-1960s and had been in charge of the land-mobile radio division since 1970. He had been involved in mobile radio and mobile telephony since the end of the 1950s, when he worked for another company. He participated in the development of one of the early Swedish mobile telephone systems, MTB (which could handle only six telephone calls simultaneously in Stockholm). SRA also had a history in the system since they supplied its base stations and telephones.[2] Lundqvist had an early vision of the importance of mobile telephony, a vision 'based on radio technology, to eliminate the wire from the regular telephony'. However, at Ericsson, SRA's vision was laughed at, and the company was considered a 'garage outfit', a 'bicycle repair shop' represented by 'cowboys'. As one manager in Ericsson's largest division, the Public Telecommunications Division put it: 'They were not really a part of us. They looked different and behaved differently.'

ERICSSON – A PUBLIC TELECOMMUNICATIONS COMPANY WITH AXE AS THE FLAGSHIP PRODUCT

The main products of Ericsson had traditionally been switching and transmission equipment. A switch, or telephone exchange, controls and operates telephone calls in a telephone network. In the early days it consisted of a manual system where an operator used pairs of plugs to connect people on a switchboard. All major R&D was invested in switching and Ericsson introduced its digital switching technology, AXE, at an early stage. It became widely known and well respected and contracts all over the world had been signed by 1980. The PTTs had historically been the principal markets for these products. Roughly a dozen telecommunications companies dominated the world market (AT&T, Ericsson, CIT-Alcatel, Fujitsu, Hitachi, ITT, NEC, OKI, Plessey, Siemens, Strowger). They competed for orders from the PTTs where markets were open. The US was still closed and the British PTT bought only from British companies. Similar arrangements prevailed in many other markets. Political considerations often played a larger role than commercial or technological ones. Once a relationship had been built with a PTT, it usually lasted for a very long time, with continuous follow-up contracts, and competition was limited. John Meurling, director of corporate relations and investor relations at Ericsson of the time:

> The vendor–customer relationship could often be described as marriage-like: once a PTT had made its system choice – or often vendor choice, which might go back to

---

[2]A base station is equipped with transmitters and receivers and covers a geographical area or a 'cell' with radio signals connecting to mobile telephones. Base stations are connected to mobile telephone switches, which in turn are linked to the fixed telephony network.

the beginning of the century – the relationship was expected to continue for a long time . . . Not many countries were supplied by one manufacturer only, but very few countries had more than two or three. For most companies it was cozy.[3]

Even if Ericsson had one of the least 'cosy' positions, because the Swedish PTT manufactured most of its own switches, their culture and way of doing business reflected the prevalent stable and semi-competitive environment. However, SRA, although quite remote both in terms of technology and products, had spent its whole 60-year history in a less protected and quite competitive business environment. Most managers at Ericsson did not know much about SRA; it was a minor, independent and pretty unglamorous business. AXE was the flagship of Ericsson and Public Telecommunications was its captain. As John Meurling described it:

> We [Public Telecom] were the biggest, the most important, and the most beautiful part of the Ericsson Group – and we knew it.[4]

THE NORDIC MOBILE TELEPHONE NETWORK

The Swedish and other Nordic PTTs were pivotal in developing and establishing mobile telephony in Sweden and the Nordic countries. They joined forces in order to develop the Nordic Mobile Telephone (NMT) network. Telecommunication equipment manufacturers were asked in 1977 to submit proposals to provide the NMT network. Ericsson and SRA and their competitors – among them NEC, Motorola, Mitsubishi and Fujitsu – were invited to bid. Ericsson, however, was not particularly enthusiastic about mobile phone systems. Its Public Telecommunications unit was not interested in providing switches for mobile systems. They finally offered switches, but it was more in order to preserve old relations with its long-term partner, the Swedish PTT, than enthusiastically to enter a new market. Ericsson did not offer its latest technology (AXE) at first. An adjusted AXE switch for mobile telecommunication was simply seen to have a limited future. The company, however, subsequently did offer AXE at the insistence of the Swedish PTT, which indicated that otherwise it might adopt the technology of NEC, the closest contestant.

Ericsson's lack of enthusiasm for mobile phone systems reflected its very small role compared with its other businesses and a belief that mobile telephony would continue to be of minor importance. Mobile telephony was seen as something more exclusive and directed towards professional use. Personal application was something not very serious – a service for the privileged. Ericsson was far from alone in its assessment of a limited mobile phone market. For example, the NMT network was initially thought to be complementary to manual mobile telephone systems. Bell Labs at AT&T, which originally

---

[3]Meurling, J. and Jeans, R. (1995) *A Switch in Time: AXE – Creating the Foundation for the Information Age*, London: Communications Week International.
[4]Meurling, J. and Jeans, R. (1994) *The Mobile Phone Book: The Innovation of the Mobile Phone Industry*, London: Communications Week International.

invented mobile telephone networks, hired a major US management consultancy firm to study mobile telephony and its market potential around this time. The firm concluded that the potential was insignificant and firmly advised against involvement in mobile telephony. Another reason for Ericsson's resistance was that in radio the company's involvement was in closed radio systems and it was questionable whether SRA had the right competences for mobile telephony. In fact, the rest of Ericsson did not think much of the SRA personnel. As one SRA manager of the time explained: 'We were considered as lacking in knowledge, stupid and inexperienced.'

At SRA, enthusiasm for the NMT venture was greater and they did have some radio technology competences. However, their mobile systems competences were limited. SRA did not yet have its own base stations, a central part of a mobile system. At first SRA was more focused on the mobile telephone itself than on the entire mobile system, but its technology in that area was inferior as well. SRA had succeeded in developing a mobile telephone, but it was not the latest technology. Instead, one of SRA's main resources at this time was its entrepreneurial spirit and, perhaps, insight compared with the rest of Ericsson and competitors. As Åke Lundqvist put it: 'We had a vision to eliminate the wire in telephony, everybody laughed at us!'

THE FIRST COMMERCIAL CELLULAR MOBILE SYSTEM IN THE WORLD

In the end, Ericsson got the order to deliver switches for the NMT network in the Nordic countries and SRA became a sub-supplier of a base station control unit for Magnetic, a local Swedish radio technology firm. SRA also supplied mobile telephones or stations for the system.[5] Since SRA needed competence in this area they acquired Sonab in 1978, a rival in radio technology and the leader in mobile stations in Sweden at that time. That company had a land mobile terminal that was upgraded to a mobile telephone. Despite winning the NMT order there was still limited interest in mobile telephone systems at Ericsson and consequently little integration of Ericsson's and SRA's products, mobile telephone switches and radio equipment, respectively.

The first commercial mobile telephony system in the world was delivered in 1981, not to the Nordic countries, but to Saudi Arabia. The NMT in the Nordic countries was not in operation until a couple of months after the Saudi première. In the late 1970s Ericsson won a major order to supply Saudi Arabia with a fixed telecommunication infrastructure. Åke Lundqvist enthusiastically took the initiative on a mobile telephony system in Saudi Arabia. Lundqvist suggested to Ericsson's CEO, Björn Lundvall: 'Can't we try to sell a mobile telephone system to Saudi Arabia? They want the latest of everything else.' Lundqvist managed to convince both the CEO and the head of Ericsson's Public

---

[5]The correct terminology here is mobile stations or terminals. At this time these were based on land-mobile products and were large and heavy units to be installed in vehicles.

Telecommunications Switching Division, Håkan Ledin, to offer the Saudis a mobile telephone system. They were prepared to go along with Lundqvist's ideas; after all, any mobile phone deal would only be small compared with the fixed network that represented the main order. Ledin actually believed a system already existed. However, SRA and Ericsson did not have a complete system at that time; even some of the core products did not exist.

The first cellular mobile systems were not without problems. The Saudi order included 8,000 mobile stations, which put pressure on production sources – there were no terminals left to sell in the Nordic home market. Competitors naturally exploited the situation. Furthermore, there were important quality problems. Among other things, the telephone station keypads melted in the hot Saudi sun, and the armour-plated limousines and cars caused installation problems. In addition, as SRA tried to get its first generation of mobile phones into production on the Nordic market, the competitors were bringing out their second generation. Flemming Örneholm, SRA's Marketing Manager at the time, referred to the situation as a disaster:

> It was a mess . . . Quality was certainly not up to expectations . . . The competitors were beating the hell out of Ericsson [SRA].[6]

TRYING TO SELL INTEGRATED MOBILE TELEPHONY SYSTEMS

At the end of the 1970s and beginning of 1980s more PTTs started to show an interest in mobile telephony. SRA began to see a sizable potential market and started to penetrate more markets, 'shooting at everything they saw' as one manager put it. They wanted to provide a more co-ordinated and integrated mobile telephony *system* of Ericsson's switches and their own radio equipment to the operators. However, the initial orders were small, and the contracts were of modest size from the viewpoint of Ericsson's corporate management and switching division. Switching merely regarded mobile telephony as another way among many others to sell switches. Attempting to exploit mobile telephony applications was more trouble than it was worth and it was out of the question that SRA, with not quite 4 per cent of total sales, would be in charge of Ericsson's flagship product AXE for mobile systems. Furthermore, it was far from obvious that mobile telephony was a promising future market. There were no indications in terms of market investigations or any other indicators and few thought that mobile telephony would grow into a mass market. Forecasts continuously underestimated the number of subscribers during the 1980s. Mobile phone network operators, governmental bodies, mobile phone infrastructure providers and mobile phone manufacturers all underestimated the tremendous growth of mobile telephony. During these early years of mobile phone networks, Ericsson and SRA continued to

---

[6]Meurling, J. and Jeans, R. (1997) *The Ugly Duckling: Mobile phones from Ericsson – putting people on speaking terms.* Stockholm: Ericsson Mobile Communications AB.

submit separate offers. And the different views on mobile system integration resulted in increased tension between the two units. However, even if there was no coherent arrangement for mobile phone systems, SRA were finally given at least the marketing responsibility for them.

A CONTRACT IN THE NETHERLANDS

SRA continued to fight dual battles for a more complete system concept, both internally, versus the Switching Division and corporate management, and in the market. This was apparent in the Netherlands, where both the Dutch PTT and Ericsson's corporate management and Switching Division had to be convinced of the advantage of the integrated system idea. From Ericsson there were separate offers as usual; the Switching Division offered switches, and SRA offered radiotechnology. The PTT wanted Ericsson's AXE switch since it had a high capacity. However, Motorola was involved in the discussion as well and suggested a combination of AXE switches and its own base stations. The Dutch PTT supported this concept. So did Ericsson at first. The arrangement could eventually lead to further AXE orders to be filled jointly with Motorola. However, Åke Lundqvist strongly disapproved. He argued that Ericsson should be a provider of integrated systems in mobile telephony, and should furnish the whole package - switches and base stations - or nothing. Lundqvist's position brought matters to a head, causing considerable distress among managers at Switching. Ericsson would risk losing the entire order and would actually be declining an opportunity to sell its principal product. This was particularly frustrating since SRA were not ready either in terms of products - their base station was not fully developed - or in terms of competence. Since Switching also supplied switches to the PTT's fixed network, relations with this customer had to be handled with care. As one manager of the time explained:

> That is a thriller, it was terrible . . . They were absolutely lost . . . They did not really understand, they made base stations and there was not much to it . . . I wondered: Can this be true?[7]

The Netherlands PTT and Motorola considered that agreement had been reached on the arrangement, which would include Motorola's base stations and Ericsson's switch. However, Lundqvist did not give up, but tried to convince the parties involved. He managed to obtain the passive approval of Ericsson's new CEO, Björn Svedberg, and consent from some Switching managers. All in all, it was not a major AXE order; and they were more concerned with the relationship with the Dutch PTT because of the supply of AXE to their fixed network which, naturally, was larger. Prompted by Motorola, the PTT now required a 'small-cell concept' (a technology where the cells - the

---

[7]McKelvey, M., Texier, F. and Alm, H. (1997) *The Dynamics of High Tech Industry: Swedish Firms Developing Mobile Telecommunication System*, Working Paper No. 187, November, Linköping University.

geographical area covered by a base station – are particularly small) to suit the topography and the density of population in the Netherlands. SRA lacked knowledge in the small-cell technology required. Nevertheless, Lundqvist continued to fight. He happened to know, and managed to recruit, one of the best US consultants in the area, Chan Rypinski. SRA and Lundqvist were playing a tough game with high stakes. First, he obtained partial consent from the CEO. Second, the Switching Division was convinced. The PTT's purchasing department, however, showed no interest in the proposal. Unconventional methods were required. When the PTT did not listen, Lundqvist became furious: he recalled: 'This was the only time I ever slammed my fist on the table while arguing with a customer.' With SRA playing the leading role, they and Ericsson finally managed to win the contract, which included a complete system of switches, base stations and cell planning services (the design and planning of the number of cells, base stations, etc.), but it was a hard sell to the PTT. Thus, SRA and Ericsson had begun to sell a more integrated system and not only separate parts of mobile telephony.

Later SRA thought that the integration had to be complete and that it had to be finally decided whether Public Telecommunications (including switching) should invest in mobile telephony or if this mission should be left to SRA alone. The discussions were heated. Although the Switching Division still saw only a limited future for AXE in mobile telephone networks, after much pressure and debate corporate management finally gave SRA the business and responsibility for the system as a whole, including base stations, switches and cell planning services. As one executive recalled: 'The reason was not lack of competence. They [Switching] simply did not believe in this.' The drive from SRA to co-ordinate proposals into a package deal and integrate the whole business had paid off. SRA and mobile telephony were now at least and at last 'an accepted, but not acceptable activity', as one SRA manager put it. However, the Switching Division was to be in charge of and manufacture the switches and sell them to SRA. While mobile telephony now was central to SRA, it was still a peripheral and negligible business for the rest of Ericsson. The entire Radio Communications business area, of which SRA was part, only accounted for 5 per cent of Ericsson's sales in 1982 and mobile telephony was only a small part of that.

ENTERING THE US

In 1983 Åke Lundqvist predicted that 'by the turn of the century, sales in Ericsson's mobile telephone business would pass those in public telecom'. John Meurling, director of corporate relations and investor relations at Ericsson of the time, replied: 'God help us, that's ridiculous!' Corporate management had their strategic focus on something completely different: information systems, the merger between computer and telecommunication technology, was the wave of the future. Ericsson was to participate in this vision in order to create the 'paperless office'. The company made a bold strategic change, forming an entirely new business area, Ericsson Information Systems (EIS), including four new divisions.[8] Beginning in 1981, EIS received considerable attention, resources, capital and manpower. Two main acquisitions were made to obtain the new technologies needed.

SRA continued its aggressive and ambitious ways of doing business. In order to acquire knowledge in mobile telephony, SRA had an active policy: 'We had a well-developed buying approach, we bought firms or consultancy services' (Åke Lundqvist). Through the consultant in the Netherlands case, Åke Lundqvist happened to meet another US-based consultant, Jan Jubon, who urged SRA to enter the US. Lundqvist was interested, and the consultant was hired to submit a market report. The SRA management made a decision to enter. The entry was initially a trial and error expedition. SRA thought the risks were reasonable in order to make a try. The organisation set up was small, in temporary offices and with staff commuting to the US. Its job was to get acquainted with the operators and present products and services. Lundqvist regarded the pioneers in the US venture as heroes:

> There were two or three persons in the US, making calls for hours. They made a superhuman accomplishment. EIS (Ericsson Information Systems) did the opposite, they had hundreds of salesmen.

SRA's US mobile system was marketed to various potential operators applying for licences to the Federal Communications Commission (FCC), the federal government body regulating public communication systems in the US. In 1982 it became clear that the SRA system had been used and specified in 30 per cent of the applications to FCC. This news did not mean that any contracts were assured, but it was positive, and somewhat surprising. The main competitors in the US market were Motorola, together with Northern Telecom, EF Johnsson, Harris Corporation and NEC. In fact, SRA and Ericsson were not awarded any contracts at first, but in May 1983 they obtained their first order for a mobile telephony network system in Buffalo in competition with Motorola and NEC. Later the same year, another important contract was won in Chicago. Subsequently the US organisation was strengthened in order to fulfil all requirements regarding planning, installation and testing. More contracts followed in other parts of the US. SRA competitors now had to take them seriously, but their market position was far from well established. Soon competitors were offering creative financing solutions, a challenge to SRA since the risks involved were high and financing was not one of the company' strengths. While this problem held SRA back at first, later a 'pay as you grow' strategy was implemented in which the operator repaid his loans as he obtained more subscribers.

SRA also experimented with various methods in order to gain contracts and they took considerable risks. In the competitive fight, Lundqvist brought up the idea of taking responsibility for filling the stock of subscribers, if the operators had not filled it themselves within a certain timeframe. It was initially quite successful, but some argued that in the end a large sum of money was

---

[8]EIS initially had four divisions: Communication Systems (business switch from Ericsson, MD 100, and network communications), Business Systems (bank terminals and mini computers), Alfaskop Terminals (computer terminals) and General Terminals (voice, text and computer systems).

almost lost. Besides entering into risky market ventures, daring actions were undertaken internally as well. When SRA entered the US they did not have the products. They developed a base station based on their prior knowledge in radio technology for the military. Åke Lundqvist recalls: 'Normally it takes 3–4 years to develop a base station. We took one that we used for military purposes; but we managed it; it had a good technical performance.' Furthermore, since the AXE switch seemed too large, especially for small networks in the US, where competitors such as Motorola and AT&T had smaller and cheaper ones, they carefully thought about building their own switch. AXE was considered too costly anyway and the trouble with the switching division could be put aside if they had their own switch. SRA had product plans, even brochures, and developed prototype versions of switches. However, these plans had to be abandoned. Another undertaking was to go for mobile telephones. It was an area where SRA had started out, but where they did not have any large market shares and did not have any products at all to offer the US market. Motorola marketed mobile phones in the markets that were up for mobile system bids and had swung decisions its way. SRA set up a new research laboratory and tried to increase sales of mobile telephones. However, the business was quite small and unprofitable through the whole decade.

Because Marconi was owned by one of Ericsson's competitors in switching (GE), Ericsson bought Marconi's interest in SRA at the turn of 1982/83. However, they still did not pay much attention to SRA: they kept their focus on EIS. However, SRA became a wholly owned company under the name of Ericsson Radio Systems AB (Inc.). ERA became part of Radio Communications, one of seven business areas that were created.

CONTINUED INTERNATIONAL EXPANSION – NEW MARKETS AND NEW STANDARDS

An opportunity in the UK appeared at the same time as the US venture. Massive resources were required in the US. An additional attempt in another market where Ericsson had limited and mostly unpleasant experience would put even more pressure on the organisation, but they entered anyway. As one ERA manager of the time explained: 'We had to choose between the US and UK markets, we decided to take them both on.' This step was a bold venture by ERA as it involved expansion from a small sales organisation to a large manufacturing and R&D company in the UK. In addition, it meant working with a new mobile telephony standard, TACS (Total Access Communications System). In 1983 Vodafone, one of two British operators, chose ERA as infrastructure supplier. The company won the contract in competition with AT&T and Motorola and it was fulfilled in 1985. As ERA entered more and more markets in Europe and North America, the company faced an increasingly complicated environment, including various uncertainties about technologies and standards, and deregulated markets involving more and more multifaceted customers. The market potential was highly unpredictable and competition intensified. ERA encountered this complexity with a business and action-oriented culture, as one ERA manager of the time explained:

> We were independent entrepreneurs . . . hunting mobile telephone technology . . .
> fighting over markets . . . and firing at everything we saw.

The Nordic PTTs decided to upgrade the NMT system in 1983. ERA, which still lacked complete base station technology and products at this time, bought the Swedish radio technology company Magnetic the same year. The two companies received orders for base stations in Sweden. A strong competitor was Radiosystem, a spin-off from Magnetic. The new NMT system was opened in August 1986. Meanwhile expansion continued into other markets. ERA was successful in Canada in 1984 and additional contracts were won in Houston and major cities in Ohio the same year and in California in 1985/86. In 1987, ERA won a prestigious contract for a network infrastructure in New York City. By now ERA had definitely established itself as a serious competitor in North America. They were also able to enter markets in the Far East – Thailand and Indonesia – and also Australia in 1985. With the mobile telephony vision as a foundation, ERA aimed at gradually moving into different technologies, standards and markets in order to 'obtain as many customers as possible and then deliver', as one ERA manager put it. When they entered the Far East they had a proactive approach, according to another ERA manager:

> Often the Asian ministries answered that they did not have 450 MHz available [the required radio frequency for ERA's system]. Our people became acquainted with these engineers and located opportunities in their frequency plans. We were very proactive.

The entrepreneurial and independent culture of ERA caused frequent friction with the more methodical and bureaucratically oriented corporate management and switching division in the Public Telecommunications business area. 'It was two completely different worlds. Ericsson was ignorant, there was animosity and competition', explained an Ericsson manager of the time. Despite their market success and growth, ERA was still regarded as a minor business and was treated accordingly by corporate management and, in particular, by managers in Switching, who 'considered us as something the cat dragged in', as one ERA manager put it. From corporate management's point of view ERA was not considered to have a strategy. The CEO of Ericsson criticised ERA's strategy for being 'completely absent'. One ERA manager of the time argued that there even seemed to be talks about getting rid of ERA altogether: 'It was most probably discussed . . . I am sure someone tried to strangle us.'

Corporate management had to keep their focus on the information systems venture (EIS), but now for reasons other than expansion. The new division, EIS, had expanded rapidly and met its goals in terms of company growth to 31 per cent of total sales in 1985, but the market growth predictions faltered immensely and so did profit expectations, and it reported a loss of SEK 806m (roughly $100m). The unit had to be fundamentally restructured, but it took several years to repair the damage. Understandably, this process required considerable attention from top management. Meanwhile, ERA and mobile telephony had been largely left aside, and when they were bothered, Åke Lundqvist, president of SRA, fought the botherers off. As one ERA manager recalls: 'He kept corporate management away when they troubled us.'

RECOGNITION AND SUCCESS OF MOBILE TELEPHONY

In 1986 Lars Ramqvist, former president of the Components business area, became one of three vice-presidents, and part of the Ericsson Corporate Executive Committee. He was assigned to examine Ericssons's corporate strategy. Ramqvist identified several core businesses. Among them all, mobile telephony was included, although the AXE switching system was clearly still the central product. As John Meurling put it:

> For the first time cellular [mobile telephony] was seen as a legitimate, worthwhile, even important, part of Ericsson's business. However, there was a great deal of lack of understanding and distrust left, even if more people saw its importance. They said 'those damn cowboys' and at ERA they said 'those damn bureaucrats'.

In 1988 ERA succeeded in their long-term internal battle and the mobile telephony business was almost fully integrated. Sales in the area had increased substantially and market growth continued to increase as well. ERA was given responsibility for the entire mobile telephone system, including switches. Nevertheless, the Switch Division within the Public Telecommunications business area controlled the research and development of digital switching. Other technological and development responsibilities for mobile system switches were shifted to ERA. Controversies continued between parts of the switch division and ERA, but more people now seemed to realise the impact of ERA and mobile telephony. The same year the Swedish base station company Radiosystem was acquired. It increased ERA's market share in base stations considerably and together with strong market growth ERA gained almost 40 per cent share of the world market for mobile telephony systems. Also in the same year Åke Lundqvist, who was considered 'too wild and unstructured' by corporate management and whose ERA still ran into conflicts with the rest of the organisation, resigned. Lars Ramqvist became the president of ERA. He came from the four-man Corporate Executive Management team and the change indicated the increased importance of ERA in Ericsson. In addition, more structure and order in the organisation followed. As explained by one ERA manager:

> When Ramqvist arrived we got more freedom. There was a reorganisation and some people disappeared then. But it is unclear if it was a strategic undertaking even at that time.

An obvious problem with various national analogue mobile telephone networks (NMT, TACS, etc.) was that terminals or telephones could not be used across borders. The standardisation organisation of western Europe's PTTs had appointed a group, GSM (Groupe Spéciale Mobile), to work on a new common standard for mobile telephony in 1982. Ericsson had a strong position in the negotiations with its involvement in both NMT and TACS. A Nordic solution, close to the system on which ERA had been working, won in a referendum among the European countries in 1987. The German and French telecommunication companies were clearly behind. Ericsson first obtained contracts in Germany, Sweden, Norway and Finland. By 1990 Ericsson had contracts with ten out of the 18 European GSM countries. Besides digital GSM, in which sales were increasing, analogue systems continued to be sold worldwide, in Mexico, eastern Europe, China, etc. Radio Communications sales, including ERA, increased by almost 70 per cent between 1988 and 1989; that year it accounted for 20 per cent of total Ericsson sales. It was a business to be taken seriously and more and more people did so, including corporate management. Lars Ramqvist was appointed new CEO of Ericsson in 1990. Kurt Hellström became the president of ERA. Some animosity continued between Radio and Switching, but it diminished after the entire responsibility for mobile telephony, including all switching development, including digital GSM, was transferred to Radio Communications and ERA in 1992. The two following years showed immense and sustained growth. 1993 was a turning point, since Radio Communications passed Public Telecommunication in sales with 40 per cent of total sales, compared with 32 per cent for PT. Mobile telephony alone (apart from other product areas in Radio Communications) had achieved sales equal to the total for Public Telecommunication, 32 per cent. Now there was no doubt that mobile telephone systems were a strategic and important part of Ericsson, as their 1994 annual report stated:

> Ericsson's success in mobile telephony is based on the very farsighted and advanced development work in the field of radio that was begun at an early stage within Ericsson Radio Systems [ERA].

Sales successes and expansion continued as ERA continued to enter into all standards as new digital ones were launched. Ericsson enjoyed repeated success when the digital standard in the US was adopted (Digital AMPS – Advanced Mobile Phone System). With digital mobile telephony in the US, Ericsson managed to increase its market share there considerably. The company also had similar successes in another digital system, the Personal Communication System (PCS), in the US. Moreover, Ericsson became a competitor in the segment based on the Japanese digital standard, Pacific Digital Cellular (PDC). In general the Asian markets expanded rapidly for Ericsson during the end of the 1990s, especially Japan and China. Other Asian markets included the Philippines, India, Indonesia, Taiwan and Korea. By 1994, Radio Communication, including ERA, accounted for more than 50 per cent of Ericsson's sales and almost 30 per cent of its workforce. Radio Communications was the main product area and mobile telephone systems was its flagship. Later, mobile telephones and terminals were to be another flagship. The tremendous growth of Mobile Systems continued and in 1997 total mobile telephony sales had reached 70 per cent of the corporate total, and the number of employees had almost quadrupled since 1992. The same year the Radio Communication business area was divided into two new business areas: Mobile Systems, including mobile system infrastructure equipment, and Mobile Phones and Terminals, with 44 and 26 per cent of total sales, respectively. Sales increased by another 10 per cent in 1998 to more than twice as much as four years earlier. The introduction to the strategy section, 'The new world of Telecom', in the 1998 annual report illustrates the importance of mobile telephony:

> Ericsson is a world leader in mobile telephony. The corporation is the largest supplier of mobile systems, with ca. 30 per cent of the world market, in dollars. The

corporation is also among the largest on the market for digital mobile telephones and public switches.

By the turn of the century Ericsson was completely dominated by the mobile telephony business. Meanwhile the Public Telecommunication business area, renamed Infocom, went through a restructuring process and some sections were outsourced and sold.

EPILOGUE

By 2001, after years of success, Ericsson was experiencing major difficulties. The *Financial Times* (29 May 2001)[9] reported:

> The group's handset business is in crisis and its infrastructure arm is being battered by global economic slowdown . . . .
>
> To be sure, Ericsson is not the only telecoms group to be hit by global slowdown and a difficult transition to third-generation (3G) mobile telephony. But its problems are not just of the market's making – and they are big enough to risk permanently damaging the group's competitive position . . . .
>
> As recently as five years ago, Ericsson's handsets business was almost neck-and-neck with Finland's Nokia, and was the world's leading supplier of digital cellular phones. By last year, it was making bigger losses than any other company in the hand-sets business – a total of SKr24bn ($2.28bn), SKr553 on each phone sold. Its market share in the first quarter of this year was a mere 7 per cent, while Nokia's had soared to nearly 40 per cent.
>
> Mr Hellström accepts that mistakes were made. The group was late to launch several new models and failed to anticipate the market shift from high-tech phones – Ericsson's speciality – to cheaper, entry-level models. 'We had the wrong profile in our portfolio,' he says.
>
> Other commentators are more critical. They say Ericsson's phones have been well engineered – indeed, over-engineered – while failing on basics such as design, usability and battery-life.
>
> 'They are simply not a consumer products company. They are a bunch of engineers who couldn't care less what the phone looks like,' says one banker.

Other sources

Ericsson Annual Reports 1978–1998.

Mölleryd, B. (1999) 'Entrepreneurship in Technological Systems – The development of mobile telephony in Sweden', Dissertation, EFI, Stockholm School of Economics.

Regnér, P. (1999) *Strategy Creation and Change in Complexity – Adaptive and creative learning dynamics in the firm.* Published doctoral dissertation. Stockholm: Institute of International Business, Stockholm School of Economics.

---

[9]Adapted from 'First aid rushed in as Ericsson bleeds', *Financial Times*, 29 May 2001, by Christopher Borwn-Humes.

Building excellence at STMicroelectronics

John Oakland

The case study presents an opportunity to examine the approaches to strategy development and business excellence used by a leading company in one of Europe's most interesting industries – semiconductors. It is an industry at the centre of recent technological advances, which have driven great changes in the lives of almost everyone in the developed world. Most readers will have some personal experience of the use of the end products from this industry.

The case examines the reasons for, and experiences with, the take-up of total quality management and business excellence as a key part of the company's strategy process in a highly competitive industry.

• • •

COMPANY BACKGROUND

STMicroelectronics (ST – formerly SGS-Thomson Microelectronics) is a global, independent semiconductor company which designs, develops, manufactures and markets a broad range of integrated circuits and discrete devices for a wide variety of microelectronic applications, including telecommunications and computer systems, consumer equipment, automotive products, industrial automation and control systems. This Franco-Italian group is Europe's largest 'chip' maker with a market value of €43.6bn ($40bn) at the beginning of 2001. It was formed in 1987 by the merger of Thomson Semiconducteur and SGS Microellecttronica.

The semiconductor industry has over 300 suppliers competing for market share through product innovation, excellence of execution and lowest operating costs. Its customers expect price reductions on an ongoing basis, as they are also operating in fiercely competitive global markets.

ST's revenues grew 50 per cent in the last quarter of 2000 and it was the only large chip maker to 'match expectations'. It is now in a better position than most of its competitors to protect its margins, with a superior product and geographical mix, and an excellent base of long-term contracts.

It has not always been thus. In the very early 1990s SGS-Thomson was a second-rank player. In order to fully appreciate the achievement of the company in the ten years or so since then, it is first necessary to consider some of the dynamics of the semiconductor industry, since these shaped ST's programme of change. Microelectronics is one of the most competitive industries in the world, with over 100 of the merchant suppliers being global players, servicing a market of more than $150bn that has long-term CAGR of about 16 per cent. Only three European companies are left in the top 20 worldwide ranking.

The economic law of microelectronics is 'when the demand goes up – prices fall; when the demand goes down – prices fall'. Technological advance is very rapid, capital intensity is high. Spending on R&D runs at about 14–16 per cent of sales, two to four times higher than most other industries. Every dollar of incremental sales requires a dollar of incremental investment, with the investment usually one year ahead of the sales.

In this environment companies tend to polarise into two groups, the broad line, global companies with market shares in the range of 4–7 per cent, and narrow niche companies with market shares of less than 1 per cent. A notable exception to this group structure is, of course, Intel, which has a narrow product base but a high market share.

In 1987 the two founder companies of ST saw themselves in a difficult position, since neither were large enough to become truly global world-class players and yet both had a reasonably broad product and technology base. The decision was taken, therefore, to merge the two bodies into one, creating a company which, in 1987, had sales of $851m, a headcount of 17,300 people and a loss after tax of $203m.

Whilst this achieved a critical mass, the company was a weak, loss-making semiconductor company ranked 15th in the world. The financial results were not encouraging and much work was clearly needed to transform the company into the organisation which was the vision of the senior management team. The first years of the programme were devoted to rationalisation and consolidation. At the same time, however, advantage was taken of the complementarity of the product and technology portfolios, customers, market strengths and production capacities. Attention was focused on eliminating the weaknesses and exploiting the strengths. Two of the early key goals were defined as being a rapid increase in sales and market share, together with a slimming down of production sites and the number of employees.

Unfortunately, as the programme developed, the market suddenly hit one of the down cycles which the industry experiences periodically and, in 1990, the improvements in financial results halted and, in fact, worsened and the company found itself back in the red. Immediately, the 'traditional' management action process was brought into play. There was a rapid 'downsizing' programme which hit people, the product portfolio and, ultimately, market share. By examining this process in action, both within ST and in other companies, the realisation rapidly dawned of the danger of it developing into a 'vicious circle'.

This brought about a review of the focus of the company and the determination to find a new way of proceeding, which would give rise to a 'virtuous spiral'. The severity of the market downturn and the highly competitive nature of the market led the CEO to believe that, if the company was to survive and compete effectively, there needed to be a radical rethink about how the company was managed. At this time the company was seriously thinking about total quality management (TQM) and the CEO and other general managers were seeing these principles as a way in which the company could be managed into the future.

TOTAL QUALITY MANAGEMENT AND BUSINESS EXCELLENCE IN ST

Against the backdrop of a downturn in a highly competitive market, and the need to improve quality and consistency of product, there was the need to get managers within the company thinking and behaving differently. Hence, it was decided in 1991 that the principles of TQM would be used as a basis for managing the company, and it should become a champion of the TQM culture.

During the early 1990s it also became clear to SGS that, whilst technological innovation was vital to future success, it was insufficient on its own. The company had to find a way to enable its customers to gain access to the innovations and be supported and satisfied in that process. The adoption of TQM was the chosen route to becoming more customer oriented, whilst retaining technological excellence, and in 1991 SGS launched an initiative based on the European Foundation for Quality Management (EFQM) model for TQM.

For more than twenty years, organisations like SGS in the UK, Europe and beyond had come under increasing pressure to improve their business performance, measure themselves against world-class standards and focus their efforts on the customer. To assist this process, many companies, especially those in the so-called 'high-tech' industries, were adopting various 'new' approaches or philosophies, including total quality management and business process re-engineering (BPR). The most advanced organisations, in this respect, were turning to frameworks or models such as the US Malcolm Baldrige National Quality Award (MBNQA) or the EFQM's TQM or 'Business Excellence' Model (BEM) – promoted in the UK by the British Quality Foundation (Exhibit 1).

The BEM, as it was in the early 1990s, illustrated the key business areas – the 'enablers' and the 'results' – typically addressed by organisations striving for superior business performance. This particular model included nine main categories, such as *customer satisfaction*, *people satisfaction* and *impact on society*, achieved through *leadership* driving *policy and strategy*, *people management*, *resources* and *processes*, leading ultimately to excellence in *business results* – both financial and non-financial. Financial measures included profit, sales, cash flow, working capital, liquidity; non-financial targets included reduction of non-quality costs, service level achievements, market share, product delivery time, batch processing time and inventory turnover time. Self-assessment to the BEM involves an organisation, such as ST, in the regular and systematic review of its enablers and results, allowing the identification of strengths and areas for improvement.

Various awards have been set up to encourage adoption of TQM/Business Excellence principles and these provide a platform for measurement or self-assessment against world-class standards. The MBNQA was launched in 1987,

Exhibit 1   The EFQM/BQF Business Excellence Model

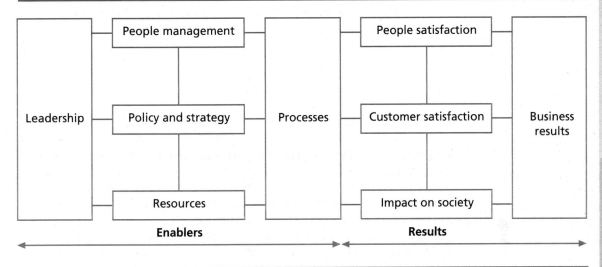

the European Quality Award was first awarded in 1992 and the UK Quality Award established in 1994. (STMicroelectronics was subsequently winner of the European Quality Award in 1997.) Guidelines exist for the implementation of business excellence and self-assessment – available from the EFQM or BQF, as are details of the revised and improved model, now known as the 'Excellence Model'.

In SGS a process of workshops and discussion groups were held throughout 1992 and, by the end of that year, it was believed that all managers were on board with Business Excellence principles. In launching this programme, there was total commitment from the CEO and all his executive staff. In fact in December 1991 Pasquale Pistorio (still the CEO in 2001) stated that: 'TQM is a mandatory way of life in the corporation. SGS-Thomson will become a champion of this culture in the Western world.' These words needed to be backed by action and resource – both financial and people. Very quickly there was a framework put in place, based on an analysis which determined that the key components of successful change implementation should be:

● Organisation
● Common framework
● Local initiatives
● Culture
● Mechanisms
● Policy deployment

Also, the 'programme' needed to be driven from the top down, not by dictate, but by example.

Exhibit 2	STMicroelectronics shared values

Mission

We are fortunate to work in a unique and vital industry. All recent and future advances in commerce, industry, science, medicine and entertainment depend, in the final analysis, on semiconductor micro-electronic circuits and components.

No advanced electronics industry can ensure its economic independence without secure access to microelectronics components and technology.

Our mission is to offer strategic independence to our partners worldwide, as a profitable and viable broad range semiconductor supplier.

Objectives

Growth: we will grow faster than our competitors, with a target of 5 per cent market share. The key to profitable growth is Total Customer Satisfaction, which is our corporate priority Number 1.

Financial: we will generate shareholder value, and return on equity better than the average of the Top Ten semiconductor suppliers.

Social: we will contribute to the well-being of our people and of every community in which we operate with particular emphasis on environmental responsibility and sustainable development.

Strategies

The following strategies provide a decision-making framework to focus our priorities in every aspect of our company's activities.

1. *Manufacturing:* to be recognised as a world-class manufacturer in the three major parameters of our activity: Quality, Service and Cost.
2. *Globalisation:* to have an integrated presence (Development, Manufacturing and Marketing) in each major macroeconomic system of the world.
3. *Innovation:* to sustain a high rate of innovation in products, processes and manufacturing capabilities, as the main fuel for our growth, supported by R&D expenditures higher and more effective than the industry average. Our innovation process will be driven by the market, through our strategic alliances with key partners. We will encourage innovation in all ways, including management methods, and we will welcome new and challenging ideas.
4. *Strategic alliances:* to form relationships with key world customers, assuring them strategic access to our technology as well as to our manufacturing capabilities, and assuring us the vital access to their market and system know-how; legally share resources and know-how with suppliers, other semiconductor manufacturers, universities and technical institutions when there is a mutual advantage to do so.
5. *Product portfolio:* to be a broad range supplier, but with different product goals.
   (a) World leadership:
       - System-on-chip;
       - Non-volatile memories;
       - Power discretes and ICs.
   (b) Among the Top Five:
       - Microcontrollers;
       - Standard linear ICs.
   (c) Profitable participation:
       - all other products provided they generate a positive cash-flow.

Exhibit 2	*Continued*

6. *Application focus:* to serve all application segments, with particular emphasis on:
- Automotive;
- Computer peripherals;
- Digital consumer;
- Smartcards;
- Wireless communications and networking.

Guiding Principles

Customer satisfaction: the key to competitive success is Total Customer Satisfaction. We will listen to *the voice of the customers* and strive to anticipate and fulfil their needs and expectations; our future relies on strong partnerships, which we can ensure if each one of us does his/her best to provide world-class Service, Quality, Time-to-Market and Value.

Business integrity: we will conduct our business with the highest ethical standards in dealing with each of our stakeholders' communities. We will dedicate ourselves to honouring our commitments, delivering on our promises, being loyal and fair, and standing up for what is right.

People: we will behave with openness, trust, simplicity and humility; we will be ready to share what we know, encourage everyone's contribution and recognise achievements; we will emphasise job enrichment and personal realisation through empowerment, teamwork and training. Each one of us will be loyal, hardworking, committed and personally involved in the continuous improvement and learning process.

Excellence: the only 'status-quo' we will accept is one of permanent change and continuous challenge, always for the better. In all aspects of our activities, we will strive for excellence, quality, competency and efficiency; we will be flexible and nimble, and we will encourage innovation and creativity in every aspect of our activities.

Profitability: the profit we generate from our activities is the main source of the funds we need to prosper and grow; profit is necessary to provide security and future opportunities for each of us, and to allow the company to meet its other social and business responsibilities.

SETTING THE DIRECTION FOR ST

There was already in existence a corporate mission statement but it was not closely linked in the minds of the staff with their day-to-day activities. Furthermore, it had been written shortly after the merger and did not totally reflect the needs of the company, the shareholders, the employees or the customers. It was, therefore, revised and became the key launching point for all the decisions affecting the future of the corporation.

The mission statement is both short and clear reading, and is still in place today:

> To offer strategic independence to our partners worldwide, as a profitable and viable broad range semiconductor supplier.

The statement had implications regarding the size and dynamics of the corporation, resulting directly from the structure and investment needs of the semiconductor industry. Following the revitalisation of the mission statement there quickly followed publication of the corporation's:

- Objectives
- Strategic guidelines
- Guiding principles
- TQM principles
- Statement of the future

All of these were published in a booklet titled 'Shared Values' which was, and still is, circulated to all employees worldwide (Exhibit 2).

These initial efforts by the corporate management team would have been in vain if the necessary resources had not been provided to support the implementation. A corporate change support group was established, budgets were allocated and the executive management, including the CEO, allocated significant time to implementation. In the initial phase, most of the time and effort went into training and communications with regular bulletins, e-mails, and brochures.

The policy deployment process allowed the corporate goals to be cascaded into local goals, which were both realistic and challenging. The training programmes, targeting 50 hours per employee per year, ensured that people had the skills to accept the goals and translate them into local action plans. The management were encouraged to recognise achievements at local, national and international level. Finally, strong efforts were made to break down the walls between the various parts of the organisation and create an atmosphere in which cross-fertilisation was not only accepted but actively encouraged, until it became a way of life.

These changes were not easily or readily accepted in all parts of the corporation. Whilst the benefits could be seen on an intellectual plane, at a cultural level some groups found it easier to move faster than others. The then corporate TQM vice-president, Murray Duffin, described the process as 'pulling down the walls and using the bricks to build bridges'. The difficulty of achieving success cannot be underestimated. ST started with the advantage that many of its European staff had a fundamentally Latin culture and many of the managers had been exposed to American culture, as a result of either working in American companies or interfacing with American customers. Also, the semiconductor industry had its own culture, which was and still is very strong. Nonetheless, cultural barriers still existed and ST had to find ways of working with many different cultures, whilst trying to overlay a common ST culture, ways of working and vision of the future.

POLICY AND DEPLOYMENT AT ST

Policy deployment (PD) is the primary method used in ST to make TQM 'the way we manage' rather than something added to operational management. In order to make it effective, ST has simplified the approach, combining as many existing initiatives as possible, to leave only one set of key improvement goals deriving from both internal and external identified needs. In this process the management of ST also provided a mechanism for 'real time' visual follow-up of breakthrough priorities to support very rapid progress.

In ST policy deployment is regarded as:

- the 'backbone' of TQM;
- the way to translate the corporate vision, objectives and strategies into concrete specific goals, plans and actions at the operative level;
- a means to focus everyone's contributions in support of employee empowerment;
- the mechanism for jointly identifying objectives and the actions required to obtain the expected results;
- a vehicle to ensure that the corporate quality, service and cost goals are given superordinate importance in annual operational planning and performance evaluation;
- the method to integrate the entire organisation's daily priority activities with its long-term goals;
- a process to focus attention on managing ST's future, rather than the past.

A policy deployment manual, addressed to all managers at every level of ST, was developed as a methodological and operative user guide for those charged with planning and achieving significant improvement goals. Examples, detailed explanations, and descriptions of tools/forms were, and still are, included in the manual.

Policy deployment operates at two levels: continuous focused improvement and strategic breakthrough – referred to as Level 1 and Level 2. The yearly plan is designed by assembling the budget and improvement plan, but also taking into account the investment plan.

All these elements must be consistent and coherent. Current year business result goals are defined in the budget and the underlying operations and capability improvement goals have to be approached using policy deployment. Among all the improvement goals, a very few (one to three per year) are then selected for a more intensive management. These are the breakthrough goals and must be managed using special attention and techniques. Policy deployment goals have to be consistent with long-term policies, and finally, everything must be consistent with and must be supported by the investment plan.

Continuously improving performance and capabilities, and especially achieving 'breakthroughs', i.e. dramatic improvements in short times, was the main task that each manager was asked to face and carry out in his/her activities. Once the importance of achieving dramatic goals was clear, the problem arose of how to identify and prioritise them. To assist, ST fixed four long-term policies (broad and generic objectives):

- become number one in service;
- be among the top three suppliers in quality;
- have world-class manufacturing capabilities;
- become a leader in TQM in the western business world.

| Exhibit 3 | Policy deployment management process in STMicroelectronics |

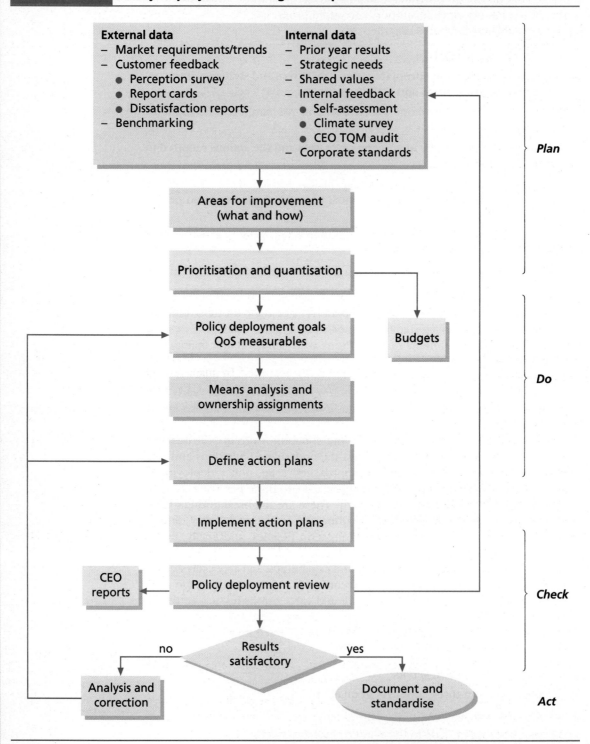

These long-term policies reflected the need to improve *strategic capabilities*. They were implemented progressively by achieving sequential sets of shorter-term goals focused on *operational capabilities*, *operational performance*, and *urgent requirements*. ST recognised that a successful enterprise ensures consistency between its short-term efforts and long-term goals.

Exhibit 3 is a high-level schematic of the yearly planning flow, relating budgeting and policy deployment (PD) in ST. The sequential deployment, at different levels, of PD goals and action plans is linked to an ST TQM 'Management Amplifier'. This illustrates four key requirements for good policy deployment:

1 a negotiation at each level to agree means and goals or targets, illustrated by the 'catch ball' approach;
2 the creation of action plans to achieve goals or targets;
3 review of action plan progress, and adjustment as necessary;
4 standardisation of improvement to 'hold the gains'.

The policy deployment tools used to help with means analysis, ownership assignments and progress assurance were explained in detail in the manual for managers.

APPROACHES TO MANAGE AND ACHIEVE THE STM GOALS

The yearly plan comprised all the goals and the performances the company had to reach during the year. Goals related to sales volume, profit and loss, inventories, standard costs, expenses etc. were generally managed by management control through the budget. In order to be more and more competitive, however, more challenging goals had to be identified each year and these goals – the ones that constitute the improvement plan – need 'Special Management' through a specific approach. This approach is policy deployment, in which a policy can be fully defined as the combination of goals/targets and means. The characteristics of the different approaches to manage the different goals (budget level and policy deployment level) are illustrated in Exhibit 4.

Policy deployment applies both to 'What' goals, i.e. mainly results oriented, and 'How' goals, which are more related to operational, technological, organisational and behavioural aspects, mainly process oriented.

- 'How' is mainly concerned with improving capabilities and 'What' is mainly concerned with improving results, deriving from improved capabilities.
- Drivers for 'What' goals are mainly corporate standards, prior results and vision statements.
- Drivers for 'How' goals are mainly vision statement, climate survey, self-assessment, customer feedback and strategic plans.
- Each level of the company (corporate, group, division) must perform its own 'Whats' deployment and 'Hows' deployment.
- 'Whats' deployment requires both targets and means deployment, where means deployment must be supported and must be coherent with 'Hows' deployment, that is, generally related to a longer-term vision.

Exhibit 4	Characteristics of approaches to managing goals

	IMPROVEMENT GOAL	IMPROVEMENT APPROACH	DRIVERS
Budget level	● Business as usual	● Maintenance growth sporadic or undefined	● Budgets ● Competition ● Customers ● SOP's routine[†] ● Tactical opportunities
Two levels of policy deployment	● Focused improvement (Policy deployment)	● Kaizen*	● Shared values ● Corporate standards ● Strategic focus ● Self-assessment ● Benchmarking
	● Breakthrough (Policy deployment and visual management)	● Quantum	● Vital priorities ● Benchmarking

* Kaizen means continuing improvement in personal life, home life, social life and working life.
[†] SOP = standard operating procedure.

In ST Microelectronics they believe that, to be a total quality company, strategy, philosophy, values and goals must be transmitted down the organisation, from level to level in a systematic way, to provide focus, clarity of direction and alignment. For them, policy deployment is the process through which goals, and the action plans to achieve them, in support of and consistent with the top-level corporate mission, strategic guidelines and objectives, are cascaded to all levels of the organisation. Effective policy deployment ensures that ST's goals and actions are aligned 'from top floor to shop floor'.

TQM ACHIEVEMENTS AND ITS FUTURE AT ST

In 1997 the company won the European Quality Award. This marked the progress made in development as a world-class organisation, and also coincided with the tenth anniversary of the formation of the company. Each time

ST wins a quality award the top management feel a deep joy and pride, being recognised as a champion of TQM culture and achieving the goal that they set in 1991, at the beginning of their initiative.

Without TQM, ST say they could never have achieved the fantastic turn-around which brought them from the status of a second-rank player to the top tier of semiconductor manufacturing and world-class performance, with ca. 30,000 employees and better than the average of the top five semiconductor companies in sales growth, market share gain, operational profit and ROI. The corporation has achieved major improvements in efficiency, sales per head, innovation (measured by the number of successful patent applications) and cash flow. They have dramatically reduced the costs of non-quality cycle time and inter-departmental friction. Last but not least, they have created a better environment from within which they are better able to serve customers, staff and shareholders, measured by customer perception surveys, the employee climate survey and financial results.

TQM is now part of life at ST but their journey has not ended yet – it never will. They recognise they must keep improving, following the directions that have already been set (teamwork, empowerment, policy deployment, etc.) and opening new roads to face the challenges of tomorrow: growing power of intellectual capital, increased mobility, speed and globalisation. The world is moving fast, the market requires fast responses to changing conditions and ST's objectives are more ambitious than ever.

TQM is no longer a new challenge for ST but it remains the primary concern. Its basic concept has not changed but is evolving at the same pace as the corporation. The real wealth of STMicroelectronics is in its people, their dedication, their expertise and their knowledge, but TQM has provided the necessary framework and set the conditions for them to develop. To quote president and CEO, Pasquale Pistorio, 'TQM is this powerful blend of values and tools to achieve excellence'. Georges Auguste, corporate vice-president TQEM, confirms, 'TQM is and will always remain the way to achieve Excellence for the entire organisation'.

Bibliography

European Centre for Business Excellence (Oakland Consulting plc, Leeds UK), *The Model in Practice*, British Quality Foundation (BQF), London, 2001.

Macdonald, John and Tanner, Steve, *Understanding Benchmarking in a Week*, Institute of Management, London, 1996.

Oakland, John S., *Total Organisational Excellence*, Butterworth-Heinemann, Oxford, 1999.

Oakland, John S., *Statistical Process Control*, 4th edn, Butterworth-Heinemann, Oxford, 1999.

Oakland, John S., *Total Quality Management – text with cases*, 2nd edn, Butterworth-Heinemann, Oxford, 2000.

Porter, Les and Tanner, Steve, *Assessing Business Excellence*, Butterworth-Heinemann, Oxford, 1996.

The pharmaceutical industry, 2000

Bernardo Bátiz-Lazo and
Sarah Holland

The case looks at the development of the modern pharmaceutical industry with an emphasis on events in the late 1990s. The various forces affecting the competitive environment around the discovery, development, production, distribution and marketing of prescription and non-prescription drugs are discussed in terms of their origins and recent developments.

● ● ●

During the 1990s, news services and other media in both developed and developing countries devoted increasing space to discussing health issues. Healthcare and the rising cost of healthcare treatments were also at the centre of the year 2000 US Presidential campaign because candidates of the main political parties regarded this as a topic of interest not only for retired people but also for the all-important (and ageing) *'baby boomer'* generation. Alongside increasing interest in the industry, pharmaceutical companies engaged in a number of high-worth (and highly publicised) amalgamations while, at the same time, the sector continued to deliver value in most stock markets around the world. How this situation came about and the role of pharmaceutical companies in the debate around healthcare provision are central topics for this case study.

ORIGINS

The origins of the modern pharmaceutical industry can be traced to the late nineteenth century, when dyestuffs were found to have antiseptic properties. Roche, Ciba-Geigy and Sandoz all started out as family dyestuff companies based near the Rhine in Basel, Switzerland. Slowly but steadily many chemical companies moved into synthetic pharmaceuticals and eventually became global players. Penicillin was a major discovery for the emergent industry during the 1940s. Throughout that decade and that of the 1950s, research and development (R&D) became firmly established within the sector, with the relative success of specific drugs making or breaking individual companies over time. For example, the use of anti-blood coagulants (i.e. beta blockers) to speed up recovery after serious injury was largely discovered by ICI, which formed major franchises out of the treatment of cardiovascular diseases. Companies such as Syntex and Boots established themselves based primarily on the discovery of products to treat swollen muscles with very lenient side-effects (i.e. non-steroidal inflammatory drugs).

The industry expanded rapidly in the 1960s, benefiting from new discoveries with permanent patent protection while the time from discovery to launch took between 3 and 5 years. Regulatory controls on development and marketing were lax, and healthcare spending boomed as economies prospered. Around this time a distinctive characteristic emerged for the pharmaceutical industry which marked its development for the following 30 years. This unique feature encompassed the final consumer (i.e. the patient) having little or no say in the choice of drug and treatment. Specialists and general practitioners were the customers of the pharmaceutical companies because they were ultimately responsible for purchasing decisions. To no surprise, pharmaceutical companies' marketing efforts targeted medical practitioners and specialists, building on individual representatives that would alert practitioners of new products through one-to-one sessions at the practitioner's office. This sales approach became known as '*muscle marketing*', and proved to be a successful approach for a fragmented customer base, while increasing the number and spread of sales representatives was an effective way to overcome challenges posed by high mobility of specialists, cramped appointment schedules and general practitioners' geographic exclusivity arrangements.

Since medical practitioners became susceptible to details provided by sales representatives, some newcomers to the industry, as well as established providers, found it attractive to devote R&D resources for the development of '*me too*' drugs, copies of a competitor's product. The attractiveness of *me too* products for manufacturers was that these drugs were traditionally priced at a premium to the existing market on the back of *muscle marketing*. Doctors would accept a premium price for a new product because it was usually perceived as offering some sort of advantage. For example, the advantage might be a less frequent dosage or the new drug might have a slightly improved side-effect profile. But with regard to its therapeutic outcome, the new product was very similar to the established product with which it was competing.

EVOLUTION

There were two major developments in the 1970s, the first being the introduction of much tighter regulatory controls on clinical trials, greatly increasing time-to-market and development costs. A second major event was the enactment of legislation allowing the introduction of '*generic*' medicines by setting a fixed period on patent protection. A *generic* product is a drug manufactured after patent expiry by another pharmaceutical company and usually sold at a cheaper price. Generics are identical in virtually every respect to the branded original and their prices normally are at the bottom of the market. Generics are neither developed nor manufactured by the original company and as such, are not backed by the manufacturer's quality control and medical information department. To a lot of medical practitioners that difference was irrelevant, whereas for others the difference was important, thus an opportunity to have '*branded generics*' opened up. Branded generics are generic products which offer a small advantage and which are sold at a price above the lowest-priced generics.

The immediate effect of legislation allowing generic products was that major pharmaceutical companies started to develop similar products by investing in similar processes and research agendas. Once patent protection of a well-selling drug was over, other manufacturers would dig into their compound library and start selling *generic* alternatives almost immediately. Since the price of generic drugs typically represents only 60 per cent of the price at launch of the branded alternative, legislation provided incentives to reduce the lag time to market, augment price competition for products in top therapeutical segments and lead to an erosion of the branded original's market share. By the end of the decade the combination of lower barriers to manufacturing generic products and more stringent controls on clinical trials was reflected through substantial increases in R&D spending.

During the early 1980s the pharmaceutical industry was unusual, as in many geographic markets there was effectively only one powerful purchaser, the government. In the 1980s, governments around the world began to focus upon pharmaceuticals as a politically easy target in their efforts to control rising healthcare expenditure. At the time there was realisation of changes in the underlying trends at the heart of healthcare provision: patients' expectations were increasing, the cost of healthcare was increasing but, at the same time, the capability of several countries to sustain such spending was not. Many countries introduced some form of price or reimbursement control, while industry participants lacked the public or political support to prevent these changes. Take the UK, for example. In 1985, the British government introduced its '*black list*', a group of patented drugs that the government would not pay for. Some products that were '*delisted*' from official supply lists, or '*blacklisted*', included anti-hypnotics such as valium and some cough syrups. The effect of *delisting* had a tremendous differential effect on the industry. Prior to the introduction of the *black list*, Roche, for one, was in the top ten companies within the pharmaceutical industry but fell to the 40s within the industry when its two major products were *delisted*.

Despite price controls or claims of increased government intervention, the pharmaceutical industry enjoyed recession-proof growth in demand. Volume business from selected ('*listed*') products during the 1980s resulted in average operating margins in the USA moving from 16 to 24 per cent, gross margins from 63 to 76 per cent and net profit margins from 10 to almost 19 per cent. Increased profitability resulted from a combination of final consumers still being protected from absorbing a significant share of total costs, together with the effects over R&D platforms and marketing strength from horizontal and vertical integration (more below).

Other key developments in the 1980s were the emergence of biotechnology firms and greater use of computer power. The appearance of small biotechnology start-up companies came about with the assistance of venture capital to exploit the myriad opportunities opened up by molecular biology. This boom was short-lived as genetically engineered products proved to be even more costly than conventional pharmaceuticals to develop and manufacture. Most start-ups also lacked the finances to cope with the huge risks involved. A few spectacular development failures took the gloss off the sector and investors became more cautious.

However, the introduction of personal computers and more sophisticated information and communication technology equipment during the 1980s had two benefits. The first benefit was the introduction of innovative ways to hold and manage growing numbers of patients' records. The second benefit was allowing for software applications to set a '*formulary*', that is, a list of drugs that encompassed those drugs most often or routinely used by the doctors in a practice, region or group of patients. The computer systems enabled purchasers to print all prescriptions in their generic form rather than a branded form. This effectively meant that if an alternative, cheaper generic drug was available then the pharmacist could prescribe it and hence save the purchaser money. The result was that the old brand loyalty, which the pharmaceutical industry had spent so much time and money developing, was threatened and could disappear. Furthermore, the viability of large salesforces became increasingly called into question.

Entering the 1990s, public and private finances faced similar challenges. Worldwide economic recession reduced cash for provision of healthcare through tax-funded systems such as those in Canada, Italy, Spain and the UK, and the social security supported systems in France, Germany and Japan, as well as the employer/privately funded systems in the US. The ageing population introduced further pressures because the over–65s consume four times as much healthcare support per head as those below 65. An ageing population combined with more expensive high-technology solutions and increasing patient expectations created an unsustainable situation: on the one hand, historically underfunded systems (such as those in Spain and the UK) were systematically in deficit, while slow or unable to introduce the latest treatments. On the other, well-funded systems were able to afford the latest innovations but, as the experience in the US suggested, lost opportunities to share those benefits with an increasing part of the population.

The year 1993 was a watershed, with the environment filled with talk about healthcare reforms across Europe and in the US. Although many proposals were never put into action, it became evident that governments would no longer tolerate spiralling healthcare costs. Events of 1993 also signalled a global shift in customer behaviour towards healthcare costs in general and pharmaceuticals in particular. In that year, sales in the German pharmaceutical market fell by 11 per cent while the four leading generics manufacturers increased their sales by between 10 and 63 per cent per year. Managed competition became the model for healthcare reform, creating a purchaser/provider split which focused attention sharply on achieving '*value for money*'.

By the end of the 1990s there was a wide variety of managed competition methods to control public spending on pharmaceuticals, with most countries using a combination of methods (as no country relied on a single approach). Some price control methods have emphasised the supply side, that is, on the manufacturer and the distributor. Supply-side methods have included negotiated prices, average prices, reference pricing, lists and other constraints over

Exhibit 1	**Effects of legislation on ethical drug's product life cycle: the product life cycle of the past**

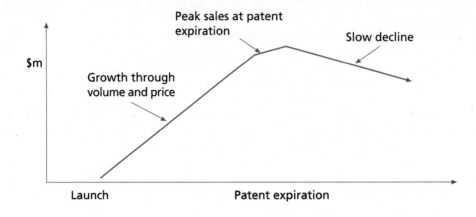

wholesalers and pharmaceuticals. Some methods have emphasised the demand side – the prescriber and the patient. These methods have included patient co-payment, guidelines, fixed budgets, and incentives to prescribe and dispense generic drugs or parallel imports. Other methods such as reimbursement systems affect both demand and supply as volume purchasers negotiate individual drug price levels with manufacturers. Reimbursement systems, therefore, have assisted in controlling prices directly (supply) and may influence demand as they could require the patient to pay a part of the charge.

PRODUCT LIFE CYCLE

The net result of all the factors introduced to manage competition was a more difficult environment for pharmaceutical companies as illustrated in Exhibits 1 and 2. The exhibits show the aggregate impact of the introduction of price controls and other legislation on the typical pharmaceutical product life cycle.

Exhibit 1 shows how, in the past, growth for drug manufacturers came through both volume and price, with peak sales at patent expiry. The decline in sales after patent expiry took years. Exhibit 2 shows how the product life cycle pattern shrinks due to external pressures on pharmaceuticals. Prudent purchasing by powerful players limits initial growth and holds down prices. The expiration of the first patent in the same drug class often results in all the members of that drug class being priced as commodities (even before the patents expire). Generic substitution speeds up the decline of sales value with time.

Differences between Exhibits 1 and 2 also help to understand why pharmaceutical marketeers have constantly sought ways to extend the product life cycle. As a product approaches patent expiry, great effort may be invested in switching patients to new, improved formulations with longer patent protection. Another strategy for appropriate drugs has been to move them from prescription-only status to over-the-counter (OTC), and encourage patients to recognise and

Exhibit 2	**Effects of legislation on ethical drug's product life cycle: reduced by future healthcare changes**

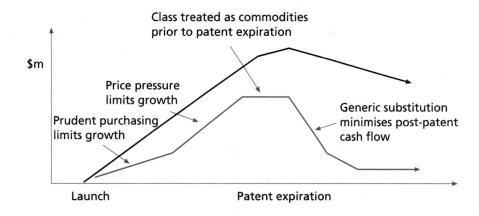

buy a familiar brands. Since OTC drugs are not reimbursed, prices may have to fall further, but that fall may be compensated for by increased volume as consumer brand loyalty can then be used as a defence against generic competition.

PARALLEL TRADE

On top of reductions in the product life cycle, pharmaceuticals have faced the growing importance of distribution. Large distribution companies with pan-European operations emerged as distributors started to source products from the lowest point of supply in Europe through the medium of parallel imports. Parallel imports are products which are available at a cheaper price in lower-fixed-cost countries. Within Europe the higher-priced markets are Germany, the UK, Sweden and Holland; the lower-priced markets are Spain, Portugal, France, Italy and Greece. It is from the lower-priced markets that wholesale distributors source parallel imports. Parallel imports grew in strength when pharmaceutical wholesalers began to consolidate internationally with cross-border mergers and acquisitions, and were quick to spot the opportunities to buy in one country and distribute in another. Hence, the creation of the Single European Market led to new problems for the industry because government-introduced controls created significant price differentials between countries. While the single market enabled parallel importers to trade ethical drugs, this resulted in minimal benefit to governments or final consumers but a very significant loss in profit for the industry because profit margins went to the parallel importers instead of being ploughed back into R&D.

Institutions such as the European Commission recognised the anomaly created by the enforcement of a free market alongside government price controls and this provided opportunities for pharmaceutical companies to influence European policy. However, there was significant divergence in the goals of the different players in the industry. Some US-based companies argued in favour of complete freedom in pricing pharmaceuticals in Europe, combined with parallel trade. Big European-based companies recognised that national controls on pricing and reimbursement would persist, but wanted a special embargo on parallel trade in pharmaceuticals. Meanwhile, smaller domestic players (who are powerful national lobbyists) simply wanted to continue with existing protective national pricing systems and did not want wholesale change of any sort. The lack of industry consensus, combined with the fundamental paradox at the heart of the problem and the determination of member states to retain national controls, meant there was unlikely to be any significant change to pharmaceutical regulation in Europe. Furthermore, the enlargement of the European Union (EU) would exacerbate parallel trade as prices in central and eastern Europe tend to be low and differentials would worsen if currencies were devalued to ensure compliance with convergence criteria.

Parallel trade was not confined to Europe. It was prevalent in the Far East and could even become a threat in the US given the price differentials with Canada. Parallel trade was a source of concern for managers in ethical drug companies because pharmaceuticals have been subject to strict regulatory controls in virtually all world markets. For example, in the US, the Federal Drug Administration (FDA) requires manufacturers to perform extensive testing to demonstrate safety and efficacy before allowing a new drug to be put on the market. The time taken for the FDA to review a new compound typically requires from 6 to 12 months but this has been a process governed by legislation and therefore, many hurdles have to be jumped before reaching that stage (more below). One could assume that complying with requirements in the US could suffice, but while FDA endorsement could be very helpful, that endorsement in itself has not guaranteed automatic approval in other countries. Regulatory authorities typically wish to ensure that the product is suitable for their population and that the product delivers improved disease outcomes when compared with the standard of care in their country. For example, Japanese authorities firmly believe that people in their country may metabolise the drug differently from western subjects and insist on separate clinical trials. Pharmaceuticals have thus been forced to develop capabilities to deal with the fact that every regulatory authority is different.

During the 1990s, a positive development for regulation and supervision of pharmaceuticals took place in Europe with the establishment of the European Medicines Evaluation Agency (EMEA) at the same time that European and non-European regulators established the International Conference on Harmonisation (ICH). EMEA is a body expected to enable more rapid approvals across Europe through a system where one country acts as *rapporteur* on behalf of the new product, recommending its approval which is then endorsed by the other member states. ICH is a body created by national supervisors from all over the world aiming to co-ordinate international policy and create uniform global standards for drug approval. But at the turn of the millennium, either one of these bodies had yet to deliver a smoother process for drug approval.

GLOBAL MARKETS

The audited world pharmaceutical market was worth $340 billion in 1999, a growth of 11 per cent over 1998, with projections showing annual global sales

| Exhibit 3 | Health spending as % of GDP, 1998 |

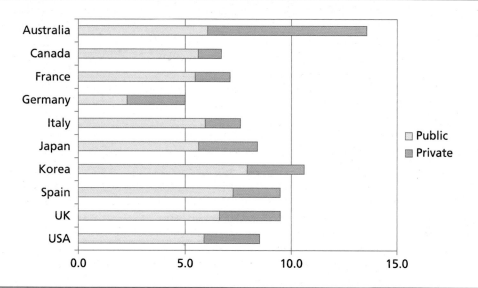

Source: OECD Health Data 2000.

growth of 8 per cent over the following five years, which would expand the global pharmaceutical market to $500 billion by 2004. The majority of sales originated in the '*Triad*' (US, EU and Japan), with nine strategic markets accounting for over 80 per cent, namely the US, Japan, France, Germany, the UK, Italy, Canada, Brazil and Spain. Of these, the US had grown the fastest since 1995, accounting for 60 per cent of the sales of drugs since then. Furthermore, in 1999 alone the US market grew 16 per cent to $133 billion in sales, so becoming the key market for international companies. See Exhibit 3.

There have been two key developments in the US market. First, the intro-duction of managed care, a system in which plan administrators set cost and reimbursement limits on healthcare services. Managed care changed the US environment but the fear that managed care would increase competition and drive down pharmaceutical prices proved somewhat illusory for several reasons: on the one hand, managed care organisations (MCOs) had more important areas of focus than the 10 per cent of expenditure on drugs. They also found it hard to refuse reimbursement retrospectively once the pharmacist had fulfilled the prescription. On the other, consumers covered by MCOs did not like restrictive drug formularies and offering pharmaceutical choice was therefore a source of differentiation. A second key development in the US mar-ket was growth fuelled by direct-to-consumer (DTC) advertising. DTC emerged as pharmaceutical companies began to recognise that patients did take a strong interest in their therapy and were prepared to ask for drugs by name, creating a powerful new '*pull*' strategy. Spending on DTC advertising amounted to $1.8 billion in 1999.

Another interesting example in world markets is Japan, which was the sec-ond single biggest market with sales of $51 billion in 1999, and together, Japan

CASE STUDIES

Exhibit 4	Total expenditure on pharmaceuticals and other medical non-durables, % GDP					
	1960	1970	1980	1990	1997	RANK*
Australia	1.0		0.6	0.7	0.9	18
Canada	0.7	0.8	0.6	1.0	1.3	5
France	0.9	1.4	1.2	1.7	2.0	1
Germany		1.0	1.2	1.2	1.3	9
Italy	0.7	0.7	1.0	1.5	1.5	8
Japan			1.4	1.3	1.5	3
Korea				1.2	0.8	25
Spain			1.2	1.2	1.5	13
UK		0.7	0.7	0.8	1.1	15
USA	0.8	0.9	0.8	1.1	1.4	2

* = total expenditure per capita in US dollars, 1997.

Source: OECD Health Data 2000.

and the US accounted for half the worldwide sales of ethical drugs. As shown in Exhibit 4, the US and Japan have also scored highly in the percentage of resources spent on healthcare. The Japanese operating environment has historically been very different from that of the US or the EU. This divergence has been observed at all levels, from medical practice, healthcare delivery and funding, to regulatory requirements, higher prices, the lack of generics, distribution, and the accepted approach to sales and marketing. Not surprisingly, the market has been dominated by domestic companies. But due to environmental turbulence during the 1990s, Japanese medical practice begun to shift towards the US model while companies based in the US and the EU began to develop presence through acquisitions.

Emerging markets have also become increasingly important. The pharmaceutical markets in Latin America have proven highly volatile, reflecting underlying economic trends. Nevertheless, they have large numbers of wealthy consumers who are able to afford branded pharmaceuticals. In 2000, the Brazilian market was the eighth largest in the world by value, but Mexico was rapidly catching up. Pacific Rim countries were also becoming important contributors to the global market. Copy products have traditionally been a significant issue in these markets, where patent protection may be absent or very difficult to police. Another problem is associated with foreign companies becoming successful in marketing high-price branded products and then finding themselves affected by parallel imports from as far afield as Belgium. The majority of the population in markets such as India and Africa have different healthcare needs from people in advanced industrialised countries because of the need to improve nutrition, sanitation and health education. Access to effective older products for common infections and diseases has also been a concern. Because the money is not there to provide a return, the research-based pharmaceutical industry has focused little R&D effort on diseases specific to these markets. The AIDS epidemic in Africa has illustrated how solutions appropriate for advanced economies are unrealistic and inappropriate for developing countries.

Nevertheless, with their enormous populations, emerging markets do offer significant long-term potential. Many have strengthened patent protection and liberalised equity controls. Pharmaceutical companies have been particularly interested in China, which has one of the most rapidly growing pharmaceutical markets. While Chinese herbal medicine has remained a core part of healthcare, the use of western medicines has been increasing dramatically in the booming coastal cities.

At the turn of the millennium, the US was predicted to continue increasing its world market share, while Japan was expected to decrease and the EU to remain static. The same projections suggested that the most populous countries such as China and India were expected to increase in importance, Mexico was likely to overtake Brazil in Latin America, and Poland to continue growing rapidly in importance. By 2010, non-Triad countries were expected to hold a third of the world market.

THERAPY CLASS

So what has determined the relative importance of market sectors in the pharmaceutical industry and leading companies within those sectors? Although the overall pharmaceutical market appears relatively fragmented, this has disguised the true level of concentration. Since both R&D and commercial franchises break down naturally along therapeutic lines, companies generally choose to compete in a selected range of therapeutic areas. The market leader within a specific area could have a market share as high as 22 per cent (AstraZeneca in gastroenterology) and a figure around 15 per cent was not uncommon. Typically the top 10 companies hold over 50 per cent of a given therapeutic area. This has emphasised the need for genuine product superiority, since price premiums and/or reimbursement levels awarded by governments are based on perceived innovativeness and superiority, penalising ‘*me too*’ drugs.

Industry intelligence has meant that companies are invariably in a race to market with each new class of drugs. Competition has been waged at the level of drug class and being late to market with an undifferentiated product is a recipe for failure. At the same time and in spite of high concentration levels within specific therapeutic areas, most pharmaceutical companies have been product-led rather than customer-led. This has probably been a consequence of the unpredictability of the R&D process because it has not been easy to develop a product to meet specific customer needs.

Another important source of success has been global reach. As the cost of developing and commercialising a new drug soared to more than $600 million per product, and 80 per cent of products did not recoup their R&D investment, it became imperative to maximise return by launching a product worldwide. Companies which lack marketing presence in key markets have been obliged to make use of licensing deals, which meant sharing profit with another company. Furthermore, a strong global marketing capability has been vital in attracting the best in-licensing candidates and co-marketing deals, thus strengthening the product pipeline. Successful drug launches strongly correlated with product superiority, high prices and high promotional spend. Interestingly, '*satisfied*' markets have not appeared to have been a barrier to success. Drugs can be successful even in the most saturated markets as products offering meaningful incremental improvements are generally more successful than drugs which are first in class. In any event, low product prices are seldom associated with success.

PRODUCT CLASS

The pharmaceutical industry can also be divided into three broad product segments. First, prescription-only medicines (i.e. '*ethical*' drugs) comprise about 80 per cent of the market by value and 50 per cent by volume. A second broad segment comprises branded and identical '*generic*' competitors. A third segment are '*over-the-counter*' medicines (OTCs), which may be purchased without prescription and may also be branded or generic. Each of these three segments has required very different strategic capabilities. Producers of branded prescription drugs require strong R&D combined with sales and marketing infrastructure. Generics companies focus on supply chain management and manufacturing cost leadership in both ethical and OTC sectors. But since OTCs are rarely reimbursed, branded OTC drugs demand direct-to-consumer marketing capability.

The market can also be segmented according to the broad uses to which drugs are put. An important distinction is between '*primary care*' and '*specialist*' products. Primary care products are generally self-administered therapies prescribed by general practitioners, whereas treatment with specialist products is typically initiated in hospitals. Sales volume, marketing spend and skills required differ for the two segments. Thus *primary care* products require mass marketing, while specialist products involve targeted relationship marketing. Therapies for common chronic diseases have been the most lucrative; the biggest sector has been cardiovascular disease, with 5.2 per cent of world audited sales in 2000 and rank 3 in terms of the number of prescriptions, as cardiovascular disease has remained the leading cause of death worldwide. The treatments for gastric ulcers, infections, central nervous system disorders, arthritis and asthma have also been important contributors. In contrast, drugs to treat cancer have made up only 1.6 per cent of the world market (in terms of audited sales in 2000) and, although with that volume of sales cancer drugs rank number 12 in importance, they hardly were in scene before the late 1990s. Moreover, even in 2000, drugs to treat cancer had a negligible volume of prescriptions when compared with top-selling products.

Changing trends in audited sales have usually been influenced by demographic patterns and medical advances. But changing trends in the late 1990s, and particularly the rise of new therapeutic classes, have been associated with patients with chronic diseases who are increasingly well satisfied with existing treatments. Pharmaceutical companies have thus found themselves forced to pursue research into niche areas, which have had a high medical need for new treatments. Up and coming areas have included cancer treatment or so-called '*lifestyle*' conditions such as impotence, obesity and hair loss. Diseases of the elderly, such as Alzheimer's disease, have also become important targets for research because drugs aimed at the ageing population have grown in importance, and encompass the two leading therapeutic classes in terms of prescriptions (i.e. product units) in 2000.

MANUFACTURING

One way to segment participants in the markets for prescription pharmaceuticals would consider the type of producer that manufactures the medicine, namely research-based sector, generic manufacturers and biotechnology companies. First, research-based pharmaceutical companies have historically been niche specialists which commercialised in mass volume markets. The typical cost structure at research-based pharmaceutical companies comprised the manufacturing of goods (25 per cent), research and development (12–21 per cent), administration (10 per cent), and sales and marketing (25 per cent). Manufacturing at research-based companies historically suffered from low utilisation, high fixed costs and low productivity. Growing costs related to R&D and marketing became an incentive for leading corporations to take steps and restructure manufacturing. Restructuring usually involved rationalising the number of production sites and placing them in strategic locations which offered tax advantages (such as Puerto Rico or the Republic of Ireland). Distribution of drugs to pharmacies and hospitals has been largely performed by specialist wholesalers, although some companies deliver directly. Companies have also made efforts to improve supply chain management and release the value previously trapped in high inventories. However, manufacturing and distribution efficiency at research-based companies has not been comparable with that at manufacturers of generics who have competed on low price and cost leadership. Research-based companies which own OTC and generics businesses generally operate them separately, frequently using another company name. Similarly, those that have acquired biotechnology companies normally leave them to operate fairly autonomously. Other companies in the research-based sector have been increasing grants to and joint ventures with research-active universities across the world.

A second type of producer is the generic manufacturer. For them size has also become critical because during the late 1990s there was a collapse of generics prices in the US. As a result, the speed and aggression of generics attacks on branded products increased sharply. The outlook for the sector has been fairly rosy given the increasing number of global brands with patent expiry looming and markets with untapped generics potential (e.g. Italy, Spain, France), with compound annual growth rate of 12 per cent predicted to deliver $30 billion dollars by 2004.

A third type of producer encompasses biotechnology companies, which rely on molecular biology and genetic engineering. Efforts in biotechnology companies opened up vast new areas of medical research but participants were soon to discover that genetically engineered products had far higher production costs than traditional pharmaceuticals, with higher prices limiting applications to low-volume, high-need areas. Many biotechnology operations originally planned to integrate and perform all functions from research to sales. However, the very high attrition rate in drug development made integration a high-risk strategy. Only three companies have succeeded in achieving this goal, namely, Amgen, Biogen and Genzyme. Of these, Amgen was the only serious global player as it ranked number 20 in terms of sales during 2000. The remaining leading players (Genentech, Chiron, Genetics Institute) were partly owned by larger firms. Biotechnology companies largely abandoned attempts to market drugs themselves (although they often try to retain US marketing rights) and use the global presence of the research-based pharmaceutical companies to leverage return on R&D investment through licensing and strategic alliances.

INTERNAL INNOVATION

Managers at research-based manufacturers, generic manufacturers and biotechnology companies have used resources at their disposal to compete and develop an advantage by accessing products which are innovative and differentiated; possess the potential for intellectual property protection; can be developed rapidly; and can be marketed successfully. Moves away from the pharmaceutical 'core' have been made by various firms in the past, the results of which have been mixed at best and usually weakening of earnings as well as stock market performance. Companies with consistently high levels of R&D spending and high productivity resulting from R&D investment have become industry leaders. For this reason, company valuations place as much importance on the R&D 'pipeline' (i.e. the products in development) as on the currently marketed products. Regarding the pipeline, the pharmaceutical industry differs from most others in its long new-product lead times. New-product development can be divided into distinct research and development phases. The research phase produces a molecule which has the desired characteristics to be an effective drug for a targeted disease process. Development encompasses all of the formulation, toxicology and clinical trial work necessary to meet stringent regulatory requirements for marketing approval. As Exhibit 5 shows, time-to-market from discovery to marketing authorisation typically takes almost 12 years.

Obtaining marketing approval has for some time no longer been the end of the road in many countries, as further hurdles must be overcome in demonstrating the value of the new drug to justify its price and/or reimbursement to cost-conscious payers. Development must also consider resources used while manufacturing and commercialising the drug (resources such as those used in market preparation activities). External and internal pressures for the industry have resulted in a shorter, flatter, product life cycle and a race to market. However, all of the evidence points to lengthening development times and a fall in R&D productivity. For instance, the time taken for drugs to move from laboratory to market increased by nearly 7 years from 1960 to 2000. During that period the time taken for regulatory review remained fairly static and the period before clinical testing rose only slightly. Most of the increase has occurred in the clinical development phase. The average number of trials and

Exhibit 5 Creating new pharmaceuticals

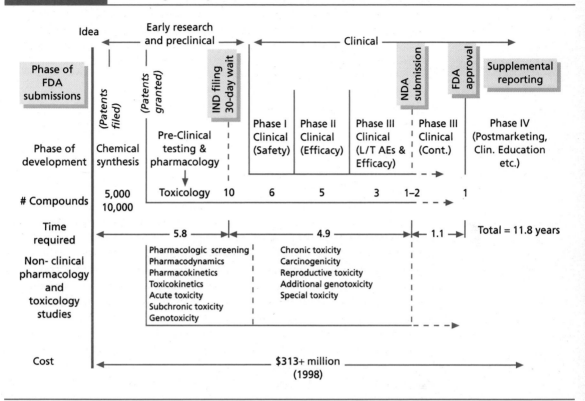

Source: Adapted from Tufts CSDD.

the number of patients for each new drug application have increased enormously, that is, from 26 trials involving 1,500 patients in 1980, to more than 65 trials involving over 4,000 patients by 1995. Not surprisingly, a combination of increasing time-to-market, together with easy drug targets (such as simple infections) having been addressed and growing spending on R&D, resulted in the number of new products reaching the market falling. For instance, in 1981, global R&D expenditure was around $5.4 billion, while it was estimated to exceed $50 billion in 2000. Conversely, 51 new chemical entities (NCE) were introduced in 1980 but only 32 in 1999.

Given the high attrition rates of NCEs it should be no surprise that '*blockbuster*' or '*megabrand*' drugs have had the potential to determine the fortunes of pharmaceutical companies. GlaxoWellcome's strength was originally derived from Zantac, for the treatment of gastric ulcers, which was superseded by Astra's Losec as the world's best-selling drug for the same indication. To become a blockbuster, a drug must normally be a chronic therapy for a common condition, offer a perceived step-change in efficacy or tolerability and be marketed globally. There has been no official definition, but as suggested in Exhibit 6, annual sales should probably exceed $1 billion for a drug to earn this

| Exhibit 6 | Individual drug sales, 1999 |

SALES PER ANNUM	% NCES ACHIEVING
$1.8bn +	1%
$920m–$1.8bn	1%
$460m–$920m	2%
$180m–$460m	6%
Less than $180m	90%

accolade. The exhibit also shows that 1 per cent or less of available drugs could be considered a blockbuster.

While blockbusters have made immense contributions to company fortunes and provided tremendous returns on R&D investment, they have been few and far between. In 1998, only 40 products achieved over $1 billion sales world-wide, and the average for all drugs has been put at $186 million. Furthermore, overdependence on a blockbuster can render a company highly vulnerable to generic competition once patent expiry looms, and one-third of the top 35 molecules (NCEs) in 2000 faced patent expiry by 2004. In other words, the global exposure to blockbusters in 2000 was nearly $45 billion, of which over 60 per cent affected the top eight companies.

EXTERNAL INNOVATION

So how have pharmaceutical companies responded to environmental change? The industry has adopted a number of strategic responses to the challenges posed by globalisation and greater R&D scale. Many pharmaceuticals introduced 'disease management' initiatives. These have involved understanding the goals of the healthcare system in addressing a specific disease area. The pharmaceutical company then aligns itself with the healthcare providers, trying to offer an integrated service which improves eventual disease outcomes, positioning its drugs as one part of the delivery process. The US market saw the brief emergence of an interesting new business model to link pharmaceuticals and healthcare providers while, at the same time, offer the potential to move pharmaceutical companies away from greater R&D scale as critical success factor: Merck acquired a Pharmacy Benefit Manager (PBM) in 1993. Merck's move was deemed interesting because PBMs cover the cost of prescriptions in exchange for insurance premiums, often paid for by employers. After Merck acquired Medco for $6 billion, in 1994 SmithKline Beecham purchased another PBM called DPS, and that same year Eli Lilly purchased PCS. The apparent logic was the conventional strategic rationale for vertical integration. But much to the surprise of managers at pharmaceuticals, barriers were quickly put in place to prevent companies from influencing PBM's formularies and removing competition. While Merck has retained ownership of Medco and has apparently benefited, both SKB and Eli Lilly were unable to create cross-links between their R&D operations and their PBM's databases, with the result of costly divestments of the PBMs in 1999.

Another common response has been to conduct pharmacoeconomic evaluations, studies that aim to demonstrate the added value offered by a new drug as a result of improved efficacy, safety, tolerability or ease of use. However, it is very difficult to conduct a health economic study that will be regarded as credible and relevant by the intended audience. The enormous variability in healthcare practice and cost, even within one country, the difficulty of using clinical trial data to model everyday reality, and the fact that industry sponsors most of the research result in most pharmacoeconomic evaluations being presumed to be biased. Health economic evaluations, therefore, have added to the costs of introducing and marketing drugs but have rarely made a significant impact on barriers to entry or pricing and reimbursement levels.

ORGANIC GROWTH VERSUS ACQUISITION

Exhibit 7 shows how alongside attempts at vertical integration, the overwhelming industry response to the need for critical mass in R&D and global marketing presence has been a wave of mergers and previously unheard-of hostile acquisitions leading to amalgamation.

Products of mergers in the late 1990s included Novartis, Aventis, AstraZeneca, Pharmacia (with Monsanto), Pfizer (with Warner-Lambert) and the planned marriage of GlaxoWellcome and SmithKline Beecham in 2001. As a result of amalgamation and as Exhibit 7 suggests, the leading global players in the pharmaceutical industry have originated from Triad countries and predominantly the US and Europe, as Japanese companies lag behind. American companies have pulled away from European companies in terms of sales growth by benefiting from a strongly growing domestic market. American companies such as Pfizer, Merck, BMS and Johnson & Johnson recorded growth exceeding 15 per cent between 1998 and 1999. At the same time, European-based companies like Novartis, Aventis and Sanofi-Synthelabo languished at around 5 per cent for that period.

There has been a strong belief that companies must have critical mass to survive in the long term. Analysis of growth rates provides some support in favour of size, with average growth rates declining with size. However, there have been exceptions to the trend such as US-based Pharmacia and Takeda from Japan, which ranked at 10 in terms of sales volume but grew at over 20 per cent in 1999. Another argument for increasing size to improve R&D productivity has been that productivity rests at least partly on 'technology platforms'; that is, companies must invest in the development of (expensive) research capabilities if they are to keep up with the industry leaders in terms of time-to-market. Managers of many pharmaceuticals, therefore, have considered that the larger the total R&D programme, the greater the number of individual projects that can benefit from the new capability, and the greater the opportunity to amortise these costs.

Exhibit 7 also suggest that merger deals completed between 1999 and 2000 among pharmaceutical companies intensified the pressure on other leading

CASE STUDIES

| Exhibit 7 | Leading global pharmaceutical companies, 1997 and 2000 |

(Top worldwide sales, retail market share and major drug mergers in the late 1990s)

1997		2000			
Company	Total sales, $bn	Company	Total sales, $bn	Share within global retail	Sales growth (1999 to 2000)
GlaxoWellcome[1] (UK)	11.6	GlaxoSmithKline[6] (UK)	22.2	7.3%	12.4%
Merck (US)	11.4	Pfizer[5] (US)	20.2	6.7%	12.0%
Novartis[2] (CH)	11.0	Merck (US)	15.5	4.4%	16.0%
Bristol-Myers Squibb (US)	9.3	AstraZeneca[4] (UK/Swe)	14.8	4.6%	4.4%
Johnson & Johnson (US)	8.7	Aventis[3] (Ger/Fra)	13.1	4.4%	15.8%
American Home Products (US)	8.4	Bristol-Myers Squibb (US)	12.0	4.1%	11.0%
Pfizer (US)	8.4	Novartis (CH)	11.6	4.1%	15.3%
Roche (CH)	8.0	Roche (CH)	11.0	3.2%	7.5%
SmithKline Beecham (UK)	7.4	Johnson & Johnson (US)	10.7	3.6%	11.8%
Hoechst (Ger)	7.4	Eli Lilly (US)	9.3	3.1%	8.7%

Notes:

Number	Created	Originating companies	
1	1995	Glaxo (UK)	Wellcome (UK)
2	1996	Sandoz (CH)	Ciba-Geigy (CH)
3	1998	Hoescht (Ger)	Rhône-Poulenc (Fra)
4	1998	Astra (Swe)	Zeneca (UK)
5	2000	Warner-Lambert (US)	Pfizer (US)
6	2000	Glaxo Wellcome (UK)	SmithKline Beecham (UK)

Source: The Economist (21 February 1998), Financial Times (6 April 2000) and own estimates.

companies to abandon organic growth strategies and consider potential partners. Exhibit 7 shows how companies formed between 1999 and 2000, such as Aventis and the new Pfizer, have overtaken Merck, which followed an organic growth strategy throughout the 1990s and dropped from second to fourth place on a revenue basis. Managers of Merck announced they were maintaining an emphasis on organic growth, but analysts doubted that the company could expand fast enough on its own to compete with GlaxoSmithKline or the new Pfizer. Similar thoughts probably crossed the minds of the management team at American Home Products and Bristol-Myers Squibb, a company that had been confined mainly to healthcare activities but covered a broad scope of products including, for example, OTC products.

According to many industry observers the next big deal could involve Novartis. This company was seen as the potential partner of choice because of a wide range of business that complemented any portfolio of pharmaceutical products. The company also had a large department for the production of generic drugs in Europe. The second partner of choice was Bristol-Myers Squibb whose sales had grown by 9 per cent on average in the second half of the 1990s and was free of patent expirations in early years of the new millennium.

Until the mid-1990s, Bristol Myers Squibb held the number one position in the US market with sales of $8.4 billion dollars in 1998; and third position in the European market, with sales of $2.9 billion dollars in 1998. In fact, the position of Bristol-Myers Squibb as a leading pharmaceutical company was effectively challenged by the round of amalgamations in 1999 and 2000 and, as a result, managers could see a need to merge in order to maintain competitive momentum.

In the course of the process of widespread amalgamation and industry change, European companies have faced tougher challenges than their US rivals. The US has been the world's biggest and fastest-growing market, while Europeans have typically consumed about half the number of pills than people in North America. Perhaps these differences in consumption could explain why only half of Germany's 1,000-plus drug companies had more than 100 workers.

But even as top organic-growth-led companies like Merck were falling in the rankings, few wanted to abandon their strategy. Arguments used by proponents of pharmaceutical firms' pursuit of organic growth involved lack of evidence to support scale contributing to greater efficiency. Furthermore, success of biotechnology companies in drug discovery suggested that great scale in R&D could actually be a disadvantage as creativity seems to work better in small groups.

Supporters of organic growth have tended to believe that portfolio management can also be problematic in merged companies: cutting too many projects in the search for *blockbusters* could result in a much higher level of risk. Cutting too few means under-resourcing potential winners and risks an over-stretched and unfocused organisation. In one analysis, the median number of projects at merged firms fell from 85 in both pre-merger companies to 56 by three years post-merger, suggesting that companies which merged during the late 1990s tended to focus on winner products or that merged companies became less productive. Definitive evidence could be years away.

Other supporters of organic growth have claimed that adding more sales power through representatives would bring diminishing returns (particularly in the US) because specialists (as opposed to general practitioner medical doctors) have continued to grow in importance and new distribution channels (such as direct-to-consumer marketing) have also increased in importance. Sales techniques have also been changing because product launches can be implemented by using *spare capacity*, contracting excess resources from big firms and thus smoothing out peaks that could emerge between drug launches and thus maximising marketing expenditure. The argument effectively evolved around those types of developments plus market segmentation between therapeutic categories, allowing medium-size companies and drug specialists to mount successful sales efforts.

Yet other proponents of organic growth claimed that marketing success develops from the right skills, resources and competences rather than from sheer size of the salesforce. For them, improving internal performance was a superior alternative because big pharmaceuticals have suffered from high employee turnover, talent has seldom been attracted outside the pharmaceutical industry, there has been poor use of technology, and sales techniques have not really changed in 35 years. Moreover, in their opinion, mergers have tended to result in slower growth, while big pharmaceuticals look more and more like specialist marketing and development outfits, increasingly subcontracting to academia and biotechnology companies.

But in any event, few could really tell whether amalgamation or organic growth would solve the pharmaceuticals' '*productivity crisis*', the challenge of expanding the revenues in the medium term because of product disappointments which severely undermined the '*pipeline*'. Pharmaceuticals have thus been challenged to sustain high valuation in the stock market once financial disposals finish and before the benefits of long-term investments (such as those made in genomics) kicked in. However, observers still disagreed whether the amalgamation of pharmaceutical companies could become a race to eliminate bloat and duplication in corporate overheads, sales and marketing. At the same time, regulators have been increasingly concerned that dwindling suppliers in the marketplace would threaten dwindling consumer choices.

EMERGING TRENDS

At the end of the 1990s, the sales representative remained decisive for successful sales and marketing in the pharmaceutical industry. There was a belief that the introduction of managed care meant that the marketing approach based on salespeople providing detailed information to individual prescribers was outdated, but the challenge was successfully surpassed by the creation of new types of salespeople to liaise with MCOs. However, those companies which stuck with the old approach and increased their salesforce size and share of voice, such as Pfizer, found that it paid off.

Nevertheless, it was also true that marketing approaches have been shifting. The term '*high compression marketing*' (HCM) was coined to describe the approach adopted by leading companies in their efforts to establish new market presence. HCM has involved simultaneous worldwide launches, global branding, and very heavy investment in promotion and share of voice around time of launch. The intention has been to create a rapid take-off curve which will maximise return from the product by creating higher peak-year sales earlier in the product life cycle. A good example was the launch of Celebrex by Searle, a subsidiary of Pharmacia, which netted $1 billion sales in the first nine months.

However, while product-led muscle-marketing seems to be the name of the game in mass pharmaceutical markets, a small number of companies have adopted a very different approach with notable success. These companies build their strategies around specific customer groups, aiming to satisfy their needs on multiple dimensions. In other words, they develop a franchise. Good examples include Elan Corporation, which has built a profitable niche business by targeting and meeting the needs of the neurology market, and Bristol-Myers Squibb, which managed to keep the top position in the specialised cancer market.

Another response to environmental change has been developed by Roche, which claims to be operating a new '*integrated healthcare*' business model. At the core of this model lies a strong diagnostics division which has to create opportunities to use '*diagnostics*' to select patient groups for treatment and thus maximise the impact of information derived from the Human Genome Project (HGP). Genomics is the study of human genes and, through a joint multinational effort known as HGP, has delivered a complete list, in order, of the chemical '*letters*' making up the DNA in human cells, discovering the location and composition of all human genes. But sequencing the genome does not equal fully understanding the function of the genes. In order to identify new opportunities for pharmaceutical intervention, it is essential to understand what genes are actually doing. So-called '*functional genomics*' is the next challenge and to develop drugs that interact with '*targets*'; for example, enzymes involved in disease processes or the cell-wall of bacteria. The total number of targets discovered up to the year 2000 by the HGP amounted to well under 1,000. Functional genomics has the potential to increase this by orders of magnitude, offering immense potential for better-targeted, more effective and less toxic therapies.

Furthermore, the HGP provided the sequence for one person's genetic make-up but only the '*plain vanilla*' version of the genome. Variations in genetic make-up (single nucleotide polymorphisms or SNPs) will also be of great interest. Understanding genetic susceptibility to disease could lead to much improved screening tests and earlier intervention (provided that effective therapies are available). Pharmacogenomics involves the use of genetic information to understand why some patient populations benefit more than others from a therapy, or why some populations experience specific side-effects. This should allow treatments to be aimed at those who will benefit most (which will appeal to healthcare payers), while pricing policies change to maintain profitability from smaller market segments. In other words, the development of drugs which target specific molecular components of the disease may require patient-specific characterisation.

The expectation is that the HGP will provide accurate molecular components if diagnostics provide relevant patient information. Roche identified this opportunity early on and repositioned itself to take advantage of it. Managers at Roche have had a strong diagnostics division, whose strategic vision was to move from seller of instruments and reagents to a health information provider, offering value through better targeted treatments, convenience and '*peace of mind*'. Managers at Roche also recognised the potential impact of surrogate markers on the speed of clinical development. Roche claimed to have developed the only company embracing these principles, having both requisite experience and all the necessary tools to lead the improvement of disease categorisation as well as lead the shift in healthcare provision offered by genomics and diagnostics. Actually, Roche owned much of the relevant intellectual property, with consequent high barriers to entry for other companies which had yet to develop similar capabilities.

Another emerging trend has evolved around the role that direct-to-consumer (DTC) advertising, predominantly on television, will take in pharmaceuticals' marketing mix. As a medium, DTC TV was one of the key drivers behind the strong volume growth of the US pharmaceutical market during the 1990s. Although the EU does not yet allow DTC advertising of pharmaceuticals, consumers with Internet access can obtain information on new products directly.

In the year 2000, health was one of the top two reasons for people to conduct searches on the Internet, with Yahoo.com/Health, Excite.com/Health and AOL.com/Health the three most visited health-related websites. These could be accessed by both US and European consumers: at the turn of the millennium, about 71 per cent of US households had Internet access, while in the EU the proportion of adults over 15 with Internet access ranged from 12 per cent in Spain to 65 per cent in Sweden. Internet access had so far largely been determined by the availability of a computer, with penetration rates increasing significantly with the advent of interactive digital television. Moreover, along with a shift of medium from print and TV to the Internet, the late 1990s also saw a noticeable shift in news coverage, with the reporting of political events giving way to health-related issues.

As the convergence of telephone, information technology and television accelerates, it has been difficult to envisage how a ban on DTC could be maintained. Furthermore, marketing surveys by pharmaceutical companies resulted in nearly half of respondents reporting that they found the Internet better than other sources for health-related information. Thanks to the Internet, consumers could become much better informed about their health and the available treatment options. Information on new drugs has been reaching consumers via company websites, independent websites and through distribution of press releases to PR services. Marketing surveys suggested that up to 75 per cent of those who search for health-related information on the Internet in the US were likely to discuss that information with their healthcare providers (while the same surveys suggested the number to be 44 per cent on average in the EU). To continue, this trend could increase the level of patient demand for new, effective, better-tolerated therapies, particularly in litigious countries such as the US. The increased transparency of information provided by the Internet has not, however, been an unmixed blessing for the pharmaceutical industry. It was also likely to raise awareness of the enormous price differentials that can exist between countries in the same region or trading bloc for the same product (such as the wide price differential between the US and Canada or between EU countries). As consumers become better informed, the industry could find it hard to maintain pricing levels. If the very significant barriers to inter-country supply were reduced, consumers could even purchase across borders, using 'intelligent agent' software to hunt down the best prices.

But in spite of the human genome project (HGP) and the Internet, emerging markets and new 'lifestyle' drugs, the challenge for the future of pharmaceutical companies at the turn of the millennium had changed little from 30 years earlier: to discover the right drug, for the right dose, in the right time. Finding new formulas for value creation will play a major role in this tough challenge, not only by providing new tools and concepts but also by helping to combat criticism as a frenzy of big deals and (for some) frequent changes of focus proved that most strategies were failing to convince analysts.

Irish ports

John Mangan and James Cunningham

The case describes the changes that have occurred in Irish port administration and outlines the industry structure in the 1990s. Major change in 1996 resulted from new legislations which forced ports to consider their strategic future as well as to address operational issues. The case study lends itself to the use of industry analysis frameworks and the consideration of strategic options and change management in a public sector context.

• • •

THE INTERNATIONAL TREND TOWARDS PORT REFORM

The tendency to reform the operational and institutional structures of ports is a matter of strategic interest within the maritime sector internationally. Ports are critical nodes which facilitate trade flows and, to a lesser extent, tourism flows. In turn, their operational efficiency can have a considerable impact upon the wider economy. Alfred Baird of Napier University in Scotland described the four different models of port administration which are in place variously in different countries and these are shown in Exhibit 1.

As can be seen from Exhibit 1, ports can have any combination of three different functions. Land ownership concerns the physical assets such as vessel berths, terminals, parking areas etc. which comprise the port. Regulation concerns vessel navigation, ensuring compliance with various regulations such as waste disposal and crew safety. Cargo handling concerns the loading and unloading of vessels, storage of freight, provision of value added services, etc.

Exhibit 1   Four models of port administration

	PORT FUNCTIONS		
MODELS	LAND OWNERSHIP	REGULATION	CARGO HANDLING
1. Pure public sector	public	public	public
2. PUBLIC/private	public	public	private
3. PRIVATE/public	private	public	private
4. Pure private sector	private	private	private

Much debate surrounded the question of what combinations of these functions should be controlled by the state and what combinations should be left to the free market and be controlled by the private sector.

STRUCTURE OF THE IRISH MARKET

The Republic of Ireland, a member of the European Union (EU) since 1973, is an island country geographically located in the north-west of Europe with a population of some 3.6 million people. The island of Ireland comprises both the Republic of Ireland, established initially as a Free State under a treaty with the United Kingdom in 1922, and Northern Ireland which remains part of the United Kingdom. A feature of the whole island of Ireland is that, since the opening of the Channel Tunnel linking England with Continental Europe, Ireland is now the only EU member country without a landlink to the rest of the EU and is thus totally dependent on both the air and maritime transport modes for external access and egress. In addition, Ireland has both a large economic dependence on external trade and is in a peripheral location *vis-à-vis* the economic centre of gravity of the EU. Consequently, ports are of special importance to the Irish economy.

The Celtic tiger

Economic conditions in Ireland in recent years have been so positive that it has been dubbed the 'Celtic tiger' (the once-vibrant economies of South East Asia were referred to as 'tiger' economies; the term 'Celtic' refers to the earliest immigrants to Ireland, the Celts, who arrived from central Europe in the period up to 150 BC and who fashioned the course of Irish life and culture for the next 1,000 years). This economic success has resulted from growth in both the manufacturing and service sectors and is a consequence of, *inter alia*, a combination of careful economic planning, investment in infrastructure, high standards of education and, not least, EU grant aid. A member of the EU since 1973, Ireland was one of the first qualifiers for European Monetary Union (EMU) and became a member of the single currency (Irish pound IR£ = €1.27). Over the last decade many multinational companies have located high-tech manufacturing facilities in Ireland. Ireland became an essential node in the global value chains of many of the world's leading manufacturers. In recent years there has been significant growth, in particular in exports of high-value products such as electronics and pharmaceuticals which are exported to diverse overseas locations. In 1997 exports were valued at ca. IR£35 billion and imports at ca. IR£26 billion, yielding a balance of trade surplus of ca. IR£9 billion. Unemployment has fallen sharply in recent years and now stands at a record low of ca. 6 per cent. Inflation, previously relatively high, has fallen to a low of 2 per cent, although there was some evidence pointing to overheating in the economy leading to potential rises. Lastly, in 1998, gross national product (GNP) stood at IR£46.8 billion (having grown by 50 per cent in real terms since 1993) and gross domestic product (GDP) per capita was US$21,500 (GDP per capita was substantially lower, however, because of profit repatriation by foreign firms and interest payments on the national debt).

Ireland's maritime past and present

Ireland has been influenced by maritime trade since the arrival of the Celts from central Europe in the period up to 150 BC. The next major influx of settlers were the Viking warriors who arrived by sea (mostly from Scandinavia) in the ninth and tenth centuries and built fortified settlements, including one at the mouth of the River Liffey, thus giving birth to what is now Dublin, Ireland's capital city, and establishing it as a centre for maritime trade. The next wave of settlers were the Normans in 1169, thus effectively beginning some 800 years of association between England and Ireland. This then was to define the basis for the development of Ireland's maritime trade which revolved largely around shipping between England/Wales and Ireland. Unlike the great maritime nations such as England, France, Spain and Portugal, Ireland was not to have a large maritime fleet and thus did not participate in overseas conquests and empire building. Indeed the domination of maritime trade by flows between Ireland and England was to continue up to and even beyond Ireland's independence from the British Empire in the twentieth century. The twentieth century saw Ireland increasingly engage in international trade, particularly since joining the EEC in 1973, and with it a growth in maritime transportation occurred.

Over 37 million tonnes of goods were handled at Irish ports in 1997 (Exhibit 2). This represents an increase of 43 per cent on the 1990 volume. Over 93 per cent of the volume handled in 1997 was at the nine corporatised ports, with the remaining volume spread over some 16 smaller ports. Over two-thirds of the goods handled at Irish ports in 1997 was 'bulk' freight (i.e. coal, oil, livestock etc.) while under one-third was unitised. The unitised freight typically comprises higher-value commodities such as electronics and is typically held in 20- or 40-foot-long boxes which are either lifted on and off vessels (LoLo) or driven on to vessels (RoRo). Over two-thirds of the volume of sea freight to and from Ireland transits ports along the eastern and southern seaboards of Ireland, reflecting their proximity to England and Wales (which was of importance when Ireland was a member of the British Empire), the current direction of trade, and their proximity to the areas of greatest economic activity in Ireland.

A significant, EU aided, programme of investment has taken place into port infrastructure in the Republic of Ireland. Between 1994 and 1999 a total EU co-financed investment of IR£163 (€207) million was made at Irish ports – one of the aims of this investment was a reduction in combined port and shipping costs to users over the period 1994 to 1999 by a cumulative minimum of 15 per cent, in real terms. Concomitant with this investment programme was a substantial programme of reform concerning the management of Irish ports. EU co-financing of port infrastructure investment has largely arisen as a result of Ireland's classification as an 'Objective 1 region' by the European Commission (i.e. a region whose GDP per capita is 75 per cent or less than the

Exhibit 2	Trade handled by the principal ports in Ireland	
	1990	1997
Arklow	275	501
Cork*	5,857	8,182
Drogheda*	1,004	826
Dublin*	6,383	12,362
Dundalk	320	218
Dun Laoghaire*	261	448
Foynes*	1,084	1,200
Galway	429	535
Greenore	491	344
Shannon Estuary*	5,933	8,359
New Ross*	1,021	1,107
Rosslare*	806	1,116
Waterford*	1,327	1,131
Wicklow	205	167
Others	676	731
Total	**26,072**	**37,227**

* Corporatised ports

EU average). Given the improvements in indigenous economic conditions, it was likely that such EU aid would be largely discontinued after 1999.

Many of the ferry companies in the Irish market who carry RoRo freight also carry passengers. Between four and five million passengers travel on RoRo ferries between Britain and Ireland each year, while in contrast over eight million travel by air; a relatively small number (approximately three hundred thousand) travel on ferries between Ireland and France. Deregulation in the air transport market has led to considerable growth in this sector and the ferry companies now face stiff competition from the air mode. One major cloud on the horizon of the passenger travel market was the intended abolition of duty-free sales in late June 1999.

GOVERNMENT POLICY

Together with the investment programme in port infrastructure there has been a substantial programme of reform concerning the management of Irish ports. Irish ports had been governed by relatively old legislation, namely the Harbours Acts 1946–1976. A government-appointed Review Group was established in 1991 to review the policy and legislation governing commercial ports in Ireland. The Review Group was chaired by Patrick Murphy, a highly successful Irish industrialist, and comprised eight other members who represented the various stakeholders' interests. The Review Group's report noted that 'Ireland's ports have been severely constrained in their ability to respond commercially because of the restricted legislation under which they operate'. Prior ministerial approval was, for example, required for matters such as setting rates and charges, borrowing money, carrying out harbour improvements, and acquiring and disposing of property. The Review Group considered four alternative structures for Irish ports in order to bring about greater commercialisation:

- privatisation;
- amalgamation/regionalisation of ports;
- a national seaports company, on the model of *Aer Rianta* (the state-owned company which operated Ireland's three main airports);
- separate state companies to operate individual ports on a commercial footing (i.e. the state remains the sole shareholder).

The Review Group recommended that commercial state companies should be set up to manage twelve key (in effect the largest) Irish ports. Consequently the Harbours Act 1996 was passed with the purpose of 'freeing Ireland's key ports from direct Departmental control and giving them the commercial freedom they need to be able to operate as modern, customer-oriented service industries'. In March 1997 the first eight ports (see Exhibit 3) out of a planned twelve ports were corporatised and vested as commercial harbour companies (previously they were known as harbour authorities). The port of Waterford was subsequently corporatised in January 1999. There were a number of reasons for the delay in corporatising Waterford, which included the port's largest customer going out of business, storm damage to two cranes (key assets in any ports infrastructure and which are not possible to replace over a short period), and an outstanding loan from the European Investment Bank (EIB). It was intended to corporatise a further three ports (Arklow, Dundalk and Wicklow) but this did not subsequently happen.

PROGRESS TO DATE

The government department responsible for the ports sector, the Department of the Marine and Natural Resources, was committed to enhancing the effectiveness of Irish maritime transport infrastructure and services, especially in the context of the critical role which maritime transport played in Ireland's geographically peripheral island economy. The Department in their strategy statement for the period 1998–2000 stressed that sea transport and port services must be efficient, adequate, responsive and competitive. Dr Michael Woods TD, the Minister for Marine and Natural Resources, stated at a national ports conference in late 1998 that 'freeing up our key ports from direct state control gave them the commercial freedom to operate as modern, customer-oriented service industries, while tightening up accountability for operational and financial procedures'. Dr Woods, a noted scientist and long-serving politician, was regarded by his peers as a hard-working minister (he also served as Minister for the Marine in a previous government) who achieved results, aided and abetted by a new breed of astute and commercially focused civil servants.

By mid-1999 the corporatised ports were enjoying significant successes, buoyed up by very healthy domestic economic conditions. Whether these ports would have been as successful had economic conditions not been so

Exhibit 3   Major ports in Ireland and the types of traffic handled

* Vested as commercial harbour company
• Multi-pupose port
■ RoRo-only port

good was a moot point. Many of the ports had made strides to becoming much more commercially focused and began to explore other value-adding and non-core commercial activities. Areas of business being developed included the development of marinas, industrial parks, transhipment facilities, car park developments, and the cruise liner business. A number of ports also introduced leading-edge navigation technologies for vessels (VTIMS) using their ports and also introduced quality standards. In addition, the corporatised ports submitted five-year development plans to the Department of the Marine and Natural Resources. Invariably, it would take some time for matters to settle and for the ports to further develop and prosper under their new status.

Under the 1946–1976 Acts individual ports were overseen by boards of 25 harbour commissioners. The boards of the corporatised ports, however, which had previously comprised 25 members under the 1946–1976 Acts, now comprised 12 members (typically a chairman, the chief executive, two worker directors and ten directors). Directors were appointed on the basis of their ability to have a strategic and commercial input into the running of the corporatised ports. In practice, many were appointed for reasons such as this, but also on the basis of their political connections. Furthermore, conflict sometimes arose between the management of corporatised ports pursuing a wholly commercial mandate and directors pursuing a more socio-political mandate. Typical examples of this would have been the question of whether to develop areas of a port for commercial or community uses or whether to provide berths for military vessels (which in practice did not have to pay harbour dues). One benefit which accrued to the Department of the Marine and Natural Resources was that the corporatised ports could now get on with their job and did not have to pester the minister and his department with mundane matters, as was the case under the 1946–1976 Acts.

The corporatised ports did, however, inherit certain difficulties with their change of status. Many port employees had been guaranteed that there would be no threat to their jobs. Pensions provisions were complex and in some instances lacking. The new corporatised ports had to deal with certain restrictive work practices and other issues such the results of a lack of investment in staff training over previous years. In addition, the corporatised ports were expected to be cognisant of various externalities which might affect the many varied stakeholder groups. Issues which arose here included noise pollution from cargo handling disturbing local communities, marine engineering works affecting aquaculture developments and fishing interests, and the introduction of new services disturbing marine leisure users. Confusion also arose over ownership of the foreshore (i.e. that part of the shore between the high- and low-tide marks) which was governed by very dated legislation, namely the 1933 Foreshore Act. Finally, difficulties with surface transport access (primarily congestion) also affected some ports.

ISSUES FOR THE FUTURE

It had been intended to corporatise a further three ports (Arklow, Dundalk and Wicklow) but this did not happen. In addition, the question arose in the late

1990s as to what should be done with the thirteen other smaller ports. This combined group of sixteen ports still operated under the rather dated 1946–1976 Harbours Acts. Exhibit 2 illustrated the relatively small volumes handled by these ports. In effect, policy makers had six options, which were not mutually exclusive, to choose from with regard to the future of these ports, namely:

1 Allow the status quo to remain and make small legislative changes as necessary to the 1946–1976 Acts (this would of course involve these ports still being quite dependent upon the Department of the Marine and Natural Resources).

2 Corporatise the ports under the 1996 Harbours Act as was done with the nine larger ports (one pragmatic issue which would have to be addressed was board remuneration: the chairman of a corporatised port received an annual fee of IR£4,000 and each director received IR£2,500; some of the smaller ports had annual revenues below IR£100,000 and could not afford such a structure. It should be noted that fees payable to directors under the 1946–1976 Acts were insignificant in comparison).

3 Transfer ownership of ports to local authorities.

4 Sell ports to the largest customer (in some instances the bulk of the traffic through the smaller ports was derived from one large customer).

5 Develop the ports jointly with the private sector on a public–private partnership (PPP) basis – there were precedents elsewhere in Ireland for such an undertaking (e.g. toll roads etc.).

6 Stipulate that mergers or alliances are made between different combinations of ports.

Key aspects of whatever strategy would be chosen included ensuring that public expenditure would be kept to a minimum, and also ensuring that traffic would not merely be displaced from one small port to another, but instead that real growth would occur and would be of benefit to the port hinterland and the wider economy. Furthermore, policy makers also decided that they would review progress under the Harbours Act 1996 with regard to the nine corporatised ports by completing statutory audits on these ports in March 2000.

References

Baird, A (1995) Privatisation of trust ports in the UK: review and analysis of the first sales. *Transport Policy*, 2 (2) 135–143.

Mangan, J. and Hannigan, K. (eds), (2000) *Logistics and Transport in a Fast Growing Economy*, Blackhall Publishing, Dublin.

The following websites are recommended for further information concerning the Irish economy:

Irish Government (with links to Government departments) *www.irlgov.ie*

Irish Economic and Social Research Institute *www.esri.ie*

Irish Central Statistics Office *www.cso.ie*

Irish Industrial Development Authority *www.idaireland.com*

Economic Review and Outlook 2000, Department of Finance, Dublin, available at *www.irlgov.ie/finance/econ2000.pdf*

The Irish Times (daily newspaper with various links) *www.ireland.com*

KPN – telecommunications strategies for the twenty-first century

D. Jan Eppink

Like most previously state-owned telecommunications companies, KPN was for many years a monopoly supplier in its small home market in the Netherlands. After deregulation the company embarked on a large number of international activities, either in the form of alliances or by taking stakes in other companies.

The case describes these developments up to the middle of 2000. Their strategy was to become one of the three leading companies in Europe in three specified fields of telecommunication (mobile telephony; IP/data; and Internet, call centres and media services). Quite an ambitious goal for a telecommunications operator from a small country.

• • •

In December 2000, Joop Drechsel had been on the executive board of KPN for almost four years. Marten Pieters had joined the board in March 2000. The two of them had direct responsibility for achieving the aims they had set for the company of becoming one of the leading three players in selected fields in the European telecommunications arena. In the eight months that had passed since the stock market was at its highest point, much had changed. The share price had taken a deep drop (along with other European telecoms stocks) and voice revenue per mobile customer was not growing as it used to in the past. New revenue from third-generation mobile broadband technology (UMTS) was uncertain and large investments were needed to gain licences. For a relatively small competitor the strategic aims were very ambitious.

BACKGROUND

KPN was born out of the public sector Post and Telecommunications corporation in the Netherlands. On 1 January 1989 the legal form of the PTT was changed from a department of the Ministry of Transportation and Public Works into a plc – initially 100 per cent government owned. From the early 1980s, various committees had studied the needs for and possibilities of liberalising mail and telecommunications. In the middle of the 1980s the Steenbergen committee proposed that the date for the privatisation be set as the first day of 1989. The mission of the new company, called KPN (Koninklijke PTT Netherlands), was stated as:

> Royal PTT Netherlands is a company that within and outside of the concession it has been granted will deliver to the business and private market a complete set of high quality products and services, concentrated around the national and international transportation of information, goods, and valuables.

The concession described the products and services that would be the exclusive domain of KPN and the 'terms of trade'. The annual report for 1989 mentioned that the progressive deregulation of markets would erode the concession. For PTT Telecom (one of the two subsidiaries, the other being PTT Post) this would mean that, for instance, it would lose its monopoly on the sales of hardware, ranging from telephones for private homes, costing a few hundred guilders, to telecom infrastructures for big companies, costing several millions. Further, in the future, new entrants in the home market would compete for existing business as well as for new growth opportunities. But deregulation would provide new opportunities also.

The change from government department into government-owned company was not just a legal one. Government decided that in view of the liberalisation of the markets and the expected increase in competition, a change of management style was also required. After a short transition period the whole executive board consisted of newcomers. The new CEO of KPN came from Unilever and another director was lured away from IBM. Also, top managers for the two divisions (Post and Telecom) were attracted from outside. The new CEO of PTT Telecom, Ben Verwaayen, was recruited from the Dutch subsidiary of Alcatel, a French company supplying to the telecoms industry. One of his main challenges was to change the culture from a bureaucratic one into an entrepreneurial one.

The 1989 annual report stated:

> External conditions change at high speed. Because of this, our company is continually confronting new challenges.

Rather than seeing these changes as threats, the company applauded them:

> PTT telecom is in favour of this deregulation, provided it is based on international reciprocity and on equal terms for all suppliers of telecom services. (Annual report 1994)

In 1994 about one-third of the shares that had been held by the government were sold to the public when the company was quoted on the Amsterdam Stock Exchange.

In 1997 KPN was split up into several companies. Of these PTT Telecom would carry the name KPN in future, whereas the mail and courier activities would be named TPG. Both companies were quoted on the Amsterdam Stock Exchange. The cable company Vision Networks was eventually sold to France Telecom.

In the years after the privatisation, the environment changed dramatically for a number of reasons. First was the gradually increasing deregulation in the international market. This was a particularly important factor. Until the early 1990s international calls were handled on the basis of bilateral agreements between countries. A call from Holland to Germany would cost a certain amount per minute and the revenue would be split between the German and Dutch operators on an agreed basis. A call from Holland to Italy would involve four national operators. There was a clearing system for making these payments. Deregulation meant that the exclusive rights of the national operators would soon disappear and that operators would start looking for the least costly way to route traffic. Second, deregulation had as an objective to stimulate competition. National governments had to make it possible and attractive for new companies to enter their markets. For companies that for decades had been monopolists this meant an enormous change in the playing field. Some entrants were relative newcomers in the telecoms business, but had quite an impact in the parts of the market they chose to enter – for example, Worldcom. Third were the technological developments that enabled the rise in the use of Internet. Particularly important in this respect were methods of increasing the speed of data transmission and data processing (microprocessors and routers). KPN started giving Internet-related issues serious top management attention early in the second half of the 1990s.

STRATEGY

The strategy of the company was stated as follows in the 1999 annual report:

> In 1999 KPN has identified its core activties: fixed telecommunication; mobile telecommunication; data communication (IP/data) and Internet, call centre, and media services (ICM) (abbr. added, DJE). In all these fields KPN wants to excel. That means: in three of the four sectors (mobile, IP/data, and Internet, call centre and media services) KPN aims for fast growth and a position in the European top three.

Joop Drechsel, responsible in the executive board for mobile and ICM, expressed a vision in which transactions in future would increasingly take place in cyberspace. He expected enormous increases in the number and value of transactions. These transactions could be in the fields of commerce, financial services, entertainment, information, etc. Cyberspace would connect suppliers and customers. Companies that facilitated such transactions could earn vast amounts of money. Customers could access cyberspace through various means, for instance cable, fixed lines (narrow band and fast lines), mobile and satellite. KPN would provide all means of access except cable. Combined with the KPN-Internet providers for the private and the business market this should give a good position for the future.

Marten Pieters, member of the executive board of KPN and responsible for IP/data, commented on the characteristics of some of the activities:

> Fixed telecommunication is basically a service for the domestic market. . . .

> Data/IP is very international . . . requires fast global or at least pan-European infra-structures . . .

... scale is very important for development of products and services for mobile. If you look at UMTS, you need not only to buy the licences, you must also offer new services, for which you need large numbers of customers. ... branding may become very important: in Germany we have the E-Plus brand.

Data/IP and mobile differ in customers and services ... technologies are converging ...

In the field of fixed telecommunication KPN aimed at maintaining its market leadership in the Netherlands and a leading position in Europe in selected segments, among which was network/DSL services.

The European expansion would mainly be achieved by means of acquisitions, joint ventures and/or partnerships. It was of major importance to have management control over these activities. Where useful because of flexibility in the market, speed, transparency and value creation, KPN would create separate entities with or without their own quotations.

CUSTOMERS

Historically, PTT Telecom had two groups of customers in its home market: private individuals and small businesses (which did not spend large amounts on telecommunications), and big companies whose telecommunication bills could run into tens of millions of guilders. The latter group was especially important for future success, for two reasons. First, it was expected that because of the ongoing internationalisation of business, telecommunications needs would increase. Second, developments such as just-in-time deliveries, enterprise resource planning systems, the Internet, and increasing size of companies (through mergers and acquisitions) were also expected to have an impact on the demand for telecommunication and the competitive situation.

In the course of the 1990s the strategy of the company changed, not only to include more and new services (mobile and Internet), but also in a geographical sense. The market was no longer just the familiar home market, but also countries nearby and far away.

STRATEGIC ALLIANCES AND PARTNERSHIPS

One of the pillars of achieving the strategic goals was the formation of strategic alliances. Initially these were relatively small-scale. In 1991 the alliance with Televerket from Sweden (now Telia) was announced just before the international Telecommunication Exhibition in Geneva. Both companies would eventually join their international activities in a new company called Unisource. Unisource would offer network and advanced fax services for larger international companies worldwide. Depending on the area and the service, Unisource would seek appropriate additional partners. In 1992 the Swiss PTT Telecom announced it would join Unisource. In that year an agreement was also signed between Unisource and US-based Sprint for the distribution of worldwide network services.

The formation of Unisource had two aims for the parents. The first was to achieve economies of scale. To give an idea of the relative size of the companies in the international arena: PTT Telecom was the sixth largest company in the field of international telecommunications, but only one-tenth of the size of the fifth largest. The other aim was to make possible 'one-stop shopping' for international businesses.

In 1993 Unisource made deals with SITA, the worldwide telecommunications systems of the airlines; an agreement was signed with KDD, a Japanese telecoms company, for the distribution of services. In 1993 Telefonica, a Spanish operator, signed an agreement for mutual support for international clients. It was agreed that in 1995 Telefonica would become the fourth equal partner in Unisource: this was effected in May 1996.

In December 1994 the European perspective was broadened when US-based AT&T and Unisource decided to start a joint venture named Uniworld. The new entity targeted large, internationally operating companies with an integrated package of worldwide data and voice services. The company offered its services via its own offices or through local providers. Uniworld also represented in Europe World Partners (the alliance of Unisource, AT&T, KDD from Japan and Singapore Telecom). In 1996 the name Uniworld was changed into AT&T-Unisource Communication Services (AUCS), in which Unisource had a 60 per cent share and AT&T a 40 per cent share.

The structure and market approach of Unisource is shown in Exhibit 1.

The alliance between Unisource and AT&T was not the only worldwide telecom alliance aimed at multinational companies. Global One had been formed in early 1996 by US-based Sprint and Europe's Atlas, which was formed by Deutsche Telekom and France Telecom (each 50 per cent). Another major alliance was Concert, formed in 1994 by British Telecom and MCI from the USA. In November 1996 BT and MCI announced that they had entered into a merger agreement. BT would offer $20 billion for the shares of MCI (in fact the merger never took place – it was overtaken by other events).

In April 1997 Telefonica, BT and MCI announced they had formed a new strategic alliance. To compensate for the damage this caused to Unisource, Telefonica had to pay several hundreds of millions of dollars to the three other Unisource partners. Finally WorldCom made a far higher bid ($37 billion) in October 1997 for MCI's shares and won the contest with BT. Telefonica was, for the time being, left without a partner. In March 1998 Telefonica, WorldCom and MCI announced a new partnership, which later was dissolved. WorldCom and Sprint announced a merger in 1999, with WorldCom offering $129 billion for the shares of Sprint (including debt); anti-trust authorities on both sides of the Atlantic blocked this in July 2000. After the Telefonica, BT and MCI partnership fell apart, BT teamed up with AT&T to form the Concert global equity joint venture. Concert aimed at the business customer with complex telecommunication needs. It installed an international IP-network.

At the end of 1997 there were rumours in the financial press that because of a possible link with Norwegian Telecom, Telia might also leave Unisource. At around the same time it was disclosed that Unisource and Telecom Italia were negotiating a deal that would tie the Italian company to the Unisource group, either as owner or as strategic partner.

CASE STUDIES

Exhibit 1

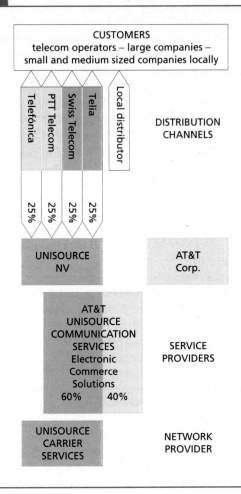

BREAKING UP

In the course of 1998 there were fundamental discussions within Unisource about the strategy the company should follow. The financial results were still negative (1998 loss of DFl 382 million on revenues of DFl 2.610 million) and the interests of the original partners seemed to be diverging. The 1998 Unisource annual report made the newly developed strategy look like a 'leap forward' rather than a split-up of Unisource:

> Unisource made a thorough analysis of what had been achieved since 1992, against the background of the rapidly changing telecommunications market. This resulted in a new strategy in which Unisource will concentrate on the segment of small- and medium-sized enterprises with a full range of products and services, but with a special focus on data services and Internet protocol (IP) services in the largest telecommunications market in Europe. We can realise this ambition only from an independent position.

Observers within KPN would remark later that Unisource missed a compelling strategic *raison d'être* and that the alliance model was not working any longer. Stronger links between companies were required.

It was decided that the three owners of Unisource would each buy the Unisource Business networks that served their home market. KPN bought the Belgian network as well. Later, other parts of Unisource were sold to other operators and parties.

In the course of 1998 AT&T decided it would withdraw from AUCS and WorldPartners. This again weakened the position of what was left of Unisource. In the same period other strategic alliances were dissolved also. Global One fell apart after France Telecom and Deutsche Telekom fought over a participation in Italy.

NEW PARTNERS

In 1998 KPN and Qwest from the USA decided to establish KPNQwest, a new jointly owned company which was quoted on exchanges in the Netherlands and USA in November of the next year. By 2001 this company was a leading pan-European provider of data-centric services based on the Internet protocol. It has an advanced 20,000 km fibre optic network, which connects 50 cities in Europe. It was one of the largest business Internet service providers (ISPs) in Europe, operating in 15 countries. The company was developing a network with a large capacity, the so-called EuroRings which will connect 50 cities. In 18 of these locations Cybercenters will provide hosted customers with unlimited bandwidth. The first CyberCenter opened in Munich in July 2000, whereas Paris and London were ready for service at the end of 2000. Milan, Frankfurt and Stockholm would be offering services in 2001. KPNQwest wants to become the highest quality and lowest costs fibre optic network in Europe.

In view of the increasing investments as well as the required scale of operations, in May 2000 KPN discussed the possibility for co-operation with Telefonica of Spain, the former partner in Unisource. But Spanish political developments were said to be an obstacle to the merger of the two companies.

At the same time KPN Mobile was discussing an agreement with NTT-DoCoMo, the immensely successful Japanese mobile operator, who could provide not only financial resources but also advanced technology for future generations of mobile telecommunications. It was decided that NTT-DoCoMo would acquire shares in KPNMobile in exchange for several billion euros. NTT-DoCoMo also bid for German UMTS licences together with KPN Mobile. Initially Hutchinson Whampoa from Hong Kong was also involved, but this company later sold its shares to KPN. KPN's share in the licences is estimated at €6.4 billion. KPN expected that another €3.5 billion would have to be invested before the network became operational.[1] On 31 October 2000 the *Financial Times* wrote that NTT-DoCoMo was discussing with AT&T the possibility of buying a 10–20 per cent share in AT&T Wireless.

---

[1] Research agency Forrester had a much higher estimate: between 4 and 6 billion euros for the infrastructure and another 2–3 billion euros for marketing efforts.

EQUITY PARTICIPATIONS AND JOINT VENTURES

The internationalisation of the Dutch PTT Telecom also was pursued in another way – through direct equity participation in existing or newly formed telecoms operators in other countries. The political changes in central and eastern Europe in the late 1980s was a trigger to explore the market possibilities in that area.

The 1990 annual report mentioned the start of joint ventures with the Czech and Slovak operators Telecomspol SRO and Isysspol SRO. A consultancy agreement was signed with the Czech partner in 1993, whereas with the Slovak partner further possibilities were under investigation. The Czech national operator SPT Telecom was privatised in 1995. Together with Swiss Telecom, PTT Telecom bought a 27 per cent stake in the SPT. At the time of purchase SPT was profitable, with growth opportunities: the number of telephones per 100 inhabitants was 20, a total of two million. In 1996, 400,000 new telephones were installed, with a similar expansion expected for 1997. The SPT share price showed a satisfactory increase. Despite the growth and good operational results of the company it became increasingly difficult in the following years to maintain management control. Because of European regulations the company would lose its monopoly in the near future. In August 2000 KPN announced that it would not bid for more shares in Cesky Telecom (formerly SPT).

In 1992 PTT Telecom participated in two joint ventures in the Ukraine. One was Utel, with the aim of modernising the national and international infrastructure. The other was UMC, a company that had to build and manage the infrastructure for mobile telecommunications in the Ukraine. As a result, the first international gateway was opened in L'vov in 1993. Owing to the bad economic situation in the Ukraine, KPN had to write off its investments in the companies in the Ukraine. No further investments were anticipated.

In 1993 a concession for mobile communication in Hungary was granted to a consortium called Pannon GSM. PTT Telecom was one of the partners in this consortium. In the course of 1994 the mobile network became operational. In the same year a licence for a regional fixed network was obtained in co-operation with Swiss Telecom and the Hungarian partner Jasz-Com. The latter participation was sold in 1999 with a profit of DFl 5 million.

At the beginning of 1998 KPN bought the shares Unisource had in Pantel, a Hungarian company with a fixed network that also provided leased lines, data communication and VPNs. Over time, the participations in Pannon and Pantel were enlarged on several occasions.

Investigations into the possibility of investments in telecoms companies in Slovakia, Romania and Bulgaria were discontinued in the course of 2000.

Besides central and eastern Europe, the focus was also on other areas. Some ventures were in small markets such as Antillean Telematics which was established in 1991 to provide telematic services in the Caribbean area. Other targets were large and fast-developing markets such as Indonesia where, in 1993, an umbrella agreement was signed with PT Telkom for joint activities and projects in Indonesia and South East Asia. The two initial projects were a trial with GSM mobile telephony in Indonesia and the building of infrastructure for companies in the Jakarta area. The next year PTT Telecom took a 30 per cent stake in PT Bakrie Electronics Company (BEC). Through this participation PTT Telecom co-operated with the national Indonesian telephone company in Ratelindo to build and manage fixed networks in Jakarta and Western Java. BEC held 55 per cent of the shares in Ratelindo.

Participation in a mobile operator was obtained in 1996 when 17 per cent of the shares of PT Telekomunikasi Selular (Telkomsel) were acquired. The company provided services on the main islands of Sumatra, Java, Bali, Lombok, Kalimantan and Sulawesi. The number of mobile phones increased beyond expectations: by the end of 1996 there were 188,000, which was 54,000 more than anticipated.

The Asian economic crisis in 1997 hit Indonesia badly. The currency devalued, which caused a loss for KPN on its participation in Telkomsel of some DFl 80 million. In 1997 the total investment in BEC was written off for similar reasons. The potential for the Indonesian market (200 million inhabitants) in the long run was still considered interesting.

In 1996 PTT Telecom formed a consortium, Comsource, with its Swedish Unisource partner Telia to acquire a 20 per cent stake in Telecom Eireann costing 500 million Dutch guilders.

The agreement with the Irish government included an option to increase the participation by a further 15 per cent not later than 1999. For the Irish partner, Comsource could make an important contribution to cost reductions and thus increase financial and commercial performance. These could be achieved by better management of existing operations but also by means of joint purchasing, and software and systems developments. For PTT Telecom the attractiveness of Ireland as a new market was the international orientation of Irish industry: the Irish partner could be a powerful distributor of Unisource products and services. Also, the relatively low penetration of telephones in Irish households provided opportunities for growth. In Holland, for 100 people there are 54 telephone connections, whereas in Ireland there were only 36.

The results of Eircom developed satisfactorily. In 1999 KPN decided to increase its share in Eircom from 12 per cent to 21 per cent. Late in 1999 KPN decided to sell its shares in Eircomm, in part because the potential of the Irish market is limited. By the end of 1999 the market value of the KPN shares was DFl 4.3 billion; the book value was DFl 2.8 billion.

By the end of 1997 PTT Telecom discussed internally a link with the Chinese People's Liberation Army in setting up a telecoms company in the biggest market in the world. It was anticipated that the initial investment would be modest, but that in future the build-up of infrastructure would run into billions of dollars. The critical issues were not commercial or technical, but political: particularly the role of the army in the Tianenmen Square massacre of 1989. In 1998 there were further discussions with Chinese companies about joint ventures. In view of the decision of summer 2000 to concentrate on western Europe, it was decided not to extend these discussions.

On many of these participations, Joop Drechsel commented:

> They have in common that as a minority partner we do not have much influence. Moreover the initial capital outlays are very high with value creation expected on the longer term. It is very difficult to achieve synergies and cost savings if you do not have management control.

On 9 December 1999, KPN announced that it had come to an agreement with BellSouth to buy 74.49 per cent of its shares in the mother company of E-Plus, the third German mobile operator (market share 16 per cent; 3.8 million subscribers). This move gave KPN an entry into the large German market of some 80 million inhabitants; €9.1 billion was paid in cash. BellSouth was given the right to convert their remaining 22.51 per cent in E-Plus into shares of KPN or KPN Mobile; BellSouth could also continue to hold the shares. To this end, KPN gave BellSouth a warrant. Furthermore, they agreed that BellSouth, until 9 December 2003, should acquire shares in KPN other than by using the warrant, and that an eventual participation of BellSouth after 9 December 2003 would not exceed 24.9 per cent. As far as KPN Mobile is concerned, BellSouth could acquire 24.9 per cent of KPN Mobile shares in addition to a possible conversion based on the warrant, but not later than 9 December 2002. In exceptional situations the periods mentioned above could be shortened.

INTERNET AND MEDIA

The beginning of an Internet strategy for KPN was in the early 1990s with an investment (19.5%) in Videotex Nederland NV. This interest was mentioned in the annual report of 1992 for the first time, in a list of subsidiaries and participations. In the report itself no further mention was made of the activities and the strategic importance of this activity. This company provided information to a personal computer via telephone lines. In the beginning the service was very slow, but later it could be used for online bank transactions.

The annual report of 1993 briefly mentioned the participation in this company in a longer list of companies in the field of tele-information services in which KPN had a participation. In 1994 KPN Multimedia was formed (a joint venture between Post and Telecom) which aimed to develop initiatives with interactive media. The next annual report mentioned the further integration of telecommunication with other services in the field of information technology, financial services and entertainment. These developments were considered major opportunities. The 1996 report for the first time mentioned the word Internet. The interest in Videotex Nederland had been increased to 53.5 per cent. In the meantime, KPN had bought Planet Internet, an independent Internet service provider. The company provided access to the Internet under the brands World Access and the Planet Internet. These two subsidiaries were merged in the autumn of 1996. Services for target groups were developed, such as for small and medium-sized enterprises. In time a third network, as well as the fixed and mobile telecommunications, would be built for Internet services. This would require considerable investment. A first step was investment to increase the capacity of existing lines by means of ISDN technology. By January 1997 all Internet acitivites were to be concentrated in a new unit for Internet services.

On 30 September 1997 Het Net was opened to the public. It was an information network for the Netherlands based on the same principle as the Internet. It was useful for companies and organisations that wanted to provide information to the public. By the end of 1997 more than 700 companies had a site on Het Net; the number of regular visitors was close to 150,000. In 1998 it became possible to transact via Het Net, including payment for goods and services. In the meantime, the number of ISDN subscribers increased: by the end of 1998 the number of ISDN channels had increased to 1.57 million. This increase was in large part due to the increase in Internet traffic. The number of analogue lines decreased by 3.5 per cent to 7.77 million. Also, the equity interest in World Access/Planet Internet was increased to 100 per cent, whereas two other ISPs were acquired: Capitol Online (12,000 subscribers) and XS4ALL (40,000) by the end of 1998.

When by the end of June 1999 Het Net became a full-blown ISP, KPN had brands of several types: Het Net, a free ISP; World Access with a moderate subscription fee; and the high-end XS4ALL. By the end of 1999 KPN's ISPs had 1.2 million subscribers in the Benelux region. As an ISP, Planet Internet co-operated with content providers as well. An exclusive contract was made with Disney for distribution of services in the Benelux region.

To accomodate the enormous increase in Internet traffic KPN built the Lambda network of 10,000 km optic fibre with a capacity to handle 20 million telephone calls and Internet sessions simultaneously. This network will be linked to the KPNQwest network, thus securing fast access to other parts of the world. It was also decided that ADSL would increasingly become available to Internet users.

As far as the services for business were concerned, KPN was active in supporting companies in implementing an e-business strategy by offering applications for Internet sites, intra- and extranets, web hosting, securing payments etc.

ORGANISATION

In 1997 the responsibility for the international activities of PTT Telecom were concentrated in the Business Development department. But its origin was the department that since 1989 had taken care of the administration of international calls, then called Business Unit International Telecommunications. This accounting-oriented department had to be turned around to become the initiator of acquisitions and international co-operation as well as the 'manager' of investments in foreign telecom companies.

In 1994 it was decided that the centralised PTT Telecom would be reorganised to become more market oriented. The changes brought with them, among other things, the reshaping of the Business Development department (BD), which was given responsibility for the international activities of PTT Telecom. To be included in BD was the former 'Business Unit International Telecommunications', which took care of the administration of international calls. There were two options for redesigning BD. One was to set it up along functional lines, the other was to create geographical 'divisions'. The latter had the disadvantage that there would be some duplication of groups such as finance and support, acquisition etc. Initially a functional form was chosen because of the scarcity of people and the need for efficiency. The following managers reported to the director for Business Development: International Acquisitions,

Exhibit 2	KPN organisation structure

Royal KPN NV

	Services via the fixed network	IP/Data	ICM	Mobile telecommunication
National	BU Fixed Telephony BU Business Communication BU Carrier Services	BU Corporate Networks	BU Telecommerce Planet Internet XS4ALL Het Net SNT	KNP Mobile
International	Eircom Cesky Telecom	KPNQwest Infonet Pantel	Planet Internet Belgium	E-Plus (G) KPN Orange (B) Pannon GSM (H) Telkomsel (Ind) UMC (Ukraine)

International Operations, and Finance and Support. Later a manager for human resources joined the management team. The BD department saw its role as orchestrator and co-ordinator of all the activities that were necessary to grow the business internationally. For this, it had to get the co-operation of many other departments and business lines within PTT Telecom. If, for instance, in a foreign project there was a need for certain types of specialists, the HRM part of Business Development had to seek them out from other parts of the company and persuade them to work abroad for a while.

Joop Drechsel and others on the executive board found the organisational set-up for BD and other parts of KPN too loosely structured and not transparent and results-oriented enough. It was expected that, in future, demands for shareholder value would increase and that a high share price was necessary to make possible future acquisitions. It was decided there should be more clarity, transparency and accountability. This led to a reorganisation of which the final result was the establishment in the course of 1997 of KPN International. This unit consisted of three regions, (1) Western Europe, The Americas and Africa, (2) Asia, (3) Central and Eastern Europe, and the product-group, (4) International Solutions Provision. KPN Telecom would deal with the national market, including the national mobile market.

The organisation in January 2000, as far as subsidiaries are concerned, is shown in Exhibit 2.

Exhibit 3   Some data about KPN

YEAR	1999	1998	1997*	1996	1995	1994	1993	1992	1991	1990	1989
Turnover (DFI million)	20,124	17,719	15,780	14,276	13,623	12,686	11,831	11,122	10,345	9,649	8,953
Gross profit	2,320	3,470	3,288	3,456	3,179	2,862	2,676	2,789	2,634	2,622	2,444
Net profit after tax	1,825	1,515	1,936	1,774	1,579	1,389	1,366	1,330	1,311	1,290	1,251
Investment in P&E	5,563	4,296	2,997	2,425	2,629	2,665	2,728	2,854	3,046	2,714	3,007
% of total assets	14.0	14.3	11.35	10.4	12.0	12.6	12.4	12.7	14.1	13.1	N/A
Investment in telecoms companies	425	498	198	620†	724‡	N/A	N/A	N/A	N/A	N/A	N/A
% of total assets of PTT Telecom	1.1	1.6	0.8	2.7	3.3	N/A	N/A	N/A	N/A	N/A	N/A
Turnover International Calls (DFI million)	3,465	2,241	1,934	2,188	2,467	2,459	2,410	2,704	2,539	2,338	2,088
% of total turnover	17.2	12.6	12.3	15.3	18.1	19.4	20.4	24.3	26.2	25.6	23.3
No. of international calls (million)	N/A	N/A	488	462	434	405	372	334	294	259	222
No. of employees (FTE)	34,753	32,547	32,088	29,690	30,548	31,671	31,981	32,327	30,819	29,262	28,977

* In the course of 1997 KPN was split up in two parts: TPG, the post and courier group, and KPN, the telecommunications company. Because of the adjustments made the data are not always entirely comparable to those of 1996.

† Includes investments in Telecom Eireann and Telkomsel (Indonesia)

‡ Includes investments in SPT Telecom (Czech Republic, DFI 624 million) and Unisource (DFI 100 million)

When the executive board of KPN was enlarged in March 2000, some of the responsibilities were reshuffled. Mr L. Roobol was made responsible for services on the fixed net when he joined the executive board. The board member responsible for IP/Data, Marten Pieters, was also made responsible for Eircom and Cesky Telecom. In an earlier position within KPN he had held operational responsibilites for the foreign operations and knew both companies and actors around them well. Joop Drechsel was responsible for all mobile and Internet, Call centre and Media (ICM) activities.

Where appropriate, parts of the company would be set up as separate entities, with the possibility of their own quotation on the stock market. This was done with KPN/Qwest and KPNMobile. The first was quoted on the stock market. In July 2000 KPN announced that it would establish a separate plc for most of its Internet, call centre and media activities (IMC). This would give subsidiaries the flexibility needed to respond quickly to developments that might unfold in the years ahead. Moreover, stock market quotations made visible the value of the separate units.

Exhibit 4   Segmentation of turnover, gross profit and investment of KPN

	1999	1998	1997	1996
Turnover**				
Fixed telephony, equipment, etc.	14,849	13,923	12,977	10,202
Mobile	3,851	3,002	2,153	1,886
International activities	3,465	2,258	1,934	2,188
Internal deliveries	−2,041	−1,464	−1,284	N/A
Total	20,124	17,719	15,780	14,276
Gross profit**				
Fixed telephony, equipment, etc.	844	2,898	2,850	2,893
Mobile	516	252	227	209
International activities	960	320	211	361
Total	2,320	3,470	3,288	3,463
Investment in Plant & Equipment**				
Fixed telephony, equipment, etc.	4,303	3,658	2,572	2,178
Mobile	900	444	378	336
International activities	360	350	48	36
Total	5,563	4,452	2,997	2,425
Investment in immaterial* and financial assets**				
Fixed telephony, equipment, etc.	N/A	150	5	13
Mobile	N/A	290	0	0
International activities	N/A	1,372	371	1,154
Total	N/A	1,812	376	1,167

* Investment in goodwill and licences.
** 1 million Dutch Guilders.

Exhibit 5	Some information on competitors		

	TURNOVER	REGION(S)	DATE OR YEAR	
Mobile telephony				
Vodatone AirTouch:				
Group turnover	£7,873m		1999/2000	
	£2,901m	UK	1999/2000	
	£2,030m	EMEA	1999/2000	
	£3,956m	USA/Asia Pacific	1999/2000	
France Telecom	£2,470m	not specified	9 months 2000	
Deutsche Telekom	£2,455m	not specified	9 months 2000	
British Telecom	£2,170m	not specified	1999/2000	
Subscribers				
Deutsche Telekom	26.5m	not specified	3rd quarter 2000	
KPNMobile	6.6m	Germany	Dec. 2000	
	4.8m	Netherlands	Dec. 2000	
British Telecom	7.4m	not specified	31 March 2000	
France Telecom	12.6m	France	31 Sept. 2000	
	22.1m	outside France	31 Sept. 2000	
Vodafone AirTouch	12m	USA, Australia, New Zealand	31 March 2000	
Internet etc.				
Tiscali	10.7m	15 countries	January 2001	Incl. World on Line + Liberty Surf
T-Online	7.0m	not specified	30 Sept. 2000	
KPN Planet	over 2m	not specified	end 2000	
France Telecom:	2.2m	not specified	30 Sept. 2000	Aims for 10m active users in 2003

Information on **Data/IP** is very difficult to extract in a consistent and reliable way.
KPN-Qwest indicates they are one of the top players.

Exhibit 6	Glossary of abbreviations

ADSL	Asynchronous digital subscriber line: an advanced technology to increase the capacity of normal telephone lines. Increases the speed of web-surfing
BD	Business Development: in the mid-1990s this department was responsible for creating new business opportunities for KPN
DSL	Digital subscier line: allows transfer of digital infomation only. Used for customers wanting to transfer large quantities of data
GSM	Second-generation technology for mobile telecommunication in use in many parts of Europe and Asia. Not used in the USA
ICM	Internet, Call centres and Media services: a 'division' of KPN
IP	Internet protocol: a standard for sending messages over the Internet
IP/Data	Divison of KPN responsible for data transmission for corporate customers
ISP	Internet service provider: company that provides acces to the Internet. May also provide addtional services, such as content
ISDN	Integrated services digital network: an early technology to increase the capacity of telephone lines
UMTS	Technology that will eventually succeed GSM as the mobile technology. Can provide fast mobile Internet access
VPN	Virtual private network: for instance an intranet that is operated by a telecoms operator

Amazon.com – from start-up to the new millennium

Gary Stockport and David Street

This case study provides an ideal example of emerging e-commerce strategic thinking because of Amazon's first-mover development and prominence, its accelerated growth and its recent and rapid emergence as a significant e-commerce player. Amazon.com's development is significant because of its strategic approach in a still emerging industry, its dominance over more traditional retailers, as well as its explosive growth in new products, services and new geographic areas. The case also provides an example of the unique problems, risks and opportunities experienced within the e-commerce environment.

• • •

INTRODUCTION

Jeff Bezos as CEO of Amazon.com, Inc. is facing a grand opportunity – to succeed in a US$5 trillion world retail market, with one major concern – the more Amazon.com sells, the greater are its losses. These losses are also expected to increase into the near future, as the competitive focus has remained clearly on gaining market share as opposed to generating profits.

This strategy is embraced by many investors who have assisted in driving Amazon.com's stock beyond any established benchmark of price-to-revenues. On the other hand, other investors believe that the price is overvalued and that the company is facing an increasing range of challenges from both local and international competitors.

Under Jeff Bezos's leadership, Amazon.com appears to be pursuing a strategy to make itself the Wal-Mart of the Internet, and in doing so is facing increasing competition on every front. Many investors believe it is spreading itself too thinly as it moves into more low-margin businesses, and expectations for the year 2001 include a significant growth in revenue, an improvement in gross margins, and decreasing operating costs as a percentage of revenue as well as an increase in marketing expenditure. Along with its growing revenue and customer base is an increasing long-term debt position combined with a growing loss per share.

This case was prepared by David Street, University of Cape Town, under the supervision of Professor Gary J. Stockport, Graduate School of Management, University of Western Australia. It is intended as a basis for class discussion and not as an illustration of either good or bad management practice. © Gary J. Stockport, 2001. Not to be reproduced or quoted without permission.

With the explosive growth in Internet companies' market capitalisation positions, the rational investor would justifiably ask whether or not some over-hyped mania is at play. But the truth is, in spite of the noise and hyperbole, the Internet is for real and the trend data clearly reveal that what is happening is nothing more than an embryo taking shape. According to Forrester Research (a company that creates, publishes and sells technology research reports), the total value of goods and services purchased over the Web exceeded US$43 billion in 1998 and is expected to increase to US$1.3 trillion in 2003 (*Amazon.com 1998 Annual Report*, 1999). Amazon.com believes it is well positioned to capitalise on this growth. According to Media Metrix (a company that provides audience measurement products and services to Internet advertisers, Internet advertising agencies, Internet properties, technology companies and financial institutions), approximately 16 per cent of Web users visited Amazon.com's stores in December 1998 (*Amazon.com 1998 Annual Report*, 1999). Many analysts are optimistic and point out that Amazon's problems, though real, do not necessarily mean that the stock is destined to fail.

Some of the achievements backing the optimism of analysts include the following:

- Amazon.com (Amazon.com, Inc., and its subsidiaries) is the Internet's No. 1 retailer. Amazon.com opened its virtual doors on the World Wide Web in July 1995 and today offers Earth's Biggest Selection, along with online auctions and free electronic greetings cards. Amazon.com seeks to be the world's most customer-centric company, where customers can find and discover anything they might want to buy online. Amazon.com lists more than 28 million unique items in categories such as electronics, kitchen products, books, music, DVDs, videos, camera and photo items, toys, software, computer and video games, tools and hardware, and lawn and patio items. Through Amazon.com zShops, any business or individual can sell virtually anything to Amazon.com's more than 25 million customers, and with Amazon.com Payments, sellers can accept credit card transactions, avoiding the hassles of offline payments.

- Amazon.com operates three international Web sites: www.amazon.fr, www.amazon.co.uk and www.amazon.de. It also operates the Internet Movie Database (www.imdb.com), the Web's comprehensive and authoritative source of information on more than 250,000 movies and entertainment titles and 1 million cast and crew members dating from the birth of film in 1891 to 2001.

- Amazon Anywhere is the leader in mobile e-commerce, providing access from anywhere in the world to Amazon.com, Amazon.co.uk and Amazon.de on personal digital assistants (PDAs) and through handheld wireless Internet devices that use HDML or the Wireless Application Protocol.

'In a very short period of time, Amazon.com has become one of the world's most recognized brands,' said Jaleh Bisharat, vice-president, marketing, Amazon.com. 'We updated our logo to match the vitality of the brand and to reflect our most important core value – customer satisfaction. We believe the new logo exudes happiness, is fresh and unique, and has the potential, over time, to join the world's great consumer marks' (Amazon.com, 2000).

With Amazon.com's current strategy combined with the ongoing recruitment of an entrepreneurial top management team for each business segment, the challenge for Amazon.com is increasingly on the strategic implementation front. With a growing customer base (exceeding 25m customers at November 2000), a well-respected brand, strong customer service and order fulfilment together with a significant cash position, Bezos appears to be bringing together the assets necessary to make Amazon.com's vision a reality.

BACKGROUND – JEFF BEZOS

Bezos had always been fascinated with technology. At the age of 14, he had admitted to wanting to be an astronaut or a physicist, or something that would allow him to use cutting-edge technology. During high school he founded his first business, DREAM Institute, a summer school programme that was aimed at stimulating creative thinking in youngsters.

At age 30, Jeff Bezos, with an electrical engineering and computer science BA from Princeton, was the youngest senior vice-president of D.E. Shaw, running a Wall Street hedge fund. At some time, Bezos came up with the statistic that the electronic world known as the World Wide Web would grow at the incredible rate of 2,300 per cent monthly. Bezos has used the term *compelled* to describe his emotional reaction to the growth figures of the World Wide Web. If he had not acted immediately, he has said, he would have regretted it his whole life: 'When something is growing that fast, every second counts.' One reporter reported Bezos saying:

> I decided that when I was eighty I wouldn't regret quitting a Wall Street job when I was thirty, but when I was eighty I might really regret missing this great opportunity.
> (Quoted in Saunders, 1999, p. 8)

In June 1994 Bezos quit his job, climbed into a Chevy Blazer with his wife, MacKenzie, and their Labrador, pointed the car west, and began driving. His last day of work at D.E. Shaw was 30 June 1994 and he arrived in Seattle on 5 July.

Bezos considered selling a variety of products and his list of top five contenders comprised computer hardware, computer software, CDs, videos and books. He eventually settled for books because the worldwide market is large (US$82 billion in 1994), the price point is low, and the range of titles is large. Web-based technologies were also described as being able to effectively organise and select information in ways that could positively enhance the sales of books.

Being unsure of the ideal location, four likely locations were identified: Portland, Oregon; Lake Tahoe, Nevada; Boulder, Colorado; and Seattle, Washington. Seattle was eventually chosen because it was the location of book distributor Ingram, which has continued to provide approximately 60 per cent of Amazon.com's books. Additional factors for choosing Seattle included its favourable sales-tax climate as well as its high-tech workforce. During the next 12 months, Bezos, his wife, and three others raised money, established relationships with shippers and wholesalers, and developed the software that would go live with the launch of the online store in July 1995.

Despite his contacts in the New York money markets, Bezos had to turn to Silicon Valley for funding for his firm. By selling on the Internet, he told his investors, he would change the economics of the book industry as a whole. Investors recall that Bezos said in their early discussions:

> I know nothing about the book industry, nothing, I want to tell you that up front. But let me just tell you this: I know that I can get the books here, and I can get them to the customer and forget about bricks and mortar.
>
> (Quoted in Saunders, 1999, p. 11)

1995/1996

In June 1995 Amazon.com, Inc. launched on the World Wide Web. Ever conscious of the need for effective branding on the Web, Bezos chose to name his site after the world's largest river, telling newsgroups that Amazon.com, in turn, would become the biggest bookstore in the world. Bezos considered branding even more important on the Internet than in traditional retailing because of the power of the Internet in continuous communication and word of mouth.

After its initial entry into the market, Amazon.com had no significant rivals and there were no dominant traditional players. Barnes & Noble had 15 per cent market share and no online presence. Despite the rapid growth of the business, the first few months found Bezos doing the manual work, loading and unloading packages in the back of his Blazer and delivering them to the post office himself.

Within one year, Amazon.com was recognised as the Web's largest and best bookstore with over 1,000,000 titles to choose from. Even at this time, Amazon.com was providing a powerful search facility as well as a host of services not provided by other online competitors. These services included:

- *Personal Notification Service* (which lets you know by e-mail when a particular book you want comes out in paperback or when your favourite author releases another book);
- *Recommendations Section* (exceeding 20 categories);
- *Awards Section* (where books that have won various prizes are listed);
- *Associate Program* (where other sites can link to Amazon.com where they sell selections from Amazon.com's database and receive a commission for each sale).

While a host of physical bookstores entering the virtual domain, there were still no large competitors competing for market share. The reality was that few retail sites on the Internet had made back their start-up costs, Amazon.com included, with Bezos warning investors not to expect a profit in the first five years. Analysts also warned of a highly volatile Internet sector with strategic plans constantly being revised and speedy growth being no guarantee of earnings, let alone of a company's long-term success.

1997

Despite aggressive competitive entry (i.e. Barnes and Noble went online in February 1997) into the e-commerce market, Amazon.com passed many milestones in 1997. They reached the 1,000,000th new customer milestone with customers in over 160 countries, exceeded 15,000 Associate Websites, signed relationship agreements with a number of key Internet players, and launched a range of new features. Probably the most notable achievement, however, was its ability to raise net proceeds of almost US$50 million in its initial public offering of 3,000,000 shares of common stock in May. These proceeds enabled aggressive investment in building the business, brand and customer base, as well as enhancing its product and service offerings.

With a growing employee base (from 151 in 1996 to 868 in 1997) Amazon.com focused on establishing its executive team, which included the recruitment of Richard Dalzell, a former Wal-Mart vice-president from their information systems division. Richard Dalzell joined Amazon.com as chief information officer during August. He brought with him experience in merchandising and logistics systems, supply chain systems, international retailing and merchandising systems, and commercial decision support and data mining systems.

Amazon.com lowered its book prices in 1997, which meant that for more than 400,000 titles, every hardcover was at least 30 per cent off and every paperback was at least 20 per cent off. Specially featured books were up to 40 per cent off. With these prices, Amazon.com offered the lowest book prices anywhere in the world, online or off. Additional discounts were also available on all audio books as well as calendars in all categories. These price reductions encouraged customers to do more of their book purchasing online with cumulative customer accounts growing to over 1,500,000 at 31 December, a growth of some 740 per cent from 180,000 customer accounts at 31 December, 1996.

The combination of Amazon.com's editorial ability, technological development, and growing customer base allowed the company to offer customers new features and services that were not available anywhere online or in physical stores. New features launched during 1997 included:

- a state-of-the-art Recommendations Centre (including recommendations to customers that other customers who shared their taste have enjoyed by tapping its extensive information about book purchasers, thereby assisting customers to find books that match their tastes);
- 22 subject browsing areas;
- the use of a proprietary technology – 1-Click Ordering – to streamline the ordering process; and
- An innovative Gift Centre to make gift-giving fast and easy, thereby augmenting its powerful recommendations centre.

Extensive promotional relationships with other dominant Internet players were concluded which reinforced Amazon.com's momentum as the leading online bookseller through the generation of substantial brand awareness and customer flow for the business. Some of these relationships were concluded with Yahoo!, Excite, America Online, Prodigy, Netscape, @Home Network and GeoCities, some of which are considered below:

- Amazon.com became the premier bookseller featured on Yahoo!. This alliance brought together Yahoo.com (the world's largest Internet navigational guide) with Amazon.com (the largest online bookseller) and provided a seamless transition for Yahoo! users researching information to be able to purchase relevant books directly from Amazon.com.

- Amazon.com made a multi-million-dollar Internet advertising purchase on Excite as well as establishing a strategic relationship where Amazon.com became Excite's exclusive bookseller integrated throughout Excite's channels. Excite, Inc. was committed to providing consumers with the most comprehensive network of directory and search services online through its four brands – Excite, Webcrawler, Excite Travel by City and Magellan.

- America Online (AOL.com) was the most visited site on the web, and the agreement provided Amazon.com the exclusive bookseller position on AOL.com and AOL's NetFind search engine. This meant immediate access to over 8 million members worldwide.

- The agreement with Prodigy Shopping Network ensured Amazon.com's prominence in the Prominent Shopping Network Mall with direct links to Amazon.com content from relevant areas inside the Prodigy Internet service. The Prodigy Shopping Network search engine is used by a large and loyal customer base to shop across a database of more than 20,000 items.

- Under the terms of the agreement with Netscape Communications Corp., Amazon.com became the exclusive bookseller on Netscape Netcentre's newly launched commerce section. Netscape Communications Corporation was a leading provider of open software for linking people and information over enterprise networks and the Internet.

- The agreement with @Home Network (the leader in high-speed Internet services via the cable infrastructure) made Amazon.com the premier bookseller throughout the @Home service.

- Amazon.com was incorporated throughout GeoCities 39 themed communities, offering GeoCities members and visitors new book features and services based on their areas of interest. GeoCities was the world's largest and fastest-growing community on the Internet.

Amazon.com opened its second distribution centre in New Castle, Delaware. The 200,000 square foot state-of-the-art distribution centre, together with the expansion of its original Seattle distribution centre, increased the company's stocking and shipping capacities to approximately six times their previous levels. The new Delaware centre positioned Amazon.com closer to its East Coast customers and publishers and provided immediate reductions in shipping times for many Amazon.com book buyers.

Amazon.com also completed a US$75 million credit facility aimed to provide the company with substantially increased resources to execute its long-term strategy. Aimed at enhancing Amazon.com's flexibility, it allowed the company to pursue its goal of extending its market position.

1998

By the end of 1998, Amazon.com had served a cumulative 6.2 million customers, exceeded the cumulative US$1 billion revenue level, exceeded 60,000 members in its *Associate Program*, launched music, video and gift stores in the US, and expanded operations into the UK and Germany. Sales grew from US$148 million in 1997 to US$610 million (an increase of 313 per cent) and cumulative customers grew by over 300 per cent. Despite this rapid customer growth, the percentage of orders placed on the Amazon.com website by repeat customers grew from over 58 per cent in the fourth quarter of 1997 to over 64 per cent in the same period in 1998.

Following the company's October launch in the UK and Germany under the Amazon.com brand and with Amazon.com technology, the combined fourth-quarter sales in the UK and German stores nearly quadrupled over the third quarter, establishing Amazon.co.uk and Amazon.de as the leading online booksellers in their markets. Twenty-five per cent of fourth-quarter sales for 1998 were derived from Amazon.co.uk, Amazon.de, as well as music, video and gift sales on Amazon.com, which were all very new businesses.

The growth in Amazon.com's infrastructure continued with a staff increase from 600 in December 1997 to over 2,100 in December 1998. This staff increase included the strengthening of the management team with the appointment of Jimmy Wright who joined Amazon.com as vice-president, chief logistics officer. Jimmy Wright joined from Wal-Mart and had more than 26 years of experience in logistics management. He became responsible for all global supply-chain activities at Amazon.com, including the management of the company's distribution centres, product purchasing, distribution and shipping.

Additional new products included *Amazon.com Advantage*, an innovative new programme designed to increase the visibility and sales of titles from independent publishers. It levelled the playing field for smaller publishers by providing tools and the framework to ensure their books appeared more often and more prominently throughout Amazon.com's catalogue of titles. *Amazon.com Kids* was also launched, which became the most comprehensive resource for children's and young adult books on the World Wide Web.

Amazon.com's expansion programme is evidence of a growth strategy via acquisitions, strategic relations and internal development. Since launching Amazon.com, Bezos has used both strategic relationships and acquisitions to grow sales, improve services and bring in new customers. Extensive relationships with other dominant Internet players concluded in 1998 reinforced its momentum as the leading online bookstore. Some of these relationships included Quicken, Intuit and Yahoo!

- The agreement with Quicken resulted in Amazon.com becoming Quicken's exclusive bookseller in the US, and the preferred provider of books in the UK and Germany. Quicken.com, a leading online personal finance site, brings together tools, resources and expertise to help empower consumers, thereby enabling them to make confident investment and financial choices.

- The agreement with Intuit meant that Amazon.com will be promoted on the desktop within select Quicken software. Intuit, a financial software and

Web-based services company, developed and marketed Quicken, the leading personal software; TurboTax, the best-selling tax preparation software; and QuickBooks, the most popular small business accounting software.

- During 1998, Yahoo!'s globally branded network of World properties included Web guides in Japan, Korea, Canada, Australia and New Zealand, France, Germany, UK and Ireland, Denmark, Sweden, Norway and Italy. It also included language-based websites, *Yahoo! Chinese* and *Yahoo! En Espanol*, as well as an English-language site based in Singapore, *Yahoo In Asia*. With a far-reaching network of globally branded Yahoo! Properties, they were in a unique position to provide Amazon.com with the ability to reach simultaneously a variety of markets and an unsurpassed worldwide audience. Amazon.com was featured on all Yahoo! World sites.

Amazon.com also expanded by acquiring leading Internet companies. Both *Bookpages* (one of the largest online bookstores in the UK) and *Telebook* (ABC Telebuck – Germany's no. 1 online bookstore) were acquired to become fundamental components of its expansion into the European marketplace. The sites made available to Europeans a vast selection, guaranteed safety of transactions, unparalleled convenience, and electronic gift certificates for worry-free gift-giving.

Amazon.de (Germany) had its headquarters and a distribution centre in Regensburg and editorial and marketing offices in Munich. The store featured 335,000 titles from German publishers, fast and easy access to 374,000 US titles, swift delivery, as well as an array of recommendation features to better serve book buyers, including instant recommendations. A Munich-based staff of expert German editors develop reviews and recommendations of German-title books.

Amazon.co.uk had headquarters and a distribution centre in Slough, England. The store carried a complete catalogue of 1.2 million UK titles in print, fast and easy access to 200,000 US titles, and speedy delivery. A staff of expert UK editors provides recommendations and reviews.

Internet Movie Database (www.imdb.com) was also acquired. Launched in 1990, Internet Movie Database was a comprehensive repository for movie and television information on the Internet and was acquired to support Amazon.com's eventual entry into online video sales.

> 'Everyone at IMDb is excited about becoming a part of Amazon.com . . . because of their similar passion for books, the Amazon.com team understands and fully supports IMDb's mission of providing the best possible information to movie lovers', said Colin Needham, IMDb Managing Director.
>
> (Amazon.com, 1999)

The company incurred total charges of approximately $55 million in connection with all three transactions (Amazon.co.uk, Amazon.de and imdb.com). Consideration comprised cash and common stock, and the company anticipated issuing an aggregate of approximately 540,000 shares of common stock as a result of these transactions.

PlanetAll and Junglee were acquired to enrich Amazon.com's e-commerce experience for customers. PlanetAll had approximately 1.5 million members and provided a unique Web-based address book, calendar and reminder service. Junglee was the leading provider of advanced Web-based virtual database technology that could assist shoppers to find millions of products on the Internet. Amazon.com acquired 100 per cent of the outstanding shares and assumed all outstanding options of Junglee and PlanetAll in exchange for equity having an aggregate value of approximately $280 million.

Additional distribution and customer service centres were opened in the UK and Germany, and the planned lease of a highly mechanised distribution centre of approximately 323,000 square feet in Fernley, Nevadas, was concluded. This latest addition more than doubled Amazon.com's distribution capacity and allowed it to further improve time-to-mailbox for customers. Inventories rose from US$9 million at the beginning of the year to US$30 million by year-end, enabling improved product availability and improved product cost through direct purchasing from manufacturers.

Amazon.com's first major product expansion took place with the launch of its music store, which became the leading online music retailer in its first full quarter. Once the addition of more than 42,000 classical and opera CDs to its music store was completed, the store's total number of CDs exceeded 200,000 – 25 times the selection of a typical music store, with everyday savings of up to 40 per cent. This addition of music was followed by the addition of video and gifts in November, and Amazon.com became the leading online video retailer in only six weeks.

It is these economics, a product of being online, that is enabling Amazon.com to rewrite the retail industry. In 1998, Amazon.com received top honours in the prestigious Computerworld Smithsonian Award competition, taking first place in Business and Related Services. The award recognises those who have demonstrated vision and leadership in the innovative use of information technology. Amazon.com was said to be 'a driving force behind e-retail, with technology that allows customers to find and purchase books in a convenient and secure manner' (Saunders, 1999, p. 15). Jeff Bezos said of the award:

'We were flattered, of course, but more important this is recognition that online commerce has arrived. Millions of people, not just the digerati, are taking advantage of the benefits of secure online shopping'.

(Quoted in Saunders, 1999, p. 16)

1999

Cumulative customer accounts exceeded 17 million in over 150 countries. Amazon.com had at the end of 1999 built the leading global e-commerce brand and platform. Repeat customer orders represented more than 73 per cent of orders. A major focus on customers helped Amazon.com continue to improve customer experience and grow its brand and extend operational reach. Amazon.com was rated as the most widely recognised e-commerce brand in the United States, as rated by online shoppers in a nationwide survey by Opinion Research Corp. Some 117.8 million adults, or 60 per cent of the adult population in the US, recognised the Amazon.com brand, according to the survey. Amazon.com was also rated as the 57th most valuable brand world-wide, just above Hilton, Guinness and Marriott, and just below Pampers, in a June study of global brands by Interbrand Newell and Sorrell. Additional achievements included ratings as:

- the No 1. Toys store, Books, Music, and Video stores, and General Merchandise store in Forrester Research's recently released PowerRankings™;
- the best online toy store in a Microsoft (MSNBC) survey, barely one month after the launch of the Amazon.com Toys Store, beating longer-established e-commerce players;
- the No. 1 place to save money on the Internet, as rated by online shoppers in a nationwide survey by Opinion Research Corp. (company provides an extensive research service);
- the No. 1 online shopping site and the No. 7 Web property during September, according to Media Metrix;
- the No. 1 Video store, the No.1 Music store, and the No. 1 Bookstore by Gomez Advisors (a company that provides support to consumers wanting to transact online and information to businesses that want to attract and retail online customers) in their most recent scorecards of online stores in these categories;
- the most-visited music store online, according to Greenfield Online's study of more than 5,000 consumers who have shopped for music online.

The company continued to build on its management strength, naming Warren C. Jenson as its senior vice-president and chief financial officer (CFO). Jenson had been executive vice-president and CFO at Delta Airlines, the largest domestic airline. Prior to Delta, Jenson was CFO of NBC, a division of General Electric. Jenson came to Amazon.com with a strong record of achievement in financial management, innovative transactions and Web-based initiatives. Jeffrey A. Wilke was named vice-president, general manager of operations. Wilke was formerly vice-president and general manager of AlliedSignal's Pharmaceutical Fine Chemicals unit. Wilke was directly responsible for 15 plants/distribution centres in the US, Europe and Asia.

Joseph Galli was named president and chief operating officer and a few months later was elected onto Amazon.com's board of directors. Galli joined Amazon.com after a highly successful 19-year career with Black & Decker where he had led resurgence in the power tools business. His exceptional performance re-established market leadership for the Black & Decker brand as he introduced new products and significantly improved customer service.

With a focus on offering its customers compelling value for money, Amazon.com launched a range of new products and services. New products during 1999 included a broad selection of toys and games ranging from new to speciality toys from hundreds of toy makers and an electronics store featuring a full range of popular electronics products and brands. Amazon.com also launched a home improvement centre that had a comprehensive range of home improvement products, as well as Amazon.com Advantage for Video where customers had access to a broad selection of hard-to-find books, CDs and videos.

zShops and Auctions were also introduced during the year. zShops made it possible for any individual or business to sell through Amazon.com, reaching more than 13 million experienced online shoppers. zShops enables anyone to offer merchandise for sale at Amazon.com, whether they are micro-manufacturers or major manufacturers, small businesses or global corporations, or specialised retailers. With the launch of zShops, Amazon.com introduced Amazon.com Payments, which allowed individuals to pay for purchases with credit cards using Amazon.com's 1-Click payment feature.

Auctions were aimed at assisting people find, discover, buy – and now sell – virtually anything online with current Amazon.com's customers being pre-registered to begin buying and selling immediately in more than 800 product categories. The new service was easy to use, with innovative and time-saving features such as Bid-Click^{SM} for hassle-free bidding. To enhance customer safety, the Amazon.com Auctions Guarantee covers purchases of up to US$250 in the event that a buyer did not receive what a seller promised. In an important innovation, sellers will automatically have their auctions cross-merchandised across Amazon.com's millions of book, CD and video product pages.

New services included *Amazon.com Cards* which consisted of a free electronic greetings card service. Cards can be sent by visiting www.amazon.com and clicking on the e-cards tab. The new site offers diverse styles of electronic greetings cards and a unique selection, with hundreds of illustrations, pictures, animated cards, and messages to choose from. Card senders also have the ability to customise their messages. *Amazon.com Anywhere* is an initiative in wireless e-commerce that allows customers to shop and check the status of auction items at Amazon.com securely when they are away from their desktop computers (with the national launch of the new Palm VII™ organiser by 3Com, Amazon.com's vast selection of merchandise is now accessible to customers anywhere, anytime).

Amazon.com also introduced *Wish List*, consisting of an advanced and extensive online gift registry (Wish List was the No. 1 customer request during 1998's holiday shopping season and since its introduction has seen faster adoption than almost any other feature Amazon.com has offered its customers). The new *All Products Search* is located in the search box on the upper-left of the Amazon.com Welcome page and helps shoppers find anything for sale on the Net, providing customers with a convenient, easy-to-use guide for finding and discovering exactly what they want among the Net's millions of offerings. An expanded and improved *Recommendations Centre* offers music fans authoritative guides to the best CDs in more than 100 music styles. Designed to help beginners and experts alike, the new features included introductions to a wide range of music styles, as well as a comprehensive guide to essential CDs by style, artist and year. *Purchase Circles*™ features thousands of bestseller lists for hometowns, workplaces, universities, and more.

A relationship between Dell and Amazon.com was concluded. Both Dell.com and Amazon.com launched links from the checkout sections of their respective sites that led to new, co-branded Dell and Amazon.com home pages. The sites recognise and welcome customers to the full www.amazon.com and www.dell.com online experience. Amazon.com is the first company Dell has linked to from its www.dell.com site, and Dell is the first computer system company Amazon.com has linked to.

Amazon.com also announced strategic investment in the following companies that it believes share its passion for bringing customers value through selection, service, convenience and community:

- Drugstore.com, an online source for thousands of brand-name health, beauty and wellness products. Amazon.com has an investment of approximately 46 per cent of Drugstore.com's outstanding shares.

- Pets.com, the leading pet-oriented company on the Internet, specialising in popular and rare pet accessories, products and food for all types of animals.

- As part of the strategic relationship with Amazon.com, Della & James's wedding gift registry is available through Amazon.com, enabling Amazon.com's 13 million customers to find wedding registries and purchase wedding gifts through Della & James. Della & James was the first company to bring together wedding registries from a broad selection of premier national retailers and local stores, creating the best way to register for and purchase wedding gifts.

- Amazon.com's investment will give it a 35 per cent stake in HomeGrocer.com and allow the online grocer, which served customers in the Seattle, Washington, and Portland, Oregon, areas, to accelerate its national rollout. HomeGrocer was the first fully integrated Internet grocery shopping and home delivery service.

- Amazon.com's investment in Gear.com gives its customers access to the only Internet store to offer 100 per cent closeout merchandise (in a company staffed by knowledgeable sports enthusiasts) in all sports categories. Sporting goods closeouts resulted from overproduction, a change of style, colour, or function, and the cancellation of pre-season orders placed by retailers. Merchandise is new and comes in mint condition and original packaging.

Amazon.com also expanded by acquiring the following Internet companies. Amazon.com acquired *Exchange.com*, the premier online marketplace for hard-to-find antiquarian books, thereby adding more than 12 million books and music items for sale and auction. *Biblinfind.com* was acquired for its range of used books while *Musicfile.com* was acquired for hard-to-find recordings and music memorabilia. Adding LiveBid's technology and services to Amazon.com Auctions expanded the breadth and types of items customers could find and gave local and regional auction houses full access to a vast Internet auction community (*LiveBid.com* was the sole provider of live-event auctions on the Internet).

Amazon.com substantially increased its customer-service capability and increased distribution square footage from roughly 300,000 square feet to over 5 million square feet in less than 12 months at several distribution centres nationwide – more than 10 times the distribution centre floor space the company had in 1998. With its IT and distribution centre investments, Amazon.com was clearly building supply ahead of demand (Exhibit 1).

| Exhibit 1 | Distribution centre locations (November 1999) |

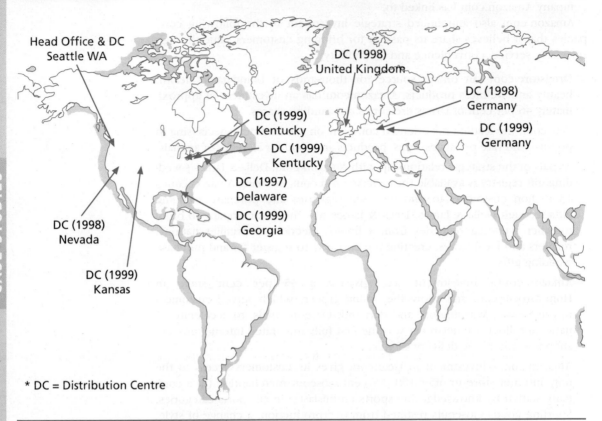

Head Office & DC
Seattle WA

DC (1998)
United Kingdom

DC (1998)
Germany

DC (1999)
Kentucky

DC (1999)
Germany

DC (1999)
Kentucky

DC (1997)
Delaware

DC (1998)
Nevada

DC (1999)
Georgia

DC (1999)
Kansas

* DC = Distribution Centre

Some of the expansion plans completed in 1999 included the leasing of a 460,000-square-foot distribution facility in Coffeyville, Kansas, which enabled faster delivery to Amazon.com customers across the Midwest and southeast United States. This was expanded to a 750,000-square-foot distribution facility with the result being that customers in such places as Chicago, St Louis, Dallas and Minneapolis would receive their orders much faster, as a consequence of deeper inventory, faster processing and shorter delivery times. Amazon.com's highly mechanised 322,560-square-foot facility in Fernley, Nevada, began shipping on a limited basis, increasing availability and improving delivery times for customers in the western US. The acquisition of two Kentucky distribution centres also played an integral role in the company's overall global logistics strategy. The existing 570,000-square-foot Campebellsville facility was expanded to approximately 770,000 square feet and the Lexington facility has a capacity of 600,000 square feet. The acquisition of a highly mechanised distribution facility in McDonough, Georgia, allowed the company to reduce standard shipping times to customers in key markets in the southeastern US This 800,000-square-foot distribution centre was the largest Amazon.com distribution facility to date. Amazon.de also leased a new distribution centre in Bad Hersfeld, Germany, which began operations during the second half of 1999.

2000

Amazon.com celebrated its five-year anniversary in July with over 23 million cumulative customers and continued to grow its customer base so that worldwide cumulative customer accounts increased to over 25 million as of September 2000. Sales per active customer for the twelve months ending 30 September 2000 were $130.00, up from $108.00 for the same period a year ago. Gross margin for the third quarter was 26 per cent, up from 20 per cent for the third quarter of 1999.

> 'Our vision remains being Earth's most customer-centric company, the best place for customers to find and discover anything they want to buy online,' said Jeff Bezos, Amazon.com founder and CEO. 'While we continue to see improvements in all of our businesses, we are especially pleased with the profitability in our U.S. Books, Music and Video group and the unusual growth in our Electronics store. For the company as a whole, we're well on our way to achieving our 2000 objectives.'
>
> *(Amazon.com 3rd Quarter 2000 Report,* 2000)

Achievements for the 2000 financial year included the following:

- The World's Most Valuable Brands 2000, Interbrand's annual survey, valued the Amazon.com brand as the 48th most valuable brand in the world, up from 57th in 1999.

- The Amazon Tools and Hardware, Toys, Video/DVD, Music, Books and Home Living stores were named the overall top stores in their respective categories in the most recent Gomez Internet Scorecard and/or Forrester Research PowerRankings.

- A first – Amazon.com partnered with Stephen King to provide online payment services for downloading instalments of *The Plant*, a new episodic novel that can be found at www.amazon.com/stephenking.

- Amazon.com, in connection with a strategic alliance with Toysrus.com, launched a co-branded toy store. The new online store combined the strengths of the two e-tailers' prior stores, to bring customers the best toy-buying experience available online;

- Microsoft Corp. (NASDAQ: MSFT) announced that its Microsoft Reader had been selected by Amazon.com as the preferred format for Amazon.com's forthcoming e-Books store.

- Amazon.com launched a Camera & Photo store, offering digital and film cameras, optical gear, and accessories, and announced an alliance with Ofoto, Inc., a premier online photography service.

- Apple (NASDAQ: AAPL) announced that it had licensed Amazon.com's 1-Click patent and trademark for use in its Apple Online Store, as part of an e-commerce patent cross-licensing agreement.

- Amazon.com launched a Computer & Video Games store, offering the largest selection of computer and video games and accessories available, online or offline, to provide a one-stop gaming destination for both casual and hard-core gaming enthusiasts.

CASE STUDIES

- Amazon.com launched a new-car buying service, providing customers with a superior car-buying experience backed by service and support from an expansive network of premier auto dealers affiliated with its partner Greenlight.com.

Amazon Anywhere, Amazon.com's mobile e-commerce initiative, extended beyond Amazon.com and Amazon.co.uk to provide easy access to Amazon.de using the Wireless Application Protocol. The global Amazon Anywhere initiative underscores Amazon.com's commitment to enhancing the customer's buying experience with the convenience, safety and speed of state-of-the-art wireless commerce.

This global mobile e-commerce initiative using WAP was one of many global initiatives. Key global expansion initiatives during 2000 included the following:

- According to the MMXI Europe May 2000 European Audience Ratings Report, the Amazon.co.uk, Amazon.de and Amazon.com sites were the top three online retail sites based on reach.
- Within the third quarter, Amazon.co.uk added Software and Video Games stores and Amazon.de added a Video Games store.
- Amazon.com launched Amazon.fr, a French-language site offering books, music CDs, DVDs and videos dedicated to customers in France and to French-speaking customers around the world. Amazon.fr was named the best overall online retailer by leading French publications *Capital*, *Le Monde* and *Journal du Net*.
- Amazon.de launched a Software store.
- Amazon.com launched Amazon.co.jp with a comprehensive catalogue of Japanese and foreign books for Japanese speakers worldwide.

Many new product and technology expansions were undertaken in 2000. Some of these selection extensions and partnerships for 2000 included:

- Amazon.com launched the Amazon Kitchen store (www.amazon.com/kitchen), featuring thousands of culinary products and accessories alongside in-depth editorial content, including original product reviews, recipes, and cooking and entertaining tips.
- Amazon.com launched a Home Living store, providing Amazon.com customers direct access to living.com from the top of Amazon.com's welcome page. Home Living visitors can shop for furniture, decorative accessories, bed and bath linens, lighting and rugs.
- Amazon.com introduced the Amazon.com NextCard Visa, offering no annual fee and the ability to purchase both online and offline while earning reward points that can be redeemed for Amazon.com gift certificates.
- Amazon.com announced the availability of more than 22,000 hours of spoken audio content from Audible, Inc. Located within the Amazon bookstore, the new audible.com Audio Downloads Store is the only place Amazon.com customers can find more than 4,700 audiobooks plus a vast array of comedy, audio newspapers, magazines, speeches, lectures, language lessons,

motivational programmes, business information and subscriptions to public radio programmes.

- Amazon Books added Spanish Language, Large Print and Gay & Lesbian stores within the Amazon bookstore.

- Amazon Music, the No. 1 online music retailer, added several new areas to its store, including Bargain Music, Music Accessories and Classical for Beginners, and it opened the Music Lovers Lounge, which features exclusive live streaming concerts, artist spotlights, interviews, digital downloads and discussion boards.

- Amazon.com entered into an agreement with Hewlett-Packard to be Amazon.com's primary Internet infrastructure provider and become an anchor tenant in the Amazon Electronics store, providing Amazon.com's customers with an even more extensive selection of HP products.

- The Amazon Electronics store also added Handspring Visor handheld computers to its ever-growing electronics selection. Handspring appointed Amazon Electronics as the exclusive online reseller for its Visor and Visor Deluxe handheld computers through July 2000.

- Amazon.com's DVD store, the largest online retailer of DVDs, has become the top retailer (online or offline) for pre-order sales of many of the industry's top DVDs, including the highly anticipated 29 August *Braveheart* DVD release, with over 26,000 units ordered to date.

- Amazon zShops introduced new storefront features that offer sellers custom browse, search, featured items, merchant photos and business description functionality.

The company continued to recruit for its management strength, naming Paul Misener vice-president of global public policy. Mr Misener joined Amazon.com from the Washington, DC, law firm of Wiley, Rein & Fielding, where he was a partner and chairman of the e-commerce and Internet practice group. He was formerly manager of telecommunications and computer technology policy at Intel Corp., where he also co-founded and led the Internet Access Coalition. Mr Misener is a 1985 graduate of Princeton University with a BSE in electrical engineering and computer science and has a JD from the George Mason University School of Law.

The company also named Diego Piacentini senior vice-president and general manager – International. From April 1997 until joining Amazon.com, he was vice-president and general manager, Europe, of Apple Computer, Inc., with responsibility for Apple Computer's operations in Europe, the Middle East and Africa. From April 1996 to April 1997, he was European sales director of Apple Computer, Inc., from May 1995 until April 1996, he was general manager of Apple Computer's Italy operations, and before that, from September 1994 to May 1995, he was Apple Computer's sales director for Italy. He joined Apple Computer in 1987. Prior to that time he held a financial management position at Fiatimpresit in Italy. Mr Piacentini received a degree in economics from Bocconi University in Milan, Italy, in 1985.

Amazon.com also announced strategic investment in the following companies that it believes share its passion for bringing customers value through

selection, service, convenience and community. The first of these is
Ashford.com, an online retailer of luxury and premium products offering new
and vintage watches, fragrances, leather accessories, sunglasses, and writing
instruments, at www.ashford.com. Another one of these was eZiba.com, a
leading online retailer of handcrafted products from around the world, at
www.eziba.com.

Sales for the final quarter of 2000 were expected to be between $950 mil-
lion and $1.05 billion. Gross margin was expected to be seasonally down com-
pared to the third quarter of 2000, although up strongly over the fourth quarter
of 1999. Pro forma operating losses are expected to be between 5 and 8 per
cent of sales. Cash and marketable securities at year-end are expected to be
over $1 billion.

2001

Some projections for the 2001 financial year include:

● Sales are expected to be approximately $4 billion.

● Pro forma loss from operations is expected to narrow to less than 5 per cent
of sales, perhaps substantially so.

● Cash and marketable securities as of 31 March 2001 are expected to be
approximately $700 million, and the company expects to generate
significant positive cash flow from operations for the nine months ended
31 December 2001.

DEFINING THE BUSINESS

It would seem that the vision behind Amazon.com has changed over the past
five years, although if anything, the vision has been expanded beyond creating
a successful online bookstore, to creating a successful cyberstore with the
world's largest selection. During 1999, Jeff Bezos outlined a vision, 'to be the
world's most customer-centric company', and in conjunction with the desire
'to be the place where people come to find and discover anything they might
want to buy online'.

Amazon.com is more formally defined as an online retailer offering a range
of products and services that are broader than its speciality retail sector
comparisons allow. Since opening for business as 'Earth's Biggest Bookstore' in
July 1995, Amazon.com has changed focus and quickly become one of the
most widely known, used and cited retail commerce sites on the Web. What
makes Amazon.com different is that it is clearly an Internet-based company
that develops proprietary software to make its retail operations work. Industry
analysts have suggested during 1999 (due to the increasing growth in product
offerings over 1998/1999) that Amazon.com's offering may soon be as various
as those offered by Wal-Mart.

Despite Amazon.com's growth over the past five years, its strategic focus has
remained on the customer. The focus is on creating a customer experience

(from the first time a potential customer types in 'amazon.com' on an Internet browser to after the package has arrived at the customer's door) that is compelling enough to get the person to return. By establishing a new business model, Amazon.com has fulfilled one of its primary goals – to change the way business is conducted. While the book market was a starting-point for Amazon.com, the company now oversees a network of Internet sites, which offer a constantly expanding host of other consumer goods.

The key components of Amazon.com's offerings include browsing, searching, reviews and content, recommendations and personalisations, 1-Click technology, secure credit card payment and availability and fulfilment:

- *Browsing*: The Amazon.com site offers visitors a variety of features arranged in a simple, easy-to-use fashion intended to enhance product search and selection.

- *Searching*: A primary feature of Amazon.com websites is their interactive, searchable catalogues of books, music CD, video, DVD, computer games and other titles. The company provides a selection of search tools to find products based on keyword, title, subject, author, artist, musical instrument, label, actor, director, publication date or ISBN. Customers can also use more complex and precise search tools such as Boolean search queries.

- *Reviews and content*: Amazon.com stores offer numerous forms of content to enhance the customer's shopping experience and encourage purchases. Various types of content are available for particular titles, including cover art, synopses, annotations, review by editorial staff and other customers, and interviews by authors and artists.

- *Recommendations and personalisations*: Amazon.com personalises its product and service offerings. These features include greeting customers by name, instant and personalised recommendations, bestseller and chart-topper listings, personal notification services, purchase pattern filtering and a number of other related features.

- *1-Click technology*: Amazon.com offers a streamlined ordering process using 1-Click technology. If a customer has previously activated 1-Click functionality, he or she can place an order by clicking one button without having to fill out an order form. The customer's shipping and billing information is automatically referenced on the company's secure server.

- *Secure credit card payment*: Amazon.com utilises secure server software for secure commerce transactions. It encrypts all of a customer's personal information, including credit card number, name and address, so that it cannot be read as the information travels over the Internet.

- *Availability and fulfilment*: Most of the company products are available for shipment within 24 hours, others are available within 2–3 days and the remainder are generally available within 4–6 weeks.

Critical organisational divisions

Amazon.com has rapidly and significantly expanded its staff both in the USA and internationally to keep pace with the operational requirements and will further expand its current staff levels to address potential growth of its product, service offerings and customer base. The expansion, training and management of employees will be crucial to its long-term profitability. Its current and planned personnel, systems, procedures and controls will continue to be under pressure to support and effectively manage its future operations. The ability to hire, train, retain, motivate and manage staff may limit its growth.

Within the company there are three critical divisions, but it is probable that as the company continues with its rapid growth, its structure is likely to change:

- **Product development**: Includes everything that involves the website as a product to customers. Departments within this area include editorial, marketing, as well as site design and site navigation.

- **Technology**: The technology drives the organisation – it is the systems that drive the functionality for the customer. The technology group consists of developers who work on e-merchandising, product databases, information technology systems (fulfilment, distribution-centre software, as well as finance and human resources software), and all the engineering that customers experience on the website, including 1-Click Shopping, a recommendations centre, and search features. While there is overlap between all departments, it can be broken down into website development and back-end fulfilment systems.

- **Supply chain and distribution**: Operations staff, together with those in the distribution centres, report to the chief logistics officer (CLO). Customer service also falls under this group. The operations business unit includes distribution, supply chain management, and the engineering and logistics related to creating distribution centres and making them work as effectively as possible. This is clearly the largest part of the company with the largest growth potential. Customer Service is a customer-focused service department that is also one of the largest in Amazon.com – and acts as a feeder for the rest of the organisation.

MARKET POSITIONING

Jeff Bezos studied the book market before choosing it as a starting point for Amazon.com. But, more importantly, he identified and took advantage of opportunities with the growth of the Internet. Bezos has stated that this know-how is Amazon's hard-earned advantage over barnesandnoble.com and borders.com. With increasing competition from a range of online players, this expertise should make for a level playing field.

Exhibit 2	Major US book retailers by revenue (Dec. 1998)			
COMPANY	98 REVENUES (US$M)	1-YR GROWTH (%)	98 NET INCOME (US$M)	1-YR GROWTH (%)
Barnes & Noble	2,796.9	14.2	53.2	3.9
Borders	2,266.0	15.7%	80.2	38.5
Amazon.com	610	413.0	(124.6)	N/A
Books-A-Million	325.8	16.6	7.0	20.7
Crown	297.5	3.4	(48.7)	N/A

Source: Wall Street Journal, 20 August 1998.

US retail market

The US retail market sales total approximately US$2.7 trillion annually in sales (1998), and of that, about a quarter comes from general merchandise, apparel and furniture sales. Taking every consumer item sold, then taking out cars, building material and food, the rest (computers, clothing, sports equipment, and so forth) falls into the total of US retail market sales. These goods are retailed in department stores, high-volume stores, and speciality stores, and via catalogues and websites.

In contrast to traditional retailers, shopping via PC screen, on the Internet, is growing at an increasing rate, despite early failures of online malls and cyber-shops. Expected to reach US$30 billion in 2000, sales via the Net are strongest for companies such as Amazon.com, Dell Computers, Gateway (computers), and FTD (floral delivery), whose products don't require help with fit or colour.

Amazon.com began in this retail and wholesale sector, with a focus on books. Amazon.com's objective is, however, far broader than books and it aims to be the leading online retailer of information-based products and services. A comparison of the major US book retailers ranked by revenues (Exhibit 2) highlights that within the retail book segment it is clear that Amazon.com has a relatively small segment of a very large market and the breakdown shown in Exhibit 3 indicates the relative market share of the different players.

Amazon.com's primary sector is that of 'services'. Its industry has been defined as 'speciality retail' although much of its competition is clearly within the electronic commerce medium. While it is difficult to detail the exact industry position of Amazon.com, there are strong signals from Jeff Bezos as the following statement made during 1999 highlights:

> 'Sixteen months ago, we were a place we could come to find books,' he said. 'Tomorrow, we will be a place to find anything, with a capital A.'

> (Amazon.com, 1999)

If Amazon.com's position is compared to other companies that are similar – all of them being Internet-based companies – it is clear that Amazon.com is one of the leading Internet-based companies in the world.

Exhibit 3	Market share of retail store sectors (Dec. 1998)	
COMPANY	% OF MARKET	AMOUNT (US$BN)
Superstores (Barnes & Noble, Borders)	25.2	4.23
Book clubs	20.0	3.36
Independent bookstores	17.2	2.89
Price clubs	6.0	1.01
Mass-merchandisers (Wal-Mart)	5.9	0.99
Amazon.com	3.0	0.6
Other	22.7	3.89
Total	100.0	16.8

Source: *Wall Street Journal*, 20 August 1998.

Geographic expansion

While Amazon.com delivers books and other products to over 160 countries throughout the world, its dominant focus remains in the US, mainly due to the growth in electronic commerce. In April 1998, Amazon.com acquired three Internet companies in the United Kingdom and Germany. In October 1998, the company relaunched two of these businesses under the Amazon.com brand. The company incorporated Amazon.com's technology and look-and-feel into the European sites, www.amazon.co.uk (United Kingdom) and www.amazon.de (Germany). Expansions into the UK and Germany have been very successful, and following expansions into France (Amazon.fr) and Japan (Amazon.co.jp) its global expansion is well under way.

BUILDING THE TEAM

Bezos has brought together a talented and diverse group of people who are enthusiastic about making Amazon.com a success. He has also given them a sense of ownership through generous stock option incentives. Amazon.com, Inc. had 2,100 employees at the 1998 financial year-end, a significant change from the 1997 year-end figure of 868 employees, and 151 in 1996. This represents a 242 per cent growth in employee numbers over the 1998 financial year.

Along with Bezos, the vice-presidents make the strategic decisions. Group directors and managers report to a vice-president. Despite this, many employees insist that Amazon.com is an extremely flat organisation. The executive-level staff are composed of highly skilled and experienced staff, many of whom came from large US organisations. The full team details can be found in Exhibit 4.

STRATEGIC CHOICES

The fact that Amazon.com has yet to make a profit has resulted in some investment managers taking their money elsewhere. Bezos has expressed

| Exhibit 4 | Senior executive staff (Nov. 2000) |

Bezos, Jeffrey P. (36)

Chairman of the Board, Chief Executive Officer, President, Chief Operating Officer

Mr Bezos became President and Chief Operating Officer on 25 July 2000 and has been Chairman of the Board of Amazon.com since founding it in 1994 and Chief Executive Officer since May 1996. Mr Bezos served as President from founding until June 1999 and Treasurer and Secretary from May 1996 to March 1997. From December 1990 to June 1994, Mr Bezos was employed by D.E. Shaw & Co., a Wall Street investment firm, becoming Senior Vice President in 1992. From April 1988 to December 1990, Mr Bezos was employed by Bankers Trust Company, becoming Vice President in February 1990. Mr Bezos is also a Director of drugstore.com, inc. Mr Bezos received his BS in Electrical Engineering and Computer Science from Princeton University.

Alberg, Tom A. (60)

Director

Tom A. Alberg has been a Director of the Company since June 1996. Mr Alberg has been a Principal in Madrona Investment Group, L.L.C., a private merchant banking firm, since January 1996. From April 1991 to October 1995, he was President and a Director of LIN Broadcasting Corporation, and from July 1990 to October 1995, he was Executive Vice President of McCaw Cellular Communication, Inc.; both companies were providers of cellular telephone services and are now part of AT&T Corp. Prior to 1990, Mr Alberg was a partner of the law firm Perkins Coie, where he also served as Chairman of the firm's Executive Committee. Mr Alberg is also a Director of Active Voice Corporation, Advanced Digital Information Corporation, Emeritus Corporation, Mosaix, Inc., Teledesic Corporation and Visio Corporation. Mr Alberg received his BA from Harvard University and his J.D. from Columbia University.

Cook, Scott D. (47)

Director

Scott D. Cook has been a Director of the Company since January 1997. Mr Cook co-founded Intuit, Inc., a leading personal finance, tax and accounting software company, in 1983, served as President and Chairman of the Board of Intuit since that time until April 1994 and has served as its Chairman of the Board since April 1994. Prior to co-founding Intuit, Mr Cook was a consultant for Bain & Company, a strategy consulting firm, and a brand manager for Proctor & Gamble. Mr Cook is also a Director of Broderbund Software, Inc. and Intuit. Mr Cook received his BA in Mathematics and Economics from the University of Southern California and his MBA from Harvard Business School.

Doerr, L. John (48)

Director

L. John Doerr has been a Director of the Company since June 1996. Mr Doerr has been a general partner of Kleiner Perkins Caufield & Byers, a venture capital firm, since September 1980. Prior to joining Kleiner Perkins Caufield & Byers, Mr Doerr was employed by Intel Corporation for five years. Mr Doerr is also a director of Intuit, Macromedia, Inc., Netscape Communications Corporation, Platinum Software, Inc. and Sun Microsystems, as well as several private companies. Mr Doerr received his MEE and BSEE from Rice University and his MBA from Harvard Business School.

Stonesifer, Patricia Q. (43)

Director

Patricia Q. Stonesifer has been a Director of the Company since February 1997. Ms Stonesifer is President and Chairman of the Board of the Gates Library Foundation, which is dedicated to partnering with public libraries to bring access to computers, the Internet and digital information for patrons in low-income communities in the United States and Canada. Prior to joining the Gates Library Foundation, Ms Stonesifer

Exhibit 4 *Continued*

ran her own management consulting firm whose clients included DreamWorks SKG. From 1988 to 1997, Ms Stonesifer worked in many roles at Microsoft, most recently as Senior Vice President of the Interactive Media Division. In that role, she managed Microsoft's investment in new online content and service products, notably MSNBC on the Internet. Ms Stonesifer is a Director of the Fund for America's Libraries and Kinko's, Inc. Ms Stonesifer received her BA in General Studies from Indiana University.

Jenson, Warren C. (42)

Senior Vice President, Chief Financial Officer, Chief Accounting Officer

Mr Jenson joined Amazon.com in September 1999 as Senior Vice President, Chief Financial Officer and Chief Accounting Officer. Before joining Amazon.com, Mr Jenson was the Chief Financial Officer and Executive Vice President for Delta Air Lines from April 1998 to September 1999. From September 1992 to April 1998, Mr Jenson served as Chief Financial Officer and Senior Vice President for the National Broadcasting Company (NBC), a subsidiary of General Electric, and participated in efforts to develop MSNBC, the cable-Internet joint news venture between NBC and Microsoft. Mr Jenson earned his Masters of Accountancy – Business Taxation, and BS in Accounting from Brigham Young University.

Piacentini, Diego (39)

Senior Vice President and General Manager International

Mr Piacentini joined Amazon.com as Senior Vice President and General Manager, International in February 2000. From April 1997 until joining Amazon.com, Mr Piacentini was Vice President and General Manager, Europe of Apple Computer, Inc., with responsibility for Apple Computer's operations in Europe, the Middle East and Africa. From April 1996 to April 1997, Mr Piacentini was European Sales Director of Apple Computer, Inc. From May 1995 until April 1996, Mr Piacentini was General Manager of Apple Computer's Italy operations, and before that, from September 1994 to May 1995, Mr Piacentini was Apple Computer's Sales Director for Italy. Mr Piacentini joined Apple Computer in 1987. Prior to that time he held a financial management position at Fiatimpresit in Italy. Mr Piacentini received a degree in Economics from Bocconi University in Milan, Italy in 1985.

Risher, John D. (34)

Senior Vice President and General Manager, US Retail Group

Mr Risher has served Amazon.com as Senior Vice President and General Manager, US Retail Group since February 2000. Mr Risher joined Amazon.com in February 1997 as Vice President of Product Development. Mr Risher served as Senior Vice President of Product Development from November 1997 to February 2000 and as Vice President of Product Development from February 1997 to November 1997. From July 1991 to February 1997, Mr Risher held a variety of marketing and project management positions at Microsoft Corporation, including Team Manager for Microsoft Access and Founder and Product Unit Manager for MS Investor, Microsoft's Web site for personal investment. Mr Risher received his BA in Comparative Literature from Princeton University and his MBA from Harvard Business School.

Peek, Mark S. (42)

Vice President – Finance

Mr Peek joined Amazon.com in March 2000 as Vice President, Finance, and has been selected to become Chief Accounting Officer beginning 1 April 2000. Prior to joining Amazon.com, Mr Peek was, since 1990, a partner at the independent public accounting firm of Deloitte & Touche LLP where he served as lead partner for a number of that firm's multinational technology clients. Mr Peek joined Deloitte & Touche in 1980. He received a BS in Accounting, Economics and International Business in 1980 from Minnesota State University.

Exhibit 4	*Continued*

Wilke, Jeffrey A. (33)

Vice President and General Manager of Operations

Mr Wilke has served as Vice President and General Manager, Operations since September 1999. Previously, Mr Wilke held a variety of positions at AlliedSignal from 1995 to 1999, including Vice President and General Manager of the Pharmaceutical Fine Chemicals unit from March 1999 to September 1999 and General Manager of the Carbon Materials and Technologies unit from August 1997 to February 1999. Prior to his employment at AlliedSignal, he was an information technology consultant with Andersen Consulting. He received a BSE in Chemical Engineering from Princeton University and has an MBA and Master of Science in Chemical Engineering from the Massachusetts Institute of Technology.

Dalzell, Richard L. (42)

Vice President, Chief Information Officer

Mr Dalzell joined Amazon.com in August 1997 as Vice President and Chief Information Officer. From February 1990 to August 1997, Mr Dalzell held several management positions within the Information Systems Division at Wal-Mart Stores, Inc., including Vice President of Information Systems from January 1994 to August 1997. From 1987 to 1990, Mr Dalzell acted as the Business Development Manager for E-Systems, Inc. Prior to joining E-Systems, Inc. he served seven years in the United States Army as a teleprocessing officer. Mr Dalzell received a BS in Engineering from the United States Military Academy, West Point.

Britto, Mark J. (35)

Vice President, Strategic Alliances

Mr Britto has served as Vice President, Strategic Alliances since August 1999. From June 1999 to August 1999, Mr Britto served as Director of Business Development. Mr Britto joined Amazon.com in June 1999 as part of the acquisition of Accept.com, which he co-founded in October 1998 and served as a Vice President. From October 1994 through October 1998, Mr Britto was Executive Vice President of Credit Policy at FirstUSA Bank, where he was responsible for their credit risk management practice. Prior to that, he served as Senior Vice President of Risk Management at NationsBank. Mr Britto received an MS in Operations Research and a BS in Industrial Engineering and Operations Research from the University of California at Berkeley.

Misener, Paul E.

Vice President, Global Public Policy

Mr Misener joins Amazon.com from the Washington, D.C., law firm of Wiley, Rein & Fielding, where he was a Partner and Chairman of the e-commerce and Internet practice group. He was formerly manager of telecommunications and computer technology policy at Intel Corp, where he also co-founded and led the Internet Access Coalition. Mr Misener is a 1985 graduate of Princeton University with a BSE in Electrical Engineering and Computer Science and has a JD from the George Mason University School of Law.

more concerns that to focus on profitability could distract the management attention from what he considers to be more critical business, which is, in his opinion, introducing more and more customers to Amazon.com. Bezos sees Amazon.com in what he calls an '*investment phase*', not unusual for a firm in its first five years. The '*harvest cycle*' will come later, he has said.

Investors point to the fact that the retailer only need bring more customers to its single online site, not build stores of bricks and mortar to raise sales. According to an interview with Jeff Bezos during 1999, he highlighted an aspect of Amazon.com's growth strategy (after being questioned on its lack of profitability) by stating that:

> We're focused on long-term returns for investors. And to throttle back on investment now would be shortsighted. When we have less opportunity that will probably happen, but as long as we have lots of opportunity, we're going to continue to invest commensurate with that opportunity in a very disciplined and methodological way, but in a long-term context. To do anything else, we believe, is irrational.
>
> (Quoted in Hof, 1999)

Amazon.com is clearly showing a commitment to long-term financial results, managing the business for ROIC and profits and not for per cent margin. Exhibits 5, 6 and 7 give consolidated statements of operations, cash flows and balance sheets for 1994–1999. Exhibit 8 shows stock trends May 1997–October 2000 and Exhibit 9 gives a market guide ratio comparison at November 2000. In conjunction with Bezos, Joy Covey (chief financial officer) stated that:

> We've always said we would sacrifice short-term profits to generate long-term value for our customers. I think investors will punish us if we stray from that. Right now, they see us making decisions consistent with what we've said.
>
> (Quoted in Koselka, 1999)

The company intends to continue developing its distribution infrastructure to increase efficiency and to support greater demand. Similarly, the company has implemented numerous site management, search, customer interaction, recommendation, transaction processing and fulfilment services and systems using a combination of its own proprietary technologies and commercially available, licensed technologies. The company's current strategy aims to focus its development efforts on creating and enhancing the specialised proprietary software that is unique to its business and to license or acquire commercially developed technology for other applications where available and appropriate.

COMPETITIVE RIVALRY

Bezos recognizes that quality service is a moving target and believes that once you satisfy customers in one area, their needs shift and Amazon.com has to be alert to these changes and innovate or adapt to meet these new needs (that may mean acquisition and strategic alliances). There is also a necessity to constantly reinvent oneself to remain competitive (as the increasing rivalry between Amazon.com and barnesandnoble.com intensifies). Bezos sees a problem with an obsession with competition:

Exhibit 5	Consolidated statement of operations (in US$'000, except per share data)

	JULY 5TH – DEC 31ST, 1994	YEAR ENDED DEC 1995	YEAR ENDED DEC 1996	YEAR ENDED DEC 1997	YEAR ENDED DEC 1998	YEAR ENDED DEC 1999
Sales	–	511	15,746	147,787	609,996	1,639,800
Cost of Sales	–	409	12,287	118,969	476,155	1,349,200
Gross Profit	–	102	3,459	28,818	133,841	290,600
Operating expenses:						
Marketing and sales	–	200	6,090	40,486	133,023	483,300
Technology & content	38	171	2,401	13,916	46,807	159,700
General and administrative	14	35	1,411	7,011	15,799	–
Merger and acquisition related costs	–	–	–	–	50,172	–
Stock-based compensation	–	–	–	–	–	–
Amortisation of goodwill & other intangibles	–	–	–	–	–	214,700
Merger, acquisiton & investment related costs	–	–	–	–	–	–
Unusual expenses (income)	–	–	–	–	–	8,100
Other operating expenses	–	–	–	–	–	30,600
Total operating expenses	52	406	9,902	61,413	245,801	2,245,600
Loss from operations	(52)	(304)	(6,443)	(32,595)	(111,960)	(1,955,000)
Interest income	–	1	202	1,901	14,053	45,500
Interest expense	–	–	(5)	(326)	(26,639)	(39,100)
Other expense, net	–	–	–	–	–	1,700
Net interest income (expense)	–	1	197	1,575	(12,586)	6,400
Loss before equity in losses of equity-method investees	(52)	(303)	(6,246)	(31,020)	(124,546)	(1,948,600)
Equity in losses of equity-method investees	–	–	–	–	–	–
Net loss	(52)	(303)	(6,246)	(31,020)	(124,546)	(1,948,600)
Basic and diluted loss per share	(0.00)	(0.00)	(0.06)	(0.24)	(0.84)	–
Shares used in computation of pro forma basic and diluted loss per share	79,146	86,364	111,271	130,341	148,172	–

Source: Amazon.com, Inc., 2000.

The obsession should be with defining the future needs of customers and translating that information into innovations that give the firm a competitive edge . . . Intel Chairman Andy Grove taught us all that only the paranoid survive, and he's right . . . but the thing that drives everything is creating genuine value for customers. Nothing happens without that.

THE FUTURE

The Internet is an increasingly significant global medium for online commerce and Amazon.com appears to be well positioned to capitalise on this growth.

Exhibit 6	Consolidated statement of cash flows (in US$'000)

	YEAR ENDED DEC 31ST, 1996	YEAR ENDED DEC 31ST, 1997	YEAR ENDED DEC 31ST, 1998	YEAR ENDED DEC 31ST, 1999
OPERATING ACTIVITIES				
Net loss	(6,246)	(31,020)	(124,546)	(719,968)
Adjustments to reconcile net loss to net cash provided by (used in) operating activities:				
Depreciation and amortisation	296	3,442	9,692	36,806
Amortisation of deferred comp . . . related to stock options	–	1,354	2,386	30,618
Non-cash merger and acquisition related costs, including amortisation of goodwill and other purchased intangibles	–	–	47,065	222,766
Equity in losses of equity-method investees	–	–	–	76,769
Non-cash revenue for advertising & promotional services	–	–	–	(5,837)
Loss on sale of marketable securities Non-cash	–	–	–	8,688
interest expense	–	64	23,970	29,171
Changes in operating assets and liabilities:				
Inventories	(554)	(8,400)	(20,513)	(172,069)
Prepaid expenses and other	(315)	(3,034)	(16,465)	(60,628)
Deposits and other	(148)	(21)	(293)	–
Accounts payable	2,756	30,172	78,674	330,166
Accrued advertising	598	2,856	9,617	42,382
Other liabilities and accrued expenses	1,603	5,274	21,448	90,261
Net cash provided by (used in) operating activities	(2,010)	687	31,035	(90,875)
INVESTING ACTIVITIES				
Maturities of marketable securities	–	4,311	332,084	4,024,551
Purchases of marketable securities	(5,233)	(122,385)	(546,509)	(4,290,173)
Purchases of fixed assets	(1,335)	(7,603)	(28,333)	(287,055)
Acquisitions, dispositions, and investments in businesses	–	–	(19,019)	(369,607)
Net cash used in investing activities	(6,568)	(125,677)	(261,777)	(922,284)
FINANCING ACTIVITIES				
Net proceeds from initial public offering	–	49,103	–	–
Proceeds from exercise of stock options	195	509	5,983	64,469
Proceeds from issuance of capital stock	8,443	3,746	8,383	–
Proceeds from long-term debt	–	75,000	325,987	1,263,639
Repayment of long-term debt	–	(47)	(78,108)	(188,886)
Financing costs	–	(2,309)	(7,783)	(35,151)
Net cash provided by financing activities	8,638	126,002	254,462	1,104,071
Effect of exchange rate changes	–	–	(35)	489
Net increase in cash	60	1,012	23,685	91,401
Cash at beginning of period	804	864	1,876	25,561
Cash at end of period	864	1,876	25,561	116,962

Source: Amazon.com, Inc., 2000.

| Exhibit 7 | Consolidated balance sheets (in US$'000, except per share data) |

	DEC 31ST, 1994	DEC 31ST, 1995	DEC 31ST, 1996	DEC 31ST, 1997	DEC 31ST, 1998	DEC 31ST, 1999	JUNE 30TH, 2000
ASSETS							
Current assets:							
Cash & cash equivalents	52	996	6,248	1,876	25,561	133,309	720,377
Marketable securities	–	–	–	123,499	347,884	572,879	187,244
Inventories	24	17	571	8,971	29,501	220,646	172,360
Prepaid expenses and other	–	14	321	3,363	21,308	85,344	86,659
Total current assets	76	1,027	7,140	137,709	424,254	1,012,178	1,166,640
Fixed assets, net	–	57	985	9,726	29,791	317,613	344,042
Deposits and other	–	–	146	169	626	–	–
Goodwill & purchased intangibles, net	–	–	–	–	186,377	730,144	596,778
Investments in equity-method investees	–	–	–	–	–	226,727	211,715
Other investments	–	–	–	–	–	144,735	88,261
Other assets	–	–	–	–	–	40,154	53,294
Deferred charges	–	–	–	2,240	7,412	–	–
Total Assets	76	1,084	8,271	149,844	648,460	2,471,551	2,460,730
LIABILITIES AND STOCKHOLDERS' EQUITY							
Current liabilities:							
Accounts payable	–	99	2,852	33,027	113,273	463,026	286,239
Accrued advertising	–	–	598	3,454	13,071	–	–
Other liabilities and accrued expenses	–	8	920	6,570	34,547	181,909	146,874
Accrued product development	–	–	500	–	–	–	–
Unearned revenue	–	–	–	–	–	54,790	115,566
Interest payable	–	–	–	–	–	24,888	41,213
Current portion of LT debt & lease	–	–	–	1,500	684	14,322	17,731
Total current liabilities	–	107	4,870	44,551	161,575	738,935	607,623
Long-term debt & portion of lease obligation	–	–	–	76,702	348,140	1,466,338	2,131,531
Commitments and contingencies Stockholders' equity:							
Preferred stock, $0.01 par value: Authorised shares – 10,000	–	–	6	–	–	–	–
Issued and outstanding shares – none	–	1,075	159	–	–	–	–
Common Stock, $0.01 par value: Authorised shares – 300,000							
Issued and outstanding shares	–	–	–	1,449	1,593	3,452	3,554
Additional paid-in capital	–	–	9,873	66,586	300,130	1,194,369	1,335,733
Note receivable from officer for common stock	–	150	–	–	(1,099)	–	–
Deferred compensation	–	–	(612)	(1,930)	(1,625)	–	–
Other gains/losses	–	–	–	–	–	(47,806)	(25,410)
Other gains/losses	–	–	–	–	1,806	(1,709)	(84,664)
Accumulated deficit	(16)	(248)	(6,025)	(37,514)	(162,060)	(882,028)	(1,507,637)
Total stockholders' equity (deficit)	8	977	3,401	28,591	138,745	266,278	(278,424)
Total liabilities and stockholders' equity	76	1,084	8,271	149,844	648,460	2,471,551	2,460,730

Source: Amazon.com, Inc., 2000.

CASE STUDIES

Exhibit 8 **Stock trends**

DATE	OPEN	HIGH	LOW	CLOSE	VOLUME	ADJ. CLOSE*
Oct-00	38.1875	38.4375	19.375	**36.625**	11,215,100	36.625
Sep-00	42.125	49.625	35.5	**38.4375**	6,686,900	38.4375
Aug-00	30.625	49.9688	29.3125	**41.5**	6,281,000	41.5
Jul-00	36.6875	43.9375	27.875	**30.125**	9,926,200	30.125
Jun-00	48.875	58.125	32.4688	**36.3125**	9,233,600	36.3125
May-00	56	62.375	40.4375	**48.3125**	5,940,300	48.3125
Apr-00	65.4375	68.625	40.8125	**55.1875**	8,526,900	55.1875
Mar-00	67.625	75.25	60	**67**	6,808,000	67
Feb-00	67.5	85.9375	63.0625	**68.875**	10,372,800	68.875
Jan-00	81.5	91.5	58.4375	**64.5625**	13,110,400	64.5625
Dec-99	87.25	113	76	**76.125**	11,254,400	76.125
Nov-99	68.0625	96.875	61	**85.0625**	13,384,200	85.0625
Oct-99	77	90	65.875	**70.625**	12,110,000	70.625
Sep-99	127	127	57.375	**79.9375**	14,792,100	79.9375
Sep-99			2:1 Stock Split (before market open)			
Aug-99	98.375	135.5625	82	**124.375**	10,433,700	62.1875
Jul-99	125.25	142.5	97.5	**100.0625**	9,253,500	50.0312
Jun-99	111.5	129.5	89.75	**125.125**	8,289,700	62.5625
May-99	166.875	167.0625	104.5	**118.75**	7,594,100	59.375
Apr-99	179.375	221.25	151	**172.0625**	8,649,600	86.0312
Mar-99	127	178	114	**172.1875**	7,195,800	86.0938
Feb-99	117.75	130	84.25	**128.125**	8,372,200	64.0625
Jan-99	327.6875	356	92.5625	**116.9375**	16,319,800	58.4688
Jan-99			3:1 Stock Split (before market open)			
Dec-98	185.5	361.875	182	**321.25**	5,486,500	53.5417
Nov-98	128.125	233.125	120.75	**192**	5,431,500	32
Oct-98	108	129.8125	80	**126.4375**	3,821,500	21.0729
Sep-98	76.125	120	65	**111.625**	5,379,600	18.6042
Aug-98	109.75	137.5	83.125	**83.75**	3,496,800	13.9583
Jul-98	101.8125	147	94.25	**110.875**	5,029,900	18.4792
Jun-98	88	104.75	41.25	**99.75**	4,392,800	16.625
Jun-98			2:1 Stock Split (before market open)			
May-98	92.75	95.875	79.75	**88.125**	728,600	7.3438
Apr-98	85.25	100	77.125	**91.75**	1,408,200	7.6458
Mar-98	75.875	88.25	70	**85.5312**	783,400	7.1276
Feb-98	59.375	79.625	57.25	**77**	572,900	6.4167
Jan-98	60	64.125	49.75	**59**	467,000	4.9167
Dec-97	50.875	60.5	49.625	**60.25**	246,100	5.0208
Nov-97	62.625	62.625	44	**49.5**	297,300	4.125
Oct-97	53.25	66	42.25	**61**	381,100	5.0833
Sep-97	28.125	57.75	27.75	**52.0625**	428,000	4.3385
Aug-97	28.125	29	23.25	**28.0625**	126,600	2.3385
Jul-97	18.5	30.875	18.125	**28.75**	411,400	2.3958
Jun-97	18.125	20.5	16.5	**18.5**	210,900	1.5417
May-97	23.625	23.75	15.75	**18**	768,100	1.5

* Adjusted for dividends and stock splits.
Source: Yahoo.com, 2000.

Exhibit 9   Market guide ratio comparison (Nov. 2000)

	AMAZON.COM	SPECIALITY RETAIL IND ...	SERVICES SECTOR	S&P 500
Valuation Ratios				
P/E Ratio (TTM)	NM	22.97	29.66	33.46
P/E High – Last 5 Yrs.	NA	50.14	50.91	49.21
P/E Low – Last 5 Yrs.	NA	15.93	16.57	17.12
Beta	2.78	1.41	0.96	1.00
Price to Sales (TTM)	5.01	1.81	4.94	6.96
Price to Book (MRQ)	NM	3.99	4.96	8.70
Price to Tangible Book (MRQ)	NM	4.42	7.65	12.17
Price to Cash Flow (TTM)	NM	17.31	19.60	25.60
% Owned Institutions	29.70	49.32	42.41	57.00
Dividents				
Dividend Yield	NA	1.88	1.98	1.57
Dividend Yield – 5 Year Avg.	NA	0.32	1.21	1.20
Dividend 5 Year Growth Rate	NM	21.31	0.93	8.96
Payout Ratio (TTM)	0.00	3.11	17.26	23.35
Growth Rates (%)				
Sales (MRQ) vs Qtr. 1 Yr. Ago	79.29	29.31	30.87	26.07
Sales (TTM) vs TTM 1 Yr. Ago	102.67	34.08	25.83	24.33
Sales – 5 Yr. Growth Rate	652.65	20.34	26.91	20.67
EPS (MRQ) vs Qtr. 1 Yr. Ago	NM	21.41	14.21	28.82
EPS (TTM) vs TTM 1 Yr. Ago	NA	26.65	18.16	26.02
EPS – 5 Yr. Growth Rate	NM	26.31	22.80	21.38
Capital Spending – 5 Yr. Growth Rate	534.11	11.90	28.47	19.26
Financial Strength				
Quick Ratio (MRQ)	1.37	0.62	1.02	1.23
Current Ratio (MRQ)	1.77	2.00	1.51	1.76
LT Debt to Equity (MRQ)	NM	0.44	0.78	0.57
Total Debt to Equity (MRQ)	NM	0.53	0.97	0.86
Interest Coverage (TTM)	−7.01	12.23	5.42	9.68
Profitability Ratios (%)				
Gross Margin (TTM)	21.06	28.92	41.48	50.37
Gross Margin – 5 Yr. Avg.	20.21	28.50	40.29	48.55
EBITD Margin (TTM)	−19.97	3.71	20.19	23.09
EBITD – 5 Yr. Avg.	−29.67	2.37	19.20	21.74
Operating Margin (TTM)	−32.13	0.34	11.13	18.37
Operating Margin – 5 Yr. Avg.	−35.46	−0.44	10.24	17.65
Pre-Tax Margin (TTM)	−34.84	0.39	10.83	18.12
Pre-Tax Margin – 5 Yr. Avg.	−35.82	−0.89	8.67	17.10
Net Profit Margin (TTM)	−34.84	−2.58	4.47	12.83
Net Profit Margin – 5 Yr. Avg.	−35.82	−2.86	2.84	10.69
Effective Tax Rate (TTM)	NM	38.16	37.12	34.71
Effective Tax Rate – 5 Yr. Avg.	NM	39.42	38.44	35.41
Management Effectiveness (%)				
Return On Assets (TTM)	−35.33	1.21	4.11	10.29
Return On Assets – 5 Yr. Avg.	−54.49	−1.89	4.82	8.89
Return On Investment (TTM)	−46.56	3.20	6.41	14.16
Return On Investment – 5 Yr. Avg.	−94.49	−4.96	6.95	14.04
Return On Equity (TTM)	NM	15.89	11.57	23.32
Return On Equity – 5 Yr. Avg.	−203.02	16.38	13.92	22.34
Efficiency				
Revenue/Employee (TTM)	324,430.00	392,990.00	377,981.00	516,316.00
Receivable Turnover (TTM)	NM	41.51	12.97	8.98
Inventory Turnover (TTM)	11.48	6.72	13.06	9.81
Asset Turnover (TTM)	1.01	2.25	0.99	1.00

Source: Yahoo.com, 1999.

While the outlook is positive, there are numerous risks and uncertainties that could negatively affect this potential.

With a limited operating history and the unpredictability of the industry, Amazon.com (currently in a highly debt-leveraged position) has an accumulated deficit and anticipated further losses. Aggressive pricing has further resulted in low product gross margins, requiring Amazon.com to generate and sustain substantially higher revenues in order to become profitable. The current growth rate may be unsustainable and the percentage growth rate is expected to decrease into the future. Amazon.com is therefore expected to incur substantial operating losses for the foreseeable future, and these losses may be significantly higher than its current losses. Combined with this is evidence that investors may be getting impatient with Amazon.com showing no signs of profit. If investor confidence continues to flag, Amazon.com could find itself gasping for capital just when it needs more to compete with a growing competitor base (*Business Week*, 1999, p. 52).

The online commerce market is new, rapidly evolving and intensely competitive. Competition in the Internet and online commerce markets is expected to intensify as various Internet market segments obtain large, loyal customer bases, and participants in those segments may use their market power to expand into markets in which Amazon.com operates. In addition, new and expanded Web technologies may increase the competitive pressure on online retailers. This increased competition may reduce Amazon.com's operating margins further, diminish its market share or impair the value of its brand. These risks will intensify as Amazon.com continues its international expansion as well as expansion into new business areas.

As Amazon.com continues to expand its operations by entering into business combinations, investments, joint ventures or other strategic alliances with other companies, so the risks increase. These include the difficulty associated with assimilating the operations, technology and personnel of the combined companies, and the additional operating losses and expenses of acquired businesses. Combined with this is the requirement for rapid technological development on a cost-effective and timely basis. Amazon.com will need to adapt quickly to changing customer requirements and industry standards. Other risks involve its reliance on key suppliers, systems reliance, and domain name risks as well as intellectual property protection.

As Amazon.com continues to develop, these factors together with broad market and industry fluctuations may adversely affect the business and its financial situation. The future may look rosy or bleak. Reflecting upon 2000, Jeff Bezos acknowledged that it had been a brutal year and during the year rumours began to circulate that Amazon.com might be taken over by Wal-Mart. Nevertheless, Amazon.com served 20 million customers in 2000, up from 14 million in 1999, and sales grew to US$2.76bn from US$1.64bn. Operating loss shrank to 6 per cent of sales in the fourth quarter 2000 from 26 per cent in the comparable 1999 period. Bezos revealed, in a letter released in a Securities and Exchange Commission filing, that his top priority was to achieve an operating profit in the fourth quarter 2001. In a separate filing, Amazon.com indicated that in 2000, Bezos had a base salary of US$81,840, the same as in 1999 and 1998. He owned 32.4 per cent of the company. During February 2001,

Amazon.com announced that it would slash up to 1,300 jobs and on 12 April 2001, Amazon.com shares closed at US$14.67. During the past 52 weeks, the stock had seen lows of US$8.10 and had moved as high as US$68.44. Reflecting upon these results as well as upon his hopes for the future, Jeff Bezos concluded:

> Online retailing won't replace in-store retailing. I've never said that. But I do think it can be a different, enriching experience . . . Our mission is to create a new level of expectation in customers, which will cause all companies to raise their level. And if we can do that, that would be truly meaningful. That'll be something we can tell our grandchildren about. That's the difference between a mission and a job. If it's a job, then you won't have stories to tell your grandchildren.

SOURCES

Alexa.com (1999) www.alexa.com.

Amazon.com (1999) *Amazon.com 1998 Annual Report*, Amazon.com, Inc.

Amazon.com (2000) *Amazon.com 1999 Annual Report*, Amazon.com, Inc.

Amazon.com (2001) *Amazon.com 2000 Annual Report*, Amazon.com, Inc.

Amazon.com (2000) *Amazon.com 3rd Quarter 2000 Report*, Amazon.com, Inc.

Amazon.com (1999) www.amazon.com

Amazon.com (2000) www.amazon.com

Amazon.com (2001) www.amazon.com

Barker, R. and McNatt, R. (1999) 'A star stumbles on Net stocks', *Business Week*, vol. 3634, pp. 8–12.

Boston Business Journal (1999) 'Bezos on business, books and bears', *Boston Business Journal*, 19(19), 3–4.

Business Week (1999) 'EBay vs Amazon.com', *Business Week*, 31 May, 49–51.

Corcoran, E. (1999) 'On-line: Amazoned', *Forbes*, March, 22.

Gibson, P. (1999) 'The sharp rise of e-commerce', *Information Today*, 16(7), 28–33.

Haylock, C.F. and Muscarella, L. (1999) *Net Success: 24 Leaders in Web commerce show you how to put the Web to work for your business*. Adams Media Corporation, Massachusetts.

Hof, R.D. (1998) 'A new chapter for Amazon.com', *Business Week*, vol. 3591, 39–41.

Hoovers Ltd (1999) www.hoovers.com.

Kalakota, R. and Robinson, M. (1999) *E-business: Roadmap for Success*. Addison Wesley Longman, Inc., Massachusetts.

Karlgaard, R. (1999) 'Digital rules', *Forbes*, 164(2), 43–44.

Koselka, R. (1999) 'A real Amazon', *Forbes*, 163(7), 50–53.

Krauss, M. (1998) 'Shifting strategies necessary on the Net', *Marketing News*, 32(21), 8–10.

Nucifora, A. (1999) 'Despite the hype, Marketing Internet's numbers adding up', *Business Press*, 12(8), 13–14.

Overstreet, J. (1999) 'Bookseller plans 600-employee Memphis centre', *Nashville Business Journal*, 15(25), 19–21.

Porter, M.E. (1985) 'The value chain and competitive advantage', in M.E. Porter *Competitive Advantage: Creating and sustaining superior performance*. The Free Press, New York.

Roth, D. (1999) 'Meg muscles Ebay uptown', *Fortune*, 140(1), 81–87.

Sacharow, A. (1998) 'Amazon calling', *Adweek*, 48(24), 70–71.

Saunders, R. (1999) *Business the Amazon.Com Way: Secrets of the world's most astonishing Web business*. Capstone Ltd, Washington.

Schwartz, N.D. (1999) 'The tech boom will keep on rocking', *Fortune*, 139(3), 64–67.

Stockport, G.J. and Street, D. (2000) 'Amazon.com: from startup to the new millennium', European Case Clearing House, 38pp, No. 300-014-1.

Stone, B. (1999) 'Amazon's pet projects', *Newsweek*, 133(25), 56-57.

Tadjer, R. (1996) 'Redefining inventory', *Communications-Week*, 626, 513-514.

USA Securities and Exchange Commission (1999) Washington DC.

Watson, R.T., Berthon, P., Pitt, L.F. and Zinkhan, G.M. (1999) *Electronic Commerce*. Dryden Press, Fort Worth.

Volgelstein, F. (1999) 'Amazon toys with success', *U.S. News & World Report*, 127(4), 43-45.

Yudkowsky, C. (1997) 'A tale of two Internet sites: a startup and a national giant who copied', *San Francisco Business Times*, 11(44), 18-20.

Car dealers in the headlights

The relative power of buyers and suppliers throughout a value chain can change considerably as a result of changes in the business environment. This article from the Financial Times *on 20 March 2001 shows the pressure being felt by car dealers in the UK as they were squeezed between the powerful car manufacturers and consumers who were exerting more buying power than ever before.*

• • •

FT

Like a vehicle in a traffic jam, Britain's car dealers are stuck between the competing interests of consumers and manufacturers.

With two well-known groups, the publicly-quoted DC Cook and privately-owned HMG, falling into receivership in recent months, the pressure is beginning to show.

Their demise is the latest in a series of setbacks in the £50bn-a-year UK car dealing market. According to some estimates, about 400 of Britain's nearly 30,000 dealerships have gone out of business in the past year.

This month, Perry Group confirmed the industry's plight by pulling out of car retailing with the sale of its 27 dealerships to management.

John Woollatt, Perry chief executive, says tough market conditions prompted its withdrawal. 'Car dealerships are just not attractive as an investment,' he says. 'Faced with heavy investments in the business and unsatisfactory returns, we decided to look for higher returns elsewhere.'

The reasons for the malaise afflicting the industry are simple: car prices have fallen sharply over the past year while dealers' costs – driven by the investment required by manufacturers – have remained the same.

This double whammy first hit car dealers last year – described by the head of a large group as the industry's *annus horribilis*.

Throughout the first half of 2000, the UK car market was unsettled by an investigation by competition authorities into claims that car prices in the UK were up to 12 per cent higher than in the rest of Europe.

In April, the inquiry found the claims – part of the 'Rip-Off Britain Campaign' launched by the Consumers' Association and supported by sections of the press – were justified and urged the government to take action.

Four months later, the government introduced measures that sparked a fall of about 10 per cent in car prices.

Richard Barber, chief executive of Quicks, one of the largest dealers, believes dealers' margins and cash flow were hit by consumers deciding to wait for the expected price cuts to buy a new car.

At the same time, the expected fall in new car prices prompted sharp cuts in the price of used cars, hitting dealers that accept old vehicles in part-exchange for new ones.

'Last year was the most problematic year I had witnessed in 26 years in the industry,' Mr Barber says.

'We had fewer customers in the showrooms as people waited for the government to curb prices. We had to increase volume at the expense of margins. The market was just out of order and there was a sense of desperation in the industry.'

However, in the last part of 2000, demand picked up, driven mainly by the fall in prices, and has carried on growing in 2001.

In February new car registrations rose by 7.3 per cent – the fifth consecutive month of growth. The market is forecast to rise by about 1.3 per cent in 2001 – slightly more than last year – partly due to further falls in prices.

Mr Barber believes the worst is over. 'DC Cook and HMG were the victims of 2000. The market is now more settled and there is more consumer confidence.'

This month [March 2001] the industry is looking forward to the introduction of the new Y number plates, which is expected to lure a large number of people into buying a car.

But many industry figures believe dealers face serious longer-term problems due to their relationship with manufacturers.

Dealers say manufacturers have too much power. They claim that the large car-makers decide which dealer will sell their cars exclusively in a particular area and have a large degree of influence on how much dealers invest on premises and training.

'The manufacturers are holding the whip hand. We need measures to even up the power between dealers and manufacturers,' says Mr Woollatt.

The carmakers reject these criticisms. 'It's unfair to lay the blame at the door of manufacturers. The motor industry is facing a tough time and margins are under pressure for everybody,' says the Society of Motor Manufacturers and Traders, the industry body.

It claims the 'block exemption' system, which allows manufacturers to grant exclusive geographical licences to dealers, ensures that it is in manufacturers' interests to have a profitable retail network.

Many dealers disagree but refuse to go public, due to what one chief executive calls 'the climate of fear instilled by manufacturers'.

The tension is set to come into the open in the coming months in the run-up to the end of the block exemption system in September next year. Several dealers want new rules, similar to the US model where contracts between manufacturers and retailers last five years, rather than two, to give them more time to absorb the cost of the investment required by carmakers.

The manufacturers are opposed to these changes and some of them, such as Ford and Mercedes, have started taking stakes or buying in their dealers in order to keep a close tab on the cost of selling their cars.

Experts believe the answer to the problems is consolidation. According to a report by market research group MBD, analysts expect the number of dealers to halve over the next two years, with smaller dealers either bought by larger groups or forced to turn to used cars.

The need for corporate activity has been noted by activist investors.

Guinness Peat Group, the investment vehicle of the corporate raider Sir Ron Brierley, has recently taken stakes in car groups such Quicks, Perry and Inchcape. Analysts say GPG could pressure management to explore merger opportunities if the shares start showing signs of weakness.

Trevor Finn, chief executive of Pendragon, one of the UK's largest dealers with 160 outlets, agrees. 'It's a difficult market and the only way to survive is to become more efficient and reduce costs through economies of scale.'

The Formula One Constructors

Mark Jenkins

*This case describes three examples of the creation of competitive advantage
in a highly competitive technological context. F1 motorsport is the pinnacle of
automotive technology and involves highly specialised constructors designing and building single-seat race cars which compete for annual championships which bring huge financial and reputational rewards. These three cases
explore the stories of three contrasting companies: Ferrari, McLaren and
Williams in terms of how they both created and lost the basis for sustained
competitive advantage.*

• • •

Between two and four on a Sunday afternoon this is a sport. All the rest of the time
it's commerce.

(Frank Williams, Managing Director, Williams F1)

In 1945 the Fédération Internationale de l'Automobile (FIA) established
Formula A as the premier level of motorsport. In the years that followed,
Formula A became referred to as Formula One and a drivers' world champion-
ship was introduced in 1950. The first world champion was Giuseppe Farina
of Italy driving an Alfa Romeo. At that time Alfa dominated the racing along
with the other Italian marques of Ferrari and Maserati. Drivers such as Juan
Fangio, Alberto Ascari, Jack Brabham, Jim Clark and Graham Hill were to take
the championship during the 1950s and 60s driving cars built by Alfa Romeo,
Ferrari, Mercedes-Benz, Lancia, Cooper and Lotus. By the mid-sixties Formula
One had moved from being a basis for car manufacturers to promote their
products and develop and test technology, to a highly specialist business
where purpose-built cars were developed through leading-edge technology to
win a TV sporting event enjoying the third highest TV audience in the world,
surpassed only by the Olympics and World Cup Soccer.

There have been between 10 and 14 race car manufacturers or constructors
competing in Formula One at any one time. The constructors themselves
can be grouped into a number of different categories. In the late nineties the
top four teams were Williams, Ferrari, McLaren and Benetton, all medium-
sized businesses turning over £30–60 million a year. Patrick Head, technical
director of Williams, estimates that it required between £25 and £30 million
capital investment in research facilities to set up the minimum basis for

being competitive. The top teams would typically have their own testing and development equipment which would include wind-tunnels and other facilities. In the 1990s McLaren, Williams and Benetton all employed around 200 people in their Formula One operations, a quarter of whom were the engineer/mechanics who travelled round the world attending Grand Prix every two to three weeks throughout the F1 season (March to November). Labour costs account for around 25 per cent of the larger teams' budgets. All the teams would have highly qualified technical staff which would include race engineers (who work with the driver to set up the car), designers, aerodynamicists, composite experts (to work with specialised carbon-composite materials) and systems specialists.

The revenues to run these operations come from a number of sources: commercial sponsorship from non-related companies such as cigarettes and clothing (e.g. Marlboro, Rothmans, Benetton, Hugo Boss); support through the provision of free products and services such as engines, fuel and lubricants (e.g. Renault, Ford, Shell, Elf and Agip) and systems support (e.g. Andersen Consulting, Bull and Sun Microsystems). In order to secure these inflows of capital and services the top teams have sophisticated marketing departments to establish and manage the relationships with these sponsors. More recently, the automotive manufacturers have become major sources of finance, with Ford, Daimler-Chrysler, BMW, Honda and Toyota all becoming major partners, and in many cases owners or equity holders of the F1 teams.

In addition, revenue is provided by prize money generated by winning championship points. A first place earns 10 points, second 6 points, third 4 points then down in single steps to sixth place earning 1 point. The prize money is a way of dividing up the royalties earned from media coverage and other revenues which is negotiated, on behalf of all the teams, by the constructors' association (FOA). In 1996 the Jordan team estimated that around £1.8 million (11 per cent) of their revenue would come from prize money.

Most of the constructors are located in what has been referred to as 'Motorsport Valley', an area of the UK covered by a broad arc from Oxfordshire, stretching into East Anglia and down into Surrey. Whilst there are other teams located in other countries such as Ferrari (Maranello, Italy), Prost (Guyancourt, near Paris, France) and Sauber (Hinwil, Switzerland), the majority of teams reside in the UK. The focus on the UK has been attributed to the network of specialist engineering talent which is fundamental to success in F1, as summarised by the MD of the Benetton team, Flavio Briartore, in 1994: 'If you like proscuitto you come to Italy. If you like champagne, you come to France. For Formula One you come to England. I don't like the English weather, but the best engineering is here.'

The Formula One Constructors provide a unique context where we can consider the competitive advantage of different multi-million-pound organisations over time. The pace of change and the basis of advantage is constantly changing, shown by the fact that since the start of the world championships, no constructor has won the championship consecutively more than four times (McLaren 1988–91) and only Ferrari (1975–77) and Williams (1992–94) have won for three consecutive years (Exhibit 1). The remainder of the case considers each of these periods of competitive dominance in chronological order.

Exhibit 1

YEAR	DRIVER	CAR	CONSTRUCTOR'S CUP
1950	Giuseppe Farina	Alfa Romeo	
1951	Juan Manuel Fangio	Alfa Romeo	
1952	Alberto Ascari	Ferrari	
1953	Alberto Ascari	Ferrari	
1954	Juan Manuel Fangio	Maserati	
1955	Juan Manuel Fangio	Mercedes-Benz	
1956	Juan Manuel Fangio	Lancia-Ferrari	
1957	Juan Manuel Fangio	Maserati	
1958	Mike Hawthorn	Ferrari	Vanwall
1959	Jack Brabham	Cooper	Cooper
1960	Jack Brabham	Cooper	Cooper
1961	Phil Hill	Ferrari	Ferrari
1962	Graham Hill	BRM	BRM
1963	Jim Clark	Lotus	Lotus
1964	John Surtees	Ferrari	Ferrari
1965	Jim Clark	Lotus	Lotus
1966	Jack Brabham	Brabham	Brabham
1967	Denny Hulme	Brabham	Brabham
1968	Graham Hill	Lotus	Lotus
1969	Jackie Stewart	Matra	Matra
1970	Jochen Rindt	Lotus	Lotus
1971	Jackie Stewart	Tyrrell	Tyrrell
1972	Emerson Fittipaldi	Lotus	Lotus
1973	Jackie Stewart	Tyrrell	Lotus
1974	Emerson Fittipaldi	McLaren	McLaren
1975	Niki Lauda	Ferrari	**Ferrari**
1976	James Hunt	McLaren	**Ferrari**
1977	Niki Lauda	Ferrari	**Ferrari**
1978	Mario Andretti	Lotus	Lotus
1979	Jody Scheckter	Ferrari	Ferrari
1980	Alan Jones	Williams	Williams
1981	Nelson Piquet	Brabham	Williams
1982	Keke Rosberg	Williams	Ferrari
1983	Nelson Piquet	Brabham	Ferrari
1984	Niki Lauda	McLaren	McLaren
1985	Alain Prost	McLaren	McLaren
1986	Alain Prost	McLaren	Williams
1987	Nelson Piquet	Williams	Williams
1988	Ayrton Senna	McLaren	**McLaren**
1989	Alain Prost	McLaren	**McLaren**
1990	Ayrton Senna	McLaren	**McLaren**
1991	Ayrton Senna	McLaren	**McLaren**
1992	Nigel Mansell	Williams	**Williams**
1993	Alain Prost	Williams	**Williams**
1994	Michael Schumacher	Benetton	**Williams**
1995	Michael Schumacher	Benetton	Benetton
1996	Damon Hill	Williams	Williams
1997	Jacques Villeneuve	Williams	Williams
1998	Mika Hakkinen	McLaren	McLaren
1999	Mika Hakkinen	McLaren	Ferrari
2000	Michael Schumacher	Ferrari	Ferrari

Bold type signifies that the constructors' championship has been won on three or more consecutive occasions

FERRARI

The period 1975–77 saw the renaissance of the Ferrari team. Their last Formula One World Championship had been won in 1964, one of the few reminders of the glorious 50s and early 60s when the bright red cars of Ferrari dominated motor racing. In the mid-70s they won 15 of the 45 races during 1975, 1976 and 1977.

Ferrari are the oldest of all the Grand Prix teams who are still racing. Their heritage gives them a special place in the hearts of all motor racing enthusiasts. Founded by Enzo Ferrari, an ex-driver and manager of the Alfa Romeo racing team in 1950, they and other Italian marques such as Maserati and Alfa dominated the sport during the 1950s. Ferraris have taken part in more than 550 Grand Prix (the next highest is McLaren with 440) and, despite the variable nature of the team's performance, drivers continue to view a contract with Ferrari as something very special. Perhaps this is why world champions such as Alain Prost, Nigel Mansell and Michael Schumacher have been attracted to the team at times when their cars have been far from the fastest or most reliable.

In an era when the majority of constructors are British specialists who buy in central components such as engines and gearboxes, Ferrari are distinctive in that they have always done everything themselves: engine, gearbox, suspension, chassis are all made at their Maranello factory, which enjoys the most up-to-date facilities in terms of designing, developing and building all the necessary components of a race car. While other constructors such as McLaren and Williams will paint their cars whatever colour required by their flagship sponsor, Ferraris always have been and, one assumes, always will be, bright red, the national motor racing colour of Italy. The cars have, until recently, displayed very little evidence of sponsorship; it has always been the Ferrari emblem – a black prancing horse – which has the most prominent position. The Italian public see Ferrari as a national icon, as observed by Niki Lauda in an interview in 1996: 'The Italians love you when you win and hate you when you lose and whatever you do, win, lose or simply break wind everyone in Italy wants to know about it!'

The influence of Enzo Ferrari, or *Il Commendatore* as he was frequently known, was total and the myths and stories surrounding him still permeate the team, despite his death in 1988. It was legendary that Ferrari himself hardly ever attended a race and very rarely left the Maranello factory where his beloved cars were made; he relied on the media and his advisers for information which often created a highly political atmosphere in the team. Ferrari's first love was motor racing; this was despite having created a very successful range of road-going cars which he saw primarily as the source of funding for his racing. The merger (or rather takeover) between Fiat and Ferrari in 1969 provided Ferrari with a huge cash injection which simply allowed Enzo, who was then 71, to concentrate on his first love, motor racing at the highest level: Formula One.

The resources which Ferrari have at their disposal have always been the envy of every other team; they had always built their own engines and have a large technical team dedicated to the task of engine design and development.

In 1971 they opened their own test track at Fiorano, literally a few hundred yards from the Maranello factory. At the time, it was the most advanced and sophisticated test circuit in the world, enabling the cars to be constantly tested and developed between the track and the factory. Ferrari himself attended most of the tests and would make sure he was kept informed as to exactly what was being tested and why. Enzo himself had always declared his love for the distinctive sound and power of a Ferrari engine, as indicated by former Ferrari driver, Nigel Mansel: 'Enzo Ferrari believed that the engine was the most important part of the race car. Colin [Chapman – head of Lotus] believed it was the chassis.'

The early seventies began shakily for Ferrari; the new ownership and influence from Fiat meant increased resources, but also increased pressure for results. In 1971 the cars were very fast, but not reliable. It got worse in 1972 and 1973 with cars only finishing every other race and rarely in the points. Enzo himself had been suffering poor health and the team seemed to be unable to turn around despite having the huge resources of Fiat at their disposal. However, through 1974 things began to change. The brilliant technician Mauro Forghieri had been recalled to Ferrari in 1973 as technical director; Forghieri had been responsible for some of the more successful Ferraris of the 1960s. It is not clear why he left, but in 1973 he returned.

In addition to the arrival of Forghieri, a new team boss was also appointed to try to turn Ferrari fortunes around. At 25 years old, a qualified lawyer and a member of Fiat's aristocratic Agnelli dynasty, Luca Montezemolo was an unlikely right-hand man for *Il Commendatore*. However, he was given a relatively free hand by Ferrari and brought much-needed management discipline to the team. While there had always been a huge supply of talent at Ferrari, particularly in the design and development of engines, gearboxes and suspension systems, it had not always reached its collective potential. Enzo's autocratic style of 'divide and rule' had created much confusion and rivalry within the team. Montezemolo defined strict areas of responsibility in order to reduce the amount of interference and internal politics. This created a situation where the various technical teams (chassis and suspension; engine; gearbox) concentrated on and were fully accountable for their own area. Montezemolo was also instrumental in the recruitment of driver Niki Lauda, of whom he was a close friend. Lauda was of Austrian aristocratic descent, but was totally committed to his racing. He had been very successful in Formula Two but was having a torrid time with the ailing BRM team in Formula One. In 1973 Enzo Ferrari told Lauda he wanted him to drive for Ferrari, an offer which very few drivers have ever refused.

In 1974 Ferrari was in the ascendant. Lauda and the design team had embarked upon an exhaustive testing and development programme at the Fiorano test track. The new car, the 312B, was very much the fastest car on the track. However, there were still reliability problems and, although Lauda was leading the championship at the British Grand Prix, the lead was lost through technical problems which resulted in Emerson Fittipaldi in a McLaren taking the eventual honours.

In 1975 the tables were turned. The fruits of Forghieri's creative ideas and the intensive testing at Fiorano was exemplified in the 312T which featured a powerful 12-cylinder engine and a revolutionary transverse (sideways mounted) gearbox which improved the balance of the car, making it handle extremely well. While the new car was not ready until the season had already started, Lauda, with the support of team-mate Regazzoni, was easily able to secure both the drivers' and constructors' world championships. The Ferraris dominated the 1975 season; with their elegant handling and the power advantage of the engine, they were in a class of their own. Because the majority of the competition all had the same engine–gearbox combination (Ford V8 and Hewland gearbox), they were unable to respond to a chassis/gearbox/engine combination which was unique to Ferrari.

In 1976 things continued in much the same vein, with Lauda and Regazzoni winning the early races. The intensive testing did not let up and new ideas and innovations, such as a revised rear suspension system, were constantly being tried out. On the management front, Montezemolo had been promoted to head up Fiat motorsport, which included the Lancia rally programme as well as Ferrari, and Daniele Audetto was moved from managing the rally team to become sporting director at Ferrari. However, things were not to go as smoothly as in 1975. At the German Grand Prix Lauda lost control of the car in the wet and crashed in flames. He was rescued by four other drivers, but not before suffering severe burns and inhaling toxic fumes. His life was in the balance for some weeks, while the Grand Prix series continued with James Hunt (McLaren) reducing Lauda's lead in the championship. Miraculously Lauda recovered from his injuries and, although still scarred, he returned to the Grand Prix series. He and Hunt went into the last Grand Prix of 1976 (Japan) with Lauda leading by three points. There was heavy rain and Lauda pulled out of the race, leaving the drivers' championship to Hunt, while Ferrari still collected the constructor's championship. While, on paper, it was a good year, by rights Ferrari should have dominated 1976 as they had 1975. Audetto who, perhaps not surprisingly, had been unable to live up to the role created by Montezemolo and had failed to develop a strong relationship with Lauda, returned to the world of rallying. Ferrari went into 1977 in a state of disarray.

In 1977 Ferrari were still the team to beat, although the testing and development lost through Lauda's six-week convalescence seemed to have reduced the crushing dominance which the team had earlier shown. The competition were also beginning to find ways of catching up. The Brabham team moved away from the Ford V8 and used an Alfa Romeo flat 12 similar to the Ferrari engine. Tyrrell launched the revolutionary P34 six-wheeled car which seemed to be the only car able to stay with the Ferrari. Ferrari themselves were not standing still and launched the 312T2 in 1976, which was a significant development of the original 312T. Ferrari won the 1977 drivers' and constructors' championship, but this was the end of the partnership with Niki Lauda; the relationship had never been the same since the Nurburgring accident. Lauda left to join Brabham but did not regain the world championship until he drove for McLaren in 1984. He retired from driving in 1985, and became a successful airline entrepreneur before returning to F1 as chief operating officer of Ford's performance motorsport group in 2001. While Lauda was not perhaps the fastest racer on the track he was always able to develop a car and build relationships with the design team, which enabled Ferrari to translate the driver's senses into reliable technical solutions.

The unprecedented run of Ferrari success continued in 1978 with the 312T3 car driven by two highly talented drivers: Argentinean Carlos Reutemann was joined by the flamboyant Gilles Villeneuve and, while they were not able to win the constructors' championship, they achieved a very strong second place. In 1979 Reutemann was replaced by South African Jody Scheckter whose consistency contrasted with Villeneuve's erratic speed. Scheckter won the driver's championship, with Ferrari taking the constructors' championship. Their greatest moment was when Scheckter and Villeneuve finished first and second at the Italian Grand Prix at Monza.

However, 1979 was the last time that Ferrari were to win a Drivers' World Championship for 21 years. The 1980 season was something of a disaster for Ferrari. Scheckter and Villeneuve were totally uncompetitive in the 312T5, which, while a significant development from the 312T4, was outclassed by the competition. Innovations in car design brought the 'ground effect' revolution, pioneered by Lotus and quickly adopted by Williams and Brabham. Here the underside of the car featured two 'venturi', or channels, either side of the driver. These were aerodynamically designed to create a vacuum which held the car to the track, allowing faster cornering. While the Ferrari's engine was one of the most powerful, it was a 'flat 12,' meaning that the cylinders were horizontal to the ground, creating a low and wide barrier which gave no opportunity to create the ground effects which were being achieved with the slimmer V8 engines. In 1978 Alfa Romeo had launched a V12 engine to replace their flat 12 for this very reason. No such initiative had been taken at Ferrari who were concentrating on a longer-term project to develop a V6 turbocharged engine. Autosport correspondent Nigel Roebuck provided a succinct overview of Ferrari's 1980 season: 'Maranello's flat-12, still a magnificent racing engine, is incompatible with modern chassis. Villeneuve and Scheckter were competing in yesterday's cars.' The lowest point came in the Canadian Grand Prix; the reigning world champion, Jody Scheckter, failed to qualify his Ferrari for the race, a bit like Italy or England failing to qualify for the World Cup. Once again the full wrath of the Italian press descended on the team.

Ferrari's longer-term view, focusing on the V6 turbo-charged engine, also paid off in 1982 and 1983 when they were able to secure the constructors' championship. In the mid-eighties more and more investment was poured into facilities but to no effect on performance. In 1986 British designer John Barnard was recruited and surprisingly allowed to establish a design and manufacturing facility near Guildford in Surrey that became known as the Ferrari GTO or Guildford Technical Office. It seemed that rather than being a unique and distinctively Italian F1 team, Ferrari were now trying to imitate the British constructors whom Enzo had once, rather contemptuously, referred to as the *Garagistes*. Enzo Ferrari's death in 1988 created a vacuum which was filled by executives from the Fiat organisation for a number of years and it wasn't until the appointment of Luca di Montezemolo as CEO in 1992 that Ferrari seriously began the journey that was to allow Michael Schumacher to retake the drivers' championship for them in 2000, fifty years from their first F1 race.

McLAREN

The period from 1988 to 1991 was highly unusual in the hypercompetitive world of Formula One where a new car is created each year and the pace of change is rarely matched in any other competitive environment. This period was notable because of the dominance of one constructor. In this four-year period the McLaren team won 38 of the 48 races; such dominance had not been seen before and will almost certainly never be seen again.

Founded by the New Zealand F1 driver Bruce McLaren in 1966, the McLaren team had their first victory in the Belgian Grand Prix of 1968. Tragically McLaren himself was killed two years later while testing a sports car for the American Can-Am series at Goodwood. Lawyer and family friend Teddy Mayer took over as team principal and the team continued to develop and in 1974 secured sponsorship from Philip Morris to promote the Marlboro brand of cigarettes. This was a partnership that was to last until 1996, probably the most enduring relationship between a constructor and a 'flagship' sponsor. In September 1980 Ron Dennis, a former mechanic, became joint team principal with Mayer, a position which he took over solely in 1982, when Mayer was 'encouraged' by Philip Morris to take a less active role in the management of McLaren. In the previous year McLaren moved from their modest site in Colnbrook to a modern facility in Woking.

Dennis was a mechanic for the highly successful Cooper team in 1966, but left to set up his own Formula Two (a smaller, less expensive formula) team in 1971. By the end of the 70s he had built up a reputation for professionalism and immaculate presentation. His Project Four company brought in designer John Barnard who had some radical ideas about using carbon fibre, rather than metal, as the basis for a race car chassis. These ideas were to provide the basis for the MP4 car (McLaren Project Four).

Before Dennis's arrival, the team had enjoyed some success during the mid-seventies, winning their first drivers' and constructors' championships with Emerson Fittipaldi in the M23 car in 1974. However, the real period of dominance which McLaren enjoyed was in the period from 1988 until 1991 when they won the driver's title (Alain Prost: 1989; Ayrton Senna: 1988; 1990; 1991) and constructor's championship for four consecutive years.

In 1986 designer John Barnard left to join the struggling Ferrari team. Barnard was considered by many to be the reason for McLaren's developing dominance. The partnership between Dennis and Barnard had been stormy but a huge amount had been achieved through the energy of these two individuals, Dennis providing the managerial and commercial acumen and Barnard highly innovative design skills (by the end of the 90s Barnard was still regarded by many as the best designer in F1). To replace Barnard, Brabham designer Gordon Murray was brought into the team, perhaps best known for developing the innovative 'fan car' for Brabham in 1978. Murray, like Barnard, was at the leading edge of F1 car design.

Halfway through 1987 McLaren announced that they had recruited two of the top drivers in F1 to their team: Alain Prost and Ayrton Senna, for the 1988 season, as reported in Motorsport:

Ayrton Senna is being moved from Lotus to McLaren to join Prost in one of the most professional and well balanced teams of all time. Prost and Senna have been announced as joint number one drivers, and McLaren International has shown in the past that it is well capable of handling two top drivers, which few other teams have managed.

Ayrton Senna, the young Brazilian, had made a name for himself as being extremely talented and totally committed, but very difficult to manage. In his previous team, Lotus, he is alleged to have blocked the recruitment of driver Derek Warwick as he regarded him too great a threat and persuaded the team to bring in the less experienced and younger Johnny Dumfries instead. Prost and Senna were real contrasts: Senna was fast and had unparalleled commitment to winning races; Prost was fast too, but a great tactician and adept at team politics, making sure that the whole team was behind him. However, it was ultimately Senna who was able to change the balance of power within the team.

In 1988 the Honda-powered MP4 car designed by John Barnard was without question the fastest and most reliable car on the circuit. This meant that effectively the only real competition for Prost and Senna was each other. In a remarkable year McLaren won 15 out of the 16 Grand Prix. This competition between two highly committed and talented drivers resulted in one of the most enduring and bitter feuds the sport has ever known. In 1988 Senna swerved at Prost as they raced wheel to wheel at 190 mph; Prost told him, 'If you want the world championship badly enough to die for it, you are welcome.' In 1990 the acrimony with Senna culminated in Prost's moving to Ferrari. Senna now had the team to himself. But the battle between them continued, reaching a dramatic climax at the Japanese Grand Prix when Senna forced Prost's Ferrari off the road, and as a consequence became world champion. Despite these darker moments, Senna's brilliance was undisputed. The accolades from the industry following his tragic death in 1994 were sincere and he is widely regarded as one of the greatest drivers of all time.

The other element in the success of the McLaren in 1988 was the fact that Ron Dennis had negotiated exclusive use of Honda engines. The engines were supported by a significant commitment from Honda in both people and resources, Honda using this as an opportunity to develop some of their most talented engineers. In 1988 Honda engines were among the most powerful and certainly the most reliable. Honda had been engine supplier to the Williams team since 1983. Sadly, team principal Frank Williams was seriously injured in a car accident in 1986 which left him tetraplegic. This caused concern in Honda over the future of the Williams team.

The combination of Prost and Senna made McLaren an attractive alternative to Williams for Honda, as identified by a journalist at the time: 'Honda, said our source, want to dominate F1 and it knows it can never do that if it does not have Prost.' Honda switched allegiance exclusively to McLaren for 1988 after also supplying the Lotus team (and driver Ayrton Senna) in 1987. This meant that Honda-powered cars had won six consecutive world championships from 1986 to 1991 (Williams: 1986 and 1987; McLaren 1988, 1989, 1990 and 1991).

Ron Dennis, with his professional management style, has been synonymous with the success of McLaren, indicating that the era of the 'one-man band' Formula One constructor was past. His record since taking over in 1982 has been unsurpassed. Eddie Jordan, principal of the Jordan team, made the following statement when planning to enter F1 in 1990:

> I know it sounds far fetched, but I want to emulate Ron Dennis. He's won that many Grand Prix, he's won that many championships, he's been on pole that many times and he's got the best drivers. Everyone hates him; but they only hate him because he's the best. I believe I'm as good as he is: I believe I'm in the same league, but only time will tell.

Dennis's negotiating and marketing abilities were legendary throughout Formula One. McLaren also created their own marketing consultancy operation where the smaller teams engaged them to find sponsors. In 1991 *Management Week* had Ron Dennis on the front cover with the question: 'Is Ron Dennis Britain's best manager?' Dennis likens the management of McLaren to that of a game of chess: '. . . you've got to get all the elements right, the overall package, the budget, the designer, the engine, the drivers, the organisation'. John Barnard once likened working with Dennis as 'being in a room with a hand grenade rolling about without its pin, about to go off and make a horrible mess.' It should also be said that Barnard himself was not particularly famous for having a long temper. Dennis's ambitions were beyond F1 and in 1988 he began a project to build a road-going car, the McLaren F1. In many ways this mirrored the development of Ferrari who had made the progression from producing dedicated race cars to also developing road-going cars. The McLaren F1 was launched in 1994 and with a price tag of £634,000 and a top speed of 231 mph became the most expensive and fastest road-going car in the world. The design skills of Gordon Murray were used heavily in the development of the car, which has a BMW engine.

However, in 1992 the slippage began. The Renault-powered Williams was developing into the fastest and most reliable car on the circuit. In September, following widespread speculation, Honda confirmed that that they were pulling out of F1 racing. Honda's reasons were simple: they had been hugely successful and achieved all of their objectives; it was now time to stand back from F1 and find some new challenges. While Dennis had been told about Honda's thinking in late 1991, it appeared that he hadn't taken it seriously enough and the team had no real engine alternatives. This meant they lost valuable winter development time as they tried to find a new engine supplier. In 1993 they competed with 'off the shelf' Ford engines available to any team who had the cash to buy them. Senna's skills still gave McLaren five victories, despite having a less than competitive car. However, at the end of 1993 Senna left the McLaren team to move to Williams, whom he saw as having the superior car and engine combination. Former world champion and adviser to Ferrari, Niki Lauda, saw this as the terminal blow: 'Senna was a leader. He told them exactly what was wrong with the car. Hakkinen (Senna's replacement) is not in a position to do that, so the reaction time is much longer. Senna motivated the designers.' John Hogan, VP of European marketing for Philip Morris and holder of the McLaren purse strings, saw the problem as design leadership and was advocating that Barnard be brought back to McLaren.

The mid-nineties were a particularly difficult period for McLaren. Having tried Peugeot engines in 1994 they moved to Mercedes in 1995. However, 1995 was perhaps best remembered for the debacle at the start when neither Nigel Mansell or Mika Hakinnen could fit into the new £50 million MP4/10 and then Mansell's alleged £4.5 million contract to race for the year fell apart when neither he nor the car came up to expectations. In 1996 the relationship between McLaren and Philip Morris came to an end, Philip Morris moving support of their Marlboro brand to Ferrari driver Michael Schumacher, while McLaren entered into a substantial agreement with German-based tobacco firm Reemtsma to support their West brand. In 1997 McLaren acquired the services of Williams designer Adrian Newey for a reputed £2 million contract. Newey's design talents coupled with a more powerful and reliable Mercedes engine meant that McLaren again became the team to beat.

WILLIAMS

If the McLaren MP4 was the dominant car in the late eighties, the Williams F1 FW15 and 16 powered by a Renault V10 was the car to beat in the early 1990s. During the period 1992–94 Williams cars won 27 out of 48 races, they secured the F1 constructors' title for all three years and the world championship for drivers was won in a Williams in 1992 (Nigel Mansell) and 1993 (Alain Prost).

Like most of the founders of the Formula One constructors, Frank Williams began as a driver, perhaps not of the same standing as Bruce McLaren or Jack Brabham, but nonetheless someone who lived, breathed and loved motor racing. His desire to remain in the sport led him to develop a business buying and selling racing cars and spare parts, and in 1968 Frank Williams (Racing Cars) Ltd was formed. A series of triumphs, tragedies and near bankruptcies led up to the establishment of Williams Grand Prix Engineering in 1977 when Frank Williams teamed up with technical director Patrick Head. Frank Williams' approach and style owes a lot to the difficult years in the seventies when he survived on his wits and very little else. His style could be described as autocratic, entrepreneurial and certainly frugal, despite the multi-million-pound funding he managed to extract from the likes of Canon, R.J. Reynolds and Rothmans. Williams saw his role as providing the resources for the best car to be built and to hire the best driver to sit in it. His long-standing relationship with Head was pivotal to the team and brought together a blend of entrepreneurial energy and technical excellence needed to succeed in F1.

The first car from this new alliance was the FW06, designed by Patrick Head with support from Saudi Airlines. The team enjoyed some success in 1980/81 by winning the constructors' championship both years and with Alan Jones winning the driver's title in 1980. Jones was a forthright Australian who knew what he wanted. His approach to working with the team was very influential. In Frank Williams' view of drivers: 'I took a very masculine attitude towards drivers and assumed that they should behave – or should be treated – like Alan.'

A similar situation occurred in 1986/87 with Nelson Piquet winning the driver's title in 1987 and Williams the constructors' title in both years. This was despite the road accident in 1996 which left Frank Williams tetraplegic and confined to a wheelchair. However, the most dominant period in the history of Williams, so far, has been the period 1992–94 when they were able to win the constructor championship for three consecutive years.

Williams' 1986/87 success had been, in part, due to the use of powerful and reliable Honda engines. However, Frank Williams' accident in 1986 caused concern at Honda over the future of the team and in 1987 they made their engines available to Lotus and withdrew from Williams (a year before the end of the contract) to supply McLaren in the 1988 season. The 1988 season was Williams' worst, as they were forced suddenly to switch to 'off the shelf' Judd V10 engines which were available to anyone who wanted one. Williams didn't win a single race, while McLaren won 15 out of the 16 Grand Prix of 1988 and a disillusioned Nigel Mansell left and went to Ferrari. Frank Williams had to search frantically for a new engine deal which he found in 1990 with Renault. In 1985 Renault had withdrawn from Formula One as a constructor, having failed to win a world championship. However, they continued their engine development activities with the aim of building a new F1 engine to meet the new non-turbo standards due to be introduced in 1989. Frank Williams was able to form an agreement for Renault to supply him with the new V10 engine. This relationship became a far-reaching and durable one, with Renault putting human and financial resources into the project with Williams. They also sought to develop the relationship further and extended their activities with Renault by running their team of saloon cars for the British Touring Car Championship.

In 1990 a lack of real driver talent meant that the team were only able to win two races. In 1991 Nigel Mansell was persuaded to return from retirement by Frank Williams and narrowly missed taking the 1991 title, but in 1992 the team dominated the circuits, effectively winning the championship by the middle of the season. Nigel Mansell went into the record books by winning the first five consecutive races of the season. This was a phenomenal achievement as it emphatically demonstrated that McLaren were no longer at the top; Williams most certainly were. However, a deterioration in the relationship between Williams and Mansell led to the driver's retirement from racing at the end of the year.

The Williams approach to design and development of a car was always the highest priority. Patrick Head had always been one of the more conspicuous and forthright of the technical directors in Formula One, a role which is often shadowed by the head of the team and driver. In a sport where personnel change teams frequently, the stable relationship between Williams and Head (and up to 1996, Adrian Newey, who was a brilliant aerodynamicist and design assistant) provided enviable continuity compared with the rest of the field. While Head's designs had often been functional rather than innovative, he had always been able to take a good idea and develop it further. These have included ground effect (originally developed by Lotus), carbon-composite monocoque (McLaren), semi-automatic gearbox (Ferrari), and active suspension (Lotus). The car development process was always a top priority at Williams and Head was supported by many designers who went on to be highly influential in Formula One, such as Neil Oatley and Adrian Newey (who left for McLaren), Frank Dernie (Ligier, Lotus and Arrows) and Ross Brawn (Benetton and then technical director at Ferrari).

This focus on developing the car and engine combination has sometimes meant that the driver took second place in the Williams philosophy, despite the fact that a good test driver, who could tell the technicians what needed to be done to the car to improve its performance, was essential to the development process. There had been a number of high-profile disputes between drivers and Williams which had, in part, been attributable to Frank Williams' 'masculine' approach to dealing with drivers. Controversy, and unpleasant hints of xenophobia from the tabloid press, broke out when the relationship between Williams and two top British drivers broke down. In 1992 Nigel Mansell left when he felt his 'number one' driver position was threatened by the recruitment of Alain Prost for 1993 (although Prost himself left the following year for the same reason regarding the hiring of Ayrton Senna). A similar situation arose when the 1996 world champion, Damon Hill, was not retained for the 1997 season and was replaced with German Heinz-Harald Frentzen. In an interview with the *Sunday Times*, Patrick Head set out the reasons for the decision not to hold on to Hill:

> We are an engineering company and that is what we focus on. Ferrari are probably the only team where you can say the driver is of paramount importance and that is because Schumacher is three-quarters of a second a lap quicker than anyone else.

This emphasis on the driver being only part of the equation was not lost on Paul Stewart who was concentrating on developing the Stewart Grand Prix entry to F1:

> If you haven't got the money none of it is possible, so money is one key to success – but what makes a difference is how the money is used. It's not down to any one thing like a driver or a engine, but the interaction that matters. If you look at the Williams team, they rely on a solid framework, their organisation, their engine, their car design is all amalgamated into something that gives a platform for everyone to work on. They don't believe putting millions into a driver is going to make all the difference.

Williams' emphatic dominance in the 1992 season was due to a number of factors: the development of the powerful and reliable Renault RS3 V10 engine was perfectly complemented by the FW15 chassis which incorporated Patrick Head's development of some of the innovations of the early nineties, namely semi-automatic gearboxes, drive-by-wire technology and their own active suspension system. As summarised by a senior manager at Williams F1:

> I think we actually were better able to exploit the technology that was available and led that technology revolution. We were better able to exploit it to the full, before the others caught up . . . it wasn't just one thing but a combination of ten things, each one giving you another 200/300th of a second, if you add them up you a get a couple of seconds of advantage.

However, other teams were also able to use these innovations and in 1993 the Benetton team made a great deal of progress with both the gearbox and suspension innovations largely attributed to the development skills of their new driver, Michael Schumacher. However, Williams' technical lead coupled with the tactical race skills of Alain Prost, supported by promoted test driver Damon Hill (due to Mansell's sudden exit), secured the 1993 world championship and constructors' championship for Williams F1.

1994 was a disastrous year, but not for reasons of performance as Williams won the constructors' championship for the third successive year (this was always their declared primary objective, with the drivers' championship very much a secondary aim). Frank Williams had, for some time, regarded Brazilian Ayrton Senna as the best driver around and, now with the obvious performance advantage of the FW15 chassis and the Renault V10 engine, Senna was keen to move to Williams. The problem was that a bitter and prolonged feud between Senna and Prost, originating from their time together at McLaren, meant that if Senna arrived Prost would leave. This was exactly what happened. Prost decided to retire (though he returned to run his own team) and Ayrton Senna was partnered by Damon Hill for the 1994 season. However, tragedy struck in the San Marino Grand Prix at Imola and Senna was killed in an accident, an event which not only devastated the Williams team but the sport as a whole. For the remainder to the season Hill found himself as lead driver supported by the new test driver, David Coulthard, and a couple of 'comebacks' from Nigel Mansell. While Williams lost the drivers' title to the rising star of German driver Michael Schumacher, amazingly despite these huge setbacks Williams retained the constructors' title for 1994.

In 1995 the Benetton team was eclipsing the Williams domination. Benetton had developed a car using many of the technological innovations used by the Williams (with the help of ex-Williams designer Ross Brawn). In addition, Renault's ambitions to match Honda's previous domination of the sport as an engine supplier from 1986 to 1991 led them to supply Benetton with their engines as well as Williams, a decision which particularly incensed Head and Williams. 1995 was the year of Benetton and Michael Schumacher, breaking the three-year domination of the Williams team. However, in 1996 Schumacher moved to the then uncompetitive Ferrari team for £27 million, putting him in third place in the Forbes chart of sports top earners. This left the way clear for Williams to dominate the season, with Benetton failing to fill the gap left by Schumacher.

Broken Hill Proprietary (BHP) Company Limited – turnaround strategy

Gary Stockport and Gary Norvall

BHP is a major international resources company with headquarters in Melbourne, Australia. The case study is an example of corporate turnaround in practice. It takes the reader through the stages of a turnaround and examines the actions the company took at each stage. The importance of hiring an external CEO with experience in turnaround management is also considered within the case. The case concludes with the announcement in March 2001 that BHP was to merge with UK-based Billiton, which would create a global resources powerhouse with dominant positions in coal and copper.

• • •

INTRODUCTION

On 27 July 2000, BHP announced its highest-ever profit with an A\$1.63 billion net profit for the 13 months to June (A\$2.03 billion excluding abnormals). This remarkable turnaround from the losses in 1998 and 1999 can be traced back to the appointment of Paul Anderson as CEO and MD in 1998.

Broken Hill Proprietary Company is a major international resources company with headquarters in Melbourne, Australia. The company was incorporated in 1885 in the State of Victoria, Australia. In 1999, the company employed some 50,000 employees and had a market capitalisation of A\$27,150m, which made it Australia's third largest company after National Australia Bank and News Corporation Ltd. BHP has interests and operations in the following sectors:

• minerals exploration, production and processing;
• oil and gas exploration and development;
• steel production and merchandising;

In 1999, the company generated A\$19.2 billion in external sales revenues to markets around the globe in Australia, Japan, America, Europe, Korea, China, Taiwan and the UK (Exhibit 1 gives BHP financial performance 1995–99 and

Exhibit 1	BHP financial performance 1995–1999

BHP Profit and loss account (A$m)

	1999	1998	1997	1996	1995
Sales	19,229	21,189	20,947	19,124	17,696
Other revenue	2,692	3,475	1,373	690	748
	21,921	24,664	22,320	19,814	18,444
less					
Operating expenses & Cost of sales	20,973	22,594	18,101	15,392	13,732
Depreciation & amortisation	2,218	2,206	1,974	1,798	1,651
Group Centre & general administrative expenses	143	161	146	134	129
Interest expense	732	716	739	477	407
	24,066	25,677	20,960	17,801	15,919
Operating profit before interest and tax	(1,413)	(297)	2,099	2,490	2,932
Operating profit before tax	(2,145)	(1,013)	1,360	2,013	2,525
less Income tax attributable to operating expense	164	518	885	752	1,014
Operating profit/(loss) after income tax	(2,309)	(1,531)	475	1,261	1,511
add Outside equity interests – operating profit after tax	(3)	57	(65)	(215)	(295)
Operating profit/(loss) after tax (including abnormals)	(2,312)	(1,474)	410	1,046	1,216
add Retained profit at beginning of the financial year	4,826	7,077	7,434	7,184	6,651
Total available for appropriation	2,514	5,603	7,844	8,230	7,867
less Dividends provided or paid for	766	777	767	744	683
Retained earnings at year end	1,748	4,826	7,077	7,486	7,184
Profit & Loss Account detailing abnormal items					
Operating profit before abnormal items	365	1,302	1,386	1,293	1,617
less Abnormal items after income tax	(2,667)	(2,776)	(976)	(247)	(401)

BHP Balance sheet items

	1999	1998	1997	1996	1995
Assets					
Current assets	5,852	7,218	8,399	6,820	6,105
Non-current assets	25,635	29,864	28,336	28,410	24,182
Total assets	31,487	37,082	36,735	35,230	30,287
Liabilities					
Current liabilities	6,194	6,175	7,328	6,503	5,357
Non-current liabilities	15,932	18,498	13,194	12,981	10,123
Total liabilities	22,126	24,673	20,522	19,484	15,480
Net assets	9,361	12,409	16,213	15,746	14,807
Shareholders' equity	9,361	12,409	16,213	15,746	14,807

BHP Financial statistics

	1999	1998	1997	1996	1995
BHP Balance sheet items					
Gearing % (a)	54.2	52.7	39.4	39.4	31.3
Capital investment expenditure	2,675	4,014	4,149	6,827	3,100
BHP profit and loss statistics					
Return on shareholders' equity	(26.7)	(12.7)	3.3	8.6	10.2
Dividend payout ratio	(negative)	(negative)	2.0	0.8	0.6
Current ratio	0.9	1.2	1.1	1.0	1.1
Earnings to interest expense	(1.9)	(0.4)	2.8	5.2	7.2
Sales to operating income (operating margin)%	–12%	–7%	2%	7%	9%

Exhibit 1	Continued				

	1999	1998	1997	1996	1995
Cash flow statistics					
Operating cash flow to sales	0.2	0.2	0.2	0.2	0.2
Operating cash flow to total assets employed	0.1	0.1	0.1	0.1	0.1
Operating cash flow to annual interest expense	4.9	5.0	5.4	6.9	10.0
Operating cash flow to total debt	0.2	0.1	0.2	0.2	0.3
Share information					
Price/earnings ratio (times)	(negative)	(negative)	75	29	22
Dividend yield %	3.3	3.7	2.7	2.7	2.7
Earnings per share (incl. abnormal)	(133.5)	(87.2)	25.0	65.1	78.7
Market capitalisation at year end	27,150	28,125	37,753	37,106	34,154
Number of employees (000's)	50	55	61	60	49

Notes
(a) Based on the borrowings (current and non-current excluding finance leases, bank overdrafts etc.) as a percentage of total borrowings and shareholders' equity

BHP Cash flows

	1999	1998	1997	1996	1995
Net operating cash flows	3,585	3,559	3,996	3,305	4,090
Net investing cash flows	(1,264)	(1,523)	(4,348)	(7,177)	(3,218)
Net financing cash flows	(2,677)	(1,515)	(32)	(3,578)	(429)
Net (decrease)/increase in cash flow	(356)	(521)	(384)	(294)	(443)
Cash & cash equivalents at beginning of year	949	363	735	883	431
Effect of exchange rate changes on cash	(20)	65	12	(34)	9
Cash & cash equivalents at end of year	573	949	363	555	883

Abnormal items

	1999	1998	1997	1996	1995
Asset write-downs					
Minerals	−2996	−2483	−739		
Other minerals	−1196	−834	−189		
Copper	−1800	−1617	−550		
Coal		−32			
Steel	−105	−246	−220	−222	
Petroleum	−210	−17	−124	−151	
Group	−13				−542
Total	−3324	−2746	−1083	−373	−542
Asset sales					
Minerals	347				
Steel					
Petroleum	121	−146	107	61	234
Services	173	99			
Group	6				
Total	647	−47	107	61	234

Source: BHP.

Exhibit 2	Revenues by geographic location and industry 1995–1999				
	1999	**1998**	**1997**	**1996**	**1995**
Revenue by geographic market					
Australia	8,430	9,375	7,415	6,790	7,051
USA	3,383	4,780	4,310	3,498	2,782
Japan	2,815	2,755	3,090	2,906	2,845
Other*	7,293	7,754	7,505	6,620	5,766
Total	21,921	24,664	22,320	19,814	18,444
Revenue by industry					
Minerals	9,235	8,303	8,465	7,316	6,105
Steel	8,096	8,320	8,217	7,531	7,155
Petroleum	3,093	5,054	4,963	4,284	4,428
Other	1,389	2,987	675	683	756
Total	21,813	24,664	22,320	19,814	18,444
Profit by industry					
Minerals	(2,288)	(1,993)	239	1,083	953
Steel	115	202	113	155	643
Petroleum	162	106	509	329	711
Other	(298)	(249)	(431)	(306)	(796)
Total	(2,309)	(1,934)	430	1,261	1,511

* Incudes South Korea, China, Taiwan, Europe, UK, New Zealand and South America.

Source: BHP.

Exhibit 2 gives a breakdown of revenue by geographic region). The company operates in 50 different countries from as diverse regions as: Yellowknife, Canada (Diamonds); the Atacama Desert in Chile (Copper); and the North West Shelf, Australia (Oil).

In fiscal 1999, the operating loss of BHP including abnormal items attributable to BHP shareholders was A$2,312m, compared with a loss of A$1,474m for fiscal 1998. The poor financial performance of the company reflected the difficult global economic environment over 1998/99 and, in particular, the severe downward pressure on commodity prices over this period. The results also reflect the BHP board's decision to close and sell off poorly performing operations and adjust the carrying value of certain assets. BHP's stock has historically traded on a premium for its management capacity and its ability to take up an opportunity in any kind of business and turn it into a stellar performer. It was the argument of former CEO, John Prescott, that the sum of BHP's components is far greater than the whole.

THE COMMODITIES BUSINESS

The commodities business is no different from any other business in that the fundamental laws of economics – demand and supply – apply. As a consequence of the immense volumes of product that are traded, minor fluctuations in either demand or supply can have major consequences on individual commodity prices and therefore, upon an individual business's bottom line.

The Asian crisis starting in late 1997 saw a major crash in the demand for commodities, and by 1999 the market had still not recovered. In 1999, the Asian markets still remained weak but showed preliminary signs of recovery. For BHP, the prices of nearly all of its major products remained depressed in 1999 and there was overcapacity in the world market of most of BHP's products. The down cycle of the commodity prices from 1997 to 1999 severely affected the bottom line of BHP and in fiscal 1999, increased the loss by some A\$1,080 million. The major products that were affected were: export steel prices declined by approximately 30 per cent; realised crude oil prices declined by 16 per cent; copper prices declined by 15 per cent; and coal prices declined by 12 per cent. Furthermore, the reduction in sales volumes through a fall in demand affected profit by A\$170 million compared with the previous period.

Based upon company projections for fiscal 2000, a US\$1 movement in the oil price would affect the BHP bottom line by A\$47 million and a US¢1 movement in the copper price by A\$16 million. The cost of doing international business can also be high, and a 1 cent currency fluctuation between the US and the Australian dollars affects profit by A\$26 million. As a consequence of the volatility of the commodity markets, companies make use of financial hedging techniques in an attempt to create some predictability in their earnings. As at May 1999, BHP had 27 per cent of their projected oil sales covered by forward contracts and swaps at an average price of US\$16.46 per barrel – on a market-to-market basis, these positions were showing an unrealised loss of US\$4 million.

Following the Asian crisis and the decrease in demand for BHP's products in the Pacific region and in Australia, BHP mitigated the impact of these adverse trading conditions by transferring its export business to alternative markets primarily in Europe and the Americas. But the increased pressure on the steel market led to the European and US steel industries protecting their markets with anti-dumping laws, which has compounded steel production in other parts of the world. Further competitive pressure has been experienced by BHP in the 1998 devaluations of the Brazilian, South African and Indian currencies which have made these countries more competitive internationally.

EARLY ATTEMPTS AT TURNAROUND

Proposals to redefine BHP and address cost structures were issues at BHP during the latter 1990s. John O'Connor, former head of Petroleum until 1998 (under whose leadership the division on most measures such as reserve growth, finding costs per barrel, development costs and operating margins had measured up to and surpassed industry benchmarks), proposed '*Project Leopard*' – a proposal to float Petroleum as an independent company. He claimed that Petroleum was subsidising other divisions of the conglomerate while it was itself being 'starved' of capital. Former CEO Prescott had also put forward a proposal to float Steel independently. The board rejected both proposals.

> The board's intentions to shelve plans to float both the petroleum and the steel divisions separately indicate a clear intention to run BHP as a portfolio, despite the clear preference of the financial markets for specialist companies rather than conglomerates.
>
> (*Business Review Weekly*, 8 March 1998)

Floating the two divisions would have cost the company and shareholders millions of dollars in capital gains tax, stamp duties and lost benefits from joint ventures. Other analysts argued that the company and the board simply had no decisive strategic vision as to where to take the company.

> But the problem the company had was that it couldn't actually work out what it wanted. Nobody could answer what it was that was going to happen to the rest of BHP. It did not have a clear idea of its own future, so the default position was don't do it.
>
> (*Business Review Weekly*, 8 March 1998)

PAUL ANDERSON

In December 1998, Paul Anderson was appointed CEO and managing director of BHP by outgoing chairman of the board, Jerry Ellis. Anderson's appointment was the result of a global search process conducted by the board and supported by the international executive recruiting firm, Heidrick & Struggles. His appointment to CEO and MD of BHP brought with it positive reactions from shareholders, analysts, the media and later BHP employees. Anderson stated that it was his first priority to restore confidence in the company with the employees and with the external public.

Anderson came to BHP with a track record of turning around companies from a position of weakness to one of strength. His experience covered mergers and acquisitions and restructuring companies to improve performance. Anderson, an engineer by trade, obtained his MBA from Stanford University in 1969. He was previously chief operating officer (COO) of Duke Energy Corporation, the world's seventh largest energy company with a market capitalisation of US$36 billion and operations in 50 different countries. Duke Energy was created after the merger of Duke Power and PanEnergy, a company he was instrumental in turning around and increasing its stock value fivefold. He has led two public offerings; been a principal in three multi-billion-dollar mergers on either side of the offering, acquirer and aquiree; fought off a hostile public tender offer; and led several dozen transactions of projects in the hundreds of millions of dollars. He is also no stranger to the steel business, having served as chief financial officer (CFO) at Inland Steel in the US.

His style is considered 'inclusive' of all employees – if any less formal it would be 'shorts and a t-shirt', and the emphasis is on teamwork and shareholder value. The difference in Anderson's style from that of former CEO John

Prescott highlighted BHP's need for a modern chief executive, not only to lead the organisation strategically, but also publicly. At BHP, Anderson is the first CEO to have any remuneration based on meeting defined achievement goals (previous CEOs have held company-provided shares). The press described his package as one of Australia's most *'unusual and creative'* remuneration deals. With a salary including benefits of A\$2.3 million, the package includes 1 million share options and 1 million performance rights, both dependent on performance. He surprised his colleagues with his determination to place much of his remuneration at risk by being performance based.

THE BIG AUSTRALIAN RENEWS

While 1998 saw the beginnings of a major cost restructuring drive by Ron McNeilly, acting CEO of BHP while the board conducted its search for a new CEO, 1999 represented a year in BHP's history of significant changes led by Paul Anderson.

> On the one hand there is a need to continue to clean up the balance sheet and non-core assets, with some minor write offs and asset sales to be completed and tweaking the remaining assets to realise their full value. On the other hand, the company must make shareholders richer, not poorer, through growth. BHP has a suite of not-insignificant new projects and expansions, but the emphasis today, will be on innovation rather than the old method of digging bigger holes. BHP has no consumer brands and operates in a depressed commodity business. It simply has to be the best.
>
> (*Business Review Weekly*, 7 February 1999)

When Anderson addressed shareholders at his first extraordinary general meeting he laid out his intent to create value for shareholders but emphasised the point that there was no magic solution to be unveiled that would create instant value and that the road to profitability would be systematic and untheatrical.

> The first priority will be to get alignment within the company and establish a workable management team. There is nothing I can do myself, we have to have a team that works together. The intent is to simplify the organisation, provide the organisational glue that pulls it together, set out clear accountabilities and responsibilities and above all to expedite decision-making. You will see a number of incremental actions – a new pace in the way we do business – a speed in bringing issues to a head.
>
> (Paul Anderson, CEO BHP, Shareholders Address, 26 February 1999)

The methodology of rebuilding BHP was structured as a three-phase process, of which, by December 1999, only phase one was complete. Phase I, in Anderson's words, was a matter of *'righting the ship'*, facing up to immediate problems and fixing them. Phase II is to take the assets that are healthy and with which the company wishes to continue and optimise their return. Phase III is to develop the overall strategy for the company and the portfolio of business units. Anderson notes that while the activities are discussed as three distinct phases, they are continuous and they overlap, but are also sequential in the priority that they receive.

PHASE I – RIGHTING THE SHIP

By May 1999, the formerly eight business units were consolidated into three distinct business units: minerals; steel; and petroleum. The multi-tiered management structure was replaced by a much smaller management structure of which only one member had been with the company for longer than four years. The board of directors appointed a new chairman, saw four resignations and appointed two new directors, both of whom had international experience. The corporate culture has been revised through the elimination of hierarchical structures, and a reorientation of compensation towards performance-based stock options and salary awards, thereby aligning employee interests firmly with those of shareholders.

Cost structure reduction

The cost structure reduction began in 1998 when Ron McNeilly, the then chief operating officer, took over in the interim as acting CEO. Through lowering overhead costs, reduction in labour, and streamlining operating costs the company saved some A$363 million during fiscal 1998 and furthermore, A$540 million during fiscal 1999 and A$290 in the first quarter of fiscal 2000.

The company further reduced its labour at the iron ore operations in Western Australia by 25 per cent, closed down the previously held corporate headquarters in San Francisco, and downsized the operating base of the Minerals exploration division by reducing field offices from 30 to 6. In steel, the company closed part of the Newcastle Steelworks, effectively taking 1.75 million tonnes or 21 per cent of BHP Australia's raw steel capacity out of the system. It thereby reduced the company's exposure to low margin exports markets while adding to the efficiency of the total steel business. In coal, over and above labour reductions and changes in work practices, the company negotiated a more equitable freight regime for the Queensland operations with the adoption of a common 7 per cent royalty for all producers. The company also cut discretionary spending on capital, adding A$26 million to the bottom line of the first quarter of fiscal 2000, and cut R&D and exploration spending in the fiscal 2000 budget by 40 per cent.

Project selection and assessment criteria

A number of countries and commodities were 'red lined' or 'blacklisted' by new BHP management to reduce risk and exposure. A Project Review Committee was set up to ration capital to all new projects and eliminate some projects early before further management time and cash were wasted on feasibility studies. Project champions were required to test their proposals against a predetermined commodity price range and a matrix of hurdle rates reflecting the nature of the business, leverage, technical and country risk. New projects had to demonstrate that they are able to achieve acceptable returns even at the bottom of the price cycle before being approved. Once the projects have been approved and are up and running, they will be independently monitored to ensure that they engage in best practice project management and that they progress according to plan; if not, they will be stopped.

Problem assets

While in the pursuit of a lower cost structure, there was also a need for the company to address both the immediate and long-term value of a number of existing projects and then assess and reshape the asset and business portfolio. The long-term strategy of the structure of this portfolio is for Phase III. Phase I dealt with the need to dispose of, or transform: those underperforming assets which were not currently profitable or would not be profitable in the foreseeable future; were non-core assets; were assets of limited strategic value; or could have more value to somebody else.

In fiscal 1999, BHP generated A$1.75 billion from restructuring, which included the successful sale of the manganese business for A$347 million and the power business for A$173 million. This also included the sale of oil assets in the Timor Sea for A$121 million and the sale of the Eastern Gas pipeline. The sale of the 1,400 km gas pipeline which supplied the BHP power station 'Pilbara Energy' in Kalgoorlie, and supplied numerous mines and projects in and around Port Headland, signalled a change in corporate strategy where BHP no longer saw a need to control the supply chain in order to get into and run projects in new markets. New Zealand Steel was subject to significant asset write-downs to reflect the market outlook.

Fiscal 2000 saw the sale of other problematic projects owned by BHP, primarily Hartley Platinum in Zimbabwe, Beenup Titanium minerals in Australia and the North American copper operations. All three operations had been part of the significant asset write-downs of fiscal 1999. These decisions to sell did not take place without BHP incurring cost both in financial terms and at a cost of some of its people. Hartley Platinum saw the retrenchment of some 3,000 people in May 1999. The mine was sold to Anglo American (Zimplats) subject to various conditions of the mining lease for only US$3 million, at a cost to BHP's profit in asset write-downs of A$300 million in fiscal 1998 and a further A$342 million in fiscal 1999. The mine lost A$31 million in operating loss in the first quarter of fiscal 1999 and was also responsible for four of the Group's six fatalities in fiscal 1999. It was considered uneconomical because of low ore grades compared with the feasibility studies as well as very unstable ground conditions. Beenup Titanium Minerals was sold in April 1999 and the decision to close Beenup followed an extensive study into the technical problems caused by the high clay content of the Beenup ore body, which had impacted upon the ability to reach profitable production levels. Beenup lost some A$8 million in the first quarter of fiscal 1999 and the cost to the Group profit in fiscal 1999 was A$134 million in asset write-downs. In August 1999, a decision to cease operations of the North American copper assets was made, which cost BHP some A\$1,800 million for fiscal 1999. The assets were all part of the Magma Copper Company purchased by BHP in 1996. The sale of these assets was primarily because of the continually depressed copper prices. The decision to close or cease operations at these three projects effectively stopped the cash bleeding from these operations, resulting in a US\$45 million favourable impact on profit in the first quarter of fiscal 2000 compared to the corresponding quarter.

PHASE II – FINE-TUNING

Phase II was considered a stage in which the company attempted to get the very best from its asset base at optimal efficiencies. Effectively, the need was to fine-tune the organisation and to increase the level of communication and co-ordination.

An incentive programme, which began in 1999 throughout the organisation and rewards the performance of individuals according to the company's ability to deliver better total shareholder return than its competitors, continues down the organisation as part of phase II. It was considered vital that management continued to optimise the system in which the company pays people, which indicated a need to place more compensation at risk.

Opportunities

Anderson felt that the improved outlook in the Asian economy in November 1999, particularly in Japan, called for a more intensified marketing effort in the East, which was expected to increase the prospects of further liquefied natural gas (LNG) sales there, as well as provide more opportunities for BHP's iron ore business. Increased market demand and sales of both these products in this region would mean viable opportunities for expansion in both LNG and iron ore for BHP. The Escondida copper mine in Chile was arguably the world's best copper mine. The last extension to the mine (Phase 3.5) was implemented on time and to budget and Escondida Phase 4 and Escondida Norte, two new developments, will rely in part on existing infrastructure and will be profitable even at low copper prices. Expansion to the successful EKATI diamond mine in Canada is also viable. While the further development of existing projects will lift performance of the business, the company also has a range of greenfield opportunities which the company is evaluating – most notably Petroleum's position in the Gulf of Mexico.

Debt restructuring

The efforts to lower costs, manage the asset portfolio and tighten control over discretionary spending have been directed towards strengthening the balance sheet. The company gearing (measured debt to debt plus equity) was 54.2 per cent at fiscal 1999 year-end. Such gearing is in part a result of major asset write-downs and also a weaker Australian dollar. The company target is mid-40 per cent and the priority was to monitor and cut spending while actively managing the asset portfolio in order to further reduce debt.

PHASE III – FUTURE STRATEGY

Beyond phase II, Anderson noted that the most significant influence driving the strategy of a resources company is globalisation, meaning the elimination of barriers to trade, economic barriers, tariffs, political barriers and institutional barriers. The reaction to globalisation of large companies like BHP has been consolidation – consolidation of institutions, companies and even countries. Financial institutions have merged and countries have consolidated, the most obvious example being Europe which has consolidated to form the euro currency. The impact of financial institutions consolidating puts a premium on liquidity and market capitalisation. The liquidity needs of 'mega' funds require 'mega' investment alternatives. The implications for BHP are that size does matter, and that the largest, most cost-efficient producer will be winner in the new environment and large capitalisation companies *will* be in demand. It is therefore imperative that in order to determine future strategy, BHP determines whether it is a 'mega' player or not. The Minerals division is one of the fourth largest minerals producers in the world, and is therefore considered 'mega'. The Petroleum and Steel businesses are not.

The BHP Steel strategy is to transform BHP's Steel business into a niche player capable of delivering its cost of capital on a sustainable basis through the peaks and troughs of the business and price cycle. The new BHP Steel will base itself on the business's existing strength in flat rolled steel and focus upon construction markets in Australia, New Zealand and Asia. It will fully utilise existing competitive advantages in its low cost base, strong market position, world-leading coating technology and the well-established distribution channels. The new BHP Steel will operate around BHP's world-class Port Kembla and New Zealand steelworks. Port Kembla is one of the world's lowest-cost producers of steel. The new BHP Steel will be a niche player in a region where it is a leader in product technology, customer service, brand marketing and has access to low-cost raw materials. BHP Steel will distribute a range of finished coated and painted products for the construction industry. The currently successful marketing brands for the coated steels ZINCALUME® and COLORBOND® will continue to be marketed. The remainder of BHP Steel assets, primarily in the US, including tube makers, merchandising, structural, pipeline and packaging products, will be divested. It is the opinion of BHP management that these assets in their current environment are constrained from performing at their peak and would be better in the hands of somebody else. This strategy primarily centres around creating shareholder value. The breaking up of Steel into separate niche competitors will hopefully create more value for shareholders. However, it reduces BHP's investment in the steel business by approximately one-half.

THE FUTURE

Looking to the future, the core of BHP's business will be natural resources. The company, according to the BHP Charter, seeks to create shareholder value through the discovery, development and conversion of natural resources. With the closure of a large portion of the company's steelworks, the weightings of the company portfolio will be increased towards the Minerals and Petroleum businesses.

The company has experienced an intense period of change, cleaning up the asset portfolio and improving productivity. The next phase of BHP's development is to chart the course for the future. This period will focus on returns and shareholder value, rather than production and growth.

> Although my preference is to grow the company, I would rather see it half the size and twice as profitable than twice the size and half as profitable. Our focus on shareholder value is on value per share, not absolute earnings.
>
> Paul Anderson, MD and CEO, BHP

Anderson concluded:

> It is a challenge to turn a resources company around during the lowest period of commodity prices in two decades. The key is to position the company so that we can make money in a down market, so we can create shareholder value when conditions are bad, but then be positioned when the market turns to shoot out of the pack – not just rise with everybody else.

On 27 July 2000, BHP announced its highest-ever profit with an A$1.63 billion net profit for the 13 months to June (A$2.03 billion excluding abnormals) and the results were driven by Petroleum whose earnings skyrocketed 471 per cent. By November 2000, BHP had spent some A$2.5 billion on new projects during the year and it was set to approve a further A$1.5 billion over the next few months. This was a consequence of the cash windfall from the rising oil prices. Their big 'to do' list at the end of 2000 included:

- Change the asset base from 25 per cent Petroleum, 30 per cent Steel and 45 per cent Minerals to 40–50 per cent Minerals, 30–40 per cent Petroleum and 20 per cent Steel.
- Restructure the executive teams, splitting strategic and operational decisions.
- Consolidate operations to reduce duplication, gain benefits of scale and ensure that all projects advance the group's goals.
- Achieve a 12 per cent return on capital for the five years to June 2004.
- Generate a net positive cash flow before dividends and funding every year.
- Cut operating costs by at least 2 per cent per year.
- Generate net operating cash flow of more than A$11 billion in the three years to June 2002.
- Raise A$4 billion from divestments by June 2001.

MERGER WITH BILLITON

During March 2001, a merger between BHP and UK-based Billiton was announced which would create a global resources powerhouse with dominant positions in coal and copper. A combined BHP-Billiton would have a market capitalisation of US$28.8bn (valued 60:40 in favour of BHP to comply with UK tax laws) which would be just short of the US aluminium giant Alcoa (US$30.3bn) but ahead of Anglo American (US$28bn). Billiton was the world's fourth largest producer of aluminium and aluminia and one of the biggest exporters of thermal coal, which would complement BHP's strength in coking coal. It was also the world's fourth largest producer of nickel. A Billiton merger would also give BHP exposure to global stock market liquidity through Billiton's primary listing in London. It was felt that the merger had parallels with Paul Anderson's marriage of the US energy companies Duke Power and Pan Energy in 1997, which created a much larger energy group but left him out of the top job. Brian Gilbertson, Billiton's CEO, was regarded as an ambitious South African and it was announced that he would succeed Anderson as CEO of BHP in December 2002. It was felt that he would provoke enormous change at the *Big Australian*.

Sources

The Age, 'Highest ever annual profit for BHP', 27 July 2000.
The Age, 'BHP has $1.5b ready to spend: Anderson', 20 November 2000.
BHP First Quarter Profit Result, Fiscal 2000.
BHP Internal Press Release, 'BHP Announce new CEO', November 1998.
BHP Internal Press Release, 'The right man for the job – the search for the new CEO ends', Kate Dunstan, November 1998.
BHP Profit Result, Fiscal 1999.
BHP website, http://www.bhp.com.au
BHP, A Profile of BHP in 1999.
BHP, Annual Reports, Description of Business and Financial Statements, 1995–1999.
BHP, Annual Reports, Report to Shareholders, 1995–1999.
Business Review Weekly, 'A tall order for the Chairman', 20, 8 March 1998.
Business Review Weekly, 'A troubled giant awaits its destiny', 20, 8 March 1998.
Business Review Weekly, 'A creative deal for BHP's new boss', 20, 11 September 1998.
Business Review Weekly, 'A good start for the new face at BHP', 20, 11 September 1998.
Business Review Weekly, 'BHP up for redefining', 20, 8 March 1998.
Business Review Weekly, 'The Big Australian renews', 21, 7 February 1999.
Business Review Weekly, 'Why BHP is hot stock', 21, 5 July 1999.
Business Review Weekly, 'After the pain, BHP is pressured to make gains', 22, 30 June 2000.
Coburn, L. (Acting CEO), Rothwell, J. (GM & President BHP Diamonds), Adams, M. (GM BHP Minerals, Cannington), Dummett, H. (Senior VP & GM Minerals Discovery), *BHP World Minerals Briefing to Financial Analysts*, 17 November 1998. *Financial Review*, 'Marriage of mining giants is mutually convenient', 22 March 2001.
Paul Anderson, BHP CEO and MD, Address to Shareholders GM, December 1998.
Paul Anderson, BHP CEO and MD, Address to Shareholders EGM, 26 February 1999.
Paul Anderson, BHP CEO and MD, Address to the Global Metals and Mining Conference, Dublin, 12 May 1999.

Paul Anderson, BHP CEO and MD, Presentation to the Australian Investment Conference, Edinburgh, October 1999.

Paul Anderson, BHP CEO and MD, Presentation to the Securities Institute of Australia, Sydney, 4 August 1999.

Stockport, G.J. and Norvall, G.R. (2000) *Broken Hill Proprietary (BHP) Company Limited: Turnaround Strategy*, European Case Clearing House, 28pp, No. 300–025–1. Website: http//www.Bloomberg.com

Viking Sewing Machines AB

Jonas Dahlqvist and Anders Melander

The history of Viking Sewing Machines is one of considerable contextual and organisational change. The case describes this and provides a basis to consider the developing strategic capability of the organisation and the process of strategic change.

• • •

A NEW BEGINNING

Sometimes, things just happen all at once. The ownership question had been lingering for quite some time before the deal was finally closed; articles that explicitly mentioned Electrolux's intention to divest its sewing activities were appearing in the Swedish business press as early as 1990. However, it was not until 1997 that Electrolux actually did sell Viking Sewing Machines AB to the investment fund Industri Kapital.[1] The deal was concluded on 6 February 1997, exactly 125 years after a decision was taken by the board of directors at Husqvarna AB to start manufacturing sewing machines.[2]

In 1996, the Electrolux Group was actively working on a sale of their sewing machine activities and had initiated discussions with Industri Kapital. During this period, the Husqvarna CEO Mr Jörgen Johansson resigned and a new CEO had to be hired. The choice fell on Mr Svante Runnquist of Volvo. Having been with Volvo for over 25 years, Mr Runnquist had worked in a number of different positions, mainly in marketing. He had also held the position as CEO of Volvo Germany for five years. Svante Runnquist commented:

> I was offered a position by Electrolux CEO Leif Johansson just before he went to Volvo – ironic, isn't it? He was in charge of hiring a new CEO in case the sewing machine activities were sold to Industri Kapital . . . I got the offer in December 1996 and accepted right away. I thought it sounded great! I started on 1 January 1997 so everything

---

[1] The full name of the formal owner is the Industri Kapital 1994 Fund. However, we will refer to the owner as Industri Kapital. Further details on the activities of Industri Kapital can be found in Appendix 2.

[2] On 30 April 1998, Husqvarna Sewing Machines AB changed its name to Viking Sewing Machines AB. Before the purchase by Electrolux in 1977 the company name was Husqvarna AB. For simplicity we will refer to Viking Sewing Machines AB, meaning the sewing machine manufacture that stems from Husqvarna AB. The brand name for products manufactured by Viking Sewing Machines is Husqvarna-Viking.

happened really fast. Suddenly I found myself in the middle of the negotiation process, but at that time it still wasn't obvious that Electrolux actually would sell.

A NEW DIRECTION

Viking Sewing Machines AB develops, manufactures, markets and sells household sewing machines. Electronic and computerised models are manufactured
at the Husqvarna plant in Sweden, while low-priced mechanical machines and
overlockers are sourced from Asian manufacturers. When the new CEO Svante
Runnquist came to Viking Sewing Machines, much of his work was directed
towards improving the company's market orientation. The number of concurrent changes in the company made for a window of opportunity to redirect
the strategic focus of the company. An intense weekend meeting in April 1997
marked the beginning of a very busy period for the top management team.
Mr Runnquist explained:

> We started off with a weekend meeting on a country resort. I didn't even bring in a
> consultant this time. I have done that in the past, but this time I was so fresh on the
> job that I was the one who could ask all those 'stupid' questions.

During the first meeting, the basic scope of the strategy document was laid out
while further refinements and changes were made during the summer of 1997.
The new mission statement[3] and the companion strategy document were presented to middle management and sales area managers in a series of seminars.
The opportunity to participate in the strategy process was a new experience to
most of the people involved and some took a dim view of the amount of time
spent away from more pressing matters such as low sales or the installation of
a new accounting system. Nevertheless, the high involvement seemed to pay
off. The strategy document was often referred to for guidance on operational
matters and the mission statement was frequently promoted in the company's
public relations. The physical appearance of the strategy document was very
plain; it consisted of folded and stapled photocopies wrapped in a two-colour
sleeve. This was indeed a reflection of the concern that the Viking management
had about setting in stone something that was inherently an ongoing process.
The strategic conversation within the top management team continued with at
least five off-site workshops a year formally dedicated to assessing the company's
current strategic position. Summing up the initial process, Mr Runnquist said:

> The first attempts were very unstructured and people were complaining about how
> it was all empty phrases and buzz words. My point is that, it is only when you engage
> in that type of discussion that you may come to realize that your thoughts aren't that
> clear after all.

MAKING IT HAPPEN

The dealers were very important to Viking Sewing Machines in their new
plans for future profitability. This crucial link to the customers became a tar-

---

[3]Please refer to the mission statement in Appendix 3.

geted area for Viking Sewing Machines with the arrival of the new CEO. One important effort in this direction was the programme to transform the retailers through 'Dealer Partnerships'. The concept included extended support for business development to encourage dealers to carry the Viking product line exclusively. Marketing associate Sofia Axelsson put it this way:

> There have been tremendous changes in Viking since Svante [Runnquist] came here, there really have. But we may change all we want; the customer only meets the dealer and as long as the dealer doesn't change, the customer won't perceive any change at all.

In the US, Viking Sewing Machines started to co-operate with Jo-Ann Fabrics & Crafts, a large retailer of fabrics with over a thousand stores nationwide, setting up small sewing machine outlets inside their fabric stores. By May 1999, Viking Sewing Machines had opened 47 exclusive dealers in the US, many in co-operation with Jo-Ann Fabrics & Crafts. Mr Runnquist explained:

> The US is our biggest market,[4] then comes Sweden. In Sweden, we have market shares touching 60 per cent of the total market and in our target segment about 75–80 per cent. This country [Sweden] is the only country where we have had exclusive retailers for a long time. In the US we only started this a couple of years ago. You can make a living on the Husqvarna-Viking brand there. In most other parts of the world we have very few exclusive Viking retailers; we're a brand among many others in the shop. A dealer in Europe typically carries 3–4 brands. Unfortunately, that's often the type that just 'peddles' machines. We don't believe that's our future.

It was in the light of the expanding after-market that dealer integration became really important, since the company's strategy expanded the core product beyond the sewing machine. The 'after-market' included services, such as training in sewing techniques, software for embroidery construction and ready-made embroidery patterns, together with spare parts and auxiliary sewing equipment. But how did the average dealer respond to Viking's proposal to expand their activities? Mr Runnquist again:

> You really can make money on training and that's what we are trying to teach the dealers. Our organisation in the USA is particularly successful. Over there, people willingly pay 5–600 dollars to be in on a three-day course with a sewing expert.

SUPPORTING THE STRATEGY

Changes in organisational structure and routines accompanied the company's claims of a new commitment to think more about the customer and less about technical 'features'. The top management team was changed to incorporate the managers of the major sales companies as well as the marketing vice-president. However, a meeting with a management team spread out over the world made logistics an issue. To mitigate the loss of time in travel, video conferencing was introduced for participant managers.

The new management structure involved not only a change at the top level, but also changes in operating systems to support the new strategic direction.

---

[4]About 45 per cent of the turnover.

One major task for the financial manager Gunnar Vidén was the installation of a new accounting system in May 1999. One important problem with the old accounting system was that it could not report profitability for each product group. Cost information was fairly well covered, but Viking had a very vague idea about how much they spent on marketing a specific product, let alone what their competitors spent. The old system may have seemed sufficient during the Electrolux period when worries tended to end at the factory gate. However, as a separate company, Viking needed to assess the accounting information in new ways to keep track of the various activities in the value chain.

On an even more concrete level, the marketing and the technical development department moved into the same office building in January 2000. Hitherto, Production and Technical Development had resided in the same building away from the rest of the departments. Looking back, it comes as no surprise that the turnaround programmes in R&D during the 1980s mainly focused on streamlining production efficiency, rather than on developing customer value by innovative functions. The new office space was located in an old brick building till recently used for production. It blended in with the other buildings of the Viking plant but was given a completely new interior with glass walls and a centrally placed multi-purpose area for business meetings as well as the usual Swedish coffee breaks.

COMPETING IN AN INTERNATIONAL ARENA

When it came to market information, the sewing machine industry lacked the transparency normally associated with a mature manufacturing industry. Since very little information was collected by official bodies, Viking participated in a co-operation between competitors to collect figures of volume in different price-brackets through a third-party intermediary. This was done in France, Germany, Sweden, Norway, and to some extent in the US. All the major manufacturers participated in this mutual exchange between competitors in order to obtain at least some rudimentary market information. Viking also collected information on competition through the sales companies and dealers. In addition, the R&D department as well as Marketing and Sales regularly compared their own machines with the ones manufactured by competitors. To the CEO Mr Svante Runnquist, the lack of market information came as a surprise:

> For me, coming from the car industry, all this lack of information is very frustrating. That was one of my first questions [when I came to Viking]: what does it [the market] look like? The industry is rather poorly monitored as to market shares. You know what models and specifications exist, but there are actually rather few that start from the customer and develop the product definition that way. So now we start asking about market shares and we discover that the information is not nearly as good as in the car industry.

In terms of volume, the demand for sewing machines in the western hemisphere had been declining for two decades. As a result, industry profitability had deteriorated. In the period 1976–81, total unit sales of sewing machines in western Europe dropped 25 per cent; the decline in the US was considerably less severe at 4 per cent. This downturn had been particularly hard on manufacturers of industrial machines and low-price mechanical machines for domestic use. In Europe and in the US, the manufacturers competing on the professional side were severely affected by the sharp drop in demand for industrial sewing machines. Firms such as Pfaff, with the production of domestic and industrial machines in the same company, experienced major difficulties in the 1990s. Pfaff, with about two-thirds of their sales in the professional market, went bankrupt in September 1999. A week later, the almost mythical Singer was on the brink of bankruptcy and filed for a Chapter 11, mainly as a result of their 80 per cent ownership in Pfaff's industrial division. After a reconstruction, Singer was up and running again but with no or little in-house manufacturing. However, their huge global net of dealers managed to stay operative in spite of the turmoil.

The aftermath of the Pfaff/Singer bankruptcy proved to be very important for the development of Viking. When news of the demise of Pfaff reached Viking, it posed new and intricate challenges to the owner Industri Kapital. The original plan for Viking was to set a good track record over a five-year period in order to get a profitable exit through an IPO.[5] The choice facing Industri Kapital was to go ahead as planned or to support a bid for Pfaff domestic sewing machine division. However, this would necessitate a postponement of the planned exit on Viking. In the past, Industri Kapital had been known to seek out structural deals to develop the companies in their portfolio. True to form, they finally decided to give the green light on the acquisition of Pfaff's division for domestic products. The deal was closed on 2 May 2000.

By 2001, Viking Sewing Machines AB and Bernina Fritz Gegauf AG were the only remaining independent manufacturers in Europe. Bernina was a fourth-generation family company located in Switzerland, enjoying a solid reputation and actively demonstrating their Swiss heritage. Their product range resembled that of Viking and their top model accepted embroidery files developed for other brands, including Viking's. The financial situation of Bernina was difficult to assess since they were not publicly owned and therefore had no obligation to inform the public about their financial position. However, the relative geographical proximity and a similar corporate situation made Bernina an important quality benchmark for Viking.

In the Far East, there existed a number of small manufacturers, primarily acting as OEMs[6] for established brands in the lower price-bracket. However, there were three competitors that set themselves apart. Brother, Janome and Juki were all major competitors to Viking; Janome alone produced over a million units a year. Not only were these companies high-volume manufacturers with complete product ranges but, more importantly, they also sported their own R&D facilities capable of developing advanced sewing-embroidery machines. Being Japanese, their location gave them access to low-cost production facilities in e.g. Taiwan, Thailand and Korea. However, this seemed to be a mixed

[5] Initial public offering. When a company sells stock to the market for the first time.
[6] Original equipment manufacturer.

blessing since the competition from local low-cost brands was fierce for modestly priced mechanical sewing machines.

Brother was a well-known manufacturer of office machinery such as labellers, typewriters, fax and copying machines. However, they were also very active in the sewing industry, both in the consumer and industrial markets. Their gross sales of domestic sewing machines during the fiscal year of 2000 amounted to $246 million.[7]

Another big player was the Juki operation. Being more specialised on sewing machines than Brother, they manufactured and marketed both industrial and domestic machines. After the Singer reconstruction, Juki made the entire range of computer-controlled machines for Singer, including their top-of-the-line embroidery models. Juki did not market these expensive models under the Juki brand in the US. Rather, the models offered as Juki were very modest in features. Total sales of Juki during fiscal year 1999 were $704 million, of which $129 million were in domestic sewing machines.

The largest competitor by volume was Janome of Japan. Their dominant activity was domestic sewing machines, although they maintained some side activities in small industrial robots. They had no manufacturing of industrial sewing machines. Total sales in the fiscal year of 1999 grossed $443 million including robotics. Janome had introduced several important industry innovations; they were the first to produce computer-controlled embroidery machines for domestic use as well as touch-screen controls, which had become an industry standard on up-market machines.

INTO CYBERSPACE BY DESIGN

When Viking presented their new top-of-the line machine in early 1999, it was meant to be a 'world's first' in several respects. The *Designer I* came out as a real engineering *tour de force* retailing at a hefty $5,000. The new model made extensive use of software to control the machine and contained no fewer than eight motors to cater for all functions. Several features were logical developments and refinements of existing solutions but the new sensor control for the presser foot with an automatic thread cutter, the built-in disk drive and a Flash memory made for a redefinition of what a sewing machine really is.

For a long time, the engineers at Viking had wanted to make a presser foot that did not need manual assistance to raise and lower itself. Some mechanical solutions to this had already been developed by competitors but were blocked by patents. Moreover, a mechanical solution did not seem to be the way forward. The way around this was to construct a unique mechanism where the pressure on the presser foot was sensed by an electronic sensor and pressure was applied by a step motor instead of using a mechanical spring. Since a step motor can be controlled by a microprocessor, this solution made it possible to

---

[7] Sales figures originally stated in yen for Brother, Juki and Janome; US dollar equivalents were calculated at rate of 110 JPY/USD.

bring one of the last mechanical functions into the realm of numerical control. The specific result of this invention was a presser foot that not only applied the same pressure regardless of fabric thickness but also raised and lowered itself automatically.

Late in the development process of the new model, the Viking engineers decided to change the processor hardware of the machine from an EPROM to a more expensive Flash memory. The difference in function was small but important; both types of memory chip were reprogrammable but the EPROM had to be upgraded by the manufacturer while the Flash memory could be upgraded by the customer. Since all the functions of the *Designer I* were now controlled by a programmable microprocessor it opened up completely new ways of customer support. One illustration was the way Viking started to make new versions of the operative system available for download via the Internet, free of charge. The customer downloaded the file from the Internet site, saved it on to a floppy and slid it into the built-in disk drive of the *Designer I*. This method of upgrading performance was well developed in the computer business, but was new for sewing machines.

When the *Designer I* was in a pre-production stage, the Viking website presented what they referred to as a 'sneak peek'. This translated into a list of features together with an interactive three-dimensional model where people who were interested could have a virtual-reality look at the new model. In conjunction with this presentation, advance orders were accepted as well as general comments. From this campaign, Viking collected about 7,000 requests for more information and a contact from a retailer.

The general e-business hype during the late 1990s and the plethora of dotcoms was the subject for recurring debates, questioning the Internet as a viable medium for distributive trades. Viking's position on this was extreme and followed the lines developed in their strategy document; since Viking tried to promote dealer partnerships, there could be no parallel mail-order distribution of Viking sewing machines. Viking was quite unique by not allowing web shops to carry the Husqvarna-Viking brand. However, Viking did sell low bulk notions and accessories such as presser feet, needles and embroidery files on their website. The service was first offered to US residents only, and like its competitors, Viking had not extended this service to Europe by early 2001.

The bonus clearing system on Internet sales was one tangible sign of Viking's intention to stay on good terms with the dealer partner. Each customer was given a unique identification code that linked her to the area dealer. The area dealers were given a bonus based on web sales to clients within the assigned area. The information on the customer was not passed on to the dealers, only the money. As Anne Jansson, the manager of Internet marketing put it:

> Up till now, we haven't had one single complaint from the dealers. I think they rather like the idea of getting a bonus automatically without any work involved.

In March 1999, Viking declared that they had acquired the small British software producer called Embroidery Networks Ltd (Emnet). This company was founded in 1988 to provided software for PC-controlled professional sewing machines and actually had only two people employed. Viking-Emnet started to co-operate in 1993 to develop software for embroidery in various degrees of sophistication. To have this activity in-house was obviously important to the Viking management team. CEO Svante Runnquist commented:

> The notion is not that far-fetched if you think about the fact that we want the after-market to grow more than the total business. We cannot do that by selling more spare parts; we will probably be selling fewer . . . It's by selling more auxiliary equipment and developing new products for the after-market that we will grow and then software will be an important part for our computer-controlled machines.

With the breakthrough of the WWW, distribution of software and embroidery files took a new turn. People could exchange embroidery patterns through the Internet or download them at the website of Husqvarna-Viking. This site was one of the most accessed corporate sites of the net, recording as many as 700,000 hits in one month by reaching people that are not the average Internet surfer.

In just five years, Viking had transformed itself from a trader of sewing machines to a customer-oriented marketing organisation, selling the joy of creative sewing. Sewing sure isn't what it used to be!

APPENDIX 1 COMPANY HISTORY OF VIKING SEWING MACHINES

An unbroken tradition of engineering and manufacturing since 1689 is something that is often emphasised in the company's own presentations of Viking Sewing Machines AB. In 1846, a machine that could sew a lock stitch, using an under-thread and a shuttle, was patented by the American engineer Elias Howe. The sewing machines of today basically use the same principle. A manufacturer of guns for 200 years, Husqvarna AB needed something to support the company's declining sales in guns and the new invention was seen as a solution that matched their skills in machining and precision casting. The company's first sewing machine appeared in 1872 but was relatively unsuccessful. Instead Husqvarna began to produce American models under licence from Weed and Singer. In 1883, the engineers of Husqvarna AB presented a new model of their own conception, the 'Freja'. It became an instant success and was manufactured for over 40 years.

In more recent times, the Husqvarna Company was early to investigate the possibilities of sintered metal technology in the 1950s and actually held the European patent rights for this special technology. Using sintered metal, the Husqvarna engineers were able to make the moving parts of a sewing machine permanently lubricated, thereby eliminating the need for oiling and greasing.[8]

A century after the their first sewing machine was produced, Husqvarna AB had become a diversified manufacturing company, producing and marketing consumer durables such as cookers and refrigerators, lawnmowers, chain saws and even cross-country motorcycles. In November 1977 the company was acquired by Electrolux, their fiercest competitor. Looking back at the twenty years of Electrolux ownership tells a story of major structural redesign of the company. The parts of Husqvarna AB that manufactured consumer durables became an integrated part of the worldwide manufacturing system of Electrolux.

Two years after Electrolux's purchase of Husqvarna AB, the company was profitable except for the sewing machine division. The Electrolux approach to this was to give some financial slack to the management of the sewing machine division who could invest in technical development despite persistent losses. This strategy seemed to pay off in 1982 when Husqvarna AB made a small profit and profitability peaked in 1986. Three years later, volumes and margins declined and in 1989, Husqvarna AB was once again in the red. This year, two important decisions were made: Husqvarna AB embarked on a cost-cutting programme while a new development programme was instituted.

A couple of years later, Husqvarna Sewing Machines AB seemed to have coped with the crises of 1989. The profitability increased in face of the slump in the Swedish business cycle. Firstly, the depreciation of the Swedish Krona slashed costs by 30 per cent overnight relative their competitors'. Secondly, a

---

[8] A sintered metal is made from a blend of metal powders that is compressed under high pressure and temperature to form a solid metal. A sintered metal can be given a number of properties (e.g. controlled porosity) that are not obtainable through traditional methods such as cast alloys. A porous metal can be permanently impregnated with oil, which gives a self-lubricating effect.

drastic reduction of in-house manufacturing of components paid off. This was a result of a turnaround programme that was started in 1989. Some of the core elements were the reduction of parts in the sewing machines to streamline production as well as sourcing parts from outside manufacturers to cut costs.

Macroeconomic variables have seemed to affect the profitability of Husqvarna AB. The first crisis in the late 1970s was concurrent with a general crisis in the Swedish industry. The improved profitability came in 1982 when the Swedish currency was devalued by 16 per cent. The profits started to dive in 1987, two years after the US dollar had started to depreciate against several of the European currencies, including the Swedish krona. Prospects were miserable in 1989 when the Swedish krona was very strong. The company's competitive edge started to look really good in 1992 when the Swedish krona depreciated 25 per cent, literally overnight. Although the antecedents of Viking Sewing Machines initiated several programmes for technological development and cost-cutting to improve profitability, the sudden changes in profitability seem highly correlated with the cost of production as set by the exchange rate.

APPENDIX 2 BRIEF DESCRIPTION OF INDUSTRI KAPITAL

In 2001 the owner of Industri Kapital Fund 1994 was a venture capital fund, managed by Industri Kapital AB. The company was originally created in 1989 and specialises in unglamorous but well-kept companies with moderate annual growth. The funds for investments come mainly from large institutional investors such as banks and insurance companies. Industri Kapital AB has offices in Stockholm, London and Hamburg. Since the start they have acquired 39 companies and manage funds to a total value of approximately €3 billion. The total turnover of the companies owned by the funds managed by Industri Kapital reached about €8 billion in 2000.

The strategy of Industri Kapital is to buy companies where they think they can contribute to increase the value of the company, either by providing management know-how or by merging companies or parts of companies in their portfolio. Industri Kapital does not have the intention to run companies indefinitely; they will typically seek an exit either by an IPO[8] or by selling to another company. When Industri Kapital buys a company, the top management group of the target company is offered to engage financially in the buy-out. In the case of Viking Sewing Machines AB, top management and other employees hold about 8 per cent of the shares.

APPENDIX 3 MISSION STATEMENT OF VIKING SEWING MACHINE

- To develop, produce, market and sell household sewing machines and related products, which enhance the joy of creative sewing.
- To grow our business by creating demand for more creative uses of sewing.

CASE STUDIES

- To be a consumer-driven company, securing growth, profitability, and success by providing superior satisfaction to the Consumer and our Dealer-Partner by continuously adding value to the Husqvarna-Viking brand.
- To provide valued employees growth opportunities in an environment of which they can be proud.
- To be recognised as the leading premium sewing machine company in the world.

APPENDIX 4 FINANCIAL OVERVIEW

Basic statistics (fiscal year 2000)

Number of employees: 1,200, of which 470 are in Sweden.

Turnover: about SEK 1.9 billion ($190 million)

Export: over 90 per cent of sales

Profitability: very good

Total numbers of sewing machines and overlockers sold: 500,000 units.

Number of sewing machines produced: 260,000 units.

Number of sourced sewing machines and overlockers: 240,000 units

Historical data 1986–98

YEAR	SALES (SEK M)	GROSS MARGIN	TURNOVER/ CAPITAL	PROFITABILITY
1986	810	>10%	~ 2	Very good
1987	790			Satisfactory
1988	775			Unsatisfactory
1989	760	<5%	~ 1.5	Unsatisfactory
1990	686	<5% [increasing]	~ 1.5	Better, but still unsatisfactory
1991	676	<5% [increasing]	~ 1.5 [increasing]	Still unsatisfactory
1992	631	<5% [increasing]	~ 2	Better, but still unsatisfactory
1993	784	>10%	~ 2.5	Very good
1994	808	>10% [increasing]	~ 2.5 [decreasing]	Very good and improving
1995	856	>10%	~ 2.5 [increasing]	Very good and improving
1996	858	>10% [decreasing]	~ 2.5 [decreasing]	Very good, but decreasing
1997	954	>10% [increasing]	~ 3	Very good, all-time high
1998	974	>10% [decreasing]	~ 3 [decreasing]	Very good, but decreasing
1999	1,200	>10% [increasing]		Very good, and improving
2000	1,900	>10% [stable]		Very good, stable

Learning the governance lessons of Tomkins

Paul Lee, Hermes Focus Asset Management

This case study is concerned with issues of corporate governance. It describes the situation which developed in the late 1990s as shareholders and investors became unhappy with the corporate strategy and performance of Tomkins, a highly diversified conglomerate. In particular, it describes the different ways in which the investors of Tomkins set about influencing the corporate strategy and management of that organisation and the consequences arising from this.

●●●

HERMES, HFAM AND CORPORATE GOVERNANCE

Hermes Investment Management Ltd is wholly owned by, and is the principal fund manager for, the British Telecom Pension Scheme, the UK's biggest. Hermes also manages money for other pension schemes, including that of Consignia (the former Post Office), and has funds under management of around £50 billion. About half of this money is held in UK equities, the vast majority of which is invested passively, which means that Hermes's clients hold around 1.2 per cent of every company in the FTSE All-Share, and will only sell those stakes if the companies are taken over or shrink so that they no longer qualify for the index. As a result of this passive investment strategy – so-called index-tracking – Hermes has for many years taken an active interest in the way UK companies are run. By ensuring that all companies follow good corporate governance, Hermes hopes that all UK companies will run themselves wholly in the best interests of their long-term shareholders.

Because of these concerns, Hermes has been extremely active in the corporate governance debate.[1] For example, it has had a policy of voting at every shareholders' meeting in the UK since 1990, and in the early 1990s its CEO Alastair Ross Goobey led a campaign against five-year rolling contracts for executive directors. These effectively guaranteed executives payments of five times their annual remuneration when they left office, even when they were

---

[1] Hermes published its latest Statement on UK Corporate Governance & Voting Policy at the start of 2001. This was sent to the chairman and company secretary of every FTSE All-Share company, and it is also available on the Internet (www.hermes.co.uk/corporate-governance/intro.htm).

sacked for underperformance. As a result of this campaign, it has become best practice in the UK for executives to have one-year rolling contracts.

Hermes argues that companies with good governance should perform better than those whose governance is flawed. At the least, because they allow vigorous discussion and debate in the boardroom, such companies should avoid substantial destruction of value. Given that Hermes's clients invest for the long run, Hermes is interested in ensuring such strong long-term performance – and, as importantly, avoidance of losses – across the market.

In 1998, Hermes decided to use the corporate governance expertise that it had built up over the years to create a new business, called Hermes Lens Asset Management now known as Hermes Focus Asset Management (HFAM). This would launch a new fund to invest in underperforming companies where there was value that wasn't being recognised because of corporate governance and or strategic problems, but which the HFAM team believed could be released by a programme of building relationships with the management and helping them to make the changes which would enable the City to reassess the business and re-rate the company. By investing in these companies, HFAM could gain the clout necessary to put its arguments in front of the board and its clients could benefit from the financial uplift which results from the success of the programme. By becoming a larger and active shareholder, HFAM could encourage change in companies where Hermes's normal governance strategies had not been able to move matters forward.

One of the companies in which HFAM[2] invested in its first year was Tomkins plc. Exhibit 1 shows the consistent decline in Tomkins's share price relative to the stock market for over seven years before HFAM's investment. While for much of that time the share price rose, it did not do so at the rate of the market as a whole, so that Tomkins's value relative to the market was virtually cut in half over the period.

TOMKINS: BACKGROUND AND STRATEGIC PROBLEMS

Tomkins was a spectacular performer in the 1980s, growing by aggressive acquisition from a tiny buckle-maker in the Midlands to a sprawling conglomerate famously stretching from buns to guns – encompassing both baker Rank Hovis McDougall (RHM) and pistol manufacturer Smith & Wesson. Its formula had been to acquire underperforming cash-cow engineering businesses and improve their operating efficiency. But the Tomkins share price had underperformed for eight years, as the company found it increasingly hard to find acquisition targets at an appropriate price, to transform the companies it acquired, and/or to develop an alternative strategy. HFAM began investing in July 1999.

The company had begun to lose investors' confidence by having been seen to overpay for its acquisition of RHM in 1992. This acquisition was a deal too far for many analysts' creating the view in the City that the management was interested in growth for its own sake. Analysts suspected that executives

---

[2]In 2001 HFAM changed its name to Hermes Focus Asset Management (HFAM).

Exhibit 1	Performance to 6 July 1999 (first investment)

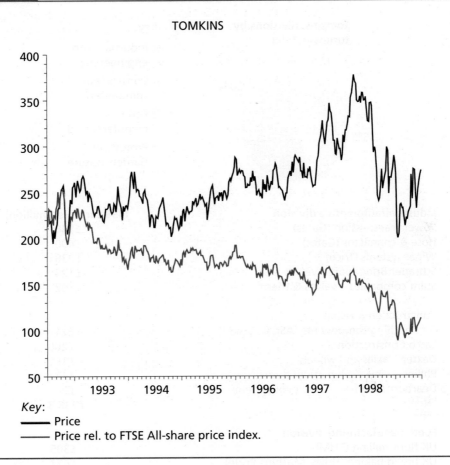

TOMKINS

Key:
—— Price
—— Price rel. to FTSE All-share price index.

Source: Datastream.

focused solely on earnings per share (EPS) growth, at the expense of (and, as it turned out, to the detriment of) long-term shareholder value.[3] Returns from the business had been below the firm's cost of capital, with inadequate improvement taking place post-acquisition.

HFAM'S ANALYSIS – STRATEGY

On the strategy side, the HFAM analysis suggested that fundamental restructuring of the company was likely to be necessary because it seemed to the team that after its initial input to acquired businesses, Tomkins headquarters added

---

[3]While EPS growth is a step towards potentially greater dividends to shareholders, it is not by itself enough to raise the share price, which depends at least as much on cash returns above the cost of capital and on confidence that management can drive profitable growth into the future.

| Exhibit 2 | Tomkins's structure |

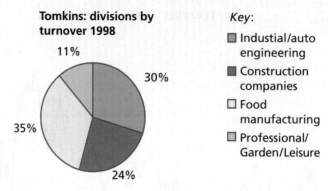

Tomkins: divisions by turnover 1998

11%
30%
35%
24%

Key:
- ■ Industial/auto engineering
- ■ Construction companies
- □ Food manufacturing
- □ Professional/ Garden/Leisure

Industrial/automotive division	1998 turnover (million)
Power transmission (Gates)	£546
Hose & connector (Gates)	£400
Wiper systems (Trico)	£236
Schrader Bridgeport – valves & sensors	£124
Stant companies – valves & thermostats	£202
Construction division	
Air handling components (ASC & Ruskin)	£212
Lasco Construction	£200
Dexter – axles and wheels	£165
Philips – vinyl & aluminium doors	£171
Dearborn/Mayfran – conveyor systems	£204
Others	£236.3
Food manufacturing division	
UK flour milling (RHM)	£305
UK bread baking (Hovis, Mothers Pride)	£577
Cakes (Mr Kipling, Cadbury, Lyons)	£288
Grocery brands (Paxo, Bisto, Sharwoods)	£323
Partnerships	£305
Professional, gardening and leisure division	
Mowing machinery etc (Hayter & Murray)	£426
Murray Bike	£64
Smith & Wesson – pistols etc.	£65

Source: HFAM.

little value, and the extremely disparate parts of the business were not adding value to each other. For many of its businesses, they doubted that Tomkins would pass the 'best parent' test.

A limited reorganisation (see Exhibit 2) – splitting the firm into four divisions, including what were called the core activities of engineering, food and construction – seemed to be largely cosmetic because each of those divisions was a mini-conglomerate. Although margins were good in comparison with those of its competitors (as might be expected from a conglomerate based on tight financial control), organic growth was very low, suggesting that there was an over-emphasis on costs and price levels at the expense of volumes. HFAM believed that this needed to be addressed to ensure that Tomkins had a successful future.

One strategic analysis would be that the company had two core businesses: the industrial and automotive group, based around the strong Gates business acquired in 1996; and a UK-oriented food company including the recent add-on acquisitions as well as RHM. In addition, there were the disparate holdings in the construction sector and gardening and leisure division. Depending on resolving tax and gun litigation issues (Smith & Wesson was at this time facing substantial law suits in the US), this last group should be sold off piecemeal over a period of time; this could be done either from the industrial and auto-motive group or from a shell Tomkins after both the other businesses had been demerged. Tomkins would be able to focus on adding value through focussed organic, as well as acquisitive growth.

HFAM'S ANALYSIS – BOARD STRUCTURE

Hermes's experience is that strategic problems rarely come to light in companies where governance is strong. Where there are enough independent-minded non-executives on a board, the right questions get asked so that potential strategic issues are addressed early and do not become problems that are obvious outside the company. In HFAM's analysis, this was not happening at Tomkins. Indeed, the fact that the board seemed content with the company's poor share price performance, that no new strategy was emerging and that there was no challenge to the existing structure was a strong indication that input from an influx of independent directors was needed to spark the changes that would unlock value for shareholders who had suffered for eight years. Not surprisingly, the existing structure was poor in corporate governance terms. Hermes had a history dating back to 1993 of raising concerns over the independence of non-executives and calling for a stronger board.

Greg Hutchings, who had created the conglomerate, filled the roles of both chairman and chief executive. The City perception was that he dominated the board. There were further signs of board problems in an apparent dis-agreement over strategy between Hutchings and deputy chairman and MD finance Ian Duncan – who was apparently arguing for some of the restructuring which HFAM believed was needed. The HFAM team worried about the strategic implications of Duncan's possible resignation, and the fact that it might unbalance the board further.

Given this, HFAM believed that the roles of chairman and chief executive should be split and that the non-executive representation on the board needed to be substantially strengthened. This seemed particularly true because of the need to take tough decisions about the structure of the company and HFAM's allied concerns that Hutchings might not be willing to preside over the division of a company which he had spent so long creating. This view was reinforced by the stories of the apparent spat with Duncan and of the increasing difficulty the centre seemed to be having in adding value to its disparate businesses. If Hutchings were to decide – or be forced – to leave, a stronger board would be needed to ensure that there was no vacuum at the top of the company.

Plans for the demerger of RHM were announced on 12 July. Duncan resigned at the same time. This made HFAM's concerns about the structure of the Tomkins board still more immediate.

THE INITIAL MEETING

In November 1999, while HFAM was still building its initial stake in the company, the team became aware of a former corporate financier who was representing certain dissatisfied shareholders. He was trying to raise wider support for a campaign to oust Hutchings, and was looking for finance to build a 10 per cent stake in Tomkins to call an EGM.

HFAM's policy had always been to meet and discuss issues with the company before taking any action, let alone action which might be seen as hostile. The team therefore made it clear that they would not have a meeting with this dissident shareholder representative until they had met with the company's executives. There were wider concerns in this instance, because HFAM thought that the timing was entirely negative: Hutchings was in the middle of negotiations on the sale of RHM and of other smaller businesses; Smith & Wesson was facing litigation in the US; and the team doubted that the board was strong enough to prevent an evaporation of value if Hutchings were ousted. In addition, the public nature of the planned attack could easily be value-destroying in itself.

The HFAM team first met with Hutchings in early February 2000. He was extremely courteous, giving a full two hours over to the meeting, and not unreceptive to the team's strategic and governance agenda. He was willing to consider the idea of splitting the roles of chairman and chief executive, with himself staying as chairman and the board appointing a new CEO. HFAM welcomed the recent addition of David Newlands, former finance director of GEC, as a first step to strengthening the board. Hutchings agreed that further additions might add value.

Following this meeting, HFAM's agenda was simple: to encourage the company to appoint an independent non-executive deputy chairman to ensure that an independent point of view was given full weight on the board; to explore what difference it would make were a new CEO to be appointed; and to encourage the company to make aggressive share buybacks. Given that the share price was so undervalued, buybacks were clearly a good way to increase shareholder value, and this seemed to HFAM by far the best use for the proceeds of the RHM sale rather than using it for further acquisitive growth.

MEETINGS WITH OTHER INTERESTED PARTIES

HFAM began its usual process of discussions with other major shareholders and with various board members to try to advance this case. The team believed it had support for its view from 25 per cent of the shareholders, including some who had apparently supported more aggressive change. So they felt they were making good progress when the board considered the HFAM proposals at a meeting on 3 May.

In late May the HFAM team also met the representative of the dissident shareholders. He had identified a chairman and chief executive to take over at the company. HFAM representatives agreed to meet his suggested team, and they seemed credible. The HFAM team again told them, however, that they were not prepared to support their activities as they were waiting for a response from the company to their proposed agenda and had the impression that response would be favourable.

Unfortunately, the share price continued to drift and HFAM was concerned that this might draw in interest from venture capitalists eager to buy at a low price. The team hoped that their plan to bolster the board would keep such moves at bay to give the new board enough time to take the actions necessary to revitalise the share price and so provide full value to long-term shareholders.

These concerns were reinforced by a slew of stories in the press suggesting that City figures were trying to oust Hutchings. This whispering campaign was particularly unfortunate because it was having a detrimental effect on the sale of RHM. The venture capitalist buyers were happy to slow down the process, because Hutchings might feel under increasing pressure to complete a deal – at whatever price – to bolster his position.

MATTERS COME TO A HEAD

The whispering campaign came to a head in early June 2000. The company had still not implemented any of the changes HFAM had suggested, and had not included shareholders in the non-executive director appointment process as they had requested. But the board did insist that the process was well under way.

In the meantime, the dissident campaign was gaining support in the City. The Tomkins board were clearly not aware of the extent of the backing that the rebels had won, and the real danger of hostile action. HFAM put the rebels in touch with Newlands so that the exact situation could be made apparent to him and to the rest of the board. HFAM made it clear that if the board made substantial changes rapidly they believed that a number of the City institutions then attracted by the rebel campaign could be won round. In the absence of prompt and substantial reforms, it was possible that rapid and perhaps unfortunate change might be forced through.

Within two weeks, Tomkins announced that Hutchings was to split the roles of chairman and CEO. However, in contrast to the former suggestions, instead of his dropping the CEO role and staying on as chairman, the plan was to install a non-executive chairman. The changes were put into effect at the prelims announcement at the end of the month. Newlands took on the role of non-executive chairman, with Hutchings staying on as CEO. In addition, the firm appointed Sir Brian Pitman – widely respected as the man who turned the flabby Lloyds Bank into one of the most efficient in the world – as a heavy-hitting new non-executive. As HFAM had expected, this news led to the collapse of the rebel campaign and to a rise in the share price.

HFAM was relieved that after a long delay the company had felt able to make the board changes which the team had argued were necessary. The moves meant that a strong board was now in place to take the tough decisions that lay ahead, and there was no risk of a vacuum at the head of the company.

The RHM sale was finally completed in September, raising £1.1 billion. The sale of the Murray and Hayter businesses for £150 million followed shortly thereafter. These two companies – predominantly focused on the lawnmower market – had formed the bulk of the professional, gardening and leisure division. Though the company's share price fell over this period, the governance improvements led Tomkins to outperform its peers, all of which were hit by a downturn in the US automotive markets.

HUTCHINGS' RESIGNATION

The Tomkins AGM was held on 29 September 2000. It was here that an event unforeseen by both Tomkins and HFAM occurred. One fund manager asked questions about the company's ownership of jets and flats in central London. Hutchings gave inaccurate answers to these questions. Tomkins promptly issued a correction and stated that it would sell the jets. But the revelation of 1980s-style corporate excesses was enough to spark wider-ranging questions. Newlands publicly acknowledged the existence of a formal investigation on 9 October. Hutchings resigned on 12 October.

HFAM was not directly involved in these events, which became a corporate governance *cause célèbre*, as facts emerged of inappropriate fringe benefits and executives' wives on the payroll. However, HFAM had helped to put in place the beginnings of a board structure which was independent enough to sanction a formal enquiry, and robust enough to ensure continuity following Hutchings' resignation. Newlands also launched a strategic review by McKinsey & Co. in October 2000.

AN EPILOGUE: by Gerry Johnson

The press picked up the story to highlight the issues of conglomerate diversity and corporate governance. For example, the *Independent*'s (13 October 2000) columnist wrote:

> . . . a combination of playing fast and loose with company assets whilst presiding over a chronically under performing share price is invariably lethal. We ought not to become too pious here. Were it not for the precipitous decline in Tomkins share price over the last five years, then most investors as well as the non-execs would probably not have noticed that the company had slipped from 'the highest standards of good corporate governance' as Mr Newlands put it yesterday whilst donning his hair shirt.
>
> Nevertheless, it is clearly right that Mr Hutchings should have gone and gone quickly. In the last year he had become part of the problem not the solution.
>
> The bigger question now is what happens to the empire he leaves behind? For all Mr Hutchings' attempts to shake-off the conglomerate tag, no-one was ever fooled

into believing that Tomkins remains anything other than a ragbag of unconnected businesses. The buns and the lawnmowers may have gone. But the guns remain, along with the jacuzzis and the rubber car seals and the household fittings and the air handling operation. That does not sound like focus to many people – Tomkins' temporary executive chairman included. Mr Newlands has promised not to rush to judgement until his strategic review is complete. But a break-up and disposal of the group is surely on the cards, if not already long overdue.

And again (*The Independent*, 14 October 2000):

But the greedy and the dodgy will crop up, and shareholders should be able to rely on non-executive directors of quoted firms, and codes of practice on corporate governance, to curb the most venal tendencies. It matters to the rest of us because of the effect of such a culture on the efficiency of the economy as a whole.

What is most disturbing about the Tomkins case is the way that it shows how weak these safeguards are, and how those clubby, mutual back-scratching old City habits still persist . . . The solution? Even making the codes statutory and trying to tighten up the rules only invites the invention of new abuses. The only answer is the vigilance of the shareholders. Rumours about Tomkins had been circulating for years before institutional investors in the company bothered to raise questions. If shareholders won't protect their own interests then it is hard to see what, apart from highlighting cases such as Tomkins, can be done.

Sheffield Theatres Trust

Gareth Morgan and Kevan Scholes

The case study concerns a charitable trust which is responsible for two of the UK's leading provincial theatres – the Crucible and Lyceum Theatres in Sheffield (plus a third stage – the Studio). It covers the period from 1971 (when the Crucible theatre opened) to 2001 by which time it had become part of Sheffield Theatres Trust together with its refurbished sister theatre – the Lyceum – and under the management of a single chief executive. During the 30-year period the theatre saw many new developments and significant changes in its environment – particularly regarding its funding. The case study shows that strategy formulation is not a simple process of matching capabilities to environmental 'requirements'. It is crucial to understand the political context within which strategies are formulated. Stakeholder mapping is a useful method of assessing this political dimension. The fact that the theatre has both commercial and public service objectives to pursue illustrates that strategy formulation usually proceeds through a process of compromise and the balancing of different stakeholder interests and not through optimisation of the needs of just one group.

● ● ●

Sheffield Theatres is a unique challenge. Often it feels like being on a high wire with no safety net. But if we can get it right, the potential is greater than for any other regional theatre.

(Grahame Morris, Chief Executive of Sheffield Theatres, September 2000)

Sheffield has two distinct theatrical traditions: a profile of high quality producing theatre (represented mainly by the Crucible) and a strong history of touring theatre (for which the main venue is the Lyceum). This distinction is fundamental: a producing theatre, through its artistic direction, commissions and finances its own productions and employs its own artistes. By contrast, a touring theatre enters into contracts with touring companies who bring their productions (and their own artistes) to the theatre concerned.

In Sheffield, these approaches are brought together in a charitable company known as the Sheffield Theatres Trust, which, with three stages in all, is unique in the UK outside London in being able to produce, co-produce and present independent productions all in one complex. Serving the population of the fourth largest English city outside London, Sheffield Theatres has around £5m income, making it one of the 500 largest charities in the UK. But the aims of creating high quality artistic work, filling sufficient seats, and working without deficits have created a constant challenge for the last ten years.

THEATRE BUILDINGS IN SHEFFIELD

The Lyceum Theatre opened in 1897; it was designed by a leading theatre architect of the day, and is now a grade II listed building. It has the rare advantage of traditional theatres of having no pillars obstructing audience views and having one of the deepest stages in the country. By the early part of the twentieth century it had established itself as one of the UK's leading touring venues, a reputation which grew further in the 1940s. In the 1950s and 60s it was especially famous for pantomime. But lack of investment and modern amenities forced the Lyceum to close as a venue for music and drama in 1968 and it subsequently became a bingo hall.

Modern producing theatre in Sheffield dates from the Sheffield Repertory Company, founded around 1923, which became 'The Playhouse' in 1938. Initially its work was purely commercial but in 1961 it first received an Arts Council grant to extend the range of productions. This marked the change from commercial to subsidised theatre, and in 1963 the Playhouse became one of only eight theatres outside London to be taken into formal association with the Arts Council.

In 1966 Sheffield Council announced its intention to sponsor the building of a new theatre of 800–900 seats, and a board of trustees was appointed, responsible for organising the public appeal and other decisions about the new building. This would be mainly a producing house, although with the demise of the Lyceum, it would also host some touring productions.

The result was the Crucible Theatre, completed in 1971 at a total cost of £884,000, on a site next door to the old Lyceum. The 'Crucible' name was chosen to reflect the design of the building and Sheffield's historically famous steel industry. After some controversy, the final building comprised a main auditorium with 980 seats around three sides of a thrust stage (which critics complained limited its use for large-scale opera and ballet), and a smaller Studio Theatre with 250 seats (now increased to allow up to 400).

The Playhouse completed its last season in 1970/71 and the Crucible opened in a blaze of local publicity. One of the most notable differences between the Crucible and the old Playhouse was the range of activities which were undertaken. Apart from the two stages, there was a restaurant, coffee bar, shop and licensed bar. Most of these services were operated throughout the day on the principle that the more people who could be enticed through the doors for whatever purpose, the stronger the theatre-going community would be. The foyer/bar was exceptionally large by most standards and was also used for exhibitions and for *ad hoc* folk music performances.

However, as early as 1981 there was a major local campaign to reopen the Lyceum as a theatre, and in 1987 Sheffield City Council agreed to redevelop it as part of the decision to build a number of first-class sporting and leisure facilities for the 1991 World Student Games. The building was by this time derelict and the renovation cost £12.4m. On completion in 1990 the restored Lyceum Theatre provided a superb example of a historic theatre, thoroughly refurbished to modern standards, and with seating for 1,100.

The Crucible and Lyceum stand physically together overlooking a paved square, and for reasons of economy of scale it was decided to form a new company, Sheffield Theatres, to run both venues. The distinctive role of each theatre was, however, to be retained, with the Crucible working largely as a producing house, and the Lyceum now hosting a new range of touring companies for the 1990s. The Studio theatre hosts a mixed programme of chamber music and drama, and is the resident home of the Lindsay String Quartet.

CONTROVERSIES

The Crucible Theatre, and more recently Sheffield Theatres as a whole, have constantly faced controversy. In 1972, less than a year after the Crucible opened, it had unprecedented losses and was at the centre of a public storm following confidential reports by the city treasurer claiming that the theatre should slash costs and run more popular shows to attract bigger audiences.

It was only in 1975 that one person became the overall 'director' of the theatre (previously it was run jointly by an administrator and an artistic director). But Peter James, who took the role, soon found himself with attendances below 50 per cent of capacity. Speaking to the *Sheffield Star* he said: 'There is a wealth of difference between what an audience thinks they want and what contemporary writers want to write about. The problem is trying to strike a balance.' In 1981 he was succeeded by Clare Venables, who said in an interview: 'A theatre that isn't controversial is dead. If people aren't talking about it and getting excited about the theatre, even if it includes criticism, then you are having no impact.'

A further financial crisis in 1982 led to an investigation by the Arts Council and Sheffield City Council. According to the *Sheffield Star* the subsequent report criticised the board for meeting only twice a year. The management committee was accused of failing to manage, and scathing comments were made about the 'ill-defined and ineffective' role of the finance committee.

Following this, structures were changed. The chair of the board resigned, and the board membership was widened to give greater representation of external and internal interests. The board was by then meeting bi-monthly and the finance and management committees were replaced by a new executive committee.

Changes were made to budgets, planning on much lower percentages of seats filled (until then the assumption had been 70 per cent – despite the fact that this had only been achieved once, back in 1974). Since 1998 this has been further developed by using a measure of 'net stage contribution' which considers attendances, revenues and costs, for every production individually.

However, budgetary changes have never been easily received, particularly when they impinge on artistic freedom. By the mid-1980s a new national climate of public finance had emerged, with no new monies from the Arts Council, and no scope for local authorities to advance substantial sums to bail the theatre out of difficulties. Despite these pressures, under Clare Venables the theatre enjoyed a considerable reputation – at least among its regular audiences – with productions that were both controversial and challenging artistically.

But then, as the *Sheffield Telegraph* subsequently noted, 'attention began to focus on the Lyceum, and suddenly the Crucible started to take a back seat'.

With the reopening of the Lyceum, a new post of chief executive of Sheffield Theatres was advertised. In January 1990, Stephen Barry was appointed to manage the overall Crucible/Lyceum complex. Clare Venables completed her final season as artistic director the same year, and a number of other staff changes took place.

The Lyceum brought big-name touring productions and popular drama and musicals to Sheffield for much of the year – previously the Crucible had hosted some touring productions (for up to 30 per cent of the year) but it was now able to concentrate almost entirely on its own work. Seats at the Lyceum sold well, with average fill at over 60 per cent of capacity, and up to 100 per cent for some shows.

But by 1991, a new crisis was emerging. In October, the *Sheffield Weekly Gazette* reported: 'The artistic director has resigned, attendances are down by 50 per cent, productions planned for the new year are cancelled, the company is heading for a £250,000 deficit'. This came after an emergency meeting of the directors to discuss the drastic fall in Crucible box office receipts following the opening of the Lyceum. However, Stephen Barry insisted that the situation could be managed. 'We are not asking for more money, nor are we trying to take audiences away from the Lyceum,' he said. 'There are different types of audiences out there and we must look at ways of attracting them to the Crucible.'

Two years later he reflected: 'In retrospect we were too defensive about the Crucible – narrowing our market appeal and attempting an over-specialist role. We did not capitalise on the single-site thinking brought about by the management structure. We knew the Lyceum would inevitably have an initial effect on the Crucible audiences – which was no doubt deepened by the recession.'

By now, a new artistic director, Deborah Paige, had been appointed, and some relaxation of the split between the role of the two theatres was agreed, with a few touring productions being accommodated in the Crucible, and occasional local productions being staged at the Lyceum. Following some good reviews, box office income appeared to be improving over 1992–93. The accounts were still showing deficits (as they had done for all but five years since the Crucible opened) but the level of deficit was around £35,000: small in relation to the total turnover.

However, attendances were overshadowed by yet another financial crisis which emerged in 1993, this time caused entirely from within. A senior member of the finance staff had, over a period of two years, embezzled nearly £0.5m of funds from the various companies under the Sheffield Theatres umbrella. The person responsible was charged and convicted by the courts, and around a third of the money was subsequently recovered. But the events of the fraud created a major trauma for everyone involved. It also worsened the overdraft in the theatre accounts, with consequent ongoing interest charges.

Once the shock of the fraud was over, it emerged that box office sales had once again fallen drastically, and in 1995–96 the average capacity fill across all performances was only 57 per cent. The 1994/95 accounts showed a deficit of £318,000, and 1995/96 showed a £353,000 deficit: considerably worse than the figure suggested in the shock headlines of 1991.

Fortunately the charity has a major asset in the form of the Crucible building (the Lyceum building is leased). Nevertheless, the accumulated deficit was such that there began to be some doubt as to whether the company was in fact a 'going concern'. If, in fact, the company continued to trade while knowingly insolvent, the board members would lose the benefits of limited liability, and would end up personally accountable for any continued losses. For each year since then the accounts have contained a special note reviewing the going concern basis. In the worst year, 1996/97, the accounts showed the company to have net assets of just £10,000, made of up a building worth £969,000 less accumulated deficits of £959,000.[1]

Crisis meetings were held in summer 1996 and a 'recovery plan' agreed, which involved drastic cost-cutting. Productions were greatly slimmed back, and key members of the permanent production staff were made redundant and offered purely seasonal contracts (the posts were eventually restored in 1999). The result was that artistic morale was extremely low and long-term planning seemed impossible: in order to control cash flow, budgets for each production could only be agreed once the outcome of preceding productions was known. The output began to be characterised by plays such as *Educating Rita* which could be mounted with two actors and a one-room set.

As a result, the reputation of the Crucible began to fall, with weak reviews and audiences less willing to travel to the theatre, resulting in even lower attendances. In its best year (1993), Sheffield Theatres had achieved combined attendances across all three stages of 450,000; by 1996 this had fallen to 240,000: no better than the best figures achieved in some years with the Crucible and Studio alone, before the reopening of the Lyceum. The problems were compounded by a couple of poor Lyceum performances with box office sales below the level of the minimum guarantee given to the touring company. In such cases, the theatres had to make a net payment to the touring company: had they known in advance, it would have been cheaper to have kept the Lyceum dark in such weeks!

A NEW STRATEGY

Until 1996, the board of the theatres was chaired by a Sheffield City Councillor, but the pressure for further change led to Norman Adsetts being asked to take

---

[1] The severity of this was softened on a day-to-day basis, because theatres receive significant cash from ticket sales in advance of productions. At Sheffield Theatres this applies both for their own productions and for tickets sold for others; moreover, grant aid is often received in advance of when it is used. So in fact, provided the theatres remained a going concern, it was possible to cover a cumulative deficit of nearly £1m with a net bank overdraft of just under £200,000. But if closure had been considered, all the advance cash would have to be repaid to third parties.

over as chair of the board in summer 1996. A prominent business leader in the city, and the former chair of governors of Sheffield Hallam University, Norman Adsetts (subsequently Sir Norman) brought a new emphasis on strategy and business planning.

Stephen Barry left in December 1996 for a new role in Edinburgh; he sadly died in autumn 2000 while his vision of a 'single site' theatre complex in Sheffield was still being taken forward by others. The new chief executive, Grahame Morris, took up his post in September 1997 and immediately had the task of presenting a new business plan for approval by the board. He brought with him experience from Plymouth of combining production and touring theatre: one of the few other UK locations to work on that basis.

The 1997 business plan, which was prepared with the support of an outside consultant, sought to unravel the various problems that the theatres had faced, and in particular stressed the need to distinguish between the historic deficit and the need to generate at least a small surplus for the years ahead. The business plan, which was agreed with the various funders, proposed many modest but significant changes over a three-year period to make the complex more profitable, by developing the marketing further, increasing the number of co-productions with other theatres, strengthening the profitability of the catering function, and giving greater opportunities to the senior management team to manage the theatres as a single venture.

In the light of this, by 1998/99 a major decision was made to reverse the decline of the previous years, and to invest in more significant productions which would attract better audiences. This was a fundamental shift of thinking in that the artistic quality and financial prudence were no longer to be seen as competing forces: commitment was obtained from the board and from funders to a policy which recognised that the only way the theatres would succeed would be to have output of a standard that would attract the audiences needed.

This bore fruit in the 1998 production of *Brassed Off* at the Crucible (based on the film of the same title) which was the most successful Sheffield production ever, generating excellent box office sales, subsequently transferring to the National Theatre, and then touring the UK (coming back, on tour, to the Lyceum as a touring production). Such spin-offs generate substantial revenue to Sheffield Theatres well beyond their life in Sheffield.

In early 2000, a new finance director, Kay Ford, took up office: she had previously been finance director of the London Symphony Orchestra, and was fully supportive of this new financial strategy. Commenting on the relationship between the financial aims and the charity's objects, she said, 'It's all about producing output of the highest quality – if you're not doing that, there's no point in being here.'

Deborah Paige left in 2000 and the post of artistic director was not replaced, but there had already been a policy of using freelance directors for some productions. One of these, Michael Grandage, created a highly successful production of *Twelfth Night* at the Crucible in late 1998, and in 1999 he was made associate (artistic) director, with a brief to develop the range and scale of productions. By 2000, a production schedule was planned and costed for a whole year ahead, enabling the theatres to market performances with long leadtimes and to invest in high quality casts including well-known actors.

In 1997/98 the financial position recovered to show a small £10,000 surplus on the year, and in 1998/99 a very respectable surplus of £87,000 was achieved – well beyond the basic aim of a charity which is usually to break even. 1999/2000 also showed a surplus of £19,000, so taking the three years together a major turnround had been achieved. But by autumn 2000 there was further disappointment that the first Crucible performance of the key 2000/01 season had achieved attendances well below expectations, and the visiting company programme was also showing disappointing sales, with internal accounts predicting a significant deficit for 2000/01. For once, no major cuts were made, but as Grahame Morris commented, 'The resolve of the board to stick to its new strategy was severely tested'.

STRUCTURES

In the early days, all the work of the Crucible was handled by one Trust board. Then from 1987 a separate Lyceum Trust was established, and a further management company was formed, providing the common support functions to both theatres. It was clear that very few people (certainly very few board members) understood the overall financial situation. It was also found that grant aid might be increased to one company whilst being withdrawn from another.

So in 1995, after extensive debate, it was agreed to transfer overall legal responsibility for the work of *both* theatres to one body, the Sheffield Theatres Trust. Sheffield Theatres Trust is a registered charity and a company limited by guarantee (with permission to omit the word 'Limited' from its title). Its charitable objects, as stated in its Memorandum of Association, are:

- To promote, maintain, improve and advance education, particularly by the production of educational plays and the encouragement of the arts of drama, mime, dance, singing and music . . .
- To receive, educate and train students in drama, dancing, music, and other arts, and to promote the recognition and encouragement of special merit in students. . . .

The Lyceum Trust continues, but it employs no staff. It leases the building to Sheffield Theatres Trust for use as a theatre for a payment of £90,000 per year – most of this money goes into a long-term building fund to cover future repairs and maintenance.

As with most charitable organisations of any size, it is necessary to have a trading subsidiary company to undertake non-charitable activities such as the sale of food and drink and commercial sponsorship: this is the role of Offstage Ltd. Offstage is wholly owned by Sheffield Theatres Trust, and at the end of each year, Offstage undertakes a gift aid payment to transfer all its profits to Sheffield Theatres Trust – this means no corporation tax is paid, and the theatres get the full benefit of all associated activities undertaken on their premises.

The board of Sheffield Theatres now operates in effect as one organisation, with overall responsibility for management of the whole complex – the board membership is shown in Appendix 2. The board members are both directors of the company and trustees of the charity; as such they are unpaid. The full board takes responsibility for the entire work; the only sub-committees are an audit committee and a nominations committee (which seeks out new trustees to replace those retiring). Staff of the two theatres, from the chief executive downwards, are employees of the board: they are not actually directors of the company even if the job title 'director' is used.

GRANT FUNDING

Since the beginning of subsidised theatre in Sheffield in 1960–61, income had shifted from purely commercial sources towards a heavy dependence on grants, primarily from the Arts Council of Great Britain and the local authorities. By 1977 some 63 per cent of the income was in the form of grants; this declined to about 55 per cent by the 1980s, to 40 per cent in 1989, and to 27 per cent by 1995, though with some one-off grants for specific initiatives the grant funding rose slightly to 31 per cent in 2000 (post-1990 figures are based on both theatres together).

The Arts Council does not give grants to touring theatres, but instead gives grants to certain touring companies towards the cost of their productions. However, Sheffield City Council makes grants towards both theatres (in the case of the Lyceum, this is simply to cover lease payments back to the Council for the Lyceum site).

The policy on public funding of the arts had changed substantially over the years. In 1985 there was an attempt to build up genuine 'centres of excellence' in the regions, and the Crucible was one of thirteen regional theatres selected as a major beneficiary. Another important policy change in the late 1980s was the introduction of 'parity funding', by which the Arts Council aimed that the total public funding of any theatre should be shared equally between themselves and the local authority. However, Sheffield City Council was unable to reach agreement with the Arts Council on this issue. David Patmore, Director of Arts for Sheffield City Council in 1992, stated that much of the problem was due to the internal structures of the Arts Council, which treated producing theatre and touring venues completely separately. As a result, the substantial money which the City Council was contributing to the Lyceum project was not recognised by the Arts Council in calculations of overall parity. 'From our point of view,' he stated, 'we'd prefer to talk to the Arts Council about our theatre policy as a whole – but their structure gets in the way of this.' The net effect was that the Crucible lost out substantially in the overall 'pecking order' of Arts Council grants, compared with other large provincial repertory theatres.

In the early 1990s, the Arts Council moved to a regional structure, which meant that most of the grant to Sheffield Theatres came from Yorkshire Arts Board rather than direct from the Arts Council of England (ACE), though the latter has continued to make grants for certain one-off projects (such as the 'How Much?' study, described below). This change meant that the Crucible was no longer in direct competition for funds with as many other theatres as previously (there being only one other producing theatre in Yorkshire of comparable size), but it also meant that the scope for Arts Council grants was influenced heavily by the initial split of the 'cake' into regional 'slices', over which the theatre had relatively little influence. The funding from Yorkshire Arts remained virtually static at around £650,000 from 1994 to 2000 – effectively a cut each year after allowing for inflation.

But in 2001, a major shift of government policy towards the arts began to emerge, with new policies to support excellence in regional theatres, and in 2001 Yorkshire Arts announced an extra award to Sheffield Theatres of £247,500 for 2002/03, and £470,000 for 2003/04, as a reward for innovative output. This meant that over just two years the Trust was due to receive a massive 72 per cent increase in its Yorkshire Arts core funding.

Sheffield City Council has continued to see the theatres as vital to the city, and relationships between the theatres and the Council are seen as good. Grant funding has been largely maintained despite heavy cuts elsewhere in the city's arts budgets: in 1999/00 the City Council grant was worth £685,000 to Sheffield Theatres (excluding amounts related to the lease-back of the Lyceum site). However, with small cuts and the effects of inflation, the theatres continue to face year-on-year reductions in the net value of this support, and financial support from two other neighbouring local authorities (Rotherham and Barnsley) together worth around £23,000 was also withdrawn during the late 1990s.

However, the launch of the National Lottery in 1994 meant a new possible source of support from the Arts Lottery Fund from around 1996 (though only for specific initiatives, usually of a capital nature); this is administered by ACE but separately from the government arts funding. Then with the election of the Labour government in 1997, some changes began to emerge in national policies towards support of the arts through the new Department of Culture, Media and Sport (DCMS).

These initiatives enabled Sheffield Theatres to secure emergency funding from ACE of £100,000 per year for 1997–99, and a one-off grant of £300,000 for audience development work and the research project on ticket pricing. Then in 1999 ACE announced the launch of its Stabilisation Programme, aimed at helping major arts bodies such a Sheffield Theatres to get on a stable footing, both in their financial structures and in their artistic output. It was recognised, for example, that whilst good management would allow the theatres to balance their budgets each year and perhaps make a small surplus, there is no way they would recover the cumulative historic deficit which was still around £790,000 in 2000 and looked set to grow again by 2001.

Confirmation was received in summer 2000 that Sheffield Theatres had been accepted on to the programme, and by spring 2001 a total award of £1.7m was confirmed: the largest single injection of funds to Sheffield Theatres since the opening of the Lyceum. £1m of this would completely wipe out the historic cumulative deficit, £130,000 was for a new stage lighting system and £140,000 for new IT infrastructure for the theatres, with the balance available as revenue funding up to 2003/04 to develop the artistic programme and educational work.

This was received with great optimism, but further funds would also be needed. The cuts of the preceding years meant that the Crucible building and much of the production equipment were in desperate need of repair or replacement, with the age of the building now approaching 30 years. Although funding was received to replace the erratic stage lighting system, the auditorium chilling system (vital for audience comfort to attract patrons during the summer months) had completely failed a year previously; and a new stage surface was required. Urgent refurbishment of the front of house was needed, and certain external maintenance was needed. Grahame Morris estimated that a minimum of £750,000 was required for emergency capital works, with as much as £8–10m needed to bring the Crucible fully up to the standard needed for the 21st century.

AUDIENCES, PRICING AND MARKETING

The largest part of Sheffield Theatres' revenue is dependent on tickets sold at the box office, and this money must meet all the remaining costs not met by grants or ancillary income. Budgeting for this is dependent upon the three issues of how seats are priced, what proportion of seats for any production are sold, and to what extent seats are sold at concessionary prices.

Seats in the Crucible (without concessions) were normally priced in the range £12 to £17, including VAT, in autumn 2000. In the Lyceum, prices varied widely according to the production, but prime seats could be as much as £28 for a major touring musical or even £40 for opera. Seats in the Studio theatre were normally priced at £10 for the theatre's own productions, but the Studio also hosts many musical concerts and smaller outside production companies. The theatres offer a range of discounts for regular theatre-goers who belong to certain membership schemes (over 2,400 households belong to one of these – they have the advantage of providing the company with a certain amount of regular committed income). Concessions were also available to those over 60, children, students, registered unemployed, disabled people and their carers. Standby seats at £5 were also widely sold on the day of each performance.

After deducting VAT from the prices, and allowing for concessions, the average yield per seat in 2000 (i.e. the net revenue to the theatres' accounts) was around £7.50 for Sheffield productions, and around £9.50 for performances mounted by visiting companies.

In the case of the visiting productions (mostly at the Lyceum) the revenue from ticket sales is distributed between Sheffield Theatres and the touring company according to a contract which is negotiated individually for each production. However, the shape of the Lyceum can be somewhat limiting in terms of revenue: with 1,100 seats it is not quite sufficient to attract the very largest touring companies, and over 300 of the seats are in the balcony, where visibility is limited.

In some cases quite complex formulae can be used to allocate the box office sales for visiting productions, but a typical split is for 70 per cent of revenue to go to the touring company and 30 per cent to be retained by the theatre. However, it is not uncommon for the touring company to have a 'first call' on all sales up to a certain level, or even a minimum guarantee (as mentioned above) which the theatres have to commit before the touring company will agree to come to Sheffield. In terms of minimising risk, the best arrangement with visiting productions is 'hire only' where the touring company simply pays a fixed fee for use of the theatre, regardless of ticket sales – but then if such productions prove to be very successful, Sheffield Theatres has no share in the profits beyond the hire fee agreed.

Even with the in-house productions, since 1998 increasing emphasis has been placed on plays which are originated at Sheffield Theatres but then transferred elsewhere (as with *Brassed Off* mentioned above), giving royalty income back to the company, or co-productions with other regional theatres where production costs are shared. However, the unique shape of the Crucible stage makes such transfers relatively difficult; it becomes more viable if productions are originated for the Lyceum. For the same reason, the Lyceum is much more suitable than the Crucible for most touring companies.

From 1996 a marketing director, Angela Galvin, was added to the senior management team, and the roles of marketing, publicity, box office, and development (fundraising) are now managed on an integrated basis, which was not always the case in the past (see structure in Appendix 1). A more systematic approach to marketing has seen attendances rise compared with the dire situation on 1996, though inevitably there are variations from year to year depending on whether a given season included any overwhelmingly successful productions.

Both the Trust and its funders have long been concerned to extend the reach of the theatres to a wider audience. By 2000, the theatres had built a database of ticket purchasers running to some 250,000 names, but surveys in the past had found that around 70 per cent of all seats were sold to a core of around 20,000 regular theatre attenders, drawn largely from those living in certain middle class suburbs of Sheffield.

To help understand the audience issues more clearly, and especially to implement one of the Labour government's aims of making theatre more attractive to young people, Sheffield Theatres successfully obtained a £300,000 Arts Council grant in 1998 for a two-year project entitled 'How Much?'. Theatre audience are often dominated by middle aged and older people: the obvious scope for audience growth is to attract more young people. Nationally, only 16 per cent of theatre audiences come from the 16–24 age group, and in Sheffield the figure was just 7 per cent, despite a large student population in the city. It was generally supposed that young people are cautious about theatre as a leisure activity, because of the twin problems of the cost of seats and unexciting productions (cinema being much more attractive). The 'How Much?' grant enabled the company to tackle this directly: 21 productions were publicised under the 'How Much?' banner with seat prices as low as £3.50 for those aged 16–24. Several new productions specifically tackled issues seen as relevant to young people, and others were marketed directly to them with headlines such as 'Sex . . . Violence . . . Brilliance . . . Shakespeare . . . all for £3.50'. With the support of the two universities in Sheffield, 'How Much?' was tackled as a major research project, also involving studies on non-theatre-attenders.

The net effect was a massive increase in seats sold to young people: for these 21 productions, 41 per cent of the audience was in the 16–24 age group, and overall, 29 per cent of the audience for these productions were new attenders. The box office coded all sales according to how the purchaser said they had heard of the production, so the marketing director knew exactly which sales came from which promotional media.

The results were seen as very exciting, but without further special grants, the theatres cannot continue to offer such low prices to young people (though student discounts and standby seats continue to apply); there was also the problem that these productions were less attractive to some of the more traditional audience. Whether productions are in-house or touring, it remains a real challenge to fill 2,500 seats of theatre capacity, across the three stages. Some local commentators have felt that Sheffield was simply unable to support this capacity of professional theatre (although there was no attempt to use all three stages for productions for 52 weeks per year). But capacity fill remains the fundamental issue in achieving sufficient box office revenue. Appendix 3 gives more details of attendances.

OTHER INCOME

In addition to the grant and box office income, Sheffield Theatres has worked hard, particularly since 1990, to generate other forms of income.

The most long-standing source of external income has been from hosting the World Snooker Championships, and to many people in the UK the Crucible became synonymous with the World Snooker Championships, which have been held there over three weeks every April/May from 1977, under the sponsorship of a tobacco company (which itself caused some controversy in the early days). Although the snooker brought in substantial revenue (including extra catering profits as well as the basic hire charge), this decision was not without its critics. One of the board members commented in 1996: 'I don't like snooker. I really object to my theatre being used as a snooker hall and it breaks up the theatre season. But it does mean that five or six times a day the *Crucible, Sheffield* is mentioned on prime time TV. And we do need the money!' Although the net revenue from hosting the snooker has fallen over the years (particularly on the catering side, due to changes in the arrangements), the overall view of the board has been that the Crucible needed the income, and in 2000, Sheffield Theatres were negotiating to continue hosting the Championships.

The profits of the restaurant, bars and gift shop form an important source of additional income, which is generated via the trading subsidiary Offstage Ltd. Significant steps were taken from 1997/98 to increase the profitability of this side of the work, by altering the staffing levels, opening hours, menus and prices. However, one of the longer-term aims of the major capital investments proposed for the Crucible will be a complete redesign of the front of house areas (at present the bar and coffee shop are not on the natural circulation route, and access to these areas for disabled people is very difficult). So although the late 1990s saw improvements in catering revenues, for the time being there is little scope to go further.

By the mid-1990s, Sheffield Theatres became increasingly successful in attracting sponsors for many Sheffield productions (and for some touring productions, too, if not already sponsored through the touring company); in particular, from 1997/98 they received support through the DCMS-promoted Arts and Business Pairing Scheme, and a further sponsor supported the education work. However, such income can be vulnerable in times of recession, as sponsorship of the arts is an obvious area for companies to reduce in times of difficulty.

The total profits of such commercial activities (catering and sponsorship) contributed about £300,000 to theatre funds in 1998/99, but this fell to £225,000 in 1999/00 (and it should be noted that the Trust does not charge Offstage a full rental for the space used by bars etc.).

In addition, as a charity, Sheffield Theatres has been active in various forms of fundraising over the years. A Programme Development Fund generated around £100,000 over four years in the mid-1990s, from individuals supporting the development of new Crucible productions. A number of charitable trusts make occasional grants to the theatres, but such grants are usually only for one-off projects.

Certain capital projects have also been supported by fundraising – in particular in 1994, £400,000 was raised for enlargement of the Studio Theatre from 250 to 400 seats and improved auditorium access for disabled people. But the need for major upgrading of the Crucible building means that a new fundraising project, possibly for up to £10m, might soon be launched, with a view to completion by 2004.

EMPLOYEES

In 2000, Sheffield Theatres employed 161 staff on ongoing contracts: 63 in selling and front of house, 45 technical (stage crews etc.), 24 in maintenance and security, and 14 administrative and secretarial. A further 56 were employed by Offstage Ltd in catering and retailing. Actors and production staff are taken on individually for each production – the average number in post at any one time was 15.

ISSUES FOR THE EARLY 2000s

For Sheffield Theatres, the principal challenge as the Crucible approached its 30th birthday in 2001 remained the ongoing requirement to maintain and develop the quality of output on the three stages, whilst attracting sufficient revenue from a combination of grants and box office sales to make this possible. Building new audiences remained crucial.

The major injection of funds won in 2001 meant that the Trust would soon see the historic deficit wiped away, giving it the long-sought financial stability (plus a big saving in interest charges). The new revenue grants from Yorkshire Arts meant that for the first time in many years the management could think about expanding the investment in productions.

Sheffield Theatres Trust recovered from the near-disastrous situation of 1997 when the company almost became insolvent, but even by 2000 the general fund remained £788,000 in deficit, the net assets were only £113,000, and the deficit was expect to worsen by 2001. Charity Commission guidance suggests that charities should have adequate reserves over and above their fixed assets to cover a reasonable period of expenditure (three months is often suggested): it would need a £2m increase in current assets for the charity to reach this level of financial security, and even with all the new funding agreed, the theatres would still be below this level.

However, there was real encouragement that new government policies towards the Arts were creating a potential where, for the first time in many years, Sheffield Theatres might really be able to move forward in the quality of its artistic output, though huge amounts management time were devoted to securing these funds, and much of the extra funding was in the form of special one-off grants so the longer-term revenue funding remained uncertain. Moreover, most of the new funding would take up to two years to come on stream, and as well as meeting the running costs, major capital investment was also urgently required to carry out urgent repairs, and in due course to bring the Crucible building up to the standards of a top-class theatre for the 21st century.

The company was moving forward in response to a comprehensive business plan, based on high levels of artistic investment, detailed research on ticket pricing, and a more strategic approach to maximising other income. There was a sense amongst staff that the new willingness to invest in larger and higher-quality in-house productions was beginning to bear fruit. But a strategy of high investment in production quality can only succeed in the long term if it leads to higher levels of attendance. Sadly, due to a combination of apparently unrelated issues, attendances in 2000/01 were disappointing both for in-house and visiting productions.

The key question which remained was whether or not, on a long-term basis, the output of the theatres could be translated into a level of sales at the box office that could give the financial stability which Sheffield Theatres so desperately needed.

APPENDIX 1 MANAGEMENT STRUCTURE, FEBRUARY 2001

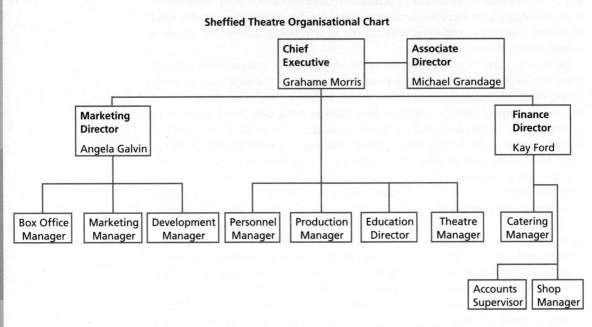

Sheffied Theatre Organisational Chart

APPENDIX 2 SUMMARY OF BOARD MEMBERSHIP, FEBRUARY 2001

Directors/Trustees (12 persons):
Nominated by Sheffield City Council – three members (two councillors and one other).
Elected – nine members including the chair (Sir Norman Adsetts). These members serve for periods of three years after which they may be re-elected for one further three-year period. The board elects its own successors.

Observers:
Sheffield City Council Arts Department – two observers (officers of the Council).
Yorkshire Arts Board – one observer.

Officers in attendance:
Chief Executive
Associate Director
Finance Director
Marketing Director

APPENDIX 3 PERFORMANCE FIGURES AND SUMMARY REVENUE ACCOUNTS (1973–2000)

MEASURE	1973	1974	1975	1976	1977	1978	1979	1980	1981	1982	1983	1984	1985	1986	1987	1988	1989	1990	1991	1992	1993	1994	1995	1996	1997	1998	1999	2000
1. Attendances																												
Crucible total ('000s) (All in-house productions from 1997 – see note 6)	190	221	246	215	227	197	183	174	201	193	176	182	176	186	232	222	192	173	180	110	139	131	92	84	88[6]	81	85	72
Studio total ('000s)	13	15	20	32	22	18	21	15	13	19	17	13	8	18	21	15	17	13	5	10	9	15	28	22	Note 6			
Lyceum total ('000s) (All visiting productions from 1997 – see note 6)	–	–	–	–	–	–	–	–	–	–	–	–	–	–	–	–	–	–	51*	316	288	299	253	219	268[6]	254	296	264
TOTAL ATTENDANCES ('000s) (excluding snooker)	203	236	266	247	249	215	204	189	214	212	193	195	184	204	253	237	209	186	236	436	436	445	373	325	356	335	381	336
2. Capacity fill																												
Mean capacity fill (%) for in-house productions – see note 6	52	69	77	49	51	62	61	49	66	55	59	71	58	63	74	74	65	58	65	41	64	63	49	40	48[6]	53	54	42
3. Financial																												
Box office (£'000s)	89	119	142	152	209	226	256	343	380	399	389	454	486	1,145[1]	1,306	1,330	1,446	1,596	2,274[2]	4,051	3,929	4,599	3,789	3,148[2]	3,298	3,026	3,395	3,098
Grants (% of income)	64	58	56	60	63	58	58	53	53	53	53	55	55	45	45	44	43	40	36[2]	25	27[3]	23	23	30	28	27	30	31
Surplus/(Deficit) (£'000s)[4]	(12)	(12)	(8)	(43)	(53)	(5)	(80)	(38)	(111)	(170)	40	(8)	(22)	54	82	(19)	40	(170)	98[2]	(31)	(36)	(115)[5]	(219)	(353)	(164)	10	87	19

Years shown relate to the financial year *ending* 31 March in the year shown – e.g. the column '1999' refers to performances for the year April 1998 – March 1999. * = Part year only.

Note 1: Catering revenue accounted differently from 1986.
Note 2: Accounting principles again changed in 1991 (to a basis similar to that used to 1985). Also, from 1990 the figures include box office sales and grants for the Lyceum (i.e. the figures from the Crucible Trust and Lyceum Trust have been amalgamated for this table). Further changes were made in 1997 in order to comply with the Statement of Recommended Practice on Accounting by Charities (see note 4).
Note 3: From 1993 the Lyceum site was the subject of a lease-back arrangement with the City Council – grants relating to lease payments are excluded from the calculation.
Note 4: The figures given from 1997 onwards are for the consolidated surplus or deficit, covering both the charity (Sheffield Theatres Trust) and its trading subsidiary (Offstage Ltd).
Note 5: The final surplus or deficit for each of the years 1991 to 1994 is affected to some extent by the fraud referred to in the text.
Note 6: From 1997, when the company began using the three stages more flexibly, figures were analysed by type of production (Sheffield productions or visiting companies) rather than by the specific stage used. Hence the 'Crucible' line shows figures for all Sheffield Productions (most of these are in the Crucible or Studio) and the 'Lyceum' line shows all touring productions (mostly, but not exclusively, in the Lyceum).

Source: Theatre records and published accounts

No one loves you, baby:
The Child Support Agency

Alex Murdock

The Child Support Agency (CSA) is an example of the problems that can occur when a new public sector agency is created. The case study demonstrates how difficult it can be for an organisation when there are multiple stakeholders and competing and often unclear objectives. The CSA, as a national agency, attracted more political and media attention than public sector organisations which are more locally oriented. The history of the creation of CSA also shows the conflict between stated goals and explicit targets (reducing the cost to the public purse of child maintenance) with implicit 'social policy' goals (better support for single-parent families).

• • •

In August 2000 the London *Times* published the story of a policeman who gassed himself in his car. His fiancée blamed the Child Support Agency for driving him to suicide. She said that he killed himself because of the 'impossible' demands made of him by the agency which asked him to pay £1,217 a month from his salary of £1,798 towards the maintenance of his teenage children by a previous relationship. 'He was happy to support his children but the amount asked for was just impossible for him,' she said. The campaign group NACSA (National Association for Child Support Action) believed that 42 suicides and eight murders can be laid at the agency's door.

That same month Faith Boardman, chief executive of the Child Support Agency, resigned to take up a senior job in local government. The new chief executive of the Child Support Agency, Doug Smith, may have reflected that he was the first man to occupy the role – the previous three having been women. Would he be able to make the agency both widely accepted and respected . . . and possibly even liked?

In the last annual report of his predecessor, Doug Smith would have found the comments:

> I am very conscious that the service we provide to our customers is still not as good as we wish it to be. But we have made considerable progress over the last three years and I believe we are now on the right track.
>
> (Foreword: Child Support Agency Annual Report 2000/2001)

However, earlier the influential Public Accounts Committee of the UK Parliament had been forthright in its criticism of the Child Support Agency. It stated that the agency had got itself into a position where nearly one-third of its current maintenance assessments were wrong and the proportion of non-resident parents who paid an incorrect amount was very nearly 50 per cent and there was no sign of any improvement. Indeed, the situation was actually getting worse with the large number of errors being made each year simply adding to the agency's 'legacy of error'.

BACKGROUND TO THE CHILD SUPPORT AGENCY (CSA)

The Agency came about following a debate about what role the state should play in maintaining single parents and their children. In 1990 Margaret Thatcher, the then prime minister, summed up the concern when she observed that 'Nearly four out of five mothers receive no maintenance from the fathers. No father should be able to escape his responsibility.' Over the period 1971-91 there had been a fivefold increase in single parents – mostly women.

This had been associated with a large increase in expenditure of state welfare benefits to support single parents. The legal system was regarded as inefficient and ineffectual in securing maintenance from the liable but absent parent and hence single parents had increasingly come to rely on state welfare benefits. Indeed, divorce settlements often presumed that the parent with care of children would receive such welfare benefits. The government Benefits Agency, which paid out welfare benefits, did not regard assessing absent parents as its prime task. A large number of absent parents, who might have been liable to contribute to the support of their children, had been able to avoid doing so.

The legislation to set up the Child Support Agency was not opposed by any of the major political parties. There was widespread agreement with the principle that absent parents should pay to support their children. The implications of the changes were described in a Parliamentary report as 'the most far reaching social changes to be made for 40 years. The assumption that in broken marriages or partnerships taxpayers should assume financial responsibility for the first family is, at long last, being challenged. The prime responsibility is placed where we believe it has always rested until recently i.e. with natural parents.'

WHAT WAS UNUSUAL ABOUT THE CSA

The Child Support Agency was unusual not only in terms of its brief to tackle the problem of child support. It was also a newly created agency. The chief executive was on a five-year contract and was given specific targets to meet. The person appointed was Ros Hepplewhite whose background was from the voluntary sector. She was used to dealing with the media and was seen as someone who would be able to bring a high level of energy and commitment to making the CSA a success.

The functioning of the Agency brought it into contact with other government agencies. It had obvious links with the Benefits Agency, a section of which had previously undertaken the role of assessing parental liability. It also linked to the Inland Revenue, the agency responsible for assessing and collecting tax.

The Agency had to recruit staff and set up an operational structure. Many of the staff recruited had little experience of the sort of work involved. Even though Ros Hepplewhite sought to downplay this aspect of the CSA's role, there was a general impression fostered by some politicians that much of the role of the CSA was to track down 'feckless fathers'.

THE EARLY HISTORY

The CSA found problems almost from the outset. The complexity of the assessment process meant that few were processed through to completion. The staff were new to the work and for the system to work efficiently it required that both parents with care and absent parents complied with a complex administrative process.

The legislation provided for a set formula for assessing liability. This formula did not take into account remarriage or children arising from new relationships. It did not take account of costs of access where there was a significant geographic distance between absent parent and children.

The Agency found that it was falling behind in its targets to complete maintenance assessments and bring in contributions. The response was to focus upon the easier cases which were those where there was already a record of maintenance being paid and where the absent parent was easier to track down and assess. Typically such parents were mature men in stable and well-paid jobs who had second marriages and mortgages. They were not at all like the 'feckless fathers'.

Another problem was that parents with care who were receiving state benefits did not gain from the CSA assessment process. Maintenance from the absent parent went to the government unless the parent with care came off benefit. A study commissioned by the Child Poverty Action Group was highly critical of this. Its title, 'Putting the Treasury First', was a clear reference to its conclusion that the CSA's implicit (if not explicit) task was to reduce social security costs rather than to put more resources into the hands of the caring parent.

STAKEHOLDERS

A number of groups had been affected by the creation and operation of the CSA. Single-parent organisations expected that the Agency would deliver more child maintenance for their members. They had been very supportive of the Agency, seeing it as representing a positive step towards addressing the inadequacies and problems inherent in the court-based system. The government had also expectations of the Agency to deliver against its targets and also implicitly to bring about changes in the nature of parental behaviour. However, the experience of the Agency operations was generally disappointing. Delays, mistakes and bureaucracy meant that cases were not being progressed. Also, some parents who had concerns about issues such as domestic violence felt pressured by the CSA to complete forms which might put them at risk of further violence or intimidation from ex-partners. In some cases this demonstrably occurred when, as a result of the CSA inquiries, women at risk of violence were tracked down by violent former partners.

The Treasury, the government department responsible for allocating resources, had a clear financial interest in the success of the Agency. They expected to improve on the collection rate of the previous section of the Department of Social Security. The targets set for the Agency in this respect were initially seen by the Treasury as reasonable and attainable.

Many divorced men with court-agreed financial settlements were shocked to find themselves the subject of the Agency. The failure of the formula to take account of second families meant that new partners (and their children) of divorced or separated men also were negatively affected by the Agency in a way they had not expected. The operations of the Agency – in particular where mistakes of attributing parenthood were made – caused great distress and brought about highly negative publicity.

REACTIONS

Organisations rapidly sprang up to oppose the operation of the Child Support Agency. Divorced and separated men (and their new partners) made common cause and were joined even by feminist groups opposed to the CSA. A letter-writing campaign swamped politicians' in-trays. Advice lines and support groups appeared, often using the Internet. Information was rapidly disseminated on ways to delay or obstruct the CSA. Some organisations whose members' incomes were relatively easy for the CSA to access, such as firefighters and police officers, campaigned even more vociferously. The *FireFighters' Magazine* was soon devoting a substantial portion of each issue to attacking the CSA.

Some of the opposition took more direct forms. CSA offices were picketed. Staff of the CSA were abused and in some cases threatened. Unpleasant and sometimes dangerous substances and materials were sent to the CSA in the post. CSA staff became liable to be treated as 'social outcasts', finding it difficult to book venues for social events. The press picked up on the issue very quickly and highlighted tragedies such as suicides of fathers confronted with sudden and apparently impossible demands for maintenance. Mistakes made by CSA staff – often in misattributing paternity – were rapidly seized upon and heavily publicised. Staff at the Agency felt 'under siege'.

The parents with care also complained that the Agency was taking an inordinate time to complete assessments and deliver on maintenance. There was a perception that mothers receiving benefit were being pressured to complete CSA forms – even when there might be a history of domestic violence. Examples where violent ex-partners had been able to trace former partners as a result of the CSA process gave rise to understandable concerns.

CSA RESPONSE

The CSA confronted a particular problem with the rigidity and complexity of the formula it was supposed to apply. Many people, unhappy with the nature of the assessment made by the CSA, complained to their Member of Parliament (MP). The avalanche of MPs' letters to the CSA led to often anodyne or pro forma responses which infuriated MPs. The Parliament Social Security Select Committee conducted some highly critical and televised investigations on the operation of the CSA and the legislation.

The lack of success in meeting its targets – particularly in completing assessments – led to an exercise called 'closing the gap'. This involved targeting the easiest cases – liable parents who were already paying maintenance and who had stable homes and regular employment. However, although this raised more revenue, the CSA was seen as punishing the most responsible parents whilst letting the 'feckless' ones get away.

The costs of second families also became a major issue effectively exploited by CSA critics. The retrospective element of the legislation was seen as particularly pernicious because it unravelled divorce settlements. The nature of the legislation gave the CSA little option in this regard.

The chief executive of the CSA, Ros Hepplewhite, adopted a highly visible role and went on the media frequently to defend the CSA and the spirit of the legislation.

The CSA annual report for 1993–94 on its first two years of operation showed it had failed to meet targets for arranging maintenance (31 per cent against a target of 60 per cent) and for making benefit savings (£418 million against a target of £530 million). However, it was successfully operating within its budget.

Ms Hepplewhite blamed the shortfalls on difficulties in setting up the new system and the campaigns against the Agency. However, she also acknowledged the distress that had been caused to many divided families and publicly apologised for this. In September 1994 (18 months before the end of her contract) she resigned as chief executive and was replaced by Ann Chant, a career civil servant from a government agency.

SUBSEQUENT HISTORY

Ann Chant took a much lower public profile than her predecessor. She focused upon addressing the operational shortcomings. However, the overall performance of the Agency continued to be disappointing, despite changes made in the Child Support Act 1995. Though the number of assessments made increased, this was in part linked to a reduction of the inflow of new applications. The backlog still remained substantial. Press coverage, although less vociferous, was still negative and critical. Although the opposition to the CSA became less vigorous, it had by no means gone away.

In 1997 Ms Chant was replaced by Faith Boardman – another career civil servant. The Conservative government lost the election and 'New Labour' took office determined to manage government efficiently and effectively. However, in February 1998 the *Observer* newspaper commented:

the agency seems to have established itself as the single most ridiculed, overworked and unsuccessful branch of the government machine. Organisations have been set up with the sole purpose of getting it abolished. It is by far the biggest cause of constituents' complaints to MPs and has been accused of simply acting as a collection agency for the Social Security Department, rather than acting to support children.

The Agency staff voted in favour of strike action and Barry Reamsbottom, the union general secretary, stated: 'Morale is very low. It's not the fault of our members that the Agency was set up in the most cack-handed way, with undue haste. It has been battered by review after review, and the fact that our members have voted for strike action is symptomatic of how they have become brassed off.'

The media coverage continued to be critical and – perhaps significantly – highlighted that opposition had grown amongst parents with care (usually mothers) who would be normally viewed as potential allies of the Agency. Ann Perkins, an informed and sympathetic observer of the CSA, writing in the *Guardian* on 21 April 1998, noted:

> An increasing number of women deserted by their husbands are refusing to co-operate with the CSA because they are baffled by the complex formula it uses to work out claims. A minister revealed . . . that 70 per cent of women on benefit now declined to reveal the name of their ex-partner – citing fear of violence. That represents an increase of 15 per cent on last year – a figure which ministers link to disillusionment with the Agency's workings rather than a genuine rise in violence.

The CSA and the government recognised that the focus of their approach had to change:

> Our agenda changed and we have moved away from numeric targets to a more balanced approach, concentrating first and foremost on the overall service we provide to our customers.
>
> (Faith Boardman, CSA Annual Report 1998)

Faith Boardman also set up a panel so that those who use the service can make suggestions as to how it can be improved. Gingerbread (an organisation campaigning for one-parent families) accepted a place on the panel which Ms Boardman chaired. The National Association of Child Support Action (NACSA) was not offered a place.

This seemed to have had some effect as shown in the report of the Independent Case Examiner – an office set up to respond to customer complaints:

> I see measurable improvements in the recognition of complaints; of much improved apologies; explanations offered and redress volunteered. Furthermore this improvement is not confined to specialised complaints handling teams alone and I have seen energetic and enthusiastic staff seeking to resolve complaints on the front line. The year was marked by improved co-operation between my office and the Child Support Agency, which recognises our mutual interest in responding well to customer complaints. This is reflected in a jointly agreed framework for improvements in standards of service to my clients.
>
> (Independent Case Examiner, Annual Report 1999–2000)

The Labour government introduced legislative proposals to replace the complex formula of the CSA with a simpler one using a fixed percentage of earnings based upon the number of children. This has generally been welcomed. However, no account was to be taken of the mother's income (where the mother has care) and in a situation where an increasing number of women earn more than their partners this is predicted to cause problems. Indeed, some commentators used the prime minister, Tony Blair, and his wife (a high-earning lawyer) as an example of the inequity that could arise.

The operations of the CSA continued to be the subject of ongoing concern. The head of the National Audit Office, the government body entrusted with examining the accounts of the CSA, noted in his report:

> the Agency's poor performance has left a legacy of error. The results of both my audit and of the Agency's internal performance measuring unit indicate that there has been no discernible improvement in the Agency's performance in 1999–2000.

Doug Smith, the new chief executive, was no stranger to working in agencies with critical or unfriendly stakeholders. He had previously spent 37 years in the Inland Revenue, the agency responsible for collecting taxes. In his new agency he had to confront a range of stakeholders with divergent and possibly opposing interests. They were very aware of the Agency's troubled history and watchful of its progress.

The government plans required him both to implement a new set of child maintenance rules and, at the same time, introduce a major new computer system to the Agency which was just beginning to feel a sense of stability after its difficult and eventful first eight years.

APPENDIX A FURTHER INFORMATION

Useful CSA-related links

www.nacsa.org.uk/

National Association of Child Support Action. This site describes itself as the 'definitive website for people affected by the United Kingdom's Child Support Agency (CSA), who want good advice, intelligent discussion and to wise up to the truth that lies behind government doubletalk'. The NACSA has been set up to represent those adversely affected by CSA decisions, and its site provides a forum for criticisms of the Agency.

www.nacsanews.org.uk/BodEntrance.htm

NACSA, using a US-hosted website, publishes this macabre site which commemorates all those whom NACSA claim have died as a result of the CSA. It does, however, give an idea of the depth of feeling associated with the CSA.

www.spig.clara.net

SPIG (Shared Parenting Information Group) – a group which indicates the complexity of modern family relationships

www.gingerbread.org.uk

Gingerbread – Support group for lone parents which is regarded as a key stakeholder by the CSA.

www.fnf.org.uk

FNF (Families Need Fathers) – a lobbying and campaigning group which has sought to present itself as 'balanced' in its comments on the CSA.

Political Parties

- Website of the UK Labour Party – www.labour.org.uk
- Website of the UK Conservative Party – www.conservative-party.org.uk
- Website of the UK Liberal Democratic Party – www.libdems.org.uk

Government

Houses of Parliament – www.parliament.uk

A key source site for political comment by politicians and which gives access to the working of parliamentary committees.

Department for work and pensions – www.dss.gov.uk

Child Support Agency and Benefits Agency website.

Inland Revenue – www.inlandrevenue.gov.uk

The government agency responsible for collecting tax.

Social Security and Child Support Commissioners – ww.hywels.demon.co.uk/commrs

A site for the Agency which handles CSA appeals.

NACAB – www.nacab.org.uk

National Association of Citizen's Advice Bureaux: a voluntary, influential and widely respected independent organisation which advises people on a range of issues.

General CSA Information

- Child Support Guide (www.dss.gov.uk/csa/csaguide.htm) provided by the Child Support Agency (www.dss.gov.uk/csa/).
- National Audit Office (www.nao.gov.uk) for the CSA's accounts.
- Independent Examiner's Report on the CSA (www.ind-case-exam.org.uk).

Thorntons plc

David Jennings

The case concerns the growth and development of Thorntons, the UK's largest manufacturer and retailer of specialist chocolates. Throughout its history the company had followed a strategy of in-house manufacture and retailing largely through the company's own shops and, to a lesser extent, through franchising. This policy presented the company with the difficulties of economically meeting seasonal demand variations in the chocolate and gift markets. The case also describes the company's attempts at diversification into the US and European markets and their disappointing conclusion.

Following this period of 'manufacturing-led' strategy the company appointed a non-family member as chief executive and a review of company activities led the directors to adopt a 'retail-led' approach to the company's further development. This included expansion of the chain of company-owned shops, the relocation of shops, and product and outlet development and experimentation. Deteriorating profits led to the replacement of this chief executive and renewed efforts to increase day-to-day sales and sales to commercial customers and to reduce the dependence on own shops whilst introducing joint shops with another company involved in the gift market.

● ● ●

FOUNDATION AND DEVELOPMENT

Thorntons, the UK's largest manufacturer and retailer of specialist chocolates, was founded in 1911 by Joseph Thornton, a commercial traveller engaged in selling confectionery. Tired of travelling, he opened his own shop in the city of Sheffield. His two sons, Norman and Stanley, joined him to combine their abilities in retailing, devising recipes, and manufacture, to provide freshly made confectionery, manufactured in the shop it was sold in.

The benefits of self-manufacture and product innovation were soon to become apparent. During the 1920s several product lines were established that have continued to the present day. In 1925 a recipe for Special Toffee, based upon cream, butter and eggs, gave the business an outstanding product. The self-manufacture of Easter eggs, decorated in the shop to include names and messages, added to the range of freshly made and fresh-tasting confectionery.

In 1953 Stanley and Norman Thornton visited Switzerland to find out how Thorntons could make what was regarded as the very best of chocolates. The visit included the Basle School for Swiss Chocolatiers and the recruitment of an outstanding student, Walter Willen, a young Swiss *confiseur*, who was to stay with Thorntons until his recent retirement. Walter Willen created the original recipes for Thorntons' Continental chocolates, a range that was to become the largest-selling specialist assortment of chocolates in the UK.

Thorntons began to develop sales outside the UK and by 1982 the value of Thorntons' exports to Europe and Australia had reached £300,000. Attracted by the prospect of further sales outside the UK, the company decided that the massive potential of the US market offered the best vehicle for expansion. Thorntons opened two shops in Chicago, with the longer-term intention of operating a 100-shop chain throughout the USA.

GOING PUBLIC

By the late 1980s Thorntons operated the largest chain of quality confectionery shops in the UK: 170 company-owned shops and 100 franchised outlets operating in towns too small to merit a Thorntons-owned shop. The company also acted as a supplier to Marks and Spencer. The product was delivered weekly to the shops from the company's own factories at Belper, Sheffield and Alfreton. In addition, the company owned the Mary Morrison chain of 25 greetings card shops in Scotland. The Mary Morrison chain was not considered to be central to Thorntons' core business and in 1990 Mary Morrison was sold to Hall of Cards for £2m.

The company had developed its product range to focus upon the rapidly growing higher value and gift market through a range of chocolate assortments, Easter eggs, special designs (such as a white chocolate 'Snowman') and liqueur chocolates. With sales of £46m and a pre-tax profit of £6m, Thorntons believed that there was scope in the UK for a further 130 retail outlets with the expansion concentrated in the south east, away from the company's heartland in the Midlands and the north. Although Thorntons were achieving success in the UK, the venture into the US, showing little prospect of profit, had recently been closed. Further opportunities for growth were anticipated through acquisitions in Europe, where markets were believed to be more similar to the UK than had proven to be the case with the venture in America.

The directors believed that the time had arrived for the stock market flotation of Thorntons. At a flotation price of 130p, with the offer of shares eight times oversubscribed, share trading began at a good premium.

1988–96: EUROPEAN AND UK DEVELOPMENTS

Within three months of flotation Thorntons had made its first European acquisition, Gartner, based in Antwerp, a specialist in high-quality chocolate and fresh-cream products with sales mainly through patisseries. With net assets of £196,000 Gartner had a turnover of £1.7m. Thorntons established an integrated manufacturing and retail operation, distributing Gartner's products through Thorntons' retail network as well as selling its own confectionery to the Belgium company's customers.

In the following year Thorntons acquired two French confectionery retailers, Candice-Martial SA and Société Nouvelle de Confiserie (SNC), for a total of £8.65m. Candice had 55 retail outlets based mainly in the Paris area selling confectionery and ice cream. SNC had 11 confectionery outlets in the Normandy and Brittany region. The French and UK factories were to contribute to the supply of each other's markets.

In the UK Thorntons had a 1 per cent share of the daily confectionery market and a 6 per cent share of the confectionery gift market, and as a consequence sales were highly dependent upon a number of seasonal events. The six weeks before Christmas provided 30 per cent of turnover. Easter, Valentine's Day and Mothering Sunday accounted for a further 25 per cent of sales. The concentration of sales into short periods of time made the company particularly vulnerable to conditions at those times. While snow might be part of the image of Christmas, poor weather conditions were only one of many factors, along with the development of superstores and Sunday trading, that could result in reduced high-street shopping activity. Unseasonably hot weather could also reduce the demand for chocolate. The comparatively short shelf-life of the company's products exacerbated the problems of seasonality. As a counter-seasonal product, Thorntons introduced a range of ice creams. However, at 5 per cent of total company sales the effect was too small to offset the periodic fall in confectionery sales.

Determined to further reduce the effect of seasonal variations in sales by expanding day-to-day sales of confectionery, the company changed its promotional message. However, finding the right marketing approach proved elusive. In 1994 the Christmas sale of speciality boxed chocolates fell compared with the previous year, a decline attributed to the use of an advertising campaign in the run-up to Christmas that was a modified version of an earlier campaign aimed at boosting daily sales of loose chocolates. While the number of customers was sustained, there was an increase in the purchase of cheaper, loose, chocolates rather than boxed.

While the majority of Thorntons' sales were made through the company's own shops, use was also made of other forms of distribution, including franchising. In certain respects franchising provided a cost-effective way to achieve distribution coverage; however, it did not provide the customer with the same experience as shopping in a Thorntons-owned shop and occasionally it could be difficult to maintain standards. Franchising could also provide surprises. In 1995 the company lost fifteen franchised outlets following their takeover by Clinton Cards, a company that did not normally sell confectionery. The retailing of greetings cards represented the principal business of a high proportion of Thorntons' franchisees.

Progress was made in developing the company's commercial customers. Thorntons had a long-standing supply arrangement with Marks and Spencer and in 1991 Sainsbury's was added to Asda as a supermarket outlet for the company's products, with the range of chocolate products broadened to suit supermarket shelves. The supply of chocolates and ice cream to commercial customers continued to increase, to £14.8m in 1992. Commercial customers' products differed by style and recipe from those provided through Thorntons' own outlets and regular customers would not be sure they were made by Thorntons.

The attempt by the group to enter the European market began to show disappointing results. Although several of the acquisitions had well-established brand names, including the well-known Martial brand, there were marked differences between the UK and French markets. While Thorntons' UK sales divided 80 per cent to chocolate and 17 per cent to toffee, the French market divided equally between chocolate (with the French consumer preferring bitter chocolate), ice cream and sugared confectionery. Sales relied less upon Christmas and Easter, with a greater emphasis upon gifts for weddings, births and christenings. In addition, the French operations demonstrated a difference in working culture.

In 1991 Thorntons (France) made a loss of £850,000. The losses continued and were worsened by high French interest rates, the severity of the downturn in the French economy and the devaluation of sterling. In 1993 the loss reached £1.8m. Thorntons' chairman and chief executive, John Thornton, concluded, 'We had a strategy that we believe would have worked in the end, but we are not a large enough company to sustain large losses over a long period'. The accumulated cost of the French initiative had reached £20m. Thorntons began to plan for the conversion of many of the remaining shops to the Thorntons brand, with the aim of increasing the synergy with the UK business.

In the UK market Thorntons continued to develop the products and packaging within the core chocolate gift ranges. The Continental range was developed to include a 'French' dark chocolate selection and a 'Belgian' milk and white chocolate selection. A new Classics traditional assortment and a Premier Selection of hand-finished chocolates were established to top the company's range. Product development was complemented by a programme of shop refurbishment to enhance both image and selling environment.

A CHANGE OF DIRECTION

Thorntons' chairman and chief executive, John Thornton, had joined the company in 1966. After holding senior positions on the production side of the business, John Thornton was appointed production director in 1977, MD of the UK business in 1982 and chairman and chief executive in 1987. During the later part of 1995 the company announced that it was seeking a new person for the position of chief executive. In January 1996 Roger Paffard became chief executive of Thorntons, with John Thornton as chairman. Roger Paffard's previous position was that of managing director of Staples UK, the office superstore joint venture between Kingfisher and Staples of the US. Joining Staples in 1993, he had presided over the expansion of the out-of-town superstore business. Announcing the appointment, John Thornton described Mr Paffard as 'energetic with a strong retail background'. Roger Paffard demonstrated his faith in the company by purchasing 73,000 shares at 135p.

Further changes to the board of directors included the appointment in 1995 of the company's first marketing director and in 1996 the appointment of the company's first retail director and a director for operations.

The new management team undertook a comprehensive review that resulted in a number of changes to the group. To improve efficiency and cut costs, packaging was to be concentrated at the Belper packing and manu-facturing site, providing annual savings of £250,000. The Belgium business, Gartner Pralines, was to be sold for a nominal sum. The third of Gartner's out-put that had been produced for the UK would be replaced by production at the group's main plant at Alfreton. Within the year a buyer was found, again for a nominal sum, for the 21 shops remaining in operation in France.

With regard to UK operations, the new chief executive concluded that the company's existing shops were 'tired and increasingly off-pitch'; many of the shops were too small and in poor locations. The chief executive concluded that the group had become a manufacturing rather than a retail-led business, that the product range had not been fully updated and that Thorntons needed to return to its retail roots. Mr Paffard had initially doubted whether Thorntons should continue manufacturing; however, a review convinced the board that the company was the only possible manufacturer for 70 per cent of its product lines. With the aid of retail consultants, Thorntons undertook a review of its UK market, concluding that there was still significant potential to increase the UK retail chain.

By October 1996 the company's three-year plan had been developed to include the closure of 126 shops and the opening of 216, taking the total from 269 to 359 shops. There was to be an emphasis on developing larger and better, prime location sites, in such locations as malls, shopping centres and small market towns. Expansion was particularly targeted towards London and the south. The aim was to provide a 60 per cent increase in total floor space by 2000, with annual sales per shop of £350,000. In addition, the product range would be developed to provide a wider range of products. Achieving these targets would require an ambitious programme of investment, averaging £17m a year for three years.

OPERATIONS

One of a number of ways in which Thorntons' confectionery was distinctive concerned the freshness of the product; at the extreme, a chocolate egg might reach the retail outlet within less than a week of manufacture. For other manu-facturers, addressing the wider chocolate market, the greater use of vegetable fat (other than cocoa butter) resulted in products with a shelf-life of up to two years. Although Thorntons' own research indicated that freshness was not the first concern for consumers when purchasing a gift of chocolates, the company believed it was essential to maintain the customer's experience of a fresh product. As a consequence, many retail outlets, corner shops, garages and some of the supermarkets were not seen as suitable for the product, even if the company wished to achieve sales through those outlets. For similar reasons care had to be taken in selecting and controlling franchised outlets.

The retail outlets provided a good quality of service and offered the inclusion of personalised messages, written in icing, on such gifts as Valentine's Day chocolate hearts and the two million Easter eggs sold by the company each year. At extra cost, products could also be purchased gift-wrapped.

The quality of the boxed chocolate selections was assured by Thorntons' use of quality ingredients (the champagne truffles contained Moët and Chandon champagne) and through the manufacturing expertise the company had developed. In-house manufacture was felt to protect the exclusivity of Thorntons' principal recipes. Products that were regarded by the company as non-core, such as solid chocolate bars, chocolate buttons, jelly beans and much of the ice cream, were largely supplied by outside producers.

Thorntons had developed manufacturing and selling activities to follow a largely in-house pattern. In 1998–99, 83 per cent of sales were made through the company's own shops (as against 67 per cent four years earlier) with sales through franchises declining. The number of franchised outlets had been intentionally reduced and was intended to account by 2001 for 28 per cent of shop outlets, as against 44 per cent in 1994. The layout and appearance of the shops were altered as often as every two weeks, with the changes developed and evaluated in the company's mock shops in Derbyshire and the south of England, prior to their high-street introduction.

The company's in-house delivery fleet served the company's outlets through a 48-hour order delivery cycle. Several reviews had been undertaken to consider the outsourcing of physical distribution. The in-house service was retained due to considerations that included the fragility of some of the products, the difficulties of access to city centre sites and issues concerning night delivery and shop security. In addition, the expanding network of outlets helped reduce the cost of distribution.

By the late 1990s new manufacturing plant included one of only four machines in the world capable of automatically manufacturing coloured chocolate figures (such as Oscar the Rabbit, a figure that included a bright orange carrot topped with a sprig of green). The manufacture of basic, liquid chocolate was potentially a capital-intensive process requiring an investment of £40–50m and reinvestment to achieve equipment updates; consequently Thorntons purchased liquid chocolate from an outside supplier. The supplier achieved buying and processing economies of scale beyond those that would be available to Thorntons. Packaging, which accounted for a large part of the product's perceived value, was designed in-house and bought in from outside suppliers.

The combination of providing a fresh product together with the need to meet a seasonal pattern of demand placed particular pressures upon the company's manufacturing facilities. A proportion of the Christmas product could be produced up to six months in advance, maintaining freshness through chilled storage. However, Thorntons' chocolates were enrobed in chocolate, rather than moulded. Their hand-made appearance made the labour-intensive process of packing boxed chocolates less open to automation than was the case for moulded chocolates (with their more uniform shape and size) produced by companies such as Cadburys. The seasonal demand for the labour-intensive task of packing required 700–800 casual workers, with consequent falls in efficiency.

Seasonal demand also required the use of temporary staff in the retail outlets to meet a sales pattern that could, within a few days, increase tenfold.

The company had continued to develop responses to the problem of seasonality. Through product development and shop relocation initiatives Thorntons sought to attract a wider range of customers, thereby increasing the importance of impulse and everyday snack purchases. The effectiveness of these initiatives in smoothing demand had been limited. In 1997–98 the tonnage produced at the low point of production remained half of that achieved at peak. While sales to outside customers might in principle be used to counteract the effects of fluctuating demand, for Thorntons the requirements of their main commercial customers were seasonal and similar to their own. The development of mail order provided an economic response to a seasonal pattern of demand, while new forms of outlet, such as Café Thorntons (combining aspects of a café and a confectionery store), offered the possibility of developing outlets with a less seasonal pattern of sales. Within manufacturing, increased automation, with its effect on reducing the overall use of labour, in some instances by 80 per cent, had helped to reduce the use of temporary employees.

1998–2000

By 1998 the company's senior management had come to see Thorntons as a market-led, retail-driven business, selling into a market that could be defined in a number of ways. As a gift, the boxed chocolates competed with a wide range of products in the £5–10 price range, provided by high-street specialist retailers, such as The Body Shop, KnickerBox and Wax Lyrical. The same market was also addressed by postal gifts such as flowers and wine. The company's Continental range of chocolate, the best-selling specialist chocolates in the UK, had no large direct competitors in the UK; however, to an extent, supermarkets, the Boots, Marks and Spencer and BHS retail chains and Woolworths, with its large range of confectionery, offered some competing products, including imported chocolates.

The company's advertising slogan ('Chocolate heaven since 1911') and shops had become a widely accepted part of UK retailing. In an independent market research survey, consumers asked to rank their typical high street, included Thorntons in fifth place. However, establishing and maintaining shops required a considerable commitment of resources. For a new shop the average cost of fitting out was £80–100,000. To account for wear and tear the shop investment was written off over a four-year period.

Thorntons' channels of distribution were targeted for further expansion to increase the total of wholly owned shops to 507 by 2001, together with 200 franchised outlets. Some of the existing franchisees had come to be seen as inappropriate through occupying a major location or an inappropriate location. In addition, while some franchisees had been very committed, others operated units that had become rather run down. Thorntons' efforts were aimed at replicating the customers' experience of the company's own shops, and to that end a new look and layout was trialled for the franchise outlets. Overall, the company's sales growth was targeted to increase by 15 per cent a year.

Thorntons had markedly increased the rate and scope of product innovation, repackaging and relaunching the Classics range, adding 'Swiss' and 'Austrian' selections to the core Continental range and introducing an Awesome American range. In 1997, 27 new countlines had been introduced, providing a fivefold increase in the range available. The ice cream range was expanded and a children's range introduced, with product themes including dinosaur eggs, fossils and Dalmatian spots. In 1998 a further 132 new and updated products were introduced. Widening the product range to include a greater emphasis on countlines, acting as a snack or impulse buy, attracted a wider range of customers but it also brought Thorntons into competition with the products of such companies as Nestlé and Cadburys. Overall, Thorntons prices ranged from a £50 Easter egg or £30 boxed assortment (previously £20 represented the top of the range), through self-selected assortments, to 19p for a single, individually boxed chocolate.

Sales from the new ranges were over £5.5m in 1998, but not all of the new products were to prove successful. Within the year 15 new products were discontinued due to their failing to reach an acceptable level of sales. In 1998 the company had begun a £3m programme to install EPOS (electronic point-of-sale) in the shops but, due to a lack of timely performance information, the loss from discontinued products was disproportionate.

During 1998, Thorntons' sales increased to £133m, with sales in the company's own shops growing to £105.9m. Sales to commercial customers had reached £17.4m, the main customer remaining Marks and Spencer. However, profits fell short of the company's own target. Partly this was due to margin erosion as a result of renting costly external warehousing space ahead of the availability in 1999 of the company's new £14m warehouse and the cost of the fifteen underperforming new product lines.

By mid-1999 the group's manufacturing had been consolidated to two factories, Belper and Alfreton, and an Internet and interactive television sales operation had been launched. The group had invested a total of £53m in new factory, warehousing and till systems. The manufacturing investment had tripled the level of potential output; however, the company's financial gearing was approaching 100 per cent.

The introduction of new products had achieved a number of beneficial effects, increasing the number of male customers, children and teenagers and lowering the overall age profile of the customers, although 50 per cent of turnover was still derived from 12–16 weeks of sales for Christmas, Easter, Valentine's Day, Mother's Day and Father's Day. Seasonal demand remained difficult to meet. During the Christmas 1998 period, consumers had tended to delay their seasonal purchases, and when demand finally occurred it ran ahead of the capacity of the shops. Tired of queuing, customers went elsewhere. Sales for the Christmas season were down by 3.8 per cent on a like-for-like basis. Roger Paffard explained: 'Christmas came very late and our shops couldn't cope, which meant people were dropping off the queues rather than waiting to buy. Demand was far greater than our shops could process. If we had had one more day before Christmas at those busy levels we would have seen a like-for-like increase.' Franchise sales for the Christmas sales period fell 13.1 per cent, and commercial revenues declined by 6.1 per cent. Profit forecasts were reduced as Mr Paffard said he anticipated continuing rough trading conditions in 1999.

Sales for Easter 1999 and Mother's Day were disappointing, leading to a warning of a reduction in profits. The chief executive announced that the group had underestimated the amount of new product necessary to stimulate sales over Mother's Day and Easter; advertising spending and new product launches were to be increased to raise the momentum of sales. The chief executive believed that a slowdown in product development during 1999 had been 'lethal' in a situation where consumers constantly expected new offerings. For the coming spring (year 2000) new products and relaunches would make up 92 per cent of items on sale for Valentine's Day, 100 per cent for Mother's Day and 91 per cent for Easter Sunday. New products for Valentine's Day were to include chocolate-scented T-shirts and underwear, and for Easter eggs on sticks that could be hidden in the garden. New and relaunched products were to be in place for the 1999 Christmas sales period, including a relaunch of the best-selling Continental selection and a range designed for the millennium celebrations, which included a chocolate champagne bottle.

Christmas and New Year sales for 1999 rose 3.7 per cent compared with 1998; however, if anything, the group had underestimated the consumer's appetite for novelty – new products such as a chocolate Millennium Bug and a Hair of the Dog model had achieved strong sales. However, in March 2000 the company announced that it was unlikely that it would achieve even the 1999 pre-tax profit of £10.5m, let alone meet stock market expectations of £12m for the year to late June 2000. In March 2000, by mutual agreement with the board, Roger Paffard left Thorntons.

RE-ADDRESSING STRATEGY

Within a month the appointment of a new chief executive, Peter Burdon, had been announced. Peter Burdon's career included Esso, McKinsey & Co. and the Boots retail group. The new chief executive announced that the management's strategy of increasing the number of stores had had a negative effect on trading performance; 'in the past Thorntons has focused a little bit too much on store openings and less on driving sales growth'. In his view the company needed to exploit its strong brand through marketing and advertising campaigns but did not need immediate changes in its product range. 'Thorntons is, and will remain, chocolate and toffee.'

Despite product developments, Easter 2000 proved disappointing; although like-for-like sales increased by 6 per cent, the increase was not as much as expected, leaving the company with 200,000 unsold chocolate eggs. Expensive adult eggs, costing more than £15, proved difficult to sell and the market for novelty eggs, such as one that contained a CD, was also weak. The unsold eggs were worth £1.4m but after marketing expenditure represented a loss of £5m. Announcement of the Easter sales performance was met by Thorntons' shares falling to a record low of 93.5p.

The company announced a change in strategy. New product development was to increase its emphasis towards day-to-day sales while the opportunity for reducing duplication within product ranges was to be examined. Opportunities to increase commercial sales were also to be explored. The capital expenditure programme was to be reduced, with expenditure focused more clearly on profit enhancement. The company would also change its accounting policy on depreciation to extend the life of shop fixtures from four to five years. The roll-out of new stores was to be slowed; however, agreement had been reached for joint shops to be developed within the Birthdays Group[1] of greetings card stores as an experiment in serving small catchment areas. The lower rents and the attractiveness of the joint offer were proving profitable.

Sales from the company's Internet operation totalled £1.1m for the half year, a doubling of sales (which included non-confectionery products) for the equivalent period in the previous year. Plans were announced to spin off the operation and the mail-order business. While Thorntons believed they did not have the necessary resources for its further development, the growth of the e-business was seen as adversely affecting the profitability of the core business. The business was to be become physically and functionally separate from the mainstream business, to become a separate corporate entity with its own dedicated management team.

---

[1]Founded in 1966 as Greetings Cards, the company had since 1986 developed the Birthdays concept, gradually diversifying the product range to include novelties, soft toys and ornaments. The number of Birthdays outlets had grown to almost 500.

APPENDIX A THORNTONS GROUP (£M)

	1990	1992	1994	1995	1996	1997	1998	1999
Sales	76.2	84.3	96.6	95.6	97.6	111.3	132.8	141.3
Operating profit	10.0	10.4	12.6	10.1	5.8	11.3	12.9	13.1
Profit after tax	7.9	6.3	7.8	6.7	(15.1)	8.6	9.0	9.7
Fixed assets	49.0	52.3	51.0	50.4	45.1	52.1	86.2	109.1
Net assets	39.1	48.0	47.3	50.1	33.3	38.4	44.8	48.1
Number of UK outlets:								
Own shops			243	263	269	300	344	390
Franchised			189	150	129	202	151	110

APPENDIX B THE UK CONFECTIONERY MARKET

UK per capita consumption of confectionery is one of the highest in the world. Within the UK market, chocolate confectionery is viewed as an affordable treat, as part of snacking or a gift. In recent years, increased consumer spending confidence has boosted demand for luxury chocolates, a trend shared with other products such as wine. The major UK confectionery manufacturers have rapidly responded to this trend by launching their own premium ranges. Premium chocolates generally have a continental image and are frequently imported from Belgium. The UK confectionery market is highly competitive with a great deal of product and packaging innovation. Manufacturers have tended to focus effort upon the chocolate sector, with its higher margins. The sector has demonstrated strong value growth. New chocolate products include larger-size countlines and premium boxed chocolates. The UK market for chocolate confectionery grew by 2.1 per cent during 1998–99 to a value of £3.86 billion.

UK confectionery sales (£m)

	TOTAL	CHOCOLATE	SUGAR
1993	4,415	3,038	1,377
1997	5,109	3,571	1,538

Chocolate market: sub-sectors

	VALUE SHARE 1999 (%)
Countlines	41
Moulded bars	16.2
Boxed chocolates	19.2
Seasonal products	12.1
Bagged selflines	10.5
Other chocolate	1

Countlines: Wrapped chocolate bars designed for one person to consume. Products include Kit Kat (Nestlé Rowntree) 16 per cent of countline sales value, Mars Bar 12 per cent. Advertising expenditure, 1996, Kit Kat £4m, Mars Bar £1–2m.

Moulded bars: Chocolate as slabs or segmented; the product can be separated to be shared.

Boxed chocolates: Sales increased by 23 per cent, 1995–99. There is competition from the increasing number of luxury products and gift goods within other sub-sectors of the chocolate market; for example, some moulded bars have been turned into suitable gift goods as 1 kg bars, combining novelty and value for money. Cadbury's Roses were the leading brand of boxed chocolates in 1997 with a 15 per cent share of sub-sector sales. Thorntons Continental had a 6 per cent share, Ferrero Rocher 5 per cent, Dairy Box (Nestlé Rowntree) 5 per cent. Advertising expenditure, 1996, Cadbury's Roses £2–3m, Ferrero Rocher, £2–3m.

Seasonal products: This product area has been the fastest-growing sector of the market, growing by 25 per cent during 1995–99. In 1997 Easter chocolate accounted for 66 per cent of the sales of seasonal chocolate, with Cadbury's having a 50 per cent share of the Easter market. In 1998 Woolworth stocked 153 different varieties of Easter egg, 79 of which were exclusive to its stores. Selection packs account for over half of Christmas chocolate sales. Increasingly, manufacturers are linking with companies, such as Disney, to use film and cartoon characters to add appeal for younger consumers.

Bagged selflines: Smaller chocolates sold in bags; examples include Smarties, M&M's, Mars Miniatures.

Chocolate confectionery: manufacturers

Market share 1999

	% VALUE
Cadburys	26.3
Nestlé UK	25.1
Mars	20.4
Kraft Jacobs Suchard	8.0
Private label	7.3
Ferrero UK	2.1
Thorntons	1.9

Leonidas, a Belgian manufacturer, has over 1,750 independently owned stores throughout the world (19 in the UK). The retailers receive supplies, at least weekly, from the company's three factories in Belgium. The retailer is allowed to add products of suitable quality produced by other companies to broaden the range of products available in the shop.

Consumers

Percentage of adults, 1999, regularly purchasing chocolate bars, chocolate slabs and boxed chocolate

	CHOCOLATE BARS (%)	CHOCOLATE SLABS (%)	BOXED CHOCOLATE (%)
Male	51	11	5
Female	53	14	7
Age			
15–24	75	10	8
25–34	60	13	7
35–54	53	15	5
55+	35	12	5

Distribution

In 1997, 45 per cent of chocolate confectionery sales were through multiple grocers (1993, 40 per cent), CTNs 19 per cent (1993, 22 per cent), department stores 10 per cent (1993, 12 per cent), garage forecourts 8 per cent (1993, 7 per cent).

Despite the predominance of sales through multiple grocers, brand sales accounted for 94.8 per cent of chocolate confectionery sales in 1997. Price cutting is most apparent in the major multiples. The average retailer margin for chocolate confectionery is 25 per cent, excluding VAT, with seasonal lines having higher margins.

Source: Marketing data source, Euromonitor.

CASE STUDIES

The Sale of Burmah Castrol to BP Amoco

Gerry Johnson

In 1999, the management team of Burmah Castrol, the lubricants and chemicals business, led by its CEO Tim Stevenson, decided to recommend to the corporate board the sale of the company to BP Amoco. In what follows, Stevenson explains how the company arrived at the point of considering this option, and why the board decided to take it.

• • •

The Burmah Oil Company was founded in 1886 by Scottish entrepreneurs interested in exploiting newly found oil deposits in Burma. Success there was followed by a milestone investment in an exploration concession across a substantial area of Iran acquired from the Shah. That company, then called the Anglo-Persian Oil Company, later became British Petroleum (BP). Burmah held a major shareholding in BP right through until the early 1970s. Indeed, after a long period operating effectively as an intermediate holding company for BP shares, the management of Burmah in the 1960s used the value of the shares as collateral to embark on an ambitious plan to turn Burmah into both a fully integrated oil company and a substantial conglomerate group. Businesses bought included Castrol and Signal Oil and Gas; other interests included major exploration licences in the North Sea, a substantial fleet of oil tankers and a raft of other activities, including high-street retailer Halfords, various chemicals companies and Quinton Hazell, an automotive component supplier. This period of expansion was brought to an abrupt halt by the recession consequent on the Yom Kippur war in 1974. Much of the company's subsequent history is the story of how this expansionist drive was gradually unwound, and a new corporate approach and concept developed.

THE STRATEGIC DEVELOPMENT OF BURMAH CASTROL

Tim Stevenson explained how the portfolio of the Burmah Castrol businesses developed and changed from the 1960s:

This case was prepared by Professor Gerry Johnson, University of Strathclyde Graduate School of Business, based on discussions with Tim Stevenson, the past CEO of Burmah Castrol, and on published sources. The author is published with the permission of BP Amoco. It is intended as a basis for class discussion and not as an illustration of either good or bad management practice. Not to be reproduced or quoted without permission.

First there was a process of divestment: selling Signal Oil and Gas, selling the tanker fleet, re-negotiating the Bahamas terminal and selling other peripheral companies like the automotive parts retailer, Halfords and Quinton Hazell.

Over time, and as the process of slimming down progressed, there emerged the concept a two-pronged Burmah Castrol, consisting of related businesses. One prong was the Castrol business which, throughout all this turmoil, was continuing to develop as a very successful global business with an increasingly powerful brand. The other prong was Chemicals, which it was planned could provide a substantial counter weight for Castrol. From the later 1970s/early 1980s onwards, a portfolio of special-ity chemicals businesses was put together, taking some of the businesses inherited from the past as the foundation and adding to them by buying in high-quality special-ity businesses as additions to the portfolio. The emerging rationale for Burmah Castrol that resulted was that the Group's business was the sale and marketing of speciality oil and chemical products. The argument was that we were good at managing Castrol and that we would be able to demonstrate to shareholders and the market that we could also very successfully manage chemical businesses whose style and approach to the market would be in certain key respects similar to that followed by Castrol. We also argued that management had skill in spotting both good managers and sound investment opportunities: the combination would enable all the Group's businesses to prosper and grow. There was sufficient similarity in terms of key factors for success between Castrol and the Chemicals businesses to enable senior management to add value across the portfolio. The idea that Burmah Castrol, as slimmed down, was a con-glomerate *per se* was resisted.

Whilst the process of simultaneous slimming down and building up the chemical portfolio proceeded, the market's response, as measured by improvement in the share price, was satisfactory. Castrol continued to perform strongly.

There was, however, internal questioning, particularly towards the end of the 80s, about where the Group was headed over the medium to long run. There was an argu-ment that Burmah as a two-legged stool needed a third to give it, overall, an appro-priate, stable shape. This led to a search for moves that might provide such balance. Included within this search were possibilities for rendering the Chemicals portfolio as a whole more substantial and therefore more able to sit comfortably alongside Castrol. This process culminated in the successful hostile acquisition of Foseco in the early 90s. The opportunity arose because Foseco had lost its way; its share price was very depressed. In fact, as it turned out, the price wasn't quite as cheap as it might later have become, because economic conditions continued to deteriorate after the purchase. This inevitably affected Foseco's short-run performance to a greater extent than Burmah Castrol had anticipated. In turn, this meant that it took somewhat longer to achieve an appropriate return on the investment than originally planned. However, vigorous restructuring work on the business and an improved economic environment in due course demonstrated the acquisition to have been sound. But in a qualitative sense the acquisition of Foseco was important because it led to some serious question-ing in the market for the first time concerning Burmah Castrol's overall *raison d'être*. Was it appropriate for Burmah to be expanding its Chemicals businesses to such a substantial extent? How usefully related was the Castrol business to the Chemicals businesses, and what was the real value in having them in the same portfolio?

There were also other issues to sort out in the Chemicals businesses where some were underperforming: work needed to be done to improve their overall operating efficiency. That was a task that was successfully set about and delivered: significantly improved ratios were achieved through cost cutting and effective focus. But that was not enough. The market response was, 'You've improved the performance but what are you going to do now?' When I took over as chief executive in 1997 a clear message from some substantial investing institutions was that management should not contemplate further substantial expansion – through acquisition – of the Chemicals portfolio. 'We don't understand why you bought Foseco. We don't understand how you think you can add value to acquisitions of that sort.'

RECONSIDERING STRATEGY AND STRUCTURE

By the mid-1990s Burmah Castrol consisted of Castrol, blending and marketing lubricants; and Chemicals with a residual Fuels retailing business – effectively the final relic of the past – which was in the process of being sold off. Until 1997 Castrol and Chemicals were run as two distinct groups of businesses. From 1997 onwards, for reasons explained below, the corporation was restructured into discrete business units. Exhibit 1 summarises the activities and performance of these business units.

In 1994 Mike Dearden, then CEO of the Chemicals businesses, had undertaken a review of the strategy and structure of those businesses. He had inherited a situation in which the acquired businesses still provided the foundation for the structure of his group. Foseco operated as Foseco; Fosroc as Fosroc, Sericol as Sericol and so on; each with its head office and often with subsidiary geographical offices. There had been no attempt within this to sort out a rationale for the Chemicals Group. The strategic review identified an underlying theme of industrial marketing and quality service as the core competences of the successful chemicals businesses. It was clear that the success of these businesses was much more to do with understanding customer needs than the production of chemicals. This conclusion resulted in a move to much greater focus on devolution of responsibility to the market-facing business units.

In 1996 Tim Stevenson, then CEO of the Castrol business, also instigated a strategic review of that side of the portfolio. The passenger car engine oil business, which represented 75 per cent of total profits, faced the prospect of more efficient engines requiring longer and longer gaps between oil changes; and therefore of potential long-term volume decline. However, the strategic review was triggered by a short-term challenge: Tim Stevenson explained:

In 1996, we had a difficult year in North America after a run of consistently good volume and profit growth; and simultaneously we started to develop worries about long-run developments in the passenger car engine oil business in Europe. Thus we believed we had the makings of a problem in the developed world concerning the sustainability of the sorts of growth achieved in the past in selling growing volumes of high-margin sophisticated lubricants into passenger car engine oil markets. And whilst we had a very successful developing world position, particularly in Asia Pacific, that was unlikely to offer sufficient to offset the difficulties we might be going to encounter over a five-year run – absent of action – in the bigger developed markets in Europe and North America.

All this provoked us into having a re-look at what was happening to our passenger engine oil business, what the medium-term market development might look like and what was going to happen to the competitor structure. The conclusion was that our old approach, unaltered, was not going to enable us to continue to grow the business at the rate previous strategic plans had assumed. We also looked at the other businesses;

Exhibit 1 The Burmah Castrol business in the late 1990s

CASTROL CONSUMER

Castrol Consumer is world leader in the supply of car and motorcycle lubricants and services, marketing to workshops and retail chains, auto accessory stores and petrol stations. Principal products are engine oils, e.g. GTX, transmission fluids and brake fluids.

Market share 11%
Market position 1
World market size 11bn litres
Main competitors:
Mobil
Shell
Texaco

CASTROL INDUSTRIAL

Castrol Industrial is the world leader in supplying metalworking fluid and services to industries such as transport and metal component manufacturers. The business also supplies process industries such as food and beverage, mining, power generation and offshore oil and gas production.

Market share 6% (metalworking)
Market position 1 (metalworking)
World market size 12bn litres
Main competitors:
Fuchs
Houghton
Milacron

CASTROL MARINE

Castrol Marine markets specialist lubricants and fluids to the international marine market. Customers range from the largest international shipowning groups, leisure and cruise operators to small fishing boat owners. Castrol Marine provides unique lubricant solutions and essential business information, increasingly through the Internet.

Market share 12%
Market position 5
World market size 2bn litres
Main competitors:
BP
Mobil
Shell

CASTROL COMMERCIAL

Castrol Commercial provides products and services principally to on and off-road vehicle fleets. Off-road business includes vehicles used in construction, quarrying, agriculture and forestry. On-road fleets cover trucks, buses and coaches. Castrol Commercial assists its customers in optimising service intervals, achieving fuel economy and improving engine efficiencies.

Market share 2%
Market position 5
World market size 11bn litres
Main competitors:
Exxon
Mobil
Shell

FOSECO FOUNDRY

Foseco Foundry is the world's leading supplier of consumable chemicals and services to the foundry industry. Foseco's products are used in the conversion of molten metal into finished castings. This enables foundries to produce castings of high quality, strength and weight whilst improving efficiency and reducing energy consumption.

Market share 19%
Market position 1
World market size £1.2bn
Main competitors:
Ashland
Borden
Huttenes-Albertus

FOSROC CONSTRUCTION

Fosroc Construction provides formulated products for the civil engineering and construction industries worldwide. Products include concrete admixtures to provide enhanced characteristics and greater cost effectiveness; a wide range of cement-based mortars and products and systems to extend the life of concrete structures.

Market share 2%
Market position 5
World market size £6bn
Main competitors:
SKW-MBT
Sika
W R Grace

SERICOL PRINTING

Sericol Printing is the world leader in screen printing inks and ancillary products. It supplies inks to the graphic, textile and speciality markets which include CDs, credit cards and snowboards. Sericol provides its customers with a high level of support, including training, computerised colour matching and environmental services.

Market share 11%
Market position 1
World market size £1.1bn
Main competitors:
Coates Screen
Nazdar

CHEM-TREND RELEASANTS

Chem-Trend Releasants is the world's largest manufacturer of specialised mould and die cast release agents. Customers range from manufacturers of tyres and car steering wheels to shoe soles for the footwear industry. Each relies on Chem-Trend's tailor-made formulations and application skills to improve quality, cost and productivity.

Market share 182%
Market position 15
World market size £270m
Main competitors:
Acheson
Acmos
Wacker

FOSECO STEEL

Foseco Steel's strong market position has been built on an ability to provide major steel producers with a total package of products and services which are vital to the safe, efficient and cost-effective production of high-quality steel.

Market share 5 %
Market position 2
World market size £1bn
Main competitors:
Thor-Didier
Stollberg
Vesuvius

Source: Burmah Castrol annual report.

the industrial lubricants business, the marine lubricants business and the commercial lubricants business. The key overall conclusion that emerged was that our internal structure for managing the global Castrol lubricants business was no longer appropriate if we were to optimise our position in each of the four markets. Our old structure had been a geographically based model, with four regional directors, the line managers responsible for over 50 country managers who ran their country businesses, very successfully hitherto, like individual fiefdoms. Within the country they were responsible for all aspects of Castrol's business, covering all the four market areas, and for sourcing of raw materials, blending, distribution, customer relationships; everything. They had to comply with central instructions in terms of the use of the brand and other broad policy areas but, subject to a relatively small number of rules of engagement, they were left to themselves.

A problem was that some of the areas of business were suffering because of the dominant culture of the passenger car engine oil business. So, for example, an opportunity for significant business development was being missed because there was no co-ordinated policy for focusing on the industrial lubricants business. The conclusion was reached that to optimise performance over the whole business, and to achieve economies of scale, we needed to move away from a geographic structure to one focusing on each of the four areas of Castrol as global businesses in their own right. We made the decision halfway through 1997 and then implemented it in 1997 and 1998. It was a very significant cultural change for the organisation. The old structure had been immensely successful. It had enabled a very strong ethic of customer focus and a strong *esprit de corps*. If you had the right man in Australia or Vietnam or Brazil, and you gave him his head, he produced strong results. So turning our backs on all of that and sweeping away the country structure was a major move. We originally planned to implement over two years, phasing it in; but in practice the job was completed in just over 12 months. It was done quickly and with minimal disruption. The results didn't suffer and on balance little of our market-facing customer focus was lost. Furthermore, the early signs were that the substantial benefits that we hoped to achieve from the change would materialise.

The logic behind these changes had two main elements. First, it gave the opportunity of unleashing potential in the industrial business and the commercial business and giving marine the proper focus that it needed. But the biggest benefit, second, was that the restructuring enabled a global focus on the passenger car engine oil business. Market trends couldn't be reversed, of course; but by having a single team to think about how we were going to manage the business globally, to take advantage of economies of scale on a regional and global basis and maximise the potential of our global branding strategy, opportunities were opened up for managing that business much more effectively in what looked as though it would become a tougher environment.

Exhibit 2 summarises the financial performance of Burmah Castrol in the late 1990s.

THE GOLDEN THREAD

In 1997 Tim Stevenson took over as CEO of the Burmah Castrol Group. He was aware that some financial institutions were looking for action at the Group level. They had witnessed and approved the restructuring of the organisation; but there remained bigger questions.

Exhibit 2   Five-year summary of Burmah Castrol financial performance

	1999 £M	1998 £M	1997 £M	1996 £M	1995 £M
Turnover net of duties:					
Continuing operations (including acquisitions)	**2,907.8**	2,761.9	2,778.6	2,853.5	2,751.3
Discontinued operations (note (i))	**35.9**	75.2	157.4	206.0	297.2
	2,943.7	2,837.1	2,936.0	3,059.5	3,048.5
Operating profit before exceptional items:					
Continuing operations (including acquisitions)					
Castrol subsidiaries	**211.4**	185.8	209.6	201.4	194.7
Share of operating profit in associates	**1.6**	1.6	1.6	3.0	4.5
Castrol	**213.0**	187.4	211.2	204.4	199.2
Chemicals	**78.6**	71.7	72.8	64.1	60.3
Fuels	**1.9**	1.7	(0.8)	(0.7)	3.4
Energy investments	**4.0**	4.0	5.9	5.1	0.7
Central management	**(13.6)**	(13.3)	(13.6)	(12.5)	(12.6)
	283.9	251.5	275.5	260.4	251.0
Discontinued operations	**0.7**	7.3	18.4	21.9	29.7
	284.6	258.8	293.9	282.3	280.7
Interest	**(25.0)**	(9.5)	(14.2)	(20.9)	(27.7)
Profit before exceptional items and taxation	**259.6**	249.3	279.7	261.4	253.0
Exceptional items:					
Continuing operations	**(76.7)**	(49.0)	(24.1)	(7.5)	
Discontinued operations	**(7.3)**	34.7	(17.9)	18.5	
Profit before taxation	**175.6**	235.0	237.7	272.4	253.0
Taxation	**(79.9)**	(86.8)	(92.2)	(97.6)	(97.8)
Profit after taxation	**95.7**	148.2	145.5	174.8	155.2
Minority interests	**(22.7)**	(19.6)	(22.2)	(19.7)	(20.2)
Profit for the financial year attributable to shareholders	**73.0**	128.6	123.3	155.1	135.0
Balance sheet					
Fixed assets	**883.1**	864.6	839.1	914.0	974.5
Net current assets	**309.4**	381.8	376.9	424.7	445.7
Total assets less current liabilities	**1,192.5**	1,246.4	1,216.0	1,338.7	1,420.2
Long-term creditors and provisions	**(603.1)**	(395.6)	(391.9)	(491.6)	(631.4)
Minority interests	**(68.7)**	(62.6)	(61.1)	(80.5)	(80.7)
Shareholders' funds	**520.7**	788.2	763.0	766.6	708.1
	pence	pence	pence	pence	pence
Statistics per ordinary share:					
Ordinary dividends (note (ii))	**47.3**	43.0	40.5	36.8	33.45
Earnings per ordinary share before exceptional items	**77.0**	66.1	75.5	71.1	66.9
Earnings per ordinary share after exceptional items	**39.0**	60.7	58.0	74.2	66.9
Shareholders' funds	**291.5**	369.4	329.6	332.6	320.8

(i) Discontinued operations relate to the results of subsidiary and associated undertakings discontinued at any time during the five year period under review.

(ii) Excluding any Foreign Income Dividend enhancement.

CASE STUDIES

CASE STUDIES

| Exhibit 3 | Relative performance of FTSE All-Share vs. Burmah Castrol, from January 1995 to July 2000 |

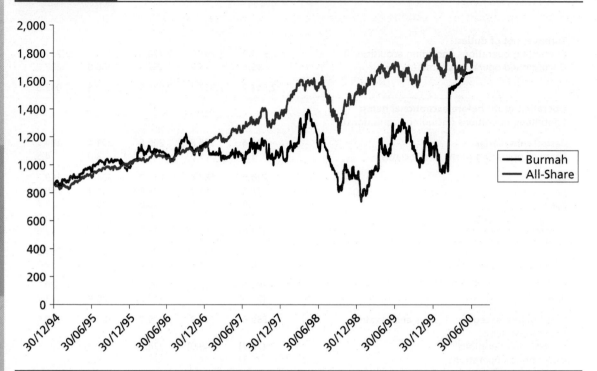

I was seen by some as an opportunity to force management to look at the business with new eyes; if you like, through their eyes in terms of how value could be released to them. Our Board had earlier discussed, in general philosophical terms, what management's objectives ought to be and whether shareholder value should be the driving force of what we were doing. There was complete agreement that that had to be the guiding force. Our share price reached £10 in the early 1990s and hadn't really moved from that level. It moved to £13 at one point and down to £7 at another, but these were the extremes of a dull range. [See Exhibit 3.] When you have a share price that is doggedly stuck, but you have high-quality assets, there is an imperative to do something about it because, if you don't, sooner or later the market will find a way of doing it for you – of delivering value to the shareholders.

At this time we argued with our shareholders that the rationale for Burmah Castrol lay in our having a 'golden thread'. Although Castrol and Chemicals were separate entities and we didn't manage them as one, there were sufficient similarities in terms of the sorts of businesses they were and the way they went to market, to enable Burmah Castrol to add value at the top level.

The 'golden thread' argument had received qualified support from a study of 21 of the most successful businesses in Burmah Castrol, spanning consumer, industrial and commercial lubricants and various chemicals businesses from different parts of the world. It concluded that the success of most of the businesses was based on competences to do with high levels of service rooted in localised knowledge of how their product applications could meet customer need. Similar to the earlier exercise on the Chemicals businesses, the conclusion was that success was not so much based on the technical aspect of product as on industrial marketing and service on a local basis. An important exception to this pattern was that part of the passenger car lubricants business which involved sale of product through retail channels. This relied a great deal more on brand and marketing push. The results of the exercise did, however, support the decision to reorganise the Group into market-facing business units. Further, it helped identify appropriate, and inappropriate, roles for the centre. The Group centre of Burmah Castrol should concentrate on developing people with the skills to work internationally but with local sensitivity; but it should avoid heavy-handed central co-ordination. The Corporate Centre was reorganised as a result of this exercise, splitting the 'corporate'-level activity off from the 'servicing' activity which was set up to be market responsive. So if operating companies did not want to buy the services the centre was offering they could go elsewhere.

There were, then, arguments that management could use in support of the proposition that Burmah Castrol businesses were linked by a 'golden thread':

> We believed we had a strong story to explain to the institutions what it was we were trying to do, and how we were going to release value.
>
> However, as we got into the streaming of Castrol into four separate business streams, this increasingly had an influence on our own thinking about the shape of the portfolio as a whole. Having split out the industrial business from the passenger car engine oil business, it further highlighted, for example, that there might be more similarities between the industrial lubricants business and the foundry chemicals business than there were between, say, the industrial lubricant business and the passenger car engine oil business. So by breaking up Castrol into business units, we had an effect on our own internal thinking.
>
> At the same time as this change within the company, a process of major consolidation in the oil industry was under way. We believed this to be a once-off process. It seemed to us that Castrol – its brand and marketing culture – would represent a great prize to a number of the major oil companies because of economies of scale and the broader coverage of the lubricants market that it would provide. This led us to believe that there could be latent potential for releasing substantial value to our shareholders by in some way putting our lubricants business together with another major lubricants business.
>
> Thus at this point there were various distinct strands of thinking. At one level we were explaining to the City that management had a clear vision for developing our Castrol and Chemicals portfolio as restructured. At another, we believed we had to explore what routes might be open to us to release the value that we believed was inherent in our businesses but which was not reflected in our share price.

THE PRESSURE FOR RELEASING SHAREHOLDER VALUE

The pressure on management to demonstrate how Burmah Castrol could release more value for shareholders remained; and there was growing concern internally about a need for greater clarity of corporate strategy:

The activism from some shareholders continued. When our share price went down to £7.50 there was particularly strong pressure from some shareholders along the lines of 'We don't want to strong-arm you but you must do something about this. You are sitting on a strong global asset in Castrol, the value of which is being dragged down by the fact that as management you continue to manage speciality chemicals businesses which are not so highly rated'. And by 1999, internally there was some feedback about the lack of vision in the corporation. We had a series of senior executive briefings in Europe, Asia Pacific and in North America; open and frank debate suggested that senior teams sought a clear banner for the future of the corporation that they could rally round. With half of the profit coming from the passenger car engine oil business, however, it was difficult to provide a really strong argument that would provide an overall cohesive umbrella that people could buy into. It was not possible for senior management to argue that there was something over and above the golden thread – which some were questioning. So at this point we had a combination of some lack of belief internally, lack of belief externally and a possibly time-limited opportunity as a result of oil industry consolidation. In addition, one of our non-executives argued consistently at board meetings that there was indeed a time-limited opportunity to release value to shareholders. 'If you leave it you will discover that it's passed you by and the opportunity for releasing value will disappear, and, worse, in some scenarios you will find, as an independent player who has not played a part in consolidation, you are increasingly squeezed by the big players.' As an executive team we came to a view that we had to explore what opportunities there were for us to play a part in the process of consolidation.

Joint venture discussions

The earliest conversations we had with a major player in the oil industry were in late '97 and the summer of '98. The argument was that at a time of consolidation you need to be aware how the big players may operate in the lubricants market. They have substantial economies of scale. If they should choose to use the advantages of those economies of scale to buy market share through cutting margins in the developed markets, that could seriously affect our business. They can make such cuts and still make good returns because they enjoy economies of scale that we don't have. If we could establish a joint venture, we would have the possibility of releasing value by locking our brand alongside another major brand, and reaping the benefits of scale. At the same time it could head off the perceived threat to our business from the process of oil industry consolidation.

We went into these discussions on the basis that what we had to offer was the premier independent premium lubricants brand in the consumer market and a strongly embedded marketing culture. Our working assumption was that we could achieve value and long-term growth security, by allying ourselves in some way with a major oil company.

Discussion about possible structures, however, raised issues about how Burmah Castrol could structure a joint venture for its Castrol business with another major international oil company in a way that would unequivocally put value into our shareholders' hands. In a joint venture with a major oil company where they would own 50 per cent of Castrol and our shareholders would own 50 per cent of Castrol, what would that then make of Burmah Castrol as a whole? An independent investor in Burmah Castrol would have a 100 per cent investment in a £800m turnover series of speciality chemicals businesses and a 50 per cent share in a major global lubricants business, the other half of which would be owned by a major oil company. Our advisers counselled that this would not be acceptable to the market. Any bid premium in our share price would go, and we would be tied in terms of flexibility for what we could do with Castrol. This led to the inevitable conclusion that release of value to shareholders through allying Castrol with another lubricants business effectively meant selling.

Other strategic options

What was the alternative to such a sale, bearing in mind the value which it could potentially release? The alternative which management developed, in considerable detail, involved breaking the Group up. This acknowledged market scepticism about the coherence of the portfolio. Although the need for radical restructuring was accepted, an issue which management did not fully resolve at this point in the process concerned how the slicing should be carried out. There were two views.

One option would be to sell Chemicals, significantly run down the Burmah Castrol head office to those functions needed to support the Castrol business, and be even more radical than we were being in terms of the way the Castrol business was run by taking out substantial cost. This would have involved major rationalisation of the whole supply chain; of the back office infrastructure throughout the world; of the way the portfolio of brands was run. In other words, turning the business into one focused on sales and marketing organisation with most other activity being outsourced.

The alternative was a variant on the theme. It was to sell parts of the Chemicals businesses but to keep those that were *automotive* based. Under this model we might have retained our foundry chemicals business, the Chem-Trend releasants business, the investment casting business and sold construction chemicals, mining, printing inks, cables, wax – all of the things that didn't obviously fit into an 'automotive products and services' model. That would have left us with a business of two parts: a passenger car engine oil business and an industrial-facing business – and with the residual possibility of in due course breaking it into two. Some work was done on the viability of this option.

THE DECISION TO SELL

On 11 August 1998, BP announced its merger with Amoco and in so doing initiated a wave of consolidation amongst the major oils. This was followed on 1 December 1998 by Exxon's announcement of a merger with Mobil, which put into play the lubricants business within the BP-Mobil joint venture in Europe.

During its early conversations with Amoco, BP had come to the realisation that there remained a strategic gap in its downstream portfolio. The small lubricants business that it would potentially inherit from Amoco in combination with BP's existing lubricants business simply would not have the critical mass to compete effectively on the world stage. After the Amoco merger, BP either had to consider maintaining a niche tactical presence or perhaps even a total withdrawal from the lubricants business, or seek other opportunities to grow the business into a material globally branded business. The thinking within BP had identified Burmah Castrol amongst others as possible opportunities to help achieve this objective.

As this thinking crystallised in mid-1999, the decision was taken within BP to take a significant strategic step in the lubricants sector first by extracting at a minimum its share of the lubricants business from the Mobil joint venture in Europe, and secondly by pursuing exploratory discussions with Burmah

Castrol. BP management saw Burmah Castrol as a vehicle for growth, delivering a global brand, world-class marketing talent and significant synergy savings as well as, importantly, growth through brand extension, cross-selling, and access to additional emerging markets. It saw no advantage in retaining the ancillary Chemicals portfolio within Burmah and resolved, if an arrangement were reached to acquire Burmah, to divest them as soon as practically possible.

In Burmah Castrol too the implications of the likely consolidation in the industry were being considered. Tim Stevenson explained:

It was clear that a knock-on effect would be a major change in the status of the European-wide pre-existing joint venture between BP and Mobil. It seemed to us, as part of our approach to examining options for combining our lubricants business with that of one of the majors, that this opened an opportunity. We approached BP with this proposition, and they responded favourably. A team was put together to examine the possibilities.

Within Burmah Castrol there was, quite rightly, considerable executive debate about the appropriateness of selling the business. The argument that something had to be done to release value to our shareholders locked up in our business but not reflected in our share price was clearly powerful. Yet there were also considerations of corporate tradition: the fact that Burmah had existed for over 100 years; the fact that we were beginning to develop an aggressive alternative to outright sale to a third party.

All acknowledged that there was a point at which we would have to sell. It came down to a discussion concerning the net present value of what management's alternative 'go it alone' option would deliver against the price BP would be prepared to pay. In the event BP's offer of £16.75 per share had to be set against that value that management's 'plan B' could deliver over time.

At the board meeting that decided to recommend the BP bid the board accepted that the company was at a crossroads; something significant had to happen. If the BP bid were not to be recommended then there would need to be a radical change to the shape of the corporation, involving the abandonment of the 'golden thread' argument The alternative option on the table at the meeting involved the plan outlined earlier: radical reshaping of the portfolio, together with substantial cost-saving measures and some aggressive new business initiatives. We had modelled this in terms of its impact on the share price over the medium term, assuming successful implementation. The board's debate concerned management's ability to carry through a radical new agenda; how quickly success would be reflected in the share price; and how this would stack up against BP's £16.75 offer.

The response from the financial institutions and the press to the board's decision to accept £16.75 was that it was the right thing to do. Internally, response was inevitably mixed. The initial response in Castrol was broadly enthusiastic. 'It's the right thing to do; taking a five-year view as an independent company we're going to come under increasing pressure. Putting the Castrol business together with the BP business gives us a much greater footprint globally around the world, particularly in Europe but also in the Far East. BP are tougher, harder managers than Burmah Castrol; very rigorous in terms of costs. Castrol needs that. They'll bring their rigour to sorting out the expense base'. In the Chemicals businesses there was inevitably some sense of betrayal; certainly disappointment and anxiety about who the new owners were going to be. But the Chemicals executives continued to manage the businesses very professionally. Results for the first six months of 2000 were excellent. Perhaps hardest hit were those people in Burmah Castrol head office: the ending of the PLC meant the end of requirement for many head office functions. They were perhaps the people who most felt we should have stayed independent and go our own way; although of course the reality was that had we not sold to BP, our own restructuring plan would likely have put many jobs in jeopardy in any event.

In July 2000 Burmah Castrol formally became part of BP Amoco. Most of the corporate board of Burmah Castrol left, including Tim Stevenson, and BP started the process of finding buyers for the Chemicals businesses.

The News Corporation

Julie E. Cooper

The case examines how the financial and business logic of an organisation's strategic development may be reinterpreted through the attitudes, values and resulting strategies of the key management officers of the business. In the fast-moving world of media it illustrates the importance of understanding the financial basis of an organisation's strategies and the development of a diversified group in terms of both business and financial logic. It also shows how the values, aspirations and style of a dominant personality, Rupert Murdoch, influenced this development.

● ● ●

For the year ending 30 June 2000, revenues at The News Corporation (TNC) reached over A$22 billion (US$14 billion). At the time, this made TNC the third largest media business in the world, eclipsed only by America's Time Warner and Disney. Yet, there was no doubting who was the leader in the media industry. What was breathtaking about TNC was its global reach, its sweeping ambition and the extent to which it was the creation of one man. Rupert Murdoch has been chief executive since 1953.

EARLY YEARS AND GROWTH TO 1980

The origins of TNC lie with the establishment in 1923 of a local newspaper, *The News*, in Adelaide, Australia, by Rupert Murdoch's father, Sir Keith. By 1980, TNC was publishing that country's only national newspaper, *The Australian*, two national magazines and over twenty provincial newspapers. Interests in book publishing and television broadcasting had also been acquired, along with film making, record production, farming and transport interests. The Murdoch family interest in the company, however, remained strong, via an equity holding of nearly 45 per cent.

The profitability of this Australian base was the springboard to multinational status. It provided the financial backing for the 1968 purchase of the UK-based News of the World Organisation, publishers of the *News of the World* (NOTW) Sunday newspaper. By 1980 the UK subsidiary was publishing not only the NOTW, but also the *Sun*, both newspapers with consistently the largest circulation in the UK, and had interests in magazine and book publishing, printing, warehousing and transport. In 1981 TNC added to its newspaper stable with the acquisition of Times Newspapers Ltd, publishers of *The Times* and *Sunday Times*. During the early 1980s, this UK subsidiary, with its newspaper interests, was the major contributor to TNC's profits.

From 1973, with the purchase of the Express publishing company of San Antonio, Texas, TNC also operated in the United States. During the 1970s, expansion here occurred in the areas of local newspaper publishing (for example, the *New York Post* was acquired in 1976) and in magazine publishing (the *Star*, a national magazine, was founded in 1974, and *Village Voice* and *New York Magazine* were acquired in 1977).

In TNC's annual report for 1980, Rupert Murdoch outlined the company's approach to its early growth and development:

> Over the years, expansion has been both by original start-up and acquisition. Typically, acquisition has been followed by a mobilisation of energies and talents to transform both the professional quality and the market performance of old or failing publications. . . . In virtually every market where [TNC] operates, it has achieved its position by first purchasing the weakest existing publication and slowly restoring its viability.

TELEVISION AND FILM MAKING

The 1980s saw TNC accelerate its real growth and development. Early expansion continued to focus on traditional product areas of newspapers and magazines and by 1984, revenues had reached nearly A$2 billion. The financial results for the period of the case are summarised in Appendix 1.

However, 1984 saw the beginnings of a major geographical and product shift. This expansion was US based. It aimed to transform TNC into a vertically integrated global media group, with a place in all parts of that industry from newspapers to television, from magazines to film. In 1984, TNC acquired the film company Twentieth Century Fox for US$575 million, and in 1985 paid US$1.9 billion for the six television stations of the Metromedia broadcasting group. These acquisitions provided the company with access to studios for making films and television programmes, to a film library of more than 2,000 titles, and to a distribution platform for that content. They were restructured into three principal operating groups:

- Fox Television Stations, formed in March 1986, which owned and operated six independent television stations, all within the top ten US television markets (and including the first three).

- Fox Broadcasting Company (FBC), launched in May 1986, which distributed programming by satellite to independent affiliated television stations. Besides the Fox Television stations, by summer 1986 FBC had signed up 92 further affiliates, giving it the ability to deliver its programmes to 80 per cent of the total US market. Although commencing with programming in prime time, late at night and at weekends, the company aimed to create a new, fourth, broadcast network to rival those of CBS, NBC and ABC.

- Twentieth Century Fox Film which financed, produced and distributed television programmes and motion pictures throughout the world to cinemas, television broadcasters (including FBC) and on video. The company encompassed DeLuxe Laboratories, a film processing subsidiary, and a 50 per cent interest in CBS/Fox home video distribution joint venture. Films produced by the company since acquisition include *Aliens*, *Die Hard*, *Wall Street* and *Home Alone*. Television programmes include *LA Law*, *The Simpsons*, *The X-Files* and *Ally McBeal*.

For Rupert Murdoch, this consolidation confirmed that:

> The News Corporation is now a multi-national, multi-media company . . . at the forefront of global marketing, ready to encourage the cross fertilisation of ideas between continents, and the different media within them. . . . The News Corporation is a citizen of the global village.

However, these purchases had two further significant implications for TNC. Revenues and operating profits increased but so too did debt levels. Rupert Murdoch had to be careful that his acquisition, and the debt associated with them, did not breach private bank loan agreements, which required total borrowings not to exceed net assets by more than 10 per cent. Furthermore, as US law prevented foreign citizens from holding more than 25 per cent of any company with a broadcasting licence, in 1985 Rupert Murdoch became a US citizen.

RUPERT MURDOCH – THE WIZARD OF OZ

> He's an expansion minded person, he's wanted to buy assets, he's wanted to take over, to move around the world, to build his media empire. But he also wants to retain control.
>
> (Australian financial analyst)

What was unique about TNC was that it was not a faceless multinational, but an organisation keenly linked to its chief executive – as a 1990 UK television programme commented, it was Rupert Murdoch's 'Empire', built on his 'vision, ruthlessness and daring'.

Rupert Murdoch disliked committees, bureaucracy and red tape. In the late 1980s, the worldwide headquarters in midtown Manhattan, US, employed barely 60 people, with hardly a memo in sight and communications kept to a bare necessity. The whole management structure was very informal with no defined responsibilities. One aide suggested that TNC was 'an emotionally driven and bonded company, where executives don't spend time guarding territories because nobody has one nailed down'. Another suggested that Rupert Murdoch's idea of management was to put in a manager and put in someone beside him, and not quite tell either of them what they were doing. A company executive confirmed 'I think he does do that. I don't think he does it to undermine the original person. I think he thinks that if the two can work off each other things will improve'.

Yet he has 'a proprietorial finger in every pie and on every pulse' (*Financial Times*, 24 April 1998) as, at the same time, his management style was supplemented by an extremely efficient reporting system. This focused on a weekly document known as the 'Flash', for which each operating unit had to provide a summary of its operating results. These had to include the budgeted figures for every aspect of its affairs set against the actual figures for the week, and then compared with the same week in the previous year. Each Thursday it was passed to headquarters, with Rupert Murdoch studying it over the weekend. Control was also achieved by detailed telephone briefings and unannounced 'parachuting-in' trips to check in person on the details of a business's activities and management, or to take personal control at key moments. As one financial manager confirmed:

> He really is the driving force and most major decisions are made by him . . . even relatively minor decisions – like whether we start our TV burst of advertising now or do we put it back three weeks. Those are the sorts of thing that would be discussed with him before the final timings are decided. He does like leading from the front and where there's likely to be a bit of excitement he'll wade in. . . . I think his biggest advantage is understanding the businesses that he's in. He can get down to the core of the business and has a lot of vision as to where that business ought to be going.

Maintaining control also required that Rupert Murdoch looked outside of the business to the regulatory environment that might constrain his activities. Most governments believed that the media was an industry whose importance required regulation, particularly regarding foreign ownership, cross-ownership and concentration. Controlling a business with a global reach, with several media products, Rupert Murdoch was likely to find himself affected by national regulatory systems. Many commentators have suggested that his political friendships have bought him influence in this area.

For example, in 1979 the Australian government amended the rules regarding the foreign ownership of television stations, from a requirement that an owner be resident in Australia to one requiring only that an owner be an Australian citizen. This enabled Rupert Murdoch to acquire Channel 10 in Melbourne although he was no longer resident in Australia. These amendments were christened 'the Murdoch amendments' by the Australian press. Again, it was suggested that the support of Murdoch's newspapers for Margaret Thatcher in the 1979 UK general election helped ensure that his acquisition of Times Newspapers in 1981 was not referred to the Monopolies and Mergers Commission, and certainly the government called a three-line whip to stop any referral.

However, as one commentator has put it: 'his personal politics are right-wing . . . but he's opportunistic in his business dealings. He doesn't support only right-wing leaders – he supports winners. And he supports people who are going to promote his business interests'.

Today, Rupert Murdoch and his family control only 30 per cent of TNC, though for practical purposes Murdoch is the company: 'For better or for worse, our company is a reflection of my thinking, my character, my values' (*Financial Times*, Profiles).

TOWARDS THE 1990S – THE SKY IS THE LIMIT?

During the second half of the 1980s, TNC continued to expand and develop its traditional product and market areas. Significant acquisitions included the US book publishers Harper & Row and Triangle Publications, and the Australian *Herald and Weekly Times* (HWT). Although the issue of convertible notes (classified as equity finance) largely funded the acquisition of HWT, the increased debt involved with the acquisition of Triangle Publications was of such magnitude that Rupert Murdoch was obliged, in 1988, to commit TNC to a significant debt reduction programme. This commitment, however, did not restrain the company from the launch in the UK on 5 February 1989 of Sky Television, a direct-to-home (DTH) satellite broadcasting television network. Satellite broadcasting represented a new approach to the distribution of programme material. Particularly, it provided the opportunity for any broadcaster to increase the 'footprint' (distribution) of any channel, allowing, for the first time, the distribution of programmes to more than one country.

Sky Television's origins went back at least as far as 1983 when, in his annual report, Rupert Murdoch disclosed that,

> In the past year, we have given careful study to the Company's options for the future, particularly in relation to the fast, emerging opportunities in electronic and satellite-assisted communications. . . . While we have every intention of continuing to build and strengthen our publishing enterprises we have reached the conclusion that at the same time we are advantageously placed for a strategic move into satellite broadcasting at an early stage in the development of that medium.

Following this, TNC took a controlling interest in Satellite Television plc (SATV) which distributed English-language television programming by satellite to cable systems in Europe. SATV was first planned to function essentially as a distribution system with programming purchased from outside sources. The acquisition of Twentieth Century Fox and the restructuring of the US subsidiaries provided the opportunity for SATV to acquire entertainment and information programming from within the group. By 1988 the company broadcast four channels – Sky Channel (a general entertainment channel aimed at a younger (15–45) audience than traditionally watches broadcast television), Sky News (news and current affairs), Sky Movies and Sky Sports – and was received by over 12 million viewers in 15 European countries.

In July 1988 Murdoch announced the launch of a new four-channel Sky service to be transmitted via a new satellite system called Astra based in Luxembourg. At the time, Sky was operating from slum offices in Foley Street in London's West End, the new Sky Broadcast Centre in Isleworth still a construction site. As for the staff involved, Murdoch 'had chosen to launch a multi-million pound venture with a handful of Australian TV cronies he had known for years – and not much else' (Andrew Neil, *Full Disclosure*, 1996).

To successfully launch Sky ahead of its rival British Satellite Broadcasting (BSB), Murdoch brought in managerial talent from across TNC. Andrew Neil, editor of the *Sunday Times*, became executive chairman in November 1988. Two further arrivals from Fox, Gary Davey, a creative programmer, and Pat Mastandrea, who knew about selling advertising in a competitive environment, strengthened the team. Tough targets were agreed and regularly monitored. The 24-hour news channel on which most of Sky's original (as opposed to bought-in) programming would appear was hastily put together:

> I insisted we take some of the programme formats of CNN and give them a British spin: they had already invented the wheel and I had no time to reinvent it. We took their popular *Crossfire*, a political debate show, and turned it into our *Target*, and

CNN's *Larry King Show*, a talk/phone-in programme, and made it our *Frank Bough Show*. I also copied ABC's *Nightline* and called it *Newsline*. Formats that would have taken the BBC or ITV months or even years to launch were being piloted within weeks.

(Andrew Neil, *Full Disclosure*, 1996)

The launch target of 5 February 1989 was met, but it was a low-key affair – it had been a rush, no one was sure it would work on the day and workers were still painting and fixing wires to the end.

Initially, the new Sky Television offered three of the 'own-brand', free-to-air, advertiser-supported channels that had been on SATV (with Sky Sports replaced by Eurosport). As before, these were distributed to cable systems throughout Europe. What made Sky Television different related to consumer hardware developments that had recently taken place. Individual satellite receiving dishes were now available at a price and size that made them afford-able and usable by millions of households across Europe. This opened up the possibility of Sky Television distributing to the consumer direct-to-home (DTH) and of moving Sky from free-to-air to a subscription-based service.

UK media regulations barred national newspaper proprietors from owning more than 20 per cent of a television company. Even though Sky's program-ming was aimed mainly at a UK audience, Murdoch was able to evade this by beaming Sky's programmes from channels rented from the Luxembourg-controlled Astra satellite.

There were fewer subscribers than expected, resulting in lower revenues. Although stringent cost reductions were implemented (one of Rupert Murdoch's maxims being that it was easier to take a million off costs than add a million to revenues), the performance of Sky Television had marked financial consequences for TNC. In the year to 30 June 1990, £134 million had been invested in the venture, yet losses of nearly £10 million per month were being incurred.

By November 1990, Sky Television had merged with its UK rival, BSB. BSB had missed its launch date, commencing broadcasting in March 1990. Start-up costs here had also been higher than expected and the purchase of satellite dishes lower than expected. The merged company, BSkyB, was jointly owned by TNC and BSB (although because BSB was a consortium, the next largest indi-vidual shareholder after TNC held only 11 per cent). However, the new com-pany came to be dominated by Sky Television. The Astra satellite channels and the technology used by Sky Television were adopted, redundancies following the merger occurred mainly among the BSB staff, and Sky executives came to dominate senior management, giving it operational and editorial control of the new company.

Other severe problems had materialised in the company in 1990. These included a protracted strike at the 50 per cent owned Ansett Airlines and a poor year at Twentieth Century Fox. The News Corporation was also investing £500 million in new printing presses in the UK. This was a heavy cash drain at a time when there was a slowing of the economies of each of TNC's three main markets. These problems resulted in a gap in working capital financed by highly expensive short-term borrowing. At the same time, banks worldwide experienced a liquidity crisis which resulted in TNC facing difficulty in refinancing maturing bank debt and in meeting working capital requirements. TNC's market value fell to less than one-fifth of its 1990 A\$11 billion net asset value, while borrowings rose to five times stock market capitalisation. It became clear that, without some form of restructuring, the company would default on loans due for repayment in 1991.

In October 1990, TNC called in Citibank of New York and began negotiations for the refinancing of its debt. At the time it was the largest and geographically most diverse corporate restructuring sought from international banks. Agreement to the restructuring was not automatic. The majority of problems developed following the discovery that original lenders had, quite legally, passed on some of their exposure to TNC to other banks, without TNC's knowledge. The result was that the company had to obtain unanimous agreement to the restructuring from a total of 146 banks. In February 1991, TNC finally entered into a three-year, near A\$9 billion debt restructuring and A\$700 million bridging loan agreement.

ON THE REBOUND

By October 1991, TNC had raised A\$2 billion through asset sales, and had announced plans for the flotation of 55 per cent of its Australian printing and magazine interests to raise a further A\$700 million. By the end of 1991, most of the A\$1 billion debt repayment due in February 1992 had been paid, and it appeared that further obligations could be met from existing cash flows without raising new money. The important issues again lay with business directions.

Rupert Murdoch himself set out his view of TNC's longer-term future in his chief executive's review of 1992. This involved 'steering a growth course' according to the following principles:

- Further strengthening the company's balance sheet.
- Improving and expanding existing businesses.
- Building new businesses.
- Nurturing and guiding the creative process as the foundation of the company's products.
- Strategic planning, involving examining opportunities for owning and operating media and entertainment ventures around the world.

Elements of the implementation of Murdoch's five principles can be seen in the progress of the company through to 1995 and beyond.

A major refinancing of all borrowing took place. This resulted in short-term private bank debt as a proportion of total debt falling from 80 to under 10 per cent, and the average maturity of public debt being extended from less than three years to over ten years. Debt repayments due in 1994 under the restructuring agreement were made early.

In August 1995, MCI Communications Corporation, the second largest US long-distance telecommunications operator, agreed to pay US\$2 billion in return for a 13.5 per cent stake in TNC. This, and other share issues, reduced the Murdoch family holding to just over 30 per cent (over which MCI was given first refusal should it be offered for sale). The terms of the alliance, however, limited MCI to a maximum of 20 per cent investment in TNC and, although having voting rights, MCI was obliged to vote with the majority.

Existing newspaper businesses in Australia and the UK benefited from the reduced production costs resulting from the completion of capital investment programmes for upgrading printing facilities. British newspapers added new sections, which offered better-targeted advertising, and initiated aggressive price competition. In Australia, the company was at the forefront of the introduction of colour printing.

In 1995, the printed world of newspapers and magazines still provided over half of TNC's profits. But increasingly, profits were coming from the screen, from films and from television.

CONTENT IS KING . . .

Sky and BSB (and the subsequent merged company, BSkyB) were first marketed primarily as movie channels, for films receiving their first-time television screening, with Sky Movies becoming the first of the BSkyB channels to be subscription based. This was still seen as important, with BSkyB securing exclusive pay-TV rights to all major Hollywood films until 2002. However, in September 1992, BSkyB launched Sky Sports channel, having secured exclusive rights to broadcast English football Premier League matches for five years. In less than six weeks, a million new subscribers were added. Rights to broadcast golfing, cricket, rugby union and rugby league were subsequently acquired. A gap in the market had been identified that was to revolutionise the nature of sport, the finances of BSkyB and the broadcasting strategy of TNC.

The unique value of sport is that it is inexpensive and easy to produce and it is best viewed live. It is therefore ideal for subscription and pay-per-view-based programming. Moreover, it is ideal for advertising, as it attracts those 'with the fattest wallet: man in the prime of life' (*The Economist*, 10 February 1996).

However, for a subscription-based broadcaster such as BSkyB it was important to be able to control the content that was received by the consumer to ensure receipt of all revenues due. This required the development of set-top decoder boxes and the use of encryption technology to securely 'scramble' and 'decode' the satellite signal. As a result the consumer was unable to watch programmes that had not been paid for and a rival content provider was unable to gain a distribution outlet. In the UK, News Datacom (NDS), a subsidiary of TNC, controlled the only established technology at the time. Using NDS's proprietary encryption code, BSkyB sent viewers a smart card which, when inserted into the decoder box, allowed programmes to be viewed.

This has ensured full and appropriate payment for services provided by BSkyB. Furthermore, as one industry executive pointed out, the company 'is in a position to skim off money from anyone who wants to start a satellite channel'. Control of encryption technology makes BSkyB a channel 'gatekeeper'. For any channel operator, getting through the gate requires the payment of significant fees. Bypassing the 'gatekeeper' requires any new channel establishing its own encryption and marketing systems. Apart from the high investment and running costs, this would require viewers to buy a new decoder box to sit on top of their television sets. As a result BSkyB now distributes the programme channels of other media companies via a series of joint ventures, owning, for example, 50 per cent of Nickelodeon UK and 25 per cent of the Paramount Channel.

The success of BSkyB's sports strategy made the company the most profitable television broadcaster in the UK. What provided value was the fact that 80 per cent of revenues came from subscription. For the future, analysts believed that the company's exclusive rights to key programmes – films and sports – would drive the subscriber base forward:

> As critical mass is achieved and additional advertising revenues obtained, the strong cash flow generated will put the group in pole position to secure further sports rights and renegotiate the movie contract, which will in turn further stimulate subscriber interests.
>
> (Barclay de Zoote Webb)

In December 1994, the company made a public offering of 20 per cent of its shares for over £4 billion. This reduced TNC's interest to 40 per cent, but its share of the flotation funds was a useful £600 million.

The strategy of sports-led programming was viewed by Murdoch as his 'battering ram' for entry into new markets and was exported to other areas. For example, in 1993 in TNC's other major television market, the US, the Fox group outbid CBS and paid US$1.6 billion to obtain the broadcast rights to the National Football League's NFC games for four years and the 1997 Super Bowl. Fox also spent US$350 million to purchase the LA Dodgers, Lakers and Kings baseball teams.

Fox has also become a dominant player in local sports by accumulating stakes in numerous regional cable sports networks that collectively own local TV rights to 70 of the 76 major league baseball, NBA and NHL teams. Thus Fox has built a national network by stitching together regional sports channels that televise local teams, often outbidding competitors in the process. Fox then wraps its national programming around these local programmes. This is an alternative strategy to that of Disney's ESPN channel, which is the market leader in sports programming, but which focuses on national programme events. Fox is therefore able to offer advertisers a unique alternative, a custom-ised package of regional advertising that could in aggregate reach an audience bigger than ESPN. Fox is also able to sell the kind of local and regional adver-tising that ESPN cannot.

The central battle for media giants is to purchase television rights to the most popular sports events – European professional soccer, the World Cup, the summer Olympics and the leading North American professional team sports. However, because the supply of existing sports events is less than the global demand, rights fees are soaring. As a result, many media companies are finding themselves involved in joint ventures in the area. For example, in 1996 Fox and Tele-Communications Inc. (TCI), the leading US cable operator, established a joint venture as equal partners to create a global sports television network.

Besides films and sport, the other programmes to gain audiences are news and animation. As with sports programming, Fox trailed one or two of the other global media giants. Global television news has been the domain of Time Warner's CNN, but in 1996 Fox introduced the Fox News Channel to the US (and later globally) to better utilise the journalistic resources of TNC as a whole.

Time Warner and Viacom have led in the global market for children's television with their respective Cartoon Network and Nickelodeon. Again, in 1996 Fox launched Fox Kids Channel. In the realm of animated feature-length films, Disney has enjoyed a virtual monopoly on output. However, animated films are ideal products for the global media market. There are no royalties to pay stars, large cross-selling and cross-promotional possibilities exist and they are easily dubbed into any foreign language. Fox (and Time Warner) has constructed new state-of-the-art digital animation studios to compete with Disney in this market. Further details of TNC's major media competitors can be found in Appendix 2.

The economics of broadcasting in the US changed dramatically during the 1990s. There has been a vast increase in the demand for content, not just from Fox but from other new entrants distributing via cable and satellite systems. As a result, good content has become increasingly expensive to produce or to purchase.

In this situation Fox has a number of advantages over the established US networks. As a start-up network, Fox could own as much of its own programming as it wanted, unlike the other networks which were hamstrung by legal limits and therefore had to buy more programming. Also, the Fox group included Twentieth Century Fox which provided television and film programming. However, while Fox had the advantage of acquiring first-run programming from Twentieth Century Fox (purchasing over 50 per cent of its television output), internal sourcing was not the only route to acquiring good programming, and costs at Twentieth Century Fox have risen significantly. Thus Fox has not been shielded from the increasing costs of programme acquisition.

As a result of this, and given that films are extremely unpredictable in respect of their profitability, the US group's biggest profit centre is its 23 (as at October 2000) owned and operated TV stations. Fox owns more stations than any of the other US networks.

In 1998 TNC restructured its US media interests into a new entity, Fox Entertainment Group Inc. (FEG). The aim was to create a clean new vehicle for investors who wanted to buy into the US entertainment industry without having to master the complexities of TNC. By June 2000 TNC owned 83 per cent of FEG which operates in five segments:

- Filmed Entertainment, which principally consists of the production and acquisition of live-action and animation motion pictures for distribution and licensing in all formats in all entertainment media worldwide, and the production of original television programming. Revenues derive from theatrical distribution, home video sales, and distribution through pay-per-view, pay-television services, broadcast and cable television.

- Television Stations, which principally consists of the operation of 23 broadcast television stations.

- Television Broadcast Network, which principally consists of the broadcasting of network programming.

- Other Television Businesses, which represents other broadcast television-related activities. The three television segments derive their revenues principally from the sale of advertising time. Viewer demographics, programme ratings and market conditions affect the sale of advertising. Adverse changes in general market conditions for advertising may also affect revenues.
- Cable Network Programming, which principally consists of the production and licensing of programming distributed through cable television systems and direct broadcast satellite (DBS) operators, and professional sports team ownership. Cable Network Programming derives revenues from monthly subscriber fees as well as from the sale of advertising time. Monthly subscriber fees are dependent on maintenance of carriage arrangements with cable television systems and DBS operators. The sale of advertising time is affected by viewer demographics, programme ratings and general market conditions.

For the year to 30 June 2000 turnover at FEG reached nearly US$8.6 billion and operating profit was over US$650 million.

. . . AND GLOBAL IS GOOD

In a speech to the International Institute of Communications in September 1988, Rupert Murdoch confessed that he did not have a very detailed strategic plan:

> If in 1980 we had attempted to chart on paper the destiny of our company, we would never have anticipated the 30 very diverse acquisitions we made on four continents, almost all of which arose from unique and unanticipated events. Business situations and business opportunities simply change too quickly for there to be much point in loading ourselves down with piles of strategic speculation.

He has, however, asked himself three questions about the globalisation of the media:

> Is a global communications network a reality? Yes. Are there really going to be worldwide networks? Yes. Is it really going to be possible for an advertiser to achieve, in practice, a single order with the media of his choice across the world? Yes.

The attraction of globalisation was based on the belief that tastes, income levels, technologies and even political philosophies around the world were converging on the American model, producing strong demand for American-style films and television programmes. For example, in 1988, for the first time in history, foreign television stations spent more on American movies than stations in the US itself.

With respect to TNC, by June 2000 the company had the means to distribute its television content to 75 per cent of the world's population.

BSkyB was the world's largest pay-television DTH satellite broadcasting operator with more than 6 million paying subscribers. A further 3 million also watched the company's content via other distribution platforms such as cable and ONdigital. The company offered ten channels in its basic package and 34 on a premium basis, with almost 60 per cent of subscribers taking the premium channels. Turnover for the year was £1,847 million with pre-tax losses of £263 million. DTH subscribers accounted for 64 per cent of revenues, cable and other distribution platforms 17 per cent, advertising 13 per cent and other 6 per cent.

BSkyB has moved to extend its position in continental Europe, acquiring a 24 per cent stake in Kirch pay-TV in Germany. Kirch is Germany's largest subscription television operator. TNC also has a 50 per cent stake in Stream, an Italian pay-television service.

As early as 1993, TNC moved into Asia with the acquisition of the Hong Kong-based satellite television company STAR TV, which broadcasted free-to-air over China, India and 51 other countries containing approximately two-thirds of the world's population. To date, this has not been a profitable venture for TNC.

Initially, STAR was planned as a pan-Asian, English-language service, which would have been cheap to produce. However, it was never profitable in this guise – there is no pan-Asian audience. With the possible exception of Hollywood feature films, regional programmes in local languages were needed to make any impact outside English-speaking elites. Murdoch's strategy therefore became a variant of the 'be global, act local' philosophy, which in media terms implies a strategy of 'narrowcasting'. To that effect, STAR acquired the world's largest contemporary Chinese movie library and entered into exclusive agreements with prominent Hong Kong film companies. TNC has subsequently launched separate satellite services with costly local programming for India, the Philippines, Indonesia and China. By June 2000 STAR was operating in 53 countries across 27 channels and reaching 80 million households.

It was also clear that STAR would not be profitable remaining as a free-to-air service. While in the UK Sky moved to being a pay-for-view network with surprisingly little difficulty, the costs of developing such a network in the immature Asian market was a further reason STAR continued to lose money.

Other problems stemmed from having to find a *modus vivendi* with Asia's political leaders. In September 1993, addressing an audience in London, Rupert Murdoch had claimed that 'advances in the technology of telecommunications have proved an unambiguous threat to totalitarian regimes everywhere'. A month after this speech the Chinese passed a law that virtually banned individual ownership of satellite dishes. In response, Murdoch sold the embarrassingly anglophile *South China Morning Post* newspaper and STAR removed the BBC World Service from its northern Asia channel. Murdoch also offered authorities the opportunity of controlling satellite programming through TNC's decoding technology. This would effectively allow censors to filter programmes to be broadcast.

Elsewhere in Asia, by June 2000 TNC owned 10 per cent of SkyPerfecTV!, which broadcasts 168 digital television channels in Japan, reaching nearly 2 million subscribers. A little further afield, TNC also has interests in pay-television services in Australia and New Zealand.

In November 1995, TNC joined with three other television, programming and distribution groups to create a satellite service covering Latin America. These partners were Globo, Brazil's biggest media group; the Mexico-based Grupo Televisa, the biggest Spanish-language programming provider in the world; and TCI International, a subsidiary of Tele-Communications Inc. of the US. By June 2000 Sky Latin America had over 1 million subscribers.

In its 2000 annual report TNC announced a restructuring of all its satellite interests into a new entity named Sky Global. This is to include BSkyB (now 37 per cent owned), STAR (100 per cent owned), Stream, Sky Mexico (40 per cent owned), Sky Multi-Country (30 per cent owned), SkyPerfecTV!, NDS Group (an 80 per cent owned artificial intelligence software developer) and the US TV Guide Inc. (a 44 per cent owned print, electronic and interactive programme listings company). The aim is to enable the management team to build on the successes of BSkyB and to migrate those to the other satellite platforms of Sky Global.

The biggest gap in TNC's global satellite operations is the US. Here Fox guarantees distribution, firstly by outright ownership of local television stations (thus giving 'gatekeeper' status) and secondly by creating an affiliated network, bound together by the quality of the programming that Fox offers. By June 2000, with this strategy, Fox Broadcasting had the ability to deliver its programming service to 98 per cent of the total US network. In the future, station ownership will increase Fox's distribution position as a result of all US television stations being required to convert to digital by 2005. Each analogue channel can convert to six digital channels, increasing station distribution potential overnight.

From 1994, Fox Broadcasting also began distributing programming via the cable network system. Fox was a late entrant to cable, with distribution and programming dominated by other major competitors. However, by June 2000 cable operations were showing a modest profit.

Satellite broadcasting services began in the US in 1995 and by 2000 had more than 15 million subscribers (cable subscribers numbered 60 million). In 1996 TNC and MCI paid US$682 million for the last unclaimed frequency and set up a new satellite television company, ASkyB. Again, TNC was a late entrant to this market in the US – Hughes' Electronics DirecTV and PrimeStar, a partnership involving Time Warner, TCI and others, were already established. Overturning such established players required even greater investment than that made in BSkyB and continuing in STAR. Furthermore, cable operators threatened not to carry Fox's cable channels if TNC began a satellite system in the US. In June 1997, therefore, TNC ceded ASkyB's assets to PrimeStar in exchange for US$1.1 billion in non-voting shares.

However, in 2000 TNC started negotiations with Hughes' Electronics (a subsidiary of General Motors) about the possibility of a merger between DirecTV (then the largest of the satellite broadcasters) and Sky Global. The proposal was that Hughes' shareholders would own 65 per cent of the new entity and TNC 35 per cent. However, as the single largest shareholder, TNC would exercise effective management control.

THE SUPERHIGHWAY

Technological development drove many of the competitive changes within the media industry throughout the 1980s and 1990s as traditional terrestrial systems of television distribution via aerial found themselves in competition with satellite and cable systems. As we have seen, TNC has been involved with both of these new systems. These technological changes went hand in hand with political changes in certain parts of the world that encouraged liberalisation and deregulation of national broadcasting monopolies or oligopolies. For the future, developments evident by the end of the twentieth century suggest that technological development will be a driver of competitive change well into the twenty-first century.

The development that has already impacted is the replacement of analogue technology with digital compression technology. Essentially, this technology allows for the distribution of significantly more data. It is a technology that can be utilised by all the currently established distribution platforms – satellite, cable and terrestrial land-based.

Digital technology (especially when combined with other technological advances with respect to satellite and cable delivery) has a number of significant effects for distributors. Firstly, it allows them to offer more programme channels (creating further demand for quality programming). By the end of 1997 most parts of the world had the opportunity to tune into at least 150 channels of digital television; in Europe the figure was over 500. Secondly, it allows for the addition of new services such as video-on-demand and interactive television, allowing the consumer to decide what to watch and when. Thirdly, it allows for the development of new products by offering Internet access via the television.

BSkyB is a prime mover responding to these new possibilities. The company plans to cease analogue transmission in June 2001. It has therefore offered a digital package to all existing and new subscribers of a free digital set-top decoder, free Internet access and a 40 per cent reduction on British Telecom (BT) call rates. Analysts calculate that this campaign will cost the company over £1 billion. The company suspended dividend payments in 1999 to help fund the cost. In October 1999, in alliance with BT, the company launched Open, currently the largest television-based e-commerce platform in the UK, and in July 2000 increased its stake to over 80 per cent.

In the autumn of 2000 in partnership with TiVo (and with plans for its own integrated set-top system) BSkyB pioneered the introduction of personal video recorders (PVRs) into the UK. PVRs are the new generation of set-top boxes that bring computer technology to the television. PVRs do not use tape; they convert television pictures into a digital format and then save them on to a hard drive spacious enough to store (currently) up to 40 hours of viewing. PVRs will store the last 30 minutes of any programme you are watching so that you can rewind, freeze frame and replay programmes as they are broadcast. A 'season pass' will automatically record every episode of a series. PVRs will learn your viewing habits and automatically record programmes of interest. They also allow you to 'buzz' past the commercials. Digital storage allows quick scanning of recordings and automatic indexing. Because the PVR contains a hard drive on which to store its picture data, it is closer to a computer than a conventional video cassette recorder. This opens up the possibility for adding further online services. Such boxes are being dubbed 'home gateways' and with their computer-like capacity are able to store movies and shopping catalogues, manage e-mail and play online games.

Tony Ball, chief executive of BSkyB, suggests the future for the company:

> Sky has built a digital platform on which many different revenue-creating services can be delivered. Pay television is merely the first. . . . Sky's New Media Strategy is to develop and distribute our content across multiple devices and platforms and monetise the traffic through e-commerce, advertising and subscription.

What is yet to make a significant impact on the consumer (although it is at the forefront of the corporate agenda) is the advent of broadband. This has been developed by the telecommunications industry under the acronym ADSL (asynchronous digital subscriber line). This offers high-speed video, voice and data transmission over existing copper telephone lines. This will allow data to be sent in the form of television pictures and Internet access, along with music, games and videos on demand – all in real time, and from anywhere in the world. Distributed to a gatekeeper set-top box, this would enable the television to fully replace the personal computer. The big attraction of this to investors is the enormous revenues expected from home shopping. The sales of goods and services bought through interactive television (t-commerce) is projected to exceed the size of all Internet consumer business (e-commerce) within five years of its inception.

For the traditional television distributors this offers the possibility of a new distribution platform – 'net casting' – the delivery of television and other products via a telephone link and the Internet. This would involve media companies becoming Internet service providers (ISPs) themselves, or in alliance with an established ISP. BSkyB, already a partner in Open, is discussing a joint venture that could result in Sky's TV channels being delivered over BT's next generation of telephone lines. Such a deal would give a BT portal content and services to attract customers, while offering Sky the opportunity to move beyond its satellite platform.

However, this technology also opens up the possibility of established ISPs becoming media distributors themselves, and integrating backwards with the purchase of content to distribute through their own portals. In this scenario the computer would replace the television. Computer software and hardware companies, in response to these changes and the impact of PVRs, are already adapting the desktop PC to accept television signals. Microsoft's 2001 version of Windows will effectively turn the computer into the equivalent of a digital TV set-top box. Microsoft has also invested US$500 million in Dreamworks, the entertainment group founded by Steven Spielberg, and is looking to invest US$4–5 billion in any new group created by the merger of Sky Global and DirecTV. In Germany in 2000, Siemens and the Japanese firm Fujitsu launched a machine, powered by Windows, which combines Internet and telephone access, and players for CD, DVD, MP3 and games, in one box.

One key to controlling these developments is control of the set-top box, which is the gateway into homes and will potentially rival the personal computer. With the economics of scale that will be made possible through Sky Global, Murdoch's vision is for a worldwide project, code-named World Box, with Microsoft Windows at the heart of the device. TNC executives are working on three kinds of World Box: a cheap introductory box which decodes multi-channel television; an intermediate box, much like the state-of-the-art

BSkyB decoder, which enables interactive services and includes a hard disk to record programmes; and a next-generation box which will be multi-functional, doing things such as running a domestic security system, reading the gas meter and such like.

AND INTO THE MILLENNIUM

The possibility of Rupert Murdoch's retirement, with all its implications for TNC's future, seemed remote in 2001. This was perhaps fortunate. Although having some stability in senior management with his two co-chief operating officers, Peter Chernin and Chase Carey, Murdoch had repeatedly quarrelled with previous potential successors. He possibly prefers the hereditary principle. In 1996, when aged 65, Murdoch was asked which of his two daughters and two sons he would like to succeed him. He was quoted as saying: 'I hope we can work it out between us'; adding, however, that he would probably make a judgement about his successor in about twenty years. Andrew Neil, a former editor of the *Sunday Times*, has said that both TNC and its founder would die together. However, at the beginning of 2000 TNC entered into arrangements with Liberty Media whereby Liberty became the second largest shareholder in TNC (after the Murdoch family) with a (non-voting) 20 per cent stake. It has been suggested that Liberty Media's chairman, John Malone, might be inserting himself to take over one day.

For the near future, the activities of TNC will continue to be linked with the motivations, personality and perceptions of Murdoch himself. It is appropriate, therefore, that he should have the last word:

> [W]e have always welcomed change. In fact, I like to think that we have helped to define the new world of media and entertainment. Our own evolution from a single newspaper to a multi-media, multi-platform global media company reflects our adaptability and agility; our constant search for new frontiers; our relentless pursuit of new and better products to serve our customers; our refusal to become complacent. Ours, indeed, is an entrepreneurial spirit.

APPENDIX 1 THE NEWS CORPORATION LTD: FINANCIAL DATA

Consolidated profit and loss accounts (summarised)

	FOR YEAR ENDING 30 JUNE (A$ MILLIONS)						
	1982	1985	1988	1991	1994	1997	2000
Turnover							
USA		829	2,540	6,560	8,068	10,054	16,665
UK		790	1,689	2,249	1,980	2,665	3,600
Australia		828	1,790	2,162	1,573	1,670	2,178
	1,250	2,447	6,019	10,971	11,621	14,389	22,443
Operating profit							
USA		26	413	1,028	1,078	1,131	1,835
UK		75	376	197	297	488	727
Australia		63	241	332	222	81	180
	64	164	1,030	1,557	1,597	1,700	2,742
Interest charges	52	(74)	(579)	(1,170)	(667)	(634)	(822)
Profit after tax	37	96	473	391	1,232	1,342	1,396
Abnormal item	(4)	51	34	(615)	136	(575)	1,102
Profit attributable to shareholders	33	147	472	(393)	1,335	720	1,921

Consolidated balance sheets (summarised)

	AS AT 30 JUNE (A$ MILLIONS)						
	1982	1985	1988	1991	1994	1997	2000
Current assets							
Cash	6	144	129	202	433	3,616	4,638
Other	346	762	1,864	3,073	3,310	5,282	8,489
Total current assets	352	906	1,993	3,275	3,743	8,898	13,127
Non-current assets							
Investments	180	581	3,408	2,999	3,396	6,152	13,806
Property, plant and equip.	275	590	1,584	3,249	3,545	4,422	5,948
Intangibles	84	1,302	5,569	12,895	13,619	18,694	27,232
Other	27	84	1,297	2,430	2,643	3,192	5,472
Total non-current assets	566	2,557	11,858	21,573	23,203	32,460	52,458
Total assets	918	3,463	13,851	24,848	26,946	41,358	65,585
Current liabilities							
Borrowings	33	16	593	749	112	12	50
Other	243	738	1,861	3,167	3,539	5,272	8,958
Total current liabilities	276	754	2,454	3,916	3,651	5,284	9,008
Non-current liabilities							
Borrowings	274	1,174	4,891	9,927	7,793	11,327	15,381
Other	16	930	725	1,298	1,039	2,513	8,536
Total non-current liabilities	300	1,350	5,616	11,225	8,832	13,840	23,917
Total liabilities	576	2,104	8,070	15,141	12,483	19,124	32,925
Net assets	342	1,359	5,781	9,707	14,463	22,234	32,660
Shareholders' equity							
Share capital							
Ordinary	32	63	133	134	926	975	4,799
Other	0	0	1,276	1,275	436	1,375	6,570
Revaluation reserve	0	482	1,290	4,262	3,806	3,606	3,143
Profit and loss	69	139	213	2,857	5,171	6,709	11,691
Other reserves	213	501	2,152	452	3,637	8,169	3,676
Minority interests	28	173	717	727	487	1,400	2,781
Total shareholders' equity	342	1,359	5,781	9,707	14,463	22,234	32,660

Consolidated statement of cash flows (summarised)

	FOR THE YEAR ENDED 30 JUNE (A$ MILLIONS)			
	1991	1994	1997	2000
Interest payments	(1,250)	(633)	(807)	(1,127)
Income tax payments	(43)	(23)	(66)	(164)
Cash provided/(used) by operating activity	526	1,387	928	533
Investing and other activity				
Property, plant and equipment	(724)	(446)	(684)	(671)
Investments	(317)	(1,153)	(1,757)	(4,157)
Proceeds from sale of non-current assets	1,090	1,064	562	3,341
Other	(13)	0	408	0
Cash provided/(used) in investing activity	36	(553)	(1,471)	(1,487)
Financing activity				
Issuance of debt	988	1,416	1,655	0
Repayment of debt	(872)	(3,193)	(990)	(1,621)
Issue of shares	0	867	1,307	444
Redemption of shares	(358)	0	(3)	(1,166)
Dividends paid	(50)	(67)	(170)	(236)
Other	(228)	(44)	(65)	(52)
Cash (used)/provided by financing activity	(520)	(1,021)	1,734	(2,631)
Net (decrease)/increase in cash	42	(187)	1,191	(3,585)
Opening cash balance	160	659	2,298	7,483
Exchange movement	0	(39)	127	740
Closing cash balance	202	433	3,616	4,638

Note: No cash flow statements prior to 1991.

Industry sector analysis

	(A$ MILLIONS)					
	1985	1988	1991	1994	1997	2000
Revenues						
Newspapers	1,600	2,569	3,088	2,894	3,158	4,448
Magazines	340	610	2,035	1,654	1,541	1,585
Television	193	564	1,331	2,103	3,700	5,843
Filmed entertainment	0	1,184	2,199	3,093	4,219	6,115
Cable network programming	0	0	0	0	0	2,005
Commercial printing	121	260	0	0	0	0
Book publishing	0	0	1,555	1,597	946	1,634
Other	193	832	762	280	825	813
	2,447	6,019	10,970	11,621	14,389	22,443
Operating profit						
Newspapers	79	479	522	436	610	870
Magazines	55	107	413	339	388	411
Television	9	83	123	466	537	1,120
Filmed entertainment	0	121	211	141	133	188
Cable network programming	0	0	0	0	0	120
Commercial printing	7	22	0	0	0	0
Book publishing	0	0	205	208	16	141
Other	14	218	83	7	(20)	(108)
	164	1,030	1,557	1,597	1,700	2,742
Identifiable assets						
Newspapers	1,327	3,735	7,633	7,301	7,440	7,656
Magazines	866	799	3,578	3,572	3,697	2,518
Television	258	2,660	4,232	6,073	13,462	16,785
Filmed entertainment	0	1,457	2,270	2,660	4,485	7,465
Cable network programming	0	0	0	0	0	7,448
Commercial printing	69	299	0	0	0	0
Book publishing	0	0	2,661	3,027	1,796	2,775
Other	362	1,493	1,475	917	710	2,495
Investments & Corporate	581	3,408	2,999	3,396	9,768	18,444
	3,463	13,851	24,848	26,946	41,358	65,585
USA	1,277	5,197	12,510	13,891	21,085	34,674
UK	854	2,106	5,172	5,193	5,703	7,293
Australia and Pacific Basin	751	3,140	4,167	4,466	4,802	5,174
Investments & Corporate	581	3,408	2,999	3,396	9,768	18,444
	3,463	13,851	24,848	26,946	41,358	65,585
Capital expenditures						
Newspapers	111	245	553	255	102	121
Magazines	15	9	8	10	7	19
Television	6	17	102	101	408	182
Filmed entertainment	0	10	29	14	103	129
Cable network programming	0	0	0	0	0	130
Commercial printing	10	13	0	0	0	0
Book publishing	0	0	30	8	5	10
Other	13	38	32	61	64	80
	155	332	724	449	689	671
USA	24	49	70	171	469	473
UK	91	192	437	79	112	109
Australia and Pacific Basin	40	91	217	199	108	89
	155	332	724	449	689	671

Significant accounting policies

Underlying principles

Financial statements are prepared in accordance with the historical cost convention, except for certain revaluations of property, plant and equipment, publishing rights, titles, television licensees and investments.

Principles of consolidation

The consolidated accounts include the financial statements of the parent entity, The News Corporation Limited, and its controlled entities (the group). They also include the group's portion of the results of associated entities over which it has significant influence.

Valuation of non-current assets

Certain non-current assets are revalued periodically. Revalued assets are shown at their latest valuation. Increments in the value of a class of assets are taken to the asset revaluation reserve.

Publishing rights, titles and television licences

As a creator and distributor of branded information and entertainment copy-rights, the group has significant and growing intangible assets, including free and cable television networks and stations, television licences, sports franchises, entertainment franchises, newspaper mastheads, publishing rights and other copyright products and trademarks. These assets are stated at cost or valuation. No amortisation is provided against these assets since, on the opinion of the directors, the life of publishing rights, titles and television licences is of such duration, and the residual value would be such that the amortisation charge, if any, would not be material.

Developing businesses

Costs incurred in the development of major new activities are capitalised until the operations are commenced on a commercial basis. At that point any readily identifiable intangibles, such as publishing rights, titles and licences are recorded at cost and accounted for in accordance with the relevant accounting policy. Any other costs are amortised over the period in which benefits are expected to be received.

Capitalisation of interest

Interest cost on funds invested in major projects with substantial development and construction phase is recorded as capital cost until production or operations commence. Thereafter, the capitalised interest is amortised over the period in which benefits are expected to be received.

Note: Share capital

Changes in ordinary share capital relate particularly to the following:

  (i) 1988: A one for one bonus issue

 (ii) 1994: A three for one bonus issue

(iii) 2000: Conversion of convertible preference shares issued in 1993 in part to fund the acquisition of STAR Television, and previously reported under other share capital

Significant elements of other share capital include issuance of the following:

  (i) Preferred limited voting ordinary shares: A$767 million (1997), A$6,080 (2000)

 (ii) Cumulative $8^5/8$ per cent guaranteed perpetual preference shares: A$358 million (1994, 1997, 2000)

(iii) Convertible notes: A$1,257 million (1988, 1991)

Note: Investments

Investments as at 30 June 2000 include the following associated entities:

50 per cent National Rugby League, an Australian rugby league football competition

50 per cent Fox Studios Australia, a film production and entertainment facility

50 per cent Stream, an Italian pay-television provider

49.7 per cent Independent Newspapers Ltd, a New Zealand newspaper publisher

49.5 per cent Fox Family Worldwide, a family television programming venture

44 per cent TV Guide Inc., a US print and electronic guidance company

41.7 per cent Queensland Press Ltd, an Australian newspaper publisher

40 per cent Regional Programming Partners, a partnership holding interests in various regional sporting networks and sporting teams and arenas

40 per cent Ventures Arena which also holds interests in sporting arena

37.6 per cent BSkyB, a UK satellite broadcaster

25 per cent FOXTEL, an Australian pay-television operation

APPENDIX 2 THE NEWS CORPORATION LTD: MAJOR COMPETITORS

Time Warner

The origins of Time Warner lie in the 1990 merger of the publishing company Time Inc. with Warner Communications a television, music and cable systems company, which created the largest entertainment group in the world. The new company then acquired Turner Broadcasting, owner of Cable News Network, in 1996.

Time Warner operates in the following business segments:

- Filmed entertainment and television production, with Warner Bros film studios and New Line Cinema.
- Cable television programming and distribution. Time Warner Cable is the second largest cable operator in the US. Time Warner's own cable channels include CNN, TNT, HBO and WB.
- Music, with the Warner Bros, Elektra, Atlantic and Sire record labels.
- Publishing, including *Time Magazine*, *People*, *Fortune*, *Life*, *Entertainment Weekly* and Book-of-the-Month Club.
- Digital media with the establishment in 1999 of Digital Media Fund designed to identify and invest in new Internet-related and digital media business.

While nearly 80 per cent of the company's revenues derive from its home market of the United States, Time Warner has international operations in the United Kingdom, Germany, Japan, Canada and France.

In January 2000 the company announced that it would merge with America Online Inc. (AOL). At the time, this was biggest merger in history, with the two groups initially being valued at US$260 billion (£158 billion). AOL is the largest Internet service provider with 22 million subscribers (including CompuServe). The company also owns Netscape Communications and ICQ Instant Messenger, which are used by 162 million users. AOL offers access to the Internet in 15 countries. One of the first priorities of the merged company will be to use Time Warner's extensive network of cable to deliver high-speed access to AOL users.

Walt Disney

With the 1994 purchase of Capital Cities/ABC, one of the top three US broadcast network and television station groups, The Walt Disney Company transformed itself from a cartoon and theme-park operation into a diversified international entertainment company.

The company now operates in the following business segments:

- Filmed entertainment and television production, with Walt Disney Pictures, Walt Disney Television, Hollywood Pictures, Touchstone and Miramax.
- Broadcasting and cable programming and distribution with the broadcast company ABC, and cable channels ESPN and The Disney Channel.

- Music with Mammouth Records.
- Theme parks and resorts, with Disneyland, Walt Disney World, Disneyland Paris, Disney Vacation Club and Disney Cruise Lines.
- Consumer products, with Disney Stores.
- Internet and direct marketing.

While nearly 85 per cent of its revenues were derived from its home market of the United States, the company also operates in Europe, Asia Pacific, Latin America, and Canada.

Viacom

Originally Viacom was an operator of cable TV systems that had been spun off by CBS. In 1987, in a reverse takeover, the 400-screen Cineplex chain acquired the company. Further acquisitions included the MTV and Nickelodeon cable channels from Warner Communications, Paramount, the movie and publishing conglomerate and the Blockbuster video stores.

In May 2000 the company merged with the network television company CBS and now operates in the following business segments:

- Filmed entertainment and television production with Paramount Pictures and Spelling.
- Broadcasting and cable programming and distribution with CBS, the number one US television network, and cable channels MTV, Nickelodeon, UPN and Showtime.
- Radio broadcasting with Infinity Radio, the number two US station.
- Publishing with Simon & Schuster, Scribner and Pocket.
- Parks and video with Paramount Parks and Blockbuster.

Vivendi Universal

Vivendi Universal was created in June 2000 by the merger of the Canadian company Seagram and the French companies Vivendi and Canal Plus. The new company is headquartered in Paris and led by Vivendi's Jean-Marie Messier as chairman and chief executive. The company initially had combined revenues of US$55 billion.

Seagram is largely known for its drinks business. However, it also encompasses a successful film business, a music business and a series of theme parks contributing approximately 52 per cent of its pre-merger revenues. Vivendi (formerly Générale des Eaux) was originally a French water company that subsequently acquired interests in cable and satellite television transmission, telephones and publishing. Publishing, media and communications currently account for 21 per cent of its pre-merger revenues. Canal Plus is Europe's largest subscription television company.

The new company currently operates in the following business segments:

- Filmed entertainment and television programming with Universal Studios.
- Cable television with Canal Plus.
- Music with MCA, Geffen, Interscope, Polygram, Island, Motown, Mercury, A&M, Def Jam, Decca, Deutche Grammophon.
- Theme parks with Universal theme parks.
- Fruit juices, spirits and wine: with Tropicana, Dole, Seagram's, Chivas Regal, Glenlivet, Martell, Perrier-Jouet and Oddbins wine merchants.
- Environmental business including water distribution, waste management, thermal energy supply, building and heavy public construction projects.

According to the merger document, the aim is to create a 'fully integrated global media and communications company for the wired and wireless world, combining compelling content across the world's most popular genres with an enormous customer and subscriber base in every access format'. Vivendi Universal therefore plans to spin off its environmental businesses and sell the drinks businesses, leaving a business consisting primarily of media and communications businesses.

Sony Corp.

Sony is known to be one of the world's foremost companies in the consumer and industrial electronics business areas. It manufactures audio/video equipment, televisions, information and communication equipment, semiconductors and other electronic components, home video and games systems. However, in 1987 Sony acquired CBS records and in 1989 acquired the Columbia film studios and music business.

The company now operates in the following business segments:

- Insurance with Sony Life Insurance, Sony Finance International.
- Electronics with Sony Handycams, DVD players, CD players, VCRs, Walkmans, stereos, radios, TVs, PCs, cellular phones, videotapes, audiotapes, semiconductors, components, broadcast equipment.
- Games and online with Sony Playstation, Sony Online Entertainment.
- Filmed entertainment, television production and retail with Columbia Pictures, Columbia TriStar TV, Loews Theatres, Sony Theatres and Cineplex Odeon.
- Music with the Columbia, Epic, 550 Music and Sony Classical labels.

Music, motion picture and television business accounted for 17 per cent of fiscal 2000 revenues. The company joined the Japanese satellite consortium SkyPerfecTV!.

The following exhibits give details of the comparative sales (US$ billions) of these companies for the years 1995 to 2000 and comparative stock market data as at 31 October 2000.

Exhibit 1   Comparative sales

	1995	1996	1997	1998	1999	2000
Time Warner	8.1	10.1	13.3	14.6	27.3	N/A
Walt Disney	12.1	18.7	22.5	23.0	23.4	N/A
Viacom	11.7	12.1	13.2	12.1	12.9	N/A
Seagram	5.9	8.9	10.6	8.4	11.4	15.2
Vivendi	20.8	21.4	21.4	27.3	35.2	N/A
Sony	36.5	42.1	51.9	61.9	62.3	61.3

Exhibit 2   Comparative stock market data

	MARKET CAPITALISATION (US$ BILLIONS)	SHARE PRICE (US$)	CHANGE ON YEAR (%)	P/E RATIO
Time Warner	95.4	75.91	+3.7	115.02
Walt Disney	71.5	35.81	+29.5	71.63
Viacom	85.5	56.88	+26.0	N/A
Seagram	N/A	N/A	+13.8	672.31
Vivendi	38.6	68.62	+12.1	29.93
Sony	80.0	87.76	+17.7	383.57
The News Corporation	43.0	10.30	+74.3	65.87

CASE STUDIES

The Royal Bank of Scotland Group

What follows is based on a speech explaining the strategy of The Royal Bank of Scotland Group by Sir George Mathewson, chairman of The Royal Bank of Scotland Group, in September 2000 at the British Academy of Management Conference in Edinburgh. In this speech he set out the group's approach to corporate strategy in an uncertain and changing business environment.

• • •

THE ROYAL BANK OF SCOTLAND GROUP

The history of The Royal Bank of Scotland Group (RBSG) extends from the Industrial Revolution to the Internet age. The Royal Bank of Scotland was founded in 1727 and can claim several innovative UK banking firsts, including overdraft coverage in 1728, direct insurance in the 1980s and the current account mortgage in the 1990s.

In 2000, RBSG purchased London-based NatWest, a bank twice its size, for £20bn. By acquiring NatWest, RBSG successfully completed the largest hostile takeover in financial services. The combined group ranks amongst the top ten of the world's banks by market capitalisation.

The Royal Bank of Scotland Group is now one of Europe's leading financial services groups and has a diversified range of businesses serving personal, business and corporate customers. It ranks first in Corporate Banking, first in Private Banking, first in Offshore Banking and second in Retail Banking in the United Kingdom.

In addition to the full range of banking services under The Royal Bank of Scotland and NatWest brands, the Group also includes other major financial services brands:

- *Lombard*, the UK leader in Asset Finance
- *Coutts*, the UK's premier private bank
- *Direct Line*, the UK market leader in direct motor insurance
- *Citizens Financial Group*, based in the USA and the second largest bank in New England
- *Ulster Bank*, the island of Ireland's third largest bank.

This case was prepared by Professor Gerry Johnson, University of Strathclyde Graduate School of Business based on a speech by Sir George Mathewson, chairman of The Royal Bank of Scotland. It is intended as a basis for class discussion and not as an illustration of either good or bad management practice. Not to be reproduced or quoted without permission.

SIR GEORGE'S SPEECH

When I hear presentations on Group Corporate Strategy, I normally see a Group Vision, various specific objectives, and clear strategies for achieving them. Certainly, it is good to know where you are going, and how you are going to get there. But, is it enough? What are you going to do if the environment changes in the meantime, what are you going to do instead? In short, will the objectives become boundaries and limit the ability of the firm to progress?

Turning to The Royal Bank of Scotland, we do not want our objectives to become boundaries. Nor do we believe that we can predict future changes in the environment. We do not have a Group Vision, in terms of a few simple words. Our Group objectives cannot be set down in terms of market shares or financial profits. Our objective is to continuously create an institution that is capable of delivering ongoing shareholder value – and as such will be capable of surviving and prospering, no matter what the future brings. Corporate strategy must be built around the constant creation of options for future growth. These strategic options will enable us to manage across boundaries, and avoid us creating boundaries for ourselves.

Background

However, before I develop my thesis, I should perhaps say a few words about The Royal Bank of Scotland Group, since I realise that many of you may not know much about us, except that in 1999 we completed a hostile bid for NatWest. In particular, I should explain our credentials to make this presentation on Group Strategy and Strategic Options. I will do this by reviewing our performance over the period from 1992 to 1999 – that is, roughly the period from when there was a substantial management change at the Royal Bank, and I became Chief Executive, until we made the bid for NatWest.

Between 1992 and 1999, we grew our Group income at 17 per cent per annum – more than any other UK bank. The Bank of Scotland and Abbey National also did well. For Barclays and NatWest, income growth was only about the average rate of inflation. *[See Exhibit 1.]*

And we grew our profits by more than any other UK bank. Here I refer to profits before bad debts, because growth in profits after bad debts, for all UK banks, was flattered to a greater or lesser extent by the decline in bad debts, over this period. *[See Exhibit 2.]*

From the end of 1991 until shortly before the bid for NatWest last September, our share price was up from under 200 pence to over 1,200 pence. We outperformed the Index by a considerable margin. *[See Exhibit 3.]*

What were the key reasons for our good performance over the period 1992 to 1999? Certainly, we had some strong strategic themes:

- Focusing on customers, and being willing to adapt our products and services in relation to their changing needs.
- Parenting our businesses – that is, restricting our activities to areas where we had competitive advantage, and could be the best owner.

| Exhibit 1 | Average growth in income 1992–99 % p.a. |

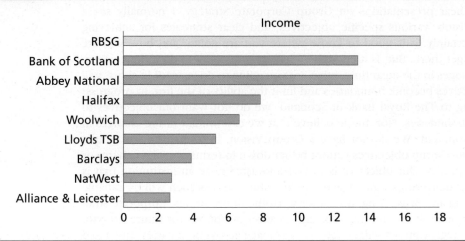

| Exhibit 2 | Average growth in profits 1992–99 % p.a. |

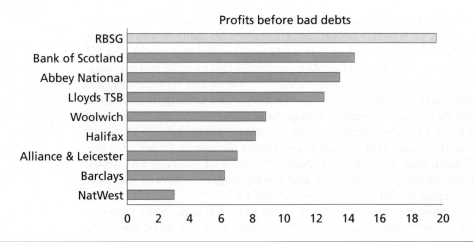

Certainly, we showed strong operational capabilities. We implemented a major business re-engineering programme, which transformed almost every part of our UK banking activities. In the earlier years, we even had a Group Vision – to be the best bank in the UK. This vision was helpful in unifying our corporate efforts, but was sometimes difficult to reconcile with creating value for our shareholders. But many other companies have good visions, strategies and operational capabilities. What additional ingredient did we have? I think it was early recognition of the scope to create additional value through strategic options. Let me give you some examples.

Exhibit 3	RBSG share price, FTSE Bank Sector Index

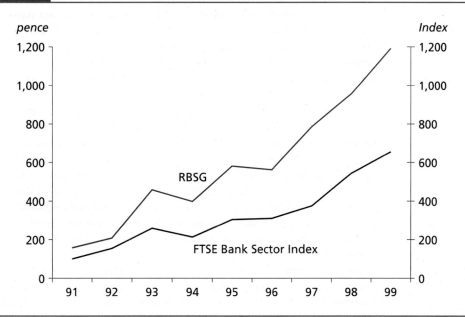

Strategic Options

Firstly, corporate banking. We have maintained a balance between retail banking and corporate banking. Not so long ago, it was suggested that disintermediation by non-banks would lead to a significant decline in corporate banking. The stock market's clear preference for retail banking was shown by the higher price/earnings ratios on retail banks, which only recently reversed. We expanded our commitment to corporate banking by developing a number of specialist corporate banking businesses, such as acquisition finance, structured finance and sophisticated treasury products, to augment our core services in payments, lending and treasury. Our commitment to corporate banking, while some other banks were becoming more cautious, was one principal reason for the strong growth in our profits. More recently, the stock market has become worried about erosion of margins in personal banking, because of intense competition between existing players and new entrants, including Internet banks. While we are still committed to retail banking, we are glad to have a strong corporate bank. Indeed, without it, we would not have had the necessary competences and potential synergies to bid for NatWest.

Secondly, retail banking. In retail banking, we have created strategic options by offering personal financial services under various brands, including our own brands The Royal Bank of Scotland and Direct Line, and joint venture brands Tesco Personal Finance and Virgin Direct Personal Finance; and through various channels: branches, phone and Internet. This approach has enabled us to appeal to various customer groups, and to offer product variants appropriate to the different brands and channels. It gives us considerable flexibility for the future: we are able to respond quickly to changing customer needs.

Initially, our multi-brand, multiple channel strategy was not particularly well received by the City or even by our own staff. City analysts asked why we did not save costs by combining our retail offerings and our staff asked why we allowed our various retail businesses to compete with each other. However, the strategy has proved successful. Between 1992 and 1999 we grew our UK personal customer base from 4 million to 8 million.

Thirdly, Europe. Our approach to Europe was an even more conscious application of strategic options. As a relatively small bank, at the edge of Europe, we recognised that it would be difficult to participate in Europe, as things were. But we saw the importance of European convergence, and wished to retain the option to participate, if at some stage it seemed appropriate for us to do so. In 1988, we formed a strategic alliance with Banco Santander – now BSCH, one of the largest banks in Europe. We took cross-shareholdings and co-operated on some successful joint ventures, and have met regularly to exchange experiences, plans and ideas. This alliance has contributed substantial value to both partners.

The stock market could never understand why we placed so much importance on this relationship, perhaps because many of its true benefits are not tangible. However, the NatWest transaction could not have been carried without both BSCH's goodwill and £1.7 billion investment in us. To my mind, our alliance with Banco Santander is a straightforward example of a low-cost strategic option which has created significant shareholder value.

NatWest

I now return to the acquisition of NatWest. Clearly this was a tough battle. It was a hostile bid for a major UK bank; as I understand it, the largest hostile bid in financial services. It was a bid for a bank more than twice our size; and a bid in competition with Bank of Scotland, which also has an excellent track record.

Strategic options are important in relation to three aspects of this transaction:

- our ability to make a credible bid;
- the way in which we are managing the integration;
- and the benefits we gain from the acquisition of NatWest.

In making the bid for NatWest, our credibility benefited from our ability to exercise a number of strategic options; among them were:

- our ability to demonstrate our own good track record – far better than NatWest's;
- our strong position in corporate banking and treasury activities – important aspects of NatWest's business;
- and our alliance with BSCH, who supported us in the transaction.

In the integration of the two banks, we have combined RBS and NatWest units in a series of customer-facing divisions: Retail Banking, Corporate Banking and Financial Markets, Wealth Management, and so on. And we have established a central Manufacturing division, which supports all our UK banking activities. This approach enables us to accelerate the integration, with minimum impact on customers. However, it also gives us important strategic options for the future:

- It enables each of our businesses to have its own appropriate culture – appropriate for its customers, and appropriate for its competitive environment.

- It enables us to respond quickly and easily to changing customer requirements and market developments.

- It enables us to maximise efficiency in our manufacturing activities – and to consider outsourcing or insourcing of manufacturing activities, where appropriate.

- It positions us well for joint ventures and acquisitions, if and when opportunities arise.

The acquisition of NatWest will also bring many benefits for our shareholders, customers and staff. In the first place, as a result of combining market shares, the combined group will have a very strong position across its core businesses in UK retail banking, corporate banking and treasury. There will also be a degree of added synergistic diversification in banking businesses. For example, we now own Coutts, the leading private bank in the UK, and Ulster Bank, which is the number two bank in Northern Ireland and number three in the Republic of Ireland. However, we sold a number of businesses, such as Gartmore, the fund managers, which were not core to us and which we believed would be worth more to 'better owners'.

Secondly, the transaction will make possible substantial cost savings and income benefits. In our bid document last year, we promised £1.2 billion per annum cost savings over three years, the largest part coming from the elimination of duplication in central functions, processing and technology. We also promised £390 million per annum income benefits – and we said we thought we could do better than this. We were always more excited about the long-term income opportunities than the one-off cost savings.

We continue to feel optimistic about achieving these targets. The synergy benefits I mentioned may seem large – but because of the similarity between the two groups across retail banking and corporate banking, this transaction can deliver more de-duplication cost savings and more overall synergies than any other combination of banks in the UK. For example, Barclays, in buying the Woolwich, is promising synergies of only about £200 million per annum. Diversification, cost savings and revenue growth are also obvious ways in which to increase shareholder value.

But we also saw an opportunity to create additional value in future through having enhanced strategic options. We always saw the bid as creating a company with a wealth of future choices and options.

I could list a number of areas in which the enlarged group has enhanced strategic options, but I shall mention just two:

CASE STUDIES

Exhibit 4	UK banks market capitalisation	
		£BN
1.	HSBC	92.1
2.	**RBSG**	**36.1**
3.	Lloyds TSB	33.8
4.	Barclays	25.7
5.	Abbey National	11.9
6.	Halifax	11.5
7.	Standard Chartered	10.8
8.	Bank of Scotland	7.4
9.	Woolwich	5.5
10.	Alliance & Leicester	2.8

Market capitalisations based on 13 September 2000 share prices.

- Acquisitions: The larger group will be more able than either the Royal Bank or NatWest alone to create value through further acquisitions, through both financial muscle and ability to achieve synergies across a variety of activities.

- Europe: Now that the Royal Bank and BSCH are two of the largest banks in Europe, we obviously have increased potential to do things there together.

The acquisition of NatWest has enabled us to cross an important boundary of size. A year ago our market capitalisation was about £12 billion and our annual profit before tax was around £1.2 billion. We had many good ideas for growing our business, but were sometimes frustrated that we could not implement them – usually because, although they would create value over a period, they would reduce our profits too much in the short term.

Following the acquisition of NatWest, our market capitalisation is now £36 billion. We are the second largest bank in the UK. Only HSBC is larger. *[See Exhibit 4.]*

And we are the fifth largest bank in Europe. We are approximately the same size as Deutsche Bank and Lloyds TSB. We are now a large bank. *[See Exhibit 5.]*

But the objective of the transaction was shareholder value, not size. Size does not in itself necessarily create value, or create strategic options. For us, it is the combination of our financial strength with our diversity and flexibility which gives us so many options to create additional value, no matter what future lies ahead.

From the particular to the general

Now, moving from the particular to the general, the examples which I discussed of the benefits RBSG gained from the acquisition of NatWest illustrate where, for any Group, strategic opportunities fit into a hierarchy of value-creating opportunities.

Exhibit 5	European banks' market capitalisation	
		£BN
1.	HSBC	92.1
2.	ING	44.3
3.	UBS	43.7
4.	Credit Suisse	40.6
5.	**RBSG**	**36.1**
6.	Deutsche Bank	35.7
7.	Lloyds TSB	33.8
8.	**BSCH**	**33.2**
9.	BBVA	33.1
10.	BNP	28.5

Market capitalisations based on 13 September 2000 share prices.

- At the bottom of the hierarchy, we have diversification – aimed at improving the quality of the Group's earnings – that is, reducing their volatility. Diversification will not by itself add to earnings growth – it will produce the weighted average of the growth rates of the two diversified activities. And diversification should not be a reason for retaining businesses which could be sold to a 'better owner'.

- Next, there is the opportunity to improve earnings growth by creating value through synergies between the two diversified activities – for example, by selling the products of one business to the customers of the other.

- Then there could be maximisation of the synergies. In this case, the Group would be the best owner, or best parent, of its subsidiaries: they would clearly be worth more to the Group than to any other owner.

- Lastly, at the top of the hierarchy, there would be the creation of strategic options. For example, ownership by the Group of the two subsidiary businesses might put it in a uniquely competitive position to make further acquisitions in the future – this value does not appear in the analysts' spreadsheets.

We believe that an organisation capable of creating long-term value is not an end point but a dynamic which can only be achieved through constant renewal. Because of this, a corporate strategy of creating ongoing shareholder value through the continuous creation of strategic options brings its own challenges for the business – there is no one goal – no one end point – it is a continuous journey – there is no ultimate arrival – goals such as the achievement of market shares or financial returns are temporary and subordinate goals – contributing to the delivery of shareholder value, but they are only the means to an end – the true objective.

Obviously shareholder value depends on the stock market. We are competing for investors' funds. Nowadays this is almost entirely decided by the investors' views of your prospects for growth – growth is the god – the holy grail. So for an organisation to create ongoing shareholder value, investors must perceive and continue to perceive that the business has growth opportunities.

Exhibit 6	UK banks share prices (1 January 1999 to 13 September 2000)	
RBSG		+41%*
Lloyds TSB		−28%
Barclays		+34%
Halifax		−40%
Abbey National		−35%
Bank of Scotland		−19%
Woolwich		0%
Alliance & Leicester		−41%

* +49% including Additional Value Shares.

They must believe that the organisation has a growth culture and has the ability to keep creating – on an ongoing basis – opportunities for growth. In time, a single focused strategy must run up against market limits or indeed regulatory limits and competition problems unless the stock market sees the market for your product as infinite – as they would currently appear to believe of some technology companies.

Companies with a single focus do not, in general, last as independent entities – unless they are very large whereupon they may continue but create little shareholder value. It is only the ongoing creation of strategic options that can ensure that opportunities for growth will continue to emerge.

I have mentioned the difficulty of communicating an option-creating strategy to a market which has, in the past, put a higher value on focus and clarity. Potential cost-cutting was valued above potential income growth, because it was more tangible. There seems to be an assumed incompatibility between focus on implementation excellence and a strategy of option creation, rather than a recognition of their mutual necessity for long-term survival. I believe some of this follows from the difficulty in valuing future choices and that this presents a challenge to the management theorists that are here today. I am aware of the work that has been recently done on real options and I think that if a method making the value of strategic options more accessible to the market could be developed it could be a significant contribution to communicating value. Although it is clearly difficult to develop a model for the valuation of strategic options, the City may now be showing greater recognition of them than I would have expected, in the valuation of shares in UK banks.

There has been concern about increased competition in retail banking, partly because of the Internet, but there has been greater awareness of the ongoing opportunities in corporate banking.

Over the period from the beginning of 1999 until 12 September 2000, the share prices of the large commercial banks, The Royal Bank of Scotland and Barclays, have both risen by over 30 per cent. The share prices of the retail banks – the converted building societies, Halifax and Abbey National – have fallen by more than 30 per cent. And Lloyds TSB, which is much more retail than corporate, has declined by 28 per cent. *[See Exhibit 6.]*

The stock market does seem to be showing some recognition of the value of strategic options.

In conclusion

In conclusion, following the NatWest acquisition, The Royal Bank of Scotland Group looks to the future with immense confidence. We never did see this acquisition as only a cost-saving opportunity. We will create shareholder value through income growth – not only through the immediate opportunities created by the acquisition but also through the greater range of options we now have for our future development – options in business lines, brands, geographies, acquisitions and so on.

We will not let this acquisition restrict us to a narrow consolidation strategy which must ultimately come to an end. Rather, it opens up a whole new range of added opportunities to create shareholder value. Our ongoing goal is not only to achieve world-class efficiency levels but to maintain an organisation with a range of strategic choices which will ensure continued growth in income and shareholder value.

NOTE TO READERS

On 1 March 2001, The Royal Bank of Scotland Group published its pro-forma results for the year ended 31 December 2000. The highlights are summarised below:

Financial highlights for the year ended 31 December 2000 – pro-forma basis

	31 DECEMBER 2000 £M	31 DECEMBER 1999 £M	INCREASE %
Total income	12,358	11,065	12
Total expenses	6,614	6,563	1
Operating profit before provisions	5,046	3,901	29
Profit before tax, goodwill amortisation and integration costs	4,401	3,359	31
Profit before tax	3,332	2,670	25
Cost: income ratio	53.5%	59.3%	N/A
Adjusted earnings per ordinary share	102.0p	78.3p	30

CASE STUDIES

CRH plc: an evolving strategy

Mike Moroney

CRH, an international building materials group headquartered in Ireland, faced crucial decisions on acquisitions at the end of 1998. This case provides the background to the acquisition prospects and the opportunity to consider the decisions the board should take.

● ● ●

In mid-December 1998, Don Godson, chief executive officer of CRH plc, and his senior management team were faced with an interesting, and potentially highly prospective, acquisition opportunity. Over the previous quarter of a century CRH, one of Ireland's largest companies and a leading international building materials group, had pursued a very successful growth strategy involving the acquisition overseas of numerous medium-sized, largely private businesses. Now, following recent stock market activity, the opportunity had arisen for CRH to purchase Ibstock plc, a quoted leading UK brick manufacturer with operations also in the US which CRH had analysed for some time. Although Godson and his team were of the judgement that the acquisition of Ibstock would be an excellent strategic fit for CRH, the likely purchase price of €550 million would be twice as large as any acquisition previously undertaken by the Group. Moreover, CRH was, at the same time, also evaluating at least one other large-scale purchase opportunity and the potential disposal, on favourable terms, of the Group's UK builders' merchanting subsidiary, Keyline. As part of their deliberations CRH management were aware of the implications that the purchase of Ibstock would have for the Group's carefully crafted and articulated strategy and how it would be perceived, particularly among CRH's loyal shareholder base. Given the dynamic situation in relation to Ibstock's shares, and the imminence of the Christmas holiday period, Godson and his colleagues were of the opinion that, if CRH was to proceed, making a move before Christmas would be the best chance of success. This would involve making a decision, obtaining board approval and executing the transaction within one week.

THE BUILDING MATERIALS INDUSTRY

The construction sector can be divided into two broad parts. Contracting and speculative development involves the physical building process – of houses,

---

Exhibit 1	UK building materials industry

END USE OF MAJOR BUILDING MATERIALS AND PRODUCTS (% *DATA, 1998*)

	NEW WORK				RMI
	RESIDENTIAL	INDUSTRIAL	COMMERCIAL	PUBLIC WORKS	
Materials					
Cement	45	20	19		16
Aggregates	19	9	22	36	14
Readymix	23	11	25	33	8
Heavyside products					
Blocks	65	15	15		5
Bricks	61	15	15		9
Glass	15	5	15		65
Plasterboard	30	10	30		30
Rooftiles	20	5	10		65
Lightside products					
Sanitaryware	23		12		65
Boilers	20		20		60
Radiators	20		20		60

Note: Aggregates comprise crushed rock and sand & gravel.

Source: Warburg Dillon Read.

factories, offices, roads and other infrastructure. Although a potentially lucrative segment, it involves considerable capital investment and a high degree of risk. By contrast, the supply of building materials is more stable. The building materials industry is involved in the manufacture and supply of materials to the construction sector, for use in contracting and other building activity. The industry's major products can be categorised as follows:

- primary materials (cement, aggregates, readymix concrete);
- 'heavyside' products which are used in the earlier stages of the building process (precast concrete and blocks, bricks, glass, plasterboard and roofing products);
- 'lightside' products used in finishing (primarily sanitaryware and heating products);
- merchanting (involving the distribution of products and materials to building contractors).

In terms of product end-use, the building materials industry can be broken down into new work and repair, maintenance and improvement (RMI). New work can be further disaggregated into residential/housing, industrial, commercial and public works (roads and infrastructure) (Exhibit 1). Although the relative importance of building products and their end-use may vary geographically according to economic development and building practice and regulation, the nature of the core products is similar across markets and has not changed significantly over time.

CASE STUDIES

Industry Characteristics

In general, construction (and, by extension, building materials) has been a cyclical, commodity business, characterised in most markets by maturity and fragmentation. In part reflecting the considerable capital investment and risk involved, resulting in the fixed and slow changing nature of supply, construction has always been a highly cyclical activity. As a general comment, industry cycles tend to be longer in duration and larger in amplitude than general economic cycles. However, the timing of cycles has varied between countries. Building materials products are largely commodities, with no proprietary technology and subject to price-based competition.

Construction is an activity that enjoys rapid growth when an economy is modernising and the population is rising, since new building activity is required to support the process of development and expansion. By contrast, once economies attain a steady-state level of economic activity and a stable population (as in the case of most of the western world currently) construction matures. In the major western economies since the 1970s, average growth in construction output has been less than half the rate of economic growth. In addition, by the late 1990s, RMI in such markets accounted for upwards of half total construction output. By contrast, in newly emerging areas of the world (Asia, eastern Europe, Latin America) and in western countries at an earlier stage of economic development (such as Ireland, Finland and Portugal), construction was a booming activity at this time. Such markets were characterised by double-digit growth in output, a high and rising share for construction in GDP (16 per cent in Ireland) and the predominance of new build as opposed to RMI. On the other hand, cyclicality in such markets had tended to be more pronounced.

Traditionally, the construction sector and building materials industry had been highly fragmented. This reflected a number of factors. Building materials and products are, by and large, characterised by a high weight to value ratio. As a result, high transport costs outweigh scale economies and determine the radius of economic activity and, therefore, of competition. In many cases, the effective arena of operation and competition can be one hundred miles or less. In addition, markets had tended to be local in nature due to differences in building regulations and activity, in business practices and in product standards. Finally, success in the business was, in many cases, determined by factors such as personal service, local contacts, close operational control and the ability to react to change. In such circumstances, it is not surprising that there were, in many areas of activity, a large number of small and medium-sized firms, often privately owned and with a sizeable proportion family-run.

Notwithstanding the traditional local nature of the industry, a number of large, international building materials companies had emerged over time. Such companies typically used the base of a dominant local market position and/or product competence as a springboard to expand into other regions and areas of activity. Chief among such companies in 1998 were Holderbank (Switzerland, cement), Lafarge (France, cement), Blue Circle (UK, cement) and CRH (Ireland, heavyside materials and products).

CRH: BACKGROUND AND HISTORY

By 1998, CRH enjoyed an established position as a leading international building materials group. Headquartered in Dublin, Ireland, the Group manufactured and supplied a broad range of products for the construction industry in the areas of primary materials (cement, aggregates, asphalt and surfacing, readymix, lime and magnesia), building products (concrete, bricks, insulation, glass and security products) and distribution (builders' merchants and DIY stores). Employing 30,000 people, CRH operated from more than 1,150 locations through over 100 local companies in 12 countries on three continents. The Group enjoyed a major presence in mature markets in Europe and North America and a growing foothold in emerging regions, including Poland and Argentina. Since its formation in 1970, CRH had delivered a consistently strong and superior track record of performance, with compound total shareholder return of around 22 per cent per annum, well in excess of its industry peers internationally. At year-end, CRH had a stock market capitalisation of €5.7 billion, making it the fourth largest company on the Irish stock exchange and the fifth largest building materials company in the world, by value.

History, growth and development

CRH's origins as a Group date from 1970. In that year, Roadstone/Wood, an Irish building products company, launched a bid for Irish Cement. When Readymix plc, a large UK building materials group, launched a counter-bid, the two Irish groups agreed to merge. The new entity was named Cement Roadstone Holdings, which was subsequently abbreviated to CRH. At the time, Group revenue was IR£21 million (€26.7 million) and pre-tax profits were IR£2 million (€2.5 million), 99 per cent of which was generated in Ireland.

In the period from formation through December 1998, CRH had four CEOs: Tom Roche (1970–July 1974), Jim Culliton (July 1974–January 1988), Tony Barry (January 1988–October 1994) and Don Godson (since October 1994). Although part of a clear chain of succession within a consistent policy framework, each CEO had his particular style and left his own legacy on the Group. During the Roche era, the newly merged group was put on a sound footing and the foundations for future success laid down. Jim Culliton enjoyed the longest tenure and during his regime the Group advanced strongly, capitalising on a boom in Irish construction during the 1970s and embarking in earnest on the acquisition-led expansion overseas that was to remain a central feature of CRH. The Barry stewardship was characterised by consolidating and building on previous success and by a move into several new product areas and regions, which by 1998 accounted for a significant proportion of Group turnover and profits. Finally, under Don Godson CRH continued to enjoy considerable success on the back of an increased level of acquisition activity, particularly in the US. At the same time, Godson led the move towards a greater articulation of strategy and a more product (as opposed to geographic) focused organisation structure.

In broad terms, the growth and development of CRH can be broken down into two periods: from formation to the late 1970s and since then. During the 1970s, Irish construction enjoyed a boom brought about by a young and rising population and the continuation of the modernisation of the economy that had commenced in the late 1950s. The newly merged CRH capitalised on this favourable environment by virtue of its vertically integrated and leading or dominant positions in virtually all areas of heavyside building materials, from cement through aggregates and road surfacing to concrete products. This gave the Group exposure to all areas of construction output: housing, commercial, industrial and public works.

In the late 1970s CRH embarked on a deliberate and major strategy of overseas expansion by acquisition. This was in part prompted by the view that it would be unwise for the Group to be almost totally reliant on the Irish market. As a general comment, CRH's growth overseas was concentrated on areas in which the Group operated in Ireland – heavyside building materials and products. Early merchanting acquisitions in the UK and the Netherlands were augmented by purchases in other product areas. The Group entered the Catalan region of Spain in the area of concrete products and aggregates in 1987 and benefited significantly in the run-up to the Barcelona Olympics. Positions in other European countries such as Germany, France, Belgium and Portugal followed during the 1990s. By far the greatest overseas success for CRH was the US. In 1977, Don Godson went to the States with 'a telephone and a cheque book'. By 1998, CRH had over 500 locations there in five major product areas, accounting for over half Group turnover and profits. In the mid-1990s, CRH took its first steps in emerging markets, acquiring a presence in clay products and aggregates in Argentina and in cement, aggregates and concrete products in Poland. Once they had attained critical mass, countries were operated on a stand-alone basis, headed by a country manager (or regional managers, in the case of the US).

On the other hand, CRH also expanded in a limited, but highly rewarding, way into new product areas. The purchases of Van Neerbos in the Netherlands in 1973 and of the Henderson chain in the UK in 1978 marked the Group's entry into merchanting. Security fencing in the Netherlands was added in 1986. Clay brick products followed, through the acquisition of Ormonde Brick in Ireland in 1988 and Kleiwarenfabriek in the Netherlands the following year. Finally, CRH entered glass fabrication in the US around 1990, a business which was subsequently built up substantially through add-on acquisitions.

CRH's expansion had been particularly strong in the period since the early 1990s. As late as the end of 1994, CRH had a total of 686 locations in eight countries. In the following four years, CRH added 487 new locations (an increase of 71 per cent) primarily as a result of acquisitions. The bulk of these new locations (315, or two-thirds) were added in the US, while new markets were entered in Belgium, Canada, Portugal and Poland. The latter two countries represented a deliberate foray by the Group into more prospective peripheral and emerging markets and built on the position established with the 1994 acquisition of CCN, a major producer of clay products in Argentina. While no new product areas were added to the 14 existing in 1994, the number of merhanting branches and DIY stores more than doubled over the

1994–98 period, while significant increases were recorded in aggregates and concrete products.

In terms of contribution, acquisition-led expansion and organic growth in the period 1994 to 1998 resulted in an increase of almost two and a half times in both Group revenue and earnings per share (EPS) (based on broker forecasts for the latter year). There were two major contributors to this exceptional level of growth. Firstly, Ireland enjoyed a boom in construction output (up two-thirds between 1994 and 1998). The impact of this increased volume on a largely fixed investment and cost base had raised Irish trading profits by a factor of three over the period. More significantly, however, the increased scale and scope of activities in the US, supported by a favourable economic and construction climate, boosted both revenue and trading profits sevenfold over the same four-year period.

CRH AS AT THE END OF 1998

Strategy

CRH's growth and development was based on a clear, explicit and unambiguous strategy. Although it had evolved and had been modified, the Group's strategic direction had remained substantively intact and consistent since CRH's first push into overseas markets in the late 1970s. Over time, the broad thrusts of this strategy had become progressively more articulated and refined, particularly since the accession of Don Godson to CEO in late 1994.

CRH's statement of strategy contained two main elements, which were outlined in full in the Group's 1997 annual report and in company documents. Firstly, CRH expressed its strategic vision to be 'an international leader in building materials, products and distribution, delivering sustained growth and superior shareholder value'. Secondly, this vision was underpinned and its achievement made possible by ten key drivers of strategy (Exhibit 2).

In summary, the core of the Group's strategy involved a focus on growth across the global building and construction industry to deliver consistently superior long-term returns to shareholders. The key to achieving this was a continuous flow of value-added acquisitions of mid-sized companies enjoying leadership positions in their markets. This was augmented by substantial post-acquisition improvement in performance using the products, management and resources of the Group. Strategy occurred within a framework of balanced product, geographic and sectoral spread. It was based, moreover, upon a strategic architecture comprising a federally devolved structure, a healthy mix and depth of management, strong corporate values, a focus on performance measurement and conservative and highly cash-generative financial management.

Products and markets

By the end of 1998, CRH had accumulated a formidable portfolio of products and markets, with 1,173 separate locations in 14 product areas (arranged into

Exhibit 2	CRH drivers of strategy

1 **Growth platforms:** a presence across the building and construction industry supply chain, from the manufacture of primary materials and building products to distribution in many countries, creates new platforms for future growth.

2 **Devolved development:** CRH encourages local entrepreneurship, through development teams that generate a continuous flow of value-adding mid-sized acquisitions and capital projects.

3 **Leadership positions:** are patiently built by paying fair prices for good companies through negotiated deals and then effectively integrating and developing these acquisitions.

4 **Unique balance:** across regions, products and all building and construction sectors helps smooth the effects of industry and economic cycles.

5 **Business builders:** CRH is an industry owner, not a trader in businesses. As a building materials industry specialist it can bring products, management and financial resources to grow the businesses it acquires.

6 **People:** a healthy mix and depth of management in core businesses keeps the organisation fresh and vital: owner-entrepreneurs who join with their companies, internally developed managers and highly qualified development professionals.

7 **Federal group:** people and companies share a common purpose and set of values, with dual citizenship and responsibilities as members of CRH and of their own local companies.

8 **Measurement:** the communication of best practice and innovative new financial performance measures throughout the Group influence behaviour.

9 **Financial strength:** conservative accounting, a strong balance sheet, a low tax charge and healthy cash flow enable the Group to avail of its many development opportunities.

10 **Total shareholder return:** is a key overall objective for the Group which focuses efforts on enhancing shareholder value. CRH has consistently delivered superior long-term returns and has the strategy, structure, people and resources to ensure continued growth.

Source: CRH annual report 1997.

three main product groups) spread across 12 different countries on three continents (Exhibits 3 and 4).

Geographically, Ireland and the US were the Group's main markets in terms of the number of operations, scope of activities and financial performance. Collectively, mainland Europe represented an important arena of activity, although no individual country (with the exception of Holland) was major in Group terms. While the UK was a significant market for CRH with regard to the number of operations and revenue, profitability had remained subdued in the light of the sluggish state of construction following the severe sector downturn of the early 1990s. Finally, although their contribution was small in 1998, emerging markets were seen to be an important element of future growth.

In product terms, merchanting and DIY accounted for around one-third of Group revenue, but less than half this proportion of trading profits, reflecting the relatively low margins available in distribution (as opposed to extraction or manufacturing). On a volume basis, aggregates were the largest single product area, by some distance. Concrete products (precast, blocks, pavers and rooftiles), road surfacing, readymix and glass fabrication were also significant areas of activity. Although cement accounted for a relatively small volume of

Exhibit 3   CRH: Products and markets at end 1998

	NUMBER OF OPERATIONS/LOCATIONS												PRODUCTION VOLUMES P.A.			
	US	CANADA	ARGENTINA	IRELAND	UK	FRANCE	PORTUGAL	SPAIN	BELGIUM	NETHERLANDS	GERMANY	POLAND	THE AMERICAS	EUROPE MATERIALS	EUROPE PRODUCTS & DISTRIBUTION	TOTAL
Materials																
Cement[1]	141			2								2		5.1		5.1
Aggregates[1]	112		2	68	12			5				2	62.5	28.1		90.6
Asphalt/Surfacing[1]				22	6								15.9	2.1		18.0
Readymix Concrete[2]	66			42	13			57				6	2.6	4.4		7.0
Lime[1]				22	1									0.5		0.5
Seawater Magnesia[1]				1										0.1		0.1
Building Products																
Precast Concrete[1]	38	1		4	3	2		14	5	5		3	1.2	0.6	1.1	2.9
Blocks & Rooftiles[1]	33	6		27	12	2		9	5	16		2	4.7	2.9	2.9	10.5
Bricks & Tiles[1]			2	1						5	8	1	0.3	0.1	0.5	0.9
Insulation[2]				2	4				1	1	3				0.9	0.9
Security[3]					6	1			1	4	3				1.1	1.1
Glass[4]	26	6							1	2	4		10.2		0.4	10.6
Distribution																
DIY Stores[5]										43					43	43
Builders Merchants[6]	88				103	23	9			47		9	88		188	276

Notes: 1. Million tonnes   2. Million cubic metres   3. Million lineal metres   4. Million square metres   5. Number of stores   6. Number of branches.

Source: CRH.

Exhibit 4	CRH: Product/market financials

Financials by geographic market

	1998 (forecast)		1997	
	€M	% OF TOTAL	€M	% OF TOTAL
Revenue				
Republic of Ireland	532	10.6	484	11.4
Britain & Northern Ireland	774	15.4	673	15.9
Mainland Europe	1,105	22.1	986	23.3
The Americas	2,600	51.9	2,091	49.4
Group Total	**5,011**	**100.0**	**4,234**	**100.0**
Trading Profit				
Republic of Ireland	100	22.8	91	25.4
Britain & Northern Ireland	34	7.8	25	7.1
Mainland Europe	75	17.1	70	19.4
The Americas	229	52.3	172	48.1
Group Total	**438**	**100.0**	**358**	**100.0**

Note: Revenue and trading profit are by destination and include share of joint ventures.

Source: CRH, Goodbody Stockbrokers.

Financials by sector

	1998 (forecast)		1997	
	€M	% OF TOTAL	€M	% OF TOTAL
Revenue				
Building Materials	3,458	69.0	2,861	67.6
Merchanting & DIY	1,553	31.0	1,373	32.4
Group Total	**5,011**	**100.0**	**4,234**	**100.0**
Trading Profit				
Building Materials	385	87.8	307	85.8
Merchanting & DIY	53	12.2	51	14.2
Group Total	**438**	**100.0**	**358**	**100.0**

Source: CRH, Goodbody Stockbrokers.

Financials by product group

	1998 (forecast)		1997	
	€M	% OF TOTAL	€M	% OF TOTAL
Revenue				
Europe Materials	938	18.7	816	19.3
Europe Products & Distribution	1,473	29.4	1,327	31.4
The Americas	2,600	51.9	2,091	49.4
Group Total	**5,011**	**100.0**	**4,234**	**100.0**
Trading Profit				
Europe Materials	129	29.4	109	30.4
Europe Products & Distribution	80	18.3	77	21.5
The Americas	229	52.3	172	48.1
Group Total	**438**	**100.0**	**358**	**100.0**

Source: CRH, Goodbody Stockbrokers.

Exhibit 4 Continued

Financials by product end-use and product group (1998 estimated)

	EUROPE MATERIALS €M	EUROPE PRODUCTS & DISTRIBUTION €M	THE AMERICAS €M	CRH €M
Revenue				
Infrastructure	206	147	1,040	1,393
% of total	*22*	*10*	*40*	*28*
Non-residential	347	442	780	1,569
% of total	*37*	*30*	*30*	*31*
Residential	385	884	780	2,049
% of total	*41*	*60*	*30*	*41*
Group Total	**938**	**1,473**	**2,600**	**5,011**

Source: CRH, Goodbody Stockbrokers.

output, its contribution in financial terms was much more substantial. This reflected the high intrinsic value of the product and CRH's dominant position in the buoyant Irish market, where the Group enjoyed a market share of the order of 60 per cent on the total island.

There were two notable characteristics of CRH's product/market portfolio. The first was leadership. In virtually every area of activity, the Group benefited from clear positions of leadership and, in certain cases, dominance (Exhibit 5). For the most part, CRH's leadership was not at national or country level, the major exception being Ireland and, to a lesser extent, the US and the Netherlands for certain product areas. Reflecting the fragmented nature of the industry, the Group focused on securing and maintaining leading positions in local or regional markets and in product segments or niches.

Exhibit 5 CRH: Market leadership positions

1. Europe Materials product group

PRODUCTS	PRESENCE	MARKET POSITION
Materials		
Cement	Ireland, Poland	No.1 producer in Ireland No.3 producer in Poland
Aggregates	Ireland, Poland, Spain	No.1 producer in Ireland
Asphalt	Ireland	No.1 producer
Readymixed concrete	Ireland, Poland, Spain	No.1 producer in Ireland Leader in Catalonia, Spain
Agricultural & Chemical Lime	Ireland	No.1 Producer
Building Products		
Concrete blocks, pavers, rooftiles	Ireland, Spain	No.1 block and rooftile producer in Ireland
Clay bricks	Ireland	No.1 producer

Exhibit 5	*Continued*

2. Europe Products & Distribution product group

PRODUCTS	PRESENCE	MARKET POSITION
Building Products		
Concrete blocks & pavers	Belgium, France, Holland, UK	No.1 patio tiles in Belgium No.1 paving products in Holland No.1 architecture masonry in UK
Precast concrete products	Belgium, France, Holland	No.2 precast flooring in Holland
Clay bricks & rooftiles	Germany, Holland, Poland, UK	No.1 clay pavers in Germany No.1 quality brick in Holland Joint No.1 facing bricks in UK
Security gates & fencing	Belgium, Germany, France, Holland, UK	No.1 security fencing in Europe
Glass fabrication, rooflights	Belgium, Germany, Holland	No.1 rooflights & ventilation in Holland
Insulation products	Belgium, Ireland, Holland, UK	No.1 PU insulation in Benelux No.1 EPS insulation in Ireland No.1 EPS insulation in UK
Distribution		
Builders merchants	France, Holland, Poland, UK	No.2 merchant in Ile de France No.1 roofing products in Holland No.1 ironmongery in Holland Top 5 builders merchant in UK
DIY stores	Holland, Portugal	Part of leading chain in Holland Joint No.1 DIY in Portugal

3. The Americas product group

PRODUCTS	PRESENCE	MARKET POSITION
Materials		
Aggregates	US	No.5 national aggregate producer No.1 materials producer in north-east, inter-mountain & northwest
Asphalt and surfacing	US	No.2 producer
Readymixed concrete	US	Top 10 producer
Building Products		
Precast concrete	US, Canada	No.1 US producer
Concrete masonry, pavers, rooftiles	US, Canada	No.1 US masonry and paving No.1 Canadian producer paving
Clay bricks, pavers, tiles	US, Argentina	No.1 northeast US bricks No.1 Argentina rooftiles No.3 Argentina wall & floor tiles
Glass fabrication	US, Canada	No.1 US custom tempered glass
Distribution		
Roofing, siding and related products	US	No.3 distributor

Source: CRH.

The other noteworthy aspect of CRH's activities was its balance. The Group was characterised by product, geographic and sectoral balance, which had been deliberately nurtured and developed during its expansion overseas since the late 1970s. Although CRH's products were almost entirely heavyside, this reflected the Group's origins, resource base and competences. Within this, however, CRH had a broad spread across materials, building products and merchanting. The Group's balance yielded significant benefits. CRH's global range insulated it from exogenous shocks in different parts of the world. Its heavyside product spread served to balance the investment intensity of its various activities. By end-use, CRH maintained an equilibrium between new build and RMI and among residential, commercial, industrial and infrastructural activities. This enabled the Group to weather periods of high interest rates and oversupply of commercial property, which had been features of many of CRH's markets in the late 1980s through the mid-1990s. CRH's balance and spread of activities was unique among its peers (Exhibit 6).

Acquisitions

Acquisitions (and their subsequent value-enhancing integration into the Group) were the primary engine of growth and success for CRH. There was a strong correlation between spending on acquisitions and growth in EPS (Exhibit 7). In the six years to December 1998, CRH had spent in excess of €1.5 billion on acquisitions and investments. The financial contribution was no less significant, with over half Group revenue growth in recent years accruing from acquisitions.

CRH's acquisition programme was based on a well-honed formula, the primary elements of which were as follows:

- Target medium-sized companies, which tended to be predominantly privately owned and many of which were family-run. In 1997 and up to December 1998, the average purchase price was in the region of €10 million.

- Assess the suitability and cultural fit of businesses prior to purchase, usually involving a long courtship.

- Acquire firms which are market leaders, are well run and, in most cases, are an add-on to one or more existing Group businesses.

- Conclude agreed deals on favourable terms. On the one hand, this meant no hostile takeovers, no auctions and no overpaying. On the other hand, in emerging regions and in new product areas, deals were often structured on the basis of low initial ownership stakes, incorporating options to increase shareholdings at minimum additional cost.

- As far as possible, retain owner-vendors and existing management in the acquired businesses.

To implement its acquisition programme, CRH had 14 development teams, spread across the Group in different product areas. This approach ensured a steady stream of purchases of well-run businesses with strong market positions acquired at prices representing low multiples of current profits. However, this

| Exhibit 6 | Comparative data: CRH vs. major UK heavyside building materials companies |

(Companies for which heavyside is the main activity or is large in absolute terms)

Geographic analysis of operating profits: 1998 (estimate) *(% data)*

Company	UK	NORTH AMERICA	GERMANY	FRANCE	HOLLAND	SPAIN	ITALY	AUSTRIA	IRELAND	OTHER
Aggregate Ind.	60	40								
Blue Circle	33	33	3	4			3			24
Hanson	51	46			3					
Ibstock	68	23								9
RMC	26	12	37	3	3	1		4	4	9
Rugby	43	29			9					20
Tarmac	77	16		2						5
CRH	8	53	2		10	2			23	2

Source: CRH, Warburg Dillon Read.

Product analysis of revenue: 1998 (estimate) *(% data)*

Company	HEAVYSIDE	LIGHTSIDE	NEW BUILD	RMI	CEMENT & LIME	AGGREGATES & READYMIX	CONCRETE PRODUCTS	BRICKS	MERCHANTING & DIY	OTHER
Aggregate Ind.	100		80	20		93	7			
Blue Circle	48	52	65	35	76					24
Hanson	100		75	25		84		16		
Ibstock	100		90	10				97		3
RMC	70	30	80	20	34	58				8
Rugby	40	60	55	45	57					43
Tarmac	100		85	15		69	11			20
CRH	100		N/A	N/A	3	53	10	1	15	18

Note: CRH product estimates are based on production volumes.

Source: CRH, Warburg Dillon Read.

level of purchases did not fully reflect CRH's acquisition activity. In many cases, CRH walked away from deals, either because the timing was not right, the required level of suitability and cultural fit did not exist, or because the asking price was too high. It was not unknown for acquisitions to represent the culmination of several years of effort and relationship. At any given time, therefore, the number of potential deals under consideration was well in excess of those actually consummated. Moreover, entire Group management, and not just the development teams, was focused on the acquisition process.

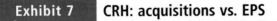

| Exhibit 7 | CRH: acquisitions vs. EPS |

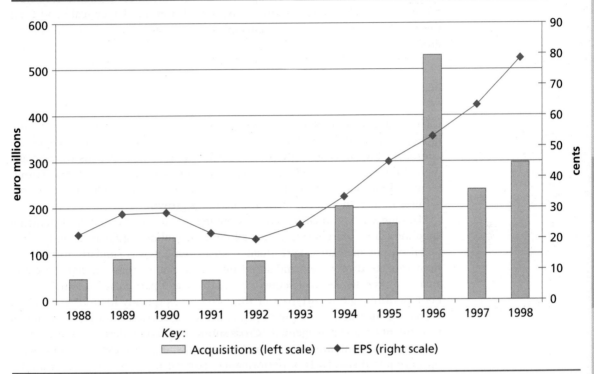

Key:

☐ Acquisitions (left scale) ◆ EPS (right scale)

Source: CRH.

A large proportion of the time of local, regional, product group and corporate management was consumed in finding, negotiating, completing and integrating acquisitions.

Integration of acquired businesses

CRH devoted considerable time and effort and resources into the integration of newly purchased businesses into the Group, a process that was facilitated by the frequent retention of vendors of firms. In monetary terms, CRH's integration effort was reflected in capital expenditure of €1 for every €2 of acquisition spend, on average. As a result, CRH benefited from a substantial and rapid uplift in the returns generated by these businesses, much of it occurring the first 12 to 18 months after purchase.

Apart from selective and targeted capital investment, CRH employed a range of approaches to boost the profitability of acquired entities. Almost immediately upon purchase, the process of co-ordinating and integrating businesses into existing Group operations, processes and systems was put in train. Opportunities for synergies, in revenue and especially in efficiency terms, were identified and exploited. Product transfers were effected. Formal programmes of benchmarking and best practice exchange were put in place. To facilitate

CASE STUDIES

these processes and ensure cultural integration, managers were rotated between entities and established operations were assigned as mentors to new businesses. Finally, acquired entities benefited from the larger scale and from the planning and control mechanisms of being part of a large multinational group.

Management of operations

CRH's management of existing operations was no less rigorous than, and indeed formed the template for, the integration of acquired businesses. In approach, CRH was strongly performance-oriented, with a focus on management by results, to which incentives were closely tied. Indeed, the Group identified measurement as a driver of strategy in its own right and as a contributor to margin improvement and earnings growth.

Planning was a formalised and deeply ingrained activity. Standard performance indicators were specified for all entities, embracing financial and operational output measures. Performance measurement was similarly formal and rigorous, based on timely and sophisticated central systems for reporting and analysis of results. As a consequence, control was a particular strength of CRH. Poor performance in any part of the Group was quickly identified, enabling corrective measures to be put in place, involving revised strategy, incremental investment or new management. Cross-subsidisation of underperforming operations was not contemplated. In the final analysis, if a business did not measure up to required standards of performance, particularly in a new area or a joint venture situation, CRH had no hesitation in divesting it. Often, this was accomplished on favourable financial terms.

This mode of management underpinned the Group's approach to organic growth, which was based on continuous improvement of existing operations. Products and processes were continually evaluated and re-engineered to yield higher returns, primarily through greater efficiencies, but also involving higher volumes where market conditions were favourable. This was achieved through an ongoing programme of development investment, incorporating new plant, capacity extensions and major plant upgrades. For example, during 1998 Marlux (the Group's high-quality concrete flags manufacturer in Belgium) successfully commissioned a new state-of-the-art production line which set new standards for productivity, quality and safety. A further example in 1998 was the large-scale, replacement concrete block factory outside Dublin for Roadstone with an annual capacity of 30 million 100 mm solid concrete blocks. In the eleven years 1988–98, CRH spent over €1 billion on capital investment of this nature.

Management and human resources

Since its inception in 1970, CRH had enjoyed stability and continuity of management. The chairman and five serving executive directors as of 1998 (CEO, finance director and managers of the three product groups) had all joined CRH at or before formation and had spent virtually their entire careers working for the Group. Together they had a wide variety of experience at different levels and in different areas of the Group totalling almost 200 years. With the exception of Harry Sheridan, the finance director, all had a scientific or engineering background, although in most cases their technical credentials were supplemented by formal postgraduate business education. Senior management was entirely Irish by nationality. At the level below senior management, however, a number of managers of either product areas or geographic regions were, by 1998, drawn from various countries, reflecting the geographic expansion of CRH's activities over the preceding 20 years.

CRH regarded its people, both managers and employees, as a strength (and a driver of strategy). The Group's managers were drawn from three areas: owner-entrepreneurs who joined with their companies, internally developed managers and highly qualified development professionals. CRH saw the depth and mix provided by these different backgrounds as an advantage and a source of vitality. Whatever the mode of entry into the Group, CRH sought similar characteristics in its management recruitment. In addition to the requisite skills and/or business potential (in relation to acquisitions), aspiring CRH managers were expected to be self-starters and team players.

CRH's development and deployment of managers was consistent with its overall management philosophy. Managers were rotated frequently across product areas and locations to broaden their experience base. Development was similarly designed to broaden perspectives and was largely 'hands-on', through early operational and profit responsibility. (The 14 development teams were viewed as a rich source of potential future line mangers). Of the Group's 30,000 employees, only around 50 worked in the Group's headquarters in Dublin: the remainder were directly employed in the Group's numerous operations. Promotion was almost entirely from within the existing management pool, the Group's rapid expansion having provided many opportunities for advancement. In common with their more senior colleagues, most managers spent long careers with CRH and turnover was low.

Structure (Exhibit 8)

CRH had always operated a federal structure, consisting of a small central headquarters and local entities with devolved operational responsibility and decision making. CRH identified this structure as being one of the ten drivers of strategy for the Group. Although a constant feature of CRH's organisation over time, the nature of the federal structure had changed over time. Until the late 1970s, when the Group's activities were largely confined to Ireland, CRH operated as effectively a single-country entity with direct contact between senior corporate management and the managers of the various Irish product-based profit centres. This changed when the process of international expansion became established and CRH evolved into a multinational group. The structure became geographically based, with country managers (regional managers in the case of the US) having management and operational responsibility for whatever product areas were in their remit.

| Exhibit 8 | **CRH organisation chart December 1998** |

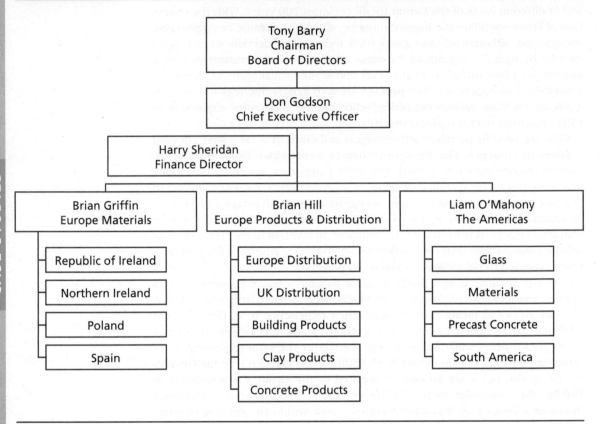

A further change took place in two stages in the 1990s to a broadly product-based structure. In 1991, CRH reorganised its US operations into four major product areas: materials, precast, architectural products, glass. (Distribution was added as a separate product area in 1996). Each product area was provided with dedicated development resources to provide a new stimulus for successful growth. In 1998, the outstanding performance of the US had indicated the benefits of this approach and a similar reorganisation was put in place in Europe. The new structure comprised two groups of comparable size. These were a Materials Group, consisting of primary materials and related products and located in Ireland, Spain and Poland, and a Building Products and Distribution Group, with operations in the Benelux, Britain, Germany, France, Portugal and Ireland (Exhibit 8). Unlike in the Americas, however, a country structure was retained within the Materials division. The objectives of the European product-based reorganisation were: to intensify the focus for business development, resulting in greater acquisition, investment and capital project activity; to facilitate the sharing of experiences and best practices; to create opportunities for managers to broaden their experiences across national frontiers.

Within CRH's structure, the corporate centre fulfilled two fundamental roles (in addition to providing central support services such as accounting, treasury, legal and public and investor relations). Firstly, headquarters performed the traditional evaluation and control function, based around policies and procedures, largely (although not exclusively) financial performance measures and resource allocation. Secondly, since the formation of the Group, senior management determined strategy. The centre also provided the framework for operational behaviour by clearly articulating CRH's vision and strategy drivers, by nurturing and developing a strong corporate culture and by its decisions in relation to the deployment and promotion of managers. In latter times, the centre was facilitated by the product groups, which by 1998 had developed specific operational measures of performance that were standardised within product groups.

Culture

Notwithstanding the fact that it was both geographically dispersed and operated across 14 separate product areas, CRH had a robust corporate culture. The 'federal group' strategy driver stated that, within the Group, 'people and companies share a common purpose and set of values, with dual citizenship and responsibilities as members of CRH and of their own local companies'.

CRH operated a number of mechanisms to give effect to this aspiration. The articulation of CRH's vision and strategy drivers was an expression of the core values of the Group and was widely disseminated throughout the organisation. Activities such as regular manager rotation and formal best practice exchange and benchmarking programmes were operational manifestations of corporate values and provided fora for interaction. Important vehicles for senior managers were the gathering in Dublin each May for the Group's AGM and the annual strategic corporate seminar, also held in Ireland. This event provided the top 100 managers at CRH with the opportunity to get to know one another better and to get together and debate strategy, based around a particular theme to which the seminar was dedicated. Topics debated during the 1990s included: customer service, the acquisition process, Group IT strategy, human resources planning and, most recently, continuous improvement – best practice. In addition, best practice and benchmarking training sessions were regularly held at product group level, facilitated by technical advisers and co-ordinated from the centre. Finally, more subtle mechanisms also existed, such as leading by example and clear norms of acceptable behaviour.

Finances

Since formation, CRH had delivered strong year-by-year financial performance. Between 1970 and 1998, compound total annual shareholder return was almost 22 per cent. Based on broker forecasts of 77.2 cents for 1998 (which were likely, on past evidence, to be exceeded), earnings per share (EPS) had grown by an average of 12.6 per cent p.a. since 1988 and by 26.1 per cent p.a.

Exhibit 9	CRH: Five-year financial summary

	1994 €M	1995 €M	1996 €M	1997 €M	1998F €M
Profit & loss					
Revenue	2,193	2,520	3,354	4,234	5,011
Trading profit	173	225	284	358	438
Net interest expense	−23	−19	−24	−32	−34
Share of joint ventures	−2	−2	−4	−4	−8
Profit before taxation	**148**	**204**	**256**	**322**	**396**
Taxation	−27	−42	−58	−76	−95
Profit after taxation	121	162	198	246	301
Earnings per share (cents)	**33.7**	**45.2**	**53.4**	**63.8**	**77.2**
Dividend per share (cents)	10.3	11.6	13.0	14.9	17.1
Cash flow per share (cents)	53.9	68.0	81.7	97.6	120.9
Key financial indicators					
Net cash/(debt)	30	(189)	(442)	(465)	(411)
Debt to equity ratio (%)	21.7	21.4	40.9	34.9	25.9
Interest cover (times)	6.8	9.0	10.3	9.9	10.4
Dividend cover (times)	3.3	3.9	4.0	4.3	4.7
Tax rate (%)	18.7	20.5	22.8	23.5	24.5
Return on average capital employed (%)	18.2	17.2	16.9	16.9	18.0
Return on average equity (%)	15.8	14.9	15.0	15.5	16.0

Note: Revenue and trading profit include share of joint ventures. Figures for 1998 are forecast values.

Source: CRH, Goodbody Stockbrokers.

since the low point of 1993 (Exhibit 9). 1998 would also represent the 16th consecutive year of higher dividends for the Group, with an increase of 15 per cent forecast in the dividend per share. Equally impressive was the consistency of the Group's performance, in an industry with notorious volatility and pronounced cyclicality. (CRH had only experienced two relatively short periods of moderately declining EPS, in the early 1980s and early 1990s.) In addition to the outstanding nature of its absolute performance, CRH's returns were superior to those of its industry peers internationally, both in terms of level and constancy (Exhibit 10).

CRH was noted for its financial management, with a strong focus on return on capital a particular hallmark. The Group's approach to accounting and financial matters was characterised as diligent, conservative and prudent. This was represented in statistics such as a debt/equity ratio of between one-quarter and one-third, double digit interest cover, a dividend cover of around four times and a tax rate of not much more than 20 per cent. The Group's financial policies reinforced this stance. Although multinational in scope, CRH minimised its exposure to any one currency by deliberately spreading its net worth across the currencies of its different operations. In addition, the Group did not trade financial instruments and fixed approximately 50 per cent of its debt. Furthermore, CRH's accounting policy stance was deliberately

Exhibit 10 Comparative financials: CRH vs. major UK heavyside building materials companies

(Companies for which heavyside is the main activity or is large in absolute terms)

PROFITABILITY AND PRODUCTIVITY	EBIT MARGIN (%)				CAPITAL EMPLOYED AS % OF SALES				RETURN ON CAPITAL EMPLOYED (%)			
	1997	1998F	1999F	2000F	1997	1998F	1999F	2000F	1997	1998F	1999F	2000F
Aggregate Ind.	10.7	12.6	13.1	13.3	118.6	121.4	116.8	111.3	9.0	10.4	11.2	11.9
Blue Circle	12.9	13.0	13.5	13.6	53.0	63.2	67.9	67.4	24.4	20.6	19.9	20.2
Hanson	9.9	11.2	13.2	13.6	90.8	110.2	124.9	121.1	10.9	10.2	10.6	11.2
Ibstock	9.7	12.4	12.9	13.4	138.6	138.3	128.4	122.7	7.0	9.0	10.1	10.9
RMC	7.8	8.0	8.3	8.6	67.8	69.1	68.7	65.8	11.4	11.6	12.1	13.1
Rugby	6.9	8.3	9.2	10.3	46.4	55.7	57.9	57.1	15.0	14.9	15.9	18.0
Tarmac	5.7	6.1	6.3	6.6	46.2	43.3	42.2	41.4	12.4	14.0	14.8	15.9
CRH	**8.4**	**8.7**	**8.9**	**9.0**	**40.0**	**40.9**	**41.3**	**40.0**	**21.1**	**21.2**	**21.6**	**22.6**
Sector average	8.3	8.7	9.2	9.5	49.0	56.4	57.2	56.0	17.0	15.5	16.1	17.0

Notes: EBIT Margin is earnings before interest, goodwill amortisation and tax as a % of sales.
Capital employed is the sum of net tangible fixed assets plus net working capital and is based on year-end, not average, numbers.
Return on capital employed is the operating return on capital employed.
Sector average includes all sector activities: materials, heavyside, lightside and merchanting.
Figures for 1998, 1999 and 2000 are forecast values.

Source: Warburg Dillon Read.

cautious. In recognition of its financial management and of its well-regarded and superbly executed investor relations programme, CRH consistently won awards for the transparency of its finances and the presentation of its financial statements.

Notwithstanding the foregoing, perhaps the most outstanding aspect of CRH's finances was its strong cash generation. On a per share basis, this was on average more than 50 per cent higher than Group EPS. A cash generative mentality informed all operations and was central to the Group's evaluation and control processes, for both new acquisitions and existing operations. CRH's cash generation had been a major factor enabling it to fund its rapid and major expansion overseas without compromising its principles of financial prudence.

CRH: FUTURE DEVELOPMENT AND DIRECTION

Industry outlook and trends

As of 1998, the outlook for the construction sector, although varying as always across markets, was somewhat brighter than it had been for several years, particularly in Europe. However, this was coming off a base of a low, or declining, level of activity and the general prognosis remained unexciting. Any pick-up in growth was expected to be modest, matching or at best marginally exceeding the rate of economic expansion. Average growth in construction output across Europe was expected to be around 3 per cent in 1999, helped by lower interest rates, rising incomes and falling unemployment (Exhibit 11). The civil engineering, non-residential and RMI segments were expected to perform best. As against this, doubts were beginning to emerge amongst commentators as to whether the unprecedentedly long growth cycle in the US could be sustained and commentators were anticipating slower growth going forward. Less developed western markets (such as Ireland), which had similarly enjoyed a prolonged period of high growth, were also expected to experience lower

Exhibit 11	Growth in construction output for CRH's key European markets (%)					
	1995	1996	1997	1998F	1999F	2000F
Belgium	1.2	−2.2	5.5	4.0	4.0	2.2
France	0.1	−3.8	−0.9	1.8	2.7	1.8
Germany	0.3	−3.1	−2.2	−1.9	1.3	1.5
Ireland	13.0	17.5	12.3	9.2	5.7	4.5
Netherlands	1.8	1.6	4.2	1.7	1.8	1.2
Poland	N/A	N/A	N/A	9.0	8.0	7.5
Spain	5.0	−1.0	2.0	5.0	4.0	3.0
UK	−0.3	2.0	2.9	3.7	3.6	3.6
Europe Total	0.8	−0.4	0.7	1.3	3.0	N/A

Note: Figure for 1998, 1999 and 2000 are forecast values.
Source: Euroconstruct Conference, Berlin, December 1998.

Exhibit 12	Concentration in UK heavyside markets 1998			

(Market shares, % data)

	CEMENT		AGGREGATES	READYMIX
Blue Circle	50.0	Tarmac	24.5	19.0
Castle	25.0	Hanson	18.0	17.0
Rugby	20.0	RMC	10.5	32.0
		Lafarge	10.5	9.0

Source: Warburg Dillon Read.

rates of growth in the near future. Emerging markets remained prospective, but risky, as the turmoil in Asia and eastern Europe in 1997 and 1998 had demonstrated.

In addition, as the millennium beckoned, a number of structural trends were emerging in the construction sector and the building materials industry, in part prompted by sustained low levels of activity. In heavyside markets (especially materials), supply-side consolidation was taking place, most particularly in the UK, which had yet to fully recover from the doldrums of the severe downturn in the early years of the decade. Significant corporate activity had occurred, resulting in the disappearance, over a number of years, of such previously well-known industry names as Steetly, Redland and Marley. In addition, other activity such as mergers (Bardon–Camas to form Aggregate Industries), joint ventures (between Tarmac and Hanson to form Midland Quarry Products) and asset swaps (involving Tarmac and Wimpey) had all taken place. As a result, major UK heavyside materials markets in 1998 had become relatively highly concentrated (Exhibit 12). The net result was substantial cost savings for the industry in excess of £100 million p.a. and improved pricing discipline and power for surviving players in a position to exercise it and benefit from it.

In parallel with this trend, there was evidence to suggest that, to a certain extent, local differences between geographic markets were eroding, prompted by a number of trends. Driven by institutional factors, such as at European Union level, a convergence of building regulations, product standards and tendering procedures was occurring. This was reinforced by a convergence in building practice across markets, resulting from mobility of workers and the increasingly multinational activity of contracting and building materials firms. Related to this development were emerging trends among the industry's customer base, which was itself consolidating. As a consequence, customers' needs were homogenising and they were becoming more demanding. Ibstock had recently experienced pricing pressures by virtue of having to deal with a smaller number of larger customers.

The competitive arena in the building materials industry had also toughened considerably by the late 1990s. The increasing international spread of a small number of large players meant that multi-market competitors existed in many areas. Such competitors had considerable resources that were not available to local players. A consequence was that the investment threshold for competing in such markets had effectively been raised, resulting in greater pressures for payback and return. There also remained the danger that efficiencies from higher investment and the process of consolidation could be competed away in the form of lower prices, particularly in the event of a severe cyclical downturn. Finally, as a result of industry consolidation (to which CRH had contributed significantly), there were fewer potential acquisition targets. As a result of this and of the appreciation in asset values generally that had occurred in the mid-to late 1990s, there was some evidence that vendors' asking prices had firmed.

Future challenges

As 1998 drew to a close and Don Godson and his team reflected on another successful year for CRH, they were aware (as ever) of the challenges they faced as the Group sought to sustain its track record of success. Looking forward, they knew it would be unwise to rely on the US and Irish construction markets to continue to deliver the high levels of growth of recent years. On the other hand, the outlook for the UK and mainland Europe was moderately brighter. However, CRH had to a certain extent been a victim of its own success in Ireland and the US and these two markets were expected to account for three-quarters of Group trading profits in 1998. This represented a departure from the traditional geographic balance that CRH had assiduously pursued since the late 1970s. Overall, it was clear that profit growth in 1999 would depend more on correcting underperforming divisions and on bringing onstream new investments in the developing areas of Poland and South America.

Structural changes in the environment posed greater uncertainties. It was unclear whether industry consolidation would remain largely confined to heavyside materials and whether it would also spread out from the UK. In addition, while the pace of rationalisation was uncertain, it did appear to be hotting up. Furthermore, the extent to which consolidation could ultimately proceed was questionable, given the underlying economic basis for the local and fragmented nature of markets. Notwithstanding this, it was certainly true that there were certain markets in which fixed investment requirements were high and where scale economies could be readily leveraged. For example, cement had always been subject to cross-border trade, albeit in a small way. Moreover, recent reductions in the cost of manufacture of cement through the use of alternative fuels and flexible work practices could be expected to facilitate this trend. Separately, it was undeniable that a trend towards the convergence of markets, customer needs and competition was occurring. How this would impact on different product/markets and what the best form of response would be remained to be seen.

The implications of environmental change for CRH were equally uncertain. If substantial change occurred along the above lines, the key success factors in the industry would undoubtedly shift fundamentally. However, it was by no means certain that such an elemental shift was in fact occurring, or whether it would necessarily take place. Nonetheless, the possibility of change of this nature, at least in certain parts of the industry, raised interesting questions for

CRH. Would the Group's core strategy, which had served it so well in the past, meet its needs going forward? How responsive were CRH and its operating units to external market changes? There was evidence from the US that, in competitive markets for glass products, service had become an important factor in competing. Finally, would CRH's Group-wide strategic architecture, which had supported and reinforced Group strategy, continue to be appropriate in its entirety in the event of significant change?

The critical area of acquisitions seemed to encapsulate many of these issues. During 1998, CRH had benefited from an increased pace of acquisition activity, with purchases of medium-sized companies running at the rate of two per month. Notwithstanding its track record and the success of its development teams, the Group would be challenged to sustain this level of activity going forward. Industry rationalisation and competition had tightened the market for well-run, medium-sized businesses. Moreover, as CRH got larger, it needed either to increase the size of individual acquisitions or to further boost the number of acquisitions undertaken in order to obtain the same proportionate benefit.

Current issues

It was against this background that the senior management of CRH considered the Ibstock situation and other potential issues. In addition, there was another specific factor pertaining to Ibstock's plc status. The imminence of euro-based stock market indices with the introduction of the euro on 1 January 1999 had resulted in investor preference for the larger stocks which would be included in such indices. As a result, the share prices of mid-capitalisation stocks had languished, including Ibstock. Such a situation provided potential opportunities for larger companies seeking to acquire smaller plcs on favourable price/earnings multiples.

The opportunity to acquire Ibstock had arisen rapidly and unexpectedly. For some time, Ibstock had had a large shareholder on its register in the form of Brierly Investments Ltd, which owned 29.9 per cent of the shares. In October 1998, the Austrian brick manufacturer Wienerberger had acquired this stake at a price of 66 pence per share, a 50 per cent premium on the previous share price. It was known that the Ibstock board was unhappy with this stake, which was likely to lead to a full bid for the company by Wienerberger in due course. The developing situation meant that Ibstock had no future as an independent entity and, therefore, it was likely to welcome an approach from a friendly suitor. CRH, which had known and admired the Ibstock business for some time, would almost certainly fall into this category.

There was no doubt that Ibstock had attractions for CRH and would represent a good strategic fit. Ibstock had a substantial clay facing brick business in the UK with annual sales of 1,000 million bricks and was the joint market leader with a share of 30 per cent. It also had a concrete masonry business in the UK that could provide critical mass to Forticrete, CRH's UK concrete products company. In the US, Ibstock's Glen Gery subsidiary sold 500 million bricks p.a. in the northeast and, merged into CRH's Architectural Products activities, would give the Group market leadership in the region. Finally, the US concrete pipe and block operations of both companies complemented each other.

On the other hand, the acquisition was not without risk. The UK clay brick market was competitive, with four large producers and a host of smaller players. Near-term growth prospects were not good, although affordability in housing (a major end-use of bricks) was at historically favourable levels and confidence appeared to be returning to the residential market after the trauma of the late 1980s. Nevertheless, clay bricks were a commodity, fixed costs of production were high and, with increasing consolidation of the customer base, there was little likelihood of product price increases in the short-term. Ibstock's financial performance had improved in recent years and pre-tax profit for 1998 was expected to be £31 million on sales of £290 million, an increase of one-third on 1997 profits of £23.4 million. As against this, margins of 14.5 per cent compared unfavourably with 20 per cent at Hanson Brick, the other joint market leader. Finally, the dynamic situation in relation to the Wienerberger stake meant that the best chances of success would be if CRH were to proceed with the acquisition of Ibstock before the Christmas holiday period, one week away.

A larger question was what implications the acquisition of Ibstock would have for CRH's carefully crafted acquisition strategy. Firstly, there was the issue of size. Ibstock would be likely to cost in the region of €550 million, twice as large as the €270 million CRH paid for the Tilcon aggregates and concrete group in the US in 1996. Moreover, this latter purchase was not, in itself, a major departure for CRH. According to Harry Sheridan, CRH's finance director, Tilcon was '60 small locations that just happened to come in one package'. In addition to size, the likely mode of purchase of Ibstock and the probable take-out price were also considerations. Notwithstanding its good relationship with the company, CRH would have to persuade the institutional shareholders to sell, which would probably require an additional premium on top of the 66 pence per share paid by Wienerberger. The possibility of an auction situation arising could not be discounted. Furthermore, the size of the deal and circumstances surrounding an acquisition might mean that cultural fit and subsequent integration of Ibstock could become issues. Finally, although CRH shareholders were very loyal and had been well rewarded for their fealty, such a perceived major departure from the Group's normal acquisition formula might cause confusion and result in an adverse share price reaction.

Although not as urgent as Ibstock, CRH management was also faced with another potential large-scale acquisition opportunity in late 1998. Arising from an EU Commission ruling that it held a dominant position, the Scandinavian cement producer Scancem was likely to be put up for sale by its two main shareholders. Scancem had two major assets that might be attractive to CRH. The first was Castle Cement, number two in the UK market with a share of 25 per cent, but no downstream activities (such as concrete products). International interest in Castle was likely to be intense and a price tag of upwards of €700 million was speculated. The second area of potential interest to CRH was Scancem's Finnsementti and Rudus businesses. Finnsementti was Finland's sole cement producer with output of 1.4 million tonnes p.a. in addition to sizeable aggregates and concrete interests, similar in profile to CRH's vertically integrated operations in Ireland. The Rudus business had substantial aggregates and readymix operations in Poland and had expanded into the Baltic states of Estonia and Latvia in 1997. The likely total purchase price for both entities would be around €400 million. The sale of Scancem would almost certainly be conducted on an auction basis.

The last major strategic issue confronting CRH's management in late 1998 related to Keyline, the Group's UK merchanting subsidiary. Heavyside merchanting in the UK had recently undergone considerable consolidation with the four largest competitors acquiring six smaller players. Keyline ranked number five in this market with a market share of 4 per cent, some way behind Meyer, the market leader with 12 per cent. Against this background, Keyline was finding it difficult to develop and grow its business. The high prices commanded in recent deals made within sector purchases difficult to justify on shareholder value grounds. The multiple of 0.66 times revenue paid by Wolseley in its recent acquisition of Hall & Co. had set a new headline in this regard. Nonetheless, Keyline's fortunes had improved considerably in recent years and 1998 would be a record year. Indications were that Keyline would make operating profits of £19.5 million on revenue of £313 million.

As Don Godson and his colleagues contemplated the strategic issues confronting CRH, only one thing was certain. They would earn their Christmas vacation.

EPILOGUE

In the first five months of 1999, CRH acquired Ibstock in addition to Finnsementti and Rudus, and disposed of Keyline. Ibstock was purchased for €552 million, following a pre-Christmas dawn raid in which CRH accumulated 50.7 per cent of the shares. Having attained an initial controlling interest, the purchase was rapidly completed. CRH immediately set about integrating Ibstock into the Group. Finnsementti and Rudus were acquired following a successful bid for €415 million. The purchase price represented a multiple of 6.5 times EBITDA (earnings before interest, tax, depreciation and amortisation) – broadly in line with other deals in the sector at the time. Finnsementti and Rudus were brought into the Europe Materials division, with CRH's existing Ozarow cement business in Poland in an overseeing role. Finally, Keyline was sold to Travis Perkins, the UK merchanting group, for €279 million, a healthy 59 per cent of sales. The sale was part of CRH's strategy of focusing on higher-margin businesses where the group had a bigger market share.

Ryanair – the low fares airline*

Eleanor O'Higgins

This case study provides a background to the development of Ryanair, Europe's first low-cost airline, and one of the fastest-growing and profitable carriers in Europe. It also discusses the increasingly competitive nature of the market and provides an overview of Ryanair's strategic initiatives. It therefore provides an opportunity to evaluate strategic options available to this company.

INTRODUCTION

Ryanair was founded in 1985 by the Ryan family to provide scheduled passenger airline services between Ireland and the UK, as an alternative to the then state monopoly carrier, Aer Lingus. Initially, Ryanair was a full-service conventional airline, with two classes of seating, leasing three different types of aircraft. Despite a growth in passenger volumes, by the end of 1990 the company had flown through a great deal of turbulence, disposing of five chief executives and accumulating losses of IR£20 million. Its fight to survive in the early 1990s saw the airline restyle itself to become Europe's first low-fares, no-frills carrier, built on the model of Southwest Airlines, the highly successful Texas-based operator. A fresh management team was appointed by Tony Ryan, headed up by Michael O'Leary. The new formula effected a turnaround in the fortunes of the company, and by 1997 the company was floated in an IPO on the Dublin Stock Exchange and on NASDAQ.

The financial arrangements which surrounded the public offering were highly advantageous to Tony Ryan, his three sons, Cathal, Declan and Shane, and to Michael O'Leary. In effect, the Ryan family had sold the company for IR£56.7 million and repurchased a 61 per cent stake for only IR£3.1 million. Michael O'Leary was allowed to purchase 17.9 per cent of the company for IR£0.9 million, partly to compensate him for the cessation of an executive bonus scheme which had netted him IR£17 million over three years. Another investment group led by David Bonderman invested IR£1 million in equity and a IR£24 million loan to Ryanair through a vehicle company, Irish Air, for a stake of 19.9 per cent. Bonderman, an entrepreneur from Texas, chairman of Continental Airlines and a partner in a Washington law firm, provided

---

*Updated by Urmilla Lawson

Exhibit 1	Comparative airline share price valuations (in euros – unless stated otherwise)			
	YEAR END	SHARE PRICE 11/04/2001	2002 FORECAST P/E	2003 FORECAST P/E
Ryanair	Mar.	10.75	29.5	23.2
British Airways	Mar.	£3.41	18.5	8.8
KLM	Mar.	20.05	5.8	6.0
Lufthansa	Dec.	20.3	11.2	N/A
Southwest	Dec.	US$18.45	18.9	N/A
easyJet	Sept.	3.82	30.2	25.5

Source: Company data; Credit Suisse First Boston (Europe) Limited estimates.

credibility for the company in the USA and was made chairman of Ryanair at its flotation. The proceeds of the flotation of IR£58 million for just under 35 per cent of the shares were used to repay loans and to purchase aircraft. It left the Ryans with 33 per cent of the company, Irish Air with 14.7 per cent and Michael O'Leary with 14.1 per cent.

Since its flotation, the company has enjoyed a premium price/earnings ratio compared with other airlines (Exhibit 1). In July 1998, the company placed 9.1 million shares on the London Stock Exchange, while the principal share-holders (the Ryan family, Michael O'Leary and Irish Air) disposed of 12.6 million shares, thereby reducing the percentage of shares held by them from almost 62 per cent to 51.4 per cent. A further disposal of 10.5 per cent of the company by the Ryans for IR£117 million, 1.5 per cent by Michael O'Leary for IR£17 million and 3.1 per cent for IR£34 million by David Bonderman, was announced in May 1999. In 2000, O'Leary sold 6m shares, reducing his stake from 10.8 to 8.6 per cent. Bonderman, together with associated investors in Irish Air General Partners, sold 4m of their holding of 8.8m shares. O'Leary has been progres-sively selling his shares in Ryanair as the airline has returned to the market annually for capital. The disposed shares were sold in a public offering in the USA, and to institutional shareholders in Europe. The continuation of Ryanair's licence as an EU carrier is conditional on a majority share ownership by EU nationals. This could limit the trading market in ordinary shares, especially in markets outside the EU. In 2001, Ryanair disclosed that not less than 54 per cent of its shares were held by EU nationals.

THE LOW-FARES AIRLINE

Ryanair's objective was to maintain its position as Europe's leading low-fares airline, operating frequent point-to-point flights on short-haul flights, mainly out of regional and secondary airports (see Exhibit 2 for market share data). The heart of its strategy was based on providing a no-frills service with low fares designed to stimulate demand, particularly from budget-conscious leisure

Exhibit 2	European low-fare airlines' market share, 2000		
AIRLINE	PASSENGERS (000)	PERCENTAGE OF LOW-COST MARKET	PERCENTAGE OF TOTAL MARKET
Ryanair	6,939	34.6	2.3
easyJet	6,262	31.2	2.1
Virgin Express	2,976	14.8	1.0
Go	2,823	14.1	0.9
Buzz	1,080	5.4	0.4
Total	20,080	100	6.7

Source: Company data, Credit Suisse First Boston (Europe) Limited estimates.

and business travellers, who might otherwise have used alternative forms of transportation, or who might not have travelled at all.

From the outset, as a budget carrier, Ryanair set itself vigorous but steady growth ambitions which it hoped to achieve in various ways. This included initiating additional routes from Dublin and London to other locations in continental Europe, new UK–Ireland routes, and new intra-UK routes, which were all served by high-cost, high-fare carriers. Ryanair also intended to increase the frequency of services on existing routes where warranted. The company's goal was to be profitable on new routes from their inception, by pitching their fares to be low enough to attract new customers but high enough to provide a satisfactory operating margin. This could be quite a challenge, given the steep marketing and advertising costs associated with the launch of a new route, especially in continental European markets where Ryanair was less well established than in Ireland. Ryanair would also consider making acquisitions, should the right opportunities become available.

In 1997, in the Ireland–UK market, Ryanair overtook Aer Lingus as the number one carrier on flights between the Republic of Ireland and the UK with 4 million passengers and a 37 per cent market share. The entry of Ryanair into the Ireland–UK market, originally dominated by Aer Lingus, was followed by more competitors, which led to substantially lower fares and significantly increased traffic on the routes serviced by Ryanair. At one stage, Ryanair put in a bid with the Irish government to carry civil servants to EU meetings in Brussels, offering an annual IR£1 million service contract instead of the IR£3 million it claimed Aer Lingus charged. This bid did not receive a response.

At first, Ryanair's successful growth was based on a perception that it was an Irish ethnic airline, relying on reciprocal visits between the large Irish population in the UK and their relatives and friends in Ireland, availing of low fares to travel more often. In fact, the term 'Ryanair generation' was coined to describe the younger educated Irish emigrant population in the UK. However, by 2001 fewer than 20 per cent of passengers originated from Ireland. By mid-2001, Ryanair's route system had expanded from its primarily Irish–UK emphasis to serve various cities in continental Europe. It had shifted the emphasis of its

Exhibit 3	Ryanair destinations, 2001				
	Aarhus Denmark	Alghero Italy	Ancona Italy	Birmingham UK	
Bournemouth UK	Bristol UK	Biarritz France	Brescia Italy	Brussels (Charleroi) Belgium	Carcassonne (Toulouse) France
Cardiff UK	Cork Ireland	Derry N. Ireland	Dinard France	Dublin Ireland	Esbjerg Denmark
Frankfurt (Hahn) Germany	Gatwick (London) UK	Genoa Italy	Glasgow Scotland	Gothenburg Sweden	Hamburg (Lübeck) Germany
Kerry Ireland	Knock Ireland	Leeds (Bradford) UK	Liverpool UK	Luton (London) UK	Malmo Sweden
Manchester UK	Nimes France	Oslo (Torp) Norway	Paris (Beauvais) France	Perpignan France	Pescara Italy
Pisa Italy	Salzburg Austria	Shannon Ireland	Stansted (London) UK	St. Etienne (Lyon) France	Stockholm (Skavsta) Sweden
Stockholm (Vasteras) Sweden	Teesside UK	Trieste Italy	Turin Italy	Venice (Treviso) Italy	

Source: Ryanair Website
(Rimini, Italy discontinued June 2001).

expansion to mainland Europe, establishing a hub at Brussels South/Charleroi Airport. Exhibit 3 describes the Ryanair route network in 2001.

The carrier claimed that it generally made its lowest fares widely available by allocating a majority of seat inventory to its two lowest-fare categories. According to the company, this meant that its no-frills services allowed it to prioritise features important to its clientele, such as frequent departures, advance reservations, baggage handling and consistent on-time services. Simultaneously, this eliminated non-essential extras that interfered with the reliable, low-cost delivery of its basic flights. The eliminated extras included advance seat assignments, in-flight meals, multi-class seating, access to a frequent flyer programme, complimentary drinks and other amenities. When the catering firm which supplied Ryanair withdrew the provision of free ice, the airline sent a memo to cabin staff advising them that ice would no longer be available for passengers' drinks, a measure that has saved the airline IR£40,000 a year.

In 1997, Ryanair dropped its cargo services, at an estimated annual cost of IR£400,000 in revenue. Without the need to load and unload cargo, the turnaround time of an aircraft was reduced from 30 to 25 minutes, according to the company. It claimed that business travellers, attracted by frequency and punctuality, comprised 40 per cent of its passengers, despite often less conveniently located airports and the absence of pampering.

Ryanair aimed to enhance its revenue through ancillary services offered in conjunction with its core airline business. These included on-board sales, charter flights, travel reservations services, travel insurance, car rentals, in-flight television advertising services, and advertising outside its aircraft, whereby a corporate sponsor paid for the right to paint an aircraft with its logo. For example, passengers might have been surprised to find themselves flying inside a giant beerglass when Kilkenny, a beer brand within the Guinness Group, turned a Ryanair airplane into a flying billboard.

In 2001, Michael O'Leary declared that by 2004, at least 10 per cent of the airline's flights would be fare-free, because ancillary revenues would increasingly be used to subsidise airfares. This was to include the availability of satellite television and Internet services on flights, allowing passengers to watch their favourite television programmes or play arcade games from their seats – for a fee. Market research suggested that these new services were expected to generate at least £1 per passenger, in addition to the average spend of £4 already being achieved, netting £9 million per year.

On within-country flights in the UK, merchandise was sold on a duty-paid basis. The company believed that longer flights encouraged higher per passenger revenues from in-flight sales, which should enhance such sales on newer routes to destinations in continental Europe, compared to the shorter Ireland–UK or within-UK routes. The EU abolished duty-free sales on intra-EU travel from 1999, contending that it was a tax distortion. This could have been a triple blow to Ryanair, since it might have entailed an irreplaceable loss of revenue as well as a loss of incentive to flight attendants. Attendants could have earned as much as one-third of their compensation from commission on the sale of beverages and duty-free goods. Some Irish and UK airports increased landing charges by 20 per cent to make up the lost revenue.

However, in fiscal year 2000, revenues from ancillary services increased by 38 per cent to IR£42.7 million, reflecting an increase in the level of car hire rentals, Internet-related revenues and other ancillary products. These, together with on-board sales of food and beverages, helped to mitigate the reduction of revenue derived from duty-free sales.

The company continued to incur significant capital expenditures in expanding its aircraft fleet in order to realise its growth ambitions. This included the purchase of new aircraft for $2 billion, refitting used aircraft, and hushkitting and rudder installation of existing aircraft to comply with EU regulations. Ryanair stated that it expected to retain all of its earnings for expansion purposes and not to pay any dividends.

Although headquartered in Ireland, Ryanair has had its operating expenses and revenues as well as assets and liabilities denominated in currencies other than the Irish pound. Fuel prices quoted in US dollars have been an especially sensitive issue. Also, the UK's delayed entry into the European Monetary Union (EMU) has been problematic for Ryanair, with so much UK-based business, but offset by a weak euro in 2001. However, its increasing operations in mainland Europe and the denomination of air traffic control charges in euros provided some currency exchange stability. Ryanair also engaged in some foreign exchange hedging in transactions involving the Irish pound/euro, UK sterling and the US dollar. Exhibits 4 and 5 provide financial data on Ryanair.

Exhibit 4	Ryanair profit and loss account (euros millions) fiscal year to March		
	1999	2000	2001 ESTIMATE
Scheduled revenues	258.87	330.5	425.3
Ancillary revenues	36.88	39.6	54.7
Total operating revenues	295.75	370.1	480.0
Staff costs	39.8	48.5	59.5
Depreciation	36.2	44.1	56.1
Fuel and oil	36.6	41.7	60.5
Maintenance, material, repairs	12.0	16.9	19.1
Marketing and distribution	24.6	32.1	20.7
Aircraft rentals	2.9	2.1	8.9
Route charges	20.8	26.3	35.1
Airport charges	29.0	43.1	66.0
Other	25.9	31.3	40.7
Total operating expenses	227.8	286.1	366.6
Operating profit	67.8	84.1	113.4
Other income	7.9	6.0	9.5
Profit before tax	75.7	90.1	122.9
Tax	−18.3	−17.6	−22.6
Net profit	57.4	72.5	100.3

Source: Ryanair Annual Report 2000; Commerzbank Securities.

Exhibit 5	Ryanair consolidated balance sheet (euros millions)	
	31 MARCH 1999	31 MARCH 2000
Fixed assets	203.54	315.06
Current assets	196.29	397.63
Total assets	399.83	712.70
Financed by:		
Current liabilities	114.40	143.65
Provisions for liabilities	11.27	15.28
Long-term debt	23.20	112.41
Shareholders' funds	250.96	441.36
Total liabilities and shareholders' funds	399.83	712.7

Source: Ryanair Annual Report 2000.

COSTS AND OPERATIONS

The company realised that the achievement of its objective of being the leading no-frills airline in Europe depended on being the lowest-cost airline. This demanded a continuous concentration on driving down costs to sustain low fares and remain profitable, even on low yields. Ryanair's cost reduction strategy focused on five areas:

- fleet commonality;
- contracting out of services;
- airport charges;
- staff costs and productivity;
- marketing costs.

Fleet commonality

Initially, Ryanair's fleet consisted principally of a single aircraft type – used Boeing 737-200s, currently the most widely flown commercial aircraft in the world, with a single class 130-seat configuration. Thus, the company was able to obtain spares and maintenance services on favourable terms, limit costs of staff training and offer flexibility in scheduling aircraft and crew assignments. In 1998, Ryanair ordered 45 Boeing 737-800 aircraft (189-seat capacity) worth $2 billion, taking delivery of five aircraft a year. The purchase of these new aircraft, to be financed by internally generated funds, borrowings and the proceeds of the July 1998 London flotation, would allow the airline to meet its goal of increasing capacity by 25 per cent a year. By 2001, Ryanair had a fleet of 36 Boeing 737s. The purchase of new, as opposed to second-hand aircraft may have reflected the growing scarcity of used aircraft on the market.

The newest aircraft would augment Ryanair's existing fleet of 20 Boeing 737-200s, with an average age of over 15 years, and a life expectancy of 25 years. The average age was considerably higher than that of the fleets of Ryanair's current or potential competitors. Older aircraft entailed higher maintenance costs and were less fuel efficient. Moreover, 14 of Ryanair's airplanes required the installation of hushkits to comply with an EU directive on noise requirements by 1 April 2002, at an estimated total cost of $19.6 million. The increased weight due to the hushkits would potentially result in a higher level of fuel consumption. The company attempted to hedge out the price it paid for fuel by contracting for a large proportion of its needs in advance. The fuel cost difficulty was compounded by foreign exchange rate fluctuations that could not be predicted or controlled, since aircraft fuel prices were denominated in US dollars.

Contracting out of services

Other than Dublin Airport where it maintained its own staff and services, Ryanair contracted out aircraft handling, ticketing, baggage handling and other functions to third parties. The company has attempted to obtain competitive rates and multi-year contracts at fixed prices, limiting exposure to cost increases. EU directives forbidding ground-handling monopolies at European airports should enable Ryanair to continue to negotiate economical contracts in these likely competitive conditions.

While Ryanair engineering staff carry out routine maintenance, repair services and checks on aircraft, engine and heavy maintenance are contracted out to third parties. Contract work is carried out under the supervision and planning of Ryanair engineering staff, enabling the company to retain control of quality and safety without incurring the cost of a specialised labour force for a modestly sized fleet. It has also allowed Ryanair to avoid the labour unrest that dogged the maintenance subsidiary of its rival, Aer Lingus, before the national carrier disposed of this loss-making unit.

Airport charges and route policy

Airport charges include landing fees, passenger loading fees, aircraft parking fees and noise surcharges. Ryanair has reduced these fees by avoiding the congested main airports, choosing secondary and regional airport destinations, which are anxious to increase passenger throughput. As with most of its continental destinations, these airports are significantly further from the city centres they served than the main airports. For example, Ryanair uses Torp which is 65 miles from Oslo, Charleroi – 37 miles from Brussels, and Beauvais – 35 miles from Paris. Ryanair has chosen Stansted rather than the more congested and expensive Heathrow or Gatwick as its main London airport. Indeed, Stansted is Ryanair's main UK headquarters. Since Ryanair has been typically able to produce high volume for airports, it has negotiated favourable access fees. Less expensive gate locations and outdoor boarding stairs rather than jetways (which also consume more turnaround time) help to keep costs down. Generally, less busy airports can be expected to provide higher rates of on-time departures, faster turnaround times and fewer terminal delays, all of which maximise aircraft utilisation and mean fewer restrictions on slot requirements and on the number of allowed take-offs and landings.

Consistent with its policy of point-to-point flights on short-haul routes, Ryanair does not interline with other airlines. This allows the airline to offer direct non-stop journeys, avoiding the costs of providing through service (baggage transfer, passenger assistance) for connecting passengers, as well as delays often caused by the late arrival of connecting flights. Unavoidable services are contracted out and charged to passengers. For example, wheelchair services cost passengers at Dublin Airport IR£8.

Many of Ryanair's contracts were for a five-year period. The carrier asserted that it would quit any airport location that raised its charges to an unacceptable level when contracts were renegotiated. However, in the name of non-discrimination, the EU regulatory authority has prepared legislation that prevents airports from offering differential deals to different airline operators. This could have the effect of undermining the favourable treatment Ryanair had previously managed to negotiate.

Although Ryanair was able to avail of 90 per cent rebates offered by the Irish Airports Authority, Aer Rianta, on incremental traffic that it generated at Dublin and Cork Airports, Michael O'Leary continues to publicly attack the airport operate. This centres on a number of issues, including an increase in airport charges and inadequate congested amenities at Dublin Airport, with parking facilities described as 'a joke'. Ryanair claims that these inadequacies are stifling its growth plans. The airline submitted a plan to build its own IR£20 million terminal at Dublin Airport, or alternatively, it would support another consortium with a proposal to build a second terminal. The latter has been challenged in the Irish High Court by Aer Rianta. In any case, Ryanair has moved its centre of gravity away from Dublin towards Great Britain and mainland Europe.

Staff costs and productivity

Since employee compensation costs are typically the most important component of total airline costs, Ryanair controls these costs through a performance-related pay structure. The company believes that its labour costs are lower than those of many established airlines. Nevertheless, despite modest base salaries, pilots and cabin crew can earn total remuneration in excess of industry norms by, for example, maximising the number of sectors flown daily within regulation limits. However, EU social/employment legislation is always subject to change, and could eventually invoke further limitations on crew working hours. In May 1998, Ryanair announced an employee share option scheme worth up to 5 per cent of the shares of the company. In 2001, Ryanair pilots and in-flight employees received an apparently generous five-year pay, productivity and share options package, with other employees expected to receive a similar package. The agreement narrowly averted a threatened strike by pilots over working schedules and conditions.

Ryanair cabin attendants earn commission on on-board sales and in-flight services, but as outlined, EU legislation has abolished intra-EU duty-free sales. Nevertheless, cabin staff still make commission on duty-paid sales and in-flight refreshments. The absence of 'free' in-flight service, normally provided by full-service airlines, has several beneficial spin-off effects – the opportunity for staff to earn commission for paid service, and a reduction in the extent to which the aircraft need cleaning between flights, so cabin crew can tidy up the cabin and allow a quicker turnaround time.

Ryanair has been a newsworthy and controversial company in Ireland with respect to its employment practices, most specifically in its refusal to recognise any trade unions. Ryanair asserts that it will only recognise trade unions when a majority of workers opt to join. The company regards the heavily unionised nature of employment in its rival Aer Lingus as a huge contributory factor to the state airline's historical lack of competitiveness. Ryanair's stance over union recognition has aroused strong feelings on both sides of the issue. The company was criticised by the EU Commissioner for Social Affairs, by members of the Irish legislature and in the press. Editorials and government ministers' statements were made, to the effect that Ryanair's behaviour posed a threat to the series of tripartite agreements involving trade unions, employers' organisations and government that had created industrial peace in Ireland for over a decade, deemed to be an important factor in the creation of a vibrant and growing economy. However, those on Ryanair's side claim that Ryanair is simply leading the way in facing the realities of international competitiveness and the growing irrelevance of trade unions to effective enterprise and workers' rights. Several hundred Ryanair employees issued a statement asserting that they are happy to work for the company.

Marketing costs

Ryanair advertises its low fares primarily on its website, in national and regional Irish and UK newspapers, on radio and on television. In 1997, Ryanair was one of the first European airlines to cut its rate of commission to travel agents, from 9 per cent to 7½ per cent. This led to a dispute with travel agencies in Ireland and the UK, which threatened a boycott on handling reservations for Ryanair flights. Ryanair subsequently won the backing of the Competition Authority in Ireland against the boycott. Travel agents remained disgruntled. Some individual agents stopped selling Ryanair tickets, claiming the low fares and low commission rates were not worth the effort. This unofficial boycott has been dubbed 'Anybody but Ryanair' in Ireland. Other airlines have since followed Ryanair's measures *vis-à-vis* travel agents' commission rates.

In a move to capture more value from its operations and improve contact with its customers, Ryanair established Ryanair Direct Limited in Dublin in 1996, transferring its reservations operations from two locations in Dublin and London. The company benefited from a package of government grants and incentives in setting up Ryanair Direct. This centralised reservations centre could be accessed by customers from anywhere in Ireland and the UK, for the price of a local call. Passengers were charged IR£3 per each credit card booking. Ryanair Direct enabled management control over customer service quality and consistency and increased sales of ancillary services such as travel insurance, car rental, and connecting rail services.

In January 2000, Ryanair launched its *www.ryanair.com* website. This has had the effect of saving money on staff costs, agents' commissions, and computer reservation charges, while significantly contributing to growth. Internet sales accounted for 65 per cent of all bookings, which, when added to Ryanair Direct, meant that over 90 per cent of bookings were taken directly. Travel agency sales accounted for just 8 per cent of bookings. By the end of 2000, the particularly strong performance of *ryanair.com* contributed to a 24 per cent decrease in marketing and distribution costs.

Ryanair did, however, accept that it could not entirely dispense with some dependency on travel agents, especially when opening up new routes in unfamiliar markets. Ryanair recognised the potential loss of business that could result from a systems breakdown on the Internet or other adverse events affecting the operation of a single centralised reservation centre. Customers experiencing difficulties on the Internet could ring a special helpline. However, telephone booking lines were often continuously engaged, especially during special price promotions. Exhibit 6 details some operating statistics for Ryanair.

Independent customer satisfaction statistics are not available for Ryanair. In an annual report, Michael O'Leary cited on-time performance (defined as up to 15 minutes after scheduled time in UK Civil Aviation Authority statistics) and baggage handling as of key importance to customers. On the latter factor, Ryanair claimed less than one bag lost per 1,000 carried, even better than the best US airline, America West, with 3.39 bags per 1,000 lost. On punctuality, Ryanair claimed a 74 per cent 'on-time' performance on the Dublin–London

| Exhibit 6 | Ryanair selected operating statistics (euros) |

	1999	2000
Passengers carried	4.8 million	5.5 million
Revenue passenger miles (RPM)	1,643 million	2,103 million
Available seat miles (ASM)	2,304 million	3,126 million
Passenger load factor	71%	67%
Break-even load factor	58%	54%
Average length of passenger haul	339 miles	382 miles
Average passenger fare	55.33 euros	60.09 euros
Average daily flight utilisation	6.47 hours	6.37 hours
Employees at period end	1,203	1,388
Employees per aircraft	57	53
Passengers per employee	4,035	3,963
Average yield per RPM	0.158 euros	0.157 euros
Average yield per ASM	0.112 euros	0.106 euros
Average passenger spend per flight	5.11 euros	3.91 euros
Adjusted cost per ASM	0.092 euros	0.085 euros
Average fuel costs per gallon	0.66 euros	0.63 euros

Source: Ryanair.

route in 2000, compared to 64 per cent for Aer Lingus, 66 per cent for British Midland, and 77 per cent for CityFlyer operated by British Airways. It was unclear whether Ryanair included departure and arrival statistics, or departures only as it has done in the past. Exhibit 7 shows some punctuality comparisons between Ryanair and some of its competitors. (Not counted in the statistics were cancelled flights; Ryanair has been known to 'consolidate' passengers by transferring them from their original flight to later or alternative routing without any notice, if passengers were unfortunate enough to have originally been booked on a low seat occupancy flight.)

RYANAIR'S COMPETITIVE ARENA – THE EUROPEAN AIRLINE INDUSTRY

Even after deregulation, the European Commission was concerned that liberalisation had been ineffective, for several reasons. For example, advertised discounted fares are often so hedged with conditions and limited in quantity that passengers actually receive little benefit. Fares continued to rise on a large number of routes, operated as monopolies and duopolies. Further, strictly allocated slots at many major airports, such as London/Heathrow and Amsterdam/Schippol, were retained by incumbent national carriers, which restricted the scope of new market entrants.

The European market continues to be characterised by higher fares and operating costs than the US, resulting from relatively high tax and excise charges on fuel, and higher landing, ground handling and air traffic control charges. These stem from less competition in services, fragmentation in air

| Exhibit 7 | Airline punctuality comparisons for January 2001 arrivals and departures |

AIRLINE AND AIRPORT	NO. OF FLIGHTS	% EARLY TO 15 MINUTES LATE	AVERAGE DELAY (MINUTES)
Ryanair – Stansted[a]	1,081	74	11
Ryanair – Luton[b]	319	85	5
Ryanair – Gatwick[c]	247	76	8
Aer Lingus – Glasgow[d]	223	87	15
easyJet – Luton[e]	1,172	55	10
Go – Stansted[f]	424	86	8
Lufthansa – Stansted[g]	364	82	18
Aer Lingus – Gatwick[h]	186	82	11
Aer Lingus – Heathrow[i]	973	73	12
Go – Glasgow[j]	232	89	5
British Airways – Gatwick[k]	348	83	0
easyJet – Glasgow[l]	377	73	7
Virgin Express – Gatwick[m]	267	80	1
KLMuk – Stansted[n]	460	91	7

a Aarhus, Biarritz, Carcassonne, Dinard, Dublin, Nimes, Toulouse, Turin.
b Dublin.
c Dublin.
d Dublin.
e Amsterdam, Geneva, Glasgow, Palma, Zurich.
f Copenhagen, Geneva, Lyon, Munich, Prague.
g Frankfurt, Munich.
h Dublin.
i Dublin, Shannon.
j Stansted.
k Lyon, Toulouse.
l Luton.
m Brussels, Berlin, Shannon (also Sabena).
n Frankfurt, Geneva, Helsinki, Lyon, Toulouse, Vienna.
Source: UK Civil Aviation Authority.

traffic control, and greater worker protection and benefits in Europe than in the USA.

Relatively short distances on intra-European routes also contribute to higher expenses on a per 'available seat mile' (ASM) basis, passed on to the traveller in higher fares. The European market is also rendered difficult for airline operators because the airports and skies of Europe are more congested than in the USA. This forces new entrants into smaller airports, which tend to be far from large metropolitan city centres, in contrast to the USA where the smaller airports are usually within 10 miles of major city centres.

Another airline sub-sector in Europe is the vertically integrated groups of tour operators and travel agents which use in-house charter airlines. Since deregulation, some of these charter airlines have entered the scheduled service sector, but are still sticking to leisure-dominated routes.

In Europe, high-speed rail travel and the construction of major tunnels and bridges, for example the Channel Tunnel across the English Channel, provide viable and often quicker transport alternatives to air travel for journeys of up to 500 km (about 300 miles). This has had a dramatic effect in some cases. For example, after a high-speed rail link was established between Madrid and Seville, the rail versus air split changed from 33 per cent rail/67 per cent air, to 82 per cent rail/18 per cent air. Airline seats sold on the route fell from over 60,000 seats a month in 1992 to under 20,000 in 1993. In the first three years of the Eurostar rail operation on the Channel Tunnel, air passenger numbers from Britain to Paris fell from 4 million in 1994 to 2.8 million in 1997. However, while high-speed rail links are being developed around Europe, it is an extremely capital-intensive business. Further complications arise because of the convergence criteria set by the EU for cross-border train links.

An issue for European airports has been the abolition of duty-free shopping within the European Union from July 1999. Aer Rianta, the state-owned Irish Airports Authority, derived a major part of its profit from duty-free retail sales, and has raised landing and other airport charges to recover the loss in revenues. The same held for UK airports, including Stansted. The loss of duty-free sales was a bigger blow to smaller regional airports whose travel was heavily dependent on intra-continental travel, as compared to larger airports which could fall back on duty-free sales to passengers travelling outside the EU. Having accepted the inevitable, some airlines put pressure on the airports not to pass on the loss of their duty-free revenues to the airlines in the form of increased airport charges. For example, Ryanair reversed its expansion plans at Dublin Airport, although it has continued its expansion programme at Stansted.

Nevertheless, on the positive side, growth in air travel in the European market is one and a half times that of the more mature American market. A study conducted by the UK Civil Aviation Authority (CAA) in 1995 identified 34 intra-European international routes with potential for a new operator. This potential, along with deregulation, attracted new entrants, as many as 30 in 1996. However, most of them were small, undercapitalised, and subject to early failure. Vicious price wars were launched by major airlines serving the same routes. As soon as the new carrier was forced out of business, the big airline raised its prices and withdrew its extra seats. Nevertheless, between 1992 and 1998, national carriers' aggregate share of intra-European routes fell from over 80 per cent to under 70 per cent. However, on routes outside the EU, national carriers' share remains over 80 per cent.

A trend among national carriers has been to form alliances amongst themselves and/or with smaller airlines. It is predicted that, by 2010, the airline industry will form into a maximum of four groupings of national airlines. These alliances could themselves be networked to smaller airlines. For example, in 1998, American Airlines (AA) inaugurated a link with Air Liberté, a subsidiary of British Airways, to interline at Paris Orly airport to fly transatlantic AA passengers to seven provincial cities in France. (Air Liberté has since been sold off by British Airways to SAir, the parent company of Swissair, and in 2001 was threatened with liquidation after incurring unsustainable losses.) Generally, large established airlines have tended to consolidate their positions in their hub airports and not to avail of EU cabotage rights, instead opting for code sharing links with smaller airlines.

BUDGET AIRLINES IN EUROPE

The 1990s saw the birth of several budget carriers in Europe, starting with Ryanair. Generally, these airlines use the tactics of offering low fares, no frills, and point-to-point routes to smaller airports. According to a 1998 UK CAA report, evidence suggested that the budget carriers were able to achieve costs as low as half those of a major network carrier. Generally, they have not confronted the large established airlines in head-to-head battles, by choosing airports that were not served by the large carriers, instead growing volumes on new routes. In instances of direct confrontation, the large carriers have reacted in a number of ways. For example, Sabena's action in response to Virgin Express' entry to the Brussels–London route was to arrange a pooling deal where VE flies Sabena customers into Heathrow, using Sabena's access to scarce slots at Heathrow. BA has responded by franchising out some of their short-haul routes.

By 2001, the other main budget airlines operating in Europe were Buzz (owned by KLM, hub in Amsterdam/Schippol), easyJet (original hub in London/Luton, and almost continually loss-making since its inception in 1985, with an IPO in autumn 2000), Go (sold off in 2001 by British Airways to 3i, a private investment group, hub at Stansted), Virgin Express (hub in main Brussels Airport, pulled out of secondary hub at Shannon, Ireland, in 2000, after only 18-month operation there) and Air One (out of Milan). However, Ryanair is by far the dominant player in the budget industry in Europe (Exhibit 2).

BUDGET AIRLINES IN EUROPE – THE CUSTOMER'S PERSPECTIVE

The cheap flight deals offered to customers are frequently confusing. Often, when passengers attempt to avail themselves of advertised bargains, they discover that the deals are hedged with conditions, and that just a small proportion of seats are offered at the bargain fares.

In view of this fact, the *Sunday Times* carried out a study of four airlines – Debonair, easyJet, Go and Ryanair. Four writers each chose a route offered by one of the airlines. They were briefed to telephone for a price one month in advance of travel and then monitor fares up to the day of departure. It would be up to them as to when to actually purchase the ticket.

The results of the study are summarised in Exhibit 8. Early booking was more likely to get a bargain, but it was not always a guarantee of the lowest fares, as prices could go down if sales stagnated, and airlines monitored each flight by means of a yield management computer program. Early Internet booking apparently resulted in the cheapest fares, and the best fares were usually available for flights that left at unsociable hours.

The survey rated the total experience, from booking through to check-in, on-board comfort, catering and punctuality. The especially poor rating of Debonair was due to a number of factors – confusing price information from the booking agents and inaccurate check-in instructions at both ends, which were deemed a 'fiasco'. Worst of all, Debonair put its own passengers on AB

Exhibit 8	Low-cost airlines – an evaluation			
	DEBONAIR	**EASYJET**	**GO**	**RYANAIR**
Route	Gatwick to Lisbon	Luton to Barcelona	Stansted to Rome	Stansted to Dublin
Lowest available fare	£129	£108	£100	£49.98
Number of cheap fares	'A reasonable amount'	'Never less than 10%'	'A substantial number'	'50% at lowest fare'
Fare quoted 4 weeks before travel	£191.40	£148	£140	£100
3 weeks before	£221.30	£148	£120	£100
2 weeks before	£191.30	Sold out	£135	£100
1 week before	£291.50	£193	£135	£110
Day of travel	£291.50	£208	£170	£110
What other passengers paid	£129	£49–£188	£100	£40–£110
Cheapest rival	£161 (BA)	£173 (BA from Gatwick)	£155 (Alitalia)	£79 (Aer Lingus)
Rating of overall experience	0/10	9/10	8/10	8/10

Source: *Sunday Times*, 18 October 1998.

Airlines flights and charged them up to £160 more than AB passengers paid. For the critic, these factors outweighed the relative comfort of the flight itself. Debonair went into liquidation in 1999.

THE FUTURE?

Ryanair was the first airline in Europe to see an opportunity for a budget airline, and in 1998 was regarded as the leader of the pack.[1] Others followed as deregulation opened the skies of Europe. The US experience suggested that not all of them would fly. However, Michael O'Leary was not worried. He blamed faulty management, not competition, for the collapse of many of the US low-fare airlines. He declared, 'The majors would have never been able to put a lot of low fare guys out of business if the low fare guys hadn't tripped themselves up by overexpansion'.[2]

In a 1998 survey of the Irish equities market, Ryanair had the highest return on capital employed (ROCE) of all shares quoted on the Irish Stock Exchange. Moreover, the company was ranked number three of 60 Irish Stock Exchange companies by analysts on the criteria of 'strategic positioning' and 'capital structure'[3] and number two for 'marketing' in 2000. The same year, Ryanair was awarded the 'Irish Company of the year' accolade by *Business & Finance*, an Irish weekly business magazine.

---

[1]C.P. Wallace, 'Leader of the low-fare pack', *Fortune*, 138 (11), Dec. 7, 1998, pp. 92–94.
[2]C.P. Wallace, 'Leader of the low-fare pack', *Fortune*, 138 (11), Dec. 7, 1998, pp. 92–94.
[3]'The Irish Stock Market', *Finance*, Nov. 1998.

CASE STUDIES

In 1999 and 2000, Ryanair won the prestigious Best Managed Airline Award organised by US *Aviation Week* and *Space Technology* magazines. The Award was based on six criteria – asset utilisation, productivity, financial stability, earnings protection, liquidity, and valuation. *Aviation Week* vice-president Kenneth Gazzola said, 'The best managed companies rankings are a report card for determining how well management is running the business in light of current and future competitive requirements.'[4] Another international award won by Ryanair in 2000 is 'Airline of the Year' from *Transport World*.

By 2001, Ryanair had increased its profits for 10 years in succession. It derived 60 per cent of its business from UK operations, 18 per cent from Ireland, and the rest from Continental Europe. Ryanair had 45 routes across 11 countries in Europe and indicated it was focusing on intensifying competitive pressure on established European flag carriers and other low-cost airlines. By summer 2001, Ryanair planned to offer more European routes from Stansted than BA served from Heathrow. The new bases would shift the focus of its next phase of growth to continental Europe, which was expected to be the source of 40 per cent of Ryanair's traffic within the next two years. O'Leary's target of 9m passengers by 2002 would make Ryanair the fifth largest airline on intra-European routes. He predicted that by 2008, Ryanair would carry 20m passengers, taking it beyond BA in European traffic terms and contesting Lufthansa for the number one spot. The challenge now was to maintain focus on its niche and to keep costs under control.

---

[4] *The Sunday Tribune*, June 6, 1999, *Business*, p.7.

BMW Automobiles

Valeriano Lencioni

Bayerische Motoren Werke (BMW) was one of Europe's top automobile makers. BMW automobiles accounted for nearly 75 per cent of the company's sales. The company's operations also included motorcycles and software: this case deals only with BMW automobiles. This case looks at the position of BMW in 2000, following the sale of Rover. BMW had sold its Land Rover SUV operations to Ford and unloaded its money-losing Rover Automobiles unit to the Phoenix Consortium (for a token £10). The case looks at the structure of the automobile industry, especially in Europe, and poses the question of the future of BMW in the highly competitive and collaborative environment of the early twenty-first century. BMW had been the subject of merger talk as the European auto industry consolidated, but the Quandts, a reclusive German family that owns 46 per cent of BMW, have downplayed such speculation.

• • •

BACKGROUND

The automobile industry in 2000

The origins of the automobile industry are rooted in the development of the petrol combustion engine, brought about principally in France in the second half of the nineteenth century. By the beginning of the twentieth century automobiles were manufactured in France, Germany, Italy, the UK and the US: the US dominated automobile production in the first half of the century through the development of large-scale production technologies; in the second half of the twentieth century, Europe and Japan had also become major producers and exporters.

Consolidation

The trends in the automobile industry present through the 1990s intensified as the industry moved into the twenty-first century. Global convergence stood out

---

as a major issue. The well-established practice of building and marketing auto-mobiles specifically designed for national countries had been bucked by Japan when they entered the international automobile market in the late 1960s. In a couple of decades the old national-based approach had virtually disappeared, and automobiles built in one region were sold, with peripheral changes, around the world. Two main forces had driven this change: the virtual disappearance of the national assemblers, squeezed out by the international giants, and the standardisation of markets across international segments, pushed by regulatory forces at regional level and fuelled by ever more intense global communica-tions. The trend applied as much to original equipment manufacturers (OEMs) or auto assemblers as to parts suppliers. It is difficult to tell where it will end, but there is little doubt that the trend is set to continue. This was bound to put pressure on the mid-sized players that were not big enough to compete with the half a dozen giants that dominated the industry, but were not small or dif-ferentiated enough to compete in a niche market. Consolidation was continu-ing, driven by overcapacity: worldwide plant utilisation in 2000 was 69 per cent, compared with 80 per cent in 1990.

Competition in the automobile industry, especially in Europe, was very fierce. Exhibit 1 shows the main producers. The level of quality attained by most manufacturers meant that opportunities for product differentiation were fewer and fewer, whilst the cost structure and the degree of rivalry made price competition a likely strategy for most automobile makers. The increasing productivity across Europe had fostered overcapacity, with capacity to pro-duce 20m automobiles a year in a 14m per annum European automobiles market. Japanese output, particularly from the British plants of Nissan, Honda and Toyota, had also increased, creating a gross oversupply. The mismatch between capacity and demand increased the price competition, whilst cost of sales was spiralling. In 1999, Ford Europe made losses of almost $117m; Fiat automobiles were just breaking even whilst Peugeot's profits plummeted. And at the same time as they were being squeezed by price pressures, European automobile makers were also having to satisfy increasingly demanding con-sumers, who sought new products, greater choice and value for money. Also, environmental concerns and petrol prices generated demand for smaller auto-mobiles, which give smaller margins. Together these trends produced heavy demands on the automobile makers' resources.

There was a great deal of consensus amongst commentators that in a few years the industry would consist of no more than six giants, with a peppering of niche players. Mergers and acquisition activity between January 1998 and May 2000 had generated $138.7bn in 875 deals, with emphasis moving from automobile manufacturers, already highly concentrated, to parts suppliers. The European automobile industry, in the last few years of the 1990s, had under-gone major changes. Ford acquired Volvo autos; GM acquired 20 per cent of Fiat automobiles division, with Fiat buying a 5.1 per cent stake in GM; BMW disposed of Rover. VW dominated the European automobile scene. Middle-sized players, such as Fiat, BMW and Peugeot, were under pressure to merge with other players to survive. The quest for cost reduction and the increasing pressure for regulatory compliance accelerated the trends towards standardisa-tion of the automobile as a product across regions.

| Exhibit 1 | Automobile production in the European Union (in units) by group at 16 June 2000 |

AUTOMOBILE GROUP	PASSENGER CARS	LIGHT COMMERCIAL VEHICLES	TRUCKS	BUSES	TOTAL
Volkswagen	2,985,715	177,890	0	0	3,163,605
PSA Peugeot Citröen	1,969,102	415,367	0	0	2,384,469
Ford*	2,079,412	198,495	0	0	2,277,907
GM	1,916,279	58,249	0	0	1,974,528
Renault	1,645,670	263,285	42,182	2,355	1,953,492
Fiat	1,402,698	217,474	66,108	4,197	1,690,477
Daimler-Chrysler	1,127,085	178,259	94,848	6,423	1,406,615
BMW Rover	1,048,046	24,155	0	0	1,072,201
Volvo	0	0	50,505	5,698	56,203
MAN	0	0	50,025	3,943	53,968
Paccar–DAF–Leyland Trucks–Foden	0	0	32,466	1,795	34,261
Scania	0	0	41,580	2,633	44,213
Porsche	46,167	0	0	0	46,167
Other European manufacturers	0	1,532	12,913	6,744	21,189
Japanese manufacturers	713,296	82,225	3,584	0	799,105
TOTAL	14,933,470	1,616,931	394,211	33,788	16,978,400

* Volvo Cars Production is included in Ford.

Source: National Associations/ACEA.

Companies left out of the big game were well aware of the vulnerability of their independence and, despite the protection given to some by the family structure of their ownership, they had endeavoured to make their position more difficult for predators to attack. Fiat had forged a link with giant GM: the deal entailed selling 20 per cent of Fiat automobiles division and acquiring 5.1 per cent of GM. The deal secured Fiat a badly needed access to the US market, and offered GM Alfa Romeo as a new brand to exploit globally. Daimler-Chrysler had acquired Mitsubishi of Japan. In general, a web of relationships linked automobile makers and parts suppliers in a very complex system, both as a drive to efficiency and as an attempt by smaller players to retain independence. Peugeot and Renault-Nissan, despite the French government having ended its financial help, seemed to be relatively safe, Renault-Nissan because of its substantial size, Peugeot because it was family controlled. BMW also looked vulnerable to predators: its position is discussed later in this case.

The pace of consolidation in Asia was less hectic but still sustained. Daimler-Chrysler acquired 34 per cent of Mitsubishi of Japan, in a deal widely considered successful despite the risk of clashes of the very different cultures. Renault acquired 36 per cent of Nissan; its likely acquisition of Samsung of South Korea would further increase the synergy of Renault-Nissan, as Samsung used Nissan technology. Toyota and Honda, like most Japanese companies, were fiercely independent; however, allying with each other would have reduced the risk of having to merge with foreign companies.

Exhibit 2	Worldwide vehicle sales and profit per vehicle, 1999	
	SALES (000)[1]	AVERAGE PROFIT PER VEHICLE (US$)
General Motors	8,786	$859
Ford	7,220	$1,170
Toyota	4,280[2]	$1,390
Chrysler	3,174	$1,657
Mercedes	1,080	$2,691
BMW	751	$2,865
Volvo	411	$0.72[4]
Lexus	333[3]	Not available
Saab	131	$645[4]

[1] Includes light trucks where applicable.
[2] Excludes Lexus.
[3] Includes Lexus models sold as Toyotas in Japan.
[4] Based on fiscal year 1998.

A well-known inhibitor of consolidation was the desire of governments to minimise the disruption caused by major mergers and acquisitions, principally in the form of the unemployment that usually accompanies post-merger cost cutting. A less well known inhibitor was the family ownership of a number of important automobile manufacturers, notably Ford, Fiat, BMW and Peugeot-Citroën. The founders of these illustrious industrial dynasties were entrepreneurs that took well-rewarded risks by investing in businesses in the emerging automobile manufacturing industry: echoes of today's dot-com start-ups are loud! However, a few generations later their successors, operating in a mature industry and in a radically different business environment, were likely to question the amount of wealth locked in giant motor corporations returning a lower than average profitability or even making a loss. Exhibit 2 shows the relative size and profitability of a selection of world automobile manufacturers in 1999.

The Internet and e-commerce

Given the importance of automobile purchasing to customers, the Internet and e-commerce were likely to play a vital role by shortening the lead time for the production of an automobile, which was 60–100 days. If, given the importance of the purchase, customers could be brought into a Web-driven relationship with automobile suppliers and manufacturers, a shortening of the lead time was a distinct possibility.

The Internet was likely to allow for a more accurate assessment of demand, not only of its volume, but also of the kind of vehicles and optional extras the market required. Toyota and GM were dreaming of a 'five-day automobile' built to order! As far as manufacturing was concerned, considering that a typical automobile was made up of more than 20,000 parts provided by about 200 suppliers, all due to be delivered 'just-in-time', a business-to-business network looked remarkably useful.

Automobile manufacturers were keen to control design and technology: major breakthroughs had been fuel injection, ABS and air bags. The pursuit of cost reduction had generated a trend towards an increased role of parts suppliers in the design of the finished product. By outsourcing more and more to suppliers, and shifting towards assembling modules, rather than parts, many automobile assemblers reduced their scope for design, thus impairing their ability to add value to the final product, or their ability to appropriate it. Supplier consolidation was set to accelerate, due to the use of Internet and business-to-business procurement to design, produce, assemble, distribute and service automobiles.

Outlook

Consensus amongst analysts was that there would be a sustained period of slowdown in the global automobile market, with exceptions in some developing countries. Despite being caught out for wrongly forecasting a slowdown in the late 1990s whilst, in fact, sales grew this time, they were likely to be right. First there was a slowdown in the economy in many parts of the world; secondly, 'Customers are burning out of buying new automobiles', according to D.B. Healy of Burnham Motors. Moreover, for many types of vehicles profit margins were shrinking.

The automobile industry was a vital part of the economy of many countries; automobile exports were essential to the health of their trade balances and, due to the number of allied industries involved, a valid source of jobs. A natural by-product of automobile industry globalisation was the diminishing importance of nation states in the decision processes affecting the automobile industry. There was a conflict of objectives: auto manufacturers pursued a maximisation of shareholder value, which did not necessarily coincide with the interests of the host country. BMW's somewhat unceremonious disposal of Rover in the UK was an example of outcomes generated by such conflict, resolved by BMW in favour of defending shareholders' value.

BMW AUTOMOBILES

Bayerische Motoren Werke (BMW), owner of the prestigious BMW brand, was one of Europe's top automakers. BMW automobiles accounted for nearly 75 per cent of the group's sales. The company's operations also included motorcycles and software. BMW's equity was controlled by the Quandts, a reclusive German family that owned 46 per cent of the BMW Group.

The turnover of the Group was over €35bn (£22bn), with BMW Automobiles accounting for about €25bn (£15.5bn), achieving over 10 per cent operating profit. BMW Automobiles employed 82,000 workers in plants in Munich and

Regensburg in Germany, Spartanburg in the US and Rosslyn in South Africa: they produced over 820,000 BMW cars. The main models produced by BMW were the 3-series, aimed at young executives, the 5-series, aimed at the executive segment, and the 7-series, aimed at the luxury market. Other models were coupés or cabriolets derived from the basic saloon models. Significant models were also the Z3 coupé, an expensive roadster, and the X5, a premium-priced SUV.

Origins

BMW was established during the First World War to manufacture engines; in 1945, the company was still Germany's leading manufacturer of aero-engines. Subsequently it diversified into what in 2000 were its main products, automobiles and motorbikes. By then BMW was one of Germany's largest and most successful companies. But BMW's road to sustained success was a troubled one and in 2000 the horizon was not all rosy. The group's activities were concentrated almost exclusively on two product ranges: high-performance saloon automobiles and motorbikes. The focus of this case is on automobiles.

The march to success

At the end of the Second World War, both its aero-engines market and its capital equipment were under serious threat. The demand for aero-engines, Germany having lost the war, had temporarily disappeared, and its main factory was now in the Soviet occupation zone. Therefore, whilst post-war West Germany experienced an economic miracle, BMW struggled. Uncertain of its destiny, the company concentrated on automobile production, but without a focus, its products ranging from small 'bubble cars', built under licence, to large limousines. In 1959 BMW faced bankruptcy, when it found a powerful shareholder, Herbert Quandt, who could see the company's inherent strengths beyond the current difficulties. The turning point came in 1961, when it launched the BMW 1500, which soon established the BMW automobile brand as one with a reputation for engineering excellence.

The BMW brand also acquired a distinctive identity as a symbol for young, affluent European professionals: most drivers perceived high-performance saloon automobiles as synonymous with BMW: '*The Ultimate Driving Machine*'.

In the twenty-first century, the scarce resources that most influence national competitiveness are likely to be the skills displayed by the workforce. One of Germany's distinctive national resources was a highly qualified labour force that could be used by German manufacturers as a source of competitive advantage. Most of such advantage went to companies that like BMW, managed to build a perception of valuable differences in the minds of their buyers.

It was difficult to single out a specific resource that underpinned BMW's success: it was rather a series of factors, and the way they combined to sustain its competitiveness powerful, reliable, luxurious but not exceptionally so. BMW's technology had been advanced, but not exceptionally innovative (when compared, for example, with Citroën). Its automobiles were conventionally designed and traditionally styled, yet they were expensive, even considering the high level of specification offered by most models, with retail margins comparatively high. The company had tightly controlled its distribution network, to the benefit of brand management and communication. Being close to the buyers had also allowed them to segment the market effectively: for example, BMW automobiles have been positioned differently and priced differently in the various national markets. BMW also exercised a firm control on the supply chain and dealings and relationships with suppliers, who mostly had maintained a long association with the company. That combination, a system of production that gave the company advantage in its chosen segment, a reputation for product quality and a brand which immediately identifies the aims and aspirations of its customers, by the mid-1990s had built BMW into one of the most profitable automobile manufacturers in the world.

THE BMW BRAND

BMW had traditionally taken great pride in the quality of its engineering, higher than was usual in most production vehicles. Whilst at the end of the 1990s most automobile assembly operations were carried out by automated assembly lines or relatively unskilled workers, BMW employed a highly skilled German labour force. The comparatively high costs were more than offset by the benefits of a reputation for high-quality products.

On the product front, until the early 1990s, BMW had stuck to its core of performance saloons, with only limited diversification into other niches, such as convertibles. In business terms, this strategy of adhesion to BMW's core values had been vindicated by the bottom line, with the 3-series saloons continuing to be especially in demand. However, what was a strategic focus could be seen as inflexibility at a time when competitors had spanned successfully across segments. Volkswagen, for example, on the back of a broad and attractive range of brands, was establishing a significant presence in most segments of the market. An attempt by BMW to dramatically broaden the range of models on offer and to increase its size was the acquisition of Rover automobiles from the UK.

THE ROVER VENTURE

In the early 1990s BMW had kept a watchful eye on the progress of Rover of the UK, a company of similar size to itself in terms of unit volume, increasingly competing in segments in which BMW was present and some segments it was planning to enter. In 1994 Mr Pischetsrieder, then CEO of the BMW group, masterminded the £800m ($1.3bn) acquisition from British Aerospace in what was one of the boldest moves in the motor industry at the time and an extraordinary step for the conservative German automobile manufacturer. Pischetsrieder was committed to an 'overlap' product strategy – developing

a full line of Rover automobiles that at the larger end would overlap with BMW models. But the second-in-command at BMW, Wolfgang Reitzle, argued that Rover should be developed as a complementary brand, and wanted to focus on Land Rover and automobiles below BMW's 3-series: i.e. the Mini and maybe MG. The overlap strategy was meant to give the discerning buyer a choice between two distinctive and classy products, clear alternatives in the same categories of vehicles. Pischetsrieder was backed by Eberhard von Kunheim, BMW's supervisory board chairman and adviser to the Quandts, who owned a 46 per cent controlling stake in the company. With Rover specialising in small, front-wheel drive vehicles, compared with BMW's larger, rear-wheel drive models, it was also hoped that the acquisition would bring complementary skills, in addition to a geographically broader market.

But the acquisition turned out to be a much more difficult venture than BMW had expected, due to Rover's inadequate manufacturing and, crucially, the strength of sterling which in the late 1990s put immense pressure on the company's already poor profitability. The strong UK currency gave an advantage to continental European carmakers such as Peugeot-Citroën, Renault and Fiat, who could use their increased profitability to boost their market share in the UK; also exports, which Rover had managed to increase, were badly squeezed.

In 2000, Joachim Milberg, a mild university professor who had joined BMW in 1993, succeeded Pischetsrieder, who had resigned as chairman of BMW management board in the wake of the worsening Rover crisis. During his time at BMW Milberg had been instrumental in creating one of the most efficient automobile plants in the world, at the company's manufacturing base in Regensburg, as well as being closely involved with the Spartanburg plant in South Carolina. He had inherited a company in need of a long-term strategy, with a thorny problem at Rover.

A major problem in the venture had been that Rover had a very high break-even point, which made it virtually impossible to achieve a profit. Another problem had been caused by BMW's management approach after the acquisition: the executives from Munich were too slow to enforce the BMW management style and press on with the integration. When they changed their approach it was too late. More crucially, BMW believed that it could turn Rover into a brand as strong as the BMW brand, but Rover products had suffered too many quality lapses, and buyers simply would not choose Rover, even if owned by BMW.

There had been an inflated expectation of the UK market, and the strong pound did the rest. So the acquisition, which had been BMW's hope for the future, in the brief space of six years had become worthless. In early 2000 BMW sold Rover to the Phoenix Consortium, which included some Rover managers, for the symbolic sum of £10. It also sold the Land Rover division (which produced Range Rover, Discovery, Defender and Freelander) to Ford: in doing so, BMW relinquished perhaps the only part of the group that could have had some future potential. BMW had not been able to make a profit from Land Rover because to emphasise the brand's exclusivity it built each model on separate platforms, rather than seeking cost efficiencies through sharing parts and platforms. As a result, the models had been priced out of the market.

BMW'S MAJOR COMPETITORS IN 2000

Volkswagen (VW), with a production of 4.9m automobiles a year from plants all over the world, was Europe's no. 1 automobile maker. VW had revamped the 'beetle', and produced models such as Jetta and Passat, which competed with BMW in the executive saloons segment. At the luxury end of the automobile market it owned such carmakers as AUDI, Lamborghini, Rolls-Royce and Bentley. Other brands included Seat (family automobiles produced in Spain) and Skoda (family automobiles produced in the Czech Republic). The company had also agreed to buy a 19 per cent stake in Scania, the Swedish truck-maker. VW had interests in consumers' finance and in automobile rental (Europcar International). The German state of Lower Saxony had a 16 per cent stake in VW.

General Motors (GM) had succeeded in remaining the world's no. 1 maker of automobiles and trucks, including brands such as Buick, Cadillac, Chevrolet, GMC, Pontiac, Saab, Saturn and Oldsmobile (which was to be discontinued). GM also produced automobiles through its Holden, Opel and Vauxhall subsidiaries. Other GM interests included Hughes Electronics (DirecTV, communications), Allison Transmission (heavy-duty automatic transmissions) and GM Locomotive (locomotives, diesel engines). GM had a 49 per cent stake in Isuzu Motors and 20 per cent stakes in Fuji Heavy Industries (Subaru), Suzuki Motor and Fiat Auto (which also included Alfa Romeo and Lancia). GMAC was GM's financial arm.

Daimler-Chrysler was the world's no. 3 automobile maker in sales (behind General Motors and Ford) and no. 5 in number of automobiles sold. It was also BMW's arch-rival, with whom it battled head-on in most of the segments in which BMW competed. Formed by the $37 billion acquisition of Chrysler by Germany's Daimler-Benz in 1998, the company made about 4 million vehicles a year (of all types). Chrysler's brands included Dodge, Eagle, Jeep and Plymouth vehicles; the Mercedes brand was limited to luxury automobiles, commercial vehicles and SUVs. Also, Daimler-Chrysler's Freightliner unit was the US's no. 1 heavy truck maker. Daimler-Chrysler, which had announced a 26,000 jobs cut over three years at its US-based Chrysler division, had a 9 per cent stake in Hyundai Motor and a 34 per cent stake in Mitsubishi Motors. Mercedes-Benz had branched away from its established image and ageing customer base. Despite the difficult start of the A-Class mini car, which had to be expensively redesigned, diversification had greatly contributed to the achievement of 1m car sales a year by 2000. But it was the Daimler-Benz parent company that had put pressure on BMW: by taking over Chrysler, it was forcing BMW to review its assumptions about its own optimum size and the economies of scale necessary to its survival as an independent company. The Daimler-Chrysler deal had left smaller, specialised carmakers looking vulnerable

When **Toyota** decided to introduce their Lexus models to compete in the luxury-automobile market, they employed a best-cost provider strategy. They did this by transferring the expertise in making high-quality Toyota automobiles at low cost to making premium-quality luxury automobiles at costs below other luxury-automobile makers. They targeted especially Mercedes and

BMW, focusing on the provision of performance features and upscale quality into Lexus models at a lower cost than other luxury-automobile manufacturers. Toyota reasoned – correctly – that with their cost advantage they could price their well-appointed Lexus cars low enough to draw price-sensitive buyers, e.g. fleet managers, away from Mercedes and BMW and perhaps induce dissatisfied Lincoln and Cadillac owners to switch to a Lexus. They also established a new network of Lexus dealers, separate from Toyota's, to provide an unprecedented level of personalised customer service.

The Lexus 400 series models competed against Mercedes' 300/400E series, BMW's 5/7-series, Nissan's Infiniti Q45, Cadillac Seville, Jaguar and Lincoln Continental. The lower-priced Lexus 300 series competed against Cadillac deVille, Acura Legend, Infiniti J30, Buick Park Avenue, Mercedes' C-Class series and BMW's 3-series. Lexus had also introduced sport-utility vehicles to compete against those from Mercedes, Lincoln, Cadillac, BMW, Infiniti, Jeep and Range Rover. Lexus's best-cost producer strategy was so successful that Mercedes, in order to become more competitive, introduced a new, lower-priced C-Class series. The Lexus LS 400 models and the Lexus SC 300/400 models have consistently ranked amongst the top 10 models in authoritative surveys.

Other competitors in the BMW traditional executive and luxury segments of the automobile market were Volvo, and increasingly brands like Jaguar, also owned by Ford.

BMW'S FUTURE

On the face of it, BMW occupied a position in the automobile industry that any automobile maker would envy. In 2000, BMW sales rose 8 per cent worldwide and 18 per cent in the US, where it outsold both Mercedes and Lexus. And although GM and Ford sold many more vehicles, BMW's average profit per car sold was more than double, with margins amongst the highest in the world – only the small and narrowly focused Porsche had a higher profitability.

But it was not a uniformly positive picture. Even though sales of the lower-margin 3-series rose 7 per cent, taking them to over 500,000 cars for the first time, and overall group sales rose 6.6 per cent, sales of BMW's top ranges, the 5-series and 7-series, fell in 1999 and 2000, by 8 and 9 per cent respectively. BMW faced strong competition from Daimler-Chrysler's C-class and from Audi's new A-class, launched late in 2000. Moreover, some analysts attributed much of the rise in BMW's operating profit to currency gains, reflecting the euro's continuing fall against the other major currencies.

Until the ruinous Rover adventure, BMW had not had an unprofitable year for 40 years: only Toyota could make a similar claim. Its shares had climbed steadily through the 1990s, from the equivalent of $8.80 a share to about $30. BMW's buyers were primarily wealthy 'baby-boomers' and up-and-coming Gen Xers – two very attractive segments. The brand's popularity was still rising, with eager buyers joining long waiting lists. Over the decades, with fanatical devotion to manufacturing quality, a single-minded focus on sporty luxury,

and careful, conservative nurturing of its brand, BMW had established a shining reputation. So in 2000 BMW was in an attractive, indeed enviable, position, but this also made it an attractive takeover target, possibly the most tempting in the automobile industry. All major car manufacturers (VW, Ford, GM) had made advances: all were rejected. BMW had no intention of being taken over by anybody. On the contrary, by taking over the Rover Group, it had attempted to grow big enough to join the ranks of the auto industry's superpowers. But that strategy failed when the Rover venture ended in tears. The failure put into serious question whether BMW was really competitive at building anything other than performance, premium cars, and exposed BMW's management weaknesses.

It is not surprising therefore that, after such painful lessons, BMW's stance for independence was re-emphasised: 'BMW Group will continue to grow under its own power, without requiring any mergers or diversification,' CEO Joachim Milberg told shareholders at the annual meeting in May 2000. 'And from now on we will pursue a strategy based on the BMW brand extending from the lower midrange segment all the way to the luxury-performance segment.' BMW's size continued to be a cause for concern. Industry wisdom sustains that to survive long-term an automobile manufacturer must build two million vehicles a year. Yet, in 2000, without Rover, BMW made only 820,000 vehicles.

Barbarians may not have been at BMW's door yet, but signs were not reassuring. A number of small and medium-sized automobile makers (Jaguar, Volvo, Mazda, Subaru, Nissan) had been taken over by bigger players; Daimler merged with Chrysler, and Volkswagen had swallowed a number of small but valuable luxury brands (Lamborghini, Bentley, Bugatti, and some rights on the Rolls-Royce brand name). But if BMW saw size as a protection of its cherished independence, was Milberg's brand extension strategy really the way for it to grow?

The strategy of independence had always been strongly supported by the Quandt family, which had controlled BMW since 1959 when Herbert Quandt snatched it from Daimler and made it into one of the most successful German manufacturers. However, circumstances were changing. The auto industry was not amongst the most profitable. Even considering the greater margins generated by BMW's premium pricing, the differentiation that justified higher than average prices came at great cost, and was time-consuming. The family may have begun to compare the dwindling margins to be had in the automobile industry with alternative investments, and be tempted to switch interest and commitment, especially after the costly Rover debacle. The public squabbling at the top of BMW's management in the wake of the failure of Rover's venture, culminating in Pischetsrieder's and Reitzle's resignations, must have been looked at with dismay by the very private family. The circumstances had also changed in other ways. The son and daughter of Herbert Quandt had joined the supervisory board when their mother stepped down: their loyalty to the company may not have been as solid as that of the previous generation. The Quandts do not comment – they never do – but some industry observers believe that they may have been working towards shaking up the management and putting the company back into shape before selling their stake. That would end the independence of the proud Bavarian group.

South African Breweries

Gerry Johnson and Urmilla Lawson

South African Breweries (SAB) has grown on the basis of its strength in developing markets, first in Africa and then in other parts of the world. This case study explains that development and the strategy of the firm as it was declared in its annual reports. It provides an opportunity to evaluate strategy based on market expansion which has led the firm from its origins in Africa to become one of the largest brewers in the world.

• • •

BACKGROUND

SAB has become one of the major beer and beverage companies in the world. It was registered in London by a syndicate of investors from the UK and South Africa in 1895. Castle Lager was launched in Johannesburg in 1898 and in the same year SAB was listed on the London stock exchange. In 1970, its primary listing was moved to the Johannesburg stock exchange and, in 1999, SAB moved this back to London. By 2001, SAB was the fifth largest brewer in the world and the fastest-growing brewer from 1996 to 2000, with brewing operations in 21 different countries and an output of 77m hectolitres of beer. Its financial performance over this time is summarised in Appendix 1.

In South Africa, SAB leads the beer market with Castle Lager. However, its wider portfolio included:

● SAB: Beer – South Africa and continental Africa with breweries for both lager and sorghum and brands such as Castle, Carling Black Label, Hansa Pilsner, Lion, Amstel, Heineken, Hoftbrau, Dakota Ice and 24 other brands.

● SABI Asia: breweries in China and India; with 18 major beer brands in China and purified water and soya milk.

● SAB Europe: breweries in the Canary Islands, Czech Republic, Hungary, Poland, Romania, Russia and Slovakia and brands including Pilsner Urquell, Gambrinus, Radegast, Keller, Ursus, Redd's, Lech and Tyskie.

● Other beverage interests: bottling plants in Africa of spring water, soft drinks, juices and sparkling water, including the Coca-Cola, Schweppes, Appletiser range.

● Southern Sun Hotels (77 hotels throughout Southern Africa) and 3 casinos.

STRATEGY

The 1998 annual report of SAB explained the Group's strategy:

SAB's international focus has been on countries in which it believes it could use its expertise, which has been gained over 100 years in South Africa, to develop beer markets in emerging economies. SAB has invested significantly in its core businesses, and has commenced brewing operations in a further 5 African countries, 3 Chinese provinces, and 4 Eastern European countries since 1995. SAB intends to continue to protect and further develop its South Africa operations, while investing for growth in its international beer business, where a profitable base, with critical mass in selected developing markets and regions, has been achieved. Incremental growth, both organic and through acquisitions, is being pursued aggressively.

This was spelled out more fully by 2000:

In the less developed world, Africa and Asia and much of Europe, brewing remained highly fragmented, with beer drinkers supplied by breweries which were never more than small-scale and localised, often producing low-quality beer. This was also the case, even under the Communist regimes, in China, Eastern and Central Europe, despite their centralising and mass production strategy for most other industries.

This fragmentation presented the opportunity for SAB from the mid-1990s to create a profitable and fast-expanding business in emerging markets with huge potential. This opportunity involves, generally, taking a share in a brewery with a local partner and, while retaining the brand because drinkers tend to have fierce attachments to their local brew, transforming the business. This starts with upgrading quality and consistency to create a beer for which people are prepared to pay more and which can give us a healthy profit margin. Then comes improvement to marketing and distribution. Next we improve productivity and capacity.

In each country we have begun by acquiring an initial local stronghold from which we can advance into regions beyond the brewery's original catchment area. We then build critical mass in the region and progress, over time, to a national basis. This is often achieved by acquiring further brewing businesses and focusing the brand portfolio. An optimum brand portfolio gives us a better overall marketing proposition, increases total sales and delivers economies of scale in production and distribution.

This process demands, on one level, great political sensitivity in dealing with governments, partners, local communities and our workforce and, on another level, the deployment of expert operational management skills learnt in South Africa. At the same time we market and promote selected premium brands, either brewed locally or imported – often our own Castle Lager, which is the biggest selling beer in Africa. Our management structure is decentralised, reflecting the local nature of beer branding and distribution.

In most emerging markets, consumption of beer is directly related to the level of disposable income at consumer level. Attractive markets thus arise in developing economies as consumer spending increases. This is often accompanied by structural changes in society, such as increasing urbanisation and the development of more varied and sophisticated lifestyles, which also encourage beer consumption.

Our businesses do not all advance at the same speed, nor have the same potential. It is characteristic of emerging markets that growth can be variable, and we are accustomed to temporary setbacks. However, the spread of our international businesses provides a 'portfolio effect', thereby reducing the impact of setbacks in one or two individual countries. For example, last year adverse climatic conditions in

Mozambique and Tanzania and economic problems in Romania were more than offset by spectacular growth in Poland and China, strong growth in Botswana and a steady improvement in more than a dozen other countries.

Since we embarked on our global expansion in 1994, the trend in sales and profits has been steadily upwards. We are confident that over time our returns will prove to be outstanding.

Appendix 2 shows the volume sales of beer by country achieved by SAB from 1997 to 2000.

SOUTH AFRICA

South Africa was the original market for SAB and remains centrally important. However, here, the company had experienced mixed fortunes. In 2000 it had suffered a 2 per cent decline in volume, but could report an increase in its margins as a result of continuing productivity initiatives. The main reason for the downturn was the domestic situation in South Africa, and in particular a switch in consumer spending. The annual report explained this as follows:

> The proportion of disposable income which the average South African spends on beverages and tobacco has fallen steadily since 1992. The 'normalisation' theory suggests that this shift in consumer expenditure will continue as a higher proportion of discretionary expenditure moves from immediate gratification to self-improvement. As home ownership is encouraged, townships are electrified and more schools are opened, so money is earmarked for mortgages, rents, consumer durables and education. Mobile phones have also become very popular with the potential to divert spending further from beer.
>
> However, the increasingly stable macroeconomic environment, which has encouraged many of these trends, provides a significant opportunity for SAB to grow volumes over the long term. Sound economic policies, which create wealth and higher employment, also result in increased consumer expenditure. We believe that absolute expenditure on beer will rise even if beer is taking a lower percentage of growing consumer spending.
>
> In the meantime, we continue to work hard to increase our market share in the total South African liquor market by making beer the alcoholic drink of first choice for more people primarily through better channel segmentation, distribution and promotions. Our percentage share of the total liquor market is in the mid-50's, so there is scope for further increase.

Upgrading of production facilities had included the expansion of the Alrode brewery to provide a capacity of 8.2 hectolitres a year and a new packaging line; and the commissioning of a new brewery in Port Elizabeth with a filling line capability of 50,000 bottles an hour – one of the largest and fastest in the world. The expectation was that the Port Elizabeth brewery would have an eventual capacity of 62,500 litres a day with a continuous 24-hour process. The aim was to continue the emphasis on productivity improvements which had already contributed to the rise in margins.

In addition, the company had launched new products, for example adding to its range of alcoholic fruit beverages, and seeking market share gains in the premium lager sector through its Amstel and imported Heineken brands.

However, there were concerns by analysts over SAB's position in South Africa. According to HSBC and ING Barings, by 2001 beer volumes in South Africa were declining at an annualised rate of about 4 per cent and there were few signs that growth in the rest of Africa was holding up. There were also concerns that costs of raw materials would rise. Other conditions in South Africa also seemed to be worrying. As well as consumer spending on beer being diverted into other products such as the lottery and mobile phones, there was real concern that the spread of AIDS was becoming 'pandemic'. SAB was dependent for turnover growth either on price increases or volume growth in the market and neither seemed very likely. There were no signs that consumer spending would increase on beer and population growth was unlikely, especially given the AIDS epidemic. In fact beer growth was averaging around 3.2 per cent in the 1990s, declining to 2.5 per cent since 1996. When it came to AIDS, UN statistics showed that around 4.2 million people (or 9 per cent of the population) were infected with HIV or full-blown AIDS. This was less than the estimates of the World Health Organisation who forecast a rise in the disease in the population of around 30 per cent by 2010. The estimate was that 8 million AIDS-related deaths could occur by that time, and that most of these would be young adults, who were the key market segment for SAB.

As for the new capacity for brewing, the fear was that SAB could be facing a situation of underutilisation by 2001. In addition, there were fears that the Castle brand was insufficiently differentiated in South Africa, potentially being 'caught in the middle'. Premium brands such as Heineken or Amstel were little more in price than Castle, while Sorghum beer, often drunk in townships, was a good deal cheaper and positioned Castle as a premium beer in relation to it.

None of these factors was much helped by the wetter and colder conditions which seemed to prevail in South Africa at the turn of the millennium and which reduced demand for beer; or the flooding experienced in 2000 in much of the country.

REST OF AFRICA

SABI operated in 13 other countries in Africa. The annual report in 1998 had stated that:

> The countries in which SABI Africa (SABIA) owns and operates breweries have in recent years, generally experienced relative political stability, steady economic progress and favourable agricultural conditions. These factors have served to support most domestic currencies and disposable incomes, with the result that SABI Africa has enjoyed volume growth and increased profitability. In many African countries, SAB's South African brands, particularly Castle Lager, are already well known and are used by SABIA to gain market share without significant additional marketing expenditure. SABI is currently pursuing a strategy to make Castle Lager the first pan-African beer. Castle Lager is currently brewed in 10 African countries. SABIA aims, where possible, to extract synergies from its operational management. SABIA's strategy is to invest in African countries with low per capita beer consumption but where SAB believes there is growth potential. SABIA have pursued a policy of expansion into other African states by acquisition and by establishing greenfield breweries.

The operations in the rest of Africa differed significantly, not least because the potential in the different countries was different. In 2000 Botswana had been particularly successful. The country had experienced a GDP growth of 10 per cent as both diamonds and other industrial areas had performed well. The result had been a growth of employment and a consequent increase in consumption of beer – both lager and sorghum. SAB's emphasis on productivity had also helped improve profit margins.

In addition, Tanzania, Mozambique and Zimbabwe had traditionally done well, but had experienced significant problems in 2000: Mozambique and Tanzania due to unfavourable climatic conditions and Zimbabwe because of major political disruption in the country in 2000. SAB believed that Kenya, Angola and Zambia had the size and potential to become profitable for them too; and that in most of these markets the business was well run and did not require significant capital expenditure in the medium term. However, there were difficulties in other countries; Lesotho continued to be depressed, the Swazi economy was growing slowly and Angola, despite its vast natural resources, continued to experience political problems.

EXPANSION OUTSIDE AFRICA

Increasingly through the 1990s SAB had expanded outside Africa. Here the strategy, too, was to acquire local breweries, improve productivity and efficiency and grow market share, often in fragmented markets.

Asia

In Asia there was an emphasis on growth in China through a joint venture with CREB. In 1998 this intended strategy was explained as follows:

> China is the second largest beer market in the world in terms of consumption and is currently growing at over 10 per cent per annum. The Chinese beer market is projected to become the largest in the world within the next five years. There are few national brands in China and SABI Asia treats each area in which it operates as an independent self-contained market. SAB believes that the Chinese beer market and the areas in which CREB operates has a strong potential for significant long term growth. CREB's strategy is to acquire and develop breweries in cities where it can obtain significant market share by focusing on the mainstream, rather than the premium beer market. Accordingly, CREB's operations are situated in areas where there is limited direct competition. CREB is actively investigating opportunities to expand its operations in China which meet these strategic criteria.

By 2000 the annual report could lay claim to major growth in China and could report that:

> SAB now sells over eight million hectolitres; last year we grew by 38 per cent. China is a fragmented market of around 200 million hectolitres a year, with vast potential for SAB. The Chinese economy has been growing at 6–7 per cent a year for some time. Beer plays an important role in Chinese social life and the government is committed to encouraging a switch away from hard liquor to beer and other beverages. Beer in China is among the cheapest in the world. SAB aims to develop mainstream

and premium beers of higher quality than the local competition, which can therefore command higher prices.

In China our aim is to develop the quality end of the mainstream brand sector. This allows us to keep the cost of capital expenditure down and avoid the expensive marketing programmes characteristic of areas such as Beijing and Shanghai, where competition is intense.

Europe

In 1998 SAB had explained its overall strategy in Europe as follows:

SABIE's strategy has been to invest in countries whose markets are developing from state-run economies to market economies, which typically leads to increased consumer demand. Due in part to the previous state ownership of many breweries and associated businesses, there had been a lack of capital investment in plants and distribution systems, and many of the working practices were inefficient and out-dated. SABIE seeks to identify existing operations where, by upgrading brewery and distribution infrastructures and augmenting the operations with SABIE management skills, it can improve marketing, product quality, and productivity so as to increase market share and profitability. Operations in each country are run autonomously.

By 2000 it would report progress in key markets as follows:

Russia

Russia is a country where beer is becoming increasingly popular and SAB sales have grown strongly. The industry is highly fragmented, most beer consumed is of poor quality from domestically owned breweries and there are no well-established national brands. All this creates a good opportunity for SAB.

SAB completed renovation and construction of its brewery at Kaluga, south-west of Moscow, in just eight months and launched its own brand 'Golden Barrel'. This brand has now provided such a great success that the Kaluga brewery's capacity is being expanded from 480,000 to 1.4 million hectolitres a year to cope with demand. Further expansion to 2.0 million hectolitres is planned. In addition to the Golden Barrel brand our portfolio will include a number of foreign brands brewed under licence, such as Staropramen, Holsten Premium and Miller Genuine Draft.

Czech Republic

In 2000 the Group also acquired Pilsner Urquell, the major brewer in the Czech Republic.

Pilsner Urquell is the national premium brand in the Czech Republic and, together with the Radegast, Gambrinus and Kozel brands, which we also acquired, immediately gave us a 44 per cent share of the Czech Republic beer market. We expect to achieve cost savings through the merger of the Pilsner Urquell and Radegast breweries. This will bring increased productivity, improved capacity utilisation, better distribution and enhanced pricing opportunities from a reorganised brand portfolio.

Pilsner Urquell is already a beer with a unique heritage and has great international appeal. We have added it to our brand portfolios in Poland and Slovakia and will be

doing so to other markets in due course. We have also acquired a brand with the stature to drive exports into important large markets such as North America and Germany, where Czech beers enjoy a great reputation.

Poland

The rapidly increasing popularity of beer, particularly among young people, has meant that beer consumption per capita, which on a drinks equivalent basis, formerly lagged well behind spirits such as vodka, had overtaken that of spirits by 1999, a trend which augurs well for SAB in the years ahead.

Poland is a very successful market for SAB. The Polish economy has been growing strongly in recent years and the compound annual growth rate of beer consumption from 1995 to 1999 was 9 per cent. In 1999 SAB merged the two beer companies which it controlled jointly with Euro Agro Centrum to create a single company, Kompania Piwowarska SAB, brewing three Polish brands (Lech, Tyskei and 10.5). This merger enabled SAB to create a unified brand portfolio, increase productivity, and make savings on aspects of the business ranging from 24-hour operations to distribution synergies.

Poland produced an exceptional individual performance following the merger, with sales volumes up 33 per cent and a sharp improvement in market share. During the year we invested US$55 million to increase our holding by 15 per cent to 69 per cent.

Pilsner Urquell will be an important addition to our brand portfolio in the premium segment.

Elsewhere in Europe

In other parts of Europe the situation was less satisfactory. Though it was a large potential market, Romania had experienced economic difficulties, with inflation running at over 40 per cent in 1999. SAB had the major brand, Ursus, though only with a 10 per cent share in a highly fragmented market. SAB had entered the Slovakian market in 1997 and had gained a 19 per cent market share. However, the economic conditions there had limited consumer spending. In Hungary SAB had well-established brands, including Dreher, but the market was fiercely competitive and there had been a considerable switch away from alcoholic drinks and a consequent decline in beer consumption. SAB had reduced its production capacity in 1999 by closing one of its two breweries, and by 2000 was in the process of reducing its distribution centres from 18 to 9.

SOUTHERN SUN HOTELS

By 2000 the hotel business was under review.

Southern Sun, our Hotel and Gaming division, has embarked on a substantial programme of development, with a major new casino and entertainment complex north of Johannesburg, scheduled to open in December 2000. There are also new hotels and a convention centre under construction, as well as applications for new gaming

licences in other urban centres in South Africa. As part of our divestment programme relating to non-core assets, we are reviewing various strategic options for Southern Sun. These options are aimed at enhancing the value of the company and include the possible listing of Southern Sun on the Johannesburg Stock Exchange.

WHERE FROM HERE?

Many commentators believed that for a brewery of its size SAB needed to have a major brand in the developed markets. It had tried to do so. It had attempted to acquire Bass Brewers but this was taken by Interbrew of Belgium. Kronenbourg had been acquired by Scottish & Newcastle. And it was known that SAB was on the lookout for such a major brand.

By 2000 the five major brewers still made up less than 30 per cent of world beer sales, which suggested that this share would grow dramatically in the future. However, the likelihood was that this would be through acquisitions. This further emphasised the need for SAB to make such an acquisition.

In 2000 SAB was listed on the London Stock Exchange (LSE) and justified this as follows:

> The Directors believed that the listing of the company on the LSE and the placing would put SAB in a strong position to pursue its strategy of growth by giving the group greater access to world capital markets and providing it with the financial resources and flexibility to pursue this strategy in an effective and competitive manner. This would enhance the ability of SAB to take advantage of increasing consolidation in the international brewing industry and to compete with other international brewers for development opportunities throughout the world. The Directors expected to use the proceeds of the placing due to the Company to continue SAB's strategy of growth worldwide and, in particular, to continue its investment in its Polish and Eastern European operations. In recent years, SAB has committed significant resources both to international acquisitions and to the reconstruction of acquired businesses. SAB intended to continue to protect and further develop its SA operations, while investing for growth in its international beer business, where a profitable base, with critical mass in selected developing markets and regions, has now been achieved. Incremental growth, both organic and through acquisitions, is being pursued aggressively.

However, the listing had its problems. It was reported that SAB's shareprice lost 15.55 per cent relative to the FTSE 100 in the year to end November 2000 (in the same period it lost 2.68 per cent on the South African stock exchange). Analysts argued, again, that this was because of the failure to make a major acquisition of a first-world brand and, thus, its over-reliance on its developing markets.

The *Financial Times* (23 November 2000) also believed that their reception in London had surprised SAB directors. They quoted John Clemmow, of the South African Investment Bank, Investec, as saying 'I think it came as a shock to them to come over here and discover how unimportant they were in the lives of the City.' The FT believed that, whilst in South Africa the firm was well known, it was necessary for SAB to spend a great deal more time explaining itself in London and that it was not sufficiently geared up to doing this. Indeed Graham Mackay, SAB's chief executive, was reported as being taken aback

by the harshness of some of the comments: 'It's more picky, to the point of cynicism and hostility, than you encounter in South Africa'.

So where would the giant brewer go next? What would the strategy be for a firm, so dominant in Africa, so extended throughout the world and yet relatively unknown in the most well-developed beer markets in the world?

Main sources

South African Breweries annual reports and website
Financial Times, 23 November 2000, 'A whole world away from Johannesburg' by Michael
    Skapinker
Reports on SAB by HSBC and ING Barings

APPENDIX 1 FIVE-YEAR FINANCIAL REVIEW FOR THE YEARS ENDED 31 MARCH

	1996 US$M	1997 US$M	1998 US$M	1999 US$M	2000 US$M	1996 RM	1997 RM	1998 RM	1999 RM	2000 RM
Income statements										
Turnover (including associates' share)	5,178	5,244	5,877	6,184	5,424	19,251	23,731	28,205	36,364	33,355
Turnover (excluding associates' share)	4,542	4,543	5,028	4,923	4,390	16,888	20,559	24,130	28,950	27,007
Operating profit (including associates' share)	689	701	707	717	844	2,562	3,170	3,394	4,213	5,196
Net interest payable	(109)	(70)	(59)	(117)	(80)	(404)	(315)	(284)	(683)	(492)
Taxation	(177)	(190)	(211)	(195)	(186)	(659)	(860)	(1,010)	(1,145)	(1,145)
Minorities	(63)	(78)	(59)	(85)	(94)	(234)	(353)	(284)	(501)	(580)
Profit for the year	340	363	378	320	484	1,265	1,642	1,816	1,884	2,979
Adjusted earnings	341	360	410	394	426	1,270	1,628	1,973	2,306	2,623
Balance sheets										
Fixed assets	2,038	2,164	2,204	2,600	3,510	8,133	9,564	11,110	16,118	22,924
Current asset inv./cash at bank and in hand	246	547	602	749	316	978	2,419	3,031	4,640	2,063
Other current assets	1,036	1,046	1,006	913	558	4,138	4,621	5,071	5,662	3,644
Total assets	3,320	3,757	3,812	4,262	4,384	13,249	16,604	19,212	26,420	28,631
Interest bearing debt	(899)	(751)	(1,052)	(953)	(602)	(3,588)	(3,321)	(5,300)	(5,909)	(3,933)
Other creditors and provisions	(986)	(1,099)	(1,604)	(1,445)	(1,223)	(3,934)	(4,856)	(8,084)	(8,954)	(8,054)
Total liabilities	(1,885)	(1,850)	(2,656)	(2,398)	(1,825)	(7,522)	(8,177)	(13,384)	(14,863)	(11,987)
Net assets	1,435	1,907	1,156	1,864	2,559	5,727	8,427	5,828	11,557	16,644
Shareholders' funds	1,131	1,593	1,098	1,703	2,161	4,514	7,039	5,536	10,556	14,042
Equity minority interests	304	314	58	161	398	1,213	1,388	292	1,001	2,602
Capital employed	1,435	1,907	1,156	1,864	2,559	5,727	8,427	5,828	11,557	16,644
Cash flow statements										
EBITDA	818	819	907	933	917	3,043	3,704	4,362	5,489	5,646
Working capital movements	51	(25)	14	(45)	(53)	188	(112)	60	(269)	(336)
Net cash inflow from operating activities	869	794	921	888	864	3,231	3,592	4,422	5,220	5,310
Net interest and dividends	(102)	(76)	(55)	(119)	(82)	(380)	(343)	(267)	(695)	(505)
Taxation	(140)	(126)	(160)	(166)	(175)	(518)	(572)	(762)	(975)	(1,075)
	627	592	706	603	607	2,333	2,677	3,393	3,550	3,730
Net capital expenditure	(352)	(278)	(374)	(544)	(401)	(1,310)	(1,261)	(1,795)	(3,198)	(2,466)
Net investments	(11)	(8)	(21)	(1)	(569)	(41)	(34)	(100)	(4)	(3,509)
Net acquisition of subsidiaries and associates	(83)	(173)	(251)	(273)	30	(306)	(781)	(1,205)	(1,558)	190
Net cash(shortfall)/surplus	181	133	60	(215)	(333)	676	601	293	(1,210)	(2,055)
Management of liquid resources	22	(8)	(152)	(419)	503	81	(38)	(732)	(2,466)	3,102
Net cash inflow from financing	(41)	158	57	256	72	(155)	713	283	1,371	443
Dividends paid	n/a	n/a	n/a	n/a	(50)	n/a	n/a	n/a	n/a	(309)
Increase/(decrease) in cash for the year	162	283	(35)	(378)	192	602	1,276	(156)	(2,305)	1,181
Performance per ordinary share (US/SA cents per share)										
Basic earnings	46.8	49.9	52.1	43.9	64.3	174.0	225.9	249.9	258.1	395.6
Diluted basic earnings	n/a	n/a	n/a	43.8	64.1	n/a	n/a	n/a	257.6	394.7
Adjusted basic earnings	46.9	49.5	56.6	54.0	56.6	174.7	223.9	271.4	315.9	348.4
Net asset value	155.6	219.1	151.0	220.1	279.3	620.9	968.3	761.5	1,364.4	1,814.9
Share statistics										
Total number of shares (million)	727.0	727.0	727.0	773.7	774.3					
Weighted average number of shares (million)	727.0	727.0	727.0	729.9	752.8					
Weighted average number of shares (diluted) (million)	n/a	n/a	n/a	731.3	754.8					
Returns and productivity										
Return on equity (%)	30.2	22.6	37.3	23.1	19.7					
Operating margin (%)	13.5	13.5	13.0	13.2	14.6					
Cash operating margin (%)	18.0	18.0	18.0	19.9	20.9					
Operating return (%)	33.5	33.5	47.7	45.1	35.3					
Cash operating return (%)	26.4	25.1	28.6	24.7	22.2					
Group turnover per employee ($000's)	97.2	94.8	101.7	100.3	91.3					
Average monthly number of employees	46,741	47,902	49,431	49,099	48,079					
Solvency and liquidity										
Net interest cover (times)	6.4	10.1	13.0	7.4	9.9					
Total borrowing to total assets (%)	27.1	20.0	27.6	22.4	13.7					
Cash flow to total borrowings (%)	96.7	105.7	87.5	93.2	143.5					

	TURNOVER					OPERATING PROFIT				
	1996 US$M	1997 US$M	1998 US$M	1999 US$M	2000 US$M	1996 US$M	1997 US$M	1998 US$M	1999 US$M	2000 US$M
Business segment analysis										
Beer South Africa	1,935	1,753	1,804	1,609	**1,608**	404	378	401	380	**407**
SAB International	831	898	1,258	1,352	**1,474**	109	112	165	190	**199**
Other Beverage Interests	850	833	920	967	**954**	76	82	98	117	**120**
Hotels and Gaming	317	279	282	276	**263**	35	36	34	42	**40**
Central administration	–	–	–	–	–	(11)	(13)	(13)	(18)	**(35)**
Continuing businesses – excluding										
exceptional items	3,933	3,763	4,264	4,204	**4,299**	613	595	685	711	**731**
PGSI	1,245	1,481	1,613	1,751	**1,125**	86	113	81	75	**61**
Group – excluding exceptional items	5,178	5,244	5,877	5,955	**5,424**	699	708	766	786	**792**
Exceptional items										
SAB International	–	–	–	229	–	–	–	–	(50)	**(11)**
Hotels and Gaming	–	–	–	–	–	–	–	–	(9)	–
PGSI	–	–	–	–	–	(10)	(7)	(59)	(10)	**(13)**
Group – including exceptional items	5,178	5,244	5,877	6,184	**5,424**	689	701	707	717	**768**

	TURNOVER					OPERATING PROFIT				
	1996 RM	1997 RM	1998 RM	1999 RM	2000 RM	1996 RM	1997 RM	1998 RM	1999 RM	2000 RM
Business segment analysis										
Beer South Africa	7,194	7,933	8,658	9,459	**9,908**	1,501	1,709	1,926	2,236	**2,507**
SAB International	3,089	4,064	6,038	8,021	**9,081**	407	509	791	1,099	**1,225**
Other Beverage Interests	3,159	3,771	4,412	5,688	**5,872**	283	370	473	688	**735**
Hotels and Gaming	1,180	1,262	1,353	1,624	**1,618**	129	164	163	245	**248**
Central administration	–	–	–	–	–	(42)	(60)	(65)	(104)	**(217)**
Continuing businesses – excluding										
exceptional items	14,622	17,030	20,461	24,792	**26,479**	2,278	2,692	3,288	4,164	**4,498**
PGSI	4,629	6,701	7,744	10,294	**6,876**	322	509	388	436	**376**
Group – excluding exceptional items	19,251	23,731	28,205	35,086	**33,355**	2,600	3,201	3,676	4,600	**4,874**
Exceptional items										
SAB International	–	–	–	1,278	–	–	–	–	(281)	**(66)**
Hotels and Gaming	–	–	–	–	–	–	–	–	(50)	–
PGSI	–	–	–	–	–	(38)	(31)	(282)	(56)	**(80)**
Group – including exceptional items	19,251	23,731	28,205	36,364	**33,355**	2,562	3,170	3,394	4,213	**4,728**

	OPERATING MARGIN					NET OPERATING ASSETS				
	1996 %	1997 %	1998 %	1999 %	2000 %	1996 US$M	1997 US$M	1998 US$M	1999 US$M	2000 US$M
Business segment analysis										
Beer South Africa	20.9	21.6	22.2	23.6	**25.3**	719	599	490	539	**509**
SAB International	13.1	12.5	13.1	14.1	**13.5**	353	493	599	781	**1,593**
Other Beverage Interests	8.9	9.8	10.7	12.1	**12.6**	220	227	198	600	**601**
Hotels and Gaming	11.0	12.9	12.1	15.2	**15.2**	89	83	109	134	**169**
Central administration	–	–	–	–	–	300	287	176	(61)	**(27)**
Continuing businesses – excluding exceptional items	15.6	15.8	16.1	16.9	**17.0**	1,681	1,689	1,572	1,993	**2,845**
PGSI	6.9	7.6	5.0	4.3	**5.5**	407	422	34	75	–
Group – excluding exceptional items	13.5	13.5	13.0	13.2	**14.6**	2,088	2,111	1,606	2,068	**2,845**

	NET OPERATING ASSETS				
	1996 RM	1997 RM	1998 RM	1999 RM	2000 RM
Business segment analysis					
Beer South Africa	2,870	2,648	2,471	3,341	**3,322**
SAB International	1,411	2,180	3,019	4,841	**10,401**
Other Beverage Interests	880	1,003	998	3,722	**3,923**
Hotels and Gaming	356	364	550	831	**1,108**
Central administration	1,197	1,269	887	(375)	**(240)**
Continuing businesses – excluding exceptional items	6,714	7,464	7,925	12,360	**18,514**
PGSI	1,623	1,865	172	466	–
Group – excluding exceptional items	8,337	9,329	8,097	12,826	**18,514**

Group turnover and group operating profit*

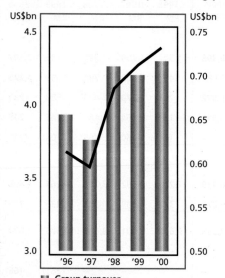

■ Group turnover
— Group operating profit

*Continuing operations –
before exceptional items

Group turnover and group operating profit*

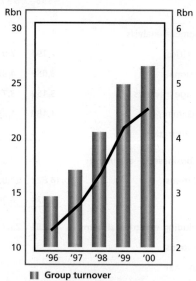

■ Group turnover
— Group operating profit

*Continuing operations –
before exceptional items

APPENDIX 2 BEER VOLUMES BY COUNTRY

	F'97 '000	F'98 '000	F'99 '000	F'00 '000
SABI (Africa)				
Botswana	306	419	491	524
Lesotho	310	399	385	374
Swaziland	245	290	250	220
Zimbabwe	1,577	1,629	1,578	1,401
Tanzania	1,267	1,492	1,643	1,596
Mozambique	385	698	764	790
Zambia	432	558	526	530
Ghana		34	203	202
Uganda		124	576	661
Angola		70	153	162
Kenya			84	217
	4,522	5,713	6,653	6,677
SABI (Asia)				
India	–	–	–	–
China				
Shenyang	2,793	2,897	3,409	3,680
Dalian	262	662	1,137	1,752
Mianyang		44	427	756
Jilin		178	1,117	1,856
Tianjin				204
Wanghua				23
Anshan				158
	3,055	3,781	6,090	8,429
SABI (Europe)				
Czech				1,527
Poland	1,542	3,860	4,083	5,443
Romania	149	989	1,217	1,076
Hungary	2,700	2,588	2,427	2,103
Slovakia		702	652	741
Russia				394
Canary Islands	927	964	955	985
	5,318	9,103	9,334	12,269
Total SABI	12,895	18,597	22,077	27,375
Beer SA	24,812	25,077	25,639	25,141
Total SAB	37,707	43,674	47,716	52,516

The Brewery Group Denmark: Faxe, Ceres and Thor

Flemming Agersnap

The case study explains the strategic moves of Brewery Group Denmark (BGD), a small Danish brewery fighting for a position in a world market. The case shows how small companies can co-exist with giant competitors in an international context and how a coherent international strategy can be built whilst allowing for different local strategies. BGD is an example of a firm which has achieved a distinctive position in a highly competitive industry by focusing on importing Danish beer into selected markets, through a network of alliances. The case provides an opportunity to consider the strengths and weaknesses of the company's strategy and options for future development.

• • •

It is better to be dominant in a small niche than to be a marginal supplier in a big market.

(Claus Nielsen, international sales director, BGD)

Denmark is a beer-drinking country with a long tradition of brewing beer. The Danish brewing industry is dominated by the Carlsberg Group, holding a market share of 70–75 per cent and a worldwide position with sales and production in many countries.

In the Danish market there were four mid-size breweries and a number of smaller ones competing with Carlsberg. In 1989 two of the mid-size breweries merged their brewing activities into a joint venture 'Bryggerigruppen', The Brewery Group Denmark (BGD). This made it the second largest brewer in Denmark and was the background to significant international expansion.

BREWERY GROUP DENMARK (BGD), FAXE, CERES AND THOR

Together BGD supplies about 15 per cent of the beer consumed in Denmark, although its share varies within the various Danish regions. Located in Aarhus, Jutland, Ceres has had a strong market position there for many years and over

| Exhibit 1 | Financial statistics for BGD, 1989–95 |

	1995	1994	1992	1990	1989
Turnover (DKK million)	2.274	2.204	1.977	1.607	1.624
Export share (%)	59	59	52	51	43
Profit before tax (DKK million)	103	93	46	16	−19
Return on equity (after tax) (%)	18	18	12	7	−8
Number of employees	1,089	1,005	1,039	824	930

the last 30 years it had merged with breweries in neighbouring towns. One of these breweries was the Thor brewery in Randers. In 1996, Thor had a strong position in the northern part of Jutland. Located on Zealand, Faxe had only a small local market, but it had long been an important supplier to restaurants and retailers in Copenhagen.

At an early stage, both Ceres and Faxe felt a need for growth in order to obtain sufficient volume gains in production and subsequent reductions in costs. They first expanded in the domestic market to become national distributors, but any substantial growth could be obtained only through exports.

Exhibit 1 shows the financial data for the years after the establishment of the joint venture.

Organisation and management

Exhibit 2 shows the organisation structure of BGD. After the merger in 1989, the positions of chief executive officer and of international sales director were filled with people without previous experience of breweries. Claus Nielsen came with a background from the international pharmaceutical industry. Hiring a manager from outside also solved the problem of choosing a candidate from one of the two existing sales organisations.

BGD was formed as a limited company, where the Faxe and the Ceres companies each owned 49 per cent and their common bank 2 per cent. All beer and soft drinks activities were transferred to BGD. The parent companies also had a few other small activities besides BGD. Both companies were listed separately on the Copenhagen Stock Exchange. The Faxe brewery had a controlling capital owned by the founding family, whereas the Ceres company had no such controlling shareholder group. Carlsberg owned 38 per cent of the predominantly non-voting B-shares of Ceres, but without a seat on the board of the company. Carlsberg declared that it had no wish for a more active role in the management of Ceres or BGD, rather its involvement was said to be an investment for financial reasons. Others argued that the investment could be seen as a defensive investment guarding against a foreign acquisition of Ceres.

| Exhibit 2 | Organisation diagram (simplified) |

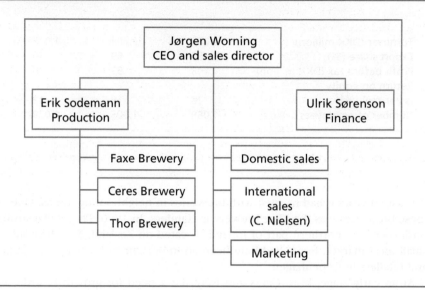

INTERNATIONAL DEVELOPMENT

Despite the dominance of Carlsberg, in its annual report BGD could lay claim to being the largest Scandinavian beer exporter. This was because Carlsberg placed emphasis on licensing agreements or local production for its foreign markets, while BGD's strategy was export led: 'Eighty-three out of every hundred bottles of beer that we produce are sold in foreign markets.' By 1995 the percentage of export sales by region of the world was as follows: western Europe 63 per cent, the Americas 10 per cent, eastern Europe 22 per cent, others 5 per cent. The development of BGD's operations in some of these markets is now reviewed.

Italy

More than 30 years ago, Ceres entered into co-operation with a slaughterhouse for pork (Tulip) in a neighbouring Jutland town. This slaughterhouse specialised in select meat cuts and canned meat for different markets. The co-operation led to export to Italy based on the transportation of meat and beers in refrigerated vans. Ceres joined this co-operative venture at the invitation of the slaughterhouse, but in 1996 beer export accounted for 75 per cent of turnover and more than 95 per cent of profit – and the joint sales company in Italy had been bought fully by BGD, though still acting as agent for the slaughterhouse.

Claus Nielsen commented:

We are the largest exporter of beer to Italy and dominate the 'duplomolto' [strong beer] segment. Our success has been largely due to our marketing strategy. For the last 30 years we have been concentrating on the on-licence trade – restaurants, discos, bars and so on. We have achieved a very strong position in such outlets, which has given us a strong brand presence in Italy. In these outlets we have strongly promoted out bottled Ceres brand at point of sale. We would prefer people who go to restaurants and discos to be holding our bottle with our brand name on than drinking draught beer out of a glass without a brand name on it. In the last ten years we have also started to develop our presence in the off-licence retail trade – the shops selling beer. As in so many markets, the retailers have become more powerful, but a good indication of our brand strength is that we are able to resist the pressure they put on us for increased discounts. If they want to press us for such discounts, we simply refuse. They can delist us if they like, but they have to come back again because of the strength of the brand.

The Italian culture also helps us. Most young men do not get married until they are about 30 and live at home until then. This means that there is a great deal of disposable income for men in their early 20s; and they spend a lot of money in restaurants, discos and bars, where we are strongly represented. They also prefer our brand, which is a premium, strong beer. The trend in Italy away from wine drinking has also helped us. It has become less common to drink wine heavily at lunch, for example. But Italians do like to have a drink and our beer is a good deal stronger than Italian beer. So they can feel good about not drinking wine, but drink a couple of Ceres instead. It looks better, but has much the same effect.

The Ceres concept in export markets such as Italy has been to emphasise the origin of the beer, that the beer is imported, and to emphasise premium and strong lager beers.

The Caribbean

Ceres also found and developed a market in the Caribbean islands for malt beer. A Ceres manager on vacation in the Caribbean observed that some of the locals were drinking a rather distinct type of beer, dark and sweet. When it was analysed back at the brewery, it turned out that the beer was very much like Danish malt beer, an almost non-alcoholic beer. Exports started and a market niche was developed in that region.

The product, Vitamalt, is rich in vitamins B and D and proteins. Claus Nielsen explained:

In the Caribbean you have two markets for beer: those who drink alcoholic beer and those who do not drink alcohol at all. Our market is for the non-alcoholic market people who do not drink because of their religious beliefs, as well as a significant percentage of women and children too. The product is also believed by some to have aphrodisiac properties.

In a few markets in the Caribbean, local production is beneficial because of high import duties, and Heineken produce Vitamalt in the Bahamas under licence. However, Vitamalt became so successful that both Heineken and Guinness approached BGD with a view to licensing the product for production elsewhere in the Caribbean.

In fact, Vitamalt has a market not only in the Caribbean, but also in many other parts of the world where there are people of Caribbean origin. Sales are high in London, Amsterdam and Paris, for example.

Germany

On the border between Germany and Denmark, a special border trade had developed, since Danes could avoid paying the high Danish duty on beer by purchasing it in Germany. At times this trade has accounted for approximately 10 per cent of Danish beer consumption. Ceres dominated the border market.

Before the joint venture, Faxe also developed a market in the wider Germany for canned beer. In the 1970s Faxe bought tapping equipment for canned beer; for environmental reasons, canned beer was not allowed to be sold in Denmark, but it is accepted in Germany. And canned beer is especially suitable for supermarket chains. This development (plus bottled beers) created a comparatively strong position for Faxe in the German market – considering the low level of German imports of beer. Its beers were sold partly in ordinary retail shops and supermarkets, but increasingly also in restaurants.

The Baltic States

The changed political and economic situation in the former Communist bloc has opened up many sales opportunities. Following the break-up of the Soviet bloc, the Baltic states of Estonia, Latvia and Lithuania wished to become more closely linked to other Nordic states, a move encouraged by the governments of the Nordic countries. Trade delegations were organised from Denmark, and BGD took part in the first of these. 'We realised all the breweries were worn out and the quality of the beer was poor, but the population liked beer.' As a result, BGD appointed two distributors in Lithuania.

> We often appoint two distributors when we start up in a country to see which will be most successful. Here we agreed that both could import the Faxe brand and compete in Lithuania; one would also export to Latvia and the other to Estonia. It has been very successful. Unfortunately we also found that a good deal of the product was crossing the border into Russia, and we got complaints from our Russian distributors about this. We have to change the contract with our distributors in the Baltic States to prevent exporting Faxe to Russia. What we did was to provide them with another brand each, providing they did not export Faxe to Russia. They also have the right to export the other brand to Russia.

Elsewhere in western Europe

In 1993 BGD bought a small British brewery, Cain's, located in Liverpool, England, and with an established local market. Besides involving a transfer of brewing technology, the acquisition of Cain's brewery opened up more possibilities for pub sales of BGD beers in that region, though still as imported beer. Similarly, Cain's traditional English beer was introduced into Denmark and other European countries as a supplement to the BGD range.

There are also markets for beers in Holland, Belgium, Austria and Switzerland. Yet, as Claus Nielsen said, 'Why bother when we know we won't get any result?' These beer markets are very competitive, but also stagnating. He continued:

> We were about to move into Spain, but I said: Stop, Stop. Look how much the others have invested. Carlsberg has lost DKK 500 million. Heineken and all the other big ones are there. Why enter that fight? Why not look to the nice neighbouring country, Portugal, where imported beers account for less than 1 per cent of beer consumption? They are an extraordinarily kind and pleasant people to work with. Let us focus on these 10 million people and try to gain a foothold there. So we were established there before anybody else with imported beer.

Brazil

A fast-growing market for BGD is Brazil. Traditionally, the Brazilian market has been protected by high import duty, varying from 8 to 60 per cent depending on the economic situation of the country. Furthermore, the Brazilian government had been very restrictive and avoided foreign capital. Big Brazilian breweries took advantage of the situation and set very high prices. But partly as a consequence of the GATT negotiations and partly to counteract inflation, the Brazilian government planned to open the country for imports. The entrance of American and European breweries into the market led to a price reduction of about 80 per cent. Claus Nielsen explained:

> There was an opening coming up and I could see there was an under supply. We took the step with imported beer before anybody else and were successful. It was a combination of timing, of finding the right partner and of the change in regulations.
>
> We thought of using our Caribbean concept, malt beers, since the northern parts of Brazil resemble the Caribbean climate and population. However, a closer study and an awareness of the culture of Brazilian society led us to act differently.
>
> Brazil is a multiethnic country, although many Brazilians get angry and agitated when one wants to distinguish between the European and African parts of the population. Such distinctions do not exist for the Brazilians. Now I have been there several times and differences do exist. For me it was like walking around in Africa and in the ethnic parts of London and Paris. Those who understand and adapt to the differences will obtain benefits in this market. And that is what we have done. So in the end we have emphasised a European approach – also because of the partner we found.
>
> We were very lucky with the partner we found. Cafe Bom Dia is a company with a distribution network covering all relevant segments of the market. It is a modern coffee roaster with ISO 9000 certification of quality; the biggest in Brazil. They have a distribution network covering coffee shops and supermarkets and delivery to 90,000 restaurants. And today our beers are placed on their vans.
>
> They know – or we tell them – that if they choose Heineken or Carlsberg, these breweries in a few years' time will start local production and take over the distribution. The big ones enter as 'big brothers'. They chose us – we have been very lucky and the sales volume is growing rapidly.
>
> There is also a benefit with regard to the cost of distribution. They are one of Brazil's biggest coffee exporters and we have arranged to use their empty containers to ship product into Brazil at a lower cost than we would normally incur.
>
> I have never – like other breweries – entered a market together with other breweries, not even local ones, in a joint operation. It may give an easy start if the partner

has the set-up, knows how to distribute the beer – and has the same target group. But one only gets the share of the market the partner allows one to get. I want to find a partner where we complement each other instead of competing. It can be a soft drinks distributor – or a coffee distributor. In India we will enter a contract with the biggest tea distributor.

Russia

By 1996 BGD was also operating in Russia.

The Russian market is huge and the demand for beer very high; but there had been no investment in the breweries and they produced very low-quality beer. In 1993 we began with a number of distributors in order to handle the problems of distribution. However, eventually it became clear there were two performing really well and we were approached by both of them for sole distribution rights. Given the way in which business is done in Russia, this is not a straightforward matter. We eventually decided on one distributor who is also a major distributor of other food products to cash 'n' carries and small shops in the cities. It also has associates who can handle distribution elsewhere in Russia; and it is a very sophisticated operation in terms of the education of their management and their computer and distribution systems. It is proving to be immensely successful: for example, we have 80 per cent retail penetration in Moscow. Russia is now our biggest export market, in terms of volume.

Initially we found problems because of transport costs to Russia. There was one major container distributor from Denmark who quoted extremely high costs of distribution. We overcame this in a rather novel way. We decided in the summer to ship our products direct to Moscow by river using barges with loads of 2 to 6 million bottles. Keeping transport costs down in beer distribution is extremely important.

China

The Chinese market for beer is growing at around 10–20 per cent per annum, and Claus Nielsen saw it as one of the most attractive markets for the future.

It is of course a huge market, but we had to be very clear about our positioning. Most of the people in China are not that wealthy, but there is a percentage of the population which is. China has become one of the largest markets for Rolex watches, Mercedes cars and French XO Cognac. We decided to position Faxe as a premium product and target geographic regions where there was high disposable income. Our distribution strategy was also important. Most western companies have tended to go through Hong Kong, where they can find English-speaking distributors. But of course it adds to costs of distribution. We wanted to export to China direct. Most organisations we contacted wanted a joint venture arrangement for manufacturing and the building of a brewery. This is of course not our strategy; we only deal with export beer, so we were not prepared to do this. We spent three years finding the right distributor and eventually did so. It is a government-owned organisation, regionally structured, selling mainly liquor and tobacco, but not beer until now, to tax-free shops throughout China. We began in September 1995 and we are doing well. We also distribute Ceres through the more traditional route via a Hong Kong distributor.

THE MARKETING CONCEPT

BGD did not intend to compete directly with the big international breweries on their major markets, with standard-type beers. It looked for niches for special forms of distribution or special products. The core of BGD's international marketing concept has been to emphasise that its beers are *imported*. There was no local production of its brands outside Denmark and its beers are alike in all countries. As Claus Nielsen says: 'The big breweries adapt their brands to the various markets. Let them have these markets. If we are to get any distinction, it must be tied to the fact that our beer is always the same Danish beer.'

So BGD emphasised the development of its sales organisation in the various markets more than price and production costs. In this way, its beers could be seen as competing more with beers like the Dutch Grolsch beer than with widely sold beers from, for example, Heineken or Carlsberg. The consumer might think of the beer as something to be chosen for a special occasion and not as a daily standard product.

The types of customer and the consumption patterns of the standard beers and of special beers were quite different. Although in a specific country the market for expensive imported beer might be small, it could be an attractive size for BGD. Furthermore, imported beers were acquiring an increasing market share worldwide, even though by 1996 they exceeded 10 per cent of the total market in only a few countries.

BGD IN DENMARK

Like Carlsberg (and Tuborg), BGD had a wide assortment of beers, ranging from non-alcoholic beers and ordinary beers to premium beers and strong beers. Alongside their traditional beers the two breweries introduced a number of specialities, such as Dortmunder beer (Ceres), draught beer in cans or special bottles (Faxe), and Christmas and Easter beers. BGD had not produced and sold discount beers to the big retail chains.

In the Danish market, Faxe had intended to launch draft beer in cans. When distribution in cans was banned, Faxe launched draft beer in special dark bottles with a different shape than ordinary beers. The dark brown colour of the bottles was necessary because the draft beer was more sensitive to sunlight than ordinary beers. It was a success at the time, since many smaller restaurants and bars did not have beer-tapping equipment. Gradually the price on this equipment has fallen and many restaurants and bars have got beer taps, so this special market has almost vanished.

In 1996 the ban on canned beer was up for reconsideration. The EU understood the environmental reasons behind the ban. However, in Sweden, canned beer has been allowed provided there is a 'pawn' on each can which is refunded when the empty can is returned. This system, which is similar to the present Danish one for bottles, ensures that the cans are recycled. It is actively debated whether, by such a system, cans represent a heavier burden on the environment than bottles. The cans have a high return rate (to cash the pawn) and are reused through a melting process. The bottles are directly reused, but the washing of the bottles requires many chemicals and considerable amounts of water.

The major reason that the EU wanted the ban lifted was that it is seen as a trade barrier. It is difficult for a foreign brewery to tap beer in the special Danish bottles and to handle the bottle return system. If the ban is lifted, canned beers are expected to account for only about 10 per cent of the market. But it would be far easier for a German brewery to enter this market niche.

In the Danish market, BGD also sells a number of soft drinks, some under its own brands and others under licence to tap and sell, such as Pepsi Cola and 7-Up.

INTERNATIONAL MANAGEMENT

With so many international opportunities to consider, Claus Nielsen commented:

> I have a well-functioning organisation with seven regional managers and their staff and the most efficient shipping/transportation department in Denmark, exporting more than 15,000 containers a year. I only want to expand at the pace of adding a new colleague each year. He or she has a chance really to get versed in the job and to get attention from the organisation. Then soon they may get their own independent area of responsibility. So physically we cannot enter all the potential markets, not even all the promising ones. We must focus on some and leave the others till we have the organisation to enter them. We aim at structured and well-studied approaches, but sometimes it is incidental information that tells us where the best potentials surface.
>
>   I like to run a very flat structure. The regional executives have total operating control over their regions. It is my job to set up new businesses around the world – I spent a lot of time in China in 1995, for example – and deal with overall strategy, price setting and yearly budgets. They then run the businesses. It does mean a lot of travel; I try to visit all major markets at least once a year. In 1995 I spent 150 days out of Denmark.

MANAGING THE BGD JOINT VENTURE

The joint venture mainly had an impact on the organisation of sales and distribution, but not on production. In the domestic market, a number of depots were merged and considerable cost savings achieved. In the international markets where Faxe had a significant export market Ceres was virtually absent and vice versa. Faxe was positioned in one way and Ceres in another, so they complemented each other without overlap. The success was evident. In 1989 exports were DKK 514m and in 1995 DKK 1,522m.

Although the sales organisation became fully merged, the production units remained separate according to the old company structures, with breweries in the towns of Faxe, Ceres and Thor, and brands exclusively brewed where they were first introduced. This was said to be necessary due to special requirements as to water and yeast as well as local knowledge of the brewing processes.

Just for fun we have tried to let the Ceres people brew some Faxe beer. It didn't taste the same. Similarly, Faxe people have tried to make Ceres Dortmunder. It didn't work either. We do not want any risk of mixing of the yeasts, so they are kept apart. The water supply is also very different. Carlsberg has a brewery in Copenhagen and one in Fredericia, Jutland, where they brew the same beer brands, but experienced brewers can tell where one of these beers is brewed.

The absence of merged activity in production was also attributed to the existing cultures and loyalties among managers and workers. Traditionally, the two breweries have been staffed at the top levels by 'brewers' – people with a pharmaceutical, chemical or engineering background at university and later trained within the trade and with formal education from the special advanced Scandinavian Brewing High School. This tradition had created a high professional standard and intimate knowledge of the trade, but had also meant a certain level of closure to other forms of training and experience from other consumer goods industries. Similarly, the experienced brewery workers had developed a competence in, for example, adjusting the beer taste and a strong attachment to the specific brewery.

This has meant that the brewers have emphasised their wish to have full discretion in running a brewery and have been reluctant to consider more integrated operations. However, the expansion in sales volume required the full use of capacity, utilising established production patterns.

THE DANISH BREWERY GROUP A/S: 1998–2000

In 1998 The Brewery Group Denmark became The Danish Brewery Group A/S. Claus Nielsen also left the company. The following extracts from the annual reports provide an explanation of developments in some key areas of their business.

1998

On 22 April 1998 and with effect from 1 January 1998, the former Brewery Denmark A/S merged with the holding companies Jyske Bryg Holding AS, Faxe Bryg Holding A/S and Rolink A/S with Jyske Bryg Holding AS as the Continuing company. After the Merger, Jyske Bryg Holding AS changed its name to The Danish Brewery Group A/S. Through this transaction, The Danish Brewery Group A/S obtained a direct listing on the Copenhagen Stock Exchange and the ownership structure was considerably simplified.

Domestic market

In general, the Danish market was affected in 1998 by the cold and rainy summer as well as the industrial dispute which culminated in a 2-week strike in the spring of 1998.

1999

At 1 July The Danish Brewery Group A/S acquired 50 per cent of the share capital of the Swiss company Drinktech Holding AG through a new issue of shares of CIIF 5.5 million. Through interests in breweries in the Caribbean, Africa and the Pacific, this investment is expected to reinforce the position of The Danish Brewery Group A/S on malt products.

During the autumn, The Danish Brewery Group A/S successively acquired a total of 95.2 per cent of the share capital of the Lithuanian brewery AB Vilniaus Tauras. At year end, the total investment in Vilniaus Tauras shares amounted to some USD 4.8 million. Also in Lithuania, a 50 per cent share of the distribution company UAB Bartos Prckyba, which handles the sale and distribution of the Faxe products in Lithuania, was acquired.

Domestic market

The decline in Danish beer consumption continued in 1999 as a 2 per cent decrease of consumption from 1998 is estimated. However, The Danish Brewery Group A/S's sales

2000

On 11 September 2000 The Danish Brewery Group submitted a cash bid to the shareholders of Albani Bryggerierne A/S. Upon the expiry of the bid period, The Danish Brewery Group held some 87.1 per cent of the share capital and some 71.8 per cent of the voting rights of Albani Bryggerierne A/S. Through the subsequent compulsory bid for the remaining shares of Albani Bryggerierne A/S and other purchases on the market, The Danish Brewery Group's share of Albani Bryggerierne A/S had by the end of 2000 been increased to 90.8 per cent of the share capital and 74.3 per cent of the voting rights.

The Danish Brewery Group acquired the remaining 50 per cent of the shares of the Swiss company Drinktech Holding AG which is now wholly-owned by The Danish Brewery Group.

Domestic market

For the Danish Brewery Group (excluding Albani Bryggerierne A/S), beer sales in Denmark went up by some 3 per cent. The Danish Brewery Group thus reinforced its market position on beer in the

Total beer sales in Denmark declined by some 7 per cent in 1998. In addition to the above-mentioned factors, Danish beer consumption is generally showing a negative trend.

The competitive situation in the Danish market has further intensified and in 1998 The Danish Brewery Group A/S had to see slightly declining market shares in the lager segment, whereas stronger beer types and duty-free beer have gained ground.

Total consumption of soft drinks is estimated to have decreased by 3–4 per cent in 1998 caused, it must be assumed, exclusively by the strike and poorer summer weather than in 1997.

increased slightly from 1998 and overall the Group's beer brands have managed to win market shares in 1999. in particular, Faxe beer and the newly launched 'ROYAL' de luxe products comprising ROYAL EXPORT, ROYAL SELECTION, ROYAL STOUT and ROYAL ALL MALT have gained significant ground.

Danish market as it is estimated that total beer sales in Denmark in 2000 declined by some 4 per cent. Increased sales of the Group's brands concern the lager products from Faxe, Ceres and Thor as well as the ROYAL series, whereas low-alcohol and alcohol-free beer have showed a decline.

Excluding Albani Bryggerierne A/S, total group sales of soft drinks in Denmark remained at the 1999 level. . . . Overall, The Danish Brewery Group has strengthened its market position as it is estimated that total soft drinks sales decreased by some 3 per cent due to, among other things, a wet and cool summer.

Russia

The year was characterised by the turbulent situation in Russia with the crisis in August obstructing continued sale of import beer – including Faxe – in the Russian market. Since that time, Faxe has not recorded any sales to this market. The loss of the Russian market is estimated to have reduced export sales by some 7 per cent of total export volumes.

Russia

The overall level of international sales in 1999 matched that of 1998 in spite of the Russian foreign exchange crisis in August 1998 putting a stop to the exportation of beer to Russia. Viewed in isolation, the loss of this significant market has resulted in a 10 per cent reduction, approximately, of international volumes in 1999.

UK

In the UK market Robert Cain & Company Ltd, recorded declining sales with a reduction of volumes from 1997 by

UK

In the UK market, Robert Cain & Company Ltd achieved considerable sales growth partly due to supplying a UK chain

UK

Excluding malt products, The Danish Brewery Group's sales in England declined by 14 per cent, and the financial results some 13 per cent, primarily due to intensified competition on brand products due to, among other factors, the strong British currency favouring imports from continental Europe. In spite of the competition, the subsidiary continued improving its operating results in 1998 primarily due to improved production efficiency. Investments in Robert Cain's brand products continued in 1998, evidenced by, among other things, the opening of another four pubs.

with a private brand, and partly due to satisfactory growth in respect of Cain's own brands.

The positive development of Robert Cain & Company Ltd continued in 1999 due to the increased level of activity and continuously improving production efficiency.

of Robert Cain & Company Ltd are not satisfactory. The sales decrease is due to a significant reduction of private brands sales to certain UK retail customers – a decrease that has not been offset by a positive development for the Cain brands, both in the (hotel, restaurant and catering) and the retail sectors, and for Faxe Premium.

Germany

The German market showed a positive trend and Faxe Premium remained the top selling import beer brand in Germany. In general, the German market is characterised by a considerable number of breweries, excess capacity and few, strong retail chains, which produces keen competition among breweries.

Germany

The Danish Brewery Group A/S's subsidiary succeeded in 1999 in increasing sales significantly due to increased distribution in retailing. Also sales to the retail trade at the German/Danish border have shown satisfactory development.

Germany

The German market is still characterised by declining beer consumption (estimated at –2 to –3 per cent), and intensified competition due to considerable excess capacity in a highly fragmented industry. . . . Sales in Germany went up by 9 per cent from 1999 (excluding Albani and Maribo). Overall and considering the keen competition in the German market, the financial results of the German activities have been satisfactory – and better than in 1999.

Italy

The sales increase in Italy continued in 1998 with both sales and earnings meeting expectations. Considerable resources have been allocated also in 1998 to strengthening the Company's brand products and product development.

Italy

In 1999 sales in Italy were more or less at the 1998 level, whereas earnings were affected by the costs of terminating agency agreements. Considerable resources are still being spent on developing the Company's brand

Italy

Developments in Italy have been highly satisfactory with a total sales growth of 8 per cent in 2000. the new product Ceres North Light, which was launched in 2000, accounts for about half of the growth, but also the main product in the

products and on product development.

market, Ceres Strong Ale, showed satisfactory growth. Accordingly, the extension of the product range has had a positive effect on the existing product portfolio.

Malt products

Sales of the Group's malt products are still on the increase in established markets such as the Caribbean and the UK as well as in developing markets in Africa, etc.

Malt products

In 1999 the development of the Group's malt products was primarily characterized by growth in Africa, where Ghana has entered into a licence agreement for the production and marketing of Vitamalt.

Malt products

Own-produced malt drinks are primarily sold in England, the Caribbean and the USA. Sales of own-produced products showed an increase of 16 per cent in 2000 (including Albani's malt sales in the fourth quarter).
Products produced under licences are sold in the Caribbean and in Africa. Volumes in the Caribbean have been slightly increasing, whereas Africa has been affected by a decline in Ghana.
Total malt drinks sales increased by 1 per cent over 1999. Sales of malt drinks amounted to 7 per cent of the total volume of international activities in 2000.
Some 140,000 hectolitres of the Vitamalt brand were produced under a licence in Nigeria in 2000 compared to 125,000 hectolitres in 1999.

Turnover from international activities amounts to DKK 1.8 billion equal to 62 per cent of the Group's total turnover. International turnover has increased by 15 per cent over 1999, including 2 per cent accounted for by the Albani and Maribo products.

Summary financial statistics, 1996–2000

KEY FIGURES (DKK MILLION)	2000	1999	1998	1997	1996
Turnover	2,849.9	2,469.5	2,453.2	2,560.7	2,293.0
Profit before tax	189.7	226.1	159.1	139.5	126.4
Return on equity after tax	19.2	27.5	20.8	16.2	14.6
Number of employees	1,731	1,282	1,119	1,142	1,096

International activities in 2000

MARKET AREA	TURNOVER 2000 DKK M	SALES 2000 – KHL	GROWTH OVER 1999 TURNOVER	SALES
Northern Europe				
Sweden	17.6	47.6	–3%	15%
Greenland/the Faroes/Iceland	12.0	58.6	7%	–11%
Other markets, Northern Europe	3.9	2.4	–54%	–18%
Total Northern Europe	*33.5*	*108.6*	*–11%*	*–2%*
Western Europe				
Italy	550.5	367.5	11%	8%
Germany	363.9	815.8	15%	13%
England	344.0	323.4	–2%	–14%
France	28.2	33.9	12%	0%
Other markets, Western Europe	23.3	60.7	189%	491%
Total Western Europe	*1,309.9*	*1,601.3*	*10%*	*8%*
Eastern Europe				
Lithuania	128.1	262.7	516%	326%
Poland	67.7	113.8	39%	41%
Other markets, Eastern Europe	1.7	5.9	–39%	–22%
Total Eastern Europe	*197.5*	*382.4*	*173%*	*154%*
Other markets				
Tax-free	56.2	110.9	–38%	–41%
Caribbean	25.0	17.5	–10%	–13%
Middle East	11.4	23.3	208%	183%
USA/Canada	9.9	12.5	169%	54%
Africa	2.4	3.9	–68%	–31%
Other markets	1.8	3.1	18%	–16%
Total other markets	*106.7*	*171.2*	*–21%*	*–26%*
Malt				
Caribbean	48.9	99.2	18%	6%
England	36.0	33.4	22%	14%
Africa	7.9	12.5	18%	–59%
USA/Canada	6.9	8.9	–9%	12%
Other markets, malt	16.1	24.6	44%	68%
Total malt	*115.8*	*178.6*	*20%*	*1%*
TOTAL	**1,763.4**	**2,442.1**	**15%**	**13%**

Source: Year-end report 2000 of The Danish Brewery Group A/S.

Barclaycard

Bernardo Bátiz-Lazo*, Jarunee Wonglimpiyarat[†] and Douglas Wood[†]

The case study is concerned with how a long-standing market leader maintains a position of advantage and develops its business in a fast-moving environment undergoing significant change. There are many different strategic options open to Barclaycard, but which will be most suitable? Will all the options be acceptable, not only in terms of the likely risk and returns but also to the major stakeholders? Will the options be feasible? The case invites readers to evaluate and compare a range of strategic options and to choose the best way forward for Barclaycard.

• • •

At the turn of the millennium, Barclaycard was operating in a sophisticated and highly competitive environment. The company, a wholly owned subsidiary of Barclays plc, aimed to provide the plastic card infrastructure for Barclays Bank and was responsible for producing, issuing and replacing all Barclay's plastic cards. It also managed directly all customer relationships for Barclay's plastic card services in the UK (a range of services which is described below). Through its Global Services Division, Barclaycard had a commitment to extending the Barclaycard brand and services across the world, providing card acceptance services to many countries, predominantly on the African continent, Middle East, Caribbean and in a few countries in South America.

By 1999 Barclaycard had over 9 million customers and employed over 5,000 people at three locations around the UK and its Northampton headquarters. Barclaycard was accepted at over 400,000 places in the UK and more than 12 million worldwide.

THE ORIGINS OF CREDIT CARDS AND BARCLAYCARD

Credit cards emerged in the first half of the twentieth century and initially cards were used as a way to simplify the process of identification and confirmation of customers when tellers required authorisation for account purchases in retail stores. The process developed and in the 1940s a number of US banks allowed

* Open University Business School   † Manchester Business School.

customers to charge purchases against their monthly bank charge account rather than to a store account. In 1950, Diners Club launched a Travel and Entertainment (T&E) card, an innovation that also led to the establishment of American Express and, separately, Carte Blanche. The issuer of the T&E card would settle the bills from hotels, restaurants or airlines and reclaim payment from the member. The T&E card, therefore, provided settlement in arrears but no rollover credit, while additional revenue for the issuer was generated from annual fees from customers and charging a commission on sales to the merchant.

It was around this time that the Franklin National Bank (based in New York) developed what is recognised as the originator of the first real credit card. This innovation considered offering rollover credit up to an authorised credit limit. Furthermore, managers at Franklin National Bank also recognised the competitive potential of credit cards by being the first to issue cards to customers of other banks. However, the localised nature of branch banking in the US meant cards were only useful in the limited area served by the issuing bank, an inconvenience to an increasingly mobile population. Nevertheless, a franchising system developed under which banks acquired the right to issue branded cards in a particular city that customers could use with collaborating merchants both locally and out of state. In 1958, Bank of America, with the advantage of its huge West Coast network, launched the blue, white and gold *BankAmericard*. By 1965 Bank of America was realising the brand value of its heavily promoted card by actively franchising other banks to issue its card and recruit merchants. In this way the network provided BankAmericard cardholders with a national (and eventually international) network of service points which was to provide the foundation for the future Visa network.

Barclays Bank was the first UK bank to recognise the potential of the credit card. After evaluating BankAmericard's operations in the US it negotiated a franchise from BankAmerica at the end of 1965. A small team was set up to plan a UK launch six months later under the brand *Barclaycard*, and by launch date 30,000 retailers had been signed up. Early promises to retailers to publish the name and address of every shop accepting Barclaycard led to what is still believed to be one of the largest-ever press advertisements. It appeared in the *Daily Mail* on 29 June 1966, extended over eight pages and carried all the 30,000 names and addresses of retailers. Successful acceptance by the British adult population meant that by the end of 1966 Barclays Bank had passed the milestone of 1 million Barclaycard holders.

THE DEVELOPMENT OF COMPETITION

Early contenders to both Visa and Barclaycard emerged from their closest competitors. In 1966, prompted by the success of the BankAmericard network, members of competing franchises formed the Interbank Card Association (ICA), later to become MasterCard International. ICA differed from BankAmericard in being an organisation controlled by member banks which took responsibility for promoting the MasterCard brand and for setting standards for security and authorisation, clearing and settlement systems between members. ICA went international in 1968 with an association with Banamex

(Mexico's biggest bank in terms of assets), an alliance in Europe with Eurocard, and the recruitment of member banks from Japan. A comparable organisation, National BankAmericard, Inc. was formed by US banks issuing BankAmericards in 1970. Later on, what was to become Visa International was formed by Bank of America's international licensees while, in parallel, ICA rebranded as MasterCard International and then as Mastercard. At this point the two card systems that between them would preside over the world credit card market for the following thirty years were in place. As open membership organisations they provided a common framework giving banks (and in due course non-banks) access to what turned out to be easily the most profitable and fastest-growing product in the portfolio of most retail banks.

Alongside the creation of two international networks and conscious of the strong position Barclaycard had created in the fast-growing UK card market, the other major UK commercial banks decided they would collaborate to reduce the risks of launching a rival card. In 1972, National Westminster (NatWest), Lloyds, Midland and The Royal Bank of Scotland/Williams & Glyn's Group established the Joint Credit Card Company Limited (JCCC). Trading began using the *Access* brand and, after merchants had been recruited, a computer program was purchased from the US (which was extensively rewritten for Access purposes) and IBM equipment installed to process payments. At the same time, Access was aligned with the network of banks that would eventually become Mastercard in the UK.

Unlike the T&E card, bank credit card usage expanded rapidly in the UK and elsewhere. For instance, between September 1967 and January 1972 growth in the US resulted in an increase of 680 per cent in the number of banks with credit card facilities. In the UK, within a year of launching, the Access group had 3.3 million cardholders and 65,000 retail or merchant outlets. That same year, Barclaycard had 1.7 million cardholders and was accepted in 60,000 merchant outlets (but this growth took place while Barclays acted as sole card-issuer and sole merchant-acquirer for its network). In comparison and in spite of the T&E card having been introduced earlier than the bank credit card, the combination of Diners Club and American Express had only 550,000 cardholders in 1979.

During the late 1960s and 1970s, therefore, a period of intense competition between Visa and Mastercard and between individual holders of each franchise to sign up merchants ensued, this against a background of an annual increase in credit card ownership of more than 20 per cent. Apart from grocery chains and other outlets where purchase values were low, acceptance of both Barclaycard/Visa and Access/Mastercard became universal, in part reflecting banks' reluctance to increase cheque guarantees above £50.

In subsequent years the demand for credit cards exploded. At the same time, outlets (merchants) were recruited by both networks, merchants began accepting American Express and Diners Club cards, and the right to issue Visa cards extended to an increasing range of bank and non-bank competitors. Moreover, duality, whereby banks could join both Visa and Mastercard networks, became possible in 1988 with the banks able to issue both cards. But by-laws of each group prevented their members from issuing the cards of third parties such as American Express or Discover, a practice that was challenged in the US by both the federal government and a powerful group of retailers at the end of the 1990s. In any event, duality further enhanced the potential for scale economies since banks could process all the Visa and MasterCard transactions of their merchants.

During the 1980s and 1990s, Barclays responded using heavy promotion and branding to retain the position of Barclaycard as market leader. This position of advantage in the UK was maintained with success and represented servicing around 9 million credit card customers in 1999.

INFORMATION TECHNOLOGY

Excluding marketing costs, Barclay's initial investment in the Bank of America franchise was low. Managers at Barclaycard were able to migrate the entire operation from the US, including computer programs, terms and conditions of service to both retailers and cardholders. However, minor modifications to the Bank of America computer program were required for UK purposes. A senior executive at Barclaycard explained:

> From Barclaycard's viewpoint, it envisaged that the complexities of adopting a US system for UK use were for example integration with feeder systems for capturing voucher details, customer payments (as the US had a radically different banking system), authorisation (which was then an intense manual process), Country Club Billing (where individual transaction slips were matched and sent out with the statement) and address formats/postcodes which were very different from the United States model.

Although some customisation was required, the original system (like its paper or cardboard-based predecessors), relied primarily on carbonless duplicate paper vouchers imprinted with details embossed on the customer's plastic card. Credit control was then managed using floor (merchant) limits combined with telephone authorisation.

Growth in card usage convinced Barclaycard that automation through a fully computer-based transaction system was required and one was commissioned in 1974 to eliminate much of the paperwork, speed up the authorisation process and provide narrative statements for cardholders. This need to accelerate service delivery time eventually led to the formation of a platform for 'real time' operations; in other words, an array of IT applications that allowed automatic credit authorisation and funds transfer to the merchant's bank using extensive communications networks to link Visa's and Mastercard's electronic fund transfer protocols as well as their 24-hour-a-day and 7-day-a-week credit authorisation systems.

Alongside development in credit card markets, banks had been issuing cash card/cheque guarantee cards to their customers and installing networks of automated teller machines (ATM) to lower the costs of delivering basic bank services. Barclays Bank led the world with the first operational ATM in 1967, while IBM introduced the magnetic stripe plastic cards in 1969. Together these innovations marked the birth of electronic banking. Bank systems then developed to implement 'real time' transactions through ATMs and these were equivalent to the transactions required to transfer funds from the credit balances of credit cardholders to transacting merchants.

Barclay's early adoption of ATMs was no coincidence because cash withdrawal through ATMs is a major use for credit cards. Initially, the heavy investment required to build an ATM network was seen as a major source of competitive advantage for large banks, so interconnection was slow to develop. But after 30 years the absurdity of terminals connected to different networks located side by side, and long after terminal density had reached saturation point, eventually resulted in a single interconnected network in 1999 for the UK. Competitive to the end, Barclays then announced that it would charge non-customers heavily for using its machines, a proposal it had to withdraw after being vilified in the press.

Given the slowness with which banks integrated their networks, it was not surprising that Visa and Mastercard standards were adopted for debit cards. Debit cards provide instantaneous transfer of funds from the cardholder's account to the transacting merchant or cash issuing bank and in the UK banks were again split between the Switch and Delta formats (Visa Delta was re-branded in due course as Visa Debit). Debit cards were a new source of growth for card-issuing banks during the late 1980s to the extent that in 1991 MasterCard, with partner Europay International, launched their global online direct debit system to provide immediate transfers from customers' accounts against transactions (Maestro). Shortly after that, a system to support direct debit for ATM cash withdrawal worldwide (MasterCard/Cirrus network) was developed.

In summary, developments in the 35 years that followed the launch of credit cards in the UK by Barclaycard have been marked by a continuing move to industry standards, interconnecting and interoperating hardware and software, and overlapping membership of the two technology platforms (i.e. Visa International and Mastercard), as well as by almost identical functionality between cards. Barclaycard's achievement over this period was that it retained the advantage gained through early entry and remained as market leader, not just with the basic credit cards but in most of the segments that evolved in the market. From scratch, Barclaycard grew to be the largest credit card business in Europe, with a presence in UK and elsewhere, including Germany, France and Spain.

CARD PROFITABILITY

Exhibit 1 summarises the revenue streams from cards and these comprise four potential sources of income:

1. annual fees charged to cardholders;
2. interest charges on customer balances outstanding beyond the free credit period;
3. merchant commissions and handling charges;
4. processing charges recovered through contracts to non-processing card issuers.

Exhibit 1	The five players in the plastic card game

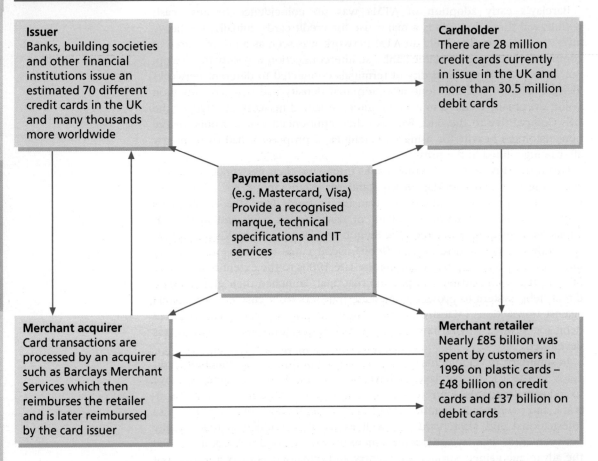

Issuer
Banks, building societies and other financial institutions issue an estimated 70 different credit cards in the UK and many thousands more worldwide

Cardholder
There are 28 million credit cards currently in issue in the UK and more than 30.5 million debit cards

Payment associations
(e.g. Mastercard, Visa) Provide a recognised marque, technical specifications and IT services

Merchant acquirer
Card transactions are processed by an acquirer such as Barclays Merchant Services which then reimburses the retailer and is later reimbursed by the card issuer

Merchant retailer
Nearly £85 billion was spent by customers in 1996 on plastic cards – £48 billion on credit cards and £37 billion on debit cards

Source: Adapted from *The 1997 Guide to Barclays Merchant Services.*

Despite being the initial, and for a considerable period the only, credit card issuer in the UK, Barclaycard made losses for the first decade of its operations as it built up its card and merchant volumes. As the market leader, it consistently priced Barclaycard at a premium, charging an annual card fee as well as the highest interest rate on credit card debt (annual percentage rate or APR) in the market. To sustain this position, management invested heavily in marketing to the point at which Barclaycard was the most recognised financial brand in the UK. Shaun Powell, a commercial director of Barclaycard until 1997, was typically opposed to anything that would dilute Barclaycard's brand: 'branding is a discipline, it is all about sustaining your premium price'.

The financial summary for the performance of Barclaycard during 18 months of trading is summarised in Exhibit 2. These figures illustrate that cards deliver a high proportion of non-interest income and are therefore attractive to banks who have to provide regulatory capital to back interest-bearing assets. Actually,

Exhibit 2	Barclaycard financial results

	HALF-YEAR ENDED		
	30.6.00	31.12.99	30.6.99
Net interest income	£269m	£247m	£241m
Net fees and commissions	£254m	£249m	£231m
Total income	£523m	£496m	£472m
Total costs	(£218m)	(£202m)	(£195m)
Provisions for bad and doubtful debts	(£110m)	(£88m)	(£82m)
Operating profit	£195m	£206m	£195m

Source: Barclays Plc Interim Statement 2000.

the growth of credit cards has been part of the reason why both international and British banks have been able to more than double the proportion of their income earned as fees and commissions over the last 30 years.

With around £4.8 billion of credit card receivables in 1999, Barclaycard was required to provide £480 million of regulatory capital. So profits of £400 million a year provided a return of close to 100 per cent on equity, a vivid contrast with a British bank's typical return on equity (ROE) of 15 per cent per annum. This was also an indication that, despite claims of increased competition, credit cards remained a remarkably profitable component in a bank's portfolio. For instance, the profitability of the card business within Citibank, the world's card market leader, was such that it was estimated to be worth 50 per cent more as a stand-alone business than the entire value of the bank.

Another element in the profit equation was the average value of balances settled outside the 'free interest period'. If a customer settled early then the issuing bank would only earn commission and fees (see Exhibit 3). This provided an incentive for issuers to have customers observing high-interest-earning balances outside the free interest period and indeed, Barclays aimed for individual customers to have at least 70 per cent of interest-earning balances outside the free interest period. So in effect, card issuers provide medium-term consumer finance. But to be able to grow credit card balances profitably issuers must entertain the possibilities under which credit risk might increase. For instance, in 2000, Barclaycard's transaction volume grew by 12 per cent while charges for bad and doubtful debts increased by 34 per cent. Financial performance thus suggested that the job for Barclaycard managers was finding customers who needed rollover credit but would not default on payments. Barclaycard's in-house skills in measuring and monitoring credit risk were, therefore, crucial to its strategy.

Exhibit 3 also portrays how, at the end of the millennium, competition in UK credit card markets had intensified and how customers encountered a wide-ranging offer as compared to Barclaycard's premium-priced cards. But a consequence of greater competition in retail financial markets (and the credit card business in particular) was that the best creditworthy customers have access to

Exhibit 3	Credit card competitors (January 2001)

ISSUER	TYPE	FEE P.A.	INTEREST-FREE DAYS	INTEREST, % APR			INSURANCE		LOYALTY SCHEME[†]
				DEBT	TRANSFERS	DAYS*	PURCHASE	TRAVEL	
Credit cards									
Barclaycard	V,M	£10	56	19.4%	9.9%	60	100 days	£50k	Rewards
RBS Advanta	V,M	£0	56	17.9%	1.9%	365	0	£50k	none
Goldfish	V,M	£0	52	18.9%	4.9%	180	0	£50k	Goldfish
Egg	V	£0	45	11.9%	0.0%	180	30 days	none	Cashback
Tesco	V	£0	56	15.9%	3.9%	180	50 days	£50k	Clubcard
Smile	V	£0	46	12.9%	8.9%	365	0	£25k	none
LloydsTSB(Adv)	M	£0	0	13.9%	9.9%	α	0	none	none
MBNA	V,M	£0	59	16.9%	2.9%	180	100 days	none	none
HSBC	V,M	£0	56	18.9%	7.9%	180	0	£50k	Choice
Amex blue	Amex	£12	56	19.5%	9.9%	α	90 days	£50k	Moneyback
GM	V,M	£0	52	19.9%	4.9%	180	0	£50k	Rebates
Gold cards									
Barclaycard Gold	V	£10	56	19.4%	7.9%	60	100 days	£100k	Rewards
HSBC Gold	V	£0	56	14.9%	7.9%	180	90 days	£100k	none

* The debt transfer rates and periods refer to the preferential rates offered to new customers with debt balances brought across from a different card issuer.
† Additional benefits such as purchase discounts, medical insurance, extended warranty and personal liability are not included for reasons of space.

credit far more cheaply than the 20–25 per cent charged by mainstream card issuers. Hence, greater competition could have made it ever more difficult for credit card transaction volumes to grow at high rates without issuers incurring an even higher provisioning for bad and doubtful debts.

COMPETITION IN PAYMENTS

Barclaycard's strategy in the card market has been associated with three continuing elements. The first was the continued growth of the credit card market shown in Exhibit 4. Over the period 1989–99 the volume of credit card transactions grew at 7.5 per cent, while debit cards grew at 40 per cent. The number of credit cards in use increased by 5 per cent per annum and the value of a transaction increased by 5.5 per cent p.a.

The second factor was the relative success of Visa, whose UK franchise was exclusively enjoyed by Barclaycard in the early years. Over the years Visa secured a position as the world's most widely used card, by 1998 accounting for $1.4 trillion dollars of purchases or 55 per cent of the global market. Although the competition between Visa and Mastercard was less clear-cut in the UK, Barclaycard's Visa cards had international acceptability with 16 million merchants worldwide. Exhibit 5 suggests that although Barclaycard lost market share somewhat faster than the other major banks, the strength of Visa's international position to some extent offset Barclaycard's premium pricing.

Exhibit 4	Growth of transactions in the UK card market, 1989–99 (millions of transactions per year)

	1989	1990	1991	1992	1993	1994	1995	1996	1997	1998	1999
Debit card	68	192	359	522	659	808	1,004	1,270	1,503	1,736	2,062
Credit and charge cards	650	690	699	724	748	815	908	1,025	1,128	1,224	1,344
Store cards	56	48	46	70	82	106	109	118	128	134	131
All card purchases	774	930	1,104	1,316	1,488	1,723	2,023	2,413	2,759	3,094	3,537
Cash issues by card	918	1,045	1,112	1,199	1,277	1,372	1,512	1,656	1,809	1,917	2,025

Source: www.apacs.com

The third factor was the ability to avoid price competition by branding and by use of new features supported by technology developments within the card networks. Although MasterCard introduced its gold card in the US in 1981 and by 1992 there were similar offerings in the UK (such as those supplied by American Express or the Co-operative Bank), Barclaycard made an attempt with Barclaycard Gold until 1995. Barclaycard acquired 90,000 Gold customers and the launch pushed its market share of new credit cards issued to over 30 per cent. It also segmented its market, improving the retention of profitable high borrowers with smaller required repayments and reduced rates for high borrowings. Non-price features like extended purchase warranties and purchase insurance were also added to the package for some cards.

With more than 1 billion cards issued worldwide, credit cards were becoming an increasingly important form of payment in many countries. But the usage of debit and credit cards issued in North America and Europe showed significant differences. The US accounted for about 40 per cent (400 million units) of the cards issued and a massive £340 billion credit card spending in 1995. This compared with the UK's £44 billion and Italy's £6 billion, while in some countries, such as France, debit cards and charge cards were dominant and the credit card market was underdeveloped.

Managers of Barclaycard then identified the unusually low penetration of credit cards in Germany as a business opportunity and by 2000 they had issued 1.1 million cards in Germany, France and Spain, with business growing at 10 per cent per annum. The potential for continued growth in these markets was signalled by figures from the Credit Card Research Group showing that credit card payments in the UK were equivalent to 8.5 per cent of GDP, while in France, Germany and Italy the equivalent figure was 1 per cent.

Barclaycard also moved quickly into e-commerce as the first UK credit card to offer Internet account services, with 250,000 cardholders registered to monitor their account status on the Barclaycard website.

However, and in spite of some card issuers having been quick to grasp opportunities opened by technological innovation, rather belatedly card issuers (and banks in particular) realised that the same technology that supported retail credit cards could also support business-to-business transactions. Europay is quoted as estimating that European businesses spend an annual £100 billion on routine business expenses, mostly by cash or cheque. Corporate cards, for

Exhibit 5	Cards issued by major banks and associated market shares						
	1994	%	1995	1996	1997	1998[E]	%
Barclays	8,464	37.2	8,944	9,273	9,429	9,561	29.4
Lloyds TSB	4,775	21.0	5,256	5,619	5,801	5,923	18.1
NatWest	3,556	15.6	3,654	3,834	4,502	4,655	14.1
Midland/HSBC	3,296	14.5	3,620	4,089	4,534	4,489	13.6
Total bank credit cards	22,692		25,216	27,455	31,829	32,793	

Source: Key Note – Credit & Other Finance Cards 1999, p. 38.

travel and subsistence costs, provide detailed reports and cost centre consolidation. With a typical cost for paper-based order processing and payment of $50 dollars and 50 per cent of total procurement spend on orders under $400, purchasing cards provide a major opportunity to stream-line purchasing procedures and save administration costs. American Express launched its Corporate Purchasing Card in the US in 1993 and in 1995 in the UK, with Visa International introducing its corporate purchasing system to the European market in 1994. Purchasing cards were attractive to business organisations by allowing paperless 'order to payment' purchasing, itemised transaction reports as well as consolidated reports by employee, supplier and purchase category.

Barclays provided both company charge cards and purchasing cards under the brand Company Barclaycard and established UK market leadership in corporate charge cards. Its four corporate cards, all Visa based, offered a combination of travel discounts and insurance, extended purchase warranties and supplier discounts and provided reporting options and VAT reporting. The Visa-based Company Barclaycard Purchasing card allowed customers to nominate a monthly statement date and provided the alternative of extended credit as well as the reporting possibilities of the Company Barclaycard corporate card. Barclays leading position in this market was underlined by its success in securing the account for a Government Procurement card with variants provided to the Ministry of Defence, Customs and Excise, the Ministry of Agriculture, Fisheries and Food and the Environment Agency.

TRANSACTION PROCESSING

The transition from paper to electronics introduced large economies of scale in processing. This innovation, however, was characterised by relatively high-level, one-off investments. The most expensive related to the linking of the point-of-sale system through leased lines and satellites, as well as with investments to develop packet-switching systems to carry and distribute messages across the network. Software, equipment and operating staff were relatively independent of volume and so offered scale economies. Barclaycard implemented the transition from paper to electronic processing using Barclaycard

Services for card issue, transaction processing and statement services. At the time, Barclaycard's share of total card transactions in the UK was 27 per cent from 9 million issued cards. Its nearest rival, Lloyds-TSB, had 5 million cardholders.

However, Barclaycard rejected the potentially profitable opportunity of servicing other card issuers through Barclaycard Services. Although others, including Bank of Scotland, Royal Bank of Scotland and NatWest, were active in supporting cards, issued by retail chains, building societies and smaller banks – who reasoned they could narrow their scale disadvantage by gaining incremental processing volume. The processing area was further complicated by the entry in the UK market of card issuers such as MBNA, who, with 16 million cardholders in the US, clearly out-scaled Barclays.

Increasingly, though, processing was determined by the two dominant card networks. By 2000, Visa's network, VisaNet, had a peak throughput of 2,700 transactions while MasterCard used AT&T to replace its transaction network infrastructure with the industry's first virtual private network. Technology improvements provided new opportunities for Barclaycard to save costs and in 1998 a change programme identified ways to eliminate 1,100 jobs over the following three years. Results were already evident by 1999 when costs fell by 4 per cent to $397 million despite the continued expansion of Barclaycard activity in Europe and especially in Germany.

All card issuers though were faced with some major changes as magnetic stripe cards began to give way to smart or chip cards which could store trans-action data without needing to access the complex networks required to handle credit cards. By 2001, Visa member banks had already issued 23 million chip cards in the market while e-commerce transactions were being supported by Visa's Secure Electronic Transaction platform. At the same time, MasterCard had bought an interest in Mondex, the smart-card-based electronic wallet developed by NatWest Bank.

The on-board chip in smart cards could handle complex security features, including biometrics, which reduced card delinquency for banks switching to the new technology. But greater security allowed credit transfers to be made direct to merchants over the telephone or Internet without the need for pro-cessing by either the cardholder's or merchant's bank. Furthermore, V-Sync, a Japanese digital content provider, developed a matchbox-sized device, CoCyph, to turn a mobile phone into a payment mechanism by a device that could scan store and transaction details, then confirm payment from a digital account through a terminal at the supplier which, at $200 per unit, cost one-tenth of a conventional online terminal. This process would deprive card processors and suppliers of the personal information they routinely obtained in a card-based transaction. At the same time, chip cards would support multiple relationships. So the strength of banks' links with their customers would be tested by many other businesses such as utility companies and petrol companies who have frequent contact with their customers and can offer direct incentives for customers to take their card rather than the bank's card.

Technological change and the open nature of the main networks thus attracted a plethora of competitors into credit card markets. But even with a flood of new entrants in the mid-1990s Barclaycard kept defection rates below

| Exhibit 6 | Market share estimates |

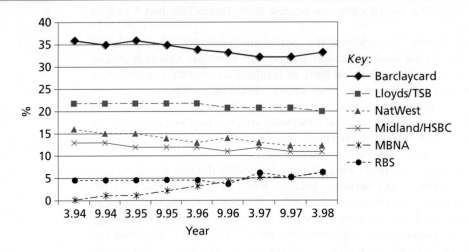

Source: RBS estimates, *Chartered Banker*, October 1998, p. 56.

5 per cent per annum. Defection rates were low thanks to the inertia of bank customers, which had been historically high. Even for credit cards, where the formalities of changing suppliers were minimal, customer retention rates were high historically. However, acquisition of new customers was a different story, with Barclaycard's share dropping to 15 per cent, well below its ongoing market share of 30 per cent of the market. Exhibit 6 further illustrates how processing specialists such as MBNA or Royal Bank of Scotland have gained ground at the expense of participants which had grown organically, while issuing cards to their own customer base.

Exhibit 7 depicts how competition intensified as a rash of new participants, including non-bank issuers, moved into the market, with variable success. But many of the new entrants found that customers acquired through intensive promotion of discount offers often moved on once the offer ended. Nevertheless, free for life offers from the Co-operative Bank for its Gold Card or Halifax for a Platinum card offering purchase protection, travel insurance, helpline and a 2.9 per cent APR on transferred balances offered large savings against even a standard Barclaycard. As a senior executive at one card issuer remarked,

> The main barrier for a new credit card provider is the fragmented nature of the business and the present focus on rate driven offers. Rates below the cost of funds are not sustainable but unless offers are competitive, it is difficult to achieve market share growth . . .

Affinity and co-branded cards also entered the market. Arrangements such as NatWest's 'air miles' offer, HFC Bank's GM card and Barclaycard's ventures with Cellnet, Eastern Electricity and Natural Gas involved revenue sharing between the affinity group and the card issuer. Nevertheless, British Gas's Goldfish card (launched with HFC Bank in 1996) was picking up 7.5 per cent

| Exhibit 7 | Changes in outstanding balances in the UK credit card market |

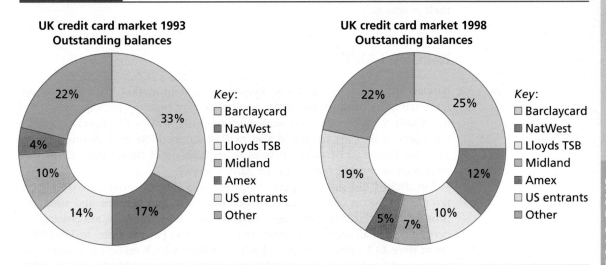

UK credit card market 1993
Outstanding balances

UK credit card market 1998
Outstanding balances

Key:
☐ Barclaycard
■ NatWest
☐ Lloyds TSB
☐ Midland
■ Amex
☐ US entrants
☐ Other

Source: Card Forum International, Jan/Feb 2000, p. 51.

| Exhibit 8 | New players in the UK credit card market in the 1990s |

TYPE OF PLAYER	NEW PLAYERS IN THE UK MARKET
1 Foreign entrants	American Express, Citibank, MBNA, HFC, Capital One, Bank One, People's Bank and The Associates
2 Non-financial institutions	Virgin, General Motors (GM) card, AT&T Universal Card
4 Specialist credit card issuers	MBNA, Capital One, and Household International
5 Retailers card and store cards	Tesco and Sainsbury, Marks & Spencer (branded loyalty card products)
6 Internet-based card suppliers	Egg, Marbles, Smile, Cahoot

of new cards (against Barclaycard's 15 per cent) within two years, while MBNA, after entering in 1994, won 5 per cent of the national card base by 1998, on the back of a massive direct mail operation. Exhibit 8 summarises the types of established and new participants in the market.

The entry of non-banks into the card business was helped by the technical support of established card processors. The cost of establishing banks like Sainsbury's Bank (Bank of Scotland), or Royal Bank of Scotland's Virgin and Tesco financial operations, is less than £40 million, with Prudential Insurance's

Egg at £200 million the exception. Supporting customers through cards, call centres and the Internet allowed these new entrants to offer cut-throat rates on their products.

BARCLAYCARD'S STRATEGY

Barclaycard's strategy was to develop and maintain market leadership by differentiating its product using the comprehensive benefits package described in Exhibit 9. As it operated semi-autonomously within the Barclays group, managers of Barclaycard could also market its products as a unique service. This differentiated Barclaycard from other high-street bank credit cards that were sold as another feature of the bank's service.

Barclaycard did not compete on price – its interest charges (APR) were not the lowest on offer. It had invested heavily in an energetic and sustained promotion/advertising campaign. Barclaycard's investment in advertising exceeded that of all other companies in the industry. For example, in 1995/96 it spent over £12 million compared with NatWest's £1.5 million and American Express's £3 million. Few in the UK will not be familiar with the long-running television advertisement series featuring Rowan Atkinson (a.k.a Mr Bean) or Angus Deayton. The message in the advertising encapsulated the essence of Barclaycard's strategy and how it planned to differentiate itself from competitors. The advertisements emphasised peace of mind – in case of an emergency such as losing your card or passport, medical problems on holiday or

Exhibit 9	Barclaycard products and services, 1998
Credit cards	• *Standard credit cards*: Visa and Mastercard • *Special privilege cards*: Barclaycard Gold, Barclaycard Premier, Company Barclaycard • *Barclaycard Sense*: For consumers new to credit cards
Free user benefits	• *Barclaycard purchase cover*: 100 days of free insurance • *Barclaycard holiday club*: Discounts for over 80 tour operators; free travel accident insurance • *Barclaycard Profiles*: 'Reward points' to be collected for gifts or cash
Advice	• *International rescue*: Cash advances, advice or local doctors, etc. • *Barclaycard assist*: advice on legal, home or roadside assistance
Online services	• *Barclaycard Call Service*: Direct debiting for calls worldwide • *Barclaycard Netlink*: Online banking services (Internet)

Exhibit 10   SWOT for Barclaycard

In 1998 Barclaycard was the subject of an MBA student project at Cranfield School of Management in the UK. The student groups produced detailed analyses of Barclaycard's strategic position, summarised as a SWOT analysis.

The *strengths* of Barclaycard were:

- Market leadership with a market share of 34 per cent in terms of credit cards issued, and 27 per cent in terms of transaction value, provided the company with a strong financial base.
- Low-cost production, resulting from accumulated experience as the first credit card issuer in the UK and economies of scale derived from its high market share. However, this was being rapidly eroded.
- Brand status. The Barclaycard name was almost a generic term for a credit card and was widely recognised by consumers.
- A well-established distribution network, through Barclays Bank and other members of Barclays plc, other financial institutions and large retail organisations which made its product available to a wide range of potential customers.
- Information technology capability, which allowed Barclaycard to develop improved products through alliances with companies such as British Telecom and Cellnet.

However, Barclaycard had at least two *weaknesses*:

- The annual transaction value per card of £1,719 was low in comparison with NatWest's figure of £2,121.
- Its typical APR of 25 per cent was twice or even three times larger than the interest rate offered by new competitors. Although defection rates were low, average transaction value was at risk of dropping further.

In the late 1990s there appeared to be a number of possible *opportunities* for Barclaycard:

- Spending on credit and debit cards amounted to 43 per cent of total retail sales, leaving scope for further development.
- Only 54 per cent of UK adults owned credit cards, leaving room for increased market penetration.
- Technological developments and new products would improve security and flexibility of payment by plastic systems.
- Company-branded cards and store cards provided access to a base of new users and the opportunity to develop loyalty-based ties. This could enable further marketing of discounts, new products, etc. Company cards also provided an opportunity to expand into the charge card market for business customers.
- The short-term macroeconomic situation in the UK was encouraging, with real income increasing, low inflation and strong economic growth. The expansion in the credit card industry was expected to continue in the foreseeable future.

However, there appeared to be a number of *threats*:

- New entrants such as building societies and non-bank providers offering similar products.
- Low APR cards were being offered by some new entrants. This included some American banks that were used to operating in a home market where APR had been driven down by 'no frills' operators who had continued to gain market share.
- The cannibalisation of the credit card market by debit cards and electronic purse (smart) cards.
- Increased availability of other forms of credit, e.g. point-of-sale interest-free credit.
- Increased opportunities for potential card fraud.
- Reliance on electronic communications – the effect of a major breakdown in national communications (e.g. a strike at British Telecom) could be catastrophic.

losing goods purchased with Barclaycard. It underlined the benefits package of support provided by Barclaycard. It also capitalised on its strong customer base by relationship marketing alliances with leading organisations in other service industries such as BT and Cellnet (telecommunications) and Marks and Spencer and J. Sainsbury (retailing).

In such a fast-moving and competitive industry there were many opportunities for all competitors to develop. It was important that Barclaycard was clear which of the various options it should itself pursue. It was also a question that others were asking: in 1998 Barclaycard was the subject of an MBA student project at Cranfield School of Management in the UK. The results of their SWOT analyses are described in Exhibit 10 and might help your deliberations too.

WH Smith plc

Bill Sutherland

This case examines a well-known retailer, WH Smith plc, and adjustments to its portfolio of business units in light of falling margins and changes to its external and competitive environments. At a time when mass retailing was coming under pressure from specialist retailers, WH Smith sought to redefine its position and improve its financial performance with special emphasis on increasing margins. A further aspect of the case reviews the company's unsuccessful attempts to change the balance of power in the wholesale magazine distribution industry – resulting in their decision to exit from that field. The case can be used to evaluate aspects of corporate strategic choices.

● ● ●

INTRODUCTION

WH Smith plc, the name of the WH Smith Group with effect from 1 February 2000, has been a familiar name in high-street retailing in the UK for many years. The change of name was intended firstly to reflect how customers commonly refer to the company; secondly, it was hoped that it would help to promote the WH Smith brand across the business. The company believes that its brand is synonymous in the high street with the concept of trust and accessibility and it hoped to build on these core values for the future. In 2000, WH Smith had sales of £2,584 million and some 26,400 employees. The business units were focused on retailing (predominantly book, magazine and stationery retailing), consumer publishing and news distribution. Although the majority of its business is UK based, the company operates in a further 10 countries, with North American, Asian, Australian and mainland European presence. WH Smith was the leading seller of books and magazines in the UK in 2000. The configuration of the business at the start of 2001 is detailed in Exhibit 1. Selected financial information is provided in Exhibit 2.

The structure of the company has rarely been static since the mid-1990s, with several businesses being acquired and others sold. There has been significant change and many tough decisions over the years to reach this point.

This case was prepared by William J. Sutherland, Aberdeen Business School, The Robert Gordon University. It is intended as a basis for class discussion and not as an illustration of either good or bad management practice. © W.J. Sutherland, 2001. Not to be reproduced or quoted without permission.

Exhibit 1	WH Smith business units in 2001	
PRINCIPAL BUSINESS UNITS	DESCRIPTION	ANNUAL TURNOVER £ MILLION (YEAR 1999/2000)
WH Smith High Street	Retail outlets primarily in high street and shopping mall locations	1,058
WH Smith Europe Travel Retail	Retail outlets located primarily in UK airports and railway stations	265
WH Smith USA Travel Retail	Retail outlets in airports and hotels	192
WH Smith Asia Travel Retail	Retail outlets primarily in Singapore, Hong Kong and Australia	12
WH Smith.co.uk	Online retailing service	7
Hodder Headline	Book publishing	105
WH Smith News Distribution	Newspaper and magazine wholesaling, marketing and distribution	945
TOTAL		2,584

THE DEVELOPMENT OF WH SMITH

The history of the business is a fascinating one. Established in 1792, WH Smith is arguably one of the best-known names in high-street retailing. The company was originally a family newsvendor business run from a small store in London. Several generations of the Smith family presided over continuous growth in the formative years. In 1848 the company opened its first bookstall at a railway station, Euston in London. These station outlets expanded rapidly, taking advantage of the growth in railways at that time. Newspaper distribution businesses and a printing works were acquired and the first overseas branch was opened in Paris in 1903. Expansion into North American markets began in Canada in the 1950s and was followed by entry to America in the 1960s. In the 1970s the company diversified into the travel agency business and do-it-yourself (DIY) stores. The 1980s and 1990s saw further acquisitions of stationers, office suppliers and the music retailer, Our Price, and joint ventures with Boots in DIY and Virgin in music retail. A controlling interest in the major specialist book retailer, Waterstone's, was achieved in 1989.

Exhibit 2 Selected financial information

BUSINESS UNIT	SALES £ MILLION						PROFIT £ MILLION						PROFIT %						% CONTRIBUTION TO GROUP PROFITS					
	2000	1999	1998	1997	1996	1995	2000	1999	1998	1997	1996	1995	2000	1999	1998	1997	1996	1995	2000	1999	1998	1997	1996	1995
WHS High Street	1,058	1,033	894	796	778	773	69	60	49	43	41	53	7	6	5	5	5	7	51	50	36	32	37	42
WHS Travel Europe	265	242	172	125	114	107	17	14	7	5	5	4	6	6	4	4	4	4	13	12	5	4	5	3
WHS Travel USA	192	178	171	150	134	127	12	13	9	10	9	7	6	7	5	7	7	6	9	11	7	7	8	6
WHS Travel Asia	12	8	4	4	2		0	0	-2	0	0		0	0	-50				0	0	-1			
Internet Trading	7	5	1				-8	-3					-114	-60					-6	-3				
TOTAL RETAIL	1,534	1,466	1,242	1,075	1,028	1,007	90	84	63	58	55	64	6	6	5	5	5	6	67	70	47	43	50	50
Publishing Businesses	105	28					16	4					15	14					12	3				
WHS News Distribution	945	897	933	946	884	793	38	39	45	45	31	36	4	4	5	5	3	4	28	33	33	33	28	28
Discontinued operations (disposals)	0	0	643	790	916	889	0	0	37	36	25	27							0	0	27	27	23	21
TOTAL GROUP	2,584	2,391	2,818	2,811	2,828	2,689	135	120	135	135	111	127	5	5	5	5	4	5						

Notes:

In 1995 and 1996, Retailing comprised WHS High Street Retail, Virgin Our Price, Waterstone's, WHS Inc. (USA), The Wall Inc. (USA), and Waterstone's Inc. (USA).

Trading accounts for years 1995 and 1996 are to 31 May, all other years to 31 August.

1995 and 1996 figures are representations of current business unit equivalents and are taken from WH Smith Group plc annual report and accounts for 1999.

Sales figures for the WHS News Distribution and Publishing Businesses exclude internal sales to WHS retailing units.

Data from published annual reports, subject to variations in reporting.

WH SMITH FROM 1995 TO 2000

Exhibit 3 provides the core business units in 1995. The performance of the business at this time came under intense scrutiny following some difficult trading conditions prompted by an economic downturn in the UK which had significant impact on the housing market and corresponding knock-on effects in the DIY sector. In 1995 the book selling and publishing industries faced some major changes following the removal of the Net Book Agreement. This agreement had until then effectively fixed the price of books in the UK. The change in legislation provided opportunities to promote special offers relating to books or to compete with lower prices. This also enabled other volume multiple retailers such as supermarkets to actively undercut the more traditional bookselling companies.

In the mid-1990s sales in the books, periodicals and newspapers segment of retailing grew by 9.7 per cent in a four-year period compared with other

Exhibit 3	WH Smith business units in 1995	
PRINCIPAL BUSINESS UNITS	**DESCRIPTION**	**ANNUAL TURNOVER £ MILLION (YEAR 1994/1995)**
Virgin Our Price	Music, games, video, multimedia retail outlets	414
Waterstone's	Book retail outlets	148
WH Smith News (Distribution)	Newspaper and magazine wholesaling, marketing and distribution	806
WH Smith Business Supplies	Acquisition and distribution of stationery supplies	165
WH Smith Retail	Book, multimedia and stationery retail outlets	916
WH Smith USA	Retail outlets in the USA including those under the brand names of The Wall (music retail), Waterstone's (book retail) and outlets in hotels and airports	240
Heathcote Books	Book wholesaler	Not specified in annual report
Do it All	Do-it-yourself chain	Not specified in annual report
	TOTAL	2,689

selected elements of the retailing sector such as floor coverings, pharmaceutical/medical and specialised stores which exhibited growth of 22, 22 and 27 per cent respectively over the same period.

The then chairman and group chief executive, Jeremy Hardie, had to explain the company's performance to its shareholders. His opening statement in the 1995 annual report did not pull any punches; it read:

> In last year's report I said that we must do better. We have done worse. The performance on which we are reporting this year is unacceptable. We fully recognise that over the next two or three years we will still have to do a lot better.
>
> A reduction of 7.6 per cent in Group profits is not cataclysmic. But against the growth plans which we had developed for the Group over the next few years and the expectations which we create among our investors, it has raised pointed questions about the calibre of the Group's senior management and the quality of our strategy.
>
> I have no doubts about our strategy for securing future growth. We recognised some time ago that our specialist retail brands – Virgin Our Price and Waterstone's – had a lot of potential. We have invested heavily in building these brands and we have made them profitable. We saw good opportunities for developing both WH Smith and our specialist brands in the USA and we have not been disappointed. Our office supplies business, despite a setback in 1994/95, should move ahead strongly over the next few years as the benefits of rationalisation are secured. WH Smith News, the oldest business in the Group, is once again proving its capacity to move with the market and will go on earning good profits.
>
> But for many months – well before the May profits warning – it has been clear that WH Smith Retail faces a formidable task. Threatened in some areas by supermarkets and in others by the specialists, some analysts argue that it no longer has a future. It is true that WH Smith will continue to face increasing competition, but so will all retailers, so that cannot of itself be fatal. The key task, having identified afresh our substantial customer base, is to serve it much better than we do now. This is the opportunity to make our profits grow.

It was clear that the company could not continue with its strategy as it had failed to deliver the key anticipated objective of improvements to margins. Changes to its strategy were required if it was to retain its place as a major force in its industry.

A major strategic review of WH Smith, its operations and customers was reported in the group's 1996 annual report. This review resulted in a rationalisation of the portfolio of the company. The overall aim of the review was to improve net margins by increasing customer satisfaction and sales. Exhibit 4 summarises the various disposals and acquisitions made by the company from 1996 to 2000.

The performance of the company could not just be blamed on changes to its business environment. The review also looked internally to streamline supply chain issues, improve supplier relationships and remove unprofitable product lines. An external benchmarking exercise was also undertaken and the top management team strengthened by employing several external directors for finance, operations management, and supply chain logistics. Stores were also revamped in response to feedback from customers.

Following the problems identified in 1995 the organisation itself adopted a flatter management structure and certain individuals in key positions were

| Exhibit 4 | Significant events in the corporate profile of WH Smith, 1996–2000 |

YEAR	PUBLISHING	BOOK AND MAGAZINE RETAILING	MUSIC AND VIDEO RETAILING	STATIONERY	OTHER
1996		Sells Heathcote Books (wholesale bookselling) to John Menzies plc		Sells the Niceday stationery company (WH Smith Business Supplies) to Guilbert of France Sells Paperchase	Sells 50% share in Do It All DIY chain to Boots
1997		Launches loyalty card 'Clubcard' scheme Enters the gaming hotel market in the USA	Closes chain of 29 Playhouse Video stores Sells 'The Wall', its US music retailing business, to Camelot		Sells stake in Virgin Cinemas
1998		Sells Waterstone's to EMI Group Purchases John Menzies retail chain Purchases the Internet Bookshop	Sells its 75% stake in Our Price music retailing to Virgin Group		
1999	Acquires Helicon Publishing (electronic publisher) Acquires book publisher Hodder Headline Purchases Wayland Publishing Ltd which specialises in books for schools	Launches Internet portal site for selling online in alliance with Telewest and Carlton			Signs up for the Open shopping channel (digital interactive TV)
2000	Appoints John Brown Contract Publishing to produce WH Smith own-brand magazines and guides	Purchases The Benjamin Company stores in the USA Acquires Hazelwood Enterprises Inc. (retail outlets in 71 hotel-based stores)			Forms Connect2U (80% holding) a business-to-business Internet trading portal in alliance with Axon Forms alliances with BT, Egg and OnDigital

replaced. The group moved to new, less costly headquarters and proposed to deliver a more commercial, customer focused culture. In 1996 the role of group chief executive was given to Bill Cockburn, with Jeremy Hardie continuing as chairman. This appointment was, however, short-lived, as Bill Cockburn resigned in 1997 and after a gap of three months Richard Handover, who was previously managing director of WH Smith News, was confirmed as his replacement.

In 1998, having disposed of its Waterstone's book chain for £300 million and its music retail businesses The Wall and Our Price for £28 million and £153 million respectively, WH Smith used some of the proceeds to purchase the high-street stores of its main competitor, John Menzies, at a cost of £70 million. Some 232 stores were purchased as part of the deal and gave WH Smith immediate access to markets in Scotland where its presence had been limited. By 2001, WH Smith's stores had sold more books than any other retailer in the UK.

Changes to the top management of the company continued, with Jeremy Hardie standing down as chairman in November 1999 and being replaced by Martin Taylor who had rejoined the board earlier that year.

The WH Smith brand

The company believed that the WH Smith brand was a powerful asset, standing as it does for associations of trust and accessibility. Richard Handover, WH Smith group chief executive, said, 'It has enormous untapped power and potential. Our products provide entertainment and learning for our customers. We aspire to create an environment and customer offer that is exciting, adventuresome and inspirational.' Other industry watchers commented that the WH Smith product was unexciting and undifferentiated given that other multiple retailers carried identical products. Some also questioned what WH Smith was actually for, given that others could satisfy the same needs, sometimes even more conveniently than the high-street retailer.

Exhibit 5 provides additional background to changes in the number of stores, retail space available and staff numbers in the late 1990s. The following paragraphs describe the business units at the start of the year 2001, with further background information on the history of their development and issues which were then being faced.

WH SMITH IN 2001

WH Smith High Street

The primary categories of merchandise in the high-street stores were books, magazines, stationery, music and video products. Books, stationery and magazines were the core markets. Exhibit 6 lists the various product and service offerings from many of these stores in 2001. UK retailing has seen significant industry consolidation in the 1980s and 1990s. The sector was dominated by

Exhibit 5	Stores, retail space and staff			

YEAR	2000	1999	1998	1997
Number of stores				
WHS High Street	529	545	558	413
WHS Travel Europe	187	183	184	105
WHS Travel USA	503	412	409	387
WHS Travel Asia	20	10	8	2
TOTALS	1,239	1,150	1,159	907
Retail selling space in square metres (000's)				
WHS High Street	271.8	275.6	277.3	208.4
WHS Travel Europe	18.6	18.1	17.9	9.9
WHS Travel USA	47.0	41.5	41.4	39.6
WHS Travel Asia	2.5	0.8	0.7	0.4
TOTALS	339.9	336.0	337.3	258.2
Number of employees				
WHS High Street	15,772	17,290	16,906	14,025
WHS Travel Europe	2,764	2,733	2,626	1,561
WHS Travel USA	3,309	2,762	3,039	3,118
WHS Travel Asia	173	89	90	45
TOTAL RETAIL	22,018	22,874	22,661	18,749
WHS News Distribution	4,397	4,278	4,406	4,749
Number of employees (FTE*)				
WHS High Street	8,036	9,012	8,935	7,419
WHS Travel Europe	1,774	1,754	1,685	978
WHS Travel USA	2,838	2,110	2,464	2,467
WHS Travel Asia	160	86	90	35
TOTAL RETAIL	12,808	12,962	13,174	10,899
WHS News Distribution	3,509	3,370	3,467	3,720

* FTE = Full Time Equivalents, i.e. the reduction of the number of people employed (including part-time staff) to full-time equivalents.

supermarkets, which, by the late 1990s, together accounted for more than 37 per cent of total retail sales. There was strong evidence that these large food multiples were expanding into other non-food market segments, with the pharmaceutical, book, clothing and home electrical sectors being particularly favoured. Many of these familiar names such as Tesco, Sainsbury, and Marks and Spencer had already diversified into services such as finance, DIY and furnishings respectively. Books were a key product area for WH Smith and it faced increasing competition in this product line from superstores and online sales companies.

WH Smith embarked on a store revamp and selectively closed old stores which it did not consider suitable for refurbishment or which were poorly positioned, such as the 21 former John Menzies stores it closed in 2000, and identified new locations such as shopping malls.

CASE STUDIES

Exhibit 6	WH Smith High Street products and services in 2001

Products
- Home entertainment, videos, CDs, DVDs
- Books, magazines and newspapers
- Home, office and fashion stationery
- Education and revision aids
- Travel guides and maps
- Art materials
- Theatre tickets
- Gift vouchers
- Gift ranges comprising activities such as wine tasting, white water rafting
- Stamps
- Batteries
- Lottery tickets
- Electronic products
- Confectionery
- Snacks and soft drinks
- Phone cards

Services (not in all stores)
- Online kiosks (for delivery to customer)
- Book ordering
- Magazine ordering
- Historic newspapers
- Photographic film processing
- CD-ROM factory – burn your own CDs
- Information screens
- Newspaper payment point (honesty box)
- Customer helpline

WHS International Travel Retail (USA, Europe and Asia)

WH Smith has provided news vending at travel centres, starting with railway stations in London and latterly at airports in the UK, USA and Hong Kong. Since becoming the first retailer at London's Heathrow Airport in 1948, it has continued a long tradition of exploiting retail opportunities in the travel business. To this has been added the development of opportunities in the hotel and gaming hotel market in the USA.

The travel retail businesses had specialised stores located at airport, train stations and hotels. In 2000, some 8 per cent of the company's turnover was earned in foreign currencies. The size of Travel Retail effectively doubled in 1998 with the purchase of the John Menzies chain. The Travel Retail business units were formed in 1998, as an organisational change which reflected the different attitude of the travelling public from the shopping public. Customers of the Travel Retail outlets, in contrast to the high street outlets, had little time to browse and required to make their purchases quickly with minimum disruption to their busy schedules. To help achieve this WH Smith introduced honesty boxes for customers to pay for their newspapers without using a till. Changing the sales mix to one with less entertainment and more books helped improve the margins in the Europe Travel business unit. Prior to 1998, these stores were considered part of the High Street business.

These airport and station outlets recognised the differing needs of their customers which were distinct from high-street customers. When time is limited, efficient store configuration is particularly important. Innovative promotions such as 'Read of the week' for books and 'Hot off the Press' for magazines stimulated sales and provided the regular travelling public with something fresh every week. Airport business performance was particularly strong in the late 1990s and the company continued to negotiate long-term contracts with major airports in the USA and elsewhere. WH Smith had a presence in nine of the top ten US airports following its acquisition of Benjamin Books. The 2000 annual report stated that the USA was seen as 'the largest English language consumer market in the world'.

The Asian market performed poorly in the late 1990s but, despite this, WH Smith continued to invest in new stores and entered the Australian market in 1999 with a contract to operate retail outlets at Sydney airport.

Europe Travel Retail was focused mainly on UK airports and railway stations. London stations showed particularly strong sales performances in 2000, up some 10 per cent on the year 1999. Forecasts from the Civil Aviation Authority and British Airports Authority estimated strong growth in the number of airport passengers at around 5 per cent per annum to the year 2005.

Publishing

WH Smith strengthened the publishing stream of its portfolio in February 1999 with the acquisition for £6 million of Helicon Publishing, the Oxford-based publisher of Hutchison Encyclopaedia. Hodder Headline, which had an educational publishing division and its own commercially focused mainstream titles, was acquired for £192 million in May 1999. The company produced educational textbooks and home learning guides, including the well-known 'Teach Yourself' brand. The thinking behind the purchases was to increase ownership of home-grown content and to improve the WH Smith own-brand titles and develop itself as a publisher of mainstream books in its own right. The publishing arm would also feed through to online content.

In rebuilding its book ranges WH Smith focused on food, travel, gardening and popular fiction. The company was also well known for its own-brand GCSE syllabus books and its range of educational books for 3–11-year-olds which were unique to the high street. According to the 2000 annual report, sales of these and other own-brand products had grown by 15 per cent across the group.

A range of electronic books (e-books) has been produced by Hodder in conjunction with Helicon. Helicon was also heavily involved with the launch of the world's first encyclopaedia for interactive digital television.

In October 2000 the group announced its intentions to enter the magazine publishing sector. It planned to launch a series of WH Smith-branded one-off guides and lifestyle titles. These gave purchasers advice on a range of issues from getting fit, to the pros and cons of purchasing a new computer or hi-fi music system. The contract for these products was given to John Brown Contract Publishing (JBCP). JBCP chief executive Andrew Hirsch denied that the new titles were in direct competition to other magazine products. 'They are not monthly newsstand titles, so they will not compete with titles that are already in store', he said.

Internet Trading

Some key acquisitions in the late 1990s provided WH Smith with its Internet presence at whsmith.co.uk. It purchased bookshop.co.uk for approximately £9.5 million. The Internet business in 2000 demonstrated a 55 per cent increase in sales – though the business unit itself was not profitable. One element of the e-business activity which was dissimilar to other online product offerings was the ability of WH Smith customers to order goods online for pick-up or return to their nearest WH Smith high street store. Internet kiosks were installed in some existing retail units. Strategic alliances were formed with BT, Open, Egg, MSN, Telewest, OnDigital (which became ITV Digital in 2001) and Carlton to extend its distribution channels.

WH Smith News Distribution

WH Smith's News Distribution division was responsible for the wholesale and delivery of magazines and newspapers to some 25,000 businesses comprising its own retail outlets and also those of other retail businesses throughout the UK. As well as distributing and delivering newspapers and magazines to its own retail stores, WH Smith News also delivered newspapers to other outlets, including independent newsagents, confectioners, tobacconists, newsagents, petrol retail forecourts and multiple retailers such as supermarkets. This process involved advising retailers of appropriate titles and appropriate quantities for their local market. Independent retailers accounted for some 40 per cent of magazine sales. By 2000 WH Smith News delivered 34 per cent of all newspapers in the UK and 36 per cent of all magazines, making WH Smith the biggest wholesaler of news in the UK.

Contracts for distribution were struck with publishers of newspapers and periodicals. In 1998 a contract with Emap valued at £47 million, which generated £6 million of profits, was lost. Some 75 per cent of turnover for the business unit came from its long-term contracts. In order to secure these long-term contracts the company came under pressure from customers to offer additional discount and as a consequence of these bulk arrangements profit margins were reduced. By the end of the century growth in the magazine market had slowed and WH Smith sought to use its logistical capabilities in other areas, such as the distribution of pre-paid mobile phone cards.

John Menzies continued to offer news distribution in Scotland, although WH Smith opened new distribution centres in both Scotland and Leeds in the north of England in 2000.

As stated earlier, WH Smith Retail is a customer of WH Smith News distribution. Of the £1,047 million sales in 2000, some £102 million of sales were attributable to WH Smith retailing businesses. This proportion of 'in house' sales had remained at a little short of 10 per cent for some four years.

The main challenges for WH Smith News was the timely distribution of newspapers and journals and the provision of sufficient quantities to match supply with demand. The implementation of SAP information systems and the launch of the Connect2U portal with its technology partner, Axon, indicated significant investment in the logistics and supporting technology to improve distribution. The portal permitted newsagents direct access to place and monitor their order through the Internet. Some 500 independent retail outlets had entered into an agreement with WH Smith for the facility, which helped the company manage and track the daily sales of some 2,500 magazine and 300 newspaper titles.

THE NEWS DISTRIBUTION SYSTEM

The distribution of newspapers and magazines in the UK is a major logistical exercise. Newspapers in particular have a limited shelf-life and it is therefore critical to ensure that they are distributed speedily and efficiently. The distribution system relies on wholesalers who are assigned exclusive distribution rights within a specific geographical area for both magazines and national newspapers. Wholesalers are in effect middlemen for the publishers of newspapers and magazines. National retailers must therefore negotiate with a variety of wholesalers up and down the country rather than with a single wholesaler for the supply of the retailer's national magazine requirement.

The distribution system itself was seen as inefficient with up to one-third of all magazines being pulped because they remained unsold. Retailers routinely either complained about getting insufficient access to supplies of magazines or claimed to be forced into taking large numbers of magazines which they did not wish to stock. In some cases retailers might sell out of the more popular periodicals in days and could not get further supplies even though there may have been unsold copies lying elsewhere in the country. WH Smith claimed that as a result of this mismatch sales of some £36 million per year were being lost. WH Smith and John Menzies had the major share of the wholesaling and distribution business, with competition from Surridge Dawson and some other smaller independents.

Arguments for change

In 2000, WH Smith embarked on a controversial agreement with Tesco, the UK's largest supermarket, which raised major concerns from all corners of the industry. In its annual report of that year, chairman Martin Taylor stated, 'WH

Smith has acted with determination in the UK to recast the magazine supply chain, which has been dominated by producer interests for too long'. This statement was backed up with action in the form of a proposed joint magazines distribution deal with the supermarket giant. What the two companies were proposing was for a single wholesaler to supply the UK's national magazine requirements for all multiple retailers.

Such an agreement would benefit national retailers like Tesco as they would have to negotiate only one contract for distribution rather than a range of locally specific ones as required under the existing scheme. Single wholesaling contracts would offer some economies of scale and also reduce the power of local wholesalers.

Tesco and WH Smith suggested that the proposed deal would improve market freedom and extend consumer choice. Lloyd Wigglesworth of WH Smith claimed that the deal would actually result in less money for WH Smith and it affirmed that the company wished to safeguard the future of independent retailers, and indeed that those retailers would welcome change in the supply chain. In response to suggestions that service levels might drop, he argued that the independents would retain the ability to complain and seek improvements.

With a national distribution system there was speculation that WH Smith, having more control, would be able to identify and focus on deals with publishers which were more lucrative. There was the possibility of the independent retailers in turn having to face higher charges from wholesalers trying to recoup lost sales.

Arguments against change

The deal was received with hostility from the publishers themselves and independent retail outlets and the proposal became the subject of a report commissioned by the Newspapers Publishing Association (NPA) by Professor Paul Dobson of Loughborough University. The results of this report were presented to Members of Parliament and other opinion formers with a view to block the proposed deal between Tesco and WH Smith (some referred to this as the WHESCO deal). At the time, Tesco accounted for some 7 per cent of sales of the £1.8 billion magazine market and WH Smith 16 per cent.

The NPA argued that the proposal would impact the industry in a variety of ways, including the abandonment of regional distribution in favour of national distribution. This would have meant that many wholesalers would have had to compete nationally for access to magazines and perhaps, if the agreement were to be extended, newspapers as well. If the deal had been approved, WH Smith News would have had effective control of over 50 per cent of the magazine distribution market.

Publishers believed that the proposed deal would adversely impact upon small publishing houses and independent retailers and that it was likely that some companies would be forced to cease trading and this, ultimately, would reduce consumer choice and restrict where periodicals could be purchased. If small newsagents disappeared this could result in localised areas across the country where access to newspapers was severely restricted. This in turn would result in lower sales and job losses in both retailing and newspaper publishing. Professor Dobson's report suggested that some 6,000 to 8,000 retail outlets might be out of business as a result of changes in magazine distribution. Regional newspapers were likely to be hardest hit because many of them had direct contracts with retail outlets and were therefore not as reliant on wholesalers. Therefore, with the possibility of a national deal, regional newspaper publishers were likely to suffer disproportionately as a result of the reduction in the numbers of these retail outlets.

Events and outcomes

A reported slip of 3 per cent in WH Smith's profits for the wholesaling business to £38 million for 2000 added to the uncertainty surrounding the distribution deal with Tesco. Richard Handover, WH Smith chief executive, insisted that rumours of a planned pull-out of magazine and newspaper wholesaling altogether were unfounded. Despite these problems Tesco and WH Smith pressed on with the proposed national distribution system and the disagreements between the companies and publishers came to a head when Grüner and Jahr (G&J), the publisher of periodicals *Prima* and *Best*, had its publications withdrawn from Tesco's shelves after it refused to sign the deal with Tesco and WH Smith. In response to this, G&J threatened to take matters to the Office of Fair Trading (OFT) and a further blow was dealt when, in November 2000, the *Daily Mail*'s publisher, Associated Newspapers, announced its decision to terminate two-thirds of its newspaper distribution contract with WH Smith. Once implemented, this would have removed approximately £100 million from WH Smith's annual revenues. This bad news was further compounded when the distributors of Emap publications and the BBC's magazines, *Front Line* and *Seymour*, threatened to terminate contracts with WH Smith. Of the £500 million total value of these contracts, WH Smith had some £140 million of the business. The company was therefore under severe pressure to abandon its proposed national system of magazine distribution and by the end of November 2000 the proposed deal with Tesco was abandoned.

Late in 2000 the Periodical Publishers Association (PPA) announced plans for an alternative new national information hub for the distribution of magazines from publishers to retailers. The PPA was considering seeking out organisations which provided similar services in other industries – such as national postal operators, or possibly a consortium of existing wholesalers. A major focus of the PPA proposal was the protection of the industry's 40,000 or so smaller retailers.

Following the withdrawal of the national distribution proposal a spokesperson for the industry said, 'WH Smith has been surprised by the power of the industry. We are delighted and are convinced that an industry-wide solution is the way forward.'

A press release on 12 April 2001 confirmed that the rumours surrounding the proposed sale of the WH Smith News Distribution business unit were in fact correct after all. Richard Handover commented, 'The decision to sell WH Smith

News is consistent with our strategy of realising the potential of the WH Smith brand through our retail and publishing businesses. Whilst WH Smith News continues to create value for the Group and is highly cash generative, over the longer term it is not central to achieving these objectives.'

Against this background of events, Richard Handover identified that the challenge for WH Smith in the new century was to maintain and build upon its history of innovation – as it had done for some 200 years. The management of WH Smith's portfolio of products and services in a rapidly changing business environment continues to test the creativity and skills of its people.

SOURCES

Bennett, N. (2000) 'Newsagents threatened by retail giants', *The Telegraph*, 6 August 2000.
Dobson, P. (2000) 'The impact of proposed national distribution developments on the UK Regional Press Industry', Loughborough University, a Report for the Newspaper Society.
Olins, R. (1997) 'Cockburn leaves WH Smith in limbo', *The Sunday Times*, 29 June 1997.
Rankine, K. (2000) 'WH Smith denies plan for wholesale pull-out', *The Telegraph*, 27 October 2000.
Rees, J. (2001) 'Press barons cut WH Smith plan to ribbons', *Scotland on Sunday*, 7 January 2001.
Stretton, M. (2000) 'Magazine publishers in revolt over distribution shake-up', *The Sunday Times*, 13 August 2000.
WH Smith plc, 'Embracing the future', 2000.
WH Smith plc Annual Report and Accounts 2000.
WH Smith Group plc Annual Report and Accounts 1999.
WH Smith Group plc Annual Report and Accounts 1998.
WH Smith Group plc Annual Report and Accounts 1997.
WH Smith Group plc Annual Report 1996.
WH Smith Group plc Annual Report 1995.

Note

Regarding figures in exhibits: Year on year comparisons of WH Smith's financial performance are complicated by the disposal and acquisition of business units, the development of an Internet business which is initially in a loss-making situation and in some years the return of capital to shareholders. Nevertheless, the exhibits provide some background data to the performance of the individual business units.

GlaxoSmithKline – a merger of equals?

Bernardo Bátiz-Lazo

This case summarises events leading to the creation of a global giant. The merger of Glaxo Wellcome and SmithKline Beecham had implications that went beyond the UK, where both companies were domiciled. The new company sought to take residence in the US but anti-trust authorities kept the companies formally apart for more than a year as they examined every aspect of the deal. The case invites readers to consider the process of integration as a general strategy, as well as the expectations, deliberations and motivation of managers and shareholders in doing so.

• • •

Exhibit 1 summarises how, during the 1990s, Europe's pharmaceutical companies were locked in a high-stakes multi-billion dollar struggle with their US rivals to stay in business beyond the first decade of the twenty-first century. The frenzy of takeover activity resulted from companies seeking economies of scale to finance spiralling research and development budgets. However reassured companies could be of going alone, each new merger deal intensified pressure on rivals either to respond with matching amalgamations or to risk falling behind in the race for market share. Merger activity during the 1990s took place while little evidence emerged to suggest that bigger research programmes were better (least of all after a merger) to replenish the 'pipeline'. For instance, the amalgamation of Hoechst (Germany) and Rhône-Poulenc (France) into Aventis reported a meagre 13 per cent annual increase in profits between 1999 and 2000. Aventis's financial performance was amongst the lowest in the industry but typical for a drugs company that had merged and had realised as much cost-saving as possible.

More representative of the industry norm were Pfizer and newly formed GlaxoSmithKline. Pfizer reported a 27 per cent annual increase in profits between 1998 and 1999 after launching Viagra. In 2001 GlaxoSmithKline reported a 29 per cent annual increase in profits from that achieved a year earlier by its originating companies. But while Pfizer's performance resulted directly from the successful launch of a new product, some questioned GlaxoSmithKline's ability to generate and sustain revenue growth. Deciding

This case was prepared by Bernardo Bátiz-Lazo, Open University Business School. It is intended as a basis for class discussion and not as an illustration of either good or bad management practice. Helpful comments from Sarah Holland, Steve Gorton and Ana María Valdes are gratefully acknowledged. © B Bátiz-Lazo, 2001. Not to be reproduced or quoted without permission.

Exhibit 1	Ethical drug sales after mergers are completed ($millions, 1998)				
COMPANY	TOTAL SALES	US SALES	RANK	EUROPEAN SALES	RANK
GlaxoSmithKline	21,227	9,504	2	5,028	2
Pfizer (including Warner-Lambert)	17,834	11,435	1	3,170	6
Aventis	15,172	3,061	12	5,526	1
Merck	12,840	6,076	4	1,864	10
AstraZeneca	11,876	5,519	5	3,422	3
Bristol-Myers Squibb	10,368	8,393	3	2,926	5
Novartis	9,534	3,995	11	3,111	4
American Home Products	8,902	4,723	8	1,398	14
Eli Lilly	8,622	4,517	9	1,006	21
Johnson & Johnson	8,562	4,857	6	1,781	11

Source: Datamonitor, 2000.

whether shareholders of GlaxoSmithKline should expect disappointing results in the medium term, however, was not so straightforward.

SMITHKLINE BEECHAM

The 1989 merger of Beecham and SmithKline Beckman led to the creation of a transcontinental pharmaceutical and healthcare firm, and also sparked a wave of mergers between pharmaceutical companies that spanned the following decade. Beecham and SmithKline Beckman were two '*also rans*', both running out of internal options: SmithKline had failed in its efforts to replace the income stream of its main '*blockbuster*' drug (Tagamet) but had an aggressive salesforce in the US. Beecham was essentially a consumer goods company that had been successful in early research on antibiotics. Beecham had neither the mass nor the competences to become a serious pharmaceutical player but it and SmithKline Beckman felt threatened as potential takeover targets.

Through amalgamation, both Beecham and SmithKline Beckman were able to keep up with critical mass in R&D, as the combined research budget doubled, but total R&D expenditure still lagged behind the likes of top firms such as Glaxo, which were outspending them two to one. However, the amalgamation resulted in a meticulous power-sharing agreement between the two management groups and brought about a new organisation with international marketing and sales presence.

People at SmithKline Beecham knew that the advantage of a friendly merger was allowing for '*equality of chances*' for those involved – a perception reinforced by Mr Bauman CEO, and his team investing substantial amount of time and effort to create a new culture (under the *Simply Better* initiative), which also transformed the way people were measured and rewarded. The amalgamation of Beecham and SmithKline Beckman was lengthy and relied on a combination of benchmarking (i.e. continuous improvement efforts) and process re-engineering. But the fairly lengthy integration process resulted in great deal of uncertainty for the workforce as stringent demands were made on individual managers, who were not given their new responsibilities until after the integration plans and new organisation structures were approved.

Jan Leschly became chief executive in 1994 and was responsible for the continuing implementation of Bauman's vision. The key element of this vision was to create a *'fully integrated healthcare provider'* through, among other things, diversifying into managed care in the US. The intent was for the pharmaceutical company to match services already offered by insurance companies, hospitals and doctors, by offering complete healthcare packages for a flat, up-front fee. Merck had been the first to integrate vertically by acquiring a pharmacy benefit manager (PBM) called Medco in 1993. This move was followed by other major pharmaceutical companies in 1994 when SmithKline Beecham and Eli Lilly purchased DPS and PCS Health Systems, respectively.

Drugs companies aimed to integrate vertically for several reasons. First, there was a potential threat in the success of the managed care model: in the US and elsewhere, pharmaceuticals could be reduced to meagre suppliers of commodity products. A second reason involved the possibility of giving preference to SmithKline drugs in formulary lists managed by DPS and substitution for SmithKline's leading prescription drugs by DPS pharmacists. Yet a third reason was an expectation that synergies would emerge from SmithKline's Clinical Laboratories division and DPS, enabling the group to offer combined pharmaceutical and diagnostic testing services to large employers. Another potential benefit was having access to detailed patient records, which would improve drug discovery processes but also benefit direct-to-consumer marketing efforts.

Through the acquisition of DPS, SmithKline inherited a six-year alliance with United Healthcare Corp., which owned several health management organisations (HMOs) with some 1.6 million members. The alliance would assure SmithKline exclusive rights among pharmaceutical and diagnostic companies, and access to medical outcome data from members of HMOs owned by United Healthcare. This would constitute a set of patient usage data, doctors' prescribing habits, and personal information that was more complete than that accessible to Merck through Medco. The alliance, therefore, would provide a potential advantage in conducting outcome studies as well as actuarial studies on patient usage patterns.

However, the validity of the managed care model was questioned in 1998 when Ely Lilly sold PCS, at a substantial financial loss. The following year SmithKline divested DPS as well as the clinical laboratory business. For the industry the divestiture of PBMs was more significant than the associated financial losses. The strategic turn around of Eli Lilly and SmithKline Beecham signalled a failure to control distribution channels through formulary lists and the inability of established pharmaceutical companies to integrate proprietary outcome and patient information into new drug discovery.

GLAXO WELLCOME

In the mid-1970s, Glaxo was a small British firm with its origins in the dried milk business and most of its sales in antibiotics, respiratory drugs and nutritional supplements. During the 1980s Glaxo grew organically and rapidly thanks to its success in researching and developing innovative new medicines. By 1994 sales totalled £5,656 million or 3.6 per cent of the world market, with earnings emerging from a strong presence in Europe and the US.

The top industry position was secured in 1995 when the industry as a whole faced yet again climbing drug discovery costs. Glaxo managers effectively engineered a takeover of Wellcome, as the Wellcome Foundation (the largest non-profit medical institution in the UK) owned a 40 per cent stake in Glaxo's Zantac and 39 per cent of Wellcome's share capital. Zantac was an anti-ulcer '*blockbuster*' product and the world's best-selling drug, commanding 35 per cent of the anti-ulceran market and achieving record sales of £2.4 billion in 1994. Zantac had been launched at the beginning of the 1980s and contributed 43 per cent of Glaxo's revenues, resulting in a large part of Glaxo's growth being based on Zantac's success. The problem was that Zantac's patent expired in 1997.

Wellcome was known for its '*academic*' approach to pharmaceuticals, with strong science but weak marketing. In 1996, and six months after the merger with Glaxo, managers already claimed that the newly created Glaxo Wellcome was fully integrated while its sales volume ranked worldwide first, it was the third largest company by market capitalisation in London and the world's largest pharmaceutical research firm with 54,000 employees. But the reality was that a severe clash had occurred between Wellcome and Glaxo's hard-nosed, commercial culture and things had worsened by the fact that few former Wellcome executives survived the takeover to serve the new Glaxo Wellcome. Organisational culture problems were exacerbated by significant overlap between product portfolios and the geographic distribution of the salesforce in key therapy classes.

Top managers thus endeavoured to rationalise the overall organisation and introduce economies of scale in R&D activities. However, executives had great difficulty holding the new company together. Russell Reynolds, a top recruitment consulting firm, was brought in to help reorganise worldwide operations. The aim was to create a levelled playing field so that few key individuals were lured away while, at the same time, the integration of different units was smooth and effective. In spite of this, there was increased middle-management turnover after coming together.

As part of its US operation, Glaxo Wellcome had developed presence in the managed care sector through a subsidiary called Wyeth-Ayerst Healthcare Systems. This company provided disease-management programmes, patient/member materials, outcomes assessment, and support for managed care marketing efforts. The incursion into the managed care sector was cautious as management believed that research, development and marketing of drugs were Glaxo Wellcome's areas of expertise. Other areas of excellence included developing world-class operations in combinatorial chemistry and a late (although successful) involvement in the biotech industry. A joint venture with Warner-Lambert, called Lambert Wellcome, had given a foothold in the prescription-to-OTC switch market and thanks to this venture Glaxo Wellcome successfully managed competition from generics at the end of Zantac's patent in 1997.

At the time of the merger with Wellcome, the chief executive at Glaxo was Sir Richard Sykes. He had been holding that job since 1994 and was a former (very successful) British academic and R&D director, as well as a firm believer in investing in R&D for company growth. One of the biggest setbacks of his career, at the top position in the new Glaxo Wellcome, was the UK government's decision in 1999 not to place Relenza, the company's new flu drug and the first real success of combinatorial chemistry research, on the National Health Service list of prescription drugs. However, he had been responsible for the diversification into emerging markets, a new organisational structure (called '*global products responding to regional needs*'), as well as joint ventures in India and Japan.

By the end of the 1990s, some analysts were sceptical about whether the merger of Glaxo with Wellcome had produced any synergies at all. It was true that sales of revitalised Wellcome products through Glaxo's marketing muscle had helped to avoid slipping in the rankings, but it was also true that the drugs '*pipeline*' was unimpressive and many new products had failed to live up to expectations. The merger had, indeed, brought Glaxo presence in certain therapeutic areas that it had not exploited before (such as anti-virals), while Wellcome benefited from greater financial discipline and focus. But both companies had been used to cash- and profit-rich years. So analysts wondered whether costs had really been brought under control, whether Glaxo Wellcome had relied too much on disposals to flatter its earnings performance and, on balance, many were disappointed that augmented R&D facilities had done little to replenish the '*pipeline*' by producing new potential '*blockbusters*'.

THE BIRTH OF GLAXOSMITHKLINE

In 1998, the merger between the two top British drugs companies seemed virtually complete, with Glaxo Wellcome shareholders having 59.5 per cent of the new group, leaving 40.5 per cent to SmithKline Beecham shareholders. With a market capitalisation of $110 billion, the deal would create the biggest pharmaceutical company and the world's third biggest corporation. The chief executive for the new group was going to be Jan Leschly, a former international pro-tennis star turned pharmaceuticals executive and SmithKline Beecham's CEO. The new chairperson would be Sir Richard Sykes, Glaxo's CEO. But after a weekend meeting of intense negotiations and to everyone's surprise, the deal was called off. The following trading day $6.6 billion or 10 per cent of SmithKline Beecham's market capitalisation was knocked off while the stock price of Glaxo lost 13 per cent. Formally, Glaxo Wellcome's directors indicated that they were not prepared to proceed on the agreed basis. Informally, SmithKline directors claimed that Glaxo Wellcome reneged on the original agreement that Leschly would be leader of the new colossus. Glaxo executives never challenged this version of the events. Neither were there comments on whether Mr Leschly's suggestion of spinning off the entire research effort into a separate capital-raising company might have been rejected by Sir Richard and Glaxo as too radical, sacrificing innovation in the pursuit of short-term cost reductions.

Both Leschly and Sykes had worked together in the past and some sort of rivalry seemed to have emerged since then. Leschly's patriarchal management style and SmithKline's financial rigour and performance-related culture seemed to have clashed with Sykes' passionate (sometimes even messianic) belief in science and Glaxo's more traditional management model. But it appears that if Leschly and his colleagues had retreated on the CEO issue, the merger would have gone through, and Leschly would have been $100 million dollars richer – the value of his shares and stock options in SmithKline, according to an estimate published in *The Economist*.

Another explanation offered for Mr Leschly's bitter reaction against the possibility that he might not be the chief executive of the new group was based on matters of principle and dignity. As CEO of SmithKline Beecham and before that as the CEO who delivered Squibb to Bristol-Myers, Leschly had done well financially. With or without the merger with Glaxo Wellcome he had already amassed enough for him and his family to fulfil any conceivable material wants. At the same time, Sykes and his management board disliked Leschly's management style and feared the merger would turn into a takeover by SmithKline people. Glaxo's management board also wanted to break with tradition (as Skyes had not led the initial move to merge) and claim the top post, because Glaxo Wellcome was the bigger of the proposed partners in terms of market capitalisation, products and R&D expenditure.

The fact remained that after the failure to merge, SmithKline still lacked the R&D funds to pursue its many leads for new drugs. Other major drugs companies continued with their plans and merged, while later that year Glaxo Wellcome still remained without a partner as managers also failed in their talks to amalgamate with Bristol-Myers Squibb.

After the first round of merger talks collapsed in acrimony in 1998, renewed interest in the merger emerged after Jan Leschly's retirement announcement in mid-1999, which effectively removed the barrier to the merger. This was also the time when industry participants learnt that Pfizer, the US drugs giant, had begun negotiating with Warner-Lambert, another US competitor, to create the world's second-largest drug maker with the potential for a 6.7 per cent global market share, $4.5 billion in R&D spent, and $287 billion in market capitalisation. Sir Richard Sykes said about his company's determination to do a deal:

> This is where two big successful organisations come together, not to protect future earnings growth but actually to increase critical mass to really outperform the industry. . . . The more effort, the more money, and the more power you can put to research, the stronger the company is going to be.[1]

Significantly, as part of the new deal, Sir Richard Sykes agreed to become non-executive chairman, a post of influence but few management responsibilities, while the chief executive of the new GlaxoSmithKline would be Jean Pierre Garnier. Known simply as 'JP', he had been raised in Normandy (in the north of France), where he grew steadily on a diet of British and US movies and music (he still claims Jimi Hendrix as a patron saint). Mr Garnier got a master's degree

---

[1] *Pharmaceutical Executive*, May 1999, p. 37.

and a doctorate from France's Université Louis Pasteur before accepting a Fulbright scholarship to Stanford University. Except for a few years in various parts of Europe, Mr Garnier's career had kept him in the US ever since, where he got a business degree. He joined SmithKline in 1990 as president of the pharmaceuticals division and moved to number one after Leschly retired.

British and European regulators were swift to give clearance to the emergence of GlaxoSmithKline, though some time after that the Federal Trade Commission (FTC), the US competition regulator, forced the groups to dispose of medicines for chemotherapy-induced nausea and herpes with annual sales of almost $400 million. At that point managers felt that the most substantive issues had been dealt with. However, the FTC continued to have concerns about the merged company's perceived domination of the US smoking-cessation market and this caused a second delay in taking the merger forward. The concerns of the FTC were based on the fact that, at the time, SmithKline had the leading over-the-counter brand and Glaxo the only approved prescription drug to help smokers quit – two key products which the FTC felt would give the combined company control over 90 per cent of that market.

For some observers, managers at GlaxoSmithKline failed to envision that creating the world's biggest pharmaceuticals firm would involve a very complicated regulatory submission process. Others argued that the arrogant approach by the new company management team to the FTC was to blame. Yet others felt that regulators were burdened with the recent wave of mega-mergers (in pharmaceuticals and elsewhere) and that they were also influenced by the US presidential race (which put the spotlight on healthcare spending). In any event, managers intimated that some regulatory delays were anticipated but it was never thought that regulatory concerns in the US over monopoly power of the new group in certain therapy classes would consume more than 10 months of negotiations and backtrack the merger process twice. Further, lengthy negotiations with US regulators prevented the early implementation of the new organisational structure. Executives were prevented from specifying how economies of scale in labs would be achieved, how performance would improve or how co-operation across business units would be implemented. Delays in getting regulatory clearance also prevented managers from stopping speculation that the company could eventually split up into separate businesses or announce how they would reckon with incompatible information technology platforms. All this, in turn, resulted in low morale and a 'brain drain' of middle managers (although occurring mainly among administrative staff). Nevertheless, developments were worrying for a corporation which had yet to be born and which was already involved in a process full of mishaps.

BUSINESS PORTFOLIO

As one of the key points of the merger, managers considered building operational headquarters in the US while corporate headquarters would remain in the UK. The new company's increasing leanings to the US in style and markets puzzled many, as Britain was home to both originating companies and the UK one of the world's leading centres for the research, development and

Exhibit 2	**Global presence and product leadership of GlaxoSmithKline (1998 pro forma sales figures)**		

	SALES (% OF TOTAL COMBINED SALES)	MARKET SHARE (% OF TOTAL SALES)	RANK
Region			
North America	45	8.9	1
Europe	34	7.6	1
Rest of the World	21		
Asia Pacific		7.5	1
Middle East/Africa		7.6	1
Latin America		4.9	4
Japan		1.9	18
Therapy class			
Anti-infectives	25	16.9	1
Central Nervous System	18	11.6	2
Respiratory	15	16.8	1
Alimentary & Metabolic	10	7.0	2
Vaccines	5	N/A	1
Consumer Health	16	N/A	N/A
Other Pharma	11	N/A	N/A

Source: Presentation to stock analysts, January 2000.

manufacture of prescription medicines. Britain's pharmaceutical output doubled between 1980 and 2000 in real terms while exports boomed and research and development of prescription drugs increasingly became a high-technology business and one of the most successful parts of the '*knowledge economy*'. But the fortune of the British pharmaceuticals industry seemed closely linked to that of its two main representatives: Glaxo Wellcome and SmithKline Beecham. When announcing the merger, Mr Garnier said that the new company was proud of its UK roots:

> But a world-class competitor cannot operate all its functions from a market that represents only 6 per cent to 8 per cent of its existence. The US, by contrast, accounts for 45 per cent of the global pharmaceutical market.[2]

Indeed, Exhibit 2 shows that that US would be an important market for GlaxoSmithKline as that market represented about half the business (based on 1998 combined pharmaceutical sales). Europe and the rest of the world would account for 34 and 21 per cent respectively. In addition to having a broad portfolio of products, the new company would lead in four of the five largest therapy classes, which together represented roughly half the global pharmaceutical market. This was complemented by a leading position in the vaccines market. The new company would also have blockbuster treatments

---

[2]*Chemical Market Reporter*, January 2000, p. 24.

for asthma, depression, AIDS and migraines. Not surprisingly, new drugs still in the *pipeline* were expected to reinforce the new pharmaceutical's position in the anti-infective group, but other strong growth products were expected in the alimentary and metabolic group as well as a new vaccine (Infantrix) and a respiratory drug (Seretide/Advair). Top managers then claimed that the new group could be expected to have a solid base in selected therapeutic markets while delivering sales of £17 billion per annum or 7.4 per cent of the world's pharmaceutical market.

Another key point to the merger were expected savings of £250 million from combined R&D operations. Those savings were to be reinvested in R&D to produce an annual research budget of £2.4 billion, the largest in the world after the new Pfizer. Top executives also expected the combined company to save an annualised £1 billion pounds after three years. These savings would come on top of previously announced restructuring at both companies, expected to cut a combined £570 million a year. But analysts of pharmaceutical companies at investment banks were puzzled by these figures. On the one hand, analysts were disappointed by the planned savings. Most estimated the figure to be between £1.1 billion and £1.5 billion, as well as some sort of immediate disposal of factories, reduction of intermediate capacity or outsourcing plan. On the other hand, analysts were encouraged by potential pay-offs that could come from the complementary research skills of the two companies. In other words, Glaxo Wellcome's investment in technology to automate the chemistry of developing drugs combined well with SmithKline's leadership in genomics (which promises a wealth of drug development opportunities). In fact, SmithKline Beecham had an existing *pipeline* of four promising drugs in the final stages of development. This was indeed very attractive to Glaxo Wellcome, who relied heavily on the generic sales of its *blockbuster* drug Zantac. However, only 7 per cent of Glaxo Wellcome's sales depended on drugs whose US patents expired before 2006 as compared with SmithKline's 33 per cent.

HUMAN RESOURCE MANAGEMENT

As part of the merger process, plans were drafted for the amalgamation of corporate and support operations of the new pharmaceutical colossus in most countries. This made labour unions unhappy because of the lack of consultation. Corporate executives claimed that there was nothing to consult about until the legal merger had taken place and thus, the newly introduced European regulation on consultation would not be broken. Nevertheless, unions feared that at least 15,000 jobs, no less than 14 per cent of the 105,000-strong combined global workforce, would be lost.

As for the 300 or so senior managers likely to be made redundant, Spencer Stuart, an international recruitment consultancy, was brought in to look into areas of potential overlap between business units rather than the universe of managers at the new corporation, and would leave the vital R&D and marketing teams intact. By bringing in a recruitment consultancy to carry out a management audit, top executives once again expected to develop a level playing field so that few key individuals were lured away. This fear was further supported by anecdotal evidence which suggested that the most valuable executives were likely to '*jump ship*' to competitors (including small, entrepreneurial biotechnology start-ups) before the merger process was over and this could be a reason why most mergers between pharmaceuticals failed to add shareholder value. As one top manager of another new big pharmaceutical said at the time:

> We learnt from other mergers to spend more time on cultural values and the way we wanted to behave in the future . . . Senior managers felt the final report captured the real competencies, and we believe we're the first merger not to have lost market share.[3]

Once the FTC approved of the merger, no divestitures were required in the smoking-cessation market and the new company revealed plans to re-engineer its R&D and marketing operations. At the time, Jean Pierre Garnier considered that organising 15,000 scientists across several time zones, with an annual budget in the billions of pounds, would require a radical new structure. This '*facilities master plan*' would allow him to assess which, if any, of the 24 global R&D sites should be closed. However, rivals such as Pfizer, Novartis or Aventis, which had already restructured their core operations, questioned how radical Garnier's plan really was.

ORGANISATIONAL STRUCTURE

The new plan considered breaking up discovery efforts through a combination of centralisation and decentralisation. Investments to generate new chemical entities (NCE) would concentrate on traditional activities and genetics while aiming to develop economies of scale. Discovery efforts would then be broken into six autonomous sub-units while aiming to maintain the excitement of a small discovery outfit. Drug development (including clinical trials) and marketing would again be co-ordinated by the central organisation.

Maintaining a single effort to discover NCEs aimed to apply scarce skills and expensive equipment across a range of diseases. There was to be two administrative divisions or the partition into Genetics Research and Drug Discovery Research. The emphasis on genetic research followed the new company's inheriting substantial investments in the use of genomics[4] in drug discovery: at its formation, GlaxoSmithKline would have over 500 patent filings for genomics-based drugs. Actually, just as merger proceedings evolved, SmithKline brought to clinical testing one genomic-based drug to treat obesity and one to treat hypertension, which were likely to take only five years to get to the market.

The plan for the new structure at GlaxoSmithKline also considered creating six sub-units (one in Italy, two in the UK and three in the US) out of the

---

[3]*Financial Times*, 23 August 2000, p. 23.
[4]Genomics, the study of genes and their function, promises to increase treatment effectiveness while limiting side effects by identifying people who would definitely respond to a specific medicine.

middle section of the *pipeline*, the part of the drug generation process considered to be where bright ideas are incorporated into drugs. The six business units, called Centres of Excellence (Cedds), were to organise the efforts of the 24 R&D sites across the world, work semi-autonomously and compete to attract financial resources from head office (and eventually from venture capitalists and even the stock market). The six sub-units were empowered to use molecules discovered within internal early research divisions, brought in from academia or from external biotechnology groups. It was hoped that as a result of the plan, the new company would avoid greater scale and associated bureaucracy while maintaining agility, entrepreneurial spirit and individual accountability in a key part of drug discovery. Moreover, it would attract talent by emulating the culture at biotechnology firms, including the introduction of big share option packages through which scientists receive royalties on the sale of medicines they helped to invent. But observers were sceptical as to how autonomous the six '*internal biotech*' would be allowed to become or whether the new structure would increase short-term productivity.

Finally, the plan for the new structure at GlaxoSmithKline also considered clinical trials and marketing to be undertaken on a massive scale, often across continents, and simultaneously complying with strict regulatory conditions. Scale at this last stage of the *pipeline* aimed to achieve corporate control and uniformity as well as capitalise on global reach. For instance, shortly after the merger was announced, two licensing agreements were signed by SmithKline Beecham while looking to strengthen links with the Japanese pharmaceuticals sector. Since marketing partnerships were seen as the only way to enter some markets (particularly for non-Americans to enter the US or for non-Japanese to enter Japan), the deals could become very important to make the best of the new organisational structure. But, at the same time, creating a difference through licensing agreements of late-stage products would not be easy. For instance, Pfizer had a successful record of marketing drugs in the US created elsewhere while many other big and medium-sized pharmaceuticals also had gone along the licensing route into Japan.

CONSUMER HEALTH

Greater scale in marketing was attractive to managers because, while regulatory approval proceeded in the US, SmithKline Beecham became the world's second-biggest toothpaste manufacturer following the completion of its acquisition of Block Drug of the US for $1.24 billion with a cash bid worth $53 per share. The deal added Block's Sensodyne toothpaste to SmithKline's range of dental care brands, which included Aquafresh, Macleans and Odol. Consumer goods sales, including toothpaste and drinks such as Lucozade, Ribena and Horlicks, would then make £2.5 billion or a third of SmithKline Beecham's sales and 15 per cent of the combined 1999 sales of Glaxo and SmithKline.

When questioned on the subject of consumer healthcare, Jean Pierre Garnier was said to be committed to the consumer health business because he saw this area as being key for GlaxoSmithKline extending the life of certain prescription pharmaceutical brands, such as *blockbuster* Tagamet, by switching them to over-the-counter sales. However, analysts at investment banks speculated that the lower-margin consumer unit could be sold and the money reinvested in pharmaceuticals assets. SmithKline Beecham had been willing to sell individual brands in the past. Opinion was thus divided as to whether the Block Drug acquisition represented greater commitment to consumer health or a strengthening of the business in preparation for a sale. Yet, for others, growth into consumer health signalled another significant acquisition for GlaxoSmithKline in the not too distant future, while questioning which were the core competences that would deliver the much-needed advantage in prescription pharmaceuticals markets.

The debate around the role of healthcare in the business portfolio of GlaxoSmithKline suggested that the new company was at a crossroads. The merger could yield a wealth of new drugs, for the good of shareholders and patients alike. And the new company seemed to have everything needed to be the best in the business, but so did Glaxo and Wellcome or Beecham and SmithKline Beckman when they merged.

Snappy Snaps

This case is taken from an article in Business FT Weekend on 28 April 2001. It explains the development of the franchise operation, Snappy Snaps, and provides an opportunity to consider the challenges faced by the owners as digital technology threatens to change the future of its market.

• • •

Twenty-one years ago in a shop in Toronto, Don Kennedy clapped eyes on the machine that was to transform his life. He was on holiday, hoping to get some photos developed. Ordinarily, he might have expected to wait a few days, but in this particular shop he discovered a machine capable of churning out prints in just an hour.

When he returned home, he got in touch with an old school friend named Tim MacAndrews. 'He thought it offered a great business opportunity,' says MacAndrews, who was initially sceptical. 'I told him it was a daft idea – until I saw the machine in action and immediately realised he was right.'

Thus was born Snappy Snaps, a Hammersmith-based business that now has roughly 400 staff working at 90 stores and an annual group turnover of £35m.

'Ten years ago, if I'd met someone at a social occasion and mentioned Snappy Snaps, they'd have said, "Who?"' claims Kennedy. 'But now we've become synonymous with high-street photography.' Better still, the organisation has for five years running been named High Street Photo Lab of the Year by *Amateur Photographer* magazine.

Even so, all is not well. In the decades since Kennedy brought MacAndrews news of the developing machine, the march of technology has, if anything, picked up speed. It's now practically impossible to visit a tourist destination without bumping into crowds of visitors armed with the latest in digital cameras. (See Exhibit 1 for an explanation of digital camera technology and capability.)

These are in the vanguard of a revolution in photography, which threatens to make old-fashioned film a thing of the past. This month, Eastman Kodak announced massive job cuts, blaming a 48 per cent fall in profits on declining sales of camera film. So what future can there be for a chain that was established precisely to process that film? Can Kennedy and MacAndrews continue to prosper? Or will the people they encounter at social occasions once again start to ask, 'Snappy who?'

Exhibit 1	'Bridging the Digital Divide' by Richard Cook

When George Eastman launched Kodak more than a hundred years ago, his proposition was simple: 'You push the button and we do the rest.' Kodak duly grew to dominate the film and processing businesses, but the company largely ignored the early days of digital photography, arguing that Kodak was a mass-market brand, while digital photography was an expensive, top-end niche.

Last month that strategy abruptly changed. Kodak used an ad in the middle of the Oscars ceremony to launch the mc3, a device that not only takes digital pictures but also records videos and plays music. The mc3 retails in the US for just $230 (£160) and some commentators are saying it could be the breakthrough piece of kit that opens up digital photography to a mass audience.

With the cost of digital cameras dropping all the time, the one stumbling block appears to be the printing process. The inkjet printers now commonly employed to make hard-copy prints of digital images are relatively inexpensive and – especially if you use glossy paper – the results look, from a few feet away, just like real photos. However, up close, the image is rather grainier and the prints fade within months, not years. What's more, you usually need a PC to process your snaps.

The answer to this may already be here. Hewlett-Packard has already developed technology that enables consumers to plug a digital camera directly into a printer and a technology called dye-sublimation printing is producing results that are indistinguishable from the best lab-processed prints. A dye-sublimation printer such as the Olympus P-400 will produce a single 10×8 inch image in just 90 seconds. The only problem is cost. Right now, the P-400 will set you back £650.

If it weren't for the advent of digital cameras, the story of Snappy Snaps could be considered a textbook example of how to turn a money-spinning idea into reality. The duo realised their dreams in a thoroughly businesslike fashion. After returning from Canada in 1980, Kennedy quit his law and accountancy studies, MacAndrews gave up his job as an accountant and the two gained the specialist experience they needed by becoming franchisees of the Kall Kwik printing-shops chain.

In September 1983, they set up the first Snappy Snaps photo lab in Queensway near the West End of London, offering a one-hour development service. First-year turnover was an impressive £300,000, thanks to the shop's prime location. Three further stores were opened over the next three years. Since then a growing army of franchisees – among them a former bank manager, a customs officer, a teacher, a City trader and a sailor – have helped turn Snappy Snaps into a nationwide concern with outlets from Brighton to Belfast and Exeter to Edinburgh, even if it is still centred on the London area.

Photo-processing has always been competitive but competition has, if anything, intensified in recent years. 'Every letter-box in the country has an envelope stuffed in it a couple of times a year, petrol stations want to do it, newsagents and supermarkets want to do it – everyone wants to get on the bandwagon,' says Kennedy, sitting at the double desk he shares with MacAndrews in their first-floor office in a converted Victorian bakery. 'Yet we're more successful than ever.'

Over the past dozen or so years, Snappy Snaps has grown by an average of around 10 per cent per annum, helped by the takeover of the 11-outlet Anglia Supercolour in 1989 and nine Express Photo Labs in 1993. Much of its success can be attributed to a drive for quality. 'We all know operations where the quality varies from outlet to outlet. That's something we were determined to avoid,' says MacAndrews.

The shop might have made their name catering for 'happy snappers', but a third of custom is now business-related. And the shops themselves offer a range of services including image-scanning and photo restoration, poster printing and the transfer of images on to CD – in addition to providing traditional developing and gifts such as picture frames.

Another keystone of Snappy Snaps' success is that it opted for the business model best suited to its needs. After opening their first few stores, Kennedy and MacAndrews experienced difficulties in motivating staff. 'We felt franchising was the best way to expand because the person running each outlet was, in effect, their own boss,' says Kennedy.

Unlike some businesses that went down the franchise route in the 1980s but expanded too quickly and went under in the recession of the early 90s, Snappy Snaps played it safe – and prospered. 'We never had grand ambitions of opening a phenomenal number of shops,' says Kennedy. 'Our strategy has always been to grow at a controlled pace.'

Choosing the right franchisees was also vital. 'If we send out 100 information packs to prospective franchisees we'd rather take on no one than take on the wrong person,' says MacAndrews. How can they be sure of picking a franchisee with the Midas touch? 'That's one question we never answer,' says Kennedy wryly. 'They obviously need to have drive, enthusiasm, a desire to succeed and a belief in our way of doing things – but the selection procedure for finding the right franchisee is our own Coca-Cola-style secret formula.'

The cost of setting up a Snappy Snaps shop is about £140,000 but the franchisee only has to stump up £30,000. In return for a 6 per cent royalty and a 2 per cent advertising royalty, Snappy Snaps helps raise the money for equipment (the main cost), negotiates discounts from suppliers, provides a business plan and training and allows use of the company name. In return, franchisees benefit from the Snappy Snaps brand and a £750,000-a-year advertising budget.

Franchisees can expect a £35,000 profit by the end of their first year in business, according to MacAndrews. But he warns: 'It's not an easy way to make money. You're not just running a corner shop and shutting up at five. You don't turn customers away at one minute past four, as happens at some high-street chains. And the busiest days are Saturday and Monday, which ruins any hope of a long weekend.'

There has been the odd failure – usually put down to a franchisee's 'inflexibility' or failure to go out and look for new business, but Kennedy says, 'No matter how you profile people, until they're doing the job you can never predict 100 per cent how they are going to cope.'

The duo are proud of their close relations with the franchisees, whose own pictures adorn the walls of their office. There are annual conferences, regional meetings and staff-training courses – all designed to foster team spirit. 'We were once franchisees ourselves so we understand their concerns,' says MacAndrews. 'But they continue to stay with us and even buy further franchises – a testament to the strength of the bond between us.'

He and Kennedy have retained the shared dream they started out with – another factor in Snappy Snaps' success. 'It's been a joint business from the beginning,' says Kennedy. 'We created Snappy Snaps, we built it and it's our baby. It really is a 50–50 partnership and if somebody asked our advice I'd like to think we'd give the same answer.' (The two laugh when I remind them how they told me they weren't interested in photography on our first meeting several years ago. But MacAndrews is quick to point out: 'Our expertise lies in franchising and business management.')

Despite the material success Snappy Snaps has brought the pair, to which Kennedy's gleaming Jaguar sports car outside the company HQ bears testament, they have no desire to sell up and spend the rest of their lives flitting between golf course and sunshine villa.

'We hope to have about 100 stores by next year,' says Kennedy when I ask about their plans. The duo are also preparing to expand overseas. 'We've had many inquiries over the years but it's something we've hitherto avoided,' says Kennedy. 'But we now believe the time is right to look abroad. We have a big enough organisation to support the training of a master licensee overseas.' MacAndrews adds: 'It won't be crash, bang, wallop, let's go and open 500 units in Poland. We'll be taking it slowly, going into one country at a time to make sure we get it right.'

Not that the future is without risk. The digital camera revolution means that it's possible to take pictures without purchasing film and, by plugging your camera into a PC, run off colour copies on a printer.

But Kennedy, who points out that Snappy Snaps offers a wider range of digital services than ever before, says: 'Film volume is being maintained despite all the digital cameras out there. The reality is that very few people are developing pictures at home because it's cumbersome, difficult and the cost per print actually works out far more than what we charge for high-quality durable prints. If anything, the new technology has boosted business because people who have spent serious money on digital cameras want serious photographs and therefore come to us.'

Surely the digital revolution poses a substantial threat in the longer term, though? 'It's impossible to predict the future,' says Kennedy cautiously. 'But I suspect the vast majority of people who buy a digital camera will use it for certain specific functions. They won't take a very expensive digital camera to a beach for instance. It's rather like camcorders. A few years ago it was predicted that lighter, cheaper camcorders would make the camera obsolete, but that hasn't happened. People use them sparingly and continue to use an ordinary camera for day-to-day stuff.'

It was, however, embracing technological change that first put Snappy Snaps in business and that's the way MacAndrews and Kennedy want to keep the company thriving. As MacAndrews bluntly puts it: 'If a business cannot adapt, it will die.'

Coopers Creek and the New Zealand wine industry

Heather Wilson and Maureen Benson-Rea

The case examines the international growth of a medium-sized New Zealand winery – Coopers Creek. It is concerned with the international strategies employed by Coopers Creek since its inception. This is set against the background of a small, rapidly internationalising economy within a global market environment and the effect upon the New Zealand wine industry. Readers are encouraged to consider the future strategic options for Coopers Creek.

• • •

INTRODUCTION

Coopers Creek, established in 1982, became one of New Zealand's more successful medium-sized wineries by following a strategy of resource leveraging via networks of co-operative relationships with other New Zealand winemakers in the domestic and export markets. This strategy allowed Andrew Hendry, the managing director, to consciously manage the growth of the company to retain the benefits of small size. However, with increasing globalisation of the wine industry, the changing nature of export markets, the early maturity of the New Zealand industry and the constrained supply facing New Zealand winemakers, Andrew Hendry was faced with the decision of how to position a smaller company for the future. He had to decide whether the network-based strategies that served the company so well continued to be appropriate under conditions of industry concentration, increasing competition and emerging globalisation.

BACKGROUND

Coopers Creek and network-based strategies

Coopers Creek was a typical entrepreneurial venture in that its development and growth had been driven by the founding entrepreneur, Andrew Hendry. From 120 tonnes of grapes crushed in 1988 and less than 1 per cent export

Exhibit 1	Comparative export figures

NZ WINE INDUSTRY FIGURES	1992	1993	1994*	1995*	1996	1997	1998	1999	2000
Total exports NZ$million	34.7	48.3	41.5	40.8	60.3	75.8	97.6	125.3	168.6[†]
% increase	37.4	39.2	−14.1	−1.7	47.8	25.7	28.8	28.4	34.6
Exports as % of sales (vol.)	13.9	18.9	21.7	20.2	25.3	25.2	28.5	30.1	n/a
% increase	15.8	36.0	14.8	−6.9	25.2	−0.4	13.1	5.6	n/a
COOPERS CREEK FIGURES	1992	1993	1994*	1995*	1996	1997	1998	1999	2000
Total exports NZ$million	.36	.76	1.1	1.0	1.2	1.8	2.0	2.3	2.1
% increase	65.0	111.1	44.7	−9.1	20.0	50.0	11.1	15.0	−8.7
Exports as % of sales (vol.)	22.4	42.9	48.9	42.4	49.2	63.3	57.9	61.5	49.1
% increase	97.3	91.5	14.0	−13.3	16.0	28.7	−8.5	6.2	−20.2

* Less wine available for export due to low cropping years (real effect of which covers 18 months).
[†] Year-end June 2000.

Source: Statistics New Zealand and Coopers Creek.

volume to 670 tonnes crushed in 1999 and greater than 49 per cent export volume, growth was achieved with minimal comparable overheads and infrastructure. Exhibit 1 contains the relative export figures for Coopers Creek and the New Zealand wine industry. A critical factor in the success of Coopers Creek was Andrew's ability to build relationships, within the context of an innovative and flexible approach, in order to leverage critical resources to pursue growth.

Andrew Hendry and his wife Cynthia purchased the land for the Coopers Creek vineyard in 1980 with seed capital from their home-made pâté business. Coopers Creek was formally established two years later with 40 per cent loan capital from a local bank and 60 per cent equity capital, 20 per cent from Andrew and 40 per cent from other shareholders. These other shareholders comprised grape growers, who were also suppliers to the business, colleagues from Andrew's former employment with Coopers and Lybrand, and the original winemaker for the company. Andrew Hendry arranged the partnership structure so that the winemaker owned one-third of the company, Andrew owned another third and the other shareholders owned the final third. Later on, as profits were generated, Andrew bought out the partnership and, by 2000, he owned 71.3 per cent of the shares of the business and the ratio of debt to equity was 1:1.5. The original winemaker partner left the business to return to the USA, selling his shareholding to Andrew. Only one grower retained a shareholding, although all of the shareholder growers experienced capital gain. Essentially the growers decided they could no longer operate on both sides of the fence: as growers they wanted to negotiate the highest price, but as shareholders they wanted to bargain for the lowest prices. Most of the other shareholders had retained or increased their shareholdings.

Coopers Creek established collaborative relationships with a group of four local competitors in the West Auckland area. These relationships were formed in 1990 on the initiative of Andrew Hendry who, on a visit to Australia, observed some Australian wineries collaborating locally. This group of Auckland companies regularly gathered in an informal committee to decide on their next collaborative efforts. Sometimes all five companies were involved, at other times only two or three went ahead with particular initiatives. The West Auckland group initially came together for joint advertising and promotions, increasing the custom from retailers, restaurateurs, wine vendors and visitors for the group of wineries beyond what they could achieve individually. The success of these marketing initiatives led to collaboration on the production side of the companies' operations, sharing equipment and processes like grape crushing at key times. Investigations made to collaborate on joint purchasing of key inputs, like barrels, corks and bottles, resulted in Coopers Creek sharing the costs of container-loads of barrels with three other wineries. Although the local collaborative grouping still existed in 2000, its configuration had changed, with one winery dropping out and a new one taking its place with its relocation to the West Auckland area. Also, one of the original wineries had been taken over by another in the grouping and, in turn, this combined winery was taken over by an Australian winery.

A feature of the more recent networks in which Coopers Creek was involved was a focus on horizontal or competitor-based co-operation. Competition in the domestic marketplace was considered to be intense, but this did not impede collaborative efforts where these were deemed more efficient or beneficial, while paying heed to the need to avoid anti-competitive behaviour. According to Andrew Hendry, there were very few secrets in the wine industry as transfer of technology and know-how between wineries was highly developed and was a source of national competitive advantage for the industry. In international markets the competition for sales and market share was seen by New Zealand wine companies to be from other countries rather than from individual firms. However, once the customer had decided to purchase New Zealand wine, Coopers Creek considered itself to be in competition with all New Zealand wineries present. The newer producing countries, such as Chile, were perceived to be the bigger threat due to rapid advancements in production quality. However, even within the international marketplace there was co-operation, with industries across countries sharing information and learning about new techniques and processes. This international learning was achieved often through informal means. For example, Coopers Creek organised exchange visits by producers and sent its winemaker to spend the off-season in northern hemisphere wineries to build connections and to benefit from low-level technology exchange.

The NZ wine industry

When Andrew Hendry established Coopers Creek, the New Zealand environment was highly regulated. By 1984, the New Zealand government had initiated a programme of deregulation, which included devaluation of the New

Zealand currency, exchange rate flotation and general anti-inflationary measures. The opening of New Zealand's domestic market meant that businesses had to improve their efficiency substantially over a short period. The agricultural sector sought out new markets, to replace the loss of their traditional dependence on the UK market with its increasing commitment to its European trading partners, and new products, reflecting a growing awareness that much of New Zealand's exports were of a commodity nature. This period saw growing exports to Australia, the United States, Japan and the rest of Asia and exports of predominantly sheep meat and dairy produce being accompanied by more fresh fruit, venison and wine. A further response to fiercer competition at home and in overseas markets was an increasingly strong focus on quality, a case in point being the New Zealand wine industry.

The New Zealand wine industry accepted the consequences of the liberalisation of the domestic economy and recognised the need to understand how ongoing changes in the international economic environment affected its prosperity and how to plan accordingly. Building from a low international base in the 1980s ($4.5 million in exports in 1987), New Zealand wine exports achieved phenomenal growth and accounted for $168 million in 2000, comfortably exceeding the $100 million by 2000 target set in 1997. The UK market was the most important export market for the industry in 2000, and at $84 million it accounted for around 50.22 per cent of total exports by value and 54.28 per cent by volume (see Exhibit 2). Europe accounted for 66 per cent of exports, with 85 per cent of that going to the UK. Four large firms, namely Corbans, Montana, Nobilo and Villa Maria, dominated the wine industry in New Zealand in 1999. The following year, Montana purchased Corbans and Nobilo was bought by BRL/Hardy of Australia. Between them, these large firms accounted for around 80 per cent of all exports in 2000, with another 17 medium-sized companies, of which Coopers Creek was one, handling 16 per cent in combination. For the most part, industry participants exported between 30 and 35 per cent of their production, but a few producers had a much higher export intensity.

All New Zealand winemakers had to belong to the New Zealand Wine Institute. In order to sell wine, companies were legally obliged to acquire a licence and take out membership of the Institute. The Institute acted as a self-regulatory body for the wine industry. Among its regulatory activities, the Institute administered the Ministry of Health's export certification procedures, which involved chemical testing and blind tastings. In 2000, there were 293 members of the Wine Institute, with the majority comprising small, 'boutique' wineries. Some Institute members with export interests in specific markets had established special interest groups, of which the UK Wine Guild was one (see later). Other groups, termed Country Action Groups, were established to share information, experiences and promotional activities relating to Germany, the USA, Canada and Australia. The groups developed marketing plans to explore and, ultimately, exploit export opportunities within the chosen markets, and these were implemented through a semi-formal funding arrangement whereby individual companies contributed to costs on a project-by-project basis. For example, only those companies interested in a particular promotion contributed to the costs of mounting it. Countries were split into Tier 1 markets,

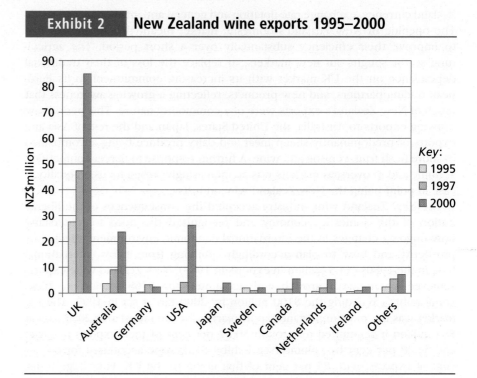

| Exhibit 2 | New Zealand wine exports 1995–2000 |

Source: Statistics New Zealand and Wine Institute of New Zealand.

where New Zealand had a strong and growing presence (UK, US and Australia) and Tier 2 markets, where there was a smaller presence and growth potential (Canada, Germany, Ireland and Japan). These markets received differential attention and funding. As well as the UK Wine Guild, Coopers Creek was actively involved in the Canadian and US Country Action Groups in terms of joint promotional efforts. In those markets where collaborative efforts had been employed, the principal aim had been jointly and effectively to sell the New Zealand label ahead of individual wine company labels. Promoting the generic New Zealand brand in this way was seen as a way of benefiting all New Zealand exporters.

With the management of the quantity and quality of the grape supply proving to be a critical resource issue within the New Zealand industry, investment in plantings had been important for the industry as a whole. Rising grape prices followed poor yields in the 1992, 1993 and 2000 seasons. Some wine producers diversified away from high-priced contract grapes and invested extensively in their own vineyard plantings. After two relatively small harvests, the 1995 and 1998 vintages produced bountiful crops. Along with the New Zealand industry entering early maturity (see later), oversupply situations caused concern that the industry would focus on the production of lower-cost wines, either by growers forming a co-operative to utilise the excess grapes and produce their own wine or by wineries focusing on low-cost competition. It was anticipated that a low-cost competitor would affect the export market more than the domestic markets, because domestic customers valued particular winery and vineyard labels while export customers were considered to be more price sensitive because they lacked this local knowledge. However, it should be borne in mind that, in the past, the liabilities of a small economic base and the vagaries of the New Zealand climate had left the industry without sufficient product to tackle export market diversification.

By 2000, the New Zealand wine industry was considered to be at an early maturity phase of its life cycle, as evidenced by a small number of takeovers and increasing concentration. Historically, the industry had focused on the production of premium wines, given its constrained supply, small scale, high cost structures and distinctive 'clean and green' growing conditions. This was in keeping with the general trend of New Zealand producers to move away from the commodity mentality to more value-added, quality products. The wine industry's strategy was to retain a focus on a quality, differentiated product, hold its premium price position, play to its strengths in white wines and introduce more red wines into its portfolio. In the UK market it obtained the highest average prices for wines, closely followed by Australia. The Wine Institute's marketing strategy was intended to maintain this position and not to compromise it by attempting to achieve volume production. Whilst the emerging global wine companies in the US, Australia and Europe[1] sought to supply reliable, consistent supermarket sales, the New Zealand producers aimed for the 'fine wine', connoisseur niche market.

In terms of the industry's structure and positioning, New Zealand was facing major challenges. As an industry facing early maturity, the number of new entrants into the smaller production end of the industry continued to grow. However, concentration was occurring among the medium and large players as a result of both local acquisitions and acquisitions by overseas purchasers. Two related challenges faced the industry: the rise of the global wine company and access to production inputs, such as grape supplies and expertise. Historically, the New Zealand industry had a small level of international ownership of wine companies. However, international wine companies from Australia, France and the Americas were becoming more active globally and in New Zealand. Of the original top four larger producers in the New Zealand wine industry, Corbans, Montana, Nobilo and Villa Maria, only one had been partly overseas owned in 1997. By 2000, only Villa Maria remained 100 per cent New Zealand owned. Whilst this international interest was motivated by portfolio ambitions, risk spreading and issues of market access, perhaps the key reason was to gain access to New Zealand's unique growing conditions and the local industry's technology, skills and talent. On the one hand, this could strengthen the resource base behind the New Zealand industry and facilitate access to increasingly concentrated distribution channels in Europe and the US, but, on the other hand, it could impact on New Zealand's unique position in world markets.

---

[1]For example: LVMH, Castel Frères, Pernod Ricard in France; E&J Gallo and R. Mondavi in the US; and Southcorp, BRL Hardy and Mildara Blass in Australia.

COOPERS CREEK

Operations

In order to keep up with growth, principally driven by exports, Coopers Creek had to increase its supply of grapes from the original four hectares west of Auckland. This was achieved by acquiring additional land for its own plantings in West Auckland and Hawkes Bay, also in the North Island, as well as buying grapes from independent growers in Gisborne in the North Island and Marlborough in the South Island. This strategy enabled the company to spread the risk of adverse weather conditions in any of the four major New Zealand growing regions. By 2000, Coopers Creek sourced 90 per cent of its grape supplies from 20 independent growers. These purchases were made on long-term contracts, which were based on the potential quality of the site and the grower's husbandry of the grapes. The company would have liked to have grown more of its own supplies, but decided to wait until prices stabilised before purchasing more land. Given this, Andrew Hendry had to plan with growers for longer-term quality plantings, especially with the company's shift in emphasis from retail sales to on-premise sales (that is, sales to restaurants). To that end, Coopers Creek had effectively leased blocks of vines from grape growers and the price per hectare was determined according to the targeted wine style for the end market. Buying in bulk wine from other wineries had enabled Coopers Creek to meet extra export demand without having to produce cheaper wines itself. Andrew Hendry's intent was to avoid being production-led and to leave the production of cheaper wine to wineries with the overhead structure to support it.

The batch production system at Coopers Creek was well set up to produce in 25–30 tonne lots, a modular approach based on grape truck load capacities. The company had the capacity to crush 100–120 tonnes of grapes a day, giving it a major competitive advantage: for example, in one year in five, wineries may have to crush all of their grapes over a short period, as Coopers Creek did in the bad cropping year of 1995. Coopers Creek also had the capacity to juice for other wineries, as outlined above. The cost difference when installing the crushing plant was insignificant so it made sense to Andrew Hendry to install the larger machinery, and one person could operate this machinery alone if necessary. The batch operation system allowed for tank traceability on each consignment or bottling run and samples were kept on hold in the winery.

Andrew Hendry considered production based on 1,000 tonnes of grapes crushed to be an optimal level for Coopers Creek. If production rose much above those levels, then the company would be moving into higher administrative costs and away from quality-based wines. In addition, lifestyle aspirations meant that Andrew Hendry had consciously avoided dilution of shareholdings to fund expansion. Future growth was to be through servicing the export market. He had a strong commitment to a rifle rather than shotgun approach to international marketing and relationship building. Coopers Creek's strategy was based on having a carefully controlled, but finite quantity of wine to sell in any one year. The company considered the requirements of each market for certain wine styles and, as the grapes came in, it looked at the targets, the price points and the maintenance of quality standards in each market. The company produced in expectation of sales (planning for which was linked to previous years' performance and also to the grape supply) and, in order to retain flexibility, the company did not label bottles of wine until it was known exactly where the product was going. Nonetheless, major decisions had to be made at the supply stage and sometimes this involved the buying of bulk wine from other New Zealand producers to keep supplies going. For example, Tesco's in the UK wanted to do a summer price promotion in 1997 on a New Zealand wine. When one of the larger New Zealand wineries failed to respond, Coopers Creek took up the challenge, although it did not have all the wine to meet Tesco's requirements. The company sourced additional wine through a commodity purchase from some local companies and even made some money from the wine purchase.

The domestic market

Andrew Hendry observed that the New Zealand marketplace had become increasingly competitive, with nearly 400 New Zealand producers and cheaper imports from Australia. Coopers Creek serviced the three segments of on-premise, liquor store and supermarket sales in the domestic market. The winery had recently employed two sales representatives, one concentrating on restaurant and inner-Auckland retail sales, the other focusing on retail sales in the outer-Auckland and local country areas. According to Andrew, the advent of supermarket wine sales, as well as the increasing competition, required more personal representation. Elsewhere in the country, Andrew continued to use commissioned sales representatives. In the Wellington region, Coopers Creek shared a representative with another winery based in Tauranga, south of Auckland, and was looking for a similar arrangement to cover sales to the South Island.

Domestically, the last few years have seen some ups and downs for Coopers Creek in terms of public relations. In November 1997 the company received a major national award for excellence in exporting. Then in March 1998 came an accusation that Coopers Creek had, in 1995, altered the composition and labelling of an export wine in breach of export regulations. In the media lax rules were blamed, together with a lack of government funding to police the compliance requirements of three different laws facing wine producers. The Wine Institute publicly expressed its concern that sloppy monitoring of wine producers was leaving the industry open to abuse and announced that it would take a more active role in policing wine standards and would act to safeguard wine authenticity. The New Zealand Ministry of Health investigated the allegations for a breach of the Food Regulations Act and the Food Act. Coopers Creek voluntarily suspended all exports pending an external audit of its vintage records, which was carried out by a senior partner of Ernst & Young. By April 1998 Coopers Creek had resumed exporting. Whilst in May 1998 the Ministry audit did find discrepancies in record-keeping and in the make-up and labelling of some 1995 and 1996 wines, no further action was taken. In an ironic twist, two of the wines which were the subject of some of the controversy later won awards at the London International Wine Challenge, and in early 2000 British Airways added Coopers Creek Reserve Pinot Noir 1998 to its first-class wine list.

The negative publicity knocked the local business back for a while, mostly in the retail sales area, but the following year's sales were up 15 per cent on the previous year and Coopers Creek's representation in the on-premise segment was stronger than ever. Andrew Hendry believed that the export sales were not really affected, although he did observe that, not unexpectedly, other New Zealand wineries distanced themselves from the issue with visiting international sales representatives. In addition, it was noted that whenever negative publicity arose for another New Zealand winery, the New Zealand press would raise the Coopers Creek case as a prior example of a problem relating to the industry.

Major international markets

The international development of Coopers Creek drew on the shared learning, marketing efforts and resources with other wineries in the New Zealand Wine Institute, the UK Wine Guild and other market development groups, although considerable individual company effort was also expended in the process. For example, in perhaps the toughest market in the major economies served by Coopers Creek, Ontario, where a 100 per cent margin is imposed on liquor prices by the state monopoly, the winery received a Trade New Zealand export commendation in 1994 as the first New Zealand wine producer to receive a general listing by all of the 630 government liquor stores. Recently, Coopers Creek had been offered two more listings by the Ontario board, which would bring exports there to a potential six thousand cases per year.

Andrew Hendry's approach to exports had been to delay efforts until the company had secured enough long-term commitments from grape suppliers and had established a firm foothold in the New Zealand market. However, Andrew found the opportunity to enter the Australian market in 1984 irresistible due to the devaluation of the New Zealand currency making New Zealand products attractive in the Australian marketplace. Entry into the Australian market was facilitated by the New Zealand Wine Institute, which co-ordinated a wine expo in Sydney. By 1987, less than 1 per cent of Coopers Creek produce was exported, mainly to Australia.

Coopers Creek initiated a serious export strategy in 1989, having delayed for one year because 1988 was a bad season for the production of grapes. The UK was the next major market targeted by the company, again in partnership with the Wine Institute. From this, the UK Wine Guild evolved. This was a partnership of Trade New Zealand, a publicly funded body concerned with promoting overseas trade, and wineries either already established in the UK export market or interested in entering this market. Established in 1992, the UK Wine Guild was supported by one-third funding from Trade New Zealand for a limited period and two-thirds funding from active exporters and collected as a 1 per cent levy on free-on-board sales. These funds were used to establish an office in London with two full-time employees to promote and support the sales of New Zealand wines. Sales and distribution remained the responsibility of the exporting firms. The overall Wine Guild administration, based in the offices of the Wine Institute in Auckland, was initially controlled by a board of directors, of whom Andrew Hendry was one. Essentially, the board provided financial and marketing expertise for the successful operation of the Guild, as well as ideas for future developments. Although a voting system was in place, decisions were usually made by consensus. By 2000, the configuration of the UK Wine Guild had changed and, with the end of government funding, the board of directors was disbanded and control came under the function of the Wine Institute. The Institute moved to a system of presenting UK promotion initiatives to members and inviting participation and payment, which, according to Andrew Hendry, resulted in the loss of feeling of involvement in the Guild.

The winery catered for buyers' own brands in the UK market and, although considered useful, this segment was not particularly profitable. Coopers Creek's own branded product was the winery's focus and, in 2000, it was anticipated that it would sell more in the USA than in the UK. Andrew Hendry was concentrating on the development of a small number of markets and selling a broad range of higher-margin wines in the on-premise segment. This focus allowed the company to reach consumers willing to pay more expensive prices as New Zealand wines became a permanent category on restaurant wine lists.

Andrew Hendry visited his overseas importers on a regular basis, spending 12 weeks per annum overseas, as much overseas contact as any other New Zealand winery regardless of size. The visits were usually linked to wine trade shows in the UK, France and the USA. Apart from the exchange of views on the state of the market, details of latest vintages and discussions on prospective new customers, the visits had proven successful in providing a constant reminder that the winery was committed to the market, encouraging the agent to focus attention on the Coopers Creek brand and making sure that export customers were very clear about the amount of product they could expect from the winery in coming years.

The UK market

By 2000, Coopers Creek was no longer selling through the same liquor chains in the UK. Its initial arrangement with Victoria Wines changed when the company was taken over by Threshers, now named Thirst Quench. Unfortunately the takeover coincided with Coopers Creek being out of stock for six months as a result of Andrew's decision to sell off the 1998 Sauvignon Blanc vintage in bulk because it was of a poor standard. This stockout, combined with the rationalisation of stock following the takeover, led to the Coopers Creek brand being dropped. Recently sales commenced with two new UK retail groups, the supermarket Aldi and a buying consortium representing 60 independent wine merchants. Meanwhile, Coopers Creek encouraged its UK distributor to set up an on-premise division in 1997, which enabled the easy realignment of the company's sales to focus on the restaurant segment. Sales through the UK distributor have picked up again after a slowdown caused by its takeover of another distributor. The winery's relationship with the Tesco supermarket chain was still strong, nearing nine years in length by 2000, with Coopers Creek producing wine for the supermarket's specific own-label requirements. This arrangement resulted from Andrew Hendry's basic inclination to conduct some personal selling in export markets in addition to his appointed agents. The winery was actively involved in the promotion of new vintage releases through the supermarket chain and was looking to extend this arrangement to the Co-operative chain of supermarkets in the UK.

The changing nature of the UK Wine Guild in New Zealand coincided with a change of staff in the London office and the perception that there were fewer attendees per winery at organised tastings. Coopers Creek was not alone in its concerns about the changes to the UK Wine Guild. A number of wineries had reduced their involvement in the Guild, including Coopers Creek, and a knock-on effect was experienced, with lost support for other Country Action Groups and initiatives of the Wine Institute. In addition, the makeup of Coopers Creek exports to the UK, with 85 per cent comprising buyers' own brands, meant that the Guild levy system caused some concern to Andrew Hendry. Essentially, the winery was in a high fees category, given the total volume of sales, but only a small percentage of these sales promoted the Coopers Creek label. As Andrew Hendry states:

> The main thing is to get New Zealand known as a big brand, once it has a following then you look at your own. New Zealand has reached that stage and it reached that stage in the UK a long time ago. It probably reached that stage in the States last year [1999].

However, Coopers Creek was involved in discussions with two other New Zealand wineries to undertake some joint promotions, possibly in the UK and other markets, taking advantage of Trade New Zealand funding that is available to groups of applicants rather than individual applicants.

The US market

A major aspect of the longer-term plan was developing the US market. An on-premise focus in the US was critical because, in the retail sector, Australian and New Zealand wines were marketed together and Australian wines were cheaper due to the ability to achieve scale economies. Coopers Creek had changed to a larger distributor with expertise in on-premise representation, being one of the top three distributors in New York servicing some 2,000 restaurants in Manhattan alone. Until recently the winery had focused on increasing its network of distributors and conducting regional tastings on a state-by-state basis, mainly focusing on the East Coast, but also California, Colorado and Wisconsin.

A new development, initiated by Andrew Hendry, had been a collaborative arrangement with a Chilean winery, a Californian winery and a US importer. Together they had shared the costs of employing a brand manager in the USA, with the importer paying half of the manager's salary and the other half being split between the three wineries on the basis of cases sold. The brand manager had begun by organising all of the US promotions and going out with the importer's sales representatives, essentially doing the same sort of job that

Andrew Hendry did on his overseas visits. Since coming up with this arrangement, Coopers Creek's sales have trebled, growing from 1,500 cases in the late 1990s to 6,000 in 2000 with anticipated sales of 10,000 cases. Coopers Creek and the Californian winery were of a similar size, selling wine at similar price points, while the Chilean winery was much larger and focused on selling cheaper wine. This arrangement had now changed and Andrew employed the brand manager to work exclusively on Coopers Creek business. By cutting out the intermediary, and distributing across 15 states from warehouses in California and New Jersey, Coopers Creek was able to reduce the cost to restaurants by 35 per cent, making its wine extremely competitive in the critical on-premise segment.

THE FUTURE

The New Zealand wine industry, despite entering early maturity, remained constrained by issues of supply. Whilst the cost of new land for grape planting was rising and more, previously marginal land became economic to grow on, the problem was still one of access to capital for these resources. Overseas investors were welcomed by the industry, so long as New Zealand's distinctiveness and competitive advantage were not compromised. The key was to lock this investment in for the long-term economic good of the industry and the country.

Andrew Hendry believed the self-funded, relationship-based approach to growth achieved good fit with the nature of the New Zealand industry, namely the strong reliance on scarce resources on an annual basis. He and Coopers Creek had bounced back from the difficulties of 1998, and indeed Andrew was enthusiastically pursuing new opportunities. However, with the local industry showing signs of concentration, should Andrew Hendry maintain a focus on building relationships with other domestic producers? Is he right to begin seeking collaborative arrangements with overseas producers given the nature of the wine industry globally? Can Coopers Creek remain independent, retain the benefits of small size and yet still achieve exceptional returns in the changing environment? Is it time for Coopers Creek, and Andrew Hendry, to fundamentally rethink the winery's dominant strategy?

Enterprise resource planning at Topps International Ltd

Frédéric Adam and Eleanor Doyle

This case illustrates the importance of a reliable information systems infrastructure in supporting the operations and the development of modern businesses. It presents a longitudinal analysis (1995–2001) of Topps International Ltd and its attempt to acquire and implement a state-of-the-art enterprise resource planning (ERP) system to increase control over its operations and to develop management information systems to improve decision making in relation to the commercial strategy of the firm. The case shows how the evolution of Topps to an internationally successful competitive situation has been enabled and facilitated by the greater control allowed by its ERP system. The case begins with a description of Topps – its line of business and its development over time – and its business strategy in 1995. The reasons that contributed to the decision to select an ERP system for Topps emerge from both the case and the consultant's report included in the Case appendix, which considers the relevance of ERP systems for Topps International Ltd in view of the general strengths and weakness of ERP systems. The teething troubles associated with the system are addressed and latest information from Topps' management on the success of the implementation concludes the case.

TOPPS INTERNATIONAL LTD, 1995

Topps International Ltd has been operating since 1977 and is a subsidiary of a US-owned multinational company, the Topps Company Inc. Topps is an international marketer of entertainment products – principally collectable trading cards, confectionery, and sticker and album collections – and was founded in 1938. Topps created *Bazooka* bubblegum in 1947 and marketed the first baseball cards in 1951. Nowadays, Topps is a major player in the children's entertainment business on the European market and describes its business as the marketing and distribution of fashion items for the children's market. Hence, Topps is not a typical manufacturing company. Some of the most famous products on which Topps success has been built, the *Bazooka* chewing gums and

This case was prepared by Frédéric Adam and Eleanor Doyle, University College Cork. They are indebited to managers at Topps for their help and support in writing this case. It is intended as a basis for class discussion and not as an illustration of either good or bad management practice. © F. Adam and E. Doyle, 2001. Not to be reproduced or quoted without permission.

the *Push-Pops* lollipops, have now become household names. Topps has also become famous for adding an entertainment component to its confectionery products in the shape of 'Casper the friendly ghost' toy containers, containing gum or sweets. Recently, Topps has been particularly successful with its purchase of the rights to make Pokémon-branded products, including the sale of stickers and albums.

The emphasis of its business has changed substantially over the years from a heavily manufacturing perspective to an approach based more on the trade of goods imported from the Far East. By 1995, 20 per cent of its products were manufactured locally, the remainder being imported from China, Thailand and other countries. This represented a significant shift from the position even five years earlier when less than 20 per cent of products were imported. This switch in business emphasis allowed sales growth to mushroom with corresponding increases in the import/export activities. The product life cycle of some of the products was extremely short so the company needed to react quickly to change, emphasising the company's requirement for accurate information that was readily available. This acceleration of the business flows was aggravated by the rapid development of the new trading element of Topps' business.

Topps products were distributed out of three warehouses – Cork (Ireland), Liverpool (UK) and Rotterdam (Holland). The Cork plant stored the products manufactured in Cork while the Rotterdam depot stored imported products and the Liverpool depot maintained stocks required to serve the UK market. All activities were managed from Cork[1] with outside companies providing warehousing and distribution facilities at both external locations. The UK was the biggest market and a team of sales representatives handled sales to multiple stores and wholesalers. Ireland and the rest of Europe were serviced through distributors in each country. Products were sold mainly on a sale or return basis, making it vital that returns were identified quickly and resold within the life cycle where possible. Sales campaigns were not launched simultaneously in all countries and regions so it was often possible to pass unsold products on to another, less saturated market.

Identifying the critical success factors for Topps in 1995

Topps' business success revolved around making correct management decisions quickly. Information technology (IT) supported the vital provision of rapid, accurate information on which to base these decisions. Spreadsheets were used extensively (on a limited number of PCs used in the company) to create mini profit and loss accounts representing scenario analyses on specific markets or for specific products and to identify windows of opportunity aimed at maximising the rotation of stock. The main business tools centred on the strategic plan and operational budgets derived therefrom which were based on a number of spreadsheet models developed in a PC-based software package. The majority of information was gathered manually and the non-strategic data

---

[1] While three separate locations existed, all activities were processed through the Cork offices.

processing services (payroll, invoicing, inventory control, and other non-strategic transactions processing systems) were provided by software supplied by an external supplier. Both the software and the computer used to run it were completely obsolete – Topps was the final customer using these services, which were becoming increasingly expensive and unreliable.

Management at Topps had repeatedly complained to its parent company about the failure of their largely manual systems, but each time clearance to purchase a new system was requested, it was refused by headquarters (in New York). Topps' management realised that too much replication and duplication was taking place and that a fully integrated financial, manufacturing and distribution system was required to both:

● support the basic business processes, and
● automate basic flows of information.

A more reliable information basis was required to speed up the reporting processes across the organisation. A need for the capability of downloading all required information from a central system into existing information systems was identified to improve and make the production of crucial management reports more reliable. Such an approach would require the implementation of a network of PCs to enable data collection and screen enquiries throughout the different business functions (new hardware), selection and implementation of appropriate financial, distribution and manufacturing modules (new software), and staff training.

In March 1995, Topps International Ltd again attempted to purchase such an integrated software package that would cover the financial, distribution and manufacturing aspects of their business. The business was growing rapidly across all European markets and it was also looking to expand into a number of South American countries. It had been mainly a manufacturing organisation, but 75 per cent of its turnover was now coming from trading in goods produced by Far East suppliers.

The most significant problem for Topps was identified as the lack of online stock control for key personnel as the basic computerised stock system used tracked only goods manufactured and stored in Cork. There were also occasional failures to meet shipping deadlines because of paperwork delays. The robustness of the cash flow was compromised by the lack of control of debtors' balances and invoice due dates. In addition, there were also problems with reporting to the US headquarters due to the unavailability of information on territory and product profitability. Compliance with requirements for regular monthly and quarterly reports on EU movements of goods was slow. As described by the then financial controller, the company was vulnerable in the shipping, credit-control and treasury departments. He concluded that too much information was contained in employees' heads rather than in the company's information systems. Reports that were written at this time pointed out that hiring extra staff would not solve these problems and that the availability of a fully integrated system of the enterprise resource planning type would be required (see, for example, the Consultants' Report in the Appendix). In addition to this operational data layer, a powerful report generation application would also be required to generate better quality managerial reporting.

At the time, a number of potential failures were threatening:

- Sales order processing required attention as it was feared that Topps might begin to lose a significant portion of the ever-growing business due to orders not being met on time or not being processed at all.

- Invoicing is always a crucial element of a business, but Topps' management sometimes had no clear idea how much had been shipped to a particular customer. In fact, some shipping deadlines were not met due to paperwork delays.

Convincing HQ

Over twenty months of time and effort (in tendering, and development) was involved in the process that culminated in the selection of the required ERP system and the local software vendor who was to supply it. Consultants had argued that local support would be a significant asset during the implementation phase as people in Topps had little experience with large computer systems (there were no full-time IT personnel in Topps at the time). The next step in the process was to commit the money to this investment of roughly £180,000 and the signs were good when the IT director at HQ responded favourably to the request and agreed with the conclusions of the final report he had been sent.

Topps' parent company then purchased Merlin Publishing, a UK-based company similar in size to Topps but operating in the complementary children's entertainment market (e.g. the production of stickers of players in the English premiership and other major European soccer leagues). Due to uncertainties regarding the sharing of business between Topps and Merlin and the relations to be developed between the two companies, HQ decided, again, to block the ERP investment in Topps. Following a number of meetings with equivalent personnel in Merlin, a new strand of reports was sent to HQ to indicate how the systems in both Topps and Merlin could operate and the processes that could be shared between the two companies. A joint report signed by Topps and Merlin was even sent to the US to emphasise the support that Merlin were ready to give Topps in its implementation of the system selected. A further series of negotiations took place but the project was put on hold while a global IT strategy for Topps was developed by the IT director at HQ. More than two years after the first reports had been written and sent to the US about the weaknesses of the systems in Topps, nothing had been done and the manual systems were still holding on. A computerised system for Topps International had never seemed so far away.

In a final attempt to demonstrate that there were no managerial grounds for postponing the commitment of Topps to the purchase of a system (software and hardware) another report was sent to HQ. The report emphasised that a global IT strategy for the company made little sense as no truly shared processes requiring integration of computer systems had been identified either between Ireland and the US or between Topps and Merlin (the computing cultures differed significantly as Merlin had full-time IT personnel and a networked IT infrastructure with its international subsidiaries; no such common processes existed between Merlin and Topps – no consolidation of financial information was required; finally, using a UK-based supplier of software services would lead to significant cost increases in IT provision). Compatibility of each organisation's systems would, however, be required to enable the smooth exchange of information, and for example, reports on the performance of various Topps and Merlin products. In addition, the implementation of a global strategy meant that Topps would have to sacrifice the possibility of using local support for the software, an added – and potentially very costly – difficulty for a company without full-time resident IT expertise. This report was to change the minds of managers in the parent company. In mid-December 1995, news from HQ indicated that management should start implementing the decision to purchase an integrated computer system covering the financial and distribution activities. Before the end of January, the cabling had been put in place and system installation began in earnest.

ERP teething troubles following implementation

Management at Topps found that committing to a solution was not the only important aspect of the decision making in relation to deciding to implement its ERP system. Actual implementation involved enacting the choices made on the basis of management expertise and consultants' advice, and raised new issues and fresh questions which were overlooked or ignored throughout the previous stages. Such difficulties have frequently been reported in the management of ERP projects around the world.

More specifically, there were problems with the support provided by the system for the manufacturing operations of Topps' business. ERP systems are an extension of the materials requirement planning (MRP) systems of the 1970s and most of them are based on some MRP logic. This means that companies should have an MRP-organised factory before they can implement an ERP system that also supports their manufacturing. At the time, Topps had reduced its manufacturing to a small number of products (most originating in the Far East) but the factory floor had never been MRP-oriented. In fact, there had never been any just-in-time requirement in the factory and it was not known how useful it would be to switch to MRP at that stage. This issue was increasingly relevant as the manufacturing operations of Topps' activities were being phased out. As a result, 'workarounds' had to be implemented at the interface between the ERP and the manufacturing activities. Workarounds were portions of business processes that had to be 'invented' in the computer system and in reality to ensure that the ERP software could be used even though it did not exactly match the way activities were carried out. Developing the workarounds was not likely to compromise the success of the ERP implementation because the products being made in the factory represented a very small fraction of Topps' turnover but it did take some time that had not been planned for.

There were also problems with the lack of familiarity of Topps' staff with the software. Such problems are very common with enterprise-wide software such as ERP and most companies who implement them find themselves on a steep learning curve from the moment their new system goes live. No amount of training is ever going to provide staff with the confidence needed to use their

ERP to its full extent from the outset. Thus, even though training was quite extensive, it took a while before staff became accustomed to the new ways of doing business through the ERP system. Topps' business, like any other, includes a certain level of idiosyncrasy and, in the ERP area, software providers can never become so familiar with a company that they would be able to anticipate every detail of the business processes. Some are replaced by new processes suggested by the package, but some remain and require workarounds that take a while to establish and to integrate into day-to-day routines. After a few weeks, staff became more comfortable with their systems, and after a few months, they became true experts at exploiting the functionality of their ERP software to develop Topps' business.

Another problem that arose was that of data migration, which is also common with ERP systems. ERP systems are organised around very large databases that contain all the data required for the systems to operate properly and to link up with other information systems the company may have decided to keep. These data must often be uploaded from previous systems (which is referred to as *migration*). This applies to the more stable data a business uses, such as bills of material (describing the recipe of the company's products), customer data, but also some much needed transactional information such as invoicing data, sales data and any other accounting-based data. In the case of Topps, the previous system was an obsolete integrated package running on an even more archaic computer. The data proved difficult to extract on account of the lack of flexibility of the old system. Also, the data did not always have the proper level of detail, as modern ERP systems offer far greater depths of information and far more schemes to classify and organise data. Thus, a substantial amount of manual data entry was originally required before the system could go live.

After a few months, however, it became clear to the managers in Topps that their ERP system was a sound investment and that the benefits obtained in terms of inventory management and acceleration of business processes would far outweigh these initial teething problems.

Using the ERP system – January 2001

According to the financial controller in 2001, the ERP project had been very useful and positive from the first year of its implementation and Topps had progressed in leaps and bounds in terms of its information systems. Before the implementation of the ERP system, production of the complete month's end results took two weeks and even then did not allow managers to drill down into products, geographical areas and activities with any flexibility. This time had been halved after the implementation of the ERP system and the system also enabled managers to investigate sales figures to a much greater level of detail, drilling down into each market and each product far more accurately than ever before. The main strength of the ERP system was that it provided managers with the full set of live data regarding the inventory and shipment elements of the business, whereas managers used to rely on suppliers to establish accurate quantities shipped. The sales function, by contrast, was not improved to the same exent, but the purchase of an additional software package (called Adaytum™) enabled managers to achieve significant improvements in this area.

This added flexibility in understanding the business and controlling the flows of goods had been achieved despite enormous growth of sales from IR£20m in 1996 to over IR£50m in 2000. The greatest advantage of the ERP system identified was how it allowed managers to control stocks, sales volumes and quality control in a way that was never possible before. Slow-moving lines were exposed, quality problems could be traced down to specific consignments and first-in first-out stock movements could be strictly enforced. Such was the accuracy of the ERP system that managers in Ireland could tell operators in the Rotterdam warehouse which cases should be shipped first and the exact location (or bin number) where they were located in the warehouse. In practice, however, they did not need to do so because the Rotterdam operators had a separate system which tallied with Topps' ERP system. A new project is currently under way which will enable staff in the Liverpool and Rotterdam facilities to access Topps' ERP system remotely through its e-business module so as to increase the integration of the companies and reduce the extent of duplication of work.

These represented very significant improvement from a quality control point of view because the appearance of sweets disimproves over time (even though they are extremely slow to perish) and become impossible to sell. Since the implementation of the ERP system, products no longer had to be destroyed on a regular basis.

As far as reporting was concerned the ERP package was not initially sufficient to cater for Topps' needs. Even though all the required information was available, the report generation capabilities of the system were not sufficiently flexible. This problem was solved in 2000 by the purchase of the additional package (Adaytum™) which used the data contained in the ERP system to provide the drill-down and reporting capabilities required by Topps' managers. Reports could then be produced on every single line or item sold by Topps and customer profitability analyses could be carried out to an extent never possible before. At this point, the ERP system could cater for all the actual orders and the Adaytum software could handle the forecasting and planning of demand. These two key sources of data could then be aggregated to produce the overall plan for the company.

CASE APPENDIX: TOPPS INTERNATIONAL LTD[2]

CONSULTANTS' REPORT (1995)

Goals of information system implementation for Topps

As an introduction, it should be acknowledged that Topps is currently a healthy organisation with a clear management structure and a very good knowledge of its market. This does not mean, however, that the performance of Topps could not be improved significantly. Topps possesses a combination of up-to-date managerial thinking but rather outdated administration. It is therefore certain that the introduction of state-of-the art computing in Topps could have a significantly positive impact on the performance of the business and create a more reliable administration of the organisation as a whole, especially given the recent increases in the volume of transactions dealt with by Topps International Ltd. Additional benefits arising from such an introduction could include:

- an advance towards ISO certification (and the potential resulting benefits);
- freeing of manpower for either higher-level analytical tasks or improved customer service;
- an administrative system less reliant on individuals, thereby providing more permanent and consistent long-run company operations.

Given that Topps' business success revolves around making correct management decisions quickly, it is important that information technology (IT) is applied more efficiently to provide the rapid, accurate information on which to base these decisions. This occurs to a degree with the extensive use of spreadsheets but these are not centrally available and sometimes are not preserved for reuse such that substantial duplication of work arises. Reports take more time to produce than they should and the standard of presentation suffers as a result. Time better spent in utilising the information creatively and efficiently to exploit opportunities and be aware of threats is currently spent on gathering basic information.

Required systems for Topps

As an initial step, the application of a modern software package would substantially improve the quality of managerial reports. However, from the investigations carried out, excessive replication and duplication of work (e.g. data entry) also need to be addressed. A fully integrated financial and distribution system would support both the basic business processes carried out at Topps and automate the basic flows of information within the organisation. All modules of the system need not be implemented simultaneously and a phased approach to implementation should suffice, once commitment to implement all modules in the medium term is established.

---

[2]The issues described in this report are expanded in Adam and Doherty, 2000.

Enterprise resource planning systems

Such a system may be classified as an enterprise resource planning (ERP) system which is an integrated enterprise-wide software package designed to support the key functional areas of the organisation. ERP systems have inherent strengths and weaknesses, and are therefore better suited to certain types of organisations and certain circumstances. Management at Topps should, therefore, understand the inherent trade-offs of an ERP system before they make any decision regarding the potential appropriateness of the ERP concept for their organisation. While many consultants and media reports are prompt to emphasise the benefits of ERP implementations, the key issue resides in understanding the specific needs of an organisation and the business model best suited to its operations.

The added difficulty in ERP projects is that few companies, if any, could possibly contemplate developing such vast applications in-house. For the majority of companies, the decision to implement ERP functionalities will mean buying a software package from one of the major suppliers on the ERP market.[3] The software selection phase is not straightforward and managers must understand what ERP packages are on offer, how they differ, and what is at stake in selecting one ERP over another. Each ERP package uses a business model as an underlying framework and can be quite different relative to competitors' products in terms of how they operate or the business processes they support. The problem for Topps' management is that not all business models fit all organisations and the cost of failing to recognise the relationship between the nature of one's business and the ERP system to be purchased can be very high indeed. Quite literally, selecting the right software package, i.e. the right blueprint for one's organisation, is a critical failure factor in ERP projects. An analysis of the strengths and weakness of ERP systems can help managers facing such decisions.

Strengths and weaknesses of ERP systems

The case for ERP systems

In many ways ERP systems represent the implementation of a managerial dream of unifying and centralising (or at least under one name) all the information systems required by the firm in one single system. Most notably, ERP systems support the recording of all business transactions from purchase orders to sales orders and the scheduling and monitoring of manufacturing activities. Most ERP systems are based on an inventory control module that records the movements of goods in and out of the company which makes them particularly suited to organisations seeking to rationalise their internal processes and obtain higher performance from their operations.

ERP systems provide employees within organisations with a common language and a common pool of data. At a practical level, ERP systems have very beneficial effects that remove the need for often disparate and unreliable end-user applications, operating and reporting procedures can be standardised and some of the key processes of the firm (e.g. order acquisition and processing or inventory control) can be optimised. In addition, these systems offer high levels of portability and reasonable flexibility in adapting to the requirements of specific organisations.

---

[3]For example, SAP, Baan, JD Edwards, Peoplesoft, Oracle or MFG/PRO.

One of the key strengths of ERP systems is that they are built on top of a relational database[4] which enables a reliable and rapid circulation of the data between the modules and eliminates the need for multiple data entry. Thus, ERP systems simplify, accelerate and automate much of the data transfers that must take place in organisations to guarantee the proper execution of operational tasks. The relational database underlying an ERP can be quite large, depending on company and operational complexity (some SAP applications implemented are reported to have in excess of *one thousand* different tables).

Currently, the case for ERP systems seems compelling and the development of more powerful and user-friendly platforms makes it now possible to integrate many large systems in a way that was not possible up to very recently. This is clear from the fact that Microsoft spent 10 months and $25m replacing 33 existing systems in 26 sites with ERP systems. Managers in Microsoft claim to save $18m annually as a result and Bill Gates reportedly expressed great satisfaction with the system. Microsoft had reportedly grown so fast that it could not keep up with itself – the number of applications developed to support the company's operations and their lack of integration meant that information systems staff had lost control over the complexity of the systems they administered. Moving to a single ERP architecture enabled better linkages between business areas as well as with suppliers and customers.

The case against ERP systems

The strengths of ERP packages are matched by the high level of risk associated with ERP projects. ERP projects are complex and require the reliance on many different types of expertise often sourced outside the organisation. Consultants often advise managers to undertake some degree of re-engineering of key processes before acquiring ERP systems and this adds to the complexity and political character of the projects. There is empirical evidence of the dangers inherent in such vast projects.[5]

These difficulties have led to some researchers taking a negative view of ERP systems. Some researchers argue that the current interest in ERP in the business community is justified more by political reasons than by sound managerial reasoning. Relevant surveys show low levels of satisfaction of firms having implemented ERP systems, with 45 per cent of firms perceiving no improvements whatever from implementation and 43 per cent claiming that no cycle reduction had been obtained.

The difficulty inherent in ERP implementations is largely due to the fact that organisations implementing them should typically only hold on to 20 per cent of their previous applications. But the extensive replacement of previous systems may be a requirement if the major benefits of ERP implementation – greater integration of functional areas and, in the case of multinational firms, greater co-ordination between entities and between sites – are to be obtained. The consequence of this 'clean slate' approach is that organisations find it virtually impossible to revert to their pre-ERP situation and, in any case, their investment either cannot be recouped or generates very low returns.

---

[4]A relational database is a collection of items organised as a set of formally described tables from which data can be accessed or reassembled in many different ways without having to reorganise the database tables.
[5]Kalatoka and Robinson (1999) detail the case of Foxmayer which went bankrupt in 1996 after three years of unsuccessful implementation of SAP – suing SAP's US subsidiary and Arthur Andersen in the process. This is illustrative of what can happen to the largest organisations when ERP implementations go wrong.

Finally, there is anecdotal evidence that many companies were pushed into ERP projects by the much-publicised fears of what might have happened to legacy systems during the year 2000 change.

Conclusions for Topps

These arguments paint a very mixed picture of the potential of ERP packages which may be portrayed as silver bullets as often as villains. The message to be taken from the potential strengths and weaknesses of ERP systems for Topps' management is that they would be well advised to conduct a detailed analysis of proposed benefits *and* costs of their ERP system prior to going down the implementation road to ensure that the system can appropriately meet the organisational requirements. Of vital importance in this process is the consideration of the business strategy needs of Topps and the specific improvements that an enterprise-wide integrated software package can provide.

Articles consulted to support report

Adam, F. and Doherty, P. (2000) 'Do ERP implementations have to be lengthy? Lessons from Irish SMEs', 5th Conference of the Information and Management Association, Montpellier, France, November.

Bancroft, N. (1996) *Implementing SAP/R3: How to introduce a large system into a large organisation*, Manning / Prentice Hall, London, UK.

Bingi, P., Sharma, M. and Godla, J. (1999) 'Critical issues affecting an ERP implementation', *Information Systems Management*, Summer, 7-14.

Forrest, P. (1999) 'Les ERP à l'épreuve de l'organisation', *Systèmes d'Information et Management*, 4(4), 71-90.

Kalatoka, R. and Robinson, M. (1999) *E-business - Roadmap to success*, Addison-Wesley, Reading, MA.

Rowe, F. (1999) 'Cohérence, Intégration informationnelle et changement: esquisse d'un programme de recherche à partir des Progiciels Intégrés de Gestion', *Systèmes d'Information et Management*, 4(4), 3-20.

Wood, T. and Caldas, M. (2000) Stripping the 'big brother': unveiling the backstage of the ERP fad, http://www.gv.br/prof_alunos/thomaz/ingles/paper5.htm.

White, B., Clark, D. and Ascarely, S. (1997) 'Program of pain', *Wall Street Journal*, 14 March 6.

General Motors Brazil

General Motors' Gravataí plant in Brazil is a test-bed for manufacturing techniques and has transformed the relationship between carmakers and suppliers.

● ● ●

The managers running the Gravataí car plant believe they run the 'most Japanese factory' in the world. That may seem an odd claim for a $554m (£390m) industrial complex on the outskirts of Porto Alegre, deep in Brazil's southernmost state. Until, that is, they describe how General Motors' most innovative assembly facility promises to revolutionise modern car production.

GM is one of several global carmakers expanding its presence in Brazil. The Gravataí project has coincided with new investment by Ford, Fiat and PSA Peugeot Citroën – among others – in Brazilian car assembly. These manufacturers have come to regard South America's largest economy as a low-cost manufacturing hub for the region, where a combination of cheap labour, state aid packages and readily available green field sites has attracted $1.8–$2.4bn of annual investment in each of the past five years.

GM's plant, code-named 'Blue Macaw' until its official opening eight months ago, represents a test-bed for manufacturing techniques. 'Almost all the new initiatives by GM are based on concepts generated here,' says Roberto Tinoco, the manufacturing director at Gravataí.

Given the mule traffic and shanty dwellings on the approach to the onetime coffee farm, it is hard to believe that the complex contains a car plant surpassing most European and US specifications. Gravataí even boasts its own banks, post offices, shops, travel agencies and restaurants. Its 40 streets, each named after a GM car such as Corsa, Vectra and Omega, connect all these amenities to the production site.

More importantly, Blue Macaw has broken ground in the relationship between carmakers and their suppliers. While most manufacturers have encouraged component groups to set up supplier parks near their assembly lines, GM has gone a step further at Gravataí by designing the plant and the car it produces in conjunction with suppliers.

The world's largest carmaker has persuaded 17 leading suppliers, including Delphi, VDO, Goodyear and Valeo, to build their own production facilities

This case is based on an article that appeared in the *Financial Times*, 10 April 2001, p. 15 by Tim Burt. It is intended as a basis for class discussion and not as an illustration of either good or bad management practice. © *Financial Times*, 2001. Not to be reproduced or quoted without permission.

inside the complex. Each supplier is located according to where its components are required on the assembly line.

That 'system sourcing concept' has made Gravatai one of the world's most productive plants, completing a car every two minutes. According to Mr Tinoco, the arrangements mean that 85 per cent of the Chevrolet models produced at Gravatai rely on components assembled on site. In most plants, 60 per cent of a car's components by value are sourced from outside the factory.

'We have broken a lot of paradigms,' says the plant manager. 'In a big company you have to fight against internal pressures.'

Mr Tinoco admits that Gravatai is regarded as something of an experiment by some GM managers. What might be acceptable in southern Brazil – where inward investment is hailed as a vote of confidence – was regarded with suspicion in Michigan. The carmaker abandoned plans for US versions of the plant, known as Project Yellowstone, amid concerted opposition by the United Auto Workers union.

Union leaders feared that suppliers would influence the employment conditions of their members. GM's senior management also wanted to avoid suggestions that they were adopting ideas pioneered by Jose Ignacio Lopez de Arriortua, the former GM purchasing chief who was accused of defecting to Volkswagen with thousands of confidential company documents.

Mr Lopez argued that suppliers should take more responsibility for assembly, allowing carmakers to concentrate on higher-margin design, engineering and distribution. The controversial purchasing manager is the subject of extradition proceedings in the US, where a federal grand jury has charged him with wire fraud and handling stolen property.

In spite of Mr Lopez's departure, Mr Tinoco acknowledges his contribution. 'Lopez made a revolution in GM,' he says. 'And we have achieved a considerable reduction in costs here.'

The Lopez vision was for suppliers to assume more and more responsibility for final assembly. Although he has now left VW, Lopez' legacy has survived at the German group's truck plant in Resende, not far from Rio de Janeiro. There, components are trucked in as at other plants but they are installed on the assembly line by their suppliers, rather than by VW.

Other carmakers are studying VW's project, notably at Ford's so-called Amazon plant in Bahia. But most have retained control of final assembly. For all practical purposes, however, Blue Macaw is following the VW trend. Employees at the plant – who have an average age of 28 – are hired by the site rather than by the individual companies within it.

The management of human resources is handled jointly by a committee representing GM and its suppliers. A network of joint committees, reporting to an executive council, oversees every aspect of the site.

The executive council has another pioneering achievement in regard to payments to suppliers. Companies such as Delphi are not paid when components are delivered; they receive payments when the finished cars reach the dealer. To make this work, GM had to simplify the whole supplier chain at Gravatai. It has done so by producing only one basic model at the plant, the Celta small car, which is badged as a Chevrolet for the Brazilian market.

The Celta, derived from GM's Corsa model, is less sophisticated than more expensive models and requires fewer complex sub-systems.

'What we did was to dis-assemble a Corsa into basic modules and then invite about 60 suppliers from all over the world to bid for supplier contracts for various parts,' recalls Mr Tinoco.

By simplifying in this way, GM can install sub-systems quickly and easily as they arrive on the line. Orange wagons, each bearing the motif of the supplier, arrive at the assembly line at the moment that the vehicle requiring the parts rolls past. A system of traffic lights automatically stops the line as each wagon of components is emptied. A new wagon is lowered into place from an overhead gantry, while the old one is rolled away.

In another area, the cars undergo an 'auto-marriage' where robots fit the Celta's engine, gearbox, fuel tank, rear axle and front suspension at a single work-station. Productivity is measured on digital screens overhead that are labelled 'Objective' and 'Actual'.

Some analysts argue that the system could not be adapted easily for more sophisticated models. 'It is typical of GM to build a well organised and impressive facility but then to make a car that does not really do it justice,' says Prof Garel Rhys, head of motor industry economics at Cardiff University business school.

Following a recent visit to Gravatai, Prof Rhys warned: 'GM really has to put in other models if the plant is to punch its weight, not least in export markets.'

But GM claims that the Celta is suited to Brazil and neighbouring Mercosur countries, because they are heavily weighted towards cheap, entry-level cars.

'We are selling everything we produce and introducing a second shift, creating another 700 jobs,' according to Mr Tinoco.

Any lack of sophistication in the Celta, he says, is more than offset by its quality: 'What we have here is a proving ground. It is a first not only for Brazil but also for the whole of GM.'

ScottishPower Learning

Mik Wisniewski and Jim McLaughlin

The case looks at an industry that has undergone major strategic and operational change over the past decade. It is primarily concerned with how ScottishPower structured itself after privatisation and the relationships between the corporate centre and the business units. These issues are viewed from the perspective of one business unit (ScottishPower Learning, SPL) that was created through the merger of a number of teams and units responsible for training and development throughout ScottishPower's UK operations. The case is about the role of SPL in relation to the company as a whole and in relationships with the other semi-autonomous operating divisions which were now its customers. It encourages readers to reflect on the different organisational structures and management processes that can be adopted by organisations and their strategic and operational implications.

● ● ●

A COMPANY TRANSFORMED

1990. The South of Scotland Electricity Board (SSEB) is part of the UK's nationalised electricity industry and with its 12,000 employees generates and supplies electricity to its customer base of fewer than 2 million customers in the south of Scotland.

2001. ScottishPower, the privatised SSEB, is one of the world's top 15 global utility businesses and rated the very best FTSE 100 company by *The Times* newspaper. The group has a turnover of over £4 billion in the UK and the USA, a customer base exceeding 7 million, around 20,000 employees and as well as electricity has moved into gas, water and wastewater, appliance retailing, telecoms and Internet services.

Strategic change and success on such a scale rarely happen by accident. A clear strategic vision and focus are required together with the development and implementation of appropriate plans at both the strategic and operational levels to turn the vision into a reality. Equally, such strategic change cannot be driven simply on a top-down basis from the centre of the organisation. Each part of the business must contribute to success.

SPL

From the time of privatisation the company had reorganised around semi-autonomous operating divisions such as Generation and Power Systems. One of the more recent divisions, established at the start of 2000, was ScottishPower Learning (SPL). The company had a number of reasons for creating such divisions: the need for a clearer strategic and operational focus in each of different parts of the company and an increased ability to respond quickly and effectively to turbulent and increasingly competitive environments in the different parts of the business. Historically, training and development had been the responsibility of each of the six major stand-alone divisions within the company, with each division having its own team of staff responsible for this. SPL was created through the merger of a number of teams and units responsible for training and development throughout ScottishPower's UK operations. In addition, the ScottishPower Learning Unit became part of SPL. This unit had been established in 1996 to promote the company's commitment to lifelong learning for its staff and to support the wider communities in which ScottishPower operated through open learning centres and by supporting learning and training for the unemployed in local communities linked to the UK government's New Deal initiative.

The creation of SPL produced a number of major opportunities for SPL but also a number of critical challenges that it had to address. These were primarily about its future role in relation to the company as a whole and in relation to the other semi-autonomous operating divisions which were now its customers. Critical tensions that needed to be managed related to the relationship between SPL and group headquarters; the relationship between SPL and the other operating divisions; the boundaries of SPL's activities; and the organisational processes critical to SPL's success.

The company's review of training and development activities in 1999 had identified this as an area of significant expenditure (over £12 million in 1999/2000) directly employing over 100 staff, as well as buying in training and development from external suppliers. There was a clear expectation that the new SPL division would contribute to the company's ongoing cost reduction targets. However, the review had also identified that the training and development environment in the company as a whole was likely to change. Some parts of ScottishPower business were being divested; there were ongoing organisational changes in the company's core businesses; there was increasing opportunity to exploit new technology in training and development delivery; there were increasing opportunities for generating external income by selling SPL's services to other organisations. The creation of SPL as a semi-autonomous division was felt to be an appropriate way to respond to these challenges and to capitalise on opportunities. Training and development had already made major contributions to the company's success since privatisation. As the chief executive, Sir Ian Robinson, said: 'In the development and evolution of ScottishPower, our people, with their drive and enthusiasm, have been the big differentiating factor.'[1] However, SPL could not afford to take the future for

---

[1] Quoted in 'When even the best isn't good enough', *Human Resources*, March 2000, pp. 30–34.

granted. To better understand SPL's position it will be worthwhile reviewing the company's strategic growth over the previous decade.

SCOTTISHPOWER STRATEGY

By its own admission, at privatisation in 1991 SSEB was dominated by a culture characterised by: a strong engineering orientation where costs, profit margin and commercial performance came second; where maintaining electricity supply at virtually any cost was seen as the prime organisational objective with little real priority given to customer service as a whole; a large, centralised, nationalised industry with diffused responsibility and no real ownership or accountability at either strategic or operational levels; being risk averse with little importance attached to entrepreneurial and innovative approaches. This culture had to change if the company was to survive, let alone be successful.

At the time of privatisation, each of the new companies (RECs, or regional electricity companies) in the UK still had a geographical monopoly for much of its customer base. In addition, the generating companies in England and Wales had also been privatised and split into two companies, Powergen and National Power (ScottishPower was vertically integrated and had both the REC responsibilities in its area as well as the generation capacity). The UK government, however, had indicated that there would be a gradual move to full competition in both the electricity and gas markets, with all customers ultimately able to choose their energy suppliers. The government had also appointed an industry regulator to ensure that RECs delivered year-on-year improvements in performance and customer service, and the regulatory regime required both operating cost reductions and price reductions as well as requiring RECs to meet service quality targets. In addition, through what was known as the government's golden share in each new company, the RECs were effectively immune from takeover until 1995.

However, much of the rest of ScottishPower's environment was highly uncertain. It was not clear how the detail of the regulatory regime would develop. It was not clear what would happen to the industry as a whole from 1995 onwards when individual RECs would be exposed to potential takeover, mergers and consolidation. Emerging from the strategic analysis undertaken by the company was a clear vision statement, '*to become a world-class multi-utility*'. The overall strategy set by the company is summarised in Exhibit 1. The first focus of the overall strategy was that of *reshaping the existing core business and exploiting existing assets*. There were two related aspects to this: a major drive to improve operational efficiency and reduce costs and ensuring that the company's assets and skills base were exploited to the maximum. By 1995 employee numbers were down from 12,000 to 8,000. However, the focus was not simply on cutting costs by cutting staff numbers. The company had made great efforts through workshops and staff briefings to ensure that all employees were aware of, and understood the implications of, the harsh commercial environment in which it now had to operate. The company also invested heavily in staff training and development to ensure that staff could contribute effectively to the overall strategy. As Paul Pagliari, group human

Exhibit 1	Company strategy

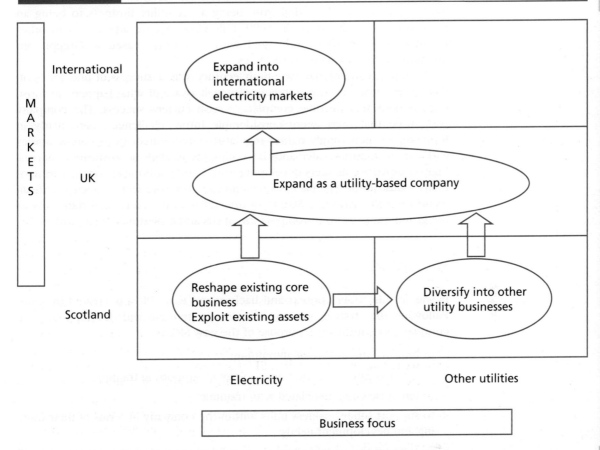

resources director, says: '*We want to make everyone improve. It's a big thing for us as a business to get everyone to move up their performance curves*'.[2] The focus was twofold: technical training to improve efficiency and productivity and to reduce operating costs; management training to help develop commercial awareness and business skills.

The second stage of the overall strategy was that of *diversifying into other utility businesses*. Two markets were specifically targeted: that of gas supply and that of telecoms, both areas where the company anticipated that considerable synergies with its traditional business existed. The third stage was expanding the company to become a *broader utility-based business*. This was achieved with the takeover of two companies. The first of these, Manweb, based around Merseyside and north–mid Wales, was another REC taken over by ScottishPower in 1995 and adding a further 1.5 million customers. The

---

[2]ScottishPower annual review 1999–2000.

second was Southern Water, based in the south of England supplying water to around 1 million customers and wastewater services to 1.7 million. The fourth stage involved moving from being a UK utility business to being an *international multi-utility*. In 1999, following abortive attempts with other US utilities, ScottishPower merged with PacifiCorp, based in Oregon but operating across six western US states.

The last decade of the twentieth century was a successful one for ScottishPower. However, the company was well aware of what happens to those organisations that become complacent with current success. The company recognised that there were considerable future challenges, particularly in terms of: an increasingly tighter regulatory environment in its core activities and markets; customer demands becoming increasingly sophisticated; increasingly competitive markets developing in the utility industries; restructuring of utility industries on a global basis. Training and development are seen as critical. As Sir Ian Robinson says, 'Staff development is all the more important now as the group expands, to encompass the needs and aspirations of employees.'[3]

SPL STRATEGY

It was in this wider context and background that SPL was created in 2000. Following the strategic review of company training and development, the company set out the core purpose of the new SPL as:

- to improve the quality of all training;
- to optimise the use of new technology in supporting training;
- to minimise costs associated with training;
- to support other business units within the company in terms of their training and development needs;
- to support the ongoing organisational and cultural changes required in all businesses and at Group level.

How this was to be achieved, however, was down to SPL itself; there was no top-down imposition of strategy other than the broad expectations set out in the purpose statement. Shortly after the company announced its creation, the senior managers from the various teams making up the new SPL division met to develop their strategic thinking. SPL was faced with an immediate task of putting together a business plan to present to the company's senior management. However, it also realised that longer-term thinking and planning were needed if SPL was to be successful. The strategic thinking and planning were not simply a matter of rolling forward each teams' activities into the future. SPL realised that its operating environment was now radically changed as a result of the larger reorganisation within the company. For the short term, each of the business divisions within ScottishPower which originally made up SPL were required, because of a corporate-level decision, to use SPL for training

---

[3]ScottishPower annual review 1999–2000.

and developing their staff. However, in the medium term there was a clear corporate expectation that divisions would ultimately be free to buy their training and development from SPL or from any other competing external supplier. SPL, in other words, would need to establish quickly some meaningful competitive advantage in the eyes of its internal customers. It decided that this could best be achieved by ensuring that the services it provided were demonstrably seen as adding value to their (internal) customers' own core business. This was also consistent with the message coming from the company HQ from Paul Pagliari, group HR director: 'I always question what an HR activity or proposal means for business performance, business efficiency and business deliverables. I think that if you can talk to line management in that language, they're quite prepared to take things on board because they do understand the real value that's been added.'[4]

The boundaries of SPL's activities were another strategic aspect to be resolved. Some parts of SPL generated external income into the business. Part of this related to technical training courses that were made available commercially to other utility companies. Part related to the activities of the ScottishPower Learning unit which attracted government grants for its work with local communities. It was recognised that this external income generation was likely to cause considerable strategic tension and conflict. On the one hand, SPL would need to ensure it was delivering a value-adding service to other ScottishPower divisions. On the other, SPL realised there were opportunities for further external income generation adding further value to the company as a whole. SPL realised it would have to agree processes and systems for managing this tension in terms of its operational planning and resourcing.

SPL also saw the business plan as an opportunity to market its services to the other internal divisions, to declare its mission in supporting other divisions and to indicate longer-term strategic direction. SPL decided that a number of key messages for various stakeholders would be communicated through the plan:

- Stressing SPL's enhanced collective capabilities and competences in terms of the range of services it could now offer other divisions. This involved SPL changing its relationships with the other divisions – moving from simply being a provider of training and development to one of business adviser, understanding how training and development could best support each division's own goals, strategies and plans.

- SPL's commitment to achieving its own performance targets in terms of reducing costs and improving service quality. This meant reducing training costs for other divisions also.

- An indication of SPL's longer-term vision. This included a commitment to 'growing the training and development business' both internally and externally, with external income used to reduce internal costs or reinvested in new technology applications; to ensuring that SPL added value to other divisions' activities through its own services; to an increasingly innovative approach to training and development (through online learning, for example).

---

[4]Quoted in 'When even the best isn't good enough', *Human Resources*, March 2000, pp. 30–34.

There were two broad parts to the plan. The first part was primarily strategic and the second operationally focused, providing the detail of SPL's services and activities for 2000/2001 for each division in ScottishPower. The plan also summarised the key actions/objectives for the coming year. These included the need:

- To identify the major long-term opportunities and challenges for SPL by completing a detailed environmental scan.

- To develop a product/service costing model so that SPL could properly cost and price its products/services (both internally and externally). This would help ensure SPL was properly competitive for the time that divisions could buy their training and development from outside the company. It also ensured that recharges to businesses were transparent and open to scrutiny, very important from a regulatory perspective.

- To review SPL operations using the costing model to enable SPL to assess costs and value of all activities.

- To arrange top-level discussions with the managing directors of the other divisions to 'sell' SPL and to start developing service level agreements (SLAs) with the individual divisions. The SLAs in particular were seen as a critical mechanism for agreeing with divisions the services and activities to be provided by SPL and the agreed cost of doing so.

- Development of a strategy for exploiting online/technology-based learning across all SPL activities.

- Developing an approach to performance measurement that demonstrated where SPL added value to the company's operations.

It is often assumed that strategic thinking and strategic management only take place at the corporate level in an organisation. The same sort of thinking, however, is also needed within the organisation, as demonstrated by the SPL division. As Jim McLaughlin from SPL comments:

> Strategy at this level is more difficult than at corporate level since the division must operate within the strategic constraints set by the company as a whole. But thinking strategically is just as appropriate and applicable in our own search for future success.

Tetra Pak Converting Technologies: A project-based organisation

Lars Lindkvist

Tetra Pak Converting Technologies Inc. is an example of an organisation which, triggered by a performance crisis, decided to abandon its traditional matrix structure and operate almost exclusively on the basis of autonomous projects. The case provides an opportunity to consider the appropriateness and viability of this approach to organising.

• • •

BACKGROUND

Tetra Pak Converting Technologies (CT) was an R&D unit within Tetra Pak, a leading company worldwide in developing and producing process, packaging and distribution systems for liquid food. Tetra Pak had about 18,500 employees and total sales in 1999 amounted to €7.3 billion. Tetra Pak was organised in a matrix structure with three business areas – Carton, Plastic and Processing – and two regions – Asia/America and Europe/Africa – including 70 market companies. CT was located in Lund, Sweden, and belonged to the Carton business area, which was the largest of the three. Within Carton there were two main R&D centres. Besides CT, which engaged in converting technologies, there was another complementary R&D unit located in Modena, Italy, which was engaged in developing filling machines. Taken together, these units employed about 250 people. Serving the entire Tetra Pak organisation was a central R&D unit, located in Lund, that was engaged in basic research and prospecting future packaging technologies.

CT developed, implemented and optimised material and converting technologies, covering the whole process (including lamination, printing, etc.) which transformed raw carton into ready-made packages. Most of its development projects were customer initiated, either by Tetra Pak factories or by market companies after agreements with external customers. But it also initiated its own R&D projects and advanced development projects with no customer attached. Although CT was legally an independent company it was financially operated as a cost centre, and received centrally allocated funds based on performance, reputation and demand for its services.

THE REORGANISATION

CT was established in 1989 but already by the beginning of the 90s it had experienced a diminishing demand for its services. At that time, Tetra Pak was decentralised in order to facilitate adaptation to different development and needs in local markets. In the new structure the factories and product companies increasingly turned to other sources, such as consultants, machine or raw materials suppliers, or they built their own capabilities to manage their development needs. In September 1994 demand was very low and the future of the unit was strongly questioned. At that time a newly appointed managing director initiated a comprehensive SWOT analysis. This resulted in several conclusions. It became obvious that the organisation was not very customer-focused. There was also a realisation that the only chance of out-competing its internal and external competitors was to build superior competences and problem-solving capabilities. To stay ahead of them it also had to be more efficient, especially in its ability to shorten and keep lead times.

At that time, CT had a traditional line-of-command structure organised along functional units, which was subdivided into smaller, technical specialist departments. The functional units were responsible for personnel, and project leaders had to engage in difficult negotiations in setting up new projects. Line managers tended to focus more on their line duties than on project goals, and they maintained great influence over how projects were carried out. This led to a reinforcement of their technical character while downplaying a customer or market focus. As a result, project leaders were accountable, but had little authority, and individual project members felt torn between the demands of the line organisation and the projects they were engaged in.

It became clear that minor changes were hardly enough. To bring about increased focus on customers, projects and competences, more profound changes in the ways of thinking and acting were needed. It was no longer deemed adequate to think in terms of functions and positions. The managing director and a team of top managers in CT thus decided to undertake a more fundamental reorganisation. The former matrix organisation dominated by the functional units was abolished, and instead a purely project-based organisation was introduced.

In the change process, functional units were dissolved, leaving individuals without a 'home base' or superiors in a traditional line-of-command sense. Instead they only belonged temporarily to projects and were subjected to new project leaders as their assignments changed. In the new structure, a number of 'competence networks' covering core technical areas were established. Each individual had a mentor, responsible for suggesting wage increases and discussing appropriate ways of furthering the individual's long-term competence development. To underline the non-hierarchical nature of the firm, the individuals were free to choose their own mentor from among those elected as nominees.

These revolutionary change efforts were successful. As a consequence, the organisation was no longer on the edge of survival, but was prospering with highly increased demand for its services, increased creativity manifested in its patent records, and more motivated members. Between 1994 and 1999 demand for its services doubled several times over, and the same was true of the number of patents registered yearly.

The characteristics of CT promoted the picture of a very flat, decentralised and loosely coupled system. This also applied to the knowledge dimension – knowledge was highly dispersed, fragmented and localised. Despite its basic feature as a distributed knowledge system, it was, however, obviously integrated enough to produce valuable services. In addition to market and technology strategies, the 'rules of the game' implied by the new organisation structure were highly significant in achieving this. CT carried out its operations in projects that were largely self-organised within goals set for quality, cost and time. Below we discuss in more detail how projects were operated and how they were complemented by the competence networks.

PROJECTS – ACTION AND INTERACTION

In the new structure, projects made up the core part of the organisation. Projects in CT were fairly short-lived and new projects all had a unique mix of different competences. Well-functioning project work was imperative to survival. The project leaders were fully accountable for attaining the project goals. To a great extent, the project leaders exerted an influence over who should work in the project. As stated by one project leader, getting the right mix of competences in the project was extremely important. It was also recognised that due to the complexity of the problem-solving processes involved, it was not possible to know the right mix with precision initially. The project leaders had to 'guess' who should be able to contribute, get a broad enough mix and hope that the team as a whole would manage the task challenge.

> . . . in development work the important thing is to collect those you believe might contribute . . . you take some of them and some of them . . . and when they start to 'thrash it out' they come up with a solution . . . but if you have forgotten any of them it does not work.

However, the team composition was not seen to be a haphazard undertaking. The potential project members had a reputation regarding professional competence, their ability to work with others, etc. acquired during earlier project engagements. Although project leaders did not know in great detail what kinds of problem might appear during the project, they had good intuition as to which individual members and which mix of members could manage a given development task.

The reliance on the capacity of the individuals to merge into a self-organised team engaged in communal problem solving also lent a distinctive emergent character to the project. Initial parameters, such as the mix of participants, a specification of goals and perhaps some general rules or policies, were set initially. But then, due to the specific competences and idiosyncrasies of the participants and the local or situational circumstances, the project, to some extent, would develop its own trajectory and take on a logic of its own.

The project team also had full discretion in project execution within certain set limits. The goals were then broken down into a more detailed project plan, identifying certain phases of the projects and milestones. Essentially, evaluations during project execution and the 'final report' that had to be written after project completion centred around the project plan measures. In addition to those feedback measures, more technical 'development reports' were written, covering testing activities – including specification of equipment used, results and conclusions. These were all stored in a central database system.

PROJECTS – KNOWLEDGE PROCESSES

The projects were conceived of as team activities bounded by certain goals. The clearness and tightness of the deadline forced the project members to engage in time-paced problem solving. This meant that swift judgement often had to replace analysis. Therefore, the project leader had to encourage 'action' and an action orientation among project members.

In projects, people had to learn how to use their expert knowledge in a practical context, where action and results as well as swiftness were the dominant governing norms or values. They had to develop their abilities to work together with others in complex problem solving, and had to learn how to become valuable employees. In doing that, they also learnt a lot about the other members' specialties and 'interface' areas between the different functional areas.

Much of the knowledge generated within the projects was hard to formalise and incorporate into the development reports, final reports or other kinds of written material. Another problem was the 'real-time-action' character of most of the project work. With the time focus being strong, reporting and ex-post reflective activities were suppressed. The goals of the projects were so strong that individual orientations as well as reporting practices were adapted to the basic project logic of moving forward towards the goals – as fast as possible.

> Projects are very focused on their goals and nothing else. It's like there is an abyss after its completion.

> . . . we write a report but it might well be insufficient . . . if there was a problem we only write we solved it, you don't write how you perhaps tried two hundred thousand other things that did not work. . . .

This did not mean that written documentation was not used at all. In setting up a new project, during the pre-study phase, many looked at previous development reports and final reports. The purpose in reading these reports was to find out who had experience of what area and with whom problems could be discussed in an informal way. Both in the start-up phase of the project and during project execution, informal communication was a major medium. This was facilitated by the fact that the organisation was relatively small and that many of the employees had been with the organisation for years. One project leader remarked: 'Should we take this [informal communication] away, it would immediately die.'

CO-ORDINATION AND CO-OPERATION

Since Tetra Pak carried out its operations in projects, concerns about producing high-quality products at low cost, time considerations and deadlines were of special importance. There was a project plan in which activities were designated to certain phases with various tollgates and milestones. Although such plans conveyed a very simplistic and unproblematic picture of projects, more or less ignoring the uncertainties and complexities of the real-world context of project work, such measures were vital in order to achieve co-ordination.

The organisational change introduced also affected the individual's relation to the organisation in fundamental ways. They no longer belonged to specific, permanent units, had no traditional boss, and no longer belonged to a competence network. With fewer instructions and guidance, they had to take more initiative themselves, both within projects and in the context of those networks. From the managing director and the mentors, they also learned that the aim was to have a truly knowledge-based organisation. Their pay was thus related to their competences and especially their ability to use their competence in solving the problems of the projects. In addition, this required that they had social competences, and a willingness to share their knowledge with others.

COMPETENCE NETWORKS

Within CT there were a number of competence networks covering the key technologies involved in the entire converting process, such as lamination, printing, automation, etc. There was also a project leadership network. Membership in those networks was voluntary. Most members were connected to one of these, but some were involved in several of them. The network members chose a leader, who had no formal authority or accountability, acting more like a 'technical mentor'. Yet it was clear that they were expected to, and did, feel responsible for developing a deep enough competence within their specialist area. This included both a concern for the total amount and depth of specialist knowledge and judgement of strength and weaknesses of each of the members. They could have also initiated development activities as well as recruitment when needed. Apart from constituting an arena for exposing a broad knowledge resource base for the projects, the network meetings were also important as arenas for discussions of current problems or experiences that members had in project work.

> . . . [knowledge] follows the individual persons leaving the project. So here we have a job in our network to recognise what we work with in different projects.

These networks constituted formalised arenas for 'cross-talk' between the projects and for discussion about more technical competence needs. Unlike project work, the networks had a longer-term orientation and were engaged in exploring new technological ideas. They were also connected to the visions or strategies about the competences of the entire organisation and their leaders met the managing director regularly in the PPM (Project Portfolio Management) group, where the technological strategies of CT were matched against the project mix and where changes in either of these were considered.

LEADERS AND MEMBERS

In CT there were leaders (a managing director, mentors, project and network leaders) but no bosses. This was the message sent by introducing the new organisation structure. Obviously this did not mean that decisions regarding strategy, recruitment and wage setting were left to the employees, with only supporting guidance from the leaders. Yet the new structure and philosophy in most other areas brought about substantial changes which affected the individuals' relation to the organisation in fundamental ways.

In the old, basically functional organisation, information flowed along hierarchical lines, with considerable selection and filtering processes involved on its way up and down. These ideas of information distribution were abandoned, and instead, every individual was made responsible for searching for the kind of information s/he needed or wanted, in the newly installed conference system and other electronic media, or elsewhere inside or outside the organisation. This reliance on the individual to be the one with the best knowledge of what information s/he needed was paralleled by the policy of everybody having access to everything, the maps of all networks, including letters, documents, etc. in uncondensed form.

This information-seeking philosophy was generally accepted, and a climate emerged in which people tended to share their knowledge with others. Opportunism in this respect was thus seen as a very minor problem.

> We work together to build a good reputation for the firm . . . and all must participate and all who know something must share this with others.

> . . . the climate now is that everybody wants to help everybody.

One explanation had to do with the change in focus from functional units to projects. In the latter context, this kind of knowledge opportunism was less likely to pay off.

> . . . in the line organisation you could keep some information to yourself and use it to your own benefit later on, but in a project you have no use for it, because it is likely to be a long time before you are in a similar position again, so all information has to come out all the time . . .

A 'helping attitude' was also rewarded in the wage-setting procedure. The mentor talked to the project leaders about employees, not only about their specialist competences, but also about their ability to use their knowledge and their social competences. Since the project work was rather public and transparent, there was thus a non-negligible risk that opportunism would be detected. Getting a reputation for such non-cooperative behaviour would have been devastating in this organisation, since that meant that nobody would ask you to participate in projects or ask for your advice.

Individuals did not seem to have a very strong sense of belonging to or identification with CT. For some individuals, the projects represented an important social collectivity, for others, the competence networks were seen as more important. Instead of relating their membership identity strongly to the organisation or parts thereof, they tended to rely primarily on their competences.

> . . . there is no longer the same need to belong to an organisational unit. People identify with their competences . . . they feel at home in their working activities . . .

Neither was there any management intention or expectation that the individual should feel more like they were integrated parts of the organisation. As expressed by one of the leaders, you should take care not to 'glorify' the organisation too much.

> . . . the focus on the organisational unit may become so strong that you forget why you are here . . . a reduction in customer focus.

In many ways, CT was a very individualised organisation. It was up to every individual to seek relevant information, and to see to it that their competences (including both specialist competences and social competences) were strong enough, and developed as needed. If they did not do so, they risked a reputation of having obsolete knowledge, lack of practical or social ability. As a result, demand for that employee's contributions tended to diminish, and nobody asked that employee to join new projects or wanted his/her advice on problematic issues. Moreover, in such a small community as CT, it was not hard to observe how this demand structure was evolving. The wage-setting procedure reinforced this emphasis on the individual's responsibility to develop appropriate and in-demand competences. The members were granted great autonomy, but it was a matter of 'freedom and responsibility', as expressed by one leader.

CT provided a highly motivating social context for the members. One leader suggested that, although people were very different, the need for confirmation seemed to be basic to most of them. Another leader noticed how these confirmation/demand issues were connected to the construction of status differences within the organisation.

> . . . a fundamental need for confirmation, when somebody asks: 'could you join our project', you feel like a prince . . .

> Status I guess is to be needed . . . The worst thing that can happen to a person is not to be needed and inversely it has to be a kind of status to be in demand. Everything else such as having an extravagant car or high salary is merely exterior signs of that.

Moreover, those working in the organisation, due to recruitment policies and self-selection mechanisms, liked to be engaged in knowledge development and to work in project teams. They all tended to emphasise strongly that they were primarily driven by curiosity, and by their own interest in discovering and learning about new things. Several also said that they got a 'kick' out of managing a difficult project, and some appreciated that project work meant that you actually finished something and could then start anew with other things. Most of the employees were happy to work in CT – and they accepted its basic philosophy and image as a project-based, knowledge-based and individual-based organisation. For the individuals, the key to their career development was to have adequate knowledge or competences and to prove that in the real-life context of project work.

KPMG (A):
Strategic change in the 1990s

Gerry Johnson

KPMG is one of the major accounting firms worldwide. In the 1990s it underwent significant strategic change. The case is primarily concerned with the management of strategic change processes in this firm during this period and includes verbatim explanations of the challenges they faced and how they were handled. The case provides a context in which to consider the extent to which these change programmes succeeded in effecting strategic change.

• • •

By 2001 KPMG was one of the largest professional services firms in the world. Its fee income for the fiscal year to September 2000 was US$13.5bn, of which Europe, Middle East and Africa accounted for US$5.7bn and the Americas $6.6bn. The UK accounted for $1.8 bn (or 13 per cent of world fee income). Within the UK, KPMG employed 11,130 staff.

KPMG was, undeniably, a success story; yet this was a business facing an increasingly competitive environment on a global basis. KPMG had experienced a decade of change: and knew that it faced more in the future.

THE PARTNERSHIP HERITAGE

KPMG was a partnership. Over the years the firm had grown, prospered and amalgamated with others to become the huge enterprise it was. From 1993 to 1997 Colin Sharman was the UK senior partner of KPMG and had been responsible for the review of strategy and the programme of change that had taken place in the UK in the 1990s.

In common with many partnerships, KPMG's legacy was an emphasis on powerful, influential individual partners, skilled in their areas of professional expertise and with strong personal relations at senior level with clients. At the beginning of the 1990s a partner would typically have been a chartered accountant who had spent 10 to 15 years in the firm working his or her way up to a senior client management position in a specialist area such as audit or

This case was prepared by Professor Gerry Johnson, University of Strathclyde Graduate School of Business. It is intended as a basis for class discussion and not as an illustration of either good or bad management practice. The author is indebted to the partners and managers in KPMG who co-operated in the preparation of this case study. © G.N. Johnson, 2001. Not to be reproduced or quoted without permission.

tax. Given a successful record in developing business with clients and providing first-class professional services, the appointment to partner might take place, provided existing partners were in agreement. Thereafter the new partner would seek to further a reputation for winning new clients, building relationships with existing clients and ensuring excellence of service, by cultivating a network of trusted managers and other partners with whom he or she would co-operate.

Attempts to formalise strategic planning in such a context were difficult. In KPMG in the past, committees had been set up to do it; or partners given special responsibility for it; but whilst planning procedures or plans themselves might appear, they did little to change the way in which the firm developed. The successful growth in the 1970s and 80s had come about on the basis of excellence of professional advice given to clients and through long-standing relationships built by experienced partners. The strategic direction emerged from this. Where there were problems or disagreements these were resolved between the partners themselves.

Colin Sharman believed that the situation had changed by the mid-1990s.

In practice, of course, we have moved a long way from the Victorian notion of partnership and we run ourselves increasingly on corporate lines. I am the senior partner, the managing director, and I have a management team who make many of the operational decisions of an executive board. But the partners have to be consulted and have to agree – or at least not disagree – with any change.

But it is not just about partnership. Over 70 per cent of our total workforce are graduates, a highly intelligent group of people who, quite rightly, need to be convinced we are following the right strategy. This is not just an issue of drawing up some sort of plan and communicating it well through the organisation, but also of winning hearts and minds.

KPMG IN THE EARLY 1990s

The review of KPMG's strategy began in 1992, when Colin Sharman took over responsibility for KPMG's largest UK region (the South East) with 300 of the UK partners at that time. He described what he inherited:

In many respects the way we did things had its benefits. It was based on a network of very bright people, professionally trained and dedicated to providing quality advice to their clients. But there were problems, especially if we remember that our primary purpose was to provide services to our clients which may not always coincide with the skills, experience and interests of the partner who dealt with that client historically.

We had a matrix structure. We had a delivery structure for services along discipline lines; different practice units for audit, for tax, for management consultants and for corporate recovery. Separately we focused on our market sectors through firm-wide multi-disciplinary groups focusing on banking, insurance, manufacturing and so on. But the dominant axis remained the discipline-based practice units, and that was the primary interface to the market.

Our mission involved providing the highest quality of services to our individual clients but our practice units were discipline based. The only way that we focused across disciplines was through our market sector groups, but they merely co-ordinated and did not run the business. Hence there was a conflict between our stated goals and our structure.

KPMG would have been characterised as professional, highly conservative and sometimes complacent. There was also an attitude that our partners can, and will, 'do anything' – different from a 'do well' culture. And also a belief from right across the firm that being a generalist, rather than a specialist, was the most desirable state.

Partners believed they should have a say in decision making. There was a widespread network of committees – the answer for most things in the organisation was to set up a committee, a retreat into collectivism at the drop of a hat. Alongside that, the responsibilities of individuals within the organisation were so ill-defined that it made achieving change very difficult. Our control systems were full of paradoxes. At lower levels our staff saw controls as bureaucratic, taking time away from the real business of being a professional services firm; but at the higher levels there was a belief that we had poor controls and poor management information to run the business. Both of those were probably right – we spent a lot of time collecting and controlling the things that didn't help us to run the business. Alongside that, we had too much poor discipline – a lack of rigour and not caring about doing it right the first time; not surprising if we were asking people to spend a lot of their time on data that were never used to manage the business. But poor discipline, endemic through an organisation, was a major barrier to new ways of working. For example, there was too little value placed on managing carefully to timescales. It was regarded as much better to whirl around in frenzied activity at the last minute. That applied whether we were serving clients or trying to do something that contributed towards managing the business. You would hear people bragging about the extremely long hours that they worked, doubtless to reinforce the air of crisis that they were managing (though never creating!).

The 'mystique of partnership' didn't always help. Promotion to partner was seen as the summit of a KPMG person's career with virtually no second prizes for those who did not make it – we had a culture of 'up or out'. Partners, once created, were quite distinct and elevated people within the organisation. There were also problems with the discipline structure of audit, tax, consultancy and so on being dominant; problems illustrated, for example, by the tales people told about how awful one of the other disciplines was. Nor was the 'cult of the individual' always helpful. The kinds of people who were lionised were mavericks – people out of the mould; people who had broken the mould; people who didn't conform – there were lots of stories about individuals. You can imagine the way some of this expressed itself; especially when it came to 'them and us' – partners and the rest or, at lower levels, senior managers and the rest. For example, in our London office we had three levels of dining room and partners got their tea brought to their desks in china pots and silver trays.

THE COMPETITIVE POSITION IN THE EARLY 1990s

Colin Sharman explained the competitive position of the firm in the early 1990s:

The accountancy profession had been in a period of turbulence and change for some time. It was threatened by litigation, subject to 'low-balling', increasingly governed by rules and regulations and lacking a recognised market leader. The market was dominated by six large firms. In the 1980s the leading firms underwent a series of international mergers and diversified into a range of professional services – corporate finance, consulting, investigations and forensic accounting. There were portfolio differences – for example, KPMG was clearly a leader in corporate finance and the only player in career consulting, but the similarities were far greater than the differences.

The players were broadly similar in size and in their range of resources, consequently there was no natural leader to direct and structure the market. Even where the professional offerings were similar, effective relationships could provide a competitive edge through understanding the business and client needs.

The ability to co-ordinate and integrate people to create a real benefit for the client would also be a distinguishing factor since this is the area that accountancy firms have been notoriously bad at. The result was that teamwork, relationship management and integration are the competences that may distinguish one firm from the pack given their equivalence in many technical aspects. One of the fascinating aspects of this struggle of the giants was that success lay not necessarily in the originality of the idea or strategy but in the ability to implement the idea effectively.

In the early 1990s the expectations of clients were changing: however, they expected their advisers to understand the problems they faced, and to be able to provide a range of services to meet their needs. The issue for KPMG was, therefore, to ensure that partners were seen as, and performed the role of, business advisers.

THE IMPETUS FOR CHANGE

Colin Sharman saw the need for change. The problem was that many – perhaps most – of his colleagues did not. After all, the firm had experienced years of growth and was, clearly, very successful. Moreover, those who did think change was needed disagreed about what it should be. Sharman explained what he did in these circumstances.

> In 1992, we organised a series of eight strategy workshops for the region's partners; around one-third went through them. Quite deliberately, those who attended the workshops, particularly the early ones, were partners with a desire for change and views about what those changes might be; and they were not necessarily my views. What those workshops did was to work through the strategic position of the firm, what the competitive strategy should be, what the blockages to change were, what the critical success factors were and crucially what actions needed to be put in place.

In fact the workshops achieved some 'ownership' of the problems the firm was likely to face if it did not change. The partners, working together in groups, came to see the extent to which the services offered by the main firms were largely undifferentiated; and the consequent likelihood of eventual 'price-based' competition leading to reduced fees was a powerful stimulus for change.

> I personally attended a de-briefing session at the end of each of the workshops. The messages that came out of them were remarkably consistent. They confirmed the need for increased client focus. Major issues of specialism and integrating our service delivery also emerged.
>
> At the end of the series of workshops I arranged for some more detailed feedback sessions for all of the partners. I held ten evening sessions with all but a small handful of partners coming to one of the sessions. There we took the main messages from

the workshops, discussed the main directions of the firm and tried to surface any real concerns. Those proved a very useful way of building the consensus that we needed and also reinforcing the fact the change was definitely coming. I also used the senior management conference, which was an annual ritual for our senior managers to complain about the firm, as a way of getting them into strategic issues. The managers worked through much the same process as the partners had done on the workshops. At the end of that, the senior managers produced a serious analysis of the issues facing the firm and the kind of actions that were needed.

I tried to capture that enthusiasm, that commitment, that sense of change by holding a series of briefing sessions for partners and senior managers together to spread some of the messages. The messages I wanted to get across were that we were serious about change; that we needed to become a much more open organisation; that we needed to involve people at all levels in the development of the organisation and that we needed to communicate very much better than we had done in the past. To make them have a real impact I had the sessions designed to reinforce the underlying message, which was that we are going to do things very differently in future. For example you might think that the visuals [see Exhibit 1] we used were pretty ordinary but my KPMG audience was accustomed to nothing more exciting than slides with a KPMG-blue background and logo. So if nothing else my pop-art images made an impact. People started talking openly about wanting to change, wanting to try new things and wanting to succeed.

The workshops had, then, helped identify the main elements of the strategy. Colin Sharman had also developed his views about the required approach to change.

The key was to get client focus into our organisation. Initially I thought that I could operate successfully by changing only the behaviour and skill sets of our people, in particular our partners. But I came to the conclusion that was not going to work. If we changed the behaviour of partners and staff to become more client focused, more market sector focused, more knowledgeable about the marketplace, that would rapidly fall apart. We would need to reinforce it by measurement systems to ensure that our people were measured by these new ways of doing things; and by a structure which aligned with what people were being asked to do. If people, accountable in one direction, were told to focus their efforts in another, it was likely that one or other would lose out; and if our measurement systems and reward systems measure something other than the new behaviour we are asking for, it is fairly clear what would happen. So I concluded that we needed what I call a virtuous circle of change consisting of three interlinking elements – structure, measurement and behaviour – all needing to operate on each other.

THE LAUNCH OF 20:20 VISION

Following the strategy workshops in February 1992, many partners within KPMG had become impatient for action. Colin Sharman was rather more cautious. He believed it might take three to four years to put proposed changes into effect. However, a plan which set out structural changes had been put together by the end of April 1992. This plan was central to the guiding vision of the future and became known as '20:20 Vision'.

The underlying strategic thrust of 20:20 Vision was to move to an industry-based focus for service delivery to clients; to develop teams of auditors,

Exhibit 1 Visuals for the presentation

Exhibit 2   **UK structure of KPMG, 1993**

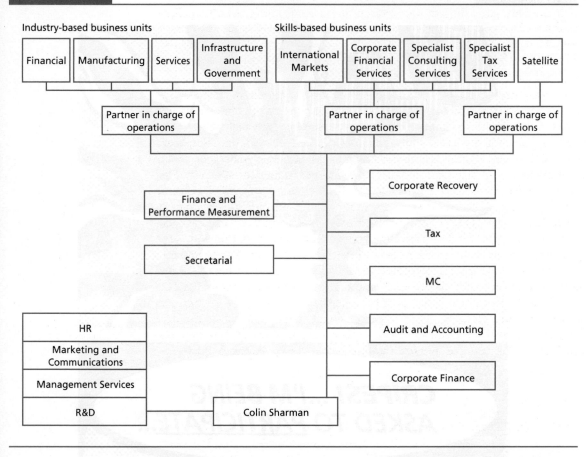

consultants, tax specialists and so on, who were experts by industry sector, not just by discipline. To do this a new structure for the firm was introduced made up of four industry-based business units and four skills-based business units, headed by senior partners reporting to two partners in charge of operations, one for Industry Units and one for Skills Units. These were directly accountable to Colin Sharman (see Exhibit 2).

There was a mixed response to these moves initially. Some parts of the firm were enthusiastic; others were not. As Alan Reid, the partner in charge of the Skills Units, explained:

> It was audit that went hell for leather into it; it was a way of getting the audit prac-tice managed. I don't think they recognised that 20:20 Vision was for the whole firm. However, on the tax side 49 out of 50 partners did not want it because they had been going through three years of change themselves, had only just come to the end of it and felt well poised to drive forward. What they thought they could do was to co-locate rather than merge. They accepted they had to work together but there was a question of whether they were managed by tax people. They had come out of

subservience to the audit practice and they thought that this was a magnificent ruse to get them back into that position. Consultancy never really debated it.

In the initial stages the staff were probably the most supportive and that's perhaps worth learning from. The staff saw the reality of the vision quicker than partners. In fact, as staff became more excited the whole thing accelerated, but quite a few partners lingered behind. I think some partners thought that all this might cancel itself out in due course.

By 1993 the structure was in place and co-location had occurred. However, the extent to which the new strategy had become accepted and put into effect was mixed. In some industry units it was being pursued energetically. One of the heads of the industry-based units established a co-located multi-disciplinary team, with team briefings, tailored training in the strategic analysis of clients for all partners and managers, whether consultants, auditors or tax specialists; and was able to demonstrate the effective working of the unit in half the time initially planned. In others it was little more than co-location at that time. As one audit manager put it: 'I had moved my office but nothing else had changed. As far as I was concerned I was dealing with the same clients in the same way.'

Changes to established control procedures were also slow. For example, it was unclear who would be allocated fee income for an assignment between business units and skills-based units where joint teams were operating. This lack of clarity was exacerbated by the concentration of some of the partners on the traditional monitoring of chargeable hours on client business. The new structure was also sometimes unclear, especially in sorting out 'turf disputes' which arose, for example, between industry-based and skills-based units.

THE LEADERSHIP PROJECT

In 1993 Colin Sharman was appointed to UK Senior Partner. At that time there were other developments taking place. At an international level in KPMG there were the beginnings of an international strategy to position KPMG as the leading 'advisory firm' rather than an audit firm. This took shape in the UK in what became known as the 'Leadership Project'.

In his address to the UK partners' meeting in October 1994, Colin Sharman announced KPMG's aim 'to become the leading accountancy firm in the UK'.

Our research shows that clients are saying: 'know me, know my business. Give me advice, help me to compete. I want frequent contact, robust and independent opinions, proactive advice and fast reactions to changes in my business. I want value for money.' . . . They want a trusted and valued relationship. If KPMG can succeed in genuinely making the transition from audit firm to business adviser, it can pull ahead of its competitors rather than being just one among the leaders . . . I want us to be indispensable to our clients because we give robust opinions, offer advice and provide business solutions that they simply could not get for themselves. I want us to attract the best people and to be the best firm to work for. The best firm because we have the most interesting clients, and the most attractive careers, the most demanding assignments. I want us to employ people who will make a real difference to their clients' business. I want us to be the firm that other leading advisers want to work with. We want the merchant banks, the lawyers, the specialist consultants to be alongside us. I want us to be the leading firm in the new markets – business transformation, forensic accounting – right at the cutting edge. I want us to foster a culture that sees opportunities and not problems, strengths not weaknesses, team work and not just individuals.

He explained how this would be put into effect:

The concept of having a leader on a client account – the lead partner – is not new. However, in KPMG, the role historically adopted has been that of a senior audit partner with the key relationship at the finance director level. It is now much more than this. The role is defined as an account management role that carries the ultimate responsibility for management of the client relationship, particularly at the chairman /chief executive level. The aim is to allow a single individual to be the integrator of all the firm's services to a client and of the people supplying those services. There is also a leadership aspect to the role as it includes responsibility for effective teamwork and managing internal relationships. This is not the role that all the partners should aspire to since specialist partners and engagement partners are essential to ensuring that the service delivery and advice are first class and this is the 'must have' of any professional service firm. It would not be commercially sensible to use the time of leading-edge specialists in what is essentially a generalist role.

Each project or piece of work performed for the client will be led by an engagement partner whose role is to deliver that specific piece of work. Take an audit for example; the audit engagement partner retains responsibility for the independent opinion. However, all services and relationships are co-ordinated through the lead partner.

HUMAN RESOURCE STRATEGY

The Leadership Project also provided a vehicle to roll out some of the changes already made in the South East to the rest of the UK and to develop human resource practices and policies in line with the changing strategy. Important here was a focus on behaviour. A competence framework was established and developed in 1993. David Westcott then (HR Partner) explained that:

The starting point for this framework was the question – what are the characteristics we need in our future partners? External consultants conducted a whole series of interviews which asked clients, partners in key positions together with younger partners what they thought the behavioural characteristics should be for the future success of the company.

From this, six categories of competence emerged (see Exhibit 3).

Reward systems were also revised. David Westcott:

Pay had been largely a matter of how long anyone had been in a particular grade. . . . We set out to introduce a pay structure and review system which sought to reward improvement and achievement rather than time in grade.

Colin Sharman explained the basis of the system:

We changed all our systems to move everybody into just five bands so that instead of having everybody promoted every year, which was the old system, we had a situation where promotion meant something. . . . Promotion would only be between the bands, on the basis of performance in terms of the competences. Eventually, we completely restructured the reward system for partners, right the way across the UK.

Exhibit 3	The Competence Framework

Client responsiveness
1. Relationship building – establishes rapport and builds long-term relationships with key decision makers.
2. Professional judgement – knows who the 'real' client is at all times and uses this knowledge to operate effectively for KPMG.

Business skills
1. Commerciality – relates all aspects of KPMG's service to client's business perspective and commercial drivers.
2. Business development – is seen by existing clients to market effectively and appropriately.

Management
1. Task management skills – controls the process of delivery to the client.
2. Team skills – encourages openness and co-operative working.
3. People development – gives staff responsibility and autonomy appropriate to their level of competence.

Personal effectiveness
1. Drive and commitment to results – goes beyond client's expressed requirements and meets their real need.
2. Resilience – recovers crisis situations; is resourceful at times of pressure and stress.

Social skills
1. Communication skills – speaks clearly and with impact.
2. Social confidence – is perceived to enjoy the company of a wide range of people.

Thinking skills
1. Analytical thinking – analyses large amounts of complex data, extracts essentials.
2. Proactive thinking – comes forward with ideas unprompted by clients.

There were problems on these changes, as David Westcott explained:

> A language problem existed because we were talking about performance, which had never really featured before. Time was no longer an issue. Disquiet around this was driven by the uncertainty many people were feeling – they knew where they were under the old system. Suddenly the whole thing was turned upside down.

Development centres were also established to which newly promoted senior managers were sent to identify personal development plans to prepare them for the role of partner. David Westcott explained their purpose:

> There had been some concern within the practice that the role of the senior manager, which is a very important one within KPMG but is largely a production and operational job, did not prepare people for partnership, which is more about relationships and social skills. So we ran a development centre as people were promoted to senior manager. It was initially seen as being to do with judgement, assessment and appraisal rather than development; but they have now been accepted and people find them very valuable.

In the past, appointment to partner was seen by many in the firm as dependent on a senior manager being seen by existing partners as 'the right sort of chap'. However, in 1994 Partner Assessment Centres were also introduced:

> Before anyone is admitted to partnership in any of the regions of the firm they have to have the approval of the UK board. The UK board had for some time expressed concern that their job had become one of a rubber stamp. Another concern was that a number of partners around the UK had been asked to leave the partnership within five years of their becoming a partner. We need something more rigorous. We needed to ensure that the competences we had defined for future partners were those in evidence or they had the potential to be. So in 1994 the board agreed to establish nationally two processes for partner admission. One was an assessment centre and the other was an interview panel which represented the board. It's much clearer now what it takes to become a senior manager and to become a partner because there is a greater openness in terms of the sort of behaviour expected of people. There are those who are upset that the patronage system has gone . . . but by and large there is a general belief that it is a better way of doing things.

Colin Sharman commented:

> It was the most unfair thing we've done really. What we were saying was the old system finishes here. Very justifiably a lot of the guys said 'until today I knew how to become a partner: you attach yourself to a powerful guy, keep your head down and you don't make mistakes; and he will see you all right'. That was the problem, there was enormous patronage in the system and at a stroke we took that away. For the first time the board was not going to accept someone bullying through his boy – and that had never happened before. Down the line people are saying 'OK the rules have changed but I know what I have to do and I can still make it even if I don't have a patron'. It is one of the key things helping us get behavioural changes.

Assessment centres were also adopted for recruitment. David Wescott:

> We asked if we were happy about the quality of the graduates that we were getting? So we introduced a new selection process, which incorporated a mini assessment centre whereas previously we, like all other firms of accountants, had relied exclusively on interviews. By introducing a new and very much more rigorous selection process for the 600 graduates that we take on we are getting a much higher acceptance rate of people we offered positions to. Our feedback from them is, (a) we seem to know what we want from a new recruit, and (b) we have made it difficult to join – and that has an attraction.

INTEGRATION INTO INDUSTRY BASED UNITS

It was Colin Sharman's belief that:

> Where we have been able to integrate things into the industry-based business units we have had unparalleled success. Consulting volumes delivered through the industry groups are growing like topsy. Where we have failed is in those bits we left in the skills groups.

There were certainly problems in integrating the consultancy practice. Alan Reid explained:

There were very few consultants put into the industry business units originally. Two consultants headed up industry units because it was important that not all the business units were headed by auditors. But I would say maybe 70–80 consultants went into industry business units and 600 were left in the skills unit. So there was a very strong force of consultants left. I don't think that they wanted to be submerged below auditors. Our auditors are very suspicious of our consultants. If you actually assess them as separate business units, some of our most talented people are in our consultancy, but audit has performed better than consultancy. It is a lot to do with their marketplace and the nature of their work. We have to win £2 million of new work every week for our consultancy – our audit practice has a more recurring base of work. There is a lot of concern that they just don't understand each other. We had also grown consultancy by just adding on services; little cottage industries and boutiques here and there. They went in and sold the service they had to a client, worked hard in doing it, then came away again and left it instead of nurturing the relationship and trying to sell other services. They acted as 35 cottage industries.

COMMUNICATIONS AND FEEDBACK

Colin Sharman believed that one of the most significant means of change was communications:

> For example, internally we now do a report on the partners' conference. In the past it would have been a paragraph in the house magazine saying we had a partners' conference. What we now do is take a video of it, interview the partners as to what they think and then we roll that right out immediately after the partners' conference to tell everyone about it. I exercise very little editorial control over that.
>
> Then there is the UK-wide staff opinion survey. Some people say 'we shouldn't ask because they will tell us we are not very good'. Interestingly enough, the survey work I have seen shows that an awful lot of them identify with what we are trying to do, but that they think some of the partners need to change their behaviour. One of the things we are doing for this year's partners' conference is to give some feedback from the staff to the partners about partner behaviour and about what the partners are doing. The other thing that is being developed is upward appraisal. That's becoming accepted throughout the organisation.

The surveys conducted at this time showed mixed results.

In 1995, an internal KPMG attitude survey on the progress of the Leadership Project showed that staff and partners saw KPMG as above average compared with the rest of the Big Six, as a firm with a successful future and that job satisfaction was above average for a professional firm. However, KPMG was not seen as a people-oriented firm and development and career opportunities were still not clear. The Leadership Project had not yet impacted in a practical way on the way most staff worked day to day. Teamwork was not yet fully effective. And whilst relationships between partners and staff were seen as good locally, barriers still existed: there was still a sense of 'us and them'. This was borne out in a survey of the consultancy operation reported in *Accountancy Age* in February 1995:

> Over half of the 74 staff questioned said they would not recommend KPMG 'as a good place to work', nor did they 'expect to be with this organisation two years from now' . . . And well over 60 per cent said they only knew what was expected of them to a 'slight' or 'moderate' extent . . . A huge 82 per cent of staff named 'avoidance' as

a key feature, involving 'shifting responsibility, procrastinating and avoiding issues'. Power was another dominant characteristic with 'empire-building' at the fore. And while 90 per cent said that 'winning is valued and staff feel they have to outperform each other', just 20 per cent believed there was any 'value placed on constructive interpersonal relationships, friendliness and openness' within the KPMG culture. Similarly, just 16 per cent felt that any regard was given to 'coaching and developing people, being supportive and constructive'.

However, Colin Sharman argued that from a client point of view the benefits were clear:

> Clients love it. We asked them what they wanted and then we were able to sell it to them and they bought more of it. We've gone back and said, 'do you like what you're getting?' and by and large our clients are very positive about what we have done. We have put six points on our market share in the last four years.

INCORPORATION

In 1995 KPMG announced that it planned to incorporate that part of its audit practice dealing with companies listed on the UK stock exchange or in the regulated financial services industry. One reason for this was the need to protect the personal assets of partners from increasing threats of litigation affecting the profession as a whole, especially in the USA. However, as the *Financial Times* reported early in 1996, KPMG believed the move would provide competitive advantages:

> KPMG felt that a stronger corporate management structure would give it an edge in competing with the looser partnerships of the other Big Six firms. With incorporation comes disclosure. Accounts will have to be published for the audit company but KPMG has pledged that it will go further – it will produce full financial results for the whole firm. This has wrong-footed the competition, most of which are still pondering a response . . . KPMG's focus on auditing is a strategy which sets it apart from many of the other big firms. While some firms have boosted volumes by entering markets such as out-sourcing and information technology – and the implementation of services – KPMG is seeking to preserve the pre-eminence of auditing. (*Financial Times*, 25 January 1996)

The FT reported the publishing of 50,000 copies of KPMG's annual report for the UK – the first major accountancy firm to do so:

> Why has KPMG become the first to disclose so much about what is still, legally, a private business? Whatever the truth, the firm's chutzpah is admired by most – albeit privately. The firm admits that it would have had to publish full results for the audit plc, but that its decision to open all the books was prompted by a desire to present a transparent business to clients and the general public. It feels the public has a legitimate interest in an organisation which audits 400 listed companies.

RESTRUCTURING: A UK FIRM

In October 1996 a new UK board was established. Its brief was strategic rather than operational, with board members selected for their ability to contribute

| Exhibit 4 | UK structure of KPMG, 1997 |

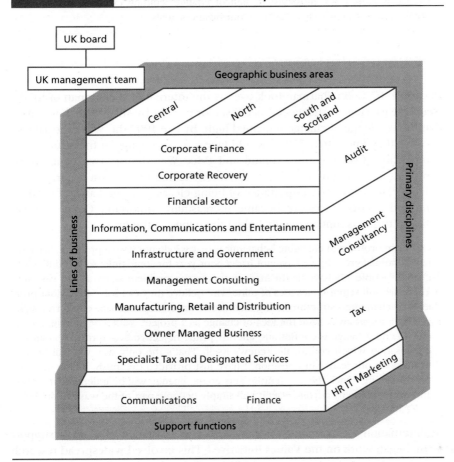

to the strategy of the firm. It was non-representational, in that it did not consist of the heads of parts of the organisation; and it institutionalised the separate role of chairman and chief executive. Colin Sharman moved to the role of chairman with Mike Rake taking over as chief executive. Following the establishment of this board, reconsideration of the structure of the firm took place with the intent of bringing the UK firm together more. The result was the structure for the UK as a whole shown in Exhibit 4. Under the UK board was established a UK management team with operational responsibilities for running KPMG UK. This structure was explained in the firm as follows:

> KPMG's move to becoming an advisory firm is about creating a clear leading position in the market. The old regional structure provided a strong presence in local geographic markets, but insufficient UK investment and focus on the industry and specialist needs of clients (our lines of business) and strong but not always consistent processes or disciplines. The challenge is to balance the matrix of geography, line of business and discipline in a way which builds on KPMG strengths. Balancing the matrix has to be complemented by better working together across the UK. This

necessitates robust UK support functions and effective reward systems. Structural change is merely the most visible sign of change; cultural changes and business-driven strategies will help us achieve our business goals.

THE VALUES INITIATIVE

In early 1997 Colin Sharman took over as the international chairman of KPMG (see Case B). He was succeeded as UK senior partner by Mike Rake. Both knew that the challenge of change remained high. By late 1997 this was especially so because they knew that KPMG would face a major change in the structure of competition. Coopers and Lybrand and Price Waterhouse, two of its major competitors, had announced their intention to merge to form a partnership twice KPMG's size. The importance of being clear about the bases of KPMG's competitive edge therefore became increasingly important. Colin Sharman believed this was fundamentally linked to change in the firm.

> Our main problem in changing behaviour is that we do not have a problem. We have had continual growth; we have not had a poor year for some time; so it is difficult to change people's behaviour. In many respects the problem starts at the very top. There are still senior colleagues of mine who believe they can solve behaviour problems by changing a structure, going on a course or sending someone else on a course. We have to get away from the idea of change as a project, with a beginning, middle and an end. Change is continuous, and my prime objective is to turn KPMG into an organisation which continually renews itself. That's the only way we will be able to maintain our leadership position. I have just provided the 'push' which gets that process going. Once the momentum gets going, change will be independent of me, and unstoppable by anyone else: it will simply become part of the way we do things in KPMG.

As International Chairman Sharman, with the assistance of a small support team, began work on the Values Initiative.* This involved widespread research into the values and behaviours in KMPG as they related to client relationships. What emerged from the research and their discussions was a clarity about KPMG's values as at 1997. Many of these were highly positive to the future direction of the firm. However, Sharman and his team recognised that each of these also led to potentially negative behaviours.

Desirable as it was, *client centredness* could sometimes mean accommodating the client or doing what the client requested without question. *Individualism* could also mean self-interest and therefore undermine teamwork. *Technical excellence* could sometimes mean lengthy attention to a technical report without enough questions as to what was of real value to the client. However, *integrity* was taken as centrally important and unquestionably positive.

The question then arose as to what, if anything, needed to change. It was out of this that the new mission statement arose. It had been:

---

*For a fuller explanation of this initiative see J. Thornbury (1999) 'KPMG: revitalising culture through values', *Business Strategy Review*, 10(4), 1–15.

KMPG shall be the world's leading accounting and consulting firm. We shall achieve this by delivering the highest quality services that provide significant added benefits to our clients and that meet or exceed their expectations. We shall thereby build enduring relationships and be always worthy of our clients', our people's and society's trust.

The view was that this was laboured and non-memorable. It was revised to:

KMPG is the global advisory firm whose aim is to turn knowledge into value for the benefit of its clients, its people and its communities.

The change team then organised a series of activities and support tools to help put the values programme into operation. This included work with partners at a series of events throughout 1997 and 1998, with a growing emphasis on the implementation of the values. Implementation support included written material as an implementation guide, with tools and techniques on issues such as leadership, team development, communications. It also included a board game – the Values Game – which was designed as a fun way of communicating the need for behaviour in line with the values across the firm.

The Values Initiative was also picked up in national firms, not least in the UK. Mike Rake had attended the Harvard programme on Leadership in Professional Services Firms. The programme convinced him, too, of the importance of powerful and enduring organisational values, and that it was important for KPMG to be clear about these values and the behaviours associated with them. Since his appointment he had spent time listening to partners and managers about what was needed. He believed that there was a consensus around the needs for a clearer vision, clear leadership and above all else, behavioural change. All of these needed to be linked to a clarity about the values of the firm. This gave rise to the Values Charter which was launched at the UK partners' conference in Birmingham in 1998. Here Mike Rake argued that success would be dependent on the ability to share values across the firm in such a way as to achieve KPMG's vision. The Charter consisted of ten key values (see Exhibit 5). At the Birmingham conference the partners worked in small groups to craft the statements in this charter and to identify the appropriate behaviours to support such values. At the end of the conference individual partners, including Mike Rake, stood up to make commitments about how they would personally change in line with the identified values and behaviours. Partners at the conference were enthusiastic: they believed that there had been a real attempt to translate values into behaviours; and to try to ensure an acceptance of this across the firm. Some admitted that the problem could be that 'they would all revert to type' but nonetheless believed it was an important step forward.

Geoff Gaines was then given responsibility for taking the values programme forward. Mike Rake charged Geoff with developing a programme to make the Values Charter a reality. Geoff explained:

How do we take values into action? If you take all these values there are synergies but there are also dilemmas. For example, bollocking someone for not sharing knowledge is rude, but it is also about encouraging knowledge sharing. I pushed the idea of this sort of dilemma being the basis of the conversation; and we developed a 'dilemma workshop' for partners and senior managers.

Exhibit 5	The Values Charter

To achieve our overall vision and apply our values, we will conduct ourselves in line with this charter.

- We will put KPMG's interests above our personal business agendas.
- We will remain courteous and good humoured in all of our dealings, thus creating an environment where cynicism, oppression and rudeness are not acceptable.
- We will be proactive and innovating with our clients, and will respond to their needs quickly, effectively and objectively.
- We will listen to and aim to understand alternative perspectives and put our own points of view across openly, honestly and constructively.
- We will support our leaders, encourage our peers and develop our people.
- We will openly and proactively share knowledge.
- We will respect all of our people and the contribution they make to the firm.
- We will obtain the facts before making judgements on people or issues.
- We will respect our own and our people's needs to balance personal and business lives.
- We will learn from our experiences and will take the time to enjoy our successes in the company of those we work with.

In early 1999, Eddie Oliver, who was developing a blueprint for the integration of the European consultancy business, asked me how the values work could help. I suggested that values could create conversations about business issues. When such conversations take place, they help identify practice, i.e. what people would really do in a given set of circumstances. We ran two events and it surfaced the sort of typical dilemma situations. The underlying idea was to relate the values to real life.

By 2000 Geoff Gaines believed the Values Charter had achieved some real benefits: but he was also conscious of outstanding issues:

It's now OK to talk about things such as work/life balance that people felt they couldn't talk about before; the level of awareness of values is still high; newcomers are attracted by our values so that would have an effect on the 'mix' over time. But it's behaviour that matters. We have to sustain the programme if we're to make an enduring impact on that. The Charter emerged out of what we do in the UK. But we need values to do with a global firm. We have to avoid those values being 'sent down' by management, rather than emerging from what is actually done in the practice. Values are not a decision: they are a discovery.

Eddie Oliver, a senior partner in the UK, added:

So far we have all the old management control levers and have added the values but some of us believe we can rely on values drivers much more than controls. There is a view that the winning organisation of the future will need to be more diverse in terms of people and more organic. The values work is of central importance to this. But, around the world, KPMG has some leaders who adhere to 'scientific management'. We need to guard against the UK getting out of step as we apply the principles of self-organising systems.

FURTHER CHANGES IN STRUCTURE

20:20 Vision had moved the firm towards a structure based on 'lines of business', which focused on particular industries or sectors. However, in the second quarter of 1999 it was announced that the day-to-day management control of the firm in the UK would be through functions: audit, tax, corporate recovery and so on. Eddie Oliver explained:

> It was only some countries that implemented 20:20 Vision; and there was a feeling that there had to be a common arrangement around the globe. KPMG's market positioning varies from country to country and we needed a framework which would accommodate this. So we decided on a structure within which resources are managed by function but go to market via lines of business. The Sharman philosophy – focus on markets and clients' needs – has not been changed but the organisation structure has.

THE SITUATION IN 2001

Mike Rake, senior UK partner and chairman of KPMG Europe, reflected on the changes he had seen in the firm over the past decade:

> The firm has changed significantly. Although we've always had very talented people, ten years ago we operated as generalists and were reliant of our past success. Today we have a more professional approach to the way we deliver services to out clients and the way we run our own business, with a particular focus on specialisation.
>
> A decade ago we were in danger of stagnation. KPMG was a great City firm but it's market share and influence were being challenged. It had to become more flexible and faster to respond to the changes happening all around.
>
> As I look back on the great strides we've made, a number of themes emerge as the key drivers to the overwhelming change to and success of the firm in the last five or six years:
>
> - **Openness**: externally, through the publication of our annual report and accounts and internally, through out communications architecture, appraisal systems and so on.
> - **Integration**: of geography, function, etc to harness our potential and focus it on our strategic priorities.
> - **Widening horizons**: as the forces of globalisation, e-business, etc. have removed the old market certainties.
> - **Values**: our values programme has helped open people's minds. We've moved from a hierarchical mindset to one focused on what the team can do to add value to our clients' businesses.
>
> It's worth mentioning a few of the specific changes we've made:

- We've integrated our network of regional partnerships into a single UK partnership and successfully moved to integrate our practice in Europe.

- We've recruited, and continue to recruit may direct-entry partners (unheard of 15 years ago).

The combined effect of these changes has been dramatic. And yet, in other ways the firm hasn't changed at all. The people are as dedicated as ever. And we still place personal integrity above all else.

I wouldn't want to give the impression that the job is done. It never is. Ten years ago KPMG was great for it's time but not ready for the future – today our challenge is to make KPMG a truly 21st century organisation.

KPMG (B):
Developing a global firm

Gerry Johnson

In the late 1990s expectations of global clients and international opportunities for development were prompting greater global co-ordination and the need for a clearer global strategy in KPMG. The case allows these developments to be considered in the light of the context of KPMG as a worldwide partnership but with a history of localised service delivery.

● ● ●

In January 1997 Colin Sharman received a telephone call from Jon Madonna, international chairman of KPMG, asking to get together for an urgent meeting. They met for breakfast the next morning in London. At this meeting Madonna announced that he was leaving KPMG within the next two weeks and was nominating Colin Sharman as the next international chairman. Sharman took over on 1 February 1997.

THE CHALLENGE OF THE GLOBAL FIRM

In 1997 KPMG had practices in 156 countries throughout the world; more than their competitors. However, the US, UK, Netherlands, Germany, France, Canada and Australia accounted for 80 per cent of fee income (see Appendix 1 for further descriptive statistics of KPMG worldwide). Exhibit 1 shows the revenue and personnel distribution for the firm internationally at that time.

In 1997 the view was that the main challenges for KPMG's international strategy into the millennium were twofold. The first was how to develop a coherent strategic approach to service delivery across the world, given the globalisation of so many existing and potential clients. The second was that many of the major opportunities for growth were in areas of the world in which neither KPMG nor their competitors had well-established practices – for example, eastern Europe.

'Standing still' was not seen as an option because, as competitors sought growth internationally, this would effectively mean losing share and market standing in the eyes of international clients. A lack of growth would also, very

Exhibit 1	KPMG revenue and presonnel, 1997

REGIONS*	REVENUE (US$M)	PARTNERS	PROFESSIONALS	ADMINISTRATIVE	PERSONNEL TOTAL
Africa	100	231	2,320	766	3,317
Asia Pacific	858	841	10,052	2,324	13,217
Europe	4,181	2,769	26,674	8,594	38,037
Latin America	203	268	3,088	1,137	4,493
Middle East	34	71	767	222	1,060
North America	3,624	2,381	16,762	6,024	25,167
Total	**9,000**	**6,561**	**59,663**	**19,067**	**85,291**

Note: All international revenue and growth figures are measured in US dollars and are affected by fluctuations in exchange rates.

* Countries: 155; cities: 844.

likely, have implications on the ability to attract the best people into the firm; slow growth would mean diminishing opportunities – or at least perceived opportunities – to advance in the firm. Sharman admitted that the growth rate of KPMG worldwide was not good enough. He explained:

> Growth will come in the developing world: in Asia Pacific, eastern Europe and Latin America. But even if we are growing at 40 per cent in those regions, the impact on our overall growth rate can be only marginal because of the composition of KPMG. If the US, the UK, the Netherlands, Germany and France are growing rapidly, that will put our growth rate right. So first and foremost, the task is to get the big practices growing quickly; especially the US where our position is not as strong competitively as it needs to be. That means that we've got to diversify into the faster-growing services in those countries.

By 1997, there were already some global initiatives under way to try to address this. Project Globe was about trying to achieve a consistent international approach in management consulting and speed up the international development of higher added value consulting projects. Audit 2000 was seeking to develop a risk-focused audit by building elements of strategic analysis into auditing. The Global Tax Vision was, again, attempting to provide a consistent international dimension on the tax practice. As far as the US was concerned, it was concentrating on organic growth and looked set to achieve a 25 per cent growth rate in 1997 (50 per cent in consultancy).

> We've then got to look at the developing areas of the world – Asia Pacific's tiger economies, the restructured economies in eastern Europe – and achieve very, very dynamic growth there.

There was also the question of the required investment internationally. Despite KPMG's size, Sharman believed that the challenge was finding the money to spend for international development and information systems infrastructure. This included the development of a global knowledge management system, automation of audit systems and up to $100 million on India and eastern

Europe alone. KPMG knew that at least one other firm had spent a similar sum developing their global consulting business.

By the end of 1997 a new mission statement had developed from the Values Initiative (see Case A):

> KPMG is the global advisory firm whose aim is to turn knowledge into value for the benefit of its clients, its people and its communities.

Sharman explained that:

> The fundamental purpose is to turn knowledge into value. We then need to consider what this means in terms of the values, product range, processes and infrastructure in the firm. To be honest, we have done very little on any of these so far. We have set up project teams to look at them. Some points are clear. As far as the product range is concerned it means we have to be clear about what we don't do as well as what we do. We shouldn't be into health systems in Manchester or car leasing in Puerto Rico or architecture in Switzerland, for example. They do not help provide a uniform image of what KPMG is about in line with our *mission.*

In an address to the International Board in May 1997 Colin Sharman made this quite clear:

> We need clear, agreed criteria by which we judge whether a service should be core to all KPMG practices worldwide, optional according to local markets, or forbidden to all practices.

As far as the infrastructure was concerned, Sharman believed it was necessary to develop quickly a more common international approach to IT, HR and marketing.

> That means that some of the bigger firms have got to have a bit of give and take. And I include the UK firm in that. We are not going to be able to have it all our own way; neither is anybody else. We've got to come to common approaches and then we've got to manage them sensibly from the centre. I don't think it's a structural issue. I think this is about behaviour. We need common processes across disciplines, because we need to get people to work the same way wherever we are. It doesn't matter whether you are a consultant in Ecuador, a registered accountant in the Netherlands, a chartered accountant in the UK, an IT specialist in Malaysia or a tax lawyer in Nigeria, you need to approach client work through a set of common processes. That melds us together as one firm. The fact that your ownership structure is different is not terribly relevant.

However, the realities of a successful federated partnership structure of KPMG had to be recognised. His view at that time was that:

> The easiest way to waste our time and energy would be to attempt to reorganise the international firm. We have seen some of our major competitors fall into this trap. We will clarify the role and responsibilities and sharpen the focus of our committees and other bodies – including the Board, Executive Committee and International HQ. We will strengthen and centralise the support functions. But we will not spend the next three years wrestling with the structure of the international firm. This would not be successful. We will aim to become a 'virtual global entity in the knowledge business'. This means we will look and act like one organisation while retaining our individual member firm structure.

A GLOBAL MERGER?

Coopers and Lybrand and Price Waterhouse announced their intention to merge in September 1997, and this prompted KPMG to consider its options. In considering the possibility of KPMG merging, Colin Sharman explained:

> In terms of our global development, the option of doing nothing was really not acceptable. In the US, for example, bigness matters. You don't get into major companies if you are not in the top four; and following merger we would have been fifth out of five; and we could not get back into a top four position through organic growth in the US. You also have to be one of the biggest to operate in eastern Europe, China and Russia. Andersen and a combined Coopers and Price Waterhouse operation would be bigger there too and with more to invest. So we would be disadvantaged in developing markets too. So the drive for us to consider a merger too was nothing to do with the UK but to do with international markets.

By the end of 1997, KPMG and Ernst & Young were in merger negotiations. Sharman explained:

> A merger with Ernst & Young seemed most sensible, particularly in the US. Ernst & Young are strong in the US; KPMG are strong in Europe. Moreover, we are both industry-focused firms. I believe we will be able to work together well with them. There are differences. They are more centrally managed than we are at KPMG, for example. They focus more on the short term than we do. Had we moved down the route of integration further there would have been problems. But I believe that if we ensure that the two practices are mixed up well and we do not leave pockets of separate activities it will work.

Not everyone saw the proposed merger in the same way. In December 1997, the FT Lex column warned:

> If the mega mergers proceed, shrinking choice, customers may be less keen to have all their eggs in the same few baskets.

The European Commission also expressed concern about both the KPMG/Ernst & Young and Coopers/PW mergers. Karel Van Miert, the EU competition commissioner, said his office 'had been overwhelmed by the amount of concern generated by the announcement'. Regulatory authorities elsewhere, particularly in the USA, were also concerned, especially about the KPMG/Ernst & Young merger which, it was argued, would give too great a share of key markets to the merged firm.

As negotiations proceeded in the first few months of 1998 it also became clear that the operationalisation of this merger was giving rise to doubt amongst partners in both firms. In March it was announced that the merger would not proceed.

LEARNING FROM THE MERGER NEGOTIATIONS

The fact that the merger was not to proceed magnified rather than diminished the need for the global development of KPMG; indeed Sharman's belief was that there was a massive momentum for change resulting from the idea of the merger. They had also seen Ernst & Young at close quarters. It faced similar challenges and it too had been through significant changes; but it was much more centralised than KPMG. As one partner said: 'It was rather like holding a mirror up to ourselves.'

By spring 1998, Sharman was sketching out what he believed had to be done:

> I believe we have learned a lot over the last few months in these merger negotiations. We have realised that we have quality in depth throughout the firm and probably more cohesion than we thought. What we need is more focus on what we do well across the world, better alignment with global strategies and greater investment in global infrastructure. We need to give attention to a number of priorities.
>
> The first is our international structure. This needs to be clearer in order to manage a global strategy more effectively. In particular we need to focus our management activities on a number of regions, with people responsible for implementing global policy, especially the development of emerging markets and identifying investment opportunities. I am also proposing we have managing partners responsible for the key services we provide. Again they will be responsible for ensuring the implementation of global strategy but from a service point of view. They should determine and manage our portfolio of services to be offered by member firms and make sure there are common business process methodologies. I believe we need full-time, international, senior-level executives for these roles. These appointments will be senior people who might be located anywhere but who will report into a central worldwide office in Amsterdam. This international executive team will report to an international board, responsible for reviewing and endorsing the vision and policy for the global firm and monitoring the implementation of strategy. The Council will be the firm's ultimate governing body.

Exhibit 2 shows the structure. In 1998, an International Executive Team, with Paul Reilly, a US partner, as CEO, was appointed with responsibility for managing the global strategy. This team reported to Sharman and his international board, which had on it senior partners from the major country-based partnerships around the world.

Sharman continued:

> We also need to clarify the agreements and arrangements we have across the world with our various partnerships and licensees. They need to have a stronger alignment to our goals, a clearer definition of their rights and responsibilities; and we need to develop their commitment to the important role they play in providing a coherent range of services internationally. I think there needs to be clarity, for example, on the use of the KPMG name and brand; the acceptance of lead partner authority for international assignments; the mandatory acceptance and delivery of core services; and we need to ensure their acceptance of global policies on investment, technology, knowledge sharing, human resource development and our business processes. Not least, we need globally enforced standards in quality, risk management and management information, and I believe we need the approval by the international board for national senior partner appointments.
>
> None of this will be possible without making quite clear what the international centre of KPMG is responsible for. I believe the priorities of the centre are:
>
> ● knowledge management across the world; and in particular means of ensuring that we extend the frontiers of our shared knowledge;

Exhibit 2	The international structure, 1998

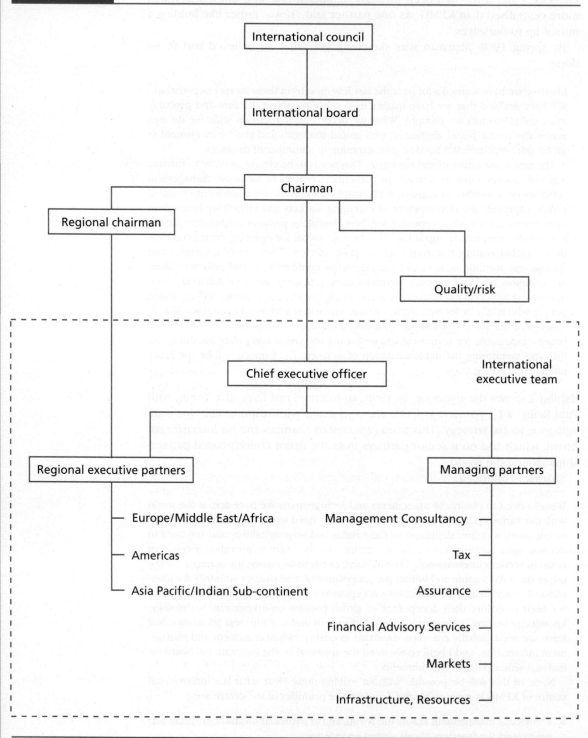

- information technology on a global basis not only for purposes of control but also to share the knowledge upon which we will develop;
- global human resource policies and, in particular, international partner development;
- marketing and, in particular, our global image and positioning;
- finance and investment planning;
- global communications both within the firm and outside.

These priorities formed the agenda for the first meeting of the International Executive Team (IET) in mid-1998: and they were priorities which continued to guide global development.

GLOBAL MARKETS

One of the major priorities the IET addressed was how to serve global clients. Responsibility for this on the IET lay with Alastair Johnston:

We decided the underlying *raison d'être* of KPMG was to serve its global clients. There had been a lack of focus on just how important that list of clients was. We decided we had to give them the very best service we possibly could and we had to grow market share at the highest level. We decided to re-focus on the major clients and targets and the sectors within which they operate.

We began by establishing best practices with regard to the management of major clients. We then brought together international client teams for training and planning sessions. These core client teams were the 8–10 key people from around the world dealing with a particular client. There were 100 of these teams and each of them went through a programme focused on identifying opportunities and building relationships. This whole programme was launched at the end of 1998 event at our Monaco partners' meeting. Since then over 1,000 partners and senior people have been through the programme.

Four global 'lines of business' were also established: financial services, consumer markets, industrial and automotive and information, communications and entertainment (ICE). Within these global lines of business are 95 per cent of our global clients. The chairs of these global lines of business report to me and, within the lines of business, global lead partners for particular global clients report to those chairs. The chairs are responsible for the plans for that line of business globally.

The role of the centre is to support the work on global clients and also to support targeting and proposals to win and retain more global clients by providing a central impetus to the energy and quality of such proposals.

For example, best practice for global client service teams had been codified, emphasising seven key principles (see Exhibit 3). Alastair Johnston believed such efforts had paid off:

In 1998 in Monaco I said that we needed to achieve a doubling of revenue on global clients. Our revenue with them in 1998 was $1.2 billion, which accounted for about 12 per cent of our fee income for the firm. In 2000, the figure will actually be $2.1 billion – not quite double, but impressive growth nevertheless.

At the next level below the Top 100 global clients, we also now have national account programmes across the world headed in each country by a national account

| Exhibit 3 | Best practice for client service teams |

1. The right team in the right place

All Lead Partners are empowered to draw on the specialist resources they need to ensure we have Client Service Teams that can exceed the expectations of our clients.

Functions and Lines of Business should be included on every Client Service Team. This should ensure that the client is aware of all our products and services, including those that are being developed.

Global and National Lead Partners are empowered to draw at any time from the top ranks of our people anywhere in the world to meet the needs of our Global and National Clients.

We also recognise that longer-term international relocation may be the best solution and Lead Partners and key members of Client Service Teams should be prepared for such moves.

2. Sharing and applying our knowledge of the client's business

Lead Partners and key members of the Client Service Team have a responsibility to keep at the forefront of their Line of Business through attendance and participation in industry conferences, trade events, KPMG's business schools and other forums where industry expertise is developed and shared. Plus encourage active use of K-World.

3. Knowing the state of our relationships

The nature of the relationship – formal or informal, demanding or relaxed, social or business – needs to be carefully matched to the culture and expectations of the client.

We can gain an impression of the state of our relationships by continuously seeking informal feedback.

4. Account planning

Systematic account planning, which takes into consideration all our current products and services, is essential if we are to serve our clients effectively and develop the account to the full.

5. Performance management

Clear and unambiguous personal targets are the foundation for success.

It is vital that we think and act globally. This is why an element of the financial remuneration of Lead Partners is now based on global as well as national peformance.

6. Communication and collaboration

Lead Partners represent to their clients a single, accessible, top-level point of contact with the power to make things happen.

A suite of collaboration tools is being made available to help Client Service Teams. For example, the Web-based software called KClient provides a powerful means of engagement management and communications with the client.

7. Sharing and adopting best practice to win business

However, it is important that our Client Service Teams seek out and make use of the best practice that is available and that the best practice they develop or come across is similarly shared. Again the use of K-World was recommended.

partner. These teams are going through the same development programme as for global clients. These arrangements are not forced on countries but it is now self-sustaining because they see the benefits. The focus has been on the quality of the relationship with the clients. It is not just about technical adequacy, which is regarded as essential, not a differentiator.

Reward systems had also been changed. Rewards for lines of business chairs and global lead partners were at least partly based on global performance. Alastair Johnston believed that it was 'recognised that a global lead partner is one of the top roles in the firm. It is no longer the case that to get to the top of KPMG you have to go into line management.'

At the International Partners' Conference in Berlin in 2000, Alastair Johnston was able to report considerable success: 100 global client teams had been set up; 200 workshops on best practice had been conducted; there were account plans for 70 per cent of global accounts and these plans crossed KPMG disciplines and functions; over 50 per cent of proposals they put forward for new clients had been won with very low attrition of current clients. He believed that the main reason for this was that they were 'getting the power of alignment: we are all more visibly singing from the same song sheet'.

KNOWLEDGE AND KNOWLEDGE MANAGEMENT

A second major priority for development by the IET was the management of knowledge across the firm. Peter Chivers, head of knowledge management in the UK, acknowledged that the attempted merger with Ernst & Young (EY) had made a significant impact in KPMG:

One realisation was that EY was much more centrally controlled. Decisions were taken at its centre which committed the world: whereas a decision in KPMG required consultation with 40 senior partners.

EY had also made high levels of investment in technology and infrastructure. What that allowed them to do was to share knowledge across the world. KPMG saw it was weak on technology and the sharing of knowledge. In KPMG there were 13 different e-mail systems at the time and lots of local knowledge management initiatives. There was me in the UK, someone in the US and in Amsterdam. That was it on knowledge management. EY had over 300 people on knowledge management in Cleveland.

Prior to the negotiations with EY, Colin Sharman had realised that knowledge management was important because there was potential for reusing and learning from what we had done. Moreover, clients were requiring that we were better informed about their industries. Also, global clients were expecting common levels of service across the world. For example, we lost SAS/Volvo audit because the client demanded that KPMG could demonstrate knowledge sharing within the firm and with them and we were seen wanting.

Following the decision not to merge, in February 1998 there was a decision taken to identify and establish what should be done. The firm has allocated $100m a year since then to develop knowledge management and K-World. K-World was to do with knowledge sharing through the Internet, collaboration with clients and the ability to communicate with clients and potential clients. It provided a facility which can be accessed by 90,000 people around the world to get at the best information available within the firm. So it is valuable from an assurance point of view. And there is tangible evidence within KPMG that we are doing something on knowledge management. There have been some real benefits: with proposals it takes five hours rather than five days to get together information. It is difficult to get measures of success: but if we didn't have it, we would be behind others. Certainly previously EY and PWC would attack us on this as a weakness.

However, there were some problems arising from what some saw as exaggerated claims for K-World by its US architects. Peter Chivers:

> There is a lack of recognition from the US of different cultures around the world. For example, some of the advanced publicity was about how great it was. My impression was that in the US if you promise a Rolls-Royce they don't expect one: but in Europe they do. In practice, the incremental benefit depended on how advanced national systems were. Those countries who had little in the way of knowledge management thought it was marvellous. Those who already had effective national arrangements found it offered little incremental benefit over what already existed except as a portal to other systems. So there was some loss of credibility.

GLOBAL RESTRUCTURING

Increasingly the potential conflict between global management of the firm and the traditional national federated structure had to be resolved. For example, Eddie Oliver recognised the achievements of the IET but commented:

> It has been a remarkable achievement under the circumstances. If you looked at KPMG's constitution you would think you could not operate globally. The fact that we do is a tremendous tribute to the individuals who achieve it. But we've got to get the global structure right so that it doesn't take such Herculean efforts to serve global clients.

Increasingly it was recognised that any form of global strategy was vulnerable to national decisions. For example, in 1999 the Canadian partnership announced that it intended to leave KPMG. It was only the timely intervention of Paul Reilly and the IET that prevented this.

There had already begun to emerge the idea that there were, in fact, three major regions within KPMG: the US, Europe and Asia Pacific. Steve Butler, who had taken over as International Chairman from Colin Sharman in 1999, announced a restructuring of the firm to transfer power from national practices to these three regions at the partners' conference in Berlin in September 2000, stating that 'the tradition of allowing national practices a high degree of autonomy was outdated and increasingly unwieldy' (*Financial Times*, 18 September 2000). In an interview with the *Financial Times* he went on to comment that 'none of the big professional services firms offered the global services increasingly demanded by clients'. He insisted that KPMG was moving towards this but there was still need to improve the ability to bring expertise together. The decision to move to the three regions would mean: 'we are not going to destroy the existing national organisations, but they are going to become less and less meaningful in terms of how we manage the business'.

In fact, in Europe, there had already been moves towards further integration: but not without its problems. Eddie Oliver explained:

In Europe there were two stages envisaged for integration. The first was establishing the Anchor Practice. The idea was that the UK, Germany, Holland and France would integrate. The second stage was that all the other European practices would join it. It is under way but is it moving fast enough? There is a shared view of where we're going but different opinions about how quickly we need to move – influenced, no doubt, by the different characteristics of national economies. The UK view is that time is of the essence.

THE CONSULTANCY IPO[1]

As this move towards global restructuring occurred, there developed another restructuring issue: the separation of the consultancy practice from the rest of KPMG. Eddie Oliver explained:

The US firm decided on an IPO of consultancy – driven by commercial and regulatory pressures. There was a need for finance for investment in systems integration and to acquire other organisations, which it wanted to pay by paper and not cash. Also in the US there was an inability to offer recruits stock options. KPMG in the US also needed money for its pension funds and an IPO was a way of getting this. Also, they saw the regulator getting more concerned not to allow audit firms to do consulting. These trends were spotted by KPMG in the US earlier than the other big firms.

They formed consultancy into a separate organisation and incorporated it. Cisco took a 20 per cent stake. The original idea was that it would still somehow be linked to KPMG. An independent firm but part of a KPMG family. Step by step we have realised that this will not be possible. They will be separate.

It then became clear that if US consulting did this, the situation became untenable for others. Our whole consultancy strategy was geared to being a UK arm of a US-led global company because so many of our clients have US headquarters or have huge interests in the US. If we cannot do US work, we cannot do global work.

At the moment, we are operating under a co-operation agreement with the US consulting firm. But we intend to bring global consulting together in a single entity. One way of achieving this would be for the US practice to buy other consulting practices. There will then be a global US-led consulting firm.

FUTURE CHALLENGES

The restructuring into regions and the IPO gave rise to significant challenges by 2001, not least for Europe. However, there were other challenges. Eddie Oliver:

If you take consulting out of KPMG US, revenues from the European firms are greater than those of the US. So KPMG is not then a US-dominated firm. The three powerful countries are the US, the UK and Germany. The big opportunity is the chance for a global firm which is not US dominated. The difficulty is that the US, the UK and Germany have to agree and there are huge cultural differences. For example, the way audit has developed is different. The accountancy profession in the US has not gained the standing that it has in the UK. In the UK we aim to be the CEO adviser: they are

---

[1]IPO = initial public offering.

a more traditional audit practice. They don't always seem to share our aspiration to move up the value chain. Corporate finance is critical to KPMG in the UK but not in the US. Some European practices have successful legal practices and we're building one in the UK. The US firm doesn't do it. These differences are barriers to globalisation and hence regionalisation makes sense.

But there were other challenges:

The world out there is US led with firms with more command and control: and I think they are all ahead of us in globalising their operations. PWC dominates the market and is US dominated. EY have sold consulting and are US led: they are ahead of us on globalisation. Deloitte-Touche is US led and is advancing strongly currently.

Some people in KPMG think that it is possible that the big five accountants will choose strategic paths which are truly distinctive and differentiated. The firms would be different in management. For example, KPMG would be non US-dominated. They may also be different on products such as whether they all continue to do statutory audits. It might also be that one goes for value added, dropping statutory audits, and another gets really smart on low margin, volume work. I could see a scenario where KPMG could be a global leader in five years or just as credibly another where it would not survive. Some of these forces are in its own hands and some are not.

One of those factors was the future of auditing: Eddie Oliver again:

If the regulators insisted on the separation of audit from everything else it would be a real problem. The present model has two key advantages. It gives clients access to multi-disciplinary services. And it enables us to offer the variety of experience that talented knowledge workers are seeking. Separated from the rest of KPMG, statutory audit would soon become a low value-add commodity.

It was an issue echoed by Peter Chivers:

In audit you will get a file electronically from the client. You will be looking for value-added services on risk, on benchmarking, on profit improvement, on profiling versus competitors. There is an issue for the profession of whether the statutory audit remains the best springboard for the provision of these value-added services.

By 2001 it was clear that the traditional accountancy profession was in a state of significant change: and change which was, in the view of Peter Chivers, highly unpredictable:

For years I thought I could see two or three years ahead. I'm doing well now if I can see much beyond six months.

(The Appendix sets out the fee split for major accountancy firms in 2000 by region and services offered.)

APPENDIX FEE SPLIT FOR MAJOR ACCOUNTANCY FIRMS IN 2000

Regional fee split for leading accountancy firms (%)

FIRM	TOTAL FEES $ MILLION	EUROPE, MIDDLE EAST & AFRICA	AMERICAS	ASIA PACIFIC	OTHER
KPMG (Sept. 2000)	13,500	42%	49%	9%	–
Arthur Andersen (Aug. 2000)	8,400	33%	49%	13%	5%
PricewaterhouseCoopers (June 2000)	21,500	41%	49%	10%	–
Ernst & Young (June 2000)	9,200	N/A	N/A	N/A	–
Deloitte Touche Tohmatsu (May 2000)	11,200	N/A	N/A	N/A	–

Notes:
KPMG: figures are taken from year end press release.

AA: figures are taken from year end press release. Corporate finance revenues are not broken down geographically and are shown in 'other'.

PwC: figures are taken from year end press release.

EY: figures are taken from year end press release; no fee split is available for DTT globally.

DTT: figures are taken from year end press release; no fee split is available for DTT globally.

International fee split for leading accountancy firms (%)

FIRM	ASSURANCE	TAX & LEGAL	CONSULTING	OTHER
KPMG (Sept. 2000)	41	21	29	9
Arthur Andersen (Aug. 2000)	45	30	19	6
PricewaterhouseCoopers (June 2000)	39	19	31	11
Ernst & Young (June 2000)	57	34	–	9
Deloitte Touche Tohmatsu (May 2000)	N/A	N/A	N/A	N/A

Notes:
KPMG: figures are taken from year end press release. The 'other' data largely comprises FAS revenues.

AA: figures are taken from year end press release. The 'other' data largely comprises CF revenues.

PwC: figures are taken from year end press release. The 'other' data includes FAS, BPO (Business Process Outsourcing) and GHRS (Global Human Resource Solutions) revenues.

EY: data is estimated by the International Accounting Bulletin. EY sold their consulting arm to Cap Gemini in May 2000.

DTT: no fee split is available for DTT globally.

Marks and Spencer

Nardine Collier

Marks and Spencer became a household name, first in the UK and then internationally. However, in the late 1990s it suffered a reversal in its fortunes. This case study gives an account of how commentators explained that decline, and how the management at Marks and Spencer sought to introduce and manage changes to improve performance.

● ● ●

Michael Marks began what was to become one of the most recognised brands in the UK and eventually across the world by establishing a penny bazaar in the late 1880s. It was a huge success, with the majority of products only costing one penny. Marks rapidly expanded his business, and soon decided that he needed a partner to help perform all the responsibilities a growing organisation brings. Tom Spencer, a cashier of Marks' supplier, was recommended and from this partnership Marks and Spencer (M&S) steadily grew.

THE M&S FORMULA FOR SUCCESS

Simon Marks took over the running of M&S from his father. He was aggressive with his ideas for the organisation, and went to America to investigate how they were running their stores. On his return to Britain he made a number of changes to the penny bazaars, firstly by turning them into stores, establishing a simple pricing policy and introducing the 'St Michael' logo as a sign of quality. There was a feeling of camaraderie and close-knit family atmosphere within the stores, and this was compounded by employing staff whom the managers believed would 'fit in' and become part of that family. The staff were also treated better and paid more than sales assistants in other organisations. The family nature of this firm dominated top management too: until the late 1970s the board was made up of family members only.

Simon Marks was renowned for his personal control over the business and his attention to detail. According to a Channel 4 TV programme (25 February 2001) his was a style of top-down management which could often take the form of shouting and even bullying. This concern for control also manifested itself in the way Marks dealt with suppliers. He always used the same UK-based suppliers and meticulously ensured that the goods were exactly to specification; a relationship designed to ensure high and consistent quality.

Until the late 1990s M&S had been hugely successful in terms of both profit and market share. It worked to achieve this esteem by applying a structured formula to all its operations and maintained it by establishing a set of fundamental principles which were held as core to the organisation and used in all of its business activities. In his book *Marks and Spencer: An anatomy of Britain's most efficiently managed company*, Tse (1982) described these principles as being:

1 to offer our customers a selective range of high-quality, well designed and attractive merchandise at reasonable prices under the brand name St Michael;

2 to encourage suppliers to use the most modern and efficient production techniques;

3 to work with suppliers to ensure the highest standards of quality control;

4 to provide friendly, helpful service and greater shopping comfort and convenience to our customers;

5 to improve the efficiency of the business, by simplifying operating procedures;

6 to foster good human relations with customers, suppliers and staff and in the communities in which we trade.

Other components of this formula were developed. M&S always used British suppliers, believing that they delivered the highest quality products, whilst most other retailers sourced merchandise from overseas to keep costs down. Its specialist buyers operated from a central buying office from which goods were allocated to the stores: a formula which stood M&S in good stead for most of its years. The store managers followed central direction on merchandising, layout, store design, training, and so on. Every M&S store was identical in the procedures it followed, leading to a consistency of image and a guarantee of M&S standards. However, it also meant conformity, with very little local discretion. Store managers were severely restricted in how they could respond to the local needs of customers and could do little that departed from central direction.

During M&S's growth period there were few changes in its methods of operation or to its strategies. It stocked generic clothing ranges with a wide appeal to the public: buyers often made choices which would outlast the current fashion and trends seen in other high street retailers. Its reputation for good quality clothing was built on basics, the essentials which every customer needed; for example, its reputation for womenswear was built on underwear, jumpers and skirts. As it did not have fitting rooms until the 1990s, all assistants carried tape measures with them and M&S would give a 'no quibble' refund to any customer who was unhappy with the product he/she had purchased. Because its products remained in the stores all year round for most of its history it never held sales. It priced its goods at a 'reasonable' level while emphasising the products' high quality: a claim which it believed was readily accepted not least because of its insistence on using British suppliers. (More than 90 per cent of the suppliers M&S used were British.) It liked this relationship as it felt it could develop the suppliers' skills and it would not be able to do this with inaccessible overseas manufacturers. It also believed its customers thought that they

Exhibit 1	Marks and spencer customer satisfaction survey results		
	MARCH 1995	**MARCH 1998**	**SEPT' 1999**
Viewed positively	71%	62%	45%
Value for money	69%	57%	45%

Source: *The Money Programme*, 1 November 2000.

received higher quality from British suppliers. This often led to the situation where the supplier was reliant on M&S as M&S bought up all the stock the supplier could manufacture: but it also meant that M&S came to be reliant on particular suppliers.

The success of M&S continued into the 1990s, with ever-rising profits and share prices. Richard Greenbury, the chief executive from 1991, explained this success as follows:

> I think that the simple answer is that we followed absolutely and totally the principles of the business with which I was embued . . . I ran the business with the aid of my colleagues based upon the very long-standing, and proven ways of running it.
>
> (Radio 4, August 2000)

This commitment from the very top to the M&S way of doing things had been evident since the time of Simon Marks and for succeeding chief executives. Indeed, chief executives of M&S were renowned for their attention to detail in terms of supplier control, merchandise and store layout; and it had seemed to work. The success of M&S under Simon Marks was often attributed to his understanding of customer preferences and trends. However, because of this same phenomenon, it could also mean that buyers tended to select merchandise which they knew chief executives would approve of. For example, the BBC's *Money Programme* (1 November 2000) reported that, since it was known that Richard Greenbury did not want M&S to be at the cutting edge of fashion, buyers concentrated on the types of product they knew he would like – 'classic, wearable fashions'.

The same programme also reported on the problems of centralised authority; on one occasion Richard Greenbury had decided that to control costs there would be fewer full-time sales assistants in stores. Although this led to an inability in stores to meet the service levels required by M&S, when Greenbury visited those stores, store managers ensured they were fully staffed by bringing in all full-time, part-time and Saturday staff so that it appeared that stores were giving levels of service that, at other times, they were not.

It also meant that there was sometimes little disagreement with policies sent down from the top, so that decisions might remain unchallenged even when executives or store operations managers were concerned about negative effects of policies and decisions. The same *Money Programme* claimed that customer satisfaction surveys which showed decreasing satisfaction throughout the late 1990s (see Exhibit 1) were kept from Greenbury by senior executives, who felt that he might be annoyed by the results.

Commenting to the *Money Programme*, Greenbury stated that he never saw the results from customer surveys, and used sales figures and visits to stores as the basis to make judgements on how M&S was operating.

A HITCH IN THE FORMULA

M&S's problems began to hit the headlines in October 1998 when it halted its expansion programme in Europe and America.

The expansion programme had begun in the early 1990s when M&S had moved into a number of overseas markets, where it implemented its tried and trusted formula. In America M&S operated as Brooks Brothers, and in Canada it opened 22 stores by entering into a joint venture. It also opened in France as a basis for expansion throughout Europe. It had previously stated that it would spend £130m a year on the expansion until 2001, as it was essential for the organisation's long-term progress. However, in 1998 it instructed its US subsidiary Brooks Brothers to cut spending. It was also known that M&S was considering whether to abandon the expansion plans in the US, where it had wanted to increase retail space by 17 per cent. Indeed, it admitted to having financial difficulties worldwide, having been hampered by tough trading conditions which had seen many retailers have sales even though their new ranges had just been released.

In November M&S announced a 23 per cent decline in first-half profits, causing its shares to fall drastically. Sir Richard Greenbury, chairman and CEO, blamed the competitive environment, saying that it was turbulent and that M&S had lost sales to its competitors. Competitors were eroding market share, from the top and bottom ends of the retail market. Competitors at the top end of the market were niche organisations such as The Gap, Oasis and Next, offering similarly priced goods, yet more design focused with up-to-date fashions, and from which obvious comparisons could be made against the more traditional M&S merchandise. Furthermore, these stores were attracting the customers who would have naturally moved on to become M&S customers. At the bottom end of the market there was competition from discount stores, such at Matalan, and supermarkets, such as the 'George' range at Asda. These stores were competing against M&S by offering essential and basic ranges of clothing, but at significantly lower prices. Moreover, Tesco and Sainsbury's moved into offering added value foods, which had been pioneered by M&S.

It was frequently reported in the press that M&S no longer understood or reacted to its customers' needs. It had misread its target market, and could not understand that those customers who purchased its food or underwear might not necessarily want to buy products from its home furnishings range.

It was seen to have been too complacent and ignoring changes in the domestic market which have now caught up with it.

(*Financial Times*, 16 January 1999)

Analysts commented that M&S had continued too long with its traditional risk-aversive formula and ignored the changes in the marketplace. Its competitors, meanwhile, were being praised for improving their performance as they quickly reacted to the changes.

Although Greenbury had blamed the competitive environment for the difficulties M&S had been experiencing, a Channel 4 programme (25 February 2001) felt that it was his focus on the day-to-day operations of the organisation rather than long-term strategy that had been the problem. The programme also highlighted that M&S was firmly placed in the 'middle ground', tied to a generalised view of the market, instead of trying to understand and tailor that offering to the various segments in the market and how they were emerging and growing.

Commentators tried to make sense of what had happened. M&S did not have a loyalty card at a time when almost every other retailer did. It was accused of having an inward-looking culture. Almost all M&S managers and executives were promoted internally, starting at the bottom of the organisation, and becoming immersed in the routines and established traditions of M&S, a culture that had been established, and continually reinforced, since the creation of M&S. Observers also pointed to the fact that, although a large proportion of M&S customers were women and much of the merchandise was womenswear, top management was hugely dominated by men. There had never been a CEO of M&S who had not been a member of the founder's family or a lifetime employee. It was believed that the culture was also strongly reinforced by Greenbury and not helped by his autocratic approach. This was, however, denied by Greenbury:

> I would strenuously deny that I was autocratic, what I would say is that I was extremely demanding, I was considered to be tough but fair. When I became chairman, I introduced to the business a method of discussion in the boardroom, and outside of the boardroom that was far reaching down the business in terms of discussing what we were doing. I was like any chairman, I had strong views and if I could persuade people of my views then obviously I tried to do . . . I was chairman and chief executive almost by accident because I was appointed chief executive in 1988 and I became chairman and chief executive in 1991.
>
> (Radio 4, August 2000)

In November 1998, after months of speculation and boardroom arguments, Greenbury announced that he would be stepping down from the CEO position. There then ensued a series of heavily publicised arguments between Keith Oates, Greenbury's deputy, and another senior director, Peter Salsbury, whom the media suggested was Greenbury's favoured successor. The in-fighting at M&S came to a conclusion when Greenbury returned to Britain after a sudden end to his holiday. Greenbury held a five-hour meeting with the board and non-executive directors to determine who would be the successor. However, at the voting the next day, Oates did not attend and elected to take early retirement. Salsbury was appointed as chief executive. This was poorly received by shareholders and the City, where M&S shares fell 25¼p. Analysts commented that, as Salsbury had only worked in womenswear, one of the worst-performing units in M&S, it might have been wiser to bring in an outsider (Channel 4, 25 February 2001).

During this period of boardroom scuffles, the problems M&S were encountering were further compounded by its £192m purchase of 19 Littlewoods department stores, on the grounds that they were situated in prime locations and complemented the existing M&S stores. M&S had acquired the stores with the aim of refurbishing them (at a cost of £100m) so that their full range of products could be stocked at city central locations. However, the difficulties began to arise during the refurbishment programme, as not only were Little-woods being refurbished but so were the existing M&S stores. The disruption caused by the double refurbishment had a far worse effect on the customers than M&S had predicted, leading Greenbury to describe the clothing section as a 'bloodbath'. In hindsight he thought that the problems M&S faced had com-pounded upon each other:

> We decided, as a board, to invest very heavily in the next decade, so from 1997 to 1999 we embarked upon a massive capital investment programme, set at well over £2 billion . . . It comprises all sorts of things: infrastructure, expenditure, distribution, tilling, it involved the purchase of selected Littlewoods stores to increase our footage in major city centres, property acquisitions, all on top of what was a fairly aggressive investment and expansion plan already. We then decided to accelerate our business overseas, so I think it is very clear that it became an even more competitive market than certainly any of us had anticipated.
>
> (Radio 4, August 2000)

In January 1999 M&S announced its second profits warning. This caused a rapid sell-off of M&S shares. M&S blamed customers, who, it believed, had been unwilling to pay full price for products over the Christmas period, espe-cially when they could buy similar clothes at cheaper prices from some of M&S's competitors. Furthermore, it overestimated its sales and bought £250m worth of stock. The excess stock then had to be heavily discounted for a quick sale so that storage space could be freed for the next season's stock. There were also a number of problems with its European operations. M&S had been pursuing a series of rapid expansion initiatives in the European market. Many of the European countries were difficult to expand in, for example Germany where M&S reacted to any opportunities for expansion that arose. However, these stores' performance had been worsening over the previous months, totalling a cost of £25m. They continued to show no signs of improvement, and so a programme was put in place to gradually close most of the European stores.

NEW TACTICS

To overcome the difficulties M&S had been facing, and in an attempt to regain confidence, Salsbury began to implement a reorganisation strategy, splitting the company into three: UK retail business, overseas business and financial services. His plans also involved establishing an organisation-wide marketing department to break down the power of the traditional buying fiefdoms which were established around product lines. Salsbury wanted the marketing depart-ment to adopt a customer-focused approach, rather than allowing the buyers to dictate what the stores should stock.

By April 1999 Salsbury had devised a large-scale promotional campaign to try to restore its image as an innovative retailer offering unique quality products.

To coincide with this, M&S launched new clothing and food ranges. Salsbury also issued a memorandum explaining that he wanted to make changes to M&S which would move the organisation away from its bureaucratic culture. One way Salsbury felt this could be achieved was by creating a decision-making environment that wasn't encumbered by hierarchy. He wanted to challenge the traditional ways that M&S operated, as he believed these could be the root cause of its problems. However, by May Salsbury was forced to announce a severe drop in trading and a halving of profits. He then outlined more measures he would take in order to alter the perception of M&S. As well as stripping away further layers of hierarchy, M&S would take a lifestyle approach to buying and presenting products. For example, previously M&S had placed together all types of trousers, even to the extent of separating suits. One analysis commented:

> M&S has behaved more like a wholesale buyer of products . . . rather than thinking about the sort of person that was buying the item and what else they could sell to that customer.
>
> (*Financial Times*, 19 May 1999)

M&S also established a property division to enable it to charge rents to the individual stores; this was done to make store managers more accountable for their branches' actions, failures and achievements.

In mid-June Greenbury retired a year earlier than in his contract; a decision which came just before the board were meant to enter a three-day meeting to discuss 'a few hundred pages of its new strategy'. Salsbury commented:

> What we are doing has moved away from his [Greenbury's] methodology and thought processes and decisions were reached without him being able to have an input.
>
> (*Financial Times*, 23 June 1999)

In another attempt to slow its decline in profits, July saw the closure of six of M&S's European stores, a reduction in the size of its head office, and the closure of all its 38 Canadian stores, which had been operating at a loss for 24 out of 25 years of trading (*Financial Times*, 10 July 1999). Meanwhile, in the UK market M&S began to implement a costly store change strategy. It commissioned design consultants to create a new store image. The pilot store displayed new lighting and flooring to create a mood which 'looks to the future with the anticipation of creating change'.

. . . AND MORE PROBLEMS

In September 1999 M&S announced further changes as a result of a strategic business review conducted over the previous 18 months. It stated that it was in the process of, or was, implementing:

- overseas sourcing while severing links with UK suppliers;
- streamlining international operations;
- diversifying into home and Internet shopping;
- creating a department dedicated to identifying new business opportunities.

Shortly after this, there followed yet another profits warning, despite the major investments which had been put into making the stores appear more friendly to customers, a new well-received fashion range, and more staff working on the shop floor to improve customer service. Customers continued to voice their concerns regarding the clothing range, however, commenting that it was difficult to see the difference in the positioning of work and casual-style clothes. Customer comments were reported in the press, such as:

> There are so many items here to find and they don't tend to segregate it out, so there's something I might like next to something my granny might like.
>
> (*Financial Times*, 28 September 1999)

In November 1999 M&S had more bad news for its shareholders when it revealed that its shares had fallen to 250¾p, the lowest price since 1991. By December there were stories of acquisitions. Some of the groups cited as being interested in acquiring M&S were Tesco, American pension fund companies, and Philip Green, the retail entrepreneur. One analyst stated:

> If it wasn't for these take-over stories the shares would be down to about 200p now and the business would be looking very vulnerable.
>
> (*Financial Times*, 14 December 2000)

However, other observers believed that an acquisition would not really be the answer. They felt that there continued to remain deep structural problems in the marketplace, as there were high costs of entry and maintenance to remain in the clothing market.

In an effort to counteract the acquisitions, and to restore the wavering faith in the company, M&S set about implementing another management restructure to become more customer focused. It attempted to achieve this by splitting into seven business units: womenswear, menswear, children's wear, lingerie, food, home, and beauty. Executives were appointed at just below board level to head the units, reporting directly to Salsbury, who believed that the flatter structure allowed it to be more responsive to market changes and customer needs.

A NEW HORIZON

January 2000 did not just bring a new millennium, but also a new chairman for M&S. Belgian-born Luc Vandevelde was appointed with a two-year contract (most executives only received one year), a £2.2m 'golden hello', and a salary of £1.3m a year plus share options. The 48-year-old Vandevelde was employed in the position of executive chairman. Salsbury was to remain in charge of the day-to-day business.

In taking the position at M&S, Vandevelde left his managing director role at Promodés, the French food retailer, which ranged from operating convenience stores to hypermarkets. There he had achieved a sixfold increase in the value of its stock, and before leaving, had finalised the sale of Promodés to Carrefour, thus creating the second largest retailer in the world. This was the first time that anyone from outside the organisation had been appointed to the position of chairman at M&S, and many commented that it showed an indication that M&S had plans to develop as more of an international retailer.

Vandevelde said that he wanted to revitalise the domestic brand and then go overseas with an extensive expansion plan. Further, he wanted M&S to become a multi-format retailer, as was Promodés. Analysts observed that this would certainly require a major culture change for the organisation.

By February, M&S promised an extra 4,000 staff who would operate on the shop floor. By directly serving and helping customers, M&S felt it was offering a more personal and improved service. It also entered into deals with two football clubs as part of its plan to tailor stores geographically and unveiled a new collection of clothes designed by haute couture fashion designers exclusively for M&S. Purchasing of the clothing range was also shifted to almost 100 per cent Asian sources.

In March 2000, M&S declared a dramatic overhaul to its brand. It planned a new corporate image. It stopped using its famous green carrier bags and downgraded the once acclaimed, and seemingly invaluable, St Michael brand, in a move which would have shocked the founders and past CEOs of the organisation. The plans encompassed a complete overhaul of the organisation, as the stores, uniforms, packaging and labelling all had to be altered to fit with the new image. Vandevelde said he thought the changes were 'evolutionary rather than revolutionary' (*Financial Times*, 13 March 2000).

M&S stated that it had identified that customers were confused about the differences between the St Michael and Marks and Spencer brands and felt that it needed to use one distinctive brand which everyone could understand. The new-look M&S brand was then displayed, in a range of colours each indicating different departments. The St Michael brand was relegated to inside clothing labels as a symbol of quality and trust.

Vandevelde also began to change M&S's supply chain. He grouped the stores on the bases of demographic characteristics and lifestyle patterns, instead of operating with the old system whereby stores were allocated merchandise dependent on floor space. Under the old system, stores of the same size were sent the same clothes regardless of location or customer profiles. This new move was widely accepted and received positively as being one of the first major steps to becoming customer focused.

Vandevelde conducted numerous interviews with widely regarded newspapers and publications in an effort to raise his and his organisation's profile and awareness, mainly with the City, investors and shareholders. In an interview with the *Financial Times* (4 April 2000) he admitted that in the past M&S had lost its way in a fast-changing market where new competitors were making the rules. He argued that the strategies he intended to implement would not involve drastic changes to the board or the structure of the organisation, and added:

> I think in the glory days of M&S everybody felt proud to be associated . . . it drove our reputation and our share price up to levels that we may not have deserved. Whereas when things started going slightly sour I guess everybody just exaggerated and we probably were punished a bit more than we deserved. Understanding that is important . . .

There is one general theme and that is that we are probably too 'push' and not enough 'pull' orientated . . . this is echoing a theme that the group was not focused sufficiently on the customers. Today it is much more difficult to come up with real unique propositions and customers are much more intelligent and have minds of their own, so they don't wait for a retailer to tell them to come by. We have got to start with the customer and work our way backwards . . .

It was only when I started getting ideas about the stores in Germany and Belgium and later on in the US that I started to have a benchmark to be able to compare practices to see what worked better and where there might be some possible leverages. I think that because of geographic distance [of the overseas stores] and because they have been less influenced by whatever atmosphere may have been created in the UK, they have probably felt free to start experimenting with a certain number of ideas that were probably difficult to get done here.

(*Financial Times*, 4 April 2000)

He explained that stores outside the UK had developed their own strategies which were tailored to the needs of the local market. Vandevelde hoped that the ideas and strategies which had been implemented overseas would provide leverages which could also be exploited in the UK stores.

In May 2000 M&S announced its figures for the year, reporting £8.2bn of sales, the same as the previous year, and a fall in profit from £628.4m to £557.2m. So despite the new measures and strategies there was no visible improvement. M&S's stakeholders were also unimpressed after receiving the first cut in their dividend, seeing it fall to 9p from 14p. Salsbury commented that they had managed to slow the sales decrease, and that customers had noticed a difference in the stores and products: the dividend cut was made so that future investment capacity was not compromised.

THE FUTURE

Vandevelde wanted to look towards the future instead of concentrating on the past. Once he had stabilised M&S in the UK he planned to relaunch the organisation internationally. He also outlined his strategy for the year, beginning with four overarching priorities, which again had the objective of moving the business closer to the customer.

1 Creating clear profit centres
2 Creating a customer-facing organisation
3 Restoring overseas profitability
4 Building the financial services sector

He was confident that this would enable M&S to start on a path of sustained recovery. He aimed to achieve these objectives by a further restructuring of the organisation into five operating divisions: UK retail; international retail; financial services; property and ventures. Within the UK retail division seven customer business units were established, and to ensure customer focus each unit would have dedicated buying and selling teams. M&S also created a Customer Insight Unit (CIU) after reviewing with customers the perceptions of the M&S brand. The CIU would perform in-depth research with customers to gain an understanding of shopping habits and their demographics. Vandevelde said that after starting in-depth research they had identified that one in five items from the clothing range was the wrong type of offering for the stores' local market.

As for the stores, a series of different formats would be launched; there would be further modernising of stores; more customer advisers on the shop floor; and the opening of three prototype stores where all new initiatives and concepts would be tested.

At the end of 2000 M&S disclosed its plans to offer clothes at a discounted price of 30 per cent in factory outlet malls. The malls would be used to sell excess stock, something which its more aggressive competitors had been doing for a number of years. Although this would mean that M&S could clear space in stores for new stock and recoup money from slow-selling items quicker than if they had to wait for sales, commentators wondered what loyal customers would think when the clothes, to which they attributed a certain standard of quality and price, were being sold 30 to 50 per cent cheaper.

WHERE FROM THERE?

In September 2000 Salsbury retired from M&S. Analysts, journalists and commentators agreed that the road ahead for Vandevelde and M&S would be a tricky one, especially when trying to serve the local needs of nearly 300 stores, while at the same time embracing the benefits of globalisation. Although Vandevelde was extremely optimistic, Greenbury did not believe M&S would ever regain the position it once held:

> Do I think in the foreseeable future that it will go back to making those kind of returns? The answer is, I think, it is extremely unlikely.

> (Radio 4, August 2000)

At the end of March 2001, M&S announced its plans to withdraw from Europe and America. Brooks Brothers was put up for sale, as were the remaining 38 branches which were operating in Europe. Its stores in Hong Kong were sold to franchises. M&S also closed its 'Direct' catalogue operations at a cost of £300m. Vandevelde explained that the disposals were necessary so that M&S could focus on its core domestic clothing. To complement this, George Davies, founder of Next and creator of the 'George at Asda' clothing range, was brought in to design a new range of clothes for M&S.

Sources

BBC2 'Sparks at Marks', *The Money Programme*, 1 November 2000.

Beaver, G. (1999) 'Competitive advantage and corporate governance: shop soiled and needing attention, the case of Marks and Spencer plc', *Strategic Change*, 8, 325–34.

Channel 4 *Inside Marks and Spencer*, 25 February 2001.

Radio 4 Interview with Sir Richard Greenbury, 22 August 2000.

Rees, Goranwy (1969) *St Michael: A history of Marks and Spencer*, Wiedenfeld and Nicolson, London.

Tse, K.K. (1985) *Marks and Spencer: Anatomy of Britain's most efficiently managed company*, Pergamon Press, Oxford.

APPENDIX MARKS AND SPENCER GROUP FINANCIAL RECORD, 1997–2000

	2000 (£M)	1999 (£M)	1998 (£M)	1997* (£M)
Profit and loss account				
Turnover	8,195.5	8,224.0	8,243.3	7,841.9
Operating profit/loss before exceptional operating costs	543.0	600.5	1,050.5	1,700.2
Exceptional operating costs	−72.0	−88.5	53.2	–
Total operating profit/loss	471.0	512.0	1,103.7	1,037.9
Profit/loss on sale of property/fixed assets	−22.3	6.2	−2.8	−1.8
Net interest payable	14.2	27.9	54.1	65.9
Profit/loss on ordinary activities before taxation	417.2	546.1	1,155.0	1,102.0
Taxation	−158.2	−176.1	−338.7	−346.1
Profit/loss on ordinary activities after taxation	259.3	370.0	816.3	755.9
Minority interests	−0.6	2.1	−0.4	−1.3
Dividends	−258.6	−413.3	−409.1	−368.6
Retained profit/loss for the year	0.1	−41.2	406.8	386.0
Balance sheets				
Fixed assets	4,298.4	4,448.7	4,034.5	3,646.5
Net current assets	3,717.1	3,355.9	3,401.5	3,204.2
Short-term creditors	2,162.8	2,029.8	2,345.0	1,775.1
Long-term creditors	804.3	772.6	187.2	495.8
Provisions for liabilities and charges	126.6	105.0	31.0	31.8
Net assets	4,921.8	4,897.2	4,872.8	4,548.0
Equity shareholders' funds	4,905.3	4,883.9	4,853.7	4,529.3
Statistics				
Earnings/loss per share (p)	9.0	13.0p	28.6p	26.7p
Adjusted earnings/loss per share (p)	13.2	15.8p	27.3p	26.7p
Dividends per share (p)	9.0	14.4p	14.3p	13.0p

* Marks and Spencer altered its accounting practices in 1998 and therefore the figures for 1997 are not strictly comparable with those from 1998, 1999 and 2000.

DOWNFALL AT XEROX

This case study is based substantially on the cover story in Business Week, *5 March 2001. It is concerned with the decline in fortunes of the Xerox Corporation; and in particular with the role of strategic leadership, CEO succession and boardroom activity in this.*

• • •

One morning in May 2000, G. Richard Thoman arrived for work to find an urgent summons from Paul A. Allaire, the man he had replaced as chief executive of Xerox Corp. just 13 months earlier. Allaire, who had remained as chairman, was waiting next door in his office at Xerox headquarters. A man of few words even on happy occasions, Allaire delivered the bad news without preamble. He said that Thoman's colleagues had lost confidence in him and that the next afternoon the board would announce his resignation. In other words, Thoman, who had left IBM in 1997 to join Xerox as heir apparent to Allaire, would be out of a job in about 30 hours. Thoman was livid, but obligingly fell on the sword Allaire handed him. Late the next day, after the board had announced Allaire's reinstatement as CEO, Thoman sat alone in a Xerox conference room and fielded calls from the press. 'The board and I agreed that it made more sense to implement our strategy with an internal team,' he told one caller. Actually, he could only guess at what his fellow directors wanted. Thoman had not been invited to the board meeting or even asked to defend himself by speakerphone. He had been fired in absentia, the bizarre but perhaps inevitable outcome of a CEO succession that had begun so promisingly yet ended in utter disaster for Allaire and Xerox no less than for Rick Thoman.

HUGE GAP

Xerox' bungled CEO succession is an object lesson in the difficulty of reinventing an old-line company. For a good 20 years now, Xerox executives have been restructuring, revamping, and repositioning virtually non-stop. But in the last analysis, Allaire's Xerox has been far better at proclaiming the need for change than actually making change. 'There was always a huge gap between the visionary aspirations the company nominally was pursuing and what it actually drove employees to do,' says a former senior Xerox executive.

Exhibit 1	Xerox' history: the highs and lows

Once synonymous with corporate success and technological innovation, Xerox is now struggling with losses and leaden stock – not to mention a reputation for fumbling high-tech opportunities.

1938: Chester Carlson produces first xerographic image in his lab in Astoria, Queens.

1959: Launches the Xerox 914, the first automatic, plain-paper office copier – which becomes the top-selling industrial product of all time.

1961: Shares listed on the New York Stock Exchange. Xerox becomes one of the great growth stocks of the go-go era.

1970: Opens Palo Alto Research Center, birthplace of the personal computer, laser printer, and ethernet; much of the technology goes unexploited by Xerox.

1982: Visionary leader David T. Kearns becomes CEO, facing a dire competitive threat from Japanese rivals pioneering low-cost copiers.

1983: Begins a disastrous foray into financial services with purchase of Crum & Forster insurance group; later buys brokerage and life insurance companies.

1990: Launches line of digital presses, creating lucrative new market; Paul A. Allaire named chief executive.

1993: Decides to quit financial services; announces first major layoffs, reducing workforce by 10 per cent.

1995: Introduces digital copier, opening vast new market and creating a $3 billion-a-year business. But success blinds it to threat of desktop printers.

1997: Rick Thoman leaves IBM to become president and COO.

1998: Sells Crum & Forster at huge loss; slashes an additional 9,000 jobs, taking $1 billion write-off.

1999: Shares hit peak of $64 as Thoman is named CEO. But quick attempts to overhaul hidebound culture backfire. Earnings and shares plummet. US inkjet printer sales hit $5.2 billion, with 50 per cent controlled by Hewlett-Packard. Xerox logs 2 per cent share.

March 2000: Announces 5,200 more layoffs.

May 2000: Allaire ousts Thoman and returns as CEO.

December 2000: Reports largest quarterly loss under Allaire. Stock hits $7.

January 2001: Announces 4,000 layoffs. Company again forced to deny it has plans to file for Chapter 11 bankruptcy. Leveraged buyout firms begin serious discussions for a minority stake in Xerox.

There was a time when Xerox embodied visionary aspirations realised. Throughout the 1960s, the company was as potent a symbol of the transformational power of technology innovation as Apple Computer Inc. and Microsoft Corp. would be later. (Exhibit 1 outlines Xerox's history.)

Xerox is descended from the Haloid Co., a photographic supply company founded in Rochester, NY, in 1906. Under Joseph C. Wilson, its long-time leader, Haloid spent 14 years and virtually all of its income to develop the 914, the first xerographic copier. Introduced in 1959, the new copier was a money machine nonpareil. By the time the 914 was retired in 1973, it was the biggest-selling industrial product of all time, and Xerox was in the dictionary as a synonym for photocopy. Success spoiled Xerox, in a sense. To sustain its rapid growth, it needed to move beyond copiers, but what could ever measure up to the 70 per cent gross profit margins of the 914? Xerox was defined as 'the copier company' in its very DNA, blinding it to the enormous commercial potential of Palo Alto Research Center's many innovations. Attempts to buy its way into new businesses were equally unsuccessful. Whether it was mainframe computers or financial services, Xerox tended to buy the wrong company at the wrong price and then run it into the ground. Novelty in any form simply was no match for the well-heeled copier bureaucracy – or 'Burox' – spawned by the phenomenal success of the 914.

CUT-PRICE COMPETITION

Burox almost was the death of Xerox. The company's xerography patents began expiring in the early 1970s, and its 95 per cent share of the market dwindled. By 1982, its portion of the US copier business had declined to 13 per cent under an onslaught of cut-price copiers imported from Japan. Through sheer force of personality, CEO David Kearns, a former IBM marketing executive, inspired the Xeroid masses to commit to elaborate Japanese-style programmes to improve product quality and pare manufacturing cost. Rejuvenated, Xerox reclaimed lost market share at home and by 1990 was even taking business away from Canon and Ricoh in Japan.

In keeping with Xerox tradition, Kearns stepped down as CEO in 1990, when he turned 60, and yielded to Allaire. The son of a Massachusetts vegetable farmer turned quarry operator, Allaire had joined Xerox in 1966 and worked his way up through the finance and administration ranks. Kearns remained as chairman, but not for long. Just nine months after Allaire became CEO, Kearns resigned from the board to accept the No. 2 spot at the Education Dept. in the Bush Administration. 'I had zero involvement in Xerox during the two years I was in Washington,' Kearns says now. 'And I never went back on the board.'

Free to act on his belief that Xerox needed new blood, Allaire remade senior management with executives imported from the outside. The two Allaire recruits who would rise to the highest rank were Romeril, formerly finance director of British Telecommunications, and William F. Buehler, an affable sales executive from AT&T. Allaire developed close relationships with both men, especially Buehler, who spent so much time with the boss socially that they were presumed inside the company to be best friends. Buehler, who recently retired, declined to be interviewed.

Kearns brought Xerox back from the abyss in the copier business only to jeopardise its future anew by putting the company into property and casualty insurance on a grand scale. By the time Allaire took over, Xerox' balance sheet had been crippled by billions of dollars in insurance liabilities. This time, Allaire saved Xerox, methodically disentangling the company from insurance and other financial-services businesses. He also got Xerox' stock moving again with a Street-pleasing mix of cost-cutting and new product introductions, including the first digital copier – Document Center. With great fanfare, Xerox rebranded itself as 'The Document Company' in 1994, signalling its ambition to move far beyond copiers as the growth of desktop computing stimulated huge increases in the number of documents being created.

In keeping with accepted management practice, Allaire had discussed succession prospects with his board a couple times a year since the early 1990s. There were several internal candidates for a time, but none panned out. In late 1996, the board decided to create the new position of president and chief operating officer and to go outside to fill it with someone who could move up to CEO in a year or two. Through the executive-recruiting firm Ramsey Beirne Associates, Xerox found Thoman, the 52-year-old chief financial officer of IBM. Says Allaire: 'We were looking for a change agent, and he seemed to be a perfect match.'

BEST SHOT

Thoman had spent his entire business career working for Louis V. Gerstner, first at McKinsey & Co., then American Express and RJR Nabisco. At IBM, Thoman ranked just below Gerstner in the hierarchy but was only a few years younger than his mentor, whose retirement was not imminent in any event. After much soul-searching, Thoman concluded that joining Xerox might be his best shot at becoming CEO of a major company. He met not only with Allaire but with several other executives and directors, impressing one and all with his knowledge and intensity. 'We had such an engaging discussion,' recalls Nicholas. 'Three hours went by like that,' he adds, snapping his fingers.

Thoman boasted a gilt-edged resumé. He had collected four advanced degrees from four different institutions of higher learning, including a PhD in international economics from Tufts University. In 1992, the French government had awarded Thoman, a devoted Francophile, the Legion of Honour for helping build American tourism in France as an executive of American Express. His breadth of business experience also set him apart at Xerox, which was filled with managers who had joined straight from college and never left. Thoman had been chief of corporate strategy at AmEx, president of Nabisco International, and the leader of IBM's restructuring of its personal-computer operation. Xerox shares rose $2 on Thoman's hiring in June 1997. Dispensing with the false modesty usually spooned out on such occasions, Thoman emphasised that he was no mere Mr Fixit. 'I see myself as more of a leader, someone who can size up a situation and act on it quickly,' Xerox' new president declared. 'I came to Xerox to be chief executive.'

BIG DISADVANTAGE

At once cerebral and passionate, Thoman is the corporate equivalent of the Washington policy wonk. Long-time colleagues say he is someone who continually walks around with a hypothesis in his head that he is only too happy to share with anyone he encounters, regardless of corporate station. Thoman likes nothing more than freewheeling, intellectually charged discussion. However, he can at times become overbearingly blunt in his criticism and, like Allaire, is all but incapable of small talk or water-cooler bonhomie. 'Rick can seem haughty,' says a former Xerox colleague generally sympathetic to Thoman. 'He is not really a warm person.'

Inbred Xerox needed Thoman's intellectual energy and outsider's perspective, but in terms of personality this charm-challenged brainiac was a bad fit, as he himself realised. 'To be successful at Xerox, you have to be liked,' he says. 'While everyone likes to be liked, for me it was more important to get things done.'

It didn't take Thoman long to start violating decorum. One of the first things he did was order up a review of the economics of the existing Xerox product line. He was presented with charts showing that Xerox was 'world class' in terms of manufacturing and development costs. 'My response was "How do you know?"' he recalls. 'They told me they'd get back to me.' The third time he got this answer, he put his foot down. It turned out that staffers had relied on a sampling of 1994 market data so limited as to exclude most of Xerox' Japanese competitors. Thoman ordered them back to the drawing board. Weeks later, he finally was presented with evidence that Xerox had failed to maintain its hard-won parity with the Japanese. Says Thoman: 'It was clear to me that we were at a large and material cost disadvantage against the Japanese across the copier market.'

There was not much that could be done to alter the underlying economics, since research and development accounted for two-thirds of total product costs. But the new president did begin agitating for sharp reductions in Xerox' bloated payroll and overhead, which, in Thoman's view, left the company dangerously exposed to price-cutting by more efficient competitors. Allaire, who had engineered a major cost-cutting early in his tenure, recognised the need for further cutbacks, but swift, pre-emptive action had never been his style. Instead, 50 different Xerox management teams spent six months hashing out a complex restructuring plan finally unveiled in April 1998. It set forth 150 different initiatives aimed at saving $1 billion a year in cost cuts and productivity gains. Some 9,000 jobs were to be eliminated, 10 per cent of Xerox' workforce.

Internal tensions were rising but did not appear to be hurting Xerox' performance. Operating income was bounding upward in regular quarterly increments, while revenues now were rising at a double-digit rate. Allaire's early 1990s decision to reorient the company's office-product strategy around digital multi-function machines (copiers that also scanned, faxed and printed) seemed about to pay big dividends.

But Thoman was uneasy just the same. For the time being, Xerox had no competition in digital copying, but the Japanese would bring their own digital machines to market soon enough and if form held, would probably offer comparable quality at lower cost. Could Xerox sustain its revenue growth when it no longer had the market to itself? The burgeoning popularity of the inkjet printer posed an equally dire threat to Document Center's rosy unit sale and revenue projections. By now, inkjet sales were exploding in the so-called SOHO (small office, home office) market, which Xerox had studiously ignored for years in maintaining its focus on high-margin, high-end equipment.

By mid-1998, Thoman had concluded that Xerox had to make changes in its business strategy to deliver on its emphatic promises of double-digit revenue growth. He wanted to push hard into colour and take on mighty HP in inkjet. At the same time, he believed that Xerox' direct-sales force had to shift emphasis from pushing hardware to selling 'output management solutions'. As Thoman envisioned it, Xerox' best long-term growth opportunity lay in helping big companies create new ways to use documents more creatively and efficiently. In practical terms, this meant signing companies to outsourcing contracts or selling them special Xerox-written software. This, in turn, required turning Xerox' box-sellers into systems consultants and reorganising the sales force around industry groups rather than geographic areas.

Some of these notions had been circulating through Xerox for years but had been acted on only sporadically because of opposition from one Burox faction or another. Thoman articulated his vision with a clarity and an urgency new to Xerox. If, after countless management meetings, Thoman's ideas eventually prevailed, it was because Allaire agreed with him, not because he had won over anything close to a majority of his colleagues. Within the ranks, opposition was steadily building, though rarely was it expressed overtly. Burox had always excelled at passive resistance. 'I kept putting groups of people in rooms to work on fixing a problem, but it wouldn't get fixed because someone would disagree and the issue would not be settled,' Thoman says.

Thoman's frustrations were momentarily forgotten when he was named CEO at Xerox' annual meeting in April 1999. 'I'll always remember it as a summit moment, a wonderful feeling of arrival,' says Thoman. The happy man hardly gave Allaire's decision to remain as chairman a second thought. This was not his only mistake. As a consolation prize for Buehler and Romeril, Allaire proposed giving each a seat on the board and the title of vice-chairman. Thoman didn't like the idea but went along. 'I felt I couldn't say no. I really thought this was Paul's way of making sure everyone felt OK with my promotion. Of course, it strait-jacketed my ability to make changes.'

Thoman was able to make some executive changes. He moved the company's European president aside to make way for Pierre Danon, a dashing Frenchman who was considered Xerox' most aggressive home-grown executive. He replaced Danon as head of retail distribution with James Firestone, a former IBM colleague. He brought in Michael Miron, a 39-year-old cellular-telephony executive as head of corporate strategy. When the head of Xerox' outsourcing subsidiary retired, Thoman recruited Michael A. Ruffolo, the 36-year-old chief information officer of NCR. These digital-savvy executives and a handful of other senior leaders believed in Thoman's change agenda but did not come close to changing the balance of power. Says one ally, who resigned even before Thoman's dismissal: 'The challenge of changing Xerox was so profound that Rick needed eight or nine senior people pushing hard along with him as a group day after day.'

INVESTOR FLIGHT

In the third quarter of 1999, Xerox posted an 11 per cent drop in income instead of the healthy gain predicted. Investors deserted Xerox in droves, slicing nearly 25 per cent off its value in a single day. It was as if everything had gone wrong at once. Document Center revenues were falling behind projections as lower-priced alternatives cut into its market share. The heavy expenses of entering the inkjet business were really starting to bite, and competitors were even beginning to eat away at Xerox' monopoly in high-end digital publishing. The Brazilian subsidiary, long the company's largest source of profit outside the US, was reeling from colossal currency translation losses and soaring interest rates. In North America, productivity was deteriorating as the sales force braced for the reorganisation scheduled to begin in January.

Xerox' business woes brought the simmering tensions between Thoman and other executives to a boil. By all accounts, there wasn't a lot of yelling and screaming. But as Buehler and Romeril complained with increasing vehemence to Allaire, the fissures within top management became apparent to the board. Says one director: 'Sure, we were alarmed – alarmed as an eight-alarm bell.' In mid-December, Allaire circulated a memo to senior management affirming his support of Thoman. The board is 'unanimously supportive of Rick' despite the 'clearly disappointing performance of the company', he wrote. Behind the scenes, though, Romeril, Buehler and other executives were coming to Allaire and threatening to resign unless Thoman was removed. In the first quarter of 2000, Xerox actually exceeded the Street's expectations, modest though they were. But the die was cast. 'There was no last straw, no flash of lightning, no thunder,' Allaire says. 'Rick had clearly lost the confidence of me, the board, and his extended management team. When that happens, you have to make a change.'

There seems little doubt that Thoman did lack feel for the human and political realities of 'the Xerox family' he had only recently joined. And he shares responsibility for the crippling strategic error of spending heavily to belatedly challenge HP at a time when Xerox would have been better off husbanding its cash. On the other hand, digital markets wait for no old-line company. It is likely that the pace of change that Thoman tried to dictate was in fact the pace Xerox needed to play in the Digital Age. 'The lesson of Xerox is that halfway measures don't work,' says a former executive. 'If you bring in a change agent, then let him make change – or don't even start.' Xerox probably will survive. It might even return to solid profitability. But its hopes of becoming an important player in the 'office of the future' probably have been dashed for good.

GLOSSARY

Acceptability is concerned with the expected performance outcomes of a strategy (p. 390)

Acquisition is where an organisation develops its resources and competences by taking over another organisation (p. 375)

Balanced scorecards combine both qualitative and quantitative measures, acknowledge the expectations of different stakeholders and relate an assessment of performance to choice of strategy (p. 437)

Barriers to entry are factors that need to be overcome by new entrants if they are to compete successfully (p. 113)

Best-in-class benchmarking compares an organisation's performance against 'best-in-class' performance – wherever that is found (p. 174)

A **business model** describes the structure of product, service and information flows and the roles of the participating parties (p. 496)

Business unit strategy is about how to compete successfully in particular markets (p. 11)

A **cash cow** is a business unit with a high market share in a mature market (p. 285)

A **change agent** is the individual or group that effects strategic change in an organisation (p. 549)

Coercion is the imposition of change or the issuing of edicts about change (p. 547)

Collaboration or *participation* in the change process is the involvement of those who will be affected by strategic change in the identification of strategic issues, the setting of the strategic agenda, the strategic decision-making process or the planning of strategic change (p. 545)

Competitive rivals are organisations with similar products and services aimed at the same customer group (p. 118)

Competitive strategy is the bases on which a business unit might achieve competitive advantage in its market (p. 319)

An organisation's **configuration** consists of the structures, processes, relationships and boundaries through which the organisation operates (pp. 420, 455)

Consolidation is where organisations protect and strengthen their position in their current markets with current products (p. 363)

Convergence is where previously separate industries begin to overlap in terms of activities, technologies, products and customers (p. 110)

Core competences are activities or processes that critically underpin an organisation's competitive advantage (p. 156)

Corporate-level strategy is concerned with the overall purpose and scope of an organisation and how value will be added to the different parts (business units) of the organisation (p. 11)

The levels of management above that of business units and therefore without direct interaction with buyers and competitors are referred to as the **corporate parent** (p. 268)

Corporate social responsibility is concerned with the ways in which an organisation exceeds the minimum obligations to stakeholders specified through regulation and corporate governance (p. 220)

Cost efficiency is a measure of the level of resources needed to create a given level of value (p. 166)

Critical success factors (CSFs) are those product features that are particularly valued by a group of customers and, therefore, where the organisation must excel to outperform competition (p. 151)

The **cultural web** is a representation of the taken-for-granted assumptions, or paradigm, of an organisation and the physical manifestations of organisational culture (p. 230)

Data mining is about finding trends and connections in data in order to inform and improve competitive performance (p. 493)

The **design lens** views strategy development as the deliberate positioning of the organisation through a rational, analytic, structured and directive process (p. 41)

Devolution concerns the extent to which the centre of an organisation delegates decision making to units and managers lower down in the hierarchy (p. 444)

A **differentiation strategy** seeks to provide products or services unique or different from those of competitors in terms of dimensions widely valued by buyers (p. 322)

Diffusion is the extent and pace at which a market is likely to adopt new products (p. 515)

Direction involves the use of personal managerial authority to establish a clear future strategy and how change will occur (p. 547)

The **directional policy matrix** positions SBUs according to (a) how attractive the relevant market is in which they are operating, and (b) the competitive strength of the SBU in that market (p. 288)

Direct supervision is the direct control of strategic decisions by one or a few individuals (p. 433)

Diversification is typically defined as a strategy which takes the organisation away from its current markets or products or competences (pp. 297, 373)

Dogs are business units with a low share in static or declining markets (p. 285)

A **dominant strategy** is one that outperforms all other strategies whatever rivals choose (p. 342)

Education and communication involve the explanation of the reasons for and means of strategic change (p. 545)

Effectiveness is the ability to meet customer requirements on product features at a given cost (p. 168)

In game theory, **equilibrium** is a situation where each competitor contrives to get the best possible strategic solution for itself given the response from the other (p. 343)

The **ethical stance** is the extent to which an organisation will exceed its minimum obligations to stakeholders and society at large (p. 216)

The **experience lens** views strategy development as the outcome of individual and collective experience of individuals and taken-for-granted assumptions (p. 43)

Feasibility is concerned with whether an organisation has the resources and competences to deliver a strategy (p. 398)

In **financial control** the role of the centre is confined to setting financial targets, allocating resources, appraising performance and intervening to avert or correct poor performance (p. 448)

The **five forces framework** helps identify the sources of competition in an industry or sector (p. 112)

A **focused differentiation** strategy seeks to provide high perceived value justifying a substantial price premium, usually to a selected market segment (p. 328)

A **forcefield analysis** provides an initial view of change problems that need to be tackled, by identifying forces for and against change (p. 544)

A **functional structure** is based on the primary activities that have to be undertaken by an organisation such as production, finance and accounting, marketing, human resources and information management (p. 422)

The **governance framework** describes whom the organisation is there to serve and how the purposes and priorities of the organisation should be decided (p. 195)

Hard human resource approaches are about how systems and procedures can be used to acquire, utilise, develop and retain people (p. 479)

Historical comparison looks at the performance of an organisation in relation to previous years in order to identify any significant changes (p. 172)

A **holding company** is an investment company consisting of shareholdings in a variety of separate business operations (p. 426)

Horizontal integration is development into activities which are competitive with, or complementary to, a company's present activities (p. 299)

A **hybrid strategy** seeks simultaneously to achieve differentiation and a price lower than that of competitors (p. 326)

Hypercompetition occurs where the frequency, boldness and aggressiveness of dynamic movements by competitors accelerate to create a condition of constant disequilibrium and change (p. 122)

The **ideas lens** sees strategy as the emergence of order and innovation from the variety and diversity which exist in and around organisations (p. 50)

Individual experience is the mental (or cognitive) models people build over time to help make sense of their situation (p. 44)

An **industry** is a group of firms producing the same principal product (p. 110)

Industry norms compare the performance of organisations in the same industry or sector against a set of agreed performance indicators (p. 172)

Intended strategy is an expression of desired strategic direction deliberately formulated or planned by managers (p. 75)

Internal development is where strategies are developed by building up an organisation's own resource base and competences (p. 374)

Intervention is the co-ordination of and authority over processes of change by a change agent who delegates elements of the change process (p. 546)

A **joint development** is where two or more organisations share resources and activities to pursue a strategy (p. 378)

Key rigidities are activities that are deeply embedded and difficult to change and out of line with the requirements of new strategies (p. 179)

Knowledge is awareness, consciousness or familiarity gained by experience or learning (p. 150)

Leadership is the process of influencing an organisation (or group within an organisation) in its efforts towards achieving an aim or goal (p. 549)

A **learning organisation** is capable of continual regeneration from the variety of knowledge, experience and skills of individuals within a culture which encourages mutual questioning and challenge around a shared purpose or vision (pp. 72, 583)

Logical incrementalism is the deliberate development of strategy by 'learning through doing' (p. 69)

A **low price strategy** seeks to achieve a lower price than competitors whilst trying to maintain similar value of product or service to that offered by competitors (p. 322)

Market development is where existing products are offered in new markets (p. 370)

Market mechanisms involve some formalised system of 'contracting' for resources (p. 438)

Market penetration is where an organisation gains market share (p. 367)

Market segmentation identifies similarities and differences between groups of customers or users (p. 127)

A **matrix structure** is a combination of structures which could take the form of product and geographical divisions or functional and divisional structures operating in tandem (p. 427)

A **mission statement** is a generalised statement of the overriding purpose of an organisation (p. 239)

A **multidivisional structure** is built up of separate divisions on the basis of products, services or geographical areas (p, 425)

A **'no frills' strategy** combines a low price, low perceived added value and a focus on a price-sensitive market segment (p. 319)

Objectives are statements of specific outcomes that are to be achieved (p. 241)

A **one-start shop** deals with client enquiries by *diagnosing* the client's needs and *referring* them to the most appropriate provider (p. 454)

A **one-stop shop** is where a physical presence is created through which all client enquiries are channelled (p. 453)

Operational strategies are concerned with how the component parts of an organisation deliver effectively the corporate- and business-level strategies in terms of resources, processes and people (p. 12)

Organisational culture is the 'basic *assumptions and beliefs* that are shared by members of an organisation, that operate unconsciously and define in a basic taken-for-granted fashion an organisation's view of itself and its environment' (p. 45)

An **organisational field** is a community of organisations that partake of a common meaning system and whose participants interact more frequently with one another than with those outside the field (pp. 126, 223)

Organisational fields are networks of related organisations which share common assumptions, values and ways of doing things (p. 46)

A **paradigm** is the set of assumptions held relatively in common and taken for granted in an organisation (p. 48)

The **parental developer** seeks to employ its own competences as a parent to add value to its businesses (p. 280)

Performance targets relate to the *outputs* of an organisation (or part of an organisation), such as product quality, prices, or its *outcomes* such as profit (p. 436)

The **PESTEL framework** categorises environmental influences into six main types: political, economic, social, technological, environmental and legal (p. 102)

Planning and control is where the successful implementation of strategies is achieved through *systems* that plan and control the allocation of resources and monitor their utilisation (p. 433)

The **political view** of strategy development is, that strategies develop as the outcome of processes of bargaining and negotiation amongst powerful internal or external interest groups (or stakeholders) (p. 66)

A **portfolio manager** is a corporate parent acting as an agent on behalf of financial markets and shareholders (p. 275)

Power is the ability of individuals or groups to persuade, induce or coerce others into following certain courses of action (p. 212)

Primary activities are *directly* concerned with the creation or delivery of a product or service (p. 160)

Product development is where organisations deliver modified or new products to existing markets (p. 368)

A **project-based structure** is one where teams are created, undertake the work and are then dissolved (p. 431)

Punctuated equilibrium is the tendency of strategies to develop incrementally with periodic transformational change (p. 77)

A **question mark** (or problem child) is a business unit in a growing market, but without a high market share (p. 285)

Realised strategy is the strategy actually being followed by an organisation in practice (p. 75)

A **recipe** is a set of assumptions held in common within an organisational field about organisational purposes and a 'shared wisdom' on how to manage organisations (p. 225)

Reinforcing cycles are created by the *dynamic interaction* between the various factors of environment, configuration and elements of strategy; they tend to preserve the status quo (p. 462)

Related diversification is strategy development beyond current products and markets, but within the value system or 'industry' in which the company operates (p. 297)

Rents result from an organisation having resources or capabilities which permit it to produce at lower cost or generate a superior product or service at standard cost, in relation to firms with inferior resources and capabilities (p. 315)

Restructurers are adept at identifying restructuring opportunities in businesses (p. 277)

Routines are the organisationally specific 'ways we do things around here' which tend to persist over time and guide people's behaviour (p. 554)

Processes of **self-control** achieve the integration of knowledge and co-ordination of activities by the direct interaction of individuals without supervision (p. 442)

A **scenario** is a detailed and plausible view of how the business environment of an organisation might develop in the future based on groupings of key environmental influences and drivers of change about which there is a high level of uncertainty (p. 107)

In a **service network** the client may access all of the services of the network through any of the constituent members of the network (p. 455)

In a **simple structure** the organisation is run by the personal control of an individual (p. 422)

Social processes are concerned with organisational culture and the *standardisation of norms* (p. 440)

Soft human resource approaches are concerned with people's behaviour, both individually and collectively (p. 479)

Stakeholder mapping identifies stakeholder expectations and power and helps in understanding political priorities (p. 208)

Stakeholders are those individuals or groups who depend on the organisation to fulfil their own goals and on whom, in turn, the organisation depends (p. 206)

A **star** is a business unit which has a high market share in a growing market (p. 285)

A **strategic business unit** is a part of an organisation for which there is a distinct external market for goods or services that is different from another SBU (p. 11)

Strategic choices involve understanding the underlying bases for future strategy at both the corporate and business unit levels and the options for developing strategy in terms of both the directions and methods of development (p. 19)

Strategic control is concerned with shaping the *behaviour* in business units and with shaping the *context* within which managers are operating (p. 448)

Strategic drift occurs when the organisation's strategy gradually moves away from relevance to the forces at work in its environment (p. 81)

Strategic fit is developing strategy by identifying opportunities in the business environment and adapting resources and competences so as to take advantage of these (p. 5)

Strategic groups are organisations within an industry with similar strategic characteristics, following similar strategies or competing on similar bases (p. 122)

Strategic intent is the desired future state or aspiration of an organisation (p. 239)

A **strategic leader** is an individual upon whom strategy development and change are seen to be dependent (p. 65)

Strategic management includes *understanding the strategic position* of an organisation, *strategic choices* for the future and turning *strategy into action* (p. 16)

In a **strategic planning style**, the relationship between the centre and the business units is one of a parent who is the *master planner* prescribing detailed roles for departments and business units (p. 446)

The **strategic position** is concerned with the impact on strategy of the external environment, internal resources and competences, and the expectations and influence of stakeholders (p. 16)

Strategy into action is concerned with ensuring that strategies are working in practice (p. 21)

Strategy is the *direction* and *scope* of an organisation over the *long term*, which achieves *advantage* for the organisation through its configuration of *resources* within a changing *environment* and to fulfil *stakeholder* expectations (p. 10)

'Stretch' is the leverage of the resources and competences of an organisation to provide competitive advantage and/or yield new opportunities (p. 8)

Structural drivers of change are forces likely to affect the structure of an industry, sector or market (p. 103)

Substitution reduces demand for a particular 'class' of products as customers switch to the alternatives (p. 115)

Suitability is concerned with whether a strategy addresses the circumstances in which an organisation is operating – the strategic position (p. 384)

Support activities help to improve the effectiveness or efficiency of primary activities (p. 161)

A **SWOT** analysis summarises the key issues from the business environment and the strategic capability of an organisation that are most likely to impact on strategy development (pp. 134, 184)

Symbols are objects, events, acts or people which express more than their intrinsic content (p. 555)

Synergy can occur in situations where two or more activities or processes complement each other, to the extent that their combined effect is greater than the sum of the parts (p. 278)

A **team-based structure** attempts to combine both horizontal and vertical co-ordination through structuring people into cross-functional teams (p. 429)

A **transnational corporation** combines the local responsiveness of the international subsidiary with the advantages available from co-ordination found in global product companies (p. 460)

Unique resources are those resources which critically underpin competitive advantage (p. 154)

Unrelated diversification is an organisation moving beyond its current value system or industry (p. 302)

The **value chain** describes the activities within and around an organisation which together create a product or service (p. 160)

A **value network** is a value system where the interorganisational relationships are more fluid (p. 165)

The **value system** is the set of inter-organisational links and relationships which are necessary to create a product or service (p. 161)

Vertical integration describes either backward or forward integration into adjacent activities in the value system (p. 298)

Virtual organisations are held together not through formal structure and physical proximity of people, but by partnership, collaboration and networking (p. 452)

INDEX OF COMPANIES AND ORGANISATIONS

GENERAL INDEX